Thomson Custom Solutions allows you to:

▶ Create a comprehensive course solution by incorporating your original content such as course notes, handouts, regional or state material, or articles in a professional and attractive format. In addition, our flexible and attractive cover options will help make your project stand apart.

▶ Make technology work for you, utilizing our skilled **Custom Media Solutions** team to match your technology to your text and course.

▶ Enrich your course with selections from one of our **Thomson Custom Solutions Collections** offering additional readings, exercises, and case selections for a wide range of subjects. Use our powerful TextChoice book-building web site, **www.textchoice.com**, to explore the options available to you.

▶ Offer students more choices in their textbook format and delivery.

Thomson Custom Solutions expert editorial team will guide you through each step and work with you to ensure your project meets your goals and objectives.

For more information about your options and our services, visit **www.thomsoncustom.com** or contact your local Thomson representative.

EFFECTIVE WRITING AND READING THROUGH UNDERSTANDING THE RHETORICAL SITUATION

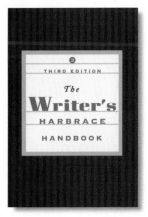

The Writer's Harbrace Handbook, **Third Edition,** is grounded in the belief that an understanding of the rhetorical situation—the writer, reader, message, context, and exigence (the reason for writing)—provides the best starting place for effective writing and reading. This edition guides student writers in employing that rhetorical understanding as they choose the most effective information to include, the best arrangement of that information, and the most appropriate language to use.

This writing-first handbook moves students through the steps that constitute successful writing, from finding appropriate topics and writing clear thesis statements to arranging ideas and developing initial drafts.

This comprehensive yet easy-to-use handbook contains a variety of features that help students develop as writers, including:

- ■ **Comprehensive coverage of the rhetorical situation throughout the entire book**—*see page 2.*

- ■ **An abundance of instructive visuals and design features, including extensive coverage of visual rhetoric**—*see page 3.*

- ■ **A reliable and accessible research, documentation, and style guide that helps students with each step of the writing process**—*see pages 4–5.*

- ■ **An exceptional selection of student and instructor resources**—*see pages 6–8.*

THOMSON

WADSWORTH

AUTHORITATIVE COVERAGE OF
THE RHETORICAL SITUATION

From writing and research to grammar and mechanics, *The Writer's Harbrace Handbook,*
Third Edition, situates all discussion of writing and reading within the rhetorical situation.
Chapter 1, "The Rhetorical Situation," lays the foundation for the entire book by explaining
the primary elements of the rhetorical situation at the
same time that it provides students with examples of the
many different types of rhetorical situations that they
will encounter in class or on the job. For example, in
Chapters 16–19, "Writing to Interpret Literature,"
"Writing in the Social Sciences," "Writing in the Natural
Sciences," and "Writing in Business," students will learn
how writers respond to a variety of rhetorical situations
using specific methods of reasoning, specialized sources
and evidence, as well as discipline-specific style and formatting conventions.

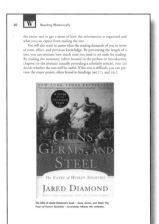

**Chapter 2, "Reading Rhetorically," teaches students
to read both words and images, applying the rhetorical situation to the interpretation of entire texts.** In
this chapter, students are guided through the analysis of
a Pulitzer Prize–winning book, focusing on the relationships among the writer, the reader, the writer's purpose,
and the context within which the writing takes place.

**"Thinking Rhetorically About …" boxes
throughout the grammar, punctuation, and
mechanics chapters ask students to
consider the impact of the choices they make
at the sentence level.** Presenting situations
where multiple options are available, these features encourage students to gauge the rhetorical
effect of the sentence-level decisions they make.

INSTRUCTIVE VISUALS THAT EMPHASIZE KEY COMPONENTS

Because visuals inundate everyday culture, *The Writer's Harbrace Handbook,* **Third Edition,** features a wide variety of instructive visuals that exemplify the material covered. For instance, in Chapter 8, "Writing Arguments," cartoons illustrate many of the rhetorical fallacies discussed. And in the research and documentation chapters, color boxes call out important information and useful tips that aid students during each step of the research and writing process.

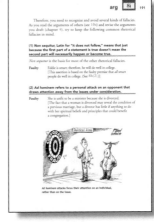

Through the use of visuals in this textbook, students come to understand the specific ways images communicate meaning to viewers in much the same way words communicate meaning to readers.

Chapter 7, "Visual Documents," introduces students to visual rhetoric, the specific ways images and text combine to communicate meaning to viewers by way of the image as a whole, the elements of the image, the arrangement of those visual elements, and the relationship between an image and the surrounding text.

Chapters 12–15 contain up-to-date style guidelines from the Modern Language Association (MLA), the American Psychological Association (APA), *The Chicago Manual of Style* (CMS), and *The CBE Manual for Authors, Editors, and Publishers* (CSE/CBE). The MLA section features over forty-five newly added citation examples—with special attention given to citations of online sources. In addition, the updated Chapter 9, "Finding Sources in Print, Online, and in the Field," walks students through each step of the research process (finding appropriate sources, forming a research question, and conducting research), using the elements of the rhetorical situation as a guide. This chapter also introduces students to various research methods, including library research, online research, and multiple kinds of field research (interviews, online discussion forums, and questionnaires or surveys).

Easy-to-follow, color-coded visual examples of each type of citation (for a book, an article, and an online source) show students the major components and exact arrangement of each citation.

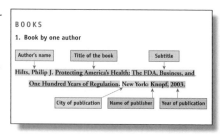

Chapter 11, "Using Sources Effectively and Responsibly," helps students establish their integrity as a writer and avoid plagiarism by presenting them with the basic methods for building a bibliography, writing an annotated bibliography, and integrating sources. Clear examples that illustrate the difference between paraphrasing, summarizing, and quoting material help students as they work with their source material. In addition, students will learn how to take notes, organize those notes, and respond to sources in terms of their role as a writer in a specific rhetorical situation.

A four-color design throughout the entire book calls out important material and useful tips, making it easy for students to quickly and accurately access information within each chapter.

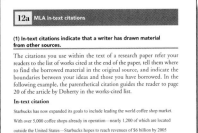

INTERACTIVE MULTIMEDIA THAT EMPHASIZE THE MOST IMPORTANT FEATURES OF GRAMMAR AND WRITING

Comp21: Composition in the 21st Century for *The Writer's Harbrace Handbook,* Third Edition, ONLINE!

Through interactive instruction, this groundbreaking online tool teaches students how to analyze the various texts that inundate their lives and demonstrates how to use rhetorical devices in their writing. Using Thomson Wadsworth's unique "Explicator" technology—which guides students in critically analyzing texts and media—students can create useful notes for their work to enhance their inquiry into their chosen topics. Ask your Thomson Wadsworth sales representative how to package **Comp21** with this text.

ThomsonNOW™ for *The Writer's Harbrace Handbook,* Third Edition

You envisioned it; we developed it. Designed *by* instructors and students *for* instructors and students, **ThomsonNOW for Glenn/Gray's *The Writer's Harbrace Handbook,* Third Edition,** is the most reliable, flexible, and easy-to-use, online suite of services and resources. With efficient and immediate paths to success, ThomsonNOW delivers the results you expect—NOW. Ask your Thomson Wadsworth sales representative how to package ThomsonNOW with this text.

Thomson's InSite for Writing and Research™

This all-in-one, online writing and research tool includes electronic peer review, an originality checker, an assignment library, help with common errors, and access to InfoTrac® College Edition. To view a demonstration, visit **http://insite.thomson.com**. Ask your Thomson Wadsworth sales representative how to package InSite with this text.

This proven online plagiarism-prevention software promotes fairness in the classroom by helping students learn to cite sources correctly and allowing instructors to check for originality before reading and grading papers. Turnitin® quickly checks student papers against billions of pages of Internet content, millions of published works, and millions of student papers and within seconds generates a comprehensive originality report. To view a demonstration, visit **http://turnitin.thomson.com**. Ask your Thomson Wadsworth sales representative how to package Turnitin with this text.

STUDENT AND INSTRUCTOR RESOURCES

Instructor's Manual Flex-Files for *The Writer's Harbrace Handbook*, Third Edition
1-4130-1683-9

Designed to give you maximum flexibility in planning and customizing your course, Flex-Files provide an abundance of instructor materials that consist of two main sections. "Part One: Questions for Teachers" raises a variety of pedagogical questions (and provides workable solutions) for you to consider in teaching your course with this handbook. "Part Two: Sample Syllabi and Activities" offers a sample syllabus with possible assignments for a semester-long course and a sample syllabus with possible assignments for a quarter-long course. Additionally, this section contains sample in-class collaborative learning activities, technology-oriented activities, and critical thinking and writing activities. The Flex-Files also include the following supplementary materials: (1) an ESL insert aimed at helping mainstream instructors teach writing effectively to their ESL students, (2) an insert on disability issues as they relate to teaching first-year composition, (3) the Answer Key for the exercises in the handbook, and (4) the Answer Key for the *College Workbook*.

Complete & Convenient Handbook—Designed Just for You

Thomson Custom Solutions makes it easier than ever to customize this or any one of our leading English Composition handbooks to create a highly personalized and convenient course resource for your students.

Tabbed for Easier Access. Tabs make it even easier and quicker to locate and find the information you need. Each section of your handbook will be separated by tabs allowing students to quickly reference the needed resources.

The First Tab Is All Yours! We have set aside the first tabbed section just for you. Include your syllabus, school policies, writing samples, style guides, or other, course-specific information. You have up to 16 pages for your content.

Add a Personal Touch with a Customized Cover. Personalize the handbook by including your course and instructor information on the front and back cover. Learn more about the available options from your local Thomson representative.

Thomson Custom Solutions' experienced editorial and design teams will be there to guide you through each step to help you create your perfect Composition handbook. For more information about our services, visit **www.thomsoncustom.com**

ADDITIONAL STUDENT AND INSTRUCTOR RESOURCES

Think About Editing: ESL Guide for *Hodges' Harbrace Handbook,* Sixteenth Edition, and *The Writer's Harbrace Handbook,* Third Edition
1-4130-1682-0

A self-editing manual for ESL writers, *Think About Editing* is designed to help intermediate to advanced students edit their writing to correct grammar and usage errors. The manual is prefaced with a correlation guide that links its units to corresponding sections in both handbooks.

College Workbook for *Hodges' Harbrace Handbook,* Sixteenth Edition, and *The Writer's Harbrace Handbook,* Third Edition
1-4130-1650-2

Twenty-seven units in five parts correspond to chapters of the handbooks and cover grammar, punctuation, usage, style, and writing. This printed workbook combines exercises with clear examples and explanations that supplement the information and exercises found in the handbooks.

English Testing Center for *Hodges' Harbrace Handbook,* Sixteenth Edition, and *The Writer's Harbrace Handbook,* Third Edition
1-4130-1681-2

Built into Thomson Learning's proprietary gradebook system, iLrn™, the Thomson Wadsworth English Testing Center includes an online version of the Diagnostic Test Package plus online tests correlated to the handbooks.

Instructor's Correction Chart for *The Writer's Harbrace Handbook,* Third Edition
1-4130-2860-8

To make marking your students' papers easier, you can prop up on your desk this oversized, laminated chart listing all of the sections of the handbook and showing the editing symbols correlated to them.

The

WRITER'S HARBRACE HANDBOOK

THIRD EDITION

The

Writer's

HARBRACE

HANDBOOK

CHERYL GLENN

The Pennsylvania State University

LORETTA GRAY

Central Washington University

THOMSON
™
WADSWORTH

Australia • Brazil • Canada • Mexico • Singapore • Spain
United Kingdom • United States

THOMSON

WADSWORTH

The Writer's Harbrace Handbook, Third Edition
Cheryl Glenn, Loretta Gray

Publisher: *Michael Rosenberg*
Senior Acquisitions Editor: *Dickson Musslewhite*
Senior Development Editor: *Michell Phifer*
Editorial Assistant: *Jonelle Lonergan*
Technology Project Manager: *Tim Smith*
Managing Marketing Manager: *Mandee Eckersley*
Marketing Assistant: *Dawn Giovanniello*
Associate Marketing Communications Manager:
  Patrick Rooney
Senior Project Manager, Editorial Production:
  Lianne Ames

Senior Print Buyer: *Mary Beth Hennebury*
Senior Permissions Editor: *Isabel Alves*
Permissions Editor: *Nora Piehl*
Production Service: *Lifland et al., Bookmakers*
Text Designer: *Linda Beaupre*
Photo Manager: *Sheri Blaney*
Photo Researchers: *Billie Porter/Cheri Throop*
Cover Designer: *Linda Beaupre*
Cover Printer: *Phoenix Color*
Compositor: *Pre-Press Company, Inc.*
Text Printer: *QuebecorWorld*

Printed in the United States of America
1 2 3 4 5 6 7 09 08 07 06

Library of Congress Control Number: 2005937962

ISBN 1-4130-1032-6

Thomson Higher Education
25 Thomson Place
Boston, MA 02210-1202
USA

For more information about our products, contact us at:
Thomson Learning Academic Resource Center
1-800-423-0563

For permission to use material from this text or product, submit a request online at
http://www.thomsonrights.com
Any additional questions about permissions can be submitted by e-mail to
thomsonrights@thomson.com

Credits appear on pages 805–808, which constitute a continuation of the copyright page.

CONTENTS

R   PART II RESEARCH

D   PART III   WRITING IN THE DISCIPLINES

G   PART IV   GRAMMAR

S | PART V EFFECTIVE SENTENCES

P PART VII PUNCTUATION

M ┃ PART VIII MECHANICS

Chapter 40 ┃ Spelling, the Spell Checker, and Hyphenation   733   sp

Chapter 41 ┃ Capitals   744   cap

Chapter 42 ┃ Italics   755   ital

What are the origins of first-year writing handbooks?

The first writing handbook of rules and conventions was Edwin A. Abbott's 1874 *How to Write Clearly*. Abbott's aim was to help his classics students at the City of London School produce more fluent English translations of their Greek and Latin lessons, and his handbook was the first college-level text to equate clear writing with the mastery of specific rules, fifty-six of them, to be precise. In the United States, *How to Write Clearly* became wildly popular—not in classics, but in English composition courses, because it provided easy-to-use, error-based rules for writers.

With the 1862 Morrill Act, the U.S. Government provided funding for the establishment of Mechanical and Agricultural Colleges (which later became the major state universities), and the country's university population exploded. Higher education was no longer reserved for the sons and daughters of the upper classes. College writing classes suddenly expanded from thirty to one hundred students—a flood of students who needed to learn how to write—and teachers desperately sought ways to handle the workload of grading weekly themes. *How to Write Clearly*, along with a number of other popular rule-governed and exercise-based handbooks, tried to meet this need. The handbook had established itself as the *sine qua non* of writing instruction.

How did the *Harbrace Handbook* get started?

The book you have in your hands is not the first handbook, but, since 1941, it has served as the paradigm for all successful handbooks. In the 1930s, John C. Hodges obtained federal funding to support his study of the frequency of errors in college students' essays. Hodges, an English professor at the University of Tennessee, collected some twenty thousand student papers that had been marked by sixteen different professors of rhetoric from all over the United States. Then, working with a cadre of graduate students, he counted and analyzed the errors in those papers, creating a taxonomy that he used to organize the 1941 *Harbrace Handbook of English* into thirty-five sections.

In the preface to that first edition, Hodges wrote:

> The *Harbrace Handbook of English* is a guide to the correction of student themes and also a text for use in class. It presents well-known subject matter in an easily usable form, and thus lightens the instructor's task of grading papers. The book contains only thirty-five major sections.

Thus, his handbook became a masterpiece of organized minimalism, easily accessible to teachers and students alike. The *Harbrace Handbook of English* captured the attention of both groups, as it responded to their needs in a material (and easy-to-use) way.

What makes *The Writer's Harbrace Handbook* so good?

Firmly established as the granddaddy of all handbooks, the *Harbrace Handbook of English* evolved into *The Writer's Harbrace Handbook, Third Edition,* which continues the Hodges' tradition of up-to-date reliability and practicality. Like all of its predecessors, this edition of *The Writer's Harbrace Handbook* responds to the material needs of teachers and students. Still providing teachers with a simplified method for marking student papers, this handbook also gives both teachers and students the ease of reference and attention to detail that have made the Harbrace handbooks the standard of reliability. Without diminishing its longstanding commitment to helping students make the best decisions in terms of grammar, style, punctuation, and mechanics, this "writing first" handbook also guides them as they develop their abilities as writers. Therefore, *The Writer's Harbrace Handbook* provides priorities for any writing course, on any topic of composition.

What's new about this edition?

This edition enhances the important changes made in the previous edition in two readily apparent ways: rhetorical principles now underpin the entire book, and the purposeful use of visuals is emphasized throughout. These changes reinforce our commitment to helping students understand the rhetorical situation as the starting point for their reading and writing and to guiding them in the interpretation and production of visuals, which are ubiquitous in contemporary culture.

- **Opening with the Rhetorical Situation** Perhaps the most significant substantive change is in the opening chapter, which now emphasizes even more strongly the constituent parts of the rhetorical situation: writer, audience, message, purpose, context, and exigence (the specific reason for writing). Decisions about the most effective information to include, the best arrangement of that information, and the most appropriate language to use all grow out of an understanding of the rhetorical situation.

  Chapter 1, "The Rhetorical Situation," lays the rhetorical foundation for the entire book, from the writing chapters through the research and grammar chapters that follow. When students are guided by the rhetorical situation, they can read and write more effectively and efficiently, whether in an English or science course or in the workplace.

  Chapter 2, "Reading Rhetorically," applies the rhetorical situation to the interpretation (rather than the production) of words by helping students focus on the relationships among the writer, the reader, the writer's purpose, and the context within which the writing takes place. In this chapter, students are guided through an analysis of a Pulitzer Prize–winning book, beginning with the front cover and the table of contents and including a sample page, an explanatory figure, and the review blurbs on the back cover. They learn to read both words and images. Students who can read rhetorically better comprehend content and can separate their understanding of what is on the page (or screen) from their personal response to that content.

- **Chapter 5, "Planning for Academic Success,"** demonstrates specific methods students can use to ease the pressures of academic reading and writing through understanding course requirements, seeking out academic support opportunities, managing deadlines, and preparing for in-class essay examinations.

- **Chapter 7, "Visual Documents,"** introduces students to visual rhetoric, the specific ways in which any visual image communicates meaning to viewers, by way of the image as a whole, the elements of the image, the arrangement of those visual elements, and the relationship between an image and the surrounding text. Students will also learn about the conventions of document design in terms of the relationships between design and function and graphics and purpose.

- **Thinking Rhetorically About . . . Boxes** New to this edition, these boxes prompt students to consider the impact of the choices they make in grammar, style, and punctuation. Many of the boxes present situations in which a writer has multiple options or in which a conventional rule may be broken. These possibilities move students away from thinking that "one rule fits all" to gauging the rhetorical effect of the sentence-level decisions they make.

■ **Revised Chapters** Attention to the rhetorical situation has invigorated all of the writing and research chapters and many of the grammar ones, whether those chapters are thoroughly revamped or completely new. The following chapters have been extensively revised in light of contemporary composition pedagogy, while maintaining those aspects of traditional rhetorical theory that are still widely respected.

Chapter 6, "Online Documents," helps students assess the rhetorical situation in the online environment, whether they are participating in electronic messaging or a discussion forum or composing documents for online presentation. The chapter covers netiquette and the use of hyperlinks to enhance online documents.

Chapter 9, "Finding Sources in Print, Online, and in the Field," guides students through the process of formulating a research question, conducting research, and choosing appropriate sources—all in terms of the elements of the rhetorical situation. The methods of conducting research presented in this chapter include traditional library research, online research, and field research (through interviews, discussion forums, and questionnaires).

Chapter 11, "Using Sources Effectively and Responsibly," reminds students of the importance of establishing an ethos as a writer, one firmly grounded in integrity. This chapter, then, helps students understand the importance of taking notes, organizing those notes, and responding to sources in terms of a specific rhetorical situation. Students are introduced to the basic methods necessary for creating a bibliography, writing an annotated bibliography, and integrating sources into a text of their own. Perhaps the most important feature of this chapter is its focus on helping students learn ways to use sources responsibly and thereby avoid plagiarism.

Chapters 16 through 19, "Writing to Interpret Literature," "Writing in the Social Sciences," "Writing in the Natural Sciences," and "Writing in Business," now emphasize how writers respond to differing rhetorical situations in various academic areas. These chapters contain information on discipline-specific ways of reasoning, uses of sources and evidence, and conventions for style and formatting.

■ **Updated Style Guides for Researched Writing** In this edition, we continue our thorough and updated coverage of the style guidelines from the Modern Language Association (MLA), the American Psycho-

Instructor's Correction Chart

To make marking your students' papers easier, you can prop up on your desk this oversized, laminated chart, which lists all of the sections of the handbook and shows the editing symbols correlated to them.

Student Supplements

The Writer's Harbrace Animated Handbook
A fully interactive version of the handbook, this online resource includes over 200 animated examples of the most important choices and conventions for writers, as well as explanations of the Beyond the Rule topics and a library of model student papers.

The Writer's Harbrace Handbook Web Site
The free companion Web site provides links, sample syllabi, quizzes and tests, sample student papers, and other student and instructor resources.

Thomson InSite™ for Writing and Research
 This all-in-one online writing and research tool includes electronic peer review, an originality checker, an assignment library, help with common errors, and access to InfoTrac® College Edition. InSite makes course management practically automatic. Visit http://insite.thomson. com.

Turnitin®
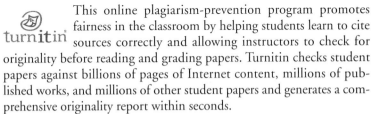 This online plagiarism-prevention program promotes fairness in the classroom by helping students learn to cite sources correctly and allowing instructors to check for originality before reading and grading papers. Turnitin checks student papers against billions of pages of Internet content, millions of published works, and millions of other student papers and generates a comprehensive originality report within seconds.

InfoTrac® College Edition
 Do in-depth research for class right from your desktop or catch up on the latest news online—using your four months of access to InfoTrac College Edition. You can search this virtual

university library's more than 18 million reliable, full-length articles from 5,000 academic and popular periodicals (including the *New York Times, Newsweek, Science, Forbes,* and *USA Today*) and retrieve results almost instantly. You can also use InfoMarks—stable URLs that you can link to articles, journals, and searches to save you time when doing research—and the InfoWrite online resource center, where you can access guides to writing research papers, grammar help, critical thinking guidelines, and much more.

College Workbook

With cross-references to sections of this handbook, the *College Workbook* covers grammar, punctuation, usage, style, and writing. This printed workbook combines exercises with clear examples and explanations that supplement the information and exercises found in the handbook.

Think About Editing: An ESL Guide

A self-editing manual for ESL writers, *Think About Editing* is designed to help intermediate to advanced students edit their writing to correct grammar, structure, and usage. The manual is prefaced with a correlation guide that links its units to corresponding sections in *The Writer's Harbrace Handbook.*

Dictionaries

The following dictionaries are available for a nominal price when bundled with the handbook: *The Merriam-Webster Dictionary,* Second Edition; *Merriam-Webster's Collegiate® Dictionary,* Eleventh Edition; *Merriam-Webster Pocket Thesaurus;* and *Heinle's Newbury House Dictionary of American English with Integrated Thesaurus.* The latter was created especially for ESL students.

Acknowledgments

Who wrote this handbook?

John C. Hodges carried forward his vision of a useful handbook for many editions of the *Harbrace Handbook*—and his influence continues with every edition. With the fifth edition, he was assisted by Mary E. Whitten (North Texas State University—now University of North Texas), who guided the book from the sixth through the tenth editions. Suzanne S. Webb (Texas Woman's University) joined the handbook on the tenth edition to enhance its rhetorical elements and add a section on logical thinking. In the eleventh edition, Winifred Bryan Horner (Texas Christian University) and Robert K. Miller (University of St. Thomas) joined the team, so that Win could add her rhetorical expertise and Bob could rework the research paper chapter.

The twelfth, thirteenth, and fourteenth editions profited from the three-person team of Sue, Win, and Bob, with remarkable results. Three new chapters, "Writing Arguments," "Reading and Thinking Critically," and "Writing under Pressure," were included in the handbook. By the fourteenth edition, the *Harbrace Handbook* appeared in three different versions to meet the growing diversity of handbook users: *Hodges' Harbrace Handbook* continued to emphasize grammar first, while *The Writer's Harbrace Handbook* and *The Writer's Harbrace Handbook,* Brief Edition, as their titles suggest, gave primary emphasis to writing, thereby rounding out the family of Harbrace handbooks.

With Win's retirement, rhetoric and composition specialist Cheryl Glenn (The Pennsylvania State University) and linguist Loretta (Lori) Gray (Central Washington University) joined Sue and Bob to produce the fifteenth edition of *Hodges' Harbrace Handbook* and the second edition of both *The Writer's Harbrace Handbook* and its briefer version.

This edition is the result of a spectacularly successful collaboration between Cheryl and Lori. They had the advantage of building on the terrific work of past Harbrace authors as they wrote what they hope is the best edition so far, one responsive to the rhetorical demands of the twenty-first century.

Who helped?

The third edition of this handbook and the other two versions took shape through extensive phone conversations and e-mail correspondence between the authors as well as with a number of members of the Thomson Wadsworth Higher Education editorial staff. For their collective ideas, enthusiasm, support, and wise counsel, we remain grateful. In particular, we thank Michael Rosenberg, Publisher, whose pride in the Harbrace family of handbooks has never wavered as he supported the two-person author team and their new ideas through many months of work. We're especially grateful to Dickson Musslewhite, Senior Acquisitions Editor, who brought Cheryl and Lori into partnership with his bolder vision for the Harbrace handbooks. On a number of occasions, he plied a tired author duo with more ideas and, therefore, more work, but he always tempered his direction with the goodwill and good sense that characterize the best of rhetors. Lianne Ames, Senior Production Project Manager, helped to bring this huge project to completion, and Jane Hoover carried out the copyediting with style and care. Linda Beaupre gave the book its clear and aesthetically pleasing interior design and cover. Without the help and support of these imaginative people, we simply could not have produced *The Writer's Harbrace Handbook.*

But it is Michell Phifer, Senior Development Editor Extraordinaire as well as friend—to whom we owe a special thanks. A scrupulously careful editor—and our constant intellectual companion—Michell successfully helped us balance our writing deadlines with our other professional commitments (teaching, for instance!). She regularly prodded us to think critically about each chapter, about our choice of images or textual examples, and especially about the project as an intellectual whole. She massaged our sometimes convoluted writing and thinking into accessible prose and challenged us to locate more effective examples of professional and student writing. Michell was always on our team, guiding our collaboration until the very last minute, until the presses rolled.

The successful completion of our work would not have been possible without the research assistance of Stacey Sherrif and Rosalyn Collings Eve, both at The Pennsylvania State University. In addition, this project benefited from the support and encouragement of those overseeing our university schedules and workloads: Patsy Callaghan, Chair of the

Department of English, and Liahna Armstrong, Dean of Arts and Humanities, both at Central Washington University; and Melanie Ekdahl, Staff Assistant in the Office of the Provost at The Pennsylvania State University. Angelique Bacon-Woodard and Rachel Smith, Administrative Fellows in Central Administration at The Pennsylvania State University, offered support, suggestions, and good company.

We would also like to thank the students whose indefatigable efforts went into the model student papers in this edition: Melissa Schraeder, Nicole Hester, and Kaitlyn Andrews-Rice, The Pennsylvania State University; Laura Klocke, Andy Pieper, Nikki Krzmarzick, and Geoffrey Rutledge, University of St. Thomas; Mike Demmon, University of Nevada, Reno; and Heather Jensen and Roxanne Kirkwood, Texas Woman's University. For writing and revising—and revising some more—we remain indebted to you. After all, good student writing, the kind that you have produced, is what this book is all about.

And we cannot forget our valued and imaginative colleagues, Stacey Sherrif (The Pennsylvania State University) and Brent Henze (East Carolina University), who served as our technology consultants for this project. Consummate professionals, they helped us envision and frame Chapter 6, "Online Documents," and Chapter 7, "Visual Documents," providing more good information than we could possibly use.

We want to thank those colleagues who reviewed *The Writer's Harbrace Handbook* throughout the course of its development. Their astute comments, frank responses, and thoughtful suggestions helped shape what is the final version—until the next edition. We thank them for taking the time out of their already busy schedules to help us.

Handbook Reviewers

James Barcus, Baylor University; Patrick Christle, University of Tennessee-Knoxville; Elaine Coney, Southwest Mississippi Community College; Laurie Cubbison, Radford University; Twyla Davis, Bladen Community College; Tiffany Griffith, University of Evansville; Terriann Gaston, University of Texas at Arlington; Richard Hay, University of Wisconsin-Milwaukee; Keith Hunter, North Idaho College; Khristian Kay, Lakeland College; Thomas Long, Thomas Nelson Community College; Margaret Loweth, Loyola University-Chicago; Kelly Martin and Peggy Vera, Collin County Community

College; Sandee McGlaun, North Georgia College and State University; Michelle Sidler, Auburn University; Allison Smith, Middle Tennessee State University; Phillip Wedgeworth and Cheryl Windham, Jones County Junior College.

Focus Group Participants

John Buckuold, Scott Downing, Laura Durnell, Janet Flood, Brenda Kilianski, Carolyn Leeb, Scott Markwell, Michael Meyer, Eileen Seifert, Salli Berg Seeley, and Christine Sneed, De Paul University; Dale Adams, Lee College; Diane Whitley Bogard, Austin Community College; Linda Brender, Macomb Community College; Hugh Burns, Texas Woman's University; Amy Childers, North Georgia College and State University; Maria Clayton, Middle Tennessee State University; Daniel Ferguson and Patricia Knight, Amarillo College; Bea Hugetz, Alvin Community College; Glen Hutchinson, University of North Carolina-Charlotte; Craig Jacobsen, Mesa Community College; Patricia Jenkins, University of Alaska-Anchorage; Martina Kusi-Mensah, Montgomery College; Marjorie Lynn, University Michigan-Dearborn; Beth Maxfield, Blinn College; Donald Pardlow, Floyd College; Carolyn Poor, Wharton County Junior College; Beverly Reed, Stephen F. Austin State University; Marti Singer, Georgia State University; Sarah Spring, Texas A&M University; Stephanie Woods, Hinds Community College.

Finally, we are grateful to our friends and families. Although our faces toward the screen meant our backs toward you, you were never far from our thoughts. After all, without you, our work would be neither possible nor worthwhile.

To all of you reading this preface and using or considering using this handbook for the first time, know that we are grateful to you too. In fact, if you have advice for how we might improve the next edition or if we can help you in any way, write us c/o Thomson Wadsworth, English Editorial Department, 25 Thomson Place, Boston, MA 02210.

Cheryl Glenn
Loretta Gray
January 2006

The

WRITER'S HARBRACE HANDBOOK

logical Association (APA), *The Chicago Manual of Style* (CMS), and *The CBE Manual for Authors, Editors, and Publishers* (CSE/CBE). (*The Writer's Harbrace Handbook* itself is edited according to *The Chicago Manual of Style,* which is the style guide used by most publishers.) We have added over forty-five new citation examples to the MLA chapter, giving special attention to the citing of sources accessed through databases. All of the documentation chapters have easy-to-follow, color-coded visual examples of each type of citation (for a book, an article, and an online source), showing the major components and their exact arrangement. In addition, tip boxes remind students of all the steps they need to follow as they compose their bibliographies.

- **More Visuals** Additional images now reinforce or demonstrate the written components of this handbook. Most chapters now feature instructive visuals. For instance, in Chapter 8, "Writing Arguments," cartoons illustrate many of the rhetorical fallacies. In the research and documentation chapters, annotated visuals, such as screen shots of databases and Web sites, help students learn how to locate in these kinds of sources the information they need for their bibliographies. In Chapter 16, "Writing to Interpret Literature," a new student paper analyzing "Everyday Use," a short story by Alice Walker, incorporates stills from the film version of the story. Most of the student-generated papers in this handbook now include some kind of visual—photograph, table, or figure. In the process of referring to the visuals in this book, students will come to understand the specific ways these features communicate meaning to an audience, meaning that supplements and enhances what words convey.

Instructor Supplements

Instructor's Flex-Files

Flex-Files, written by Professors Wendy Sharer (East Carolina University) and Eve Weiderhold (University of North Carolina, Greensboro), are designed to give you maximum flexibility in planning and customizing your course. Providing an abundance of materials, the Flex-Files are organized in two main sections. "Part One: Questions for Teachers" raises a variety of pedagogical questions (and gives possible solutions) for you to consider when teaching your course with this handbook. "Part Two: Sample Syllabi and Activities" offers sample syllabi with possible assignments for a semester-long course and for a quarter-long course. Additionally, this section contains sample in-class collaborative learning activities, technology-oriented activities, and critical thinking and writing activities. The Flex-Files also include the following supplementary materials: (1) an ESL insert aimed at helping mainstream instructors teach writing effectively to their ESL students, (2) an insert on disability issues as they relate to teaching first-year composition, (3) the Answer Key for the exercises in the handbook, and (4) the Answer Key for the *College Workbook.*

ThomsonNOW™

Help your students boost their writing skills by empowering them with this Web-based, multimedia, writing assessment and learning program—ThomsonNOW. This study system helps students understand what they know, as well as what they don't know, and build study strategies to "fill in the gaps" and master the crucial rudimentary concepts of writing. Using a variety of technologies to accommodate many learning styles, ThomsonNOW covers all aspects of writing, arming students with interactive learning tools, such as *Diagnostic Quizzes, Personalized Study Plans,* a direct link to vMentor™ tutoring, and *Multimedia Tutorials.* These tools will help students master the fundamentals of writing and build their confidence as they become more effective writers.

WRITING AND THE RHETORICAL SITUATION

Elements of the rhetorical situation.

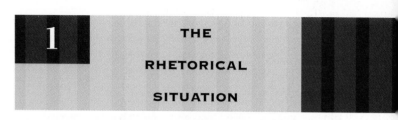

1

THE

RHETORICAL

SITUATION

Rhetoric, the purposeful use of language, pervades your daily activities. You cannot read your mail, fill out an employment application, or answer an exam question without using rhetoric to analyze what you are reading or to produce language that others will understand. Every day, you use rhetoric as you read and write—whether you are reading class assignments, directions for your stereo system, course syllabi, or e-mails or submitting written assignments, answering questions in class, instant messaging with your friends, or writing a memo to your professor. Every day, you are surrounded by rhetoric and rhetorical opportunities, and you have been reading, writing, and speaking rhetorically for most of your life.

This chapter explains reading and writing rhetorically as processes, each a series of sometimes overlapping steps that help you understand these four elements of the rhetorical situation (**1a**):

- exigence (**1b**),
- purpose (**1c**),
- audience (**1d**), and
- context (**1e**).

Writing rhetorically helps you to fulfill a variety of class assignments, some of which are discussed in this handbook:

- an essay from personal experience (**4h**),
- an argument from personal experience and research (**8j**),
- an argument based on research (chapters **9–15**),
- an interpretation of a literary text (**16g**),
- a field report and a lab report (**17d**, **18d**),
- a Web page for an organization (**6e–f**),
- a business letter and a résumé (**19b**, **19d**), and
- a business plan (**19f**).

Whatever form an assignment takes, writing rhetorically (just like reading rhetorically) involves a process of active engagement, an ability to interact with a text, step by step, until it fulfills its purpose, transferring its meaning to its audience.

1a Understanding the rhetorical situation

As a communicator, you use visual and verbal language purposefully, every day, in terms of a **rhetorical situation,** the context in which you are interpreting a reading or composing a piece of writing or a visual (see fig. 1.1). When you read and write rhetorically—whether in or out of school, as the sender or the receiver—you have a clear sense of the rhetorical situation and the specific elements that constitute it.

Fig. 1.1. The rhetorical situation.

The **writer** in a rhetorical situation is the person who identifies the **exigence,** the reason or problem that impels that person to write in the first place. When purposeful language can resolve the exigence, the situation is rhetorical. The writer then prepares a **message** (information delivered through visual or verbal means) with the **purpose** of resolving that exigence. But to fulfill that purpose, the writer must gauge the message in terms of the intended **audience,** the reader or readers who have the capability of resolving the exigence or problem. Whether or not that audience works to resolve the exigence, it reads, hears, or sees the message within a specific **context,** the constraints (obstacles) and resources (positive influences) in the environment surrounding the rhetorical situation. Those constraints and resources include whatever else has already been said on the subject; when, where, and through what medium the transaction between writer and audience takes place; and the writer's relationship with the audience, the writer's credibility (or believability), and the appropriateness of the message in terms of both content and delivery.

Reading and writing rhetorically offer you the opportunity to consider each of these elements separately as well as in combination. You can actively engage a text by establishing the writer's credibility, purpose, intended audience, context, and overall message and establishing the necessary interdependence of these elements. For instance, a writer's purpose must be appropriate for the intended audience and the context; the writer's choice of audience might change according to the purpose or context; the context affects the audience and the writer's purpose (see 1e).

By reading and writing rhetorically, you can also evaluate the thesis statement, the key points, and the amount of support each point merits, as well as what needs to be said and what is purposefully left unsaid. Therefore, when you *read* rhetorically, you read more efficiently and effectively—and you can talk knowledgeably about what you have read (see chapter 2). When you *write* rhetorically, you generate new ideas and communicate them clearly and concisely to your audience (see chapters 3 and 4)—and you improve your understanding of what you have read.

1b Writing to an exigence

The exigence is the particular problem or situation that calls for words. A parking violation, a birth, a college application, and an engagement—these are all events that compel people to write. Words—either spoken or written—can resolve the problem of fining a parking violator, announcing a birth, awarding college admission, or inviting wedding guests. Once you determine the exigence for your writing—the reason that impels you to write—you will be better able to gauge all the elements of your writing (from word choice to organizational pattern) in terms of your overall purpose.

Natural disasters provide exigencies for writing and speaking, often with the purpose of stimulating fundraising and relief efforts.

BEYOND THE RULE

EXIGENCE

Historical events of varying significance often serve as the exigencies for writing. When, over the past few years, the football teams of the University of Oregon, the University of Southern California, and Auburn University were excluded from the national championship, journalists and fans alike complained to Bowl Championship Series officials. The December 2004 earthquake and tsunami disaster in southeast Asia provided many people—from journalists to schoolchildren—with a reason to write and speak. For more information, see **www.harbrace.com**.

1c Writing with a specific purpose

As soon as you know that words can resolve an exigence or address a particular need or situation, you can concentrate on the general purpose of those words. Writers must clarify their purpose, and readers should be influenced according to that purpose—whether the writer wants to express feelings about something, amuse or entertain, report information, explain or evaluate the significance of information, analyze a situation, clarify a point, invite the audience to consider alternative points of view, or argue for or against a course of action.

Depending on the writer's overall purpose, then, the message (whether composed or read) can be classified as expressive, expository, or argumentative. Any of these types of writing can be used to help fulfill a writer's overall purpose.

(1) Expressive writing emphasizes the writer's feelings and reactions to people, objects, events, or ideas.

Personal letters and journals are often expressive, as are many essays and short stories. The following example (paragraph 1) comes from an essay designed to convey how the author feels about the relationship he had with his father. (For ease of reference, each of the sample paragraphs in this chapter is numbered.)

1   At just about the hour when my father died, soon after dawn one February morning when ice coated the windows like cataracts, I banged my thumb with a hammer. Naturally I swore at the hammer, the reckless thing, and in the moment of swearing I thought of what my father would say: "If you'd try hitting the nail it would go in a whole lot faster. Don't you know your thumb's not as hard as that hammer?" We were both doing carpentry that day, but far apart. He was building cupboards at my brother's place in Oklahoma; I was at home in Indiana putting up a wall in the basement to make a bedroom for my daughter. By the time my mother called with the news of his death—the long distance wires whittling her voice until it seemed too thin to bear the weight of what she had to say—my thumb was swollen. A week or two later a white scar in the shape of a crescent moon began to show above the cuticle, and month by month it rose across the pink sky of my thumbnail. It took the better part of a year for the scar to disappear, and every time I noticed it I thought of my father.

—SCOTT RUSSELL SANDERS, "The Inheritance of Tools"

(2) Expository writing focuses more on objects, events, or ideas than on the writer's feelings about them.

Textbooks, news accounts, scientific reports, and encyclopedia articles are usually expository, as are many of the essays students are expected to write in college. When you report, explain, clarify, or assess, you are practicing exposition. Paragraph 2 is excerpted from a book that explains how paleoanthropologists—in this case, a paleoanthropologist named Mac—discover their prizes.

2　　Searching only in the most promising areas isn't the key to [Mac's] success; perseverance is. He walks the same territory over and over again, changing courses around obstacles, and he tells his people to do the same. If you walked to the left around this bush yesterday, then walk to the right today. If you walked into the sun yesterday, then walk with the sun at your back today. And most of all, walk, walk, walk, and *look* while you are doing it. Don't daydream; don't scan the horizon for shade; ignore the burning sun even when the temperature reaches 135°F. Keep your eyes on the ground searching for that elusive sliver of bone or gleaming tooth that is not just any old animal, fossilized and turning to rubble, but a hominid. Those are the prizes we seek; those are the messengers from the past.

　　　　　—ALAN WALKER AND PAT SHIPMAN, *The Wisdom of the Bones*

(3) Argumentative writing is intended to influence the reader's attitudes and actions.

Most writing is to some extent an argument. Through the choice and arrangement of material, even something as apparently straightforward as a résumé can be an argument for an interview. However, writing is usually called argumentative if it clearly supports a specific position (see chapter 8). In paragraph 3, note how the writer calls for students to claim their own educations.

3　　The first thing I want to say to you who are students, is that you cannot afford to think of being here to *receive* an education; you will do much better to think of yourselves as being here to *claim* one. One of the dictionary definitions of the verb "to claim" is: *to take as the rightful owner; to assert in the face of possible contradiction.* "To receive" is *to come into possession of; to act as receptacle or container for; to accept as authoritarian or true.* The difference is that between acting and being acted-upon, and . . . it can literally mean the difference between life and death.　　—ADRIENNE RICH, "Claiming an Education"

Writers need to identify their overall purpose for each piece of writing, knowing that they can tap various methods of development (such as narration, description, and cause-and-effect analysis; see 3g) to work toward that goal. Whether you are the reader or the writer, however, you must assess the rhetorical purpose. For instance, when you are the reader, you want to assess the overall purpose of the writing in order to know how best to respond. If you can identify specific words or passages that convey the writer's purpose, you can discern whether the writer wants you to be entertained, informed, or persuaded. When you are the writer, you want to compose a message that responds to an exigence and fulfills a purpose while also alerting your intended audience to that purpose. If you are writing in response to a specific assignment, talk with your instructor or examine your assignment sheet to review which elements of the rhetorical situation (purpose, context, and audience) have already been set for you (see 5a(2)).

CHECKLIST for Assessing Purpose

- Has your instructor provided a purpose for your writing, or are you defining a purpose on your own? Are you trying primarily to express how you feel?

- Are you writing to improve your self-understanding or trying to help others understand you better?

- Are you trying to be entertaining or inspiring? How easily does your topic lend itself to your purpose? What examples or choice of words will help you fulfill that purpose?

- Are you writing primarily to convey information? Are you trying to teach others something they do not know or to demonstrate that you have knowledge in common?

- Are you writing primarily to argue for or against a course of action? Do you want your readers to stop a certain behavior, to undertake a specific action, or to consider alternative points of view?

- Do you have more than one purpose in writing? Which one is primary? How can the other purposes help you achieve your primary one? Or are some of your purposes in conflict?

Exercise 1

Select one of the following subjects, and write two paragraphs that begin to develop an expressive, expository, or argumentative essay on that subject.

1. your finances
2. your generation
3. your career goals
4. your computer expertise
5. your favorite musical group
6. volunteer work
7. a memorable lesson
8. music or dance performances
9. student housing
10. your closest relative

1d Considering audience

A clear understanding of the audience—its values, concerns, and knowledge—helps writers tailor their writing in terms of length, quality and quantity of details, the kind of language used, and the examples that will be most effective. Of course, the audience is anyone who reads the text, but that broader audience includes the writer's intended audience, those people whom the writer considers capable of being influenced by the words or who are capable of bringing about change. Some writers like to plan and draft essays with their purpose and their audience clearly in mind; others like to focus first on purpose and attend to their audience when they are revising. (See chapters 2 and 3.) As a writer, you will need to think clearly, at some point, about who exactly will be reading what you write and ask yourself whether your choices are appropriate for that audience.

(1) A specialized audience is predisposed to the message.

A **specialized audience** has a demonstrated interest in the subject. If a relative died as the result of drunk driving, you might become a member of a specialized audience: people whose lives have been affected by alcohol abuse. You would probably be interested in alcohol-abuse information that is specifically geared to people who have had experiences like yours. And if you decided to write about the harm done through alcohol abuse, you would probably direct your text to members of an organization such as Alcoholics Anonymous or Mothers Against Drunk Driving, who constitute a specialized audience.

Any group (such as nutritionists, police officers, or social workers) that has an area of expertise, an agenda, or a specific interest can be a specialized audience, one that you will want to address accordingly. Depending on the topic, then, you can usually assume that every member of a specialized audience has an interest in your subject and some knowledge of it.

You will want to consider your specialized audience—what they know that you do not, how much and what sorts of information you might provide them, and how best to develop your information—in terms of your overall purpose. You will be writing to readers with some degree of expertise, so you will want to establish common ground with them by mentioning areas of agreement, acknowledging their expertise, and adjusting your tone and language choices to their knowledge and attitudes. (See 4a(3) and chapter 32.) You will also want to provide your audience with new information—or a new way of understanding information with which they are already familiar.

A general reader might be surprised by the emotional content of the following excerpt, which was created for a specialized audience, one already familiar with the dire consequences of drunk driving.

When writing to a specialized audience, take into account the needs, interests, and values of its members.

4   Early on Sunday morning, September 18, 1999, Jacqueline Saburido, 20, and four friends were on their way home from a birthday party. Reggie Stephey, an 18-year-old star football player, was on his way home from drinking beer with some buddies. On a dark road on the outskirts of Austin, Texas, Reggie's SUV veered into the Oldsmobile carrying Jacqui and the others. Two passengers in the car were killed at the scene and two were

rescued. Within minutes, the car caught fire. Jacqui was pinned in the front seat on the passenger side. She was burned over 60% of her body; no one thought she could survive. But Jacqui lived. Her hands were so badly burned that her fingers had to be amputated. She lost her hair, her ears, her nose, her left eyelid and much of her vision. She has had more than 50 operations since the crash and has many more to go.

In June 2001 Reggie Stephey was convicted of two counts of intoxication manslaughter for the deaths of Jacqui's two friends. He was sentenced to seven years in prison and fined $20,000.

—**TEXAS DEPARTMENT OF TRANSPORTATION**, "Jacqui's Story"

Even knowing the meaning of every word in the preceding paragraphs does not guarantee that you will be interested in what the author is arguing or that you will make any changes in your drinking habits. Nevertheless, the passage is aimed at a specialized audience of people, who are committed to ending drunk driving.

Many of the essays you will be assigned to write in college—in English, history, economics, psychology, and the sciences, for example—are for a specialized audience, and often that audience is your instructor, who is already familiar with the subject matter. For example, if you are writing an essay about molecular mapping for your biology instructor, it is not necessary to define *chromosomes*. Instead, use your essay to communicate your understanding of the molecular process or of its connections with various physical characteristics. (See chapter **18**.)

Writing for a specialized audience does not mean that you have to know more than the members of that audience, nor does it mean that you have to impress them with your interpretation. Since no one knows everything about a subject, members of a specialized audience will usually appreciate thinking about their subject in a new way, even if they are not learning new information.

(2) A diverse audience represents a range of expertise and interest.

A **diverse audience** consists of readers with differing levels of expertise and varying interest in your subject. For example, if you are writing about upgrading computer software in a report that will be read by all the department heads of a company, you should be aware that some of your readers probably know more about software than others, including you. But you can also assume that all of your readers share a willingness to learn about new material if it is presented clearly and respectfully by someone who is establishing common ground with them.

Paragraph 5 helps a diverse audience of readers understand an unusual illness that put a young man in the hospital.

5   I first met Greg in April 1977, when he arrived at Williamsbridge Hospital. Lacking facial hair, and childlike in manner, he seemed younger than his twenty-five years. He was fat, Buddha-like, with a vacant, bland face, his blind eyes roving at random in their orbits, while he sat motionless in his wheelchair. If he lacked spontaneity and initiated no exchanges, he responded promptly and appropriately when I spoke to him, though odd words would sometimes catch his fancy and give rise to associate tangents or snatches of song and rhyme. Between questions, if the time was not filled, there tended to be a deepening silence; though if this lasted for more than a minute, he might fall into Hare Krishna chants or a soft muttering of mantras. He was still, he said, "a total believer," devoted to the group's doctrines and aims.

—**OLIVER SACKS,** "The Last Hippie," *An Anthropologist on Mars*

Oliver Sacks writes to a diverse audience. Although its members share an interest in science writing, and medical stories in particular, they come to Sacks's essay with varying levels of expertise. Therefore, Sacks describes a medical condition in words easily understood by a wide audience. When you are writing to a diverse audience, you too need to establish what the members are likely to have in common in order to make appropriate word choices (see chapters 32–34) and include appropriate details (see 3f(1)).

There will be times, however, when you simply will not know much about your audience, even though your purpose for writing might be to evaluate a product or argue for a course of action. When this is the case, it may help you to imagine a thoughtful audience of educated adults, with whom you may even share common ground. Such an audience is likely to include people with different backgrounds and cultural values (see 8e(2)), so be careful not to assume that you are writing for readers who are exactly like you (see 32d). To a considerable extent, the language you use will determine whether diverse readers feel included in or excluded from your work. Be careful to avoid jargon or technical terms that would be understood only by a specialized audience. If you must use a specialized term, explain what you mean by it. (See 32c and 32e.)

(3) Multiple audiences read for different reasons.

Writers often need to consider multiple audiences, a task related to—yet different from—addressing a diverse audience. When you address a diverse audience, you try to reach everyone. When you consider multiple audiences, you gauge your choice of words and tone according to your primary audience, knowing that a secondary audience might have access to your text. At work, for instance, you address your research report, employee evaluation, or proposal to your boss. But if you know that she will circulate the text among your colleagues, you adjust your words and tone accordingly. You might not be as frank in writing as you would be in person; you might omit potentially hurtful information or temper your words. If you are asked to evaluate the performance of an employee under your supervision, you might be asked to send the evaluation to your boss, who is looking to see whether you are a competent supervisor, and a copy of it to the employee, who is looking for praise. When you know that your rhetorical situation includes multiple audiences, you can better select your words.

 The use of e-mail for communication (see **6b**) has increased the likelihood of writing for multiple audiences because messages can be forwarded easily—and not always with the writer's permission. Other electronic texts, such as those generated by listserv dialogues or online conversations through a Web site, also reach multiple audiences. When writing for electronic submission, consider whether anyone outside your primary audience might read your work.

When writing essays in college, you may also find yourself writing for multiple audiences. For example, you may use an English essay as the foundation for developing another essay for your psychology or history class. You may take a linked or team-taught course in which you submit written work for evaluation by two instructors (your two primary audiences). Or you may write an essay for a general audience (which constitutes your secondary audience) and submit it to an instructor who is a specialist in your subject (and your primary audience).

In each of these cases, you are writing for multiple audiences. This kind of writing requires that you consider a variety of attitudes and positions (see 8d–e). Considering different points of view is helpful when planning an essay and also when reading what you have drafted as you prepare to revise it (see chapter 4). The following checklist may also help you assess your audience.

CHECKLIST for Assessing the Audience

- Who is going to be reading what you write?
- What do you know about the members of your audience? What characteristics can you safely assume they have? What do they have in common? How are they different?
- What values do you share with them? How do you differ from them?
- How much do they already know about your topic?
- What kind of language is appropriate or inappropriate for this audience?
- How open are the members of this audience to views that may be different from their own?
- What level of expertise will they expect from you?
- What do you *not* know about this audience? What assumptions would be risky?
- Are you writing with a primary audience in mind but expecting a secondary audience to also read what you have written? If so, have you clearly identified the primary audience so that you can address that audience specifically, while recognizing the expectations of the secondary audience?

Exercise 2

Examine an introductory and an advanced textbook in a discipline of your choice, and locate a passage in each devoted to the same issue or concept. Photocopy these passages, and prepare a class presentation in which you explain how they reveal differences in audience.

1e   Sending and receiving a message within a context

Context includes time and place, writer and audience, and the medium of delivery—the circumstances under which writer and reader communicate. Social, political, religious, and other cultural factors influence context, as do the constraints and resources of the rhetorical situation. Therefore, what you are able to produce in writing is always influenced (positively or negatively) by the context.

Your background and beliefs often shape the stance (or attitude) you take when writing. An essay written shortly before your school's winter break, for example, could be influenced by both your anticipation of a combined religious holiday and family reunion and your uncertainty as to whether your audience shares that anticipation. Or an international crisis, such as the war in Iraq or the tsunami in southeast Asia, might prompt you to reconsider the purpose of an essay you are drafting for your international economics course. Writers who consider the time, place, and other factors of the context in which they are writing, as well as their audience, are more likely to communicate their ideas effectively.

The medium in which you are writing is also part of the context. Writing material for a Web page or another online medium requires you to think differently about organization, design, and style than does writing a traditional academic essay or business letter. Depending on your familiarity with and aptitude in using the technology, writing electronically may demand a good deal more time from you, too. Considering the method of delivery for a Web page, for example, requires making different kinds of rhetorical decisions than you would make for a text in a wholly static print medium. (See chapter 6.)

When you read the work of other writers, you will sometimes find that the context is specifically stated, as in the following passage. You can tell the time, place, and event that Churchill refers to in this one sentence.

6   In the twenty-second month of the war against Nazism we meet here in this old Palace of St. James, itself not unscarred by the fire of the enemy, in order to proclaim the high purposes and resolves of the lawful constitutional Governments of Europe whose countries have been overrun; and we meet here also to cheer the hopes of free men and free peoples throughout the world.   —**WINSTON CHURCHILL**, "Until Victory Is Won"

Often, however, the context must be inferred. Whether the context is announced or not, it is important that writers and readers identify and consider it.

CHECKLIST for Assessing the Context

- Under what circumstances of time and place are you writing?
- Under what circumstances will your writing probably be read? Will it be one among many texts or documents being received, or is your particular message eagerly awaited? In either case, how can you help your reader quickly see the purpose and thrust of your work under these circumstances?
- How has your response to the task been influenced by other events in your life, your country, or the world?
- Have you been asked to write a text of a specific length? If length has not been specified, what seems appropriate for your purpose and audience?
- What document design (see chapter 7) is appropriate given the context for your writing?

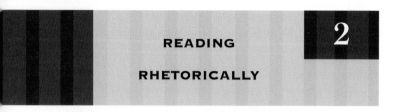

Reading is more pleasurable and profitable when undertaken as a series of steps. Every time you pick up a newspaper, glance over the headlines, turn to the sports section, skim over the first page, and then go back to read the story that most intrigues you, you are reading rhetorically. Sometimes, as with an article about baseball players who claim that they and many of their teammates use steroids, you find yourself rereading the text to make sure that you understand the differences between what the sportswriter is reporting and what the baseball players (whom the writer quotes) are alleging.

Whether you are reading the sports pages, a church bulletin, or your biology assignment, you are reading rhetorically every time you find yourself previewing a text, reading for content, responding, and rereading. When you follow these steps, you can more easily determine how difficult the text will be to understand, what you are likely to learn from it, and how useful it will be to you—assessments that will improve your reading comprehension. In addition, you can use these steps to consider the features of the rhetorical situation (writer, audience, exigence, purpose, and context).

This chapter explains the process of reading rhetorically and describes ways for you to monitor your personal and intellectual responses to a text. Whether **chronological** (in order of occurrence) or **recursive** (alternating between moving forward and looping back), reading rhetorically is a process of

- previewing (**2a**),
- reading for content (**2b**), and
- rereading (**2c**).

This chapter will not only help you move through the process but will also

- help you distinguish between actual content and your personal response to that content (**2d**) and
- encourage you to write daily about your reading (**2e**).

Powered by **Clickability**

 Click to Print

SAVE THIS | EMAIL THIS | Close

Caminiti comes clean

Ex-MVP says he won award while using steroids

Posted: Tuesday May 28, 2002 4:16 PM

ATLANTA (CNNSI.com) -- Former major leaguer Ken Caminiti says he was on steroids when he won the National League Most Valuable Player Award in 1996, according to an exclusive report in this week's issue of *Sports Illustrated.*

But even though it left him with health problems that continue to this day, Caminiti defended his use of steroids and told SI's Tom Verducci the practice is now so rampant in baseball that he would not discourage others from doing the same. Caminiti told Verducci that he continued to use steroids for the rest of his career, which ended last season when he hit .228 with 15 home runs and 41 RBIs for the Texas Rangers and the Atlanta Braves.

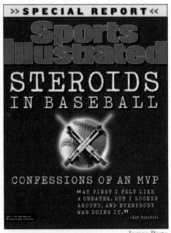

>> SPECIAL REPORT <<

STEROIDS IN BASEBALL

CONFESSIONS OF AN MVP

"AT FIRST I FELT LIKE A CHEATER, BUT I LOOKED AROUND, AND EVERYBODY WAS DOING IT." —Ken Caminiti

James Porto

•SI Report: Caminiti comes clean

An article about a controversial situation or issue may require careful rereading.

2a Previewing for an initial impression

You often preview reading material—when you thumb through a news-paper or a magazine looking for articles that stir your interest. A system-atic preview, though, gives you more reliable results and makes your reading more efficient. When reading rhetorically, you systematically preview a text by reading the author's name and the title, then skimming the entire text to get a sense of how the information is organized and what you can expect from reading the text.

You will also want to assess what the reading demands of you in terms of time, effort, and previous knowledge. By previewing the length of a text, you can estimate how much time you need to set aside for reading. By reading the summary (often located in the preface or introductory chapter) or the abstract (usually preceding a scholarly article), you can decide whether the text will be useful. If the text is difficult, you can preview the major points, often found in headings (see 17c and 18c).

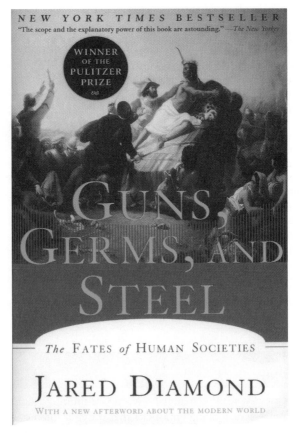

The title of Jared Diamond's book—*Guns, Germs, and Steel: The Fates of Human Societies*—accurately reflects the contents.

FEATURES OF A TEXT FOR PREVIEWING

Title

The title (and subtitle, if any) often reveals the focus of a text and sometimes even its thesis (see 3c). When a title does not provide much information, look at the chapter titles or section headings to get a clearer sense of the work as a whole as well as to gauge how much you may already know about the subject.

Author

If you know anything about the author, you may have an idea about the expertise or tone being brought to the topic. If Dave Barry is the author, you can expect the essay to be humorous, but if Anna Quindlen is the author, you can expect the essay to be timely and political. Jared Diamond's science writing is highly respected and widely read, for he has earned a Pulitzer Prize (for *Guns, Germs, and Steel*), membership in the MacArthur Foundation fellowship (otherwise known as a "genius award"), and a National Medal of Science.

Length

Considering a text's length allows you to estimate how much time you should set aside for reading. By checking length, you can also estimate whether a work is long enough to include useful content or so short that it might only skim the surface of the subject it addresses.

Directories

In addition to previewing title and author, you will also want to examine various directories. The **table of contents** identifies the chapters and main sections within a book, and the **index**, at the back, lists in alphabetical order the specific topics covered. A **bibliography**, or list of research sources and related works, indicates how much research was involved in writing the book and can also direct you to additional sources. Checking these directories can help you determine whether the book has the kind of information you are looking for, where you can find it, and how much or what sections of the book you want to read.

Visual Aids

The extent to which visual aids are useful varies, but a quick check for graphs and other illustrations can help you decide whether the work has the kind of information you need, depending on the topic you are researching.

(Continued on page 22)

(Continued from page 21)

Summaries

Both books and articles often contain summaries, and reading a summary can help you decide whether the work as a whole will be helpful. Reading a summary can also help you follow a difficult text because the summary tells you the major points. Summaries can often be found in the preface of a book, as well as in introductory and concluding chapters. Scholarly articles often begin with a summary identified as an abstract (see **9c** and **10b(2)**). Within other kinds of articles, the introductory and concluding paragraphs often include summaries (see **9c**). Sometimes, book summaries can be found on the inside or back cover.

CONTENTS

5

The table of contents shows how the material in Diamond's book is arranged and indicates how fully that material is developed.

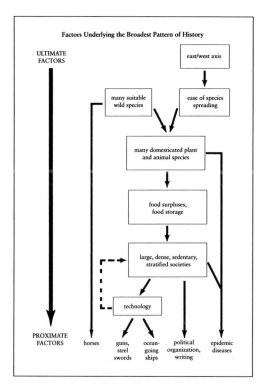

In chapter 4, Diamond uses a visual aid to map out the causal chain of factors that he believes underlies patterns of history—especially the development of steel and guns and the spread of germs.

In addition to assessing the title, author, length, directories, visual aids, and summary of a text you are previewing, assess how much you already know about the subject. If you are unfamiliar with the subject matter, you might want to start with a less demanding treatment of the topic, either in print or online. Finally, if you know that your values or opinions differ greatly from those of the author, you will want to pay close attention to passages in the text that you might be tempted to dismiss without reading carefully.

Previewing helps make your reading easier and helps you select appropriate research materials (see chapter 9). But remember that previewing a text is not the same as reading it for understanding.

SCIENCE

OVER 1 MILLION COPIES SOLD

"Fascinating. . . . Lays a foundation for understanding human history."
—Bill Gates

"Artful, informative, and delightful. . . . There is nothing like a radically new angle of vision for bringing out unsuspected dimensions of a subject, and that is what Jared Diamond has done."   —William H. McNeill,
New York Review of Books

"This is a brilliantly written, passionate, whirlwind tour through 13,000 years of history on all the continents—a short history of everything about everybody. The origins of empires, religion, writing, crops, and guns are all here. By at last providing a convincing explanation for the differing developments of human societies on different continents, the book demolishes the grounds for racist theories of history. Its account of how the modern world was formed is full of lessons for our own future. After reading the first two pages, you won't be able to put it down."   —Paul R. Ehrlich, Bing Professor of
Population Studies, Stanford University

"An ambitious, highly important book." —James Shreeve, *New York Times Book Review*

"A book of remarkable scope, a history of the world in less than 500 pages which succeeds admirably, where so many others have failed, in analyzing some of the basic workings of culture process. . . . One of the most important and readable works on the human past published in recent years."   —Colin Renfrew, *Nature*

WINNER OF THE PHI BETA KAPPA AWARD IN SCIENCE

JARED DIAMOND is professor of geography at UCLA and author of the best-selling and award-winning *The Third Chimpanzee*. He is a recipient of a MacArthur Foundation fellowship and has been awarded a 1999 National Medal of Science.

With a new afterword extending the book's significance to today's economies and geopolitics

Cover design by Calvin Chu

Cover painting: Sir John Everett Millais, *Pizarro seizing the Inca of Peru*, 1845. Victoria & Albert Museum, London/Art Resource, NY

ISBN 0–393–31755–2
51695

9 780393 317558

W. W. NORTON
NEW YORK • LONDON

$16.95 USA $24.99 CAN.
www.wwnorton.com

The reviewers have summarized Diamond's book as well as evaluated its importance.

CHECKLIST for Previewing a Reading Selection

- What do you already know about this subject that you can use to connect with the text?
- What do the title and subtitle reveal about the way the subject is being treated?

- How long is this work, and how is it organized? What do the major divisions indicate to you?
- What information do the table of contents and the index provide about the book?
- Does the article include an abstract, or does the book include a summary?
- What do you know about this author that contributes to his or her credibility? If the author is unfamiliar, what biographical information could help you assess that credibility? (See 8c and 10a.)
- If there are graphs, figures, or other visual aids, what do they illustrate?
- Is there a bibliography that indicates how extensive and current the research is?
- Is the text suited to your level of understanding, or should you start with a simpler treatment of the same subject?
- Do you have strong feelings about this subject that could interfere with your ability to understand how it is treated in this text? (See 2d.)

2b Reading for content

Effective readers pay close attention to the words on the page and develop specific strategies for increasing their comprehension as well as for working through misunderstandings. After previewing a text, you should be able to determine what the author wants to communicate, to whom, and for what specific purpose. In other words, you can begin to read for content.

As you read, you will want to note the author's major points, perhaps by underlining or highlighting them. Particular words and key phrases often signal those important points: "There are *three* advantages to this proposal. . . . The *first* is . . . . The *second* is . . . ." The phrase *in other words* signals that the author is about to paraphrase a point—because it is important. And *in this article* (or *chapter*) introduces a statement of the author's focus or purpose, whereas *in summary, in conclusion,* and *the point I am making* place a significant emphasis on the information just presented. Thus, transitional words or phrases indicating sequencing (see 4d) or movement within a text help you

Eurasia's diverse and protein-rich cereals; hand planting of individual seeds, instead of broadcast sowing; tilling by hand instead of plowing by animals, which enables one person to cultivate a much larger area, and which also permits cultivation of some fertile but tough soils and sods that are difficult to till by hand (such as those of the North American Great Plains); lack of animal manuring to increase soil fertility; and just human muscle power, instead of animal power, for agricultural tasks such as threshing, grinding, and irrigation. These differences suggest that Eurasian agriculture as of 1492 may have yielded on the average more calories and protein per person-hour of labor than Native American agriculture did.

amazing— all by hand

interesting

Such differences in food production constituted a major ultimate cause of the disparities between Eurasian and Native American societies. Among the resulting proximate factors behind the conquest, the most important included differences in germs, technology, political organization, and writing. Of these, the one linked most directly to the differences in food production was germs. The infectious diseases that regularly visited crowded Eurasian societies, and to which many Eurasians consequently developed immune or genetic resistance, included all of history's most lethal killers: smallpox, measles, influenza, plague, tuberculosis, typhus, cholera, malaria, and others. Against that grim list, the sole crowd infectious diseases that can be attributed with certainty to pre-Columbian Native American societies were nonsyphilitic treponemas. (As I explained in Chapter 11, it remains uncertain whether syphilis arose in Eurasia or in the Americas, and the claim that human tuberculosis was present in the Americas before Columbus is in my opinion unproven.)

oh! I want to hear more

This continental difference in harmful germs resulted paradoxically from the difference in useful livestock. Most of the microbes responsible for the infectious diseases of crowded human societies evolved from very similar ancestral microbes causing infectious diseases of the domestic animals with which food producers began coming into daily close contact around 10,000 years ago. Eurasia harbored many domestic animal species and hence developed many such microbes, while the Americas had very few of each. Other reasons why Native American societies evolved so few lethal microbes were that villages, which provide ideal breeding grounds for epidemic diseases, arose thousands of years later in the Americas than in Eurasia; and that the three regions of the New World supporting urban

So contact w/livestock/ animals was a major factor w/ disease

When you annotate a printed text—that is, talk back to it—you read it actively and rhetorically.

grasp content. Transitional expressions—especially those indicating purpose, result, summary, repetition, exemplification, and intensification (see page 77)—alert you to important points. Such phrases identify opportunities for you to talk back to the text itself, as though you were carrying on a conversation with the author.

When reading from a book or periodical (a magazine or professional journal) that you own, you can underline, highlight, or add comments to passages that interest or confuse you, or that you question. Write in the margins and annotate key passages whenever you have something to say or a question to pose. If you have borrowed a book, you can use sticky notes to highlight and annotate the text. With an electronic text, you can print out a hard copy and annotate it or use your word-processing program to respond directly on the screen.

Reading for content means making sure you understand the words on the page. When you encounter a word that is new to you, the meaning may be defined in the text itself, or you may be able to infer the meaning from the way the word has been used. Whenever a new term appears in a critically important position such as a thesis statement (see 3c) or a conclusion (4b(2)), look it up in a college-appropriate dictionary (32e). But even language that is well chosen can sometimes be misleading because words have different specific meanings (**denotations**) as well as strong associations (**connotations**) that vary from reader to reader (see 33a) and culture to culture (see chapter 32)—depending on the rhetorical situation.

Your challenge as a reader, then, is to try to understand what exactly the author wanted the words to mean within the particular rhetorical situation, to understand as much as you can but to keep that understanding flexible enough to accommodate what will come. If you are reading a twenty-page chapter, you probably need a preliminary understanding of the first ten pages if you are going to understand the next ten. But if you later reread the entire chapter, your understanding of all the material is likely to deepen. Accordingly, effective readers usually reread texts that are important to them in order to master the content.

2c Rereading for understanding

Rereading is the easiest way to check your understanding of the content. Effective readers use their second pass through the material to determine the author's specific purpose and to note how the information is organized and how supporting ideas are developed (see chapter 3 and 6e). In addition to noting these general features, you can also scan the first and last sentences in every paragraph. The central idea of a paragraph, which suggests a sense of content and overall organization, can occur anywhere in the paragraph (see 4c), but it often appears in one of those two sentences.

2d Recognizing a personal response

Critical readers consciously work to keep their personal responses from interfering with their ability to understand. So, in addition to reading for content, they also keep track of what they think about or how they are reacting to this content. That is not to say that they read passively. Reading rhetorically means reading actively, noting where you agree or disagree, become frustrated or intrigued, sympathetic or annoyed—and keeping track of what feature of the writing (or of yourself) triggered each response: was it the writer's tone (see 4a(3)), an example that evoked a personal memory, a lapse in the organization (3d), the topic itself (3b), or a visual element such as a photo or illustration?

As you read, try to determine what the author thinks and why he or she holds that opinion. Then determine what *you* think and why *you* hold your opinion. In other words, what information do you agree or disagree with—and why? What passages brought to mind your own experience or expertise? What have you learned from your reading? What about this text confuses you? What would you like to know more about?

By noting personal responses and recognizing that they are independent of a work's content even if they are inspired by it, you can increase your understanding of the purposeful choices writers make when communicating with readers. Personal responses often serve as the basis for your own writing (see 2e). Often, good readers and writers use techniques from the following list.

TIPS FOR RECORDING PERSONAL RESPONSES

- Note passages that capture your attention. Underline or highlight your own copy; highlight with color when reading on a computer screen.

- Put a question mark in the margin when you do not understand a passage—or if you question its accuracy.

- Put an exclamation point in the margin when a statement or an example surprises you.

- Write *yes* or *no* in the margin when you agree or disagree. When a passage reminds you of another passage (or something else you have read), note that association in the margin. Keep a reading journal (see 3a(1)). Include at least one question or reservation about something you read each day.

- Correspond by e-mail with other people who are reading the same material (see chapter 6).

2e Writing daily about your reading

Effective readers write daily about their reading. Whether you keep a personal journal, a writer's notebook, or a reading journal (or, in some classes, participate in an online discussion forum; see 6c), you are taking the opportunity to write about your reading in terms of content and personal response. When you respond to a text in this way—listening to it, arguing with it, extending it, connecting it with your own experience—you will be more likely to engage the text, understand it, and remember it. Writing regularly about your reading, then, helps you increase your comprehension and identify responses that could be the seeds from which larger pieces of writing subsequently grow.

You can design your reading journal in such a way that you will benefit in terms of comprehension and creativity. One way to do this is to keep a **double-entry notebook,** a journal in which each entry has two distinct parts: summary and response. For example, if you keep your journal in a spiral notebook, you can use the left side of each page to summarize your understanding of what you have read (see 11b) and the right side to record your responses to it. (Or you might prefer to format word-processing files into columns.)

A first-year student created a double-entry notebook for her world geography course. When she read the substantial prologue to Diamond's book, she summarized his views about the course of history on the left-hand side of a page and responded to his thinking on the right-hand side:

Summary	Response
Diamond gives an overview of the reasons why history has "proceeded very differently for peoples all over the globe." He mentions the rise of literacy in comparison to illiteracy, the development of metal tools in some societies and stone tools in others, and he uses these comparisons to explain why some societies have so easily been able to infiltrate and conquer other ones. Then he moves to his meeting with local New Guinean politician Yali, who had many questions, all of which can be summarized in the following: "Why is it that you white people developed so much cargo and brought it to New Guinea, but we black people had little cargo of our own?" Diamond uses the rest of the prologue to map out a response having to do with the inequalities of wealth and power in the modern world, which he plans to explain. He decides to work within the confines of genetics, climate, irrigation systems, and so on. Finally, he summarizes his book in this way: "History followed different courses for different peoples because of differences among peoples' environments, not because of biological differences among peoples themselves."	Diamond demonstrates a deep global and historical perspective about the course of history for different people, yet part of me still wonders if he's being "politically correct." He writes that he and Yali "both knew perfectly well that New Guineans are on the average at least as smart as Europeans" (14). Yet despite the equality of intelligence, by A.D. 1500 the die had been cast: "empires with steel weapons were able to conquer or exterminate tribes with weapons of stone and wood" (16). I see that he's not justifying the outcome; rather he's trying to understand it so that things don't always work out that way: the whites don't continue to dominant nonwhite people. In fact, he writes that he's going to explain how white people picked up the technologies that became the basis of "civilization." He's also going to talk about racism, about how people from all over the world (from the Japanese to the Australians) think about aboriginal people as uncivilized. What I find really interesting is his explanation of why the New Guineans he knows seem, on the whole, smarter than the European people he knows. He explains the differences as survival on the part of New Guineans and as genetic resistance on the part of Europeans. In other words, dumb New Guineans probably died off, whereas dumb Europeans have been protected by social and medical advances, so they grow up, reproduce, and continue to depend on their resistance. I'm pretty sure he's using the word "European" to mean "whites."

Like this student, you will want to keep the entries devoted to summarizing content separated from those devoted to your personal response. This separation will come in handy when you need to review what you have written. When you are preparing for a written examination (see 5f), for example, you will be able to easily identify the entries that will help you remember content. And when you are involved in the brainstorming necessary for drafting an essay (see chapter 3), you can turn to those entries in which you recorded your own ideas, interpretations, questions, or reflections.

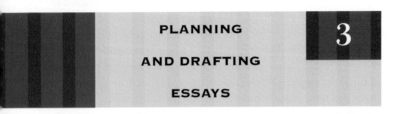

Experienced writers understand that writing is a process. Think of the writing you do out of school, and you will realize how experienced you already are at the process. When you compose an e-mail, for instance, you consider the audience, the message, and the tone you wish to convey. Even though you are writing quickly, you stop often to draft, cut and paste, and delete—just as you do when you are writing more slowly to fulfill an academic assignment. Whether you are writing in or out of school, you do so in terms of your purpose, audience, and context (see 1a), revising and editing all along the way.

This chapter will help you understand writing as a process and

- find good topics (3a),
- focus your ideas (3b),
- write a clear thesis statement (3c),
- organize your ideas (3d),
- express your ideas in a first draft (3e), and
- use various strategies to develop effective paragraphs and essays (3f and 3g).

Effective writers know they cannot do everything at once, so they generate, organize, develop, and clarify their ideas as well as polish their prose during a series of sometimes separate—but often overlapping—steps.

The writing process is **recursive,** which means that as you plan and draft an essay, you may need to return to a specific activity several times. For example, drafting may help you see that you need to go back and collect more ideas, modify your thesis, or even start over with a new one. Experienced writers expect the writing process to lead to new ideas as well as uncover passages in need of improvement.

Despite the infinite variations of the writing process, writing usually involves four basic, recursive stages, described below.

STAGES OF THE WRITING PROCESS

- **Prewriting** is the initial stage of the writing process. As soon as you begin thinking about a specific writing task, consider what is expected of you in terms of your intended audience, purpose, and context. Then start exploring your topic by talking with others working on the same assignment, keeping a journal, freewriting, or questioning. In short, do whatever it takes to energize your thinking and jump-start your writing.

- **Drafting** involves writing down your ideas quickly, writing as much as you can, without worrying about being perfect or staying on topic. The more ideas you get down on paper, the more options you will have as you begin to clarify your thesis and purpose for writing, organize, and revise. Progress is your goal at this stage, not perfection.

- **Revising** offers you the opportunity to focus your purpose for writing, establish a clear thesis statement (see 3c), and organize your ideas toward those ends (3d). This is the time to start stabilizing the overall structure of your essay as well as the structure of the individual paragraphs (3f and 4c) and to reconsider your introduction and conclusion (4b). Remember that revising means producing another draft for further revision and editing.

- **Editing** focuses on surface features: punctuation, spelling, word choice and Standardized English, grammar, and sentence structure (see 4f). As you prepare your work for final submission, consider reading it aloud to discover which sentence structures and word choices could be improved.

3a Selecting worthwhile subjects for writing

Whether you are assigned a subject or are free to respond to an exigence of your own choosing, you must consider what you already know—or would like to learn about—and what is likely to interest your audience (see 1d). The first step toward engaging an audience is to be interested in the subject yourself, so consider your interests and experience. Often the best subject is one drawn from your specific knowledge of hobbies, sports, jobs, or places. When subjects are important to you, they usually interest readers, especially when you write with a clear purpose and well-chosen details (see 1c and 3f(1)).

More often, however, you will be asked to write essays about subjects outside your personal experience but within your academic coursework.

If, for instance, you are assigned an essay for a course in ancient history, you may be responsible for choosing your topic—but it will have to be related to the course. In order to find material that interests you, look in your textbook, particularly in the sections listing suggestions for further reading. Go through your lecture notes, your reading journal, or any marginal annotations you have made for the course (see **2e**). Ask yourself whether any details of the subject have surprised, annoyed, or pleased you—if there is something you feel strongly about and would like to explore further. Writing about a subject is one of the best ways to learn about it, so use a writing assignment not only to impart information to your audience but also to satisfy yourself.

(1) Keeping a journal is one way to explore a subject.

Keeping a journal is a good way to generate subjects for essays. In a **personal journal,** you reflect on your experiences, using writing as a means to explore how you feel about what is happening in your life or in the world around you. You might focus on external events, such as what you think about a book or a film, or on your inner life, such as changes in your moods or attitudes. Writers who keep a personal journal usually write for their own benefit, but in the process of writing the journal—or reading it—they may discover subjects and exigencies they can use for essays.

Like a personal journal, a double-entry notebook (see **2e**) includes responses to experiences. In this case, however, the emphasis is on recording and exploring material for future projects. You might list quotations and observations that invite development; then, when time allows, you might also draft the opening pages of an essay, outline an idea for a story, or experiment with writing a poem.

Some writers prefer to keep a reading journal (see **2e**). You may find it convenient to keep your journal in a word-processing file on your computer, especially if you use a laptop. Whichever type of journal you keep or method you use to record your thoughts, feel free to write quickly, without worrying about spelling or grammar.

(2) Freewriting offers a risk-free way to explore a subject.

When **freewriting,** writers record whatever occurs to them, without stopping, for a limited period of time—often no more than ten minutes. They do not worry about whether they are repeating themselves or getting off track; they simply write to see what comes out. Freewriting is another good way to generate ideas for a writing assignment because no matter what you write, it will contain ideas and information you did not realize you had. Some writers use colored marking pens (or change the font in their word-processing program) to identify different topics generated by this activity.

In **directed freewriting,** you begin with a general subject and record whatever occurs to you about this subject during the time available. When Melissa Schraeder's English instructor asked her to write for five minutes, assessing some of the main challenges to being a happy and successful college student, she produced the freewriting shown below. (This freewriting represents the first step toward Melissa's essay, three different versions of which appear in chapter 4.)

Sometimes I feel like being successful in school and remaining sane are incompatible goals. Schoolwork's stressful, especially when working on those classes that I don't like, such as my math or science. This is why I have had to be creative in my study habits and patterns. One of the small compromises I make with myself is to invite a friend along to study with me. Studying seems less gloomy when done in pairs since it is comforting and motivating to know that you are not the only one who is working hard. The biggest challenge I face in maintaining my success and happiness as a college student though is balancing school and work. With tuition so high and all the extra expenses such as books and technology fees, most students have to work in order to stay afloat and I am certainly not exempt. I usually only work around 15 hours a week, but those 15 hours are crucial in the midst of exams and papers with strict deadlines. I always try to put my schoolwork first, so there are some weeks where I wish I didn't have to work at all!

As the color shading shows, Melissa's freewriting generated three possible strands of development for an essay about being a successful college student: managing stress, finding creative approaches to studying, and balancing work and school. Some of these strands overlap; all of them have to do with managing time and stress. But notice that she mentions the necessity of working while in school; she eventually decided to focus her essay on balancing the demands of her much-needed job with those of her schoolwork.

(3) Questioning pushes the boundaries of your subject.

You can also explore a subject by asking yourself some questions. The simplest questioning strategy for helping you explore a subject comes from journalism. **Journalists' questions**—*Who? What? When? Where? Why?* and *How?*—are easy to use and can help you discover ideas about any subject. Using journalists' questions to explore the subject of balancing schoolwork and a job could lead you to think about it in a number of ways: *Who* typically has to work part-time while in college? *What* should college students look for in a part-time job? *When* should students work? *Where* should students work? *Why* can part-time work be an important part of the college experience? And *how* can students balance part-time work with good schoolwork; *how* can a part-time job influence a student's attitude about schoolwork?

3b   Focusing a subject idea into a specific topic

By exploring your subject, you can discover productive strategies for development as well as a specific focus for your topic. As you prewrite, you will decide that some ideas seem worth pursuing but others seem inappropriate for your purpose, audience, or context. You will find yourself discarding ideas even as you develop new ones and determine your topic.

A simple analogy helps explain focus: when you take a picture of a landscape, you cannot photograph all that your eye can take in. You must focus on just part of it. As you aim the camera, you look through the viewfinder to make sure the subject is correctly framed and in focus. At this point, you may wish to move in closer and focus on one part of the scene, or you may decide to change the angle, using light and shadow to emphasize certain features of the landscape. You can think of your writing the same way—you focus and direct your ideas just as you focus and direct the lens of a camera, moving from a general subject to a more specific topic.

In addition to reviewing the ideas you have generated through strategies such as freewriting and questioning, you can also focus by thinking in terms of how the various rhetorical methods you might use for developing your ideas (see 3g) might take you in different directions. Responding to the exigence of "balancing a part-time job with schoolwork," Melissa needed to focus her subject into a narrow topic. Thus, she considered the subject in terms of the following rhetorical methods of development:

Like photographers, writers need to focus their ideas, moving from a general subject to a more specific topic.

- *Narration.* What kind of story can I tell about part-time work for college students?
- *Description.* What kind of part-time job do I have? What is my place of work like? How do my employers treat me?
- *Process analysis.* How have I gone about balancing my own part-time job with my schoolwork?
- *Cause-and-consequence analysis.* What have been the causes of my success in balancing my job with my schoolwork? Concentration? Commitment? What were some of the consequences when I made mistakes in balancing these two in the past? Exhaustion? Frustration? What is the primary cause? What are contributory causes?
- *Comparison and contrast.* How do my study habits and academic skills compare with those of students who do not work and those of students who do? How does my work-and-school lifestyle compare to my previous school-only lifestyle?
- *Classification and division.* How can I classify the different types of jobs that college students take on? How can I divide up the desirable qualities of jobs and employers? How many college students feel they must take a job?
- *Definition.* How do I define "success" in college? Is career experience as important as good grades? What constitutes a "good attitude" toward your education?

The following sentence suggests a focus on comparison and contrast:

Before I came to college and took on a part-time job, I spent all of my free time either studying or hanging out with friends.

This sentence focuses on cause and consequence:

> Now that I'm working part-time and taking classes full-time, I have little free time to spend with my friends or relax.

Sometimes a combination of strategies leads to a focus:

> When I think of how much leisure time I had before I came to college, I almost get depressed. I used to spend Saturdays hanging out with my friends at the mall and Sunday afternoons reading a novel. Now that I'm in college, working part-time and carrying a full load of classes, I have little time to hang out with my friends, and no time for pleasure reading. So instead of getting depressed, I try to concentrate on the positive consequences of working while attending school.

Because writing is a form of thinking and discovering, your focus might not emerge until after you have written your first draft. When you compare the draft of Melissa's essay on working while attending school (see pages 83–87) with the final version of it (pages 96–99), you will see how drafting and revising can sharpen a writer's focus.

Whatever method you use to bring a topic into focus, your choice should be determined not only by your interests but also by your purpose, the needs of your audience, and the time and space available. The following checklist may help you assess your topic.

CHECKLIST for Assessing a Topic

- Are you interested in the topic?
- Is the topic appropriate for your audience?
- Can you interest the audience in your topic?
- What is your purpose in writing about this topic?
- Can you do justice to the topic in the time and space available to you? Or should you narrow it down or expand it?
- Do you know enough about the topic to write a paper of the length your instructor requires? If not, how will you get additional information?
- Are you willing to learn more about the topic?

Use the journalists' questions to generate more ideas about a concept or subject that interests you. Then consider how you might focus that general subject into a specific topic appropriate for an essay.

3c Conveying a clearly stated thesis

Once you have focused your subject into a topic, you have come a long way toward developing the main idea you want to convey. By this point, you have probably also established your purpose for writing, whether to explain, teach, analyze, argue, or compare. Your subject, purpose, supporting information, and focus all come together in a controlling idea, or **thesis,** which is appropriate for your audience and context (see chapter 1). In the first draft or two, your thesis may be only tentative. By your final draft, however, you will have developed a clear thesis statement.

Most pieces of writing have a **thesis statement,** an explicit declaration (usually in one sentence) of the main idea. Your thesis statement, then, will convey a single idea, clearly focused and specifically stated. A thesis can be thought of as a central idea stated in the form of an assertion, or **claim** (see 8d), which indicates what you believe to be true, interesting, or valuable about your topic.

An explicitly formulated thesis statement helps keep your writing on target. It identifies the topic, the purpose, and, in some cases, the plan of development. Notice how the following thesis statements fulfill their purpose. The first is from an expressive essay.

> Dave Rahm was a stunt pilot, the air's own genius.   —**ANNIE DILLARD**

With this simple statement, the author establishes that the topic is Dave Rahm and indicates that she will discuss his genius as a stunt pilot. She conveys enthusiasm and awe about his expertise.

The following thesis statement (in two sentences) for an expository essay divides student excuses into five kinds, using humor to make a point.

> With a show of energy and creativity that would be admirable if applied to the (missing) assignments in question, my students persist, week after week, semester after semester, year after year, in offering excuses about why their

work is not ready. Those reasons fall into several broad categories: the family, the best friend, the evils of dorm life, the evils of technology, and the totally bizarre.

> —**CAROLYN FOSTER SEGAL,** "The Dog Ate My Disk, and Other Tales of Woe"

The main idea in an argumentative essay usually carries a strong point of view, as in the following, which unmistakably argues for a specific course of action.

Amnesty International opposes the death penalty in all cases without exception.

> —**AMNESTY INTERNATIONAL,** "The Death Penalty: Questions and Answers"

It is just as important to allow your thesis statement to remain tentative in the early stages of writing as it is to allow your essay to remain flexible through the first and second drafts. Rather than starting with a preconceived thesis, which you must struggle to support, you should let your final thesis statement grow out of your thinking and discovery process as you draft and revise. The following tips might help you develop a thesis statement that is neither too obvious nor too general.

TIPS FOR DEVELOPING A THESIS STATEMENT

- Decide which feature of the topic interests you most.
- Write down your point of view or assertion about that feature.
- Mark the passages in your freewriting, journal, or rough draft that support your position.
- Draft a thesis statement, and consider whether you can address the full scope of this tentative thesis in your essay or whether it is still too broad to be developed sufficiently.
- After your first or second draft, ask yourself whether your thesis is too broad for your essay (or vice versa). Revise your thesis to widen or narrow its scope in the direction your essay has taken.
- If you are unhappy with the results, start again with the first tip, and be even more specific.

A clear, precise thesis statement helps unify what you write; it directs your readers to the writing that follows. Therefore, as you write and revise, check your thesis statement frequently to see whether you have drifted away from it. It should guide your decisions about which details to keep and which to toss out as well as your search for appropriate additional information to strengthen your points or support your assertions. In addition, as you write and revise, test all of your supporting material against the thesis statement and scrupulously discard anything that does not pertain to it.

A thesis is usually stated in a declarative sentence with a single main clause—that is, in either a simple or a complex sentence (see **21d**). If your thesis statement presents two or more coordinate ideas, as a compound sentence does, be sure that you are not losing direction and focus. For example, the following thesis statement, composed of two sentences, coordinates and focuses two ideas, indicating a discussion that will contrast men's and women's use of language.

> Male students are more likely to be comfortable attacking the readings and might find the inclusion of personal anecdotes irrelevant and "soft." Women are more likely to resist discussion they perceive as hostile, and, indeed, it is women in my classes who are most likely to offer personal anecdotes.
>
> —**DEBORAH TANNEN**, "How Male and Female Students Use Language Differently"

If you wish to sharpen a thesis statement by adding information that qualifies or supports it, subordinate such material to the main idea:

> Many who today hear me somewhere in person, or on television, or those who read something I've said, will think I went to school far beyond the eighth grade. This impression is due entirely to my prison studies.
>
> —**MALCOLM X**, "Prison Studies"

As you clarify your thesis statement, resist using such vague qualifiers as *interesting, important,* and *unusual,* which can signal that the topic lacks interest or focus. For example, in the thesis statement "My education has been very unusual," the vague word *unusual* may indicate that the idea itself is weak and that the writer needs to find a sharper focus. However, this kind of vague thesis may disguise an idea of real interest that simply needs to be made specific: "Our family grew closer after my parents decided to teach me at home." The following examples show how vague thesis statements can be clarified and sharpened.

Vague   It is hard to balance work with school.

Better   Hardworking students who balance a part-time job with success in schoolwork can grow in maturity and self-confidence.

Vague   People wonder about the connection of thinking styles with intelligence.

Better   Thinking styles are largely distinct from intelligence or aptitude.

Vague   Harry Truman was an important president.

Better   President Truman's executive order in 1948 became an important step in the long-term struggle for civil rights.

The thesis statement most often appears in the first paragraph of an essay, although you can put yours anywhere that suits your purpose—occasionally even in the conclusion. The advantage of putting the thesis statement in the first paragraph is that readers know from the beginning what you are writing about and where the essay is going. Especially appropriate in academic writing, this technique helps readers who are searching for specific information to locate it easily. If the thesis statement begins the introductory paragraph, the rest of the sentences in the paragraph usually support or clarify it, as is the case in paragraph 1. (For ease of reference, each of the sample paragraphs in this chapter is numbered.)

1   *America is suffering from overwork.* Too many of us are too busy, trying to squeeze more into each day while having less to show for it. Although our growing time crunch is often portrayed as a personal dilemma, it is in fact a major social problem that has reached crisis proportions over the past 20 years.   —**BARBARA BRANDT**, "Less Is More"

If the thesis statement is the last sentence of the opening paragraph, the preceding sentences will build toward it, as is the case in paragraph 2.

2   The story of zero is an ancient one. Its roots stretch back to the dawn of mathematics, in the time thousands of years before the first civilization, long before humans could read and write. But as natural as zero seems to us today, for ancient peoples zero was a foreign—and frightening—idea. An Eastern concept, born in the Fertile Crescent a few centuries before the birth of Christ, zero not only evoked images of a primal void, it also had dangerous mathematical properties. *Within zero there is the power to shatter the framework of logic.*   —**CHARLES SEIFE**, *Zero: The Biography of a Dangerous Idea*

Most of the writing done for college courses contains an obvious thesis statement. The following checklist may help you assess the thesis of your essay.

CHECKLIST for Assessing a Thesis

- Does your thesis make a clear comment about your topic?
- Is your thesis an accurate reflection of what you believe to be true about your topic?
- Does your thesis match your essay in terms of focus and coverage?
- What two assertions can you make to support your thesis?
- What specific examples, illustrations, or experiences support your assertions?
- How does your thesis relate to the interests of your audience? To your purpose? To the context of your essay?
- Where is your thesis located in your essay? Would your readers benefit from having it stated earlier or later?

3d Arranging or outlining ideas

Many writers need a working plan to direct their ideas and keep their writing on course. Various plans of arrangement might be determined for them by their instructor, by the discipline in which they are writing, or by tradition.

Some writers quickly compose informal lists, which grow out of a collection of ideas. The ideas in these lists can overlap, be discarded, or lead to a tentative thesis statement, conclusions, and the beginning of an overall organizational plan. Other writers, however, rely on outlines. Either method (list or outline) can be especially helpful when you are writing lengthy papers (see chapters 8 and 9) and when you are writing under pressure (see chapter 5). Whatever method you choose for arranging your ideas, remember that you can always alter your arrangement to accommodate any changes your writing undergoes during the process.

You can simplify your thinking about arrangement if you accept Aristotle's claim that every speech needs "a beginning, a middle, and an end." Even the simplest outline offers an essay a structure, much like the basic framework of a house. And, like the framework of a house, a simple outline can quickly become more elaborate and detailed. As you work and think, you might introduce indentations, letters, and numbers into your rough outline to indicate various levels of subordination and coordination in your material. Thus, an outline becomes a visual map of your thinking. The main points form the major headings, and the supporting ideas form the subheadings. An outline of Melissa's essay might look something like the following.

TENTATIVE THESIS STATEMENT: Balancing a part-time job with success in school-work is not only a manageable task, but also a valuable experience contributing to growth as a student and as an individual.

I. Balancing work with school is manageable
  A. Your own sacrifices will determine success
    1. Time with friends
    2. Use breaks at work wisely
    3. Get a good handle on your school schedule and determine how far ahead you need to start assignments
  B. Best if you have an understanding employer
    1. An employer who puts school first and values scholarship
    2. Take advantage of university-run work programs
  C. Flexibility in scheduling hours
    1. Plan ahead around exam and paper weeks
    2. Often need to sacrifice weekend time in order to get in hours
II. Balancing work with school is valuable experience for students
  A. Provides discipline
    1. In prioritizing schoolwork, those students who work part-time jobs often have a good handle on their academic schedules and stay on top of their studies
    2. Working students learn the importance of time management and set realistic goals and time lines for themselves
  B. Working to pay for education leads students to place more value on their education
    1. More serious about schoolwork
    2. Realize the importance of timely completion of degree
      a. Sleep becomes a priority
      b. Exercise seems less important
  C. Part-time work can offer career experience
    1. Internships
    2. Career-related work

D. Part-time work can motivate students to achieve excellence in school as a means of moving beyond the scope of part-time work

1. Face boredom or monotony in job
2. Face low wages
3. Constructive use of potential negativity

However streamlined or detailed your outline, you will need enough headings to develop your topic fully within the boundaries stated in your thesis.

3e Getting your ideas into a first draft

When writing a first draft, get your ideas down quickly. Spelling, punctuation, and correctness are not important in the first draft; ideas are. Experienced writers know that the most important thing about a first draft is to have done it, for it gives you something to work on—and against. If you are not sure how to begin, look over some of the journal writing, listing, or outlining you have already done, and try to state a tentative thesis. Then write out some main points you would like to develop, along with some of the supporting information for that development. Keep your overall plan in mind as you draft. If you find yourself losing track of where you want to go, stop writing and reread what you have already done. Talk with someone working on the same assignment, or write in your journal. You may find that you need to revise your plan—or you may need to rethink your topic. Experienced writers expect a change in plan as they write and revise.

If you feel stuck, move to another part of your essay and draft paragraphs that might appear later (see 5e). Doing so may help you restart your engine, for when you are actually writing, you think more efficiently. You can then move on to another part that is easier to write, such as sentences that develop another supporting idea, an introduction, or a conclusion. But do not worry about writing a provocative introduction or a sensible conclusion at this point. Later, when you are revising, you can experiment with ways of polishing those sections of an essay (see 4b). What is important at this stage is to begin writing, and then keep writing as quickly as you can. Save this early work so that you can refer to it as you revise (see chapter 4).

Finally, remember that writing is a form of discovering, understanding, and thinking. As you draft, you are likely to discover that you have more to say than you ever thought you would. So, whenever drafting leads you in a direction you did not intend, allow yourself to explore if you sense that this side trip may hold a useful discovery. You can consider whether to integrate or suppress this new material when you prepare to revise.

3f Drafting well-developed paragraphs

You compose a draft by developing the information that will constitute the paragraphs of your essay. If you are working from an informal list (see 3d), you will have a sense of where you want to take your ideas but may be uncertain about the number and nature of the paragraphs you will need. If you are working from an outline (see 3d), you can anticipate the number of paragraphs you will probably write and what you hope to accomplish in each paragraph. In the first case, you enjoy the freedom to pursue new ideas that occur as you draft. In the second, you enjoy the security of a clear direction. In both cases, however, you need to develop each paragraph fully and then ask yourself whether any additional paragraphs (or additional supporting information within any paragraph) would help your audience understand the main idea of your essay.

Paragraphs have no set length. Typically, they range from 50 to 250 words, and paragraphs in books are usually longer than those in newspapers and magazines. There are certainly times when a long paragraph makes for rich reading, as well as times when a long paragraph exhausts a single minor point, combines too many points, or becomes repetitive. On the other hand, short, one-sentence paragraphs can be effectively used for emphasis (see chapter 30) or to establish transition (see 4d). Short paragraphs can also, however, indicate inadequate development. There will be times when you can combine two short paragraphs as you revise (see chapter 4), but there will be many more occasions when you need to lengthen a short paragraph by developing it with specific details or examples.

Experienced writers do not worry much about paragraph length; rather, they concentrate on getting words on the paper or on the screen, knowing that all paragraphs can be shortened, lengthened, merged, or otherwise improved later in the writing process. So think of revising and developing your paragraphs as a luxury, an opportunity to articulate exactly what you want to say without anyone interrupting you—or changing the subject.

(1) You can develop a paragraph with details.

A good paragraph developed with details brings your idea to life. Consider the following well-developed paragraph by Alice Walker.

3 I stood in front of the mirror and looked at myself and laughed. *My hair was one of those odd, amazing, unbelievable, stop-you-in-your-tracks creations—not unlike a zebra's stripes, an armadillo's ears, or the feet of the electric-bluefooted boobie—that the Universe makes for no reason other than to express its own limitless imagination.* I realized I had never been given the opportunity to appreciate hair for its true self. That it did, in fact, have one. I remembered years of enduring hairdressers—from my mother onward—doing missionary work on my hair. They dominated, suppressed, controlled. Now, more or less free, it stood this way and that. I would call up my friends around the country to report on its antics. It never thought of lying down. Flatness, the missionary position, did not interest it. It grew. Being short, cropped off near the root, another missionary "solution," did not interest it either. It sought more and more space, more light, more of itself. It loved to be washed; but that was it.

   —ALICE WALKER, "Oppressed Hair Puts a Ceiling on the Brain"

Notice how the series of details in paragraph 3 supports the main idea (italicized), the topic sentence (see 4c). Readers can easily see how one sentence leads into the next, creating a clear picture of the hair being described.

(2) You can develop a paragraph by providing examples.

Like details, examples contribute to paragraph development by making specific what otherwise might seem general and hard to grasp. **Details** describe a person, place, or thing; **examples** illustrate an idea with information that can come from different times and places. Both details and examples support your ideas in terms of the rhetorical situation.

  The author of paragraph 4 uses several closely related examples (as well as details) to support the main idea with which he begins.

4   *Illiterates live, in more than literal ways, an uninsured existence.* They cannot understand the written details on a health insurance form. They cannot read the waivers that they sign preceding surgical procedures. Several women I have known in Boston have entered a slum hospital with the intention of obtaining a tubal ligation and have emerged a few days later after having been subjected to a hysterectomy. Unaware of their rights, incognizant of jargon, intimidated by the unfamiliar air of fear and atmosphere of ether that so many of us find oppressive in the confines even of the most attractive and expensive medical facilities, they have signed their names to documents they could not read and which nobody, in the hectic situation that prevails so often in those overcrowded hospitals that serve the urban poor, had even bothered to explain.

—JONATHAN KOZOL, "The Human Cost of an Illiterate Society"

Exercise 2

Examine some of your own writing—such as an essay you have recently drafted, e-mail messages that are still on file, or entries in your journal—and select one paragraph that holds potential interest. Write out (by hand) the original paragraph, and then rewrite it, developing it with additional details or examples.

3g   Employing rhetorical methods of development

When drafting essays, you can develop a variety of paragraphs using **rhetorical methods,** mental operations that help you think through various types of rhetorical problems—having to do with establishing boundaries (definition), making sense of a person, place, or event (description and narration), organizing concepts (classification and division), understanding or thinking critically about a process (process or cause-and-consequence analysis), or needing to convince someone (argumentation). The strategies used for generating ideas, focusing your topic (see 3b), developing paragraphs and essays, and arranging ideas are already second nature to you. Every day, you use one or more of them to define a concept, narrate a significant incident, supply examples for an assertion, classify or divide information into specific parts, compare two or more things, analyze a process, or identify a cause or consequence.

When drafting an essay, you may discover that you need to define a term or explain a process before you can take your readers further into your topic. Writers have the option of tapping one, two, or several rhetorical methods to fulfill their overall purpose, which might be to explain, entertain, argue a point, or evaluate a situation.

(1) Narrating a series of events tells readers what happened.

A **narrative** discusses a sequence of events, normally in **chronological order** (the order in which they occur), to develop a particular point or set a mood. This rhetorical method, which often uses a setting, characters, dialogue, and description, usually uses transition words or phrases such as *then, later, that evening,* or *the following week* to guide readers from one incident to the next. Whatever its length, a narrative must remain focused on the main idea. Drawn from Charles Darwin's journal, written during his voyage on the *Beagle,* paragraph 5 uses narrative to convey a sense of wonder at the power of nature.

5   The day has been memorable in the annals of Valdivia, for the most severe earthquake experienced by the oldest inhabitant. I happened to be on shore, and was lying down in the wood to rest myself. It came on suddenly, and lasted two minutes, but the time appeared much longer. The rocking of the ground was very sensible. The undulations appeared to my companion and myself to come from due east, whilst others thought they proceeded from the southwest. This shows how difficult it sometimes is to perceive the direction of vibrations. There was no difficulty in standing upright, but the motion made me almost giddy; it was something like the movement of a vessel in a little cross-ripple, or still more like that felt by a person skating over thin ice, which bends under the weight of his body.

           —**CHARLES DARWIN**, "Great Earthquake"

(2) Describing how something looks, sounds, smells, or feels adds useful detail.

By describing a person, place, object, or sensation, you can make your material come alive. Often descriptions are predominantly visual, but even visual descriptions can include the details of what you hear, smell, taste, touch; that is, descriptions appeal to the senses.

    Description should suit your purpose and audience. In describing your car, for example, you would emphasize certain features to a

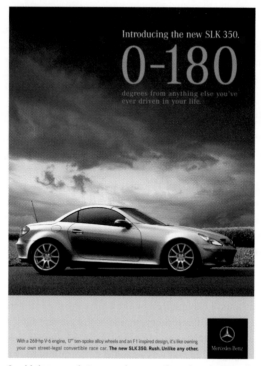

Introducing the new SLK 350.

0-180

degrees from anything else you've ever driven in your life.

With a 268-hp V-6 engine, 17" ten-spoke alloy wheels and an F1 inspired design, it's like owning your own street-legal convertible race car. **The new SLK 350. Rush. Unlike any other.**

Mercedes-Benz

Combining appeals to several senses, through a photograph and descriptive words, brings information alive for the reader (and potential buyer).

potential buyer, others to a mechanic who was going to repair it, and still others to a friend whom you wished to impress. In paragraph 6, Judith Ortiz Cofer employs vivid descriptive details to convey her ideas about cultural influences on adolescent striving and embarrassment.

6   I came to remember Career Day in our high school, when teachers told us to come dressed as if for a job interview. It quickly became obvious that to the barrio girls, "dressing up" sometimes meant wearing ornate jewelry and clothing that would be more appropriate (by mainstream standards) for the company Christmas party than as daily office attire. That morning I had agonized in front of my closet, trying to figure out what a "career girl" would wear because, essentially, except for Marlo Thomas on TV, I had no models on which to base my decision. I knew how to dress for school: at the

Catholic school I attended we all wore uniforms; I knew how to dress for Sunday mass, and I knew what dresses to wear for parties at my relatives' homes. Though I do not recall the precise details of my Career Day outfit, it must have been a composite of the above choices. But I remember a comment my friend (an Italian-American) made in later years that coalesced my impressions of that day. She said that at the business school she was attending the Puerto Rican girls always stood out for wearing "everything at once." She meant, of course, too much jewelry, too many accessories. On that day at school, we were simply made the negative models by the nuns who were themselves not credible fashion experts to any of us. But it was painfully obvious to me that to the others, in their tailored skirts and silk blouses, we must have seemed "hopeless" and "vulgar." Though I now know that most adolescents feel out of step much of the time, I also know that for the Puerto Rican girls of my generation that sense was intensified. The way our teachers and classmates looked at us that day in school was just a taste of the culture clash that awaited us in the real world, where prospective employers and men on the street would often misinterpret our tight skirts and jingling bracelets as a come-on.

—JUDITH ORTIZ COFER, "The Myth of the Latin Woman:
I Just Met a Girl Named María"

(3) Explaining a process shows readers how something happens.

Process paragraphs, in explaining how something is done or made, often use both description and narration. You might describe the items used in a process and then narrate the steps of the process chronologically. Add an explanation of a process to a draft if doing so will illustrate a concept that might otherwise be hard for your audience to grasp. In

Descriptions of a process, such as boat building, often combine description and narration.

paragraph 7, Bernice Wuethrich explains the process by which a scientist studied the effects of alcohol on brain cells.

7   Mark Prendergast, a neuroscientist at the University of Kentucky, recently revealed one way these hyperactive receptors kill brain cells. First,

he exposed rat hippocampal slices to alcohol for 10 days, then removed the alcohol. Following withdrawal, he stained the tissue with a fluorescent dye that lit up dead and dying cells. When exposed to an alcohol concentration of about .08 percent, cell death increased some 25 percent above the baseline. When concentrations were two or three times higher, he wrote in a recent issue of *Alcoholism: Clinical and Experimental Research,* the number of dead cells shot up to 100 percent above the baseline.

—**BERNICE WUETHRICH**, "Getting Stupid"

(4) Analyzing cause or consequence establishes why something happens or predicts results.

Writers who analyze cause or consequence raise the question *Why?* and must answer it to the satisfaction of their audience, differentiating the **primary cause** (the most important one) from **contributory causes** (which add to but do not directly cause a situation) or the **primary consequence** (the most important one) from **secondary consequences** (which occur because of an event but are less important than the primary consequence). Writers who analyze cause or consequence usually link events along a time line, just as you would if you were describing a traffic accident to a police officer. Always keep in mind, though, that just because one event occurs before—or after—another event does not necessarily make it a cause—or a consequence—of that event. In paragraph 8, undergraduate student Robyn Sylves analyzes some causes of credit card debt among college students.

Although companies push credit cards on many campuses, some students do not realize that a possible consequence of card use is debt.

8   Experts point to several factors for excessive credit card debt among college students. High on the list is students' lack of financial literacy. The credit card representatives on campus, the preapproved applications that arrive in the mail several times a week, and the incessant

phone offers for credit cards tempt students into opening accounts before they really can understand what they are getting themselves into. The people marketing these cards depend on the fact that many students don't know what an annual percentage rate is. Credit card companies count on applicants' failing to read the fine print, which tells them how after an "introductory" period, the interest rate on a given card can increase two to three times. The companies also don't want students to know that every year people send money (in the form of interest charges) to these companies that there is no need to send. That annual fee that credit card companies love to charge can be waived. I think that many people, students and nonstudents alike, might be surprised how often and easily it can disappear if people call the company to say they don't want to pay it.

—**ROBYN SYLVES**, "Credit Card Debt among College Students: Just What Does It Cost?"

Writers can also demonstrate consequences, as in paragraph 9, which explores the effects automobiles have had on our society by asking us to imagine life without them.

9   Let us imagine what life would be like in a carless nation. People would have to live very close together so they could walk, or, for healthy people living in sunny climes, bicycle to mass transit stops. Living in close quarters would mean life as it is now lived in Manhattan. There would be few freestanding homes, many row houses, and lots of apartment buildings. There would be few private gardens except for flowerpots on balconies. The streets would be congested by pedestrians, trucks, and buses, as they were at the turn of the century before automobiles were common.

—**JAMES Q. WILSON**, "Cars and Their Enemies"

(5) Comparing or contrasting helps readers see similarities or differences.

A **comparison** points out similarities, and a **contrast** points out differences—to reveal information. When drafting, consider whether a comparison might help your readers see a relationship they might otherwise miss or whether a contrast might help them establish useful distinctions. In paragraph 10, Jane Tompkins uses descriptive details in her revealing comparison of her two kindergarten teachers.

10   The teachers, Miss Morget (pronounced *mor-zhay*) and Miss Hunt, were tall and thin but unalike in every other way. Miss Hunt was young and

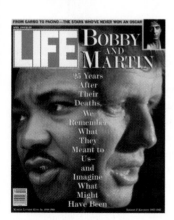

This magazine cover suggests a comparison of Martin Luther King, Jr., and Robert F. Kennedy as influential political leaders, while inviting a contrast of their individual backgrounds.

attractive. She had chestnut brown hair, stylishly rolled, hazel eyes, and a prominent chin. At first, her smart outfits and polished good looks fooled me into thinking she was the nice one. But there was a twist to her mouth sometimes and a troubled look in her eyes that frightened me, and when she spoke to the children, there was iron in her voice. Miss Morget was old and kind. Her frizzled white hair stuck out, softening her sharp nose; and her pale eyes, which held a twinkle, made me pretty sure she wasn't going to do or say anything mean. She spoke in a gentle, cracked voice that was never angry; but the children knew when she meant business, and they minded.

—JANE TOMPKINS, *A Life in School*

Two valuable kinds of comparisons are metaphors and analogies. A **metaphor** is a figure of speech that makes an indirect comparison of one thing to another, as in "He was a lion in uniform." (See 33a.) An **analogy,** on the other hand, makes a direct comparison of the similarities between two things. Although analogies can invigorate your writing, you must remember that two things that are alike in some ways are rarely alike in all ways. (See 8i(7) on false analogy.) In paragraph 11, Nelson Mandela uses a metaphor to compare leadership and gardening.

11   In some ways, I saw the garden as a metaphor for certain aspects of my life. A leader must also tend his garden; he, too, plants seed, and then watches, cultivates, and harvests the result. Like the gardener, a leader must take responsibility for what he cultivates; he must mind his work, try to repel enemies, preserve what can be preserved, and eliminate what cannot succeed.

—NELSON MANDELA, "Raising Tomatoes and Leading People"

(6) Classifying and dividing can give order to material.

To classify is to place things into groups based on shared characteristics. **Classification** is a way to understand or explain something by establishing how it fits within a category or group. For example, a book reviewer might classify a new novel as a mystery—leading readers to expect a plot based on suspense. **Division,** in contrast, separates an object or group into smaller parts and examines the relationships among them. A novel can also be discussed according to components such as plot, setting, and theme (see chapter **16**).

Classification and division represent two different perspectives: ideas can be put into groups (classification) or split into subclasses (division). As a strategy for organizing (or developing) an idea, classification and division often work together. In paragraph 12, for example, classification and division work together to clarify the differences between the two versions of the cowboy icon. Like most paragraphs, this one mixes rhetorical methods; the writer uses description, comparison and contrast, and classification to make her point.

12   First, and perhaps most fundamentally, the cowboy icon has two basic incarnations: the cowboy hero and the cowboy villain. Cowboy heroes often appear in roles such as sheriff, leader of a cattle drive, or what I'll call a "wandering hero," such as the Lone Ranger, who appears much like a frontier Superman wherever and whenever help is needed. Writers and producers most commonly place cowboy heroes in conflict either with "Indians" or with the cowboy villain. In contrast to the other classic bad guys of the Western genre, cowboy villains pose a special challenge because they are essentially the alter ego of the cowboy hero; the cowboy villain shares the hero's skill with a gun, his horse-riding maneuvers, and his knowledge of the land. What distinguishes the two, of course, is character: the cowboy hero is essentially good, while the cowboy villain is essentially evil.

—**JODY M. ROY,** "The Case of the Cowboy"

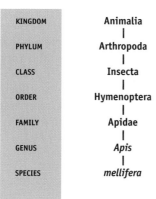

KINGDOM	**Animalia**
	|
PHYLUM	**Arthropoda**
	|
CLASS	**Insecta**
	|
ORDER	**Hymenoptera**
	|
FAMILY	**Apidae**
	|
GENUS	*Apis*
	|
SPECIES	*mellifera*

The scientific identification of the honeybee (*Apis mellifera*) requires a classification in the genus *Apis* and a division within that genus, into the species *mellifera*.

(7) Defining an important concept or term clarifies meaning.

By defining a concept or a term, writers efficiently clarify their meaning and develop their ideas. By defining a word for your readers, you can immediately connect with them; they know what you are and are not talking about. Definitions are usually constructed in a two-step process: the first step locates a term by placing it in a class; the second step differentiates this particular term from other terms in the same class. For instance, "A concerto [the term] is a symphonic piece [the class] consisting of three movements performed by one or more solo instruments accompanied at times by an orchestra [the difference]." A symphony belongs to the same basic class as a concerto; it too is a symphonic piece. However, a symphony is differentiated from a concerto in two specific ways: a symphony consists of four movements, and its performance involves the entire orchestra.

Paragraph 13 defines volcanos by putting them into a class ("landforms") and by distinguishing them ("built of molten material") from other members of that class. The definition is then clarified by examples.

13   Volcanos are landforms built of molten material that has spewed out onto the earth's surface. Such molten rock is called lava. Volcanos may be no larger than small hills, or thousands of feet high. All have a characteristic cone shape. Some well-known mountains are actually volcanos. Examples are Mt. Fuji (Japan), Mt. Lassen (California), Mt. Hood (Oregon), Mt. Etna and Mt. Vesuvius (Italy), and Paricutín (Mexico). The Hawaiian Islands are all immense volcanos whose summits rise above the ocean, and these volcanos are still quite active.   —JOEL AREM, "Rocks and Minerals"

Use the rhetorical methods just described to make your essay as a whole more understandable to your audience. Make sure, however, that you are using these methods to support your thesis and fulfill your overall purpose. If a paragraph or two developed with one of the methods is contributing to the main idea of your essay, then it is contributing to your purpose. If the development of a paragraph does not support the thesis, then you need to revise or delete it (see 4c and 4f).

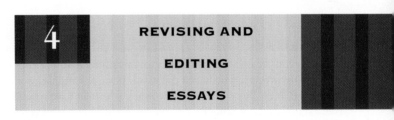

Revising, which literally means "seeing again," lies at the heart of all successful writing. When you see again, you see with a different set of eyes—those of the reader instead of the writer. **Revising** entails rethinking what you have already written in terms of your overall purpose: how successfully you have addressed your audience, how clearly you have stated your thesis, how effectively you have arranged your information, how thoroughly you have developed your assertions. **Editing,** on the other hand, focuses on issues that are smaller in scale. When you are editing, you are polishing your writing: you choose words more precisely (see chapter 33), shape prose more distinctly (chapter 34), and structure sentences more effectively (chapters 27–31). While you are editing, you are also **proofreading,** focusing even more sharply to eliminate surface errors in grammar, punctuation, and mechanics. Revising and editing often overlap (just as drafting and revising do), but they are distinct activities that concentrate on large-scale and small-scale issues, respectively. Usually revising occurs before editing, but not always. Edited passages may be redrafted, rearranged, and even cut as writers revise further.

As you revise and edit your essays, this chapter will help you

- consider your work as a whole (4a(1–2)),
- evaluate your tone (4a(3)),
- compose an effective introduction and conclusion (4b),
- strengthen the unity and coherence of paragraphs (4c),
- improve transitions (4d),
- benefit from a reviewer's comments (4e),
- edit to improve style (4f),
- proofread to eliminate surface errors (4g), and
- submit a final draft (4h).

4a The essentials of revision

In truth, you are revising throughout the planning and drafting stages of the writing process, whether at the word, phrase, sentence, example, or paragraph level. But no matter how much you may have revised during those stages of the writing process, you will still do most of your revising after you have completed a draft. You may rewrite specific sentences and paragraphs as well as reconsider the draft as a whole. A few writers prefer to start revising immediately after drafting, while their minds are still fully engaged by their topic. But most writers like to let a draft "cool off," so that when they return to it, they can assess it more objectively, with fresh eyes. Even a twenty-four–hour cool-off period will provide you more objectivity as a reader and will reveal more options to you as a writer.

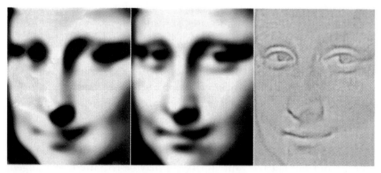

Just as changing the focus on the face in the portrait known as *Mona Lisa* alters viewers' perception of it, successful revision can alter your writing in effective ways.

Most newer word-processing programs enable you to track your revisions easily, a feature that is especially useful if your instructor requires you to submit all drafts or if a peer group is reviewing your drafts. Go to your toolbar, and click on Tools in order to see the pulldown menu. Track Changes will be listed on that menu. If your word-processing program does not have this feature, you can save each new version of your work in a separate file and date each one. By opening two or more of those files on your computer screen, you can easily compare the different versions.

(1) Anything and everything on the page can be revised.

As you reread your essay as a whole, you will want to recall your purpose, restate your thesis, and reconsider your audience. Does your main point come through clearly in every paragraph, or do some paragraphs digress, repeat information, or contradict what has come before (see 3c)?

In addition to sharpening your main idea, you will also want to revise in terms of audience expectations. Revising demands that you gauge what you have written to the audience you are addressing (see 1d). How will your audience respond to your thesis statement? Which of your assertions will your audience immediately understand or accept? Which examples or details will interest your audience? Which of your language choices were aimed expressly at this audience? In other words, revising successfully requires that you examine your work both as a writer and as a reader. As a writer, you must ask yourself whether your words accurately reflect your intention and meaning. As a reader, you must ask yourself whether what is clear and logical to you will also be clear to others.

(2) What is not on the page can be more important than what is on the page.

Writers are always on the lookout for what they have put on the page—and what they may have left out. What information might the audience be expecting? What information might strengthen your thesis? Your best ideas will not always surface in your first draft; you will sometimes have an important new idea only after you have finished that draft and taken a good look at it. No matter how complete a draft seems, ask yourself whether something is missing. You might use questioning strategies to discover what is missing (see 3a(3)). Or you might share your draft with a classmate or colleague who is working on the same assignment, asking that person to mark confusing or unclear passages (see 4e).

(3) Your tone helps you fulfill your purpose.

Tone reflects a writer's attitude toward a subject, so you will want to make sure that your tone is appropriate to your purpose, audience, and context (see 1a). Decide what you intend your tone to be (how you want to "sound"), and then read your piece aloud to see if it sounds the way you want it to. You want to present yourself as confident, well informed, and fair-minded, so you will want all of your words and sentences to convey that tone. If some passages sound defensive, self-centered, or apologetic, revise them. Such tones rarely sustain a reader's interest, let alone goodwill. Your challenge is to make sure that your tone contributes to eliciting from your readers the desired response—to you as well as to the information you are presenting.

Consider the tone in paragraph 1, written by a celebrated contemporary writer who grew up in Kentucky and is describing the consumer patterns of the typical U.S. family. (For ease of reference, each of the sample paragraphs in this chapter is numbered.)

1 I think a lot about those thirty citizens of India who, it's said, could live on the average American's stuff. I wonder if I could build a life of contentment on their material lot, and then I look around my house and wonder what they'd make of mine. My closet would clothe more than half of them, and my books—good Lord—could open a branch in New Delhi. Our family's musical instruments would outfit an entire (if very weird) village band, featuring electric guitars, violin, eclectic percussion section, and a really dusty clarinet. We have more stuff than we need; there is no question of our being perfect. I'm not even sure what "perfect" means in this discussion. I'm not trying to persuade my family to evaporate and live on air. We're here, we're alive, it's the only one we get, as far as I know, so I am keenly inclined to take hold of life by

The expressive tone of Dorothea Lange's photograph of a poor mother and children added depth and richness to a photodocumentary of the Great Depression.

its *huevos*. As a dinner guest I gratefully eat just about anything that's set before me, because graciousness among friends is dearer to me than any other agenda. I'm not up for a guilt trip, just an adventure in bearable lightness. I approach our efforts at simplicity as a novice approaches her order, aspiring to a lifetime of deepening understanding, discipline, serenity, and joy. Likening voluntary simplicity to a religion is neither hyperbole nor sacrilege. Some people look around and declare the root of all evil to be sex or blasphemy, and so they aspire to be pious and chaste. Where I look for evil I'm more likely to see degradations of human and natural life, an immoral gap between rich and poor, a ravaged earth. At the root of these I see greed and overconsumption by the powerful minority. I was born to that caste, but I can aspire to waste not and want less.

—**BARBARA KINGSOLVER**, "Lily's Chickens"

Exercise 1

Establishing your own tone, create a paragraph about the expectations for consuming or conserving in your family. Identify specific words and phrases from paragraph 1 that helped you with your version. Be prepared to read your paragraph aloud and share your findings with the rest of the class.

When Melissa Schraeder revised the first draft reprinted later in this chapter (see pages 83–87), she decided to change her tone in response to a comment from one of her readers that she sounded too breezy about her ability to balance work and school. Although she did not want to sound as though balancing work and school were impossible, Melissa surely did not mean to imply that doing so could be easy. A consistently easygoing tone was not appropriate for her rhetorical situation (see 1a).

 The thesaurus and grammar checker in your word-processing program may give you advice that can affect the tone of your writing. Go to the toolbar, and click on Tools; the pulldown menu will reveal the spelling and grammar checkers and usually a dictionary and a thesaurus as well. These tools are easy to find and use; however, only you can make the choices that enhance the tone you wish to create. For example, a grammar checker may suggest that you change a word, one you have intentionally repeated in order to achieve a specific effect and create a certain tone. If you are using these features of your word-processing program as you revise your writing, give careful consideration to the suggestions they make.

4b Guiding readers with your introduction and conclusion

Your introduction and conclusion play a special role in helping readers understand your essay as a whole. In fact, readers look for these parts of an essay and read them carefully, expecting guidance and clarification from them.

(1) An effective introduction arouses your reader's interest and establishes your topic and tone.

Experienced writers know that the opening paragraph is important; it is their best chance to arouse the reader's interest with provocative information, establish the topic and writer as worthy of consideration, and set the tone. Effective introductions make readers want to read on. In paragraph 2, Nancy Mairs speaks directly to her readers—shocking them—in order to get their attention:

2   The other day I was thinking of writing an essay on being a cripple. I was thinking hard in one of the stalls of the women's room in my office building, as I was shoving my shirt into my jeans and tugging up my zipper. Preoccupied, I flushed, picked up my book bag, took my cane down from the hook, and unlatched the door. So many movements unbalanced me, and as I pulled the door open I fell over backward, landing fully clothed on the toilet seat with my legs splayed in front [of] me: the old beetle-on-its-back routine. Saturday afternoon, the building deserted, I was free to laugh aloud as I wriggled back to my feet, my voice bouncing off the yellowish tiles from all directions. Had anyone been there with me, I'd have been still and faint and hot with chagrin. I decided that it was high time to write the essay.   **—NANCY MAIRS,** "On Being a Cripple"

Mairs's unsettling introduction takes her readers off guard: they are in the bathroom with a cripple—and a witty one at that. Her especially strong introduction orients readers to the direction her essay will take: she will candidly reveal her daily humanity in order to remind her readers that "cripples" are people, too.

Introductions have no set length; they can be as brief as a couple of sentences or as long as two or more paragraphs. Although introductions always appear first, they are often drafted and revised much later in the writing process—for introductions as well as the thesis statements they so often contain (see 3c) evolve naturally as writers revise their material, sharpening its focus and developing it to fulfill the overall purpose. You may wish to try several different introductions as you revise, to determine which is most effective.

You can arouse the interest of your audience by writing introductions in a number of ways.

(a) Opening with an unusual fact or statistic

3   In the course of a hundred days in 1994 the Hutu government of Rwanda and its extremist allies very nearly succeeded in exterminating the country's Tutsi minority. Using firearms, machetes, and a variety of garden implements, Hutu militiamen, soldiers, and ordinary citizens murdered some 800,000 Tutsi and politically moderate Hutu. It was the fastest, most efficient killing spree of the twentieth century.

—SAMANTHA POWER, "Bystanders to Genocide"

Figure 1. Estimated Numbers of Persons Aged 12 to 20 (in Thousands) Reporting Past Month Alcohol Use or Binge Alcohol Use: 2001

Opening with a thought-provoking statistic can be an effective introduction.

(b) Opening with an intriguing statement

4   In Afghanistan, nothing is ever what it seems. Including surrender.

—ALEX PERRY, "Inside the Battle at Qala-i-Jangi"

(c) Opening with an anecdote or example

5   Every morning, she wakes up earlier than everyone else in her family so she can pour a tiny bit of cereal and milk in her bowl, place the bowl and spoon in the sink, and slink upstairs to get ready for school. When she comes back down to catch the bus, she tells her mother that she's already eaten cereal and doesn't want anything else. She skips lunch at school, telling her friends that she doesn't like cafeteria food—and, besides, she eats lunch as soon as she gets home. But she doesn't. Instead, she goes home and drinks water as a way to fill up her stomach and give her a false sense of satisfaction before she sits down with her family to eat supper. She eats a little bit of food, but she spends most of her energy pushing the food around on her plate or cutting it up into small pieces so it looks like she ate some. She always leaves the table feeling hungry, but she's still angry at herself for eating anything at all. Her entire day is planned around what and when to eat, how to avoid eating, and mostly how to avoid confrontations with her mother. She is almost perfect—at deception. She has an eating disorder.

—LAUREN A. MAKUCH, "What Can We Do to Prevent Eating Disorders?"

(d) Opening with a question your essay will answer

6   You ask me what is poverty? Listen to me. Here I am, dirty, smelly, and with no "proper" underwear on and with the stench of my rotting teeth near you. I will tell you. Listen to me. Listen without pity. I cannot use your pity. Listen with understanding. Put yourself in my dirty, worn out, ill-fitting shoes, and hear me.   **—JO GOODWIN PARKER,** "What Is Poverty?"

(e) Opening with an appropriate quotation

7   Wordsworth said we "half perceive and half create" the beauty we find in nature, and I guess that's what I'm saying, too. On the one hand I see the forest differently now because of the ideas and knowledge I bring to it. I accept it because I know more and am more confused about notions I used to take for granted. On the other hand my sense of this landscape, my pleasure in it, seems to come from outside, too, unbidden and uncontrolled, surprising. I didn't expect to feel the way I do and even resisted it. Satisfaction is the feeling actually produced in me when I walk here over time. Enjoyment is what I experience in the presence of these trees and these openings, just empirically, prior to thoughts and theories.

—**CHRIS ANDERSON,** "Life on the Edge"

(f) Opening with general information or background about the topic

8   I fell in love with it—college basketball, that is—at a drafty old barn in Lincoln Square in Worcester, Massachusetts, not far from where one of my great-uncles once owned a saloon. This Worcester Memorial Auditorium was square and huge, and it had towering murals depicting men loading shells into the big guns of a dreadnought and firing artillery along the banks of the Somme. You had to walk up broad staircases to see the murals in their entirety, and I didn't have the courage for that until I was nearly ten. I continued to love it—the whole raucous, tumbling parade of it—through my undergraduate days at Marquette University, where Al McGuire put together a delightfully rambunctious program. I even loved it when I covered it for five years, more or less full-time, for the *Boston Herald*. I have missed one Final Four since 1982, and I can tell you exactly where and when I stopped loving college basketball: I stopped loving it in a hotel in Indianapolis in 1999, on a Saturday afternoon, before the national semifinals.

—**CHARLES P. PIERCE,** "ConMen"

(g) Opening with a thesis, simply stated

9   Complaining was great when I was a kid. Well, maybe not great, just better than now. When you are a kid, your sense of entitlement is more intact. At least that's how it seems from this distance. Things are supposed to be a certain way—*yours*. Oh sure, things are supposed to go your way as an adult, but it's not always appropriate to mention this.

        —**CARRIE FISHER,** "The Art of Complaining"

Whatever type of introduction you choose to write, use your opening paragraph to indicate your topic, engage your readers' attention, set your tone, and establish your credibility (see **8f(1)**).

(2) An effective conclusion helps readers understand the most important points of your essay and why they are significant.

Just as a good introduction tantalizes readers, a good conclusion satisfies them. It helps readers recognize the important points of your essay and the significance of those points while, at the same time, wrapping up the essay in a meaningful, often thought-provoking way. As you draft and revise, you may want to keep a list of ideas for your conclusion, especially ones that go beyond a simple restatement of the thesis (see **3c**). Some suggestions for writing effective conclusions follow, beginning with the technique of restating the thesis and main points.

(a) Rephrasing the thesis and summarizing the main points

10   The Endangered Species Act should not take into account economic considerations. Economics doesn't know how to value a species or a forest. Its logic drives people to exploit resources to the point of extinction. The Endangered Species Act tells us that extinction is morally unacceptable. It was enacted by a Congress and president in a wise mood, to express a higher value than a bottom line.

        —**DONELLA MEADOWS,** "Not Seeing the Forest for the Dollar Bills"

(b) Calling attention to larger issues

11   Nonetheless, the greatest growth industry in this country is the one dedicated to the mirage of good grooming as the road to immortality. Immigrants past built bridges and schools, gilded the cherubim in the corners of churches. Today an entire immigrant class makes a living painting

toenails and opening pores. Advances in science and medicine have combined to offer this: the tattooing of permanent eyeliner, the bleaching of teeth, the lasering of sun spots. The waning days of a great nation can be charted only in hindsight. But surely it is a danger sign of some sort when a country is no longer able to care for its own cuticles.

—ANNA QUINDLEN, "Leg Waxing and Life Everlasting"

(c) Calling for a change in action or attitude

12   Our medical care system is in trouble and getting worse. While the experts try to figure out how to achieve utopian goals at affordable prices, let's do something practical about the suffering on our doorsteps. Primary care is the most affordable safety net we can offer our citizens. By all means, let's continue the debate about universal, comprehensive insurance to cover all medical costs, but, in the meantime, let's provide primary health care to all uninsured Americans—now!

—GORDON T. MOORE, "Caring for the Uninsured and Underinsured"

(d) Concluding with a vivid image

13   At just past 10 a.m., farm workers and scrap-yard laborers in Somerset County looked up to see a large commercial airliner dipping and lunging as it swooped low over the hill country of southern Pennsylvania, near the town of Shanksville. A man driving a coal truck on Route 30 said he saw the jet tilt violently from side to side, then suddenly plummet "straight down." It hit nose first on the grassy face of a reclaimed strip mine at approximately 10:05 Eastern Daylight Time and exploded into a fireball, shattering windowpanes a half-mile away. The seventy-two-year-old man who was closest to the point of impact saw what looked to him like the yellow mushroom cloud of an atomic blast. Twenty-eight-year-old Eric Peterson was one of the first on the scene. He arrived to discover a flaming crater fifty feet deep. Shredded clothing hung from the trees, and smoldering airplane parts littered the ground. It did not look much like the site of a great American victory, but it was.   —RANDALL SULLIVAN, "Flight 93"

(e) Connecting with the introduction

The introduction

14   Here's a memory. On an overcast morning in February, 1996, I received in the mail from my mother, in St. Louis, a Valentine's package containing

one pinkly romantic greeting card, two four-ounce Mr. Goodbars, one hollow red filigree heart on a loop of thread, and one copy of a neuropathologist's report on my father's brain autopsy.

In the essay that follows this introduction, Jonathan Franzen focuses on what Alzheimer's takes away from the human brain—from his father's brain, in particular. His conclusion loops back to his mom, his dad, and that autopsy report.

The conclusion

15   After we'd kissed him [Franzen's father] goodbye and signed the forms that authorized the brain autopsy, my mother sat down in our kitchen and uncharacteristically accepted my offer of undiluted Jack Daniel's. "I see now," she said, "that when you're dead you're really dead." This was true enough. But, in the slow-motion way of Alzheimer's, my father wasn't much deader now than he'd been two hours or two weeks or two months ago. We'd simply lost the last of the parts out of which we could fashion a living whole. There would be no new memories of him. The only stories we could tell now were the ones we already had.

                      —JONATHAN FRANZEN, "My Father's Brain"

Whatever technique you choose for your conclusion, provide readers with a sense of closure. Bear in mind that they may be wondering, "So what? Why have you told me all this?" Your conclusion gives you an opportunity to address that concern. If there is any chance that readers may not understand your purpose, use your conclusion to clarify why you have asked them to read what they have just read.

Exercise 2

Thumb through a magazine you enjoy, and skim the introductions of all the articles. Select two introductions that catch your attention. Copy them, word for word, and then consider the reasons *why* they interest you. What specific techniques for an introduction did the authors use? Next, look through the same or another magazine for two effective conclusions. Copy these, and analyze their effectiveness as well. Be prepared to share your findings with the rest of the class.

4c Revising for unified and coherent paragraphs

When revising the body of an essay, writers are likely to find opportunities for further development within each paragraph (see **3f** and **3g**) and to discover ways to make each paragraph more **unified** by relating every sentence within the paragraph to a single main idea (**4c(2)**), which might appear in a topic sentence. After weeding out unrelated sentences, writers concentrate on **coherence,** ordering the sentences so that ideas progress logically and smoothly from one sentence to the next. A successful paragraph is well developed, unified, and coherent.

(1) The topic sentence expresses the main idea.

Much like the thesis statement of an essay, a **topic sentence** states the main idea of a paragraph and comments on that main idea. Although the topic sentence is usually the first sentence in a paragraph, it can appear in any position within the paragraph. Sometimes, the topic sentence is implied by something in all of the sentences. If you need to work at improving the unity and coherence of your paragraphs, you might want to keep your topic sentences at the beginning. Not only will they serve to remind you of your focus, but they will also be obvious to your readers, who will grasp your main ideas immediately. More experienced writers may avoid repeating the same paragraph patterns by organizing their sentences differently within different paragraphs.

When you announce your general topic and then provide specific support for it, you are writing **deductively.** Your topic sentence appears first, like the one in italics in paragraph 16, which announces that the author will offer evidence as to why we are suspicious of rapid cognition.

16   *I think we are innately suspicious of . . . rapid cognition.* We live in a world that assumes that the quality of a decision is directly related to the time and effort that went into making it. When doctors are faced with a difficult diagnosis, they order more tests, and when we are uncertain about what we hear, we ask for a second opinion. And what do we tell our children? Haste makes waste. Look before you leap. Stop and *think.* Don't judge a book by its cover. We believe that we are always better off gathering as much information as possible and spending as much time as possible in deliberation. We really only trust conscious decision making. But there are moments, particularly in

times of stress, when haste does not make waste, when our snap judgments and first impressions can offer a much better means of making sense of the world. —MALCOLM GLADWELL, *Blink*

If you want to emphasize the main idea of a paragraph or give its organization some extra support, you can begin and conclude the paragraph with two versions of the same idea. This strategy is particularly useful for long paragraphs because it gives readers whose attention may have wandered a second chance to grasp the main idea. In paragraph 17, which is remarkably long, both the first sentence and the last convey the idea that the things the soldiers carried weighed heavily upon them.

17   *The things they carried were largely determined by necessity.* Among the necessities or near necessities were P-38 can openers, pocket knives, heat tabs, wrist watches, dog tags, mosquito repellant, chewing gum, candy, cigarettes, salt tablets, packets of Kool-Aid, lighters, matches, sewing kits, Military Payment Certificates, C rations, and two or three canteens of water. Together, these items weighed between fifteen and twenty pounds, depending upon a man's habits or rate of metabolism. Henry Dobbins, who was a big man, carried extra rations; he was especially fond of canned peaches in heavy syrup over pound cake. Dave Jensen, who practiced field hygiene, carried a toothbrush, dental floss, and several hotel-size bars of soap he'd stolen on R&R in Sydney, Australia. Ted Lavender, who was scared, carried tranquilizers until he was shot in the head outside the village of Than Khe in mid-April. By necessity, and because it was SOP [standard operating procedure], they all carried steel helmets that weighed five pounds including the liner and camouflage cover. They carried the standard fatigue jackets and trousers. Very few carried underwear. On their feet they carried jungle boots—2.1 pounds—and Dave Jensen carried three pairs of socks and a can of Dr. Scholl's foot powder as a precaution against trench foot. Until he was shot, Ted Lavender carried six or seven ounces of premium dope, which for him was a necessity. Mitchell Sanders, the RTO [radio telephone operator], carried condoms. Norman Bowker carried a diary. Rat Kiley carried comic books. Kiowa, a devout Baptist, carried an illustrated New Testament that had been presented to him by his father, who taught Sunday school in Oklahoma City, Oklahoma. As a hedge against bad times, however, Kiowa also carried his grandmother's distrust of the white man, his grandfather's old hunting hatchet. Necessity dictated. Because the land was mined and booby-trapped, it was SOP for each man to carry a steel-centered, nylon-covered flak jacket, Simonov carbines and black-market Uzis and .38 caliber Smith &

Wesson handguns and 66 mm LAWs and shotguns and silencers and blackjacks and bayonets and C-4 explosives. Lee Strunk carried a slingshot; a weapon of last resort, he called it. Mitchell Sanders carried brass knuckles. Kiowa carried his grandfather's feathered hatchet. Every third or fourth man carried a Claymore antipersonnel mine—3.5 pounds with its firing device. They all carried at least one M-18 colored smoke grenade—twenty-four ounces. Some carried CS or teargas grenades. Some carried white-phosphorus grenades. *They all carried all they could bear, and then some, including a silent awe for the terrible power of the things they carried.*

—**TIM O'BRIEN**, *The Things They Carried*

As you prepare to revise a draft, try underlining the topic sentences you can identify. If you cannot find a topic sentence, add a sentence stating the main idea of that paragraph. If you find that you open every paragraph with a topic sentence, you might try experimenting with another pattern, revising a paragraph so that the topic sentence appears at the end, as in paragraph 18.

18   I have been to big-money tribal casinos on both coasts and in Minnesota, and they tend to run together in the mind. They are of a sameness—the vast parking lots, the low, mall-like, usually windowless buildings, the arbitrary Indianish décor, the gleeful older gamblers rattling troves of quarters in their bulging pants pockets, the unromantic expressions in the employees' eyes. Also, going to a major Indian casino is so much like going to a non-Indian one, in Atlantic City or someplace, that you may have to remind yourself exactly why Indian casinos enjoy tax advantages non-Indian casinos don't. The idea of Indian tribal sovereignty, a bit elusive to begin with, can fade out entirely behind the deluge of generic gambling dollars. In the last few years, some state and federal legislators have begun to view tribal casinos in just this skeptical way. Their renewed attacks on tribal sovereignty usually include a lot of rhetoric about the supposed great gambling wealth of Indian tribes nowadays. Regrettably, the resentment against Indian casinos, whose largest benefits go to only a few tribes, may end up threatening the sovereignty of all tribes. Many Indians have worried more about loss of sovereignty since the casino boom began. Some say that entering into compacts with the states is itself a wrong idea, because it accepts state jurisdiction where none existed before. Concern for sovereignty has been a main reason why the Navajo have rejected casino gambling. *A Navajo leader said that tribes who accept outside oversight of their*

gambling operations have allowed a violation of tribal sovereignty; he added, "The sovereignty of the Navajo nation and the Navajo people is not and should never be for sale." —IAN FRAZIER, *On the Rez*

Placing the topic sentence toward or at the end of the paragraph works well when you are moving from specific supporting details to a generalization about those ideas—that is, when you are writing **inductively.** Effective writers try to meet the expectations of their readers, which often include the anticipation that the first sentence will be the topic sentence; however, writers and readers alike enjoy an occasional departure from the expected. And writers need to adjust their paragraph organization according to the rhetorical purpose of each paragraph.

(2) In a unified paragraph, every sentence relates to the main idea.

Paragraphs are **unified** when every sentence relates to the main idea; unity is violated when something unrelated to the rest of the material appears. Consider the obvious violation in paragraph 19.

19   The Marion, Ohio of my childhood offered activities to suit any child's taste. In the summer, I could walk to the library and spend the afternoon browsing or reading. On the way home, I could stop by Isaly's dairy and buy a skyscraper ice cream cone for twenty-five cents. I could swim every afternoon in our neighborhood swimming pool, where kids played freely and safely. If I wanted, I could meet up with my cousin Babs and walk downtown for a movie matinee or a grilled-cheese sandwich at Woolworth's lunch counter. *It's hard to find a good grilled-cheese sandwich these days.* If we didn't want to stay within walking distance, we could take a city bus out to the roller rink or, if something big was going on, out to the fairgrounds.

Easy to delete, the italicized sentence about today's grilled-cheese sandwiches violates the unity of a paragraph devoted to childhood activities in a small town. If the overall purpose of the essay includes a comparison of small-town life then and now, the writer could simply develop the idea of what is "hard to find" into a separate paragraph.

As you revise your paragraphs for unity, the following tips may help you.

TIPS FOR IMPROVING PARAGRAPH UNITY

Identify	Identify the topic sentence for each paragraph. Where is each located?
Relate	Read each sentence in a paragraph, and decide if and how it relates to the topic sentence.
Eliminate	Any sentence that violates the unity of a paragraph should be cut (or saved for use elsewhere).
Clarify	Any sentence that "almost" relates to the topic sentence should be revised until it does relate. You may need to clarify details or add information or a transitional word or phrase to make the relationship clear.
Rewrite	If more than one idea is being conveyed in a single paragraph, either rewrite the topic sentence so that it includes both ideas and establishes a relationship between them or split the paragraph into two.

(3) Clearly arranged ideas contribute to coherence.

Some paragraphs are unified (see 4c(2)) but not coherent. In a unified paragraph, every sentence relates to the main idea of the paragraph. In a **coherent** paragraph, the relationship among the ideas is clear and meaningful, and the progression from one sentence to the next is easy for readers to follow. Paragraph 20 has unity but lacks coherence.

Lacks coherence

20   The inside of the refrigerator was covered with black mold, and it smelled as if something had been rotting in there for years. I put new paper down on all the shelves, and my roommate took care of lining the drawers. The stove was as dirty as the refrigerator. *When we moved into our new apartment, we found that the kitchen was in horrible shape.* We had to scrub the walls with a brush and plenty of Lysol to get rid of the grease. The previous tenant had left behind lots of junk that we had to get rid of. All the drawers and cabinets had to be washed.

Although every sentence in this paragraph concerns cleaning the kitchen after moving into an apartment, the sentences are not arranged coherently. This paragraph can easily be revised so that the italicized topic sentence controls the meaningful flow of ideas—from what the roommates saw to what they did.

Revised for coherence

21 *When we moved into our new apartment, we found that the kitchen was in horrible shape.* The previous tenant had left behind lots of junk that we had to get rid of. The inside of the refrigerator was covered with black mold, and it smelled as if something had been rotting in there for years. The stove was as dirty as the refrigerator. [New sentence:] So we set to work. All the drawers and cabinets had to be washed. I put new paper down on all the shelves, and my roommate took care of lining the drawers. We had to scrub the walls with a brush and plenty of Lysol to get rid of the grease.

Paragraph 21 is coherent as well as unified.

To achieve coherence and unity in your paragraphs, study the following patterns of organization (chronological, spatial, emphatic, and logical), and consider which ones you might use in your own writing.

(a) Using chronological order, according to time

When you use **chronological order,** you arrange ideas according to the order in which things happened. This organizational pattern is particularly useful in narrations.

22 When everyone was finished, we were given the signal to put our silverware on our plates. Each piece of silverware had its place—the knife at the top of the plate, sharp edge toward us; then the fork, perfectly lined up next to the knife; then the spoon—and any student who didn't put the silverware in the right place couldn't leave the table. Lastly, our napkins were refolded and put in their original spot. When we stood, we pushed our chair under the table and waited for the signal to turn right. Then we marched outside, single file, while the kitchen staff started to clean the dining room.

—ANNE E. BOLANDER AND ADAIR N. RENNING, *I Was #87*

(b) Using spatial order, according to the movement of the eyes

When you arrange ideas according to **spatial order,** you orient the reader's focus from right to left, near to far, top to bottom, and so on. This organizational pattern is particularly effective in descriptions. Often the organization is so obvious that the writer can forgo a topic sentence, as in paragraph 23.

23 The stores on Tremont Avenue seemed to be extensions of my domestic space. Each one had sensory memories that I associate with my mother. On the corner was the delicatessen. From its counter, which was like a bar

complete with a brass footrest, came the deeply dark smell of cured meats, the tang of frankfurters, with the steaming background scent of hot knishes on the griddle. —**LENNARD J. DAVIS**, *My Sense of Silence*

(c) Using emphatic order, according to importance

When you use **emphatic order,** you arrange information in order of importance, usually from least to most important. Emphatic order is especially useful in expository and persuasive writing, both of which involve helping readers understand logical relationships (such as what caused something to happen or what kinds of priorities should be established). In paragraph 24, the writer emphasizes the future as the most important arena for change.

24   Among the first things Goldsmith had taught the executive was to look only to the future, because, whatever he had done to make people angry, he couldn't fix it now. "Don't ask for feedback about the past," he says. Goldsmith has turned against the notion of feedback lately. He has written an article on a more positive methodology, which he calls "feedforward." "How many of us have wasted much of our lives impressing our spouse, partner, or significant other with our near-photographic memory of their previous sins, which we document and share to help them improve?" he says. "Dysfunctional! Say, 'I can't change the past—all I can say is I'm sorry for what I did wrong.' Ask for suggestions for the future. Don't promise to do everything they suggest—leadership is not a popularity contest. But follow up on a regular basis, and you know what's going to happen? You will get better." —**LARISSA MACFARQUHAR**, "The Better Boss"

(d) Using logical order, moving from specific to general or from general to specific

Sometimes the movement within a paragraph follows a **logical order,** from specific to general or from general to specific. A paragraph may begin with a series of details and conclude with a summarizing statement, as paragraphs 18 and 25 do, or it may begin with a general statement or idea, which is then supported by particular details, as in paragraphs 21 and 26.

25   This winter, I took a vacation from our unfinished mess. Getting back to it was tough, and one morning, I found myself on my knees before the dishwasher, as if in prayer, though actually busting a water-pipe weld. To my

right were the unfinished cabinets, to my left the knobless backdoor, behind me a hole I'd torn in the wall. There in the kitchen, a realization hit me like a 2-by-4: for two years I'd been working on this house, and there was still no end in sight. It had become my Vietnam.

—**ROBERT SULLIVAN,** "Home Wrecked"

26   It was not the only disappointment my mother felt in me. In the years that followed, I failed her so many times, each time asserting my own will, my right to fall short of expectations. I didn't get straight As. I didn't become class president. I didn't get into Stanford. I dropped out of college.

—**AMY TAN,** "Two Kinds"

4d   Transitions within and between paragraphs

Even if the sentences are arranged in a seemingly clear sequence, a single paragraph may lack internal coherence and a series of paragraphs may lack overall coherence if transitions are abrupt or nonexistent. When revising your writing, you can improve the coherence by using pronouns, repetition, conjunctions, and transitional words or phrases (see also **23d**).

(1) Pronouns help establish links between sentences.

In paragraph 27, the writer enumerates the similarities of identical twins raised separately. She mentions their names only once, but uses the pronouns *both, their,* and *they* to keep the references to the twins always clear.

27   Jim Springer and Jim Lewis were adopted as infants into working-class Ohio families. **Both** liked math and did not like spelling in school. **Both** had law enforcement training and worked part-time as deputy sheriffs. **Both** vacationed in Florida, **both** drove Chevrolets. Much has been made of the fact that **their** lives are marked by a trail of similar names. **Both** married and divorced women named Linda and had second marriages with women named Betty. **They** named **their** sons James Allan and James Alan, respectively. **Both** like mechanical drawing and carpentry. **They** have almost identical drinking and smoking patterns. **Both** chew **their** fingernails down to the nubs.   —**CONSTANCE HOLDEN,** "Identical Twins Reared Apart"

(2) Repetition of words, phrases, structures, or ideas can link a sentence to those that precede it.

In paragraph 28, the repetition of the key word *never* links sentences to preceding sentences and also provides emphasis. (See **30d**.)

28   ***Never*** is the most powerful word in the English language, or perhaps any language. It's magic. Every time I have made an emphatic pronouncement invoking the word ***never***, whatever follows that I don't want to happen happens. ***Never*** has made a fool of me many times. The first time I remember noticing the powerful effect of this word I was a student at Indian school. My best friend, Belinda Gonzalez, and I were filling out our schedules for spring semester. She was Blackfeet, a voice major from Yakima, Washington. I was a painting major and checking out times for painting and drawing courses. She suggested I sign up for drama class with her. I said, no I will **never** go on stage. Despite my initial protest I did sign up for drama and dance troupes in the country, and now I make my living performing. ***Never*** is that powerful.

—**JOY HARJO**, "The Power of Never"

In this case, the author wished to stress the expectations many people hold when they declare "never." By repeating the word five times in one paragraph, Harjo emphasizes its power.

Parallelism, another kind of repetition, is a key principle in writing coherent sentences and paragraphs (see chapter **29**).

(3) Using conjunctions and other transitional words or phrases also contributes to coherence.

Conjunctions and other transitional words or phrases demonstrate the logical relationship between ideas. In the following sentences, in which two clauses are linked by different conjunctions, notice the subtle changes in the relationship between the two ideas.

The dog ran, **and** she threw the frisbee.

The dog ran **while** she threw the frisbee.

The dog ran **because** she threw the frisbee.

The dog ran, **so** she threw the frisbee.

The dog ran; **later** she threw the frisbee.

The following list of frequently used transitional connections, arranged according to the kinds of relationships they establish, can help you with your critical reading as well as your writing.

TYPES OF TRANSITIONAL CONNECTIONS

Addition	and, and then, further, furthermore, also, too, again, in addition, besides
Alternative	or, nor, either, neither, on the other hand, conversely, otherwise
Comparison	similarly, likewise, in like manner
Concession	although this may be true, even so, still, nevertheless, at the same time, notwithstanding, nonetheless, in any event, that said
Contrast	but, yet, or, and yet, however, on the contrary, in contrast
Exemplification	for example, for instance, in the case of
Intensification	in fact, indeed, to tell the truth, moreover, even more important, to be sure
Place	here, beyond, nearby, opposite to, adjacent to, on the opposite side
Purpose	to this end, for this purpose, with this objective, in order to, so that
Repetition	as I have said, in other words, that is, as has been noted, as previously stated
Result or cause	so, for, therefore, accordingly, consequently, thus, thereby, as a result, then, because, hence
Sequence	next, first, second, third, in the first place, in the second place, finally, last, then, afterward, later
Summary	to sum up, in brief, on the whole, in sum, in short
Time	meanwhile, soon, after a few days, in the meantime, now, in the past, while, during, since

The following checklist can guide you in revising your paragraphs.

CHECKLIST for Revising Paragraphs

- Does the paragraph have a clear (or clearly implied) topic sentence (4c(1))?
- Do all the ideas in the paragraph belong together? Do sentences link to previous and later ones? Are the sentences arranged in chronological, spatial, emphatic, or logical order, or are they arranged in some other pattern (4c(2))?
- How does the paragraph link to the preceding and following ones (4d)?
- Are sentences connected to each other with effective transitions (4d(2))?
- What evidence do you have that the paragraph is adequately developed (3f)? What idea or detail might be missing (4a(1))? What rhetorical methods have been used to develop each of the paragraphs (3g)?

When revising an essay, you must consider the effectiveness of the individual paragraphs at the same time as you consider how those paragraphs work (or do not work) together to achieve the overall purpose. Some writers like to revise at the paragraph level before addressing larger concerns; other writers cannot work on the individual paragraphs until they have grappled with larger issues related to the rhetorical situation (overall purpose, attention to audience, and context; see 1a) or have finalized their thesis (3c). All experienced writers use a process to write, but they do not all use exactly the same process. Since there is no universal, predetermined order to the writing process, you can follow whichever steps work best for you each time you are revising. Be guided by the principles and strategies discussed in this chapter, but trust also in your own good sense.

4e The benefits of peer review

Because writing is a form of communication, writers check to see whether they are communicating their ideas effectively to their readers. Instructors are one set of readers, but they are often the last people to see your writing. Before you submit your work to an instructor, take advantage of other opportunities for getting responses to it. Consult with readers—at the writing center, in your dorm, in your classes, or from online writing groups—asking them for honest responses to your concerns.

(1) Clearly defined evaluation standards help both writers and reviewers.

Although you will always write within a rhetorical situation (see 1a), you will often address that situation in terms of an assigned task with specific evaluation standards. Instructors usually indicate their evaluation standards in class, on assignment sheets, or on separate handouts (see 5a(2)). Whether you are working with a small writing group from class or a single reader, such as a classmate or a writing center tutor, you need to review the evaluation criteria at the beginning of a working session and use them to determine where you should focus your attention. For example, if your instructor has told you that your essay will be evaluated primarily in terms of whether you have a clear thesis (see 3c) and adequate support for it (3f and 3g), then those features should be your primary focus. Your secondary concerns may be sentence length and variety (see chapter 31) and the effectiveness of your introduction (4b(1)).

Although evaluation standards or guidelines do not guarantee useful feedback every time, they help. They help you focus on the advice you want to ask for in a writer's memo (see 4e(2)), and they help your reviewers focus on what kinds of advice to give. Reviewers can refer to the guidelines as they carefully and slowly read and reread your draft. They will then be able to respond with specifics and with respect. If a reviewer sees a problem that the writer did not identify, the reviewer should ask the writer if she or he wants to discuss it and should abide by the writer's decision. A reviewer's comments should point out what the writer has done well as well as suggest how to improve particular passages. For instance, the reviewer may frame recommendations in terms of personal engagement with the text (see page 85): "You say 'you should' a few times. How about changing this to 'I would recommend' or 'based on my experiences, the following methods have been helpful' in order to make your tone less presumptuous?" A reviewer can be honest and helpful simultaneously. Ultimately, however, the success of the essay is the responsibility of the writer, who will evaluate the reviewer's advice, rejecting any comments that would take the essay in a different direction and applying any suggestions that help fulfill the rhetorical purpose (see 1c).

If you are developing your own criteria for evaluation, the following checklist can help you get started. Based on the elements of the rhetorical situation, this checklist can be easily adjusted so that it meets your specific needs for a particular assignment.

CHECKLIST for Evaluating a Draft of an Essay

- What is your purpose in the essay (1c)? Does the essay fulfill the assignment?
- Does the essay address a specific audience (1d)? Is that audience appropriate for the assignment?
- What is the tone of the essay (4a(3))? How does the tone align with the overall purpose, the intended audience, and the context for the writing (1c–e)?
- Is your topic sufficiently focused (3b)? What is the thesis statement (3c)?
- What assertions do you make to support the thesis statement? What specific evidence do you provide to support these assertions?
- Are paragraphs arranged in an effective sequence (3d and 4c(3))? What pattern of organization are you using? Is each paragraph thoroughly developed (3f and 3g)?
- Is the introduction effective (4b(1))? How do you engage the reader's attention?
- Is the conclusion appropriate for the essay's purpose (4b(2))? Does it draw the essay together, or does it seem disconnected and abrupt?

---

(2) You can help your reviewers by telling them about your purpose and your concerns.

When submitting a draft for review, you can increase your chances of getting the kind of help you want by introducing your work and indicating what your concerns are. You can provide such an orientation orally to a writing group, tutor, or peer reviewer in just a few minutes. Or, when doing so is not possible, perhaps because you are submitting a draft online, you can attach to your draft a cover letter consisting of a paragraph or two—sometimes called a **writer's memo.** In either case, adopting the following model can help ensure that reviewers will give you useful responses.

SUBMITTING A DRAFT FOR REVIEW

Topic and Purpose

State your topic and your exigence for writing (see 1b). Indicate your thesis (3c) and purpose (1c). Providing this information gives reviewers useful direction.

Strengths

Mark the passages of the draft you are confident about. Doing so directs attention away from areas you do not want to discuss and saves time for all concerned.

Concerns

Put question marks by the passages you find troublesome, and ask for specific advice wherever possible. For example, if you are worried about your conclusion, say so. Or if you suspect that one of your paragraphs may not fit the overall purpose, direct attention to that particular paragraph. You are most likely to get the kind of help you want and need when you ask for it specifically.

Melissa's writer's memo follows.

Topic and purpose: I'm focusing on the good and bad consequences of working part time while attending school full time. Given that tuition is on the rise nationally, while employment opportunities are on the decline, I am imagining that more and more college students will have to hold a job while attending school. My purpose is to explain that doing this is hard, but it's doable, and, besides, when done well, it makes the college student a better, more responsible and grateful human being.

Concerns: My biggest concern is sounding like I think juggling the obligations of school and work is easy if you're organized. And I know from experience that that is not true. So I guess it's my tone that I'm worried about—tone plus examples.

Melissa Schraeder submitted the draft on pages 83–87 for peer review in a first-year writing course. She worked with a classmate, who was working on the same assignment, and a peer tutor from the university writing center, using a set of criteria that she had prepared. Because these students were learning how to conduct peer evaluations, their comments represent the range of responses you might receive in a similar situation. As members of writing groups gain experience and learn to employ the strategies outlined in this section, their advice usually becomes more helpful.

Some instructors may require students to do peer reviewing online, using e-mail or a computer network. You should always check with your instructor for specific peer-review guidelines and procedures, but here are some general suggestions for online reviewing.

- If you are responding to a classmate's draft via e-mail, reread your comments before sending them to be sure that your tone is appropriate and that you have avoided the kinds of misunderstandings that can occur with e-mail (see **6b** and **6d**).
- Always save a copy of your comments in case your e-mail message is lost or inadvertently deleted.
- If you are responding to a classmate's draft using an online course-management program, such as WebCT, Angel, or Blackboard, remember that your comments may be read by other classmates, too.
- Follow the advice in **4e(1)**, just as you would if you were commenting on a paper copy of your classmate's draft.

As you read the assignment and then Melissa's draft, remember that it is only a first draft—not a model of perfect writing—and also that this is the first time the peer reviewers, Bob Geiger and Michelle Clewell, responded to it. Melissa sent her draft electronically to Bob and Michelle, who used the Track Changes function of their word-processing program to add suggested changes and comments throughout the essay.

The assignment   Draft a three- to four-page, double-spaced essay in which you analyze the causes or consequences of a choice you have had to make in the last year or two. Whatever choice you analyze, make sure that it concerns a topic you can develop with confidence and without violating your own sense of privacy. Moreover, consider the expectations of your audience and whether the topic you have chosen will help you communicate something meaningful to readers. As you draft, then, establish an audience for your essay, a group that might benefit from or be interested in any recommendation that grows out of your analysis.

Draft—Working toward a Degree   Bob   *Michelle*

When I first decided to pursue my college education at Penn State University, a key factor in my decision was that as a state university, Penn State offered a relatively low tuition. *This first sentence doesn't seem to have much grounding. Maybe develop your own experience with choosing a school more, or use a different opening?* Adding this factor to the giving financial support of my parents and my fortune at receiving several grants and scholarships, I initially believed that my college education would be easily affordable. When I started classes however, I soon found that with all the additional expenses of school such as the cost of books, technology fees, and spending money, going to school meant finding a job. Though hesitant at first about how holding a job might affect my studies, I soon took on a part-time job ~~where I worked,~~ *working* about fifteen hours a week. *Up until this point your sentences seem sort of long. Maybe you can condense these introductory sentences into a central idea that will get us more quickly to your thesis statement. See my suggestion.* Based on my own experience, I feel confident in saying that balancing a part-time job with success in schoolwork is not only a manageable task, but also a valuable experience contributing to growth as a student and as an individual. ~~Since so many students of today need to work while going to school, I hope to show them that while holding a part-time job and doing well in school may seem difficult at first, in many ways these two undertakings are quite compatible.~~ *This sentence seems repetitive to me—I don't think it is needed.*

If you have the right attitude and some good advice about finding a part-time job, you will find that working while going to school *does not have to be a scary experience* ~~is not as scary as it may sound at first~~. As college students, the most important thing ~~that we need~~ to remember is that ~~our~~ schoolwork must always be ~~our~~ *your* first priority. *I think you should keep your pronouns consistent. Since you started with the second-person voice, why not stick with it?* Keeping this in mind, as with most things in life, your own individual sacrifices in this balancing act will determine your success. One of the sacrifices that you might have to make is the need to limit or carefully schedule the time that you spend with your friends. Since you are trying to show how work at school is both manageable and beneficial for a college student, maybe you shouldn't begin your evidence with such a negative example. Keep a consistent tone. Not all sacrifices need to be so difficult though. A small sacrifice you can make is to bring your schoolbooks along with you to work and utilize your work breaks to get a ~~heads up~~ head start on your nightly schoolwork. In addition, ~~since part of your time is already committed to your employers, You~~ you will need to get a good handle on your school schedule and plan ahead ~~to determine the time you need to work on various assignments~~. *This section seems kind of vague. I think it would be better if you gave some of your own personal experiences with planning in order to show specific examples of this point.* This sacrifice however will have positive repercussions as it will encourage you to form early study and time management habits. This is a good point, but I wonder if it might fit better on page 3 where you begin to discuss the positive repercussions of part-time work on the college experience.

While it is important to make such sacrifices in balancing a part-time job with success in school, you need not put all of the pressure on yourself. In fact, a key factor in minimizing such pressure is to choose a job where you work for an understanding employer. I don't like the way this is worded, it implies that you are putting pressure on the employer. Maybe rephrase "there are ways to limit the pressure that you might feel." This is not always an easy task and is certainly easier said than done. You can, however, take advantage of the resources available to you such as older students, advisors, and internship coordinators in finding a student-friendly employer. You should look for an employer that understands the need to put schoolwork first and who values scholarship in employees. A good place to look for such an employer is in university-run businesses where supervisors are advised to view employees as students first and foremost. Planning ahead around exam or paper weeks, you should also look for a job that offers flexibility and variability in scheduling hours. Again, this is a feature that can be found in most university-related businesses or services since many of these follow the academic calendar in their hours of operation. For the understanding and flexibility that such jobs offer, you should take advantage of the many positions available within your own college or university. *This paragraph seems to repeat itself a little bit. I think you should condense this material and use a personal experience to drive home your point about university employment.* This paragraph is where you start to sound too "preachy." You say "you should" a few times. How about changing this to "I would recommend" or "based on my experiences, the following methods have been helpful" in order to make your tone less presumptuous?

Now that I have shown how college students can manage their schoolwork with a part-time job, I want to move on to demonstrating the ways in which the challenge of balancing work with school can be a valuable learning and growing experience for college students. First, this challenge provides students with a degree of self-discipline as working students need to prioritize their schoolwork carefully, thus learning the importance of realistic goal-setting and time management. *The tone of this is too definite. Remember that your previous paragraphs give good examples but are not the ultimate method for everyone.* Second, students who work to support their own education often develop a heightened sense of respect, value, and responsibility for that education. *Great point!* This means that working students often take their studies rather seriously and realize the importance of a timely completion of their degree. These two examples represent large-scale attitudes and outlooks on education, but part-time work can also have more immediate effects on the academic career of a college student.

Such immediate effects of part-time work can be categorized into two types of experiences ~~with part-time work~~, work which offers career experience and work which fuels academic and career motivation. The former category includes but need not be limited to arranged, paid internships or focused work programs implemented or overseen by your college or university. Career experience is also found in more unexpected ways, such as when a management student gets to observe her manager at work or when a communications student practices his skills in a sales job. While many students will be fortunate to have such experiences, others will find themselves working at jobs that have very little to do with their projected career goals. In such cases, there are still valuable lessons to be learned. Certain types of part-time work, such as factory, food service, or maintenance work, while less directly valuable to the education process, often have positive motivating effects on students' academic attitudes. A working student who faces boredom, monotony, or low wages in her or his part-time job, will often be motivated to achieve academic excellence as a means of moving beyond the scope of this part-time work. *I think you should add some personal experience here. Did you work at a job related to your major or that was monotonous yet motivating?*

With the right attitude and outlook, part-time work can have many positive effects on the experiences of a college student. Even the potential negativity of facing boredom or monotony at work can be used constructively to motivate students to do their best schoolwork. If your college years are the best and most important of your life, I assure you that combining work with academics will enrich that importance, as it will give you a greater appreciation for the education you worked doubly hard to receive. I like your conclusion. I think it is good that it ends on a very positive note and that it relates back to your title about "Working toward a Degree."

Melissa,

Generally, I think this is a very good essay. The overall progression of the paper going from "how to work and do well in school" to "why it is beneficial to work while in school" makes logical sense to me. I like that you emphasize the benefits of holding a job beyond just the obvious point of making money. I also think that you have strong credibility and show good will since you have personal experience with your topic. This credibility makes for a strong argument. Maybe it would behoove you to include specific examples of your working experiences in college. Although your credibility is strong, you might want to avoid being too "preachy" in your tone. I feel that this self-assured tone tends to weaken your argument. I do like, however, the way you note in your paper that not all work has to apply directly to your major in order for it to be valuable. And the way your working experiences reinforce this point. Finally, I like the point you make in the concluding paragraph about monotonous work motivating students to appreciate schooling and thus work harder at their education, as this is something that many college students don't think about. This is especially true for freshmen since many often take attending college for granted as they see it as the next logical step following high school.

—Bob Geiger

Melissa,

Your paper is well thought out and focused, yet combining several sentences and limiting the wordiness would intensify your point. The validity of the paper is strengthened because of your personal experience of holding a part-time job while attending college— tie some of these specific examples into your paper rather than using generic and general examples. This is a great draft—keep working, developing, and improving. Here are some specific suggestions for improvement.

- *First paragraph suggestion: "Because I decided to attend a state university, was fortunate to receive several grants and scholarships, and had the financial support of my parents, I initially believed my college education would be easily affordable. However, with all the additional expenses, such as the cost of books, technology fees, and spending money, going to school meant finding a part-time job."*
- *Paper has good structure and flow.*
- *Limit prepositional phrases and repeating yourself.*
- *Great points made about time management and valuing one's education.*
- *First half of the paper "you" is used talking directly to the student reading the paper, but the second half is written in a more generic third person. Try to be consistent with point of view.*
- *Add personal experiences and examples to strengthen points.*

—Michelle Clewell

Before revising, Melissa considered the comments she received from Bob and Michelle. Since she had asked both of them to respond to her introduction, conclusion, and organization, she had to weigh all the comments—relevant and irrelevant—and use the ones that seemed to be most useful for her next draft. For Melissa's own response to this draft, see pages 88–91. For Melissa's final draft, see pages 96–99.

Exercise 3

Reread "Working toward a Degree" and the comments it received. Identify the comments you think are the most useful, and explain why. Which comments seem to be less useful, even hurtful? Explain why. What additional comments would you make if Melissa asked you to review her draft?

After Melissa had time to reconsider her first draft and to think about the responses she received from readers (including the ones reprinted here), she made a number of large-scale changes concerning her attention to audience, improved her introduction and conclusion, and edited some of her paragraphs to make them more effective and clear. She also dealt with sentence-level issues of punctuation and word choice. The following pages show what her paper looked like midway through its revision. Melissa used the Track Changes function of her word-processing program as she revised so that she could see her changes.

Working toward a Degree

When I first decided to pursue my college education at Penn State University, a key factor in my decision was that as a state university, Penn State offered a relatively low tuition compared to other schools in the state, Temple, Pitt, Penn (of course), and many of the private schools. ~~That, together with my parents' support and the scholarships I'd won made me think that college would be easily affordable.~~ The relatively lower tuition, together with the generous financial support of my parents and my fortune to have received several grants and scholarships, led me to believe that my college education would be easily affordable. **When I started classes,** though ~~however,~~ I soon **discovered that unexpected expenses meant I'd have to find a job.** What with the cost of books, technology fees, and simple spending money, I realized that, for me, going to school meant going to work. ~~I was shocked by how many unexpected expenses I continued to have at Penn State. I knew I was going to have to find a job.~~ Though initially nervous about how a job would affect my schoolwork, ~~Soon,~~ I took on a part-time job at the Penn State Creamery where I worked about 15 hours a week—and I continue to do ~~still did~~ well in my coursework. ~~So I can now say that balancing a part-time job with success in schoolwork is not only manageable but valuable for students. Since so many students of today need to work while going to school, I hope to show them that while holding a part-time job and doing well in school may seem difficult at first, in many ways these two undertakings are quite compatible.~~ Based on my own experience, I feel confident in assuring you hardworking students that not only can you, too, balance a part-time job with success in schoolwork, but that the experience can be a valuable, life-long lesson for you.

If you think it through and try to keep a positive attitude, you~~'ll~~ will find that working while going to school is not as scary as it may sound at first. As college students, the most important thing we all need to remember is that our schoolwork must always be our first priority. ~~Keeping this in mind, as with~~ After all, like most things in life, ~~y~~our own individual sacrifices in this balancing act will determine ~~y~~our success. One of the first sacrifices you ~~must~~ might have to make is to ~~cut out time~~ limit, schedule, or reimagine the free time you spend with your friends~~—or schedule time with them (more about that below)~~. After you start working, you won't be able to spend long hours in the coffee shop with your friends, but you can spend study time with them. Not all sacrifices are difficult, though. Another small sacrifice might be to take ~~You can bring~~ your schoolbooks along with you to work and ~~utilize~~ consistently think of **your work** breaks ~~to get a heads up on~~ as pre-scheduled time to spend on **your nightly schoolwork**. Using work breaks for study time will also help you plan ahead in terms of your various assignment deadlines. ~~Besides, since you're already committed to work anyway, you'll need to get a handle on your school schedule and assignment deadlines. This sacrifice however will have positive repercussions early on because you'll immediately form better work and study habits.~~ Such small sacrifices can lead to big gains: you can learn quickly how to manage your time so you work and study efficiently.

While it is important to make such sacrifices in balancing a part-time job with success in school, you need not put all of the pressure on yourself. One key factor in reducing pressure will be your ability (or luck) in finding a job that includes ~~A key factor in reducing pressure is to find~~ an understanding employer.

Doing so is not easy, but is surely easier said than done, so you might want to take advantage of some of the on-campus or campus-sponsored job opportunities. Older students, academic advisors, and internship coordinators can help you locate student-friendly employers, an employer who expects you to be a reliable employee at the same time that she accepts the fact that your major responsibility is schoolwork. In fact, it was my academic advisor who told me about openings at the Creamery, a ~~This is not always easy. So take advantage of the resources available to you on campus. You should look for an employer that understands your need to put schoolwork first. A good place to look is in~~ university-run business where supervisors are advised to view employees as students first and foremost. The Creamery is one of a number of on-campus businesses that offer ~~You should also look for a job that offers~~ flexibility and variability in scheduling hours, ~~so take advantage of the many positions available within your own college or university,~~ especially during holiday breaks and finals' week. Again, this is a feature that can be found in most university-related businesses or services since they usually follow the academic calendar in their hours of operation. For these reasons, you should consider taking advantage of on-campus job opportunities.

Once you meet the challenge of balancing your schoolwork with the obligations of a part-time job, you'll find that the balancing act has its own rewards. First of all, this challenge provides you with self-discipline, the self-discipline that comes with prioritizing your schoolwork, setting realistic goals, managing your time, and becoming a reliable worker. ~~Now that I've shown how college students can manage their schoolwork with a part-time job, I want to move on to demonstrate the ways in which the challenge of balancing work with school can be a valuable learning experience for college students. First, this challenge provides students with self-discipline as they prioritize their schoolwork and learn to set realistic goals and time management.~~ Second, working students like us often value our education more because we've worked and paid (or helped pay) for it. Sometimes, we take more responsibility for our educations as well, which means that we study seriously enough to get out on time, even early. We understand the importance of a timely completion of our degree. ~~students who work value their education more. This means that working students take their studies seriously and realize the importance of a timely completion of their degree.~~ These two examples represent ~~large-scale~~ long-range attitudes and outlooks on education, but part-time work can also have more immediate effects on ~~the~~ your academic career as well. ~~of a college student.~~

Such immediate effects can be categorized into two types of experiences with part-time work~~,~~: work ~~which~~ that offers career experience and work ~~which~~ that fuels academic and career motivation. The former category includes but need not be limited to arranged, paid internships or focused work programs implemented or overseen by your college or university. Career experience is also found in more unexpected ways, such as when a management student gets to observe her manager at work or when a communications student practices his skills in a sales job. While many student~~s-workers~~ will be fortunate to have such experiences, others, like me, will find themselves working at jobs that have very little to do with their projected career goals. In such cases, there are still valuable lessons to be learned. While I'm grateful for my work environment, I don't plan to dip ice cream forever. Thus, ~~c~~Certain types of part-time work, such as factory, food service, or maintenance work, while less directly valuable to the education process, ~~often~~ can have positive motivating effects on your ~~students'~~ academic attitude. ~~If you're a~~ A working student who faces boredom, monotony, or low wages in ~~her or his~~ your part-time job, you might ~~will~~ be motivated to achieve academic excellence as a means of moving beyond the scope of this part-time work.

With the right attitude and outlook~~s~~ toward your part-time work, you might gain work experiences that are as positive as your academic ones. You can use the ~~can have many positive effects on the experiences of a college student. Even the potential negativity of facing~~ boredom at work as motivation ~~can be used constructively to motivate students~~ to do your ~~their~~ best schoolwork in order to move steadily through your requirements and graduate on time. You may also appreciate your career goals much more than someone who didn't work their way through school. Everyone tells us that our college years are the best years of our life—and I think they're right. By combining work with academics, we're earning a greater appreciation for our education, one we've worked doubly hard to receive.

After several more revisions, more peer review, and some careful editing and proofreading, Melissa was ready to submit her essay to her instructor. Her final draft is on pages 96–99.

 4f   Editing for clearer ideas, sentences, and paragraphs

If you are satisfied with the revised structure of your essay and the content of your paragraphs, you can begin editing individual sentences for clarity, effectiveness, and variety (see chapters 27–34). The following checklist for editing contains cross-references to chapters where you can find more specific information.

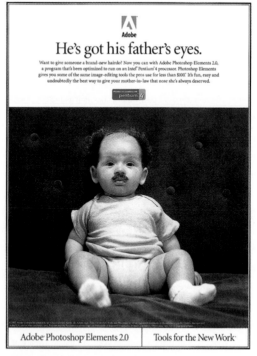

Just as photographic manipulation makes this image arresting, effective editing can make your writing more engaging.

CHECKLIST for Editing

① Sentences

- What is the unifying idea of each sentence (27)?

- Are the sentences varied in length? How many words are in your longest sentence? Your shortest sentence?

- How many of your sentences use subordination? Coordination? If you overuse any one sentence structure, revise for variation (31).

- Which sentences have or should have parallel structure (29)?

- Do any sentences contain misplaced or dangling modifiers (24)?

- Do any of your sentences shift in verb tense or tone (26c)? Is the shift intentional?

- Does each verb agree with its subject (26f)? Does every pronoun agree with its antecedent (25c)?

② Diction

- Have you repeated any words? Is your repetition intentional?

- Are your word choices exact, or are some words vague or too general (33)?

- Is the vocabulary you have chosen appropriate for your audience, purpose, and context (1a and 32)?

- Have you defined any technical or unfamiliar words for your audience (32c(4))?

| 4g | Proofreading for an error-free essay |

Once you have revised and edited your essay, it is your responsibility to format it properly (see chapter 7) and proofread it. Proofreading means making a special search to ensure that the final product you submit is free from error, or nearly so. An error-free essay allows your reader to read for meaning, without encountering incorrect spelling or punctuation that can interfere with meaning. As you proofread, you may discover problems that call for further revision or editing, but proofreading is usually the last step in the writing process.

With a computer, you can easily produce professional-looking documents. Showing that you care about presentation indicates respect for your audience. (See chapter 7.) However, no matter how professional your paper looks when you print it, proofread it carefully. Mechanical mistakes can undermine your credibility.

Because the eye tends to see what it expects to see, many writers miss errors—especially minor ones, such as a missing comma or apostrophe—even when they think they have proofread carefully. To proofread well, then, you need to read your work more than once and read it aloud. Some people find it useful to read through the paper several times, checking for a different set of items on each pass. Other writers rely on peer editors to provide help with proofreading.

The proofreading checklist that follows refers to chapters and sections in this handbook where you will find detailed information to help you. Also, keep your dictionary (see 32e) at hand to look up any words whose meaning or spelling you aren't sure of.

CHECKLIST for Proofreading

1 Spelling (40)

- Have you double-checked the words you frequently misspell and any the spell checker may have missed (for example, homophones or misspellings that still form words, such as *form* for *from*)?

- If you used a spell checker, did it overlook homophones (such as *there/their, who's/whose,* and *it's/its*) (40c)?

- Have you double-checked the spelling of all foreign words and all proper names?

2 Punctuation (35–39) and Capitalization (41)

- Does each sentence have appropriate closing punctuation, and have you used only one space after each end punctuation mark (39)?

- Is all punctuation within sentences—commas (35), semicolons (36), apostrophes (37), other internal marks of punctuation

(35d–i), and hyphens (40f)—used appropriately and placed correctly?

- Are direct quotations carefully and correctly punctuated (38a)? Where have you placed end punctuation with a quotation (38d)? Are quotations capitalized properly (38a and 41c(1))?
- Are all proper names, people's titles, and titles of published works correctly capitalized (41a and 41b)?
- Are titles of works identified by either quotation marks (38b) or italics (42a)?

4h The final draft

After producing the intermediate draft reprinted on pages 88–91, Melissa continued to revise and edit her essay. Each subsequent draft became stronger. The essay that Melissa ultimately submitted to her teacher follows.

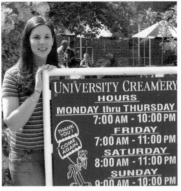

Melissa Schraeder successfully combined a part-time job with her college studies. Her hard work paid off—at graduation.

Melissa A. Schraeder

English 15

Professor Glenn

Working toward a Degree

With many private universities approaching $40,000 per year for tuition, it is all too obvious that getting a higher education is expensive. Fortunately, financial aid programs and state-funded schools, where tuition costs are normally less than half those of the average private school, have made higher education more affordable for Americans. When I decided to attend Penn State University, I was fortunate to receive several grants and scholarships as well as the promise of financial support from my parents. Little wonder that I initially believed that my college education would be easily affordable. When I started classes, however, I soon found that with all the additional expenses of school such as the cost of books, technology fees, and spending money, going to school meant finding a job—even for someone with financial support. Though hesitant about how holding a job might affect my studies, I soon took on a part-time job at the Penn State Creamery where I work about fifteen hours a week—and continue to do well in my coursework. Based on my experience, I feel confident in assuring hardworking students that not only can they balance a part-time job with success in schoolwork, but that the experience can be a valuable, life-long lesson, contributing to their growth as students and individuals.

If you have the right attitude and some good advice about finding a part-time job, you will find that working while going to school does not have to be an overwhelming experience. As a college student, the most important thing to remember is that schoolwork must always be your first priority. After all, like most things in life, your individual sacrifices in this balancing act will determine your success. One of the first sacrifices you might have to make is to limit, schedule, or reimagine the free time you have with your friends. After you start working, you

won't be able to spend long hours in the coffee shop with your friends, but you can

study with them. Not all sacrifices are difficult, though. Another small sacrifice

might be to take your schoolbooks along with you to work and consistently think of

your work breaks as pre-scheduled time to spend on your nightly coursework.

Using work breaks for study time will also help you plan ahead in terms of your

various assignment deadlines. I usually set up a calendar where I indicate the dates

of all my major exams and due dates for papers and then tailor my work schedule

around these dates. Such small sacrifices can lead to big gains: you quickly learn

how to manage your time so you work and study efficiently.

While it is important to make such sacrifices in balancing a part-time job

with success in school, you need not put all of the pressure on yourself. One key

factor in reducing pressure will be your ability (or luck) in finding a job that

includes an understanding employer. Doing so is not easy, so you might want to

take advantage of some of the on-campus or campus-sponsored job opportunities.

Older students, academic advisors, and internship coordinators can help you

locate a student-friendly employer, one that expects you to be a reliable employee

at the same time that the employer accepts the fact that your major responsibility

is your studies. In fact, it was my academic advisor who told me about openings at

the Creamery, a university-run business where supervisors are advised to view

employees as students first and foremost. Supervisors at the Creamery release a

monthly newsletter in which they highlight the academic achievements of student

employees as a means of encouragement. The Creamery is also one of a number

of on-campus businesses that offer flexibility and variability in scheduling hours,

especially during holiday breaks and finals' week. This scheduling feature can be

found in most university-related businesses or services since they usually follow

the academic calendar in their hours of operation. For the understanding and

Schraeder 3

flexibility that such jobs offer, I recommend that you try to take advantage of the many positions available within your own college or university.

Once you meet the challenge of balancing your college studies with the obligations of part-time work, you'll find that the balancing act has its own rewards: it can be a valuable learning and growing experience for you. First, this challenge can provide you with self-discipline, the self-discipline that comes with prioritizing your schoolwork, setting realistic goals, managing your time, and becoming a reliable employee. Second, students who work to support their own education often develop a heightened sense of respect, value, and responsibility for that education because we've worked and paid (or helped pay) for it. Because we take more responsibility for our educations, we usually study seriously enough to graduate on time, even early. We realize the importance of the timely completion of a degree. These two examples represent forward-looking attitudes and outlooks, but part-time work can also have more immediate effects on your academic career as well.

Such immediate effects of part-time work can be categorized into two types of experiences with part-time work: work that offers career experience and work that fuels academic and career motivation. The former category includes but need not be limited to arranged, paid internships or focused work programs implemented or overseen by your college or university. But career experience can also be found in more unexpected ways, such as when a management student gets to observe her manager at work or when a communications student practices his skills in a sales job. While many student-workers will be fortunate to have such experiences, others, like me, will find themselves working at jobs that have very little to do with their projected career goals. My experiences with work at college have fallen into the latter category, but there are still valuable lessons to be learned. Although the food service work I perform at the Creamery has little relevance to my English and history majors, I enjoy my time there as a release from my studies. Working at the

Schraeder 4

Creamery has also motivated me to do my best schoolwork, since I recognized that a food service job would not be fulfilling to me as a life-long career. If you find that the part-time work available to you is not directly related to your education, such work can still have positive motivating effects on your academic attitudes. A working student who faces boredom, monotony, or low wages in her or his part-time job will often be motivated to achieve academic excellence as a means of moving beyond the scope of this part-time work.

With the right attitude, you might gain work experiences that are as positive as your academic ones. There are likely to be many jobs available within your university community that are student friendly and may even be directly related to your major area of studies. If that is not the case, you can use the less-than-fulfilling aspects of the work as motivation to do your best academic work in order to move steadily through your requirements and graduate on time. Any kind of employment may help you appreciate your career goals more than someone who isn't working their way through school. Everyone tells us that our college years are the best years of our life—and so far I think they're right. By combining part-time work with academics, we're not only earning a greater appreciation for our education, one we've worked doubly hard to receive, but we are also helping to pay for that education.

Exercise 4

Compare the three versions of "Working toward a Degree" reprinted in this chapter, and write a two-paragraph summary describing how Melissa revised her work. If she had shown her final draft to you, asking for your advice before submitting it for a grade, what would you have told her? Write a one-paragraph response to this draft.

PLANNING FOR

ACADEMIC

SUCCESS

5

You will not always have the luxury of planning, drafting, revising, getting feedback on, and editing a piece of writing over a stretch of days or weeks. Frequently, your college instructor or employer will ask you to produce an essay or a report during a class period or within a day or two. And the need for a timely response to current events or disasters often gives rise to an unscheduled writing assignment (a quickly prepared report, proposal, or analysis).

No matter what their time line, most writers feel some pressure. But when they are asked to write quickly or on demand, that pressure intensifies. The focus of this chapter is how to write well when faced with time constraints, especially when you feel as though you have only one shot at success. This chapter will help you

- ease the pressures of academic reading and writing (5a),
- take advantage of academic support services (5b),
- manage deadlines (5c),
- abbreviate the writing process (5d),
- manage writer's block (5e), and
- plan for essay examinations (5f).

The key to academic success is to use the available time as efficiently as possible.

5a   Easing the pressures of academic reading and writing

Successful college students develop an understanding of the rhetorical situation of every class by reading carefully every course syllabus and assignment sheet—written texts that establish student rights and responsibilities.

(1) The syllabus states course requirements and the plan for meeting them.

On the first day of class, an instructor usually passes out a **syllabus,** a concise description of the course, which includes the readings, due dates, and sometimes the assignment sheets. You will want to become familiar with the syllabus, reading it carefully as you prepare for each class meeting and every assignment.

CHECKLIST for Reading a Syllabus

- Note your instructor's name, office number, and office hours. See whether your instructor has included an e-mail address and indicated any preferred method for getting in touch with her or him outside of class.

- Note the texts required for the course. Editions of textbooks change often, so be sure you purchase the correct one, new or used.

- Look closely at what the syllabus says about assignments. How much reading and writing does the course require? When are assignments due? Are there penalties for turning in papers late? Are there opportunities for revision?

- When are exams scheduled (see 5f)? If there are quizzes, will they be announced in advance?

- Does the syllabus indicate that some assignments will be given more weight than others? If not, how will your final grade be determined?

- Does the syllabus indicate an attendance policy? Are there penalties for missing class or being late?

- Will there be a Web site or other online component for the course? If so, how will it be used, and how can you access it?

Many instructors post their syllabi on Web sites created for their courses. An electronic syllabus is easier for the instructor to modify once the course gains momentum. Be sure to review a course's electronic syllabus from time to time or, if your instructor uses a print syllabus, keep track of any changes. Every course Web site is different, but there are basic guidelines to follow.

Coding for Corporate Survival
IST 301 & ENGL 202C

Next Class Meeting: JanuaryEleven

CourseRoster - CodingSchedule - SyllaBus - DueDates - GroupFormations - WakkaFormatting - DiscussionPapers - SemesterLongProject - ProjectTopics - TwoExams - SoYouThinkYouCanWriteaFinalExam? - LogoContest -

Web sites, such as this one constructed by instructor Jeff Pruchnic, have become a common source of course information—from reading and writing assignments to recommendations for outside reading and study-group times.

CHECKLIST for Using a Course Web Site

- Access the course Web site immediately to find out which Web browser properly displays the site, including its specific links and other elements, and whether your Internet connection works quickly enough. See your instructor if you have any problems.

- Learn whether the course Web site contains information and resources that are not included on the syllabus. If an instructor briefly describes a writing assignment on the syllabus but includes extensive guidelines and deadlines only on the course Web site, it is vital that you have easy access to and the ability to navigate that site.

- Check the links on the course Web site. There may be a link to a Web-based newsgroup for the course or to a required reading. It is essential that such links work properly on your browser.

(2) Reading assignments rhetorically is essential to academic success.

Instructors write out assignments so that they receive the kind of writing they want to read; therefore, you will want to respond to each assignment exactly as directed in terms of length, focus, format, and purpose. Do not risk misunderstanding an assignment because you read it too quickly. Rather, read every assignment carefully, and concentrate on fulfilling what your instructor has asked you to do. Ask questions if you have any uncertainty about what is expected.

Discussion Papers

The discussion paper should both prepare students for solving problems in class and lead to better problem results. To quickly apply knowledge from the readings while working on the problems in class, students need to have synthesized the material for it to serve as an effective resource.

Instructions

1. Read the assigned question.

2. Read each article with the question in mind, and prepare a summary of each (for yourself, not to hand in).

3. Compare the summaries and identify how each article relates to the question.

4. Develop a thesis that is related to the question (this will often narrow the scope of the question).

5. Write a 600-700 word (about one single spaced page) response and post it to the wiki. This response should explain your thesis (in three sentences or less) and support this thesis primarily with evidence from the readings as well as, if appropriate, personal experiences or knowledge gained from other classes.

Grading

Clear thesis statement (two points)
Effective application of assigned reading(s) (two points)
Organization and arrangement (two points)

Assignment sheets, such as this one devised by Jeff Pruchnic, provide information that is crucial for successfully fulfilling instructors' assignments. Note that this sheet includes information on how the assignment will be evaluated.

Whether you are asked to submit an essay, an argument, a research paper, or another form of writing, you have a better chance of completing your project successfully if you read the assignment sheet with the following concerns in mind.

CHECKLIST for Reading an Assignment Sheet

- What does this assignment require you to do? Are there subject, formatting, or length restrictions? Are there guidelines for making choices?
- Have purpose, audience, context, and exigence been supplied for you, or will you choose these components of your assignment?
- What strengths can you bring to this assignment? What do you still need to learn if you are going to complete this assignment successfully?
- How much time should you devote to this assignment? When should you get started?
- How might a visit to the writing center help you? (See 5b(2).)
- Are you expected to submit all of your process writing along with your final copy?

5b Taking advantage of academic support opportunities

One of the biggest advantages of studying at a college or university is the availability of academic support services and trained personnel. All students inevitably need academic support at some point in their college careers. Too often, though, students do not get the help they need because they do not know what resources are available, where those resources are located, and—most important—how to use them for their own benefit. Successful students seek out the multiple means of support offered on their campus.

(1) Your instructor can clarify course assignments and requirements.

Your instructor should be able to help you with most of your course-related questions, whether they concern a reading assignment, the due date for an essay, or a concept essential to the subject matter. Although you can get answers or clarifications for most of your questions either in class or immediately afterward, you are likely to get more time and attention when you visit your instructor during office hours. The checklist that follows includes tips for making your office visit a productive one.

In addition to conferring with instructors in their offices, you may also be able to consult with them by e-mail or through a Web site created especially for a class. The course syllabus may include an e-mail (or other online) address as well as a policy about communicating online. If not, ask whether such communication is possible and under what circumstances it would be appropriate. Most instructors are happy to answer short questions online; however, questions needing longer answers probably merit an office visit.

CHECKLIST for Getting Help from Your Instructor

- Learn the instructor's office hours and the location of his or her office.

- Make an appointment during office hours, and then appear on time. Before the visit, write out your questions and concerns. What do you need to take away with you for the meeting to be productive?

- If you are planning to discuss a specific reading or writing assignment, bring a copy of it to the meeting.

- Tell your instructor what information or help you need.

- Once you have clearly stated your questions and concerns, pay close attention to the answers you receive, writing them down if necessary. Do not hesitate to return.

---

(2) Writing centers offer help from tutors.

Regardless of their major, many successful college writers benefit from visits to their school's writing center, where they can discuss their work-in-progress with fellow students who are trained to assist them with their writing. Because writing tutors usually represent many majors, they bring to their work a wide range of writing experiences from virtually all disciplines. Your school most likely has a writing center where this kind of student-to-student consultation takes place on a regular basis. The writing center probably maintains a Web site where you can get information about services, hours of operation, and additional resources for writing. Students who visit a writing center are demonstrating their commitment to writing well and to reaching their own writing goals. They do not expect tutors to write or correct an essay for them.

TIPS FOR VISITING A WRITING CENTER

- Learn when the center is open, whether you can drop in or need to make an appointment, and how long tutoring sessions last.

- If you are working on a specific assignment, bring the material with you: your assignment sheet and whatever you have already written, whether notes, an outline, or a draft.

- Be prepared to explain your understanding of the assignment to your tutor and to indicate the specific kind of help you need. If you bring along the instructor's comments or previously graded assignments, the tutor can use specific information from them to help you.

- Some students find that they benefit from a visit early in the writing process, after they have written a detailed outline or an initial draft. Others find that they benefit more toward the end of the process, during revision and before they are ready to edit and proofread.

- Recognize that tutors are ready to help you with your *writing;* rarely will they serve as proofreaders or editors. In fact, they may ask you to read aloud what you have written so that *you* can catch your own surface errors and organizational weaknesses. For this reason, you will want to visit the center at least a day or two before your assignment is actually due.

- If you have a good session with a tutor, learn his or her name so that you can develop a working relationship. Many writing centers encourage weekly meetings with the same tutor so that writer and tutor can develop a collaborative learning relationship.

- If you have a frustrating experience with a tutor, ask for someone else on your next visit, and do not judge the entire staff by a single bad experience.

5c Managing deadlines

You will almost always be working with deadlines—whether for essays, business plans, grant proposals, or other time-sensitive documents. Preparing ahead of time always helps. Even though an in-class essay exam may not be scheduled until midterm, start preparing on the first day of class. As you read your assignments and participate in class discussions, try to determine what is most important about the material you are learning. Pay attention to indications that your instructor considers certain material especially important. Whenever an instructor

gives you instructions or assignments, read them carefully, asking questions until you know exactly what is expected of you.

The best preparation for a writing assignment with a longer deadline, such as a research project, is to start early. If you are choosing your own topic, begin as soon as you can to narrow down your ideas (see **3b**). The sooner you identify a subject, the sooner you can discuss it with your instructor. You can make deadlines work for you by establishing your own time line. For an important project, you might even set yourself intermediate deadlines for writing an introduction with a thesis statement, composing a first draft, meeting with a classmate for review, revising your draft, and editing. If you carry a small notebook or hand-held computer with you, you will always have a place to jot down notes and ideas.

5d Abbreviating the writing process

Students and employees are often expected to write well with little notice. When faced with a short deadline, try to narrow the topic to a manageable scope or to relate the assignment to your academic or work experiences or personal knowledge. If you give your topic a sharp focus, you can write a thoughtful, in-depth analysis, rather than skimming the surface of a broader topic. Once you have a focused topic, organize your ideas. The following tips will help you abbreviate the writing process.

TIPS FOR ABBREVIATING THE WRITING PROCESS

- Generate ideas about the assignment or topic with a friend or colleague who is facing or has faced the same kind of deadline. That person can help you clarify your line of reasoning and develop counterarguments. Take notes.

(Continued on page 108)

(Continued from page 107)

- Draft an introductory paragraph that frames your position or approach and includes a clear thesis statement. E-mail your paragraph to your instructor or to a classmate to make sure that you are on the right track.

- If your thesis statement and basic approach are on track, write down your main points; then flesh them out with examples and supporting text until you have a first draft.

- Read your draft aloud, slowly. Make sure that your topic sentences are clear. Reading aloud will help you locate passages that need transitional words or phrases to help your reader along.

- Write a conclusion that reiterates your main points and suggests their implications, the directions in which they may point.

- Read over your text to make sure that it fulfills the assignment. Reread your introduction and conclusion to see whether they frame your piece. Examine your topic sentences and supporting paragraphs to make sure that they help you fulfill your purpose and are appropriate for your audience.

- Proofread one last time. Submit your work on time.

You can use your computer to help you manage writing tasks efficiently.

- If you do not have much time for revising and editing, you can use the grammar checker and spell checker of your word-processing program to help you proofread, even while you are drafting.

- A program such as Microsoft's Outlook can be used to schedule tasks and keep a calendar. You can set the Alarm function of this type of program to remind yourself to complete certain tasks for a writing assignment in time to meet the overall deadline.

- Many on-campus writing centers can receive drafts of student writing via e-mail or through a Web site, and writing tutors will often respond to a draft within twenty-four hours. If the writing center on your campus offers such a service, you can use it to get helpful advice on short notice when you have a tight deadline.

5e   Managing writer's block

Writer's block can affect any writer at any time, no matter how experienced, no matter what the writing assignment. Many experienced and successful writers suffer from **writer's block,** which is nothing more than the inability to begin or continue writing for reasons other than lack of skill or commitment. Sometimes, it helps to stay put at the computer and keep typing away. Sometimes, it helps to focus on completing one small section of the writing assignment at a time. Other times, it helps to step away from the work.

A number of factors can contribute to writer's block: you may not think you are a very good writer; you may want the words to be "just right"; you cannot decide on a thesis statement, because there seem to be so many angles you could take; you find it difficult to organize information; or you may procrastinate.

One of the most common causes for writer's block is striving for perfection. Of course, you want your writing to be as good as it can be, in terms of grammar, spelling, structure, and development. But you will be better off turning in completed work that is less than perfect than submitting no work at all. In other words, do the very best you can, given your circumstances, and then move on. The deadline is a reality that must be honored by all writers.

CHECKLIST for Managing Writer's Block

- Allot your time with thought and care.
- Prioritize your responsibilities, and allow time for each activity.
- Establish regular writing habits, including when and where you write.
- For an out-of-class assignment, draft without worrying about structure, content, or surface errors. You can revise later.
- For an essay exam, read each question slowly and jot ideas in the margin as you read down the page.

5f	Preparing for essay examinations

If your instructor has posed a clear question and provided explicit instructions, you are (almost) home free. Write out your answer, framing it with a thesis statement, main points, and supporting arguments or examples. If a question does not make clear what is called for, ask your instructor for clarification. The steps described in the following sections will help you improve your ability to take essay examinations.

(1) Set up a time schedule.

If the exam has more than one question, figure out how much time to allot to each one. If you are faced with two questions that are worth the same number of points, give half the time to one and half to the other. When certain questions are weighted more heavily than others, however, you need to divide your time accordingly. However you allocate your time, allow ten minutes for final revising and proofreading.

Stick to your time allotment for each question. If you do not finish, leave room to complete it later and move on to the next question. Partial answers to *all* questions usually gain you more points than complete answers to only *some* questions. Besides, you can use the ten minutes you saved to put the finishing touches on any incomplete answers, even if you have to draw arrows to the margins or to the back of the page, or if you have to supply rough notes (see 5f(3)). Your instructor will probably appreciate the extra effort.

(2) Read instructions and questions carefully.

Students who take time to read instructions and questions carefully almost always do better than those who do not. Invest a few minutes in studying each question, putting that question in your own words, and then jotting down a few notes in the margin next to it. If you have been given a choice of questions to answer, choose those that best suit your knowledge yet do not overlap.

Most questions contain specific instructions about how, as well as what, to answer. Be alert for words such as *compare, define,* and *argue,* which identify the writing task and provide specific cues for organizing your response. Other words, such as *discuss* and *explain,* are less specific, so try to determine exactly what it is your instructor wants you to do. When these more general directions appear, be tuned in to such accompanying words as *similar* or *different* (which signal, respectively, a comparison or a contrast), *identify* (which signals a definition or description), and *why* (which signals the need to identify causes). You will also want to be clear as to whether you are being asked to call up course-related information from memory or to respond with your own ideas. Words such as *think, defend,* and *opinion* signal that you are to frame a thesis and support it.

Most essay exam questions begin with or contain one of the words in the following list and end with a reference to the information you are to discuss. Understanding these terms and framing your answer in response to them will help you focus on what is being asked.

TERMS USED IN ESSAY QUESTIONS

Compare	Examine the points of similarity (compare) or difference (contrast) between two ideas or things ($3g(5)$).
Define	State the class to which the item to be defined belongs, and clarify what distinguishes it from the others of that class ($3g(6)$).
Describe	Use details in a clearly defined order to give the reader a clear mental picture of the item you are being asked to describe ($3g(2)$).
Discuss	Examine, analyze, evaluate, or state pros and cons. This word gives you wide latitude in addressing the topic and is thus more difficult to work with than some of the others in this set, since you must choose your own focus. It is also the one that, unfortunately, appears most frequently on exam questions.
Evaluate	Appraise the advantages and disadvantages of the idea or thing specified (chapter 8).
Explain	Clarify and interpret ($3g(3)$), reconcile differences, or state causes ($3g(4)$).
Illustrate	Offer concrete examples or, if possible, create figures, charts, or tables that provide information about the item.
Summarize	State the main points in a condensed form; omit details, and curtail examples.
Trace	Narrate a sequence of events that show progress toward a goal or comprise a process ($3g(1)$ and $3g(4)$).

(3) Decide how to organize your response.

Even under time constraints, you should be able to draft a rough outline or jot down a few phrases for an informal list (see 3d). Identify your thesis; then list the most important points you plan to cover. You might decide to rearrange ideas later, but the first step is to get some down on paper. Before you begin to write the answer, quickly review the list, deleting any irrelevant or unimportant points and adding any better ones that come to you (keeping in mind how much time you have allotted to the specific question). Number the points in a logical sequence determined by chronology (reporting events in the order in which they occurred), by causation (showing how one thing led to another), or by order of importance (going from the most important point to the least important). Although arranging points in order of increasing importance is often effective, it can be risky in an exam situation because you might run out of time and not get to your most important point.

Following is a thesis statement and a list of supporting points that was quickly composed and edited during the first few minutes of an essay exam. Biology major Trish Parsons was responding to the following question: "Discuss whether the term 'junk DNA' is an appropriate name for the nucleic DNA that does not code for proteins."

THESIS: The term "junk" applied to DNA with no apparent purpose is a misnomer; there are many possible purposes, both past and present, for the allegedly "junk" DNA.

1a.

1b. Though junk DNA sequences do not code for specific proteins, they may play an important role in DNA regulation. ⟶ go to point #5

2. Microbiology technology has had many amazing advances since the discovery of DNA. ~~Indeed,~~ DNA itself was not immediately recognized as the "plan for life." Further technological advances that are sure to come may find a definite purpose for "junk" DNA.

3. Junk DNA may have coded for proteins in our evolutionary past and a mechanism for disposing of it ~~never has~~ ∧ evolved. (yet to evolve)

4. During DNA replication, the possibilities for mistakes are endless. The junk (filler) DNA decreases the chances of the more important, protein-coding DNA being mutated during this process.

5. Junk DNA may yet play an important role in the new field of eugenics, where it has been found that certain traits are heritable, but not directly coded for (possible relation to DNA regulation role in point # 1)

← 1a Many terms have been applied in genetics that end up creating confusion because scientists came to conclusions too quickly — e.g., dominant and recessive alleles are too simplistic. b/c genetics is a relatively new field we have only recently begun to understand. (BEGIN WITH THIS ONE)

Sometimes, the language of the question will tell you how you should organize your answer. Consider this example:

> Discuss how the two-party political system of the United States influenced the outcome of the Bush-Gore presidential election.

At first glance, this exam question might seem to state the topic without indicating how to organize a discussion of it. *To influence*, however, is to be responsible for certain consequences. In this case, the two-party political system is a cause, and you are being asked to identify its effects (see 3g(4)). Once you have recognized this, you might decide to discuss different effects in different paragraphs.

Here is another example:

> Consider Picasso's treatment of the human body early and late in his career. How did his concept of bodily form persist throughout his career? How did it change?

The reference to two different points in the artist's career, along with the words *persist* and *change*, indicates that your task is to compare and contrast. You could organize your response to this question by discussing Picasso's concept of the bodily form when his paintings were realistic and when they were cubist—preferably covering the same points in the same order in each part of the response. Or you could begin by establishing similarities and then move on to discuss differences. There is almost always more than one way to organize a thoughtful response. Devoting at least a few minutes to organizing your answer can help you better demonstrate what you know.

(4) State your main points clearly.

If you state your main points clearly, your instructor will see how well you have understood. Make your main points stand out from the rest of the answer to an exam question by identifying them. For instance, you can make a main point be the first sentence of each paragraph. Or you can use transitional words such as *first, second,* and *third.* You might even create headings to separate your points. By the time you have outlined your essay exam answer, you should know which points you want to highlight, even if the points change slightly as you begin writing. Use your conclusion to summarize your main points. If you tend to make points that differ from those you had in mind when you started, try leaving space for an introduction at the beginning of the answer and then writing it after you have written the rest. Or simply draw a line pointing into the margin (or to the other side of the paper), and write the introduction there.

(5) Stick to the question.

Always answer each essay exam question as precisely and directly as you can, perhaps using some of the instructor's language in your thesis statement. If your thesis statement implies an organizational plan, follow that plan as closely as possible. If you move away from your original thesis because better ideas occur to you as you write, simply go back and revise your thesis statement (see 3c). If you find yourself drifting into irrelevant material, stop and draw a line through it.

If you find yourself facing a vague or truly confusing question, construct a clear(er) question and then answer it. Rewriting the instructor's question can seem like a risky thing to do, especially if you have never done it before. But figuring out a reasonable question that is related to what the instructor has written is actually a responsible move if you can answer the question you have posed.

(6) Revise and proofread each answer.

Save a few minutes to reread each answer. Make whatever deletions and corrections you think are necessary. If time allows, ask yourself if there is anything you have left out that you can still manage to include (even if you have to write in the margins or on the back of the page). Unless you are certain that your instructor values neatness more than knowledge, do not hesitate to make additions and corrections. Simply draw a caret (∧), marking the exact place in the text where you want an addition or correction to be placed. Making corrections will allow you to focus on improving what you have already written, whereas recopying your answer just to make it look neat is an inefficient use of time (and you may have recopied only half your essay when the time is up). Finally, check spelling, punctuation, and sentence structure.

6

ONLINE

DOCUMENTS

Word-processing software makes it easy to capture and arrange ideas for writing, plan a writing task, compose, revise, edit, proofread, and produce professional-looking documents. In addition to word-processing capabilities, computers offer you the opportunity to communicate with a wider, often global, audience when you compose for Web sites and other online forums and documents, such as chat rooms, listservs, and instant messages.

Online writing is often **interactive** (that is, a message is related to one or more previous or subsequent messages), and it can dramatically expand the audience, context, and style and presentation options for your work. Because composing in this medium differs somewhat from writing essays or research papers delivered in hard copy, it calls for different skills—many of which you already have. This chapter will help you

- assess the rhetorical situation for e-writing (6a),
- use electronic messaging effectively (6b),
- participate in online discussions (6c),
- understand conventions for electronic communication (6d),
- compose effective Web documents (6e), and
- manage visual elements of a Web site (6f).

6a Assessing the online rhetorical situation

Whenever you compose material for a Web page, engage in an online discussion forum, or instant-message a classmate, you are using rhetoric, or purposeful language, to influence the outcome of your interaction (see 1a). In each case, you are responding to an online rhetorical situation that can be markedly different from that for a static, print medium.

Because the Web gives you access to so many different audiences, the unique nature of the online rhetorical situation becomes instantly evident when you begin composing for a Web site or a newsgroup posting. If you are constructing a Web page for a course assignment, your primary audience is probably your instructor and classmates. But as soon as you put your composition online, you open up your work to a variety of secondary audiences (see 1d(3)), whose responses you will also want to consider as you compose.

Keep in mind that primary or secondary audiences for online documents may be specialized, diverse, or multiple (1d). When writing a message for a listserv (an e-mail–based discussion forum organized around a particular subject), you are addressing a specialized audience and can assume that its members share an interest in and some knowledge of your topic. When creating a Web page about an important historical event or place, such as the 1929 stock market crash that led to the Great Depression or Booker T. Washington's Tuskegee Institute, however, you should write for a diverse audience, whose members have varying levels of knowledge, understanding of specialized terms, and interest in your subject matter.

When responding to an online rhetorical situation, you also want to specify your purpose clearly. Your purpose for writing an online document is often much like that for writing a paper document: to express how you feel about something, create a mood, or amuse or motivate your audience. For example, for a Web site such as the one developed by The Green Belt Movement (shown in fig. 6.5), the purpose is to inform and then motivate the audience to become involved. Because readers may encounter your composition in a number of different ways—by having an e-mail message forwarded to them, by finding your Web page through a search engine, or by entering an online discussion forum—you need to take extra care to clarify your purpose and make it readily apparent.

Composing online also requires a greater responsiveness to context than you may have become used to for conventional academic writing projects (see 1e). In the rhetorical situation for online composition, the boundary between writer and audience is often blurred, because participants are writing and responding simultaneously. In addition, the accessibility of electronic messaging and online discussion forums (see 6b–c) encourages many people to add to or comment on a composition. This flow of new material contributes to an always evolving rhetorical situation, requiring you to be familiar with the preceding discussion and understand the conventions of the forum in order to compose effectively.

In addition, many Internet users have come to expect online compositions to be especially timely, given the relative ease of updating an electronic document compared to a print-based publication. For example, a Web site about tsunamis produced before the December 2004 disaster in Southeast Asia surely differed from one produced after that date. In the first place, chances are that many more people became familiar with the meaning of the word *tsunami* in December 2004. Second, the later Web site was more likely to take into account the international efforts to understand, avoid, and communicate the warning signs of an impending tsunami.

6b Using electronic messaging effectively

You probably write e-mails or instant messages on a daily basis, though you may never have thought of them as online documents. Both of these media are now widely used for sharing ideas and information with coworkers and classmates, for exchanging documents, and for discussing course-related, business-related, and personal issues. Ease and speed define electronic messaging and, at the same time, compromise the user's ability to establish a fitting tone—an essential feature of effective communication in any context. In deciding on the appropriate language and style for an electronic message, you need to consider elements of the rhetorical situation as you would for any document (see 1a): who is your audience, and what do you hope to accomplish with your message? Conversational style may be acceptable for a message to a discussion group for your writing class, but a more formal style is required for a message to your instructor about the grade you received on an assignment. (See also 6c(2).)

(1) The basic rhetorical unit of e-mail is the screen (not the paragraph or the page).

Although computer screens come in a range of sizes, you can anticipate having only about twenty lines in which to present an e-mail message.

I hate to disagree with both Emily and Valerie, but I think the first real dictionary was published in 1604 (Kersey's didn't come out until 1702).

If you look on page 10 of the notes, under the first heading called "Dictionaries" you will find "Earliest English-to-English dictionary 1604." Then the notes explain it.

Also, the second-to-the-last paragraph on page 236 in the text talks about the 1604 dictionary.

Kersey's dictionary is discussed later on page 10 of the notes under the heading "Dictionaries between 1604 and Johnson's Dictionary." Kersey's was the "first English-English dictionary to contain everyday words." And yes, I agree with Valerie that Bailey's was the "best dictionary before Johnson's" because it was the "first to show stress placement."

BUT, the big clue for me that the 1604 dictionary is the first real dictionary of English is that both Kersey's and Bailey's are under the heading "Dictionaries between 1604 and Johnson's Dictionary." Therefore, 1604 was the first.

Does anyone agree with me or am I the only one who feels this way?

Meg Barry

I hate to disagree with both Emily and Valerie, but I think the first real dictionary was published in 1604 (Kersey's didn't come out until 1702). If you look on page 10 of the notes, under the first heading called "Dictionaries" you will find "Earliest English-to-English dictionary 1604." Then the notes explain it. Also, the second-to-the-last paragraph on page 236 in the text talks about the 1604 dictionary. Kersey's dictionary is discussed later on page 10 of the notes under the heading "Dictionaries between 1604 and Johnson's Dictionary." Kersey's was the "first English-English dictionary to contain everyday words." And yes, I agree with Valerie that Bailey's was the "best dictionary before Johnson's" because it was the "first to show stress placement." BUT, the big clue for me that the 1604 dictionary is the first real dictionary of English is that both Kersey's and Bailey's are under the heading "Dictionaries between 1604 and Johnson's Dictionary." Therefore, 1604 was the first. Does anyone agree with me or am I the only one who feels this way?

Meg Barry

Fig. 6.1. The top e-mail message uses white space advantageously in response to the rhetorical situation. The bottom one does not.

Keeping the length of your message to only one screen is especially important when your audience is work-related and your purpose is to inform or question. People tend to read only one screen of an e-mail message, so get to your point quickly: compose a message that fits on a single screen yet has the white space necessary for easy reading.

Because most people who use e-mail on a regular basis receive a large volume of messages, they have become used to scanning, quickly responding to, and deleting these communications. Clearly announcing your message in the subject line and then arranging and presenting it in concise, readable chunks help ensure that important information is not overlooked. In the e-mail shown in fig. 6.1, for example, Meg Barry's audience is her editing group from a course on the history of the English language; the exigence for her message is that the group is preparing for a midterm, and the context includes Meg's careful attention to tone ("I hate to disagree . . ."), her references to the textbook, and her purpose for sending the message—to make sure that the group has the right information. The content of the message responds to the features of the specific rhetorical situation and not only demonstrates Meg's logical and careful work but also enhances her credibility by showing her concern for her fellow students.

(2) Instant messaging reflects the speed and practical limits of real-time message entry.

Many users of instant messaging (IM), especially those using their cell phones, are able to read just a few lines of text at a time, so keep each message you send brief and to the point. Because instant messaging is **synchronous** (the text and multimedia elements are visible to the recipient at the moment the message is posted), messages sent between two users sometimes overlap, becoming disconnected from their original context (see 6c(2)). To avoid confusion, especially when it is important that your message be clear (as when setting up a meeting or explaining the purpose of a project), allow a time delay when you respond. Consider pasting in "reminder" text from previous e-mails or messages in order to provide the context for a response. Remember, however, that because most IM users have come to expect immediate responses to their messages, you should notify the recipient if you are pausing in a given messaging exchange or leaving your computer.

BEYOND THE RULE

WHO OWNS YOUR ELECTRONIC MESSAGES?

Your e-mail is not necessarily private or secure. Employers have been vindicated in cases where they were charged with privacy violations for reading employees' e-mail, and university legal counsels and administrators have "confiscated" the e-mails of teachers and students when complaints were lodged about grades. Be sure to check your school's or employer's policy with regard to the use of electronic messaging. For additional information, visit **www.harbrace.com**.

TIPS FOR SENDING ATTACHMENTS WITH ELECTRONIC MESSAGES

E-mail

- Before you send an attachment, consider the size of the file—many inboxes have limited space and cannot accept or store the large files that contain streaming video, photographs, and sound clips.

- If you want to send a file larger than 500K or multiple files whose combined size is larger than that, call or e-mail your recipient first to ask permission. A large file could crash the recipient's e-mail program.

- If you do not know the type of operating system or software installed on your recipient's computer, send text-only documents in **rich text format (rtf)**, which preserves most formatting and is recognized by many word-processing programs.

Instant Messaging

- Take the same care when attaching files to and including graphical elements in instant messages as with e-mails, so that you do not unintentionally send someone an inappropriate file or virus.

- Most instant-messaging programs use **file transfer protocol (ftp)** to transmit files. To protect your computer from viruses, make sure that the preferences on the program you are using are set so that you have to approve a file before it is downloaded. Then, open only files you are expecting or ones from users you know, and be sure to run a virus scan on all downloaded files before opening them. Or, in order to control what you receive, you might set your preferences to accept messages only from those on your buddy list.

Viruses

- Because attachments are notorious for transmitting computer viruses, never open an attachment sent by someone you do not know.

- Before opening attachments, make sure that you are working on a computer with antivirus software that will scan all incoming attachments for viruses.

- Check Web sites such as www.symantec.com for information and updates on viruses. You can also get virus-related updates and alerts on the Web site of the manufacturer of your computer or software (such as Apple or Microsoft).

6c The community of online discussion groups

Participating in online discussion groups is a good way to learn more about topics that interest you and to develop your writing skills. However, just as you evaluate information in print sources, you need to evaluate the information and advice you get from online forums (see chapter 10). There are two main types of online discussion groups: asynchronous and synchronous forums.

(1) Asynchronous forums allow easy access, regardless of time and place.

Some examples of asynchronous forums are listservs, newsgroups, and blogs. A **listserv** is an e-mail–based discussion forum organized around a specific subject, such as short story writing, American history, or computer gaming, and distributed from a central e-mail address to everyone who has subscribed to the forum. Many listservs archive messages (as well as shared photographs, links, calendars, and membership lists), giving you the option of reading that information on a Web site rather than in your e-mail. A **newsgroup** (sometimes called a **bulletin board**) keeps messages on a server, organized by topic (or **thread**) so that users can search for, read, and respond to messages on particular features of the subject covered by the group (see fig. 6.2). A **blog** (from the phrase

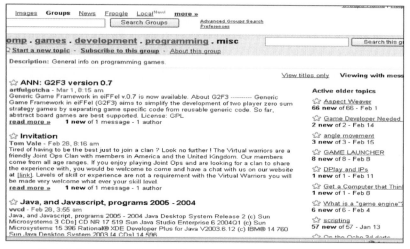

Fig. 6.2. A newsgroup allows participants to access and contribute to an online discussion at any time.

"Web log") is a Web site that is part online diary and part community forum; a blog allows users to post their responses to its creator's opinions and usually maintains archives of past postings. Some blogs also post "blogrolls" of other blogs that the original author recommends (see fig. 6.3).

The delay between posting and viewing contributions to an asynchronous forum often leads to thoughtful discussions because it emphasizes the importance of *responding* to the existing rhetorical situation. Before joining a listserv or newsgroup or responding to a blog, you might want to **lurk,** that is, remain anonymous while you read previous and current postings to understand the various topics of discussion and the histories of the different "conversations." When you have a good sense of the rhetorical situation, you can add your own comments to an existing thread or start a new one—always keeping in mind the information and overall tone in the messages posted by other users.

(2) Synchronous forums allow discussion in real time.

Synchronous forums, including chat rooms, electronic meeting software, and instant-messaging conferences, show the posted text (and any

Fig. 6.3. Some bloggers update their blogs on a daily basis, adding text and visuals.

multimedia elements) in real time. Such discussions resemble face-to-face interactions. They may or may not be archived, depending on their formality and the technology used to communicate.

Synchronous discussion groups offer a convenient way for people who are in different physical locations to interact. In business, for example, a project team in New York City can "meet" with members of another team in Los Angeles by using a program such as NetMeeting. Some academic courses use courseware (such as WebCT or Blackboard) to host synchronous discussion forums to supplement class meetings or to hold classes exclusively online. Offering not only a text-based environment but also voice and video capability, synchronous forums have the advantages of immediacy and a sense of physical presence.

Engaging in real-time online discussion can be disconcerting initially. Several different threads are usually being explored simultaneously, and it can take time to get used to having all the comments from current participants appear on your screen as though they were part of a single conversation (see fig. 6.4). Successful participation in a synchronous

ses963psu (8:32:24 PM):
rhosarhetor (8:32:26 PM): ahem
rhosarhetor (8:32:38 PM): in any case, we have a list of several "issues" for sloop.
rhosarhetor (8:32:39 PM): mo?
raenalynn (8:32:40 PM): How does Signdefwegwqrhgwethwrty having problems with comptr
rhosarhetor (8:32:48 PM): i'd say
sallysarahfl (8:33:02 PM): *these conversations move so quickly, quicker than i think!*
rhosarhetor (8:33:06 PM): what an image i have in my mind: of both of you falling off your chairs!
ses963psu (8:33:09 PM): btw, i couldn't find the this american life show reference i heard! damn.
raenalynn (8:33:12 PM): yea for me too.
xkaren08 (8:33:20 PM): speaking of KB
rhosarhetor (8:33:29 PM): we can keep looking. in our spare time.
ses963psu (8:33:31 PM): they move fast and are fun...and fun and theory isn't bad
rhosarhetor (8:33:41 PM): fun isn't bad theory
xkaren08 (8:33:52 PM): what were you thinking we should focus on in RoM?
rhosarhetor (8:34:27 PM): the reason i thought of faigley earlier -- FRAGMENTS OF RATIONALITY -- is that he does a solid foucaudian and althusserian thing with this kind of mediated comm. it's vvvv early ... and kinda wrong. but it was powerful at the time
pplwhoh8snowcanstudyinfl (8:34:44 PM): The *speed* doesn't annoy me as much as the plurality of conversations--we can be discussing more than one thing at a time and I have to do investigative work to figure out which comments go with which conversations

Fig. 6.4. Participants in an instant-messaging discussion use different colors to distinguish their responses.

forum entails concentrating on who is participating and which thread each participant is pursuing, at the point you enter the discussion. Given the speed of these discussions, convention dictates that comments be short and to the point, much more so than in newsgroups or listservs. Successful users join the discussions judiciously, taking care not to overwhelm other participants with too many messages or unannounced changes of the subject under discussion.

Both asynchronous and synchronous forums are used by a variety of online communities—social groups, scholarly or special-interest groups, and business groups. Both kinds of forums can also be used for course-related online discussions, as extensions of the classroom discourse. But remember that when you work, volunteer, or take classes with the other people in an online group, your rhetorical situation is somewhat different from that for online interactions with groups of strangers. You may want to lurk for a while so that you can learn the conventions of an unfamiliar online forum; however, when you know the other participants in an online community, you can plunge right in, remembering to take along your netiquette (see **6d**).

Exercise 1

Join a listserv or online discussion forum devoted to a subject you are currently interested in or researching. Lurk for a few days to a week. Then, introduce yourself to the members of the group, and ask a question related to one of the topics they have been discussing. After reading the responses, write a paragraph describing the experience.

6d Netiquette and online documents

Netiquette (from the phrase "Internet etiquette") is a set of social practices that was developed by Internet users in order to regulate online language and manners. For the most part, you will find electronic communication pleasurable, especially if you try to convey respect.

TIPS FOR NETIQUETTE IN ELECTRONIC MESSAGES AND ONLINE DISCUSSION FORUMS

Audience

- Keep in mind the potential audience(s) for your message: those for whom it is intended and others who may read it.
- Make the subject line of your message as descriptive as possible so that your reader(s) will immediately realize the topic.
- Use a signature line for e-mail to identify yourself and your institution or company.
- Keep your message focused and brief. The recipient's time and bandwidth may be limited, so delete anything that is not essential (previous messages, for instance) when replying.
- Give people adequate time to respond.
- Consider the content of a message, especially anything that the sender might prefer to keep private, before forwarding it to others. When in doubt, seek the sender's permission before forwarding a message.

(Continued on page 126)

(Continued from page 125)

- Respect copyright. Never send something written by someone else or pass it off as your own.
- Do not send junk mail, such as chain letters, petitions, and jokes, unless you know the recipient likes that kind of material.

Style and Presentation
- Take care to establish a tone appropriate for your message and your audience.
- Be sure of your facts.
- Present ideas clearly and logically.
- Pay attention to spelling and grammar.
- Use emoticons (such as :>)) and abbreviations (such as IMHO for "in my humble opinion") only when you are sure your audience will understand them and find them appropriate.
- Do not use all capital letters. OTHERWISE, YOU WILL SEEM TO BE SHOUTING.
- Abusive or profane language is never appropriate.

Context
- Observe what others say and how they say it before you engage in an online discussion; note what kind of information participants find appropriate to exchange.
- If someone is abusive, ignore that person or change the subject. Do not participate in **flaming** (online personal attacks).
- Understand that sarcasm and irony may appear to be personal attacks.

Credibility
- Do not use your school's or employer's network for personal business.
- Be respectful of others even when you disagree, and be kind to new members of an online community.

6e Composing Web documents

The Web offers you the chance to communicate to many different audiences for a variety of purposes. More than an electronic library for information and research, the Web is also a kind of global marketplace, allowing people all over the world to exchange ideas. For example, the home page of The Green Belt Movement (fig. 6.5) presents to an international audience themes that are conveyed throughout the Web site,

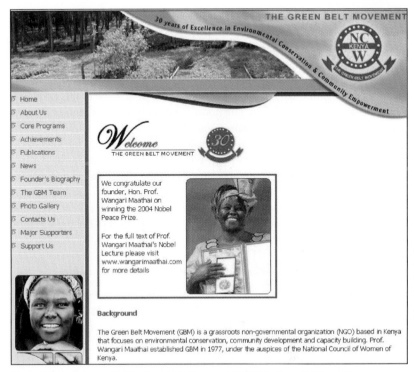

Fig. 6.5. The home page for The Green Belt Movement highlights the activities of the founder, Wangari Maathai, and emphasizes the group's values and focus: volunteerism, environmental conservation, accountability, and empowerment.

emphasizing the group's values and mission. The text on the page is designed to appeal to a diverse audience, from environmental activists to people interested in international development to conservationists planning to start their own grass-roots organizations. Even though the group is based in Kenya, its Web site strives for international appeal by highlighting the founder's Nobel Peace Prize, offering multiple ways of contacting the organization, and providing the option of making an online donation in various currencies.

Your intentions for Web composing may well be more modest than those of The Green Belt Movement. Nevertheless, you will want to remember that Web sites (and other online compositions) are available to diverse audiences, and so their composition should be given as much forethought as possible in terms of context, purpose, and message (see **1a**).

The home page of The Green Belt Movement introduces eleven main topics—from "About Us" to "Support Us"—each of which is the subject of a separate Web page. The **arrangement** (the pattern of organization of the ideas, text, and visual elements in a composition) of the site is clear. The site is thus easy to use: every page maintains the list of main topics in a navigation bar on the left. Arrangement also involves the balance of visual elements and text. The home page is unified by the use of several shades of green for the background, links, and headings, and the entire site is given coherence by the appearance of the organization's logo in the upper-right corner of every page. Finally, the trees shown in the bar that runs across the top of the home page create a visual link to one of The Green Belt Movement's key activities: planting trees as a means of fostering environmental consciousness and concern for the local environment. That visual link combines arrangement and **delivery** (the presentation and interaction of visual elements with content).

(1) Effective Web documents take advantage of the unique features of electronic composition.

Because of the flexible nature of electronic composition, you can have fun planning, drafting, and revising your Web documents.

(a) There are three basic kinds of Web documents.
You will find three types of documents on the Web:

- True electronic documents are constructed as Web pages or sites from the outset and are never intended to appear in print form.
- Print documents are frequently converted to Web pages or sites (for example, an article in the *New York Times* is placed on the newspaper's Web site).
- Electronically created documents (created with Adobe Acrobat or Illustrator, for instance) can be accessed on the Web but are often designed for printing out on paper.

A true electronic document contains **hypertext,** which includes links to other online text, graphics, and animations, as an integral part of its arrangement and content. That is, such a document is created and delivered with text, graphics, and animations integrated into the content. Although print documents converted for use on the Web can have hyperlinks as well as text and images (see 7f–j), these documents are not truly hypertextual compositions because they were not originally created with online capabilities in mind.

**(b) Hypertext allows users to customize their approach
to a Web document.**

As you work to create an effective Web document, you need to consider
the influences of hypertext on the use of that document. Basically, the
inclusion of hyperlinks transfers control over the sequence of information from you (the writer) to your audience (the user). In other words,
Web documents offer unlimited options for ordering the content, as
users may click on links in any order they choose. Clearly, the individual interests and personalities of those who read your Web document
will lead them to navigate it in different ways. Therefore, you will want
to consider how users' differences may affect the intended purpose of
your document and try to arrange your document accordingly.

You generally want to plan and compose a Web page or site with a
more fluid arrangement of material than is typical of a print document.
However, you can create some measure of consistency, as well as help
orient users, by carefully placing design elements (such as a logo and
color) and by including links to the home page on all other pages.

The visual elements included on a Web page or site create important
associations among the concepts and ideas that underlie your online
composition. For instance, the central image on The Green Belt Movement's home page (see fig. 6.5) is a photo of the organization's founder,
which immediately creates an association for users who already know
about Professor Maathai as well as connecting the organization to
African women more generally.

Using HTML

To create a Web page, you do not have to understand the computer code
(HTML) that allows a browser to display text. Programs such as Front-
Page and Netscape Composer, referred to generally as WYSIWYG (What
You See Is What You Get) HTML editors, will do such coding for you automatically.
But some writers find that knowledge of the basic HTML commands can be useful
for troubleshooting and editing a Web page. A number of tutorials on the use of
HTML are available on the Web.

**(c) Creating accessible Web documents requires attention
to audience.**

Because the Web gives you access to a wide variety of audiences, it is
important to be sure to make your Web document accessible to users

who do not have a fast Internet connection or who will access your online composition differently because of limitations in seeing, hearing, or keyboarding. To make your online document accessible, you may wish to simplify the design by using a limited number of graphic elements and to facilitate downloading by using low-resolution images (which have smaller file sizes). To accommodate users with physical disabilities or different means of accessing Web documents (for example, visually impaired users who employ talking computer programs that "read" Web pages), you may want to incorporate basic accessibility features such as **alt tags** (descriptive lines of text for each visual image that can be read by screen-reading software). Such accommodations will make your Web documents accessible to the greatest number of users.

BEYOND THE RULE

EVALUATING A WEB SITE FOR ACCESSIBILITY

Resources are available on the Web to help you evaluate whether your site is accessible to the users you want to reach. In the United States, the federal government's Access Board, in conjunction with the Departments of Education and Justice, has developed standards for electronic and online documents. Called Section 508 guidelines, these are available at **www.access-board.gov**. For more information, visit **www.harbrace.com**.

(2) Planning a Web site involves working out an arrangement for presenting ideas.

As you develop your Web document, you need to keep all the elements of the rhetorical situation in mind. Depending on your audience and purpose, you must decide which ideas or information to emphasize and then work out how best to arrange your Web document to achieve that emphasis. While you are generating the textual content, you need to consider the supplementary links that will help you achieve your overall purpose. But you do not have to do everything at once; fine-tuning the visual design can wait until the content is in place.

When you are planning a Web site, you may find it helpful to create a storyboard or other visual representation of the site's organization.

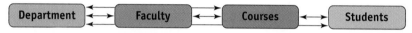

Fig. 6.6. Linear pattern for organizing a Web site.

You can sketch a plan on a sheet of paper or in a word-processing file if your site is fairly simple, or you can use index cards tacked to a bulletin board if it is more complex. If you have some time to devote to the planning process, you may want to learn how to use software such as Web Studio or FrontPage to help you map out your site (such Web site design programs are often available on computers in school labs).

Three basic arrangement patterns—linear, radial, and hierarchical—serve as starting points for planning your Web site. A linear site is easy to set up (see fig. 6.6). Hierarchical and radial arrangements are more complex to develop and may be better suited to group projects. The hierarchical arrangement branches out at each level (see fig. 6.7), and the radial arrangement, in which individual pages can be linked in a variety of sequences, allows the user to determine the sequence in which pages are viewed (see fig. 6.8).

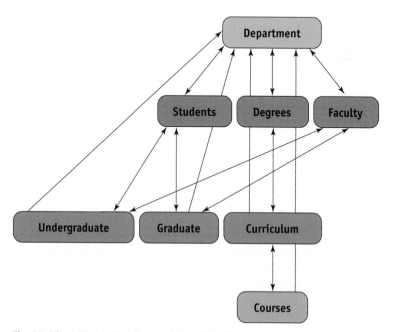

Fig. 6.7. Hierarchical pattern for organizing a Web site.

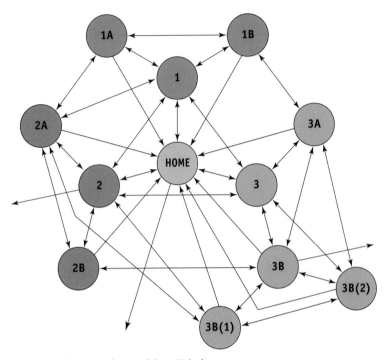

Fig. 6.8. Radial pattern for organizing a Web site.

The possibilities for organizing a Web site are endless. The most important consideration is how the arrangement of your site will affect a user's experience in navigating it. However you decide to organize your site, be sure to represent each main element in your plan. A good plan will be invaluable to you as you draft text, incorporate visual and multimedia elements, and refine your arrangement.

(3) Hyperlinks help fulfill the rhetorical purpose of a Web document.

You are probably accustomed to navigating Web sites by clicking on hyperlinks, one of the distinguishing features of online documents. However, you may not have thought about how valuable hyperlinks can be as tools for Web site development. Some basic principles can help you use hyperlinks effectively in your Web documents.

(a) Hyperlinks enhance the coherence of a Web document.

Hyperlinks should be a vital part of your organizational plan. Considering the ways in which users can exploit these links is an important part of your rhetorical strategy. You need to use hyperlinks purposefully to connect related ideas and to provide additional information. A site map is essential for a large site and helpful for a compact one. Refer again to the home page for The Green Belt Movement (fig. 6.5). Notice that the main sections of the site are featured as a list of links in a navigation bar running along the left side of the home page. A link to a relevant external site—Wangari Maathai's professional Web site—appears within the text. Hyperlinks to the individual pages of a site can provide transitions based on key words or ideas or logical divisions of the document. Because these links provide coherence and help users navigate your Web site, they are powerful rhetorical tools that aid you in creating an effective arrangement.

(b) Hyperlinks can be textual or graphical, linking to internal or external material.

You can use individual words, phrases, or even sentences as textual hyperlinks. Your hyperlinks can also be icons or other graphical elements, such as pictures or logos. If you do use graphical links, be sure that their appearance is appropriate for the transitions you are indicating. In addition, you must get permission for text, graphics, or multimedia elements you draw from other sources. Such material is often free online, but it still requires acknowledgment (see 10c).

Internal hyperlinks are those that take the user between pages or sections of the Web site in which they appear. When choosing hyperlinks that take the user to content *external* to your Web site (such as a hyperlink in a Web page about tsunamis that links to a meteorologist's Web site), be sure to select sites containing relevant, accurate, and well-presented information. You should also use any contact information provided on a site to ask permission to link to it, and you should check your links periodically to be sure that they are still active.

(c) Hyperlinks have rhetorical impact.

Textual and graphical links establish persuasive rhetorical associations (see chapter 8) for the user. Compare the rhetorical impact of linking an image of the Twin Towers in New York City to a page about public memorials with that of linking the same image to a page about global terrorism. Because hyperlinks serve various rhetorical purposes, you will want to evaluate the impact of any you include on your Web document as you plan, compose, and revise it. You will also want to evaluate the rhetorical impact of the hyperlinks on Web documents you are reading or using.

(4) Drafting Web documents can transform your composing process.

As you plan, draft, arrange, and revise a Web document, you will undoubtedly discover better material to include as well as better ways to organize that material. You may draft text for a linear arrangement and then later break the text into separate sections for different pages, which you link in sequence. However, you may find that arrangement and delivery issues related to online documents force you to change your drafting process significantly. You may find that composing a Web site requires you to write the text in chunks. You might write the text for a single page, including hyperlinks, and then move on to the next page. Or you might wait until you revise to add hyperlinks or to replace some of your initial text links with graphical ones. When you replace text with graphics, the visual aspects of your site have become part of your composing process rather than merely decorative elements that are added later.

Once you have drafted and revised your site, get feedback from your classmates or colleagues, just as you would for an essay or report. Since a Web site can include many pages with multiple links and images, you may want to ask for feedback not only about the content of your site but also about layout, graphics, and navigation (see 6f).

Professional Web developers often put a site that is still in a draft stage on the Web and solicit reactions from users, a process called **usability testing.** The developers then use those reactions to refine the site. Because Web sites are more interactive than printed texts, it is a good idea to seek input from users during site development. To solicit feedback, you may want to specify on your home page how users can contact you. Be careful, though, to consider your own security—you may want to use a free e-mail account through Yahoo! or Hotmail or allow users to post comments directly on your site.

The following checklist will help you plan a Web site and develop ideas for each page.

CHECKLIST for Planning and Developing a Web Site

- What information or ideas should a user take away from your site?
- How does the arrangement of your site reflect your purpose? How does it assist your intended users in understanding your purpose?
- How would you like a user to navigate your Web site? How might different users navigate within the arrangement of your site? To what purpose?
- Should you devote each page to a single main idea or combine several ideas on one page?
- How will you help users return to the home page and find key information quickly?
- What key connections between ideas or pieces of information might be emphasized through the use of hyperlinks?
- Will a user who follows external links be able to get back to your page?
- To ensure that your Web site has more impact than a paper document, have you used Web-specific resources—such as hyperlinks, sound and video clips, and animations—in creating it? How do those multimedia elements help you achieve your purpose?
- Do you need graphics—charts, photos, cartoons, clip art, logos, and so on—to enhance the site so that it will accomplish your purpose? Where should key visual elements be placed to be most effective?
- How often will you update your site?
- How will you solicit feedback for revisions to your site?

Exercise 2

Plan and compile information for a Web page that supports a paper you are writing for one of your classes. If you have access to a program that converts documents to Web pages, try starting with that. Then, critique your Web page.

6f Visual elements and rhetorical purpose

Visual design sends messages to users, inviting them to explore a Web site at the same time as it conveys the rhetorical purpose (see chapter 7). All the design elements of an online document, like the tone and style of a printed one, are rhetorical tools that help you achieve your purpose and reach your intended audience. For instance, if a user has a negative reaction to a photograph of dead seals on a Web site devoted to protecting wildlife, that reaction is likely to affect the user's view of the site in general. When you choose visual elements such as photographs, try to anticipate how your audience may react.

(1) Adhering to basic design principles makes an online document visually pleasing and easy to navigate.

A number of basic principles apply to the visual design of all documents, including those presented on the Web.

- **Balance** involves the way in which design elements used in a document are spatially related to one another. Web pages with a symmetrical arrangement of elements convey a formal, static impression, whereas asymmetrical arrangements are informal and dynamic.
- **Proportion** has to do with the relative sizes of design elements. Large elements attract more attention than small ones and will be perceived as more important.
- **Movement** concerns the way in which our eyes scan a page for information. Most of us look at the upper-left corner of a page first and the lower-right corner last. Therefore, the most important information on a Web page should appear in those locations. Vertical or horizontal arrangement of elements on a page implies stability; diagonal and zigzagging arrangements suggest movement.
- **Contrast** between elements can be achieved by varying their focus or size. For instance, a Web page about the Siberian Husky might show a photo of a dog of this breed in sharp focus against a blurred background; the image of the dog might also be large relative to other elements on the page. In text, you can emphasize an idea by presenting it in a contrasting font—for example, a playful display font such as **Marker Felt Thin** or an elegant script font such as *Edwardian Script*. (Remember, though, that older Web browsers may not display all fonts properly.) An easy-to-read font such as Arial, however, should be used for most of the text on a Web page.

- **Unity** refers to the way all the elements (and pages) of a site combine to give the impression that they are parts of a complete whole. For instance, choose a few colors and fonts to reflect the tone you want to convey, and use them consistently throughout your site. Creating a new design for each page of a Web site makes the site seem chaotic and thus is ineffective.

(2) Color and background play an important rhetorical role in online composition.

Like the other elements of a Web document, color and background are rhetorical tools that can be used to achieve various visual effects. Current Web standards allow the display of a wide array of colors for backgrounds, text, and frames. You can find thousands of background graphics on the Internet or create them with special software.

Designers recommend using no more than three main colors for a document, although you may use varying intensities, or shades, of a color (for example, light blue, dark blue, and medium blue) to connect related materials. Using more than three colors may create confusion on your Web pages. Besides helping to organize your site, color can have other specific effects. Bright colors, such as red and yellow, are more noticeable and can be used on a Web page to emphasize a point or idea. In addition, some colors have associations you may wish to take advantage of. For instance, reds can indicate danger or an emergency, whereas brown shades such as beige and tan suggest a formal atmosphere. Usually, textual hyperlinks appear in a color different from that of the surrounding text on a Web page. Also, links that have not yet been clicked usually appear in one color, and links that have been clicked change to a different color. Select the colors for textual hyperlinks to fit in with the overall color scheme of your document.

Background, too, contributes to a successful Web site. Although a dark background can create a dramatic appearance, it often makes text difficult to read and hyperlinks difficult to see. A dark background can also cause a printout of a Web page to be blank. If you do use a dark background, be sure that the color of the text is bright enough to be readable on screen and that you provide a version that will print clearly. Similarly, a background with a pattern can be dramatic but can obscure the content of a Web page or other online document. For example, the Web page in fig. 6.9 is difficult to read because of the background's busy appearance, which contributes nothing to the purpose or the content of

W

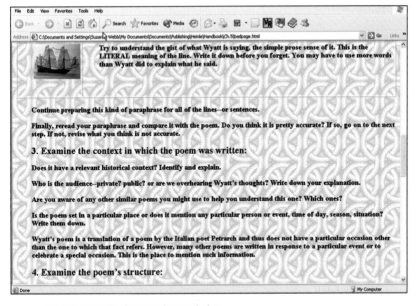

File   Edit   View   Favorites   Tools   Help

Back · · · Search · Favorites · Media

Address C:\Documents and Settings\Suzan\ Webb\My Documents\Documents\Publishing\Heinle\Handbook\Ch. 5\badpage.html

> Try to understand the gist of what Wyatt is saying, the simple prose sense of it. This is the **LITERAL** meaning of the line. Write it down before you forget. You may have to use more words than Wyatt did to explain what he said.

Continue preparing this kind of paraphrase for all of the lines—or sentences.

Finally, reread your paraphrase and compare it with the poem. Do you think it is pretty accurate? If so, go on to the next step. If not, revise what you think is not accurate.

3. Examine the context in which the poem was written:

Does it have a relevant historical context? Identify and explain.

Who is the audience—private? public? or are we overhearing Wyatt's thoughts? Write down your explanation.

Are you aware of any other similar poems you might use to help you understand this one? Which ones?

Is the poem set in a particular place or does it mention any particular person or event, time of day, season, situation? Write them down.

Wyatt's poem is a translation of a poem by the Italian poet Petrarch and thus does not have a particular occasion other than the one to which that fact refers. However, many other poems are written in response to a particular event or to celebrate a special occasion. This is the place to mention such information.

4. Examine the poem's structure:

Done   My Computer

Fig. 6.9. Example of poor Web page design.

the page. Intended to teach close reading of a poem, this page inadvertently sends the message that poetry is as difficult to read as the page itself. If you want to use a pattern for your background, check the readability of the text. You may need to change the color of the text or adjust the pattern of the background to make the page easier to read.

Use different background colors or patterns for different pages of your online document only if you have a good rhetorical reason for doing so (as you might, for instance, if you were using a different color for each of several related categories of information). When you do this, follow the other design principles in **6f(1)** strictly so that your site appears coherent to your audience.

For examples and more information on Web site design and usability, you may want to check out the following:

Jakob Nielsen's *Alertbox* (www.useit.com/alertbox/9605.html),

Killersites.com (www.killersites.com/gettingStarted.jsp),

and design guru Jeff Glover's *Sucky to Savvy* (jeffglover.com/ss.html).

CHECKLIST for Designing an Online Document

- Have you chosen the background and text colors so that users can print copies of your pages if they wish?

- Have you used no more than three colors, but perhaps varied the intensity of one or more of them?

- Does a background pattern on your page make the text difficult or easy to read?

- Have you chosen a single, easy-to-read font such as Arial for most of your text? Are the type styles (bold, italic, and so on) used consistently throughout the document?

- Have you used visual elements sparingly? Are any image files larger than 500K, making it likely that they will take a long time to transfer? If so, can you shrink them by using a lower resolution or a smaller size?

- Have you indicated important points graphically by using bullets or numbers or visually by dividing the text into short blocks?

- Is any page or section crowded? Can users scan the information on a single screen quickly?

- Does each page include adequate white space for easy reading?

- Have you made sure that all links work?

- Have you identified yourself as the author and noted when the site was created or last revised?

- Have you run a spell checker and proofread the site yourself?

VISUAL DOCUMENTS

7

So far, your education has focused mostly on the production and interpretation of written or spoken words. For years, you have been taking writing and public speaking classes, and most of your other courses have required you to use words to communicate your ideas and knowledge. In your daily experiences, however, whether in school or out, you interpret images at least as often as you interpret words. After all, you experience the barrage of images that advertisers use to sell their products, the striking visual works that artists create to express their ideas, the often compelling pictures that various news sources employ to depict important events and people, and even the commonplace images of traffic signs that alert you to potential driving dangers, such as steep hills, winding roads, children at play, or railroad crossings.

All of us derive meanings from visual messages every day—even if we do not know exactly how we "read" images. Just as important as understanding how we make sense of visuals is understanding how we can use them to communicate meaning to others in the texts we compose. In this chapter, you will learn the basic principles of "reading" and using images. This chapter will help you

- express meaning through visual representations (7a),
- use principles of visual rhetoric to examine images (7b),
- consider the entire image (7c),
- analyze the visual elements of an image (7d),
- consider the presentation and arrangement of visual elements (7e),
- consider relationships between images and accompanying text (7f),
- adapt document design to purpose (7g),
- recognize conventions of document design (7h),
- use design to serve a function (7i), and
- use graphics to achieve a particular purpose (7j).

7a   Visual representations of meaning

What constitutes an "image"? Are images limited to visual representations reproduced on a surface (such as a sheet of paper, a t-shirt, or a computer screen)? Is anything we see an image, or is an image nothing more than an idea—a mental representation that may or may not be associated with an actual object? After all, we frequently speak of things we imagine or "see" with our "mind's eye." For the purposes of this chapter, an **image** is any visual representation that expresses meaning, such as a photograph, painting, etching, sketch, illustration, or diagram. **Visual elements** refer to specific features of images, such as the people or things portrayed. Visual elements also refer to design and layout features of the larger documents in which images appear.

Just as we study a verbal text to understand a writer's messages, we can study a visual representation to understand the message communicated by the image's creator or designer. In many cases, visual and verbal elements appear together in a document, calling for analysis of how the two work together to convey a message. The growth of the Internet has made the purposeful integration of words and visuals more prevalent. Information that was traditionally text-heavy in its print form has become graphics-heavy on the Internet.

7b   Examining images using principles of visual rhetoric

Some of the rhetorical principles for understanding the meanings of verbal texts also apply to visual representations. For instance, we can ask questions about the rhetorical situation—the exigence, audience, purpose, and context—of a specific image. We can analyze the image in order to determine its theme, organization, or style. We can even assess whether it makes an argument or seeks to persuade its viewers—and, if so, what rhetorical appeals it uses to argue or persuade.

Despite the extensive overlap of the methods and the terminology for analyzing words and images, we require some specific interpretive tools to examine images. We experience visual representations differently than we do verbal texts, often making different assumptions about how and why the two types of texts were created. When reading verbal texts, for instance, we are accustomed to making distinctions between the various rhetorical methods of development (such as description or argument), but in a visual text, we look for different kinds of clues. As the following sections show, the process of analyzing and interpreting an image requires looking at the image as a whole, the parts of the image, and the context in which it appears.

7c   Considering the whole image

Like a verbal text, an image operates within a specific rhetorical situation. So, before analyzing the individual elements of any image, you want to consider the image as a whole, within its rhetorical situation: What exigence does it respond to? Who is the primary audience? What other audiences might have been anticipated? What purpose does the image carry? An illustration in a children's book, for instance, is clearly intended to be seen by children. But another important audience is parents who purchase the book and then read it to their children.

The purpose of any image may be obvious, unclear, or multiple. Consider the cover of a children's book in fig. 7.1. An obvious purpose of this image is to introduce the book's main character and theme, but it fulfills additional purposes as well: it attracts potential readers to pick up the book and entices parents to buy it for their children. Just as context shapes our interpretation of a verbal message, it informs our interpretation of a visual message. If the image on the cover appeared within the book, it would fulfill a different purpose within a different context. Hang the image in a

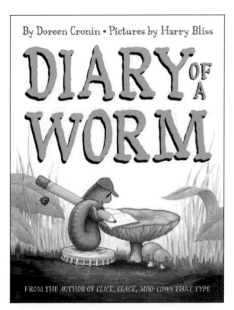

Fig. 7.1. A book's cover image can fulfill multiple purposes.

museum gallery or include it in a scholarly book on the uses of illustration, and the purpose changes again—once more within a different context.

7d Analyzing the elements of an image

After considering the image as a whole, in context, you need to analyze its elements: the participants and the lines and spaces, which work together to convey the meaning of the image to the viewers. **Analysis** is the process of separating a whole into its constituent parts (see chapter 8), so you examine the individual parts of the image as well as their relationships to one another and how each contributes to the whole.

As you conduct an analysis of an image, you need to remember that images are composed by people who wish to communicate with others. Composing is basic to paintings and sketches, and it is also essential to naturalistic photography, which produces images that seem to spring directly from the real world. A photographer chooses where to point the camera, how to set the focus and lighting, when to snap the picture, and how to crop it. In some cases, the photographer may have no direct influence on the positions of objects within the frame; in others, the photographer selects the arrangement and camera angle, making numerous decisions to emphasize certain objects and deemphasize others.

(1) Participants include the image's characters and objects.

Participants, the people, animals, or things that an image depicts, are much like characters in a narrative. The image tells a story about the participants, about their relationships to one another and to the scene in which they are placed. The broader category of participants is divided into **characters** (people, animals, and things that have been personified) and **objects** (inanimate, unthinking things). The nonhuman characters in images often assume human characteristics, prompting viewers to identify with those characters in ways they do not generally identify with objects. Keep in mind that objects (elements that are neither people nor animals) can also function as characters in an image, often because they exhibit human features or are portrayed as having consciousness. In the SpeeDee advertisement in fig. 7.2, for example, an oil can is personified

Fig. 7.2. In many images, objects are personified to enhance their appeal.

as a cheery character, moving forward rapidly and wearing an oil-funnel cap on its "head."

(2) Lines can be used to unite or divide elements of an image.

Lines indicate relationships, connections, or boundaries in an image. A single line may appear as a distinct feature (a pen mark in a cartoon sketch or a brushstroke in a painting); a line or series of lines may constitute one or more of the participants (the straight line formed by the rail of a bridge in a travel magazine photo, a line of picketers photographed in front of a factory, or the curved line of a river in an aerial photograph). Thus, lines may be used to indicate boundaries (the aforementioned line of picketers), connections (two riverbanks joined by the bridge in the magazine photo), or some more abstract relationship among characters (between God and a human in Michelangelo's *The Creation of Adam*, as shown in fig. 7.3).

Just as lines express abstract as well as concrete relationships among objects and characters, **spaces** (unmarked or uninhabited areas of an image) indicate such relationships as well. A large area of space between two objects, for example, may emphasize their difference or isolation from one another. Conversely, two objects placed near one another,

Fig. 7.3. The relationship between God and Adam is expressed by the line of the characters' outstretched arms.

particularly within a larger and otherwise empty space, can be interpreted as belonging together, as being members of the same group.

(3) The viewer is also an element of any image.

Although not a part of the image itself, the **viewer** is another element of the image, since the elements of an image are always positioned in relation to the viewer's viewpoint. When we view an image, we often assume that the objects and characters within it are simply relating to one another, when, in fact, they are also relating to us. The relationship of the image to the viewer is perhaps most powerful in portraits, where the figure portrayed usually appears to be staring directly at the viewer (see fig. 7.4). Clearly, the position of the figure in a portrait—the orientation of body,

Fig. 7.4. Viewers of Escher's self-portrait look up at the figure—but the figure is also looking down at the viewers.

head, and eyes—is determined by assumptions the painter makes about the viewer's position.

7e | The presentation and arrangement of visual elements

Once you have identified the most important elements of an image, you also consider characteristics of form, position, visual balance, and surface.

(1) Characteristics of form are shape and size.

Form concerns the shape and size of visual elements. What shapes are dominant in the image, and what impressions or cultural associations do these shapes communicate? Rounded, curving forms may suggest beauty, tranquility, or a natural state, whereas sharp angles and straight lines may suggest strength, industry, or aggressiveness. An image with contrasting forms might suggest a conflict between two different states—for example, the clash of nature with technology. Tall, skinny shapes can often seem less stable than short, stocky shapes. As viewers, we are apt to apply these interpretations whether the forms are humans, personifications, or abstractions.

The sizes of different forms may also provide clues about the image's message. Generally, larger objects are considered dominant, more important to the image's meaning. However, there are exceptions. In the image in fig. 7.11 (on page 152), for example, the focal point is the car. Although it is one of the smaller objects in the photo, the car's centrality is established by its position and its marked contrast to the elements surrounding it.

(2) Characteristics of position are relation, pointers, grouping, and order.

Visual elements can be interpreted according to where and how they are positioned in the image. **Relation** refers to the affiliation of different elements to one another and to space. Consider first the focal point of the image—which participant or space initially captures your attention? How is that element related to others in the image? If more than one element draws your attention, what pathway does your eye follow from one element to another?

Relation also involves the placement of participants with respect to the viewer of the image: which elements are in the foreground, closer to the viewer, and which are in the background, further away? Foreground participants are often, though not always, dominant, intended to be the focus of the viewer's attention. However, in images that use deep perspective (landscapes, for example), the background elements are often most prominent, while the foreground elements serve as a frame that draws the viewer's attention into the image. You will also want to think about the point of view the image creates for the viewer: are the image's elements positioned so that they are viewed from a point directly in front of them, from above or below, or from one side?

The elements in photos, paintings, and drawings do not actually move, but they may act as **pointers,** indicating movement or directing the viewer's gaze in a particular direction. For example, arrows, fingers, and other things that point imply movement between areas of the image that are related somehow. Similarly, the positioning of objects or characters often guides the viewer's attention in a particular direction. In fig. 7.5, notice how the woman's position on an overlook and her outstretched arms and upturned head direct attention toward the blue sky and the scenic valley beyond her.

Fig. 7.5. The woman's position and gesture point toward Virginia's natural beauty, thereby encouraging tourism in that state.

Elements that slant toward one side of an image can also suggest instability, and this principle applies to real objects as well. For instance, viewers of the Leaning Tower of Pisa and Hanging Rock often feel anxious.

Other characteristics of position provide clues to an image's meaning as well. Similar items placed near each other are often assumed to belong together, as members of a group. Dissimilar items grouped together usually lead to a different assumption. In the composition in fig. 7.6, all of the boats stand out from the deep blue water. However, the eye quickly separates the white powerboat from the colored kayaks, not only because of the dissimilarity of color but also because of the positioning of the

Fig. 7.6. A number of boats constitute the composition of this photograph.

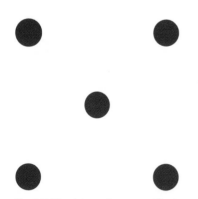

Fig. 7.7. Five dots can be arranged in the pattern of an X.

kayaks. Even though the kayaks have several colors and two sizes, their similar shapes and their clustering lead us to see them as a group.

As viewers, we also notice when elements of an image appear to be arranged in a significant order, in the pattern of a straight line, a circle, a square, a curve, or an X. We tend to interpret an ordered relationship among individual elements, such as the five dots in fig. 7.7, which we perceive as forming two intersecting lines and perhaps even as residing within a square border, as on one side of a die. As we try to make sense of visual elements, we often mentally match them to some familiar pattern rather than seeing them as randomly arranged.

(3) Visual balance can be achieved through symmetry or asymmetry.

In analyzing how elements of an image work together, you need to consider each element in the context of the others. Sometimes, a characteristic of one part of the image can be interpreted only in light of a characteristic of some other part of the image. In fig. 7.6, for example, the bright white powerboat is a prominent element partly because it stands out against the deep blue water, yet the water relates the boat to the other elements in the photo. The powerboat and the cluster of kayaks are two elements that balance each other by virtue of their positions (at opposite ends of the image) and their visual "weight" (both stand out from the blue background). The powerboat is larger, and its whiteness provides a stronger color contrast with the blue of the water. However, the repetitiveness of the kayaks sets off the singularity of the powerboat, and the bright but cool white of the powerboat differs from the generally warmer colors of the kayaks. Thus, overall, the image has balance.

(a) Symmetrical images tend to convey stability.

An image has **symmetry** when its elements are very similar in number, arrangement, form, or other characteristics on both sides of an **axis** (an imaginary horizontal or vertical line that splits an image into two separate parts). Images need not have identical halves to achieve symmetry; many natural forms, such as trees, flowers, and people, appear to be symmetrical, despite minor variations that add visual interest and variety (see fig. 7.8). Small differences between the two parts of an image create visual interest by asking the viewer to study the image more carefully than he or she might do if the image were perfectly symmetrical.

Fig. 7.8. This image of two girls is symmetrical, despite the small differences in the girls' appearance.

(b) Asymmetrical images achieve a more active kind of balance.

Balance in an image can also be achieved through asymmetry of position, color, brightness, size, or other characteristics. In fig. 7.9, for

Fig. 7.9. The right edge of the gravel road provides a diagonal axis.

instance, the right edge of the gravel road provides a strong diagonal axis that cuts the image into two roughly triangular areas, one containing the road itself (which is mostly in the foreground), and the other containing the small white building, which is the image's only other foreground object.

The dramatic tension in the image in fig. 7.9 is immediately apparent. The dominant object on the left is the road, which sweeps from the lower third of the frame nearly to the upper-left corner. But because the right edge of the road begins in the lower-right corner, the road also seems to encroach on the right side of the picture, nearly dominating the image with its detail and breadth. A road has thematic significance, as well; it acts as a pointer, suggesting transition, motion, or even progress. Because the road recedes into the distance, we imagine ourselves traveling through the scene, placing ourselves in the same position the photographer occupied. In balance to the road is the house, sitting peacefully near the center of the large triangular area in the upper right of the photograph. Although the road occupies most of the lower-left half of the photo, it is uniformly gray. The small house, on the other hand, stands in vivid contrast to the tall grass around it, and this high contrast compensates for its small size. Thus, the road and house achieve equal prominence, giving the image balance. The road suggests motion and progress; the house, sitting quietly alongside the deserted road, suggests repose and timelessness. In this case, asymmetry is used to achieve balance.

(c) Imbalance can also be used to express meaning.

Visual balance makes many images effective, but some images are effective precisely because they convey a sense of imbalance, which may communicate change, motion, instability, or unresolved tension. Of course, an image may lack balance simply because the creator has tried but failed to achieve it. As a viewer, you should consider whether a lack of balance is part of an image's message (perhaps because it is reinforced by other aspects of the image) or is instead a sign that the image simply fails to communicate its message.

(4) Characteristics of surface are color, brightness (or intensity), and texture.

Images also possess characteristics of surface that may affect our interpretations. Color, brightness (or intensity), and texture can communicate different messages. Brightly colored objects, for instance, may suggest happiness, youth, liveliness, or even chaos. Reds and oranges suggest heat, energy, or intensity, while blues and greens suggest coolness, stillness, or serenity. Some colors have cultural associations as well. Longstanding symbolic associations with color (such as the western European association of white with virtue and the Chinese association of white with death) may lead different viewers to read the same image differently.

Often, the color or brightness of an individual object is less important than how that characteristic relates to the same feature of surrounding objects. For instance, the brightly colored tree in fig. 7.10 takes center stage because it contrasts in both color and texture with the dim, foggy background; the same tree would be almost invisible if it were located in the midst of a forest of other trees with red leaves and black trunks. In addition, the crisp leaves and rough bark of the tree have much more surface texture than does the soft blurred background of sky, grass, and other trees. Even in the absence of distinct colors or textures, we notice the varying intensity among shaded elements in an image.

Fig. 7.10. A bright tree contrasts with its foggy background.

7f The relationships between image and accompanying text

Although it is worthwhile to know how to analyze images in isolation, most images are accompanied by text. Whether text is placed within an image or an image is inserted into text, combined text-and-image messages address various rhetorical situations and, therefore, can fulfill a variety of purposes. Combinations of text and image are delivered in a wide range of documents, from corporate reports, assembly manuals, and health brochures to comic strips, t-shirts, and billboards.

Your knowledge of the type and purpose of a document will help you interpret the relationship between image(s) and text and the ways in which specific techniques are used to convey meaning. Like any rhetorical analysis, then, analysis of a text-and-image document must begin by determining the basic facts about the rhetorical situation: To what exigence might the creator of the document be responding? Who is the creator? Who makes up the intended audience? What are the resources and constraints of the context? What is the document's purpose?

Whether you are examining a fiscal report, an article in a sports magazine, an advertisement, or a children's book, you want to account for any relationship between text and image in terms of the rhetorical situation of the document as a whole. You need to determine if the image illustrates, reinforces, contradicts, or reiterates the text. For instance, the images in a set of product-assembly instructions are meant to reinforce a process analysis and make assembly easier for the reader. Either words or images might suffice in this case, but, together, they offer more support to the reader. In other cases, however, words and images are a necessary bundle; neither can fulfill the document's purpose alone.

In fig. 7.11, the words and image of the advertisement work together to argue that the reader should consider buying a particular car. The image depicts three vehicles parked in a row in a clearing surrounded by stately trees. A large tree is stretched across the vehicles; the tree appears to have fallen, crushing the two large sport-utility vehicles at either end

Fig. 7.11. Both words and image are necessary to communicate this message.

of the row. The car in the middle, much shorter, is untouched. Considering the image alone, a viewer can see that the small vehicle is the focal point: prominently placed at the center of the frame, its unscathed body provides a strong contrast to the dramatically crushed vehicles on either side. The setting also contributes to the analysis, as the tall trees (one of which has fallen on the bigger, more rugged vehicles) convey an outdoorsy, back-to-nature mood. Ironically, the large vehicles are destroyed; the smaller vehicle remains intact. Along with the compelling image, the advertisement has three elements of verbal text. The first, printed on the license plate of the small car, is "ELECTRIC," a word that alerts the reader to the car's energy efficiency. Second, the sentence "HELLO, PARKING KARMA" appears below that car, the only ecologically sensitive vehicle in the image. Finally, the small type at the bottom of the image reads, "With the right car, everything's better. Introducing the electric ZAP Worldcar L.U.V.," followed by the company's contact information and logo.

Without the accompanying text, the image in fig. 7.11 might convey the message that the center car was lucky to have been parked between two bigger vehicles. But bundled with the three text elements, the message is clarified: the electric vehicle is environment-friendly, whereas the larger vehicles are gas hogs that burn fossil fuel and pollute the environment. The sentence about parking karma strongly suggests that the falling of the tree was not accidental but was, in fact, an ethical consequence; that is, nature is punishing the gas hogs and sparing the electric vehicle. The argument of this advertisement is clear: pick the "right car," one that is compact and environmentally sound, and you will be rewarded.

Any analysis of a document that combines image and text must take into account where the document appears and for whom it is intended. The ZAP Worldcar advertisement would probably work very well in magazines such as *National Geographic* and *Outside*, which cater to ecology-oriented readers for whom nature-friendly arguments are persuasive. If the same advertisement were printed on an urban billboard, on the other hand, its information about the car's compact size—particularly how easy it is to park—might be the most effective part of the message. On the other hand, either message might be completely lost on readers of *Off-Road* magazine, since they are unlikely to accept (or appreciate) the advertisement's criticism of large sport-utility vehicles.

Exercise 1

Select a print image that has caught your attention. Write for five to ten minutes in response to that image. Then, analyze it in terms of its elements and its rhetorical situation. Be prepared to share your image and analysis with the rest of the class.

7g Document design and rhetorical purpose

As the volume of information in a particular document increases, so does the importance of its delivery. After all, document design provides readers with necessary cues for acquiring information, whether that information is presented in verbal or visual form. For print as well as Web-based documents, design shapes the reader's first impression and ongoing experience. Effective design addresses the organization of the content, its readability, and the relationship between text and images.

Document design is important from the moment a written communication is conceptualized. Like the arrangement of ideas for an essay (see 3d), design helps you develop, organize, and present information in a document so as to meet the needs of your audience and fulfill your rhetorical purpose. At first glance, even before reading a word of a document, you see design features that immediately orient you to the document's content, style, quality, and purpose. These first impressions guide your interpretation and greatly influence whether the document achieves its purpose.

Effective document design involves attending to the rhetorical situation and understanding the design conventions for the particular type of document, that is, the physical, spatial, textual, and visual characteristics that reinforce the document's purpose.

7h The conventions of document design

Most academic papers share certain conventions of document design; for example, they have titles, paragraph indents, line spacing, and legible fonts (see the sample papers in 4h and 8j). The conventions that apply to academic writing work well in most classroom contexts: they are easy to learn and convenient to produce, and they make reading and commenting easier for instructors. However, when you are producing an academic paper that replicates a real-world communication task in the natural and social sciences or in business (see chapters **17–19**), you may be expected to use the design conventions for that type of professional document. Assignments such as business proposals, scientific research reports, newsletters, and résumés may require you to use specialized headings and even tables, charts, or illustrations. As a writer, you should become familiar with the document design conventions of the various academic disciplines you encounter. Knowing these conventions will help you to produce better documents for courses in these disciplines and in your professional life.

The scientific research report in section **18d** illustrates one set of specialized design conventions. The major sections are signaled by left-aligned, fully capitalized headings (such as "ABSTRACT," "INTRO-DUCTION," and "RESULTS"). In the results section, the writer includes italicized subheadings (for instance, "*INTERPHASE*" and "*PROPHASE*") to indicate divisions within the section. The use of specific section headings (Abstract, Introduction, Materials and Methods, Results, Discussion, and References) is a convention of scientific research reports; it is also customary in these papers to use subsections when the content within a section can be made clearer by further division. The specific formatting of the section and subsection headings may vary slightly from situation to situation (for instance, some instructors may ask for section titles to be underlined rather than printed in capital letters), but using the system of sections is a firm convention. The example paper demonstrates other conventions, too, such as the use of figures and tables to communicate data and results, and the positions of the figure and table titles (see pages 434–436).

You may be familiar with the conventions called for in some rhetorical situations, but not others. In terms of classroom assignments, for instance, you already possess basic knowledge about how to format and organize your papers. Without consciously learning them, you picked up certain conventions of academic writing—such as printing on white, unlined 8½-by-11-inch paper and using left-aligned paragraphs—from your experiences with such writing. Résumés call for different conventions regarding text placement, paper type, and paragraph structure than do academic papers, and the design conventions for year-end business reports may vary from company to company. Beyond these context-related variations, you may find that different audiences and different purposes call for further adaptations. You know that novice computer users, for instance, need plenty of diagrams in order to set up their new computers, and general readers often find shorter, more reader-friendly paragraphs more attractive than do members of a specialized audience.

Like most conventions of writing, document design conventions vary somewhat according to the rhetorical situation. Therefore, you will want to evaluate the audience, purpose, and context for your document while you are making design choices. You will also want to consult examples of successful documents to see what design choices have worked for others.

7i   Document design and function

Document design choices should support the document's message and purpose; they always arise from an understanding of the rhetorical situation. In fact, many of the principles of visual rhetoric discussed in 7a through 7f apply to document design, since readers perceive the pages of documents as visual objects. The following sections will help you make effective choices when designing documents.

(1) Simple, consistent document design reinforces organization, indicating differences and establishing unity.

One of the guiding principles of organization (see 3c–d and 4c–d) is to group the parts of a document that go together. In an essay, you use a thesis statement and transitions to show how ideas fit together. You can also use document design principles to reinforce the grouping of ideas, for example, using text formatting to highlight the connections between related sections or placing text sections to establish hierarchical relationships among different types of content.

Many professional documents use ordered relationships to draw together different types of information. Major sections contain subsections; subsections contain paragraphs or lower-level subsections; details may be presented in a bulleted list. Various levels of organization and types of content are signaled by such document design techniques.

Skillful use of these techniques not only reveals differences between types of content but also expresses their hierarchical relationships.

You want to use design elements that are distinctive enough to indicate differences among the document's parts but maintain enough consistency to indicate the overall unity of the document. For instance, headings should be more visually prominent than subheadings, whether that visual prominence results from a larger font, a different color, bolder type, more prominent positioning, or graphical accents (such as lines, boxes, or icons). But it is not necessary to vary every characteristic (font, color, placement on the page, and so on) for each type of content. Too much variety in typeface or other characteristics can actually make a document less effective. After all, if everything is varied, nothing will stand out.

You are already familiar with the ways simple document design choices express hierarchical relationships while emphasizing overall unity. The three-level system of headings used in this book provides a simple example: the numbered and lettered level-one headings, the numbered level-two subheadings, and the lettered level-three subheadings set up a clear hierarchy.

7a Level-one headings introduce major sections in a chapter.

(1) Level-two subheadings introduce topics within the chapter's major sections.

(a) Level-three subheadings are sometimes used to break topics into more specific subtopics.

Despite the ways in which these headings differ, however, they maintain strong connections. All use the same typeface (which is different from that used for the body text) and are boldfaced (so the headings stand out from the body text). All are left-aligned at the edge of the text, and all use **down-style capitalization** (which means that only the first word in a heading is capitalized, rather than capitalizing all the important words). In addition, the headings all use a labeling system involving numbers and letters. The ultimate effect is a coherent system of hierarchically related headings and subheadings, distinctive but clearly belonging to the same "family."

(2) Page design choices organize content into visual blocks.

Page design involves choices about the balance of elements on the page: the use of margins, columns, and grids to position major text elements; the use of lists and tables to organize certain types of information; and the use of white space, lines, shading, and boxes to organize space.

The conventional formats for academic papers will restrict your use of some page design elements (such as lines and boxes, multicolumn layouts, and centered text blocks). For many other writing projects, however, you can use a variety of these elements to improve a document's readability and visual interest. As in all areas of document design, you should base your page design decisions on how well your choices will support the document's purpose rather than how they serve as decoration.

(a) Page grids and columns structure usable areas of the page.

Compare a page from a standard college essay (such as the example in **4h**) with a typical newspaper front page (fig. 7.12). The first thing you might notice is that the newspaper uses images to illustrate the most important stories on the page. Next, you might notice that the text is laid out in multiple columns, not in the single-column format of academic papers. Both characteristics (the use of images and the arrangement of text into columns) work to organize the page into distinct areas. In fact, despite how tightly the text is packed on a newspaper page, you can very quickly separate one story from another by "reading" the visual and spatial clues available to you. Each article begins with a prominent title that spans the columns devoted to that story, and thin vertical lines highlight the boundaries between stories. Even more important, short segments of multiple columns are "chunked" together for each article. Although the page uses a six-column grid, articles extend across multiple columns rather than running from top to bottom along a single column, a technique that emphasizes the distinctiveness and unity of each story and supports readers' habit of reading newspaper articles individually rather than reading the entire page from top to bottom.

A newspaper's page design supports the specific ways in which readers typically use this kind of document. The chunking technique makes it easier to read an article while the paper is folded. The prominent images, the article titles, the text columns, and the compact, single-

Fig. 7.12. The front page of the *New York Times* is designed for ease in reading.

spaced lines all work together to organize the reader's view of the densely packed content. This page design helps readers move from story to story easily and in whatever order they wish, rather than directing them to read from left to right, top to bottom, and page to page (as readers of an academic essay would do).

(b) Lines, boxes, and white space establish borders.

Borders, formed from lines or boxes, help to distinguish one area of a page from another. Borders can also be formed from **white space** (blank areas around blocks of text) or with the use of background shading that highlights blocks of text. Prominent headings (such as those in fig. 7.12) imply borders, as do the folds of a brochure (particularly in combination with other techniques such as background shading or the placement of headings).

(3) Text elements are the basic building blocks of document design.

The most basic level of document design is the textual level. Text elements include typeface, type size, type color or highlighting, leading (the amount of space between lines), and kerning (the amount of space between letters in a word).

Some research has indicated that many readers prefer **serif** typefaces (those with little "feet" at the ends of letters) for large sections of text, either because newspapers and books have traditionally used such typefaces or because the shapes of serif letters are more readily recognized. Document designers often select a clear and readable serif typeface (such as Times New Roman, Palatino, or Garamond) for the body of the document and a **sans serif** (meaning "without feet") typeface (such as Arial, Century Gothic, or Tahoma) for headings, figure titles, and other visual accents.

Although word-processing software makes it easy to use a variety of fonts and type sizes on a single page, excessive font variation detracts from your content and distracts readers. It is better to use a single, highly legible font for the body text of a document, possibly complemented by a different font for headings and labels (if your document uses these elements). In addition, except for purely decorative purposes, avoid the more elaborate, hard-to-read display fonts, such as Old English and *Script*.

The color of type can also affect legibility. Although ink-jet printers offer the option of printing text in color, you should not do so in academic papers unless your instructor has specifically indicated that this formatting is acceptable. (Some documents such as flyers or announcements can be made more effective by the use of colored type.) Most instructors prefer that you use black ink (and a font such as Times Roman) for traditional academic assignments because it produces clear, dark text that is easy to read.

Word-processing software makes it easy to use italics for titles and foreign words and phrases, but you should resist the temptation to use italics or boldfacing for emphasizing words or phrases within lines of text. (See 42f.) With respect to the use of italics, follow the recommendations of the style manual for the specific discipline in which you are writing.

Compare the two versions of a short document presented in fig. 7.13. The first version uses a hard-to-read typeface, no highlighting of any text or headings, uniform double-spaced lines, and uniformly indented paragraphs. With its undifferentiated lines of text, this document is harder to read than the other. A few modest design changes improve the layout and readability of the second version.

The typeface in the first version (Courier, once a typewriter standard) is replaced in the second version by Palatino, a more space-efficient typeface. The headings in the second version are set in Tahoma to distinguish them from the rest of the content; boldfacing reinforces this distinction. The body text is single-spaced, with an extra line space between paragraphs. This use of extra space makes the paragraphs stand apart from one another more clearly and also makes it unnecessary to indent the first line of each paragraph. Finally, a horizontal line between the memo header and the memo body reinforces the boundary between these two parts of the document. These subtle changes improve readability, while at the same time they make the text more space-efficient; space efficiency and legibility do not have to work at cross purposes.

7j Graphics and purpose

In addition to enhancing the visual characteristics of the text, document designers often incorporate visual displays, or **graphics,** into their documents. Graphics can be used to illustrate a concept, present data, provide visual relief, or simply attract readers' attention. Different types of graphics—tables, charts or graphs, and pictures—serve different purposes, and some may serve multiple purposes in a given document. Any of these types of graphics can enable readers to capture a message more quickly than they would by reading long sections of text. However, if there is any chance that readers might not receive the intended message, it is a good idea to supplement graphics with text discussion.

DATE: Friday, September 19, 2003
TO: Statewide Insurance Corporation
FROM: John Doe, Policy #H24-6802-46
SUBJECT: Hurricane Isabel Damage Report, Claim #: 12345-678-901234-56

The following damage to property insured by Policy #H24-6802-46 has resulted from Hurricane Isabel.

Rain has leaked through the roof to the vaulted ceiling in the living room. Three water marks have appeared on the ceiling, covering approx. 6' x 4' area. Damage is also apparent in the flashing at the chimney base.

Several shingles are missing or broken on both sides of the roof.

Water has entered the attic from the west end gable vent, soaking the wall sheathing and insulation on one end wall.

Date: Friday, September 19, 2003

To: Statewide Insurance Corporation

From: John Doe, Policy #H24-6802-46

Subject: Hurricane Isabel Damage Report, Claim #: 12345-678-901234-56

The following damage to property insured by Policy #H24-6802-46 has resulted from Hurricane Isabel.

Rain has leaked through the roof to the vaulted ceiling in the living room. Three water marks have appeared on the ceiling, covering approx. 6' x 4' area. Damage is also apparent in the flashing at the chimney base.

Several shingles are missing or broken on both sides of the roof.

Water has entered the attic from the west end gable vent, soaking the wall sheathing and insulation on one end wall.

Fig. 7.13. Two versions of an insurance agent's memo.

(1) Tables organize data so that they can be easily accessed and compared.

Tables use a row-and-column arrangement to organize data (numbers or words) spatially; they are especially useful for presenting great amounts of numerical information in a small space, enabling the reader to draw direct comparisons among data or even to locate specific pieces of data. When you design a table, be sure to label all of the columns and rows accurately and to provide both a title and a number for the table. Table number and title traditionally appear above the table, as table 7.1 demonstrates, and any notes or source information should be placed below it.

Most word-processing programs have settings that let you insert a table wherever you need one. You can determine how many rows and columns the table will have, and you can also size each row and each column appropriately for the information it will hold.

TABLE 7.1
Modified Monthly Tornado Statistics

Month	2002 Prelim.	2001 Final	2000 Final	1999 Final	3-Year Average
Jan	8	5	16	212	77
Feb	2	30	56	22	32
March	30	34	103	56	66
April	114	131	136	177	140
May	130	235	241	311	256
June	?	147	135	289	219
Jul	?	123	148	102	128
Aug	?	69	52	79	62
Sep	?	85	47	56	58
Oct	?	121	63	17	60
Nov	?	112	48	7	37
Dec	?	?	26	15	16
Total	290	1212	1071	1343	1151

Source: National Weather Service.

(2) Charts and graphs provide visual representations of data.

Like tables, charts and graphs display relationships among statistical data in visual form; unlike tables, they do so using lines, bars, or other visual elements rather than just letters and numbers. Data can be displayed in several different graphic forms: pie charts, line graphs, and bar charts are the most common examples.

Pie charts are especially useful for showing the relationship of parts to a whole (see fig. 7.14), but they can only be used to display data that add up to 100 percent (a whole).

Line graphs show the relationship between one variable (measured on the vertical y axis) and another variable (measured on the horizontal x axis) that changes in a regular way. The most common x-axis variable is time. Line graphs are very good at showing how a variable changes over time. A line graph might be used, for example, to illustrate progression of sleep stages during one night (see fig. 7.15), increases or decreases in student achievement from semester to semester, or trends in financial markets over a number of years.

Bar charts show correlations between two variables that do not involve smooth changes over time. For instance, a bar chart might illustrate gross national product for several nations, the relative speeds of various computer processors, or statistics about the composition of the U.S. military (see fig. 7.16).

In addition to charts, graphs, and tables, a variety of other graphics can be used to clarify complex ideas or to illustrate relationships among

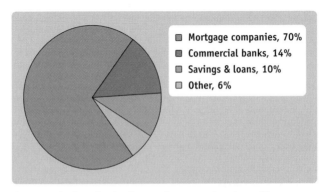

Fig. 7.14. Pie chart showing issuers of mortgage-based securities.

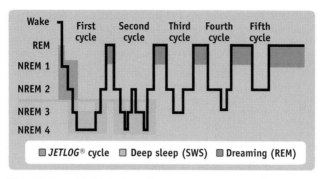

Fig. 7.15. Graph of nightly sleep stages.

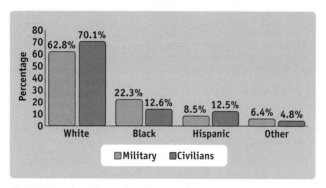

Fig. 7.16. Bar chart illustrating the composition of the U.S. military.

concepts. Figure 7.17 (a process diagram of the water cycle) uses a simple graphical convention (superimposing arrows and labels on a semirealistic drawing) to present information that, in textual form, would require a great deal of space. This process diagram shows the movement of water in different forms through the environment.

(3) Pictures illustrate how objects appear.

Pictures include photos, sketches, technical illustrations, paintings, icons, and other visual representations. Photographs are often used to reinforce textual descriptions or to show a reader exactly what something looks like. Readers of a used-car ad, for instance, will want to see exactly what the car looks like, not an artistic rendition of its appearance. Likewise, a Costa Rican travel brochure

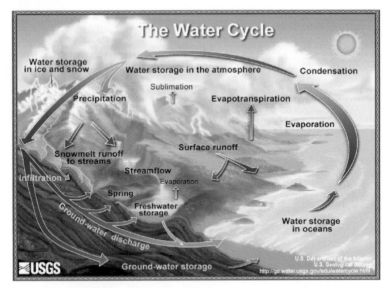

Fig. 7.17. Process diagram of the water cycle.

will contain lots of full-color photos of dazzling beaches, verdant forests, and azure water.

But photographs are not always the most informative type of picture. Compare the two parts of fig. 7.18: a photograph of a printer and a line drawing of the same printer. While the photograph is a more realistic image of the actual printer, the lines of the illustration reveal more clearly the printer's important features: buttons, panels, and so forth. With its simple lines and clear labels, the illustration is well suited to its purpose: to help the viewer set up and start to use the printer. Line drawings enable the designer of a document such as a user manual to highlight specific elements of an object while deemphasizing or eliminating unnecessary information. The addition of arrows, pointers, and labels adds useful detail to such an illustration.

Your ability to interpret images and use them in documents is greater than you might imagine. You have had years of practice at doing just those things—from responding to advertising to composing class papers, science projects, and 4-H exhibits. Consciously applying your knowledge to these tasks will help make your interactions with documents more productive.

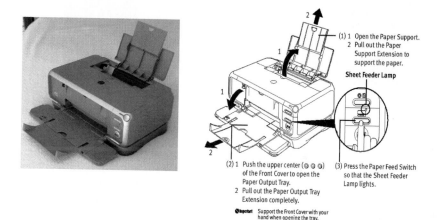

Fig. 7.18. A photo and a line drawing of the same printer.

Exercise 2

If you can locate a document that contains one or more images and that you composed for another class or an extracurricular activity, bring it to class or photograph it. Be prepared to explain how you created the document and chose the image(s). If you cannot locate a copy of such a document, write for ten to fifteen minutes, reconstructing the process by which you created the document, including what you knew how to do before you started and what you learned as you progressed.

WRITING

ARGUMENTS

8

You write arguments on a regular basis. When you send your business partner a memo to tell her that a client needs to sign a contract, when you e-mail your parents to ask them for a loan, when you petition your academic advisor for a late drop, or when you demand that a mail-order company refund your money, you are writing an argument. You are expressing a point of view and then using logical reasoning to invite a specific audience to accept that point of view or adopt a course of action. *Argument* and *persuasion* are often used interchangeably, but they differ in two basic ways. Traditionally, **persuasion** has referred to winning or conquering with the use of emotional reasoning, whereas **argument** has been reserved for the use of logical reasoning to convince listeners or readers. But because writing often involves some measure of "winning" (even if it is only gaining the ear of a particular audience) and uses both emotion and reason, this book uses *argument* to cover the meanings of both terms.

When writing arguments, you follow the same process as for all your writing: planning, drafting, and revising, as well as attending to

Argumentation is about problem solving.

audience and context (see 1d–e). Argumentative writing is distinct from other kinds of writing in its emphasis on the inseparability of audience and purpose. Recognizing and respecting the beliefs, values, and expertise of a specific audience is the only way to achieve the rhetorical purpose of an argument, which goes beyond victory over an opponent. Argument can be an important way to invite exchange, understanding, cooperation, consideration, joint decision making, agreement, or negotiation of differences. Thus, argument serves three basic and sometimes overlapping purposes: to analyze a complicated issue or question an established belief, to express or defend a point of view, and to invite or convince an audience to change a position or adopt a course of action.

This chapter will help you

- determine the purpose of an argument (8a),
- consider different viewpoints (8b),
- distinguish fact from opinion (8c),
- take a position or make a claim (8d),
- provide evidence to support a claim (8e),
- use the rhetorical appeals to ground an argument (8f),
- arrange ideas (8g),
- use logical reasoning (8h),
- avoid rhetorical fallacies (8i), and
- analyze an argument (8j).

As you proceed, you will understand the importance of determining your purpose, identifying your audience, marshaling your arguments, arguing ethically, and treating your audience with respect.

8a Determining the purpose of your argument

To what exigence are you responding? What is your topic? Why are you arguing about it? What is at stake? What is likely to happen as a result of making this argument? How important are those consequences? Who is in a position to act or react in response to your argument?

When writing an argument, you need to establish the relationships among your topic, purpose, and audience. The relationship between audience and purpose is particularly significant because the audience often shapes the purpose.

- If there is little likelihood that you can convince members of your audience to change a strongly held opinion, you might achieve a great deal by inviting them to understand your position.
- If the members of your audience are not firmly committed to a position, you might be able to convince them to agree with the opinion you are expressing or defending.
- If the members of your audience agree with you in principle, you might invite them to undertake a specific action—such as voting for the candidate you are supporting.

No matter how you imagine those in your audience responding to your argument, you must establish **common ground** with them, stating a goal toward which you both want to work or identifying a belief, assumption, or value that you both share. In other words, common ground is a necessary starting point, regardless of your ultimate purpose.

8b　Considering differing viewpoints

If everyone agreed on everything, there would be no need for argument, for taking a position or questioning one held by anyone else. But everyone doesn't agree. Thus, a good deal of the writing you will do in school or at work will require you to take a position on a topic, an arguable position. The first step toward finding a topic for argumentation is to consider issues that inspire different opinions.

Behind any effective argument is a question that can generate more than one reasonable answer. If you ask "Is there racism in the United States?" almost anyone will agree that there is. But if you ask "Why is there still racism in the United States?" or "What can Americans do to eliminate racism?" you will hear different answers. Answers differ because people approach questions with various backgrounds, experiences, and assumptions. As a consequence, they are often tempted to use reasoning that supports what they already believe. As a writer, you, too, will be tempted to employ such reasoning, and doing so is a good place to start. But as you expand and shape your argument, you will want to demonstrate not only that you are knowledgeable about your topic but also that you are aware of and have given fair consideration to other views about it. To be knowledgeable and yet respectful of others' views constitutes a worthy goal.

When you write an argument, you are trying to solve a problem or answer a question—with or for an audience. When you choose a topic for argumentation, you will want to take a stance that allows you to question, that provides you an exigence (or reason) for writing. First, you focus on a topic, on the part of some general subject that you will address in your essay (see 3b), and then you pose a question about it. As you craft your question, consider the following: (1) your own values and beliefs with respect to the question, (2) how your assumptions might differ from those of your intended audience, and (3) how you might establish common ground with members of your audience, while at the same time respecting any differences between your opinion and theirs. The question you raise will evolve into your **thesis,** an arguable statement.

The most important criterion for choosing an arguable statement for an essay is knowledge of the topic, so that you will be an informed writer, responsive to the expectations of your audience. When you are in a position to choose your own topic, you can draw on your knowledge of current events, politics, sports, fashion, or a specific academic subject. Topics may present themselves on television or the Web, as you find yourself agreeing or disagreeing with what you hear and read.

To determine whether a topic might be suitable, make a statement about the topic ("I believe strongly that . . . " or "My view is that . . . ") and then check to see if that statement can be argued.

TIPS FOR ASSESSING AN ARGUABLE STATEMENT ABOUT A TOPIC

- What reasons can you think of to support your belief about the topic? List those reasons.

- Who or what groups might disagree with your statement? Why? List those groups.

- Do you know enough about this topic to discuss other points of view? Can you find out what you need to know?

- What are other viewpoints on the topic and reasons supporting those viewpoints? List them.

- What is your purpose in writing about this topic?

- What do you want your audience to do in response to your argument? In other words, what do you expect from your audience? Write out your expectation.

If you can answer all these questions to your satisfaction, you should feel confident about your topic. As you move further into the writing process, researching and exploring your topic in the library or on the Web (see chapter 9), you may be able to clarify your purpose and improve your thesis statement.

8c Distinguishing between fact and opinion

When you develop your thesis statement into an argument, you use both facts and opinions. It is important to distinguish between these two kinds of information so that you can use both to your advantage, especially in terms of establishing your credibility (see 8f(1)), an essential feature of successful argumentation. **Facts** are reliable pieces of information that can be verified through independent sources or procedures. **Opinions,** on the other hand, are assertions or inferences that may or may not be based on facts. Opinions that are widely accepted, however, may seem to be factual when they are not.

Just because facts are reliable does not mean that they speak for themselves. Facts are significant only when they are used responsibly to support a claim; otherwise, a thoughtful and well-informed opinion might have more impact. To determine whether a statement you have read is fact or opinion, ask yourself questions like these: Can it be proved? Can it be challenged? How often is the same result achieved? If a statement can consistently be proved true, then it is a fact. If it can be disputed, then it is an opinion.

Fact   Milk contains calcium.
Opinion   Americans should drink more milk.

To say that milk contains calcium is to state a well-established fact: it can be verified by consulting published studies or by conducting laboratory tests. Whether or not this fact is significant depends on how a writer chooses to use it. As an isolated fact, it is unlikely to seem significant. But to say that Americans need to drink more milk is to express an opinion that may or may not be supported by facts. When considering the statement "Americans should drink more milk," a thoughtful reader might ask, "How much calcium does a human need? Why do humans need calcium? Is cow's milk good for humans? Might leafy green vegetables provide a richer source of calcium?" Anticipating questions such as these can help you develop an argument. These sorts of questions also help you recognize the evidence that will best support your argument, where you can obtain such evidence, and what to do if you discover conflicting evidence.

The line between fact and opinion is not always clear. Therefore, writers and readers of arguments should always be prepared to interpret and assess the reliability of the information before them, evaluating the beliefs supporting the argument's stance, the kinds of sources used, and the objections that could be made to the argument.

Exercise 1

Determine which of the following statements are fact and which are opinion. In each case, what kind of verification would you require in order to accept the statement as reliable?

1. Toni Morrison won the Nobel Prize in literature in 1993.
2. Women often earn less money than men who hold the same positions.
3. *The Lion King* was the best movie ever made about animals.
4. Writing well is a gift, like musical genius.
5. A college degree guarantees a good job.
6. Santa Fe is the oldest U.S. city that is a state capital.
7. Running is good for your health.
8. The United States won World War II.
9. In combination, ammonia and chlorine bleach result in a poisonous gas.
10. Researchers will find a cure for AIDS.

8d Taking a position or making a claim

When making an argument, a writer takes a position on a particular topic. Whether the argument analyzes, questions, expresses, defends, invites, or convinces, the writer needs to make clear his or her position. That position, which is called the **claim**, or **proposition**, clearly states what the writer wants the audience to do with the information being provided. The claim is the thesis of the argument and usually appears in the introduction and sometimes again in the conclusion.

(1) Effective writers claim no more than they can responsibly support.

Claims vary in extent; they can be absolute or moderate, large or limited. Absolute claims assert that something is always true or false, completely good or bad; moderate claims make less sweeping assertions.

Absolute claim	College athletes are never good students.
Moderate claim	Most colleges have low graduation rates for their athletes.
Absolute claim	Harry Truman was the best president we have ever had.
Moderate claim	Truman's domestic policies helped advance civil rights.

Moderate claims are not necessarily superior to absolute claims. After all, writers frequently need to take a strong position in favor of or against something. But the stronger the claim, the stronger the evidence needed to support it. Be sure to consider the quality and the significance of the evidence you use—not just its quantity.

(2) Types of claims vary in terms of how much they encompass.

(a) Substantiation claims assert that something exists.
Without making a value judgment, a **substantiation claim** makes a point that can be supported by evidence.

> The job market for those who just received a PhD in English is limited.
> The post office is raising rates again.

(b) Evaluation claims assert that something has a specific quality.
According to an **evaluation claim,** something is good or bad, effective or ineffective, attractive or unattractive, successful or unsuccessful.

> The graduation rate for athletes at Penn State is very high compared with that at the other Big Ten universities.
> The public transportation system in Washington, DC, is reliable and safe.

Sometimes, writers use evaluation claims as a way to invite their audience to consider an issue.

> It is important for us to consider the graduation rate of college athletes.

(c) Policy claims call for a specific action.
When making **policy claims,** writers call for something to be done.

> We must find the funds to hire better qualified high school teachers.
> We need to build a light-rail system linking downtown with the airport and the western suburbs.

Much writing involves substantiation, evaluation, and policy claims. When writing about the job market for those with new PhDs in English, you might tap your ability to substantiate a claim; when writing about literature (see chapter 16), you might need to evaluate a character. Policy claims are commonly found in arguments about social issues such as health care, social security, and affirmative action. These claims often grow out of substantiation or evaluation claims: first, you demonstrate that a problem exists; then, you establish the best solution for that problem.

Policy claims, such as the one made by this famous Army recruiting poster, call for a specific action.

TIPS FOR MAKING A CLAIM ARGUABLE

- Write down your opinion.
- Describe the situation that produced your opinion.
- Decide who constitutes the audience for your opinion and what you want that audience to do about your opinion.
- Write down the verifiable and reliable facts that support your opinion.
- Using those facts, transform your initial opinion into a thoughtful claim that considers at least two sides to the issue under discussion.
- Ask yourself, "So what?" If the answer to this question shows that your claim leads nowhere, start over, beginning with the first tip.

As an example of transforming an opinion into an arguable claim, consider the following scenario. Helen thinks that air pollution is a problem. She describes the situation that has inspired her opinion: she was jogging on a busy street and had difficulty breathing because of the excessive car exhaust. Describing this situation helps Helen focus her opinion. She decides to narrow her topic to reducing automobile emissions. Next, she imagines an audience for her topic, an audience who can do something about this issue. She decides to write to automobile manufacturers. Helen knows that she needs to do some research on this topic in order to write a convincing argument, so she researches the physics of automobile emissions and realizes that, with just a small amount of effort, car manufacturers could improve the efficiency of most automobile engines—and thereby reduce emissions. She also conducts a survey of fellow students and learns that most of them would prefer to buy cars with more efficient engines. Helen now has a specific audience, a specific claim for their consideration, and a specific reason for her audience to agree with her claim: despite a slight increase in automobile price, automobile manufacturers should work to produce more efficient engines; if they do so, young adults will be more likely to purchase their automobiles.

Exercise 2

The following excerpt is from an argument analyzing racial strife in the United States, written by Cornel West, a scholar specializing in race relations. Evaluate the claims it presents. Are they absolute or moderate? Can you identify a substantiation or evaluation claim? What policy claim is implicit in this passage?

[1]To engage in a serious discussion of race in America, we must begin not with the problems of black people but with the flaws of American society— flaws rooted in historic inequalities and longstanding cultural stereotypes. [2]How we set up the terms for discussing racial issues shapes our perception and response to these issues. [3]As long as black people are viewed as a "them," the burden falls on blacks to do all the "cultural" and "moral" work necessary for healthy race relations. [4]The implication is that only certain Americans can define what it means to be American—and the rest must simply "fit in."   —CORNEL WEST, *Race Matters*

8e Providing evidence for an effective argument

Effective arguments are well developed and supported. You should explore your topic in enough depth to have the evidence to support your position intelligently and ethically, whether that evidence is based on personal experience or research (see chapters 3 and 9). You will want to consider the reasons others might disagree with you and be prepared to respond to those reasons.

(1) An effective argument clearly establishes the thinking that leads to the claim.

If you want readers to take your ideas seriously, you must communicate the reasons that have led to your position, as well as the values and assumptions that underlie your thinking. When you are exploring your topic, make a list of the reasons that have led to your belief (see **3d** and **3f**). For example, when Laura Klocke was working on her argumentative essay (at the end of this chapter; see pages 198–204), she listed the following reasons for her belief that fair trade coffee should be used exclusively at her school:

1. The average price of coffee is $12.00/lb., while the average coffee grower is paid only 20–40 cents/lb.
2. The average latte costs $3.50, while the average coffee farmer makes $3.00/day.
3. The University of St. Thomas is committed to producing "morally responsible individuals who combine cultural awareness and intellectual curiosity." St. Thomas could easily support only fair trade coffee.

Although it is possible to base an argument on one good reason (such as "Buying fair trade coffee is the right thing to do"), doing so can be risky. If your audience does not find this reason convincing, you have no other support for your position. When you show that you have more than one reason for believing as you do, you increase the likelihood that your audience will find merit in your argument. Sometimes, however, one reason is stronger—and more appropriate for your audience—than several others you could advance. To develop an argument for which you have only one good reason, explore the bases underlying your reason: the values and assumptions that led you to take your stand. By demonstrating the thinking behind the single reason on which you are building your case, you can create a well-developed argument.

Whether you have one reason or several, be sure to provide sufficient evidence from credible sources to support your claim:

- facts,
- statistics,
- examples, and
- testimony, from personal experience or professional expertise.

This evidence must be accurate, representative, and sufficient. Accurate information should be verifiable by others (see 8c). Recognize, however, that a writer may provide you with information that is accurate but neither representative nor sufficient, because it was drawn from an exceptional case, a biased sample, or a one-time occurrence. If, for example, you are writing an argument about the advantages of using Standardized English but draw all of your supporting evidence from a proponent of the English-Only movement, your evidence represents only the views of that movement. If you draw all of your evidence from just one person (Bill Cosby, for instance, has strong views on the use of Standardized English, especially as a means to stamp out the Ebonics movement), your evidence is neither representative of all the support for the use of Standardized English, nor is it sufficient to support a thoughtful argument. In order to represent a wider viewpoint, you should gather supporting evidence from sociolinguists, speakers of other dialects and languages, education specialists, professors, and other experts. In other words, consult more than a single source. (See chapter 9.)

When gathering evidence, be sure to think critically about the information you find. If you are using the results of polls or other statistics or statements by authorities, determine how recent and representative the information is and how it was gathered. Consider, too, whether the authority you plan to quote is qualified to address the topic under consideration and is likely to be respected by your readers.

Whatever form of evidence you use—facts, statistics, examples, or testimony—you need to make clear to your audience exactly *why* and *how* the evidence supports your claim. As soon as the relationship between your claim and your evidence is clear to you, make that connection explicit to your readers, helping them understand your thinking.

(2) Effective arguments respond to diverse views.

Issues are controversial because good arguments can be made on all sides. Therefore, effective arguments consider and respond to other points of view, fairly and respectfully. In order for your argument to be effective and convincing, your audience must realize that you are knowledgeable about points of view other than your own. The most common strategy for addressing opposing points of view is referred to as **refutation:** you introduce diverse views and then respectfully demonstrate why you disagree with each of them. As you consider opposing points of view, you are likely to discover some you cannot refute, perhaps because they are based in a belief system markedly different from your own. You are also likely to discover that some of the other views have real merit. If you understand the reasons behind opposing viewpoints but remain unconvinced, you will need to demonstrate why.

When you find yourself agreeing with a point raised on another side of the issue, you can benefit from offering a **concession.** By openly admitting that you agree with opponents on one or more specific points, you demonstrate that you are fair-minded (see **8f(1)**) and at the same time increase your credibility. Concessions also increase the likelihood that opponents will be inclined to find merit in your argument.

Whether you agree or disagree with other positions, work to recognize and assess them. It is hard to persuade people to agree with you if you insist that they are entirely wrong. If you admit that they are partially right, they are more likely to admit that you could be partially right as well. In this sense, then, argument involves working with an audience as much as getting them to work with you.

Exercise 3

The following paragraph is taken from an argument by Martin Luther King, Jr., in which he defends the struggle for civil rights against public criticism from a group of prominent clergymen. Write a short analysis of this paragraph in which you note (a) an opposing viewpoint to which he is responding, (b) a refutation he offers to this viewpoint, (c) a concession he makes, and (d) any questions this excerpt raises for you.

[1]You express a great deal of anxiety over our willingness to break laws. [2]This is certainly a legitimate concern. [3]Since we so diligently urge people to obey the Supreme Court's decision of 1954 outlawing segregation in the public schools, at first glance it may seem rather paradoxical for us consciously to break laws.

⁴One may well ask: "How can you advocate breaking some laws and obeying others?" ⁵The answer lies in the fact that there are two types of laws, just and unjust. ⁶I would be the first to advocate obeying just laws. ⁷One has not only a legal but a moral responsibility to obey just laws. ⁸Conversely, one has a moral responsibility to disobey unjust laws. ⁹I would agree with St. Augustine that "an unjust law is no law at all."

—**MARTIN LUTHER KING, JR.**, "Letter from Birmingham Jail"

8f Using the rhetorical appeals to ground your argument

Effective arguments always incorporate several appeals to the audience simply because logical reasoning—providing good reasons—is rarely enough (see **8e** and **8h**). Human beings do not believe or act on the basis of facts or logic alone; if we did, we would all agree and act accordingly. In reality, we believe and act on the basis of our own concerns, experiences, and needs. When we do not listen to another point of view, we simply do not want to change our minds. An effective argument, then, is one that gets a fair hearing. If you want your views to be heard, understood, and maybe even acted on, you need to follow the necessary steps to gain a hearing.

(1) Three rhetorical appeals can shape any argument.

Aristotle, a Greek philosopher who lived over two thousand years ago, was the first to help speakers shape effective arguments through a combination of three persuasive strategies: the **rhetorical appeals** of ethos, logos, and pathos. **Ethos** (an ethical appeal) establishes the speaker's or writer's credibility and trustworthiness. An ethical appeal demonstrates goodwill toward the audience, good sense or knowledge of the subject at hand, and good character. Establishing common ground with the audience is another feature of ethos. But ethos alone rarely carries an argument; therefore, you also need to use **logos** (a logical appeal). Logos demonstrates an effective use of reason and judicious use of evidence, whether facts, statistics, comparisons, anecdotes, expert opinions, personal experiences, or observations. You employ logos in the process of supporting claims, drawing reasonable conclusions, and avoiding rhetorical fallacies (see **8i**). Aristotle also taught that persuasion comes about only when the audience feels emotionally stirred by the topic under discussion. Therefore, **pathos** (an emotional appeal) involves using language that will stir the feelings of the audience. If you misuse pathos in an attempt to manipulate your audience, it can backfire. But pathos can be used successfully when it establishes empathy and authentic understanding. Thus, the most effective arguments combine these three persuasive appeals responsibly and knowledgeably.

In the next three subsections, excerpts from Martin Luther King, Jr.'s "Letter from Birmingham Jail" illustrate how a writer can use all three of the classical rhetorical appeals.

(a) Ethical appeals establish a writer's credibility.

In his opening paragraph, King shows that his professional life is so demanding that he needs more than one secretary. He also indicates that he wishes to engage in "constructive work," thereby establishing common ground with his audience, whom he characterizes as being well-intentioned and sincere. He also establishes that he will argue in good faith.

1   My Dear Fellow Clergymen:

While confined here in the Birmingham city jail, I came across your recent statement calling my present activities "unwise and untimely." Seldom do I pause to answer criticism of my work and ideas. If I sought to answer all the criticisms that cross my desk, my secretaries would have little time for anything other than such correspondence in the course of the day, and I would have no time for constructive work. But since I feel that you are men of genuine good will and that your criticisms are sincerely set forth, I want to try to answer your statement in what I hope will be patient and reasonable terms.

(b) Logical appeals help an audience clearly understand the writer's ideas.

To help his audience understand why segregation is wrong, King defines key terms:

2   Let us consider a more concrete example of just and unjust laws. An unjust law is

As a writer and a speaker, Martin Luther King, Jr., successfully used the rhetorical appeals of ethos, logos, and pathos.

a code that a numerical or power majority group compels a minority group to obey but does not make binding on itself. This is difference made legal. By the same token, a just law is a code that a majority compels a minority to follow and that it is willing to follow itself. This is sameness made legal.

(c) Emotional appeals can move the audience to a new way of thinking or acting.

As he moves toward his conclusion, King evokes feelings of idealism as well as guilt:

3   I have travelled the length and breadth of Alabama, Mississippi, and all the other southern states. On sweltering summer days and crisp autumn mornings I have looked at the South's beautiful churches with their lofty spires pointing heavenward. I have beheld the impressive outlines of her massive religious-education buildings. Over and over I have found myself asking: "What kind of people worship here? Who is their God? . . . Where were their voices of support when bruised and weary Negro men and women decided to rise from the dark dungeons of complacency to the bright hills of creative protest?"

—**MARTIN LUTHER KING, JR.,** "Letter from Birmingham Jail"

The full text of King's argument includes other examples of ethos, logos, and pathos.

Although ethos is often developed in the introduction, logos in the body, and pathos in the conclusion, these classical rhetorical appeals often overlap and appear throughout an argument.

(2) Rogerian appeals show other people that you understand them.

Rogerian argument derives from the work of Carl R. Rogers, a psychologist who believed that many problems are the result of a breakdown in communication. Rogers claimed that people often fail to understand each other because of a natural tendency to judge and evaluate, agree or disagree, without really listening to, let alone understanding, what is being said. His model calls for suspending judgment until you are able to restate fairly and accurately what others believe. When each person in a conflict demonstrates this ability, the likelihood of misunderstanding is significantly reduced.

Skills such as paraphrasing and summarizing (see **11d(3)–(4)**) are essential to the Rogerian approach. Although this model can be used to achieve a number of goals, it is especially useful for building consensus. To demonstrate that you have given fair consideration to the views of others, you begin a Rogerian argument by paraphrasing these views and demonstrating that you understand the thinking behind them. Then, you introduce your own position and explain why you believe it has merit. Because the Rogerian model is designed to build consensus, you conclude your argument by showing how everyone concerned about the issue could benefit from adopting your proposal. This emphasis on being fair-minded and nonconfrontational gives ethos (see **8f(1)**) an essential place in a Rogerian argument.

The summary of benefits with which a Rogerian argument concludes gives you the opportunity to draw your threads together and appeal to your audience without simply restating what you have already said. In the following conclusion to an argument on public education, notice how the author cites benefits for students, teachers, and the public at large if her proposal is adopted.

4   Reducing the maximum class size in our secondary schools from thirty students to twenty-five will not solve all the problems in our system, but it will yield important benefits. Students will get more individualized instruction. Better able to give their full attention to the students who remain with them, teachers will gain greater job satisfaction. And in an era when events like the recent killings in Littleton, Colorado, raise legitimate concerns about the safety of public schools, an improved student-teacher ratio reduces the risk of a troubled student being overlooked—a comfort to parents as well as educators. Finally even those citizens who do not have children will benefit, because in the long run everyone benefits from living in a community where people are well educated.

—**LAURA BECHDEL,** "Space to Learn"

8g   Purposefully arranging an effective argument

No single arrangement is right for every written argument. Unless your instructor asks you to demonstrate a particular type of arrangement, the decisions you make about arrangement should be based on several factors: your topic, your audience, and your purpose. You can develop a good plan by simply listing the major points you want to make (see **3d**), deciding what order to put them in, and then determining where to include refutation or concession (see **8g(3)**). You must also decide whether to place your thesis statement or claim at the beginning or the end of your argument. Once you sort out the reasons supporting your claim, you need to develop each reason with a separate paragraph (unless, of course, you're summarizing your reasons in the conclusion).

No matter which arrangement you use, your conclusion should move beyond a mere summary of what has already been stated and instead emphasize your emotional connection with your audience, a connection that reinforces your rhetorical purpose: the course of action you want your audience to take, an invitation to further understanding, or the implications of your claim (see **8h**). The student paper by Laura Klocke at the end of this chapter (see pages 198–204) ends with a conclusion that not only reinforces her purpose but links her purpose with the stated mission of her university.

In addition, there are a few basic principles that may be useful.

(1) Classical arrangement works well if your audience has not yet taken a position on your issue.

One way to organize your argument is to follow the plan recommended by classical rhetoric, which assumes that an audience is prepared to follow a well-reasoned argument.

FEATURES OF THE CLASSICAL ARRANGEMENT

Introduction	Introduce your issue, and capture the attention of your audience. Try using a short narrative or a strong example. (See **3f(2)** and **3g**.) Begin establishing your credibility (using ethos) and common ground.
Background information	Provide your audience with a history of the situation, and state how things currently stand. Define any key terms. Even if you think the facts speak for themselves, draw the attention of your audience to those points that are especially important, and explain why they are meaningful.
Proposition	Introduce the position you are taking: present the argument itself, and provide the basic reasons for your belief. Frame your position as a thesis statement or claim. (See **3c** and **8d**.)

Proof or confirmation	Discuss the reasons that have led you to take your position. Each reason must be clear, relevant, and representative. Provide facts, expert testimony, and any other evidence that supports your claim.
Refutation	Recognize and disprove the arguments of people who hold a different position and with whom you continue to disagree.
Concession	Concede any point with which you agree or that has merit; show why this concession does not damage your own case.
Conclusion	Summarize your most important points, and appeal to your audience's feelings, making a personal connection. Describe the consequences of your argument in a final attempt to encourage your audience to consider (if not commit to) a particular course of action.

(2) Rogerian arrangement can help calm an audience strongly opposed to your position.

To write an argument informed by Rogerian appeals, use the following plan as your guide.

FEATURES OF THE ROGERIAN ARRANGEMENT

Introduction	Establish that you have paid attention to views different from your own. Build trust by stating these views clearly and fairly.
Concessions	Reassure the people you hope to persuade by showing that you agree with them to some extent and do not think that they are completely wrong.
Thesis	Having earned the confidence of your audience, state your claim, or proposition.
Support	Explain why you have taken this position and provide support for it.
Conclusion	Conclude by showing how your audience and other people could benefit from accepting your position. Indicate the extent to which this position will resolve the problem you are addressing. If you are offering a partial solution to a complex problem, concede that further work may be necessary.

For a sample student paper organized as a Rogerian argument, visit www.harbrace.com.

(3) Refutation and concession are most effective when placed where readers will accept them.

Classical arrangement places refutation after the proof or confirmation of the argument, an arrangement that works well for an audience familiar with this organizational model. Sometimes, however, that refutation can come too late. Readers unfamiliar with classical arrangement may have decided that you are too one-sided—and may even have stopped reading. Therefore, when you are taking a highly controversial stand on an emotionally loaded subject, strive to establish common ground, and then acknowledge opposing viewpoints and respond to them. This variation on classical arrangement assumes that readers will be unwilling to hear a new proposition unless they are first shown what is weak or incomplete about their current thinking.

In a Rogerian argument, a writer begins by reporting opposing views fairly and identifying what is valuable about them. The strategy here is not to refute the views in question but to concede that they have merit—thus putting the audience at ease before introducing a thesis or claim that might be rejected if stated prematurely.

However, sometimes readers may react negatively to a writer who responds to opposing views before offering any reasons to support his or her own view. These readers want to know from the start where an argument is headed. For this reason, writers often choose to state their position at the beginning of the argument and offer at least one strong reason to support it before turning to opposing views. They sometimes keep at least one other reason in reserve (often one responsibly laden with emotion, or pathos), so that they can present it after responding to opposing views, thereby ending with an emphasis on their confirmation.

Unless you are required to follow a specific arrangement, or organizational plan, you should respond to opposing views wherever your audience is most likely either to expect this discussion or to be willing to hear it. If your audience is receptive, you can place refutation and concession after your confirmation. If your audience adheres to a different position, you should respond to their views toward the beginning of your argument. You might also want to keep in mind that if you open a paragraph with an opposing view, you will want to move quickly to your response to that view so that your readers make only one shift between differing views. Your goal is to keep your readers focused on your line of thinking.

Read the editorial pages of several consecutive issues of your community or college newspaper. Look for editorials that analyze or question an established belief, express or defend an opinion, invite consideration, or try to convince. Choose an editorial that strikes you as well argued, well developed, and well organized—even if it does not change your belief or action (it may only have changed your level of understanding). Bring several copies of the editorial to class, and be prepared to discuss its purpose, audience, use of appeals, and conclusion.

8h Using logic to argue effectively and ethically

Because writers cannot argue on the basis of ethos alone, they need to understand the ways in which **logic**—the reasoning behind an argument—enhances or detracts from the argument. Logic is a means through which you can develop your ideas, realize new ones, and determine whether your thinking is clear enough to persuade readers to agree with you. By arguing logically, you increase the likelihood that your arguments will be taken seriously.

(1) Inductive reasoning is the process of using a number of specific facts or observations to draw a logical conclusion.

You use inductive reasoning on a daily basis. If you get a stomachache within fifteen minutes of eating ice cream, you might conclude that there's a connection. Perhaps you are lactose-intolerant. This use of evidence to form a generalization is called an **inductive leap,** and the leap should be in proportion to the amount of evidence gathered.

Inductive reasoning involves moving (or leaping) from discovering evidence to interpreting it, and it can help you arrive at probable, believable conclusions (but not absolute, enduring truth). Making a small leap from evidence (a stomachache) to a probable conclusion (lactose intolerance) is more effective and ethical than using the same evidence to make a sweeping claim that could easily be challenged (ice cream is bad for everyone) (see **8d**). Generally, the greater the weight of the evidence, the more reliable the conclusion.

When used in argument, inductive reasoning often employs facts (see **8c**) and examples (see **3f(2)** and **3g**). When writers cannot cite all the information that supports their conclusions, they choose the evidence that is most reliable and most closely related to the point they are making.

(2) Deductive reasoning is the process of applying a generalization (or generalized belief) to a series of specific cases.

At the heart of a deductive argument is a **major premise** (a generalized belief that is assumed to be true), which the writer applies to a specific case (the **minor premise**), thereby yielding a conclusion, or claim. For example, if you know that all doctors must complete a residency and that Anna is in medical school, then you can conclude that Anna must complete a residency. This argument can be expressed in a three-part structure called a **syllogism.**

Major premise	All doctors must complete a residency. [generalized belief]
Minor premise	Anna is studying to become a doctor. [specific case]
Conclusion	Anna must complete a residency. [claim]

Sometimes premises are not stated, for the simple reason that the writer assumes a shared belief with the audience.

> Anna has graduated from medical school, so she must complete a residency.

In this sentence, the unstated premise is that all doctors must complete a residency. A syllogism with an unstated premise—or even an unstated conclusion—is called an **enthymeme.** Frequently found in written arguments, enthymemes can be very effective because they presume shared beliefs or knowledge. For example, the argument "We need to build a new dormitory because the present overcrowded dorms are unsafe" contains the unstated premise that we should approve proposals that reduce unsafe overcrowding.

(3) The Toulmin model of reasoning provides an alternative to inductive and deductive reasoning.

To create a working system of logic suitable for the needs of all writers, philosopher Stephen Toulmin defined *argument* as a logical progression, from the **data** (accepted evidence or reasons that support a claim), to the **claim** (a debatable or controversial statement), based on the **warrant** (the underlying assumption, like the major premise). If the warrant is controversial, it requires **backing** (independent support or justification). Writers who assume that they are drawing their evidence from reliable authorities should be able to cite the credentials of those authorities. And writers who base an argument on the law or another written code that has been widely agreed upon (a university's mission statement, for instance) should be able to cite the exact statute, precedent, or regulation in question or even include the law or code in the essay itself.

Like deductive reasoning, Toulmin's method establishes a reasonable relationship between the data and the claim. The following argument may help explain the progression:

Fair trade coffee should be served at the University of St. Thomas because doing so would foster social justice.

Data	Purchasing fair trade coffee promotes social justice.
Claim	The University of St. Thomas should purchase and serve only fair trade coffee.
Warrant	The University of St. Thomas believes in promoting social justice.

The warrant establishes a relationship with the data, providing a reasonable link with the claim that follows (see fig. 8.1).

Of course, few arguments are as simple as this example. For instance, the University of St. Thomas may wish to promote social justice but be unable to follow through on every opportunity to do so. In such cases, writers must make allowances for exceptions. Qualifiers such as *usually, probably, should,* and *possibly* show the degree of certainty of the conclusion, and rebuttal terms such as *unless* indicate exceptions.

Since the University of St. Thomas seeks to promote social justice, it **should** purchase and serve only fair trade coffee, **unless** doing so would cause other problems.

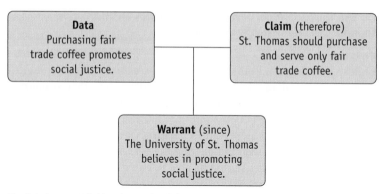

Fig. 8.1. A warrant linking data and a claim.

When using the Toulmin model to shape your arguments, you may be able to identify the claim, the data, and the qualifiers more easily than the warrant. Like the unstated premise in an enthymeme (see **8h(2)**), the warrant is often assumed and backed up by something left unsaid. In the example above, the backing is the university's mission statement, which calls for commitment to social justice. To determine the backing for a warrant in an argument you are writing, trace your thinking back to the assumptions with which you began. As you do so, remember that backing can take different forms. It may be a law or regulation (such as a university regulation about student housing), a belief that the data came from a reliable source or that what is true of a sample is true of a larger group, or a moral, political, or economic value that is widely accepted in your culture.

8i　Avoiding rhetorical fallacies

Logical reasoning not only enhances the overall effectiveness of an argument, it also enhances the ethos of the speaker or writer. Almost as important as constructing an argument effectively is avoiding errors in argument, or **rhetorical fallacies.** Rhetorical fallacies signal to your audience that your thinking is not entirely trustworthy and that your argument is not well reasoned.

Therefore, you need to recognize and avoid several kinds of fallacies. As you read the arguments of others (see **10a**) and revise the arguments you draft (chapter **4**), try to keep the following common rhetorical fallacies in mind.

(1) *Non sequitur,* Latin for "it does not follow," means that just because the first part of a statement is true doesn't mean the second part will necessarily happen or become true.

Non sequitur is the basis for most of the other rhetorical fallacies.

Faulty   Eddie is smart; therefore, he will do well in college.
[This assertion is based on the faulty premise that *all* smart people do well in college. (See **8h(2)**.)]

(2) *Ad hominem* refers to a personal attack on an opponent that draws attention away from the issues under consideration.

Faulty   She is unfit to be a minister because she is divorced.
[The fact that a woman is divorced may reveal the condition of a previous marriage, but a divorce has little if anything to do with her spiritual beliefs and principles that could benefit a congregation.]

Ad hominem attacks focus their attention on an individual, rather than on the issue.

(3) *Appeal to tradition* is an argument that says something should be done a certain way simply because it has been done that way in the past.

Faulty   Because they are a memorable part of the pledge process, fraternity hazings should not be banned.
[Times change; what was considered good practice in the past is not necessarily considered acceptable now.]

"I don't know how it started, either. All I know is that it's part of our corporate culture."

These two employees have accepted an appeal to tradition: they don't question established corporate practices.

(4) *Bandwagon* is an argument saying, in effect, "Everyone's doing or saying or thinking this, so you should, too."

Faulty   Everyone drives over the speed limit, so why shouldn't we raise the limit?
[The majority is not always right.]

Not everyone wants to jump on the bandwagon.

(5) *Begging the question* **is an argument that assumes what in fact needs to be proved.**

Faulty   We need to fire corrupt officials in order to reduce the city's crime rate.
[If there are corrupt officials in city government, this point needs to be established.]

"Nothing important—nothing on fax, nothing on voice mail, nothing on the Internet. Just, you know, handwritten stuff."

Although the secretary says that the handwritten stuff is not important, that assertion has not been proved.

(6) *Equivocation* **is an assertion that falsely relies on the use of a term in two different senses.**

Faulty   We know this is a natural law because it feels natural.
[In the first use, *natural* means "derived from nature or reason"; when used again, it means "easy or simple because of being in accord with one's own nature."]

(7) *False analogy* **is the assumption that because two things are alike in some ways, they must be alike in others.**

Faulty   The United States lost credibility with other nations during the war in Viet Nam, so we should not get involved in the Middle East, or we will lose credibility again.
[The differences between the war in Southeast Asia in the 1960s and 1970s and the current conflict in the Middle East may well be greater than their similarities.]

(8) *False authority* is the assumption that an expert in one field can be credible in another.

Faulty   We must stop sending military troops into Afghanistan, as Bruce Springsteen has argued.
[Springsteen's expertise in music does not automatically qualify him as an expert in foreign policy.]

(9) *False cause* is the assumption that because one event follows another, the first is the cause of the second—sometimes called *post hoc, ergo propter hoc* ("after this, so because of this").

Faulty   When Coach Joe Paterno turned 75, Penn State's football team had a losing season.
[The assumption is that Paterno's age is solely responsible for the losing season, with no consideration given to the abilities and experience of the football players themselves.]

(10) *False dilemma* (sometimes called the *either/or fallacy*) is a statement that only two alternatives exist, when in fact there are more than two.

Faulty   We must either build more nuclear power plants or be completely dependent on foreign oil.
[Other possibilities exist.]

(11) *Guilt by association* is an unfair attempt to make others responsible for a person's beliefs or actions.

Faulty   Jon's father and grandfather were gamblers; therefore, Jon must be one, too.
[Several people can graduate from the same school, practice the same profession or religion, belong to the same family, or live in the same neighborhood without engaging in the same behavior.]

(12) *Hasty generalization* is a conclusion based on too little evidence or on exceptional or biased evidence.

Faulty   Ellen is a poor student because she failed her first history test.
[Her performance may improve in the weeks ahead or be good in all her other subjects.]

In a clear case of guilt by association, Uncle Sam is stopped by airport security guards who are profiling men with beards.

(13) Oversimplification is a statement or argument that leaves out relevant considerations in order to imply that there is a single cause or solution for a complex problem.

Faulty   We can eliminate unwanted pregnancies by teaching birth control and abstinence.
[Teaching people about birth control and abstinence does not guarantee the elimination of unwanted pregnancies.]

This cartoon begs the question "Are children brain-damaged?" It also oversimplifies the potential causes of that damage.

(14) *Red herring* **(sometimes called** *ignoring the question***) means dodging the real issue by drawing attention to an irrelevant one.**

Faulty   Why worry about violence in schools when we ought to be worrying about international terrorism?
[International terrorism has little if any direct relationship with school violence.]

(15) *Slippery slope* **is the assumption that if one thing is allowed, it will be the first step in a downward spiral.**

Faulty   Handgun control will lead to a police state.
[Handgun control has not led to a police state in England.]

Be alert for rhetorical fallacies in your writing. When you find such a fallacy, be sure to moderate your claim, clarify your thinking, or, if necessary, eliminate the fallacious statement. Even if your argument as a whole is convincing, rhetorical fallacies can damage your credibility (see **8d** and **10a**).

Applying a slippery slope argument, this cartoon suggests that removing one potentially offensive word from the Pledge of Allegiance will result in removing almost all the words.

Exercise 5

For each of the following statements, write one or two sentences in which you identify and explain the faulty reasoning. Next, describe circumstances under which you might find these statements convincing. Finally, rewrite each statement so that it avoids rhetorical fallacies, regardless of the circumstances (if possible).

1. We must either build more dormitories or double up students in existing dormitories.

2. If we censor neo-Nazi demonstrations, we will ultimately lose freedom of speech.

3. If women dressed more conservatively, they would earn as much money as men.

4. We should cut social services because people on welfare are getting too many benefits.

5. Children would do a lot better at school if they didn't spend so much time watching television.

8j Studying a sample argument written by a student

The following paper was Laura Klocke's response to an assignment in argumentative writing. She was asked to write an essay that pointed to a specific problem in her living quarters, on her campus, in her town, or in the world at large and then recommended a solution for that problem.

As you read Laura's essay, consider whether—and how—she argued her case effectively. Note her use of classical rhetorical appeals (ethos, logos, and pathos) and arrangement and her inductive reasoning. Also, identify the kinds of evidence she uses (facts, examples, testimony, or authority).

Klocke 1

Just Coffee: A Proposal in the Classical Arrangement

Laura Klocke

Introduction

From the local café and the multinational chains to the gas station and the grocery store, you can buy lattes, cappucinos, fresh drip, and espresso. Everywhere and anywhere, it seems, coffee is "the best part of waking up."

Approximately 20 to 25 million people grow coffee for the world's drinkers and rely solely on coffee production for their income and survival. Coffee is a world beverage of choice, and this is perhaps most clearly evident in the United States, which consumes one-third of the world's coffee. Roughly $18 billion dollars is spent on coffee itself; almost just as much is invested in coffee equipment in the United States. It's not surprising, then, that coffee is the second-largest commodity traded on the market in the entire world, following oil (Dicum and Luttinger 3). With these large dollar figures and millions of cups of coffee in mind, you might wonder where all the money goes. Or, better yet, to whom?

Background
information

The answer has mostly to do with coffee plantations known as fincas, a modern-day version of pre-Civil War Southern plantations. The coffee grown and processed is taken from the fincas and enters into what is called the "coffee chain." This chain continues from the finca and its workers to a local speculator, or "coyote." The coyote draws up a contract with an exporter, and the chain proceeds to the roaster, distributor, retail outlet, and, finally, your cup. The goal of this chain, like the goal of most business transactions, is to maximize the final profit. Unfortunately for those at the beginning—the peasant farmers of the finca—their livelihood is not a consideration of their employer; the maximization of profit is the employer's sole concern. Grocery store gourmet coffee costs as much as

Klocke 2

$12.00 per pound, and yet some <u>finca</u> workers are paid only twenty to forty cents per pound. When considering that the average <u>finca</u> coffee farmer makes $3.00 a day, and the average latte is priced at $3.50 or more, it is clear that something doesn't add up in this coffee chain system (Rice and McLean 22). And, because the workers do not own the land, though they live and work on it in each stage of the coffee-growing production, they have relatively little say in their pay. Something akin to the sharecroppers of the past, the situation for those living on <u>fincas</u> is a present-day injustice. The emphasis for the world's production of coffee is on profit, and a speedy profit at that, which I will explain below.

When fair trade coffee organizations are part of the coffee-growing and coffee-selling equation, the emphasis is not only on speed and profit. Fair trade coffee organizations establish personal, gradually developing, and long-term buying relationships with coffee growers and encourage the farmers to organize into

Coffee is produced by many fair trade farms or organizations like this one. (Photo © AP Photo/Kent Gilbert/Wide World Photos)

cooperatives, where they are free to live, work, and grow coffee in a community supported by a guaranteed fair and livable wage. Fair trade coffee eliminates the middle people in the chain and thereby allocates the money that had gone to the coyotes to the growers themselves. Instead of the twenty to forty cents per pound they earned on the <u>fincas</u>, the workers can earn a minimum of $1.20 per pound. This pay raise is accomplished by eliminating the middle people and ensuring that the workers are paid fairly for their labor—not by raising the price of coffee noticeably. With the guarantee of a livable wage, many farmers would be able to put money into their community, building schools, recreation centers, churches, and businesses, improving the lives of everyone in the region.

Though I have never traveled to a <u>finca</u>, I am aware that my purchases are just one of the many ways that I can demonstrate my recognition of the inherent dignity of all people. Therefore, I do not want to support knowingly any flawed financial system with my purchases. My university is also working to make positive steps in its purchasing practices; however, with regard to fair trade food products, particularly coffee, the University of St. Thomas is not yet up to speed. In order to be fully engaged in ethical buying practices, St. Thomas must support a fully fair trade coffee supplier. Though the whole world may never be converted to the philosophy of fair trade, the sizable amount of money the university spends on coffee can still make a difference and set an example that other universities may want to follow.

Proposition

Since the university can choose between selling fair trade or unfairly traded coffee at every food service location on campus, I advocate that our university sell only that coffee that has been provided from fair trade organizations. Such a university-wide decision will reflect the ethics and politics of the university's buying power as well as align with the commitment of our University Mission Statement.

Proof

The switch from coffee drinker to conscientious coffee drinker is not difficult. The mission of the University of St. Thomas includes a commitment to "develop morally responsible individuals who combine . . . cultural awareness and intellectual curiosity." In addition, the tradition of

Klocke 4

the school seeks to foster "a value-oriented education needed for complete human development and for responsible citizenship in contemporary society"; an "international perspective"; and an "appreciation for cultural diversity." Finally, "the university embraces its role and our responsibilities in the world community," a statement that clearly connects the University of St. Thomas and the fair trade issue. The commitment to ethical activities in the university supports not only a continuation of international learning and experience, but also reflects an understanding of the inherent dignity of work and the workers that grow and process the coffee the university serves. Not only are the workers valuable as members of the human race, but their work, also, has value to them, and to the world.

Many other groups already support the fair trade coffee movement, including the Audubon Society and the MacArthur Foundation, so the University of St. Thomas would join a wide movement of people and organizations who recognize that drinking fair trade coffee is in good taste—financially, politically, and ethically (Rice and McLean 38).

Unfortunately, this proposal for a change to a completely fair trade coffee offering at the University of St. Thomas has been met with several concerns from the administration. St. Thomas does not desire to terminate its contract with Dunn Brothers Coffee, a local Twin Cities company that currently provides several varieties of certified fair trade coffee, including Guatemalan and Mexican. Though Dunn Brothers offers these choices, they are not a solely fair trade coffee company. Through a gradual approach of switching to an entirely fair trade coffee company, Dunn Brothers would be given a chance to improve their offerings as well as help St. Thomas to address some of its major concerns, in particular, those from a cost standpoint. As a student of this university, and given my

Refutation

Klocke 5

support of this mission statement, I prefer to approach this issue from an ethical stand. However, it is easy to show that the serving of fair trade coffee makes sense from a financial perspective as well.

First, however, to answer the concerns of the university is necessary. University administrators argue that, by supporting a small local company like Dunn Brothers, they are still using university money in an acceptable way. I argue that the university could use its money in an even better way. The fact that Dunn Brothers is not a solely fair trade company puts them at odds with the university mission. Besides, there are several local fair trade companies—Cloud Forest Initiatives and Peace Coffee, to name just two— that are small enough for the university to support at the same time that it does more with its buying power.

Next, the cost difference between fair trade and unfair trade coffee is an understandable concern for St. Thomas. While the movement continues to grow, fair trade coffee has the potential to cost slightly more (though hardly noticeably more) per pound than unfairly traded coffee. However, with an institution-sized order, many coffee cooperatives could be in a position to provide a contract that could work in the best way, financially, for both the growers and, in this case, the university. A worst-case scenario would be an increase of almost five cents more per cup. In answering this argument, however, the University of St. Thomas should recognize that the price difference for fair trade coffee is negligible when compared to the cost of unfairly traded coffee for communities, farmers, and families.

The last concern the administration of St. Thomas has expressed is the fear of losing the recognizable Dunn Brothers' name. The administration understandably wants to continue to sell coffee that is successfully marketed and doesn't yet know if students will support the move to fair trade coffee if there's no name recognition. To that objection, I would respond that relatively few students have taken an active interest in the coffee served at the University of St. Thomas (fair trade or otherwise). It is unlikely that once the switch to fair trade coffee is realized, my fellow students will notice—let alone protest against it. It seems that, at the heart, there is a discrepancy between the bottom lines in this issue. The University of St. Thomas would like to make the bottom line about cost, and yet the mission statement and foundation of the university clearly states otherwise. Also in response to this argument, it is worth mentioning that students are rarely consulted about the buying choices of the university. We live in a closed market system on campus, meaning, we have no choice about many of our food products (for example, the university is a "Pepsi" campus, and only Pepsi products are sold in beverage vending machines).

We at the University of St. Thomas have the chance not only to have our concerns answered but to affirm our mission statement and be a leader in the intra-campus community. We would convey a strong message with our purchase and sales of fair trade coffee, demonstrating that we are a community of concerned citizens. Our mission guides us in decisions that affect our local community as well as our global community. St. Thomas should be a leader in social justice as well as in academics.

Conclusion

We must support fair trade coffee growers and their communities, and, thereby, as a university, adhere to the mission that we profess. By helping to guarantee coffee growers a livable wage, the commitment to fair trade coffee at the University of St. Thomas is clearly the just choice.

Klocke 7

Works Cited

Dicum, Gregory, and Nina Luttinger. <u>The Coffee Book: Anatomy of an Industry from Crop to the Last Drop</u>. New York: New Press, 1999.

Rice, Paul D., and Jennifer McLean. "Sustainable Coffee at the Crossroads." <u>CCC Coffee Program</u>. 15 Oct. 1999. Consumer's Choice Council. 23 Oct. 2001.
<http://www.consumerscouncil.org/coffee/coffeebook/coffee.pdf>.

University of St. Thomas. "Mission Statement."
<http://www.stthomas.edu>.

Exercise 6

Reread Laura Klocke's essay to establish her claim and proof. What values does Klocke reveal as she argues for the use of fair trade coffee? What personal experiences have shaped Klocke's values?

R

RESEARCH

Primary sources, such as a report from an archeological dig, are useful for many research projects.

9 FINDING SOURCES IN PRINT, ONLINE, AND IN THE FIELD

When you hear the word *research*, you might think of laboratory experiments, archaeological digs, or hours spent in the library—forgetting about the ordinary research you yourself do every day as you decide what to buy, how to fix something, how to perform a function on your computer, which books to read, or where to spend your vacation. Research is common to everyone's experience. To conduct useful research efficiently, you must first develop skills in accessing information. This chapter will help you

- use the rhetorical situation to frame your research (9a),
- find books (9b),
- find articles (9c),
- find Web-based sources (9d), and
- conduct field research (9e).

9a Research and the rhetorical situation

To make the most of the time you spend doing research, determine your rhetorical situation early in the research process. By understanding your exigence, audience, and purpose, you can gather relevant sources efficiently.

(1) Identifying an exigence can help you form a research question.

The starting point for any writing project is your exigence—the issue or problem that has prompted you to write (see 1b). For research assignments, the exigence also prompts you to find more information before you write. Once you are sure of the exigence, craft a question to guide your research. Your research will then become a quest to answer that question (in essence, to resolve your exigence).

Research questions often arise when you try to relate what you are studying for a course to your own experience. For instance, you may start wondering about voting regulations and procedures while reading about past elections for a history class and at the same time noticing the number of news stories about the role technology plays in elections or the unfair practices reported in some states. Such observations may prompt you to find more information. Each observation, however, may give rise to a different question. Focusing on the influence of technology may prompt you to ask, "What are the possible consequences of having electronic ballots only?" If, instead, you focus on unfair voting practices, you may ask, "How do voting procedures differ from state to state?" Because you can ask a variety of research questions about any topic, choose the one that interests you the most and that allows you to fulfill your assignment.

To generate research questions, you may find it helpful to ask yourself about causes, consequences, processes, definitions, or values, as in the following examples.

Questions about causes

Why did the United States invade Iraq?

What causes power outages in large areas of the country?

Questions about consequences

What are the consequences of taking antidepressants for a long period of time?

How would the climate in a school change if a dress code were established?

Questions about processes

How can music lovers prevent corporations from controlling the development of new music?

How are presidential campaigns funded?

Questions about definitions

How do you know if you are addicted to something?

What kind of test is "the test of time"?

Questions about values

Should the Makah tribe be allowed to hunt gray whales?

Would the construction of wind farms be detrimental to the environment?

If you have trouble coming up with a research question, you may need a jump start. The following tips can help you.

TIPS FOR FINDING A RESEARCH QUESTION

- Can you remember an experience that you did not understand fully or that made you feel uncertain? What was it that you did not understand? What were you unsure of?
- What have you observed recently (on television, in the newspaper, on campus) that piqued your curiosity? What were you curious about?
- What widely discussed local or national problem would you like to help solve?
- Is there anything (lifestyles, political views, fashion preferences) that you find unusual or intriguing and would like to explore?

Research and writing require a commitment of time and effort, so you will find these tasks more pleasant, and maybe easier, when you are sincerely interested in your question. By talking with other people, you may discover that they are interested in it too. On the other hand, they may help you see that you need to narrow your question or change it in some other way. After talking about your question with other people, you may even decide that it does not interest you very much. To get a conversation about your ideas started, have a friend or classmate ask you the following questions. You may also use these questions to initiate a focused freewriting exercise.

- Why is it important for you to answer this research question? Why is it important for your audience to know the answer to the question?
- Does the answer to your question require research? (There should not be a simple or obvious answer to the question.)
- What types of research might help you answer your question?
- Will you be able to carry out the necessary research in the amount of time allowed?

Each of the following subjects would need to be narrowed down for a research paper. To experiment with framing a research question, compose two questions about each subject that could be answered in a ten-page paper (refer to the list on pages 208–209 for examples of questions).

1. terrorism
2. the job market
3. gender differences
4. globalization
5. civil rights
6. health care

(2) Research can help you address your audience and achieve a specific purpose.

Your audience and your purpose are interconnected. In general terms, your purpose is to have an impact on your audience; in more specific terms, your purpose may be to entertain your readers, to inform them, to explain something to them, or to persuade them to do something. Research can help you achieve any of these goals.

A research paper often has one of the following rhetorical purposes.

- *To inform an audience.* The researcher reports current thinking on a specific topic, including opposing views, without analyzing them or siding with a particular position.

  Example   To inform an audience about current nutritional guidelines for children

- *To analyze and synthesize information and then offer possible solutions.* The researcher analyzes a topic and synthesizes the available information about it, looking for points of agreement and disagreement and for gaps in coverage. Thus, part of the research consists of finding out what other researchers have written about the topic. After presenting the analysis and synthesis, the researcher sometimes offers possible ways to address any problems found.

  Example   To analyze and synthesize various national health care proposals

- *To convince or issue an invitation to an audience.* The researcher states a position and backs it up with data, statistics, testimony, corroborating texts or events, or supporting arguments. The researcher's purpose is to persuade or invite readers to take the same position.

Example   To persuade people to support a political candidate

A researcher presenting results from an original experiment or study must often achieve all of these purposes. In the introduction of a lab report, for example, the researcher analyzes and synthesizes previous work done on the same topic and locates a research niche—an area needing further study. The researcher then attempts to convince the readers that his or her current study will help address the need for more research. The body of the report is informative, describing the materials used, explaining the procedures followed, and presenting the results. In the conclusion, the researcher may try, based on the results of the experiment or study, to persuade the audience to take some action (for example, give up smoking, eat fewer carbohydrates, or fund future research).

(3) The sources you use may be primary, secondary, or both.

As you proceed with research, be aware of whether your sources are primary or secondary. **Primary sources** for researching topics in the humanities are generally documents—such as old letters and records—and literary works. In the social sciences, primary sources can be field observations, case histories, and survey data. In the natural sciences, primary sources are generally empirical—field observations or measurements, experimental results, and the like.

Secondary sources are commentaries on primary sources. For example, a review of a new novel is a secondary source, as is a discussion of adolescence based on survey data. Experienced researchers usually consult both primary and secondary sources, read them critically, and draw on them carefully.

A report from an archaeological dig is considered a primary source.

Just as you consider your rhetorical situation when you write, the authors of the sources you use have responded to their rhetorical situations. They have specified a goal for their work, a group of readers who might be interested in their findings, and a document form that best expresses their ideas. Thinking about the rhetorical situations that underlie the sources you consider will help you locate those most useful to you, read them with a critical eye, and incorporate them into your paper appropriately.

BEYOND THE RULE

PRIMARY, SECONDARY, AND TERTIARY SOURCES

Descriptions of types of research sources vary. To see examples of various descriptions of primary, secondary, and even tertiary sources (those that draw on secondary sources), visit **www.harbrace.com**.

9b Finding books

Three types of books are commonly used in the research process. **Scholarly books** are written by experts to advance knowledge of a certain subject. Most include original research. Before being published, these books are reviewed by scholars in the same field as the author(s). **Trade books** may also be written by experts or scholars, though they may be authored by journalists or freelance writers instead. But the audience and purpose of trade books differ from those of scholarly books. Rather than addressing other scholars, authors of trade books write to inform a general audience of research that has been done by others. **Reference books** such as encyclopedias and dictionaries provide factual information. These secondary sources contain short articles or entries written and reviewed by experts in the field. Their audience includes both veteran scholars and those new to a field of study.

(1) An online catalog helps you locate books.

The easiest way to find books related to your research question is to consult your library's online catalog. Once you are logged on, navigate

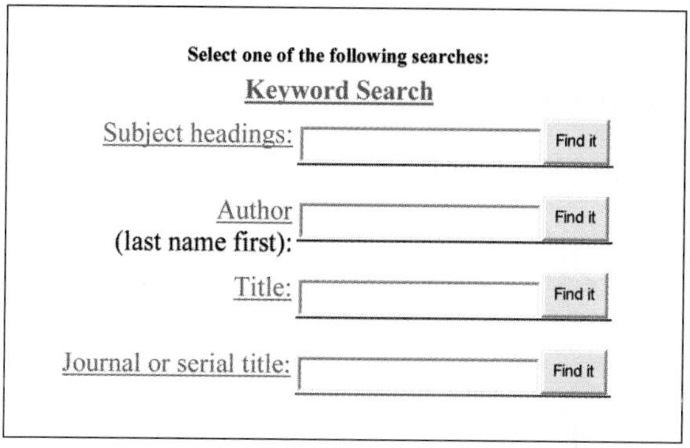

Fig. 9.1. Search boxes from a university library's Web page.

to the Web page with search boxes similar to those in fig. 9.1. When a research area is new to you, you can find many sources by doing either keyword searches or subject searches. To perform a **keyword search,** choose a word or phrase that you think might be found in the title of a book or in notes in the catalog's records. Some online catalogs allow users to be quite specific. The keyword search page in fig. 9.2 provides options for specifying a language, a location in the library, a type of book (or type of material other than a book, such as a brochure or government document), the way the results should be organized, the publisher, and the date of publication. The keyword search page in fig. 9.2 also provides some recommendations for entering words. By using a word or part of a word followed by asterisks, you can find all sources that include that root, even when suffixes have been added. For example, if you entered *environment***, you would find not only sources with *environment* in the title, subject headings, and content notes, but also sources with *environments, environmental,* or *environmentalist* in those locations. This search technique is called **truncation.**

You can also enter multiple keywords in search boxes by using **logical operators** such as *and, or, not,* and *near* (*and, or,* and *not* are sometimes called **Boolean operators**). These words narrow or broaden a search. They are used in electronic searches for books and for other documents such as articles and government brochures.

Although you will probably begin your research by using keyword searches, you may employ **subject searches** as well. To perform a successful subject search, you will have to enter words that correspond

Type the **WORD(S)** you want, then click Submit Search

Material Type: ANY ▼

Language: ANY ▼

Book/Serial: ANY ▼

Location: ANY ▼   Search and Sort: Date ▼

Publisher: [   ]

Year: After [   ] and Before [   ]

Search

SIMPLE
SEARCH   START
OVER

	Type in Words to search:	EXAMPLES
ADJACENCY	Multiple words are searched together as one phrase.	United States supreme court
TRUNCATION	Words may be right-hand truncated using an asterisk. Use a single asterisk * to truncate from 1-5 characters. Use a double asterisk ** for open-ended truncat ion.	environment* polic* fyodor dost**
OPERATORS	Use "and" or "or" to specify multiple words in any field, any order. Use "and not" to exclude words. Parentheses group words together when using Boolean operators.	(annotated bibliography) and child* (alaska or canada) and (adventure and not vacation)
PROXIMITY	Use "near" to specify words close to each other, in any order. Use "within #" to specify terms which occur within # words of each other in the record.	California near university america within 3 econom*

Fig. 9.2. Keyword search page from a university library's Web site.

LOGICAL OPERATORS

The words *and, or, not,* and *near* are the most common logical operators. However, online catalogs and periodical databases have various instructions for using them. If you have trouble following the guidelines presented here, check the instructions for the particular search box you are using.

and	narrows a search ("Starbucks **and** Vienna" returns only those records that contain both keywords.)
or	broadens a search ("Starbucks **or** Vienna" finds all records that contain information about either keyword.)
not	excludes specific items ("Starbucks **and** Austria **not** Vienna" excludes any records that mention Austria's capital city.)
near	finds records in which the two keywords occur in close proximity, within a preset number of words, and excludes those in which the keywords are widely separated ("Starbucks **near** globalization" lists only those records in which references to both *Starbucks* and *globalization* occur in close proximity.)

to the subject categories established by the Library of Congress. The best strategy for performing this type of search is to first enter words familiar to you. If, for some reason, the search does not yield any results, ask a reference librarian for a subject-heading guide. Author searches and title searches can also be useful, though only when you already have a particular author or title in mind.

Once you find the online catalog record for a book you would like to use, write down its **call number.** This number appears on the book itself and indicates where the book is shelved. The online record will reveal the status of the book, letting you know whether it is currently checked out or has been moved to a special collection. To find the book, consult the key to your library's shelving system, usually posted throughout the library. Library staff can also help you find books.

(2) Specialized reference books are listed in your library's online catalog.

A specialized encyclopedia or dictionary can often provide background information on people, events, and concepts related to the topic you are researching. To find such sources using an online search page, enter the type of reference book and one or two keywords identifying your topic. For example, entering "encyclopedia of alcoholism" resulted in the following list of titles.

> *Encyclopedia of Drugs, Alcohol, and Addictive Behavior*
> *Encyclopedia of Drugs and Alcohol*
> *The Encyclopedia of Alcoholism*

USEFUL REFERENCE BOOKS

For a detailed list of reference books and a short description of each, consult *Guide to Reference Books* by Robert Balay and *American Reference Books Annual* (*ARBA*). A few widely used reference books are listed here.

Special Dictionaries and Encyclopedias

- *Dictionary of American History*
- *Dictionary of Art*
- *Encyclopedia of Bioethics*
- *Encyclopedia of Higher Education*
- *Encyclopedia of Psychology*

Collections of Biographies

- *American National Biography*
- *Dictionary of Scientific Biography*
- *Notable American Women*
- *Who's Who in America*

---

(3) You may need to consult books not listed in your library's online catalog.

If you cannot find a particular book in your library, you have several options. Frequently, libraries have links to the catalogs of other libraries. By using such links, you can determine whether another library has the book you want and then order it through your library's interlibrary loan service. In addition, your library may have the database WorldCat, which locates books as well as images, sound recordings, and other materials. You may also access reference, fiction, and nonfiction books at Bartleby.com.

Exercise 2

Choose a research question, perhaps one you composed in exercise 1. Find the titles of a scholarly book, a trade book, and a reference book related to your choice.

9c Finding articles

Articles can be found in various **periodicals** (publications that appear at regular intervals). Because they are published daily, weekly, or monthly, periodicals offer information that is often more recent than that found in books. **Scholarly journals** usually contain reports of original research written by experts to an academic audience. **Trade magazines** feature articles written by staff writers or industry specialists. Because they are written for members of a particular trade, these articles address on-the-job concerns. **Popular magazines** and **newspapers** are generally written by staff writers for the general public. These periodicals carry a combination of news stories that attempt to be objective and essays that reflect the opinions of editors or guest contributors. The following are examples of the various types of periodicals.

Scholarly journals: *The Journal of Developmental Psychology, The Journal of Business Communication*

Trade magazines: *Farm Journal, Automotive Weekly*

Magazines (news): *Time, Newsweek*

Magazines (public affairs): *The New Yorker, National Review*

Magazines (special interest): *National Geographic, Discover*

Newspapers: *The New York Times, The Washington Post*

(1) An electronic database can help you find articles.

Your library's online catalog lists the titles of periodicals; however, it does not provide the titles of individual articles within these periodicals. The best strategy for finding print articles is to use an **electronic database,** which is a collection of articles compiled by a company that indexes them according to author, title, date, keywords, and other features. The electronic databases available in libraries are sometimes called **database subscription services, licensed databases,** or **aggregated databases.** Similar to an online catalog, an electronic database allows you to search for sources by author, title, keyword, and so on. However, such databases focus on specific subject areas.

A database search will generally yield an **abstract,** which is a short summary of an article. By scanning the abstract, you can determine whether to locate the complete text of the article, which can often be downloaded and printed. You can access your library's databases by using its computers or, if you have a password, by using an Internet link from a remote computer. College libraries subscribe to a wide variety of database services, but the following are the most common.

ERIC: Articles related to education

JSTOR: Articles from journals in the arts, humanities, ecology, and social sciences

PsycINFO: Articles related to psychology

You may be able to access the search boxes for databases directly, or you may have to access the databases through the search boxes of a vendor such as OCLC, InfoTrac, LexisNexis, or EBSCO. For example, OCLC's FirstSearch offers access to a number of databases (see fig. 9.3). To use this resource, you must first choose from a list of broad topics (such as

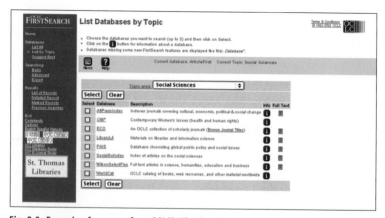

Fig. 9.3. Example of a screen from OCLC's FirstSearch.

"Arts and Humanities" and "Business and Economics") or specialized databases (such as MEDLINE and GeoRefS). FirstSearch also prompts you to enter keywords related to your topic.

If you were using FirstSearch to research the role of Starbucks in globalization, as Andy Pieper did for his paper (see **12c**), you could select one of the following topics: "General," "Business and Economics," or "Consumer Affairs and People." To research the status of African Americans in the U.S. military, as Nicole Hester did for her paper (see **14b**), you could select "General" or "Public Affairs and Law." To research the relationship between sleep and academic performance among college students, as Nikki Krzmarzick did for her paper (see **13c**), you could select "Life Sciences" or "Social Sciences." (Note that OCLC also provides access to books and Web resources through its WorldCat feature.)

The databases available through FirstSearch vary from one library to another. Similarly, the appearance of the opening screen for FirstSearch differs from one school to another. The example shown in fig. 9.3 is from the library system through which Nikki Krzmarzick conducted her search.

TIPS FOR CONDUCTING A SEARCH FOR PERIODICAL LITERATURE

- Identify keywords that clearly represent the topic.
- Determine the databases to be searched.
- Perform your search, using logical operators (see **9b(1)**).
- Refine your search strategy if the first search returned too many or too few citations, or (worse) irrelevant ones.
- Download and print the relevant articles.

---

(2) Print indexes provide essential information not found in electronic databases.

Before computers were widely used, researchers relied on **print indexes.** These bound volumes still provide essential backup when computers are out of service as well as access to older articles that may not be included in electronic databases. Some of the most useful print indexes, with their dates of beginning publication, are as follows.

Applied Science and Technology Index. 1958– .

Art Index. 1929– .

Biological and Agricultural Index. 1946– .

Business Periodicals Index. 1958– .

Cumulative Index to Nursing and Allied Health Literature (CINAHL). 1982– .

General Science Index. 1978– .

Humanities Index. 1974– .

Index to Legal Periodicals. 1908– .

Music Index. 1949– .

Philosopher's Index. 1967– .

Public Affairs Information Service (PAIS) Bulletin. 1915– .

Social Sciences Index. 1974– .

When they publish electronic versions of their indexes, some publishers change the title: *Current Index to Journals in Education (CIJE)* and *Resources in Education (RIE)* are the bound volumes for research in education, and ERIC is the electronic version. Consult the front of any bound volume for a key to the abbreviations used in individual entries.

(3) InfoTrac College Edition provides easy access to articles.

With InfoTrac College Edition and a passcode, you can conveniently search for articles with the Web browser on your own computer. You do not have to be networked to your library's Web site. InfoTrac College Edition indexes articles in over 3,800 journals and magazines and provides the full text of these articles. The InfoTrac screens in figs. 9.4 and 9.5 illustrate part of the research Nikki Krzmarzick conducted for her paper (see **13c**). Clicking in the box labeled "Mark" next to the article on the relationship between sleep and grade-point average, as shown in fig. 9.4, and then clicking on "text and full content retrieval choices" brought up the complete article, whose first page appears in fig. 9.5.

Exercise 3

Choose a research question, perhaps one from exercise 1. Find the titles of a scholarly article, a magazine article, and a newspaper article related to your choice.

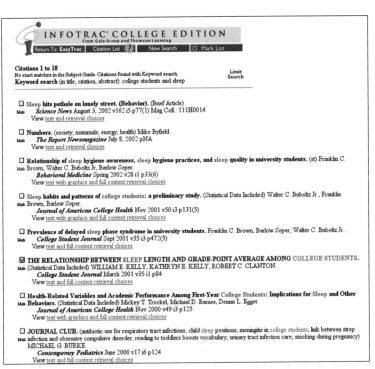

Fig. 9.4. Example of an InfoTrac screen.

9d Finding online sources

Through the Internet, you can find not only text files but also audio and video files. Most researchers start their online research by using search engines, meta-search engines, or subject directories. **Search engines** are electronic indexes of words and terms from Web pages. To use them effectively, you should understand their features. Always consult the Help feature to learn how to perform an advanced search so that you will not waste time weeding out results that are not of interest to you. Advanced searches with a search engine are performed in much the same way as searches in online catalogs and databases. You can

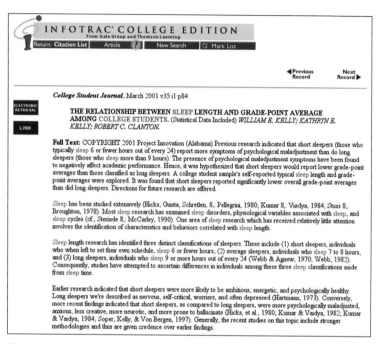

Fig. 9.5. First page of an article found through InfoTrac.

specify which words or phrases to use, how close words should be, which words should be excluded, and whether any word should be truncated. (See 9b(1).) The following are the addresses for some commonly used search engines.

Google	www.google.com
Infoseek	infoseek.go.com
Lycos	www.lycos.com
MSN Search	search.msn.com
WebCrawler	www.webcrawler.com

If you are looking solely for news stories, consider using the following.

| Google News | www.google.com/news |
| TotalNEWS | www.totalnews.com |

Meta-search engines are also useful research tools. *Meta-* means "transcending" or "more comprehensive." Meta-search engines check a number of search engines, including those previously listed. Try the following for starters.

Dogpile	www.dogpile.com
MetaCrawler	www.metacrawler.com

Unlike search engines, **subject directories** are collections of Web sources arranged topically. Yahoo! (www.yahoo.com) offers a subject directory under "Web Directory" on its home page: it includes categories such as "Arts," "Health," and "Education." Some researchers find subject directories easier to use because most of the irrelevant Web sites have been weeded out. The following are some other useful subject directories for academic and professional research.

Academic Info	www.academicinfo.net
The Internet Public Library	www.ipl.org/ref
Librarians' Index to the Internet	lii.org
The WWW Virtual Library	vlib.org

Although searching the Web is a popular research technique, it is not the only technique you should use. Search engines cover only the portion of the Internet that allows free access. You will not find library books or database materials through a Web search because library and database services are available only to paid subscribers (students fall into this category). When you search the Web, remember that no single search engine covers the entire Web and that surprisingly little overlap occurs when different search engines are used to find information on the same topic. Thus, using more than one search engine is a good idea.

(1) Knowing your location on the Web will help you keep track of your sources.

It is easy to get lost on the Web as you click from link to link. You can keep track of your location by looking at the Web address, or **URL (uniform resource locator),** at the top of your screen. Web addresses generally include the following information: server name, domain name, directory (and perhaps subdirectory) name, file name, and file type.

Sometimes when you click on a link, you will end up at a totally different Web site, so be sure to check the server and domain names when you are unsure of your location.

If you find that a URL has changed, which is likely if a site is regularly updated, you may still be able to find the site you are looking for by dropping the last part of the address and trying again. You may need to do this several times. If this strategy does not work, you can also run a search or look at the links on related Web sites.

Because sites change and even disappear, scholarly organizations such as the Modern Language Association (see chapter 12) and the American Psychological Association (see chapter 13) require that bibliographic entries for Web sites include both the **access date** (the date on which the site was visited) and the **posting date** (the date when the site was last modified or updated). When you print out material from the Web, the access date usually appears at the top or bottom of the printout. The posting date generally appears on the site itself. Some sites do not show a posting date, however, and printouts sometimes will not have an access date. Keeping a separate record of this information can help you when you need to verify information on a site or list it in a bibliography. If a site does not have a posting date, note that it is undated; doing so will establish that you did not accidentally omit a piece of information.

A convenient way to keep track of any useful Web site you visit is to create a **bookmark**—a record of a Web address you may want to return to in the future. The bookmarking function of a Web browser is usually labeled Bookmarks or Favorites.

Exercise 4

Perform a database search and a Web search using the same keywords for each. Print the first screen of the hits (results) you get for each type of search. Compare the two printouts, describing how the results of the two searches differ.

(2) The U.S. Government provides vast amounts of public information.

If you need information on particular federal laws, court cases, or population statistics, U.S. Government documents may be your best sources. You can find these documents by using online databases such as Congressional Universe, MARCIVE, LexisNexis Academic Universe, Census 2000, and STAT-USA. In addition, the following Web sites are helpful.

FirstGov	www.firstgov.gov
U.S. Government Printing Office	www.gpoaccess.gov
U.S. Courts	www.uscourts.gov
FedWorld	www.fedworld.gov

(3) Your rhetorical situation may call for the use of images.

If your rhetorical situation calls for the use of images, as did Andy Pieper's (see 12c) and Nikki Krzmarzick's (13c), the Internet offers you billions from which to choose. However, if an image you choose is copyrighted, you will need to contact the author, artist, or designer for permission to use it. Figure 9.6 is an example of an image with a caption and a permission statement. You do

Fig. 9.6. A researcher monitors a participant's sleep patterns. (Photo reproduced courtesy of Charles Gupton/Corbis.)

not need to obtain permission to use public domain images or those that are cleared for reuse.

Many search engines allow you to search for images. On the search pages for Google and AltaVista, you must first click on the Image button. For MetaCrawler, you must choose Images from the pull-down menu. Collections of specific images are available at the following Web sites.

Advertisements

Ad*Access — scriptorium.lib.duke.edu/adaccess

Adflip — www.adflip.com

Advertising World — advertising.utexas.edu/world

Art

The Artchive — www.artchive.com

The Web Gallery of Art — www.wga.hu

Clip art

The Icon Browser — www.ibiblio.org/gio/iconbrowser

Webclipz — www.webclipz.com

Photography

The New York Public Library Picture Collection Online — digital.nypl.org/mmpco

Smithsonian Images — smithsonianimages.com

9e Field research

Although much of your research will consist of reading, viewing, or listening to sources, you may also find it helpful to conduct **field research**—to gather information in a natural setting. Interviews, discussions, questionnaires, and observations are the most common methods for such research.

(1) Consider interviewing an expert.

After you have consulted some sources on your topic, you may find that you still have questions that might best be answered by someone who has firsthand experience in the area you are researching. Consider contacting a teacher, government official, business owner, or other person with the relevant background to see whether it would be possible to schedule an interview. Most people welcome the opportunity to discuss their work, especially with a student who shows genuine interest. Because you will have done some reading on your topic before your meeting, you will be prepared to conduct a well-informed interview.

To arrange an interview, introduce yourself, briefly describe your project, and then explain your reasons for requesting the interview. Most people are busy, so try to accommodate the person you hope to interview by asking him or her to suggest an interview date. If you intend to tape your interview, ask for permission ahead of time.

Start preparing your list of questions before the day of the interview. Effective interviews usually contain a blend of open (or broad) questions and focused (or narrow) questions. Here are a few examples.

Open questions

What do you think about _____?

What are your views on _____?

Why do you believe _____?

Focused questions

How long have you worked as a/an _____?

When did you start _____?

What does _____ mean?

If you ask a question that elicits just a "yes" or "no," reformulate the question so that it begins with *why, when, what, who, where,* or *how.* By doing so, you give your interviewee a chance to elaborate. If you know that the person you are interviewing has published articles or a book on your topic, ask questions that will advance your knowledge, rather than questions that the author has already answered in print.

Preparing a list of questions before an interview is essential, but do not just recite your questions during the meeting. An interview is a special kind of conversation. Although you will be guiding it, the person you are speaking with is likely to say something you did not expect but would like to know more about. Do not be afraid to ask questions that are not on your list but come to mind during the interview. Along with your list of questions, be sure to bring pen and paper so that you can take notes and a tape recorder with fresh batteries and an extra tape cassette if you will be recording the interview.

After the interview, take some time to review your notes. It will be hard to take down everything that is said during the interview, so expand on the notes you do have. If you recorded the interview, transcribe the relevant parts of the recording. The next step is to write extensively about the interview. Ask yourself what you found most important, most surprising, and most puzzling. You will find this writing especially worthwhile when you are able to use portions of it in your final paper.

(2) Consider participating in an online discussion group.

Less formal than an interview, a discussion with other people interested in your topic can also be useful. Online discussion groups, or forums (see 6c), allow you to read messages posted to all the members of a group interested in a specific topic and to post messages or questions yourself. For instance, a writing teacher may belong to a specialized e-mail list, or **listserv,** that is operated by the Alliance for Computers and Writing and called ACW-L. Participants in this online forum discuss issues related to using computers to teach writing. Someone on the ACW-L list can send e-mail messages to the **listserv address,** which redistributes them to hundreds of other writing teachers around the world, and then receive replies from any of those teachers. You can find addresses of online discussion groups at either www.forumone.com or groups.google.com. Your instructor may even have created a discussion forum especially for your class.

(3) Consider using a questionnaire to gather information from a large number of people.

Whereas an interview elicits information from one person whose name you know, a questionnaire provides information from a number of anonymous people. To be effective, a questionnaire should be short and focused. If the list of questions is too long, people may not be willing to take the time to answer them all. If the questions are not focused on your research topic, you will find it difficult to integrate the results into your paper.

Questionnaires elicit information in a variety of ways, through several types of questions. The types of questions you decide to use depend on the purpose of your survey. The first four types of questions below are the easiest for respondents to answer. Open questions, which require much more time to answer, should be asked only when the other types of questions cannot elicit the information you want.

EXAMPLES OF TYPES OF SURVEY QUESTIONS

Questions that require a simple yes-or-no answer:

Do you commute to work in a car? (Circle one.)

Yes   No

Multiple-choice questions:

How many people do you commute with? (Circle one.)

0   1   2   3   4

Questions with answers on a checklist:

How long does it take you to commute to work? (Check one.)

___ 0–30 minutes   ___ 30–60 minutes   ___ 60–90 minutes   ___ 90–120 minutes

Questions with a ranking scale:

If the car you drive or ride in is not working, which of the following types of transportation do you rely on? (Rank the choices from 1 for most frequently used to 4 for least frequently used.)

___ bus   ___ shuttle van   ___ subway   ___ taxi

Open questions:

What aspect of commuting do you find most irritating?

Be sure to begin your questionnaire with an introduction stating what the purpose of the questionnaire is, how the results will be used, and how many questions it contains or approximately how long it should take to complete. In the introduction, you should also assure participants that their answers will remain confidential. To protect survey participants' privacy, colleges and universities have **institutional review boards (IRBs)** set up to review questionnaires. Before you distribute your questionnaire, check with the institutional review board on your campus to make certain that you have followed its guidelines.

Administering a questionnaire can sometimes be problematic. Many questionnaires sent through the mail are never returned. If you do decide to mail out a questionnaire, provide a self-addressed envelope and directions for returning it. It is a good idea to send out twice as many copies as you would like returned because the proportion of responses is generally low. Questionnaires can sometimes be distributed in college dormitories or in classes, but this procedure must be approved by school officials. Listservs (6c(1)) can also be used to conduct surveys. Just remember that a survey limited to people who have a strong interest in a topic will not yield results representative of other groups, such as the students at your school or the citizens of your state.

Once the questionnaires have been completed and returned, tally the results for all but the open questions on an unused copy. To find patterns in the responses to the open questions, first read through them all; you might find that you can create categories for the responses. For example, the open question "What aspect of your commute do you find most irritating?" might elicit answers that fall into such categories as "length of time," "amount of traffic," or "bad weather conditions." By first creating categories, you will find it easier to tally the answers to the open questions.

CHECKLIST for Creating a Questionnaire

- Does each question relate directly to the purpose of the survey?
- Are the questions easy to understand?
- Are they designed to elicit short, specific responses?
- Are they designed to collect concrete data that can be analyzed easily?
- Have respondents been given enough space to write their answers to open questions?
- Do you have access to the group you want to survey?
- Have you asked a few classmates to "test-drive" your questionnaire?

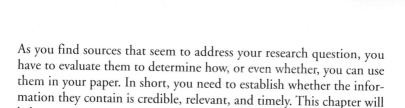

10
EVALUATING PRINT
AND ONLINE SOURCES

As you find sources that seem to address your research question, you have to evaluate them to determine how, or even whether, you can use them in your paper. In short, you need to establish whether the information they contain is credible, relevant, and timely. This chapter will help you

- assess an author's credibility (10a),
- evaluate a publisher's credibility (10b),
- evaluate online sources (10c), and
- determine the relevance and timeliness of a source (10d).

10a Credibility of authors

To be considered credible, authors must be trustworthy. They can attain such status by presenting information honestly, logically, fairly, and respectfully. That is, credible authors present facts accurately, support their opinions with evidence, connect their ideas reasonably, and demonstrate respect for any opposing views. To evaluate the credibility of the authors of your sources, find out what their credentials are, consider what worldview informs their ideas, and note how other readers respond to their work.

(1) Credentials help establish an author's credibility.

When evaluating sources, consider whether the authors have credentials that are relevant to the topics they address. Although many works have only one author, some are composed collaboratively, so be sure to take into account the credentials of all of the authors responsible for the material in the sources you use.

Credentials take various forms, including academic or professional training, publications, and experience. A college biology professor who specializes in genetics is likely to be credible when writing about genes, for example, and a civil engineer who specializes in bridges should have credibility when writing about how a particular bridge could be strengthened. However, given their areas of specialization, the biologist would not necessarily be considered a credible source of information on the foraging habits of black bears, and the engineer would not have credibility concerning the design of hydroelectric power plants.

To find information about the credentials of an author whose work you want to use, look

- on the jacket of a book,
- on a separate page near the front or back of the book,
- in the preface of the book,
- in a note at the bottom of the first or last page of an article in print, or
- on a separate page of a periodical or a Web page devoted to providing background on contributors.

As you read about an author, ask yourself the following questions.

CHECKLIST for Assessing an Author's Credentials

- Does the author's education or profession relate to the subject of the work?
- With what institutions, organizations, or companies has the author been affiliated (see 10b)?
- What awards has the author won?
- What other works has the author produced?
- Do other experts speak of the author as an authority (see 10a(3))?

---

(2) An author's work reflects a specific worldview.

An author's values and beliefs about the world constitute his or her **worldview,** which underpins any article, book, or Web site he or she produces. To determine what these values and beliefs are, consider the author's purpose and intended audience.

It might be easiest to start by identifying the audience. For example, of the following four excerpts about malpractice lawsuits, excerpts 1 and 2 are intended for physicians, while 3 and 4 are written for patients.

1   Just as quickly as medical knowledge and disease treatment options increase, so too do advances in the strategies lawyers use to bring medical malpractice suits.

Last year, an Ohio jury awarded $3.5 million to the family of a man who died of a heart attack.

His family claimed that the physician didn't do enough to help the man lose weight and stop smoking, given that physicians now know how smoking and excess weight contribute to heart disease and given the significant advances in treatment.

—**TANYA ALBERT**, "Lawyers Try New Tacks in Malpractice Suits"

2   A new study led by Wendy Levinson, Professor in Medicine, suggests that the most important reason a patient with a bad outcome decides to sue his or her doctor for malpractice is not medical negligence but how the doctor talks with the patient.

—"Bad Rapport with Patients to Blame for Most Malpractice Suits," *University of Chicago Chronicle*

3   Medical malpractice suits are legal claims that are filed against a medical professional whose actions or negligence causes injury to a patient under [his or her] care. It is estimated that 800,000 people are the victims of medical malpractice every year, though only one in eight file medical malpractice suits. Medical malpractice suits can be filed against a medical professional whose actions range from negligence (or inaction/substandard action) that causes injury to the willful and malicious abuse of patients undergoing medical care.

—"Medical Malpractice Suits," www.onlinelawyersource.com

4   A growing number of doctors fed up with skyrocketing malpractice insurance premiums are calling on their patients to bear part of the burden.

Some physicians are requiring patients to sign waivers promising not to sue for "frivolous" reasons or, in some cases, for any reason at all. Others are billing for telephone consultations, paperwork and other services that once were free.

Perhaps the most controversial—and possibly illegal—approach is charging user, or administrative, fees. Patients increasingly are protesting paying more—on top of their copayments, deductibles and premiums—for medical services already covered by their health plans.

—**CAROLE FLECK,** "Doctors' Fees Try Their Patients"

Published on a news Web site for doctors, excerpt 1 focuses on the frivolous nature of some malpractice suits. The second excerpt, taken from a university newspaper (no author is identified), highlights the research of a medical professor at that university: her findings downplay the role of negligence in malpractice suits and highlight the role of doctor-patient rapport. In contrast to the first two excerpts, the next two are sympathetic toward patients. Appearing on a commercial Web site that helps patients locate medical malpractice lawyers, excerpt 3 emphasizes the large number of malpractice cases that go unfiled. In excerpt 4, taken from a news bulletin for retired people, the reporter questions whether doctors have the right to pass on the high costs of malpractice insurance to their patients.

As you read and use sources, keep in mind that they reflect the worldviews of the authors and often of the audience for whom they were written. By identifying these various values and beliefs, you can responsibly represent and report the information in your sources. When you find yourself referring to information that reveals economic, political, religious, or social biases, you should feel free to question or argue with the author, as does Natalie Angier when she questions the views of Robert Wright and a few other evolutionary psychologists.

5   Now, it makes sense to be curious about the evolutionary roots of human behavior. It's reasonable to attempt to understand our impulses and actions by applying Darwinian logic to the problem. We're animals. We're not above the rude little prods and jests of natural selection. But evolutionary psychology as it has been disseminated across mainstream consciousness is a cranky and despotic Cyclops, its single eye glaring through an overwhelmingly masculinist lens. I say masculinist rather than male because the view of male behavior promulgated by hardcore evolutionary psychologists is as narrow and inflexible as their view of womanhood is.

—**NATALIE ANGIER,** *Woman: An Intimate Geography*

The following questions may help you determine the worldview of an author whose work you hope to use.

CHECKLIST for Determining an Author's Worldview

- What is the author's educational and professional background?
- What are the author's and publisher's affiliations; that is, with what types of organizations do they align themselves?
- What is the editorial slant of the organization publishing the author's work? Where does it lie on the political spectrum from conservative to liberal?
- Can you detect any signs of bias on the part of the author or the publisher?
- Is the information purported to be factual? Objective? Personal?
- Who advertises in the source?
- To what types of Web sites do any links lead?
- How can you use the source? As fact? Opinion? Support? Authoritative testimony? Material to be refuted?

(3) Online sources, book reviews, and texts written by other authors can provide additional information about an author.

You can learn more about authors by searching the Internet for information about them. For example, the Nobel e-Museum provides biographical information about Nobel laureates (see fig. 10.1). To find Internet sources, use a general search engine such as Google or AltaVista or a specialized search engine such as the People search option offered by Lycos (www.whowhere.lycos.com). Either type of engine will locate sites containing background information on the author or bibliographical information about his or her other works.

Book reviews, many of which are available online, often include information that is useful for determining whether an author is credible. When you read reviews, though, remember that a work by a credible author may get some negative responses. Look for the main point of a review, and decide whether that main point amounts to a positive or negative response to the book as a whole. For example, if an author is described as "entertaining but unreliable," the negative adjective is more important than the positive one. Or if an author is described as "dry but nevertheless informative," the praise outweighs the complaint. Being a credible source does not mean being a perfect source. However, dismiss from further consideration any writer whom more than one

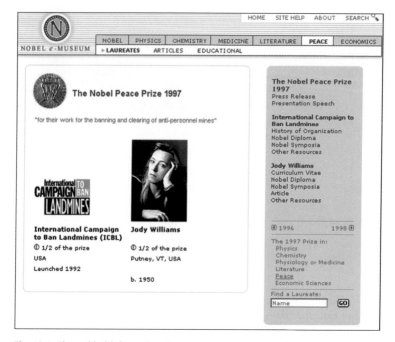

Fig. 10.1. Biographical information about Nobel laureates may be found on the Nobel e-Museum Web site.

reviewer characterizes as ill-informed, careless with facts, biased, or dishonest in any way. Keep in mind, though, that few writers please all reviewers all the time, so your responsibility is to read reviews critically.

As you research a topic, you will find that writers often refer to the work of other writers. To gain insight into how an author influences the work of others, keep track of who is being discussed or cited by whom. If several well-known writers offer negative evaluations of an author's work or do not mention the work at all, that author's contribution is likely considered insignificant or unreliable. If, on the other hand, several writers praise or build on the work of the author you are evaluating, you can be confident in the credibility of your source.

Exercise 1

Choose a book you plan to use for your research paper. Locate at least two reviews of this book. Then, write a one-page report of what the reviews have in common and how they differ.

10b Credibility of publishers

Credible sources are published by reliable institutions, organizations, and companies. When you are doing research, consider not only the credibility of authors but also the credibility of the media through which their work is made available to you. Some publishers hold authors accountable to higher standards than others do.

(1) Book publishers are either commercial or academic.

When evaluating books, you can usually assume that publishers associated with universities (university presses) demand a high standard of scholarship. Although some university presses have better reputations than others, the works such publishers produce are generally considered trustworthy—in great part because of the publishers' requirement that books be reviewed by experts before publication. Books published by commercial presses, in contrast, typically do not undergo the same type of review. Thus, to determine how a trade book has been received by others writing in the same area, you have to rely on book reviews (see **10a(3)**).

(2) Periodicals are written for an academic audience or for the general public.

Periodicals are published periodically—daily, weekly, or monthly (see **9c**). They include scholarly journals, magazines (trade, news, public affairs, and special interest), and newspapers. An article published in a scholarly journal is generally considered more credible than one published in a magazine because it has usually been both written and reviewed by an expert. Authors of these journal articles are expected to include both in-text citations and bibliographies so that other researchers can consult the sources used (see chapters **12–15**).

Articles that appear in magazines and newspapers may be reliable, but keep in mind that they are usually written quickly and chosen for publication by someone on the magazine's staff—not by an expert in the field. Because magazines and newspapers often report research results that were initially published elsewhere, you should try to find the original source to ensure the accuracy of their reports. This is not always an easy task, though, especially since in-text citations and

Forum defends right to know

By MIKE JOHNSTON
associate editor

Changes to the Clean Air Act

THE ASSOCIATED PRESS

Fig. 10.2. Examples of bylines for a staff writer of a local newspaper (left) and a wire service (right).

bibliographies are rarely provided in these periodicals. Your best bet for finding the original source is to use a search engine.

When evaluating an article in a magazine or newspaper, also take into account the reputation of the publication itself. To gauge the credibility of magazines and newspapers, you can examine several issues and consider the space devoted to various stories, the tone of the commentary on the editorial pages, and the extent to which staff members (as opposed to wire services) are responsible for stories. Figure 10.2 shows an example of a byline for a staff writer and an example of a byline for a wire service.

10c   Online sources

If you are evaluating a periodical source that you obtained online, you can follow the guidelines for print-based sources (see 10a–b). But if you are evaluating a Web site, you also need to consider the nature of the site and its sponsor. Although many sites are created by individuals working on their own, many others are sponsored by colleges or universities, professional or nonprofit organizations, and commercial enterprises. The type of sponsor is typically indicated in the site's address, or URL, by a suffix that represents the domain. Colleges and universities are indicated by the suffix .edu, government departments and agencies by .gov, professional and nonprofit organizations by .org, network sites by .net, and businesses by .com. Depending on the nature of your research paper, you can access any or all of the various types of sites. But, as you evaluate their content, remember that every site is shaped to achieve a specific purpose and to address a target audience.

Suppose, for example, you were writing a paper about how a corporate bankruptcy revealed serious irregularities in the practices of a major energy company. An education site could provide a scholarly analysis of the practices in question; a government site could contain data compiled by the Securities and Exchange Commission (SEC); an organization site could give you the viewpoint of an association of accountants; and a business site could convey information from the energy company in question. Each of these sites would offer different content, which would be shaped by the rhetorical situation as envisioned by each site's sponsor. For example, the SEC is an agency of the federal government that reports to the U.S. Congress, which, in turn, represents American citizens. Accordingly, the purpose of the SEC's Web site is to show its audience that the agency is providing careful oversight of business practices (see fig. 10.3). The commercial site of an energy company such as Enron, on the other hand, has a vested interest in making the company look good to current customers and potential clients.

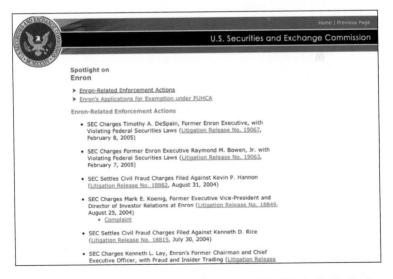

Fig. 10.3. The Securities and Exchange Commission site provides links to the details of the Enron case. If you visited www.enron.com you would get a more positive view of the company.

You can find out more about the sponsor of a Web site by using navigational buttons or links such as "About Us" or "Our Vision." The following is an excerpt from a Web page for National Public Radio, found by clicking on "About NPR" on the organization's home page (www.npr.org).

What is NPR?

NPR is an internationally acclaimed producer and distributor of noncommercial news, talk, and entertainment programming. A privately supported, not-for-profit, membership organization, NPR serves more than 770 independently operated, noncommercial public radio stations. Each member station serves local listeners with a distinctive combination of national and local programming.

This passage provides information not only on NPR's radio programming but also on its status as a nonprofit organization.

For a summary of criteria you can use to evaluate both online and print sources, see pages 242 and 243.

Exercise 2

Find Web sites that have three different kinds of sponsors but contain material relevant to a specific subject, such as global warming or disaster efforts. Explain the differences and similarities among the three sites you choose.

10d Relevance and timeliness

A source is useful only when it is relevant to your research question. Given the huge and ever-growing amount of information available on most topics, you should be prepared to put aside a source that will not help you answer your research question or achieve your rhetorical purpose. There are plenty of other sources, which you can locate by using the search strategies discussed in chapter 9. Some writers get off track when they cannot bring themselves to abandon a source they like, even if it is no longer relevant—as often happens when their focus has changed during the process of conducting research, drafting the paper, and revising it. It is better to abandon an irrelevant source than to write a poorly focused paper.

You may reject some sources altogether. You are also likely to use only parts of others. Seldom will an entire book, article, or Web site be useful for a specific research paper. A book may have just a chapter or a section or two on your topic. The table of contents can lead you to these relevant chapters or sections, and the index can lead you to relevant pages. Web sites have hyperlinks or buttons that you can click on to locate relevant information. Once you find potentially useful material, read it with your research question and rhetorical purpose in mind.

Useful sources are also timely. You should always seek up-to-date information. However, if you are writing about a specific era in the past, you should also consult sources written during that period. To determine when a source was published, look for the date of publication. In books, it appears with other copyright information on the page following the title page (see page 279). Dates of periodicals appear on their covers and frequently on the top or bottom of pages throughout each issue (see page 284). The date on which a Web site was established or last updated frequently appears on the site, and the date on which you access it will usually appear on any hard copy you print out (see page 294). Do not confuse the access date with the posting date.

CHECKLIST for Establishing Relevancy and Timeliness

- Does the table of contents, index, or directory of the work include key words related to your research question?
- Does the abstract of a journal article contain information on your topic?
- If an abstract is not available, are any of the article's topic sentences relevant to your research question?
- Do the section heads of the source include words connected to your topic?
- On a Web site, are there hyperlinks or buttons that can lead you to relevant information?
- Is the work recent enough to provide up-to-date information?
- If you need a source from another time period, is the work from the right period?

Criteria for Evaluating Sources

TYPE OF SOURCE	PURPOSE	AUTHORS/PUBLISHERS
Scholarly books	To advance knowledge among experts	Experts/University presses
Trade books	To provide information of interest to the general public	Experts, journalists, professional writers/ Commercial presses
Reference books	To provide factual information	Experts/Commercial presses
Articles from scholarly journals	To advance knowledge among experts	Experts/Publishers associated with professions or universities
Articles from magazines or newspapers	To report current events or provide general information about current research	Journalists and professional writers (sometimes experts)/ Commercial presses
Editorials from newspapers	To state a position on an issue	Journalists/ Commercial presses
Sponsored Web sites	To report information	Often a group author
Interviews with experts	To report views of an expert	Professional or student writer reporting views of expert

SOURCES DOCUMENTED?	PRIMARY AUDIENCE	CHIEF ADVANTAGE
Yes	Other experts	Reliable because they are written and reviewed by experts
Sometimes	Educated public	Accessible because the language is not overly technical
Yes	Other experts and educated public	Reliable because the entries are written by experts
Yes	Other experts	Reliable because the entries are written and reviewed by experts
No	General public	Accessible because the language is not overly technical
No	General public	Current because they are published daily
No	General public	Accessible by computer
No	General public	Reliable because the interviewee is an expert

USING SOURCES EFFECTIVELY AND RESPONSIBLY

11

To use sources effectively, you need to remember that you are a *writer*, not simply a compiler of data. Yours is the most important voice in a paper that has your name on it. To use sources responsibly, you need to acknowledge others' ideas and words when you incorporate them into a paper you write. This chapter will help you

- consider your rhetorical situation (**11a**),
- organize notes effectively (**11b**),
- compose a working bibliography or an annotated bibliography (**11c**),
- integrate sources (**11d**),
- avoid plagiarism (**11e**), and
- respond to sources (**11f**).

11a The rhetorical situation and the research paper

Like any other paper, a research paper should originate in an exigence and have a purpose appropriate for a particular audience and context. It should not be a mere compilation of research findings or a list of works consulted. Rather, in a research paper, you discuss what others have discovered, thus creating a conversation in which you play an essential role: your sources interact with one another, and, because you yourself are a source, you talk back to them.

By studying the following introductory paragraphs to a research article, you can see how the author, Timothy Quinn, chooses words, sentence types, organization strategies, and citation conventions according to his rhetorical situation. In the first paragraph, he alludes to his exigence: the increasing presence of coyotes in areas inhabited by people and the lack of a clear explanation for this presence. Because he states a problem with no easy solution, Quinn finds his own research niche. At the end of the second paragraph, Quinn states his purpose: to document coyotes' typical diet and assess changes in that diet caused by human population and land use. Quinn shows his understanding of audience and context by citing other researchers' work according to the appropriate convention of providing the name(s) of author(s) and the year of publication.

> Coyotes (*Canis latrans*) are becoming increasingly common in human-modified habitats throughout North America (Atkinson and Shackleton 1991, MacCracken 1982). One possible explanation for this trend is that human-dominated areas produce abundant food sources for coyotes. Coyotes living in urban habitats have relatively small home ranges (Atkinson and Shackleton 1991, Shargo 1988), which may indicate abundant food resources. However, little is known about the diet of coyotes in these areas. MacCracken's (1982) description of the annual diet of coyotes in residential habitats was based on a small number of scats ($n = 97$) collected during a single month. Atkinson and Shackleton (1991) described the diet of coyotes in an area that was mostly agricultural (>50% of the study area) and Shargo's (1988) description of urban coyote diet was based on 22 scats. Additionally, none of these studies looked at diet as a function of human density.
>
> Coyotes may play an important role in human-modified landscapes. Soulé et al. (1988) suggested that coyotes may reduce the abundance of house cats (*Felis catus*) and other small mammalian carnivores that prey on songbirds and thus indirectly contribute to the maintenance of native avifauna. My objectives were to document the annual diet of coyotes in three types of urban habitat of western Washington and to qualitatively assess how coyote diets changed as a function of land use patterns and human density.
>
> —**TIMOTHY QUINN**, "Coyote (*Canis latrans*) Food Habits and
> Three Urban Habitat Types of Western Washington"

As you work toward providing an appropriate response to your rhetorical situation, be sure to present yourself as thoughtful and informed. Whether your audience consists of a single instructor or some larger group, you must establish that you are a credible author (see 10a). By conducting research and citing sources, you demonstrate that you have

- educated yourself about your topic,
- drawn accurately on the work of others (including diverse points of view),
- understood what you have discovered,
- integrated research data into a paper that is clearly your own, and
- provided all the information readers will need to consult the sources you have used.

The rest of this chapter and chapters 12–15 will help you fulfill these responsibilities.

11b Organizing notes

Taking thorough and organized notes is critical when you are preparing to write a research paper in which you attribute specific words and ideas to others while taking credit for your own ideas. Some researchers are most comfortable taking notes in notebooks. Others like to write notes directly on pages they have photocopied or printed out from an online source (see 2d). Still others write notes on index cards or type them into computer files—two methods that allow notes to be rearranged easily. Each method has advantages and disadvantages, and your choice should be guided by the requirements of your project and your own working style.

(1) Organizing notes in a ring binder or folder

When using a ring binder, you can combine pages of notes with photocopies or printouts of relevant source material. Moreover, you can add, remove, and rearrange material easily. Remember to identify the source on every page of notes and to use a fresh page for each new source. Be sure to distinguish direct quotations from paraphrases or summaries (see 11d), and keep your working bibliography (11c) separate from your notes.

(2) Taking notes on photocopies and printouts

An easy way to take notes is to use photocopies of articles and excerpts from books or printouts of sources from the Web. On a printout or photocopy, you can mark quotable material while also jotting down your own ideas in the margins (see fig. 11.1). This method reduces the risk of including inaccurate quotations in your paper, because you have eliminated the step of copying quotes exactly as they appear in the original source. Make sure to record the source on a photocopy if this information is not shown on the original page(s). Printouts from the Web almost always indicate the source and the date of access, but you should also note the date on which the site was posted or last updated (see 9d(1)).

It was the authors of the Declaration of Independence who stated the principles that all men are created equal in their rights, and that <u>it is to secure these rights that governments are instituted among men.</u>

= the purpose of gov't according to Truman

It was the authors of the Constitution who made it clear that, under our form of government, <u>all citizens are equal before the law,</u> and that the Federal Government has a duty to guarantee to every citizen equal protection of the laws.

= a radical idea for many Americans at the time

The Civil Rights Committee did more than repeat these great principles. It described a method to put these principles into action, and to make them a living reality for every American, regardless of his race, his religion, or his national origin.

background on the Civil Rights Committee link to Fahy

<u>When every American knows that his rights and his opportunities are fully protected and respected by the Federal, State, and local governments, then we will have the kind of unity that really means something.</u>

what Truman is after

Public Papers of the Presidents of the United States: Harry S. Truman, 1945–53, vol. 4 (Washington, D.C.: U.S. Government Printing Office, 1964), 923–5.

Fig. 11.1. Photocopied source with notes.

The example in fig. 11.1 comes from the work Nicole Hester did for her research paper on the desegregation of the U.S. military (see **14b**).

(3) Organizing notes in computer files

You may find it efficient to use a computer for taking notes—recording them quickly and storing them safely. Then, later, you can easily copy and paste information into various files and ultimately into a draft of your paper. Given the ease of computer use, though, it is important to remember to identify which records are direct quotations (see **11d(2)**), which are paraphrases (**11d(3)**), and which are your own thoughts. Always provide necessary bibliographic information so that you will not have trouble finding the source later. The following tips can help you use your computer efficiently when taking and filing notes for a research paper.

TIPS ON USING A COMPUTER TO ORGANIZE NOTES

- Create a separate master folder (or directory) for the paper.
- Create folders within the master folder for your bibliography, notes, and portions of drafts.
- Keep all the notes for each source in a separate file.
- Use a distinctive font or a different color to distinguish your own thoughts from the ideas of others (see fig. 11.2).
- Place direct quotations in quotation marks.
- When taking notes, record exactly where the information came from.
- When you discover new sources, add them to your working bibliography (see **11c**).
- Consider using the Annotation or Comment feature of your word-processing program to make notes on documents you have downloaded.

```
Scott, Alwyn
"Shot of Americana"
FI

Some coffee shops in Europe are Starbucks spin-offs. Some even
have American names—Chicago Coffee, San Francisco Coffee,
Coffee Shop. Scott says European imitators "suggest American
style, if not Seattle." Seems like traditional coffee cultures
are competing with Starbucks AND Starbucks imitators.
```

Fig. 11.2. The researcher used green to distinguish his response to a quotation from one of his sources.

(4) Arranging notes on note cards

Taking notes on index cards (also known as three-by-five cards) can be useful if you are working in a library without a laptop or if you prefer handwritten notes that you can rearrange as your research proceeds. Each index card should show the author's name (and a short title if the bibliography contains more than one work by that author), the exact page number(s) from which the information is drawn, and a brief comment on how you intend to use the information or a reflection on what you think about it. By putting a heading of two or three key words at the top of each card, you can easily arrange your cards as you prepare to draft your paper.

Whatever method you use to create your notes, consider the points in the following list.

TIPS FOR TAKING NOTES

- Identify the source for every note.
- Put the full bibliographic citation on the first page of every photocopy.
- Copy verbatim any useful passage you think you may quote. Put quotation marks around quoted words. In computer files, you can also use different fonts or different colors to identify quoted text.
- When a source has stimulated your thinking, identify both the source and the fact that the note is your own idea based on that source.

11c Working bibliography and annotated bibliography

A **working bibliography,** or preliminary bibliography, contains information (titles, authors, dates, and so on) about the materials you think you might use. Creating a working bibliography can help you evaluate the quality of your research. If you find that your most recent source is five years old, for example, or that you have relied exclusively on information from magazines or Web sites, you may need to find some other sources.

Some researchers find it convenient to put each bibliographic entry on a separate index card; this makes it easy to add or drop a card and to arrange the list alphabetically without recopying it. Others prefer to use a computer, which can sort and alphabetize automatically, making it easier to move material directly to the final draft.

It is also a good idea to follow the bibliographical format you have been instructed to use in your paper right from the start. This book covers the most common formats:

Modern Language Association (MLA), chapter 12

American Psychological Association (APA), chapter 13

The Chicago Manual of Style (CMS), chapter 14

The Council of Science Editors (CSE), chapter 15

The examples given in the rest of this chapter follow the MLA's bibliographical and documentation style.

If you are asked to prepare an **annotated bibliography,** you should list all your sources alphabetically according to the last name of the author. Then, at the end of each entry, summarize the content of the source in one or two sentences.

Zimmer, Carl. Soul Made Flesh: The Discovery of the Brain—and How It Changed the World. New York: Free, 2004. This book is a historical account of how knowledge of the brain developed and influenced ideas about the soul. It covers a span of time and place, beginning four thousand years ago in ancient Egypt and ending in Oxford, England, in the seventeenth century.

11d Integrating sources

You can integrate sources into your own writing in a number of ways— quoting exact words, paraphrasing sentences, and summarizing longer pieces of text or even entire texts. Whenever you borrow others' ideas in these ways, be careful to integrate the material—properly cited—into your own sentences and paragraphs. Once you have represented source material accurately and responsibly, you will be ready to respond to it.

(1) Writers introduce the sources they use.

When you borrow textual material, introduce it to readers by establishing the source, usually an author's name. You may also need to include additional information about the author, especially if the author's name is unfamiliar to your audience. For example, in a paper on medications given to children, the following statement becomes more credible if the audience is given the added information about Jerome Groopman's background.

professor of medicine at Harvard University,

According to Jerome Groopman,∧ "Pediatricians sometimes adopt extraordinary measures to insure that their patients are not harmed by treatments that have not been adequately studied in children" (33).

Phrases such as *According to Jerome Groopman* and *from the author's perspective* are called **attributive tags** because they attribute, or ascribe, information to a source. Most attributive tags in academic writing consist of the name of an author (or a related noun or pronoun) and a verb in order to report what that author has said, written, thought, or felt. Verbs commonly found in attributive tags are listed below. For a list of the types of complements that follow such verbs, see **27d(3)**.

VERBS USED IN ATTRIBUTIVE TAGS

admit	disagree	observe
advise	discuss	point out
argue	emphasize	reject
believe	explain	reply
claim	find	state
concede	imply	suggest
conclude	insist	think
deny	note	

When you integrate sources, be sure to find out whether it is appropriate to add evaluative remarks. If your assignment requires that you be objective, refrain from injecting your own opinions when introducing the ideas of another writer. You can convey your opinion of the material when responding to it (see **11f**). If, on the other hand, your assignment allows you to voice your opinion when presenting ideas, you can easily add an adverb to one of the verbs on the list to indicate your attitude toward the material: *persuasively* argue, *strongly* oppose, *inaccurately* represent.

If you decide to integrate graphics as source material, you must label them as figures and assign them arabic numbers. You can then refer to them within the text of your paper in a parenthetical comment, as in this example: "The red and black bands of the Western coral snake are bordered by narrower bands of yellow or white (see fig. 11.3)." You may also want to include a title or caption with the figure number.

Fig. 11.3. Western coral snake.

(2) Direct quotations draw attention to key passages.

Include a direct quotation in a paper only if

- you want to retain the beauty or clarity of someone's words,
- you need to reveal how the reasoning in a specific passage is flawed or insightful, or
- you plan to discuss the implications of the quoted material.

Keep quotations as short as possible, and make them an integral part of your text.

Quote *accurately.* Any quotation of another person's words should be placed in quotation marks or, if longer than four lines, set off as an indented block. (See 12a(2).) If you need to clarify a quotation by changing it in any way, place square brackets around the added or changed words.

"In this role, he [Robin Williams] successfully conveys a diverse range of emotion."

If you want to omit part of a quotation, replace the deleted words with ellipsis points. (See 39h.)

"Overseas markets . . . are critical to the financial success of Hollywood films."

When modifying a quotation, be sure not to alter its essential meaning.

CHECKLIST for Using Direct Quotations

- Have you copied all the words and punctuation accurately?
- Have you attributed the quotation to a specific source?
- Have you used ellipsis points to indicate anything you omitted? (See 39h.)
- Have you used square brackets around anything you added to or changed in a direct quotation? (See 39g.)
- Have you used quotations sparingly? Rather than using too many quotations, consider paraphrasing or summarizing the information instead.

(3) Paraphrases convey another person's ideas in different words.

A **paraphrase** is a restatement of someone else's ideas in approximately the same number of words. Paraphrasing allows you to demonstrate that you have understood what you have read; it also enables you to help your audience understand it. Paraphrase when you want to

- clarify difficult material by using simpler language,
- use another writer's idea but not his or her exact words,
- create a consistent tone (see 4a(3)) for your paper as a whole, or
- interact with a point that your source has made.

Your paraphrase should be almost entirely in your own words and should accurately convey the content of the original passage.

(a) Use your own words and sentence structure when paraphrasing.

As you compare the source below with the paraphrases that follow, note the similarities and differences in both sentence structure and word choice.

Source

Zimmer, Carl. <u>Soul Made Flesh: The Discovery of the Brain—and How It Changed the World</u>. New York: Free, 2004. 7.

The maps that neuroscientists make today are like the early charts of the New World with grotesque coastlines and blank interiors. And what little we do know about how the brain works raises disturbing questions about the nature of our selves.

Inadequate paraphrase

The maps used by neuroscientists today resemble the rough maps of the New World. Because we know so little about how the brain works, we must ask questions about the nature of our selves (Zimmer 7).

If you simply change a few words in a passage, you have not adequately restated it. You may be committing plagiarism (see **11e**) if the wording of your version follows the original too closely, even if you provide a page reference for the source.

Adequate paraphrase

Carl Zimmer compares today's maps of the brain to the rough maps made of the New World. He believes that the lack of knowledge about the workings of the brain makes us ask serious questions about our nature (7).

In the second paraphrase, both vocabulary and sentence structure differ from those in the original. This paraphrase also includes an attributive tag ("Carl Zimmer compares") and a page reference.

(b) Maintain accuracy.

Any paraphrase must accurately maintain the sense of the original. If you unintentionally misrepresent the original because you did not understand it, you are being *inaccurate.* If you deliberately change the gist of what a source says, you are being *unethical.* Compare the original statement below with the paraphrases.

Source

Kolbert, Elizabeth. "Ice Memory." New Yorker 7 Jan. 2002: 37.

Humans are a remarkably resourceful species. We have spread into every region of the globe that is remotely habitable, and some, like Greenland, that aren't even that. The fact that we have managed this feat in an era of exceptional climate stability does not diminish the accomplishment, but it does make it seem that much more tenuous.

Inaccurate or unethical paraphrase

Human beings have to be resourceful in order to inhabit a wide range of remote areas. This accomplishment is remarkable in a time when our climate is constantly changing (Kolbert 37).

Accurate paraphrase

Elizabeth Kolbert believes that the spread of humans throughout the world, even to remote places like Greenland, demonstrates not only that we are resourceful but also that our achievement, however remarkable, has not yet been threatened by climate change (37).

Although both paraphrases include a reference to an author and a page number, the first focuses only on the greatness of the human achievement mentioned by Kolbert, failing to note its tenuous nature.

(4) Summaries convey ideas efficiently.

When you summarize, you condense the main point(s) of your source. Although a summary omits much of the detail the writer uses in the original, it accurately reflects the essence of that work. In most cases, then, a **summary** reports a writer's main idea (see 3c) and the most important support given for it.

Whereas the length of a paraphrase (see 11d(3)) is usually close to that of the original material, a summary is shorter than the material it reports. When you paraphrase, you restate an author's ideas in order to present or examine them in detail. When you summarize, you present just the gist of the author's ideas, without including background information and details. Summaries can include short quotations of key phrases or ideas, but you must always enclose another writer's exact words in quotation marks when you blend them with your own.

Source

Kremmer, Christopher. <u>The Carpet Wars</u>. New York: HarperCollins, 2002. 197.

Iraq was once, like the United States today, a country of firsts. Sedentary society emerged in Mesopotamia around 5000 BC when people learned to plant, irrigate and harvest crops. Three thousand years before Christ, writing based on abstract symbols was invented to label the fruits of agricultural surplus. When a potter's wheel was turned on its side and hitched to a horse, modern transportation was born. It was where time was first carved into sixty minutes and circles into three hundred and sixty degrees. When in the ninth century the Arab caliph Haroun al-Rashid wanted to demonstrate his society's superiority over Europe, he sent Charlemagne a clock.

Summary

Iraq was once a center of innovation, where new methods of agriculture, transportation, writing, and measurement were generated (Kremmer 197).

This example reduces six sentences to one, retaining the key idea but eliminating specific examples such as the clock. A writer who believes that the audience needs examples might decide to paraphrase the passage instead.

Exercise 1

Find a well-developed paragraph in one of your recent reading assignments. Rewrite it in your own words, varying the sentence structure of the original. Make your paraphrase approximately the same length as the original. Next, write a one-sentence summary of the same paragraph.

11e Avoiding plagiarism

The purpose of this chapter has been to help you use the work of others responsibly. To ensure that your audience can distinguish between the ideas of other writers and your own contributions, give credit for all information you gather through research. It is not necessary, however, to credit information that is **common knowledge,** which includes well-known events and other facts such as the following: "The *Titanic* hit an iceberg and sank on its maiden voyage." This event has been the subject of many books and movies, so some information about it has become common knowledge.

If, however, you are writing a research paper about the *Titanic* and wish to include the ship's specifications, such as its overall length and gross tonnage, you will be providing *un*common knowledge, which must be documented. After you have read a good deal about a given subject, you will be able to distinguish between common knowledge and the distinctive ideas or interpretations of specific writers. If you have been scrupulous about recording your own thoughts as you took notes, you should have little difficulty distinguishing between what you knew to begin with and what you learned through your research.

Taking even part of someone else's work and presenting it as your own leaves you open to criminal charges. In the film, video, music, and software businesses, this sort of theft is called **piracy.** In publishing and education, it is called **plagiarism.** Whatever it is called, it is illegal, and penalties range from failing a paper or course to being expelled from school. Never compromise your integrity or risk your future by submitting someone else's work as your own.

BEYOND THE RULE

PLAGIARISM

If you follow the news, you may be aware of cases in which well-established writers have been accused of plagiarism. These stories demonstrate that plagiarism is not just an academic problem. For information about some of these cases, visit **www.harbrace.com**.

Although it is fairly easy to copy material from a Web site or even to purchase a paper on the Web, it is just as easy for a teacher or employer to locate that same material and determine that it has been plagiarized. Many teachers routinely use Internet search tools such as Google or special services such as InSite (available from Thomson Wadsworth) if they suspect that a student has submitted a paper that was plagiarized.

To review how to draw responsibly on the words and ideas of others, consider the following examples.

Source

McConnell, Patricia B. The Other End of the Leash. New York: Ballantine 2002. 142.

Status in male chimpanzees is particularly interesting because it is based on the formation of coalitions, in which no single male can achieve and maintain power without a cadre of supporting males.

Paraphrase with documentation

Patricia B. McConnell, an authority on animal training, notes that by forming alliances with other male chimpanzees, a specific male can enjoy status and power (142).

This example includes not only the original author's name but also a parenthetical citation, which marks the end of the paraphrase and provides the page number on which the source can be found.

Quotation with documentation

Patricia B. McConnell, an authority on animal training, argues that male chimpanzees achieve status "based on the formation of coalitions, in which no single male can achieve and maintain power without a cadre of supporting males" (142).

Quotation marks show where the copied words begin and end; the number in parentheses indicates the exact page on which those words appear. Again, the author is identified in the sentence, although her name could have been omitted at the beginning of the sentence and noted within the parenthetical reference instead:

An authority on animal training argues that male chimpanzees achieve status "based on the formation of coalitions, in which no single male can achieve and maintain power without a cadre of supporting males" (McConnell 142).

If, after referring to the following checklist, you cannot decide whether you need to cite a source, the safest policy is to cite it.

CHECKLIST of Sources That Should Be Cited

- Writings, both published and unpublished
- Opinions and judgments that are not your own
- Statistics and other facts that are not widely known
- Images and graphics, such as works of art, drawings, charts and graphs, tables, photographs, maps, and advertisements
- Personal communications, such as interviews, letters, and e-mail messages
- Public electronic communication, including television and radio broadcasts, motion pictures and videos, sound recordings, Web sites, and online discussion groups or forums

Exercise 2

After reading the source material, decide which of the quotations and paraphrases that follow it are written correctly and which would be considered problematic. Be prepared to explain your answers.

Source

Polsby, Daniel D. "Second Reading." <u>Reason</u> Mar. 1996: 33.

Generally speaking, though, it must be said that even among enthusiasts who think about the Second Amendment quite a lot, there has been little appreciation for the intricate and nuanced way in which constitutional analysis is practiced, and has to be practiced, by judges and lawyers.

1. People who care about the Second Amendment do not really understand how hard judges and lawyers have to work (Polsby 33).

2. Daniel Polsby has claimed that nobody understands the Second Amendment (33).

3. Daniel Polsby has claimed that public debate over the meaning of the Second Amendment seldom includes a deep understanding of the careful analysis judges and lawyers practice when interpreting the Constitution (33).

4. Those who tout the rights of the Second Amendment may not have a deep understanding of the careful analysis judges and lawyers practice when interpreting the Constitution (33).

5. According to Daniel Polsby, "there has been little appreciation for the intricate and nuanced way in which constitutional analysis is practiced, and has to be practiced, by judges and lawyers."

6. Few enthusiasts of the Second Amendment appreciate the nuanced ways in which constitutional analysis is practiced by judges and lawyers (33).

11f Responding to sources

When incorporating sources, not only will you summarize, paraphrase, quote, and document them, you will often respond to them as well. To prepare for interacting with your sources, you may find it useful to make notes in the margins of whatever you are reading. Next to relevant passages, jot down your agreement, disagreement, surprise, questions, and so on (see **2d**).

Readers of academic research papers or articles expect the authors of those works to be critical. They want to know whether facts are accurate or erroneous, whether logic is strong or weak, whether the organization is well planned or ill conceived, and whether conclusions are valid or doubtful. Researchers, therefore, critique the sources they use to ensure that their readers' concerns are being addressed. However, they also evaluate the strengths and weaknesses of sources in order to motivate a line of research. For example, they may try to show that previous research is insufficient in some way so that they can establish an exigence for their own research.

For your own paper, consider responding to your sources by examining their timeliness, coverage, reliability, and reasoning.

(1) Considering the currency of sources

Depending on the nature of your research, the currency of sources may be an important consideration. Using up-to-date sources is crucial when researching most topics. Historical research may call for sources from a specific period in the past as well. When you consider the currency of a source, start by looking for the date of its publication. Then, examine any data reported. Even though a source is published in the same year that you are doing research, it may include data that are several years old and thus possibly irrelevant. In the following example, the writer questions the usefulness of an out-of-date statistic mentioned in a source.

According to Jenkins, only 50% of all public schools have Web pages (23); however, this statistic is taken from a report published in 1997. A more recent count would likely yield a much higher percentage.

(2) Noting the thoroughness of research

Coverage refers to the comprehensiveness of research. The more comprehensive a study is, the more convincing are its findings. Similarly, the more examples an author provides, the more compelling are his or her conclusions. Claims that are based on only one instance are often criticized for being merely anecdotal or otherwise unsubstantiated. The writer of the following response suggests that the author of the source in question may have based his conclusion on too little information.

Johnson concludes that middle-school students are expected to complete an inordinate amount of homework given their age, but he bases his conclusion on research conducted in only three schools. To be more convincing, Johnson needs to conduct research in more schools, preferably located in different parts of the country.

(3) Checking the reliability of findings

Research, especially when derived from experiments or surveys, must be reliable (see 18b). Experimental results are considered **reliable** if they can be reproduced by researchers using a similar methodology. Results that cannot be replicated in this way are unreliable because they are supported by only one experiment.

Reliability is also a requirement for reported data. Researchers are expected to report their findings accurately and honestly, not distorting them to support their own beliefs or claiming others' ideas as their own. To ensure the reliability of their work, researchers must also report all relevant information, not intentionally excluding any that weakens their conclusions. When studies of the same phenomenon give rise to disputes, researchers should discuss conflicting results or interpretations. The writer of the following response focuses on the problematic nature of her source's methodology.

Jamieson concludes from her experiment that a low-carbohydrate diet can be dangerous for athletes, but her methodology suffers from lack of detail. No one would be able to confirm her experimental findings without knowing exactly what and how much the athletes consumed.

(4) Examining the author's reasoning

When a source is logical, its reasoning is sound. Lapses in logic may be the result of using evidence that does not directly support a claim, appealing to the reader's emotions, or encouraging belief in false authority. Faulty reasoning is often discussed in terms of rhetorical fallacies. A list of these fallacies, along with examples, can be found on pages 191–196.

MLA DOCUMENTATION

12

The Modern Language Association (MLA) provides guidelines for documenting research in literature, languages, linguistics, and composition studies. The *MLA Handbook for Writers of Research Papers* is published specifically for undergraduates. Updates to the handbook's content can be found at www.mla.org. This chapter includes

- guidelines for citing sources within the text of a paper (**12a**),
- guidelines for documenting sources in the works-cited list (**12b**), and
- a sample student paper (**12c**).

12a MLA in-text citations

(1) In-text citations indicate that a writer has drawn material from other sources.

The citations you use within the text of a research paper refer your readers to the list of works cited at the end of the paper, tell them where to find the borrowed material in the original source, and indicate the boundaries between your ideas and those you have borrowed. In the following example, the parenthetical citation guides the reader to page 20 of the article by Doherty in the works-cited list.

In-text citation

Starbucks has now expanded its goals to include leading the world coffee shop market.

With over 5,000 coffee shops already in operation—nearly 1,200 of which are located

outside the United States—Starbucks hopes to reach revenues of $6 billion by 2005

(Doherty 20).

Works-cited entry

Doherty, Jacqueline. "Make It Decaf: Despite Heavy Revenue Gains, Starbucks' Earnings

Growth Is Slowing." <u>Barrons</u>. 20 May 2002: 20.

The MLA suggests reserving numbered notes for supplementary comments—for example, when you wish to explain a point further, but the subject matter is tangential to your topic. When numbered notes are used, superscript numbers are inserted in the appropriate places in the text, and the notes are gathered at the end of the paper on a separate page titled "Notes." You can create a superscript number in Microsoft Word by typing the number, highlighting it, pulling down the menu for Format, clicking on Font, and then clicking in the box next to Superscript. Other word-processing programs have similar procedures for creating superscript numbers.

In-text note number

To reach its goals, Starbucks will have to enter new markets in Africa, Asia,

and the Middle East,[1] and especially in Europe, where coffee is a staple of many

countries.

Notes entry

[1] It should be noted that in Saudi Arabia, Starbucks, along with other multinational

corporations, tries to conform to the existing cultural mores.

An in-text citation usually provides two pieces of information about borrowed material: (1) information that directs the reader to the relevant source on the works-cited list, and (2) information that directs the reader to a specific page or section within that source. An author's last name and a page number generally suffice. To create an in-text citation, either place both the author's last name and the page number in parentheses or introduce the author's name in the sentence and supply just the page number in parentheses.

Some recent union negotiations have been successful (Craig and Kaupa 234).

Craig and Kaupa describe recent successful union negotiations (234).

When referring to information from a range of pages, separate the first and last pages with a hyphen: (34-42). If the page numbers have the same hundreds or thousands digit, do not repeat it when listing the final page in the range: (234-42) or (1350-55) but (290-301) and (1395-1402). If you refer to an entire work, no page number is necessary.

The following examples are representative of the types of in-text citations you might be expected to use. For more details on the placement and punctuation of citations, including those following long quotations, see pages 269–271.

1. Work by one author

Set on the frontier and focused on characters who use language sparingly, Westerns often reveal a "pattern of linguistic regression" (Rosowski 170).

OR

Susan J. Rosowski argues that Westerns often reveal a "pattern of linguistic regression" (170).

2. More than one work by the same author(s)

When your works-cited list includes more than one work by the same author(s), provide a shortened title in your in-text citation that identifies the relevant work. Use a comma to separate the name (or names) from the shortened title when both are in parentheses. For example, if you listed two works by Antonio Damasio on your works-cited page, then you would cite one of those within your text as follows:

According to one neurological hypothesis, "feelings are the expression of human flourishing or human distress" (Damasio, Looking for Spinoza 6).

OR

Antonio Damasio believes that "feelings are the expression of human flourishing or human distress" (Looking for Spinoza 6).

3. Work by two or three authors

Some environmentalists seek to protect wilderness areas from further development so that they can both preserve the past and learn from it (Katcher and Wilkins 174).

Use commas to separate the names of three authors: (Bellamy, O'Brien, and Nichols 59).

4. Work by more than three authors

Use either the first author's last name followed by the abbreviation *et al.* (from the Latin *et alii,* meaning "and others") or all the last names. (Do not italicize or underline the abbreviated Latin phrase.)

In one important study, women graduates complained more frequently about "excessive control than about lack of structure" (Belenky et al. 205).

OR

In one important study, women graduates complained more frequently about "excessive control than about lack of structure" (Belenky, Clinchy, Goldberger, and Tarule 205).

5. Works by different authors with the same last name

When your works-cited list includes works by different authors with the same last name, provide a first initial, along with the last name, in parenthetical citations, or use the author's first and last name in the text. For example, if your works-cited list included entries for works by both Richard Enos and Theresa Enos, you would cite the work of Theresa Enos as follows.

Pre-Aristotelian rhetoric still has an impact today (T. Enos 331-43).

OR

Theresa Enos mentions the considerable contemporary reliance on pre-Aristotelian

rhetoric (331-43).

If two authors have the same last name and first initial, spell out each author's first name in a parenthetical citation.

6. Work by a corporate author

A work has a corporate author when individual members of the group that created it are not identified. If the corporate author's name is long, you may use common abbreviations for parts of it—for example, *Assn.* for "Association" and *Natl.* for "National."

Strawbale constructions are now popular across the nation (Natl. Ecobuilders

Group 2).

7. Two or more works in the same citation

When two sources provide similar information or when you combine information from two sources in the same sentence, cite both sources, separating them with a semicolon.

Agricultural scientists believe that crop productivity will be adversely affected by solar

dimming (Beck and Watts 90; Harris-Green 153-54).

8. Multivolume work

When you cite material from more than one volume of a multivolume work, include the volume number (followed by a colon and a space) before the page number.

Katherine Raine claims that "true poetry begins where human personality ends"

(2: 247).

You do not need to include the volume number in a parenthetical citation if your list of works cited includes only one volume of a multivolume work.

9. Anonymous work

The Tehuelche people left their handprints on the walls of a cave, now called Cave of the

Hands ("Hands of Time" 124).

Use the title of an anonymous work in place of an author's name. If the title is long, provide a shortened version. For example, the shortened title for "Chasing Down the Phrasal Verb in the Discourse of Adolescents" is "Chasing Down."

10. Indirect source

If you need to include material that one of your sources quoted from another work because you cannot obtain the original source, use the following format (*qtd.* is the abbreviation for "quoted").

The critic Susan Hardy Aikens has argued on behalf of what she calls "canonical

multiplicity" (qtd. in Mayers 677).

A reader turning to the list of works cited should find a bibliographic entry for Mayers, the source consulted, but not for Aikens.

11. Poetry, drama, and sacred texts

When you refer to poetry, drama, or sacred texts, you should give the numbers of lines, acts and scenes, or chapters and verses, rather than page numbers. This practice enables readers to consult an edition other than the one you have used. Act, scene, and line numbers (all arabic numerals) are separated by periods with no space before or after them. The MLA suggests that biblical chapters and verses be treated similarly, although some writers prefer to use colons instead of periods in such citations. In all cases, the progression is from larger to smaller units.

The following example illustrates a citation referring to lines of poetry.

Emily Dickinson alludes to her dislike of public appearance in "I'm Nobody! Who Are

You?" (lines 5-8).

Use *line* or *lines* in the first parenthetical citation; subsequent citations require only numbers. For more details on quoting poetry, see **16f(4)**.

The following citation shows that the famous "To be, or not to be" soliloquy appears in act 3, scene 1, lines 56–89 of *Hamlet*.

In <u>Hamlet,</u> Shakespeare presents the most famous soliloquy in the history of the English

theater: "To be, or not to be . . ." (3.1.56-89).

Citations of biblical material identify the book of the Bible, the chapter, and the pertinent verses. In the following example, the writer refers to the creation story in Genesis, which begins in chapter 1 with verse 1 and ends in chapter 2 with verse 22.

The Old Testament creation story (<u>New American Standard Bible</u>, Gen. 1.1-2.22), told with remarkable economy, culminates in the arrival of Eve.

Mention in your first citation which version of the Bible you are using; list only book, chapter, and verse in subsequent citations. Note that the names of biblical books are neither underlined nor enclosed in quotation marks.

BEYOND THE RULE

ABBREVIATIONS FOR IN-TEXT CITATIONS

The MLA provides standard abbreviations for the works of Shakespeare and Chaucer, for certain other literary works, and for the parts of the Bible. You can find these abbreviations at **www.harbrace.com**.

12. Constitution

When referring to the Constitution, use these common abbreviations:

United States Constitution	US Const.
article	art.
section	sec.

The testimony of two witnesses is needed to convict anyone of treason (US Const., art. 3, sec. 3).

13. Works with numbered paragraphs or screens

If an electronic source does not have page numbers, provide paragraph or screen numbers instead. If paragraphs are numbered, cite the number(s) of the paragraph(s) after the abbreviation *par.* (for one paragraph) or *pars.* (for more than one). If a screen number is provided, cite that number after the word *screen* (or *screens* for more than one).

Alston describes three types of rubrics for evaluating customer service (pars. 2-15).

Hilton and Merrill provide examples of effective hyperlinks (screen 1).

If an electronic source includes no numbers distinguishing one part from another, you should cite the entire source. In this case, to establish that you have not accidentally omitted a number, avoid using a parenthetical citation by providing what information you have within the sentence that introduces the material.

Raymond Lucero's <u>Shopping Online</u> offers useful advice for consumers who are concerned about transmitting credit card information over the Internet.

(2) The MLA offers guidelines for placing and punctuating in-text citations and quotations.

(a) Placement of in-text citations

When you acknowledge your use of a source by placing the author's name and a relevant page number in parentheses, insert this parenthetical citation directly after the information you used, generally at the end of a sentence but *before* the final punctuation mark (a period, question mark, or exclamation point).

Oceans store almost half the carbon dioxide released by humans into the atmosphere (Wall 28).

However, you may need to place a parenthetical citation earlier in a sentence to indicate that only the first part of the sentence contains borrowed material. Place the citation after the clause containing the material but before a punctuation mark (a comma, semicolon, or colon).

Oceans store almost half the carbon dioxide released by humans into the atmosphere (Wall 28), a fact that provides hope for scientists studying global warming but that alarms scientists studying organisms living in the oceans.

(b) Lengthy quotations

When a quotation is more than four lines long, set it off from the surrounding text by indenting all lines one inch (or ten spaces) from the left margin. The first line should not be indented further than the others. The right margin should remain the same. Double-space the entire quotation.

In <u>Nickel and Dimed</u>, Barbara Ehrenreich describes the dire living conditions of the working poor:

> The lunch that consists of Doritos or hot dog rolls, leading to faintness before the end of the shift. The "home" that is also a car or a van. The illness

> or injury that must be "worked through," with gritted teeth, because there's
> no sick pay or health insurance and the loss of one day's pay will mean no
> groceries for the next. These experiences are not part of a sustainable
> lifestyle, even a lifestyle of chronic deprivation and relentless low-level pun-
> ishment. They are, by almost any standard of subsistence, emergency situa-
> tions. And that is how we should see the poverty of millions of low-wage
> Americans—as a state of emergency. (214)

A problem of this magnitude cannot be fixed simply by raising the minimum wage.

Note that the period precedes the parenthetical citation at the end of
an indented (block) quotation.

Rarely will you need to quote more than a paragraph, but if you do,
distinguish between the paragraphs by indenting the first line of each
an extra quarter of an inch (or three spaces).

(c) Punctuation

Punctuation marks clarify meaning in quotations and citations. The
following list summarizes their common uses.

- A colon separates volume numbers from page numbers in a
  parenthetical citation.

  (Raine 2: 247)

- A comma separates the author's name from the title when it is
  necessary to list both in a parenthetical citation.

  (Kingsolver, Animal Dreams)

  A comma also indicates that page or line numbers are not sequential.

  (44, 47)

- Ellipsis points indicate an omission within a quotation.

  "They lived in an age of increasing complexity and great hope; we in an age of . . .
  growing despair" (Krutch 2).

- A hyphen indicates a continuous sequence of pages or lines.

  (44-47)

- A period separates acts, scenes, and lines of dramatic works.

  (3.1.56)

A period also distinguishes chapters from verses in biblical citations.

(Gen. 1.1)

■ A question mark placed inside the final quotation marks indicates that the quotation is a question. Notice that the period after the parenthetical citation marks the end of the sentence.

Peter Elbow asks, "What could be more wonderful than the pleasure of creating or appreciating forms that are different, amazing, outlandish, useless—the opposite of ordinary, everyday, pragmatic?" (542).

When placed outside the final quotation marks, a question mark indicates that the quotation is part of a question posed by the writer of the paper.

What does Kabat-Zinn mean when he advises people to practice mindfulness "as if their lives depended on it" (305)?

■ Square brackets enclose words that have been added to the quotation as clarification and are not part of the original material.

"The publication of this novel [Beloved] establishes Morrison as one of the most important writers of our time" (Boyle 17).

12b MLA list of works cited

All of the works you cite should be listed at the end of your paper, beginning on a separate page with the heading "Works Cited." Use the following tips as you prepare your list.

TIPS FOR PREPARING A LIST OF WORKS CITED

- Center the heading "Works Cited" one inch from the top of the page.
- Arrange the list of works alphabetically by the author's last name.
- If a source has more than one author, alphabetize the entry according to the last name of the first author.
- If you use more than one work by the same author, alphabetize the works by the first major word in each title. For the first entry, provide the author's

complete name (last name given first), but substitute three hyphens (---) for the name in subsequent entries.

- For a work without an author, alphabetize the entry according to the first important word in the title.
- Type the first line of each entry flush with the left margin and indent subsequent lines one-half inch or five spaces (a hanging indent).
- Double-space equally throughout—between lines of an entry and between entries.

Directory of MLA-Style Entries for a Works-Cited List

BOOKS

ARTICLES

OTHER PRINT SOURCES

LIVE PERFORMANCES AND DIGITAL RECORDINGS

IMAGES

ONLINE BOOKS, ARTICLES, AND DOCUMENTS

ONLINE RECORDINGS AND IMAGES

WEB SITES

ADDITIONAL TYPES OF WORKS-CITED ENTRIES

For the following additional types of works-cited entries, visit
www.harbrace.com.

- Article in a series
- Article in a special issue of a journal
- Book with two publishers
- Course home page
- Home page for academic department
- Manuscript, print
- Musical composition

- Online book with editor
- Online book with translator
- Online letter to the editor
- Online manuscript
- Patent
- Personal photograph
- Synchronous communication
- Work from personal subscription service, such as America Online

When writing down source information for your bibliography, be sure to copy the information directly from the source (e.g., the title page of a book). (See fig. 12.1, on page 279.)

General Documentation Guidelines for Print-Based Sources

Author, Artist, or Editor

One author or artist. Place the last name before the first, separating them with a comma. Add any middle name or initial after the first name. Use another comma before any abbreviation or number that follows the first name. Indicate the end of this unit of the entry with a period.

Halberstam, David.
Johnston, Mary K.
King, Martin Luther, Jr.

Two or more authors or artists. List names in the same order used on the title page of the book. The first person's name is inverted (that is, the last name appears first); the others are not. Separate all names with commas, placing the word *and* before the final name.

West, Nigel, and Oleg Tsarev.
Green, Bill, Maria Lopez, and
  Jenny T. Graf.

Four or more authors or artists. List the names of all the authors or artists, or provide just the first person's name (inverted) and the abbreviation *et al.* (for *et alii*, meaning "and others").

Quirk, Randolph, Sidney
  Greenbaum, Geoffrey Leech,
  and Jan Svartvik.
OR
Quirk, Randolph, et al.

Corporate or group author. Omit any initial article *(a, an,* or *the)* from the name.

Institute of Medicine.
Department of Natural Resources.

Editor. If an editor or editors are listed instead of an author or authors, include the abbreviation *ed.* for "editor" or *eds.* for "editors."

Espinoza, Toni, ed.
Gibb, Susan, and Karen Enochs, eds.

Title

Underlined titles. Underline the titles of books, magazines, journals,

<u>Newsweek</u>.
<u>Hamlet</u>.

newspapers, plays, films, and Web sites. Capitalize all major words (nouns, pronouns, verbs, adjectives, adverbs, and subordinating conjunctions). Make underlining continuous, not separate under each word. Do not underline the period completing this unit of the entry.	<u>Weird English</u>. <u>The Aviator</u>.
Titles in quotation marks. Use quotation marks to enclose the titles of short works such as journal or magazine articles, short stories, and songs. (See 38b.)	"Three Days to See." "Selling the Super Bowl." "Generations."
Subtitles. Always include a subtitle if the work has one. Use a colon to separate a main title and a subtitle.	<u>Lost in Translation: Life in a New Language</u>. "Silence: Learning to Listen."
Titles within titles. When an underlined title includes the title of another work normally underlined, do not underline the embedded title.	<u>Essays on</u> The Death of a Salesman. BUT <u>The Death of a Salesman</u>.
If the embedded title normally requires quotation marks, it should be underlined as well as enclosed in quotation marks.	<u>Understanding "The Philosophy of Composition" and the Aesthetic of Edgar Allan Poe</u>. BUT "The Philosophy of Composition."
When a title in quotation marks includes the title of another work normally underlined, retain the underlining.	"A Salesman's Reading of <u>The Death of a Salesman</u>."
If the embedded title is normally enclosed in quotation marks, use only single quotation marks.	"The European Roots of 'The Philosophy of Composition.' "

(continued on page 278)

Publication Data

City of publication. If more than one city is listed on the title page, mention only the first. Place a colon after the name of the city.

Boston:
New York:

If the work was published outside the United States and the city of publication is unfamiliar, add an abbreviation for the country or for the province if the work is Canadian.

Norwich, Eng.:
Prince George, BC:

Publisher's name. Provide a shortened form of the publisher's name, and place a comma after it. To shorten the name of the publisher, use the principal name.

Knopf (for Alfred A. Knopf)
Random (for Random House)

For books published by university presses, abbreviate *University* and *Press* without periods.

Harvard UP (for Harvard University Press)

If two publishers are listed, provide the city of publication and the name of the publisher for each. Use a semicolon to separate the two.

Manchester, Eng.: Manchester UP; New York: St. Martin's

Publisher's imprint. You will sometimes need to list both a publisher's name and an imprint. The imprint is usually listed above the publisher's name on the title page. In a works-cited entry, use a hyphen to separate the two names: imprint-publisher.

Quill-HarperCollins
Vintage-Random

Copyright date. Although the copyright date may be found on the title page, it is usually found on the next page—the copyright page (see fig. 12.2). Place a period after the date.

Fig. 12.1. The title page includes most, if not all, of the information needed for a bibliographic entry.

PROTECTING
AMERICA'S
HEALTH

Title

•

The FDA, Business, and One Hundred
Years of Regulation

Subtitle

PHILIP J. HILTS

Author

Publisher
(shorten to
Knopf)

Alfred A. Knopf   New York   2003

Date of
publication

City of
publication

Fig. 12.2. If the title page does not give the book's date of publication, turn to the copyright page, which is usually on the back of the title page.

Copyright
year
Copyright ©2002 by Anna Reid

All rights reserved. No part of this book may be
reproduced or transmitted in any form or
by any means, electronic or mechanical, including photocopying,
recording, or by any information storage and retrieval system,
without permission in writing from the Publisher.

First published in the United States of America in 2003 by
Walker Publishing Company, Inc.;
originally published in Great Britain in 2002 by
Weidenfeld & Nicolson

BOOKS

1. Book by one author

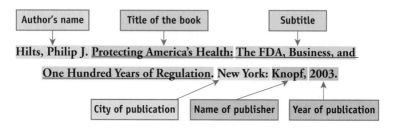

2. Book by two authors

West, Nigel, and Oleg Tsarev. <u>The Crown Jewels: The British Secrets at the Heart of the KGB Archives</u>. New Haven: Yale UP, 1999.

3. Book by three authors

Spinosa, Charles, Ferdinand Flores, and Hubert L. Dreyfus. <u>Disclosing New Worlds: Entrepreneurship, Democratic Action, and the Cultivation of Solidarity</u>. Cambridge: MIT P, 1997.

4. Book by more than three authors

Bullock, Jane A., George D. Haddow, Damon Cappola, Erdem Ergin, Lissa Westerman, and Sarp Yeletaysi. <u>Introduction to Homeland Security</u>. Boston: Elsevier, 2005.

OR

Bullock, Jane A., et al. <u>Introduction to Homeland Security</u>. Boston: Elsevier, 2005.

5. Book by a corporate author

Institute of Medicine. <u>Blood Banking and Regulation: Procedures, Problems, and Alternatives</u>. Washington: Natl. Acad., 1996.

6. Book by an anonymous author

<u>Primary Colors: A Novel of Politics</u>. New York: Warner, 1996.

Begin the entry with the title. Do not use *Anonymous* or *Anon.*

7. Book with an author and an editor

Stoker, Bram. <u>Dracula</u>. Ed. Glennis Byron. Peterborough, ON: Broadview, 1998.

Include both the name of the author and the name of the editor (preceded by *Ed.*). Note that this book was published in Ontario, Canada, so the abbreviation for the province is included (see page 278).

8. Book with an editor instead of an author

Kachuba, John B., ed. How to Write Funny. Cincinnati: Writer's Digest, 2000.

9. Edition after the first

Murray, Donald. The Craft of Revision. 4th ed. Boston: Heinle, 2001.

10. Introduction, preface, foreword, or afterword to a book

Olnos, Edward James. Foreword. Vietnam Veteranos: Chicanos Recall the War. By Lea

Ybarra. Austin: U of Texas P, 2004. ix-x.

The name that begins the entry is the author of the foreword or other section, not of the entire book. Instead of *Foreword*, type *Preface, Afterword,* or *Introduction* if you are citing from one of these sections.

11. Anthology (a collection of works by different authors)

Buranen, Lisa, and Alice M. Roy, eds. Perspectives on Plagiarism and Intellectual

Property in a Postmodern World. New York: State U of New York P, 1999.

Include the name(s) of the editor(s), followed by the abbreviation *ed.* (or *eds*). For individual works within an anthology, consult the following two models.

12. A work originally published in an anthology

Rowe, David. "No Gain, No Game? Media and Sport." Mass Media and Society. 3rd ed.

Ed. James Curran and Michael Gurevitch. New York: Oxford UP, 2000. 346-61.

Use this form for an article, essay, story, poem, or play that was published for the first time in the anthology you are using. Place the title of the anthology after the title of the individual work, noting the edition if it is not the first. Provide the name(s) of the editor(s) after the abbreviation *Ed.* for "edited by." List the publication data for the anthology and the range of pages on which the work appears. (See pages 283–284 for information on noting inclusive page numbers.)

If you cite more than one work from an anthology, provide only the name(s) of the author(s), the title of the work, the name(s) of the editor(s), and the inclusive page numbers in an entry for each work. Then, also provide an entry for the entire anthology, in which you include the relevant publication data (see the sample entry for an anthology in item 11).

Clark, Irene L. "Writing Centers and Plagiarism." Buranen and Roy 155-67.

Howard, Rebecca Moore. "The New Abolitionism Comes to Plagiarism." Buranen and Roy 87-95.

13. A work from a journal reprinted in a textbook or an anthology

Shaugnessy, Mina P. "Diving In: An Introduction to Basic Writing." College Composition and Communication 27.3 (1976): 234-39. Rpt. in Cross-Talk in Comp Theory. Ed. Victor Villanueva. Urbana: NCTE, 1997. 289-95.

Use the abbreviation *Rpt.* for "Reprinted."

14. A work from an edited collection reprinted in a textbook or an anthology

Brownmiller, Susan. "Let's Put Pornography Back in the Closet." Take Back the Night: Women on Pornography. Ed. Laura Lederer. New York: Morrow, 1980. 252-55. Rpt. in Conversations: Readings for Writing. 4th ed. By Jack Selzer. New York: Allyn, 2000. 578-81.

See item 12 for information on citing more than one work from the same anthology.

15. Translated book

Garrigues, Eduardo. West of Babylon. Trans. Nasario Garcia. Albuquerque: U of New Mexico P, 2002.

Place the abbreviation *Trans.* for "Translated by" before the translator's name.

16. Republished book

Alcott, Louisa May. Work: A Story of Experience. 1873. Harmondsworth, Eng.: Penguin, 1995.

Provide the publication date of the original work after the title.

17. Multivolume work

Young, Ralph F., ed. <u>Dissent in America</u>. 2 vols. New York: Longman-Pearson, 2005.

Cite the total number of volumes in a work when you have used material from more than one volume. Include the year the volumes were published. If the volumes were published over a span of time, provide inclusive dates: (1997-99) or (1998-2004).

If you have used only one volume, include that volume's number (preceded by the abbreviation *Vol.*) in place of the total number of volumes.

Young, Ralph F., ed. <u>Dissent in America</u>. Vol. 1. New York: Longman-Pearson, 2005.

Note that the publisher's name in this entry is hyphenated: the first name is the imprint; the second is the publisher.

18. Article in a multivolume work

To indicate a specific article in a multivolume work, provide the author's name and the title of the article in quotation marks. Note the page numbers for the article after the date of publication.

Baxby, Derrick. "Edward Jenner." <u>Oxford Dictionary of National Biography</u>. Ed.

    H. C. G. Matthew and Brian Harrison. Vol. 30. Oxford: Oxford UP, 2004. 4-8.

If required by your instructor, include the number of volumes and the inclusive publication dates after the page numbers: 382-89. 23 vols. 1962-97.

19. Book in a series

Sumner, Colin, ed. <u>Blackwell Companion to Criminology</u>. Blackwell Companions to

    Sociology 8. Malden: Blackwell, 2004.

When citing a book that is part of a series, provide the name of the series and, if one is listed, the number designating the work's place in it. The series name is not underlined. Abbreviate words in the series name according to the MLA guidelines; for example, the word *Series* is abbreviated *Ser.*

ARTICLES

A **journal** is a publication written for a specific discipline or profession; a **magazine** is written for the general public. You can find most of

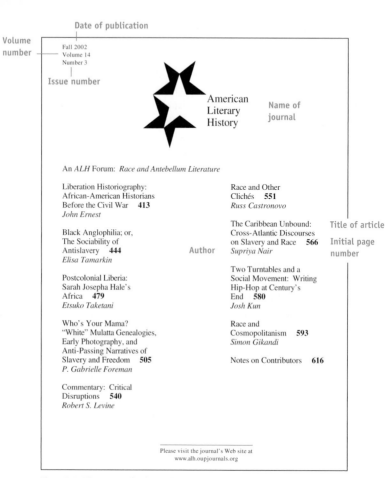

Date of publication

Volume number

Issue number

Fall 2002
Volume 14
Number 3

American
Literary
History

Name of journal

An *ALH* Forum: *Race and Antebellum Literature*

Liberation Historiography:
African-American Historians
Before the Civil War   **413**
John Ernest

Black Anglophilia; or,
The Sociability of
Antislavery   **444**
Elisa Tamarkin

Author

Postcolonial Liberia:
Sarah Josepha Hale's
Africa   **479**
Etsuko Taketani

Who's Your Mama?
"White" Mulatta Genealogies,
Early Photography, and
Anti-Passing Narratives of
Slavery and Freedom   **505**
P. Gabrielle Foreman

Commentary: Critical
Disruptions   **540**
Robert S. Levine

Race and Other
Clichés   **551**
Russ Castronovo

The Caribbean Unbound:
Cross-Atlantic Discourses
on Slavery and Race   **566**
Supriya Nair

Two Turntables and a
Social Movement: Writing
Hip-Hop at Century's
End   **580**
Josh Kun

Race and
Cosmopolitanism   **593**
Simon Gikandi

Notes on Contributors   **616**

Title of article

Initial page number

Please visit the journal's Web site at
www.alh.oupjournals.org

Fig. 12.3. First page of a journal.

the information required for a works-cited entry on the first page of
the journal or sometimes in the footer of the article you are citing. (See
fig. 12.3.)

Title of article and name of periodical

Put the article title in quotation marks with a period inside the closing
quotation marks. Underline the name of the periodical. Capitalize all

major words (nouns, pronouns, verbs, adjectives, adverbs, and subordinating conjunctions).

"Staring into the Political Abyss." <u>U.S. News and World Report</u>.

Volume and issue numbers

In an entry for an article from a journal, provide the volume number. For a journal with continuous pagination, include only the volume number after the name of the journal. For a journal whose issues are paginated separately, put a period after the volume number and add the issue number.

<u>Contemporary Review</u> 194   <u>Studies in the Literary Imagination</u> 26.3

A journal paginated *continuously* uses the number 1 to identify only the first page of the first issue in a volume. The first page of a subsequent issue in that volume is numbered to follow the last page of the first volume, and so on. In contrast, a journal paginated *separately* uses the number 1 to identify the first page of each issue in a volume.

Date

For journals, place the year of publication in parentheses after the volume or issue number. For magazines and newspapers, provide the date of issue after the name of the periodical. Note the day first (if provided), followed by the month (abbreviated except for May, June, and July) and year.

Journal	<u>Journal of Marriage and Family</u> 65 (2003)
Magazine	<u>Economist</u> 13 Aug. 2005
Newspaper	<u>Chicago Tribune</u> 24 July 2002

Page numbers

Use a colon to separate the date from the page number(s). Note all the pages on which the article appears, separating the first and last page with a hyphen: (21-39). If the page numbers have the same hundreds or thousands digit, do not repeat it when listing the final page in the range: (131-42) or (1680-99). Magazine and newspaper articles are often interrupted by advertisements or other articles. If the first part of an article appears on pages 45 through 47 and the rest on pages 92 through 94, give only the first page number followed by a plus sign: 45+.

20. Article in a journal with continuous pagination

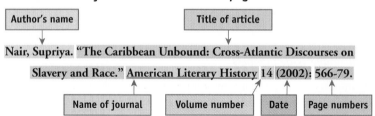

Author's name

Title of article

Nair, Supriya. "The Caribbean Unbound: Cross-Atlantic Discourses on Slavery and Race." American Literary History 14 (2002): 566-79.

Name of journal | Volume number | Date | Page numbers

21. Article in a journal with each issue paginated separately

Andrews, William L. "Postmodern Southern Literature: Confessions of a Norton
Anthologist." Studies in the Literary Imagination 35.1 (2002): 105-12.

When you use an article from a journal paginated separately, include the issue number as well as the volume number. In this example, 35 is the volume number, and 1 is the issue number.

22. Article in a monthly magazine

Keizer, Garret. "How the Devil Falls in Love." Harper's Aug. 2002: 43-51.

23. Article in a weekly magazine or newspaper

Klotowitz, Alex. "The Trenchcoat Robbers." New Yorker 8 July 2002: 34-39.

24. Article in a daily newspaper

Moberg, David. "The Accidental Environmentalist." Chicago Tribune 24 Sept. 2002, final
ed., sec. 2: 1+.

When not part of the newspaper's name, the name of the city where the newspaper is published should be given in brackets after the title: Star Telegram [Fort Worth]. If a specific edition is not identifed on the masthead, put a colon after the date and then provide the page reference. Specify the section by inserting the section letter as it appears in the newspaper (A7 or 7A, for example).

25. Unsigned article or wire service article

"View from the Top." National Geographic July 2001: 140.

26. Editorial in a newspaper or magazine

Beefs, Anne. "Ending Bias in the Human Rights System." Editorial. New York Times 22
May 2002, natl. ed.: A27.

27. Book or film review in a magazine

Denby, David. "Horse Power." Rev. of <u>Seabiscuit</u>, dir. Gary Ross. <u>New Yorker</u> 4 Aug.

2003: 84-85.

Include the name of the reviewer, the title of the review (if any), the phrase *Rev. of* (for "Review of"), the title of the work being reviewed, and the name of the editor, author, or director.

28. Book or film review in a journal

Graham, Catherine. Rev. of <u>Questionable Activities: The Best</u>, ed. Judith Rudakoff.

<u>Canadian Theatre Review</u> 113 (2003): 74-76.

OTHER PRINT SOURCES

29. Encyclopedia entry

Robertson, James I., Jr. "Thomas Jonathan Jackson." <u>Encyclopedia of the American Civil</u>

<u>War: A Political, Social, and Military History</u>. Ed. David S. Heidler and Jeanne T.

Heidler. 5 vols. Santa Barbara: ABC-CLIO, 2000.

When the author of an encyclopedia article is indicated only by initials, check the table of contents for a list of contributors. If an article is anonymous, begin the entry with the article title.

Full publication information is not necessary for a well-known reference work that is organized alphabetically. Along with the author's name, the title of the article, and the name of the encyclopedia, list the edition and year of publication in one of two ways: 5th ed. 2004 or 2002 ed.

Petersen, William J. "Riverboats and Rivermen." <u>The Encyclopedia Americana</u>. 1999 ed.

30. Dictionary entry

When citing a specific dictionary definition for a word, use the abbreviation *Def.* (for "Definition"), and indicate which one you used if the entry has two or more.

"Reactive." Def. 2a. <u>Merriam-Webster's Collegiate Dictionary</u>. 10th ed. 2001.

31. Sacred text

Begin your works-cited entry for a sacred text with the title of the work, rather than information about editors or translators.

<u>New American Standard Bible</u>. Anaheim: Foundation, 1997.

<u>The Qur'an</u>. Trans. Muhammad A. S. Abdel Haleem. Oxford: Oxford UP, 2004.

32. Government publication

United States. Office of Management and Budget. <u>A Citizen's Guide to the Federal Budget</u>. Washington: GPO, 1999.

When citing a government publication, list the name of the government (e.g., United States or Minnesota) and the agency that issued the work. Underline the title of a book or pamphlet. Indicate the city of publication. Federal publications are usually printed by the Government Printing Office (GPO) in Washington, DC, but be alert for exceptions.

When the name of an author or an editor appears on a government publication, insert that name after the title and introduce it with the word *By* or the abbreviation *Ed.* to indicate the person's contribution.

33. Law case

Chavez v. Martinez. No. 01-1444. Supreme Ct. of the US. 27 May 2003.

Include the name of the first plaintiff, the abbreviation *v.* for "versus," the name of the first defendant, the case number preceded by the abbreviation *No.,* the name of the deciding court, and the date of the decision. Although law cases are underlined in the text of a paper, they are *not* underlined in works-cited entries.

34. Public law

No Child Left Behind Act of 2001. Pub. L. 107-110. 8 Jan. 2002. Stat. 115.1425.

Include the name of the act, its public law number, the date it was enacted, and its Statutes at Large cataloging number. Notice the use of abbreviations in the example.

Although no works-cited entry is needed for familiar sources such as the U.S. Constitution, an in-text citation should still be included (see page 268).

35. Pamphlet or bulletin

<u>Stucco in Residential Construction</u>. St. Paul: Lath & Plaster Bureau, 2000.

If the pamphlet has an author, begin with the author's name, as you would for a book.

36. Published dissertation

Fukuda, Kay Louise. <u>Differing Perceptions and Constructions of the Meaning of</u>
    <u>Assessment in Education</u>. Diss. Ohio State U, 2001. Ann Arbor: UMI, 2002.

After the title of the dissertation, include the abbreviation *Diss.,* the
name of the university granting the degree, the date of completion, and
the publication information. In the example, *UMI* stands for "University Microfilms International," which publishes many dissertations.

37. Published letter

In general, treat a published letter like a work in an anthology, adding
the date of the letter and the number (if the editor assigned one).

Helen Hunt Jackson. "To Thomas Bailey Aldrich." 4 May 1883. <u>The Indian Reform</u>
    <u>Letters of Helen Hunt Jackson, 1879-1885</u>. Ed. Valerie Sherer Mathes. Norman: U
    of Oklahoma P, 1998. 258-59.

LIVE PERFORMANCES AND DIGITAL RECORDINGS

38. Play performance

<u>Proof</u>. By David Auburn. Dir. Daniel Sullivan. Walter Kerr Theater, New York. 8 Oct. 2002.

Cite the date of the performance you attended.

39. Lecture or presentation

Guinier, Lani. Address. Barbara Jordan Lecture Series. Schwab Auditorium. Pennsylvania
    State U., University Park. 4 Oct. 2004.

Scheiber, Andrew. Class lecture. English 215. Aquinas Hall, U of St. Thomas, St. Paul.
    30 Apr. 2003.

Identify the site and the date of the lecture or presentation. Use the title
if available; otherwise, provide a descriptive label.

40. Interview

Furstenheim, Ursula. Personal interview. 16 Jan. 2003.

Sugo, Misuzu. Telephone interview. 20 Feb. 2003.

For an interview you conducted, give only the name of the person you interviewed and the date of the interview. If the interview was conducted by someone else, add the name of the interviewer, as well as a title, if there is one, or a descriptive label, and the name of the source.

Harryhausen, Ray. Interview with Terry Gross. <u>Fresh Air</u>. Natl. Public Radio. WHYY,

Philadelphia. 6 Jan. 2003.

41. Film

<u>My Big Fat Greek Wedding</u>. Dir. Joel Zwick. IFC, 2002.

The company that produced or distributed the film (IFC, in this case) appears before the year of release. It is not necessary to cite the city in which the production or distribution company is based.

When you want to highlight the contribution of a specific person, list the contributor's name first. Other supplementary information may be included after the title.

Gomez, Ian, perf. <u>My Big Fat Greek Wedding</u>. Screenplay by Nia Vardalos. Dir. Joel

Zwick. IFC, 2002.

42. Radio or television program

When referring to a specific episode, place quotation marks around its title. Underline the title of the program.

"'Barbarian' Forces." <u>Ancient Warriors</u>. Narr. Colgate Salsbury. Dir. Phil Grabsky.

Learning Channel. 1 Jan. 1996.

To highlight a specific contributor, begin the entry with that person's name.

Finch, Nigel, dir. "The Lost Language of Cranes." By David Leavitt. Prod. Ruth Caleb.

Great Performances. PBS. WNET, New York. 24 June 1992.

43. DVD

<u>A River Runs through It</u>. Dir. Robert Redford. Screenplay by Richard Friedenberg. 1992.

DVD. Columbia, 1999.

Cite relevant information about the title and director as you would for a film. Note the original release date of the film, the medium (i.e., DVD), and the release date for the DVD. If the original company producing the film did not release the DVD, list the company that released the DVD instead.

44. Multidisc DVD

<u>More Treasures from American Film Archives, 1894-1931: 50 Films</u>. Prod. Natl. Film

Preservation Foundation. DVD. 3 discs. Image Entertainment, 2004.

List the number of discs after noting the medium. For a particular segment from a multidisc DVD, indicate the title of the work, relevant information about the author or director, and the date the work was initially released. In place of the number of discs, indicate the number of the disc used.

<u>A Bronx Morning</u>. By Jay Leyda. 1931. <u>More Treasures from American Film Archives,</u>

<u>1894-1931: 50 Films</u>. Prod. Natl. Film Preservation Foundation. DVD. Disc 2.

Image Entertainment, 2004.

45. Sound recording on CD

Franklin, Aretha. <u>Amazing Grace: The Complete Recordings</u>. Atlantic, 1999.

For a sound recording on another medium, identify the type (*Audiocassette* or *LP*).

Raitt, Bonnie. <u>Nick of Time</u>. Audiocassette. Capitol, 1989.

When citing a recording of a specific song, begin with the name of the performer, and place the song title in quotation marks. Identify the author(s) after the song title. If the performance is a reissue from an earlier recording, provide the original date of recording (preceded by *Rec.* for "Recorded").

Horne, Lena. "The Man I Love." By George Gershwin and Ira Gershwin. Rec. 15 Dec.

1941. <u>Stormy Weather</u>. BMG, 1990.

IMAGES

46. Work of art

Gauguin, Paul. <u>Ancestors of Tehamana</u>. 1893. Art Institute of Chicago, Chicago.

Identify the artist's name, the title of the work (underlined), the organization or individual holding the work, and the city in which the work is located. The date of creation is optional but, if included, should follow the work's title. For a photograph of a work of art, provide publication information for its source after the name of the city in which the original is located.

47. Cartoon or comic strip

Cheney, Tom. Cartoon. <u>New Yorker</u> 9 June 2003: 93.

Trudeau, Garry. "Doonesbury." Comic strip. <u>Daily Record</u> [Ellensburg] 21
     April 2005: A4.

After the creator's name, place the title of the work (if given) in quotation marks and include the descriptor *Cartoon* or *Comic strip*.

48. Map or chart

<u>Cincinnati and Vicinity</u>. Map. Chicago: RAND, 1996.

Include the title and the appropriate descriptor, *Map* or *Chart*.

49. Advertisement

Nu by Yves Saint Laurent. Advertisement. <u>Allure</u> June 2003: 40.

The name of the product and/or that of the company being advertised is followed by the designation *Advertisement*.

ONLINE BOOKS, ARTICLES, AND DOCUMENTS

Many of the guidelines for documenting online sources are similar to those for print sources. In fact, if a document exists in print as well as online, you must provide the information required for that type of print-based source before providing information about the document's online publication and access. For a source found only in electronic form, provide just the information about its online publication and access.

Electronic publication information

Indicate the title of an Internet site, the date of publication (or most recent update), and the site's sponsoring organization, usually found at the bottom of the site's home page. (See fig. 12.4.)

Title of site

Date of last update   Date of publication

Fig. 12.4. The home page for the Art Institute of Chicago indicates the title of the site (which is also the name of the sponsoring organization), the date of the last update, and the date of publication.

Access information

State the date of access and the URL (Internet address) for a Web site. You can find this information by printing out a page you are using. The date you accessed the site and the URL can be found at the top or the bottom of the printed page. (See fig. 12.5.)

By providing your readers with a complete URL, including the protocol, or access identifier (http, ftp, telnet, news), all punctuation marks, and both path and file names, you tell them how to locate the source.

<http://stanfordmag.org.marapril99/>

<ftp://beowulf.engl.uky.edu/pub/beowulf>

Fig. 12.5. When you print a page from a Web site, the URL and the date of access usually appear at the top or bottom of the page.

Place the address within angle brackets, < >, so that it is clearly separated from any other punctuation in your citation. Divide the address after a slash when it does not fit on a single line. Make sure that the address is accurate; Web browsers (such as Netscape) distinguish between uppercase and lowercase letters in a URL, and they will not be able to find a site if marks such as hyphens and underscores are missing. If the URL for the specific page you want to cite is extremely long, you may use the URL for the site's search page instead. If there is no search page, cite the site's home page, followed by the word *Path,* a colon, and the sequence of links you used. Separate the links with semicolons.

<http://www.essentialsofmusic.com>. Path: Eras; Classical; Composer; Mozart.

Also keep in mind that Internet addresses often change, so double-check the URLs you list before submitting your work. Because sites may disappear, it is wise to print out a hard copy of any material you use as a source.

50. Online book

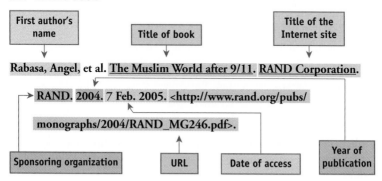

Because there are more than three authors, the abbreviation *et al.* has been used in the example, but listing all names is also acceptable: Rabasa, Angel, Cheryl Benard, Peter Chalk, C. Christine Fair, Theodore W. Karasik, Rollie Lal, Ian O. Lesser, and David E. Thaler. Note that in this example the name of the sponsoring organization is in the title of the Internet site.

When the book has an editor or a translator, list that name after the title. The name of a site editor follows the title of the site.

Flaubert, Gustave. <u>Madame Bovary</u>. Trans. Eleanor Marx Aveling. New York: Modern

Library, 1918. <u>Electronic Text Center</u>. Ed. David Seaman. 2001. Alderman Lib., U of

Virginia. 7 Jan. 2005 <http://etext.lib.virgina.edu/toc/modeng/public/FlaBova.html>.

51. Online book with separate date of print publication

Rohrbough, Malcolm J. <u>Days of Gold: The California Gold Rush and the American</u>

<u>Nation</u>. Berkeley: U of California P, 1997. <u>History E-book Project</u>. American

Council of Learned Societies. 2005. Scholarly Publication Office, U of Michigan

Lib. 17 Feb. 2005 <http://name.umdl.umich.edu/HEB00571>.

52. Part of an online book

Strunk, William, Jr. "Elementary Rules of Usage." <u>The Elements of Style</u>. Ithaca:

Humphrey, 1918. <u>Bartleby.com: Great Books Online</u>. Ed. Steven van Leeuwen.

1999. 6 June 2003 <http://www.bartleby.com/141/strunk.html>.

53. Online encyclopedia entry

"Iran." <u>Encyclopaedia Britannica Online</u>. 2002. Encyclopaedia Britannica. 6 Mar. 2004

<http://search.eb.com/>.

54. Encyclopedia entry from a library subscription service

Turk, Austin T. "Terrorism." <u>Encyclopedia of Crime and Justice</u>. 2nd ed. Ed. Joshua

Dressler. 4 vols. New York: Macmillan Reference USA, 2002. <u>Gale Virtual</u>

<u>Reference Library</u>. Thomson Gale. Pennsylvania State U, Pattee Lib., University

Park. 7 Feb. 2005 <http://find.galegroup.com/gvrl/>.

Include the name of the service (Thomson Gale), the name of the subscriber (Pennsylvania State U, Pattee Lib.), and the subscriber's location (include a state abbreviation if the state is not part of the subscriber's name).

55. Online journal article

Harnack, Andrew, and Gene Kleppinger. "Beyond the MLA Handbook: Documenting

Sources on the Internet." <u>Kairos</u> 1.2 (1996). 14 Aug. 1997 <http://www.english.ttu/

acw/kairos/index.html>.

56. Article from a scholarly archival database

Winnett, Susan. "The Memory of Gender." <u>Signs: Journal of Women and Culture in
    Society</u> 28.1 (2002): 462-63. <u>JSTOR</u>. 14 Nov. 2004 <http://www.jstor.org/search>.

Include the name of the database following all the information about the article. JSTOR and Project Muse are frequently used databases.

57. Online abstract

Landers, Susan J. "FDA Panel Findings Intensify Struggles with Prescribing of
    Antidepressants." <u>American Medical News</u> 47.37 (2004): 1-2. Abstract. ProQuest
    Direct. Washington State U Lib., Pullman. 7 Feb. 2005 <http://proquest.umi.com/>.

Add the word *Abstract* after the page numbers.

58. Online magazine article

Plotz, David. "The Cure for Sinophobia." <u>Slate</u> 4 June 1999. 15 June 1999 <http://
    www.slate.com/StrangeBedfellow/99-06-04/StrangeBedfellow.asp>.

The first date is the publication date; the second is the date of access.

59. Online newspaper article

"Tornadoes Touch Down in S. Illinois." <u>New York Times on the Web</u> 16 Apr. 1998. 20
    May 1998 <http://www.nytimes.com/aponline/a/AP-Illinois-Storms.html>.

When no author is identified, begin with the title of the article. If the article is an editorial, include *Editorial* after the title: "America's Promises." Editorial.

60. Review in an online newspaper

Parent, Marc. "A Father, a Son and an Ideal That's Painfully Tested." Rev. of <u>Scout's
    Honor,</u> by Peter Applebome. <u>New York Times on the Web</u> 6 June 2003. 12 June
    2003 <http://www.nytimes.com/2003/06/06/books/06BOOK.html>.

61. Article from a library subscription database

You can find most of the information you need for a works-cited entry on the abstract page of the article you select. (See fig. 12.6.)

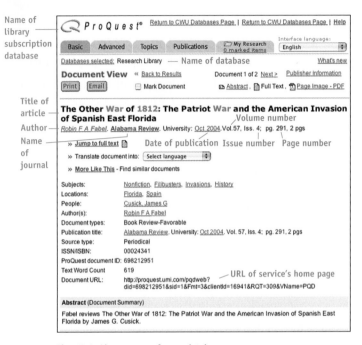

Fig. 12.6. Abstract page from a database.

a. ERIC

Holmes, Julie A. "The Least Restrictive Environment: Is Inclusion Best for All Special
　　Needs Students?" (1999): 1-12. <u>ERIC</u>. Inst. of Education Sciences, Dept. of
　　Education, Washington. ED437760. 6 Nov. 2004 <http://www.eric.ed.gov/>.

Be sure to include the ERIC database number.

b. EBSCO

Folks, Jeffrey J. "Crowd and Self: William Faulkner's Sources of Agency in <u>The Sound</u>
　　<u>and the Fury</u>." <u>Southern Literary Journal</u> 34.2 (2002): 30- . Academic Search
　　Premier. EBSCO. Wright State U, Dunbar Lib., Dayton, OH. 6 June 2003
　　<http://www.epnet.com/>.

For sources that list only the page number on which a work begins,
include that number and a hyphen. Leave a space before the period.

c. LexisNexis

Suggs, Welch. "A Hard Year in College Sports." The Chronicle of Higher Education 19

   Dec. 2003: 37. Academic Universe: News. LexisNexis. U of Texas at Austin, U

   Texas Lib., Austin. 17 July 2004 <http://www.lexis-nexis.com/>.

Provide the name of the LexisNexis database (e.g., Academic Universe or State Capitol) in which you found the article. Add a colon, and then indicate the path you followed for your search (e.g., News, Business, or Legal). Underline both name and path.

d. ProQuest

Fabel, Robin F. A. "The Other War of 1812: The Patriot War and the American Invasion of

   Spanish Florida." Alabama Review. AMA Titles. ProQuest. Central Washington U,

   Brooks Memorial Lib., Ellensburg. 8 Mar. 2005 <http://proquest.umi.com/>.

e. InfoTrac

Priest, Ann-Marie. "Between Being and Nothingness: The 'Astonishing Precipice' of

   Virginia Woolf's Day and Night." Journal of Modern Literature 26.2 (2002-03):

   66-80. InfoTrac College Edition. Gale. Alabama Virtual Library. 12 Jan. 2004

   <http://www.galegroup.com/>.

62. Online congressional document

United States. Cong. Senate. Special Committee on Aging. Global Aging: Opportunity or

   Threat for the U.S. Economy? 108th Cong., 1st sess. S. Hrg. 108-30. Washington:

   GPO, 2003. 7 Jan. 2005 <http://frwebgate.access.gpo.gov/cgibin/

   getdoc.cgi?dbname=108_senate_hearings&docid=f:86497.wais.pdf>.

Provide the number and session of Congress and the type and number of publication. (*S* stands for "Senate"; *H* or *HR* stands for "House of Representatives.")

Bills	S 41, HR 82
Reports	S. Rept. 14, H. Rept. 18
Hearings	S. Hrg. 23, H. Hrg. 25
Resolutions	S. Res. 32, H. Res. 52
Documents	S. Doc. 213, H. Doc. 123

63. Online document from a government office

United States. Dept. of State. Bur. of Democracy, Human Rights, and Labor. <u>Guatemala</u>
<u>Country Report on Human Rights Practices for 1998</u>. Feb. 1999. 1 May 1999
<http://www.state.gov/www/global/human_rights/1998_hrp_report/guatemal.html>.

Begin with the name of the country, state, or city whose government is responsible for the publication and the department or agency that issued it. If a subdivision of the larger organization is responsible, name that subdivision. If an author is identified, provide the name between the title and the date of issue of the document. Place the word *By* before the author's name.

64. Online law case

Tennessee v. Lane. No. 02-1667. Supreme Ct. of the US. 17 May 2004. 28 Jan. 2005
<http://www.usdoj.gov/osg/briefs/2003/3mer/2mer/2002-1667.mer.aa.pdf>.

65. Online public law

Individuals with Disabilities Education Act. Pub. L. 105-17. 4 June 1997. Stat. 104.587-
698. 29 Jan. 2005 <http://www.ed.gov/policy/spece/leg/idea/idea.pdf>.

66. Online sacred text

<u>Sama Veda</u>. Trans. Ralph T. H. Griffith. 1895. <u>Sacred-Texts.com</u>. Ed. John B. Hare. 2 Feb.
2005. 6 Mar. 2005 <http://www.sacred-texts.com>.

ONLINE RECORDINGS AND IMAGES

67. Online music

Moran, Jason. "Jump Up." <u>Same Mother</u>. Blue Note, 2005. 7 Mar. 2005
<http://www.bluenote.com/detail.asp?SelectionID=10376>.

68. Online speech

Malcolm X. "The Ballot or the Bullet." Detroit, 12 Apr. 1964. <u>American Rhetoric: Top</u>
<u>One Hundred Speeches</u>. Ed. Michael E. Eidenmuller. 2005. 14 Jan. 2005
<http://www.americanrhetoric.com/speeches/malcomxballot.htm>.

"12 Apr. 1964" is the date the speech was delivered, "2005" is the year of the speech's electronic publication, and "14 Jan. 2005" is the date of access.

69. Online video

Riefenstahl, Leni, dir. <u>Triumph of the Will</u>. 1935. <u>Movieflix.com</u>. 2005. 17 Feb. 2005
     <http://www.movieflix.com/movie_info.mfx?movie_id=404>.

"1935" is the year in which the movie was originally released, "2005" is the year in which it was made available online, and "17 Feb. 2005" is the date of access.

70. Online television or radio program

"Religion and the American Election." Narr. Tony Hassan. <u>The Religion Report</u>. Radio
     National. 3 Nov. 2004. Transcript. 18 Feb. 2005 <http://www.abc.net.au/rn/talks/
     8.30/relrpt/stories/s1243269.htm>.

If the source is a transcript rather than the visual or audio broadcast, include the word *Transcript* between the date the program aired and the date of access.

71. Online interview

McLaughlin, John. Interview with Wolf Blitzer. <u>CNN</u>. 14 July 2004. 21 Dec. 2004
     <http://www.cnn.com/2004/US/07/14/transcript.mclaughlin/index.html>.

72. Online work of art

Vermeer, Johannes. <u>Young Woman with a Water Pitcher</u>. c. 1660. Metropolitan Museum
     of Art, New York. 2 Oct. 2002 <http://www.metmuseum.org/collection/
     view1.asp?dep_11&item_89%2E15%2E21>.

73. Online photograph

Lange, Dorothea. <u>Migrant Mother</u>. 1936. Prints and Photographs Division, Lib. of
     Congress, Washington. Digital id. fsa 8b29516. 9 Feb. 2005 <http://www.loc.gov/
     rr/print/list/128_migm.html>.

The identification number for a photograph, such as "Digital id. fsa 8b29516" in the example, is included if it is available.

74. Online map or chart

"Virginia 1624." Map. <u>Map Collections 1544-1996</u>. Library of Congress. 26 Apr. 1999
<http://memory.loc.gov/cgibin/map_mp/_ammmem_8kk3::&title_Virginia++>.

"Daily Cigarette Smoking among High School Seniors." Chart. National Center for
Health Statistics. 27 Jan. 2005. Centers for Disease Control and Prevention, US
Dept. of Health and Human Services. 25 Feb. 2005 <http://www.cdc.gov/nchs/
images/hp2000/hdspr/hdslide13.gif>.

75. Online advertisement

Milk Processor Education Program. "Got Milk?" Advertisement. 16 Feb. 2005
<http://www.milkpep.org/programs/lebron.cfm>.

76. Online cartoon or comic strip

Cagle, Daryl. "Social Security Pays 3 to 2." Cartoon. <u>Slate.com</u>. 4 Feb. 2005. 5 Feb. 2005
<http://cagle.slate.msn.com/politicalcartoons/>.

WEB SITES

77. Web site

<u>The Rossetti Archive</u>. Ed. Jerome McGann. 2002. Institute for Advanced Technology in
the Humanities, U of Virginia. 4 June 2003 <http://www.iath.virginia.edu/
rossetti/index.html>.

Include the title of the site (underlined), the name of the editor or editors (if listed), the version number (if given), the date of publication or
of the last update, the name of the sponsoring organization or institution, and the URL. (See pages 293–294.)

78. Web site with incomplete information

<u>Breastcancer.org</u>. 2 Feb. 2005. 5 Feb. 2005 <http://www.breastcancer.org/>.

If a Web site does not provide all the information usually included in a
works-cited entry, list as much as is available.

79. Section of a Web site

Altman, Andrew. "Civil Rights." 3 Feb. 2003. <u>Stanford Encyclopedia of Philosophy</u>. Ed.
    Edward N. Zalta. Spring 2003 ed. Center for the Study of Lang. and Information,
    Stanford U. 12 June 2003 <http://plato.stanford.edu/archives/spr2003/entries/
    civilrights/>.

Mozart, Wolfgang Amadeus. Concerto No. 3 for Horn, K. 447. <u>Essentials of Music</u>. 2001.
    Norton and Sony. 18 Feb. 2005 <http://www.essentialsofmusic.com>. Path: Eras;
    Classical; Composer; Mozart.

If the URL does not vary for different pages of a site, indicate how you
accessed your source by listing the sequence of links after the word *Path*
and a colon.

80. Personal home page

Gladwell, Malcolm. Home page. 8 Mar. 2005 <www.gladwell.com>.

After the name of the site's creator, provide the title or include the
words *Home page*.

ONLINE COMMUNICATIONS

81. E-mail

Peters, Barbara. "Scholarships for Women." E-mail to Rita Martinez. 10 Mar. 2003.

The entry begins with the name of the person who created the
e-mail. Put the subject line of the e-mail message in quotation
marks. The recipient of the message is identified after the words
E-mail to. If the message was sent to you, use *the author* rather than
your name.

82. Discussion group or forum

Schipper, William. "Re: Quirk and Wrenn Grammar." Online posting. 5 Jan. 1995.
    Ansaxnet. 12 Sept. 1996 <http://www.mun.ca/Ansaxdat/>.

Provide the name of the forum (in this case, Ansaxnet) between the
date of posting and the date of access.

83. Newsgroup

May, Michaela. "Questions about RYAs." Online posting. 19 June 1996. 29 June 1996
    <news:alt.soc.generation-x>.

The name of a newsgroup (in angle brackets) begins with the prefix *news* followed by a colon.

84. Web log (blog)

Cuthbertson, Peter. "Are Left and Right Still Alright?" <u>Conservative Commentary</u>.
    7 Feb. 2005. 18 Feb. 2005 <http://concom.blogspot.com/2005/02/
    are-left-and-right-still-alright.html>.

OTHER SOURCES ACCESSED BY COMPUTER

85. CD-ROM

"About <u>Richard III</u>." <u>Cinemania 96</u>. CD-ROM. Redmond: Microsoft, 1996.

Indicate which part of the CD-ROM you are using, and then provide the title of the CD. Begin the entry with the name of the author if one has been provided.

Jordan, June. "Moving Towards Home." <u>Database of Twentieth-Century African American
    Poetry on CD-ROM</u>. CD-ROM. Alexandria: Chadwyck-Healey, 1999.

86. Work from a periodically published database on CD-ROM

Parachini, John V. "Combating Terrorism: The 9/11 Commission Recommendations and
    the National Strategies." <u>RAND Electronically Distributed Documents</u>. CT-231-1.
    CD-ROM. Disc 8. RAND. 2004.

87. DVD-ROM

Klein, Norman M. <u>Bleeding Through: Layers of Los Angeles, 1920-1986</u>. DVD-ROM.
    Karlsruhe: ZKM Center for Art and Media, 2003.

88. Multidisc publication

<u>CDA: The Contextual Data Archive</u>. 2nd ed. CD-ROM. 7 discs. Los Altos: Sociometrics,
    2000.

12c Sample MLA-style paper

(1) Submit a title page if your instructor requires one.

The MLA recommends omitting a title page and instead providing the identification on the first page of the paper (see page 307). Some instructors require a final outline with a paper; this serves as a table of contents. If you are asked to include an outline, prepare a title page as well. A title page usually provides the title of the paper, the author's name, the instructor's name, the name of the course with its section number, and the date—all centered on the page. A sample title page is shown in fig. 12.7.

Starbucks in Vienna: Coffee Cultures at a Crossroads

Andy Pieper

Professor Miller

English 299, Section 1

27 November 2002

Fig. 12.7. Sample title page for an MLA-style paper.

(2) Studying a sample MLA-style paper prepares you to write your own.

Interested in the effects of globalization, Andy Pieper decided to focus his paper on what happens when Starbucks opens coffee shops overseas. As you study his paper, notice how he develops his thesis, considers more than one point of view, and observes the conventions for an MLA-style paper.

TIPS FOR PREPARING AN MLA-STYLE PAPER

- Number all pages (including the first one) with an arabic numeral in the upper-right corner, one-half inch from the top. Put your last name before the page number.

- On the left side of the page, one inch from the top, type your name, the name of your professor, the course number, and the date of submission.

- Double-space between the heading and the title of your paper, which should be centered on the page. If your title consists of two or more lines, double-space them and center each.

- Double-space between your title and the first line of text.

- Indent the first paragraph, and every subsequent paragraph, one-half inch (or five spaces).

- Double-space throughout.

½ inch

1 inch

Pieper 1

The writer's last name and the page number

Andy Pieper   Heading

Professor Miller

English 299, Section 1

27 November 2002

Starbucks in Vienna: Coffee Cultures at a Crossroads

Center the title.

From St. Paul to Sao Paulo, from Rome to Riyadh, and from Johannesburg to Jakarta, world citizens are increasingly being pushed toward a global culture. We are being affected internationally through the media we experience, the food we eat, and the products we consume as multinational corporations act on a world stage (Rothkopf 38). People with disposable incomes can watch MTV in India, catch a Hollywood-produced movie in Australia, purchase a Mickey Mouse doll in Oman, use an Icelandic cell phone to call a friend in Malaysia, send an e-mail from an IBM computer in Russia, and purchase a bucket of Kentucky Fried Chicken in Japan.

Double-space throughout.

All of these examples are signs of <u>globalization,</u> a term coined to describe the increasingly prominent role of large companies in the world marketplace. At the forefront of globalization is the multinational corporation, which David Korten, author of <u>When Corporations Rule the World</u>, defines as a business that takes "on many national identities, maintaining relatively autonomous production and sales facilities in individual countries, establishing local roots and presenting itself in each locality as a good local citizen" (125). Many of these multinationals originate and are headquartered in the United States or other Western nations, but they have means of production or outlets in countries all over the world.

Background information

Use one-inch margins on both sides of the page.

Proponents of globalization claim that this process is advantageous because it makes business efficient and helps foster international ties. Opponents argue that local cultures are damaged and that globalization primarily benefits wealthy

Indent paragraphs five spaces.

1 inch

Pieper 2

corporations in nations already rich. The Starbucks Coffee Corporation is one

example of a multinational company involved in globalization. No matter what

the long-term advantages or disadvantages of globalization prove to be,

Thesis investigating how a Western company like Starbucks establishes itself overseas

shows that a multinational corporation can succeed in offering its own brand of

culture, despite the strength or longevity of the local culture it enters. The

introduction of Starbucks to Vienna illustrates this point because Starbucks offers

an American-style coffee shop experience to a city that is already rich in its own

coffee traditions.

  Throughout the 1990s, Starbucks sought to dominate the American

coffee shop market, and it succeeded. The company has skyrocketed since its

stock debuted in 1992, and within ten years went from revenues of $92 million

to $2.6 billion at the end of fiscal year 2001. Today, it has achieved status as

an American brand that is nearly as familiar as Coca-Cola and McDonald's.

Starbucks has now expanded its goals to include leading the world coffee

shop market. With over 5,000 coffee shops already in operation--nearly

1,200 of which are located outside the United States--Starbucks hopes to

reach revenues of $6 billion by 2005 (Doherty 20). In order to accomplish

this, the coffee corporation intends to open an additional 5,000 stores

worldwide (Scott 1). To reach its goals, Starbucks will have to enter new

A superscript markets in Africa, Asia, and the Middle East,[1] and especially in Europe, where

number

indicates an coffee is a staple of many countries. From the sidewalk cafés of Paris to the

endnote. espresso bars of Venice, Europeans have maintained a long love affair with

coffee--not only with the beverage itself, but also with their own coffeehouses.

Therefore, the continent represents both a challenge and an opportunity for

Starbucks.

  As part of its expansion plan, Starbucks had already opened European

outlets in Great Britain, Germany, and Switzerland by the time it opened a store

in Vienna, the capital of Austria, in the spring of 2002. Under this plan,
Starbucks typically enters into a joint-venture agreement with a local firm,
initially holding a minority stake in the foreign operation, usually twenty percent.
This arrangement shields Starbucks from any large losses incurred when stores
are first opened. In this way, Starbucks presents itself as a local company, when in
fact it is a multinational with similar operations throughout the globe. The local
firm then sets up a few outlets, buying prime real estate and strategically placing
stores near symbols of historic and cultural significance[2]--as in Vienna, where the
first outlet opened across from the city's famous opera house. Once some success
is accomplished, Starbucks buys enough of the foreign-owned branch to control
the company, and proceeds to enlarge rapidly throughout the country (Burke,
Smith, and Wosnitza 47).

> The writer connects a local issue to a worldwide concern.

> Citation of a work by three authors

Vienna, considered by many to be the birthplace of the coffeehouse
tradition, is legendary for its coffee culture. The first Viennese coffeehouses
appeared after invading Turks left sacks of coffee outside the city walls as
they fled in 1683 (Pendergast 10). Intellectual life abounded in elegant cafés
by the nineteenth century, as they became meeting places for early modernists
such as Sigmund Freud and Gustav Klimt, as well as for notable exiles such
as Vladimir Lenin and Leon Trotsky. In Vienna, the people take pride in
the history and enjoy the culture that surrounds the coffeehouse tradition.
Austrians received the opening of Starbucks with mixed emotions:

> Many Viennese sniff that their culture has been infected, that Viennese
> use their 1,900 or so coffee shops to linger and meet, smoke and
> drink, savor the wonders of pastries with cream and marzipan, ponder
> the world, write books and read free newspapers. They drink from
> china cups and order from a waiter, usually in a stained black dinner
> jacket. (Erlanger B3)

> Block quotation

Pieper 4

Skeptics found it difficult to believe that an American brand such as Starbucks could survive in an environment steeped in its own local history of coffee and pride in its heritage, but these skeptics seem to have underestimated Starbucks.

There are several fundamental differences between the Starbucks experience and the traditional experience found in Viennese coffeehouses. Instead of ordering through a server, Starbucks patrons order at an American-style coffee bar. As opposed to more traditional offerings such as Sachertorte and hot goulash, Starbucks sells American-style sweets like blueberry muffins and chocolate-chip cookies. Furthermore, patrons are not allowed to smoke in any Starbucks outlet in order to allow the aroma of coffee to fill each store. Smoking, however, is a large part of the European coffeehouse experience.

These differences add up to two coffee cultures at a crossroads in Vienna. Traditional American offerings are pitted against the offerings of Viennese coffeehouses that have conducted business for centuries. Both Starbucks and independent Viennese coffeehouses sell good coffee, so the primary product being sold is fairly similar. But two essentially different aesthetic experiences and cultures are involved, and they now compete within the same locality. If Austrians had wanted the Starbucks experience previously, they would have had to seek it in other countries. Now, the Viennese cannot help but notice Starbucks. The two coffee cultures have thus become intertwined--competing against each other across not oceans, but streets.

The writer describes and analyzes an image. Illustrating these differences is the following picture of a ticket seller for the opera house across from the first Viennese Starbucks. On break from work, the man is dressed in aristocratic attire from the eighteenth century, but he is sipping his Starbucks coffee out of a paper cup rather than from the kind of

Pieper 5

china cup he would have received in a traditional
Viennese coffeehouse. Moreover, he is smoking a
cigarette outside instead of inside the store, as is
customary in nearly all European coffeehouses.
At first glance, this image appears harmless; it is
a combination of new and old. Upon further
examination, however, it is more than that. The
Starbucks logo, the international symbol of the
American company, hangs above the young man,
with the angle of the photograph making him appear
to be in a Starbucks advertisement. The similar color
green in both the man's jacket and the Starbucks
logo melts the two together even further. Also, the

Photo courtesy of Roland Schlager.

reflection of another man dressed in a business suit can be seen facing the
subject of the photo. The businessman seems to be walking straight toward the
ticket seller. The image can be interpreted as a sign of the times: Starbucks and
its corporate chain of coffee shops, extending their reach and marching straight
into the traditional independent cultures of other countries. The photograph also
shows the apparent willingness of locals to embrace the products and service
Starbucks provides even if it means abandoning a long-established cultural
tradition of their own.

  Starbucks has seen initial success in its Austrian operations with an
estimated 100,000 patrons in its first two months of operation (Erlanger A1).
This result is not uncommon since the market trend over the past decade has
worked overwhelmingly in Starbucks' favor. The company has not failed in any
of the markets into which it has introduced itself. A large part of the reason its
expansion plans are on schedule in Europe is that Starbucks represents

Citation of a
newspaper
article

something different but nevertheless nonthreatening. In this case, a familiar product is being sold from one Western nation to another. The primary difference is in how that product is offered and what other products are offered along with it.

Starbucks also has played an inadvertent role in a movement that now exists throughout Europe, in which coffee shops are opening with an atmosphere noticeably reminiscent of Starbucks. Alwyn Scott, of the <u>Seattle Times</u>, writes, "For proof of Starbucks' impact, look no further than its army of European imitators. New coffee chains are springing up with names--Chicago Coffee, San Francisco Coffee, Coffee Shop--that suggest American style, if not Seattle" (F1). Therefore, the traditional coffee cultures that reside in countries like Austria, France, and Italy compete with American culture from two fronts: Starbucks and its imitators.

The writer examines an opposing claim and refutes it.

Competition alone is not necessarily bad. It is essential to capitalist economies. Without competition, there is no freedom of choice, and little innovation. People are left with the same options over and over again, while nothing new emerges. Free-market competition encourages companies to adapt to the changing needs and wants of populations. By opening stores in cities like Vienna, Starbucks could claim that it is simply offering the Viennese a choice that responds to their changing needs and that they are not compelled to accept this choice. It could even claim that it fosters diversity by increasing the options for consumers and creating an expanded coffee culture that includes not only the traditional coffeehouses but also the Americanized experience found in Starbucks and its imitators. However, Starbucks wields an immense amount of power in the regions where it establishes itself. This power is seen in its brand name--familiar from South Korea to Mexico--and in its wealth. Its coffee shops also present a powerful cultural experience, one that immerses the consumer in an

American-style environment. By expanding its base to include countries all over the world, Starbucks is expanding the role of American culture abroad. This expansion diversifies the cultures of other countries, provides competition for existing coffee cultures, and offers new options to consumers. But, at some point, competition could become hegemony. In other words, the exportation of American culture occurs right along with the exportation of American products. Such expansion of American goods and services could overwhelm another culture, creating a more homogenous, Americanized culture that blurs the distinctiveness of the native one. Increasingly, foreign markets are becoming saturated with Western goods from multinational corporations, which have spread their products--whatever they may be--to places around the globe. Some suggest that this occurrence is working toward the establishment of a single global culture. According to Hugh Mackay, of the Open University, "that 'global culture' is not something which draws in any even or uniform way on the vast diversity of cultures in the world . . . but, rather, consists of the global dissemination of US or Western culture--the complete opposite of diversity" (60).

Three ellipsis points mark an omission.

So far, Starbucks has been able to coexist with the traditional coffee culture in Vienna; the city's architecture, art, and beauty are likely to remain intact no matter how many stores Starbucks opens there. Because a relatively familiar product is passing from one Western nation to another in this case, and people have both the means to buy it and the freedom to reject it, cultural change may be limited to the Viennese getting used to drinking coffee out of paper cups and standing in the street to smoke. The social and economic effects of globalization may be more serious, as Mackay suggests, when multinational corporations operate in developing nations and limited means give people fewer choices. The lasting effects of globalization have yet to be seen. But it is clear that

The writer's conclusion is drawn from research reported on previous pages.

the already ubiquitous green mermaid, like the pervasive golden arches, is going to become even easier to find. And if Starbucks can flourish in an environment with a well-established local coffee culture of its own, then it is feasible that other multinational corporations will export not only their products but also the cultural experience that accompanies those products, no matter how strong the local culture may be.

1 inch

Notes   Center the heading.

[1]It should be noted that in Saudi Arabia, Starbucks, along with other

multinational corporations, tries to conform to the existing cultural mores. Upon

its introduction into Riyadh, Starbucks changed its logo (normally a crowned

mermaid in a green circle) to one that did not include a depiction of a female

since any representations of females are considered pornography (King,

"Sellout"). In addition, stores make women enter through separate doors as well

as drink their coffee in separate areas. The company has defended itself by stating,

"While Starbucks adheres to the local customs by providing separate entrances,

service and seating, all our stores provide equal amenities, service, menu and

seating to both men and women" (King, "Arabia's" A27).

[2]In the fall of 2000, Starbucks opened an outlet in Beijing's Forbidden City,

which was built early in the fifteenth century and listed as the world's largest

imperial palace. Administrators of the site agreed to rent space to the Starbucks

Chinese affiliate as a way of improving services. After news of the opening

spread, a survey indicated that "over 70 percent of nearly 60,000 people surveyed

were opposed to the café's entry . . . the main reason being the damaging effects to

Chinese cultural heritage and its atmosphere" ("Starbucks").

Numbers
on notes
match the
superscript
numbers in
the body of
the paper.

1 inch

Center the heading.   Works Cited

Alphabetize entries according to the authors' last names.

Burke, Greg, Stacey Vanek Smith, and Regine Wosnitza. "Whole Latte Shakin':
Can U.S. Gourmet Coffee Chain Starbucks Convert Continental Europe's
Café Society? It's Ready to Try." <u>Time International</u>. 9 Apr. 2001: 47.

Doherty, Jacqueline. "Make It Decaf: Despite Heavy Revenue Gains, Starbucks'
Earnings Growth Is Slowing." <u>Barrons</u>. 20 May 2002: 20.

Indent subsequent lines of each entry one-half inch or five spaces.

Erlanger, Steven. "An American Coffeehouse (or 4) in Vienna." <u>New York Times</u>.
1 June 2002: A1+.

King, Colbert I. "Saudi Arabia's Apartheid (Cont'd)." Editorial. <u>Washington Post</u>.
19 Jan. 2002, final ed.: A27.

Three hyphens indicate the same author as in the preceding entry.

---. "The Saudi Sellout." Editorial. <u>Washington Post</u>. 26 Jan. 2002, final ed.: A23.

Korten, David C. <u>When Corporations Rule the World</u>. West Hartford: Kumarian,
1995.

Mackay, Hugh. "The Globalization of Culture?" <u>A Globalizing World? Culture,
Economics, Politics</u>. Ed. David Held. New York: Routledge, 2000. 47-84.

Pendergast, Mark. <u>Uncommon Grounds: The History of Coffee and How It
Transformed Our World</u>. New York: Basic, 1999.

Rothkopf, David. "In Praise of Cultural Imperialism?" <u>Foreign Policy</u> 107
(1997): 38-52.

Scott, Alwyn. "A Shot of Americana; Starbucks Jolts Europe's Coffeehouses."
<u>Seattle Times</u>. 19 May 2002: F1.

"Starbucks Café in Forbidden City Under Fire." <u>People's Daily Online</u>. 24 Nov.

Place a URL within angle brackets.

2000. 3 June 2002 <http://english.peopledaily.com.cn/200011/24/
eng20001124_56044.html>.

13

APA DOCUMENTATION

The American Psychological Association (APA) publishes a style guide entitled *Publication Manual of the American Psychological Association.* Its documentation system (called an *author-date system*) is used for work in psychology and many other disciplines, including education, economics, and sociology. Updates to the style guide are provided at www.apastyle.org. This chapter includes

- guidelines for citing sources within the text of a paper (13a),
- guidelines for documenting sources in a reference list (13b), and
- a sample student paper (13c).

13a APA-style in-text citations

APA-style in-text citations usually include just the last name(s) of the author(s) of the work and the year of publication. However, be sure to specify the page number(s) for any quotations you use in your paper. The abbreviation *p.* (for "page") or *pp.* (for "pages") should precede the number(s). If you do not know the author's name, use a shortened version of the source's title instead. If your readers want to find more information about your source, they will look for the author's name, or in its absence, the title of the work, in the bibliography at the end of your paper.

You will likely consult a variety of sources for your research paper. The following examples are representative of the types of in-text citations you can expect to use.

1. Work by one author

A prominent neurologist has concluded, "Pushing back the age at which the widespread form of Alzheimer's strikes—from, say, age 70 to age 90—would be nearly tantamount to a cure" (Kosik, 1999, p. 17).

OR

Kosik (1999) maintains, "Pushing back the age at which the widespread form of Alzheimer's strikes—from, say, age 70 to age 90—would be nearly tantamount to a cure" (p. 17).

Use commas within a parenthetical citation to separate the author's name from the date and the date from the page number(s). Include a page number or numbers only when you are quoting directly from the source.

2. Work by two authors

Whether or not children spend time in day care, their development in early childhood is determined primarily by the nature of the care they receive from parents (Darvas & Walsh, 2002).

Use an ampersand (&) to separate the authors' names.

3. Work by more than two authors

The speech of Pittsburgh, Pennsylvania is called *Pittsburghese* (Johnstone, Bhasin, & Wittkofski, 2002).

For works with three to five authors, cite all the authors the first time the work is referred to, but in subsequent references give only the last name of the first author followed by *et al.* (meaning "and others"): Johnstone et al. For works with six or more authors, provide only the last name of the first author followed by *et al.*, even in the first citation.

4. Anonymous work

Use a shortened version of the title to identify an anonymous work.

Chronic insomnia often requires medical intervention ("Sleep," 2003).

This citation refers to an article identified in the bibliography as "Sleep disorders: Standard methods of treatment."

If the word *Anonymous* is used in the source itself to designate the author, it appears in place of an author's name.

The documents could damage the governor's reputation (Anonymous, 2001).

5. Two or more works by different authors in the same parenthetical citation

In informal conversation, a speaker might use the word *like* to focus the listener's

attention (Eriksson, 1995; Ferrar & Bell, 1995).

Use a semicolon to separate citations, and arrange them in alphabetical order.

6. Two or more works by the same author in the same parenthetical citation

The amygdala is active when a person experiences fear or anger (Carey, 2001, 2002).

Bayard (1995a, 1995b) discusses the acquisition of English in New Zealand.

Order the dates of publication of works by the same author from earliest to most recent; however, if the works have the same publication date, distinguish the dates with lowercase letters (*a, b, c,* and so on) assigned according to the order in which the entries for the works are listed in your paper's bibliography (see page 320).

7. Personal communication

State educational outcomes are often interpreted differently by teachers in the same

school (J. K. Jurgensen, personal communication, May 4, 2003).

Personal communications include letters, memos, e-mail messages, personal interviews, and telephone conversations. These sources are cited in the text only; they do not appear in the reference list.

13b APA-style reference list

All of the works you cite should be listed at the end of your paper, beginning on a separate page with the heading "References." The following tips will help you prepare your list.

TIPS FOR PREPARING A REFERENCE LIST

- Center the heading "References" one inch from the top of the page.
- Include only those sources you explicitly cited in your paper. Do not, however, include entries in your reference list for any personal communications you cited.
- Arrange the list of works alphabetically by the author's last name.
- If a source has more than one author, alphabetize by the last name of the first author.
- If you use more than one work by the same author(s), arrange them according to the date of publication, placing the entry with the earliest date first. If two or more works by the same author(s) have the same publication date, the entries are arranged so that the titles of the works are in alphabetical order, according to the first important word in each title; lowercase letters *a, b, c,* and so on are then added to the date to distinguish the works.
- When an author's name appears both in a one-author entry and first in a multiple-author entry, place the one-author entry first.
- For a work without an author, alphabetize the entry according to the first important word in the title.
- Type the first line of each entry flush with the left margin and indent subsequent lines one-half inch or five spaces (a hanging indent).
- Double-space throughout—between lines of each entry and between entries.

Whether you are submitting an APA-style paper in a college course or preparing a manuscript for publication, you can be guided by the format of the following sample entries. For additional types of entries, including those documenting sources found through InfoTrac, visit www.harbrace.com.

Directory of APA-Style Entries for the Reference List

The following guidelines are for books, articles, and most electronic sources. For additional guidelines for documenting electronic sources, see page 332.

When preparing entries for your reference list, be sure to copy the bibliographic information directly from the sources (e.g., the title page of a book). (See fig. 13.1, on page 326.)

General Documentation Guidelines for Print-Based Sources

Author or Editor

One author. Use the author's first initial and middle initial (if given) and his or her last name. Place the last name before the initials, and follow it with a comma. Include a space between the first and middle initials. Any abbreviation or number that is part of a name, such as *Jr.* or *II*, is placed after a comma following the initials. Indicate the end of this information unit with a single period.

Walters, D. M.
Thayer-Smith, M. S.
Villa, R. P., Jr.

Two to six authors. Invert the last names and initials of all authors. Use a comma to separate names from initials, and use an ampersand (&) (in addition to the comma) before the last name of the last author.

Vifian, I. R., & Kikuchi, K.
Kempf, A. R., Cusack, R., & Evans, T. G.

Seven or more authors. List the names of the first six authors, but substitute *et al.* for the remaining names.	Bauer, S. E., Berry, L., Hacket, N. P., Bach, R., Price, T. M., Brown, J. B., et al.
Corporate or group author. Provide the author's full name.	Hutton Arts Foundation. Center for Neuroscience.
Editor. If a work has an editor or editors instead of an author or authors, include the abbreviation *Ed.* for "editor" or *Eds.* for "editors" in parentheses after the name(s).	Harris, B. E. (Ed.). Stroud, D. F., & Holst, L. F. (Eds.).

Publication Date

Books and journals. Provide the publication date in parentheses, placing a period after the closing parenthesis. For books, this date can be found on the copyright page, which is the page following the title page (see fig. 13.2, on page 327). For journals, the publication date can be found at the bottom of the first page of the article (see fig. 13.3, on page 328). For a work that has been accepted for publication but has not yet been published, place *in press* in parentheses. For a work without a date of publication, use *n.d.* in parentheses.	(2004). (in press). (n.d.).
Magazines and newspapers. For monthly publications, provide both the year and the month, separated by a comma. For daily publications, provide the year, month, and day. Use a comma between the year and the month.	(2005, January). (2004, June 22).
Conferences and meetings. If a paper presented at a conference, symposium, or professional meeting is published, the publication date is given as the year only, in parentheses.	(2004). (2004, September).

(continued on page 324)

Publication Date *(continued from page 323)*

For unpublished papers, provide the year and the month in which the gathering occurred, separated by a comma.

Title

Books. Capitalize only the first word and any proper nouns in a book title. Italicize the entire title, and place a period at the end of this information unit.

Language and the mind.
Avoiding work-related stress.

Journals, magazines, or newspapers. Capitalize all major words in the name of a journal, magazine, or newspaper. Italicize the entire name and place a comma after it.

Journal of Child Psychology,
Psychology Today,
Los Angeles Times,

Articles and chapters. Do not italicize the titles of short works such as journal articles or book chapters. In a bibliographic entry, titles of articles and chapters appear before book titles and the names of journals, magazines, or newspapers. Capitalize only the first word of the title and any proper nouns.

Treating posttraumatic stress disorder.

Subtitles. Always include any subtitle provided for a source. Use a colon to separate a main title and a subtitle. Capitalize only the first word of the subtitle and any proper nouns.

Reading images: The grammar of visual design.
Living in Baghdad: Realities and restrictions.

Volume, Issue, Chapter, and Page Numbers

Journal volumes and issue numbers. A journal paginated *continuously* designates only the first page of the first issue in a volume as page 1. The first page of a subsequent issue in the same volume is given the page number that follows the last page number of the previous issue. In contrast, each issue of a journal paginated

Journal of Applied Social Psychology,
32,
Behavior Therapy, 33(2),

separately begins with page 1. When you use an article from a journal paginated continuously, provide only the volume number (italicized). When you use an article from a journal paginated separately, include the issue number (placed in parentheses) as well as the volume number. Only the volume number is italicized. A comma follows this unit of information.

Book chapters. Provide the numbers of the first and last pages of the relevant chapter preceded by the abbreviation *pp.* (for "pages"). Use an en dash (a short dash) between the page numbers, and place them in parentheses after the title of the book.

New communitarian thinking (pp. 126–140).

Articles. List the page numbers after the comma that follows the volume or issue number.

TESOL Quarterly, 34(2), 213–238.

Publication Data

City and state. Identify the city in which the publisher of the work is located. If two or more cities are given on the title page, use the first one listed. Add the two-letter U.S. Postal Service abbreviation for the state unless the city is one of the following: Baltimore, Boston, Chicago, Los Angeles, New York, Philadelphia, or San Francisco. If the publisher is a university press whose name mentions a state, do not include the state abbreviation. When a work has been published in a city outside the United States, add the name of the country unless the city is Amsterdam, Jerusalem, London, Milan, Moscow, Paris, Rome,

Boston:

Lancaster, PA:

University Park: Pennsylvania State University Press.

Oxford, England:

(continued on page 326)

Publication Data *(continued from page 325)*

Stockholm, Tokyo, or Vienna—in these cases, the name of the city alone is sufficient.

Publisher's name. Provide only enough of the publisher's name so that it can be identified clearly. Omit words such as *Publishers* and abbreviations such as *Inc.* However, include *Books* and *Press* when they are part of the publisher's name. The publisher's name follows the city and state or country, after a colon. A period ends this unit of information.

New Haven, CT: Yale University Press.

New York: Harcourt.

Cambridge, England: Cambridge University Press.

Title	Working with People with Learning Disabilities
Subtitle	Theory and Practice
Authors	*David Thomas and Honor Woods*

Publisher	Jessica Kingsley Publishers
Cities of publication	London and New York

Fig. 13.1. The title page of a book provides most of the information necessary for creating a bibliographic entry for a research paper.

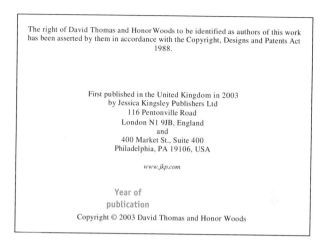

The right of David Thomas and Honor Woods to be identified as authors of this work has been asserted by them in accordance with the Copyright, Designs and Patents Act 1988.

First published in the United Kingdom in 2003
by Jessica Kingsley Publishers Ltd
116 Pentonville Road
London N1 9JB, England
and
400 Market St., Suite 400
Philadelphia, PA 19106, USA

www.jkp.com

Year of
publication

Copyright © 2003 David Thomas and Honor Woods

Fig. 13.2. Look for a book's date of publication on the copyright page, which follows the title page.

BOOKS

1. Book by one author

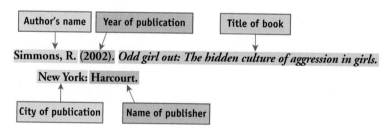

Author's name   Year of publication   Title of book

Simmons, R. (2002). *Odd girl out: The hidden culture of aggression in girls.*

New York: Harcourt.

City of publication   Name of publisher

2. Book by two or more authors

Thomas, D., & Woods, H. (2003). *Working with people with disabilities: Theory and practice.* London: Jessica Kingsley.

If there are more than six authors, list the first six names and use the abbreviation *et al.* in place of the remaining names (see page 323).

Title **Work Attitudes of American Indians**

Author CHARLES N. WEAVER[1]
School of Business and Administration
St. Mary's University

Analysis of 22 samples representative of the labor force of the continental United States shows few differences in 13 work attitudes between American Indians ($n = 732$) and European Americans ($n = 12,810$). American Indians were more insecure in their jobs and were less satisfied with their financial situation. They were more likely to prefer a job that offers a high income and chances for promotion. As their increasing earnings reach parity and the effects of discrimination and prejudice lessen, these few differences should diminish.

There are many remarkable features about American Indians that could attract the attention of social scientists. Their population fell by an astonishing 97% from 10 million in 1492 (Dobyns, 1976) to less than 250,000 in 1900 (U.S. Census Bureau, 1993), leading many to believe that they were on the verge of extinction (Office of American Indian Trust, 1999). But, their numbers grew slowly to 377,000 in 1950 (U.S. Census Bureau, 1993), at which time they were the worst fed, worst clad, worst housed, and worst schooled, and received the poorest medical care and government services of any racial group in the United States (Embry, 1956). In 1950, life expectancy was 68 years for Whites and 60 years for Blacks, but only 17 years for reservation Indians (Embry, 1956). Then, from 1950 to 1990, their population accelerated to almost 2 million (U.S. Census Bureau, 1993), and from 1990 to 1997, it grew 12% to 2.3 million, making them the fastest growing segment of the United States population (U.S. Census Bureau, 1997). "Today, [they] are in a period of social, cultural, economic, and political revitalization" (Office of American Indian Trust, 1999, p.1). Their number is expected to be 4.4 million by 2050 (U.S. Census Bureau, 1997).

The main source of demographic and labor force information about American Indians is the federal government. Since the first complete census of American Indians in 1890 (U.S. Census Bureau, 1993), they have been classified for reporting purposes in various ways, such as the 25 largest tribes; American Indians, Eskimos, and Aleuts; and American Indians and Alaska Natives. From reports based on these various methods of classification, a unique and interesting profile of today's American Indian emerges. About half of them live on either side of

[1]Correspondence concerning this article should be addressed to Charles N. Weaver, School of Business and Administration, One Camino Santa Maria, St. Mary's University, San Antonio, TX 78228-8607.

Year of
publication ——— Volume number

Name of journal

432

————Issue number

Journal of Applied Social Psychology, 2003, 33, 2, pp. 432-443.——Page numbers

Fig. 13.3. The first page of a journal article provides the information needed to complete a bibliographic entry for that source.

3. Book with editor(s)

Antony, M. M., Rachman, S., Richter, M. A., & Swinson, R. P. (Eds.). (1998). *Obsessive-compulsive disorder.* New York: Guilford Press.

4. Book with a corporate or group author

U.S. War Department. (2003). *Official military atlas of the Civil War*. New York: Barnes & Noble.

When the author and the publisher of a book are the same, use the publisher's name at the beginning of the entry and *Author* at the end.

American Psychiatric Association. (1995). *American Psychiatric Association capitation handbook*. Washington, DC: Author.

5. Edition after the first

Cember, H. (1996). *Introduction to health physics* (3rd ed.). New York: McGraw-Hill.

Identify the edition in parentheses immediately after the title. Use abbreviations: *2nd, 3rd,* and so on for the edition number and *ed.* for "edition."

6. Translation

Freud, S. (1999). *The interpretation of dreams* (J. Crick, Trans.). New York: Oxford University Press. (Original work published 1899)

A period follows the name of the publisher but not the parenthetical note about the original publication date.

7. Multivolume work

Doyle, A. C. (2003). *The complete Sherlock Holmes* (Vols. 1 & 2). New York: Barnes & Noble.

If the multivolume work was published over a period of more than one year, use the range of years for the publication date.

Hawthorne, Nathaniel. (1962–1997). *The centenary edition of the works of Nathaniel Hawthorne* (Vols. 1–23). Columbus: Ohio University Press.

8. Government report

Executive Office of the President. (2003). *Economic report of the President, 2003* (GPO Publication No. 040-000-0760-1). Washington, DC: U.S. Government Printing Office.

9. Selection from an edited book

Wolfe, A. (1996). Human nature and the quest for community. In A. Etzioni (Ed.), *New communitarian thinking* (pp. 126–140). Charlottesville: University Press of Virginia.

Italicize the book title but not the title of the selection.

10. Selection from a reference book

Wickens, D. (2001). Classical conditioning. In *The Corsini encyclopedia of psychology and behavioral science* (Vol. 1, pp. 293–298). New York: John Wiley.

ARTICLES IN PRINT

11. Article with one author in a journal with continuous pagination

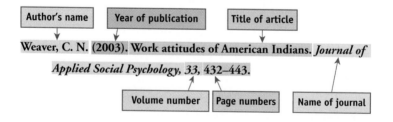

Figure 13.3 (on page 328) shows where the information for this type of entry is found on the first page of an article.

12. Article with two authors in a journal with each issue paginated separately

Rudisill, J. R., & Edwards, J. M. (2002). Coping with job transitions. *Consulting Psychology Journal, 54*(1), 55–62.

13. Article with three to six authors

Frost, R. O., Steketee, G., & Williams, L. (2002). Compulsive buying, compulsive hoarding, and obsessive-compulsive disorder. *Behavior Therapy, 33*(2), 201–213.

14. Article with more than six authors

Reddy, S. K., Arora, M., Perry, C. L., Nair, B., Kohli, A., Lytle, L. A., et al. (2002). Tobacco and alcohol use outcomes of a school-based intervention in New Delhi. *American Journal of Health Behavior, 26,* 173–181.

15. Article in a monthly, biweekly, or weekly magazine

Winson, J. (2002, June). The meaning of dreams. *Scientific American, 12,* 54–61.

For magazines published weekly or biweekly, add the day of the issue: (2003, May 8).

16. Article in a newspaper

Liptak, A. (2002, June 16). Polygamist's custody fight raises many issues. *The New York Times,* p. A20.

Include the letter indicating the section with the page number.

17. Letter to the editor

Mancall, M. (2002, June 17). Answer to cynicism [Letter to the editor]. *The New York Times,* p. A20.

After the title, indicate within brackets that the work is a letter to the editor.

18. Book review

Kamil, M. L. (2002). The state of reading research [Review of the book *Progress in understanding reading: Scientific foundations and new frontiers*]. *American Journal of Psychology, 115,* 451–458.

SOURCES PRODUCED FOR ACCESS BY COMPUTER

The APA guidelines for electronic sources are similar to those for print sources. Exceptions are explained after the sample entries that follow. Information about when and how the source was retrieved appears at the end. Notice that the period that normally ends an entry is omitted after a URL because trailing periods can cause difficulty in retrieving files. If a URL has to continue on a new line, break it before a period or after a slash.

19. Article in a journal published only online

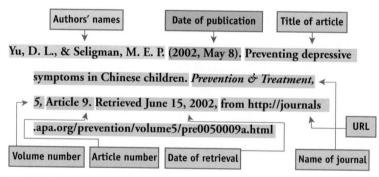

| Authors' names | Date of publication | Title of article |

Yu, D. L., & Seligman, M. E. P. (2002, May 8). Preventing depressive symptoms in Chinese children. *Prevention & Treatment,* 5, Article 9. Retrieved June 15, 2002, from http://journals .apa.org/prevention/volume5/pre0050009a.html

| Volume number | Article number | Date of retrieval | Name of journal | URL |

20. Online article based on a print source

Lindsay, D. S., & Poole, D. A. (2001). Children's eyewitness reports after exposure to misinformation from parents [Electronic version]. *Journal of Experimental Psychology: Applied, 7*(1), 27–50.

The words in square brackets indicate that the article came from the electronic version of a journal that is also published in print.

21. Article in an online newspaper

McGrath, C. (2002, June 15). Father time. *New York Times.* Retrieved June 15, 2002, from http://nytimes.com/pages/science/index.html

22. Message posted to a newsgroup

Korniejczuk, V. (2002, June 11). Clinical psychology and psychiatry—what's the

difference? [Msg 4]. Message posted to news://sci.psychology.theory

Provide the message number within square brackets after the message title.

23. Message posted to a forum or discussion group

Vellenzer, G. (2004, January 24). Synonyms of entreaty [Msg 2]. Message posted to

http://groups.google.com/groups?selm=MPG.1a7cacccd54e9c27989b95%40news

.CIS.DFN.DE&output=gplain

24. Article from a database

Kim, Y., & Seidlitz, L. (2002). Spirituality moderates the effect of stress on emotional and

physical adjustment. *Personality & Individual Differences, 32*(8), 1377–1390.

Retrieved December 6, 2004, from PsycINFO database.

Most of the information you will need for documenting an article from a database can be found on the abstract page (see fig. 13.4). Do not confuse the vendor of the database (EBSCO), also referred to as a library subscription service, with the name of the database (PsycINFO).

25. Authored document from a Web site

Harvey, S. (1994, September). *Dynamic play therapy: An integrated expressive arts*

approach to the family treatment of infants and toddlers. Retrieved December 28,

2003, from http://www.zerotothree.org/aboutus/dialogue.html

When the document is from a large Web site, such as one sponsored by a university or government body, provide the name of the host organization before the URL.

Darling, C. (2002). *Guide to grammar and writing.* Retrieved September 12, 2003, from

Capital Community College Web site: http://cctc2.commnet.edu/grammar/

modifiers.htm

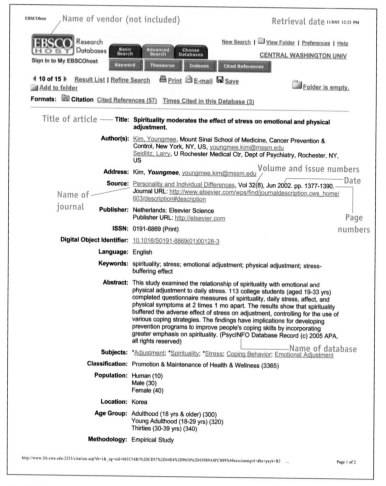

Fig. 13.4. Computer printout of an abstract page.

26. Document with no identified author from a Web site

American School Counselor Association. (2004). *Ethical standards for school*

    counselors. Retrieved December 6, 2004, from http://www.schoolcounselor.org/

    content.asp?contentid=173

Use the name of the organization hosting the Web site as the author of the document. In fig. 13.5, the name of the organization appears in the upper-left corner. If a date is provided (as there is on the printout in fig. 13.5, just before the preamble), place it in parentheses. If there is no date listed, use the abbreviation *n.d.* The date of retrieval and the URL are located at the bottom of the computer printout in fig. 13.5, but they will sometimes appear at the top.

27. Online government publication from GPO Access database

U.S. General Accounting Office. (2000, April). Federal prisons: Containing health care

    costs for an increasing inmate population (Publication No. GAO/T-GGD-00-112).

    Retrieved August 24, 2005, from General Accounting Office Reports Online via

    GPO Access: http://www.gpoaccess.gaoreports/index/html

28. Personal communication

Personal communications such as e-mail messages, letters, telephone conversations, and personal interviews do not appear in the reference list but should be cited in the text as follows: (S. L. Johnson, personal communication, September 3, 2003).

OTHER SOURCES

29. Motion picture

Smith, M. (Producer/Writer), & Gaviria, M. (Producer/Director). (2001). *Medicating kids*

    [Motion picture]. (Available from the Public Broadcasting Service, 1320 Braddock

    Place, Alexandria, VA 22314)

Begin with the primary contributor(s), identifying the nature of the contribution. Follow with the release date, the title, and the descriptive label in square brackets. For a film with limited distribution, provide,

Organization hosting the site

Title of document

URL http://www.schoolcounselor.org/content.asp?contentid=173

Retrieval date

Fig. 13.5. Computer printout of a Web document with no identified author.

within parentheses, information about how it can be obtained. For a widely distributed film, indicate the country where it was produced and the name of the studio, after the descriptive label: [Motion picture]. United States: Paramount Pictures.

30. Television program

Holt, S. (Producer). (2002, October 1). *The mysterious lives of caves* [Television

broadcast]. Alexandria, VA: Public Broadcasting Service.

Give the title of the program in italics. If citing an entire series (e.g., *Nova* or *The West Wing*), cite the producer for the series as a whole, and use the descriptive label *Television series* in the square brackets.

13c APA-style student paper

The APA recognizes that a paper may have to be modified so that it adheres to an instructor's requirements. The following boxes offer tips for preparing a title page and an abstract page for a typical student paper. For tips on preparing a reference list, see page 320.

↕ ½ inch

Place the page header five spaces from the page number.

Running Head: SLEEP AND MEMORY

The running head includes no more than fifty characters.

←——————→

Use 1-inch margins on both sides of the page.

If required, the course name and number replace the affiliation.

The Sleep and Memory Connection

Nikki Krzmarzick

University of St. Thomas

TIPS FOR PREPARING THE TITLE PAGE OF AN APA-STYLE PAPER

- Place the number 1 (to indicate that this is the first page) an inch from the right side of the paper and a half inch from the top.

- Place a **manuscript page header** (the first two or three words of the title) in the upper-right corner, five spaces before the page number. The manuscript page header should appear on all subsequent pages along with the appropriate page number.

- Below the page header but on the left side of the page, list the **running head,** a shortened version of the title (no more than fifty characters). Use *all* uppercase letters for the running head.

- Place the title in the center of the page, with your name below it. You may include your affiliation and a course name or number if your instructor requests one. Double-space these lines.

1 inch

½ inch

Sleep and Memory   2

Abstract

Center the heading.

Current research indicates that sleep plays a role in learning and memory. Results of research cited within the paper suggest that sleep affects the acquisition of knowledge and skills needed to perform perceptual, critical, and creative-thinking tasks. This topic's relevance to college students is addressed, and practical applications of findings to that end are discussed. Further research is necessary to establish how the brain acquires, consolidates, and organizes information for later retrieval.

The maximum length for an abstract is 120 words.

TIPS FOR PREPARING THE ABSTRACT AND THE BODY OF AN APA-STYLE PAPER

- Place the number 2 an inch from the right side of the paper and a half inch from the top on the abstract page.
- Place a manuscript page header five spaces to the left of the page number.
- Center the word *Abstract* one inch from the top of the paper.
- Be sure that the abstract (a short summary) is no more than 120 words. For advice on summarizing, see **11d(4)**.
- Double-space throughout the body of the abstract. Do not indent the first line of the abstract.
- Place the number 3 on the first page of the body of the paper, along with the manuscript page header.
- Center the title of the paper one inch from the top of the page.
- Use one-inch margins on both the left and right sides of your paper.
- Double-space throughout the body of the paper, indenting each paragraph one-half inch or five to seven spaces.

1 inch

Center the
title.

The Sleep and Memory Connection

Double-space
throughout.

It is finals week. In 24 hours, Kyle Rosemount has a biology exam. He is not

sure he is on track to pass the class, so a good grade is essential. He regrets not

starting earlier in the week but has resolved to stay up all night reviewing course

material. This method will afford him almost 16 hours of study time. Rosemount

reasons that this amount of time will be sufficient and is almost positive he would

Use 1-inch
margins on
both sides.

not have spent more hours with the material had he started exam preparations the

previous week.

This scenario is all too familiar to college students, and many have used the

same logic as Rosemount in thinking that the total number of hours spent

studying is more critical than when that studying takes place. It seems to make

sense that the more time one spends studying the subject matter, the better one

will retain the information. But current research on the possibility of a

relationship between sleep and memory suggests that this assumption is not

necessarily true. In fact, irregular sleep patterns and cram sessions may actually

be sabotaging students' efforts.

Thesis and
background
information

If there is a connection between sleep and memory, then getting regular sleep

may be essential for memory consolidation and for optimal performance on both

critical- and creative-thinking tasks. An exploration of this possibility requires a basic

understanding of the sleep cycle. To an observer, a sleeping person appears passive,

unresponsive, and essentially isolated from the rest of the world and its barrage of

stimuli. While it is true that humans are unaware of most of what is happening

around them during sleep, the brain is far from inactive. It can be as active during

sleep as in a waking state. When it is asleep, the rate and type of neuronal firings

(electrical activity) change. The brain cycles through four sleep stages before moving

into REM sleep. All of this occurs at relatively predictable intervals while a person is

asleep. Generally, it takes about 90 minutes to cycle through the four stages of sleep

Citation of a
work by one
author

and one REM episode, each with distinct neuronal characteristics (Hobson, 1989).

Figure 1 graphs these stages for an 8-hour sleep period.

Sleep and Memory 4

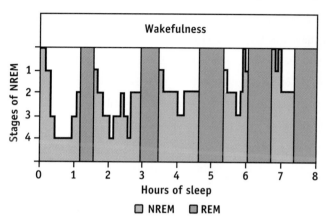

Figure 1. Sleep stages. *Note.* From *Good sleep, good learning, good life,*
by Piotr Wozniak, July 2000. Retrieved September 19, 2002, from
http://www.supermemo.com/articles/sleep.htm. Reprinted with permission.

The writer
contacted the
copyright
holder for
permission to
reproduce
this figure.

The first two stages of sleep are characterized by high-amplitude, low-
frequency neural waves, aptly named slow-wave sleep. During these phases, the
brain is relatively inactive and fires at a baseline rate. Wave III and wave IV sleep
are known as fast-wave sleep, recognized on an electroencephalogram readout by
low-amplitude, high-frequency neuronal activity. REM sleep is characterized by
rapid motion of the eyes beneath closed lids. This is the stage of sleep associated
with vivid dreams, and it is thus sometimes called dream sleep. Some dreams may
occur within other stages as well, but they lack the rich visual and emotional
content of REM dreams. The function of this fascinating phenomenon remains at
least a partial mystery.

Current research examines links between sleep, or stages of sleep, and
memory or learning. Some studies suggest that all-night cram sessions, such as the
one Rosemount is planning, do not improve performance and may even have the
opposite effect (Kelly, Kelly, & Clanton, 2001; Pilcher & Walters, 1997). The idea
that sleep is linked to learning is supported by studies showing that certain types of

The writer
focuses on a
specific
problem.

A semicolon separates sources. All five authors are listed in the first citation of their work.

learning are hampered by sleep disruption or deprivation (Horne, 1988; Karni, Tanne, Rubenstein, Askenasy, & Sagi, 1994).

Some studies implicate REM sleep as having a particularly important role in memory consolidation (Karni et al., 1994). Early research showed the importance of REM sleep for rats. Hunt (1989) summarizes a few of these early studies that

Discussion of research findings

indicate the importance of the timing of REM sleep:

A quotation of forty or more words is set off as a block quotation.

> Over the past few years Carlyle Smith (1981) has studied the REM augmentation following learning in rats over several days and has found that these increases occur as regular "windows" that climb steadily over a six-day period (Smith and Lapp, 1984). Deprivation of REM during these specific windows of augmentation was at its most effective in disrupting prior learning between 48 and 60 hours after training (Smith and Kelly, 1986). (p. 28)

The writer uses *et al.* in a subsequent reference to a five-author source.

Research involving human participants has yielded similar results. Karni et al. (1994) showed that performance on a procedural task improves "neither during nor immediately after practice but rather 8 to 10 hours after a training session has ended" (p. 679). Hunt reports confirmation of the "window" phenomenon by noting that in 1985 Epstein found participants in his study reporting life events as dream

Authors' names followed by publication dates in parentheses

content 2 or 3 days after the experiences (Hunt, 1989). Epstein's findings differ in nature from those of Karni et al. (1994) in that they are more difficult to quantify because his data depend on dream recall, which is subjective. While Epstein's observations are not the most scientifically sound support for optimal timing of REM sleep, they are worth noting and could be significant when pooled with other findings supporting the idea that the brain processes new information and experiences over the course of a few days. In addition to the timing of sleep following training, the amount of REM sleep may play a role. Toward the end of the entire sleep cycle, time spent in REM sleep increases. When people are deprived of REM sleep, their brains react by going into REM sleep more frequently or by staying at the REM stage longer during a sleep-recovery phase (Hobson, 1989).

Although there is no definitive answer as to which type of sleep is needed for memory consolidation, studies show that lack of sleep hinders learning in various ways. Pilcher and Walters (1997) noted its negative impact on participant performance on a test of cognitive ability. Horne (1988) found that participants performed creative-thinking tasks at a decreased capacity when compared with a control group. Karni et al. (1994) observed the damaging effect of sleep deprivation on perceptual learning.

Some studies include a self-report measure for perceived effort, concentration and the like (e.g., Buboltz, Brown, & Soper, 2001; Pilcher & Walters, 1997). Participants are asked to report how confident they are in their performance and to rate that performance. Findings from these self-report measures are somewhat disturbing. It appears that the tendency exists, when a person is sleep deprived, to overestimate performance. Surprisingly, although Pilcher and Walters (1997) noted that sleep deprivation negatively affected the ability of participants to perform on a test, the participants overestimated their performance. They also rated themselves as having expended more effort than participants in the control group did. Perhaps such skewed perception partially explains why college students often deprive themselves of sleep. If their perception is that performance is not hindered, there is no incentive to make sleep a priority.

The studies outlined above illustrate multiple types of learning and memory that may be affected by sleep. It is noteworthy that many of these studies used variables and methodologies that are realistic: They involve tasks similar to those that college students are asked to perform. For example, it is common for students to be asked to employ creative problem-solving skills in a classroom setting. Visual discrimination tasks, too, are common in college courses. Most students have experienced tests in which they must recognize a painting or a literary passage and then name its painter or author. This line of research offers an obvious link between science and real-life situations.

Clearly there is a need for more research on this topic. The fact that an adequate amount of sleep is necessary for a person's health and well-being is well established. We now have sufficient evidence to warrant a closer look at just how important the role of sleep is. Further research may find that all stages of sleep play an important role in optimal functioning, or that one or two stages are particularly important. The exact relationship between sleep and memory is not yet known.

Application of findings to research question

College students have notoriously bad sleeping habits, often because they are attempting to balance schoolwork, part-time jobs, extracurricular activities, and a social life. Known for their irregular sleep patterns, they are often sleep-deprived and/or suffer from some type of disturbed sleep (e.g., difficulty falling, or staying, asleep) (Hicks, Fernandez, & Pellegrini, 2001).

Based on the current body of research literature, it appears that there is a link between sleep and optimal functioning. For this reason, it is important for college students to manage their time in a way that allows them to study material over a period of a couple of days or longer and to have adequate sleep time in order to maximize retention. The consequences of inadequate sleep go beyond simply feeling sleepy. It is alarming that the self-reported sleep habits and quality of sleep of over 1,500 college students have worsened over the last decade (Hicks et al., 2001), indicating that necessary precautions are not being taken to ensure that at the very least students are educated regarding the importance of sleep.

Conclusion

It is evident that Kyle Rosemount is not doing himself any favors by delaying his studying until the last minute. Ideally, Rosemount should have studied in shorter blocks of time over a week, or at least a couple of days, allowing more time to process the information and commit it to memory. It may be that the sleep deprivation college students inflict upon themselves, particularly around finals time, may lead them to overestimate performance while actually hindering it.

References

Buboltz, W. C., Brown, F. C., Jr., & Soper, B. (2001). Sleep habits and patterns of college students: A preliminary study. *Journal of American College Health, 50*(3), 131–135.

Hicks, R. A., Fernandez, C., & Pellegrini, R. J. (2001). The changing sleep habits of university students: An update. *Perceptual and Motor Skills, 93*(3), 648.

Hobson, J. A. (1989). *Sleep.* New York: Scientific American Library.

Horne, J. A. (1988). Sleep loss and divergent thinking ability. *Sleep, 11*(6), 528–536.

Hunt, H. T. (1989). *The multiplicity of dreams: Memory, imagination, and consciousness.* New Haven, CT: Yale University Press.

Karni, A., Tanne, D., Rubenstein, B. S., Askenasy, J. M., & Sagi, D. (1994, July 29). Dependence on REM sleep of overnight improvement of a perceptual skill. *Science, 265*, 679–682.

Kelly, W. E., Kelly, K. E., & Clanton, R. C. (2001). The relationship between sleep length and grade-point average among college students. *College Student Journal, 35*, 84–86.

Pilcher, J. J., & Walters, A. S. (1997). How sleep deprivation affects psychological variables related to college students' cognitive performance. *Journal of American College Health, 46*(3), 121–126.

Wozniak, P. (2000, July). *Good sleep, good learning, good life.* Retrieved September 19, 2002, from http://www.supermemo.com/articles/sleep.htm

Center the heading.

Alphabetize the entries according to the first author's last name.

Indent subsequent lines of each entry one-half inch or five spaces.

No period follows a URL.

CMS DOCUMENTATION

14

The Chicago Manual of Style (CMS), published by the University of Chicago Press, provides guidelines for writers in history and other subject areas in the arts and humanities. The manual recommends documenting sources by using either footnotes or endnotes and, for most assignments, a bibliography. Updates to the manual can be found at www.press. uchicago.edu/Misc/Chicago/cmosfaw/cmosfaq.html. For questions about college-level papers unanswered in the manual, the editors of CMS direct the reader to Kate L. Turabian's *Manual for Writers of Term Papers, Theses, and Dissertations.* This chapter includes

- guidelines for citing sources within a CMS-style research paper and documenting sources in a bibliography (14a) and
- a sample student paper (14b).

14a CMS note and bibliographic forms

According to CMS style, in-text citations take the form of sequential numbers that refer to **footnotes** (notes at the bottom of each page) or **endnotes** (notes at the end of the paper). The information in these notes is condensed if a bibliography lists all the sources used in the paper. The condensed, or short, form for a note includes only the author's last name, the title (shortened if longer than four words), and the relevant page number(s): Eggers, *Court Reporters,* 312–15.

When no bibliography is provided for a paper, the full note form is used. For either footnotes or endnotes, a superscript number is placed in the text wherever documentation of a source is necessary. The number should be as close as possible to whatever it refers to, following the punctuation that appears at the end of the direct quotation or paraphrase. You can create a superscript number in Microsoft Word by highlighting the number, pulling down the menu for Format, clicking on Font, and then placing a checkmark next to Superscript. Other word-processing programs perform this function similarly.

TIPS FOR PREPARING FOOTNOTES

- Most word-processing programs will footnote your paper automatically. In Microsoft Word, pull down the Insert menu and choose Footnote. A superscript number will appear next to the relevant text. A box will also appear at the bottom of your page, in which you can insert the requisite information.

- If you do not have access to a word-processing program, be sure to leave enough space for footnotes on the bottom of the page to which they refer. After the last line of text on that page, create a separator—a solid line that stretches across one-third of the page. Leave one line space after the separator before typing the footnote.

- Each note begins with a full-size number followed by a period and a space.

- Use the abbreviation *Ibid.* (not italicized) to indicate that the source cited in an entry is identical to the one in the preceding entry. Include page numbers if they differ from those in the preceding entry: Ibid., 331–32.

- Indent the first line of a note five spaces.

- Single-space lines within a footnote.

- Double-space between footnotes when more than one appears on a page.

- No bibliography is necessary when the footnotes provide complete bibliographic information for all sources.

TIPS FOR PREPARING ENDNOTES

- Place endnotes on a separate page, following the last page of the body of the paper and preceding the bibliography (if one is included).

- Center the word *Notes* (not italicized) at the top of the page.

- Use the abbreviation *Ibid.* (not italicized) to indicate that a source cited in an entry is identical to the one in the preceding entry. Include page numbers if they differ from those in the preceding entry: Ibid., 331–32.

- Indent the first line of a note five spaces.

- Single-space between lines of an endnote and leave one blank line between endnotes.

- No bibliography is necessary when the endnotes provide complete bibliographic information for all sources used in the paper.

TIPS FOR PREPARING A BIBLIOGRAPHY

- Start the bibliography on a separate page, following the last page of the body of the paper if footnotes are used or following the last page of endnotes.

- Center the word *Bibliography* (not italicized) at the top of your paper. Some instructors may prefer that you use *Works Cited*.

- Alphabetize entries in the bibliography according to the author's last name.

- If a source has more than one author, alphabetize by the last name of the first author.

- For a work without an author, alphabetize the entry according to the first important word in the title.

- To indicate that a source has the same author(s) as in the preceding entry, begin an entry with a three-em dash (———) instead of the name(s) of the author(s). (If you do not know how to create this mark, search for *em dash*, using the Help function on your word processor.)

- Indent the second and subsequent lines of an entry five spaces.

- Single-space between lines of an entry and leave one blank line between entries.

Directory of CMS Note and Bibliographic Forms

BOOKS

General Documentation Guidelines for Print-Based Sources

The following guidelines are for books and articles. Both full note forms and bibliographic forms are provided. Remember that a short note form consists of just the author's last name, the title (shortened if longer than four words), and relevant page numbers.

Author or Editor

One author—note form. Provide the author's full name, beginning with the first name and following the last name with a comma. For the short note form, use only the last name(s) of author(s) or editor(s).

Full note form
1. Jamie Desler,

One author—bibliographic form. Invert the author's name so that the last name appears first. Place a period after the first name.

Bibliographic form
Desler, Jamie.

Two authors—note form. Use the word *and* between the names.

Full note form
1. Pauline Diaz and Edward Allan,

(continued on page 350)

Author or Editor *(continued from page 349)*

Two authors—bibliographic form. Invert the first author's name only. Place a comma and the word *and* after the first author's name. A period follows the second author's name.

Bibliographic form
Diaz, Pauline, and Edward Allan.

Three authors—note form. Use commas after the names of the first and subsequent authors. Include *and* before the final author's name.

Full note form
2. Joyce Freeland, John Bach, and Derik Flynn,

Three authors—bibliographic form. Invert the order of the first author's name only. Place a comma after this name and after the second author's name. Use *and* before the final author's name.

Bibliographic form
Freeland, Joyce, John Bach, and Derik Flynn.

Corporate or group author—note and bibliographic forms. Provide the full name of the group in all forms—full note, short note, and bibliographic.

Note form
3. Smithsonian Institution,
Bibliographic form
Smithsonian Institution.

Editor—note and bibliographic forms. Place the abbreviation *ed.* after the editor's name.

Full note form
4. Peggy Irmen, ed.,
Bibliographic form
Irmen, Peggy, ed.

Titles

Italicized titles. Italicize the titles of books, magazines, journals, newspapers, and films. Capitalize all major words (nouns, pronouns, verbs, adjectives, adverbs, and subordinating conjunctions). A book title is followed by a comma in a note form and by a period in the bibliographic form. In the short note form, a title

Full note form
The Great Design of Henry IV from the Memoirs of the Duke of Sully,
Short note form
Great Design of Henry IV,
Bibliographic form
The Great Design of Henry IV from the Memoirs of the Duke of Sully.

longer than four words is shortened by omitting any article at its beginning and using only important words from the rest of the title.

Titles in quotation marks. Use quotation marks to enclose the titles of journal or magazine articles, selections from anthologies, and other short works. (See 38b.) In the note form, a title of a short work is followed by a comma. In the bibliographic form, it is followed by a period.

Full note form
"The Humor of New England,"
Bibliographic form
"The Humor of New England."

Subtitles. Include subtitles in the full note and bibliographic forms but not in the short note form.

Full note form
Appreciations: Painting, Poetry, and Prose,

Bibliographic form
Appreciations: Painting, Poetry, and Prose.

Journal volume and issue numbers. Whenever possible, include both the volume number and the issue number for any journal article you use. The volume number should appear after the title, and the issue number should appear after the volume number (preceded by the abbreviation *no.*). Use a comma to separate the two numbers.

American Naturalist 154, no. 2

Publication Data

List the city of publication, publisher's name, and date. A colon follows the city of publication, and a comma follows the publisher's name. In the full note form, this information should be placed within parentheses. No

Full note form
(New York: Alfred A. Knopf, 2005),
Bibliographic form
New York: Alfred A. Knopf, 2005.

(continued on page 352)

Publication Data *(continued from page 351)*

parentheses are needed for the bibliographic form. The short note form
does not include publication data.

For a journal, place the year of
publication in parentheses after the
volume or issue number. For a
magazine, provide the full date of
publication.

International Social Work 47 (2004)
Journal of Democracy 14, no. 1
   (2003)
Time, January 24, 2005

City and state. Identify the city of
publication. If the city is not widely
known, add a two-letter state abbreviation (or, for a city outside the United
States, a province or country abbreviation). If the city of publication is
Washington, include the abbreviation
for the District of Columbia, *DC.*
When two cities are listed on the title
page, use only the first in the bibliographic entry unless both are located
in the same state.

Baltimore
Carbondale, IL
Waterloo, ON
Harmondsworth, UK
Carbondale and Edwardsville:
   Southern Illinois Press

Publisher's name. Provide either the
full name of each publisher, as given
on the title page, or an abbreviated
version. The style chosen must be consistent throughout the notes and bibliography. Even when the full name is
provided, some words may be omitted:
an initial *The* and words such as
Company or *Corporation* or abbreviations such as *Co.* or *Inc.* The word
University may be abbreviated to *Univ.*

Univ. of Chicago Press
Penguin Books
HarperCollins

Page Numbers

If you are citing information from a
specific page or pages of a book or article, place the page number(s) at the
end of the footnote or endnote. If
you are citing more than one page,

separate the first and last page with an en dash (or short dash): 35–38. If the page numbers have the same hundreds or thousands digit, do not repeat it when listing the final page in the range: 123–48. Page numbers are not included in a bibliographic entry for a book. A bibliographic entry for an article ends with the range of pages on which the article appears.

The following list contains entries for the full note form and the bibliographic form. The short note form is provided only for a book with one author. For more examples of short forms, see the endnotes of the sample student paper (pages 372–373).

BOOKS

1. Book with one author

Full note form

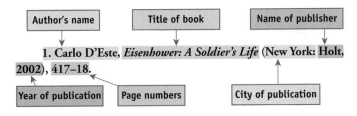

Short note form

1. D'Este, *Eisenhower*, 417–18.

Bibliographic form

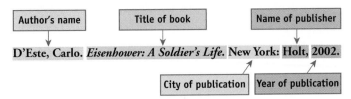

2. Book with two authors
Full note form

    2. Cathy Scott-Clark and Adrian Levy, *The Stone of Heaven* (Boston: Little, Brown, 2001), 28.

Bibliographic form

Scott-Clark, Cathy, and Adrian Levy. *The Stone of Heaven.* Boston: Little, Brown, 2001.

3. Book with three authors
Full note form

    3. Xue Litai, John W. Lewis, and Sergei N. Goncharov, *Uncertain Partners: Stalin, Mao, and the Korean War* (Palo Alto, CA: Stanford Univ. Press, 1993).

Bibliographic form

Litai, Xue, John W. Lewis, and Sergei N. Goncharov. *Uncertain Partners: Stalin, Mao, and the Korean War.* Palo Alto, CA: Stanford Univ. Press, 1993.

4. Book with more than three authors
Full note form

    4. Mike Palmquist and others, *Transitions: Teaching Writing in Computer-Supported and Traditional Classrooms* (Greenwich, CT: Ablex, 1998), 153.

In the note form, just the first person's name is used, followed by *and others.* The bibliographic form should include all the authors' names.

Bibliographic form

Palmquist, Mike, Kate Kiefer, James Hartvigsen, and Barbara Goodlew. *Transitions: Teaching Writing in Computer-Supported and Traditional Classrooms.* Greenwich, CT: Ablex, 1998.

5. Book with an editor

Full note form

    5. Hanna Schissler, ed., *The Miracle Years* (Princeton, NJ: Princeton Univ. Press, 2001).

Bibliographic form

Schissler, Hanna, ed. *The Miracle Years.* Princeton, NJ: Princeton Univ. Press, 2001.

6. Book with an author and an editor

Full note form

    6. Ayn Rand, *The Art of Fiction,* ed. Tore Boeckmann (New York: Plume, 2000).

Use the abbreviation *ed.* for "edited by."

Bibliographic form

Rand, Ayn. *The Art of Fiction.* Edited by Tore Boeckmann. New York: Plume, 2000.

Write out the words *Edited by.*

7. Translated book

Full note form

    7. Murasaki Shikibu, *The Tale of Genji,* trans. Royall Tyler (New York: Viking, 2001).

Use the abbreviation *trans.* for "translated by."

Bibliographic form

Shikibu, Murasaki. *The Tale of Genji.* Translated by Royall Tyler. New York: Viking, 2001.

Write out the words *Translated by.*

8. Edition after the first

Full note form

8. Edward O. Wilson, *On Human Nature,* 14th ed. (Cambridge: Harvard Univ. Press, 2001).

Bibliographic form

Wilson, Edward O. *On Human Nature.* 14th ed. Cambridge: Harvard Univ. Press, 2001.

9. One volume in a multivolume work

Full note form

9. Thomas Cleary, *Classics of Buddhism and Zen,* vol. 3 (Boston: Shambhala Publications, 2001), 116.

Bibliographic form

Cleary, Thomas. *Classics of Buddhism and Zen.* Vol. 3. Boston: Shambhala Publications, 2001.

10. Government document

Full note form

10. U.S. Bureau of the Census, *Statistical Abstract of the United States,* 120th ed. (Washington, DC, 2000), 16.

Bibliographic form

U.S. Bureau of the Census. *Statistical Abstract of the United States.* 120th ed. Washington, DC, 2000.

11. Selection from an anthology

Full note form

11. Elizabeth Spencer, "The Everlasting Light," in *The Cry of an Occasion,* ed. Richard Bausch (Baton Rouge: Louisiana State University Press, 2001), 171–82.

Bibliographic form

Spencer, Elizabeth. "The Everlasting Light." In *The Cry of an Occasion,* edited by
Richard Bausch, 171–82. Baton Rouge: Louisiana State University Press, 2001.

When only one selection from an anthology is used, inclusive page numbers precede the publication data in the bibliographic entry.

12. Published letter

Full note form

12. Lincoln to George McClellan, Washington, DC, 13 October 1862, in *This Fiery Trial: The Speeches and Writings of Abraham Lincoln,* ed. William E. Gienapp (New York: Oxford Univ. Press, 2002), 178.

Bibliographic form

Lincoln, Abraham. Abraham Lincoln to George McClellan, Washington DC, 13 October
1862. In *This Fiery Trial: The Speeches and Writings of Abraham Lincoln,* ed.
William E. Gienapp, 178. New York: Oxford Univ. Press, 2002.

13. Indirect (secondary) source

Full note form

13. Toni Morrison, *Playing in the Dark* (New York: Vintage, 1992), 26, quoted in Jonathan Goldberg, *Willa Cather and Others* (Durham, NC: Duke Univ. Press, 2001), 37.

Bibliographic form

Morrison, Toni. *Playing in the Dark,* 26. New York: Vintage, 1992. Quoted in Jonathan
Goldberg, *Willa Cather and Others* (Durham, NC: Duke Univ. Press, 2001), 37.

Cite both the original work and the secondary source in which you found it quoted. Begin with the name of the author you have quoted, and provide information about the work (which should be available in the notes or bibliography of the indirect source you used). Then provide information about the secondary source.

ARTICLES

14. Article in a journal

Full note form

> 14. A. Schedler, "The Menu of Manipulation," *Journal of Democracy* 13, no. 2 (2002): 48.

Use initials for an author's first and/or middle names only when they are used in the original publication.

Bibliographic form

Schedler, A. "The Menu of Manipulation." *Journal of Democracy* 13, no. 2 (2002): 36–50.

15. Article in a popular (general-circulation) magazine

Full note form

> 15. John O'Sullivan, "The Overskeptics," *National Review,* June 17, 2002, 23.

For a magazine published monthly, include only the month and the year, with no comma between them.

Bibliographic form

O'Sullivan, John. "The Overskeptics." *National Review,* June 17, 2002, 22–26.

16. Article from an online journal

Full note form

> 16. Lars Wik and others, "Quality of Cardiopulmonary Resuscitation during Out-of-Hospital Cardiac Arrest," *Journal of the American Medical Association* 293, no. 3 (2005), http://jama.ama-assn.org/cgi/content/full/293/3/299 (accessed January 28, 2005).

Place the URL along with the date of access (in parentheses) after the date of publication.

Bibliographic form

Wik, Lars, Jo Kramer-Johansen, Helge Myklebust, Hallstein Sorebo, Leif Svensson, Bob Fellows, and Petter Andreas Steen. "Quality of Cardiopulmonary Resuscitation during Out-of-Hospital Cardiac Arrest." *Journal of the American Medical Association* 293, no. 3 (January 19, 2005), http://jama.ama-assn.org/cgi/content/full/293/3/299 (accessed January 28, 2005).

Include the full date of publication as well as the date of access.

17. Article from a journal database

Full note form

17. Samuel Guy Inman, "The Monroe Doctrine and Hispanic America," *Hispanic America Historical Review* 4, no. 4 (1921): 635, http://links.jstor.org/sici?sici=0018-2168%28192111%294%3A4%3C635%3ATMDAHA%3E2.0.CO%3B2-8.

A URL that runs onto a second line may be broken *after* a single or double slash or *before* a comma, a period, a hyphen, a question mark, a percent symbol, a number sign (#), a tilde (~), or an underscore (_). It can be broken either before or after an ampersand (&) or an equals sign. Include an access date in parentheses between the URL and the final period if the material you are using is time-sensitive or if an access date is required by your discipline.

Bibliographic form

Inman, Samuel Guy. "The Monroe Doctrine and Hispanic America." *Hispanic America Historical Review* 4, no. 4 (1921): 635–81. http://links.jstor.org/sici?sici=0018-2168%28192111%294%3A4%3C635%3ATMDAHA% 3E2.0.CO%3B2-8.

18. Article from an online magazine

Full note form

18. Mark Frank, "Judge for Themselves: Why a Supreme Court Ruling on Sentencing Guidelines Puts More Power Back on the Bench," *Time*, January 24, 2005, http://www.time.com/time/magazine/printout/0,8816,1018063,00.html.

Bibliographic form

Frank, Mark. "Judge for Themselves: Why a Supreme Court Ruling on Sentencing
Guidelines Puts More Power Back on the Bench." *Time*, January 24, 2005. http://
www.time.com/time/magazine/printout/0,8816,1018063,00.html.

19. Newspaper article

Full note form

19. Rick Bragg, "An Oyster and a Way of Life, Both at Risk," *New York Times,*
June 15, 2002, national edition, sec. A.

If the city of publication is not part of the newspaper's name, it should
be added at the beginning and italicized as if part of the name: *St. Paul
Pioneer Press.* If the city is not well known or could be confused with
another city with the same name, add the state name or abbreviation
within parentheses after the city's name. If the paper is a well-known
national one, such as the *Wall Street Journal,* it is not necessary to add
the city of publication.

Bibliographic form

Bragg, Rick. "An Oyster and a Way of Life, Both at Risk." *New York Times.* June 15,
2002, national edition, sec. A.

If the name of the newspaper and the date of publication are
mentioned in the text of the paper, no bibliographic entry is needed.

OTHER SOURCES

20. Interview

Full note form

20. Yoko Ono, "Multimedia Player: An Interview with Yoko Ono," interview by
Carolyn Burriss-Krimsky, *Ruminator Review,* no. 10 (Summer 2002): 28.

Bibliographic form

Ono, Yoko. "Multimedia Player: An Interview with Yoko Ono." By Carolyn Burriss-

Krimsky. *Ruminator Review,* no. 10 (Summer 2002): 26–29.

If you are required to list interviews, each entry should include the name of the person being interviewed, the title of the interview, the name of the person who conducted it, and any available publication data.

21. Videocassette or DVD

Full note form

21. *Araby,* VHS, produced and directed by Dennis J. Courtney (Los Angeles: American Street Productions, 1999).

Bibliographic form

Araby. VHS. Produced and directed by Dennis J. Courtney. Los Angeles: American Street

Productions, 1999.

Place *VHS* (for videocassette) or *DVD* after the title.

14b CMS-style paper

The following student paper addresses an important development in the Civil Rights movement. Because it includes a full bibliography, the endnotes are written in short form (see page 346). Although CMS does not provide guidelines for a title page for a student paper, one is shown in fig. 14.1 as a sample.

RACE IN THE U.S. ARMY:

AN EXECUTIVE ORDER FOR HOPE

BY

NICOLE HESTER

AMERICAN HISTORY 257

DR. MELISSA HILL

DECEMBER 6, 2002

Figure 14.1. Sample title page for a CMS-style paper.

1

RACE IN THE U.S. ARMY: AN EXECUTIVE ORDER FOR HOPE

While students of the Civil Rights movement are often familiar with the
Supreme Court decision *Brown v. The Board of Education,* which acknowledged
the inherent inequality in separate but equal practices, that decision would not
happen until 1955, nearly eight years after President Harry S. Truman issued an
executive order to integrate the federal government and, in particular, the United
States military. Although the earlier Thirteenth (1865), Fourteenth (1868), and
Fifteenth (1870) Amendments redefined freedom, citizenship, and voting,
these amendments were diluted by Supreme Court decisions in the nineteenth
and early twentieth centuries. In cases like *Plessy v. Ferguson,* the court
established the precedent of "separate but equal," which legally allowed the
separation of races in public facilities.[1] Thus, Truman's executive order in 1948
became an important step in the long-term struggle for civil rights.

Like American schools, the United States Army was segregated, and this
segregation remained in place until after the Second World War (1941–1945). In
July of 1948, by executive order, President Truman demanded equal treatment and
equal opportunity in the armed forces, setting into motion a series of events that
would force change, however slow it might be:

> It is hereby declared to be the policy of the President that there shall
> be equality of treatment and opportunity for all persons in the armed
> services without regard to race, color, religion or national origin. This
> policy shall be put into effect as rapidly as possible, having due regard
> to the time required to effectuate any necessary changes without im-
> pairing efficiency or morale.[2]

With such language as "all persons" and "as rapidly as possible," Truman
showed that his statement was more than a publicity stunt. While understanding the
scale of the change he was demanding, Truman was also aware of the sentiment of the
American people and numerous government officials. Examining the desegregation of

2

President Truman reviews Black troops.

the Army from the viewpoints of those who sought to keep the races segregated and those who wanted integration leads to understanding how the law can begin to secure the pathways to justice and freedom.[3] Truman's executive order in 1948 illustrates how the government can be a vehicle for social change.

Historically, approximately 200,000 Blacks enlisted to fight in the Civil War, but their involvement was strongly influenced by the need for manpower.[4] After the Civil War, the Army maintained only four Black regiments. Although there were 380,000 Blacks in the Army during the First World War, no more than 42,000 actually served in combat units; most Blacks served as laborers.[5] The end of the First World War ushered in a time of analysis and redefinition of the roles of Blacks in the armed forces. The Selective Service Act of 1940 would forbid discrimination because of race with regard to enlisting and being inducted into the armed forces.[6] However, in October 1940, Robert P. Patterson, the Secretary of War, stated that the Selective Service Act would not eliminate segregation within the armed forces; instead, it would allow Blacks to serve in segregated units:[7]

> The policy of the War Department is not to intermingle colored and white enlisted personnel in the same regimental organizations. This policy has been proven satisfactory over a long period of years and to make changes would produce situations destructive to morale and detrimental to the preparations for national defense.[8]

Patterson's statement followed the idea of "separate but equal" and ultimately undercut any effect the Selective Service Act could have had on integration. The enlistment of Blacks was increasing, but their advancement was not, no doubt because they were restricted to separate units. The existence of segregation, stemming from earlier war practices and later defined by War Department policy, would become the norm in the Second World War. From the perspective of those in the War Department, the policy was working effectively, and to "experiment" with its segregated structure would be detrimental to all within military ranks.[9]

These beliefs were reinforced by unreliable data. Supporting the policy outlined by the War Department, results from the U.S. Army General Classification Tests (AGCT), which tested general learning ability, showed 45 percent of Blacks and only 5 percent of Whites in the lowest class of exam scores. However, the War Department did not assess any reasons *why* the test results showed the deficit. Because of the "differences in opportunity and background," Blacks generally did not receive the same level of educational opportunity as Whites, so a difference in overall level of performance in standardized testing was bound to exist.[10] Although the Army was correct in its statement about the difference in test results, it ignored the direct effect that segregation and social constraints were having on the academic performance of Black Americans.

The testing issue, however, was only an excuse for preventing integration. For those who believed that segregation was *right,* allowing Blacks equal opportunities in the armed services would enable them to "achieve equality in America by force."[11] Simply put, separatists were afraid that the growing political power of Blacks would lead to a revolt, bringing about the end of segregation, which threatened what separatists thought was right. More importantly, the Army did not believe the government should intervene, forcing desegregation within an otherwise segregated nation. In January 1948, nearly seven months before Truman's executive order, a Gallup poll showed that 81 percent of Southerners had heard of Truman's civil rights plan, and 58 percent felt that it should *not* be passed in Congress, compared to the 14 percent in the New England and Middle Atlantic region who felt that Truman's civil rights initiative should not be passed. In the same survey, Southern Whites responded 5-to-1 in an overwhelming show of support for segregation.[12] In a memorandum from December 1941, when the United States entered the Second World War, Chief of Staff General George C. Marshall reflected the sentiment that existed in the country and explained the Army's resistance to promote social change. In his words, integrating the U.S. Army

> would be tantamount to solving a social problem which has perplexed the American people throughout the history of this nation. The army cannot accomplish such a solution, and should not be charged with the undertaking. The settlement of vexing racial problems cannot be permitted to complicate the tremendous task of the War Department and thereby jeopardize discipline and morale.[13]

When Truman asked for the equal treatment of soldiers regardless of "race, color, religion, or national origin,"[14] he was essentially asking the government to ignore the widespread sentiment of White Americans. Undoubtedly, there were significant numbers of Blacks, Whites, and others craving freedom, but the nation as a whole was not ready for what Truman demanded. After so many years of segregation and prejudice, Truman was fighting a widely supported status quo.

Knowing the greatness of the change he had demanded, Truman established a committee that would be known as the Fahy Committee. Named after its chairman, Charles H. Fahy, the multiracial committee consisted of seven men, including Black leader Lester Granger and the executive secretary of the Urban League, John H. Sengstacke, who were responsible for examining the existing procedures and practices of the armed forces to devise a way to carry out the president's new policy.[15] The Fahy Committee set out to show the ways in which segregation was hurting the "effectiveness" of the armed forces and to establish the positive results that would follow from integrating the armed forces, particularly the Army.[16]

5

The Fahy Committee wrestled tirelessly with the Army to put an end to the quota system, which limited the number of Black enlistees to 10 percent, as well as the segregation that prevented the advancement of Blacks within the Army.[17] Essentially the Army needed to use every individual within its ranks as effectively as possible, regardless of race, but the quota system and segregation made this impossible.[18] Because the skills of Black soldiers could be used only in Black units, White units sometimes had to leave essential positions unfilled.

When the Army could no longer deny the statistical and practical truth that segregation was inefficient and ineffective, Adjutant General of the Army Edward F. Witsell finally announced on March 27, 1950, that *all* appointments would be open to *all* applicants without regard to race or color.[19] As Mershon and Schlossman discuss in *Foxholes and Color Lines,* by assessing the integration of the armed forces, the Fahy Committee helped Truman to fight segregation and essentially prepare Americans for change.[20] Having the law on their side, Blacks were encouraged in their pursuit of equal opportunity. They began to hope that the equality being fostered in the federal government would eventually affect state practices, and that prejudice and bigotry would soon fade.

However, changing the minds of individuals is an entirely different task from changing the laws. Lee reports the statement of an unnamed White officer requesting relief in 1945 from the Ninety-Second Division, an engineer battalion where Black troops worked with Whites:

> Although I can still find such interest in a few specific individuals, for the rank and file I can feel only disgust for their inherent slovenliness, and their extreme indolence, indifference and frequent insolence. . . . I am likewise convinced that with few exceptions colored officers with whom I have come into contact are thoroughly incompetent, and for the most part are to be viewed in a light little different from enlisted men.[21]

This statement shows that while the law can create an environment in which freedom can exist, the law cannot change racist hearts and minds.

Knowing that legal equality was far off and that a deeply changed society was a hope for the distant future, Blacks in the military were then faced with daunting questions about their dual role as Blacks and as Americans. From their perspective, they enlisted to defend a country that would not defend them. For what reason should Blacks then enlist? What were they fighting for? Who were they really fighting against? The simplified answer to these questions came for Blacks in what would become known as the Double V Campaign: victory abroad and victory at home. In early 1942, this campaign was explained in the Black newspaper the *Courier* as a "struggle to remove the contradiction between the claims of American democratic ideology and the racial inequalities evident in American life."[22] Blacks were fighting for what they knew America was capable of, and ultimately created for, even while being bound by the racial policies of the Army; they still had a larger vision of what America could truly be. Fighting on the battlefields of foreign countries for a nation that rejected them in so many ways, the pursuit of freedom and equality came at a high emotional cost for Blacks in the Army. Hubert Humphrey used a quotation by James Baldwin, who served in the Second World War, to exemplify the Black experience and struggle:

> You must put yourself in the skin of a man who is wearing a uniform of his country, is a candidate for death in its defense, and who is called a "nigger" by his comrades-in-arms and his officers . . . and who watches German prisoners of war being treated by Americans with more human dignity than he has ever received at their hands. And who, at the same time, as a human being, is far freer in a strange land than he has even been at home. HOME! The very word begins to have a despairing and diabolical ring. You must consider what happens to this citizen, after all he has endured, when he returns—home; search, in his

7

> shoes, for a job, for a place to live; ride, in his skin, on segregated
> buses; see, with his eyes, the signs saying "White" and "Colored," and
> especially the signs that say "White Ladies" and "Colored Women" . . .
> imagine yourself being told to "Wait." And all of this happening in the
> richest and freest country in the world, and in the middle of the
> twentieth century.[23]

Between fighting for the freedom of others in the war and hoping justice would
permeate the policies and social hierarchies in America, Black soldiers had an
immense struggle that would not end after the war.

However, Blacks were not alone, there were others fighting along with them,
and President Truman was certainly one of them. By issuing executive order 9981
in 1948, Truman clearly established his position concerning racial bias within the
government by "tak[ing] significant unilateral action to alter the stance of the
federal government toward minority groups . . . demonstrat[ing] dedication to the
legal equality for racial minorities without waiting for congressional approval."[24]
In short, Truman's order required action within the armed forces to end racial bias
and to do so within a reasonable amount of time.[25] Sidestepping a conservative
Congress and the prejudice of many Americans, Truman supported Blacks in
their struggle for advancement and equality in the armed forces, even though
he moved the law to a place where the American people were not necessarily
ready to follow.

Understanding Truman's order concerning segregation, we are left to
wonder why he would take such a political risk. Why should Truman be any
different from other government officials or separatists that surrounded him?
What could Truman gain from alienating himself from the legislative branch? Of
course, Truman undoubtedly gained the support of Black voters because of his
bold stance concerning race, but could that be the entirety of his motivations?
What Truman *really* thought or felt is something we can never know, but in

8

October 1948 in an address in Harlem, New York, where he would receive the Franklin Roosevelt Award, Truman had this to say:

> It was the authors of the Declaration of Independence who stated the principle that all men are created equal in their rights, and that it is to secure these rights that governments are instituted among men.
> It was the authors of the Constitution who made it clear that, under our form of government, all citizens are equal before the law, and that the Federal Government has a duty to guarantee to every citizen equal protection of the laws.[26]

In his own words, Truman stated what the founding documents of this nation intended, and he was determined to see those principles put into action. Truman's biographer, David McCullough, describes Truman as "the kind of president the founding fathers had in mind for this country."[27] Yet Truman himself reveals that growing international concerns such as the Cold War were also influencing him:

> Today the democratic way of life is being challenged all over the world. Democracy's answer to the challenge of totalitarianism is its promise of equal rights and equal opportunities for all mankind.
> The fulfillment of this promise is among the highest purposes of government.
> Our determination to attain the goal of equal rights and equal opportunity must be resolute and unwavering.
> For my part, I intend to keep moving toward this goal with every ounce of strength and determination that I have."[28]

Simply, Truman effected the change in government because he was compelled by the same truth that compelled individuals in the Civil Rights movement and that compels individuals today to stand against injustice and discrimination.

9

        Despite politics and despite the prevailing attitudes of many Americans, Truman initiated change. Beginning a process that would affect the Civil Rights movement, Truman established the grounds by which the government could step beyond the stance of most White Americans. Truman's executive order in 1948 showed how the action of one president can work against injustice and encourage those in the midst of a growing struggle for freedom. Legally free to advance in all branches of the armed forces, Blacks were able to prove the truth that they had been proclaiming for so long—that equality in humanity transcends racial differences.

Notes

1. *Plessy v. Ferguson,* 163 U.S. 537 (1896).

2. Merrill, *Documentary History,* 11:741.

3. It is beyond the scope of my paper to discuss all the non-Whites who were affected by Truman's order. In this essay, I focus on the effect of Truman's order on people whom I refer to as Black.

4. Lee, *Employment of Negro Troops*, 4.

5. Ibid., 73–74.

6. Mershon and Schlossman, *Foxholes and Color Lines*, 44–45.

7. Ibid., 73–77.

8. Nalty and MacGregor, *Blacks in the Military*, 108.

9. Ibid.

10. Lee, *Employment of Negro Troops,* 141.

11. Reddick, "Negro Policy," 12.

12. Gallup, *Public Opinion 1935–1971,* 2:782–83.

13. Nalty and MacGregor, *Blacks in the Military,* 114–15.

14. Merrill, *Documentary History,* 11:741.

15. Gardner, *Truman and Civil Rights*, 114.

16. Billington, "Freedom to Serve," 273.

17. Mershon and Schlossman, *Foxholes and Color Lines,* 209.

18. Nalty and MacGregor, *Blacks in the Military,* 289.

19. Ibid., 269.

20. Mershon and Schlossman, *Foxholes and Color Lines,* 217.

21. Lee, *Employment of Negro Troops,* 187.

22. Osur, *Blacks in the Army Air Forces*, 11–12.

23. Quoted in Hubert H. Humphrey, *Beyond Civil Rights*, 19. Humphrey provides no indication of the source of Baldwin's statement, and I have been unable to track it down.

11

24. Mershon and Schlossman, *Foxholes and Color Lines,* 167–68.

25. Mayer, *Stroke of a Pen*, 4.

26. Truman, *Public Papers*, 4:923–25.

27. McCullough, *Truman*, 991.

28. Truman, *Public Papers,* 4:923–25.

Bibliography

Billington, Monroe. "Freedom to Serve: The President's Committee on Equality of Treatment and Opportunity in the Armed Forces, 1949–1950." *Journal of Negro History* (1966): 262–74. http://links.jstor.org/ sici?sici500222992%28196610%2951%3A4%3C262%3AFTSTPC%.

Gallup, George H. *The Gallup Poll: Public Opinion 1935–1971.* Vol. 2. New York: Random House, 1972.

Gardner, Michael R. *Harry Truman and Civil Rights: Moral Courage and Political Risks.* Carbondale and Edwardsville: Southern Illinois Univ. Press, 2002.

Humphrey, Hubert H. *Beyond Civil Rights: A New Day of Equality.* New York: Random House, 1968.

Lee, Ulysses. *The Employment of Negro Troops.* Washington, DC: Center of Military History, 1963.

Mayer, Kenneth. *With the Stroke of a Pen: Executive Orders and Presidential Power.* Princeton: Princeton Univ. Press, 2001.

McCullough, David. *Truman.* New York: Simon & Schuster, 1992.

Merrill, Dennis, ed. *Documentary History of the Truman Presidency.* Vol. 11. Bethesda, MD: University Publishers of America, 1996.

Mershon, Sherie, and Steven Schlossman. *Foxholes and Color Lines.* Baltimore: Johns Hopkins University Press, 1998.

Nalty, Bernard C., and Morris J. MacGregor. *Blacks in the Military.* Wilmington, DE: Scholarly Resources, 1981.

Osur, Alan M. *Blacks in the Army Air Forces During World War II.* Washington, DC: Office of Air Force History, 1941.

Plessy v. Ferguson, 163 U.S. 537 (1896).

Reddick, L. D. "The Negro Policy of the United States Army, 1775–1945." *Journal of Negro History* 34, no. 1 (1949): 9–29. http://www.jstor.org/ search/8dd55340.10427454971/110?configsortorder5SCORE& frame5noframe&dpi53&config5jstor.

Truman, Harry. *Public Papers of the Presidents of the United States: Harry S. Truman, 1945–53.* Vol. 4. Washington, DC: GPO, 1964.

15

CSE DOCUMENTATION

The Council of Science Editors (CSE), formerly the Council of Biology Editors (CBE), has established guidelines for writers in the life sciences, the physical sciences, and mathematics. The CSE/CBE manual—*Scientific Style and Format: The CBE Manual for Authors, Editors, and Publishers*—covers both general style conventions for spelling, punctuation, capitalization, and so forth and specific scientific conventions for such items as chemical names and formulas. In addition, the manual presents two formats for citing and documenting research sources: the citation-sequence system and the name-year system. You can find updates to the manual's contents at www.cbe.org. This chapter includes

- guidelines for citing sources within a CSE-style research paper and documenting sources on the references list (15a) and
- a sample student paper (15b).

15a CSE citation-sequence and name-year systems

As you prepare to write your paper, be sure to find out which format your instructor prefers—the citation-sequence system or the name-year system. Because these systems differ significantly, it is important to know which you will be expected to use before you get started. Once you know your instructor's preference, follow the guidelines in one of the following boxes as you prepare your in-text citations and references list.

TIPS FOR PREPARING CITATION-SEQUENCE IN-TEXT CITATIONS

- Place a superscript number after each mention of a source or each use of material from it. This number corresponds to the number assigned to the source on the references list.

- Be sure to place the number immediately after the material used or the word or phrase indicating the source: Herbert's original method[1] was used.

- Use the same number each time you use material from or refer to the source.

- Order the numbers according to the sequence in which sources are introduced: Both Li[1] and Holst[2] have shown. . . .

- If a phrase refers to more than one source, use commas to separate the corresponding numbers; note that there is no space after each comma. Use an en-dash between two numbers to indicate a sequence of sources: The early studies[1,2,4–7]. . . .

TIPS FOR PREPARING NAME-YEAR IN-TEXT CITATIONS

- Place the author's last name and the year of publication in parentheses after the mention of a source: In a more recent study (Karr 2002), these findings were not replicated. Using the author's last name, the reader will be able to find the corresponding entry in the references list.

- Omit the author's name from the parenthetical citation if it appears in the text preceding it: In Karr's study (2002), these findings were not replicated.

- Use semicolons to separate multiple citations within a set of parentheses. Order these citations chronologically when the year differs but alphabetically when the years are the same: (Li 1998; Holst 2001) but (Lamont 1998; Li 1998).

TIPS FOR PREPARING A REFERENCES LIST

- Place the heading "References" or "Cited References" next to the left margin.

- If you are using the citation-sequence system, list the sources in the order in which they were introduced in the text. See page 387 for an example.

- If your paper employs the name-year system, your references list should be ordered alphabetically according to the author's last name. See page 384 for an example.

- Entries for the two types of references lists differ only in the placement of the year of publication: the name-year system calls for the date to be placed after the author's name; the citation-sequence system calls for the date to be placed after the publisher's name in entries for books and after the periodical's name in entries for articles.

Use the following directory to find sample bibliographic entries for the citation-sequence system.

Directory of CSE Citation-Sequence Bibliographic Entries

BOOKS

ARTICLES

ELECTRONIC SOURCES

General Documentation Guidelines

The following guidelines are for both books and articles.

Author or Editor

One author. Begin the entry with the author's last name and the initials for the first and middle name (if one is given) and then a period. Notice that there is no comma after the last name and no period or space between initials.

Klemin TK.
Laigo MS.

Two or more authors. Invert the names and initials of all authors, using commas to separate the authors' names.

Stearns BL, Sowards JP.
Collum AS, Dahl PJ, Steele TP.

Organization as author. Whenever possible, use an abbreviation or acronym for the name of the organization.

AMA.
UNICEF.
Canadian Society for Chemistry.

Editor. Add the word *editor* or *editors* after the last name.

Walter PA, editor.
Mednick VB, Henry JP, editors.

Titles

Books. Use the title given on the book's title page. Titles are neither underlined nor italicized. Capitalize only the first word of the title and any proper nouns or adjectives. Subtitles are not capitalized.

The magpies: the ecology and behaviour of black-billed and yellow-billed magpies.

If the book is a second or subsequent edition, follow the title with a period and then the number of the edition: 3rd ed.

Genetics. 5th ed.

Journals, magazines, and newspapers. For journal titles of more than one word, use standard abbreviations

J Mamm (for *Journal of Mammology*)
National Geographic
New York Times

(for example, *Sci Am* for *Scientific American*). Standard abbreviations are listed in Appendix 1 of *Scientific Style and Format*. They can also be found at www.library.uq.edu.au/faqs/endnote/biosciences.txt. Use full names of magazines and newspapers, omitting any initial *The*.

Publication Data

Books. Include the place of publication, the publisher's name, and the year of publication. The place of publication can usually be found on the title page. If more than one city is mentioned, use the first one listed. If the city is not well known, clarify the location by including an abbreviation for the state, province, or country in parentheses after the name of the city. The publisher's name should be listed next, separated from the place of publication by a colon and one space. (Standard abbreviations for publishing companies may be used. These are listed in Appendix 2 of *Scientific Style and Format*.) After the publisher's name, if you are using the citation-sequence system, list the year of publication, separating it from the publisher's name with a semicolon and one space.

London: Chatto & Windus; 2004.
Orlando (FL): Harcourt; 2005.

Journals. Use one space after the journal title; then indicate the date of publication and the volume and issue numbers. Place a semicolon between the date of publication and the volume number. Put the issue number in parentheses. An issue number is not required for articles in journals with continuous pagination.

Journal with separate pagination
Nature 2002;420(6911)
Journal with continuous pagination
Am Nat 2004;164

(Continued on page 380)

Publication Data *(continued from page 379)*

Note that there are no spaces separating the year, the volume number, and the issue number.

Magazines and newspapers.
Place the year, month, and day of publication (if any) after the name of the magazine or newspaper.

Magazine
National Geographic 2002 Nov
Newspaper
New York Times 2004 Oct 26

Page Numbers

Books. At the end of the entry, provide the total number of pages, excluding preliminary pages with roman numerals. Use the abbreviation *p* for *pages*: 431 p.

Journals and magazines. Page numbers should be expressed as a range, with the second number shortened as much as possible: 237–45 or 430–4.

Newspapers. Include the section letter, the page number, and the column number: Sect A:2(col 1).

Electronic Sources

Because the CSE manual was last published in 1994, it refers users who need guidance in documenting electronic sources to another scientific manual: *National Library of Medicine Recommended Formats for Bibliographic Citation.* According to this guide, entries for electronic sources are similar to those for books and articles; however, they include three additional pieces of information:

Ollerton J, Johnson SD, Cranmer L, Kellie S. The pollination ecology of an assemblage of grassland asclepiads in South Africa. Ann Bot [Internet]; 2003 [cited 2005 May 13];92(6): 807–34. Available from: http://aob.oupjournals.org/cgi/content/full/92/6/807

See pages 382–383 for other examples.

1. The word *Internet* is placed in square brackets after the title of the book or the name of the journal to indicate that the work is an online source.
2. The date of access, preceded by the word *cited*, is given in square brackets after the date of publication.
3. The Internet address (URL) is included at the end of the entry.

BOOKS

1. Book with one author

Citation-sequence system

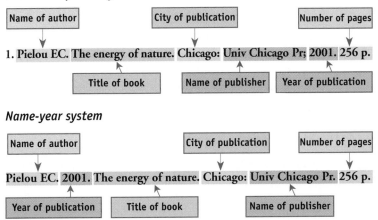

Name of author   City of publication   Number of pages

1. Pielou EC. The energy of nature. Chicago: Univ Chicago Pr; 2001. 256 p.

Title of book   Name of publisher   Year of publication

Name-year system

Name of author   City of publication   Number of pages

Pielou EC. 2001. The energy of nature. Chicago: Univ Chicago Pr. 256 p.

Year of publication   Title of book   Name of publisher

2. Book with two or more authors

2. McPherson GR, DeStefano S. Applied ecology and natural resource management.

Cambridge: Cambridge Univ Pr; 2002. 180 p.

3. Book with an organization (or organizations) listed as author

3. Seattle Times. Natural wonders: the flora, fauna & formations of Washington. Seattle:

Seattle Times; 2003. 150 p.

4. Book with editor(s)

4. Pimentel D, Westra L, Noss RF, editors. Ecological integrity. Washington: Island Pr; 2000. 428 p.

5. Chapter or part of an edited book

5. Hall SJ, Raffaelli DG. Food web patterns: what do we really know? In: Gange AC, Brown VK, editors. Multitrophic interactions in terrestrial systems. Oxford: Blackwell Science; 1997. p 395–418.

ARTICLES

6. Article in a journal with continuous pagination

6. Crickett A, Morgan D, Gulik S. New insights into chimpanzees, tools, and termites from the Congo Basin. Am Nat 2004;164:567–81.

7. Article in a journal with issues paginated separately

7. Milad MR, Quirk GJ. Neurons in medial prefrontal cortex signal memory for fear extinction. Nature 2002;420(6911):70–3.

8. Article in a popular (general-circulation) magazine

8. Morell V. Kings of the hill? National Geographic 2002 Nov:100–20.

9. Article in a newspaper

9. O'Connor A. Heart attack risk linked to time spent in traffic. New York Times 2004 Oct 26;Sect F:9(col 4).

ELECTRONIC SOURCES

10. Online book

10. Nielsen C. Interrelationships of the living phyla [Internet]. New York: Oxford Univ Pr; 1995 [cited 2002 Oct 30]. 467 p. Available from: http://emedia.netlibrary.com/reader/reader.asp?product_id522950

11. Article in an online journal

11. Van Lunteren E, Torres A, Moyer M. Effects of hypoxia on diaphragm relaxation rate during fatigue. J Appl Physiol [Internet] 1997 [cited 2002 Dec 2]; 82(5):1472–8. Available from: http://jap.physiology.org/cgi/content/full/82/5/1472

12. Article in an online newspaper

12. Forero J. As Andean glaciers shrink, water worries grow. New York Times on the Web [Internet] 2002 Nov 23 [cited 2002 Dec 7]:[about 31 paragraphs]. Available from: http://www.nytimes.com/2002/11/24/international/americas/ 24BOLI.html?pagewanted51

13. Web site

13. Corvus corax [Internet]. Bay Shore (NY): Long Island Ravens MC; c2000–2002 [updated 2001 Dec 3; cited 2003 Jan 3]. Available from: http://www.liravensmc.org/ About/about_ravens.htm

14. Listserv posting

14. Reed T. Patient Safety News. In: MEDLIB-L [Internet]. [Chicago: Medical Library Assoc]; 2002 Nov 18, 9:46am [cited 2002 Nov 30]:[1 paragraph]. Available from: MEDLIB-L@LISTSERV.ACSU.BUFFALO.EDU

Name-year system

The following sample entries for a references list in the name-year format correspond to those listed in the section on the citation-sequence system. However, the list is ordered alphabetically. The individual entries for books and articles differ from those in citation-sequence format only in the placement of the date. According to the name-year system, the date follows the author's name. Because the National Library of Medicine provides only one format for online sources, the entries for these sources are not repeated in this list.

References

Crickett A, Morgan D, Gulik S. 2004. New insights into chimpanzees, tools, and termites from the Congo Basin. Am Nat 164:567–81.

Hall SJ, Rafaelli DG. 1997. Food web patterns: what do we really know? In: Gange AC, Brown VK, editors. Multitrophic interactions in terrestrial systems. Oxford: Blackwell Scientific. p 395–418.

McPherson GR, DeStefano S. 2002. Applied ecology and natural resource management. Cambridge: Cambridge Univ Pr. 180 p.

Milad MR, Quirk GJ. 2002. Neurons in medial prefrontal cortex signal memory for fear extinction. Nature 420(6911):70–3.

Morell V. 2002 Nov. Kings of the hill? National Geographic:100–20.

O'Connor A. 2004 Oct 26. Heart attack risk linked to time spent in traffic. New York Times;Sect F:9(col 4).

Pielou EC. 2001. The energy of nature. Chicago: Univ Chicago Pr. 256 p.

Pimental D, Westra L, Noss RF, editors. 2000. Ecological integrity. Washington: Island Press. 428 p.

Seattle Times. 2003. Natural wonders: the flora, fauna & formations of Washington. Seattle: Seattle Times. 150 p.

15b CSE-style paper

Papers written for courses in the natural sciences often take the form of reports of study results and are generally divided into six main sections: **abstract, introduction, methods and materials, results, discussion,** and **references** (see 18c(2) and 18d). The following sample report, written by Geoff Rutledge for a course in comparative anatomy and physiology, includes excerpts from his abstract and introduction along with the references list. Because the CSE guidelines were not intended to be applied to undergraduate papers, you should follow your instructor's directions for formatting a title page similar to the one shown here. To read the complete report, visit www.harbrace.com.

The Effect of Nicotine Chewing Gum on Cardiovascular Function in Nonsmokers

Geoff Rutledge

Comparative Anatomy and Physiology 350

April 26, 2002

1

Abstract

Nicotine, the primary addictive substance in tobacco, affects cardiovascular function primarily through its binding to sympathetic postganglionic nicotinic acetylcholine receptors. This binding stimulates the release of norepinephrine, which in turn stimulates heart rate, ventricle contraction strength, and vasoconstriction of blood vessels. This study examined the cardiovascular effects in nonsmokers who chewed gum containing 4 mg of nicotine for 20 min.

[The abstract continues.]

Introduction

Nicotine, the primary addictive substance found in tobacco,[1] is a drug known to have both stimulant and depressant impacts, thus producing complex changes in the body.[2] However, in most clinical settings, nicotine's sympathetic impact has been found to strongly dominate any parasympathetic activity.[3] Nicotine's stimulatory mode of action involves activating a release of catecholamines directly through the adrenal medulla and also stimulating postganglionic sympathetic nerve endings.[3] These postganglionic sympathetic nerve endings are normally stimulated by a release of acetylcholine (Ach) from the preganglionic neuron. However, nicotine mimics Ach and binds to the nicotinic acetylcholine receptors, thus stimulating the release of the sympathetic neurotransmitter norepinephrine (Nor) into the body.[3] In addition to producing this release of Nor from the sympathetic nervous system, nicotine also produces a release of Nor and the sympathetic neurotransmitter epinephrine (Epi) from the adrenal medulla, thus strengthening the stimulatory mode of action.[2]

[Text omitted.]

This experiment tested the effects of nicotine chewing gum on cardiovascular function in nonsmoking individuals. Previous studies have shown significant increases in heart rate, systolic blood pressure, and diastolic blood pressure of smokers within 30 min of being exposed to nicotine from cigarettes, oral snuff, chewing tobacco, and nicotine gum.[5] This study investigated the effect of nicotine chewing gum on nonsmokers, in order to determine the effects of isolated nicotine (free from other toxins present in cigarette smoke) on human cardiovascular systems not acclimated to its presence. Because of the stimulatory effects of nicotine on the sympathetic release of Nor and Epi, the hypothesis tested was that individuals exposed to nicotine would experience increases from normal testing values in both heart rate and blood pressure.

[The introduction continues and is followed by the remainder of the paper.]

11

References

1. Tanus-Santos JE, Toledo JCY, Cittadino M, Sabha M, Rocha, JC, Moreno H. Cardiovascular effects of transdermal nicotine in mildly hypertensive smokers. Am J Hypertens 2001;14:610–4.

2. Goodman LS, Gilman A. The pharmacological basis of therapeutics. 5th ed. New York: Macmillan; 1975. 1704 p.

3. Haass M, Kuhler W. Nicotine and sympathetic neurotransmission. Cardiovasc Drug Ther 1997;10:657–65.

4. Silverthorn DU. Human physiology: an integrated approach. 2nd ed. Upper Saddle River (NJ): Prentice Hall; 2001. 816 p.

5. Benowitz NL, Porchet H, Sheiner L, Jacob P. Nicotine absorption and cardiovascular effects with smokeless tobacco use: comparison with cigarettes and nicotine gum. Clin Pharmacol Ther 1988;44:23–8.

6. Nyberg G, Panfilov V, Sivertsson R, Wilhelmsen L. Cardiovascular effects of nicotine chewing gum in healthy nonsmokers. Eur J Clin Pharmacol 1982;23:303–7.

7. Benowitz NL, Gourlay SG. Cardiovascular toxicity of nicotine: implications for nicotine replacement therapy. J Am Coll Cardiol 1997;29:1422–31.

Researchers in the social and natural sciences often collect data through observation.

16 WRITING TO INTERPRET LITERATURE

You have been interpreting and writing about literature—talking about plot, characters, and setting—ever since you wrote your first book report. When you write about literature in college—whether the work is fiction, drama, poetry, essays, manifestos, or memoirs—you will still discuss plot, characters, and setting. But you will also apply many of the same strategies you use when writing about other topics: you will respond to an exigence, explore and focus your subject, formulate a thesis statement that can be supported from the literary work itself, address an audience, and arrange your thoughts in the most effective way. In short, you will respond to the rhetorical situation.

Figure 16.1 (on page 392) shows how the elements of the rhetorical situation apply to a specific piece of writing about literature: an article on Henry James by literary critic Sarah A. Wadsworth. In response to the accepted belief that James invented the character type described as "the American woman abroad" in his novel *Daisy Miller,* Wadsworth argues that James's portrayal reshaped rather than invented the type.

This chapter will help you

- recognize the various genres of literature (16a),
- use the specialized vocabulary for discussing literature (16b),
- employ various critical approaches for interpreting literature (16c),
- realize the value of a careful reading (16d),
- understand specific terms that define the purpose of an interpretation (16e), and
- apply the special conventions for writing about literature (16f–g).

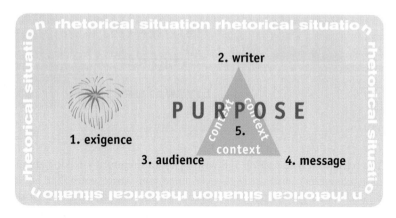

1. Recognition of the character type "the American woman abroad" in works prior to *Daisy Miller*
2. Sarah A. Wadsworth, Ph.D.
3. Scholars interested in Henry James and nineteenth-century women's issues and female characters in literature
4. *Daisy Miller* reshaped rather than reinvented the character type "the American woman abroad."
5. Dispute over James's place in the nineteenth-century literary canon

Fig. 16.1. Sample rhetorical situation for literature.

16a　Literature and its genres

Like all specialized fields, literature can be divided into categories, which are referred to as **genres.** A genre can be identified by its particular features or conventions. Some genres are timeless and universal (drama and poetry, for instance); while others are context-specific and develop within a specific culture (detective fiction is a recent Western cultural phenomenon).

Just as you can recognize film genres—action, suspense, horror, comedy, animated, Western, and science fiction—you can identify various literary genres: from poetry and drama to essays and narratives. Just as film genres sometimes overlap (for example, when an action film is partially animated), so do literary genres: some poems are referred to as prose poems, whereas some plays are written in poetic verse. But even when genres overlap, the identifiable features of each genre are still evident.

Some of the most widely studied literary genres are fiction, drama, and poetry, though many forms of nonfiction (including personal essays and memoirs, literacy narratives, and manifestos) are being studied in college courses on literature. All imaginative literature can be characterized as fictional, but the term **fiction** is applied specifically to novels and short stories.

Drama differs from all other imaginative literature in one specific way: it is meant to be performed—whether on stage, on film, or on television—with the director and actors imprinting the lines with their own interpretations. In fact, the method of presentation distinguishes drama from fiction, even though the two genres share many of the same elements (setting, character, plot, and dialogue). In a novel, you often find extensive descriptions of characters and setting, as well as passages revealing what characters are thinking. In a play, you learn what a character is thinking when he or she shares thoughts with another character in dialogue or presents a **dramatic soliloquy** (a speech delivered to the audience by an actor alone on the stage). And like fiction, nonfiction, and poetry, drama can be read; in which case, you bring your interpretative abilities to the printed page rather than to a performance of the work.

Poetry shares many of the components of fiction and drama. It, too, may have a narrator with a point of view. Dramatic monologues and narrative poems sometimes have a plot, a setting, and characters. But poetry is primarily characterized by its extensive use of connotative language, imagery, allusions, figures of speech, symbols, sound, and rhythm.

16b Vocabulary for discussing literature

Like all specialized fields, literature has a unique vocabulary, which describes the various features of literary texts and concepts of literary analysis. As you learn this vocabulary, you will learn more than just a list of terms: you will learn how to understand, interpret, and write about literature.

(1) Characters carry the plot forward.

The **characters** are the humans or humanlike personalities (aliens, creatures, robots, animals, and so on) who carry the plot forward; they

Understanding how a particular character moves the plot forward will help you interpret the work as a whole.

usually include a main character, called a **protagonist,** who is in external conflict with another character or an institution or in internal conflict with himself or herself. This conflict usually reveals the **theme,** or the central idea of the work (see **16b(7)**).

Because writing about literature often requires character analysis, you need to understand the characters in any work you read. You can do so by paying close attention to their appearance, their language, and their actions. You also need to pay attention to what the narrator or other characters say about them. Whether you are writing about characters in a novel, in a play, or in a poem, you will want to concentrate on what those characters do and say—and why.

(2) Imagery is conveyed by descriptive language.

The imagery in a piece of literature is conveyed by **descriptive language,** or words that describe a sensory experience. Notice the images in "Portrait," a prose poem by Pinkie Gordon Lane that focuses on the life—and death—of a mother.

> My mother died walking along a dusty road on a Sunday morning in New Jersey. The road came up to meet her sinking body in one quick embrace. She spread out like an umbrella and dropped into oblivion before she hit the ground. In that one swift moment all light went out at the age of forty-nine. Her legacy: the blackened knees of the scrub-woman who ransomed her soul so that I might live, who bled like a tomato whenever she fought to survive, who laughed fully when amused—her laughter rising in one huge crescendo—and whose wings soared in dark despair. . . .
>
> —**PINKIE GORDON LANE,** *Girl at the Window*

The dusty road, the sinking body, the quick embrace—these images convey the loneliness and swiftness of death. The blackened knees, bleeding tomato, and rising laughter, in contrast, are images of a life of work, struggle, and joy.

(3) The narrator tells the story.

The **narrator** of a literary work tells the story, and this speaking voice can be that of a specific character (or of characters taking turns), can seem to be that of the work's author (referred to as the **persona,** which should not be confused with the author), or can be that of an all-knowing presence (referred to as an **omniscient narrator**) that transcends both characters and author. Whatever the type of voice, the narrator's tone reveals his or her attitude toward events and characters and even, in some circumstances, toward readers. By determining the tone and the impact it has on you as a reader, you can gain insight into the author's purpose. (See 4a(3).)

Through the voices of her characters, her narrators, and herself, prominent American author Alice Walker speaks to the importance of preserving Black culture.

(4) Plot is the sequence of events and more.

The **plot** is what happens in the story, the sequence of events (the narrative)—and more. The plot establishes how events are patterned or related in terms of conflict and resolution. Narrative answers "What comes next?" and plot answers "Why?" Consider this example:

Narrative   The sister returned home to visit her family and left again.

Plot   The city sister visited her country family, for whom she had no respect, and they were relieved when she left again.

Plot usually begins with a conflict, an unstable situation that sets events

In Alice Walker's "Everyday Use," Dee and her boyfriend come to the country to visit her mother and sister.

in motion (for instance, the state of tension or animosity between the city sister and her country family). In what is called the **exposition,** the author introduces the characters, setting, and background—the elements that not only constitute the unstable situation but also relate to the events that follow. The subsequent series of events leads to the **climax,** the most intense event in the narrative. The climax is also referred to as the **turning point** because what follows is **falling action** (or **dénouement**) that leads to a resolution of the conflict and a stable situation.

(5) Setting involves place and time.

Setting involves place—not just the physical setting, but also the social setting (the morals, manners, and customs of the characters). Setting also involves time—not only historical time, but also the length of time

covered by the narrative. Setting includes atmosphere, or the emotional response to the situation, often shared by the reader with the characters. For example, San Francisco in the nineteenth century is a markedly different setting from the same city in the twenty-first century. Not only has the physical appearance of the city changed, but so has the social setting and the atmosphere. Being aware of the features of the setting will help you better understand the story, whether it is written as fiction, drama, or poetry.

This nineteenth-century street scene, illustrating a time when both people and vehicles moved more slowly, suggests the spirit of early San Francisco.

(6) Symbols resonate with broader meaning.

Frequently used by writers of literature, a **symbol** is an object, usually concrete, that stands for something else, usually abstract. For example, at the beginning of *A Streetcar Named Desire,* a play by Tennessee Williams, one of the main characters buys a paper lantern to cover a naked light bulb. During the scenes that follow, she frequently talks about light, emphasizing her preference for soft lighting. At the end of the play, another character tears off the lantern, and a third character tries to return the ruined lantern to the main character as she is being taken away to a mental hospital. Anyone seeing this play performed or reading it carefully would note that the paper lantern is a symbol. It is an object that is part of the setting and the plot, but it also stands for something more than it is (a character's avoidance of harsh truths).

When you write about a particular symbol, first note where it appears in the literary work. To determine what the symbol might mean, consider why it appears in those places and to what effect. Once you have an idea about the meaning, trace the incidents in the literary work that reinforce it.

(7) The theme is the main idea of a literary work.

The main idea of a literary work is its **theme.** Depending on how they interpret a work, different readers may identify different themes. To test whether the idea you have identified is central to the work in question, check to see if it is supported by the setting, plot, characters, and symbols. If you can relate these components to the idea you are considering, then that idea can be considered the work's theme. The most prominent literary themes arise out of conflict: person versus person, person versus self, person versus nature, or person versus society.

When you believe you have identified the theme, state it as a sentence—and be precise. A theme conveys a specific idea; it should not be confused with a topic.

Topic	family heritage
Vague theme	Alice Walker's "Everyday Use" is about family heritage.
Specific theme	"Everyday Use" reveals a conflict between a sister who puts her heritage on display and a sister who puts her heritage to use, every day.

BEYOND THE RULE

OTHER USEFUL LITERARY TERMS

As you draft and revise your essays about literature, you may want to use some of the literary terms, such as *antagonist, local color,* and *climax,* defined at **www.harbrace.com.**

CHECKLIST for Interpreting a Literary Work

- From whose point of view is the story told?
- Who is the protagonist? How is his or her character developed?
- With whom or what is the protagonist in conflict?
- How are the other characters depicted and distinguished through dialogue?
- What is the theme? How does the author use setting, plot, characters, and symbols to establish that theme?
- What symbols, images, or figures of speech does the author use? To what effect?

16c Approaches to interpreting literature

Writing a paper about a literary work usually requires you to focus on the work itself and to demonstrate that you have read it carefully—a process known as **close reading.** (Compare close reading with reading rhetorically; see chapter 2.) Through close reading, you can offer an **interpretation,** an explanation of what you see in a work. An interpretation can be shaped by your personal response to what you have read, a specific type of literary theory, or the views of other readers, whom you wish to support or challenge.

Literary theory, the scholarly discussion of how the nature and function of literature can be determined, ranges from approaches that focus almost exclusively on the text itself (its language and structure) to approaches that show how the text relates to author, reader, language, society, culture, economics, or history. Familiarity with literary theory enriches your reading of literature as well as your understanding of the books and essays about literature that you will discover when you do research (see chapter 9). Literary theory can also help you decide how you want to focus your writing about literature.

Although the most popular theoretical approaches to literature overlap somewhat, each has a different primary focus: the reader, some feature of the social or cultural context, the text itself, or the author or characters. Interpreting literature involves a responsible reliance on one or more of these approaches—*for whatever your interpretation, the text should support it.*

(1) Reader-response theory focuses on the reader.

According to **reader-response theory,** readers construct meaning as they read and interact with the elements within a text, with each reader bringing something different (intellectual values and life experiences) to the text on every reading. Thus, meaning is not fixed *on* the page; it depends on what each reader brings *to* the page. Furthermore, the same reader can have different responses to the same literary work when rereading it after a number of years: a father of teenagers might find Gwendolyn Brooks's "we real cool" more disturbing than it had seemed when he first read it in high school. Although a reader-response approach to literature encourages diverse interpretations, you cannot simply say, "Well, that's what this work means to me" or "That's my interpretation." You must demonstrate to your audience how each element of the work supports your interpretation.

(2) Both feminist and gender-based literary theories focus on issues related to gender and sexuality.

The significance of sex, gender, or sexual orientation within a particular social context is the interpretive focus of **feminist** and **gender-based literary theories.** These theories enable a reader to analyze the ways in which a work (through its characters, theme, or plot) promotes or challenges the prevailing intellectual or cultural assumptions of its day regarding issues related to gender and sexuality, including patriarchy and compulsory heterosexuality. For instance,

Like the early suffragists, many feminist literary critics focus on prevailing social and cultural constraints affecting women.

Edith Wharton's *The Age of Innocence* compares two upper-class nineteenth-century women in terms of the specific social pressures that shaped and constricted their lives and loves. A feminist critic might emphasize the oppression of these women and the repression of their sexuality. On reading Henry James's *The Bostonians*, another critic, using a gender-based approach, might focus on the positive features of the domestic relationship between the financially independent Olive and Verena. That same critic might also try to explain why Jake Barnes in Ernest Hemingway's *The Sun Also Rises* bonds with some men and is contemptuous of others.

(3) Race-based literary theory focuses on issues related to race relations.

Frederick Douglass's *Narrative* details his encounters with racism, both as a victim of slavery and as a free man.

A useful form of race-based literary criticism, **critical race theory** focuses on the significance of race relations (race, racism, and power) within a specific historical and social setting in order to explain the experience and literary production of any people whose history is characterized by political, social, and psychological oppression. Not only does this theoretical approach seek out previously neglected literary works, but it also illuminates the ways in which race, ethnicity, and the imbalance of power inform many works. Previously neglected works such as Zora Neale Hurston's *Their Eyes Were Watching God*, Rudolpho Anaya's *Bless Me, Ultima,* and Frederick Douglass's *Narrative,* which demonstrate how racism affects the characters' lives, have taken on considerable cultural value in the last twenty years. **African American literary criticism,** for example, has been particularly successful in invigorating the study of great African American writers, whose works can be more fully appreciated when readers consider how literary elements of some of these works have been informed by the social forces that helped produce them. Closely associated with critical race theory is **postcolonial theory,** which takes into account the relationship of the colonized with the colonizer and the challenge a text can direct at the dominant powers at a particular time and place, asserting a drive toward the liberation of oppressed social groups. Joseph Conrad's *Heart of Darkness,* Jean Rhys's *Wide Sargasso Sea,* Daniel Defoe's *Robinson Crusoe,* and E. M. Forster's *A Passage to India* can all be read productively through the lens of postcolonial theory.

(4) Class-based literary theory focuses on socioeconomic issues.

To explain the conflict between literary characters or between a character and a community or institution, **class-based literary theory** draws on the work of Karl Marx, Terry Eagleton, and others who have addressed the implications of social hierarchies and the accompanying economic tensions. These theorists argue that differences in socioeconomic class—in the material conditions of daily life—divide people in profoundly significant ways, more so than differences in race, ethnicity, culture, and gender. Thus, a class-based approach can be used to explain why Emma Bovary is unhappy, despite her "good" (that is, financially advantageous) marriage, in Gustave Flaubert's *Madame Bovary,* why Bigger Thomas gets thrown into such a confused mental state in Richard Wright's *Native Son,* or why a family loses its land in John Steinbeck's *The Grapes of Wrath.*

(5) Text-based literary theory focuses on the work itself.

Text-based literary theory demands concentration on the piece of literature itself; with this approach, only the use of concrete, specific examples from the text validates an interpretation. The reader must pay careful attention to the elements within the literary work—plot, characters, setting, tone, dialogue, imagery, and so on—to evaluate their interaction, overall effect, and meaning. Nothing more than what is contained within the text itself—not information about the author's life or about his or her culture or society—is needed to understand and appreciate the text's unchanging meaning. Readers may change, but the meaning of the text does not. A close reading of the work is essential, then, in order to account for all of its particularities, including the ways in which the language and the structure fit within a specific literary genre.

(6) Context-based literary theory focuses on the time and place in which a work was created.

Context-based literary theory considers the historical period during which a work was written and the cultural and economic patterns that prevailed during that period. For example, recognizing that Willa Cather published *My Ántonia* during World War I can help account for the darker side of that novel about European immigrants' harsh life in the American West; similarly, understanding that Arthur Miller wrote *The Crucible* in response to the accusations of the House Un-American Activities Committee in the 1950s helps explain why that play generated so much excitement when it was first produced. Critics who use a context-based and class-based approach known as **cultural studies** consider how a literary work interacts with economic conditions, socioeconomic classes, and other cultural artifacts (such as songs or fashion) from the period in which it was written.

(7) Psychoanalytic theories focus on psychological factors affecting the writing and the reading of literature.

This ancient stone sculpture, called the Venus of Willendorf, represents an archetype known as the earth mother.

By focusing on the psychological states of the author and the characters as well as the reader, **psychoanalytic theories** seek to explain human experience and behavior in terms of sexual impulses and unconscious motivations (drives, desires, fears, needs, and conflicts). When applied to literature, these theories (based on the work of Nancy Chodorow, Hélène Cixous, Sigmund Freud, Melanie Klein, and Jacques Lacan, among others) help readers discern the motivations of characters, envision the psychological state of the author as implied by the text, and evaluate the psychological reasons for their own interpretations. Readers may apply the psychoanalytic approach to explain why Hamlet is deeply disturbed by his mother's remarriage, why Holden Caulfield rebels at school (in J. D. Salinger's *The Catcher in the Rye*), or why Rochester is blinded (in Charlotte Brontë's *Jane Eyre*).

Theorists who use the work of psychiatrist Carl Jung to explore **archetypes** (meaningful images that arise from the human unconscious and that appear as recurring figures or patterns in literature) are also using a psychoanalytic approach to interpret literature, whether the literary form is a fairy tale, fable, epic poem, Greek drama, postmodern novel, or movie script. Archetypal figures include the hero, the earth mother, the scapegoat, the outcast, and the cruel stepmother; archetypal patterns include the quest, the initiation, the test, and the return.

16d Active reading and literary interpretation

As you read, trust your own reactions. Were you amused, moved, or confused? Which characters interested you? Were you able to follow the plot? Did the work remind you of any experience of your own? Did it introduce you to a different world in terms of historical or geographical setting, or did you encounter a familiar cast of characters? These first impressions can provide the seeds from which strong essays will grow, especially when they are later modified as you consider the work further.

(1) You can understand your response by considering how it is shaped by your identity.

When reflecting on your response to some element of a work of literature, you can consider how your reading might be shaped by the factors that make you who you are. For example, if you find yourself responding positively or negatively to a character in a novel or play, you could ask yourself whether this response has anything to do with your

- psychological makeup,
- political beliefs,
- gender or sexual orientation,
- race,
- social class,
- religion,
- geographic location, or
- conscious or unconscious theoretical approach.

Thinking along these lines can help you decide how to focus your essay and prepare you for using one or more theoretical approaches as the basis for your interpretation.

(2) After choosing a topic, develop it, based on evidence in the text.

If you are choosing your own topic, your first step is to reflect on your personal response, focusing on that response as you formulate a tentative thesis statement. Next, consider what specific evidence from the text will best explain and support your interpretation and thesis statement.

Because most readers will be interested in what *you* think, you need to discover a way to demonstrate your originality in terms of a topic you can develop adequately, by applying one or more rhetorical methods (see 3g). You might define why you consider a character heroic, classify a play as a comedy of manners, or describe a setting that anchors a work's meaning. Perhaps you can compare and contrast two poems on a similar subject or explore cause-and-effect relationships in a novel. Why, for example, does an apparently intelligent character make a bad decision? Or you might show how the description of a family's house in a novel defines that family's values or reveals the effects of an underlying conflict.

(3) Research can reveal the ways other readers have responded to a literary work.

You will undoubtedly anchor your essay in your personal response or interpretation. But if you read works of literary theory, visit online discussion groups or forums (see 6c), participate in class discussions, or become active in a book club, you can engage in a dialogue that can enrich your own ideas. Many instructors prefer that you advance your own ideas at the same time as you use and give credit to outside sources. Although it is tempting to lean heavily on the interpretations of experts, remember that your readers are mainly interested in your interpretation and in your use of the sometimes conflicting interpretations of others (including the other members of your class) to support your own points.

To locate material on a specific writer or work, consult your library's catalog (see 9b–c) and *The MLA International Bibliography*, an index of books and articles about literature that is an essential resource for literary studies and that can be consulted in printed volumes or online.

In addition to having books and articles about specific writers, your school or public library also possesses a number of reference books that provide basic information on writers, books, and literary theory. Works such as *Contemporary Authors, The Oxford Companion to English Literature,* and *The New Princeton Handbook of Poetic Terms* can be useful when you are beginning your research or when you have encountered terms you need to clarify.

16e Types of literary interpretation

An interpretation that attempts to explain the meaning of one feature of a literary work is called an **analysis.** To analyze a work of literature, a writer focuses on one of its elements, such as the setting or the main character, and determines how that one element contributes to the work's overall meaning. A common form of analysis is **character**

analysis, in which a writer interprets one or more aspects of a single character. An analysis can also focus on a single scene, symbol, or theme.

An interpretation that attempts to explain every element in a literary work is called an **explication** and is usually used only with poetry. When explicating William Wordsworth's "A Slumber Did My Spirit Seal," a writer might note that the *s* sound reinforces the hushed feeling of sleep and death in the poem. But it would also be necessary to consider the meanings of *slumber, spirit,* and *seal.*

An **evaluation** of a work gauges how successful the author is in communicating meaning to readers. The most common types of evaluation are book, theater, and film reviews. A writer can also evaluate a work by focusing on how successfully one of its parts contributes to the meaning conveyed by the others. Like any other interpretation, an evaluation is a type of argument in which a writer cites evidence to persuade readers to accept a clearly formulated thesis. (See chapters 3 and 8.) An evaluation of a literary work should provide evidence of its strengths as well as its weaknesses, if any.

Although summarizing a literary work can be a useful way to make sure you understand it, do not confuse a summary with an analysis, an explication, or an evaluation. Those who have read the work do not need to read a summary of it. Do not submit one unless your instructor has asked for it.

Exercise 1

Attend a film, a play, or a poetry reading at your school or in your community. Write a two- to three-page essay evaluating the work, using one of the theoretical approaches discussed in this chapter.

16f Conventions for writing about literature

Writing about literature involves adhering to several conventions.

(1) The first person is typically used.

When writing your analysis of a piece of literature, you can use the first-person singular pronoun, *I*:

Although some critics believe Anaya's novel to be about witchcraft, I think it is about the power of belief.

By doing so, you indicate that your opinion about a work differs from a popular one. To own an opinion, belief, or interpretation, though, you must support it with specific evidence from the text itself.

(2) The present tense is used in discussions of literary works.

Use the present tense when discussing a literary work, since the author of the work is communicating to the reader at the present time. (See **26b(1)**.)

In "A Good Man Is Hard to Find," the grandmother reaches out to touch her killer just before he pulls the trigger.

Similarly, use the present tense when reporting how other writers have interpreted the work you are discussing.

As Henry Louis Gates demonstrates in his analysis of . . . .

(3) Documentation of sources follows certain formats.

When writing about a work assigned by your instructor, you may not need to give the source and publication information. However, if you are using an edition or translation that may be different from the one your audience is using, you should indicate this. One way of doing so is to use the MLA format for listing works cited, as explained in section **12b**, although your bibliography in this case will consist of only a single work—the one you are discussing. An alternative way of providing documentation for a single source is by acknowledging the first quotation from the work in an explanatory note on a separate page at the end of your paper and then giving parenthetical page numbers in the body of the paper for all subsequent references to the work.

[1]Dorothy Allison, "Believing in Literature," *Skin: Talking about Sex, Class, and Literature* (Ithaca: Firebrand, 1994) 165-82. All subsequent references to this work will be identified with page numbers within the text.

If you use this note form, you may not need to repeat the bibliographical information on a list of works cited, nor will you need to include the author's name in subsequent parenthetical references. Check with your instructor about the format he or she prefers.

When you use a bibliography to provide publication data, you must indicate specific references whenever you quote a line or passage. According to MLA style, such bibliographic information should be placed in the text in parentheses directly after the quotation, and a period, a semicolon, or a comma should follow the parentheses. (See 12a(1) and 38d(1).) Quotations from short stories and novels are identified by the author's name and page number.

"A man planning to spend money on me was an experience rare enough to feel odd"

(Gordon 19).

Quotations from poems are referred to by line number.

"O Rose, thou are sick!" (Blake 1).

And quotations from plays require act, scene, and line numbers.

"How much better it is to weep at joy than to joy at weeping" (*Ado* 1.1.28).

This reference indicates that the line quoted is from act I, scene I, line 28 of Shakespeare's play *Much Ado about Nothing*.

(4) Quoting poetry involves several conventions.

For poems and verse plays, type quotations involving three or fewer lines in the text and insert a slash (see 39i) with a space on each side to separate the lines.

"Does the road wind uphill all the way? / Yes, to the very end" (Rossetti 1-2). Christina Rossetti opens her poem "Uphill" with this two-line question and answer.

Quotations of more than three lines should be indented one inch from the left-hand margin and double-spaced. Do not use slashes at the ends of lines, and make sure to follow the original text for line breaks, special indenting, or spacing. For this type of block quotation, place your citation outside the final punctuation mark.

(5) Authors' names are referred to in standard ways.

Use the full name of the author of a work in your first reference and only the last name in all subsequent references. For instance, refer to

"Charles Dickens" or "Willa Cather" the first time, and after that, use "Dickens" or "Cather." Never refer to a female author differently than you do a male author. For example, use "Robert Browning and Elizabeth Barrett Browning" or "Browning and Barrett Browning" (not "Browning and Mrs. Browning" or "Browning and Elizabeth").

16g A student essay interpreting a work of literature

In the following essay, undergraduate English major Kaitlyn Andrews-Rice analyzes Alice Walker's short story "Everyday Use." In addition to reading the story, she watched a dramatization of it on DVD. Andrews-Rice had the opportunity to choose her own topic, so she focused (see 3b) on the ways two sisters use their heritage, showing that everyday use is the best way.

Kaitlyn Andrews-Rice

Dr. Glenn

English 100

7 March 2005

Honoring Heritage with Everyday Use

"Everyday Use," one of the short stories in Alice Walker's <u>In Love & Trouble:</u> <u>Stories of Black Women</u>, vividly demonstrates how three women, Mrs. Johnson and her two daughters, regard their heritage.[1] Through the eyes of Mrs. Johnson, the story unfolds when her older daughter returns to her country home, mother, and sister. Throughout the story, Walker emphasizes the shared heritage of these three women and the different ways they use it. In "Everyday Use," an authentic appreciation of heritage does not come from showcasing fashionable artifacts or practices; rather, it comes from embracing that heritage every day.

Walker's physical description of the sisters illustrates the different ways each puts her heritage to use. The beautiful, sophisticated Dee embraces her heritage by showcasing the fashionable Afrocentric sentiment of the time. Her mother describes her as wearing "a dress so loud it hurts my eyes. There are yellows and oranges enough to throw back the light of sun," and her hair "stands straight up like the wool on a sheep" (52). But in addition to her African style, Dee also has "neat-looking" feet, "as if God himself had shaped them with a certain style" (52). That she's stylish comes as no surprise, for even before she appears in the story, the reader is told that "at sixteen, she had a style of her own, and knew what style was" (50). Dee is a book-smart city woman, who uses her knowledge of fashion and style to enhance her physical attributes: she is "lighter than [her sister] Maggie, with nicer hair and a fuller figure" (49). Maggie, on the other hand, replicates her Southern black heritage every day, by helping her mother clean up the dirt yard (raking, lifting, sweeping), in preparation for Dee's homecoming. In addition, Maggie works hard churning butter, cooking over a wood-burning stove, and using the outhouse. She's darker skinned, "homely and ashamed of the burn scars down her arms and legs" (47), and her simple country clothes, "pink skirt and red blouse" (49), are in sharp contrast with Dee's fancy garb.

The filmed version of the story allows the viewer to see Dee arrive home with her boyfriend, Hakim-a-barber, both in their African clothes, exchanging glances of superiority and amusement as they take Polaroid snapshots of the unsophisticated mother

Dee wants to capture the living conditions of her mother and sister.

and sister and their shabby house, as though Dee was completely separated from such living conditions, that heritage, her family.

Another way that Walker illustrates the divide between Dee's understanding of her heritage and her family's is through the use of names. When Dee arrives, she announces that she is "Not 'Dee,' Wangero Leewanika Kemanjo!" (53). According to the interview with Walker that accompanies the Wadsworth Original Film Series in Literature's filmed version of "Everyday Use," the changing of one's name to a more Afrocentric name was common during this time (Everyday Use). In Dee's mind, this fashionable African name is yet another way she is honoring her roots, embracing her heritage, and she tells her family that she "couldn't bear it any longer, being named after the people who oppress [her]" (53). Ironically, her given name carried with it a rich inheritance, that of a long line of Dees or Dicies. Yet Dee is the daughter who denies her Southern heritage and is embarrassed by her Southern family, especially by Maggie, who has taken no steps to "make something of [herself]" (59) other than a wife to local John Thomas Dee. At this point in the story, though, Mrs. Johnson and Maggie agree to go along with Dee's ways and continue to try to please her, even if they do not understand her. It is not until later in Dee's visit that they come to realize the way Dee has embraced a heritage she does not fully understand or appreciate.

To further emphasize the differences among the ways these women understand their heritage, Walker focuses on their educations. Mrs. Johnson describes the way Dee would read to them before she left for college: "She washed us in a river of make-believe, burned us with a lot of knowledge we didn't necessarily need to know" (50). Even though she's somewhat puzzled by Dee's knowledge, she maintains pride in her daughter, especially since Mrs. Johnson never had an education, and Maggie "knows she is not bright" and can read only by "stumbling along good-naturedly" (50). But when Dee accuses Maggie of being "backward," Mrs. Johnson realizes how little Dee's education has taught her about appreciating her heritage.

The focus on family-made quilts at the end of the story shines light on Walker's final take on how heritage is used differently by these women. Mrs. Johnson explains that Dee was offered these quilts before she left for college but refused them because they were "old-fashioned, out of style" (57). Now that the quilts are stylish, Dee wants them in her life. She wants to hang them on her walls, displaying them alongside the butter churn top that she plans to use as a "centerpiece on the alcove table" and dasher that she will do "something artistic" (56) with. For Dee, these artifacts should be on display, not used. But for Maggie and her mother, the quilts represent not only a direct link with their ancestors but a distinct form of African American expression. These particular quilts are made from scraps of Grandma Dee's dresses and from a scrap of fabric from Great Grandpa Ezra's uniform "that he wore in the Civil War" (56). The piecing together of these scraps to form a quilt is a testament to their importance in the heritage of this family. As Dee holds the quilts, she repeats "Imagine!" (57), as if it is so difficult to think of a time when all the stitching was done by hand, something that Maggie is capable of doing every day because "it was Grandma Dee and Big Dee who taught her how to quilt"

Every time Maggie uses the quilts, she feels connected to her family.

(58). When Dee asks to take some quilts back to the city to hang on the wall, her mother resists, saying that Maggie planned to use them. Only then does Dee reveal her prejudices, accusing her sister of being "backward enough to put them [the quilts] to everyday use" (57), right before she storms out of the house.

At this point, when she's been denied the quilts, Dee accuses her family of not understanding their true heritage, saying "It's really a new day for us. But from the way you and Mama still live you'd never know it" (59). She considers herself to be forward looking, because of her African style and name, her education, her cultural displays. In Dee's eyes, her "backward" family does not understand their heritage because they do not display the quilts or the butter churn, they *use* them every day. As Dee drives away, Maggie smiles, and it is "a real smile, not scared" (59), because she knows she embraces, lives, and understands her heritage in a very intimate way.

Andrews-Rice 5

Notes

[1]Alice Walker, "Everyday Use," <u>In Love & Trouble: Stories of Black Women</u> (New York: Harcourt, 1973) 47-59. All subsequent quotations from this work will be identified by page numbers.

Andrews-Rice 6

Works Cited

<u>Everyday Use</u>. Dir. Bruce Schwartz. Perf. Karen ffolkes, Rachel Luttrell, and Lyne Odums. 2003. DVD. Thomson Wadsworth, 2005.

Walker, Alice. <u>In Love & Trouble: Stories of Black Women</u>. New York: Harcourt, 1973. 47-59.

Exercise 2

Based on your reading of Kaitlyn Andrews-Rice's paper on "Everyday Use," what personal or political values do you think she brought to her interpretation of that text? Which of the theoretical approaches to literature did she use as the basis for her interpretation (see 16c)? Write a one- to two-page paper analyzing her interpretation of the story.

WRITING

IN THE

SOCIAL SCIENCES

17

The **social sciences** include psychology, sociology, political science, economics, business, education, and some areas of environmental science. Researchers in the social sciences primarily study how humans behave as members of groups—families, peer groups, ethnic communities, political parties, and many others. Their goal is to state how and why a person or a group tends to behave in a certain way under a particular set of circumstances. Some social scientists, however, study the behavior of animals other than humans.

In courses in the social sciences, you will most often be asked to write observation reports, applications of theory, and library research reports. Given this variety of possible assignments, you will find it beneficial to analyze each rhetorical situation before you start writing. Figure 17.1 illustrates how the elements of the rhetorical situation underpin "What Makes You Who You Are," a newspaper article written in the context of the nature versus nurture debate. Claiming that both nature (genes) and nurture (environment) have a role in shaping human behavior, Matt Ridley describes how genetic and environmental influences interact.

This chapter will help you

- determine the audience, purpose, and research question for a paper in the social sciences (**17a**),
- decide which types of evidence, sources, and reasoning to use in such a paper (**17b**), and
- follow appropriate style, formatting, and documentation conventions when writing the paper (**17c–d**).

1. A newspaper article in which environmental influences were said to be more important than genetic make-up
2. Matt Ridley, author of *Nature via Nurture*
3. Lay readers interested in understanding human behavior
4. Genes and environmental influences interact.
5. The debate over the impacts of nature (genetic make-up) and nurture (environmental influences) on human behavior

Fig. 17.1. Sample rhetorical situation for the social sciences.

17a Audience, purpose, and the research question

The first step to take in completing a writing assignment for a course in the social sciences is to determine your audience and purpose. Your audience will always include your instructor, but it could include students in your class as well. You may also be writing for others outside your class. For example, you may have the opportunity to present your work at a student research conference. Identifying your audience will help you decide how much background information to present, how much technical language to include, and what types of reasoning and evidence (sources) to use.

Most researchers in the social sciences write either to inform or to persuade. If they are simply reporting the results of a study, their purpose is informative. However, if they urge their audience to take some action, their purpose is persuasive. Once you know what your purpose is and to whom you are writing, you can craft a research question that will help you find sources, evaluate them, and use them responsibly (chapters 9–11). Here are some examples of different types of research questions that could be posed about the topic of community service by students:

Questions about causes
Why do students perform community service?

Questions about consequences
What do students believe they have learned through their community service activities?

Questions about process
How do college instructors set up community-service opportunities?

Questions about definitions or categories
What does community service entail?

Questions about values
What values do instructors hope to cultivate by offering community-service opportunities?

17b Evidence, sources, and reasoning

Because researchers in the social sciences try to explain behavior, they commit themselves to observing the activities of humans and other animals, either as individuals or in groups. In order to make accurate observations, these researchers either design controlled laboratory experiments or conduct field research. Interviews and surveys are the two most common techniques for gathering data in the field, although observations and interviews are also widely used. (See 9e.) Both laboratory experiments and field research yield data that social science researchers can use as evidence to make statements (or claims) about human behavior.

Researchers in the social sciences distinguish between quantitative studies and qualitative studies. **Quantitative studies,** such as laboratory experiments and surveys, yield data that can be presented in numerical form, as statistics. Using statistical data and formulas, researchers show how likely it is for a behavior or consequences of the behavior to occur. If you decide to undertake a quantitative study, you should turn your research question into a **hypothesis,** a prediction of what the results of your experiment or survey will be. The study you design, then, will be based on this hypothesis, which should be as objective as possible. Obviously, you cannot entirely eliminate the influence of your own preconceptions, but you can strive to be impartial by avoiding any value judgments. The results of your study will either prove or disprove your hypothesis. Be prepared to provide possible explanations for either result.

Researchers who perform **qualitative studies,** such as observations and interviews, are interested in interpreting behavior by first watching, listening to, or interacting with individuals or a group. If you decide to conduct a qualitative study, you will not reason *from* a hypothesis; you will reason *to* a hypothesis. You will observe a phenomenon and note what you see or hear. Then, instead of reporting numbers as evidence, you will provide detailed descriptions and discuss their significance. Although you may not be able to demonstrate the degree of impartiality prescribed for quantitative research, you should still strive to maintain an objective stance.

Researchers in the social sciences recognize that some studies, such as the field report in 17d, contain both quantitative and qualitative features. They also expect to use both primary and secondary sources (see 9a(3)) in many research projects. Primary sources comprise data derived from experiments, observations, surveys, or interviews. Secondary sources are articles or case studies written about a research topic.

17c Special conventions for reports in the social sciences

(1) Writers in the social sciences follow conventions specified by the style manuals they use.

The language and grammatical structures you use will depend on the style manual prescribed by the discipline in which you are writing. Most of the social sciences follow the guidelines presented in the

Publication Manual of the American Psychological Association (APA; see chapter 13). This manual stresses the importance of writing prose that is clear, concise, unbiased, and well organized. The following specific tips can help you write in the style recommended by the APA manual.

TIPS FOR PREPARING A PAPER IN THE SOCIAL SCIENCES

- Use the active voice as often as possible, although the passive voice may be acceptable for describing methodology. (See page 589.)

- Choose verb tenses carefully. Use the present tense to discuss results and present conclusions (as in "The findings suggest . . ."). Reserve the past tense for referring to specific events in the past and for describing your procedures (as in "Each participant signed a consent form . . .").

- Use a first-person pronoun rather than referring to yourself or to any coauthor(s) and yourself in the third person.

  I
  ~~The experimenter~~ described the procedure to each participant.
  ∧

  We
  ~~The experimenters~~ retested each participant after a rest period.
  ∧

- Clarify noun strings by placing modifiers after the main noun.

  the method for testing literacy NOT the literacy testing method

---

(2) Information is presented in a specific order.

Writing assignments in the social sciences require you to state a research question, thesis, or hypothesis, to discuss research that has already been published about your topic, and, then, in many cases, to describe your methodology and present your conclusions or results. Specific formats are discussed in the following sections.

(a) Library research report

Writing a library research report requires that you read a wide variety of sources on a specific topic and then summarize, critique, and integrate those sources (see chapter 11). These reports generally include the following elements, in this order:

- Statement of the research question or thesis
- Presentation of background information, using sources
- Discussion of major findings presented in the sources
- Application of those findings to the specific research question
- Conclusions
- References

An excerpt from a library research report is shown in fig. 17.2. Author P. A. Blissitt includes an abstract and uses headings to identify the sections of her report. Notice that Blissitt maintains a neutral stance that conveys an impression of impartiality, although she clearly and strongly states her point of view. Another example of a library research report is Nikki Krzmarzick's paper on sleep and memory (see 13c).

Abstract: The relationship of sleep to memory and learning is complex. Sleep affects memory, and memory must be present for learning to occur. A number of studies have been conducted to increase our understanding of their relationship. In addition to the numerous scientific investigations of each concept separately, sleep, memory, and learning have been studied together to determine (a) the effect of sleep on memory and learning, (b) the effect of sleep deprivation in general on memory and learning, (c) the effect of rapid eye movement (REM) sleep deprivation on memory and learning, (d) the effect of memory and learning on REM sleep, and (e) the effect of non-REM sleep loss on memory and learning. Neuro-anatomic correlates have been pursued as well with most attention to the hippocampus. Despite considerable efforts to date, many of the studies reveal contradictory or inconclusive findings. Much remains unknown, and additional work is needed. Implications for nursing include those that have a direct effect on the patient, the nurse, and nursing science.

Sleep, memory, and learning are most often studied as individual concepts. As separate unrelated concepts, much remains unknown about each of them. Yet, despite our lack of knowledge about each individually, the relationship of sleep to memory and learning has been and continues to be investigated in animals and humans. As result of these studies, our knowledge of the relationship of sleep to memory and learning is increasing. This article reviews knowledge about the relationship of sleep to memory, including (a) the effect of sleep on learning and memory, (b) the relationship of sleep deprivation in general to memory, (c) the effect of rapid eye movement (REM) sleep deprivation on memory, (d) the effect of memory and learning on REM sleep, (e) the effect of non-REM sleep deprivation on memory and learning, (f) neuro-anatomic correlates, and (g) implications for nursing practice and research. Only human studies are included. Studies conducted on patients with insomnia are not included because their pattern of cognitive deficits may be different [27]

Sleep, Memory, and Learning

Sleep, memory, and learning are each complex multidimensional biobehavioral systems. Sleep, for example consists of several distinct phases: Stage 1--transitional sleep, Stage 2--light sleep, Stages 3 and 4--slow wave sleep, and Stage 5--REM sleep. Together, Stages 1-4 are called non-REM sleep. Non-REM sleep often is compared with REM sleep. Each of these stages occurs five to six times nightly with a complete cycle of stages lasting 60-90 minutes. One sleep cycle consists of a progression from Stage 1 through Stage 4 of non-REM sleep followed by a return to Stages 3 or 2 of non-REM sleep, then REM sleep. [38, 42] The amount, type, timing, and quality of sleep are all important considerations.

Fig. 17.2. Excerpt from a library research report.

(b) Application of theory

When your assignment calls for an **application of theory,** you will use a specific theory to interpret the behavior of some person or group. Your report should include these sections:

- Introduction to the research question
- Discussion of previous research
- Description of the theory to be applied
- Identification of the participant(s) in the study
- Discussion of how the theory applies to the behavior of the participant(s)
- Concluding statement about the participant(s) and/or the theory

(c) Observation report

An **observation report** such as Mike Demmon's field report on diving ducks (see **17d**) contains certain standard elements. If you write an observation report, include the sections described below; however, check with your instructor to see whether you should make any modifications.

Many researchers in the social sciences collect data through observation.

- Introduction: The writer establishes the need for the current study and presents a hypothesis.
- Methodology: The writer describes how the study was performed (so that other researchers can replicate it). This section may include subsections that describe the participants, the materials used, and so forth.
- Results: The writer presents findings, often using charts or graphs.
- Discussion: The writer discusses the significance of the findings, relating them to the original hypothesis and to other research done on the topic.

(3) A reference list provides detailed information about the sources used.

At the end of any paper you write for a course in the social sciences, you should include a list of all the sources you used. By doing so, you provide your readers with the details they need to consult these sources on their own. You can find guidelines for creating a reference list in 13b.

17d Sample student field report

Mike Demmon's field report for an advanced environmental science course is an example of a paper that presents original research. (Environmental science is often considered a natural science, but Demmon's report is included here because it is a report on animal behavior.) His report includes a description of the research objectives and procedures, a table listing the data, and a discussion of the findings. Because Demmon's work was original field research, he was not required to use secondary sources, so his report does not include a reference list. Although Demmon calls his report a quantitative analysis, it includes some qualitative elements as well. For example, his subjective voice is evident when he uses the word *surprisingly* to qualify his observation about how late it was when the ducks began to be active. As you read Demmon's report, you may note that the headings and order differ from those described on page 420. Demmon adjusted the headings and organization to accommodate his instructor's directions.

Mike Demmon

Avian Ecology and Management

December 11, 2000

Quantitative Analysis of Diving Ducks

Statement
of method

Methodology

Follow a specific duck for a 10-minute time period and record diving

patterns, times, and frequency of dives. Stagger the species being watched to

create an equal representation of each species within the data. Try not to follow

the same duck in any two 10-minute intervals.

Statement
of goals

Objectives

To determine whether any of the species have evolved to share limited

resources of the environment. To look for evidence of these species having

evolved within the same environment.

Description
of procedure

Procedures

During the class field trip to Eagle Lake, I participated in a quantitative

evaluation of several diving duck species. During this time we monitored

several different variables to see whether feeding practices were staggered

between species, whether frequencies of dives were different between species,

and whether any of the species interacted with each other. The three species we

studied were the Ruddy Duck (*Oxyura jamaicensis*), the Redhead Duck

(*Aytheya americana*), and the Bufflehead Duck (*Bucephala albeola*).

Avian Ecology   2

Data

Time	Species	Sex	Number of Dives	Dive Time (seconds, respectively)	Other Activities
8:30–8:40	Bufflehead	Male	0	N/A	Preening & sleeping
8:45–8:55	Bufflehead	Female	1	Lost after 4 minutes	Preening & followed by 2 males
9:00–9:10	Ruddy	Female	4	21, 27, 33, 19 lost after 5 minutes	Paired with 2 females, ran males off, preening
9:15–9:25	Redhead	Male	13	45, 46, 13, 49, 17, 13, 24, 14, 33, 47, 49	N/A
9:30–9:40	Ruddy	Male	3	6, 33, 17	Following a female
9:45–9:55	Bufflehead	Female	7	9, 13, 11, 22, 20, 29, 19	Followed by 2 males
10:00–10:10	Redhead	Female	8	12, 14, 14, 13, 18, 21, 18, 26	N/A
10:15–10:25	Redhead	Female	11	17, 13, 14, 22, 19, 20, 17, 21, 24, 23, 19	Following 2 males
10:30–10:40	Bufflehead	Female	3	21, 11, 17	Sleeping & following 1 male
10:45–10:55	Ruddy	Male	7	9, 12, 22, 27, 16, 11, 15	N/A
11:00–11:10	Redhead	Male	10	10, 18, 22, 11, 19, 27, 10, 31, 17, 14	N/A
11:15–11:25	Ruddy	Female	6	15, 13, 21, 29, 18	Preening
11:30–11:40	Bufflehead	Male	4	12, 18, 15, 19	Followed a female

Discussion
of data

Conclusions

As the data above show, there is no evidence that these species practice any variation in diving time or frequency of dives, or that any of the species directly and intentionally interact. Surprisingly, the data do seem to show that activities do not begin until mid-morning. When we arrived, about 8 a.m., a large percentage of the birds were still sleeping. Once the birds awaken, it appears as though they ritually preen themselves before feeding. With the exception of human-induced movements, it appeared that there were no significant interactions between any of the species. As may have been expected, the Buffleheads also appeared to be courting at times. The data above also show that the majority of the birds that were paired or followed by the other sex were Buffleheads.

Discussion
of
possibilities
for further
research

Adjustments for Future Research

In order to refine this study, it would be advantageous to develop a better, easier method to follow each individual bird. I found that it was very difficult to follow a diving duck for prolonged periods of time. Also, looking through a monocular spotting scope for 10-minute segments can be very aggravating. It would also be advantageous to get closer to the birds being observed. Finally, the study time is possibly too long. It should be possible to observe more specimens and get a better sampling in half the time.

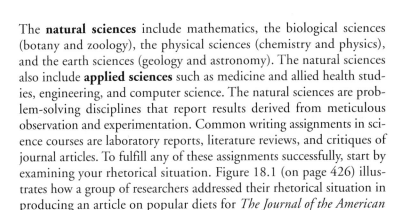

18 WRITING IN THE NATURAL SCIENCES

The **natural sciences** include mathematics, the biological sciences (botany and zoology), the physical sciences (chemistry and physics), and the earth sciences (geology and astronomy). The natural sciences also include **applied sciences** such as medicine and allied health studies, engineering, and computer science. The natural sciences are problem-solving disciplines that report results derived from meticulous observation and experimentation. Common writing assignments in science courses are laboratory reports, literature reviews, and critiques of journal articles. To fulfill any of these assignments successfully, start by examining your rhetorical situation. Figure 18.1 (on page 426) illustrates how a group of researchers addressed their rhetorical situation in producing an article on popular diets for *The Journal of the American Medical Association.*

This chapter will help you

- determine the audience, purpose, and research question for a paper in the natural sciences (18a),
- decide which types of evidence, sources, and reasoning to use in such a paper (18b), and
- follow appropriate style, formatting, and documentation conventions when writing the paper (18c–d).

18a   Audience, purpose, and the research question

Before you start working on a writing assignment for a course in the natural sciences, be sure to determine your audience and your purpose. Your instructor will always be one of your readers, but you may be asked to share your work with other readers as well. If you are enrolled

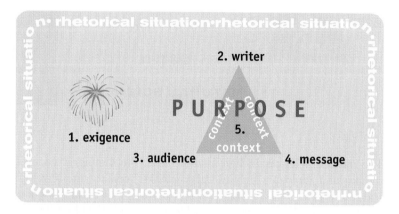

1. Lack of data on the health effects of popular diets (Atkins, Ornish, Weight Watchers, and Zone)
2. Michael L. Dansinger, Joi Augustine Gleason, John L. Griffith, Harry P. Selker, and Ernest J. Schaefer
3. Physicians
4. Each diet helped participants reduce their weight and their cardiac risk factor; the degree of adherence to the diet was correlated with the reductions in weight and cardiac risk factor.
5. The widespread use of popular diets, some of which depart from conventional medical recommendations

Fig. 18.1. Sample rhetorical situation for the natural sciences.

in an advanced class, you may be expected to present your work at a local, regional, or national conference. By knowing who your audience is, you will be able to gauge how much background information is adequate, how much technical language is appropriate, and what types of evidence and reasoning are necessary.

Researchers in the sciences generally write to inform their readers by discussing studies pertaining to a specific topic or by reporting the results of an experiment. However, their purpose may be evaluative if they are critiquing a journal article or argumentative if they are encouraging readers to take a specific action. After you have determined your purpose and audience, craft a research question that will guide you to sources and help you use them responsibly (see chapters 9–11). The following examples of research questions focus on global warming.

Questions about cause
What causes global warming?

Questions about consequences
What are the effects of global warming?

Questions about process
How can global warming be stopped?

Questions about definitions or categories
What types of greenhouse gases are responsible for global warming?

Questions about values
What are a scientist's responsibilities to the public in the face of global warming?

Research questions in the sciences are often narrowed to enable precise measurements.

Questions about length, distance, frequency, and so on
How far has Mendenhall Glacier receded each year for the past decade, and do the values show any trend?

Questions about comparisons and correlations
How are emission intensities related to the total amount of emissions?

18b Evidence, sources, and reasoning

Researchers in the natural sciences attempt to quantify and understand phenomena in the world around them. They look for **empirical evidence**—facts that can be measured or tested—to support their claims. Most of their investigations, then, are set up as experiments. If you conduct an experiment for a course in the natural sciences, you will be expected to start with a **hypothesis,** a prediction that serves as a basis for experimentation. To test the hypothesis, you will follow a procedure, either one established in another study or specified by your instructor or one designed by yourself. The results of your experiment will either validate your hypothesis or show it to be in error. This systematic way of proceeding from a hypothesis to verifiable results is called the **scientific method.** Consisting of six steps, this method helps ensure the objectivity and accuracy of experimental findings.

THE SCIENTIFIC METHOD

1. *State a problem*: When you state the problem, you establish the exigence (the reason for your writing).

2. *Collect evidence*: Close observation is the most important skill for collecting evidence. Be sure to record all details as accurately as you can. Alternatively, you may read the reports of other researchers who have addressed a problem similar to yours. If you draw on observations and experiments, you are using primary sources; if you use scientific articles and statistical charts, you are using secondary sources.

3. *Form a hypothesis*: A hypothesis is a tentative claim, or prediction, about the phenomenon you are studying.

4. *Test the hypothesis*: Although you have conducted some research before formulating the hypothesis, you now continue that research through additional observation or experimentation.

5. *Analyze the results*: Look at your results in light of your hypothesis. Attempt to find patterns, categories, or other relationships.

6. *State the conclusion*: If you have validated your hypothesis, explain why it accounts for *all* of your data. If your hypothesis is disproved, suggest revisions to it or offer a new one.

18c Special conventions for reports in the natural sciences

(1) Writers in the natural sciences follow conventions specified by the style manuals they use.

Scientific writing consists mainly of the clear and accurate presentation of facts, each with a specific source—your own experiments, studies published by other researchers, surveys, and so on. Scientific writing is also objective, keeping the writer's actions and responses in the background. In this way, the focus of the writing remains on the data (as in "The data reveal . . . ") instead of on the researcher (as in "I found . . . ").

The conventions you will follow in writing a paper for a science course, especially when documenting your sources, depend on the style manual used in the specific discipline. The following list presents a few of the most common manuals.

Style Books and Manuals for the Sciences

American Chemical Society. *The ACS Style Guide: A Manual for Authors and Editors.* 2nd ed. Washington DC: American Chemical Society, 1998.

American Institute of Physics. *AIP Style Manual.* 4th ed. New York: American Institute of Physics, 1990.

American Mathematical Society. *A Manual for Authors of Mathematical Papers.* Rev. ed. Providence, RI: American Mathematical Society, 1990.

American Medical Association. *American Medical Association Manual of Style.* 9th ed. Baltimore: Williams, 1997.

Council of Biology Editors. *Scientific Style and Format: The CBE Manual for Authors, Editors, and Publishers.* 6th ed. New York: Cambridge University Press, 1994.

United States Geological Society. *Suggestions to Authors of the Reports of the United States Geological Survey.* 7th ed. Washington, DC: US Government Printing Office, 1991.

You can find a sampling of the documentation requirements of the Council of Science Editors (formerly the Council of Biology Editors) in chapter 15. This group of editors expects scientific writing to be "accurate, clear, economical, fluent, and graceful" (p. 101 of *The CBE Manual*). The Council of Science Editors also addresses the difficulty that nonspecialists may have in reading scientific prose: the solution is to avoid the excessive use of abstract nouns, long noun phrases, abbreviations, undefined technical vocabulary, and conversational jargon (for example, using *reefer* instead of *refrigerator*).

BEYOND THE RULE

OBJECTIVITY AND SUBJECTIVITY

Researchers today hesitate to claim that any reporting can be completely objective. Everything we do is affected by our perception of ourselves, others, and the world around us. Although scientists want to control their experimental methods to filter out as much bias as possible, even that desire is subjective in some respects. For more information, visit **www.harbrace.com**.

(2) The format of a laboratory report reflects the scientific method.

The most frequent writing assignment in the natural sciences is the **laboratory report** (or perhaps a **lab summary,** an informal version of a laboratory report). The format of this type of report follows the steps of the scientific method by starting with a problem and a hypothesis and concluding with a statement proving, modifying, or disproving the hypothesis.

- The **abstract** states the problem and summarizes the results. (You may not have to include an abstract if your report is short or if your instructor does not require it.)
- The **introduction** states the research question or hypothesis clearly and concisely, explains the scientific basis for the study, and provides brief background material on the subject of the study and the techniques to be used. The introduction usually includes citations referring to relevant sources.
- The **methods and materials** section is a narrative that describes how the experiment was conducted. It lists the materials that were used, identifies where the experiment was conducted, and describes the procedures that were followed. (Your lab notes should help you remember what you did. Anyone who wants to repeat your work should be able to do so by following the steps described in this section.)
- **Results** are reported by describing (but not interpreting) major findings and supporting them with properly labeled tables or graphs showing the empirical data.
- The **discussion** section analyzes the results, showing how they are related to the goals of the study and commenting on their significance. This section also reports any problems encountered and offers suggestions for further testing of the results.
- **References** are listed at the end of the paper. The list includes only works that were referred to in the report. The comprehensiveness and the accuracy of this list allow readers to evaluate the quality of the report and put it into a relevant context.

An example of scientific writing (Heather Jensen's lab report for a first-year biology course) appears in the next section. This paper is representative of a report based on an experiment outlined in a lab manual. It includes section headings and graphics—drawings of the various stages of mitosis and a graph showing the results. The Council of

Science Editors approves two documentation formats (see chapter 15): the citation-sequence format and the name-year format. Jensen uses the citation-sequence format.

18d Sample student laboratory report

A specific format is used for a laboratory report so that the various parts of an experiment can be easily located and so that the experiment can be **replicated** (repeated in order to verify the results). When you write a laboratory report for a science course, you will likely follow a format created by your instructor or other scientists. The grade you receive for your work will depend on how well you execute the experiment, follow the prescribed format, and maintain impartiality. Study Heather Jensen's report to get a sense of the style and format generally expected.

Observations and Calculations of Onion Root Tip Cells

Heather Jensen

Biology 101

June 7, 2002

Summary of experiment

ABSTRACT

This laboratory experiment examined *Allium* (onion) root tip cells in the five stages of mitosis. The five stages of mitotic division were identified and recorded, and a 50-cell sample was chosen for closer examination. Of those 50 cells, 64% were found to be in interphase, 20% in prophase, 6% in metaphase, 6% in anaphase, and only 4% in telophase. The results showed that onion root tip cells spend the majority of their life cycle in a rest period (interphase). Prophase was calculated to be the longest phase of active division, while telophase was the shortest. These results were consistent with the experiments completed by other students and scientists.

Introduction describing the purpose of the experiment

INTRODUCTION

This lab report outlines a laboratory experiment on mitosis, the division of the nucleus of a cell to form two new cells with the same number of chromosomes as the parent cell. Mitotic cell division consists of five visually identifiable stages: interphase, prophase, metaphase, anaphase, and telophase. The purpose of this laboratory experiment was to identify and observe cells in each phase of mitosis, as well as to calculate an estimation of the real time involved in each stage of mitosis in an onion root tip cell. The onion root tip was chosen for this experiment because of

Superscript number referring to the first source

easy availability and rapid growth. Rapid root growth resulted in an easy opportunity to observe multiple cells in the phases of mitosis in a small sample, on one or two slides. Onion root cells complete the entire cycle of division in 80 minutes,[1] and it

1

was expected that larger numbers of cells would be found in interphase because the majority of a life cycle is spent performing normal cell functions.

MATERIALS AND METHODS

    The materials required for this experiment include a compound microscope and prepared slides of a longitudinal section of *Allium* (onion) root tip. First, the slides were placed on a compound microscope under low power, a 40x magnification level. The end of the root tip was located; then the cells immediately behind the root cap were examined. These cells appeared as a darker area under low power. This area of cells was identified as the apical meristem,[1] an area of rapid growth and division in the onion root tip. This area of cells was examined while keeping the microscope on low power, to find and identify cells in interphase, prophase, metaphase, anaphase, and telophase.[2] Then high power, a 400x magnification, was used to further examine and record the appearance of these cells.

    After the multiple phases of mitosis were observed, a large area of 50 cells in mitosis was selected for further examination. This area was located under low power in order to assess rows of cells in an easily countable space. Then the number of cells in each stage of mitosis was counted. These numbers were divided by the total number of cells examined, or 50 cells, and multiplied by 100 in order to calculate the percentage of cells in each phase of mitosis. For example, if 10 cells were observed in interphase, then $10/50 = 0.20$ and $0.20 \cdot 100 = 20\%$ of cells were in interphase. The actual time of each phase of mitosis in this sample of cells was calculated by multiplying the percentage by the total time of the division cycle, 80 minutes for the onion root tip cell.[1] For example, if 20% of the cells were observed in interphase, then 20% $(20/100) \cdot 80$ minutes = 16 minutes total time spent in interphase.

List of materials and description of methodology

Superscript number referring again to the first source

Superscript number referring to the second source

Description of phases with labeled drawings as support

Superscript number referring to the third source

RESULTS

Drawings and Observations

INTERPHASE

    This phase lasts from the completion of a division cycle to the beginning of the next cycle. All regular cell functions occur in this phase (except reproduction).[3]

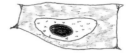

Figure 1   Two cells observed in interphase

PROPHASE

    Technically the first phase of mitosis, this stage is marked by the thickening and shortening of chromosomes, which makes them appear visible under a compound microscope. The nucleus appears grainy at first and then the chromosomes appear more clearly defined as prophase progresses.

Figure 2   Two cells observed in prophase

METAPHASE

    This phase is identified by the lining up of double chromosomes along the center line, the equator, of the cell.

3

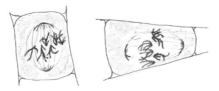

Figure 3   Two cells observed in metaphase

ANAPHASE

This phase is classified by the separation of the double chromosomes. They will begin to pull apart to opposite poles of the cell.

Figure 4   Two cells observed in anaphase

TELOPHASE

In telophase, the chromosomes have reached the opposite poles of the cell, and the connection between the chromosomes begins to break down as the nuclear membrane begins to form around each chromosomal clump. At the end of telophase, cytokinesis, or the division of the cytoplasm, takes place. In plant cells, a cell plate begins to form in the center of the cell and then grows outward to form a new cell wall, completely dividing the old cell into two new cells, both with a complete set of chromosomes.

Figure 5   Two cells observed in telophase

Table 1 shows the number of cells found in each phase of mitosis.

Table 1   Number of cells in each phase

Interphase	Prophase	Metaphase	Anaphase	Telophase
32 cells	10 cells	3 cells	3 cells	2 cells

Table 2 shows the calculated percentage of cells in each phase of mitosis.

Table 2   Percentage of cells in each phase

Interphase	Prophase	Metaphase	Anaphase	Telophase
64% of cells	20% of cells	6% of cells	6% of cells	4% of cells

Figure 6 shows the actual time cells spent in each phase of mitosis.

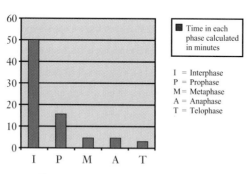

Figure 6   Time spent in each phase of mitosis

5

DISCUSSION

    This laboratory experiment provided firsthand experience with the phases of cell division. The five phases became more easily recognizable as each cell was examined and classified. Cells often looked like they could be classified in interphase or prophase or like they were between phases. Observation led to the confirmation that mitosis is a fluid process and not just a series of distinct phases. During the experiment, difficulties with overdyed and gray areas caused uncertainty because visual indications of phase were impossible to detect. This problem was lessened through the careful selection of clear patches of cells for observation. The expectation that a large number of cells would be found in interphase was confirmed by the numbers of cells counted in the cell sample of the onion root tip. Online comparison of the results of this experiment to those of other similar experiments confirmed the results found here as typical of an onion (*Allium*) root tip.[4] This indicated that the careful selection of clear patches of cells for sampling proved an effective method for eliminating error that might have been caused by the incorrect labeling of cells or the poor visibility of cells in overdyed or gray areas. Further studies might include larger samples of cells. Experiments with larger numbers of cells would offer additional evidence to confirm the results found in this experiment.

    Explanation of how the experiment's results fulfilled its purpose

    Description of a problem that was encountered

    Superscript number referring to the fourth source

List of
references
in citation-
sequence
format

REFERENCES

1. Schraer WD, Stoltze H. Biology: the study of life. 4th ed. Needham (MA): Prentice Hall; 1991. Mitosis and asexual reproduction. p 397–415.

2. Smith DW, Maier CGA. Plant biology lab manual. Dubuque (IA): Kendall/Hunt; 1995. Topic 5, The plant cell. p 52–66.

3. Alexander GM, Goodson P, Hanneman PJ, Melear, CT. Scott, Foresman biology. Glenview (IL): Scott, Foresman; 1985. Information storage and transfer in cells. p 117–43.

4. Yesnik A, Jaster K. The bio 1 super virtual lab book [Internet]. Washington DC: Sidwell Friends School; 1998 [modified 2002; accessed 2002 Jun 7]. Mitosis lab. Available from: http://www.sidwell.edu/us/science/vlb/mitosis/.

19 WRITING IN BUSINESS

Writing in business requires the same attention to audience, purpose, and context as does writing in any other situation or discipline. However, the nature of authorship differs: although you are the writer, you must project both your own image and that of your employer as credible and reliable. To do so, you need to follow the conventions and formats expected by the business community.

If you take business courses, you will receive a variety of assignments; letters, memos, business plans, and grant proposals are some of the more common. To complete such assignments successfully, start by analyzing the rhetorical situation. Figure 19.1 (on page 440) illustrates the rhetorical situation addressed by Yuka Hayashi in writing an article for the *Wall Street Journal,* titled "Fund Firms Get High-Level Rebuke—SEC's Campos Says They Acted Nonchalantly Despite Stock Scandals."

This chapter will help you

- recognize the stylistic conventions of standard business writing (**19a**),
- write a business letter (**19b**),
- prepare a business memo (**19c**),
- compose a résumé and a letter of application (**19d–e**), and
- develop a business plan (**19f**).

A sample grant proposal and information on how to write one can be found at www.harbrace.com.

19a Stylistic conventions of business writing

Whether you are writing e-mail messages, memos, letters, or a business plan, you need to meet fixed as well as unexpected deadlines. You might even find yourself working to meet several deadlines at once. The

1. Decreasing confidence in the stock market following corporate scandals
2. Yuka Hayashi, correspondent for the *Wall Street Journal*
3. Readers who buy and sell mutual funds
4. The Securities and Exchange Commissioner has told the mutual funds industry that measures need to be taken to protect investors.
5. The current discourse regarding business ethics and corporate responsibility

Fig. 19.1. Sample rhetorical situation for business writing.

strategies described in this section will help you produce comprehensive and well-organized documents on time.

(1) Consider your purpose and audience.

Determine what, exactly, your piece of writing should do; then, focus your attention on fulfilling that obligation. For example, if you are writing a recommendation letter for an employee seeking promotion, describe the employee's accomplishments, strengths, and limitations, but avoid using valuable time and space to write about the company's philosophy or your own role in mentoring the employee. If you have questions about a writing assignment, make the inquiries necessary to form a clear picture of what you are being asked to write, for whom—and why.

(2) Determine the format for your writing.

Business writing follows established formats. Business letters, résumés and letters of application, and business plans all conform to certain formats (see 19b–f). You may be able to save time if you keep beside you a sample of the kind of writing you are doing so that you can use it as a model for your own document.

(3) State points clearly.

Business writing conforms to basic formats, primarily so that it can be read efficiently. By stating your main points clearly, and sometimes emphatically, you will be able to achieve that goal. Whether you make your main points in an introductory abstract, in topic sentences, or in bulleted lists, they should stand out from the rest of your text.

19b Business letters

Business letters serve a variety of purposes—to inquire, to inform, to complain, to respond. (For letters of application, see 19e.) Regardless of the purpose, a business letter usually fits onto a single sheet of paper, single-spaced.

TIPS FOR COMPOSING BUSINESS DOCUMENTS

Be direct.

- State the purpose of your document in your opening sentence or paragraph.
- Write straightforward sentences, beginning with a subject and an active verb (see 26d(2)).
- Use technical language sparingly, unless the document is intended for a specialized audience (see 32c(4)).

Be concise.

- Compose direct sentences that are neither too long nor too complicated.
- Include only necessary details.
- Use numbers, bullets, or descriptive headings that help readers locate information easily.
- Use graphs, tables, and other visual elements that convey information succinctly.

Use conventional formatting.

- Follow the standard formats developed for your type of business or for your company, or use those outlined in this chapter (19b–f).
- Avoid using informal language, unless you know that a casual tone is acceptable.

It also follows a standard block format: each element is typed flush with the left margin, with no indentations to indicate new paragraphs. A paragraph break is indicated by double-spacing between paragraphs.

ELEMENTS OF A STANDARD BUSINESS LETTER

- **Return address.** Your employer may require that you use letterhead stationery. If not, type your mailing address one inch from the top of the paper, flush left on a one-inch margin, and single-spaced.

- **Date.** Type the date beneath your return address. If you are using letterhead stationery, type the date one or two lines below the letterhead's last line.

- **Recipient's name and address.** Provide the full name and address of the recipient. Single-space these lines, and allow an extra line space above them. If you do not know the person's name, try to find it by checking the company's Web site or phoning the company. If you cannot find the recipient's name, use an appropriate title such as *Personnel Director* or *Customer Service Manager*.

- **Greeting.** Type your greeting two lines below the last line of the recipient's address. The conventional greeting is *Dear* _____ followed by a colon. If you and the recipient use first names to address each other, use the person's first name. Otherwise, use *Mr., Ms., Mrs.,* or *Miss* and the last name. (Choose *Ms.* when you do not know a woman's preference.) If you do not know the recipient's name, you can use an appropriate title, such as *Personnel Director*.

- **Body of the letter.** Begin the first paragraph two lines below the greeting. Single-space lines within a paragraph; double-space between paragraphs. If your letter runs onto a second page, provide the recipient's last name, the date, and the page number in three single-spaced lines at the top left on the second page.

- **Closing.** Close your letter two lines after the end of the body with an expression such as *Sincerely* or *Cordially* followed by a comma.

- **Signature.** Type your full name four lines below the closing. Then, in the space above your typed name, sign your full name, using blue or black ink. If you have addressed the recipient by his or her first name, sign just your first name.

- **Additional information.** If you are enclosing extra material such as a résumé, type *Enclosure* or the abbreviation *Enc.* two lines below your name. If you would like the recipient to know the names of people receiving copies of the letter, use the abbreviation *cc* (meaning "copies") and a colon followed by the other recipients' names. Place this element on the line directly below the enclosure line or, if there is no enclosure, two lines below your name.

The following sample **letter of inquiry** (a letter designed to elicit information) contains all the parts of a typical business letter.

Letter of inquiry

550 First Avenue
Ellensburg, WA 98926
February 4, 2004

Return address and date

Mr. Mark Russell
Bilingual Publications
5400 Sage Avenue
Yakima, WA 98907

Name and address of recipient

Dear Mr. Russell:

Greeting

I am a junior in the Bilingual Education Program at Central Washington University. For my coursework in bilingual careers, I am investigating positions in publishing that include the use of two languages. Your name and address were given to me by my instructor, Marta Cole, who worked for you from 1999 through 2004.

Body of letter

I have consulted your Web site to see what kind of publishing you do. I am most interested in your publication of dual documents—one in English and one in Spanish. Could you please send me samples of such documents so that I can have a better idea of the types of publications you produce?

I am also interested in finding out what qualifications I would need to work for a business like yours. I am fluent in both Spanish and English and have taken a course in translation. If possible, I would like to ask you a few questions about your training and experience. Would you have time for an interview?

Sincerely,

Chris Humphrey
Chris Humphrey

Closing
Signature

19c Business memos

A **memo** (short for *memorandum*) is a short document sent within a business to announce a meeting, set a schedule, or request information or action. Because it is circulated internally, a memo is usually less formal than a letter, but it should still be direct and concise. The following guidelines for formatting a memo are fairly standard, but note that a particular organization may establish its own format.

ELEMENTS OF A STANDARD BUSINESS MEMO

- **Heading.** On four consecutive lines, type *To* followed by a colon and the name(s) of the recipient(s), *From* followed by a colon and your name and title (if appropriate), *Date* followed by a colon and the date, and *Subject* followed by a colon and a few words identifying the memo's subject. (The abbreviation *Re,* for "regarding," is sometimes used instead of *Subject*.) This information should be single-spaced. If you are sending copies to individuals whose names are not included in the *To* line, place those names on a new line beginning with *cc* and a colon.

- **Body.** Use the block format (see **19b**), single-spacing lines within each paragraph and double-spacing between paragraphs. Double-space between the heading and the body of the memo.

Business memo

Heading

To: Intellectual Properties Committee
From: Leo Renfrow, Chair of Intellectual Properties Committee
Date: March 15, 2005
Subject: Review of Policy Statement

Body of memo

At the end of our last meeting, we decided to have our policy statement reviewed by someone outside our university. Clark Beech, chair of the Intellectual Properties Committee at Lincoln College, agreed to help us. Overall, as his review shows, the format of our policy statement is sound. Dr. Beech believes that some of the content should be further developed, however. It appears that we have used some ambiguous terms and included some conditions that would not hold up in court.

Early next week, my assistant will deliver a copy of Dr. Beech's review to each of you. Please look it over by our next meeting, on March 29. If you have any questions or comments before then, please call me at ext. 1540.

19d Résumés

A **résumé** is essentially an argument (chapter 8) designed to emphasize a person's job qualifications by highlighting his or her experience and abilities. Along with its accompanying letter of application (see 19e), a résumé should command attention. If you create and save your résumé as a word-processing file, you can easily tailor it for each position you seek.

 You may find it helpful to use a software program that allows you to select the kind of résumé you need and then prompts you to complete the various sections. Such software also allows you to view your completed document in its entirety and redesign any or all of it.

The first step in writing a résumé is listing the jobs you have had, the activities and clubs you have participated in, and the offices you have held. Be sure to include dates, job titles, and responsibilities. Omit tangential information, such as a list of hobbies. You can organize your résumé in two ways. A **chronological résumé** lists positions and activities in *reverse* chronological order; that is, your most recent experience comes first. This format works well if you have a steady job history and want to emphasize your most recent experience because it is closely related to the position for which you are applying. An alternative way to organize a résumé is to list experience in terms of job skills rather than jobs held. This format, called an **emphatic résumé,** is especially useful when you have the required skills but your work history in the particular field is modest or you are just starting your career.

Regardless of the design and format you choose, remember that your résumé is, in effect, going to someone's office for a job interview. Make sure that it is dressed for success. If possible, design the résumé to fit on a single page. Use good-quality paper (preferably white or off-white) and a laser printer. Use boldface type for headings. Resist the impulse to make the design unnecessarily complicated, however. When in doubt, opt for simplicity.

Emphatic résumé

Karen Tran
10363 East 10th Avenue
Little Rock, AR 72204
(501) 328-6974
ktran@hotmail.com

CAREER OBJECTIVE:

A full-time management position specializing in food and
beverage services.

MANAGEMENT SKILLS:

Familiarity with all contemporary models of effective
management; good writing and communication skills; experience
with planning and evaluating food service operations; experience
with operating a coffee shop.

EXPERIENCE IN FOOD SERVICE:

Assisted in the transfer of data on development of new
restaurant locations for a major restaurant development firm;
developed and provided customer service information to
employees; worked for three years in food service.

ADDITIONAL EXPERIENCE:

Worked with students, parents, and faculty at Western Ozark
University as an information specialist; helped edit the yearbook;
gave campus tours.

EDUCATION:

Western Ozark University, B.S. with honors, 2002; majored in
Business Administration with an emphasis in Management;
minor in Nutrition; Phi Beta Kappa.

EXTRACURRICULAR:

Active in Management Club and yearbook.

References available on request.

BEYOND THE RULE

ONLINE RÉSUMÉS

Some job applicants create Web-based versions of their résumés, which may include links to their relevant work. They also create non-Web versions that can be downloaded and then printed out or scanned into a résumé database. To learn about writing online résumés, visit **www.harbrace.com**.

TIPS FOR RÉSUMÉ WRITING

- Include your name, address, telephone number, and an e-mail address or fax number, if available.

- Identify your career or job objective simply, without elaborating on future goals. Reserve details about your plans until asked about them during an interview. Try to match your qualifications to the employer's needs.

- List your college or university degree and any pertinent areas in which you have had special training.

- Do not include personal data such as age and marital status.

- Even if an advertisement or posting asks you to state a salary requirement, any mention of salary should usually be deferred until an interview.

- Whenever possible, establish a clear relationship between jobs you have had and the job you are seeking.

- The names and addresses of **references** (people who have agreed to speak or write on your behalf) are not usually listed on a résumé. Instead, job candidates are advised to take a list of references to interviews. Make sure that the individuals on your list understand the nature of the position you are seeking. The list should include their names and addresses as well as their telephone numbers and/or e-mail addresses.

- To show that you are well organized and thoughtful, use a clean, clear format.

- Proofread your résumé before sending it. Errors in spelling, punctuation, word choice, or grammar can ruin your chances of getting an interview.

BEYOND THE RULE

THE APPLICATION PACKAGE

An application package consists of a résumé and a letter of application. Both of these documents are important for any job search. To see a sample chronological résumé and get further information on application letters, résumés, and interviews, visit **www.harbrace.com**.

19e Letters of application

Writing a letter of application is an essential step in applying for a job. A prospective employer gets a first impression of you from your letter of application. Because this letter usually accompanies a résumé (see **19d**), it should do more than simply repeat information that can be found there. Your letter of application provides you with the chance to sound articulate, interesting, and professional. Make the most of it.

Address your letter to a specific person. If you are responding to an advertisement that mentions a department without giving a name, call the company and find out who will be doing the screening and how that person spells his or her name. If you cannot obtain a specific name, use an appropriate title such as *Human Resource Director.* You can assume that the recipient will be screening many applications, so try to keep your letter to one page.

Model letter of application

10363 East 10th Avenue
Little Rock, AR 72204
April 19, 2003

Return address
and date

Ms. Roxanne Kirkwood
Roxy's Coffee Shop
1819 South University Avenue
Little Rock, AR 72204

Name and
address of
recipient

Dear Ms. Kirkwood:

Greeting

I am writing to apply for the position of Business Manager of Roxy's Coffee Shop
advertised in this morning's *Arkansas Democrat-Gazette*. My education and experience
are well suited to this position; I'd welcome the chance to work full-time at making a
new business successful.

Body of letter

As you can see from my résumé, I majored in Business Administration with an
emphasis in management; I am continuing my education by pursuing an MBA at
UALR. Whenever possible, I have found campus activities and jobs that would give me
experience in working with people. As an assistant in the Admissions Office at Western
Ozark University, I worked successfully with students, parents, alumni, and faculty. The
position required both a knowledge of university regulations and an understanding of
people with different needs.

I also benefited from working as an intern last summer for Brinker Enterprises, a
firm that has established many different restaurant chains around the country. While
an employee there, I helped develop a new template for customer service. More
important, I improved my knowledge of what it takes to make a food service business
successful.

I am interested in putting my training to use at Roxy's because it is close to school
and I can draw upon skills I already have. The location makes it possible for me to
fulfill two objectives at the same time. I hope that we can schedule an interview
sometime during the next few weeks. I will be here in Little Rock except for the week
of May 7, but I will be checking my phone and e-mail messages daily when I am out
of town. You should have no difficulty reaching me.

Sincerely,

Karen Tran
Karen Tran

Closing
Signature

Enc.

Enclosure

In your opening paragraph, you should identify the position you are applying for, explain how you learned about it, and—in a single sentence—state why you believe you are qualified to fill it. In the paragraphs that follow, describe the experience and abilities that qualify you for the job. If your experience is extensive, establish that fact and then focus on how you excelled in one or two specific situations. Mention that you are enclosing a résumé, but do not summarize it. Your goal is to get a busy person, who will not want to read the same information twice, to look at your résumé.

In addition to stating your qualifications, your letter of application can also indicate why you are interested in working for the company or organization to which you are applying. Demonstrating that you already know something about it will help you appear to be a serious candidate. Extensive information on most companies is available in their annual reports. You can also find information by searching the Web (see **9d**).

In your closing paragraph, offer any additional useful information, and make a direct request for an interview. Be sure to specify how and where you can be reached. Indicate that you would enjoy the opportunity to exchange information.

19f Business plans

Business plans have three main purposes: (1) to ensure that the writer of the plan has considered all the potential risks as well as benefits of the business venture, (2) to persuade lenders and potential investors that their money will be safely invested because the writer has planned realistically and has sufficient expertise, and (3) to help the new business stay on track during its early development. To fulfill these purposes adequately, a business plan should be well researched, clearly written, and complete—that is, it should provide all the information a loan officer or investor might need.

When Roxanne Kirkwood received an assignment in a management course that required her to research and write a proposal for an actual business, she chose to write about opening a coffee shop where people could order coffee and something light to eat. Because the plan was a course assignment, she was not required to include her personal worth in the financial data or to supply the supporting documents that would be important elements of an actual plan. Though brief, her business plan contains all of the other required elements. With minor modifications, it could be used as part of a loan application.

ELEMENTS OF A BUSINESS PLAN

- **Cover page.** Include the name and address of the business.
- **Table of contents**
- **Executive summary.** State briefly the objectives of the business plan, and describe the business. Indicate who will own the business and under what form of ownership (partnership, corporation, or sole proprietorship). Finally, explain why the business will be successful. Write the summary *after* you have completed the following sections.
- **Description of business.** Identify the kind of business (service or retail), explain why the business is distinctive, and briefly describe its market.
- **Business location.** Discuss lease or sale terms, the need for and costs of renovation, and features of the neighborhood.
- **Licenses and permits.** Explain what kinds of licenses and permits must be obtained and whether the business name is registered.
- **Management.** Include information about managers' experience and education, the organizational structure, proposed salaries and wages, and any other pertinent management resources (accountant, attorney, and so on).
- **Personnel.** List the personnel needed—full-time or part-time, skilled or unskilled—and explain whether training will be required and how it will be provided.
- **Insurance.** Describe insurance needs and potential risks.
- **Market.** Characterize the market—its size and potential for growth and the typical customers. Describe how the business will attract customers—advertising, pricing, product quality, and/or services.
- **Competition.** Analyze competitors, and describe how the business addresses a market need.
- **Financial data.** Include a current balance sheet and income statement and projected (or actual) income statements by month and quarter for two years, as well as cash flow and balance sheet projections.
- **Supporting documents.** Include résumés, financial statements, and letters of reference for the owner(s) as well as letters of intent from suppliers, leases, contracts, deeds, and other legal documents.

Cover page
with
business's
name and
address

BUSINESS PLAN

FOR

ROXY'S COFFEE SHOP

1819 South University Avenue

Little Rock, AR 72204

Roxanne Kirkwood
Telephone number: (501) 847-2539
Fax number: (501) 847-2540
E-mail address: roxys@aol.com

Table of
contents to
help readers
find
information

Table of Contents

Section	Page Number
Executive Summary	3
Description of Business	4
Business Location	4
Licenses and Permits	5
Management	6
Personnel	6
Insurance	6
The Market	6
Competition	7
Financial Data	8

Executive Summary

Overview of the business plan

Roxy's Coffee Shop will provide a desirable service for students, staff, and faculty at the University of Arkansas at Little Rock (UALR) as well as for area residents. The purpose of this business plan is to secure financial backing for the shop's first year of operation. Roxanne Kirkwood will be the sole proprietor of the business and will be the general manager. She will hire an experienced coffee shop manager to oversee the actual operation of the business.

Students, staff, and faculty at UALR have requested an establishment like Roxy's for many years. The UALR campus is near a main shopping area and several working-class neighborhoods that are being revitalized. There is also a major hospital a block away on University Avenue. Roxanne Kirkwood is asking for a loan of $60,000 to open the shop and help with operating expenses until it makes a profit. The loan will be repaid in monthly installments beginning in the first month of the second year of business and will be secured using the borrower's home as collateral. Roxy's Coffee Shop will offer a useful, desirable service to a university community that continues to grow as well as to a revitalized neighborhood that has the potential for providing more consumers.

Roxy's will offer a somewhat limited menu. Focusing on coffee as the main sale item will allow for the greatest amount of profit. Serving a few other high-demand hot and cold drinks, as well as some desserts, will support the main focus on coffee. The shop will intentionally be kept small to provide the best service with the lowest prices while offering excellent quality. The research carried out for this proposal shows that Roxy's has an ideal location, a practical plan, and a product that is in demand.

Description of Business

Detailed
description
of the
business

Roxy's will be a small, independently owned coffee shop serving regular and specialty coffee. Although juice, smoothies, hot chocolate, tea, bottled water, carbonated beverages, fruit, and desserts such as pie, cake, cookies and brownies will also be served, premium quality, fair trade coffee will be marketed at a reasonable price as the primary menu item. Although Little Rock has a number of coffee shops, none are easily accessible from the UALR campus.

Roxy's primary market will be UALR students, faculty, and staff, since the restaurants on campus all close by 7:00 in the evening and the campus coffee kiosk closes at 2:00 in the afternoon. People who live close to the campus in the surrounding neighborhoods will form a secondary market. These people will benefit from having a place nearby to enjoy coffee. In addition, Roxy's will appeal to shoppers and businesspeople frequenting the nearby malls and businesses. Situated on University Avenue, Roxy's will have an ideal location on a main thoroughfare going through the center of UALR campus, so it is convenient for morning commuter traffic.

Once financial backing for the company has been secured, all suppliers are willing to begin delivery. Restaurant supplies will be obtained through AbestKitchen.com, and a merchant account will be provided by Redwood Internet.

Business Location

Details
about the
location of
the
business

Roxy's will be located at 1819 S. University Avenue, a main thoroughfare in Little Rock. This location is one block from the main campus on University Avenue, near Highway 630, which runs through the heart of Little Rock. This location is ideal because UALR students, staff, and faculty can walk to the coffee

Roxy's   5

shop from campus. In addition, tourists and businesspeople can find the location easily and park without trouble. Roxy's will be open most of the hours that the UALR library is open.

The 250-square-foot space will be leased for one year at $2,500 a month, with the option to renew and renegotiate terms at the end of that time. No walls will be moved, and electrical service and plumbing lines are to be left as they are. Renovations will involve only surface changes such as wall treatments, decorations, and furniture. The estimated cost for these changes, as noted in the financial data section of this business plan, is projected to be $5,000. Although the rent may seem high, the location of the building—only a couple of blocks from a major intersection in Little Rock offering access to traffic and potential customers—makes the cost worthwhile. This freestanding building with an adjacent parking lot is located directly on the street. The building is convenient not only for UALR students, staff, and faculty, but also for shoppers from the two major malls in Little Rock as well as for staff and visitors from a major hospital located on University Avenue. On either side of University Avenue are neighborhoods consisting of mostly working-class homes. Owners are struggling to rejuvenate these neighborhoods and keep them from being overtaken by commercial and business properties. Homeowners, attempting to keep a neighborhood feel, should welcome a local spot such as Roxy's as a place to meet socially.

Licenses and Permits

All necessary licenses and permits will be obtained. The State of Arkansas leaves most decisions up to the county in which the business is located. The Little Rock Small Business Administration is gathering information on licenses and permits.

Management

Roxy's general manager will be Roxanne Kirkwood. A business manager will be hired to assist with business operation and marketing. The general manager will work 40 hours a week for an annual salary of $30,000. The general manager will alternate day and night shifts with the business manager Monday through Friday. The business manager will work 40 hours a week for an annual salary of $25,000. Salaries will increase only when the business becomes clearly profitable.

Personnel

Other than the managers, Roxy's will hire two part-time employees who will work 15 hours per week at $8.00 an hour. These employees will be responsible for the shop 16 hours on Saturdays and 14 hours on Sundays, including getting ready to open and cleaning up before closing. Managers will be on call.

Insurance

Roxy's will have the standard liability and property insurance. Although exact numbers are still being negotiated, costs are estimated at $100 per month. Roxy's main insurance needs include liability coverage for any accident on the property affecting customers or employees and coverage for property losses resulting from fire, theft, or vandalism. The business will not provide health insurance for employees.

The Market

Roxy's target market is UALR students, staff, and faculty. Although the campus has on-site food vendors, including a coffee vendor, these vendors close early. A large portion of UALR's student body attends night classes, which begin

Roxy's   7

long after the coffee vendor's closing time of 2:00 in the afternoon. Many of these students visit the library, which is open until 11:00 on weeknights. In addition, a large neighborhood surrounds the campus, and a main street borders the campus, moving a large amount of traffic right past Roxy's. Because of Roxy's location near the intersection of Highway 630 and University Avenue, the ability to attract shoppers, tourists, and hospital staff and visitors is guaranteed.

Competition

Identification of competing businesses

Little Rock has not yet been inundated with coffee shops as many American cities have. There is one chain, Coffey Beanery, which has a stand in one mall and one shop halfway across town in West Little Rock, off Chenal. There are no Starbucks and only a few independently owned establishments. The other independently owned shops are located in neighborhoods nowhere near UALR or University Avenue.

Table summarizing projected financial data for the first year of operation

Financial Data

Table 1

Estimated Expenses for First Year of Operation

Expense	Startup Only	Monthly	Yearly
Equipment including crockery	X		$15,000
Furniture, fixtures and remodeling	X		10,000
Inventory including coffee beans and food		$2,000	24,000
Rent		2,500	30,000
Insurance		100	1,200
Advertising	$800	100	2,000
Utilities		1,000	12,000
Licenses and permits			500
Miscellaneous		200	2,400
General manager			30,000
Business manager		2,083.33	25,000
Part-time employees		960	11,520
Total needed for first year	$800	$8,943.33	$163,620
Total needed for startup costs		$80,000	(approximately 3 months operating costs, plus a small emergency reserve)
Total supplied by borrower		$20,000	
Total supplied by lender		$60,000	

BOBOLI

Directions

1. Preheat oven to 450°F.
2. Spread 1 pouch of sauce on 1 large (12") BOBOLI® Pizza Crust.
3. Top with cheese, vegetables – whatever you like!
4. Bake 8-10 minutes on oven rack or ungreased cookie sheet until crust is crisp and cheese is melted.

Package directions often include abbreviated sentences.

USING A GRAMMAR CHECKER

Most word-processing programs have features that help writers identify grammar errors as well as problems with usage and style. But these grammar checkers have significant limitations. Because they are programmed according to specific rules, they search for violations of those rules. A grammar checker will usually identify

- fused sentences, sometimes called run-on sentences (chapter 23),
- some misused prepositions (33c),
- wordy or overly long sentences (chapters 28 and 34), and
- missing apostrophes in contractions (37b).

However, a grammar checker will frequently miss subtle stylistic problems as well as

- sentence fragments (chapter 22),
- problems with adverbs or adjectives (24a),
- dangling or misplaced modifiers (24c–d),
- problems with pronoun-antecedent agreement (25c),
- errors in subject-verb agreement (26f), and
- misused or missing commas (chapter 35).

Since these problems can weaken your credibility as a writer, you should never rely solely on a grammar checker to find them. Furthermore, grammar checkers cannot distinguish between true errors and choices you make deliberately to suit your rhetorical situation. As a result, they often flag words or phrases that you have chosen intentionally.

Used carefully, a grammar checker can be a helpful tool, but keep the following advice in mind.

- Use a grammar checker only in addition to your own editing and proofreading. When in doubt, consult the appropriate chapters in this handbook.
- Always evaluate any sentences flagged by a grammar checker to determine whether there is, in fact, a problem.
- Carefully review the revisions proposed by a grammar checker before accepting them. Sometimes the proposed revisions create entirely new errors.
- Adjust the settings on your grammar checker to look only for errors you make frequently. (However, even if used in this way, a grammar checker may miss some errors.)

SENTENCE ESSENTIALS 20

When you think of the word *grammar,* you might also think of the word *rule*—a regulation that you must obey unless you are prepared to get into trouble. But *rule* has another meaning: "a description of what is true in most cases." A grammar rule, then, is a statement of how language is commonly or conventionally used. However, language use, as you know, varies according to the rhetorical situation. You are probably already aware of varying your own speech or writing for a special audience or occasion. Because language allows such variety, you have many options to consider as you draft and revise—a number of words and word arrangements at your disposal. By learning some basic grammatical terminology and concepts, you will understand what your options are and how to make the most of them. This chapter will help you

- identify the parts of speech (**20a**),
- recognize the essential parts of a sentence (**20b**),
- identify predicates (**20c**),
- identify subjects and complements (**20d**), and
- recognize basic sentence patterns (**20e**).

20a Parts of speech

When you look up a word in the dictionary, you will often find it followed by one or more of these labels: *adj., adv., conj., interj., n., prep., pron.,* and *v.* (or *vb.*). These are the abbreviations for the traditional eight parts of speech: *adjective, adverb, conjunction, interjection, noun, preposition, pronoun,* and *verb.* The definition of a word depends on which of these labels applies to the word. For example, when labeled as a noun, the word *turn* has several meanings, one of which is "curve": We were surprised by the *turn* in the road. When *turn* is labeled as a verb, one of its possible meanings is "to change color": The leaves have *turned.*

By learning the eight parts of speech, not only will you be able to use a dictionary effectively, you will also better understand the feedback your teacher, supervisor, or peers give you as well as provide fellow writers with specific recommendations. Someone reading your work, for example, may suggest that you use more action verbs. And you may note, as you read another's work, that it would be improved by balancing abstract nouns such as *nutrition* with concrete nouns such as *spinach.*

BEYOND THE RULE

COUNTING PARTS OF SPEECH

Prior to the eighteenth century, only two parts of speech—nouns and verbs—were counted. Now, in addition to the eight traditional parts of speech established in that century, others such as *determiners* and *expletives* are widely recognized. To learn more about the history of the parts of speech, visit **www.harbrace.com**.

(1) Verbs usually express action or being.

Thousands of verbs are **action verbs.** Just think of everything you do in one day: wake, eat, drink, wash, walk, drive, study, work, laugh, smile, talk, and so on. In contrast, only a few verbs express being or experiencing. Called **linking verbs,** these include *be, seem, become,* and the sensory verbs *look, taste, smell, feel,* and *sound.* Both action verbs and linking verbs are frequently accompanied by **auxiliary verbs**—verbs that add meaning to a main verb, such as information about time, ability, or certainty (*have studied, will study, can study, must be studying*). These verbs are sometimes called **auxiliaries** or **helping verbs.**

The base form of most action verbs fits into this frame sentence:

We should _____ (it). [With some verbs, *it* is not used.]

The base form of most linking verbs fits into this frame sentence:

It should _____ good (terrible, fine).

Writers of travel brochures often choose action verbs to create images of fun-filled vacations.

THINKING RHETORICALLY ABOUT

VERBS

Decide which of the following sentences evokes a clearer image.

The team captain **was** absolutely ecstatic.

Grinning broadly, the team captain **shot** both her arms into the air.

You probably chose the sentence with the action verb (*shot*) rather than the sentence with *was*. Most writers avoid using the verb *be* in any of its forms (*am, is, are, was, were,* or *been*) when their rhetorical situation calls for vibrant imagery. Instead, they use vivid action verbs. For more information on choosing effective words, see chapters 32–34.

(2) Nouns usually name people, places, things, and ideas.

Proper nouns are specific names and are capitalized: *Bill Gates, Redmond, Microsoft Corporation.* **Common nouns,** also called **generic nouns,** refer to any member of a class or category: *person, city, company.* Common nouns that have singular and plural forms are called **count nouns** because the entities they name can be counted: *book, books; car, cars.* **Noncount nouns** have only one form because they name things that cannot be counted: *furniture, air.* **Collective nouns** such as *team, committee,* and *faculty,* which comprise individual members, are either singular or plural, depending on the context (see 26f(7)).

Most nouns fit into this frame sentence:

(The) _____ is (are) important (unimportant, interesting, uninteresting).

THINKING RHETORICALLY ABOUT

NOUNS

Nouns like *entertainment* and *nutrition* are **abstract nouns.** They refer to concepts. Nouns like *guitar* and *tofu* are **concrete nouns.** They refer to things perceivable by the senses. When your rhetorical situation calls for the use of abstractions, balance them with tangible details conveyed through concrete nouns. For example, if you use the abstract nouns *impressionism* and *cubism* in an art history paper, also include concrete nouns that will enable your readers to see the colors and brushstrokes of the paintings you are discussing. To learn more about how your choice of nouns can enhance your writing, see chapters 32 and 33.

(3) A pronoun usually takes the place of a previously mentioned noun or noun phrase.

Most **pronouns** are words that substitute for nouns or noun phrases (see **21a(1)**). The nouns or noun phrases to which pronouns refer are called **antecedents.** *Dan* and *the old, decrepit house* are the antecedents in the following sentences.

<u>Dan</u> said **he** will have the report done by Friday.

They bought <u>the old, decrepit house</u> because they thought **it** had charm.

A pronoun and its antecedent may be in either the same sentence or separate, but usually adjacent, sentences.

<u>The students</u> worked in the field for an entire semester. At the end of the school year, **they** presented their findings at the Undergraduate Research Conference.

The pronouns in the preceding examples are called **personal pronouns.** However, there are other types of pronouns as well: indefinite, possessive, relative, interrogative, intensive, and reflexive. For a detailed description of pronouns, see chapter 25.

THINKING RHETORICALLY ABOUT

PRONOUNS

Why is the following passage somewhat unclear?

> The study found that students succeed when they have clear directions, consistent and focused feedback, and access to help. This led administrators to create a tutoring center at our university.

The problem is that the pronoun *this* at the beginning of the second sentence could refer to all of the information provided by the study or just to the single finding that students need access to help. If you discover that the referent for a pronoun you have used is vague, replace it with clarifying information:

> **The results of this study** led administrators to create a tutoring center at our university.

(4) An adjective modifies a noun or a pronoun.

Adjectives most commonly modify nouns: *spicy* food, *cold* day, *special* price. Sometimes they modify pronouns: *blue* ones, anyone *thin*. Most adjectives answer one of these questions: Which one? What kind of . . . ? How many? What color (or size or shape, and so on)? Although adjectives usually precede the nouns they modify, they occasionally follow them: *enough* time, time *enough*. Adjectives may also follow linking verbs (such as *be, seem,* and *become*):

The <u>moon</u> is **full** tonight.

<u>He</u> seems **shy.**

When an adjective follows a linking verb, it modifies the subject of the sentence (see **20d(3)**).

Nouns sometimes function as adjectives.

> The **marble** is from Italy. [*Marble* is a noun functioning as a noun.]
>
> An incredible **marble** statue was hidden in the basement. [*Marble* is a noun functioning as an adjective.]

Most adjectives fit into one of these frame sentences:

He told us about a/an _____ dog (person, object, idea).

The dog (person, object, idea) is very _____.

Articles, classified either as **determiners** (see Glossary of Terms) or as a subclass of adjectives, indicate that the word that follows is a noun. English has three articles: *a, an,* and *the.*

ARTICLE USAGE

Indefinite Articles, *a* and *an*

The indefinite articles *a* and *an* classify the singular nouns they precede. Use *a* before a consonant sound (*a* yard, *a* university). Use *an* before a vowel sound (*an* apple, *an* hour). Indefinite articles are used for classification (that is, to refer to a certain type or class) in the following common contexts.

- With the first mention of a noun. Use an indefinite article when you introduce a singular noun for the first time.

    I bought **a** writing journal for my English class. It was not very expensive.

- With the expletive *there.* Use an indefinite article when you introduce a topic that includes a singular noun.

    There is **a** good reason for using a journal to improve your English.

- For a generalization. When you are referring to a singular noun in a general way, use an indefinite article.

    A writing journal is a notebook in which you can write down ideas without worrying about grammar.

    If a noun is plural or if it cannot be counted, then no article is needed.

    Journals are useful.   **Writing** is an important skill.

Definite Article, *the*

The definite article *the* can precede singular or plural nouns as well as noncount nouns. It is used for identification in the following common contexts.

■ For a subsequent mention. Once a noun has been introduced, use the definite article before it later in the same sentence or paragraph.

> I wrote about two of my favorite possessions—a guitar and a flute. I received **the** guitar as a gift from my parents.

A subsequent mention does not always include exact repetition of a noun. However, the noun chosen must be close in meaning to a word or phrase in the previous clause or sentence.

> The teacher **grades** us on each assignment, but **the grade** isn't based solely on grammatical correctness. [The noun *grade* is close in meaning to the verb *grades*.]

■ For something that is unique. When referring to something that is unique in everyone's shared experience, use the definite article.

> One teacher asked her students to write about **the** moon in their journals.

Other nouns like *moon* include *universe, solar system, sun, earth,* and *sky.* A noun may be considered unique as long as the audience will recognize the referent. For example, *airport* may be preceded by *the* when only one airport would come to mind in the specific context.

> My friend wrote about her experience at **the** airport.

■ For an abstract class. *The* is used with a noun that refers to an abstract class.

> **The** writer's journal has become a mainstay in the composition classroom.

(5) Adverbs modify verbs, adjectives, and other adverbs.

Adverbs most frequently modify verbs. They provide information about time, manner, place, and frequency, thus answering one of these questions: When? How? Where? How often?

The conference starts **tomorrow.** [time]

I **rapidly** calculated the cost. [manner]

We met **here.** [place]

They **often** work late on Thursdays. [frequency]

Adverbs that modify verbs can often move from one position in a sentence to another. Compare the positions of *yesterday* and *carefully* in the following sentences.

> **Yesterday** the team traveled to St. Louis.
>
> The team traveled to St. Louis **yesterday.**
>
> He **carefully** removed the radio collar.
>
> He removed the radio collar **carefully.**

Most adverbs that provide information about how an action is performed fit into this frame sentence:

They _____ moved (danced, walked) across the room.

Adverbs also modify adjectives and other adverbs by intensifying or otherwise qualifying the meanings of those words.

> I was **somewhat** <u>surprised</u>. [modifying an adjective]
>
> He was **unusually** <u>generous</u>. [modifying an adjective]

> The changes occurred **quite** <u>rapidly</u>. [modifying an adverb]
>
> The team played **surprisingly** <u>well</u>. [modifying an adverb]

For more information on adverbs, see **24a.**

THINKING RHETORICALLY ABOUT

ADVERBS

What do the adverbs add to the following sentences?

> The scientist **delicately** places the slide under the microscope.
>
> "You're late," he scolded **vehemently.**
>
> She is **wistfully** hopeful.

Adverbs like these can help you portray an action, indicate how someone is speaking, and add detail to a description.

(6) Prepositions set up relationships between words.

A **preposition** combines with a pronoun, noun, or noun phrase to create a **prepositional phrase.** A prepositional phrase functions as an adjective or an adverb.

> The tour **of the old city** has been postponed. [adjectival, modifying *the tour*]
>
> The editor wrote comments **in the margin**. [adverbial, modifying *wrote*]

Common one-word prepositions are *on, in, at, to, for, over,* and *under.* Common **phrasal prepositions** (prepositions consisting of more than one word) are *except for, because of, instead of,* and *according to.* For a list of prepositions and more information on prepositional phrases, see **21a(4)**.

(7) Conjunctions are connectors.

Coordinating conjunctions connect similar words or groups of words; that is, a coordinating conjunction generally links a noun to a noun, an adjective to an adjective, a phrase to a phrase, and so on.

> The game was dangerous **yet** appealing. [connecting adjectives]
>
> They foraged for food at dawn **and** at dusk. [connecting prepositional phrases]

There are seven coordinating conjunctions. Use the made-up word *fanboys* to help you remember them.

F	A	N	B	O	Y	S
for	*and*	*nor*	*but*	*or*	*yet*	*so*

Correlative conjunctions, or **correlatives,** consist of two parts. The most common correlatives are *both . . . and, either . . . or, neither . . . nor,* and *not only . . . but also.*

> The defeat left me feeling **both** sad **and** angry. [connecting adjectives]
>
> **Either** Pedro **or** Jeanie will introduce the guest speaker. [connecting nouns]

For more information on coordinating and correlative conjunctions, see **21c(1–2)**.

A **subordinating conjunction** introduces a clause that depends on a main (independent) clause.

The river rises **when** <u>the snow melts</u>.

Common subordinating conjunctions are *because, although, when,* and *if.* For a longer list of subordinating conjunctions and more information on independent and dependent clauses, see **21b(2)** and **21c(3)**. To learn how to use coordination and subordination to improve sentences, see chapter **28**.

(8) Interjections are expressions of surprise or strong feeling.

Interjections are most commonly used either before a sentence or at the beginning of a sentence to indicate surprise, dread, or some other strong emotion. Interjections are generally followed by an exclamation point or a comma.

Wow! Your design is astounding.

Oh no, you can't be telling the truth.

Exercise 1

Identify the part of speech for each word in the sentences below.

1. After we finished lunch, we piled into a minivan and explored the valley.
2. A narrow river runs through it.
3. The tour guide drove very slowly because the road was old and rutted.
4. We stopped at a roadside stand for fresh figs. Oh, were they good!
5. While we were there, we bought flowers for the guide.

20b Subjects and predicates

A sentence consists of two parts:

SUBJECT + PREDICATE

The **subject** is generally someone or something that either performs an action or is described. The **predicate** expresses the action initiated by the subject or gives information about the subject.

> The <u>quarterback</u> + <u>passed</u> the ball to his wide receiver.
> The <u>landlord</u> + <u>has renovated</u> the apartment.
> [The subject performs an action; the predicate expresses that action.]

> <u>He</u> + <u>is</u> talented.
> Their <u>plans</u> + <u>had sounded</u> reasonable.
> [The subject is described; the predicate gives information about the subject.]

The central components of the subject and the predicate are often called the **simple subject** (the main noun or pronoun) and the **simple predicate** (the main verb and any auxiliary verbs). They are underlined in the example sentences above. Compound subjects and compound predicates include a connecting word (a conjunction) such as *and, or,* or *but.*

> The Republicans <u>and</u> the Democrats are debating the issues.
> [compound subject]

> The candidate **stated his views on abortion <u>but</u> did not discuss stem-cell research.** [compound predicate]

THINKING RHETORICALLY ABOUT

SUBJECTS AND PREDICATES

Generally, sentences have the pattern subject + predicate. However, writers often vary this pattern to provide emphasis or cohesion.

> He + elbowed his way into the lobby and paused. [subject + predicate]
> From a far corner came + shrieks of laughter. [predicate + subject]

In the second sentence, the predicate contains information related to the first sentence and is thus placed at the beginning. The placement of the subject at the end of the second sentence puts emphasis on the information it conveys. To learn how writers commonly vary sentence structure, see chapters 31 and 32.

Exercise 2

Identify the subject and the predicate in each sentence, noting any compound subjects or compound predicates.

1. Magicians are in our oceans.
2. They are octopuses.
3. Octopuses can become invisible.
4. They just change color.
5. They can also change their shape.
6. These shape-changers look frightening.
7. Octopuses can release poisons and produce spectacles of color.
8. The blue-ringed octopus can give an unsuspecting diver an unpleasant surprise.
9. Researchers consider the poison of the blue-ringed octopus one of the deadliest in the world.
10. Octopuses and their relatives have been living on Earth for millions of years.

20c Predicates

The central part of the predicate is the verb. A verb may be a single word, or it may consist of a main verb accompanied by one or more auxiliary verbs. The most common auxiliaries are *be (am, is, are, was, were, been), have (has, had),* and *do (does, did).* Others, including *can, may,* and *might,* are called **modal auxiliaries.**

> They **work** as volunteers. [single-word verb]
>
> They **have been working** as volunteers. [verb with two auxiliaries]
>
> They **might work** as volunteers. [verb with modal auxiliary]

Occasionally, an adverb intervenes between the auxiliary and the main verb.

> They **have <u>always</u> worked** as volunteers.
>
> **Have** you <u>ever</u> **volunteered?**

Exercise 3

Review the sentences in exercise 2, identifying all main verbs and auxiliary verbs.

20d Subjects and complements

Subjects and complements take different positions in a sentence. In most sentences, the subject refers to someone or something performing an action or being described. It usually appears before the verb.

The <u>chair</u> of the committee presented his plans for the new year.

Complements are parts of a sentence required by the verb to make the sentence complete. For example, the sentence *The chair of the committee presented* is incomplete without the complement *his plans.* There are four types of complements: direct objects, indirect objects, subject complements, and object complements.

Subjects and complements are generally pronouns, nouns, or noun phrases. Because a pronoun can replace an entire noun phrase, you can use an easy pronoun test to help you recognize noun phrases that are subjects or complements: simply substitute a pronoun for the corresponding group of words. Common pronouns used for this test are *he, she, it, they, him, her, them, this,* and *that.*

The chair of the committee introduced **the members.**

(1) Subjects are usually pronouns, nouns, or noun phrases.

Grammatically complete sentences contain a subject, which generally takes the form of a pronoun, noun, or noun phrase. An imperative sentence, however, is written without the understood subject, *you.*

> **My best friend** is a nutritionist. [noun phrase]
> **She** works at a clinic. [pronoun]
> Eat plenty of fruits and vegetables. [understood *you*]

To identify the subject of a sentence, find the verb and then use it in a question beginning with *who* or *what,* as shown in the following examples.

Jennifer works at a clinic.   Meat contains cholesterol.

Verb: **works**   Verb: **contains**

WHO works? **Jennifer**   WHAT contains? **Meat**

[not the clinic] **works.**   [not cholesterol] **contains.**

Subject: **Jennifer**   Subject: **Meat**

Some sentences begin with an **expletive**—*there* or *it.* Such a word occurs in the subject position, forcing the true subject to follow the verb.

There were **no exercise machines.**

A subject following the expletive *it* is often a clause rather than a phrase. You will learn more about clauses in chapter 21.

It is essential **that children learn about nutrition at an early age.**

Beginning a Sentence with *There*

In sentences beginning with the expletive *there,* the verb comes before the subject. The verb *are* is often hard to hear when it follows *there,* so be careful that you do not omit it.

are
There ˄ many good books on nutrition.

---

(2) Direct and indirect objects are usually pronouns, nouns, or noun phrases.

Objects complete the meaning begun by the subject and verb.

My roommate writes **movie scripts.** [The object *movie scripts* completes the meaning of the sentence.]

Whether an object is required in a sentence depends on the meaning of the verb. Some sentences have no objects at all; others have one or even two objects.

The robins are migrating. [A sentence with no object.]

She lent **me** her **laptop.** [*Me* is one object; *laptop* is another.]

(a) Direct objects

The **direct object** of an action verb either receives the action or shows the result of the action.

I. M. Pei designed **the East Building of the National Gallery.**

Steve McQueen invented **the bucket seat** in 1960.

Compound direct objects include a connecting word, usually *and.*

Thomas Edison patented **the phonograph <u>and</u> the microphone.**

To identify a direct object, find the subject and the verb and then use them in a question ending with *what* or *whom.*

Marie Curie discovered radium.	They hired a new engineer.
Subject and verb:	Subject and verb:
Marie Curie discovered	**They hired**
Marie Curie discovered WHAT?	They hired WHOM?
radium	**a new engineer**
Direct object: **radium**	Direct object: **a new engineer**

Some direct objects are clauses (see **21b**).

Researchers found **that patients responded favorably to the new medication.**

(b) Indirect objects

Some sentences can have both a direct object and an **indirect object.** Indirect objects are typically pronouns, nouns, or noun phrases that name the recipient of the direct object. Indirect objects commonly appear after the verbs *bring, buy, give, lend, offer, sell,* and *send.*

The supervisor gave **the new employees** computers.

She sent **them** contracts in the mail.

Like subjects and direct objects, indirect objects can be compound.

She offered **Elena <u>and</u> Octavio** a generous benefits package.

(3) Subject and object complements are usually pronouns, nouns, noun phrases, adjectives, or adjectival phrases.

Complements can be pronouns, nouns, or noun phrases; however, they can also be adjectives or **adjectival phrases**—phrases in which the main word is an **adjective** (a word that classifies or describes a noun or pronoun). The adjective may be accompanied by a word that softens or intensifies its meaning (such as *somewhat, very,* or *quite*).

(a) Subject complements

A **subject complement,** which identifies, classifies, or describes the subject, follows a linking verb (see 20a(1)). The most common linking verb is *be* (*am, is, are, was, were, been*). Other linking verbs are *become, seem, appear,* and the sensory verbs *feel, look, smell, sound,* and *taste.*

The game is **a test of endurance.** [noun phrase]

The winner is **you.** [pronoun]

The game rules sound **quite complicated.** [adjectival phrase]

(b) Object complements

An **object complement** identifies or describes the direct object. Object complements help complete the meaning of verbs such as *call, elect, leave, make, name,* and *paint.*

Sports reporters called <u>the rookie</u> **the best player of the year.** [noun phrase]

News of the strike left <u>the fans</u> **somewhat disappointed.** [adjectival phrase]

Exercise 4

In the sentences in exercise 2, identify all direct objects, indirect objects, subject complements, and object complements.

20e Basic sentence patterns

Understanding basic sentence patterns and variations will help you recognize subjects and complements. The six basic sentence patterns presented in the following box are based on three verb types. You have already been introduced to linking verbs (such as *be, seem, sound,* and *taste*). These verbs are followed by a subject complement or an adverbial phrase, such as a prepositional phrase indicating place. Verbs that are not linking are either transitive or intransitive (see **26d(1)**). Notice that *trans* in the words *transitive* and *intransitive* means "over or across." Thus, the action of a **transitive verb** carries across to an object, but the action of an **intransitive verb** does not. Intransitive verbs have no complements, although they are often followed by adverbs or adverbial phrases.

BASIC SENTENCE PATTERNS

Pattern 1 SUBJECT + INTRANSITIVE VERB

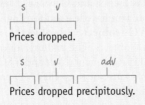

Prices dropped.

Prices dropped precipitously.

Pattern 2 SUBJECT + TRANSITIVE VERB + DIRECT OBJECT

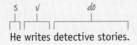

He writes detective stories.

Pattern 3 SUBJECT + TRANSITIVE VERB + INDIRECT OBJECT + DIRECT OBJECT

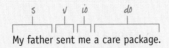

My father sent me a care package.

(Continued on page 480)

(Continued from page 479)

Pattern 4 SUBJECT + TRANSITIVE VERB + DIRECT OBJECT + OBJECT COMPLEMENT

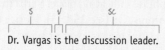

The new leaders declared the country a separate nation.

Pattern 5 SUBJECT + LINKING VERB + SUBJECT COMPLEMENT

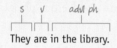

Dr. Vargas is the discussion leader.

Pattern 6 SUBJECT + LINKING VERB + ADVERBIAL PHRASE

They are in the library.

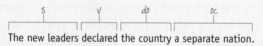

Word Order
Some languages, such as French and Cantonese, have sentence patterns similar to those you have learned for English. These languages are called **SVO (subject-verb-object) languages,** even though not all sentences have objects. The patterns for other languages vary. SOV (subject-object-verb) languages and VSO (verb-subject-object) languages are also common. Keep the SVO pattern in mind to help you understand English sentences.

When declarative sentences, or statements, are turned into questions, the subject and the auxiliary verb are sometimes inverted; that is, the auxiliary verb is moved to the front of the sentence, before the subject.

Statement: A Chinese skater (has) won a gold medal.

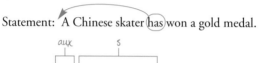

Question: Has a Chinese skater won a gold medal?

Often, a question word such as *what* or *why* opens an interrogative sentence. As long as the question word is the object of the sentence, the auxiliary verb comes before the subject.

Question: What has a Chinese skater won?

If a statement does not include an auxiliary verb or a form of the linking verb *be,* then a form of *do* is added to create the corresponding question. Once again, the auxiliary verb (in this case, *do*) is placed in front of the subject.

Statement: A Chinese skater won a gold medal.

Question: Did a Chinese skater win a gold medal?

You have learned six basic sentence patterns in this section. However, as you study sentences more closely, you will find other patterns as well. For example, some patterns require mention of a destination or location. The sentence *I put the documents* is incomplete without a phrase such as *on your desk.* Other sentences have phrases that are not essential but do add pertinent information. These phrases can sometimes be moved. For example, the phrase *on Friday* can be placed either at the beginning or at the end of a sentence.

I finished my assignment **on Friday.**

On Friday, I finished my assignment.

To learn how to write effective sentences by varying their structure, see chapter 31.

Inverting the Subject and the Verb in Questions
English is one of a few languages in which the subject and the verb are inverted in questions. Most languages rely on intonation to indicate that a question is being asked, without a change in word order. (English speakers occasionally use uninverted questions to ask for clarification or to indicate surprise.) In many languages other than English, an option for making a statement into a question is to add a particle, such as the Japanese *ka.*

THINKING RHETORICALLY ABOUT

SENTENCE PATTERNS WITH DIRECT OBJECTS

If you want to intensify a feeling or emphasize a contrast, alter the sentence pattern by placing the direct object at the beginning of the sentence. A comma is sometimes used after the direct object in such sentences.

They loved the queen. They despised **the king.**

They loved the queen. **The king,** they despised.

I acquired English at home. I learned **French** on the street.

I acquired English at home. **French** I learned on the street.

Exercise 5

a. Identify the basic pattern of each sentence in exercise 2.
b. Write a question corresponding to each of the sentences in exercise 2. Put a check mark next to the questions in which a subject and a verb are inverted.

Exercise 6

Shift the emphasis in each of the underlined sentences by moving the direct object to the front of the sentence.

1. Leah considers her medical studies her priority. <u>She calls her rock band a hobby</u>.
2. He learned to play the clarinet when he was eight. <u>He mastered the saxophone later on</u>.
3. They renovated the state house. <u>They condemned the old hotel</u>.
4. We played volleyball in the fall. <u>We played basketball in the winter</u>.
5. They named their first child Theodore. <u>They named their second child Franklin</u>.

21   PHRASES AND

CLAUSES

IN SENTENCES

Within a sentence, groups of words form phrases and clauses. Like single words, these larger units function as specific parts of speech: nouns, verbs, adjectives, or adverbs. By understanding how word groups function, you will be able to make your sentences clear, concise, and complete. You will also be able to vary sentence structure so that your paragraphs are rhythmic and cohesive. This chapter will help you

- recognize phrases (**21a**),
- recognize clauses (**21b**),
- recognize words that connect words, phrases, and clauses (**21c**), and
- identify sentence forms and functions (**21d–e**).

BEYOND THE RULE

DEFINITION OF *PHRASE*

There are two definitions of the word *phrase*. The traditional definition is that a **phrase** is a sequence of grammatically related words without a subject, a predicate, or both. However, linguists define a **phrase** as a unit that has one word as its main part. The traditional definition allows only multiword groupings to be phrases; the linguists' definition also allows single-word phrases. In most composition handbooks, including this one, the traditional definition is used. For more information on phrases, visit **www.harbrace.com**.

21a Phrases

(1) A noun phrase consists of a main noun and its determiners and modifiers.

Noun phrases serve as subjects and complements. They can also be objects of prepositions, such as *in, of, on, at,* and *to.* (See 21a(4) for a longer list of prepositions.)

The heavy frost killed **many fruit trees.** [subject and direct object]

My cousin is **an organic farmer.** [subject and subject complement]

His farm is in **eastern Oregon.** [subject and object of the preposition *in*]

THINKING RHETORICALLY ABOUT

NOUN PHRASES

In the sentences above, the articles *the* and *an* as well as the adjectives *heavy, organic,* and *eastern* add specificity. For example, the noun phrase *an organic farmer* tells the reader more than the word *farmer* alone would. By choosing nouns and noun phrases carefully, you will make your sentences more precise and cohesive.

Much of Greenland lies within the Arctic Circle. ~~The area~~ ^This large island is owned by Denmark. Its ^native name is Kaballit Nunaat.

[*The area* could refer to either Greenland or the area within the Arctic Circle. *This large island* clearly refers to Greenland. *Its native name* is more precise than just *Its name.*]

Nouns and Determiners

The determiners *a, an, this,* and *that* are used with singular nouns. Other determiners, such as *some, few, these,* and *those,* are used with plural nouns.

an/that opportunity [determiners and singular count noun]

some/few/those opportunities [determiners and plural count noun]

The determiners *less* and *much* precede noncount nouns.

less time, **much** energy [determiners used with noncount nouns]

Abstract and plural generic nouns are rarely preceded by determiners.

Patience is a virtue. [abstract noun]

Customers can be demanding. [plural generic noun]

In other languages, determiners may not be used as they are in English. For example, in Italian, the definite article, equivalent to the English *the,* is used with abstract nouns.

La pazienza è una virtù. [The definite article *la* precedes the noun *pazienza.*]

(2) A verb phrase is essential to the predicate.

The predicate says something about the subject and contains a word that expresses action or state of being—a verb (see **20a(1)**). Besides a main verb, a **verb phrase** also includes an auxiliary, or helping verb, such as *be, have, do, will,* or *should.*

The flight **is arriving.** [auxiliary verb + main verb]

The passengers **have deplaned.** [auxiliary verb + main verb]

For a complete discussion of verb structure, see chapter **26**. For more information on using verbs to convey meaning effectively, see **27d(3)**, **30e**, and **31c**.

(3) Verbals may be used as nouns or as modifiers.

Verb forms used as nouns or modifiers (adjectives or adverbs) are called **verbals.** Because of their origin as verbs, verbals in phrases often have their own objects and modifiers.

> He wanted **to finish the task quickly.**
> [The object of the verbal *to finish* is *the task. Quickly* is a modifier.]

Phrases with verbals are divided into three types: gerund phrases, participial phrases, and infinitive phrases.

Central to a **gerund phrase** is the *-ing* verb form (see **26a(1)**). A gerund phrase functions as a noun, usually serving as the subject or object in a sentence.

> <u>**Writing**</u> **a bestseller** was her only goal. [subject]
> My neighbor enjoys <u>**writing**</u> **about distant places.** [object]

Because gerund phrases act as nouns, pronouns can replace them.

> **That** was her only goal.
> My neighbor enjoys **it.**

THINKING RHETORICALLY ABOUT

GERUNDS

What is the difference between the following sentences?

> They bundle products together, which can often result in higher consumer costs.
> Bundling products together can often result in higher consumer costs.

In the first sentence, the actor, *they,* is the focus. In the second sentence, the action of the gerund phrase, *bundling products together,* is the focus. As you revise sentences, ask yourself whether you want to emphasize actors or actions.

Participial phrases include either a present participle (*-ing* form) or a past participle (*-ed* form for regular verbs or another form for irregular verbs). (See **26a** for more information on verb forms.)

> <u>**Planning**</u> **her questions carefully,** she was able to hold fast-paced and engaging interviews. [present participle]

Known for her interviewing skills, she was asked to host her own radio program. [past participle]

Participial phrases function as modifiers. They may appear at various points in a sentence: beginning, middle, or end.

Fearing a drought, all the farmers in the area used less irrigation water.

All the farmers in the area, **recognizing the signs of drought,** used less irrigation water.

Farmers used less irrigation water, **hoping to save it for later in the season.**

The commas setting off the participial phrases in the preceding examples signal that the phrases are not essential for readers to understand who is using less irrigation water. Instead, the phrases add descriptive details or reasons to the sentences. Sometimes, however, a participial phrase provides additional information that specifies who or what is being discussed. In this case, the phrase is not set off by commas.

The reporter **providing the most accurate account of the war** was once a soldier. [The participial phrase distinguishes this reporter from others.]

For more advice on using punctuation with phrases containing verbals, see **35b(2)** and **35d(1)**.

THINKING RHETORICALLY ABOUT

PARTICIPIAL PHRASES

If some of your sentences sound monotonous or choppy, try combining them by using participial phrases.

The ecstatic fans crowded along the city streets. They were celebrating their team's first state championship.

REVISED:

Crowded along the city streets, the ecstatic fans celebrated their team's first state championship.

OR

Celebrating their team's first state championship, the ecstatic fans crowded along the city streets.

A present participle (*-ing* form) cannot function alone as the main verb in a sentence. When an *-ing* form is the main verb, it is generally preceded by a form of *be* (*am, is, are, was,* or *were*).

They _∧ **thinking** about the future.
are

Infinitive phrases serve as nouns or as modifiers. The form of the **infinitive** is distinct—the infinitive marker *to* followed by the base form of the verb.

The company intends **<u>to hire</u> twenty new employees.** [direct object]

<u>To attract</u> customers, the company changed its advertising strategy. [modifier of the verb *changed*]

We discussed his plan **<u>to use</u> a new packing process.** [modifier of the noun *plan*]

BEYOND THE RULE

SPLIT INFINITIVES

Some instructors advise against putting words between the infinitive marker *to* and the base form of the verb.

Be sure to ~~carefully~~ proofread your paper_∧.
carefully

This is good advice to remember if the intervening words create an awkward sentence.

Under the circumstances, the
_∧~~The~~ jury was unable to~~, under the circumstances,~~ convict the defendant.

However, most writers today recognize that an adverb splitting an infinitive can provide emphasis.

He never planned to actually publish his work.

For more information on split infinitives, visit **www.harbrace.com**.

VERBS FOLLOWED BY GERUNDS OR INFINITIVES
Some verbs in English are followed by a gerund, some are
followed by an infinitive, and some are followed by either.

Verbs Followed by a Gerund

admit   avoid   consider   deny   dislike   enjoy   finish   suggest

Example: She **enjoys playing** the piano.

Verbs Followed by an Infinitive

agree   decide   deserve   hope   need   plan   promise   seem

Example: She **promised to play** the piano for us.

When an infinitive follows a form of *make* or sometimes a form of *have*,
the marker *to* is omitted.

Example: The teacher **had** the student **repeat** the song.

Verbs Followed by a Pronoun, Noun, or Noun Phrase and an Infinitive

advise   encourage   order   require
cause   invite   persuade   teach

Example: Her father **taught** her **to play** the piano.

Verbs Followed by Either a Gerund or an Infinitive

begin   like   prefer   stop
continue   love   remember   try

Examples: She **likes to play** the piano. She **likes playing** the piano.

Although both gerund phrases and infinitive phrases can serve as direct
objects, their meanings may be different.

We **stopped discussing** the plan. [The discussion has ended.]

We **stopped to discuss** the plan. [The discussion has not yet started.]

Good dictionaries provide information on the use of gerunds and
infinitives (see **32e(1)** for a list of recommendations).

(4) Prepositional phrases are generally used as modifiers.

Prepositional phrases provide information about time, place, cause,
manner, and so on.

With great feeling, Martin Luther King expressed his dream **of freedom.**
[*With great feeling* describes the way the speech was delivered, and *of freedom* specifies the topic of the dream.]

King delivered his most famous speech **at a demonstration in Washington, DC.**
[Both *at a demonstration* and *in Washington, DC* provide details about place.]

A **prepositional phrase** consists of a **preposition** (a word such as *around, at,* or *near*) and a noun, noun phrase, or pronoun (**object of the preposition**). A prepositional phrase generally modifies another element in the sentence.

The professor's lecture **on censorship** stirred controversy.

Everyone **in the class** was upset.

Some students met the professor **after class.**

A prepositional phrase occasionally serves as a subject.

After supper is too late!

When the object of the preposition is a pronoun such as *whom* or *what,* the preposition may follow rather than precede its object, especially in questions.

What was the book **about?** [The object of the preposition is *what.*
COMPARE: The book was about what?]

SOME COMMON PREPOSITIONS

about	behind	except	of	to
above	beside	for	on	toward
after	between	from	out	under
around	by	in	over	until
as	despite	into	past	up
at	down	like	since	via
before	during	near	through	with

Phrasal prepositions consist of more than one word.

Except for the last day, it was a wonderful trip.

The postponement was **due to** inclement weather.

PHRASAL PREPOSITIONS

according to	due to	in spite of
apart from	except for	instead of
as for	in addition to	out of
because of	in case of	with regard to
by means of	in front of	with respect to

Prepositions in Collocations

Some verbs, adjectives, and nouns combine with prepositions to form **collocations** (see also **33c**).

verb + preposition	adjective + preposition	noun + preposition
apply to	fond of	interest in
rely on	similar to	dependence on
trust in	different from	fondness for

For other information about prepositions, consult the Glossary of Usage or a specialized dictionary (see **32e(1)**).

(5) An appositive can expand the meaning of a noun or a noun phrase.

Appositives (usually nouns or noun phrases) identify, explain, or supplement the meaning of other nouns or noun phrases. Thus, they add detail and variety to sentences.

When an appositive provides essential information, no commas are used.

Jonathan Weiner's book ***The Beak of the Finch*** won a Pulitzer Prize. [The appositive identifies the book being referred to.]

When an appositive provides extra details, commas set it off.

The Beak of the Finch, **a book by Jonathan Weiner,** won a Pulitzer Prize. [The appositive provides an extra detail about the book.]

For more information on how to punctuate nonessential appositives, see **35d(2)**.

(6) Absolute phrases provide descriptive details or express causes or conditions.

An **absolute phrase** is usually a noun phrase modified by a participial phrase or a prepositional phrase.

She left town at dawn, **all her belongings packed into a Volkswagen Beetle.**

Her guitar in the front seat, she pulled away from the curb.

The preceding absolute phrases provide details; the following absolute phrase expresses cause.

More vaccine having arrived, the staff scheduled its distribution.

To learn how to punctuate absolute phrases, see **35b(2)** and **35d(3)**.

Exercise 1

Label the underlined phrases in the following sentences as noun phrases, verb phrases, prepositional phrases, or verbal phrases. For verbal phrases, specify the type: gerund, participial, or infinitive. Next, identify any appositive phrases or absolute phrases in the sentences.

1. <u>Most museums</u> acquire, preserve, and exhibit objects <u>with artistic, historical, or scientific value</u>.

2. <u>Nontraditional museums</u> abound <u>in the United States and Canada</u>.

3. <u>Established in 1849</u>, the Mutter Museum in Philadelphia displays <u>pathological specimens</u>.

4. Some of the paintings in <u>the Museum of Bad Art</u> <u>were donated</u>.

5. You <u>can learn</u> the history of <u>the potato</u> <u>at The Food Museum Online</u>.

6. For those interested in various methods for <u>making toast</u>, the Cyber Toaster Museum can be visited <u>via the Internet</u>.

7. <u>Located within the Science Museum of Minnesota</u>, the Museum of Questionable Medical Devices displays objects <u>ranging from weight-reduction glasses to the age-reversing McGregor Rejuvenator</u>.

8. <u>To learn more about funeral vehicles</u>, consider <u>visiting the National Museum of Funeral History</u>, <u>a museum dedicated to providing the public with information on a common cultural ritual</u>.

9. A large collection <u>of footwear</u>, including a pair <u>of Queen Victoria's ballroom slippers</u>, is on display at <u>the Bata Shoe Museum</u>.

10. <u>Their curiosity piqued</u>, some tourists travel <u>great distances</u> <u>to see collections of unusual objects</u>.

Exercise 2

Add details to the following sentences by adding prepositional phrases, verbal phrases, appositive phrases, or absolute phrases. After you finish, label the phrases you added.

1. The students filed into the classroom.

2. My friend delivered the bad news.

3. The driver stopped abruptly.

4. I attended the lecture.

5. Jennifer clicked Send.

21b Clauses

(1) An independent clause can stand alone as a complete sentence.

A **clause** is a group of related words that contains a subject and a predicate. An **independent clause,** sometimes called a **main clause,** has the same grammatical structure as a simple sentence: both contain a subject and a predicate. (See **20b.**)

The students earned high grades.

Other clauses can be added to independent clauses to form longer, more detailed sentences.

(2) A dependent clause is attached to an independent clause.

A **dependent clause** also has a subject and a predicate. However, it cannot stand alone as a complete sentence because of the word introducing it—usually a relative pronoun or a subordinating conjunction.

The athlete **who placed first** grew up in Argentina.
[relative pronoun]

She received the gold medal **because she performed flawlessly.**
[subordinating conjunction]

If it is not connected to an independent clause, a dependent clause is considered a sentence fragment (see **22c**).

(a) Dependent clauses can be used as subjects or objects.

Dependent clauses that serve as subjects or objects are called **noun clauses** (or **nominal clauses**). They are introduced by *if, that,* or a *wh-* word such as *why, what,* or *when.* Notice the similarity in usage between noun phrases and noun clauses.

Noun phrases	Noun clauses
The testimony may not be true. [subject]	**What the witness said** may not be true. [subject]
We do not understand **their motives.** [direct object]	We do not understand **why they did it.** [direct object]
Send the money to **a charity.** [object of the preposition]	Send the money to **whoever needs it most.** [object of the preposition]

When no misunderstanding would result, *that* can be omitted.

> The scientist said **she was moving to Australia.** [*that* omitted]

However, *that* should always be retained when there are two noun clauses.

> The scientist said **that she was moving to Australia** and **that her research team was planning to accompany her.** [*that* retained in both noun clauses]

(b) Dependent clauses can be used as modifiers.

Two types of dependent clauses—adjectival (relative) clauses and adverbial clauses—serve as modifiers. An **adjectival clause,** or **relative clause,** answers one of these questions about a noun or pronoun: Which one? What kind of . . . ? Such clauses, which nearly always follow the words they modify, usually begin with a **relative pronoun** (*who, whom, that, which,* or *whose*) but sometimes start with a **relative adverb** (*when, where,* or *why*). Notice the similarity in usage between adjectives and adjectival clauses.

Adjectives	Adjectival clauses
Nobody likes **malicious** gossip. [answers the question "What kind of gossip?"]	Nobody likes news reports **that pry into someone's private life.** [answers the question "What kind of news reports?"]
Some **diligent** students begin their research early. [answers the question "Which students?"]	Students **who have good study habits** begin their research early. [answers the question "Which students?"]
The **public** remarks were troubling. [answers the question "Which remarks?"]	The remarks **that were made public** were troubling. [answers the question "Which remarks?"]

THINKING RHETORICALLY ABOUT

ADJECTIVAL CLAUSES

If your sentences sound monotonous or choppy, try using an adjectival clause to combine them.

Dub is a car magazine. It appeals to drivers with hip-hop attitudes.

Dub is a car magazine **that appeals to drivers with hip-hop attitudes.**

A Hovercraft can go where many vehicles cannot. It is practically amphibious.

A Hovercraft, **which can go where many vehicles cannot,** is practically amphibious.

Relative pronouns can be omitted as long as the meaning of the sentence is still clear.

Mother Teresa was a woman **the whole world admired.**
[*Whom,* the object in the adjectival clause, is omitted.]

She was someone **who cared more about serving than being served.**
[*Who,* the subject in the adjectival clause, cannot be omitted.]

The relative pronoun is not omitted when the clause is set off by commas.

Mother Teresa, **whom the whole world admired,** cared more about serving than being served.

Although writers have traditionally used *that* at the beginning of restrictive clauses, *which* has become acceptable if, as in the following example, it does not cause confusion. Grammar checkers, however, do not recognize this option and will instruct you to change *which* to *that.*

The committee opposes spending which would increase the deficit.

An **adverbial clause** usually answers a question about a verb: Where? When? How? Why? In what manner? Adverbial clauses are introduced by subordinating conjunctions such as *because, although,* and *when.* (For a list of subordinating conjunctions, see **21c(3)**.) Notice the similarity in usage between adverbs and adverbial clauses.

Adverbs	**Adverbial clauses**
Occasionally, the company hires new writers. [answers the question "How frequently does the company hire new writers?"]	**When the need arises,** the company hires new writers. [answers the question "How frequently does the company hire new writers?"]
She acted **selfishly.** [answers the question "How did she act?"]	She acted **as though she cared only about herself.** [answers the question "How did she act?"]

THINKING RHETORICALLY ABOUT

ADVERBIAL CLAUSES

In an adverbial clause that refers to time or establishes a fact, both the subject and any form of the verb *be* can be omitted. Using such **elliptical clauses** will make your writing more concise.

While fishing, he saw a rare owl.
[COMPARE: **While he was fishing,** he saw a rare owl.]
Though tired, they continued to study for the exam.
[COMPARE: **Though they were tired,** they continued to study for the exam.]

Be sure that the omitted subject of an elliptical clause is the same as the subject of the independent clause. If not, revise either the adverbial clause or the main clause.

While $_\wedge$ reviewing your report, a few questions occurred to me. [*I was* inserted]

OR

While reviewing your report, $_\wedge$ a few questions ~~occurred to me~~. [*I thought of* inserted]

For more information on the use of elliptical constructions, see **34c**.

21c Conjunctions and conjunctive adverbs

(1) Coordinating conjunctions join words, phrases, or clauses.

In the following examples, note that coordinating conjunctions (see 20a(7)) link grammatical elements that are alike. Each conjunction, though, signals a specific meaning.

> tired **yet** excited [*Yet* joins two adjectives and signals contrast.]
>
> in the boat **or** on the pier [*Or* joins two phrases and marks them as alternatives.]
>
> We did not share a language, **but** somehow we communicated. [*But* joins two independent clauses and signals contrast.]

Coordinating conjunctions also join independent clauses standing alone as sentences.

> In the more open places are little lavender asters, and the even smaller-flowered white ones that some people call beeweed or farewell-summer. **And** in low wet places are the richly flowered spikes of great lobelia, the blooms an intense startling blue, exquisitely shaped.
>
> —**WENDELL BERRY**, *Home Economics*

(2) Correlative conjunctions also join words, phrases, or clauses.

Correlative conjunctions (see 20a(7)), consisting of two or more words, join single words, phrases, or clauses. However, they do not join sentences.

> **either** you **or** I [*Either . . . or* joins two words and marks them as alternatives.]
>
> **neither** on Friday **nor** on Saturday [*Neither . . . nor* joins two phrases and marks them both as false or impossible.]
>
> **Not only** did they run ten miles, **but** they **also** swam twenty laps. [*Not only . . . but also* joins two independent clauses and signals addition.]

Generally, a correlative conjunction links similar structures. The following sentence has been revised because the correlative conjunction was linking a phrase to a clause.

> **Not only** ~~saving~~ *did he save* the lives of the accident victims, **but** he **also** prevented many spinal injuries.

(3) Subordinating conjunctions introduce dependent clauses.

A subordinating conjunction introduces a dependent clause and carries a specific meaning. For example, it may indicate cause, concession, condition, or purpose.

> She studied Spanish **so that** she would be able to work in Costa Rica.
> [*So that* signals a purpose.]

> **Unless** the project receives more funding, the research will stop.
> [*Unless* signals a condition.]

SUBORDINATING CONJUNCTIONS

after	how	than
although	if	though
as if	in case	unless
as though	in that	until
because	insofar as	when, whenever
before	once	where, wherever
even if	since	whether
even though	so that	while

(4) Conjunctive adverbs link independent clauses.

Conjunctive adverbs—such as *however, nevertheless, then,* and *therefore*—link independent clauses. These adverbs signal relationships such as cause, condition, and contrast. All conjunctive adverbs can be used at the beginning of an independent clause. Some may appear in the middle or at the end of a clause.

> Heat the oil; **then,** add the onions. [*Then* begins the clause and signals another step in a sequence.]

> He made copies of the report for members of the committee. He **also** sent copies to the city council. [*Also* appears in the middle of the clause and signals an additional action.]

> My mother and father have differing political views. They rarely argue, **however.** [*However* ends the clause and signals contrast.]

For more about the use of conjunctive adverbs, see 23c. For information on punctuating linked independent clauses, see 35a and 36a.

Exercise 3

First, identify the dependent clauses in the following paragraph; then, identify all coordinating conjunctions, correlative conjunctions, subordinating conjunctions, and conjunctive adverbs.

¹With the goal of crossing both the North Pole and the South Pole alone, Børge Ousland started his 1,240-mile trek on March 3, 2001. **²**He had already crossed the South Pole in 1997, so this time he planned to walk, ski, and swim across the North Pole. **³**When he left Cape Arkticheskiy in Russia, he weighed 214 pounds. **⁴**When he reached Ward Hunt Island in Canada on March 23, he weighed only 177 pounds. **⁵**Although Ousland had prepared for the most grueling triathlon imaginable, he had no way of predicting what he would have to endure. **⁶**One night huge chunks of ice forced upward from the packed surface almost destroyed his camp, and the next morning he had to search hard for snow that he could melt into fresh water. **⁷**About a week into his trip, Ousland's sledge started to break down. **⁸**Ousland considered canceling his trip at that point, but instead he steeled himself and ordered a new sledge, which did not arrive until several days later. **⁹**Ousland also had to swim across leads, shoot at approaching polar bears, and endure the pain of frostbite and strained tendons. **¹⁰**Despite all the misery, Ousland continually took cues from his surroundings. **¹¹**Whenever he came to a lead, he asked himself what a polar bear would do. **¹²**When crossing treacherous pack ice, he thought as a fox would, making each step count. **¹³**Ousland said the most important lesson from the journey was perseverance. **¹⁴**He never gave up.

21d Sentence forms

You can identify the form of a sentence by noting the number and kind of each clause it contains.

(1) A simple sentence consists of a single independent clause.

> ONE INDEPENDENT CLAUSE

A **simple sentence** is equivalent to one independent clause. Essentially, then, it must have a subject and a predicate.

The lawyer presented her final argument.

However, you can expand a simple sentence by adding one or more prepositional phrases or verbal phrases.

> The lawyer presented her final argument **in less than an hour.**
> [A prepositional phrase adds information about time.]
>
> **Encouraged by the apparent sympathy of the jury,** the lawyer presented her final argument. [A verbal phrase adds detail.]

(2) A compound sentence consists of at least two independent clauses but no dependent clauses.

> INDEPENDENT CLAUSE + INDEPENDENT CLAUSE

The independent clauses of a compound sentence are most commonly linked by a coordinating conjunction. However, punctuation may sometimes serve the same purpose. (See **36a** and **39d**.)

> The Democrats proposed a new budget, **but** the Republicans opposed it.
> [The coordinating conjunction *but* links two independent clauses and signals contrast.]
>
> The Democrats proposed a new budget; the Republicans opposed it.
> [The semicolon serves the same purpose as the coordinating conjunction.]

(3) A complex sentence has one independent clause and at least one dependent clause.

> INDEPENDENT CLAUSE + DEPENDENT CLAUSE

A dependent clause in a complex sentence can be a noun clause, an adjectival clause, or an adverbial clause.

> **Because he was known for architectural ornamentation,** no one predicted **that the house <u>he designed for himself</u> would be so plain.** [This sentence has three dependent clauses. *Because he was known for architectural ornamentation* is an adverbial clause. *That the house he designed for himself would be so plain* is a noun clause, and *he designed for himself* is an adjectival clause within the noun clause. The relative pronoun *that* has been omitted from the beginning of this adjectival clause.]

(4) A compound-complex sentence consists of at least two independent clauses and at least one dependent clause.

> INDEPENDENT CLAUSE + INDEPENDENT CLAUSE +
>
> DEPENDENT CLAUSE

The combination of a compound sentence and a complex sentence is called a **compound-complex sentence.**

> **Because it snowed heavily in October that year,** the ski resorts opened early, **and** the skiers flocked to them. [*Because* introduces the dependent clause; *and* connects the two independent clauses.]

THINKING RHETORICALLY ABOUT

SENTENCE FORMS

If one of your paragraphs has as many simple sentences as the one below, try combining some of those sentences into compound, complex, or compound-complex sentences. As you do, you might need to add extra detail as well.

> I rode the school bus every day. I didn't like to, though. The bus smelled bad. And it was always packed. The worst part was the bumpy ride. Riding the bus was like riding in a worn-out sneaker.

REVISED:

> As a kid, I rode the school bus every day, but I didn't like to. I hated the smell, the crowd, and the ride itself. Every seat was filled, and many of the kids took their shoes off for the long ride home down a road so bumpy you couldn't even read a comic book. Riding that bus was like riding inside a worn-out sneaker.

Exercise 4

Identify each sentence in the paragraph in exercise 3 as simple, compound, complex, or compound-complex.

Exercise 5

Vary the sentence forms in the following paragraph. Add details as needed.

We arrived at the afternoon concert. We were late. We couldn't find any seats. It was hot, so we stood in the shade. We finally found seats under an umbrella. The shade didn't help, though. We could feel our brains melting. The music was cool, but we weren't.

21e Sentence functions

Sentences serve a number of functions. Writers commonly state facts or report information with **declarative sentences.** They give instructions with **imperative sentences.** They use questions, or **interrogative sentences,** to elicit information or to introduce topics. And they express emotion with **exclamatory sentences.**

Declarative   The runners from Kenya won the race.

Imperative   Check their times.

Interrogative   Wasn't it an incredible race?

Taking note of end punctuation can help you identify sentence types. Generally, a period marks the end of a declarative or an imperative sentence, and a question mark ends an interrogative sentence. An exclamation point indicates that a sentence is exclamatory.

Exclamatory   The runners from Kenya won the race! Check their times!
                    What an incredible race!

Imperatives are also easy to identify because the subject is always understood to be *you.* Because an imperative is directed to another person or to other people, the subject *you* is implied:

Look over here! [COMPARE: You look over here.]

Advertisers often use imperatives to draw in readers.

BEYOND THE RULE

SENTENCE FUNCTIONS

Each type of sentence can be used for a variety of purposes. For example, imperative sentences are used not only to give directions, but also to make suggestions ("Try using a different screwdriver."), to issue invitations ("Come in."), to extend wishes ("Have a good time."), and to warn others ("Stop there."). Furthermore, a single purpose, such as getting someone to do something, can be accomplished in more than one way.

Imperative	Close the window, please.
Declarative	We should close the window.
Interrogative	Would you please close the window?

For further discussion of the connection between the form and the function of sentences, see **www.harbrace.com**.

THINKING RHETORICALLY ABOUT

SENTENCE TYPES

One type of interrogative sentence, the **rhetorical question,** is not a true question because an answer is not expected. Instead, like a declarative sentence, a rhetorical question is used to state an opinion. However, a positive rhetorical question can correspond to a negative assertion, and vice versa.

Rhetorical questions	Equivalent statements
Should we allow our rights to be taken away?	We shouldn't allow our rights to be taken away.
Isn't it time to make a difference?	It's time to make a difference.

Because they are more emphatic than declarative sentences, rhetorical questions focus the reader's attention on major points.

Exercise 6

Identify the function of each of these sentences.

1. Who is going to the concert?
2. Go early to get good seats.
3. The concert was six hours long.
4. What an amazing song that was!

22

SENTENCE

FRAGMENTS

As its name suggests, a **sentence fragment** is only a piece of a sentence; it is not complete. This chapter can help you

- recognize sentence fragments (**22a**) and
- revise fragments resulting from incorrectly punctuated phrases and dependent clauses (**22b–c**).

Do not rely on a grammar checker to flag all the fragments in your writing. The grammar checker used in producing this chapter recognized only half of the fragments serving as examples. Instead of relying on a grammar checker, use the methods described in this chapter. Also refer to **Using a Grammar Checker** on page 461.

22a Recognizing sentence fragments

A complete sentence consists of a subject and a predicate (see **20b**), but a fragment may be missing either or both of these parts and thus require revision.

Magazines often include articles about alternative medicine. ~~Usually~~ **, usually** **covering both the benefits and the drawbacks of particular methods.**

Sometimes, alternative medical treatment includes hypnosis. ~~The~~ **, the** **placement of a patient into a sleeplike state.**

Alternatively, a fragment may have the essential sentence components but begin with a subordinating conjunction or a relative pronoun (see **21b(2)**).

Subordinating conjunction beginning a fragment

Most people can be hypnotized easily~~.~~ , although ~~**Although**~~ **the depth of the trance for each person varies greatly.**

Relative pronoun beginning a fragment

Hypnosis is usually induced by a hypnotist~~.~~ , who ~~**Who**~~ **gives repetitive, monotonous commands.**

Note that imperative sentences (see **21e**) are not considered fragments. In these sentences, the subject, *you,* is not stated explicitly. Rather, it is implied. In fact, the subject of an imperative sentence is often called the **understood you.**

Find out as much as you can about alternative treatments.
[COMPARE: *You* find out as much as you can about alternative treatments.]

Subject Pronouns

In some languages, subject pronouns are dropped when there is no risk of misunderstanding. In Japanese, a sentence such as *Sushi o tabemasu* ("Eat sushi") is permissible when the subject pronoun can be determined from the context. In Spanish, the verb form reveals information about the subject; unless needed for clarity or emphasis, a subject pronoun can be omitted, as in *Trabajo en un banco* ("I work in a bank"). In English, however, subject pronouns must be included in all except imperative sentences.

FOUR METHODS FOR IDENTIFYING FRAGMENTS

Fragments may be difficult to find within the context of neighboring sentences. If you have trouble recognizing fragments, try one or more of these methods:

1. Read each paragraph backwards, sentence by sentence. When you read your sentences out of order, you may more readily note the incompleteness of a fragment.
2. Locate the essential parts of each sentence. First, find the main verb and any accompanying auxiliary verbs. Remember that verbals cannot function

(Continued on page 508)

(Continued from page 507)

as main verbs (see $26a(5)$). After you find the main verb, find the subject by asking "Who?" or "What?" (see $20d(1)$). Finally, check to see that the sentence does not begin with a relative pronoun or a subordinating conjunction (see $21b(2)$).

Test sentence: Striving to provide educational opportunities for African Americans.

Test: Main verb? *None.* "Striving" and "to provide" are both verbals.

Subject? *None.*

[Because there is no subject or main verb, this test sentence is a fragment.]

Test sentence: Striving to provide educational opportunities for African Americans, Mary McLeod Bethune opened a small school in 1904.

Test: Main verb? *Opened.*

Subject? *Mary McLeod Bethune.*

Relative pronoun or subordinating conjunction? *None.*

[This test sentence contains a subject and a verb, and it does not begin with a relative pronoun or subordinating conjunction. It is therefore complete.]

3. Put any sentence you think might be a fragment into this frame:

They do not understand the idea that _____.

Only a full sentence will make sense in this frame. If a test sentence, other than an imperative, does not fit into the frame, it is a fragment.

Test sentence: Depending on availability of food.

Test: They do not understand the idea that *depending on availability of food.*

[The sentence does not make sense, so the test sentence is a fragment.]

Test sentence: The number of tiger sharks grows or shrinks depending on availability of food.

Test: They do not understand the idea that *the number of tiger sharks grows or shrinks depending on availability of food.*

[The sentence does make sense, so the test sentence is complete.]

4. Rewrite any sentence you think might be a fragment as a yes/no question. Only full sentences can be rewritten this way.

Test sentence: Which is made from the leaves of the foxglove plant.

Test: *Is which made from the leaves of the foxglove plant?*

[The question does not make sense, so the test sentence is a fragment.]

Test sentence: Some heart patients take digitalis, which is made from the leaves of the foxglove plant.

Test: *Do some heart patients take digitalis, which is made from the leaves of the foxglove plant?*

[The question does make sense, so the test sentence is complete.]

Exercise 1

Identify the sentence fragments in the following paragraph. Be prepared to explain how you identified each fragment. Revise the fragments by attaching them to related sentences or by recasting them as full sentences.

¹One of the most versatile American sculptors of the twentieth century, Alexander Calder (1898–1976) is best known for his mobiles. ²Playfully balanced arrangements of abstract or organic forms. ³As a young man, Calder first studied mechanical engineering. ⁴Even though he came from a family of sculptors. ⁵It was not until four years after he earned his degree that he enrolled in an art school. ⁶Shortly thereafter, Calder moved to Paris. ⁷Where his wire sculptures won him worldwide recognition. ⁸During the 1930s, he began to experiment with motion. ⁹Eventually developing the mode of sculpture that most people think of when they hear the name *Calder*.

22b Phrases as sentence fragments

A phrase (see 21a) may be mistakenly written as a sentence fragment. You can revise such a fragment by attaching it to a related sentence, usually the one preceding it. This method creates a strong link between the fragment and the independent clause it follows. If you are unsure of the correct punctuation to use with phrases, see **35b** and **35d**.

Verbal phrase as fragment

Early humans valued color. , creating ~~C~~reating permanent colors with natural pigments.

Prepositional phrase as fragment

For years, the Scottish have dyed sweaters with soot. , originally ~~O~~riginally from the chimneys of peat-burning stoves.

Compound predicate as fragment

Arctic foxes turn white when it snows. and ~~A~~nd thus conceal themselves from prey.

Appositive phrase as fragment

During the Renaissance, one of the most highly valued pigments was ultramarine. —an ~~A~~n extract from lapis lazuli.

Appositive list as fragment

In order to derive dyes, we have always experimented with what we find in nature. : shells, ~~S~~hell**s**, roots, insects, flowers.

Absolute phrase as fragment

The deciduous trees of New England are known for their brilliant autumn color. , sugar ~~S~~ugar maples dazzling tourists with their deep orange and red leaves.

Instead of attaching a fragment to the preceding sentence, you can recast the fragment as a full sentence. This method of revision elevates the importance of the information conveyed in the fragment.

Fragment: Early humans valued color. **Creating permanent colors with natural pigments.**

Revision: Early humans valued color. They created permanent colors with natural pigments.

Fragment: Humans painted themselves for a variety of purposes. **To attract a mate, to hide themselves from game or predators, or to signal aggression.**

Revision: Humans used color for a variety of purposes. For example, they painted themselves to attract a mate, to hide themselves from game or predators, or to signal aggression.

Exercise 2

Revise each fragment by attaching it to a related sentence or by recasting it as a full sentence.

1. The first person to produce an artificial dye commercially was William Perkin. A nineteen-year-old Englishman.

2. At one time in Europe, mummy was a popular pigment. Made by crushing the remains of Egyptian mummies.

3. Many food producers package their products in red. Believing that it attracts consumers.

4. Red causes the release of adrenaline in humans. As well as in other animal species.

5. Crayola assigns the colors of crayons unusual names. Including Outer Space and Pig Pink.

6. There are three colors on the Italian flag. Green on the left side, red on the right side, and white in the center.

7. One of Marie Antoinette's favorite shades was puce. The French word for "flea."

8. At times, the pigment saffron was quite popular. And worth its weight in gold.

9. The pigment carmine was in high demand. Spanish conquistadors making vast fortunes on its production.

10. Sir Isaac Newton showed that white light comprised all the visible colors of the spectrum. By passing a beam of sunlight through a prism.

22c Dependent clauses as sentence fragments

Dependent clauses that are punctuated as if they were independent clauses are sentence fragments. An adverbial clause or an adjectival clause (see **21b(2)**) is a common culprit. Such a fragment can be revised by attaching it to a related sentence, usually the sentence preceding it. By linking the fragment to the independent clause, you explicitly indicate their relationship—cause and effect, for example.

Adverbial clause as fragment

The iceberg was no surprise. ~~Because~~ *because* the *Titanic*'s wireless operators had received reports of ice in the area.

Adjectival clause as fragment

More than two thousand people were aboard the *Titanic*. ~~Which~~ *, which* was the world's largest ocean liner in 1912.

The shipbuilders first constructed the keel. ~~Which~~ *, which* was considered the backbone of the ship.

Two other methods can be used to revise these types of fragments. You can recast the fragment as a full sentence by removing the subordinating conjunction or relative pronoun and supplying any missing elements. This method of revision draws more attention to the information conveyed in the fragment. Compare the following revised sentences with those above.

Revision: The iceberg was no surprise. The *Titanic*'s wireless operators had received reports of ice in the area.

Revision: More than two thousand people were aboard the *Titanic*. In 1912, this ocean liner was the world's largest.

You can also reduce the fragment to a phrase (see **21a**) and then attach the phrase to a related sentence. When you link a phrase to a sentence, you establish a certain relationship between the two. Unlike clauses, however, participial and appositive phrases suggest relationships less directly because they do not include subordinating conjunctions or relative pronouns.

Revision: The shipbuilders first constructed the keel—considered the backbone of the ship. [dependent clause reduced to a participial phrase]

Revision: More than two thousand people were aboard the *Titanic*, the world's largest ocean liner in 1912. [dependent clause reduced to an appositive phrase]

If you are unsure of the correct punctuation to use with phrases or dependent clauses, see chapter 35.

THINKING RHETORICALLY ABOUT

FRAGMENTS

When used judiciously, fragments—like short sentences—emphasize ideas, add surprise, or enhance the rhythm of a paragraph. Fragments are not appropriate for all types of writing, however. They are generally permitted only when the rhetorical situation allows the use of an intimate or playful tone.

> The room is full of sunlight. **Yellow. Cream. Gold. White.** These colors cover two-thirds of its surface, which is also awash with lavenders and reds falling in sun-filled stripes from the curtains, the walls, the man, the table, the chair, the dresser. —**ELAINE SCARRY**, *On Beauty and Being Just*

> Narrow, shoulderless highway 61 looked as if a tar pot had overturned at the summit and trickled a crooked course down. **A genuine white-knuckled road.**
> —**WILLIAM LEAST HEAT-MOON**, *Blue Highways*

BEYOND THE RULE

ABBREVIATED SENTENCES

You encounter sentence fragments every day—in conversations, in e-mail messages, and even in some instructional materials. In conversation, someone might ask you, "Going anywhere tonight?" And you might respond, "Maybe."

(Continued on page 514)

(Continued from page 513)

To end an e-mail message, you might write, "See you later." When preparing a meal, you have probably read instructions similar to these: "Just heat and serve." "Cook to golden brown." The writers of such instructions expect you to know what is to be heated or browned. These kinds of fragments, in which words that can be understood from the context are omitted, are called **abbreviated sentences.** For other examples of abbreviated sentences, visit **www.harbrace.com**.

BOBOLI

Directions

1. Preheat oven to 450°F.
2. Spread 1 pouch of sauce on 1 large (12") BOBOLI® Pizza Crust.
3. Top with cheese, vegetables – whatever you like!
4. Bake 8-10 minutes on oven rack or ungreased cookie sheet until crust is crisp and cheese is melted.

Package directions often include abbreviated sentences.

Exercise 3

Revise each fragment by attaching it to a related sentence or by recasting it as a full sentence.

1. The iceberg was hard to see. Because there was no wind causing waves to splash against it.
2. The lookouts on the *Titanic* did not spot the iceberg. Until it was too late.

3. The name given to the large ocean liner was *Titanic*. Which means "of great size."

4. One of the most reliable eyewitnesses was Jack Thayer. Who gave his report shortly after he was rescued.

5. Moviegoers raved about the film *Titanic*. Which was based on the ship's story.

Exercise 4

Advertisements often contain sentence fragments. Find a newspaper or magazine advertisement that contains several fragments. Rewrite the advertisement so that it consists of complete sentences; then, write a short paragraph explaining why you think the advertiser may have used the fragments.

Exercise 5

Follow the guidelines in this chapter to locate and revise the fragments in the following passage. If you find it necessary, make other changes to enhance the paragraph as well. Be prepared to explain your revisions.

1A giant hairy animal has caught the fascination of many people. **2**Including normally skeptical citizens and scientists. **3**They are all interested in the phenomenon of Sasquatch. **4**Also commonly called Big Foot. **5***Sasquatch* comes from the Salish word *saskehavas*. **6**The North American Sasquatch has a counterpart. **7**The Himalayan Yeti. **8**Both have been studied by cryptozoologists. **9**Who research undiscovered animals. **10**In our country, most sightings of Sasquatch occur in the Pacific Northwest. **11**From northern California to central Alaska. **12**Although reports have come from almost every state. **13**During the settlement of the United States, stories of hairy ape-men were told by Native Americans. **14**And later on by trappers. **15**Teddy Roosevelt recorded one such story.

COMMA SPLICES	**23**
AND	
FUSED SENTENCES	

Comma splices and fused sentences are sentence-level mistakes resulting from incorrect or missing punctuation. Both are punctuated as one sentence when they should be punctuated as two sentences (or two independent clauses). By revising comma splices and fused sentences, you indicate sentence boundaries and connections and thus make your writing more coherent. This chapter will help you

- review the rules for punctuating independent clauses (**23a**),
- recognize comma splices and fused sentences (**23b**), and
- learn ways to revise them (**23c–d**).

A **comma splice,** or **comma fault,** refers to the incorrect use of a comma between two independent clauses (see **36a**).

Most stockholders favored the merger, ^but^ the management did not.

This kind of error can be easily fixed. Because a comma is a weak mark of punctuation, usually placed between words or phrases (see chapter **35**), it is not conventionally used to join independent clauses. For this purpose, you should use connecting words, stronger marks of punctuation, or both.

A **fused sentence** consists of two independent clauses run together without any punctuation at all. This type of sentence is sometimes called a **run-on sentence.**

The first section of the proposal was approved ^;however,^ the budget will have to be resubmitted.

Revising a fused sentence is also easy. All you have to do is include appropriate punctuation and any necessary connecting words.

23a Punctuating independent clauses

In case you are unfamiliar with or unsure about the conventions for punctuating independent clauses, here is a short review.

A comma and a coordinating conjunction can join two independent clauses (see **35a**). The coordinating conjunction indicates the relationship between the two clauses. For example, *and* signals addition, whereas *but* and *yet* signal contrast. The comma precedes the conjunction.

> INDEPENDENT CLAUSE**, and** INDEPENDENT CLAUSE.

The new store opened this morning, **and** the owners greeted everyone at the door.

A semicolon can join two independent clauses that are closely related. A semicolon generally signals addition or contrast.

> INDEPENDENT CLAUSE**;** INDEPENDENT CLAUSE.

One of the owners comes from this area**;** the other grew up in Costa Rica.

A semicolon may also precede an independent clause that begins with a conjunctive adverb such as *however* or *nevertheless.* Notice that a comma follows this type of connecting word.

The store will be open late on Fridays and Saturdays**; however,** it will be closed all day on Sundays.

BEYOND THE RULE

PUNCTUATION IN SENTENCES CONTAINING CONJUNCTIVE ADVERBS

A comma used to set off a conjunctive adverb is sometimes omitted when there is no risk of misreading.

(Continued on page 518)

(Continued from page 517)

The sea was unusually hot; **thus** the coral turned white.
[No misreading is possible, so the comma can be omitted.]

He was so nervous that his stomach was churning; **however,** he answered the question calmly and accurately.
[The comma is needed. Without it, *however* might be interpreted as meaning "in whatever way" rather than "in contrast." COMPARE: However he answered the question, he would offend someone.]

For more examples, visit **www.harbrace.com**.

A colon can join two independent clauses. The second clause usually explains or elaborates the first.

> INDEPENDENT CLAUSE: INDEPENDENT CLAUSE.

The owners extended a special offer: anyone who makes a purchase during the opening will receive a 10 percent discount.

A period separates clauses into distinct sentences.

> INDEPENDENT CLAUSE. INDEPENDENT CLAUSE.

The store is located on the corner of Pine Street and First Avenue. It was formerly an insurance office.

Occasionally, commas are used between independent clauses, but only when the clauses are short, parallel in form, and unified in meaning.

They came, they shopped, they left.

Commas are also used to separate a statement from an attached question (also called a **tag question**).

You went to the grand opening, **didn't you?**

For more information on punctuating sentences, see chapters 35, 36, and 39.

23b Two methods for identifying comma splices and fused sentences

If you have trouble recognizing comma splices or fused sentences, try one of the following methods.

1. Locate a sentence that might have one of these problems. It may have a comma or no punctuation at all. Put the sentence in this frame:

   They do not understand the idea that _____.

   Only complete sentences will make sense in the frame. If just part of a test sentence fits into the frame, you have probably located a comma splice or a fused sentence.

   Test sentence: The wild Bactrian camel, a two-humped camel living in the Gobi Desert, can drink salt water.

   Test: They do not understand the idea that *the wild Bactrian camel, a two-humped camel living in the Gobi Desert, can drink salt water.*

   [The sentence makes sense. No revision is necessary.]

   Test sentence: Male proboscis monkeys have oddly shaped large noses, they also have unusual webbed paws.

   Test: They do not understand the idea that *male proboscis monkeys have oddly shaped large noses, they also have unusual webbed paws.*

   [The sentence does not make sense because there are two sentences completing the frame, rather than one, so the test sentence needs to be revised.]

   Revision: *Male proboscis monkeys have oddly shaped large noses. They also have unusual webbed paws.*

2. Try to rewrite a possibly incorrect sentence as a question that can be answered with *yes* or *no*. If just part of the sentence makes sense, you have likely found a comma splice or a fused sentence.

   Test sentence: The Arctic tern migrates from the Arctic to Antarctica.

   Test: *Does the Arctic tern migrate from the Arctic to Antarctica?*

   [The question makes sense. No revision is necessary.]

   Test sentence: Meerkats use their claws to forage for food they frequently prey on scorpions.

   Test: *Do meerkats use their claws to forage for food they frequently prey on scorpions?*

[The question does not make sense because only one of the two sentences has been made into a question. The test sentence should be revised.]

Revision: *Meerkats use their claws to forage for food. They frequently prey on scorpions.*

Once you have identified a problematic sentence, you can simply correct it (see **23c**), or you can deepen your analysis by determining whether the problem is a comma splice or a fused sentence. To make such a determination, follow these steps.

1. Notice how many pairs of grammatical subjects and verbs are in the sentence (see **20b**).

   a. Find the verbs.

   b. Match verbs to subjects.

   (1) Male proboscis <u>monkeys</u> <u>have</u> oddly shaped large noses, <u>they</u> also <u>have</u> unusual webbed paws. [two pairs]

   (2) <u>Meerkats</u> <u>use</u> their claws to forage for food <u>they</u> frequently <u>prey</u> on scorpions. [two pairs]

2. Look for the punctuation that separates the pairs of subjects and verbs (if there are at least two). Sentence (1) has a comma. Sentence (2) has no punctuation.

3. If no punctuation separates the pairs, you have found a fused sentence, unless there is a dependent clause present (see **21b(2)**). Sentence (2) is a fused sentence.

   Meerkats use their claws to forage for food ⋀. They they frequently prey on scorpions.

   Notice, however, that the following sentence includes a dependent clause and thus is not fused.

   Meerkats use their claws to forage for food, which frequently consists of scorpions and beetles.

4. If a comma separates the pairs of subjects and verbs, you may have found a comma splice.

a. If the comma is followed by a coordinating conjunction or a nonessential (nonrestrictive) dependent clause (see **35d**), the sentence does not contain a comma splice.

Male proboscis monkeys have oddly shaped large noses, and they also have unusual webbed paws.

A male proboscis monkey has an oddly shaped large nose, whose size may attract mates.

b. If there is neither a coordinating conjunction nor a nonrestrictive dependent clause, as in sentence (1), the sentence contains a comma splice.

Male proboscis monkeys have oddly shaped large noses, ~~they~~ also have unusual webbed paws. [handwritten correction: . They]

You can also find comma splices and fused sentences by remembering that they commonly occur in certain circumstances:

■ With transitional words and phrases such as *however, therefore,* and *for example* (see also **23c**)

Comma splice: The director is not able to meet with you this week, [handwritten: ;] however, [handwritten: '] next week she will have time on Monday and Tuesday.

[Notice that a semicolon replaces the comma.]

■ When an explanation or an example is given in the second sentence

Fused sentence: The cultural center has a new collection of spear points ~~many~~ of them were donated by a retired anthropologist. [handwritten correction: . Many]

■ When a positive clause follows a negative clause

Comma splice: A World Cup victory is not just an everyday sporting event, ~~it~~ is a national celebration. [handwritten correction: . It]

■ When the subject of the second clause is a pronoun whose antecedent is in the preceding clause

Fused sentence: Lake Baikal is located in southern Russia ~~it~~ is 394 miles long. [handwritten correction: . It]

23c Revising comma splices and fused sentences

If you find comma splices or fused sentences in your writing, try one of the following methods to revise them.

(1) Use a comma and a coordinating conjunction to link clauses.

By linking clauses with a comma and a coordinating conjunction (such as *and* or *but*), you signal the relationship between them (addition or contrast, for example).

, and

Fused sentence: Joseph completed the first experiment ∧ he will complete the other by Friday.

but

Comma splice: Some diplomats applauded the treaty, ∧ others opposed it vehemently.

(2) Use a semicolon or a colon to link clauses or a period to separate them.

When you link independent clauses with a semicolon (see chapter **36**), you signal their connection indirectly. There are no explicit conjunctions to use as cues. The semicolon usually indicates addition or contrast. When you link clauses with a colon (see **39d(1)**), the second clause serves as an explanation or an elaboration of the first. A period (see **39a(1)**) indicates that each clause is a complete sentence, distinct from surrounding sentences.

Comma splice: Our division's reports are posted on our Web page, hard copies are available by request.

Revision 1: Our division's reports are posted on our Web page; hard copies are available by request.

Revision 2: Our division's reports are posted on our Web page. Hard copies are available by request.

:

Fused sentence: His choice was difficult ∧ he would either lose his job or betray his ethical principles.

(3) Rewrite one clause as a phrase or as a dependent clause.

A dependent clause (**21b(2)**) includes a subordinating conjunction such as *although* or *because*, which indicates how the dependent and independent clauses are related (in expressing cause and effect, for example). Phrases that do not include prepositions (see **21a**) suggest relationships less directly because they do not include explicit connecting words.

> Comma splice: The wind had blown down trees and power lines, the whole city was without electricity for several hours.

> Revision 1: **Because of the downed power lines,** the whole city was without electricity for several hours. [using a phrase]

> Revision 2: **Because the wind had blown down power lines,** the whole city was without electricity for several hours. [using a dependent clause]

(4) Integrate one clause into the other.

When you integrate clauses, you generally retain the important details but omit or change some words.

> Fused sentence: The proposal covers all but one point it does not describe how the project will be assessed.

> Revision: The proposal covers all the points except assessment procedures.

(5) Use transitional words or phrases to link independent clauses.

Another way to revise comma splices and fused sentences is to use transitional words (conjunctive adverbs) or transitional phrases (see the lists that follow). You can use these words or phrases to begin new sentences.

> Fused sentence: Sexual harassment is not just an issue for women ⟨. After all,⟩ men can be sexually harassed too.

You can also use them to join two clauses into one sentence.

> Comma splice: The word *status* refers to relative position within a group ⟨; however,⟩ it is often used to indicate only positions of prestige.

CONJUNCTIVE ADVERBS

also	however	next
anyhow	incidentally	otherwise
anyway	indeed	similarly
besides	instead	still
consequently	likewise	then
finally	meanwhile	therefore
furthermore	moreover	thus
hence	nevertheless	

TRANSITIONAL PHRASES

after all	even so	in fact
as a result	for example	in other words
at any rate	in addition	on the contrary
at the same time	in comparison	on the other hand
by the way	in contrast	that is

A transitional word or phrase may either begin an independent clause or take another position within it. When it appears within the clause, the transitional word or phrase is generally set off by commas.

> She believed that daily exercise has many benefits; **however,** she couldn't fit it into her schedule. [The conjunctive adverb begins the second independent clause and is positioned after a semicolon and before a comma (see also 36a).]

> She believed that daily exercise has many benefits. She couldn't, **however,** fit it into her schedule. [The conjunctive adverb appears later in the second clause. In this position, it is set off by commas.]

The following checklist will help you find and fix comma splices and fused sentences.

CHECKLIST for Comma Splices and Fused Sentences

① Common Sites for Comma Splices or Fused Sentences

- With transitional words or phrases such as *however, therefore,* and *for example*
- When an explanation or an example occurs in the second sentence
- When a positive clause follows a negative clause
- When the subject of the second clause is a pronoun whose antecedent is in the preceding clause

② How to Identify a Comma Splice or a Fused Sentence

a. Notice how many pairs of subjects and verbs (see **20b**) are in the sentence.
   (1) Find the verbs.
   (2) Match the verbs to their subjects.
b. Look for the punctuation that separates the pairs of subjects and verbs (if there are at least two).
c. If no punctuation separates the pairs and no dependent clause is present, you have found a fused sentence.
d. If a comma separates the pairs, you may have found a comma splice.
   (1) If there is a coordinating conjunction or a nonessential dependent clause, there is no comma splice.
   (2) If there is no coordinating conjunction or nonessential dependent clause, there is a comma splice.

③ How to Fix Comma Splices and Fused Sentences

- Link the clauses with a comma and a coordinating conjunction.
- Link the clauses, using a semicolon or a colon.
- Separate the clauses by punctuating each as a sentence.
- Make one clause dependent.

(Continued on page 526)

(Continued from page 525)

- Reduce one clause to a phrase.
- Rewrite the sentence, integrating one clause into the other.
- Use transitional words or phrases to link the clauses.

As you edit fused sentences and comma splices, you will refine the connections between your sentences, making them clearer and more coherent. By taking the time to revise, you will be helping your readers follow your train of thought. For more information on joining clauses, see chapter 28.

Exercise 1

Connect each pair of sentences in two of the following ways: (a) join them with a semicolon or colon, (b) join them with a coordinating conjunction, (c) reduce one to a phrase or dependent clause (see 21c(3) for a list of subordinating conjunctions), or (d) integrate one clause into the other.

1. Our national parks offer a variety of settings. They attract millions of visitors every year.
2. The Grand Teton National Park includes a sixteen-peak mountain range. It offers extensive hiking trails and wildlife-viewing opportunities.
3. Yellowstone National Park is generally full of tourists. The geysers and cliffs are worth the visit.
4. Hikers especially enjoy their vacations at Yellowstone National Park. The park consists of two million acres of backcountry perfect for hiking.
5. Vacationers enchanted by cascading water should visit Yosemite National Park. The waterfalls at Yosemite reach heights of more than two thousand feet.

Exercise 2

Connect each pair of sentences by including a transitional word or phrase and any necessary punctuation.

1. Discoveries in neuroscience have yielded many benefits. Researchers have developed medication for schizophrenia and Tourette's syndrome.
2. The average human brain weighs about three pounds. The average brain of a sperm whale weighs seventeen pounds.
3. Researchers studying brain hemispheres have found that many professional musicians process music in their left hemisphere. The notion that musicians and artists depend on the right side of their brain is considered outmoded.
4. The brain needs water to function properly. Dehydration commonly leads to lethargy and hinders learning.
5. The body of a brain cell can move. Most brain cells stay put, extending axons outward.

23d Divided quotations

When you divide quotations (see also **11d** and chapter **38**) with attributive tags such as *he said* or *she asked,* be sure to use a period between independent clauses.

Comma splice: "Beauty brings copies of itself into being," states Elaine

Scarry, "it makes us draw it, take photographs of it, or describe it to other

people."

[Both parts of the quotation are complete sentences, so the attributive tag is attached to the first, and the sentence is punctuated with a period. The second sentence stands by itself.]

A comma separates two parts of a single quoted sentence.

> "Musing takes place in a kind of meadowlands of the imagination," writes Rebecca Solnit, "a part of the imagination that has not yet been plowed, developed, or put to any immediately practical use." [Because the divided quotation is a single sentence, a comma is used.]

Exercise 3

Revise the following paragraph so that no comma splices remain. Some sentences may not need revision.

[1]In the introduction to his book of true stories, *I Thought My Father Was God,* Paul Auster describes how he was able to collect these accounts of real and sometimes raw experience. [2]In October 1999, Auster, in collaboration with National Public Radio, began the *National Story Project,* during an interview on the radio program *Weekend All Things Considered,* he invited listeners to send in their stories about unusual events—"true stories that sounded like fiction." [3]In just one year, over four thousand stories were submitted, Auster read every one of them. [4]"Of the four thousand stories I have read, most have been compelling enough to hold me until the last word," Auster affirms, "Most have been written with simple, straightforward conviction, and most have done honor to the people who sent them in." [5]Some of the stories Auster collected can now be read in his anthology, choosing stories for the collection was difficult, though. [6]"For every story about a dream or an animal or a missing object," explains Auster, "there were dozens of others that were submitted, dozens of others that could have been chosen."

24

MODIFIERS

Modifiers are words, phrases, or clauses that modify; that is, they qualify or limit the meaning of other words. For example, if you were to describe a sandwich as "humdrum" or "lacking sufficient mustard" or as something "that is eaten only under duress," you would be using modifiers. Modifiers enliven writing with details; if they are not placed correctly, however, they can disrupt coherence. As you revise, be sure to place your modifiers close to the words they modify. This chapter will help you

- recognize modifiers (24a),
- use conventional comparative and superlative forms (24b),
- place modifiers effectively (24c–d), and
- revise double negatives (24e).

24a Recognizing modifiers

The most common modifiers are adjectives and adverbs. **Adjectives** modify nouns and pronouns; **adverbs** modify verbs, adjectives, and other adverbs. (See 20a(4–5).) You can distinguish an adjective from an adverb, then, by determining what type of word is being modified.

Adjectives	**Adverbs**
She looked **curious.** [modifies pronoun]	She looked at me **curiously.** [modifies verb]
productive meeting [modifies noun]	**highly** productive meeting [modifies adjective]
a **quick** lunch [modifies noun]	**very** quickly [modifies adverb]

In addition, consider the form of the modifier. Many adjectives end with one of these suffixes: *-able, -al, -ful, -ic, ish, -less,* or *-y.*

accept**able**   rent**al**   event**ful**   angel**ic**   sheep**ish**   effort**less**   sleep**y**

Adjective Suffixes in Other Languages
In some languages, adjectives and nouns agree in number. In Spanish, for example, when a noun is plural, the adjective is plural as well: *vistas claras.* In English, however, adjectives do not have a plural form: *clear views.*

Present and past participles are most frequently used in verb phrases (see **26a(5)**), but they can also be used as adjectives.

a **determining** factor
[present participle]

a **determined** effort
[past participle]

Be sure to include the complete *-ed* ending of a past participle.

Please see the ~~enclose~~ *enclosed* documents for more details.

THINKING RHETORICALLY ABOUT

ADJECTIVES

When your rhetorical situation calls for vivid images or emotional intensity, choose appropriate adjectives to convey these qualities. That is, instead of describing a movie that you did not like with the overused adjective *bad* or *boring,* you could say that it was *tedious* or *mind-numbing.* When you sense that you might be using a lackluster adjective, search for an alternative in a thesaurus. If any of the words listed there are unfamiliar, be sure to look them up in a dictionary so that you do not misuse them.

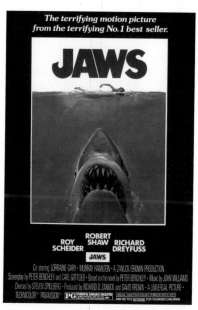

Movie ads include descriptive adjectives.

Using Participles as Adjectives

Both present participles and past participles are used as adjectives; however, they cannot be used interchangeably. For example, when you want to indicate an emotion, use a present participle with a noun referring to someone or something that is the cause of the emotion. In the phrase *the exciting tennis match,* the tennis match is the cause of the excitement. Use a past participle with a noun referring to someone who experiences an emotion. In the phrase *the excited crowd,* the crowd is experiencing the excitement.

Here is a list of commonly confused participles:

annoying, annoyed	frustrating, frustrated
boring, bored	interesting, interested
confusing, confused	surprising, surprised
embarrassing, embarrassed	tiring, tired

The easiest type of adverb to identify is the **adverb of manner** (see 20a(5)). It is formed by adding *-ly* to an adjective.

careful**ly**   unpleasant**ly**   silent**ly**

If an adverb is formed from an adjective ending in *-y,* the *y* is changed to *i* before *-ly* is added.

eas**y** [adjective]   eas**ily** [adverb]

If the adverb is formed from an adjective ending in *-le,* the *-e* is changed to *-y.*

simp**le** [adjective]   simp**ly** [adverb]

However, not all adverbs end in *-ly.* Adverbs that indicate time or place (*today, tomorrow, here,* and *there*) do not have the *-ly* ending. In addition, not all words that end in *-ly* are adverbs. Certain adjectives that are formed from nouns have the *-ly* ending (*cost, costly; friend, friendly*).

A few words—*fast* and *well,* for example—can function as either adjectives or adverbs.

They like **fast** cars. [adjective]

They ran **fast** enough to catch the bus. [adverb]

(1) Nouns can be modifiers.

Adjectives and adverbs are the most common modifiers, but nouns can also be modifiers (***movie** critic, **reference** manual*).

Noun Modifiers
In noun combinations, the first noun is the modifier. Different word orders produce different meanings.

A *company phone* is a phone that belongs to the company.

A *phone company* is a company whose business involves phones.

(2) Phrases and clauses can be modifiers.

Participial phrases, prepositional phrases, and some infinitive phrases are modifiers (see 21a(3–4)).

> **Growing in popularity every year,** mountain bikes now dominate the market. [participial phrase]
>
> Mountain bikes first became popular **in the 1980s.** [prepositional phrase]
>
> Some people use mountain bikes **to commute to work.** [infinitive phrase]

Both adjectival clauses and adverbial clauses are modifiers.

> BMX bicycles have frames **that are relatively small compared to those of other types of bikes.** [adjectival clause]
>
> **Although mountain bikes are designed for off-road use,** many people ride them on city streets. [adverbial clause]

Exercise 1

Underline the modifiers in the following paragraph.

> ¹Although it seems unbelievable, there once was a race of little people. ²The first skeleton of *Homo floresiensis* was found in September 2003 on an island near Bali. ³Archaeologists working in the area excavated the skeleton from a limestone cave. ⁴They believe that this species of human is a version of *Homo erectus*, who arrived on the island and became small to adapt to its conditions.

(3) Adjectives and adverbs are sometimes confused.

An adjective used after a sensory linking verb (such as *look, smell, taste, sound,* or *feel*) modifies the subject of the sentence. A common error is to use an adverb after this type of linking verb.

> I felt ~~badly~~ bad about missing the rally. [The adjective *bad* modifies *I*.]

These sensory verbs are confusing because they can be either linking verbs, as in the previous example, or action verbs. When they are action verbs, they should be modified by adverbs.

She looked ~~angry~~ *angrily* at the referee. [The adverb *angrily* modifies *looked*.]

BUT She looked angry. [The adjective *angry* modifies *she*.]

Good and *well* are easy to confuse. In academic rhetorical situations, *good* is considered an adjective and so is not used with action verbs.

The whole team played ~~good~~ *well*.

Another frequent error is the dropping of *-ly* endings from adverbs. Although you may not hear the ending in spoken sentences, be sure to include it when you write.

We were looking for the ~~local~~ *locally* known island protected as a wildlife refuge.

Exercise 2

Revise the following sentences to use adverbs considered conventional in academic writing.

1. My brother said he was real nervous.
2. He did not think he could drive good enough to pass the driver's test.
3. I told him that to pass he would just have to drive reasonable well.
4. He looked calmly as he got into the tester's car.
5. As I knew he would, my brother passed his test easy.

24b   Comparatives and superlatives

Many adjectives and adverbs change form to show degrees of quality, quantity, time, distance, manner, and so on. The **positive form** of an adjective or adverb is the word you would look for in a dictionary: *hard, urgent, deserving*. The **comparative form,** which either ends in *-er* or is preceded by *more* or *less,* compares two elements: I worked *harder* than I ever had before. The **superlative form,** which either ends in *-est* or is preceded by *most* or *least,* compares three or more elements: Jason is the *hardest* worker I have ever met.

Positive	Comparative	Superlative
hard	harder	hardest
urgent	more/less urgent	most/least urgent
deserving	more/less deserving	most/least deserving

The following guidelines can help you decide when to add the suffix *-er* or *-est* to show degree and when to use *more/less* or *most/least.*

GUIDELINES FOR FORMING COMPARATIVES AND SUPERLATIVES

- One-syllable words generally take *-er* and *-est* endings: *fast, faster, fastest.*
- Two-syllable adjectives ending in a consonant and *-y* also generally take *-er* and *-est* endings, with the *y* changed to an *i*: *noisy, noisier, noisiest.*
- Two-syllable adjectives ending in *-ct, -nt,* or *-st* are preceded by *more/less* or *most/least*: *less exact, least exact; more recent, most recent; more honest, most honest.*
- Adverbs of manner ending in *-ly* are preceded by *more/less* or *most/least*: *more fully, most fully.*
- Two-syllable adjectives with the suffix *-ous, -ish, -ful, -ing,* or *-ed* are preceded by *more/less* or *most/least*: *more/most famous; more/most squeamish; less/least careful; more/most lasting; less/least depressed.*
- Two-syllable adjectives ending in *-er, -ow,* or *-some* take either *-er* and *-est* or one of the preceding qualifiers: *tenderer, tenderest, more/less tender, most/least tender; narrower, narrowest, more/less narrow, most/least narrow; handsomer, handsomest, more/less handsome, most/least handsome.*
- Words of three or more syllables are preceded by *more/less* or *most/least*: *less/least fortunate; more/most intelligent.*
- Some modifiers have irregular comparative and superlative forms:

    little, less, least
    good/well, better, best

(Continued on page 536)

(Continued from page 535)

> bad/badly, worse, worst
>
> far, further/farther, furthest/farthest

(See also the Glossary of Usage.)

(1) Effective comparisons are complete and logical.

When you use the comparative form of an adjective or adverb, be sure to indicate what two elements are being compared. The revision of the following sentence makes it clear that the metropolitan area is currently bigger than it was in the past.

The metropolitan area is much **bigger** ~~*now than it was five years ago*~~.

Without this revision, the reader may wonder whether the metropolitan area is bigger than a rural area or some other area. Occasionally, the second element in a comparison is implied. The word *paper* does not have to be repeated after *second* in the sentence below.

> She wrote two papers, and the instructor gave her a **better** grade on the second.

A comparison should also be logical. The following example illogically compares *population* and *Wabasha*.

The **population** of Winona is larger than **Wabasha.**

This faulty comparison can be revised in three ways:

- Repeat the word that names what is being compared.

  The **population** of Winona is larger than the **population** of Wabasha.

- Use a pronoun that corresponds to the first element in the comparison.

  The **population** of Winona is larger than **that** of Wabasha.

- Use possessive forms.

  Winona's population is larger than **Wabasha's.**

(2) A double comparative or superlative is redundant.

Use either an ending or a preceding adverb, not both, to form a comparative or superlative.

The first bridge is **more narrower** than the second.

The **most narrowest** bridge is in the northern part of the state.

B E Y O N D   T H E   R U L E

ABSOLUTE MODIFIERS

Dictionaries list comparative forms of many adjectives or adverbs that have absolute meanings, as in *a more perfect society, the deadest campus,* and *less completely exhausted.* Such comparisons are rarely found in academic writing. For more information, visit **www.harbrace.com**.

Exercise 3

Provide the correct comparative or superlative form of each modifier within parentheses.

1. Amphibians can be divided into three groups. Frogs and toads are in the (common) group.
2. Because they do not have to maintain a specific body temperature, amphibians eat (frequently) than mammals do.
3. Reptiles may look like amphibians, but their skin is (dry).
4. During the Devonian period, (close) ancestors of amphibians were fish with fins that looked like legs.
5. In general, amphibians have (few) bones in their skeletons than do other animals with backbones.
6. Color markings on amphibians vary, though the back of an amphibian is usually (dark) than its belly.

24c Placement of modifiers

Your modifiers will be effective if you choose those with precise meanings and place them so that they add to the clarity and coherence of your sentences. A modifer whose placement confuses the meaning of a sentence is called a **misplaced modifier.**

(1) Place a modifier as close as possible to the relevant word or word group.

Modifiers such as *almost, even, hardly, just,* and *only* are clearest when they are placed right before the words they modify. Altering placement can alter meaning.

> The committee can **only** nominate two members for the position.
> [The committee cannot appoint or elect the two people to the position.]

> The committee can nominate **only** two members for the position.
> [The committee cannot nominate more than two members.]

> **Only** the committee can nominate two members for the position.
> [No person or group other than the committee can nominate members.]

(2) Place prepositional phrases and adjectival clauses as close as possible to the word or word group they modify.

Readers expect phrases and clauses to modify the nearest grammatical element. Misplaced phrases and clauses cause confusion.

> She recorded ₜhe song from the movie ~~that was her favorite~~.
> *(her favorite)*

OR

> She recorded a song from her favorite movie.

The following sentence is fine as long as Jesse wrote the proposal, not the review. If he wrote the review, the modifying clause should be moved, or the sentence should be recast.

> I have not read the review of the proposal Jesse wrote.

I have not read the review ^of the proposal ~~Jesse wrote~~.

Jesse wrote [handwritten, inserted above]

OR

I have not read ^the review of the proposal ~~he wrote~~.

Jesse's [handwritten, inserted above]

(3) Revise squinting modifiers so that they modify only one element.

A **squinting modifier** is one that might be interpreted as modifying either what precedes it or what follows it. Sentences containing such modifiers can confuse readers. To avoid such lack of clarity, reposition the modifier and/or provide appropriate punctuation.

> Even though Erikson lists some advantages **overall** his vision of a successful business is faulty.
>
> Revision: Even though Erikson lists some **overall** advantages**,** his vision of a successful business is faulty. [word repositioned; punctuation added]
>
> Revision: Even though Erikson lists some advantages**, overall,** his vision of a successful business is faulty. [punctuation added]

Ordering Adjectives That Modify the Same Noun

In English, two or more adjectives modifying the same noun are used in a particular order based on their meanings. (The use of more than three consecutive adjectives is rare.) The following list shows the usual order of adjectives and gives examples.

Size	*large, small, tiny, miniscule*
Evaluator	*fascinating, painful, content*
Shape	*square, round, triangular*
Age	*young, old, aged, newborn, antique*
Color	*black, white, green, brown*
Nationality or geography	*Arabian, Cuban, Peruvian, Slavic*
Religion	*Jewish, Catholic, Protestant, Buddhist*
Material	*silk, paper, plastic, steel*

(Continued on page 540)

(Continued from page 539)

We visited a **fascinating Italian** village.

Marquita showed us her **new black** scarves.

Adverbs of Frequency

Adverbs of frequency (such as *always, never, sometimes,* and *often*) appear before one-word verbs.

He **rarely** <u>goes</u> to horror movies.

However, these adverbs appear after a form of *be* when it is the main verb.

Movies based on Stephen King novels <u>are</u> **always** popular.

When a sentence contains more than one verb in a verb phrase, the adverb of frequency is placed after the first auxiliary verb.

My friends <u>have</u> **never** <u>seen</u> *The Shining*.

I <u>have</u> **seldom** <u>been</u> frightened by a movie.

Exercise 4

Improve the clarity of the following sentences by moving the modifiers. Some sentences may not require editing.

1. In 1665, Sir Isaac Newton devised three laws about moving objects that are still discussed today.
2. According to one of the laws, an object only moves when force is applied.
3. Once in motion, something must force an object to slow down or to speed up; otherwise, it will continue at a constant speed.
4. Another law explains the variables affecting an object's movement.
5. Another of Newton's contributions is the law about action and reaction that engineers use to plan rocket launchings.
6. Scientists still use the laws of motion formulated by Newton over three hundred years ago to understand moving objects.

24d Revising dangling modifiers

Dangling modifiers are words, phrases, or reduced clauses that lack an appropriate noun, noun phrase, or pronoun to modify. To avoid including dangling modifiers in your essays, look carefully at any sentence that begins with a modifier. Be sure that the noun, noun phrase, or pronoun being modified is the subject of the sentence. Sometimes, a dangling modifier contains a form of an action verb, but the sentence has no clear actor performing that action or the actor is not in the subject position. Other times, a dangling modifier consists of adjectives that are modifying an object in the sentence rather than the subject. You can revise sentences that contain dangling modifiers in one of these ways:

- Provide a noun or pronoun.

  we increased
  Working overtime, our earnings ~~increased~~ dramatically.

  [According to the original sentence, the earnings worked overtime.]

- Move the modifier

  The   *crouched and ugly*
  ~~Crouched and ugly,~~ the young boy gasped at the phantom moving across the stage.

  [According to the original sentence, the young boy was crouched and ugly.]

- Reword the modifier.

  After Richie gave his speech,
  ~~After listening to Richie's speech,~~ the mood in the room changed.

  [According to the original sentence, the mood listened to the speech.]

Sentence modifiers and absolute phrases are not considered to be dangling.

Marcus played well in the final game, **on the whole.**

Considering all she's been through this year, Marge is remarkably cheerful.

Exercise 5

Revise the following sentences to eliminate misplaced and dangling modifiers. Some sentences may not require editing.

1. Climbing a mountain, fitness becomes all-important.
2. Getting to the top must be in doubt to make the climb a true adventure.
3. Having set their goals, the mountain must challenge the climbers.
4. In determining an appropriate challenge, considering safety precautions is necessary.
5. Taking care to stay roped together, accidents are less likely to occur.
6. Even when expecting sunny weather, rain gear should be packed.
7. Knowing how to rappel is necessary before descending a cliff.
8. Although adding extra weight, climbers should not leave home without a first-aid kit.
9. Climbers should not let themselves become frustrated if they are not immediately successful.
10. By taking pains at the beginning of a trip, agony can be averted at the end of a trip.

24e Double negatives

Most words that express negation are modifiers. The term **double negative** refers to the use of two negative words within a clause to express a single negation.

He did**n't** keep ⟨*any*⟩ **no** records.

OR

He ⟨*kept*⟩ ~~did**n't** keep~~ **no** records.

Because *hardly, barely,* and *scarcely* denote severely limited or negative conditions, using *not, nothing,* or *without* with any of these modifiers creates a double negative.

I could**n't hardly** quit in the middle of the job.

OR

I could**n't** ~~**hardly**~~ quit in the middle of the job.

The motion passed with ~~**not**~~ **scarcely** a protest.

OR

The motion passed with ᴧ ~~**not scarcely**~~ a protest. *little*

Occasionally, emphasis requires the use of two negatives in a sentence. Such a construction is not considered a double negative.

It would**n't** be safe **not** to install smoke detectors. [This construction is permissible when *not* is being emphasized. Otherwise, the sentence should be revised. COMPARE: It would be dangerous not to install smoke detectors.]

Negation in Other Languages

The use of two negative words in one sentence is common in languages such as Spanish:

*Yo **no** compré **nada**.* [I didn't buy anything.]

If your native language allows this type of negation, be especially careful to check for and revise any double negatives you find in your English essays.

Exercise 6

Using what you have learned in this chapter, revise the following sentences to remove modifier errors.

1. As a woman in the twentieth century, the life of Gertrude Bell was unusual.
2. Young, wealthy, and intelligent, many people were impressed by the red-headed Bell.
3. Among the first women to graduate from Oxford, she couldn't hardly be satisfied with domestic life.

4. Instead, Bell traveled to what were considered the most remotest countries in the world, saw the wonders of the Ottoman Empire, and explored the desert of Iraq.

5. Several of the Arab sheiks who knew Bell thought that she acted bold.

6. The war in Iraq didn't give Bell no time to pursue her research.

7. She became an Arab rebellion supporter.

8. While traveling in Iraq, meetings with important politicians took place.

9. In 1921, Winston Churchill invited Bell to a conference in the Middle East because the other Great Britain conference participants knew little about Iraq.

10. When the photo of the conference participants was taken, Bell looked elegantly in her feathered hat and silk dress among the thirty-six black-suited males.

25

PRONOUNS

When you use pronouns effectively, you add clarity and coherence to your writing. However, if you do not provide the words, phrases, or clauses that make the pronoun reference clear, you might unintentionally cause confusion. As you revise your work, be on the lookout for pronouns that do not have conventional forms or specific antecedents. This chapter will help you

- recognize various types of pronouns (25a),
- determine the forms of pronouns (25b),
- make sure that pronouns agree with their antecedents (25c), and
- provide clear pronoun references (25d).

25a Recognizing pronouns

A **pronoun** is commonly defined as a word that refers to either a noun or a word group acting as a noun. The noun, noun phrase, or noun clause being referred to by a pronoun may be in the same sentence or in nearby sentences. English has several types of pronouns: personal, relative, interrogative, and reflexive/intensive pronouns.

(1) Personal pronouns are identified according to person, number, and case.

To understand the uses of personal pronouns, you must first be able to recognize person, number, and case. **Person** indicates whether a pronoun refers to the writer (**first person**), the reader (**second person**), or any other entity being discussed (**third person**). **Number** reveals whether a pronoun is singular or plural (see also 26b). **Case** refers to the form a pronoun takes depending on its function in the sentence. Pronouns can be subjects, objects, or possessives. When they function as subjects (see 20d(1)), they are in the subjective case; when they function as objects (see 20d(2)), they are in the objective case; and when they are possessives, they are in the possessive case (see 37a). Possessives can be divided into two groups based on whether they are followed by nouns. The possessive determiners *my, your, his, her, its, our,* and *their* are all followed by nouns; the possessive pronouns *mine, yours, his, hers, ours,* and *theirs* are not.

Their budget is higher than **ours.** [*Their* is a possessive determiner; *ours* is a possessive pronoun.]

CASE:	Subjective		Objective		Possessive	
NUMBER:	Singular	Plural	Singular	Plural	Singular	Plural
First person	I	we	me	us	my mine	our ours
Second person	you	you	you	you	your yours	your yours
Third person	he, she, it	they	him, her, it	them	his, her, hers, its	their theirs

THINKING RHETORICALLY ABOUT

PRONOUNS

As you write, consider which pronouns are called for by your rhetorical situation. In some situations, you will be expected to use *I*; in others, you will not. In some situations, you will address the reader as *you* (as is done in this handbook), but in others, you will avoid addressing the reader directly. Whatever pronouns you decide to use, be sure to use them consistently.

First, ~~one~~ you must determine your priorities.

OR

First, one must determine one's priorities.

(2) A relative pronoun usually relates an adjectival clause to a noun or noun phrase in the main clause.

An adjectival clause (or relative clause) ordinarily begins with one of these relative pronouns: *who, whom, which, that,* or *whose.* To provide a link between this type of dependent clause and the main clause, the relative pronoun corresponds to a word or words in the main clause called the **antecedent.**

The students talked to **a reporter who** had just returned from overseas.

Notice that if you rewrite the dependent clause as a separate independent clause, you use the antecedent in place of the relative pronoun:

A reporter had just returned from overseas.

Who, whose, and *whom* ordinarily refer to people; *which* refers to things; *that* refers to either people or things. The possessive pronoun *whose* (used in place of the awkward *of which*) sometimes refers to things.

The poem, **whose** author is unknown, has recently been set to music.

	Refers to people	Refers to things	Refers to either
Subjective	who	which	that
Objective	whom	which	that
Possessive			whose

Knowing the difference between an essential clause and a nonessential clause will help you decide whether to use *which* or *that.* A clause that a reader needs in order to identify the antecedent correctly is an **essential clause.**

The person who presented the award was last year's winner.

If the essential clause were omitted from this sentence, you would not know which person was last year's winner.

A **nonessential clause** is *not* needed for correct identification of the antecedent and is thus set off by commas. A nonessential clause often follows a proper noun (a specific name).

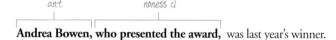

Andrea Bowen, who presented the award, was last year's winner.

Notice that even if the nonessential clause were removed from this sentence, you would still know who last year's winner was.

According to a traditional grammar rule, *that* is used in essential adjectival clauses, and *which* is used in nonessential adjectival clauses.

I need a job **that** pays well.

I took a job, **which** pays well enough.

However, some professional writers do not follow both parts of this rule. Although they will not use *that* in nonessential clauses, they will use *which* in essential clauses.

According to Trask, *nonverbal communication* refers to "any aspect of communication **which** does not involve words."

(3) Interrogative pronouns introduce questions.

Interrogative pronouns are question words that appear in the same positions that nouns do. *What* and *which* can be either subjects or objects. *Who* is used as a subject, and its counterpart, *whom*, is used as an object. *Whose* is a possessive interrogative pronoun.

Subjective interrogative pronoun	**Who** won the award?
Objective interrogative pronoun	**Whom** did you consult?
Possessive interrogative pronoun	**Whose** is it?

(4) Reflexive pronouns direct the action back to the subject; intensive pronouns are used for emphasis.

Myself, yourself, himself, herself, itself, ourselves, yourselves, and *themselves* are used as either **reflexive pronouns** or **intensive pronouns.** Both types of pronouns are objects and must be accompanied by subjects. Reflexive pronouns are used when the actor and the recipient of the action are the same. Intensive pronouns are used to provide emphasis.

Reflexive pronoun   **He** was always talking to **himself.**

Intensive pronoun   **I, myself,** delivered the letter.

Avoid using a reflexive pronoun as a subject. A common error is using *myself* in a compound subject.

Ms. Palmquist and ~~myself~~ discussed our concern with the senator.
(I)

Hisself and *theirselves* are inappropriate in college or professional writing. Instead, use *himself* and *themselves.* Attempts to create a gender-neutral singular reflexive pronoun have resulted in such forms as *themself;* these forms are also inappropriate in college or professional writing.

Each student completed a project by ~~themself.~~
(himself or herself)

25b Pronoun case

The term *case* refers to the form a pronoun or determiner takes to indicate its relationship to other words in a sentence. There are three cases: subjective, objective, and possessive. The following sentence includes all three.

He [subjective] wants **his** [possessive] legislators to help **him** [objective].

(1) Pronouns in the subject or subject complement position are in the subjective case.

A pronoun that is the subject of a sentence, even when it is part of a compound subject (see **20b**), is in the subjective case. To determine which pronoun form is correct in a compound subject, say the sentence using the pronoun alone, omitting the noun. For the following sentence, notice that "*Me* solved the problem" sounds strange.

and I
~~Me and~~ Marisa ∧ solved the problem.

Also, remember that when you use the pronoun *I* in a compound subject, you should place it last in the sequence. If the compound subject contains two pronouns, test each one by itself to ensure that you are using the appropriate case.

He
∧~~Him~~ and I joined the club in July.

A subject complement renames the subject (see **20d(3)**). Pronouns functioning as subject complements should also be in the subjective case.

I
The first to arrive were Kevin and ∧~~me~~.

In conversational English, "It's *me*" (or *him, her, us,* or *them*) is acceptable.

Noun or Pronoun as Subject
In some languages, a noun in the subject position may be followed by a pronoun. In Standardized English, though, such a pronoun should be omitted.

My roommate ~~he~~ works in the library for three hours a week.

---

(2) Pronouns functioning as objects are in the objective case.

Whenever a pronoun is an object—a direct object, an indirect object, or the object of a preposition—it takes the **objective case.**

Direct object	Miguel loves **her**.
Indirect object	Miguel gave **her** his love.
Object of a preposition	Miguel cares deeply for **her**.

Pronouns in compound objects are also in the objective case.

me
They will appoint you or ∧~~I~~. [direct object]

me
They lent Tom and I money for tuition. [indirect object]

me
He gets nowhere by scolding Jane or I. [direct object of the gerund]

me
Dad wanted Sheila and I to keep the old car. [direct object of the
sentence; subject of the infinitive phrase (see **25b(c)**)]

me
Janice sat between my brother and I. [object of the preposition]

To determine whether to use the subjective or objective case, remember
to say the sentence with just the pronoun. Notice that "Dad wanted
I to keep the old car" does not sound right. Another test is to substitute
we and *us*. If *we* sounds natural, use the subjective case. If *us* sounds better, use the objective case, as in "Janice sat between *us*."

(3) Possessive forms are easily confused with contractions.

Its, their, and *whose* are possessive forms. Be sure that you do not confuse them with common contractions: *it's* (*it is*), *they're* (*they are*), and
who's (*who is*).

(4) Appositive pronouns are in the same case as the nouns they rename.

If the noun that an appositive pronoun renames is in the subjective
case, the appositive pronoun should be in the subjective case.

I
The red team—Rebecca, Leroy, and me—won by only one point.

Likewise, if the noun is in the objective case, the appositive pronoun
should be in the objective case.

me
A trophy was presented to the red team—Rebecca, Leroy, and I.

When the order is reversed and a pronoun is followed by a noun, the
pronoun still must be in the same case as the noun.

We
Us students need this policy.

us
The director told we extras to go home.

To test the case of a pronoun that is followed by an appositive, remove the appositive.

We need this policy.

The director told **us** to go home.

 Grammar checkers often provide minimal help in identifying case errors. A grammar checker found nothing wrong with this sentence: Carol and me agree that Mark is a good athlete. In addition, grammar checkers miss as many errors involving *who/whom* as they find (see 25b(5)), and they almost never find problems with pronoun-antecedent agreement (25c). See Using a Grammar Checker on page 461.

Exercise 1

Revise the following paragraph, using appropriate cases for pronouns. Some sentences may not require editing.

¹When I was twelve, my family lived in Guatemala for a year. ²My parents taught English at a university; me and my younger brother went to a local school. ³Although the Spanish language was new to both Sam and I, we learned to speak it quickly. ⁴At first, we couldn't understand much at all, but with the help of a tutor, who we met every day after school, we started learning "survival" Spanish. ⁵Sam had better pronunciation than me, but I learned vocabulary and grammar faster than him. ⁶After we learned to ask and answer some basic questions, we started making friends, whom eventually introduced us to they're own version of Spanish. ⁷They taught us slang words that our tutor didn't even know. ⁸However, though Sam and me benefited from all our Spanish lessons, we learned the language so quickly because, unless we were with our parents or by ourself, we listened to it, read it, wrote it, and spoke it all day long.

(5) Who/whoever and whom/whomever are often misused.

You may be able to avoid confusion about the correct usage of *who/whoever* and *whom/whomever* if you remember that the case of these pronouns is determined by their grammatical function in a dependent clause. A pronoun functioning as the subject in a dependent clause takes the subjective case, even if the whole clause is used as an object.

> I remembered **who** won the Academy Award that year. [*Who* is the subject of the clause *who won the Academy Award that year.* The clause is the object of the verb *remembered.*]

> She offered help to **whoever** needed it. [*Whoever* is the subject of the clause *whoever needed it.* The clause is the object of the preposition *to.*]

When the pronoun is an object in a dependent clause, use w*hom* or *whomever.*

> They helped **whom** they liked. [direct object]

> Gabriel happily greeted **whomever** he met that day. [direct object]

> No one knew for **whom** the song was written. [*Whom* is the object of the preposition *for.*]

Whom may be omitted in sentences where no misunderstanding would result.

> The friend he relied on moved away. [*Whom* has been omitted after *friend.*]

Such expressions as *I think, he says, she believes,* and *we know* can follow either *who* or *whom.* The case of the pronoun still depends on its grammatical function in the clause. To make sure that you have used the correct form, delete the intervening phrase.

> Walter picked Jan, **who** he knows speaks well.
> [*Who* is the subject of the verb *speaks.*]

> Walter picked Jan, **whom** he knows we all respect.
> [*Whom* is the object of the verb *respect.*]

BEYOND THE RULE

WHO/WHOEVER OR *WHOM/WHOMEVER*

Although many writers still prefer *whom* or *whomever* as object pronouns, dictionaries have also approved the use of *who* or *whoever* in informal contexts.

I wonder **who** she voted for.

Give the campaign literature to **whoever** you see.

Who do you plan to vote for?

In college writing, though, it is better to use *whom* or *whomever* as the object pronoun.

Whom will they elect president?

For additional information, visit **www.harbrace.com**.

Exercise 2

Following the guidelines for college and professional writing, choose the appropriate form of each pronoun in parentheses.

1. Separate the white chess pieces from the black pieces, and decide (who/whom) will play with the white pieces.
2. The opening move is made by (whoever/whomever) has received the white game pieces.
3. (Whoever/Whomever) the black pieces were given to makes the following move.
4. The player (who/whom) can put the other player's king in check is close to becoming the winner.
5. (Whoever/Whomever) is unable to free his king must concede the game.

(6) Pronouns in the objective case precede and follow infinitives; possessive determiners precede gerunds.

A pronoun grouped with an infinitive, either as its subject or as its object, takes the objective case.

> The director wanted **me** to help **him.**

A **gerund** (*-ing* verb form functioning as a noun) is preceded by a possessive determiner.

> I appreciated **his** helping Denise. [COMPARE: I appreciated **Tom's** helping Denise.]

Notice that the possessive case is used before a gerund, but not before a **present participle** (*-ing* verb form functioning as an adjective).

> I saw **him** helping Diane.

(7) Knowing what is omitted in elliptical constructions is essential in choosing pronoun case.

The words *as* and *than* frequently introduce **elliptical constructions**—clauses in which the writer intentionally omits words. To check whether you have used the correct case in an elliptical construction, read the written sentence aloud, inserting any words that have been omitted from it.

> She admires Clarice as much as **I.** [subjective case]
> Read aloud: She admires Clarice as much as *I do.*

> She admires Clarice more than **I.** [subjective case]
> Read aloud: She admires Clarice more than *I do.*

> She admires Clarice more than **me.** [objective case]
> Read aloud: She admires Clarice more than *she admires me.*

Exercise 3

Revise the following sentences, using appropriate pronouns and determiners. Some sentences may not require editing.

1. The board of directors has asked you and I to conduct a customer survey.
2. They also recommended us hiring someone with extensive experience in statistical analysis.
3. You understand statistics better than me.
4. Although the board asked me to be in charge, I would like you to recruit and interview candidates.
5. The directors recognize your expertise and will surely approve of you taking the lead.

25c Pronoun-antecedent agreement

A pronoun and the word or word group to which it refers, the antecedent, agree in number (both are either singular or plural).

The **supervisor** said that **he** would help.
[Both antecedent and pronoun are singular.]

My **colleagues** said that **they** would help.
[Both antecedent and pronoun are plural.]

A pronoun also agrees with its antecedent in gender (masculine, feminine, or neuter).

Joseph claims that **he** can meet the deadline. [masculine antecedent]

Anna claims that **she** can meet the deadline. [feminine antecedent]

The **committee** claims that **it** can meet the deadline. [neutral antecedent]

Possessive Determiners

A possessive determiner (*his, her, its, their, my, our,* or *your*), traditionally labeled a possessive pronoun, agrees with its antecedent, not with the noun it precedes.

Ken Carlson brought ⌃*his* ~~her~~ young daughter to the office today.

[The possessive determiner *his* agrees with the antecedent, *Ken Carlson*, not with the following noun, *daughter*.]

(1) Indefinite pronouns can serve as antecedents.

Although most antecedents for pronouns are nouns, they can be **indefinite pronouns.** Most indefinite pronouns are considered singular.

anyone	anybody	anything
everyone	everybody	everything
someone	somebody	something
no one	nobody	nothing
each	either	neither

Notice that an indefinite pronoun takes a singular verb form.

Everyone **has** [not *have*] the right to an opinion.

Difficulties arise, however, because *everyone* seems to refer to more than one person. Thus, the definition of grammatical number and our everyday notion of number conflict. In conversation and informal writing, a plural pronoun or determiner is often used with the singular *everyone.* Nonetheless, when you write for an audience that expects you to follow traditional grammar rules, make sure to use a third-person singular pronoun or determiner.

Each of these companies has ~~their~~ *its* books audited.

Everyone has the combination to ~~their~~ *his or her* private locker.

You can avoid the awkwardness of using *his or her* by using an article instead, by making the antecedent noun and the possessive determiner both plural, or by rewriting the sentence using the passive voice (see 26d(3)).

Everyone has the combination to **a** private locker. [article]

Students have combinations to **their** private lockers. [plural antecedent]

The combination to a private locker **is issued** to everyone. [passive voice]

(2) An antecedent sometimes refers to both genders.

When an antecedent is a noun that can refer to people of either gender, rewrite the sentence to make the noun plural or, if not too cumbersome, use *he or she* or *his or her.*

Plural	**Lawyers** represent their clients.
Singular	A lawyer represents the clients **he or she** has accepted.
	A lawyer represents **his or her** clients.

(See **32d** for more information on using inclusive language.)

Be careful not to introduce errors into your writing when you are trying to avoid sexist language. (See **32d(1)**.)

Whenever ~~a driver lets~~ *drivers let* their ~~license~~ *licenses* expire, they have to take a driving test.

(3) The pronoun agrees with the nearer of two antecedents joined by *or* or *nor*.

If a singular and a plural antecedent are joined by *or* or *nor*, place the plural antecedent second and use a plural pronoun.

> Either Jennifer **or** her <u>roommates</u> will explain how <u>they</u> chose their majors.

> Neither the president **nor** the <u>senators</u> stated that <u>they</u> would support the proposal.

(4) When a collective noun is the antecedent, the number of the pronoun depends on the meaning of the noun.

When an antecedent is a collective noun, determine whether you intend the noun to be understood as singular or plural. Then, make sure that the pronoun agrees in number with the noun.

> The choir decided that *it* ~~they~~ would tour during the winter rather than in the spring. [Because the choir decided as a unit, *choir* should be considered singular. The singular form, *it*, replaces the plural, *they*.]

> The committee may disagree on methods, but *they* ~~it~~ must agree on basic aims. [Because the committee members are behaving as individuals, *committee* is regarded as plural. The plural form, *they*, replaces the singular, *it*.]

Exercise 4

Revise the following sentences so that pronouns or determiners agree with their antecedents.

1. A researcher relies on a number of principles to help him make ethical decisions.
2. Everyone should have the right to participate in a study only if she wants to.
3. A team of researchers should provide its volunteers with informed-consent forms, in which they describe to the volunteers the procedures and risks involved in participation.
4. Every participant should be guaranteed that the information they provide will remain confidential.
5. Institutions of higher education require that a researcher address ethical issues in their proposal.

25d Clear pronoun reference

The main rhetorical principle to keep in mind regarding pronoun reference is clarity. In the following sentence, the pronoun *they* clearly refers to the noun *cattle*—its antecedent.

> Our ranching operation keeps **cattle** year-round in the same pastures where **they** are bred, born, and raised.

A pronoun may refer to two or more antecedents.

> **Jack and I** knew **we** were late.

Sometimes a pronoun refers to a noun that follows it.

> When **she** turned nineteen, **Cindy** decided to leave home.

The meaning of each pronoun in a sentence should be immediately obvious.

(1) Ambiguous or unclear pronoun references can confuse readers.

When a pronoun can refer to either of two antecedents, the ambiguity may confuse readers. To make the antecedent clear, replace the pronoun with a noun or rewrite the sentence.

> Mr. Anderson told Mr. Eggers that ⌃*Mr. Eggers* he would be in charge of the project.

OR

> Mr. Anderson put Mr. Eggers in charge of the project.
> [In the unrevised sentence, it is not clear who will be in charge of the project.]

(2) Remote or awkward references can cause readers to misunderstand.

To help readers understand your meaning, place pronouns as close to their antecedents as possible. The following sentence needs to be revised so that the relative pronoun *that* is close to its antecedent, *poem*.

> The **poem** ⌃*that was originally written in 1945* has been published in a new book ~~that was originally written in 1945~~.

Notice, however, that a relative pronoun does not always have to follow its antecedent directly. In the following example, there is no risk of misunderstanding.

> We slowly began to notice the **changes** in our climate **that** were forecast several years ago.

(3) Broad or implied references can make writing vague.

Pronouns such as *it, this, that,* and *which* may refer to a specific word or phrase or to the sense of a whole clause, sentence, or paragraph.

> The weight of the pack was manageable, once I became used to **it**.
> [*It* refers specifically to *weight*.]

> Large corporations may seem stronger than individuals, but **that** is not true.
> [*That* refers to the sense of the whole first clause.]

When used carelessly, broad references can interfere with clear communication. Unless the meaning is clear, avoid reference to the general idea of a preceding clause or sentence. Instead, state clearly what *this* or *that* refers to.

> When class attendance is compulsory, some students feel that education is
> being forced on them. This ⌃ *perception* is unwarranted. [*This* has no clear antecedent.]

Remember to express an idea explicitly rather than merely implying it.

> *Teaching music*
> My father is a music teacher. ⌃ It is a profession that requires much patience.
> [*It* has no expressed antecedent.]

Be especially careful to provide clear antecedents when you are referring to the work or possessions of others. In the following sentence, the possessive noun *Jen Norton's* might seem like it could be an antecedent for *she*; however, because it is a modifier and not a noun, it does not qualify as a true antecedent.

> *her* *Jen Norton*
> In ⌃ ~~Jen Norton's~~ article, ⌃ ~~she~~ argues that workplace conditions need
> improvement.

(4) The use of the expletive *it* can result in wordiness or ambiguity.

The expletive *it* does not have a specific antecedent (see **20d(1)**). Instead, it is used to postpone, and thus give emphasis to, the subject of the sentence. A sentence that begins with this expletive can sometimes be wordy or awkward. Revise such a sentence by replacing *it* with the postponed subject.

> *Trying to repair the car* *useless*
> ⌃ It was ⌃ ~~no use~~ ~~trying to repair the car~~.

Avoid placing one *it* near another *it* with a different meaning.

> *Staying in the old apartment*
> ⌃ It would be simpler ~~to stay in the old apartment~~, but it is too far from my
> job. [The first *it* is an expletive (see the **Glossary of Terms**); the second *it*
> refers to *apartment*.]

Exercise 5

Edit the following sentences to make all references clear. Some sentences may not require editing.

1. It is remarkable to read about Lance Armstrong's victories.

2. A champion cyclist, a cancer survivor, and a humanitarian, it is no wonder that Lance Armstrong is one of the most highly celebrated athletes in the world.

3. Armstrong's mother encouraged his athleticism, which led to his becoming a professional triathlete by age sixteen.

4. Though you might not believe it, Armstrong was only a senior in high school when he started training for the Olympic developmental team.

5. By the time he was twenty-five, Armstrong was ranked as the top cyclist in the world.

6. Not long afterward, because of intense pain, he sought medical attention, and they told him he had testicular cancer.

7. The cancer had spread to his lungs and brain; thus, they said his chances for recovery were slim.

8. Armstrong underwent dramatic surgery and aggressive chemotherapy; this eventually helped him recover.

9. Armstrong started training five months after their diagnosis and went on to win major championships, including the Tour de France.

10. For Lance Armstrong, it hasn't been only about racing bikes; he has become a humanitarian as well, creating the Lance Armstrong Foundation to help cancer patients and to fund cancer research around the world.

26

VERBS

Choosing verbs to convey your message precisely is the first step toward writing clear and effective sentences. The next step is to ensure that the verbs you choose conform to the conventions your audience expects you to follow. This chapter will help you

- identify conventional verb forms (**26a**),
- use verb tenses to provide information about time (**26b**),
- use verb tenses consistently (**26c**),
- distinguish between the active voice and the passive voice (**26d**),
- use verbs to signal the factuality or likelihood of an action or event (**26e**), and
- ensure that subjects and verbs agree in number and person (**26f**).

26a Verb forms

Most English verbs have four forms, following the model for *walk*.

> *walk, walks, walking, walked*

However, English also includes irregular verbs, which may have as few as three forms or as many as eight:

> *let, lets, letting   be, am, is, are, was, were, being, been*

(1) Regular verbs have four forms.

A regular verb has a **base form.** This is the form you find in a dictionary. *Talk, act, change,* and *serve* are all base forms.

The second form of a regular verb is the **-s form.** To derive this form, add to the base form either *-s* (*talks, acts, changes, serves*) or, in some cases, *-es* (*marries, carries, tries*). See 40d for information on spelling changes that accompany the addition of *-es.*

The third form of a regular verb is the **-*ing* form,** also called the **present participle.** It consists of the base form and the ending *-ing* (*talking, acting*). Depending on the verb, spelling changes may occur (*changing, chatting*). (See 40d.)

The fourth form of a regular verb consists of the base form and the ending *-ed* (*talked, acted*). Again, spelling may vary when the suffix is added (*changed, served, chatted*). (See 40d.) The *-ed* form has two names. When it is used without the auxiliary verb *have* or *be,* it is called the **past form** (We *talked* about the new plan). In contrast, when the *-ed* form is used with one of these auxiliary verbs, it is called the **past participle** (We *have talked* about it several times. A committee *was formed* to investigate the matter).

Verb Forms of Regular Verbs

Base Form	-*s* Form (Present Tense, Third Person, Singular)	-*ing* Form (Present Participle)	-*ed* Form (Past Form and Past Participle)
work	works	working	worked
watch	watches	watching	watched
apply	applies	applying	applied
stop	stops	stopping	stopped

When verbs are followed by words with similar sounds, you may find the verb endings (-*s* and -*ed*) difficult to hear. In addition, these verb endings may seem unfamiliar because your dialect does not have them. Nonetheless, you should use -*s* and -*ed* when you write for an audience that expects you to include these endings:

     seems
She **seem** satisfied with the report.
     ^

     supposed
We were **suppose** to receive the results yesterday.
     ^

(2) Irregular verbs have from three to eight forms.

Most irregular verbs, such as *write,* have forms similar to some of those for regular verbs: base form (*write*), *-s* form (*writes*), and *-ing* form (*writing*). However, the past form (*wrote*) and the past participle (*written*) vary from the regular forms. In fact, some irregular verbs have two acceptable past forms and/or past participles (see *awake, dive, dream,* and *get* in the following chart). Other irregular verbs have only three forms because the same form serves as the base form, the past form, and the past participle (see *set* in the chart). If you are unsure about verb forms not included in the chart, consult a dictionary.

Verb Forms of Irregular Verbs

Base Form	-s Form (Present Tense, Third Person, Singular)	-ing Form (Present Participle)	Past Form	Past Participle
arise	arises	arising	arose	arisen
awake	awakes	awaking	awaked, awoke	awaked, awoken
bear	bears	bearing	bore	borne, born
begin	begins	beginning	began	begun
bite	bites	biting	bit	bitten
break	breaks	breaking	broke	broken
bring	brings	bringing	brought	brought
buy	buys	buying	bought	bought
choose	chooses	choosing	chose	chosen
come	comes	coming	came	come
dive	dives	diving	dived, dove	dived
do	does	doing	did	done
dream	dreams	dreaming	dreamed, dreamt	dreamed, dreamt

(Continued on page 566)

(Continued from page 565)

Base Form	-s Form (Present Tense, Third Person, Singular)	-ing Form (Present Participle)	Past Form	Past Participle
drink	drinks	drinking	drank	drunk
drive	drives	driving	drove	driven
eat	eats	eating	ate	eaten
fall	falls	falling	fell	fallen
forget	forgets	forgetting	forgot	forgotten
forgive	forgives	forgiving	forgave	forgiven
get	gets	getting	got	gotten, got
give	gives	giving	gave	given
go	goes	going	went	gone
hang (suspend)	hangs	hanging	hung	hung
hang (execute)	hangs	hanging	hanged	hanged
hold	holds	holding	held	held
keep	keeps	keeping	kept	kept
know	knows	knowing	knew	known
lay (see the Glossary of Usage)	lays	laying	laid	laid
lead	leads	leading	led	led
lie (see the Glossary of Usage)	lies	lying	lay	lain

Base Form	-s Form (Present Tense, Third Person, Singular)	-ing Form (Present Participle)	Past Form	Past Participle
lose	loses	losing	lost	lost
pay	pays	paying	paid	paid
rise (see the Glossary of Usage)	rises	rising	rose	risen
say	says	saying	said	said
see	sees	seeing	saw	seen
set (see the Glossary of Usage)	sets	setting	set	set
sink	sinks	sinking	sank	sunk
sit (see the Glossary of Usage)	sits	sitting	sat	sat
speak	speaks	speaking	spoke	spoken
spend	spends	spending	spent	spent
stand	stands	standing	stood	stood
steal	steals	stealing	stole	stolen
swim	swims	swimming	swam	swum
take	takes	taking	took	taken
teach	teaches	teaching	taught	taught
tell	tells	telling	told	told
throw	throws	throwing	threw	thrown
wear	wears	wearing	wore	worn
write	writes	writing	wrote	written

The verb *be* has eight forms.

be	**Be** on time!
am	I **am** going to arrive early tomorrow.
is	Time **is** of the essence.
are	They **are** always punctual.
was	The meeting **was** scheduled for 10 a.m.
were	We **were** only five minutes late.
being	He is **being** delayed by traffic.
been	How long have we **been** here?

Omission of Forms of *Be* in Other Languages
Forms of the verb *be* can be omitted in some languages.
In English, however, they are necessary.

Sentence without an auxiliary verb: The population ˄*is* growing.

Sentence without a linking verb: It ˄*is* quite large.

(3) A phrasal verb consists of a main verb and a particle.

A **phrasal verb** is a combination of a verb and a particle such as *up, out,* or *on*. Such a verb + particle unit is often idiomatic, conveying a meaning that differs from the common meanings of the individual words. For example, the definitions that first come to mind for the words *blow* and *up* are not likely to help you understand the phrasal verb *blow up* when it means "to enlarge": She *blew up* the photograph so that she could see the faces better. However, the meanings of other phrasal verbs are similar to common definitions; the particles just add a sense of completion: They *finished up* the report by six o'clock. The particle *up* in *finish up* does not refer to a direction; instead, it emphasizes the completion of the report. Still other phrasal verbs retain the common meanings of the verb and the particle: The protesters *hung up* a banner.

The parts of most phrasal verbs may be separated by a short noun phrase or a pronoun.

She **called** the meeting **off.**

The student **turned** it **in** yesterday.

Some phrasal verbs are not separable, however.

The group **went over** the proposal.

I **came across** an interesting fact.

Particles that add little meaning are often deleted, especially if they seem redundant.

I **sent out** the invitations.

Phrasal Verbs
If you cannot find phrasal verbs in a conventional dictionary, use a specialized dictionary that provides both definitions and information about the separability of these verbs. See **32e** for a list of dictionaries.

(4) Auxiliary verbs combine with main verbs.

The auxiliary verbs *be, do,* and *have* combine with main verbs, both regular and irregular:

be	*am, is, are, was, were surprised*
	am, is, are, was, were writing
do	*does, do, did call*
	doesn't, don't, didn't spend
have	*has, have, had prepared*
	has, have, had read

When you combine auxiliary verbs with main verbs, you alter the meanings of the main verbs in some subtle ways. The resulting verb combinations may provide information about time, emphasis, or action in progress. (See **26b**.)

Be, do, and *have* are not just auxiliary verbs, though. They may be used as main verbs as well.

be   I **am** from Texas.

do   He **does** his homework early in the morning.

have They **have** an apartment near a park.

A sentence may even include one of these verbs as both an auxiliary and a main verb.

They **are being** careful.

Did you **do** your taxes by yourself?

She **has** not **had** any free time this week.

Another type of auxiliary verb is called a **modal auxiliary.** By combining a modal auxiliary such as *will, should,* or *could* with the base form of a main verb, you can make a request (*could* you help), give an instruction (you *should* attend), or express certainty (we *shall* overcome), necessity (she *must* sleep), obligation (they *should* laugh), possibility (you *can* dream), or probability (it *could* happen).

Modal Auxiliaries and Main Verbs

Although English verbs are often followed by the infinitive marker *to* (as in *want to go* and *plan to leave*), modal auxiliaries do not follow this pattern.

We **should to** finish our report by Friday.

Each modal auxiliary has more than one meaning. For example, *may* can indicate permission or probability.

The instructor said we **may** have an extension. [permission]

The weather **may** improve by tomorrow. [probability]

The following list provides examples of the common meanings conveyed by modal auxiliaries.

COMMON MEANINGS OF MODAL AUXILIARIES

Meaning	Modal Auxiliary +	Main Verb	Example
Ability	can, could	afford	They *can afford* to buy a small house.
Certainty	will	leave	We *will leave* tomorrow.
Obligation	must	return	You *must return* your books by the due date.
Advice	should	talk	He *should talk* with his counselor.
Permission	may	use	You *may use* the computer in the main office.

When a modal auxiliary occurs with the auxiliary *have* (*must have forgotten*, *should have known*), *have* frequently sounds like the word *of*. When you proofread, be sure that modal auxiliaries are not followed by *of*.

They **could** ~~of~~ have **taken** another route.

Writers generally do not combine modal auxiliaries unless they want to portray a regional dialect.

We **might** ~~could~~ be able to plan the meeting for after the holidays.

Phrasal Modals
English also has **phrasal modals,** or auxiliary verbs consisting of more than one word. They have meanings similar to those of one-word modals.

be able to (ability): We **were able to** find the original document.

have to (obligation): You **have to** report your test results.

(Continued on page 572)

(Continued from page 571)

Other common phrasal modals are *be going to, be supposed to, had better, used to,* and *ought to.* Most of these auxiliary verbs have more than one form (*am able to, is able to, were able to*). Only *had better, ought to,* and *used to* have a single form.

(5) Participles are accompanied by auxiliary verbs.

Present participles (*-ing* verb forms) are used with the auxiliary verb *be:* We *were waiting* for the next flight. Depending on the intended meaning, past participles can be used with either *be* or *have:* We *have waited* for an hour. The first flight *was canceled.* If a sentence contains only a participle, it is probably a fragment (see **22b**).

I sit on the same bench every day. ̶D̶r̶e̶a̶m̶i̶n̶g̶ , *dreaming* of far-off places.

When a participle is part of a verbal phrase, it often appears without an auxiliary verb (see **21a(3)**).

Swatting at mosquitoes and **cursing** softly, the campers quickly packed up their gear.

Exercise 1

Supply the correct form of each verb in parentheses.

1. I (awake) early that morning.
2. Jason said we were (suppose) to leave at 5:00 a.m.
3. I wasn't (use) to getting up before dark, but I (manage) to be at the bus stop on time.
4. The sun was just (begin) to rise.
5. My backpack (be) heavy, so I (lay) it next to the other gear that was (lie) in a heap.
6. Without my pack on, though, I (be) cold.
7. I had (forget) how chilly mornings (be) in the desert.
8. Jason (see) me shivering and (lend) me his jacket.
9. "(Be) you okay?" he (ask).
10. "Yes," I (lie). It (be) early, it (be) cold, and I (be) nervous.

Exercise 2

Revise the following sentences. Explain any changes you make.

1. Any expedition into the wilderness suffer its share of mishaps.
2. The Lewis and Clark Expedition began in May 1804 and end in September 1806.
3. The Fates must of smiled on Meriwether Lewis and William Clark, for there were no fatalities under their leadership.
4. Lewis and Clark lead the expedition from St. Louis to the Pacific Ocean and back.
5. President Thomas Jefferson commission the expedition in 1803 in part because he was interest in finding the Northwest Passage—a hypothetical waterway connecting the Atlantic and Pacific Oceans.
6. By 1805, the Corps of Discovery, as the expedition was call, included thirty-three members.
7. The Corps might of lost all maps and specimens had Sacajawea, a Native American woman, not fish them from the Missouri River.
8. Sacajawea could of went off with her own people in Idaho, but she accompany Lewis and Clark to the Pacific.
9. When the Mandans had finish inspecting York, William Clark's African American servant, they assume he was the expedition's leader.
10. The success of the expedition depend on its members' willingness to help one another.

26b Verb tenses

Verb tenses provide information about time. For example, the tense of a verb may indicate that an action took place in the past or that an action is ongoing. Verb tenses are labeled as present, past, or future; they are also labeled as simple, progressive, perfect, or perfect progressive. The chart shows how these labels apply to the tenses of *walk*.

Verb Tenses

	Present	Past	Future
Simple	walk, walks	walked	will walk
Progressive	am, is, are walking	was, were walking	will be walking
Perfect	has, have walked	had walked	will have walked
Perfect progressive	has, have been walking	had been walking	will have been walking

Some of the tenses have more than one form because they depend on the person and number of the subject. **Person** refers to the role of the subject. First person (*I, we*) indicates that the subject of the verb is the writer or writers. Second person (*you*) indicates that the subject is the audience. Third person (*he, she, it, they*) indicates that the subject is someone or something other than the writer or audience. **Number** indicates whether the subject is one or more than one (*I/we, building/ buildings*). In the following subsections, conjugation tables are used to show how person and number influence the forms of the regular verb *work*.

(1) Simple tenses have many uses, not all related to specific points in time.

The conjugation for the simple present tense includes two forms of the verb: the base form and the *-s* form. Notice that the third-person singular form is the only form with the *-s* ending.

Simple Present Tense

	Singular	Plural
First person	I **work**	We **work**
Second person	You **work**	You **work**
Third person	He, she, it **works**	They **work**

Tense is not the same as time. Although the words *present, past,* and *future* may lead you to think that these tenses refer to actions happening now, in the past, and in the future, this strict separation does not always hold. For example, the simple present tense is used to indicate a current state, a habitual action, or a general truth.

We **are** ready. [current state]

Dana **uses** common sense. [habitual action]

The sun **rises** in the east. [general truth]

The simple present tense is also commonly used to add a sense of immediacy to historical actions and to discuss literary and artistic works (see fig. 26.1).

Fig. 26.1. In his painting *Sun Rising through Vapor,* J. M. W. Turner divides the canvas into areas of light and dark. (Notice the use of the simple present tense—"divides"—to describe an artistic work.)

In 1939, Hitler's armies **attack** Poland. [historical present]

Joseph Conrad **writes** about what he sees in the human heart. [literary present]

On occasion, the simple present tense is used to refer to a future event.

My bus **leaves** in twenty minutes.

The simple past tense of regular verbs has only one form: the base form with the *-ed* ending. The past tense for irregular verbs varies (see 26a(2)).

Simple Past Tense

	Singular	Plural
First person	I **worked**	We **worked**
Second person	You **worked**	You **worked**
Third person	He, she, it **worked**	They **worked**

The simple past tense is used to refer to completed past actions or events.

> He **traveled** to the Philippines. [past action]
>
> The accident **occurred** several weeks ago. [past event]

The simple future tense also has only one form: the base form accompanied by the auxiliary *will.*

Simple Future Tense

	Singular	Plural
First person	I **will work**	We **will work**
Second person	You **will work**	You **will work**
Third person	He, she, it **will work**	They **will work**

The simple future tense refers to future actions or states.

> I **will call** you after work today. [future action]
>
> The video **will be** ready by Friday. [future state]

(2) Progressive tenses indicate that events have begun but have not been completed.

The present progressive tense of a verb consists of a form of the auxiliary verb *be* and the present participle (*-ing* form) of the main verb.

Present Progressive Tense

	Singular	Plural
First person	I **am working**	We **are working**
Second person	You **are working**	You **are working**
Third person	He, she, it **is working**	They **are working**

Notice that the present participle remains the same regardless of person and number, but the auxiliary *be* appears in three forms: *am* for first-person singular, *is* for third-person singular, and *are* for the other person-number combinations.

The present progressive tense signals an activity in progress or a temporary situation.

> The doctor **is attending** a conference in Nebraska. [activity in progress]

> We **are living** in a yurt right now. [temporary situation]

The present progressive tense can refer to a future event when it occurs with a word or phrase indicating future time.

> Tomorrow we **are leaving** for Alaska. [*Tomorrow* indicates a time in the future.]

Like the present progressive, the past progressive tense is a combination of the auxiliary verb *be* and the present participle (*-ing* form) of the main verb. However, the auxiliary verb is in the past tense, rather than in the present tense.

Past Progressive Tense

	Singular	Plural
First person	I **was working**	We **were working**
Second person	You **were working**	You **were working**
Third person	He, she, it **was working**	They **were working**

The past progressive tense signals an action or event that occurred in the past and was repeated or ongoing.

The new member **was** constantly **interrupting** the discussion. [repeated past action]

We **were eating** dinner when we heard the news. [ongoing past action]

The future progressive tense has only one form. Two auxiliaries, *will* and *be,* are used along with the *-ing* form of the main verb.

Future Progressive Tense

	Singular	Plural
First person	I will be working	We will be working
Second person	You will be working	You will be working
Third person	He, she, it will be working	They will be working

The future progressive tense refers to actions that will occur over some period of time in the future.

She **will be giving** her report at the end of the meeting. [future action]

Verbs Not Used in the Progressive Form
Some verbs that do not express actions but rather mental states, emotions, conditions, or relationships are not used in the progressive form. These verbs include *believe, belong, contain, cost, know, own, prefer,* and *want.*

　　　　　contains
The book ~~is containing~~ many Central American folktales.

　　　knows
He ~~is knowing~~ many old myths.

(3) Perfect tenses indicate action performed prior to a particular time.

The present perfect tense is formed by combining the auxiliary *have* with the past participle of the main verb.

Present Perfect Tense

	Singular	Plural
First person	I **have worked**	We **have worked**
Second person	You **have worked**	You **have worked**
Third person	He, she, it **has worked**	They **have worked**

The participle remains the same regardless of person and number; however, the auxiliary has two forms: *has* (for third-person singular) and *have* (for the other person-number combinations). The present perfect tense signals a time prior to the present. It can refer to a situation originating in the past but continuing into the present. It can also refer to a past action that has current relevance.

> They **have lived** in New Zealand for twenty years. [situation originating in the past and still continuing]

> I **have read** that book already. Do you have another? [past action that is completed but currently relevant]

The past perfect tense is also formed by combining the auxiliary *have* with the past participle. However, the auxiliary is in the past tense. There is only one form of the past perfect for regular verbs.

Past Perfect Tense

	Singular	Plural
First person	I **had worked**	We **had worked**
Second person	You **had worked**	You **had worked**
Third person	He, she, it **had worked**	They **had worked**

The past perfect tense refers to an action completed at a time in the past prior to another past time or past action.

> Before 1990, he **had worked** in a shoe factory. [past action prior to a given time in the past]

> I **had studied** geology before I transferred to this school. [past action prior to another past action]

The future perfect tense consists of two auxiliaries, *will* and *have,* along with the past participle of the main verb. There is only one form of the future perfect tense.

Future Perfect Tense

	Singular	Plural
First person	I **will have worked**	We **will have worked**
Second person	You **will have worked**	You **will have worked**
Third person	He, she, it **will have worked**	They **will have worked**

The future perfect tense refers to an action that is to be completed prior to a future time.

By this time next year, I **will have finished** medical school.

(4) Perfect progressive tenses combine the forms and meanings of the progressive and the perfect tenses.

The present perfect progressive tense consists of two auxiliaries, *have* and *be,* plus the present participle (*-ing* form) of the main verb.

Present Perfect Progressive Tense

	Singular	Plural
First person	I **have been working**	We **have been working**
Second person	You **have been working**	You **have been working**
Third person	He, she, it **has been working**	They **have been working**

The form of the auxiliary *have* varies with person and number. The auxiliary *be* appears as the past participle. The present perfect progressive signals that an action, state, or event originating in the past is ongoing or incomplete.

I **have been feeling** tired for a week. [ongoing state]

We **have been organizing** the conference since April. [incomplete action]

The past perfect progressive tense follows the pattern *had* + *been* + present participle (*-ing* form) of the main verb. The auxiliary *have* is in the past tense.

Past Perfect Progressive Tense

	Singular	Plural
First person	I **had been working**	We **had been working**
Second person	You **had been working**	You **had been working**
Third person	He, she, it **had been working**	They **had been working**

The past perfect progressive tense refers to a situation or action occurring over a period of time in the past and prior to another past action or time.

She **had been living** so frugally all year that she saved enough money for a new car. [past situation prior to another action in the past]

The future perfect progressive tense follows the pattern *will* + *have* + *been* + present participle (*-ing* form) of the main verb.

Future Perfect Progressive Tense

	Singular	Plural
First person	I **will have been working**	We **will have been working**
Second person	You **will have been working**	You **will have been working**
Third person	He, she, it **will have been working**	They **will have been working**

The future perfect progressive tense refers to an action that is occurring in the present and will continue to occur for a specific amount of time.

In one more month, I **will have been working** on this project for five years.

(5) The auxiliary verb *do* is used to question, negate, or emphasize.

Unlike *be* and *have,* the auxiliary verb *do* is not used with other verbs to indicate tense. Instead, it is used to question, negate, or emphasize.

Do you have any questions? [question]

I **do** not have any questions. [negation]

I **do** have a few questions. [emphatic sentence]

The auxiliary *do* occurs only in the simple present (*do, does*) and the simple past (*did*).

Exercise 3

Explain what the verb tenses used in the following paragraph reveal about the time or duration of the actions expressed by the main verbs.

¹Professor Alex Cohen and his literature students are leaving on Friday for Oxford University. ²While there, they will study Keats and Wordsworth. ³Although they have been studying these poets since September, Professor Cohen believes that the students will gain greater insight into English poetry because they will have access to important archives. ⁴Professor Cohen studied in Oxford when he was an undergraduate, earning a degree in English and classics. ⁵This is the first trip he has planned for students. ⁶However, with the help of a university grant, he will be planning many more. ⁷He is already exploring the possibility of taking students from his mythology class to Greece next year.

Exercise 4

For each sentence, explain how the meaning of the sentence changes when the verb tense changes.

1. In "Fiji's Rainbow Reef," Les Kaufman (describes/described) the coral reefs of Fiji and (discusses/discussed) the factors affecting their health.

2. Rising water temperatures (damaged/have damaged/did damage) the reefs in 2000 and 2002.

3. The algae that (provide/provided) color (do not survive/did not survive) in the warmer water.

4. The lack of algae (has left/had left) the coral "bleached."

5. Strangely, though, new life (is flourishing/was flourishing/has been flourishing) in some of these areas.

6. Scientists (study/will study) this area to understand its resilience.

Exercise 5

In a paragraph from one of your recent writing assignments, underline all the verbs and identify the tenses you used. Explain why they are appropriate.

(6) Tense forms help convey the duration or time sequence of actions or events.

When you use more than one tense form in a single sentence, you give readers information about how actions or events are related in time and duration.

> Whenever he **calls** on me, I **stutter** nervously. [Both forms indicate habitual actions.]

> When the speaker **had finished,** everyone **applauded.** [The past perfect tense *had finished* indicates a time before the action expressed by *applauded.*]

Infinitives and participles (see 21a(3)) can be used to express time relations within a sentence. The present infinitive (*to* + base form) of a verb generally expresses action occurring later than the action expressed by the main verb.

> They **want to design** a new museum. [The action of designing will take place in the future.]

The perfect infinitive (*to* + *have* + past participle) signals that an action, state, or event is potential or hypothetical or that it did not occur.

> She **hopes to have earned** her degree by the end of next year.
>
> The governor **would like to have postponed** the vote. [The postponement did not occur.]

The present participle (*-ing* form) indicates simultaneous or previous action.

> **Laughing** loudly, the old friends **left** the restaurant arm in arm. [The friends were laughing as they were leaving.]
>
> **Hearing** that she was distressed, I **rushed** right over. [The action of hearing occurred first.]

The perfect participle (*having* + past participle) expresses action completed before that conveyed by the main verb.

> **Having learned** Spanish at an early age, she **spoke** to the Mexican diplomats in their native language.

The past participle can be used to express either simultaneous action or previous action.

> **Led** by a former Peace Corps worker, the volunteers **provided** medical assistance. [Both actions occurred simultaneously.]
>
> **Encouraged** by job prospects, he **moved** to Atlanta. [The encouragement preceded the move.]

Exercise 6

Revise the following sentences so that all verbs express the appropriate time sequences.

1. We expected the storm to have bypassed our town, but it didn't.
2. We would like to have prior notice; however, even the police officers were taken by surprise.
3. Not having known much about flooding, the emergency crew was at a disadvantage.
4. Having thrown sandbags all day, the volunteers had been exhausted by 5 p.m.
5. They went home, succeeding in preventing a major disaster.

26c Consistency of verb tenses

The tenses of a verb have two features: time frame and aspect. **Time frame** refers to whether the tense is present, past, or future. **Aspect** refers to whether it is simple, progressive, perfect, or perfect progressive. (See 26b.) Consistency in the time frame of your verbs, though not necessarily in their aspect, ensures that your sentences link together logically. In the following paragraph, notice that the time frame remains the past, but the aspect is either the simple, the perfect, or the progressive.

In the summer of 1983, I **had** just **finished** my third year of architecture *[past perfect]* school and **had** to find a six-month internship. *[simple past]* I **had grown** up and **gone** *[past perfect (compound predicate)]* through my entire education in the Midwest, but I **had been** to New York *[past perfect]* City once on a class field trip and I **thought** it **seemed** like a pretty good *[simple past] [simple past]* place to live. So, armed with little more than an inflated ego and my school portfolio, I **was** off to Manhattan, *[simple past]* oblivious to the bad economy and the fact that the city **was overflowing** with young architects. *[past progressive]*

—**PAUL K. HUMISTON**, "Small World"

If you do need to shift to another time frame, you can signal the change in tense by using a time marker:

now, then, today, yesterday
in two years, during the 1920s
after you finish, before we left

For example, in the following paragraph, the time frame shifts back and forth between present and past—between today, when Edward O. Wilson is studying ants in the woods around Walden Pond, and the nineteenth century, when Thoreau lived there. The time markers are circled.

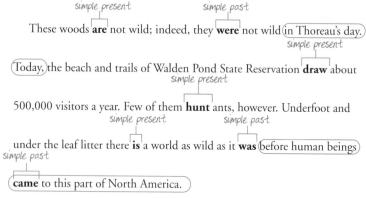

These woods **are** not wild; indeed, they **were** not wild (in Thoreau's day.)

(Today,) the beach and trails of Walden Pond State Reservation **draw** about

500,000 visitors a year. Few of them **hunt** ants, however. Underfoot and

under the leaf litter there **is** a world as wild as it **was** (before human beings)

came to this part of North America.

—JAMES GORMAN, "Finding a Wild, Fearsome World beneath Every Fallen Leaf"

On occasion, a shift in time is indicated implicitly—that is, without an explicit time marker. A writer may change tenses without including a time marker for any of these reasons: (1) to explain or support a general statement with information about the past, (2) to compare and contrast two different time periods, and (3) to comment on a topic. Why do you think the author of the following paragraph varies the verb tenses?

> Thomas Jefferson, author of the Declaration of Independence, **is** considered one of our country's most brilliant citizens. His achievements **were** many, as **were** his interests. Some historians **describe** his work as a naturalist, scientist, and inventor; others **focus** on his accomplishments as an educator and politician. Yet Jefferson **is** best known as a spokesman for democracy.

Except for the two uses of *were* in the second sentence, all verbs are in the present tense. The author uses the past tense in the second sentence to provide evidence from the past that supports the topic sentence.

Exercise 7

Determine whether the shifts in tense in the following paragraph are effective. Be prepared to explain your reasoning.

[1]The statement that clothing **is** a language, though occasionally made with the air of a man finding a flying saucer in his backyard, **is** not new. [2]Balzac, in *Daughter of Eve* (1839), **observed** that for a woman dress **is** "a continual manifestation of intimate thoughts, a language, a symbol." [3]Today, as semiotics **becomes** fashionable, sociologists **tell** us that fashion too **is** a language of signs, a nonverbal system of communication. . . .   —ALISON LURIE, "Clothing as a Sign System"

26d Voice

Voice indicates the relationship between a verb and its subject. When a verb is in the **active voice,** the subject is generally a person or thing performing an action. When a verb is in the **passive voice,** the subject is the *receiver* of the action.

> Susan Sontag **wrote** the essay. [active voice]
>
> The essay **was written** by Susan Sontag. [passive voice]

(1) Transitive verbs, but not linking or intransitive verbs, can be used in the passive voice.

A **linking verb** relates the subject and a word referring to the subject (the complement). (See **20d(3)**.) A linking verb may be a verb referring to the senses (such as *feel, look, smell, sound,* or *taste*) or a verb that indicates being (*be*), seeming (*seem, appear*), remaining (*remain, keep, stay*), or becoming (*become, grow, turn*).

> Morgan **is** studious.
>
> He **sounds** authoritative.
>
> He **seems** responsible.

Linking verbs are used only in the active voice.

An **intransitive verb** does not take an object. In other words, there is no noun or pronoun following the verb and receiving its action.

> Claudia **studies** hard.

Like linking verbs, intransitive verbs are used only in the active voice.

In contrast, a **transitive verb** takes a direct object; that is, a noun or pronoun follows the verb and receives its action.

Claudia **wrote** the prize-winning essay.

Transitive verbs can usually be used in either the active or the passive voice. When the voice is passive, the recipient of the action expressed by the verb is the subject, not the direct object, of the sentence.

The prize-winning essay **was written** by Claudia.

(2) Sentences in the active voice emphasize actors and actions.

Sentences in the active voice are generally clearer and more vigorous than their passive counterparts. To use the active voice for emphasizing an actor and an action, first make the actor the subject of the sentence, and then choose a verb that will help your readers see what the actor is doing.

Passive voice   The graduation ceremony was planned by a group of students. A well-known columnist was invited to give the graduation address.

Revised   A group of students planned the graduation ceremony. They invited a well-known columnist to give the graduation address.

For more information on using the active voice to write forceful sentences, see 30e.

(3) The passive voice highlights the recipient of the action.

The passive voice differs from the active voice in three ways. First, the subject in a passive sentence is the recipient of the action, not the actor.

The **construction** of the Guggenheim Museum was finished in 1959.

Second, if an actor is mentioned, that noun or pronoun is placed in a prepositional phrase beginning with the preposition *by.*

The Guggenheim Museum was designed by **Frank Lloyd Wright.**

Finally, the verb form is different. A verb in the passive voice consists of a form of the auxiliary verb *be* and the past participle. Depending on the verb tense, the auxiliaries *have* and *will* may appear as well. The following are the most common tense forms of the passive voice for *call.*

Simple present: *am called, is called, are called*
Simple past: *was called, were called*
Simple future: *will be called*
Present progressive: *am being called, is being called, are being called*
Past progressive: *was being called, were being called*
Present perfect: *has been called, have been called*
Past perfect: *had been called*
Future perfect: *will have been called*

THINKING RHETORICALLY ABOUT

THE PASSIVE VOICE

Use the passive voice when you want to stress the recipient of an action, rather than the actor, or when the actor's identity is unimportant or unknown. For example, you could use the passive voice to emphasize the topic of a discussion.

Tuition increases **will be discussed** at the next board meeting.

Or you could use it when you do not know who performed some action.

The lights **were left on** in the building last night.

Writers of scientific prose often use the passive voice to highlight the conditions of an experiment rather than the experimenter.

Alcohol use **was defined** as the number of days (during the past 30 days) that respondents drank alcohol. Shorter recall periods have yielded more reliable and valid self-reports when assessing behavior (Kauth, St. Lawrence, & Kelly, 1991); thus, a retrospective 30-day period **was selected.**

—CATHERINE DAVIS, student

Grammar checkers cannot distinguish between a true passive construction, such as *have been seen,* and a form of *be* followed by an adjective, such as *have been healthy.* Thus, they incorrectly flag the latter as a passive construction. In addition, they cannot tell when passive constructions are appropriate and so generally advise writers to "correct" them. For more information about grammar checkers, see Using a Grammar Checker on page 461.

Exercise 8

Identify the voice in each sentence as active or passive.

1. In a recent *National Geographic* report, Tom O'Neill describes the discovery of ancient art in Guatemala.
2. Archaeologist William Saturno recently discovered the oldest known Maya mural.
3. The mural was found in a tunnel used by looters.
4. The tunnel was actually a small room attached to a pyramid.
5. The small room was covered with debris; its exact dimensions were hard to gauge.
6. The archaeologist found the mural by accident.
7. The mural was dated to about 150 years before the beginning of the Maya Classic Period.
8. For protection from further looting, the research crew posted guards outside the small room.
9. Pigments and wall plaster were gathered for analysis.
10. The details of the mural have not yet been interpreted.

Exercise 9

Rewrite the sentences in exercise 8, making active verbs passive and passive verbs active. Add or delete actors when necessary. If one version of a sentence is better than the other, explain why.

26e Mood

The **mood** of a verb expresses the writer's attitude toward the factuality of what is being expressed. The **indicative mood** is used for statements and questions regarding fact or opinion. The **imperative mood** is used to give commands or directions. The **subjunctive mood** is used to state requirements, make requests, express wishes, and signal hypothetical situations.

Indicative   We will be on time.

Imperative   Be on time!

Subjunctive   The director insists that we be on time.

By using moods correctly, you can show your readers how you feel about the content of your sentences—certain, confident, doubtful, hesitant, ambivalent, and so on.

(1) Verb forms signal moods.

Verb forms for the indicative mood are described in **26b**. The verb form for the imperative is simply the base form. A verb in the subjunctive mood can be present subjunctive, past subjunctive, or perfect subjunctive. The **present subjunctive** is the base form of the verb.

> The doctor recommended that he **go** on a diet.

> The curator requested that I **be** at the museum by five o'clock.

In the passive voice, the present subjunctive form consists of *be* and the past participle of the main verb.

> We demanded that you **be reimbursed.**

The **past subjunctive** has the same form as the simple past (for example, *had, offered, found,* or *wrote*). However, the past subjunctive form of *be* is *were,* regardless of person or number.

> If they **offered** me the job, I would take it.

> She acts as if she **were** the employer rather than the employee.

The past subjunctive form in the passive voice consists of *were* and the past participle.

> Even if he **were given** a large amount of money, he would not change his mind.

Although it is called "past," the past subjunctive refers to the present or the future.

The **perfect subjunctive** has the same form as the past perfect tense: *had* + past participle. The perfect subjunctive signals that a statement is not factual.

I wish I **had known** about the scholarship competition.

To use the passive voice of a perfect subjunctive form, add the past participle of the main verb to the auxiliaries *had been.*

If she **had been awarded** the scholarship, she would have quit her part-time job.

(2) The subjunctive mood is mainly used in dependent clauses.

Although you may not use the subjunctive mood when speaking with your friends, using it in your writing shows your readers how you feel about your claims. In addition, your audience may expect you to follow the conventions for formal writing. The following guidelines should help you avoid pitfalls in the use of the subjunctive.

TIPS FOR USING THE SUBJUNCTIVE

- In clauses beginning with *as if* and *as though,* use the past subjunctive or the perfect subjunctive.

  were
  He acts as if he ~~was~~ the owner.

  had
  She looked at me as though she ~~heard~~ this story before.

- In nonfactual dependent clauses beginning with *if,* use the past subjunctive or the perfect subjunctive. Avoid using *would have* in the *if* clause.

  were
  If I ~~was~~ rich, I would buy a yacht.

  had
  If the driver ~~would have checked~~ his rearview mirror, the accident would not have happened.

  Note that *if* does not always mark a clause as nonfactual.

If it is sunny tomorrow, I'm going fishing. [indicative mood]

■ In dependent clauses following verbs that express wishes, requirements, or requests, use the past subjunctive or the perfect subjunctive.

I wish I ~~was~~ *were* taller.

My brother wishes he ~~studied~~ *had* studied harder years ago.

BEYOND THE RULE

DECLINE OF THE SUBJUNCTIVE

Some linguists believe that certain subjunctive forms are disappearing from the English language. For more information, visit **www.harbrace.com**.

Exercise 10

Use subjunctive verb forms to revise the following sentences.

1. The planners of *Apollo 13* acted as if the number 13 was a lucky number.
2. Superstitious people think that if NASA changed the number of the mission, the astronauts would have had a safer journey.
3. They also believe that if the lunar landing would have been scheduled for a day other than Friday the Thirteenth, the crew would not have encountered any problems.
4. The crew used the lunar module as though it was a lifeboat.
5. If NASA ever plans a space mission on Friday the Thirteenth again, the public would object.

26f Subject-verb agreement

A verb must agree with its subject in number. That is, when a subject is plural, the verb must have a plural form; when the subject is singular, the verb must have a singular form. The subject and verb must also agree in person. First-person subjects require first-person verb forms, second-person subjects require second-person verb forms, and third-person subjects require third-person verb forms. Notice in the following examples that the singular third-person subject takes a singular verb (*-s* form) and that the plural third-person subject takes a plural verb (base form). (If you cannot easily recognize verbs and their subjects, see **20b–d**.)

Singular   The **car** in the lot **looks** new. [*Car* and *looks* are both singular.]
Plural   The **cars** in the lot **look** new. [*Cars* and *look* are both plural.]

You can refer to the following subsections for guidance on ensuring subject-verb agreement in particular situations:

- when words come between the subject and the verb (**26f(1)**),
- when two or more subjects are joined by conjunctions (**26f(2)–(3)**),
- when word order is inverted (**26f(4)**),
- when the subject is a relative pronoun (**26f(5)**), an indefinite pronoun (**26f(6)**), or a collective noun or measurement word (**26f(7)**),
- when the subject is a noun that is plural in form but singular in meaning (**26f(8)**),
- when the subject is singular but its complement is plural (**26f(9)**), and
- when the subject is a noun clause beginning with *what* (**26f(10)**).

Adding -s to Nouns and Verbs

Standardized English requires the addition of *-s* to mark most nouns as plural but most verbs as third-person singular in the present tense. (Modal auxiliaries are the exception.) Be careful not to confuse the verb ending and the noun ending.

The **students** need attention. [noun + *-s*]

The student **needs** attention. [verb + *-s*]

Except for *be*, verbs have different forms to indicate third-person singular and third-person plural only in the simple present tense.

Simple present tense of *be*: *am, is, are*

Simple past tense of *be*: *was, were*

Simple present tense of other verbs: base form or base form + *-s* or *-es*, as in *read/reads* or *push/pushes*

When the third-person singular verb form (*-s* form) is confused with the third-person plural form (base form), the subject and verb will not agree in number. As you edit your writing, watch for the potential pitfalls described in the following subsections.

(1) Agreement errors are likely when other words come between the subject and the verb.

The **rhythm** of the pounding waves **is** calming. [*Waves* is not the subject; it is the object of the preposition *of*.]

Certain phrases commonly occur between the subject and the verb; however, they do not affect the number of the subject or the form of the verb:

accompanied by	as well as	not to mention	including
along with	in addition to	no less than	together with

Her **salary,** together with tips, **is** just enough to live on.

Tips, together with her salary, **are** just enough to live on.

(2) Subjects joined by *and* usually take a plural verb.

Writing on a legal pad and writing with a computer are not the same at all.

A compound subject that refers to a single person or thing takes a singular verb.

The **founder and president** of the art association **was** elected to the board of the museum.

Red beans and rice is the specialty of the house.

(3) Agreement errors are common when subjects are joined by *or* or *nor*.

When singular subjects are linked by *or, either . . . or,* or *neither . . . nor,* the verb is singular as well.

> The **provost or** the **dean** usually **presides** at the meeting.
>
> **Either** his **accountant or** his **lawyer has** the will.
>
> **Neither** the **car nor** the **motorcycle is** for sale.

If one subject is singular and one is plural, the verb agrees in number with the subject closer to the verb.

> Neither the basket nor the **apples were** expensive. [plural]
>
> Neither the apples nor the **basket was** expensive. [singular]

The verb also agrees in person with the nearer subject.

> Either Frank or **you were** going to make the announcement. [second person]
>
> Either you or **Frank was** going to make the announcement. [third person]

(4) Inverted word order may lead to agreement errors.

In most sentences, the subject precedes the verb.

The large **cities** of the Northeast **were** the hardest hit by the storm.

The subject and verb can sometimes be inverted for emphasis; however, they must still agree.

Hardest hit by the storm **were** the large **cities** of the Northeast.

When the expletive *there* begins a sentence, the subject and verb are also inverted; the verb still agrees with the subject, which follows it (see **20d(1)**).

There **are** several **cities** in need of federal aid.

(5) Clauses with relative pronouns are common sites for agreement errors.

In an adjectival (relative) clause (see **21b(2)**), the subject is generally a relative pronoun (*that, who,* or *which*). To determine whether the relative pronoun is singular or plural, you must find its antecedent (the word or words it refers to). When the antecedent is singular, the relative pronoun is singular; when the antecedent is plural, the relative pronoun is plural. In essence, the verb in the adjectival clause agrees with the antecedent.

sing ant   *sing*

The person who reviews proposals is out of town this week.

pl ant   *pl v*

The director met with the **students who are** studying abroad next quarter.

pl ant   *pl v*

The Starion is one of **the new models that include** air conditioning as standard equipment.

BEYOND THE RULE

ONE AS A POSSIBLE ANTECEDENT

According to traditional grammar rules, in sentences containing the pattern *one + of +* plural noun + adjectival clause (such as the sentence just before this box), the antecedent for the relative pronoun (*that,* in this case) is the plural noun (*models*). The verb in the adjectival clause is thus plural as well. However, professional writers often consider *one,* instead of the plural noun, to be the antecedent of the relative pronoun and thus make the verb singular:

The Starion is **one** of the new models **that includes** air conditioning as standard equipment.

For more information on this variation, visit **www.harbrace.com**.

(6) Agreement errors frequently occur with indefinite pronouns.

The indefinite pronouns *each, either, everybody, one,* and *anyone* are considered singular and so require singular verb forms.

> **Either** of them **is willing** to lead the discussion.

> **Each has bought** a first-class ticket.

> **Everybody** in our apartment building **has** a parking place.

Other indefinite pronouns, such as *all, any, some, none, half,* and *most,* can be either singular or plural, depending on whether they refer to a unit or quantity (singular) or to individuals (plural).

> pl ant   pl v
>
> My sister collects **books; some are** quite valuable.

> sing ant   sing v
>
> My sister collects **jewelry; some** of it **is** quite valuable.

Singular subjects that are preceded by *every* or *each* and joined by *and* require a singular verb.

> **Every** cat **and** dog in the county **has** to be vaccinated.

> **Each** fork **and** spoon **has** to be polished.

However, placing *each* after a plural subject does not affect the verb form. The verb should agree with the plural subject.

> Colleges and vocational schools **each have** their advantages.

When an indefinite pronoun is followed by a prepositional phrase beginning with the preposition *of* (see **21a(4)**), the verb agrees in number with the object of the preposition.

> pl obj pl v
>
> **None** of **those are** spoiled.

> sing obj sing v
>
> **None** of **it is** spoiled.

More than **half** of the **population** in West Texas **is** Hispanic.

sing obj *sing v*

More than **half** of the **people** in West Texas **are** Hispanic.

pl obj *pl v*

BEYOND THE RULE

AGREEMENT WITH *NONE*

Some grammarians reason that, like *no one*, *none* is singular and thus should be followed by a singular verb:

None of the grant requests **has** been rejected.

Nonetheless, many reputable writers have used *none* with plural verbs, leading to the widespread acceptance of this usage:

None of the grant requests **have** been rejected.

For more information, visit **www.harbrace.com**.

(7) Collective nouns and measurement words often cause agreement difficulties.

Collective nouns and measurement words require singular verbs when they refer to groups or units. They require plural verbs when they refer to individuals or parts.

Singular (regarded as a group or unit)	Plural (regarded as individuals or parts)
The **majority rules.**	The **majority** of us **have voted** already.
Ten million gallons of oil **is** more than enough.	**Ten million gallons** of oil **were spilled.**
The **number is** insignificant.	A **number** of workers **were** absent.

Although the use of *data* and *media* as collective nouns has gained currency, treat *data* and *media* as plural in most academic writing. (See the Glossary of Usage.)

> The data **are** in the appendix.

> The media **have** shaped public opinion.

(8) Words ending in -s are sometimes singular.

Individual titles that are plural in form are treated as singular because they refer to a single book, movie, recording, or other work.

> *Coffee and Cigarettes* **is** now available on DVD.

A reference to a word is also considered singular.

> *Beans* **is** a slang word for "a small amount": I don't know beans about football.

A few nouns ending in *-s* are actually singular. Examples are *linguistics, news,* and *Niagara Falls.*

> The **news is** encouraging.

Some nouns (such as *athletics, politics, electronics, measles,* and *deer*) can be either singular or plural, depending on their meanings.

Singular	Plural
Statistics is an interesting subject.	**Statistics are** often misleading.

(9) Verbs agree with subjects, not with subject complements.

Some sentences may have a singular subject and a plural subject complement, or vice versa. In either case, the verb agrees with the subject.

> Her primary **concern is** rising health-care **costs.**

> **Croissants are** the bakery's **specialty.**

THINKING RHETORICALLY ABOUT

AGREEMENT OF RELATED SINGULAR AND PLURAL NOUNS

When a sentence has two or more nouns that are related, use either the singular form or the plural form consistently.

The **student** raised her **hand.**

The **students** raised their **hands.**

Occasionally, you may have to use a singular noun to retain an idiomatic expression or to avoid ambiguity.

They kept their **word.**

The **participants** were asked to name their favorite **movie.**

(10) An agreement error may occur when the subject of a sentence is a noun clause beginning with *what.*

In noun clauses, *what* may be understood as either "the thing that" or "the things that." If it is understood as "the thing that," the verb in the main clause is singular.

What we need **is** a new policy. [*The thing that* we need is a policy.]

If *what* is understood as "the things that," the verb in the main clause is plural.

What we need **are** new guidelines. [*The things that* we need are guidelines.]

Often the main noun in the subject complement of a sentence in which *what* is used in this way will help you determine whether a singular or a plural verb should be used. In the example sentences above, *policy* and *is* are singular; *guidelines* and *are* are plural.

BEYOND THE RULE

WHAT IN NOUN CLAUSES AND VERB AGREEMENT

According to traditional grammar rules, a singular verb should be used in both the noun clause containing *what* and the main clause.

What **is** needed **is** new guidelines.

However, many current writers and editors consider this rule outmoded. For more information, see **www.harbrace.com**.

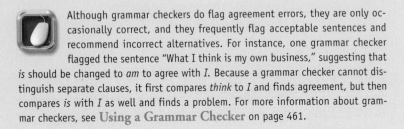

Although grammar checkers do flag agreement errors, they are only occasionally correct, and they frequently flag acceptable sentences and recommend incorrect alternatives. For instance, one grammar checker flagged the sentence "What I think is my own business," suggesting that *is* should be changed to *am* to agree with *I*. Because a grammar checker cannot distinguish separate clauses, it first compares *think* to *I* and finds agreement, but then compares *is* with *I* as well and finds a problem. For more information about grammar checkers, see Using a Grammar Checker on page 461.

Exercise 11

In each sentence, choose the correct form of the verb in parentheses. Make sure that the verb agrees with its subject according to the conventions for academic and professional writing.

1. There (is/are) at least two good reasons for changing motor oil: risk of contamination and danger of additive depletion.
2. Reasons for not changing the oil (include/includes) the cost to the driver and the inconvenience of the chore.
3. What I want to know (is/are) the number of miles I can drive before changing my oil.
4. My best friend and mechanic (says/say) three thousand miles.

5. But my brother says every three thousand miles (is/are) too often.

6. Each of the car manuals I consulted (recommends/recommend) five-thousand-mile intervals.

7. Neither the automakers nor the gas station attendants (know/knows) how I drive, however.

8. Recommendations for changing oil (is/are) based on the assumption that normally we all drive between 40 and 65 mph on good highways when it is not too hot or too cold.

9. I am one of those drivers who on hot days (speeds/speed) along at 70 mph on interstates or (bumps/bump) along at 45 mph on a dusty road.

10. I need an oil-life monitor that (tells/tell) me when it is time to change my oil.

Exercise 12

Complete the following sentences, making sure that subjects and verbs agree.

1. Applying for college and enrolling in courses . . .
2. Erik is one of the students who . . .
3. Either of them . . .
4. Neither the president nor the senators . . .
5. The list of volunteers . . .
6. There . . .
7. Hidden beneath the stairs . . .
8. The teacher, along with her students, . . .
9. Ten months . . .
10. Politics . . .
11. Their hope for the future . . .
12. What we requested . . .

EFFECTIVE

SENTENCES

S

Variety adds interest to texts and images.

THINKING RHETORICALLY ABOUT

SENTENCE STYLE

Most professional writers and readers use the following words to describe effective sentences.

- *Exact*. Precise words and word combinations ensure exactness and enable readers to come as close as they can to a full understanding of the writer's message.
- *Conventional*. Sentences are conventional when they conform to the usage expectations of a particular community. For most academic assignments, you will be expected to use Standardized English.
- *Consistent*. A consistent writing style is characterized by the use of the same types of words and grammatical structures throughout a piece of writing. A style that is inconsistent jars the readers' expectations.
- *Parallel*. Related to consistency, parallelism refers to the placement of similar ideas into similar grammatical structures.
- *Concise*. Concise prose is free of meaningless redundancies.
- *Coherent*. Coherence refers to clear connections between adjacent sentences and paragraphs.
- *Varied*. To write appealing paragraphs, a writer uses both short and long sentences. When sentences vary in length, they usually also vary in structure, rhythm, and emphasis.

In the following chapters, you will learn to identify the rhetorical options considered effective by most academic and professional writers. Remember, though, that expectations as to what is appropriate may vary across rhetorical situations. You may find that it does not make sense to apply a general rule such as "Use the active voice" in all circumstances. For example, you may be expected to write a vigorous description of an event, detailing exactly what happened, but find that you need to use the passive voice when you do not know who was responsible for the event: Several of the campaign signs *were defaced*. Or, as another example, you may need to set aside the rule calling for Standardized English if you are writing dialogue in which the speakers use regional dialects. By analyzing your rhetorical situation, rather than always following general rules, you will write sentences that make sense to you and to your audience.

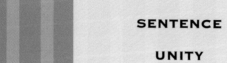

SENTENCE

UNITY

27

Effective academic and professional writing comprises sentences that are consistent, clear, and complete. By carefully crafting your sentences, you demonstrate concern for your audience and thus have a better chance of achieving your rhetorical purpose. This chapter can help you

- choose and arrange details (27a),
- include necessary words (27b),
- revise mixed metaphors (27c),
- relate sentence parts (27d), and
- complete comparisons (27e) and intensifiers (27f).

27a Choosing and arranging details

Well-chosen details add interest and credibility to your writing. As you revise, you may occasionally notice a sentence that would be clearer and more believable with the addition of a phrase or two about time, location, or cause.

Missing important detail	An astrophysicist from the Harvard-Smithsonian Center has predicted a galactic storm.
With detail added	An astrophysicist from the Harvard-Smithsonian Center has predicted **that** a galactic storm **will occur within the next 10 million years.**

Without the additional information about time, most readers would wonder when the storm was supposed to hit. Knowing that the storm is predicted for millions of years in the future will help them accept the information presented.

Missing important detail	The cataclysm in the Milky Way will result in radiation levels capable of killing nearby organisms, but it will not affect Earth.
With detail added	The cataclysm in the Milky Way will result in radiation levels capable of killing nearby organisms, but it will not affect Earth, **which is 25,000 light-years away.**

The additional information in the second sentence about location helps readers understand why the Earth will be unaffected by a cataclysm in the Milky Way.

The details you choose will help your readers understand your message. If you provide too many details within a single sentence, though, your readers may lose sight of your main point. When you revise, be sure that the details you included in your first draft are still meaningful. The writer of the following sentence deleted the mention of her uncle as she revised because this detail was irrelevant to the main idea of her essay.

> When I was only sixteen, I left home to attend a college in California ~~that my uncle had graduated from twenty years earlier~~.

When considering how much detail to include, you may sometimes want to write a long and fairly complex sentence. Just be sure that every detail contributes to the central thought, as in the following excerpt.

> A given mental task may involve a complicated web of circuits, which interact in varying degrees with others throughout the brain—not like the parts in a machine, but like the instruments in a symphony orchestra combining their tenor, volume, and resonance to create a particular musical effect.
>
> —JAMES SHREEVE, *Beyond the Brain*

By using parallel structures (see chapter 29) and careful punctuation, this writer has created a long, yet coherent, sentence.

Besides choosing details purposefully, you also need to indicate a clear connection between the details and the main idea of your sentence.

Unrelated	Many tigers facing possible extinction live in India, **where there are many people.**
Related	Many tigers facing possible extinction live in India, **where their natural habitat is shrinking because of population pressure.**

Exercise 1

Rewrite the following sentences so that the details clearly support the main idea. You may need to combine sentences or add words.

1. Firefighting is a dangerous job, but there are many high-tech devices and fire-resistant materials.
2. Wildfires can trap firefighters. Fire shelters are being developed to withstand temperatures as high as 2,000 degrees.
3. NASA developed Uninhabited Aerial Vehicles. Firefighters need to get accurate information fast.
4. Firefighters have difficulty seeing through smoke. A thermal imaging camera detects differences in heat and distinguishes between humans and surrounding objects.
5. Opticom is a traffic-control system, so firefighters can get to a fire quickly. They can change a red light to green from 2,000 feet away.

27b Including necessary words

When we speak or write quickly, we often omit small words. As you revise, be sure to include all necessary articles, prepositions, verbs, and conjunctions. Without the added article, the following sentence is incomplete.

> *an*
> The ceremony took place in ∧ auditorium.

Even though prepositions are sometimes omitted in speech, they should always be included in writing.

> *of*
> We discussed a couple ∧ issues at the meeting.

When a sentence has a **compound verb** (two verbs linked by a conjunction), you may need to supply a different preposition for each verb to make your meaning clear.

> *in*
> He neither **believes** ∧ nor **approves of** exercise.

All verbs, both auxiliary and main (see 26a(4)), should be included to make sentences complete.

has
She ∧ seen the movie three times.

been
Voter turnout has never ∧ and will never be 100 percent.

In sentences with two short clauses in which the second verb is exactly the same as the first, the second can be omitted.

The wind **was** fierce and the thunder [was] deafening.

Include the word *that* before a clause when it makes the sentence easier to read. Without the added *that* in the following sentence, a reader may stumble over *discovered the fossil* before understanding that *the fossil* is linked to *provided*.

that
The paleontologists discovered ∧ the fossil provided a link between the dinosaur and the modern bird.

That should always be retained when a sentence has two parallel clauses.

The graph indicated **that the population had increased** but **that the number of homeowners had not.**

A grammar checker will sometimes alert you to a missing word, but it will just as often fail to do so. It may also tell you that a word is missing when it is not. You are better off proofreading your work yourself.

27c Revising mixed metaphors

When you use language that evokes images, make sure that the images are meaningfully related. Unrelated images are called **mixed metaphors.** The following sentence includes incompatible images.

incurred a large
As he climbed the corporate ladder, he ~~sank into a sea of~~ debt.

The combination of two images—climbing a ladder and sinking into a sea—could create a picture in the reader's mind of a man hanging onto a ladder as it disappears into the water. The easiest way to revise such a sentence is to replace the words evoking one of the conflicting images.

27d Relating sentence parts

(1) Mixed constructions are illogical.

A sentence that begins with one kind of grammatical structure and shifts to another is a **mixed construction.** To untangle a mixed construction, make sure that the sentence includes a conventional subject—a noun, a noun phrase, a gerund phrase, an infinitive phrase, or a noun clause. Prepositional phrases and adverbial clauses are not typical subjects.

> *Practicing*
> ~~By practicing~~ a new language daily will help you become proficient.
> [A gerund phrase replaces a prepositional phrase.]

> *Her scholarship award*
> ~~Although she won a scholarship~~ does not give her the right to skip classes.
> [A noun phrase replaces an adverbial clause.]

If you find a sentence that has a mixed construction, you can either revise the subject, as in the previous examples, or leave the beginning of the sentence as a modifier and add a new subject after it.

> By practicing a new language daily, **you** will become more proficient.

> Although she won a scholarship, **she** does not have the right to skip classes.

(2) Sentence parts are linked together logically.

When drafting, writers sometimes compose sentences in which the subject is said to be something or to do something that is not logically possible. This breakdown in meaning is called **faulty predication.** Similarly, mismatches between a verb and its complement can obscure meaning.

(a) Mismatch between subject and verb
The joining of a subject and a verb must create a meaningful idea.

Mismatch	The absence of detail screams out at the reader.
	[An *absence* cannot scream.]
Revision	The reader immediately notices the absence of detail.

(b) Illogical equation with *be*

When a form of the verb *be* joins two parts of a sentence (the subject and the subject complement), these two parts should be logically related.

Speed
~~The importance of speed~~ is essential when you are walking on thin ice.

[*Importance* cannot be essential.]

(c) Mismatches in definitions

When you write a formal definition, be sure that your subject and predicate (see **20b**) fit together grammatically. The term being defined should be followed by a noun or a noun phrase, not an adverbial clause. Avoid using *is when* or *is where*.

Ecology is ~~when you~~ the study of the relationships among living organisms and between living organisms and their environment.

Exploitative competition is ~~where~~ the contest between two or more organisms ~~vie~~ vying for a limited resource such as food.

(d) Mismatch of *reason* with *is because*

You can see why *reason* and *is because* are a mismatch by looking at the meaning of *because*: "for the reason that." Saying "the reason is for the reason that" is redundant. Thus, revise any sentence containing the construction *the reason is . . . because.*

The ~~reason the~~ old train station was closed ~~is~~ because it had fallen into disrepair.

(e) Mismatch between verb and complement

A verb and its complement should fit together meaningfully.

Mismatch	Only a few students used the incorrect use of *there*.
	[To "use an incorrect use" is not logical.]
Revision	Only a few students used *there* incorrectly.

To make sure that a relative pronoun in the object position is connected logically to a verb, replace the pronoun with its antecedent. In the following sentence, *the inspiration* is the antecedent for *that*.

Mismatch   The inspiration that the author created touched young writers.
[To "create an inspiration" is not logical.]

Revision   The author inspired young writers.

(3) Verbs used to integrate information are followed by specific types of complements.

Attributive tags are phrases used to identify sources of information (see 11d(1)). Most verbs in attributive tags are followed by a noun clause beginning with *that* or a *wh-* word (21b(2)). A few common verbs and their typical complements are listed below. (Some verbs such as *explain* fall into more than one category.)

VERBS FOR ATTRIBUTION AND THEIR COMPLEMENTS

Verb + *that* noun clause

agree	claim	explain	report	suggest
argue	demonstrate	maintain	state	think

Example: The researcher **reported that the weather patterns had changed.**

Verb + noun phrase + *that* noun clause

convince	persuade	remind	tell

Example: He **told the reporters that he was planning to resign.**

Verb + *wh-* noun clause

demonstrate	discuss	report	suggest
describe	explain	state	wonder

Example: She **described what had happened.**

Exercise 2

Revise the following sentences so that each verb is followed by a conventional complement.

1. The committee chair discussed that funding requests had specific requirements.
2. He persuaded that mass transit was affordable.
3. The two groups agreed how the problem could be solved.
4. Brown and Edwards described that improvements had been made to the old building.
5. They wondered that such a catastrophe could happen.

27e Completing comparisons

A comparison has two parts: someone or something is compared to someone or something else. As you revise your writing, make sure that your audience knows who or what is being compared. To revise incomplete comparisons, add necessary words, phrases, or clauses.

Printers today are quite different~from those sold in the early 1990s~.

His first novel was better~than the one just published~.

After you are sure that your comparisons are complete, check to see that they are also logical.

Her test scores are higher than ~those of~ the other students.

In the original sentence, *scores* were being compared to *students*. You could also rewrite this sentence as follows:

Her test scores are higher than the other students'.

Because *test scores* have already been mentioned, it is clear that *students'* (with an apostrophe) is short for *students' test scores.*

27f | Completing intensifiers

In speech, the intensifiers *so, such,* or *too* are used to mean "very," "unusually," or "extremely."

> That movie was **so** funny.

In academic and professional writing, however, the intensifiers *so, such,* and *too* require a completing phrase or clause.

> That movie was **so** funny **that I watched it twice.**
>
> Julian has **such** a hearty laugh **that it makes everyone else laugh with him.**
>
> The problem is just **too** complex **to solve in one day.**

Exercise 3

Revise the following sentences to make them clear and complete.

1. By studying the villains' faces in the *Star Wars* movies can reveal popular notions about the look of evil.
2. To design the character of Darth Maul for *The Phantom Menace,* Iain McCaig started by illustrating a picture of his worst nightmare.
3. He drew generic male face with metal teeth and long red ribbons of hair falling in front of it.
4. Ralph McQuarrie sketched designs for R2D2 and Darth Vader, including his mask. McCaig wanted to create something scarier.
5. When after arriving at many dead ends, McCaig finally had an idea of what he wanted to do.
6. He designed a face that looked as though it been flayed.
7. The evil visage of Darth Maul was so horrible. To balance the effect, McCaig added elegant black feathers.
8. However, the need to add beauty was not shared by others on the production team, and the feathers eventually became small horns.

28 SUBORDINATION AND COORDINATION

Subordination and coordination both refer to the joining of grammatical structures. **Subordination** is the linking of grammatically unequal structures (usually a dependent clause to an independent clause). **Coordination** is the linking of structures that have the same grammatical rank (two independent clauses, for example). By using subordination and coordination, you indicate connections between ideas as well as add variety to your sentence style (see chapter 31). This chapter will help you

- use subordination effectively (28a),
- use coordination effectively (28b), and
- avoid faulty or excessive subordination and coordination (28c).

28a Using subordination effectively

Subordinate means "being of lower rank." A subordinate grammatical structure cannot stand alone; it is dependent on the main (independent) clause. The most common subordinate structure is the dependent clause (see 21b(2)), which usually begins with a subordinating conjunction or a relative pronoun.

(1) Subordinating conjunctions

A **subordinating conjunction** specifies the relationship between a dependent clause and an independent clause. For example, it might signal a causal relationship.

The painters finished early **because they work well together.**

Here are a few of the most frequently used subordinating conjunctions:

Cause	*because*
Concession	*although, even though*
Condition	*if, unless*
Effect	*so that*
Sequence	*before, after*
Time	*when*

By using subordinating conjunctions, you can combine short sentences and indicate how they are related.

After the *, we*
~~The~~ crew leader picked us up early on Friday. ~~We~~ ate breakfast together at a local diner.

If the subjects of the two clauses are the same, the dependent clause can often be shortened.

eating
After ~~we ate~~ our breakfast, we headed back to the construction site.

(2) Relative pronouns

A **relative pronoun** (*who, whom, which, that,* or *whose*) introduces a dependent clause that, in most cases, modifies the pronoun's antecedent. (See **25a(2)**.)

The temple has a <u>portico</u> **that faces west.**

By using a **relative clause**—that is, a dependent clause introduced by a relative pronoun—you can embed details into a sentence without sacrificing conciseness.

, which has sold well in the United States
Japanese automakers have produced a hybrid car.

A relative clause can be shortened, as long as the meaning of the sentence remains clear.

The runner ~~who was~~ from Brazil stumbled just before the finish line.

A relative clause beginning with *which* sometimes refers to an entire independent clause rather than modifying a specific word or phrase. Because this type of reference can be vague, you should avoid it if possible.

~~As~~
he should have
~~He~~ is a graduate of a top university, ~~which should provide him with~~ many opportunities.

28b Using coordination effectively

Coordinate means "being of equal rank." Coordinate grammatical elements have the same form. For example, they may be two words that are both adjectives, two phrases that are both prepositional, or two clauses that are both dependent or both independent.

a **stunning** and **satisfying** conclusion [adjectives]

in the attic or **in the basement** [prepositional phrases]

so that everyone would be happy and **so that no one would complain** [dependent adverbial clauses]

The company was losing money, yet **the employees suspected nothing.** [independent clauses]

To indicate the relationship between coordinate words, phrases, or clauses, choose an appropriate coordinating conjunction.

Addition	*and*
Alternative	*or, not*
Cause	*for*
Contrast	*but, yet*
Result	*so*

By using coordination, you can avoid unnecessary repetition and thus make your sentences more concise.

and
The hike to the top of Angels Landing has countless switchbacks ~~. It also has~~ long drop-offs.

Choosing Conjunctions
In English, use either a coordinating conjunction or a subordinating conjunction, but not both, to signal a connection between clauses.

Even though I took some aspirin, ~~but~~ I still have a sore shoulder.

Because he had a severe headache, ~~so~~ he went to the health center.

Alternatively, the clauses in these two example sentences can be connected with coordinating conjunctions, rather than subordinating conjunctions.

I took some aspirin, **but** I still have a sore shoulder.

He had a severe headache, **so** he went to the health center.

Exercise 1

Using subordination and coordination, revise the sentences in the following paragraph so that they emphasize the ideas you think are important.

¹The Lummi tribe lives in the Northwest. ²The Lummis have a belief about sorrow and loss. ³They believe that grief is a burden. ⁴According to their culture, this burden shouldn't be carried alone. ⁵After the terrorist attack on the World Trade Center, the Lummis wanted to help shoulder the burden of grief felt by others. ⁶Some of the Lummis carve totem poles. ⁷These carvers crafted a healing totem pole. ⁸They gave this pole to the citizens of New York. ⁹Many of the citizens of New York had family members who were killed in the terrorist attacks. ¹⁰The Lummis escorted the totem pole across the nation. ¹¹They made stops for small ceremonies. ¹²At these ceremonies, they offered blessings. ¹³They also offered songs. ¹⁴The Lummis don't believe that the pole itself heals. ¹⁵Rather, they believe that healing comes from the prayers and songs said over it. ¹⁶For them, healing isn't the responsibility of a single person. ¹⁷They believe that it is the responsibility of the community.

28c Avoiding faulty or excessive subordination and coordination

(1) Precise conjunctions enhance readability.

Effective subordination requires choosing subordinating conjunctions carefully. In the following sentence, the use of *as* is distracting because it can mean either "because" or "while."

Because
~~As~~ time was running out, I randomly filled in the remaining circles on the exam sheet.

Sometimes you may need to add a subordinating conjunction to a phrase for clarity. Without the addition of *although* in the revision of the following sentence, the connection between being a new player and winning games is unclear.

Although   *he won*
Chen was a new player, ~~winning~~ more than half of his games.

Your choice of coordinating conjunction should also convey your meaning precisely. For example, to indicate a cause-and-effect relationship, *so* is more precise than *and*.

so
The rain continued to fall, ~~and~~ the concert was canceled.

(2) Excessive subordination and coordination can confuse readers.

As you revise your writing, make sure that you have not overused subordination or coordination. In the following ineffective sentence, two dependent clauses compete for the reader's focus. The revision is clearer because it eliminates one of the dependent clauses.

Ineffective

Although researchers used to believe that ancient Egyptians were the first to domesticate cats, they now think that cats may have provided company for humans 5,000 years earlier **because** the intact skeleton of a cat has been discovered in a Neolithic village on Cyprus.

Revised

Although researchers used to believe that ancient Egyptians were the first to domesticate cats, they now think that cats may have provided company for humans 5,000 years earlier. They base their revised estimate on the discovery of an intact cat skeleton in a Neolithic village on Cyprus.

Overuse of coordination results in a rambling sentence in need of revision.

Ineffective

The lake was surrounded by forest, and it was large and clean, so it looked refreshing.

Revised

Surrounded by forest, the large, clean lake looked refreshing.

Exercise 2

Revise the following sentences to eliminate faulty or excessive coordination and subordination. Be prepared to explain why your sentences are more effective than the originals.

1. The Duct Tape Guys usually describe humorous uses for duct tape, providing serious information about the history of duct tape on their Web site.

2. Duct tape was invented for the U.S. military during World War II to keep the moisture out of ammunition cases because it was strong and waterproof.

3. Duct tape was originally called "duck tape" as it was waterproof and ducks are like that too and because it was made of cotton duck, which is a durable, tightly woven material.

4. Duck tape was also used to repair jeeps and to repair aircraft, its primary use being to protect ammunition cases.

5. When the war was over, house builders used duck tape to connect duct work together, and the builders started to refer to duck tape as "duct tape" and eventually the color of the tape changed from the green that was used during the war to silver, which matched the ducts.

29

PARALLELISM

Parallelism is the use of grammatically equivalent structures to clarify meaning and to emphasize ideas. Parallel structures often occur in a series.

> Their goals are **to raise awareness of the natural area, to build a walking path near the creek running through it,** and **to construct a nature center at the east end of the parking lot.**

This chapter will help you

- recognize parallel elements (**29a**),
- create parallelism by repeating words and grammatical forms (**29b**),
- use parallel elements to link sentences (**29c**),
- link parallel elements with correlative conjunctions (**29d**), and
- use parallelism for emphasis in introductions and conclusions (**29e**).

29a Recognizing parallel elements

Two or more elements are considered parallel when they have similar grammatical forms—for example, when they are all nouns or all prepositional phrases. Parallel elements are frequently joined by a coordinating conjunction (*and, but, or, yet, so, nor,* or *for*). In the examples that follow, the elements in boldface have the same grammatical form.

Words	The dean is both **determined** and **dedicated.**
Phrases	She emphasized her commitment to **academic freedom, professional development, cultural diversity,** and **social justice.**

Phrases	Her goals include **publicizing student and faculty research,** **increasing the funding for that research,** and **providing adequate research facilities.**
Clauses	Our instructor explained **what the project had entailed** and **how the results had been used.** He said **that we would conduct a similar project** but **that we would likely get different results.**
Sentences	When I interviewed for the job, <u>I tried not to sweat.</u> When I got the job, <u>I managed not to shout.</u>

Exercise 1

Write two sentences that illustrate each of the following structures: parallel words, parallel phrases, parallel clauses, and parallel sentences. Use the examples in this section as models.

29b Repeating words and grammatical forms

(1) The repetition of words often creates parallel elements.

By repeating a preposition, the infinitive marker *to,* or the introductory word of a clause, you can create parallel structures that will help you convey your meaning clearly, succinctly, and emphatically.

Preposition	For about fifteen minutes, I have been pacing in my office, hands **on** my hips, a scowl **on** my face, and a grudge **on** my mind. My embarrassment stemmed not **from** the money lost but **from** the notoriety gained.
Infinitive marker *to*	She wanted her audience **to remember** the protest song and **to understand** its origin.
Introductory word of a clause	The team vowed **that** they would support each other, **that** they would play their best, and **that** they would win the tournament.

(2) Parallel structures can be created through the repetition of form only.

Sometimes parallel structures are similar in form even though no words are repeated. The following example includes the *-ing* form (present participle) of three different verbs.

People all around me are **buying, remodeling,** or **selling** their houses.

The next example includes a compound dependent clause, each part of which has a two-word subject and a one-word predicate.

Whether **mortgage rates rise** or
building codes change, the real estate market should remain
strong this spring.

29c   Linking two or more sentences

Repeating a pattern emphasizes the relationship of ideas. The following two sentences come from the conclusion of "Letter from Birmingham Jail."

If I have said anything in this letter <u>that overstates the truth and indicates an unreasonable impatience,</u> I beg you to forgive me. **If I have said anything** <u>that understates the truth and indicates my having a patience</u> that allows me to settle for anything less than brotherhood, I beg God to forgive me.   —MARTIN LUTHER KING, JR.

Almost every structure in the second sentence is parallel to a structure in the first. To create this parallelism, King repeats words and uses similar grammatical forms. But the second sentence would still be parallel with the first even if more of its words were different. For example, substituting *written* for *said* and *reveals* for *indicates* ("If I have written anything that understates the truth and reveals my having a patience . . . ") would result in a sentence that was still parallel with the first sentence. Such changes, though, would lessen the impact of this particular passage because they would detract from the important substitution of "God" for "you" in the second sentence.

THINKING RHETORICALLY ABOUT

PARALLELISM

Parallel elements make your writing easy to read. But consider breaking from the parallel pattern on occasion to emphasize a point. For example, to describe a friend, you could start with two adjectives and then switch to a noun phrase.

My friend Alison is **kind, modest,** and **the smartest mathematician in the state.**

29d Using correlative conjunctions

Correlative conjunctions (or **correlatives**) are pairs of words that link other words, phrases, or clauses (see **20a(7)** and **21c(2)**).

both . . . and
either . . . or
neither . . . nor
not only . . . but also
whether . . . or

Notice how the words or phrases following each conjunction in the pair are parallel.

He will major in **either** <u>biology</u> **or** <u>chemistry</u>.

Whether <u>at home</u> **or** <u>at school</u>, he is always busy.

Be especially careful when using *not only . . . but also*.

His team not only practices

~~Not only practicing~~ at 6 a.m. during the week~~,~~ but ~~his team~~ also scrimmages on Sunday afternoons.

OR

does his team practice   it

Not only ~~practicing~~ at 6 a.m. during the week, but ~~the team~~ also scrimmages on Sunday afternoons.

29e Emphasizing key ideas in introductions and conclusions

By expressing key ideas in parallel structures, you emphasize them. However, be careful not to overuse parallel patterns, or they will lose their impact. Parallelism is especially effective in the introduction to a paragraph or an essay. The following passage from the introduction to a chapter of a book on advertising contains three examples of parallel forms.

> While **men are encouraged to fall in love with their cars, women are more often invited to have a romance,** indeed an erotic experience, with **something closer to home, something that truly does pump the valves of our hearts**—the food we eat. And the consequences become even more severe as we enter into the territory of **compulsivity** and **addiction.**
>
> —JEAN KILBOURNE, *Deadly Persuasion*

Parallel structures can also be effective in the conclusion to an essay.

> **Because these men work** with **animals,** not **machines, because they live** outside in landscapes of torrential beauty, **because they are confined** to **a place** and **a routine** embellished with awesome variables, **because calves die** in the arms that pulled others into life, **because they go** to the mountains as if on a pilgrimage to find out what makes a herd of elk tick, **their strength** is also **a softness, their toughness, a rare delicacy.**
>
> —GRETEL EHRLICH, "About Men"

BEYOND THE RULE

PARALLELISM AND POLITICS

Because parallelism helps make ideas easy to grasp and remember, it is frequently used by politicians when giving speeches. Some parallel structures have been used so often that they have become clichés. But others have helped to win elections or defined important moments in world history. For examples, visit **www.harbrace.com**.

Exercise 2

Make the structures in each sentence parallel. In some sentences, you may have to use different wording.

1. Helen was praised by the vice president, and her assistant admired her.

2. Colleagues found her genial and easy to schedule meetings with.

3. When she hired new employees for her department, she looked for applicants who were intelligent, able to stay focused, and able to speak clearly.

4. At meetings, she was always prepared, participating actively yet politely, and generated innovative responses to department concerns.

5. In her annual report, she wrote that her most important achievements were attracting new clients and revenues were higher.

6. When asked about her leadership style, she said that she preferred collaborating with others rather than to work alone in her office.

7. Although dedicated to her work, Helen also recognized that parenting was important and the necessity of cultivating a life outside of work.

8. She worked hard to save money for the education of her children, for her own music lessons, and investing for her retirement.

9. However, in the coming year, she hoped to reduce the number of weekends she worked in the office and spending more time at home.

10. She would like to plan a piano recital and also have the opportunity to plan a family vacation.

30

EMPHASIS

In any rhetorical situation, some of your ideas will be more important than others. You can direct the reader's attention to these ideas by emphasizing them. This chapter will help you

- place words where they receive emphasis (**30a**),
- use cumulative and periodic sentences (**30b**),
- arrange ideas in climactic order (**30c**),
- repeat important words (**30d**),
- choose between active voice and passive voice (**30e**),
- invert word order in sentences (**30f**), and
- use an occasional short sentence (**30g**).

You can also emphasize ideas by using subordination and coordination (chapter **28**), parallelism (chapter **29**), and exact word choice (chapter **33**).

30a Placing words for emphasis

Words at the beginning or the end of a sentence—especially the end—receive emphasis. Notice how the revision of the following sentence adds emphasis to the beginning to balance the emphasis at the end.

~~In today's society, most good~~ *Good* jobs *today* require a college education.

You can also emphasize an important idea by placing it after a colon or a dash. (See also **39d–e**.)

By "power" I mean precisely the capacity to do what force always does: coerce assent. —**CYNTHIA OZICK**

By 1857, miners had extracted 760 tons of gold from these hills—and left behind more than ten times as much mercury, as well as devastated forests, slopes and streams.   —REBECCA SOLNIT

Exercise 1

Find the most important idea in each set of sentences. Then combine each set into one sentence so that the most important idea is emphasized. Be prepared to explain your changes.

1. Snowboarding is a new sport. It debuted at the Olympics in 1998. The Olympics were held in Nagano, Japan, that year.

2. Snowboarders came from around the world. Some competed in the giant slalom. Others participated in the halfpipe.

3. Snowboarding has increased in popularity. Each year, more and more people go snowboarding. It attracted 50 percent more participants in 2000 than it did in 1999.

4. Snowboarding is a fast-growing sport. The number of snowboards sold each year has increased dramatically.

5. However, the inventor of the snowboard is hard to identify. People have been sliding down hills on sleds for a long time.

6. Some sources credit M. M. "Jack" Burchet. Burchet tied his feet to a piece of plywood in 1929.

7. Sherman Poppen is most frequently cited as the inventor of the snowboard. His Snurfer went into production in 1966. (The name is a combination of the words *snow* and *surfer*.)

8. Poppen created the Snurfer for his daughter. He bound two skis together. He also fixed a rope at the front end.

9. Snowboarding originated as a sport for kids. It eventually became a competitive sport.

10. The United States snowboarding team won two medals in the 1998 Olympic Games. The team won five medals in the 2002 Olympic Games.

30b Using cumulative and periodic sentences

In a **cumulative sentence,** the main idea (the independent clause) comes first; less important ideas or supplementary details follow.

> **The day was hot for June,** a pale sun burning in a cloudless sky, wilting the last of the irises, the rhododendron blossoms drooping.
>
> —ADAM HASLETT

In a **periodic sentence,** however, the main idea comes last, just before the period.

> In a day when movies seem more and more predictable, when novels tend to be plotless, baggy monsters or minimalist exercises in interior emotion, **it's no surprise that sports has come to occupy an increasingly prominent place in the communal imagination.**   —MICHIKO KAKUTANI

Both of these types of sentences can be effective. Because cumulative sentences are more common, however, the infrequently encountered periodic sentence tends to provide more emphasis.

30c Ordering ideas from least to most important

By arranging your ideas in **climactic order**—from least important to most important—you build up suspense. If you place your most important idea first, the sentence may seem to trail off. If you place it in the middle, readers may not recognize its full significance. If, however, you place it at the end of the sentence, it will not only receive emphasis but also provide a springboard to the next sentence. In the following example, the writer emphasizes a doctor's desire to help the disadvantaged and then implies that this desire has been realized through work with young Haitian doctors.

> While he was in medical school, the soon-to-be doctor discovered his calling: to diagnose infectious diseases, to find ways of curing people with these diseases, and **to bring the lifesaving knowledge of modern medicine to the disadvantaged.** Most recently, he has been working with a small group of young doctors in Haiti.

THINKING RHETORICALLY ABOUT

CLIMACTIC ORDER

Placing the least important idea at the end of the sentence can be effective when you are trying to be humorous, as in the following example:

> Contemporary man, of course, has no such peace of mind. He finds himself in the midst of a crisis of faith. He is what we fashionably call "alienated." He has seen the ravages of war, he has known natural catastrophes, he has been to singles bars. —**WOODY ALLEN**

30d Repeating important words

Although effective writers avoid unnecessary repetition, they also understand that deliberate repetition emphasizes key words or ideas.

> We **forget** all too soon the things we thought we could never **forget.** We **forget** the loves and betrayals alike, **forget** what we whispered and what we screamed, **forget** who we are. —**JOAN DIDION**

In this case, the emphatic repetition of *forget* reinforces the author's point—that we do not remember many things that once seemed impossible to forget. If you decide to repeat a word for emphasis, make sure that the word you choose conveys one of your central ideas.

30e Choosing between the active voice and the passive voice

(1) Sentences in the active and passive voices differ in form.

A sentence in the **active voice** emphasizes an actor and an action by having the actor as the subject. The **passive voice** emphasizes the receiver or the result of the action, with the actor often omitted entirely. (See **26d**.) If a reference to an actor is included in a passive sentence, this reference appears in a prepositional phrase beginning with *by.* The verb phrase in the passive voice also differs from its active counterpart: it includes the auxiliary verb *be* and the past participle of the main verb.

Active   Bob Dylan wrote that song.

Passive   That song **was written by** Bob Dylan.

(2) Sentences in the active voice highlight actors and actions.

The author of the following excerpt uses the active voice to describe the passage of an airplane and the passengers inside it.

> [1]The tiny red light of an airplane **passes** through the sky. [2]It **soars** past a low cloud, the North Star, the bold white W of Cassiopeia—vanishing and reappearing, winking in a long ellipsis. [3]Inside, its passengers **read** glossy periodicals, **summon** flight attendants, and **unhitch** the frames of their safety belts. [4]They **gaze** from the panes of double windows and **float** away in a tight red arc.   —KEVIN BROCKMEIER, "Space"

Notice how much less effective the third sentence is when written in the passive voice, with the emphasis on the actors removed.

> Inside, glossy periodicals **are read,** flight attendants **are summoned,** and the frames of safety belts **are unhitched.**

(3) Sentences in the passive voice emphasize recipients or objects of actions.

In a paragraph from a government-sponsored Web page that warns against the use of illicit drugs, the passive voice is used to discuss the drug methamphetamine. Paragraphs on users and producers of the drug are written primarily in the active voice, but the paragraph about the drug itself and the various ways in which it is used is written in the passive voice. Drug users and producers are not mentioned in this paragraph because the drug itself is the focus.

> Methamphetamine **can be ingested, inhaled,** or **injected.** It **is sold** as a powder or in small chunks which resemble rock candy. It **can be mixed** with water for injection or sprinkled on tobacco or marijuana and smoked. Chunks of clear, high-purity methamphetamine ("ice," "crystal," "glass") **are smoked** in a small pipe, much as "crack" cocaine **is smoked.**
>
> —UTAH ATTORNEY GENERAL'S OFFICE

Because whoever or whatever is responsible for the action is not the subject of a sentence in the passive voice, such a sentence is often imprecise. Politicians sometimes favor the passive voice because it allows them to avoid responsibility by saying, for example, "Taxes will have to be raised" or "A few miscalculations were made."

Grammar checkers flag all uses of the passive voice they find, usually suggesting that they be changed to the active voice. Be sure to determine for yourself whether the active voice or the passive voice is more appropriate for your rhetorical situation.

30f Inverting word order

Most sentences begin with a subject and end with a predicate. When you move words out of their normal order, you draw attention to them.

> <u>**At the back of the crowded room**</u> sat **a newspaper reporter.**
> [COMPARE: **A newspaper reporter** sat <u>**at the back of the crowded room.**</u>]

> <u>**Fundamental to life in New York**</u> is **the subway.**
> [COMPARE: **The subway** is <u>**fundamental to life in New York.**</u>]

A sentence with inverted word order will stand out in a paragraph containing other sentences with standard word order. Notice the inverted word order in the second sentence of the following passage.

> [1]The Library Committee met with the City Council on several occasions to persuade them to fund the building of a library annex. [2]So successful were their efforts that a new wing will be added by next year. [3]This wing will contain archival materials that were previously stored in the basement.

The modifier *so successful* appears at the beginning of the sentence, rather than in its normal position, after the verb: Their efforts were *so successful* that . . . . The inverted word order emphasizes the committee's accomplishment.

Inverting Word Order

English sentences are inverted in various ways. Sometimes the main verb in the form of a participle is placed at the beginning of the sentence. The subject and the auxiliary verb(s) are then inverted.

part   *aux*   *s*

Carved into the bench **were someone's initials.**

[COMPARE: Someone's initials were carved into the bench.]

An adjective may also begin a sentence. In this type of sentence, the subject and the linking verb are inverted.

adj   *link v*   *s*

Crucial to our success **was the dedication of our employees.**

[COMPARE: The dedication of our employees was crucial to our success.]

In other inverted sentences, the auxiliary verb comes before the subject. Sentences beginning with a negative adverb (such as *never, seldom,* or *rarely*) require this type of inversion.

neg adv   *aux*   *s*   *v*

Rarely have we experienced such bad weather!

30g   Using an occasional short sentence

In a paragraph of mostly long sentences, try using a short sentence for emphasis. To optimize the effect, lead up to the short sentence with an especially long sentence.

> After organizing the kitchen, buying the groceries, slicing the vegetables, mowing the lawn, weeding the garden, hanging the decorations, and setting up the grill, I was ready to have a good time when my guests arrived. **Then the phone rang.**

Exercise 2

Add emphasis to each of the following sentences by using the strategy indicated. You may have to add some words and/or delete others.

1. (climactic order) In the 1960 Olympics, Wilma Rudolph tied the world record in the 100-meter race, she tied the record in the 400-meter relay, she won the hearts of fans from around the world, and she broke the record in the 200-meter race.

2. (periodic sentence) Some sports reporters described Rudolph as a gazelle because of her beautiful stride.

3. (inversion) Rudolph's Olympic achievement is impressive, but her victory over a crippling disease is even more spectacular.

4. (final short sentence) Rudolph was born prematurely, weighing only four and one-half pounds. As a child, she suffered from double pneumonia, scarlet fever, and then polio.

5. (cumulative sentence) She received help from her family. Her brothers and sister massaged her legs. Her mother drove her to a hospital for therapy.

6. (inversion) Her siblings' willingness to help was essential to her recovery, as were her mother's vigilant care and her own determination.

7. (periodic sentence) Her passions became basketball and track after she recovered, built up her strength, and gained self-confidence.

8. (climactic order) Rudolph set a scoring record in basketball, she set the standard for future track and field stars, and she set an Olympic record in track.

9. (active voice) Many female athletes, including Florence Griffith Joyner and Jackie Joyner-Kersee, have been inspired by Wilma Rudolph.

VARIETY

To make your writing lively and distinctive, include a variety of sentence types and lengths. Notice how the sentences in the paragraph below vary in length (short and long), form (simple, compound, and compound-complex), and type (statements, questions, and commands). This assortment of sentences makes this paragraph about pleasure pleasurable to read.

> Start with the taste. Imagine a moment when the sensation of honey or sugar on the tongue was an astonishment, a kind of intoxication. The closest I've ever come to recovering such a sense of sweetness was secondhand, though it left a powerful impression on me even so. I'm thinking of my son's first experience with sugar: the icing on the cake at his first birthday. I have only the testimony of Isaac's face to go by (that, and his fierceness to repeat the experience), but it was plain that his first encounter with sugar had intoxicated him—was in fact an ecstasy, in the literal sense of the word. That is, he was beside himself with the pleasure of it, no longer here with me in space and time in quite the same way he had been just a moment before. Between bites Isaac gazed up at me in amazement (he was on my lap, and I was delivering the ambrosial forkfuls to his gaping mouth) as if to exclaim, "Your world contains *this?* From this day forward I shall dedicate my life to it." (Which he basically has done.) And I remember thinking, this is no minor desire, and then wondered: Could it be that sweetness is the prototype of *all* desire? —**MICHAEL POLLAN,** *The Botany of Desire*

This chapter will help you

- revise sentence length and form (**31a**),
- vary sentence openings (**31b**), and
- use an occasional question, command, or exclamation (**31c**).

If you have difficulty distinguishing between various types of sentence structures, review the fundamentals in chapters **20** and **21**.

31a   Revising sentence length and form

(1) Combine short sentences.

To avoid the choppiness of a series of short sentences, consider using one of the following methods to combine some of the sentences into longer sentences.

(a) Use coordinate or correlative conjunctions.

Try combining ideas using coordinate conjunctions (*and, but, or, for, nor, so,* and *yet*) or correlative conjunctions (*both . . . and, either . . . or, neither . . . nor,* and *not only . . . but also*).

Simple sentences	Minneapolis is one of the Twin Cities. St. Paul is the other. They differ in many ways.
Combined	Minneapolis **and** St. Paul are called the Twin Cities, **but** they differ in many ways.
Simple sentences	The company provides health insurance. It also provides dental insurance.
Combined	The company provides **both** health insurance **and** dental insurance.

(b) Use relative pronouns or subordinating conjunctions.

The relative pronouns *who, which, whose,* and *that* can be used to combine simple sentences.

Simple sentences	Today, lawmakers discussed some new legislation. This legislation would promote the safety of rocket passengers.
Combined	Today, lawmakers discussed some new legislation **that** would promote the safety of rocket passengers.

You can also use subordinating conjunctions such as *because, so that,* and *even though* to join simple sentences. For a full list, see page 499.

Simple sentences	Legislation on space tourism has not been passed. Plans for a commercial rocket service are going forward anyway.
Combined	**Although** legislation on space tourism has not been passed, plans for a commercial rocket service are going forward anyway.

You may also decide to use both a subordinating and a coordinating conjunction.

Simple sentences	Private rockets have been involved in very few accidents. Legislators are discussing safety issues, though. They have not agreed on any regulations yet.
Combined	**Although** private rockets have been involved in very few accidents, legislators are discussing safety issues, **but** they have not agreed on regulations yet.

Although a grammar checker will flag long sentences, it cannot determine whether they contribute to variety. You will have to decide whether you have used them effectively. See Using a Grammar Checker on page 461.

THINKING RHETORICALLY ABOUT

SHORT SENTENCES

Occasionally, a series of brief sentences produces an intended effect. For example, a writer may have a rhetorical reason for conveying a sense of abruptness; thus, what might seem choppy in one situation could be considered dramatic in another. The short sentences in the following passage capture the quick actions taking place as an accident is about to occur.

"There's a truck in your lane!" my friend yelled. I swerved toward the shoulder. "Watch out!" she screamed. I hit the brakes. The wheel locked. The back of the car swerved to the right.

Exercise 1

Convert each set of short sentences into a single longer sentence. Use no more than one coordinating conjunction in the revised sentence.

1. It was the bottom of the ninth inning. The score was tied. The bases were loaded. There were two outs.
2. A young player stepped up to the plate. This was his first season. He had hit a home run yesterday. He had struck out his last time at bat.
3. He knew the next pitch could decide the game. He took a practice swing. The pitcher looked him over.
4. The pitch came in high. The batter swung low. He missed this first pitch. He also missed the second pitch.
5. He had two strikes against him. The young player hit the next ball. It soared over the right-field fence.

(2) Avoid the overuse of coordinating conjunctions.

In early drafts, some writers overuse the coordinating conjunctions *and* and *but*, so the pattern of long compound sentences becomes tedious. The use of coordinating conjunctions can also be ineffective if the relationship the writer is signaling is vague. The following strategies should help you revise ineffective uses of coordinating conjunctions.

(a) Use a more specific subordinating conjunction or conjunctive adverb.
You can often replace *and* with a more specific subordinating conjunction or conjunctive adverb (see **21c**).

I worked all summer to earn tuition money, ~~and I didn't~~ *so that I wouldn't* have to work during the school year.

OR

I worked all summer to earn tuition money and **thus** didn't have to work during the school year.

(b) Use a relative clause to embed information.

Seafood ~~is nutritious, and it is low in fat, and it~~ *, which is nutritious and low in fat,* has become available in greater variety.

(c) Allow two or more verbs to share the same subject.

Marie quickly grabbed a shovel, ~~and then she~~ ran to the edge of the field, and ~~then she~~ put out the fire before it could spread to the trees.

(d) Place some information in an appositive phrase.

, a researcher in astronomy at Johns Hopkins University,

Karl Glazebrook ˄ ~~is a researcher in astronomy at Johns Hopkins University, and he~~ has questioned the conventional theory of galaxy formations.

(e) Place some information in a prepositional or verbal phrase.

In the thick snow,

˄ ~~The snow was thick, and~~ we could not see where we were going.

After pulling   the plane

˄ ~~The plane pulled~~ away from the gate on time, ~~and then it~~ sat on the runway for two hours.

OR

The plane, after pulling away from the gate on time, sat on the runway for two hours.

In the last example, the subject, *plane*, and the verb, *sat,* are separated. Although it is usually best to keep the subject next to the verb so that the relationship between them is clear, breaking this pattern on occasion can add variety without sacrificing clarity.

Exercise 2

Revise the following paragraph, using any of the methods for revising the ineffective use of coordinating conjunctions.

¹Onions are pungent, they are indispensable, and they are found in kitchens everywhere. **²**China is the leading producer of this vegetable. **³**Libya is the leading consumer, and on average a Libyan eats over sixty-five pounds of onions a year. **⁴**One hundred billion pounds of onions are produced each year, and they make their way into a variety of foods. ⁵Raw onions add zest to salads, but they also add zest to burgers and salsas. ⁶Cooked onions give a sweetness to pasta sauces, and they can also be added to soups and curries. ⁷The onion is a ubiquitous ingredient, yet its origin remains unknown.

31b Varying sentence openings

Most writers begin more than half of their sentences with the subject. Although this pattern is common, relying on it too heavily can make writing sound dull. Experiment with the following alternatives for beginning your sentences.

(1) Begin with an adverb or an adverbial clause.

Immediately, the dentist stopped drilling and asked me how I was doing. [adverb]

When the procedure was over, he explained that I should not eat or drink anything for an hour. [adverbial clause]

(2) Begin with a prepositional or verbal phrase.

In the auditorium, voters waited in silence before casting their ballots. [prepositional phrase]

To win, candidates need to convey a clear message to voters. [infinitive phrase]

Reflecting on the election, we understood clearly how the incumbent defeated the challenger. [participial phrase]

(3) Begin with a connecting word or phrase.

In each of the following examples, the connecting word or phrase shows the relationship between the ideas in the pair of sentences. (See also 4d.)

Many restaurants close within a few years of opening. **But** others, which offer good food at reasonable prices, become well established.

Difficulty in finding a place to park keeps some people from going out to lunch downtown. **However,** that problem may be alleviated with the construction of a new underground parking garage.

Independently owned restaurants struggle to get started for a number of reasons. **First of all,** they have to compete against successful restaurant chains.

(4) Begin with an appositive or absolute phrase.

A town of historic interest, Santa Fe also has many art galleries. [appositive phrase]

History, art, and the color of the sky—these drew her to Santa Fe. [appositive series]

Her face turned to the sky, she absorbed the warmth of the sun. [absolute phrase]

(5) Begin with a direct object or a predicate adjective.

I was an abysmal football player. **Soccer,** though, I could play well. [direct object]

Vital to any success I had were my mother's early lessons. [predicate adjective]

Exercise 3

Rewrite each sentence so that it does not begin with a subject.

1. John Spilsbury was an engraver and mapmaker from London who made the first jigsaw puzzle in about 1760.
2. He pasted a map onto a piece of wood and used a fine-bladed saw to cut around the borders of the countries.
3. The jigsaw puzzle was first an educational toy and has been a mainstay in households all over the world ever since its invention.
4. The original puzzles were quite expensive because the wooden pieces were cut by hand.
5. Most puzzles are made of cardboard today.

31c Using questions, commands, and exclamations

When you have written a long series of declarative statements, you can vary the paragraph by introducing another type of sentence: a question, a command, or an exclamation (see **21e**). The sentence that varies from the others will catch the reader's attention.

Just as variety in the elements of an image draws the viewer's attention, variety in sentences catches the reader's attention.

(1) Raise a question or two for variety.

If people could realize that immigrant children are better off, and less scarred, by holding on to their first languages as they learn a second one, then perhaps Americans could accept a more drastic change. What if every English-speaking toddler were to start learning a foreign language at an early age, maybe in kindergarten? What if these children were to learn Spanish, for instance, the language already spoken by millions of American citizens, but also by so many neighbors to the South?

—ARIEL DORFMAN

You can either answer the question or let readers answer it for themselves, in which case it is called a **rhetorical question** (see **21e**).

(2) Add an exclamatory sentence for variety.

But at other moments, the classroom is so lifeless or painful or confused— and I so powerless to do anything about it—that my claim to be a teacher seems a transparent sham. Then the enemy is everywhere: in those students from some alien planet, in the subject I thought I knew, and in the personal pathology that keeps me earning my living this way. What a fool I was to imagine that I had mastered this occult art—harder to divine than tea leaves and impossible for mortals to do even passably well!

—PARKER PALMER, *The Courage to Teach*

Although you can make your sentences emphatic without resorting to the use of exclamation points (see chapter 30), the introduction of an exclamatory sentence can break up a regular pattern of declarative sentences.

(3) Include a command for variety.

> Now I stare and stare at people shamelessly. Stare. It's the way to educate your eye. —WALKER EVANS

In this case, a one-word command, "Stare," provides variety.

Exercise 4

Explain how questions and commands add variety to the following paragraph. Describe other ways in which this writer varies his sentences.

[1]The gods, they say, give breath, and they take it away. [2]But the same could be said—couldn't it?—of the humble comma. [3]Add it to the present clause, and, of a sudden, the mind is, quite literally, given pause to think; take it out if you wish or forget it and the mind is deprived of a resting place. [4]Yet still the comma gets no respect. [5]It seems just a slip of a thing, a pedant's tick, a blip on the edge of our consciousness, a kind of printer's smudge almost. [6]Small, we claim, is beautiful (especially in the age of the microchip). [7]Yet what is so often used, and so rarely recalled, as the comma—unless it be breath itself?

> —PICO IYER, "In Praise of the Humble Comma"

An inclusive advertisement appeals to a diverse audience.

GOOD USAGE

Using the right words at the right time can make the difference between having your ideas taken seriously and seeing them brushed aside. In academic or professional writing, it is important to sound well informed and respectful. In conversation with friends, it is just as important to sound casual; otherwise, your friends may think that you are cold or snobbish. Whatever the occasion, choosing the right words will help you connect with your audience. This chapter will help you

- understand how word choice is related to the rhetorical situation (32a),
- write in a clear, straightforward style (32b),
- choose words that are appropriate for your audience, purpose, and context (32c),
- use inclusive language (32d), and
- realize the benefits of dictionaries (32e) and thesauruses (32f).

32a Usage and the rhetorical situation

The words you use vary from situation to situation. How you talk to a loan officer differs from how you talk to your best friend. A discussion with a loan officer is likely to be relatively formal, while a conversation with a friend will be less so. Understanding such differences in tone and making word choices that reflect them are essential in writing because readers cannot see your body language, hear the inflections of your voice, or interrupt to say that they are having trouble following you. Instead, readers respond to the words on the page or the screen. You can help them understand your ideas by choosing words that they know or that you can explain to them. When drafting, use words that come immediately to mind. Some of these words will be good choices. Others you can replace as you revise. Remembering your rhetorical situation will help you use the right word at the right time.

32b Clear style

Although different styles are appropriate for different situations, you should strive to make your writing clear and straightforward. An ornate and wordy style takes more time to read and could make you seem stuffy or pretentious. To achieve a clear style, first choose words that your audience understands and that are appropriate for the occasion.

Ornate　　　The majority believes that achievement derives primarily from the diligent pursuit of allocated tasks.

Clear　　　Most people believe that success results from hard work.

When you write clearly, you show your readers that you are aware of the time and effort it takes to read closely. If you want readers to take your writing seriously, you must show them respect by not using obscure words when common words will do and by not using more words than necessary. Using words that are precise (see **33a**) and sentences that are concise (see chapter **34**) can also help you achieve a clear style.

Exercise 1

Revise the following sentences for an audience that prefers a clear, straightforward style.

1. Expert delineation of character in a job interview is a task that is not always possible to achieve.
2. In an employment situation, social pleasantries may contribute to the successful functioning of job tasks, but such interactions should not distract attention from the need to complete all assignments in a timely manner.
3. Commitment to an ongoing and carefully programmed schedule of physical self-management can be a significant resource for stress reduction in the workplace.

32c Appropriate word choice

Unless you are writing for a specialized audience and have good reason to believe that this audience will welcome slang, colloquial expressions, or jargon, the following advice can help you determine which words to use and which to avoid.

(1) Slang is effective in only a few rhetorical situations.

The term **slang** covers a wide range of words or expressions that are considered casual, facetious, or fashionable by people in a particular age group, locality, or profession. Although such words are often used in private conversation or in writing intended to mimic conversation, they are usually out of place in academic or professional writing. If your rhetorical situation does call for the use of slang, be sure that the words or expressions you choose are not so new that your audience will be unable to understand what you mean and not so old that your use of them makes you seem out of touch with popular culture.

(2) Conversational (or colloquial) words are usually too informal for academic and professional writing.

Words labeled *colloquial* in a dictionary are fine for casual conversation and for written dialogues or personal essays on a light topic. Such words are sometimes used for special effect in academic writing, but you should usually replace them with more appropriate words. For example, conversational words such as *dumb* and *kid around* could be replaced by *illogical* and *tease.*

 Because contractions (such as *you'll* for "you will" and *she's* for "she is") reflect the sound of conversation, you can use them in some types of writing to create a friendly tone. However, some of your instructors or supervisors may consider them too informal for academic or professional writing.

(3) Regionalisms can make writing vivid.

Regionalisms—such as *tank* for "pond" and *sweeper* for "vacuum cleaner"—can make writing lively and distinctive, but they are effective only when the audience can understand them in a specific context.

Moreover, many readers consider regionalisms too informal for use in academic and professional writing. Consider your rhetorical situation before using regionalisms.

(4) Technical words are essential when writing for specialists.

When writing for a diverse audience, an effective writer will not refer to the need for bifocals as *presbyopia*. However, technical language is appropriate when the audience can understand it (as when one physician writes to another) or when the audience would benefit by learning the terms in question.

Jargon is technical language tailored specifically for a particular occupation. Jargon can be an efficient shortcut for conveying specialized concepts, but you should use it only when you are sure that you and your readers share an understanding of the terms. *Splash,* for example, does not always refer to water or an effect (as in *making a splash*); the word also signifies a computer screen that can appear after you click on a Web site but before you view its opening page.

BEYOND THE RULE

FROM JARGON TO ACCEPTABILITY

Terms that originate as jargon sometimes enter mainstream usage because nonspecialists begin to use them. As computer use has grown, for example, technical terms such as *download* and *mouse* have become commonly understood. For additional examples of widely adopted jargon, visit **www.harbrace.com**.

32d Inclusive language

By making word choices that are inclusive rather than exclusive, you invite readers into your writing. Advertisers follow a similar principle when they choose images that appeal to a diverse audience. Prejudiced or derogatory language has no place in academic or professional writing; using it undermines your authority and credibility as a writer.

Even if you are writing for one person you think you know well, do not assume that you know everything about that person. A close colleague at work might have an uncle who is gay, for example, or his sister might be married to someone of a different race or religion. Do not try to justify demeaning language on the grounds that you meant it as a joke. Take responsibility for the words you use.

An inclusive advertisement appeals to a diverse audience.

(1) Nonsexist language indicates respect for both men and women.

Effective writers show equal respect for men and women. For example, they avoid using *man* to refer to people in general because they feel that the word excludes women.

> Achievements [OR Human achievements]
> **Man's** achievements in science are impressive.

Sexist language has a variety of sources, such as contempt for the opposite sex and unthinking repetition of words used by others. Stereotyping can also lead to sexist language. Women, like men, can be *firefighters* or *police officers*—words that are increasingly used as gender-neutral alternatives to *firemen* and *policemen*.

A grammar checker can find sexist words ending in -ess *(authoress)* or -man *(policeman)* and almost always flags *mankind*. Unfortunately, grammar checkers also erroneously identify as sexist many appropriate uses of the words *female, woman,* and *girl,* but not similar uses of *male, man,* and *boy.*

Being alert for sexist language and knowing how to revise it will help you gain acceptance from your audience, whatever its demographics. Use the following tips to ensure that your writing is respectful.

TIPS FOR AVOIDING SEXIST LANGUAGE

When you review your drafts, revise the following types of sexist language.

- **Generic *he:*** A doctor should listen to *his* patients.

  A doctor should listen to **his or her** patients. [use of the appropriate form of *he or she*]

  Doctors should listen to **their** patients. [use of plural forms]

  By listening to patients, **doctors obtain important diagnostic information.** [elimination of *his* by revising the sentence]

- **Occupational stereotype:** Glenda James, a *female* engineer at Howard Aviation, won the best-employee award.

  Glenda James, an engineer at Howard Aviation, won the best-employee award. [removal of the unnecessary gender reference]

- **Terms such as *man* and *mankind* or those with *-ess* or *-man* endings:** Labor laws benefit the common *man. Mankind* benefits from philanthropy. The *stewardess* brought me some orange juice.

  Labor laws benefit **working people.** [replacement of the stereotypical term with a gender-neutral term]

  Everyone benefits from philanthropy. [use of an indefinite pronoun]

  The **flight attendant** brought me some orange juice. [use of a gender-neutral term]

- **Stereotypical gender roles:** I was told that the university offers free tuition to faculty *wives.* The minister pronounced them *man* and wife.

  I was told that the university offers free tuition to faculty **spouses.** [replacement of the stereotypical term with a gender-neutral term]

The minister pronounced them **husband** and wife. [use of a term equivalent to *wife*]

- **Inconsistent use of titles:** *Mr. Holmes* and his *wife,* Mary, took a long trip to China.

  Mr. and Mrs. [or Ms.] Holmes took a long trip to China. [consistent use of titles]

  OR **Peter and Mary Holmes** took a long trip to China. [removal of titles]

  OR **Peter Holmes** and **Mary Wolfe** took a long trip to China. [use of full names]

- **Unstated gender assumption:** Have your *mother make your costume* for the school pageant.

  Have your **parents provide you with a costume** for the school pageant. [replacement of the stereotypical words with gender-neutral ones]

Exercise 2

Make the following sentences inclusive by eliminating sexist language.

1. The ladies met to discuss the company's current operating budget.
2. The old boys run the city's government.
3. Mothers should read to their small children.
4. Some fans admired the actress because of her movies; others praised her for her environmental activism.
5. For six years, he worked as a mailman in a small town.

(2) Nonracist language promotes social equity.

Rarely is it necessary to identify anyone's race or ethnicity in academic or professional writing. However, you may need to use appropriate racial or ethnic terms if you are writing a demographic report, an argument against existing racial inequities, or a historical account of a particular event involving ethnic groups. Determining which terms a particular group prefers can be difficult because preferences sometimes vary within a group and change over time. One conventional way to refer to Americans of a specific descent is to include an adjective before the word *American*: *African American, Asian American, European*

American, Latin American, Mexican American, Native American. These words are widely used; however, members of a particular group may identify themselves in more than one way. In addition to *African American* and *European American, Black* (or *black*) and *White* (or *white*) have long been used. People of Spanish-speaking descent may prefer *Chicano/Chicana, Hispanic, Latino/Latina, Puerto Rican,* or other terms. Members of cultures that are indigenous to North America may prefer a specific name such as *Cherokee* or *Haida,* though some also accept *American Indian.* An up-to-date dictionary that includes notes on usage can help you choose appropriate terms.

(3) Writing about any type of difference should be respectful.

If a writing assignment requires you to distinguish people based on age, ability, geographical area, religion, or sexual orientation, show respect to the groups or individuals you discuss by using the terms they prefer.

(a) Referring to age

Although some people object to the term *senior citizen,* a better alternative has not been provided. When used respectfully, the term refers to a person who has reached the age of retirement (but may not have decided to retire) and is eligible for certain privileges granted by society. However, if you know your audience would object to this term, find out which alternative is preferred.

(b) Referring to disabilities or illness

A current recommendation for referring to disabilities and illnesses is "to put the person first." In this way, the focus is placed on the individual rather than on the limitation. Thus, *persons with disabilities* is preferred over *disabled persons.* For your own writing, you can find out whether such person-first expressions are preferred by noting whether they are used in the articles and books (or by the people) you consult. Be aware, though, that some writers and readers think that these types of expressions sound unnatural, and others maintain that they do not serve their intended purpose because the last word in a phrase can carry the greater weight, especially at the end of a sentence.

(c) Referring to geographical areas

Certain geographical terms need to be used with special care. Though most frequently used to refer to people from the United States, the term *American* may also refer to people from Canada, Mexico, and Central or South America. If your audience may be confused by this term, use *people from the United States* or *U.S. citizens* instead.

The term *Arab* refers to people who speak Arabic. If you cannot use specific terms such as *Iraqi* or *Saudi Arabian,* be sure you know that a country's people speak Arabic and not another language. Iranians, for example, are not Arabs because they speak Farsi.

British, rather than *English,* is the preferred term for referring to people from the island of Great Britain or from the United Kingdom.

(d) Referring to religion

Reference to a person's religion should be made only if it is relevant to your rhetorical situation. If you must mention religious affiliation, use only those terms considered respectful. Because religions have both conservative and liberal followers, be careful not to make generalizations about political stances (see 8i(12)).

(e) Referring to sexual orientation

If your rhetorical situation calls for identifying sexual orientation, choose terms used by the people you are discussing. The words *gay, lesbian,* and *bisexual* are generally used as adjectives. Their use as nouns to refer to specific people may be considered offensive.

CHECKLIST for Assessing Usage within a Rhetorical Situation

- Do your words convey the meaning you intend?
- Can your audience understand the words you have used?
- Do you explain any words your audience might not understand?
- Have you used any words that could irritate or offend members of your audience?
- Do any of your words make you sound too casual or too formal?
- Do your words help you to fulfill your rhetorical purpose?
- Are your words appropriate for the context in which you are writing?
- Are your words appropriate for the context in which they will be read?

32e Dictionaries

A good dictionary is an indispensable tool for writers. Desk dictionaries such as *The American Heritage Dictionary* and *Merriam-Webster's Collegiate Dictionary* do much more than provide the correct spellings of words; they also give meanings, parts of speech, plural forms, and verb tenses, as well as information about pronunciation and origin. In addition, a reliable dictionary also includes labels that can help you decide whether words are appropriate for the purpose, audience, and context of your writing. Words labeled *dialect, slang, colloquial, nonstandard,* or *unconventional,* as well as those labeled *archaic* or *obsolete* (meaning that they are no longer in common use), are generally inappropriate for college and professional writing. If a word has no label, you can safely assume that it can be used in writing for school or work. But whether the word is appropriate depends on the precise meaning a writer wants to convey (see 33a). Because language is constantly changing, it is important to choose a desk dictionary with a recent copyright date. Many dictionaries are available—in print, online, or on CD-ROM. Pocket dictionaries, which are useful for checking spellings and definitions, omit important information on usage and derivation. The dictionaries incorporated into most word-processing programs are equivalent to pocket dictionaries and may provide insufficient information.

(1) Consulting an unabridged or special dictionary can enhance your understanding of a word.

An **unabridged dictionary** provides a comprehensive survey of English words, including detailed information about their origins. A **specialized dictionary** presents words related to a specific discipline or to some aspect of usage.

Unabridged Dictionaries

The Oxford English Dictionary. 2nd ed. 20 vols. 1989– . CD-ROM. 1994.

Webster's Third New International Dictionary of the English Language. CD-ROM. 2003.

Specialized Dictionaries

The American Heritage Dictionary of Idioms. 1997.

The American Heritage Guide to Contemporary Usage and Style. 2005.

The BBI Dictionary of English Word Combinations. 1997.

The New Fowler's Modern English Usage. 3rd ed. 2000.

Merriam-Webster's Dictionary of English Usage. 1994.

Dictionaries and Other Resources
The following dictionaries are recommended for nonnative speakers of English.

Collins Cobuild New Student's Dictionary. 2002.

Longman Advanced American English. 2000.

Heinle's Newbury House Dictionary of American English. 4th ed. 2003.

Two excellent resources for ESL students are the following:

Longman Language Activator. 2003. (A cross between a dictionary and a thesaurus, this book supplies definitions, usage guidelines, and sample sentences.)

Swan, Michael. *Practical English Usage.* 3rd ed. 2005. (This is a practical reference guide to problems encountered by those who speak English as a second language.)

---

(2) Dictionary entries provide a range of information.

Figure 32.1 shows sample entries from the tenth edition of *Merriam-Webster's Collegiate Dictionary.* Notice that *move* is listed twice—first as a verb, then as a noun. The types of information these entries provide can be found in almost all desk dictionaries, though sometimes in a different order.

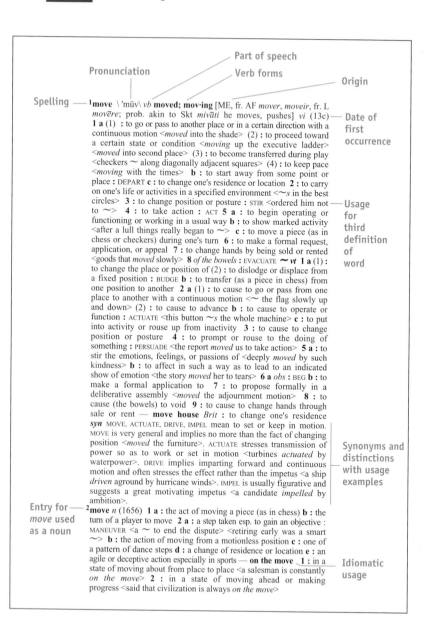

Spelling

Pronunciation

Part of speech

Verb forms

Origin

Date of first occurrence

Usage for third definition of word

Synonyms and distinctions with usage examples

Entry for *move* used as a noun

Idiomatic usage

¹**move** \ 'müv\ *vb* **moved; mov·ing** [ME, fr. AF *mover, moveir*, fr. L *movēre*; prob. akin to Skt *mivāti* he moves, pushes] *vi* (13c) **1 a** (1) : to go or pass to another place or in a certain direction with a continuous motion <*moved* into the shade> (2) : to proceed toward a certain state or condition <*moving* up the executive ladder> <*moved* into second place> (3) : to become transferred during play <checkers ~ along diagonally adjacent squares> (4) : to keep pace <*moving* with the times> **b** : to start away from some point or place : DEPART **c** : to change one's residence or location **2** : to carry on one's life or activities in a specified environment <~*s* in the best circles> **3** : to change position or posture : STIR <ordered him not to ~> **4** : to take action : ACT **5 a** : to begin operating or functioning or working in a usual way **b** : to show marked activity <after a lull things really began to ~> **c** : to move a piece (as in chess or checkers) during one's turn **6** : to make a formal request, application, or appeal **7** : to change hands by being sold or rented <goods that *moved* slowly> **8** *of the bowels* : EVACUATE ~ *vt* **1 a** (1) : to change the place or position of (2) : to dislodge or displace from a fixed position : BUDGE **b** : to transfer (as a piece in chess) from one position to another **2 a** (1) : to cause to go or pass from one place to another with a continuous motion <~ the flag slowly up and down> (2) : to cause to advance **b** : to cause to operate or function : ACTUATE <this button ~*s* the whole machine> **c** : to put into activity or rouse up from inactivity **3** : to cause to change position or posture **4** : to prompt or rouse to the doing of something : PERSUADE <the report *moved* us to take action> **5 a** : to stir the emotions, feelings, or passions of <deeply *moved* by such kindness> **b** : to affect in such a way as to lead to an indicated show of emotion <the story *moved* her to tears> **6 a** *obs* : BEG **b** : to make a formal application to **7** : to propose formally in a deliberative assembly <*moved* the adjournment motion> **8** : to cause (the bowels) to void **9** : to cause to change hands through sale or rent — **move house** *Brit* : to change one's residence **syn** MOVE, ACTUATE, DRIVE, IMPEL mean to set or keep in motion. MOVE is very general and implies no more than the fact of changing position <*moved* the furniture>. ACTUATE stresses transmission of power so as to work or set in motion <turbines *actuated* by waterpower>. DRIVE implies imparting forward and continuous motion and often stresses the effect rather than the impetus <a ship *driven* aground by hurricane winds>. IMPEL is usually figurative and suggests a great motivating impetus <a candidate *impelled* by ambition>.

²**move** *n* (1656) **1 a** : the act of moving a piece (as in chess) **b** : the turn of a player to move **2 a** : a step taken esp. to gain an objective : MANEUVER <a ~ to end the dispute> <retiring early was a smart ~> **b** : the action of moving from a motionless position **c** : one of a pattern of dance steps **d** : a change of residence or location **e** : an agile or deceptive action especially in sports — **on the move 1** : in a state of moving about from place to place <a salesman is constantly *on the move*> **2** : in a state of moving ahead or making progress <said that civilization is always *on the move*>

Fig. 32.1. Examples of dictionary entries.

TYPES OF INFORMATION PROVIDED BY DICTIONARY ENTRIES

- **Spelling, syllabication (word division), and pronunciation**
- **Parts of speech and word forms.** Dictionaries identify parts of speech—for instance, with *n* for "noun" or *vi* for "intransitive verb." Meanings will vary depending on the part of speech identified. Dictionaries also identify irregular forms of verbs, nouns, and adjectives: *fly, flew, flown, flying, flies; child, children; good, better, best.*
- **Word origin**
- **Date of first occurrence**
- **Definition(s).** Generally, the oldest meaning is given first. However, meanings can also be ordered according to common usage.
- **Usage.** Quotations show how the word can be used in various contexts. Sometimes a comment on usage problems is placed at the end of the entry.
- **Idioms.** When the word is part of a common idiom (see **33c**), the idiom is listed and defined, usually at the end of the entry.
- **Synonyms.** Some dictionaries provide explanations of subtle differences in meaning among a word's synonyms.

Exercise 3

Study the definitions for the pairs of words in parentheses. Then choose the word you think best completes each sentence. Be prepared to explain your answers.

1. Sixteen prisoners on death row were granted (mercy/clemency).
2. The outcome of the election (excited/provoked) a riot.
3. The young couple was (covetous/greedy) of their neighbors' estate.
4. While she was traveling in Muslim countries, she wore (modest/chaste) clothing.
5. The president of the university (authorized/confirmed) the rumor that tuition would be increasing next year.

32f Thesauruses

A **thesaurus** provides alternatives for frequently used words. Unlike a dictionary, which explains what a word means and how it evolved, a thesaurus provides only a list of words that serve as possible synonyms for each term it includes. A thesaurus can be useful, especially when you want to jog your memory about a word you know but cannot recall. You may, however, use a word incorrectly if you simply pick it from a list in a thesaurus. If you find an unfamiliar yet intriguing word, make sure that you are using it correctly by looking it up in a dictionary. Several print thesauruses are available. Among them are *Roget's International Thesaurus* (2002) and *Merriam-Webster's Collegiate Thesaurus* (1994). Most word-processing programs include a thesaurus, and other thesauruses are available online.

Exercise 4

Review two or three of your recent papers, and find a word you used frequently. Look up that word in a thesaurus, and then check each possible synonym in a dictionary. Use one of these synonyms appropriately in a sentence, and explain why your usage is correct.

33

EXACTNESS

Make words work for you. By choosing the right word and putting it in the right place, you can communicate exactly what you mean and make your writing memorable. When drafting, choose words that express your ideas and feelings. Then, when revising, make those words precise and fresh. Use the words that you already know effectively, but add to your vocabulary regularly so that you can pick the exact words to suit your purpose, audience, and context. This chapter will help you

- master the denotations and connotations of words (**33a**),
- use fresh, clear expressions (**33b**),
- understand how to use idioms and collocations (**33c**),
- use the first- and second-person pronouns appropriately (**33d**), and
- compose clear definitions (**33e**).

33a Accurate and precise word choice

(1) A denotation is the literal meaning of a word.

Denotations are definitions of words, such as those that appear in dictionaries. For example, the noun *beach* denotes a sandy or pebbly shore. Select words whose denotations convey your point exactly.

Yosemite National Park ~~is really great.~~ *astounds even an indifferent tourist like me.*

[Because *great* can mean "extremely large" as well as "outstanding" or "powerful," its use in this sentence is imprecise.]

The speaker ~~inferred~~ *implied* that the team attracted many new fans this year.

[*Imply* means "to suggest," so *implied* is the exact word for this sentence. *Infer* means "to draw a conclusion from evidence": From the figures before me, I *inferred* that the team attracted many new fans this year.]

(2) A connotation is the indirect meaning of word.

Connotations are the associations evoked by a word. *Beach,* for instance, may connote natural beauty, surf, shells, swimming, tanning, sunburn, and/or crowds. The context in which a word appears affects the associations it evokes. In a treatise on shoreline management, *beach* has scientific and geographic connotations; in a fashion magazine, this word is associated with bathing suits, sunglasses, and sunscreen. Most readers carry with them a wealth of personal, often emotional, associations that can influence how they respond to the words on a page. The challenge for writers is to choose the words that are most likely to spark the appropriate connotations in their readers' minds.

Mr. Kreuger's ~~relentlessness~~ *persistence* has earned praise from his supervisors.

[*Relentlessness* has negative connotations, which make it an unlikely quality for which to be praised.]

I love the ~~odor~~ *aroma* of freshly baked bread.

[Many odors are unpleasant; *aroma* sounds more positive, especially in association with food.]

Connotations
Your ability to recognize connotations will improve as your vocabulary increases. When you learn a new word that seems to mean exactly what another word means, study the context in which each word is used. Then, to help yourself remember the new word, create a phrase or a sentence in which that word is used in the context you studied. If you are confused about the connotations of specific words, consult an ESL dictionary (see page 659).

(3) Specific, concrete words provide readers with helpful details.

A **general word** is all-inclusive, indefinite, and sweeping in scope. A **specific word** is precise, definite, and limited in scope.

General	Specific	More Specific/Concrete
food	fast food	cheeseburger
entertainment	film	*The Aviator*
place	city	Atlanta

An **abstract word** refers to a concept or idea, a quality or trait, or anything else that cannot be touched, heard, or seen. A **concrete word** signifies a particular object, a specific action, or anything that can be touched, heard, or seen.

Abstract	democracy, evil, strength, charity
Concrete	mosquito, hammer, plastic, fog

Some writers use too many abstract or general words, making their writing vague and lifeless. As you select words to fit your context, you should be as specific and concrete as you can. For example, instead of the word *bad,* consider using a more precise adjective.

bad neighbors: rowdy, snobby, nosy, fussy, sloppy, threatening

bad meat: tough, tainted, overcooked, undercooked, contaminated

bad wood: rotten, warped, scorched, knotty, termite-ridden

To test whether or not a word is specific, you can ask one or more of these questions about what you want to say: Exactly who? Exactly what? Exactly when? Exactly where? Exactly how? In the following examples, notice what a difference concrete words can make in expressing an idea and how adding details can expand or develop it.

Vague	She has kept no reminders of performing in her youth.
Specific	She has kept no sequined costume, no photographs, no fliers or posters from that part of her youth. **—LOUISE ERDRICH**

Vague	He realized that he was running through the cold night.
Specific	He found himself hurrying over creaking snow through the blackness of a winter night. **—LOREN EISELEY**

As these examples show, sentences with specific details are often longer than sentences without them. But the need to be specific does not necessarily conflict with the need to be concise. (See chapter 34.) Sometimes substituting one word for another can make it far easier for your readers to see, hear, taste, or smell what you are hoping to convey.

> I had an accident while trying to catch a fish.

with the handwritten annotations: fell out of a canoe (above "had an accident" which is struck through) and land a muskie (above "catch a fish" which is struck through).

Writers use general and abstract words successfully when such words are vital to communicating ideas, as in the following sentence about what happens when a plague comes to an end.

> We expect a catharsis, but we merely find a transition; we long for euphoria, but we discover only relief, tinged with, in some cases, regret and depression.
> —ANDREW SULLIVAN

(4) Figurative language contributes to exactness.

Figurative language is the use of words in an imaginative rather than a literal sense. Similes and metaphors are the chief **figures of speech.** A **simile** is a comparison of dissimilar things using *like* or *as.* A **metaphor** is an implied comparison of dissimilar things, without *like* or *as.*

Similes
He was **like a piece of rare and delicate china which was always being saved from breaking and finally fell.** —ALICE WALKER

She sat **like a great icon** in the back of the classroom, tranquil, guarded, sealed up, watchful. —REGINALD MCKNIGHT

Metaphors
His **money was a sharp pair of scissors** that snipped rapidly through tangles of red tape. —HISAYE YAMAMOTO

The injured **bird was a broken handled flag** waving in the grass.
—TRACY YOUNGBLOM

Single words can be used metaphorically.

> These roses must be **planted** in good soil. [literal]

> Keep your life **planted** wherever you can put down the most roots. [metaphorical]

Similes and metaphors are especially valuable when they are concrete and describe or evoke essential relationships that cannot otherwise be communicated. Similes or metaphors can be extended throughout a paragraph of comparison, but be careful not to mix them. (See **27c**.)

Exercise 1

Study the passage below, and prepare to discuss in class your response to the author's use of exact and figurative language to communicate her ideas.

[1]The kitchen where I'm making dinner is a New York kitchen. [2]Nice light, way too small, nowhere to put anything unless the stove goes. [3]My stove is huge, but it will never go. [4]My stove is where my head clears, my impressions settle, my reporter's life gets folded into *my* life, and whatever I've just learned, or think I've learned—whatever it was, out there in the world, that had seemed so different and surprising—bubbles away in the very small pot of what I think I know and, if I'm lucky, produces something like perspective.   —JANE KRAMER, "The Reporter's Kitchen"

Exercise 2

Choose five of the items below, and use them as the bases for five original sentences containing figurative language.

1. the look on someone's face
2. a cold rainy day
3. studying for an exam
4. your favorite food
5. buying textbooks
6. a busy street
7. waiting in a long line for a movie
8. the way someone talks

33b Evocative language

Fresh expressions can capture the attention of readers, but when forced or overused, they lose their impact. Sometimes writers coin expressions as substitutes for words and phrases that have coarse or indelicate connotations. These expressions are called **euphemisms;** they occasionally become standardized. To talk about death or dying, for example, you might use words such as *pass away* or *being terminally ill*. However, although euphemisms may be pleasant sounding, they have a dark side.

They can be used by writers who want to obscure facts or avoid negative reactions by others. Euphemisms such as *revenue enhancement* for *tax hike* and *collateral damage* for *civilian deaths during a war* are considered insincere or deceitful.

BEYOND THE RULE

DOUBLESPEAK

In his novel *1984*, George Orwell coined the term *doublespeak* to refer to language used intentionally to obscure the facts surrounding bad news. William Lutz has continued in Orwell's steps, keeping track of language used to sugarcoat harsh realities. To find current examples of doublespeak, visit **www.harbrace.com**.

The expressions *bite the dust, breath of fresh air,* and *smooth as silk* were once striking and thus effective. Excessive use, though, has drained them of their original force and made them **clichés.** Newer expressions such as *put a spin on something* and *think outside the box* have also lost their vitality because of overuse. Nonetheless, clichés are so much a part of the language, especially the spoken language, that nearly every writer uses them from time to time. But effective writers often give a fresh twist to an old saying.

> I seek a narrative, a fiction, to order days like the one I spent several years ago, on a gray June day in Chicago, when I took a roller-coaster ride on the bell curve of my experience. —**GAYLE PEMBERTON**

> [Notice how much more effective this expression is than frequent references elsewhere to "being on an emotional roller coaster."]

Variations on familiar expressions from literature, many of which have become part of everyday language, can often be used effectively in your writing.

> Now is the summer of my great content. —**KATHERINE LANPHER**

> [This statement is a variation on Shakespeare's "Now is the winter of our discontent . . . ."]

Good writers, however, do not rely too heavily on the words of others; they choose their own words to communicate their ideas.

BEYOND THE RULE

CLICHÉS

Some scholars have defended clichés on the grounds that they convey widely accepted ideas in a direct way and can thus help writers to communicate effectively with certain readers in specific rhetorical situations. For information about this position, visit **www.harbrace.com**.

Exercise 3

From the following list of overused expressions, select five that you often use or hear and suggest creative replacements. Then, use each replacement in a sentence.

EXAMPLE

beyond the shadow of a doubt   *undoubtedly* OR *with total certainty*

1. an axe to grind
2. hit the nail on the head
3. see the light
4. business as usual
5. climb the walls

6. eat like a pig
7. beat around the bush
8. bite the bullet
9. breathe down someone's neck
10. strong as an ox

33c | Idioms and collocations

Idioms are fixed expressions whose meanings cannot be entirely determined by knowing the meanings of their parts—*bear in mind, fall in love, in a nutshell, stand a chance.* **Collocations** are combinations of words that frequently occur together. Unlike idioms, they have meanings that *can* be determined by knowing the meanings of their parts—*depend on, fond of, little while, right now.* Regardless of whether you are using an idiom or a collocation, if you make even a small inadvertent change to the expected wording, you may distract or confuse your readers.

She tried to keep a ~~small~~ profile. [*low*]

They had ~~an invested~~ interest in the project. [*a vested*]

As you edit your writing, keep an eye out for idioms or collocations that might not be worded correctly. Then check a general dictionary, a dictionary of idioms (see page 659), or the **Glossary of Usage** at the end of this book to ensure that your usage is appropriate. Writers sometimes have trouble with the following collocations, all of which contain prepositions.

CHOOSING THE RIGHT PREPOSITION

Instead of	Use
abide **with**	abide **by** the decision
according **with**	according **to** the source
accused **for**	accused **of** the crime
bored **of**	bored **by** it
comply **to**	comply **with** rules
conform **of/on**	conform **to/with** standards
differ **to**	differ **with** them
in accordance **to**	in accordance **with** policy
independent **to**	independent **of** his family
happened **on**	happened **by** accident
plan **on**	plan **to** go
superior **than**	superior **to** others
type **of a**	type **of** business

Understanding and Using Idioms
The context in which an idiom appears can often help you
understand the meaning. For example, if you read "When they
learned that she had accepted illegal campaign contributions,
several political commentators raked her over the coals," you would
probably understand that *to rake over the coals* means "to criticize severely."
As you learn new idioms from your reading, make a list of those you might
want to use in your own writing. If you are confused about the meaning of
a particular idiom, check a dictionary of idioms (see page 659).

Exercise 4

Write a sentence using each of the following idioms and collocations
correctly.

1. pass muster, pass the time
2. do one's best, do one's part, do one's duty
3. in a pinch, in a rut, in a way
4. cut down, cut back, cut corners
5. make time, make sure, make sense

33d First-person and second-person pronouns

Using *I* is appropriate when you are writing about personal experience. In academic and professional writing, the use of the first-person
singular pronoun is also a clear way to distinguish your own views
from those of others or to make a direct appeal to readers. However,
if you frequently repeat *I feel* or *I think,* your readers may suspect that
you do not understand much beyond your own experience or that
you are more interested in talking about yourself than about your
topic.

We, the first-person plural pronoun, is trickier to use correctly. When
you use it, make sure that your audience can tell which individuals are
included in this plural reference. For example, if you are writing a paper

for a college course, does *we* mean you and the instructor, you and your fellow students, or some other group (such as all Americans)? If you are using *we* in a memo to co-workers, are you intending to include the entire company, your group within it, or you and a specific individual? Because you may inadvertently use *we* in an early draft to refer to more than one group of people, as you edit, check to see that you have used the first-person plural pronoun consistently.

BEYOND THE RULE

WHO IS PART OF *WE*?

Writing specialists have been discussing how the use of *we* can blind writers to differences of gender, race, religion, region, class, and sexual orientation. Readers sometimes feel excluded from works in which the first-person plural pronoun has been used carelessly. For more information about this debate, visit **www.harbrace.com**.

If you decide to address readers directly, you will undoubtedly use the second-person pronoun *you* (as has been done frequently in this book). There is some disagreement, though, over whether to permit the use of the indefinite *you* to mean "a person" or "people in general." Check with your instructor about this usage. If you are told to avoid using the indefinite *you*, recast your sentences. For example, use *one* instead of *you*.

Even in huge, anonymous cities, ~~you find~~ ^one finds^ community spirit.

However, owing to the formality of *one*, it might not always be the best choice. Changing the word order is another possibility.

Community spirit can be found even in huge, anonymous cities.

If you are unsatisfied with either of these strategies, use different words.

Community spirit arises even in huge, anonymous cities.

For additional advice on using pronouns, see chapter 25.

Exercise 5

Revise the following paragraph to eliminate the use of the first- and second-person pronouns.

¹In my opinion, some animals should be as free as we are. **²**For example, I think orangutans, African elephants, and Atlantic bottle-nose dolphins should roam freely rather than be held in captivity. **³**We should neither exhibit them in zoos nor use them for medical research. **⁴**If you study animals such as these you will see that, like us, they show emotions, self-awareness, and intention. **⁵**You might even find that some use language to communicate. **⁶**It is clear to me that they have the right to freedom.

33e Clear definitions

Because words often have more than one meaning, you must clearly establish which meaning you have in mind in a particular piece of writing. By providing a definition, you set the terms of the discussion.

> In this paper, I use the word *communism* **in the Marxist sense of social organization based on the holding of all property in common.**

A **formal definition** first states the term to be defined, then puts it into a class, and finally differentiates it from other members of that class.

> A *phosphene* [term] is **a luminous visual image** [class] that **results from applying pressure to the eyeball** [differentiation].

A short dictionary definition may be adequate when you need to convey a special meaning that may be unfamiliar to readers.

> Here, *galvanic* means **"produced as if by electric shock."**

Giving a synonym may also clarify the meaning of a term. Such synonyms are often used as appositives.

> *Machismo,* **confidence with an attitude,** can be a pose rather than a reality.

Writers frequently show—rather than tell—what a word means by giving examples.

> Many homophones (**such as** *be* **and** *bee,* *in* **and** *inn,* **or** *see* **and** *sea*) are not spelling problems.

You can also formulate your own definition of a concept you wish to clarify.

Clichés could be defined as **thoughts that have hardened.**

When writing definitions, do not confuse readers by placing a predicate with a subject that is not logically connected to it. (See **27d.**) Constructions that combine *is* or *are* with *when, where,* or *because* are often illogical because forms of *be* signify identity or equality between the subject and what follows.

Faulty   The Internet is when you look at text and images from across the world.

Revised   The Internet allows you to look at text and images from across the world.

Exercise 6

Using your own words, define any four of the following terms in full sentences.

1. collaboration   3. party   5. globalization
2. honesty   4. style   6. terrorism

34

CONCISENESS

To facilitate readers' understanding, effective writers generally convey their thoughts clearly and efficiently. This does not mean that they always write short sentences; rather, they use each word wisely. This chapter will help you

- make each word count (34a),
- avoid unnecessary repetition (34b), and
- use elliptical constructions (34c).

34a Eliminating wordiness and other redundancies

After writing a first draft, review your phrasing to make sure that you have not been vague or repetitive. If you draft quickly or if you are worried about the length requirement for the assignment, you may write rambling sentences that obscure your message rather than clarify it.

(1) Redundancy contributes to wordiness.

Restating a key point in different words can help readers understand it. But there is no need to rephrase readily understood terms. If you do, your work will suffer from **redundancy**—repetition for no good reason.

Ballerinas auditioned ~~in the tryouts~~ for *The Nutcracker.*

Each student had a unique talent ^for^ ~~and ability that he or she uses in his or her~~ acting.

You should also avoid grammatical redundancy, as in double subjects (*my sister [she] is*), double comparisons (*[more] easier than*), and double negatives (*could[n't] hardly*).

Using Relative Pronouns
Review your sentences to make sure that no clause includes both a personal pronoun (**25a(1)**) and a relative pronoun (**25a(2)**) referring to the same antecedent (**25c**).

The drug **that** we were testing ~~it~~ has not been approved by the Food and Drug Administration.

The principal investigator, **whom** we depended on ~~her~~ for guidance, had to take a medical leave before the project was completed.

(2) Delete unnecessary words, and recast wordy phrases.

One exact word often says as much a several inexact ones.

spoke in a low and hard-to-hear voice	**mumbled**
a person who gives expert advice	**consultant**

Some unscrupulous brokers are ʌ~~taking money and savings from~~ elderly *cheating*

people ʌ~~who need that money because they planned to use it as a retirement~~ *out of their pensions.*

~~pension.~~

As you edit a draft, delete words that add no significant meaning to adjacent words, and replace wordy expressions with single words whenever possible.

If
ʌ~~In the event that~~ taxes are raised, ʌ~~expect complaints on the part of the~~ *voters will complain.*

~~voters.~~

In addition, watch for empty or vague words such as *area, aspect, element, factor, feature, field, kind, situation, thing,* and *type.* They may signal wordiness.

Effective
ʌ~~In an employment situation, effective~~ communication is essential at work.

USELESS WORDS IN COMMON PHRASES

yellow [in color]

at 9:45 A.M. [in the morning]

[basic] essentials

bitter[-tasting] salad

connect [up together]

because [of the fact that]

[really and truly] fearless

circular [in shape]

return [back]

rich [and wealthy] nations

small[-size] potatoes

[true] facts

was [more or less] hinting

by [virtue of] his authority

REPLACEMENTS FOR WORDY EXPRESSIONS

at this moment (point) in time	now, today
due to the fact that	because
in view of the fact that	because
for the purpose of	for
it is clear (obvious) that	clearly (obviously)
there is no question that	unquestionably, certainly
without a doubt	undoubtedly
beyond the shadow of a doubt	certainly, surely
it is my opinion that	I think (believe)
in this day and age	today
in the final analysis	finally

(3) The constructions *there are* and *it is* can often be deleted.

There or *it* followed by a form of *be* is an **expletive**—a word that signals that the subject of the sentence will follow the verb. (See **20d(1)**.) Writers use expletives to create a sentence rhythm that emphasizes words that would not be emphasized in the typical subject-verb order. Notice the difference in rhythm between the following two sentences:

> Three children were playing in the yard.

> There were three children playing in the yard.

However, expletives are easily overused. If you find that you have drafted several sentences that begin with expletives, look for ways to revise a few of them.

> *Hundreds*
> ~~There were hundreds~~ of fans *were* crowding onto the field.

> *Joining the crowd*
> It was frightening ~~to join the crowd~~.

> OR

> I was afraid to join the crowd.

(4) Some relative pronouns can be deleted.

When editing a draft, check whether the relative pronouns *who, which,* and *that* can be deleted from any of your sentences. If a relative pronoun is followed by a form of the verb *be* (*am, is, are, was,* or *were*), you can often omit both the relative pronoun and the verb.

> The change ~~that~~ the young senator proposed yesterday angered most legislators.

> Bromo, ~~which is~~ Java's highest mountain, towers above its neighbors.

> The Endangered Species Act, ~~which was~~ passed in 1973, protects the habitat of endangered plants and animals.

When deleting a relative pronoun, you might have to make other changes to a sentence as well.

> *handling*
> The Tsukiji fish market, ~~which handles~~ 2,000 tons of seafood a day, rates as the world's largest.

Exercise 1

Rewrite the sentences below to make them less wordy.

1. He put in an application for every job offered.
2. Prior to the time of the ceremony, he had not received an award.
3. The library is located in the vicinity of the post office.
4. The fans who were watching television made a lot of noise.
5. There was nobody home.
6. The release of certain chemicals, which are called *pheromones*, is a very primitive form of communication.
7. It is important to register early.
8. The road was closed because of the fact that there were so many accidents.

34b Avoiding unnecessary repetition

Repetition is useful only when it contributes to emphasis, clarity, or coherence.

> ~~One week was like the next week.~~ Each week was as boring as the last.
>
> She hoped Alex understood that ~~the complaint she made did not mean she was complaining because she disliked him.~~ her complaint did not reflect her feelings about him.

In the preceding examples, repetition serves no useful purpose; in the following example, however, it provides emphasis.

> We will not rest until we have pursued **every** lead, inspected **every** piece of evidence, and interviewed **every** suspect. [The repetition of *every* is effective because it emphasizes the writer's determination.]

Instead of repeating a noun or substituting a synonym, you can use a pronoun as long as the reference is clear.

> Teddy Roosevelt earned a reputation as the "conservation President."
>
> During his two terms, ~~Roosevelt~~ he designated over 200 million acres as public land.

34c Using elliptical constructions

An **elliptical construction** is one that deliberately omits words that can be understood from the context. In the following sentence, the word group *is the goal* can be taken out of the second and third clauses without affecting the meaning. The revised sentence is more concise than the original.

> Speed is the goal for some swimmers, endurance ~~is the goal~~ for others, and relaxation ~~is the goal~~ for still others.

Sometimes, as an aid to clarity, commas mark omissions in elliptical constructions.

> My family functioned like a baseball team: my mom was the coach; my brother, the pitcher; and my sister, the shortstop. [Be sure to use semicolons to separate items with internal commas (see 36b).]

As these examples show, parallelism reinforces elliptical constructions. (See chapter 29.)

Exercise 2

Revise this paragraph to eliminate wordiness and needless repetition.

¹When I look back on my high school career, I realize that I was not taught much about international affairs in the world in spite of the fact that improved communications, the media, the Internet, travel, trading with different foreign countries, and immigration have made the world smaller. ²Nonetheless, because both international affairs and business interest me, I decided to major in political science now that I am in college and to study marketing as my minor. ³There are advantages to this combination of a major and a minor in my job situation at work as well, for I am now currently working part-time twenty hours a week for a company that imports merchandise into the United States and exports products to other countries. ⁴Eventually, at some future time, when I have graduated and received my bachelor's degree, I may go on to law school and pursue my interest in politics, unless, on the other hand, my supervisor makes the recommendation that I develop my skills in marketing by spending time overseas in one of the company's foreign offices. ⁵The opportunity to work overseas would provide me with a knowledge, an understanding, and an appreciation of the world economy. ⁶Such an understanding is essential for anyone hoping to succeed in business.

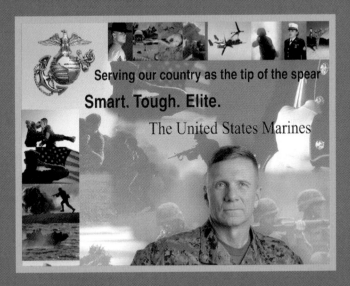

The use of the period, a strong mark of punctuation, with the words
"Smart. Tough. Elite." reinforces the strength of the image.

35

THE COMMA

Punctuation signals meaning. It lends to written language the flexibility that facial expressions, pauses, and variations in voice pitch give to spoken language. For instance, a pause after *called* in the first of the following examples would make it clear that the spoken sentence refers to only two people: the recruiter and Kenneth Martin. In the second example, a pause after *Kenneth* would let the listener know that the sentence refers to three people: the recruiter, Kenneth, and Martin. In written text, the same meanings can be established by commas.

When the recruiter called, Kenneth Martin answered.

When the recruiter called Kenneth, Martin answered.

But pauses are not a reliable guide for comma use because commas are often called for where speakers do not pause, and pauses can occur where no comma is necessary. A better guide is an understanding of some basic principles of comma usage.

This chapter will help you use commas to

- separate independent clauses joined by coordinating conjunctions (35a),
- set off introductory words, phrases, and clauses (35b),
- separate items in a series (35c),
- set off nonessential (nonrestrictive) elements (35d),
- set off geographical names and items in dates and addresses (35e), and
- set off direct quotations (35f),

as well as help you to

- recognize unnecessary or misplaced commas (35g).

35a   Before a coordinating conjunction linking independent clauses

Use a comma before a coordinating conjunction (*and, but, for, nor, or, so,* or *yet*) that links two independent clauses. An **independent clause** is a group of words that can stand as a sentence (see **21b(1)**).

INDEPENDENT CLAUSE**,** **CONJUNCTION** INDEPENDENT CLAUSE.

and

but

for

Subject + predicate**,**   **nor**   subject + predicate.

or

so

yet

Most Southwestern pottery comes from Arizona and New Mexico**,** **but** some also comes from Nevada, Utah, Colorado, and Texas.

Studying such pottery seemed simple at first**,** **yet** it has challenged archaeologists and art historians for decades.

No matter how many clauses are in a sentence, a comma comes before each coordinating conjunction.

No one knows exactly how many types of Southwestern pottery there are**,** **nor** is there a list of even the most common**,** **but** scientists are working to change that.

When the independent clauses are short, the comma is often omitted before *and, but,* or *or.*

I collect pottery **and** my sister collects jewelry.

If a coordinating conjunction joins two parts of a compound predicate, the conjunction is not normally followed by a comma. (See **20b** and **35g(3)**.)

Archaeologists have developed a classification system ⌃ and have established a comprehensive time line for pottery production.

Sometimes a semicolon, instead of a comma, follows a conjunction separating two independent clauses, especially when the second clause already contains commas or when it reveals a contrast. (See also 36b.)

Most archaeologists study the pottery of just one culture⁏ **but** it should be possible, according to Russell, to study one type of pottery across several cultures.

Exercise 1

Combine each of the following pairs of sentences by using coordinating conjunctions and inserting commas where appropriate. (Remember that coordinating conjunctions do not always link independent clauses and that *but, for, so,* and *yet* do not always function as coordinating conjunctions.) Explain why you used each of the conjunctions you chose.

1. Dinosaurs lived for 165 million years. Then they became extinct.
2. No one knows why dinosaurs became extinct. Several theories have been proposed.
3. Some theorists believe that a huge meteor hit the earth. The climate may have changed dramatically.
4. Another theory suggests that dinosaurs did not actually become extinct. They simply evolved into lizards and birds.
5. Yet another theory suggests that they just grew too big. Not all of the dinosaurs were huge.

35b After introductory words, phrases, or clauses

(1) A comma follows an introductory dependent clause.

If you begin a sentence with a dependent (subordinate) clause, you should place a comma after it to set it off from the independent (main) clause.

> **INTRODUCTORY DEPENDENT CLAUSE,** INDEPENDENT CLAUSE.

Although the safest automobile on the road is expensive, the protection it offers makes the cost worthwhile.

(2) A comma often follows an introductory phrase.

By placing a comma after an introductory phrase, you set it off from the independent clause.

> **INTRODUCTORY PHRASE,** INDEPENDENT CLAUSE.

(a) Introductory prepositional phrases

Despite a downturn in the national economy, the number of students enrolled in this university has increased.

If you begin a sentence with a short introductory prepositional phrase, you may omit the comma as long as the resulting sentence is not difficult to read.

In 2006 the enrollment at the university increased.

BUT

In 2006, 625 new students enrolled in courses.

[A comma separates two numbers.]

A comma is not used after a phrase that begins a sentence in which the subject and predicate are inverted.

With travel came responsibilities.

[COMPARE: Responsibilities came with travel.]

(b) Other types of introductory phrases

If you begin a sentence with a participial phrase or an absolute phrase, place a comma after it.

Having traveled nowhere, she believed the rest of the world was like her own small town; **having read little,** she had no sense of how other people think. [participial phrases]

The language difference aside, life in Germany did not seem much different from life in the United States. [absolute phrase]

(3) A comma often follows an introductory word.

> **INTRODUCTORY WORD,** INDEPENDENT CLAUSE.

Use a comma to set off words such as interjections, **vocatives** (words used to address someone directly), or transitional words.

> **Oh,** I forgot about the board meeting. [interjection]
>
> **Bob,** your design impressed everyone on the board. [vocative]
>
> **Moreover,** the new design will increase efficiency in the office. [transitional word]

Some adverbs and transitional words do not need to be set off by a comma if the omission does not affect the reader's understanding (see also 36a).

> **Sometimes** even a good design is rejected by the board. [A comma is not necessary.]

Exercise 2

Insert commas wherever necessary in the following paragraph, and explain why each comma is needed. Some sentences may not require editing.

¹If you had to describe sound would you call it a wave? ²Although sound cannot be seen people have described it this way for a long time. ³In fact the Greek philosopher Aristotle believed that sound traveling through air was like waves in the sea. ⁴Envisioning waves in the air he hypothesized that sound would not be able to pass through a vacuum because there would be no air to transmit it. ⁵Aristotle's hypothesis was not tested until nearly two thousand years later. ⁶In 1654 Otto von Guericke found that he could not hear a bell ringing inside the vacuum he had created. ⁷Thus Guericke established the necessity of air for sound transmission. ⁸However although most sound reaches us through the air it travels faster through liquids and solids.

35c Separating elements in a series

A **series** contains three or more parallel elements. To be parallel, elements must be grammatically equal; for example, all must be phrases, not combinations of phrases and clauses. (See chapter 29.)

(1) Commas separate words, phrases, or clauses in a series.

A comma appears after each item in a series except the last one.

Ethics are based on **moral, social,** or **cultural** values. [words]

The code of ethics includes **seeking criticism of work, correcting mistakes,** and **acknowledging the contributions of everyone.** [phrases]

Several circumstances can lead to unethical behavior: **people are tempted by a desire to succeed, they are pressured into acting inappropriately by others,** or **they are simply trying to survive.** [clauses in a series]

If elements in a series contain internal commas, you can prevent misreading by separating the items with semicolons.

A researcher's code of ethics calls for disclosing all results, without omitting any data; indicating various interpretations of the data; and making the data and methodology available to other researchers, some of whom may choose to replicate the study.

THINKING RHETORICALLY ABOUT

COMMAS AND CONJUNCTIONS IN A SERIES

How do the following sentences differ?

We discussed them all: life, liberty, **and** the pursuit of happiness.

We discussed them all: life **and** liberty **and** the pursuit of happiness.

We discussed them all: life, liberty, the pursuit of happiness.

The first sentence follows conventional guidelines; that is, a comma and a conjunction precede the last element in the series. The second and third sentences, because they veer from convention, do more than convey information. Having two conjunctions and no commas, the second sentence slows the pace of the reading, causing stress to be placed on each of the three elements in the series. Lacking any conjunctions, the third sentence speeds up the reading, as if to suggest that the rights listed do not need to be stressed because they are so familiar. To get a sense of how your sentences will be read and understood, try reading them aloud to yourself.

(2) Commas separate coordinate adjectives.

Two or more adjectives that modify the same noun are called **coordinate adjectives.** To test whether adjectives are coordinate, either interchange them or put *and* between them. If the meaning does not change, the adjectives are coordinate and so should be separated by a comma or commas.

> Crossing the **rushing, shallow** creek, I slipped off a rock and fell into the water.
> [COMPARE: a rushing and shallow creek OR a shallow, rushing creek]

The adjectives in the following sentence are not separated by a comma. Notice that they cannot be interchanged or joined by *and*.

> Sitting in the water, I saw an **old wooden** bridge.
> [NOT a wooden old bridge OR an old and wooden bridge]

Exercise 3

Using commas where necessary, write sentences in which coordinate adjectives modify any five of the following words.

EXAMPLE

metric system   *Most countries use the familiar, sensible metric system to measure distances.*

1. bagel
2. music
3. truck
4. painting
5. software
6. college

35d With nonessential elements

Nonessential (nonrestrictive) elements provide supplemental information, that is, information not needed to understand the central meaning of a sentence. Use commas to set off a nonessential word or word group: one comma separates a nonessential element at the end of a sentence; two commas set off a nonessential element in the middle of a sentence.

> The Feast and Fest Party, **planned for the last day of school,** should attract many students.

In this sentence, the phrase placed between commas conveys nonessential information: the reader does not need to know when the party will occur to realize which party is being referred to because the name of the party is given. Note, however, that in the following sentence, the same phrase is necessary for identification of the party. It specifies that the party is the one planned for the last day of school (not one planned for any other day).

> The party **planned for the last day of school** should attract many students.

In this sentence, the phrase is an **essential (restrictive) element** because the reader needs the information it provides in order to know which party the writer has in mind. Essential elements are not set off by commas; they are integrated into the sentence.

(1) Commas set off nonessential elements used as modifiers.

(a) Adjectival clauses

Nonessential modifiers are often **adjectival (relative) clauses**—those clauses introduced by relative pronouns (see **21b**). The most common relative pronouns are *who*, *which*, and *that*. In the following sentence, a comma sets off the adjectival clause because the content of that clause is not needed to identify the mountain.

> We climbed Mt. McKinley, **which is over 20,000 feet high.**

(b) Participial phrases

Nonessential modifiers also include **participial phrases**—those phrases introduced by present or past participles. (See also **21a(3)**.)

Mt. McKinley, **towering above us,** brought to mind our abandoned plan for climbing it. [participial phrase beginning with a present participle]

My sister, **slowed by a knee injury,** rarely hikes anymore. [participial phrase beginning with a past participle]

(c) Adverbial clauses

An adverbial clause beginning with a subordinating conjunction signaling cause (*because*), consequence (*so that*), or time (*when, after,* or *before*) is usually considered essential and is thus not set off by commas when it appears at the end of a sentence.

Dinosaurs may have become extinct **because their habitat was destroyed.**

In contrast, an adverbial clause that provides nonessential information, such as an extra comment, should be set off from the main clause. (See also **21b(2)**.)

Dinosaurs are extinct, **though they are alive in many people's imaginations.**

(2) Commas set off nonessential appositives.

Nonessential appositives provide extra details about nouns or pronouns. In the following sentence, the name of the person is mentioned, so the appositive is not essential for the reader to identify him. Thus, the appositive is set off by commas.

Even Milo Papadupolos, **my friend,** let me down.

If *my friend* precedes the specific name, that name is an appositive and might be necessary for identifying the particular friend. In this case, the appositive is essential and so is not set off by commas.

Even my friend **Milo Papadupolos** let me down.

Abbreviations of titles or degrees after names are treated as nonessential appositives.

Was the letter from Frances Evans, PhD, or from Francis Evans, MD?

Increasingly, *Jr.* and *Sr.* are being treated as part of a name, rather than as appositives, and so the comma after the name is occasionally omitted.

William Homer Barton, Jr.   OR   William Homer Barton Jr.

Exercise 4

Set off nonessential clauses, phrases, and appositives with commas.

1. Maine Coons long-haired cats with bushy tails have adapted to a harsh climate.
2. These animals which are extremely gentle despite their large size often weigh twenty pounds.
3. Most Maine Coons have exceptionally high intelligence which enables them to recognize language and even to open doors.
4. Unlike most cats Maine Coons will play fetch with their owners.
5. According to a legend later proven to be false Maine Coons developed from interbreeding between wildcats and domestic cats.

(3) Commas set off absolute phrases.

An **absolute phrase** (the combination of a noun and a modifying word or phrase) provides nonessential details and so should be separated from the rest of the sentence by a comma or commas. (See also 21a(6).)

The actor, **his hair wet and slicked back,** began his audition.

The director stared at him, **her mind flipping through the photographs she had viewed earlier.**

(4) Commas set off transitional expressions and other parenthetical elements.

Commas customarily set off transitional words and phrases such as *for example, that is,* and *namely.*

An airline ticket, **for example,** can be delivered electronically.

Because they generally indicate little or no pause in reading, transitional words and phrases such as *also, too, at least,* and *thus* need not be set off by commas.

My dislike of travel has **thus** decreased in recent years.

Use commas to set off other parenthetical elements, such as words or phrases that provide commentary you wish to stress.

Over the past year, my flights have, **miraculously,** been on time.

(5) Commas set off contrasted elements.

Commas set off sentence elements in which words such as *never* and *unlike* express contrast.

A planet, **unlike** a star, reflects rather than generates light.

In sentences in which contrasted elements are introduced by *not only . . . but also,* place a comma before *but* if you want to emphasize what follows it. Otherwise, you can omit the comma.

Planets not only vary in size, **but also** travel at different speeds. [comma added for emphasis]

35e With geographical names and items in dates and addresses

Use commas to make geographical names, dates, and addresses easy to read.

(1) City and state

Nashville, Tennessee, is the largest country-and-western music center in the United States.

(2) Day and date

Martha left for Peru on **Wednesday, February 12, 2006,** and returned on March 12.

OR

Martha left for Peru on **Wednesday, 12 February 2006,** and returned on 12 March.

In the style used in the second example (which is not as common in the United States as the style in the first example), one comma is omitted because *12* precedes rather than follows *February.*

(3) Addresses

Although the name of the person or organization, the street address, and the name of the town or city are all followed by commas, the abbreviation for the state is not.

The codes were sent to **Ms. Melanie Hobson, Senior Analyst, Hobson Computing, 2873 Central Avenue, Orange Park, FL 32065.**

Exercise 5

Explain the reason for each comma used in the following sentences.

1. Alvar Nuñez Cabeza de Vaca, unlike most other Spanish conquistadors, came to perceive Native Americans as equals.
2. On February 15, 1527, Cabeza de Vaca was appointed to an expedition headed for the mainland of North America.
3. The expedition landed near what is now Tampa Bay, Florida, sometime in March 1528.
4. Devastated by misfortune, the expedition dwindled rapidly; Cabeza de Vaca and three other members, however, survived.
5. His endurance now tested, Cabeza de Vaca lived as a trader and healer among Native Americans of the Rio Grande Basin, learning from them and eventually speaking on their behalf to the Spanish crown.

35f With direct quotations accompanied by attributive tags

Many sentences containing direct quotations also contain attributive tags (see **11d(2)**). Use commas to set off these tags whether they occur at the beginning, in the middle, or at the end of a sentence.

(1) Attributive tag at the beginning of a sentence

Place the comma directly after the attributive tag, before the quotation marks.

> According to Jacques Barzun, "It is a false analogy with science that makes one think latest is best."

(2) Attributive tag in the middle of a sentence

Place the first comma inside the quotation marks that precede the attributive tag; place the second comma directly after the tag, before the next set of quotation marks.

> "It is a false analogy with science," claims Jacques Barzun, "that makes one think latest is best."

(3) Attributive tag at the end of a sentence

Place the comma inside the quotation marks before the attributive tag.

> "It is a false analogy with science that makes one think latest is best," claims Jacques Barzun.

35g Unnecessary or misplaced commas

Although a comma may signal a pause, not every pause calls for a comma. As you read the following sentence aloud, you may pause naturally at several places, but no commas are necessary.

> Heroic deeds done by ordinary people inspire others to act in ways that are not only moral but courageous.

(1) A comma does not separate a subject and its verb or a verb and its object.

Although speakers often pause after the subject or before the object of a sentence, such a pause should not be indicated by a comma.

> In this climate, rain at frequent intervals⌐produces mosquitoes. [no separation between subject (*rain*) and verb (*produces*)]

> The forecaster said⌐that rain was likely. [no separation between verb (*said*) and direct object (the noun clause *that rain was unlikely*)]

(2) A comma does not follow a coordinating conjunction.

Avoid using a comma after a coordinating conjunction (*and, but, for, nor, or, so,* or *yet*).

> We worked very hard on her campaign for state representative, but⌐the incumbent was too strong in the northern counties. ∧

(3) A comma does not generally separate elements in a compound predicate.

Avoid using a comma between two elements of a compound predicate.

> I read the comments carefully⌐and then started my revision.

If you want to slow the reading in order to place stress on the second element in a compound predicate, you can place a comma after the first element. Use this option sparingly, however, or it will lose its effectiveness.

I read the comments word by word, and despaired.

(4) Commas set off words, phrases, and clauses only if they are clearly nonessential.

In the following sentences, the elements in boldface are clearly essential and so should not be set off by commas. (See also **35d**.)

Zoe was born in Chicago in 1985.

Perhaps the thermostat is broken.

Everyone **who has a mortgage** is required to have fire insurance.

Someone **wearing an orange wig** greeted us at the door.

(5) A comma does not precede the first item of a series or follow the last.

Make sure that you place commas only between elements in a series, not before or after the series.

She was known for her photographs, sketches, and engravings.

The exhibit included her most deliberate, exuberant, and expensive photographs.

Exercise 6

Explain the use of each comma in the following paragraph.

¹Contrails, which are essentially artificial clouds, form when moisture in the air condenses around particles in jet exhaust. ²Like ordinary clouds, contrails block incoming sunlight and trap heat radiated from Earth's surface. ³This process reduces daytime highs and increases nighttime lows, narrowing the temperature range. ⁴Multiple contrails can cluster together and obscure an area as large as Iowa, Illinois, and Missouri combined, magnifying the effect. ⁵Although they may not alter the overall climate, contrails could still have environmental consequences. —**LAURA CARSTEN**, "Climate on the Wing"

36

THE SEMICOLON

When you use a semicolon—instead of a comma or a period—you are making a rhetorical choice; you are clarifying the relationship you want readers to make between ideas in your sentence. The semicolon most frequently connects two independent clauses when the second clause supports or contrasts with the first. The semicolon also separates grammatically equal elements that contain internal commas. This chapter will help you understand that semicolons

- link closely related independent clauses (36a) and
- separate parts of a sentence containing internal commas (36b), but
- do not connect independent clauses with phrases or dependent clauses (36c).

36a Connecting independent clauses

A semicolon placed between two independent clauses indicates that they are closely related. The second of the two clauses generally supports or contrasts with the first.

> For many cooks, basil is a key ingredient; it appears in recipes worldwide. [support]
> Sweet basil is used in many Mediterranean dishes; Thai basil is used in Asian and East Indian recipes. [contrast]

Although a coordinating conjunction (preceded by a comma) can also signal these kinds of relationships between independent clauses, consider using an occasional semicolon for variety.

Sometimes, a transitional expression such as *for example* or *however* (see 4d(3)) accompanies the semicolon and further establishes the exact relationship between the ideas.

> Basil is omnipresent in the cuisine of some countries**;** **for example,** Italians use basil in salads, soups, and many vegetable dishes.
>
> The culinary uses of basil are well known**;** **however,** this herb also has medicinal uses.

A comma is usually inserted after a transitional word; however, it can be omitted if doing so will not lead to a misreading.

> Because *basil* comes from a Greek word meaning "king," it suggests royalty; **indeed** some cooks accord basil royal status among herbs and spices.

36b Separating elements that contain commas

In a series of phrases or clauses containing commas, semicolons indicate where each phrase or clause ends and the next begins.

> To survive, mountain lions need a large, open area in which to range**;** a steady supply of deer, skunks, raccoons, foxes, and opossums**;** and the opportunity to find a mate, establish a den, and raise a litter.

In this sentence, the semicolons help the reader distinguish the three separate phrases.

Exercise 1

Revise the following sentences, using semicolons to separate independent clauses or elements that contain internal commas.

1. Homelessness used to be typical only of the chronically unemployed, it is becoming more frequent among the working poor, some of whom earn just the minimum hourly wage of $5.15.
2. The last time the minimum wage was raised was in 1997, however, housing costs went up an average of about 20 percent in one year, which means they could have doubled since the last time the minimum wage was increased.
3. In some homeless families, even though both adults work full-time, their pay is low, they often cannot afford even the least

expensive housing, and they require state assistance, a form of welfare, to provide minimum shelter in a motel room for their children.

4. Such families are very crowded, living four, five, or six to a room, rarely having more than two double beds, a chair, and perhaps a roll-away bed, and lacking a place to keep the children's toys and school books.

5. These families eat at soup kitchens, they have no money for anything other than rent and basic clothing.

36c Revising common semicolon errors

Semicolons do not set off phrases or dependent clauses. (See **21a** and **21b(2)**.) Use commas for these purposes.

We consulted Alinka Kibukian; ,the local horticulturalist.
            ∧

Needing summer shade; ,we planted two of the largest trees we could afford.
            ∧

We learned that young trees need care; ,which meant we had to do some extra chores after dinner each night.   ∧

Our trees have survived; ,even though we live in a harsh climate.
            ∧

Exercise 2

Replace any semicolon used to set off a phrase or a dependent clause. Do not change properly used semicolons.

1. Every morning I take vitamins; a multivitamin and sometimes extra vitamin C.

2. I used to believe that I could get my vitamins from a balanced diet; then I found out that diet may not provide enough of some vitamins, such as folic acid.

3. By eating a balanced diet, getting plenty of exercise, and keeping stress to a minimum; I thought I would stay healthy.

4. New research suggests that multivitamins are beneficial; when our diets do not provide all the recommended amounts of every vitamin every day; our health can suffer.

5. Although taking one multivitamin tablet a day is a healthy habit; we do not need to buy the most potent or most expensive vitamins available.

Exercise 3

Find or compose one sentence to illustrate each of the following uses of the semicolon.

1. To link two related independent clauses
2. To separate clauses in a sentence containing a conjunctive adverb such as *however* or *therefore*
3. To separate phrases or clauses that contain commas

37

THE APOSTROPHE

Apostrophes serve a number of purposes. For example, you can use them to show that someone owns something *(my neighbor's television)*, that someone has a specific relationship with someone else *(my neighbor's children)*, or that someone has produced or created something *(my neighbor's recipe)*. Apostrophes are also used in contractions *(can't, don't)* and in certain plural forms *(B.A.'s, M.D.'s)*. This chapter will help you use apostrophes to

- indicate ownership and other relationships (37a),
- mark omissions of letters or numbers (37b), and
- form certain plurals (37c).

37a Indicating ownership and other relationships

An apostrophe most commonly indicates ownership or origin.

> Fumi's computer, the photographer's camera [ownership]
>
> Einstein's ideas, the student's decision [origin]

An apostrophe indicates other relationships as well. For example, you use an apostrophe to show how people are related or what physical or psychological traits they possess.

> Linda's sister, the employee's supervisor [human relationships]
>
> Mona Lisa's smile, the team's spirit [physical or psychological traits]

An apostrophe also indicates traits or features of animals, plants, objects, and abstract nouns.

> the dog's ears, the tree's branches, the chair's legs, tyranny's influence

Words used to identify certain tools, buildings, events, and other things also include apostrophes.

> tailor's scissors, driver's license, bachelor's degree
>
> St. John's Cathedral, Parkinson's disease, Valentine's Day

You can also use an apostrophe with some forms of measurement.

> a day's wages, an hour's delay, five dollars' worth of chocolates

A noun usually follows a word with an apostrophe. However, occasionally, the noun is omitted when it is understood from the context.

> Is this Ana's or LaShonda's? [COMPARE: Is this Ana's book or LaShonda's book?]

Word with Apostrophe and *s* or Phrase Beginning with *of*

In many cases, you can use either a word with an apostrophe and an *s* or a prepositional phrase beginning with *of.*

Louise Erdrich's novels OR the novels **of** Louise Erdrich

the plane's arrival OR the arrival **of** the plane

However, the ending *-'s* is more commonly used with nouns referring to people, and the prepositional phrase is used with most nouns referring to location.

> my **uncle's** workshop, **Jan's** car, the **student's** paper [nouns referring to people]
>
> the **end of** the movie, the **middle of** the day, the **front of** the building [nouns referring to location]

---

(1) Most singular nouns, indefinite pronouns, abbreviations, and acronyms require -'s to form the possessive case.

the dean's office	Yeats's poems	anyone's computer

Walter Bryan Jr.'s letter [To avoid confusion, no comma precedes *Jr.'s* here. *Jr.* is sometimes set off by a comma, however; see **35d(2)**.]

the NFL's reputation	OPEC's price increase

Unlike the possessive forms of nouns and indefinite pronouns, possessive pronouns and determiners *(my, mine, our, ours, your, yours, his, her, hers, its, their, theirs,* and *whose)* are not written with apostrophes (see **25b(3)**).

Japanese democracy differs from **ours.**

The committee concluded **its** discussion.

Be careful not to confuse possessive pronouns and determiners with contractions. Whenever you write a contraction, you should be able to substitute the complete words for it without changing the meaning.

Possessive pronoun	Contraction
Its motor is small.	**It's** [It is] a small motor.
Whose turn is it?	**Who's** [Who is] representing us?

To form the possessive of most singular proper nouns, you add an apostrophe and an *s: Iowa's governor.* When a singular proper noun already ends in *-s,* though, you need to consult the publication guide for the discipline in which you are writing. The *MLA Handbook for Writers of Research Papers* recommends always using *-'s,* as in *Illinois's legislature, Dickens's novels, Ms. Jones's address,* and *Descartes's reasoning.* The *Chicago Manual of Style,* however, notes some exceptions to this rule. An apostrophe without an *s* is used under the following circumstances: (1) when a name ends in a syllable pronounced "eez" *(Sophocles' poetry),* (2) when a singular common noun ends in *-s (physics' contribution),* and (3) when the name of a place or organization ends in *-s* but refers to a single entity *(United States' foreign aid).*

(2) Plural nouns ending in -s require only an apostrophe for the possessive form.

the boys' game   the babies' toys   the Joneses' house

Plural nouns that do not end in *-s* need both an apostrophe and an *s.*

men's lives   women's health   children's projects

An apostrophe is not needed to make a noun plural. To make most nouns plural, add *-s* or *-es*. Add an apostrophe only to signal ownership, origin, and other similar relationships.

protesters

The protesters' met in front of the conference center.

The protesters' meeting was on Wednesday.

Likewise, to form the plural of a family name, use *-s* or *-es,* not an apostrophe.

Johnsons

The Johnson's participated in the study. [COMPARE: The Johnsons' participation in the study was crucial.]

Jameses

The trophy was given to the James's. [COMPARE: The Jameses' trophy is on display in the lobby.]

(3) To show collaboration or joint ownership, add -'s or an apostrophe to the second noun only.

the carpenter and the **plumber's** decision [They made the decision collaboratively.]

the Becks and the **Lopezes'** cabin [They own one cabin jointly.]

(4) To show separate ownership or individual contributions, add -'s or an apostrophe to each noun.

the **Becks'** and the **Lopezes'** cars [Each family owns a car.]

the **carpenter's** and the **plumber's** proposals [They each made a proposal.]

(5) Add -'s to the last word of a compound noun.

my brother-in-**law's** friends, the attorney **general's** statements [singular]

my brothers-in-**law's** friends, the attorneys **general's** statements [plural]

To avoid awkward constructions such as the last two, writers often rephrase them using a prepositional phrase beginning with *of: the statements of the attorneys general.*

(6) Add -'s or an apostrophe to a noun that precedes a gerund.

Lucy's **having** to be there seemed unnecessary. [singular noun preceding gerund]

The family appreciated the lawyers' **handling** of the matter. [plural noun preceding gerund]

Sometimes you may find it difficult to distinguish between a gerund and a participle (see 21a(3)). A good way to tell the difference is to note whether the emphasis is on an action or on a person. In a sentence containing a gerund, the emphasis is on the action; in a sentence containing a participle, the emphasis is on the person.

Our successful completion of the project depends on **Terry's providing** the illustrations. [gerund]

I remember my **brother telling** me the same joke last year. [participle]

Gerund Phrases
When a gerund appears after a noun that ends with -'s or with just an apostrophe, the noun is the subject of the gerund phrase.

Lucy's having to be there [COMPARE: **Lucy** has to be there.]
The lawyers' handling of the matter [COMPARE: **The lawyers** handled the matter.]

The gerund phrase may serve as the subject or the object in the sentence (see 20d).

s
Lucy's having to be there seemed unnecessary.

obj
The family appreciated **the lawyers' handling of the matter.**

(7) Follow an organization's preference for its name or the name of a product; follow local conventions for a geographical location.

Consumers Union	Actors' Equity	Shoppers Choice	Taster's Choice
Devil's Island	Devils Tower	Devil Mountain	

Whether an apostrophe is used in a brand name is determined by the organization owning the name.

Exercise 1

Following the pattern of the examples, change the modifier after each noun to a possessive form that precedes the noun.

EXAMPLES

proposals made by the committee   *the committee's proposals*

poems written by Keats   *Keats's poems*

1. the day named after St. Patrick
2. a leave of absence lasting six months
3. the position taken by HMOs
4. the report given by the eyewitness
5. the generosity of the Lees
6. an article coauthored by Gloria and Alan
7. the weights of the children
8. the spying done by the neighbors
9. the restaurants in New Orleans
10. coffee roasted by Starbucks

37b Marking omissions of letters or numbers

Apostrophes mark omissions in contractions, numbers, and words mimicking speech.

they're [they are]   class of '06 [class of 2006]
y'all [you all]   singin' [singing]

Contractions are not always appropriate for formal contexts. Your audience may expect you to use full words instead (for example, *cannot* instead of *can't* and *will not* instead of *won't*).

 A grammar checker will often flag possessives, marking them as "possible" errors but not telling you whether the apostrophe goes before the *s* or after it, or if an added *s* is needed at all. A grammar checker is usually right, however, about missing apostrophes in contractions such as *can't* and *don't*.

37c Forming certain plurals

Although an apostrophe was used in the past for forming the plurals of numbers, abbreviations, and words used as words, it is used only rarely for this purpose today. These plurals are generally formed by simply adding *-s*.

1990s   fours and fives   YWCAs   two *and*s   the three Rs

Apostrophes are still used, however, with lowercase letters and with abbreviations that include internal periods or a combination of uppercase and lowercase letters.

x's and y's   B.A.'s   Ph.D.'s

The MLA differs from this style in recommending the use of apostrophes for the plurals of uppercase letters (*A*'s and *B*'s).

Insert apostrophes where needed in the following sentences. Be
prepared to explain why they are necessary.

1. Whose responsibility is it to see whether its working?
2. Hansons book was published in the early 1920s.
3. They hired a rock n roll band for their wedding dance.
4. NPRs fund drive begins this weekend.
5. Youll have to include the ISBNs of the books youre going to
   purchase.
6. Only three of the proposals are still being considered: yours, ours,
   and the Wilbers.
7. Few students enrolled during the academic year 98–99.
8. There cant be more *x*s than there are *y*s in the equation.
9. The students formed groups of twos and threes.
10. The M.D.s disagreed on the patients prognosis.

Add the apostrophes that are missing from the following paragraph.

[1]In his book *A Day in the Life: The Music and Artistry of the Beatles,*
Mark Hertsgaard describes what he found in the archives of Londons
Abbey Road Studios. [2]Although the Beatles released barely eleven
hours worth of music in their eight-year studio career, the archives
contain over four hundred hours of recordings from the 1960s,
including a master tape of each song put out by EMI Records. [3]Also
found in the archives are the working tapes that reveal each songs
evolution. [4]For instance, to Hertsgaard, the first run-through of the
song "A Day in the Life" sounds more like a folk ballad than the art
song it became. [5]Used as the title of the book, this song is notable in
other regards as well. [6]Hertsgaard shows how it reveals the
collaboration of John Lennon and Paul McCartney. [7]Though the song
could be called Johns because he came up with the narrative and its
melody, it was Paul who made it a complete composition by providing
the middle passage. [8]Yet perhaps the song is most significant because

of its message. [9]When the British Broadcasting Corporation (BBC) accused the Beatles of promoting drugs and refused to play the recording, Paul McCartney responded to the BBCs ban by saying that the groups purpose was to turn people on "to the truth" rather than to drugs. [10]According to Hertsgaard, in "A Day in the Life," the Beatles were expressing their belief that the world could be released from the hold of power and greed: it could be rejuvenated.

38

QUOTATION MARKS

Quotation marks enclose sentences or parts of sentences that play a special role. For example, quotation marks indicate that you are quoting someone else's words or that you are using a word or phrase in an unconventional way. This chapter will help you use quotation marks

- with direct quotations (**38a**),
- with titles of short works (**38b**),
- for words or phrases used ironically or unconventionally (**38c**), and
- in combination with other punctuation (**38d**).

38a Direct quotations

Double quotation marks set off direct quotations, including those in dialogue. Single quotation marks enclose a quotation within a quotation.

(1) Double quotation marks enclose direct quotations.

Quotation marks enclose only the quotation, not any expression such as *she said* or *he replied.* When a sentence ends with quoted material, place the period inside the quotation marks. For guidelines on comma placement, see **38d(1)**.

> "Like branding steers or embalming the dead," writes David Sedaris, "teaching was a profession I had never seriously considered."

When using direct quotations, reproduce all quoted material exactly as it appears in the original, including capitalization and punctuation. To learn how to set off long quotations as indented blocks, see **12a(2)** and **16f(4)**.

(2) Quotation marks are not used for indirect quotations.

An indirect quotation is a restatement of what someone else has said or written.

> David Sedaris claims that he never wanted to become a teacher, any more than he wanted to become a cowboy or a mortician.

(3) Single quotation marks enclose quotations within quotations.

If the quotation you are using includes another direct quotation, use single quotation marks for the embedded quotation.

> According to Anita Erickson, "when the narrator says, 'I have the right to my own opinion,' he means that he has the right to his own delusion."

However, if a quotation appears in a block quotation, use double quotation marks.

Anita Erickson claims that the narrator uses the word *opinion* deceptively.

> Later in the chapter, when the narrator says, "I have the right to my own opinion," he means that he has the right to his own delusion. Although it is tempting to believe that the narrator is acting according to a rational belief system, his behavior suggests that he is more interested in deception. With poisonous lies, whose concoction he savors, he has already deceived his business partner, his wife, and his children.

(4) Dialogue is enclosed in quotation marks.

When creating or reporting a dialogue, enclose in quotation marks what each person says, no matter how short. Use a separate paragraph for each speaker, beginning a new paragraph whenever the speaker changes. Expressions such as *he said,* as well as related narrative details, can be included in the same paragraph as a direct quotation.

> Farmer looked up, smiling, and in a chirpy-sounding voice he said, "But that feeling has the disadvantage of being . . ." He paused a beat. "Wrong."
>
> "Well," I retorted, "it depends on how you look at it."
>
> —**TRACY KIDDER**, *Mountains Beyond Mountains*

When quoting more than one paragraph by a single speaker, put quotation marks at the beginning of each paragraph. However, do not place closing quotation marks at the end of each paragraph—only at the end of the last paragraph.

(5) Thoughts are enclosed in quotation marks.

Quotation marks set off thoughts that resemble speech.

> "His silence on this topic has surprised everyone," I thought as I surveyed the faces of the other committee members.

Thoughts are usually marked by such phrases as *I thought, he felt*, and *she believed*. Remember, though, that quotation marks are not used with thoughts that are reported indirectly (see 38a(2)).

> I wondered why he didn't respond.

(6) Short excerpts of poetry included within a sentence are enclosed in quotation marks.

When quoting fewer than four lines of poetry, enclose them in quotation marks and use a slash to indicate the line division (see also 39i).

> After watching a whale swim playfully, the speaker in "Visitation" concludes, "What did you think, that joy / was some slight thing?"

To learn how to treat longer quotations of poetry, see 16f(4).

38b Titles of short works

Quotation marks enclose the title of a short work, such as a story, essay, poem, or song. The title of a larger work, such as a book, magazine, newspaper, or play, should be italicized (or underlined if you are using MLA style).

> "The Green Shepherd" first appeared in *The New Yorker*.

Short story	"The Lottery"	"The Fall of the House of Usher"
Essay	"Living Like Weasels"	"Play-by-Play"
Article	"Disneyland with the Death Penalty"	"Arabia's Empty Quarter"
Book chapter	"The Neurologist Vanishes"	"Spirits of Blood, Spirits of Air"

Short poem	"Orion"	"Mending Wall"
Song	"Lazy River"	"The Star-Spangled Banner"
TV episode	"An Englishman Abroad"	"The Last Time"

Use double quotation marks around the title of a short work embedded in a longer italicized (or underlined) title.

> *Interpretations of* "*A Good Man Is Hard to Find*" [book about a short story]

Use single quotation marks for a shorter title within a longer title that is enclosed in double quotation marks.

> "Irony in 'The Sick Rose' " [article about a poem]

Differing Uses of Quotation Marks

If you read a book published in Great Britain, you will notice that the use of quotation marks differs in some ways from the style presented here. For example, single quotation marks are used to set off the titles of short works, and a period is placed outside a quotation mark ending a sentence. Nevertheless, when writing in the United States, follow the rules for American English.

British usage	In class, we compared Wordsworth's 'Upon Westminster Bridge' with Blake's 'London'.
American usage	In class, we compared Wordsworth's "Upon Westminster Bridge" with Blake's "London."

38c For ironic tone or unusual usage

Writers sometimes use quotation marks to indicate that they are using a word or phrase ironically. The word *gourmet* is used ironically in the following sentence.

> His "gourmet" dinner turned out to be processed turkey and instant mashed potatoes.

Avoid using quotation marks around words that may not be appropriate for your rhetorical situation. Instead, take the time to choose suitable words. The revised sentence in the following pair is more effective than the first.

Ineffective He is too much of a "wimp" to be a good leader.
Revised He is too indecisive to be a good leader.

Similarly, putting a cliché (see **33b**) in quotation marks could make readers conclude that you do not care enough about expressing your meaning to think of a fresh expression.

38d With other punctuation marks

To decide whether to place some other punctuation mark inside or outside quotation marks, identify the punctuation mark and note whether it is part of the quotation or part of the surrounding context.

(1) With commas and periods

Quoted material is usually accompanied by an attributive tag such as *she said* or *he replied*. When your sentence starts with an attributive tag, place a comma after it to separate the tag from the quotation.

> She replied, "There's more than one way to slice a pie."

If your sentence starts with the quotation instead, place the comma inside the closing quotation marks.

> "There's more than one way to slice a pie," she replied.

Place the period inside closing quotation marks, whether single or double, if the quotation ends the sentence.

> Jason admitted, "I didn't understand 'An Algorithm for Life.'"

When quoting material from a source, provide the relevant page number(s). If you are following MLA guidelines, note the page number(s) in parentheses after the final quotation marks, and place the period that ends the sentence after the final parenthesis, unless the quotation is a block quotation. (See **12a(2)**.)

According to Diane Ackerman, "Love is a demanding sport involving all the muscle groups, including the brain" (86).

(2) With semicolons and colons

Place semicolons and colons outside quotation marks.

His favorite song was "Cyprus Avenue"; mine was "Astral Weeks."

Because it is repeated, one line stands out in "The Conductor": "We are never as beautiful as now."

(3) With question marks, exclamation points, and dashes

If the direct quotation includes a question mark, an exclamation point, or a dash, place that punctuation *inside* the closing quotation marks.

Jeremy asked, "What is truth?"

Gordon shouted "Congratulations!"

Laura said, "Let me tell—" Before she could finish her sentence, Dan walked into the room.

Use just one question mark inside the quotation marks when a question ends with a quoted question.

Why do children keep asking "Why?"

If the punctuation is not part of the quoted material, place it *outside* the closing quotation marks.

Who wrote "The Figure a Sentence Makes"?

You have to read "Awareness and Freedom"!

She called me a "toaster head"—understandable under the circumstances.

Exercise 1

Insert quotation marks where they are needed in the following sentences. Do not alter sentences that are written correctly.

1. Have you read Ian Buruma's essay The Joys and Perils of Victimhood?

2. Buruma writes, The only way a new generation can be identified with the suffering of previous generations is for that suffering to be publicly acknowledged, over and over again.

3. When my reading group met to talk about this essay, I started our discussion by noting that the word *victim* is defined in my dictionary as anyone who is oppressed or mistreated.

4. So how can we tell who the real victims are? asked Claudia.

5. Cahit responded, I think that both the Israelis and the Palestinians are victims of violence.

6. Yes, agreed Claudia, I worry especially about the women and children in that part of the world. I wish I could say to them, Do not give up hope!

7. According to Tony, the situation in the Middle East would improve if people could learn to live and let live.

8. Using the events of September 11, 2001, as an example, Kyle argued that victims can be of any race, nationality, religion, or gender.

9. Rachel agreed but added that victims can be of different ages as well, pointing out that child abuse is a growing concern.

10. I see many victims of abuse when I volunteer at the Center for the Family, Mai explained, but we must be careful not to confuse abuse with discipline.

39 THE PERIOD AND OTHER PUNCTUATION MARKS

To indicate the end of a sentence, you can use one of three punctuation marks: the period, the question mark, or the exclamation point. Your choice depends on the meaning you wish to convey.

Everyone passed the exam.

Everyone passed the exam? [informal usage]

Everyone passed the exam!

Other punctuation marks also clarify meaning and ease reading. Colons, dashes, parentheses, square brackets, ellipsis points, and slashes help your readers understand the message you want to convey. (For use of the hyphen, see **40f**.)

This chapter will help you use

- end punctuation marks (the period, the question mark, and the exclamation point) (**39a–c**),
- the colon (**39d**),
- the dash (**39e**),
- parentheses (**39f**),
- square brackets (**39g**),
- ellipsis points (**39h**), and
- the slash (**39i**).

> To accommodate computerized typesetting, both CMS and the APA style manual call for only one space after a period, a question mark, an exclamation point, a colon, and each of the periods in ellipsis points. According to these manuals, there should be no space preceding or following a hyphen or a dash. The MLA style manual recommends using only one space after end punctuation marks but allows two spaces if they are used consistently.

39a The period

(1) A period marks the end of a sentence.

Use a period at the end of a declarative sentence.

> Many adults in the United States are overfed yet undernourished.
> Soft drinks account for 7 percent of their average daily caloric intake.

In addition, place a period at the end of an instruction or recommendation written as an imperative sentence (see **21e**).

> Eat plenty of fruits and vegetables. Drink six to eight glasses of water a day.

Indirect questions are phrased as statements, so be sure to use a period, rather than a question mark, at the end of such a sentence.

> I wonder why people eat so much junk food.
> [COMPARE: Why do people eat so much junk food?]

(2) Periods follow some abbreviations.

> Dr.   Jr.   a.m.   p.m.   vs.   etc.   et al.

Only one period follows an abbreviation that ends a sentence.

> The tour begins at 1:00 p.m.

Periods are not used with many common abbreviations (for example, *MVP, mph,* and *FM*). (See chapter **43**.) A dictionary lists the conventional form of an abbreviation as well as any alternatives.

39b The question mark

Place a question mark after a direct question.

> How does the new atomic clock work? Who invented this clock?

Use a period, instead of a question mark, after an indirect question—that is, a question embedded in a statement.

> I asked whether the new atomic clock could be used in cell phones.
> [COMPARE: Can the new atomic clock be used in cell phones?]

Indirect Questions

Indirect questions are written as declarative sentences. The subject and verb are not inverted as they would be in the related direct question.

We do not know when ~~will~~ the meeting ^will^ end.

[COMPARE: When will the meeting end?]

Place a question mark after each question in a series of related questions, even when they are not full sentences.

Will the new atomic clock be used in cell phones? Word processors? Car navigation systems?

If a direct quotation is a question, place the question mark inside the final quotation marks.

Tony asked, "How small is this new clock?"

In contrast, if you include quoted material in a question of your own, place the question mark outside the final quotation marks.

Is the clock really "no larger than a sugar cube"?

If you embed in the middle of a sentence a question not attributable to anyone in particular, place a comma before it and a question mark after it.

When the question, how does the clock work? arose, the researchers described a technique used by manufacturers of computer chips.

The first letter of such a question should not be capitalized unless the question is extremely long or contains internal punctuation.

To indicate uncertainty about a fact such as a date of birth, place a question mark inside parentheses directly after the fact in question.

Chaucer was born in 1340 (?) and died in 1400.

39c The exclamation point

An exclamation point often marks the end of a sentence, but its primary purpose is rhetorical—to create emphasis.

Whoa! What a game!

When a direct quotation ends with an exclamation point, no comma or period is placed immediately after it.

"Get a new pitcher!" he yelled.

He yelled, "Get a new pitcher!"

Use the exclamation point sparingly so that you do not diminish its value. If you do not intend to signal strong emotion, place a comma after an interjection and a period at the end of the sentence.

Well, no one seriously expected this victory.

Exercise 1

Compose and punctuate brief sentences of the following types.

1. a declarative sentence containing a quoted exclamation
2. a sentence beginning with an interjection
3. a direct question
4. a declarative sentence containing an indirect question
5. a declarative sentence containing a direct question

39d The colon

A colon calls attention to what follows. It also separates numbers in time references and in parts of scriptural references and titles from subtitles. Leave only one space after a colon.

(1) A colon directs attention to an explanation, a summary, or a quotation.

When a colon appears between two independent clauses, it signals that the second clause will explain or expand on the first.

> For I had no brain tumor, no eyestrain, no high blood pressure, nothing wrong with me at all: I simply had migraine headaches, and migraine headaches were, as everyone who did not have them knew, imaginary.
>
> —JOAN DIDION

A colon is also used after an independent clause to introduce a direct quotation.

> Marcel Proust explained the importance of mindfulness this way: "The true journey of discovery consists not in seeking new landscapes but in having fresh eyes."

The rules for using an uppercase or a lowercase letter to begin the first word of an independent clause that follows a colon vary across style manuals.

MLA	The first letter should be lowercase unless (1) it begins a word that is normally capitalized, (2) the independent clause is a quotation, or (3) it begins a rule or principle.
APA	The first letter should be uppercase.
CMS	The first letter should be lowercase unless (1) it begins a word that is normally capitalized, (2) the independent clause is a quotation, or (3) two or more sentences follow the colon.

Although an independent clause should always precede the colon, a phrase may sometimes follow it.

> I was finally confronted with what I had dreaded for months: the due date for the final balloon payment on my car loan.

All of the style manuals advise using lowercase letters for the first letter of a phrase following a colon.

(2) A colon may signal that a list follows.

Writers frequently use colons to introduce lists.

> Three students received internships: Asa, Vanna, and Jack.

Avoid placing a colon between a verb and its complement or after the words *including* and *such as*.

> The winners were: Asa, Vanna, and Jack.

> Many vegetarians do not eat dairy products such as: butter and cheese.

(3) A colon separates a title and a subtitle.

Use a colon between a work's title and its subtitle.

Collapse: How Societies Choose to Fail or Succeed

(4) Colons are used in certain numbers.

Colons are used between numbers in time designations and scriptural references.

11:45 a.m.   3:00 p.m.

Psalms 3:5   Gen. 1:1

However, MLA requires the use of periods in numbers referring to scripture.

Psalms 3.5   Gen. 1.1

(5) Colons have specialized uses in business correspondence.

A colon follows the salutation of a business letter and any notations.

Dear Dr. Horner: Dear Maxine: enc:

A colon introduces the headings in a memo.

To: From: Subject: Date:

Exercise 2

Insert colons where they are needed in the following sentences.

1. Before we discuss marketing, let's outline the behavior of consumers consumer behavior is the process individuals go through as they select, buy, or use products or services to satisfy their needs and desires.

2. The process consists of six stages recognizing a need or desire, finding information, evaluating options, deciding to purchase, purchasing, and assessing purchases.

3. Many consumers rely on one popular publication for product information *Consumer Reports*.

4. When evaluating alternatives, a consumer uses criteria; for example, a house hunter might use some of the following criteria price, location, size, age, style, and landscaping design.

5. The postpurchase assessment has one of two results satisfaction or dissatisfaction with the product or service.

39e The dash

A dash (or em dash) marks a break in thought, sets off a nonessential element for emphasis or clarity, or follows an introductory list or series. You can use your keyboard to form such a dash by typing two hyphens with no spaces between, before, or after the hyphens. Most word-processing programs can be set to convert these hyphens automatically to an em dash. Dashes signal a specific meaning, so use them purposefully rather than as mere substitutes for commas, semicolons, or colons. (For use of the short dash, or en dash, see 43g.)

(1) A dash marks a break in the normal flow of a sentence.

Use a dash to indicate a shift in thought or tone.

> I was awed by the almost superhuman effort Stonehenge represents—but who wouldn't be?

(2) A dash or a pair of dashes sets off a nonessential element for emphasis or clarity.

> Dr. Kruger's specialty is mycology—the study of fungi.

> The trail we took down into the Grand Canyon—steep, narrow, winding, and lacking guardrails—made me wonder whether we could call a helicopter to fly us back out.

(3) A dash follows an introductory list or series.

If you decide to place a list or series at the beginning of a sentence in order to emphasize it, the main part of the following sentence (after the dash) should sum up the meaning of the list or series.

> Eager, determined to succeed, and scared to death—all of these describe how I felt on the first day at work.

THINKING RHETORICALLY ABOUT

COMMAS, DASHES, AND COLONS

Although commas, dashes, and colons may be followed by explanations, examples, or illustrations, is their rhetorical impact the same?

> He never failed to mention what was most important to him, the bottom line.

> He never failed to mention what was most important to him——the bottom line.

> He never failed to mention what was most important to him: the bottom line.

The comma, one of the most common punctuation marks, barely draws attention to what follows it. The dash, in contrast, signals a longer pause and so causes more emphasis to be placed on the information that follows. The colon is more direct and formal than either of the other two punctuation marks.

39f Parentheses

Use parentheses to set off information that is not closely related to the main point of a sentence or paragraph but that provides an interesting detail, an explanation, or an illustration. Parentheses used for this purpose indicate that the material they contain is an aside.

> If we refuse to talk "like a lady," we are ridiculed and criticized for being unfeminine. ("She thinks like a man" is, at best, a left-handed compliment.)
>
> —ROBIN LAKOFF

In addition, place parentheses around an acronym or abbreviation when introducing it after its full form.

> The Search for Extraterrestrial Intelligence (SETI) uses the Very Large Array (VLA) outside Sicorro, New Mexico, to scan the sky.

If you use numbers or letters in a list within a sentence, set them off by placing them within parentheses.

Your application should include (1) a current résumé, (2) a statement of purpose, and (3) two letters of recommendation.

For information on the use of parentheses in bibliographies and in-text citations, see chapters **12–15**.

THINKING RHETORICALLY ABOUT

DASHES AND PARENTHESES

Dashes and parentheses are both used to set off a nonessential element in a sentence, but they differ in the amount of emphasis they signal. Whereas dashes call attention to the material they set off, parentheses usually deemphasize the information they enclose.

Sylvia—an avid video-game player—is in front of her computer when she is not at her controls.

Sylvia $($ an avid video-game player $)$ is enrolled in the flight technology program.

39g Square brackets

Square brackets set off additions or alterations used to clarify quotations. In the following example, the bracketed name specifies who "he" is.

Parker Pilgrim has written, "If he $[$ Leonard Aaron $]$ ever disapproved of any of his children's friends, he never let them know about it."

If your rhetorical situation calls for the exact replication of directly quoted material, use square brackets to indicate that a letter has been changed from uppercase to lowercase, or vice versa.

$[$ I $]$ f the network was ever going to become more than a test bed . . . , word of its potential had to spread.   —**KATIE HAFNER** AND **MATTHEW LYON**

To avoid the awkwardness of using brackets in such a way, consider rewording the sentence so that no change in capitalization is needed.

Hafner and Lyon note that "if the network was ever going to become more than a test bed . . . , word of its potential had to spread."

Square brackets are also used within parentheses to avoid the confusion of having two sets of parentheses.

Not every expert agrees. (See, for example, Katie Hafner and Matthew Lyon's *Where Wizards Stay Up Late* [New York: Simon, 1996].)

Angle brackets (< >) are often used to enclose Web addresses so that punctuation in the sentence is not confused with the dot(s) in the URL: <http://www.harbrace.com>.

39h Ellipsis points

Ellipsis points indicate an omission from a quoted passage or a reflective pause or hesitation.

(1) Ellipsis points mark an omission within a quoted passage.

Whenever you omit anything from material you quote, replace the omitted material with ellipsis points—three equally spaced periods. Be sure to compare your quoted sentence to the original, checking to see that your omission does not change the meaning of the original. The following examples illustrate how to use ellipsis points in quotations from a passage by Patricia Gadsby.

Original

Cacao doesn't flower, as most plants do, at the tips of its outer and uppermost branches. Instead, its sweet white buds hang from the trunk and along a few fat branches, popping out of patches of bark called cushions, which form where leaves drop off. They're tiny, these flowers. Yet once pollinated by midges, no-see-ums that flit in the leafy detritus below, they'll make pulp-filled pods almost the size of rugby balls.

—**PATRICIA GADSBY**, "Endangered Chocolate"

Omission within a quoted sentence

Patricia Gadsby notes that cacao flowers "once pollinated by midges . . . make pulp-filled pods almost the size of rugby balls."

Omission at the beginning of a quoted sentence

Do not use ellipsis points to indicate that you have deleted words from the beginning of a quotation, whether it is run into the text or set off in a block. The first word of the original sentence has been omitted in the following quotation.

> According to Patricia Gadsby, cacao flowers will become "pulp-filled pods almost the size of rugby balls."

Note that the first letter of the integrated quotation is not capitalized.

Omission at the end of a quoted sentence

To indicate that you have omitted words from the end of a sentence, put a space after the last word and before the three spaced ellipsis points. Then add the end punctuation mark (a period, a question mark, or an exclamation point). If the quoted material is followed by a parenthetical source or page reference, the end punctuation comes after the second parenthesis.

> Claiming that cacao flowers differ from those of most plants, Patricia Gadsby describes how "the sweet white buds hang from the trunk and along a few fat branches . . . ." OR "branches . . ." (2).

Omission of a sentence or more

To signal the omission of a sentence or more (even a paragraph or more), place an end punctuation mark (usually a period) before the ellipsis points.

> Patricia Gadsby describes the flowering of the cacao plant: "its sweet white buds hang from the trunk and along a few fat branches, popping out of patches of bark called cushions, which form where leaves drop off. . . . Yet once pollinated by midges, no-see-ums that flit in the leafy detritus below, they'll make pulp-filled pods almost the size of rugby balls."

If, in addition to omitting a full sentence, you omit part of another and that part ends in a comma, colon, or semicolon, place the relevant punctuation mark before the ellipsis points.

> Patricia Gadsby describes the flowering of the cacao plant: "its sweet white buds hang from the trunk and along a few fat branches, . . . Yet once pollinated by midges, no-see-ums that flit in the leafy detritus below, they'll make pulp-filled pods almost the size of rugby balls."

To signal the omission of a full line or more in quoted poetry, use spaced periods covering the length of either the line above it or the omitted line.

The yellow fog that rubs its back upon the window-panes,

. . . .

Curled once about the house, and fell asleep.

—**T. S. ELIOT**, "The Love Song of J. Alfred Prufrock"

To avoid excessive use of ellipses, replace some of the direct quotations with paraphrases. (See 11d(3).)

(2) Ellipsis points show that a sentence has been intentionally left incomplete.

Read aloud the passage that begins "The yellow fog . . ."

(3) Ellipsis points can mark a reflective pause or a hesitation.

Keith saw four menacing youths coming toward him . . . and ran.

A dash can also be used to indicate this type of a pause.

39i The slash

A slash between words, as in *and/or* and *he/she*, indicates that either word is applicable in the given context. There are no spaces before and after a slash used in this way. Because extensive use of the slash can make writing choppy, consider using *or* instead. (If you are following MLA conventions, avoid using the slash in formal prose.)

A slash is also used to mark line divisions in quoted poetry. A slash used in this way is preceded and followed by a space.

Wallace Stevens refers to the listener who, "nothing himself, beholds / Nothing that is not there and the nothing that is."

Exercise 3

Add dashes, parentheses, square brackets, and slashes at appropriate places in the following sentences. Be ready to explain the reason for every mark you add.

1. Researchers in an exciting field Artificial Intelligence AI are working on devices to assist the elderly.
2. One such device is Pearl a robotic nurse that helps around the house.
3. Another application is cooking software that checks for missing and or incorrect ingredients.
4. Researchers are even investigating Global Positioning Systems GPS as a way to track Alzheimer's patients' daily routines.
5. The actual cost of such devices expensive now but more affordable later is yet to be determined.

Exercise 4

Punctuate the following sentences with appropriate end marks, commas, colons, dashes, and parentheses. Do not use unnecessary punctuation. Give a justification for each mark you add, especially where more than one type of mark (for example, commas, dashes, or parentheses) is acceptable.

1. Many small country towns are very similar a truck stop a gas station a crowded diner and three bars
2. The simple life a nonexistent crime rate and down-home values these are some of the advantages these little towns offer
3. Why do we never see these quaint examples of pure Americana when we travel around the country on the interstates
4. Rolling across America on one of the big interstates I-20 I-40 I-70 I-80 or I-90 you are likely to pass within a few miles of a number of these towns
5. These towns almost certainly will have a regional or perhaps an ethnic flavor Hispanic in the southwest Scandinavian in the north
6. When I visit one of these out-of-the-way places I always have a sense of well really a feeling of safety
7. There's one thing I can tell you small-town life is not boring
8. My one big question however is what do you do to earn a living in these towns.

Advertisers frequently use capitalization to highlight
important words.

40

SPELLING, THE SPELL

CHECKER, AND

HYPHENATION

When you first draft a paper, you might not pay close attention to spelling words correctly. After all, the point of drafting is to generate and organize ideas. However, proofreading for spelling mistakes is essential as you near the end of the writing process. Your teachers, employers, or supervisors will expect you to submit polished work.

You can train yourself to be a good proofreader by checking a dictionary every time you question the spelling of a word. If two spellings are listed, such as *fulfill* and *fulfil*, either form is correct, although the first option provided is generally considered more common. Whatever spelling you choose in such cases, use it consistently. You can also learn to be a better speller by studying a few basic strategies. This chapter will help you

- use a spell checker (40a),
- spell words according to pronunciation (40b),
- spell words that sound alike (40c),
- understand how prefixes and suffixes affect spelling (40d),
- use *ei* and *ie* correctly (40e), and
- use hyphenation to link and divide words (40f).

40a Spell checker

The spell checker is a wonderful invention, but it does not relieve you of the responsibility for spelling words correctly. A spell checker finds errors by checking the words in a document against the words in its dictionary. When it finds a word that does not match any words in its dictionary, it flags that word as misspelled.

A spell checker will usually catch

- misspellings of common words,
- some commonly confused words (such as *affect* and *effect*), and
- obvious typographical errors (such as *tge* for *the*).

However, a spell checker generally will *not* catch

- specialized vocabulary or foreign words not in its dictionary,
- typographical errors that are still correctly spelled words (such as *was* for *saw*), and
- misuses of words that sound alike but are not on the spell checker's list of words commonly confused (such as *here* and *hear*).

The following strategies can help you use a spell checker effectively.

TIPS FOR USING A SPELL CHECKER

- Keep a separate file of words you tend to misspell. When you edit a document, use the Find feature of your word-processing program to search for and correct any misspellings of these words.

- If a spell checker regularly flags a word (or a name) that is not in its dictionary but is spelled correctly, add that word to its dictionary by clicking on the Add button. From that point on, the spell checker will accept the word you added.

- Reject any offers the spell checker makes to correct all instances of a particular error.

- Use a dictionary to evaluate the alternative spellings the spell checker provides because some of them may be erroneous.

- Always proofread your writing yourself; never rely on a spell checker to locate all of your spelling errors.

40b Spelling and pronunciation

Many words in English are not spelled the way they are pronounced, so pronunciation is not a reliable guide to correct spelling. Sometimes, people skip over an unstressed syllable, as when *February* is pronounced "Febwary," or they slide over a sound that is hard to articulate, as when *library* is pronounced "libary." Other times, people add a sound—for instance, when they pronounce *athlete* as "athalete." And people also switch sounds around, as in "irrevelant" for *irrelevant*. Such mispronunciations can lead to misspellings.

You can help yourself remember the spellings of some words by considering the spellings of their root words—for example, the root word for *irrelevant* is *relevant*. You can also teach yourself the correct spellings of words by pronouncing them the way they are spelled, that is, by pronouncing each letter mentally so that you "hear" even silent letters. You are more likely to remember the *b* in *subtle* if you pronounce it when spelling that word. Here are a few words typically misspelled because they include unpronounced letters:

condem*n*   for*eign*   lab*o*ratory   mus*c*le   solem*n*

Here are a few more that include letters that are often not heard in rapid speech, though they can be heard when carefully pronounced:

can*d*idate   dif*f*erent   enviro*n*ment   gover*n*ment   sep*a*rate

The words *and, have,* and *than* are often not stressed in speech and are thus misspelled. A spell checker will not catch these misspellings.

They would rather ~~of~~ written two papers ~~then~~ taken midterm ~~an~~ final exams.

have / than / and

40c Words that sound alike

Pairs of words such as *forth* and *fourth* or *sole* and *soul* are **homophones:** they sound alike but have different meanings and spellings. Some words that have different meanings sound exactly alike (*break/brake*), others sound alike in certain dialects (*marry/merry*), and still others are only similar in sound, especially in rapid speech (*believe/belief*). A spell checker cannot identify words that are correctly spelled but incorrectly used. If you are unsure about the difference in meaning between any two words that sound alike, consult a dictionary. A number of frequently confused words are listed with explanations in this handbook's Glossary of Usage.

Single words and two-word phrases that consist of the same letters but have different meanings can also be troublesome. The following are examples.

Everyday life was grueling.	She attended class **every day.**
They do not fight **anymore.**	They could not find **any more** evidence.

Other examples are *awhile/a while, everybody/every body, everyone/every one, maybe/may be, sometime/some time,* and *nobody/no body.*

A lot and *all right* are still spelled as two words. *Alot* is always considered incorrect; *alright* is also considered incorrect except in some newspapers and magazines. (See the Glossary of Usage.)

Singular nouns ending in *-nce* and plural nouns ending in *-nts* are easily confused.

Assistance is available.	I have two **assistants.**
His **patience** wore thin.	Some **patients** waited for hours.

Contractions, possessive pronouns, and possessive determiners are also often confused. In contractions, an apostrophe indicates an omitted letter (or letters). In possessive pronouns or determiners, there is no apostrophe. (See also 25b and 37a(1).)

Contraction	Possessive
It's my turn next.	Each group waited **its** turn.
You're next.	**Your** turn is next.
There's no difference.	**Theirs** is no different.

TIPS FOR SPELLING WORDS THAT SOUND ALIKE

- Be on the lookout for words that are commonly confused (*accept/except*).
- Distinguish between similar sounding single words and two-word phrases (*maybe/may be*).
- Use *-nts,* not *-nce,* for plural words (*instants/instance*).
- Mark contractions, but not possessive pronouns, with apostrophes (*who's/whose*).

40d Prefixes and suffixes

When a prefix is added to a base word (often called the **root**), the spelling of the base word is unaffected.

necessary, **un**necessary   moral, **im**moral

Adding a suffix to the end of a base word often changes the spelling.

beauty, beau**tiful**   describe, descri**ption**   BUT   resist, resis**tance**

Although spellings of words with suffixes are irregular, they follow certain conventions.

(1) Dropping or retaining a final *e* depends on whether the suffix begins with a vowel.

- If a suffix begins with a vowel, the final *e* of the base word is dropped: bride, brid**al**; come, com**ing**; combine, combin**ation**; prime, prim**ary.**
- If a suffix begins with a consonant, the final *e* of the base word is retained: entire, entire**ly**; rude, rude**ness**; place, place**ment**; sure, sure**ly.** Some exceptions are *argument, awful, ninth, truly,* and *wholly.*
- To keep the /s/ sound in *ce* or the /j/ sound in *ge*, retain the final *e* before *-able* or *-ous:* courag**eous,** manag**eable,** notic**eable.**

(2) A final consonant is usually doubled when a suffix begins with a vowel.

- If the consonant ends a one-syllable word with a single vowel or a stressed syllable with a single vowel, double the final consonant: stop, sto**pped,** sto**pping**; omit, omi**tted,** omi**tting.**
- If there are two vowels before the consonant, the consonant is not doubled: loop, loop**ed,** loop**ing**; remain, remain**ed,** remain**ing.**
- If the final syllable is not stressed, the consonant is not doubled: edit, edit**ed,** edit**ing**; picket, picket**ed,** picket**ing.**

(3) A final *y* is changed or retained depending on whether it is preceded by a vowel.

- Change a final *y* to *i* when adding a suffix (except *-ing*): defy, def**ies,** def**ied,** def**iance** BUT defy**ing**; modify, modif**ies,** modif**ied,** modif**ier** BUT modify**ing.**

- Retain the final *y* when it is preceded by a vowel: stay, stay**s**, stay**ed;** obey, obey**s**, obey**ed;** gray, gray**ish.**
- Some verb forms are irregular and thus can cause difficulties: *lays, laid; pays, paid.* For a list of irregular verbs, see page 565.

(4) A final *l* is retained when -*ly* is added.

cool, coo**lly**   formal, forma**lly**   real, rea**lly**   usual, usua**lly**

Exercise 1

Add the specified suffixes to the words that follow. Be prepared to explain the reason for the spelling of each resulting word.

EXAMPLE

-ly: late, casual, psychological   *lately casually psychologically*

1. -ing: put, admit, write, use, try, play
2. -ment: manage, commit, require, argue
3. -ous: continue, joy, acrimony, libel
4. -ed: race, tip, permit, carry, pray
5. -able: desire, read, trace, knowledge
6. -ly : true, sincere, normal, general

---

(5) A noun is made plural by adding -s or -es to the singular.

- If the sound in the plural form of a noun ending in *f* or *fe* changes from /f/ to /v/, change the ending to -*ve* before adding -*s:* thie**f,** thie**ves;** life, li**ves** BUT roof, roo**fs.**
- Add -*es* to most nouns ending in *s, z, ch, sh,* or *x:* box, box**es;** peach, peach**es.**
- If a noun ends in a consonant and *y,* change the *y* to *i* and add -*es:* company, compan**ies;** ninety, ninet**ies;** territory, territor**ies.**
- If a noun ends in a consonant and *o,* add -*es:* hero, hero**es;** potato, potato**es.** However, note that sometimes just -*s* is added (photo, photo**s;** memo, memo**s**) and other times either an -*s* or -*es* suffix can be added (motto**s,** motto**es;** zero**s,** zero**es**).
- Certain nouns have irregular plural forms: woman, wom**en;** child, child**ren;** foot, f**eet.**

■ Add -*s* to most proper nouns: the Lee**s**; the Kennedy**s.** Add -*es* to most proper nouns ending in *s, z, ch, sh,* or *x:* the Rodriguez**es,** the Jones**es** BUT the Bachs.

BEYOND THE RULE

WORDS BORROWED FROM OTHER LANGUAGES

Words borrowed from Latin or Greek generally form their plurals as they did in the original language.

Singular	criterion	alumnus, alumna	analysis	datum	species
Plural	criteria	alumni, alumnae	analyses	data	species

When a word with such an origin is in the process of changing, two different forms will be listed as acceptable in the dictionary: *syllabus/syllabuses, syllabi.* For further information, visit **www.harbrace.com**.

Exercise 2

Provide the plural forms for the following words. If you need extra help, check a dictionary.

1. virus
2. committee
3. phenomenon
4. copy
5. delay
6. embargo
7. self
8. belief
9. foot
10. portfolio
11. cactus
12. census

40e Confusion of *ei* and *ie*

An old rhyme will help you remember the order of letters in most words containing *e* and *i:*

Put *i* before *e*
Except after *c*
Or when sounded like *a*
As in *neighbor* and *weigh.*

Words with *i* before *e:* bel**ie**ve, ch**ie**f, pr**ie**st, y**ie**ld

Words with *e* before *i,* after *c:* conc**ei**t, perc**ei**ve, rec**ei**ve

Words with *ei* sounding like *a* in *cake:* **ei**ght, r**ei**n, th**ei**r, h**ei**r

Words that are exceptions to the rules in the rhyme include *either, neither, species, foreign,* and *weird.*

American and British Spelling Differences

Spelling systems originating in the United States and Great Britain differ in a few minor ways. Spelling in other English-speaking countries varies according to the system adopted in each. Although most words are spelled the same in both systems, there are some differences, including the following.

| **American** | check | realize | color | connection |
| **British** | cheque | realise | colour | connexion |

Use the American spelling system when writing for an audience in the United States.

40f   Hyphens

Hyphens link two or more words functioning as a single word, separate word parts to clarify meaning, and divide words at the ends of lines. They also have many conventional uses in numbers, fractions, and measurements. Do not confuse the hyphen with the em dash, which is keyboarded as a double hyphen with no spaces before and after, or the en dash, which is keyboarded by hitting Option and the hyphen. (See **39e** and **43f**.)

(1) Hyphens sometimes link two or more words that form a compound.

Some compounds are listed in the dictionary with hyphens (*eye-opener, cross-examine*), others are written as two words (*eye chart, cross fire*), and still others are written as one word (*eyewitness, crossbreed*). If you have questions about the spelling of a compound word, a dictionary is a good resource. However, it is also helpful to learn a few basic patterns.

- If two or more words serve as a single adjective before a noun, they should be hyphenated. If the words follow the noun, they are not hyphenated.

  You submitted an **up-to-date** report. The report was **up to date.**

  A **well-known** musician is performing tonight. The musician is **well known.**

- When the second word in a hyphenated expression is omitted, the first word is still followed by a hyphen.

  They discussed both **private-** and **public-sector** partnerships.

- A hyphen is not used after adverbs ending in *-ly* (*poorly planned event*), in names of chemical compounds (*sodium chloride solution*), or in modifiers with a letter or numeral as the second element (*group C homes, type IV virus*).

(2) Hyphens can be used to separate words into parts to clarify meaning.

- To avoid ambiguity or an awkward combination of letters or syllables, place a hyphen between the base word and its prefix: *anti-intellectual, de-emphasize, re-sign the petition* [COMPARE: *resign the position*].
- Place a hyphen between a prefix and a capital letter and between two or more related words: *anti-American, non-self-promoting.*
- Place a hyphen after the prefix *all-, e-, ex-,* or *self-: all-inclusive, e-commerce, ex-husband, self-esteem.* Otherwise, most words with prefixes are not hyphenated.

(3) Hyphens are frequently used in numbers, fractions, and units of measure.

- Place a hyphen between two numbers when they are spelled out: *thirty-two, ninety-nine.* However, no hyphen is used before or after the words *hundred, thousand,* and *million: five hundred sixty-three, forty-one million.*
- Hyphenate fractions that are spelled out: *three-fourths, one-half.*
- When you form a compound modifier that includes a number and a unit of measurement, place a hyphen between them: *twenty-first-century literature, twelve-year-old boy, ten-year project.*

Grammar checkers can identify many compound words and suggest correct spellings, such as *double-space* instead of *doublespace*. Grammar checkers can also alert you to missing hyphens in most fractions (*one-fourth*) and compound numbers (*twenty-seven*) but not to those missing from a compound noun or adjective (*mother-in-law, high-quality*) or to those used to avoid ambiguity (*re-cover* versus *recover*).

Exercise 3

Convert the following word groups into hyphenated compounds.

EXAMPLE

a movie lasting two hours   *a two-hour movie*

1. a man who is fify years old
2. a seminar that lasted all day
3. a street that runs only one way
4. history from the twentieth century
5. roads that are covered by ice and snow
6. a paper that is well written

Exercise 4

Edit the following paragraph to correct mistakes in spelling and the usage of hyphens. Be prepared to explain any changes you make.

[1]Profesor Alan S. Brown, from Southern Methodist University, is studying the phenomena of déjà vu—the allusion of having seen some thing or been some where before. [2]As part of his research in to such second time around experiences, Brown read both literary and psychlogical accounts from the Victorian era. [3]Some of these nineteenth century explanations, he beleives, are still relevent today. [4]Brown also describes a few curius findings about the people most likly to experience déjà vu. [5]For instants, people who travel are more likly to have déjà vu then those who stay at home, political librals report déjà vu more often then conservetives, and as people age déjà vu ocurs less frequently. [6]Brown admits that all the experiences that fall under the

label of déjà vu may actualy be five or six phenomenon and thus have varius causes. [7]He is currantly testing hypothesis that may shed some light on what is happenning in are brains when we feel that uncanny sense of familarity. [8]His results may make us re-consider notions about the nature of our preceptions and memorys.

41

CAPITALS

When you look at an advertisement, an e-mail message, or even a paragraph in this book, you can easily pick out capital letters. These beacons draw your attention to significant details—for example, the beginnings of sentences or the names of particular people, places, and products. Although most capitalization conventions apply to any rhetorical situation, others are specific to a discipline or a profession. In this chapter, you will learn the conventions expected in most academic and professional settings. This chapter will help you

- use capitals for proper names (41a),
- capitalize words in titles and subtitles of works (41b),
- capitalize the first letter of a sentence (41c),
- use capitals for computer keys, menu items, and icon names (41d), and
- avoid unnecessary capitalization (41e).

BEYOND THE RULE

CAPITALIZATION STYLES

You may have noticed that different capitalization styles are used in various types of publications. For instance, the word *president* is always capitalized in documents published by the U.S. Government Printing Office, but it is capitalized in most newspapers only when it is followed by a specific name:

The delegates met with **P**resident Truman.

The delegates met with the **p**resident.

To learn more about capitalization styles, visit **www.harbrace.com**.

Advertisers frequently use capitalization to highlight important words.

41a Proper names

When you capitalize a word, you emphasize it. That is why names of people and places are capitalized, even when they are used as modifiers (*Mexico, Mexican*). Some words, such as *college, company, park,* and *street,* are capitalized only if they are part of a name (*a university* but *Oregon State University*). The following names and titles should be capitalized.

(1) Names of specific persons or things

Zora Neale Hurston	Flight 224	Honda Accord
John Paul II	Academy Award	USS *Cole*
Skylab	Nike	Microsoft Windows

A word denoting a family relationship is capitalized only when it substitutes for the person's proper name.

> I told **Mom** about the event. [I told Catherine about the event.]
>
> I told my **mom** about the event. [NOT I told my Catherine about the event.]

(2) Titles accompanying proper names

A title is capitalized when it precedes the name of a person but not when it follows the name or stands alone.

Governor Peter Dunn	Peter Dunn, the governor
Captain Ray Machado	Ray Machado, our captain
Uncle Rory	Rory, my uncle
President Lincoln	Abraham Lincoln, the president of the United States

(3) Names of ethnic or cultural groups and languages

Asians	African Americans	Latinos/Latinas	Poles
Arabic	English	Korean	Spanish

(4) Names of bridges, buildings, monuments, and geographical features

Golden Gate Bridge	Empire State Building	Lincoln Memorial
Arctic Circle	Mississippi River	Grand Canyon

When referring to two or more geographical features, however, do not capitalize the generic term: *Lincoln and Jefferson memorials, Yellowstone and Olympic national parks.*

(5) Names of organizations, government agencies, institutions, and companies

B'nai B'rith	National Endowment for the Humanities
Phi Beta Kappa	Internal Revenue Service
Howard University	Ford Motor Company

When used as common nouns, *service, company,* and *university* are not capitalized. However, some institutions, such as universities or corporations, capitalize their shortened names.

> The policies of Hanson **U**niversity promote the rights of all individuals to equal opportunity in education. The **U**niversity complies with all applicable federal, state, and local laws.

(6) Names for days of the week, months, and holidays

> Wednesday   August   Fourth of July

The names of the seasons—spring, summer, fall, winter—are not capitalized.

Capitalizing Days of the Week
Capitalization rules vary according to language. For example, in English, the names of days and months are capitalized, but in some other languages, such as Spanish and Italian, they are not.

(7) Designations for historical documents, periods, events, and movements

> Declaration of Independence   New Deal   Renaissance
> Impressionism   Stone Age   World Series

A historical period that includes a number is not capitalized unless it is considered a proper name.

> twentieth century   the Roaring Twenties
> the eighteen hundreds   the Gay Nineties

(8) Names of religions, their adherents, holy days, titles of holy books, and words denoting the Supreme Being

> Buddhism, Christianity, Islam, Judaism
> Buddhist, Christian, Muslim, Jew
> Bodhi Day, Easter, Ramadan, Yom Kippur
> Sutras, Bible, Koran, Talmud BUT biblical, talmudic
> Buddha, God, Allah, Yahweh

Some writers always capitalize personal pronouns and possessive determiners referring to the Supreme Being; others capitalize such words only when capitalization is needed to prevent ambiguity:

> The Lord commanded the prophet to warn His people.

(9) Words derived from proper names

Americanize [verb] Orwellian [adjective] Marxism [noun]

When a proper name becomes the name of a general class of objects or ideas, it is no longer capitalized. For example, *zipper*, originally a capitalized trademark, now refers to a class of fastening devices and is thus written with a lowercase letter. A word derived from a brand name, such as *Xerox*, *Kodak*, or *Kleenex*, should be capitalized. Because the corporations that own these brand names object to their use for generic purposes, use *photocopy, camera,* or *tissue* instead. If you are not sure whether a proper name or derivative has come to stand for a general class, look up the word in a dictionary.

(10) Abbreviations and acronyms

These forms are derived from the initial letters of capitalized word groups:

AMEX AT&T CBS CST JFK NFL OPEC UNESCO YMCA

(See also 39a(2) and chapter 43.)

(11) Military terms

Names of forces and special units are capitalized, as are names of wars, battles, revolutions, and military awards.

United States Army Marine Corps Eighth Air Force Green Berets
Russian Revolution Gulf War Operation Overlord Purple Heart

Military words such as *army, navy,* and *war* are not capitalized when they stand alone.

> My sister joined the navy in 2002.

STYLE SHEET FOR CAPITALIZATION

Capitals	No capitals
the West [geographical region]	driving west [compass point]
a Chihuahua [a breed of dog named after a state in Mexico]	a poodle [a breed of dog]
Washington State University [a specific institution]	a state university
Revolutionary War [a specific war]	an eighteenth-century war
U.S. Army [a specific army]	a peacetime army
Declaration of Independence [title of a document]	a declaration of independence
May [specific month]	spring [general season]
Memorial Day [specific day]	a holiday
two Democratic candidates [refers to a political party]	democratic procedures [refers to a form of government]
a Ford tractor [brand name]	a farm tractor
Parkinson's disease [a disease named for a person]	flu, asthma, leukemia
Governor Clay [a person's title]	the governor of our state

41b Titles and subtitles

The first and last words in titles and subtitles are capitalized, as are major words—that is, all words other than articles (*a, an,* and *the*), coordinating conjunctions (*and, but, for, nor, or, so,* and *yet*), prepositions (see the list on page 490), and the infinitive marker *to.* (See also 38b and 42a.)

From Here to Eternity

"To Be a Student or Not to Be a Student"

APA guidelines differ slightly from other style guidelines: the APA recommends capitalizing any word in a title, including a preposition, that has four or more letters.

> *Southwestern Pottery from Anasazi to Zuni* [MLA and CMS]
>
> *Southwestern Pottery From Anasazi to Zuni* [APA]

MLA, APA, and CMS advise capitalizing all words in a hyphenated compound, except for articles, coordinating conjunctions, and prepositions.

> "The Arab-Israeli Dilemma" [compound proper adjective]
>
> "Stop-and-Go Signals" [lowercase for the coordinating conjunction]

However, when a hyphenated compound containing a prefix appears in a title or subtitle, MLA and APA advise capitalizing both elements when (1) the second element is a proper noun or adjective (*Pre-Columbian*) or (2) the compound contains a doubled letter that could be hard to read (*Anti-Intellectual*). CMS recommends capitalizing the second element only if the word is a proper noun or adjective.

> "Pre-Columbian Artifacts in Peruvian Museums" [MLA, APA, and CMS]
>
> "Anti-Independence Behavior in Adolescents" [MLA and APA]
>
> "Anti-independence Behavior in Adolescents" [CMS]

41c Beginning a sentence

It is not difficult to remember that a sentence begins with a capital letter, but there are certain types of sentences that deserve special note.

(1) Capitalizing the first word in a quoted sentence

If a direct quotation is a full sentence, the first word should be capitalized.

> When asked to name the books she found most influential, Nadine Gordimer responded, "**I**n general, the works that mean most to one— change one's thinking and therefore maybe one's life—are those read in youth."

Even if you interrupt the quoted sentence with commentary, just the first letter should be capitalized.

> "**O**ddly," states Ved Mehta, "like my earliest memories, the books that made the greatest impression on me were the ones I encountered as a small child."

However, if you integrate someone else's sentence into a sentence of your own, the first letter should be lowercase.

> Nadine Gordimer believes that "**i**n general, the works that mean most to one—change one's thinking and therefore maybe one's life—are those read in youth."

(2) Capitalizing the first word in a freestanding parenthetical sentence

If you place a full sentence inside parentheses, and it is not embedded in a sentence of your own, be sure to capitalize the first word.

> Lance Armstrong has won the Tour de France a record-breaking seven times. (**P**revious record holders include Jacques Anquetil, Bernard Hinault, Eddy Merckx, and Miguel Indurain.)

If the sentence inside the parentheses occurs within a sentence of your own, the first word should not be capitalized.

> Lance Armstrong has won the Tour de France a record-breaking seven times (**p**reviously, he shared the record with four other cyclists).

(3) Lowercasing or capitalizing the first word in an independent clause following a colon

According to *The Chicago Manual of Style*, if there is only one independent clause (see **21b**) following a colon, the first word should be in lowercase. However, if two or more independent clauses follow the colon, the first word of each clause is capitalized.

> The ear thermometer is used quite frequently now: **t**his type of thermometer records a temperature more accurately than a glass thermometer.

> Two new thermometers are replacing the old thermometers filled with mercury: **T**he digital thermometer uses a heat sensor to determine body temperature. **T**he ear thermometer is actually an infrared thermometer that detects the temperature of the eardrum.

APA and MLA provide different style guidelines for this kind of situation. The APA manual recommends capitalizing the first word of any independent clause following a colon. The MLA manual advises capitalizing the first word only if the independent clause is a rule or principle.

> Think of fever as a symptom, not as an illness: **I**t is the body's response to infection. [APA]

> He has two basic rules for healthy living: **E**at sensibly, and exercise strenuously at least three times a week. [APA and MLA]

A grammar checker will flag a word at the beginning of a sentence that should be capitalized, but it will not be able to determine whether a word following a colon should be capitalized.

(4) Capitalizing the first word of an abbreviated question

When a series of abbreviated questions follows an introductory element, the first words of all questions are capitalized when the intent is to draw attention to the questions. Otherwise, such questions begin with lowercase letters.

> How do we distinguish the legal codes for families? For individuals? For genetic research?

> Are interest rates on car loans down to six percent? five? three?

41d Computer keys, menu items, and icon names

When referring to specific computer keys, menu items, and icon names, capitalize the first letter of each.

> To find the thesaurus, press Shift and the function key F7.

> Instead of choosing Copy from the Edit menu, you can press Ctrl+C.

> For additional information, click on Resources.

41e Unnecessary capitals

(1) Unnecessary capitalization of common nouns

The same noun can be either common or proper, depending on the context. A **proper noun** names a specific entity. A **common noun,** which is usually preceded by a determiner such as *the, a, an, this,* or *that,* is not capitalized.

> a speech course in theater and television
> [COMPARE: Speech 324: Theater and Television]
>
> a university, this high school
> [COMPARE: University of Michigan, Hickman High School]

(2) Overusing capitalization to signal emphasis

Occasionally, a common noun is capitalized for emphasis.

> The motivation of many politicians is Power.

If you use capitals for emphasis, do so sparingly; overuse will weaken the effect. For other ways to achieve emphasis, see chapter **30**.

(3) Signaling emphasis online

For online writing in academic and professional contexts, capitalize as you normally do. Be careful not to capitalize whole words for emphasis because your reader may think that you are SHOUTING—the term used to indicate the rudeness of this practice.

Exercise 1

Write a sentence using each of the following words correctly.

1. president	4. Company	7. street	10. Republican
2. President	5. east	8. Street	11. river
3. company	6. East	9. republican	12. River

Exercise 2

Edit the capitalization errors in the following paragraph. Be prepared to explain any changes that you make.

[1]Diana taurasi (Her teammates call her dee) plays basketball for the Phoenix mercury. [2]She has all the skills she needs to be a Star Player: She can pass and shoot, as well as rebound, block, and steal. [3]While playing for university of connecticut huskies, she won the Naismith award twice and ranked in the majority of the big east's statistical categories. [4]Shortly after the huskies won their third straight ncaa title, taurasi was drafted first overall by the Phoenix mercury. [5]In april of 2004, taurasi played on the u.s. national team against japan, and, in the Summer of 2004, she made her olympic debut in Athens.

ITALICS

When you use italics, you let readers know that you are treating a word or a group of words in a special way. For example, the following sentence is ambiguous.

> The linguistics students discussed the word stress.

Does this sentence mean that the students discussed a particular word or that they discussed the correct pronunciation of words? By italicizing *stress,* the writer indicates that it was the word, not an accent pattern, that the students discussed.

> The linguistics students discussed the word *stress.*

This chapter will help you use italics for

- the titles of separate works (42a),
- foreign words (42b),
- the names of legal cases (42c),
- the names of ships, submarines, aircraft, spacecraft, and satellites (42d),
- words, letters, or figures used as such or as statistical symbols or variables in algebraic expressions (42e), and
- words receiving emphasis (42f).

Word-processing programs make it easy to use italics. In handwritten or typewritten documents, you can indicate italics by underlining.

> Edward P. Jones's novel <u>The Known World</u> won a Pulitzer Prize.

Although the use of italics instead of underlining is widely accepted in business writing, conventions for academic writing vary. MLA recommends underlining, but APA and CMS prefer italics. Remember that in e-mail and on Web pages, an underlined word or phrase often indicates a hyperlink. If you are not able to format your e-mail or other electronic text with italics, use an underscore before and after words you would normally italicize.

Edward P. Jones's novel _The Known World_ won a Pulitzer Prize.

42a Titles of works published or produced separately

Italics indicate the title of a work published or produced as a whole rather than as part of a larger work. A newspaper, for example, is a separate work, but an editorial in a newspaper is not; thus, different conventions are used for indicating the title of the newspaper and the title of the editorial. (See also **38b.**) These conventions help readers realize the nature of a work and sometimes its relationship to another work.

Helen Keller's "Three Days to See" originally appeared in the *Atlantic Monthly*. [an essay in a magazine]

The titles of the following kinds of separate works are italicized.

Books	*The Hours*	*The God of Small Things*
Magazines	*Wired*	*National Geographic*
Newspapers	*USA Today*	*Wall Street Journal*
Plays, films, videotapes	*Death of a Salesman*	*Master and Commander*
Television and radio shows	*American Idol*	*A Prairie Home Companion*
Recordings	*Kind of Blue*	*Great Verdi Overtures*
Works of art	*American Gothic*	*David*
Long poems	*Paradise Lost*	*The Divine Comedy*
Pamphlets	*Saving Energy*	*Tips for Gardeners*
Comic strips	*Peanuts*	*Doonesbury*

When an italicized title includes the title of a separate work within it, the embedded title is not italicized.

The class read various selections from *Modern Interpretations of* Paradise Lost. [COMPARE: We studied various interpretations of *Paradise Lost*.]

Titles should not be placed in italics or between quotation marks when they stand alone on a title page, a book cover, or a newspaper masthead. Likewise, neither italics nor quotation marks are necessary for titles of major historical documents, religious texts, or Web sites.

> The Bill of Rights contains the first ten amendments to the U.S. Constitution.

> The Bible, a sacred text just as the Koran or the Torah is, begins with the Book of Genesis.

> Instructions for making a cane-and-reed basket can be found at Catherine Erdly's Web site, Basket Weaving.

According to MLA and CMS guidelines, an initial *the* in a newspaper or periodical title is not italicized. It is not capitalized either, unless it begins a sentence.

> The story was leaked to a journalist at the *New York Times.*

Also recommended is the omission of an article (*a, an,* or *the*) at the beginning of such a title when it would make a sentence awkward.

> The report will appear in Thursday's ~~the~~ *Wall Street Journal.*

42b Foreign words

Use italics to indicate foreign words.

> Side by side, hunched low in the light rain, the two outcasts dip up *tsampa,* the roasted maize or barley meal, ground to powder and cooked as porridge or in tea, that is subsistence food in the Himalaya. **—PETER MATTHIESSEN**

A foreign word used frequently in a text should be italicized only once—at its first occurrence.

The Latin words used to classify plants and animals according to genus and species are italicized.

> *Homo sapiens*   *Rosa setigera*   *Ixodes scapularis*

Countless words borrowed from other languages have become part of English and are therefore not italicized.

> bayou (Choctaw)   karate (Japanese)   arroyo (Spanish)

If you are not sure whether a word has been accepted into English, look for it in a standard dictionary (see **32e**).

42c   Legal cases

Italics identify the names of legal cases.

> *Miranda v. Arizona*   *Roe v. Wade*

The abbreviation *v.* (for "versus") may appear in either italic or nonitalic type, as long as the style is used consistently. Italics are also used for the shortened name of a well-known legal case.

> According to the *Miranda* decision, suspects must be informed of their right to remain silent and their right to legal advice.

Italics are not used to refer to a case by other than its official name.

> All the major networks covered the O. J. Simpson trial.

42d   Names of ships, submarines, aircraft, spacecraft, and satellites

Italicize the names of specific ships, submarines, aircraft, spacecraft, and satellites.

> USS *Enterprise*   USS *Hawkbill*   *Enola Gay*   *Atlantis*   *Aqua*

The names of trains and the trade names of aircraft are not italicized.

> Orient Express   Boeing 747   Concorde

42e   Words, letters, or figures referred to as such and letters used in mathematical expressions

When you discuss a specific word, letter, or figure as itself, not as its referent, you should italicize it.

> The word *love* is hard to define.
>
> The *p* in *ptarmigan* is silent.
>
> The *8* on the sign has faded, and the *5* has disappeared.

Statistical symbols and variables in algebraic expressions are also italicized.

The Pythagorean theorem is expressed as $a^2 + b^2 = c^2$.

42f Words receiving emphasis

Used sparingly, italics can emphasize words. When you think a sentence may be misunderstood, italicize words that you want readers to stress.

These *are* the right files. [*Are* receives more stress than it normally would.]

Italics can also emphasize emotional content.

We have to go *now.* [The italicized word signals urgency.]

If overused, italics will lose their impact. Instead of italicizing words, substitute more specific words (see chapter 33) or vary sentence structures (chapter 31).

Exercise 1

Identify all words that should be italicized in the following sentences. Explain why italics are necessary in each case.

1. Information about museum collections and exhibits can be found in art books, museum Web sites, and special sections of magazines and newspapers such as Smithsonian Magazine and the New York Times.
2. The Web site for the Metropolitan Museum of Art has pictures of Anthony Caro's sculpture Odalisque and Charles Demuth's painting The Figure 5 in Gold.
3. The title page of William Blake's Songs of Innocence is included in Masterpieces of the Metropolitan Museum of Art.
4. This book includes a photograph of a beautiful script used in the Koran; the script is known as the maghribi, or Western, style.
5. The large Tyrannosaurus rex discovered by Sue Hendrickson in South Dakota is on display at the Field Museum.

6. The International Museum of Cartoon Art provides information about the designers of such comic strips as Blondie, Peanuts, Mutt and Jeff, and Li'l Abner.

7. The Great Train Robbery, It Happened One Night, and Grand Illusion are in the collection at the Celeste Bartos Film Preservation Center.

8. In 1998, the Songwriters Hall of Fame honored John Williams, who has written music for such movies as Jaws, Star Wars, and E.T.

9. The Smithsonian Institution's National Air and Space Museum houses an impressive collection of aircraft and spacecraft, including Spirit of St. Louis and Gemini 4.

10. The digital collection listed on the Web site Experience Music Project includes music from the albums Fresh Cream and Bluesbreakers with Eric Clapton.

43 ABBREVIATIONS, ACRONYMS, AND NUMBERS

Abbreviations, acronyms, and numbers facilitate easy recognition and effective communication in both academic papers and business documents. An **abbreviation** is a shortened version of a word or phrase: *assn.* (association), *dept.* (department), *et al.* (*et alii* or "and others"). An **acronym** is formed by combining the initial letters and/or syllables of a series of words: *AIDS* (**a**cquired **i**mmune **d**eficiency **s**yndrome), *sonar* (**so**und **na**vigation **r**anging). This chapter will help you learn

- how and when to abbreviate (43a–d),
- when to explain an acronym (43e), and
- whether to spell out a number or use numerals (43f–g).

43a Proper names

Some abbreviations, such as *Ms., Mr.,* and *Mrs.,* appear before proper names.

Ms. Gretel Lopez	Mrs. Adrienne Marcus	St. Peter
Mr. Julio Rodriguez	Dr. Thomas Redshaw	Prof. Sue Li
Capt. Margaret Hoffner	Sen. Edward Kennedy	Rev. Kevin Burns

Others, such as *Jr., Sr., III,* and *MD,* appear after proper names.

Samuel Levy, Jr.	Deborah Hvidsten, MD	Henry VIII
Mark Ngo, Sr.	Erika C. Schuerer, PhD	Putman Amory III

In the past, periods were customarily used in abbreviations for academic degrees, but MLA and CMS now recommend omitting periods from abbreviations such as *MA, PhD,* and *MD.*

Abbreviated brand names create instant recognition for products.

Avoid redundant designations.

Dr. Carol Ballou OR Carol Ballou, MD [NOT Dr. Carol Ballou, MD]

Most abbreviations form plurals by adding *-s* alone, without an apostrophe: *Drs. Ballou and Hvidsten.* Exceptions are made when adding *-s* would create a different abbreviation, such as for *Mr.* and *Mrs.*

43b Addresses in correspondence

The names of states and words such as *Street, Road, Company,* and *Corporation* are usually written out when they appear in a letter, including in the address at the top of the page. However, they are abbreviated when used in the address on an envelope.

Sentence   Derson Manufacturing Company is located on Madison Street in Watertown, Minnesota.

Address   Derson Manufacturing Co.
200 Madison St.
Watertown, MN 55388

When addressing correspondence within the United States, use the abbreviations designated by the U.S. Postal Service for the names of the states. (No period follows these abbreviations.)

BEYOND THE RULE

POSTAL ABBREVIATIONS

Facilitating efficient delivery, the abbreviations of states' names required for U.S. mail consist of just two characters. Connecticut, for example, is CT, not Conn. For a list of these abbreviations, visit **www.harbrace.com**.

43c Abbreviations in source documentation

MLA, APA, and CMS all provide lists of abbreviations for writers to use when citing research sources in bibliographies, footnotes, and endnotes. Common abbreviations include the following (not all citation styles accept all of these abbreviations).

Bibliographies and Notes

anon., Anon.	anonymous, Anonymous
biog.	biography, biographer, biographical
bull.	bulletin
c. or ca.	circa, about (for example, *c. 1920*)
col., cols.	column, columns
cont.	contents OR continues, continued
et al.	*et alii* ("and others")
fig.	figure
fwd.	foreword, foreword by
illus.	illustrated by, illustrator, illustration
inc., Inc.	including; incorporated, Incorporated
intl.	international
introd.	introduction, introduction by
ms., mss.	manuscript, manuscripts

(Continued on page 764)

(Continued from page 763)

natl.	national
n.d.	no date
n.p.	no page number
no., nos.	number, numbers
p., pp.	page, pages
P, Pr.	Press
pref.	preface
pt., pts.	part, parts
trans. or tr.	translation, translated by
U, Univ.	University

Computer Terms

FTP	file transfer protocol
HTML	hypertext markup language
HTTP	hypertext transfer protocol
MB	megabyte
MOO	multiuser domain, object-oriented
URL	uniform resource locator

Divisions of Government

Cong.	Congress
dept.	department
div.	division
govt.	government
GPO	Government Printing Office
HR	House of Representatives

For abbreviations of Latin terms used in writing, see 43d(7).

43d Acceptable abbreviations in academic and professional writing

Abbreviations are usually too informal for use in sentences, but some have become so familiar that they are considered acceptable substitutes for full words.

(1) Using abbreviations for special purposes but not in sentences

The names of months, days of the week, and units of measurement are usually written out (not abbreviated) when they are included in sentences, as are words such as *Street* and *Corporation.*

> On a Tuesday in September, we drove ninety-nine miles to San Francisco, California, where we stayed in a hotel on Market Street.

In bibliographies, the months May, June, and July are never abbreviated. Except for September, the remaining months are abbreviated to their first three letters (*Jan., Mar., Dec.*). September is abbreviated as *Sept.*

Similarly, words such as *volume, chapter,* and *page* are written out within sentences, even though they are abbreviated in bibliographies and in citations of research sources.

> I read the introductory chapter and pages 82–89 in the first volume of the committee's report.

(2) Abbreviations in place names and of titles of address

Some abbreviations are commonly used in sentences: *St.* for Saint (*St. Louis*) or *Mt.* for mount or mountain (*Mt. Hood*), and *Mr., Mrs., Ms.,* and similar titles of address.

(3) Clipped forms

Because it functions as a word, a **clipped form** does not end with a period. Some clipped forms—such as *rep* (for representative), *exec* (for executive), and *info* (for information)—are too informal for use in college writing. Others—such as *exam, lab,* and *math*—have become acceptable because they have been used so frequently that they no longer seem like shortened forms.

(4) Abbreviations for time periods and zones

> 82 BC [OR BCE] for before Christ [OR before the common era]
>
> AD 95 [OR 95 CE] for *anno Domini,* "in the year of our Lord" [OR the common era]
>
> 7:40 a.m. for *ante meridiem,* before noon
>
> 4:52 EST for Eastern Standard Time

Words designating units of time, such as *minute* and *month,* are written out when they appear in sentences. They can be abbreviated in tables or charts.

sec.   min.   hr.   wk.   mo.   yr.

(5) The abbreviation for the United States (U.S. or US) as an adjective

the U.S. Navy, the US economy [COMPARE: The United States continues to enjoy a strong economy.]

The abbreviation *U.S.* or *US* should be used only as an adjective in academic and professional writing. When using *United States* as a noun, spell it out. The choice of U.S. or US will depend on the discipline in which you are writing: MLA lists US as the preferred form, but APA uses U.S., and CMS accepts either form.

(6) Individuals known by their initials

JFK   LBJ   E. B. White   B. B. King

In most cases, however, first and last names should be written out in full.

Oprah Winfrey   Tiger Woods

(7) Some abbreviations for Latin expressions

Certain abbreviations for Latin expressions are common in academic writing.

cf. [compare]   et al. [and others]   i.e. [that is]
e.g. [for example]   etc. [and so forth]   vs. OR v. [versus]

43e Acronyms

The ability to identify a particular acronym will vary from one audience to another. Some readers will know that NAFTA stands for the North American Free Trade Agreement; others may not. By spelling out acronyms the first time you use them, you are being courteous and clear.

Introduce the acronym by placing it in parentheses after the group of words it stands for.

> The Federal Emergency Management Administration (FEMA) was criticized by many after Hurricane Katrina.

Using Articles with Abbreviations, Acronyms, or Numbers

When you use an abbreviation, an acronym, or a number, you sometimes need an indefinite article. Choose *a* or *an* based on the pronunciation: use *a* before a consonant sound and *an* before a vowel sound.

A picture of **a UN** delegation is on the front page of today's newspaper. [*UN* is pronounced as two letters.]

I have **an IBM** computer. [*IBM* is pronounced as three letters.]

The reporter interviewed **a NASA** engineer. [*NASA* is pronounced as one word.]

My friend drives **a 1964** Mustang. [*1964* is pronounced "nineteen sixty-four."]

Exercise 1

Place a check mark next to those forms that are appropriate for use in the sentences of a college essay. Correct those that are not.

1. after 8 p.m.
2. 457 *anno Domini*
3. on St. Clair Ave.
4. two blocks from Water Street
5. in Aug.

6. in the second mo. of the yr.
7. in Calif.
8. at the UN
9. Ms. Lydia Snow
10. for a prof.

43f General uses of numbers

Depending on their uses, numbers are treated in different ways. In general, MLA and CMS recommend spelling out numbers from one through one hundred (*nine employees, ninety-one employees*). If one of these numbers is followed by a word such as *hundred, thousand,* or *million,* it may also be spelled out (*nine hundred years, ninety-one million years*). Use a numeral for any other number, unless it begins a sentence.

The register recorded 164 names.

APA advises spelling out only numbers below ten. All three of these style manuals recommend using words rather than numerals at the beginning of a sentence.

One hundred sixty-four names were recorded in the register. [Notice that *and* is not used in numbers greater than one hundred. NOT One hundred and sixty-four names . . . .]

In a discussion of related items involving both single- and double- or triple-digit numbers, use numerals for all numbers.

Only 5 of the 134 delegates attended the final meeting.

In scientific or technical writing, use numerals before measurement abbreviations (*2 L, 30 cc*).

43g Special uses of numbers

(1) Expressing specific times of day in either numerals or words

Numerals or words can be used to express times of day. They should be used consistently.

4 p.m. OR four o'clock in the afternoon

9:30 a.m. OR half-past nine in the morning OR nine-thirty in the morning [Notice the use of hyphens.]

(2) Using numerals and words for dates

In a text, months are written as words, years are written as numerals, and days and decades are written as either words or numerals.

May 20, 1976 OR 20 May 1976 [NOT May 20th, 1976]

the fourth of December OR December 4

the fifties OR the 1950s

from 1999 to 2003 OR 1999–2003 [Use an en dash, not a hyphen, in number ranges.]

Different Ways of Writing Dates
Many cultures invert the numerals for the month and the day: *14/2/2006* or *14 February 2006*. In publications from the United States, the month generally precedes the day: *2/14/2006* or *February 14, 2006.*

(3) Using numerals in addresses

Numerals are commonly used in street addresses and zip codes.

25 Arrow Drive, Apartment 1, Columbia, MO 78209
OR, for an envelope, 25 Arrow Dr., Apt. 1, Columbia, MO 78209

(4) Using numerals for identification

A numeral may be used as part of a proper noun.

Channel 10   Edward III   Interstate 40   Room 311

(5) Referring to pages and divisions of books and plays

Numerals are used to designate pages and other divisions of books and plays.

page 15   chapter 8   part 2 in act 2, scene 1 OR in Act II, Scene I

(6) Expressing decimals and percentages numerically

Numerals are used to express decimals and percentages.

a 2.5 average   12 percent   0.853 metric ton

(7) Using numerals for large fractional numbers

Numerals with decimal points can be used to express large fractional numbers.

5.2 million inhabitants   1.6 billion years

(8) Different ways of writing monetary amounts

Monetary amounts should be spelled out if they occur infrequently in a piece of writing. Otherwise, numerals and symbols can be used.

| two million dollars | $2,000,000 |
| ninety-nine cents | 99¢ OR $0.99 |

Commas and Periods with Numerals
Cultures differ in their use of the period and the comma with numerals. In American usage, a decimal point (period) indicates a number or part of a number that is smaller than one, and a comma divides large numbers into units of three digits.

7.65 (seven and sixty-five one-   10,000 (ten thousand)
hundredths)

In some other cultures, these usages of the decimal point and the comma are reversed.

7,65 (seven and sixty-five one-   10.000 (ten thousand)
hundredths)

Exercise 2

Edit the following sentences to correct the usage of abbreviations and numbers.

1. A Natl. Historic Landmark, Hoover Dam is located about 30 miles s.e. of Las. Vegas, Nev.

2. The dam is named after Herbert Hoover, the 31st pres. of the U.S.

3. It is administered by the U.S. Dept. of the Interior.

4. Built by the fed. gov. between nineteen thirty-three and 1935, this dam is still considered one of the greatest achievements in the history of civ. engineering.

5. Construction of the dam became possible after several states in the Southwest (namely, AZ, CA, CO, NV, NM, UT, and WY) agreed on a plan to share water from the river.

6. The concrete used in the dam would have built a highway 16 ft. wide, stretching all the way from San Francisco to NYC.

7. 3,500 men worked on the dam during an average month of construction; this work translated into a monthly payroll of $500,000.

8. Spanning the Colorado River, Hoover Dam created Lake Mead— a reservoir covering 247 sq. miles.

9. A popular tourist attraction, Hoover Dam was closed to the public after terrorists attacked the U.S. on 9/11/01.

10. Today, certain pts. of the dam remain closed to the public as part of the effort to improve U.S. security.

GLOSSARY

OF

USAGE

The term *usage* refers to the ways words are used in specific contexts. As you know from speaking and writing every day, the words you choose depend on your audience and your purpose. For example, you might use *guys* when you are at lunch with your friends but choose *people, classmates, employees,* or another more formal or precise word when you are writing a report. By learning about usage in this glossary, you will increase your ability to use words effectively. Many of the entries are context-specific; others distinguish between words that sound or look similar.

The definitions and guidelines in this glossary will help you write clear and precise prose. Nonetheless, you should be aware that the idea of standard usage potentially carries with it the assumption that words not considered standard are inferior. Words labeled "nonstandard" are commonly condemned, even though they may be words some people have grown up hearing and using. A better way to discuss usage is to label what is conventional, or accepted practice, for a specific context. Thus, words commonly used in one context may not be appropriate in another. The following labels will help you choose appropriate words for your rhetorical situation.

Conventional	Words or phrases listed in dictionaries without special usage labels; generally considered appropriate in academic and professional writing.
Conversational	Words or phrases that dictionaries label *informal, slang,* or *colloquial;* although often used in informal speech and writing, not generally appropriate for formal writing assignments.
Unconventional	Words or phrases not generally considered appropriate in academic or professional writing and often labeled *nonstandard* in dictionaries; best avoided in formal contexts.

Agreement on usage occurs slowly, often after a period of debate. In this glossary, entries are marked with an asterisk (*) when new usages have been reported by dictionary editors but may not yet be accepted by everyone.

Grammar checkers may identify some common usage errors (such as *its* instead of *it's*), but they will not find more subtle problems. Grammar checkers also rarely distinguish between words that are spelled similarly but have different meanings. For example, a grammar checker found nothing wrong with the following sentence, even though *capitol* is used incorrectly: The capitol of Minnesota is St. Paul.

a lot of *A lot of* is conversational for *many, much,* or *a great deal of:* They do not have ~~a lot of~~ **much** time. *A lot* is sometimes misspelled as *alot.*

a while, awhile *A while* means "a period of time." It is often used with the prepositions *after, for,* and *in:* We rested for **a while.** *Awhile* means "a short time." It is not preceded by a preposition: We rested **awhile.**

accept, except The verb *accept* means "to receive": I **accept** your apology. The verb *except* means "to exclude": The policy was to have everyone wait in line, but mothers and small children were **excepted.** The preposition *except* means "other than": All **except** Joe will attend the conference.

adapt, adopt *Adapt* means "to adjust" or "to change for a purpose": We will **adapt** to the new conditions. The author will **adapt** his short story for television. *Adopt* means "to take as one's own": They will **adopt** a new policy.

advice, advise *Advice* is a noun: They asked their attorney for **advice.** *Advise* is a verb: The attorney **advised** us to save all relevant documents.

affect, effect *Affect* is a verb that means "to influence": The lobbyist's pleas did not **affect** the politician's decision. The noun *effect* means "a result": The **effect** of his decision on the staff's morale was positive and long lasting. When used as a verb, *effect* means "to produce" or "to cause": The activists believed that they could **effect** real political change.

agree on, agree to, agree with *Agree on* means "to be in accord with others about something": We **agreed on** a date for the conference. *Agree to* means "to accept something" or "to consent to do something": The customer **agreed to** our terms. The negotiators **agreed to** conclude talks by midnight. *Agree with* means "to share an opinion with someone" or "to approve of something": I **agree with** you on this issue. No one **agreed with** his position.

all The indefinite pronoun *all* is plural when it refers to people or things that can be counted: **All** were present. It is singular when it refers to things that cannot be counted: **All** is forgiven.

all ready, already *All ready* means "completely prepared": The rooms are **all ready** for the conference. *Already* means "by or before the time specified": She has **already** taken her final exams.

* **all right** *All right* means "acceptable": The students asked whether it was **all right** to use dictionaries during the exam. *Alright* is not yet a generally accepted spelling of *all right,* although it is becoming more common in journalistic writing.

all together, altogether *All together* means "as a group": The cast reviewed the script **all together.** *Altogether* means "wholly, thoroughly": That game is **altogether** too difficult.

allude, elude *Allude* means "to refer to indirectly": The professor **alluded** to a medieval text. *Elude* means "to evade" or "to escape from": For the moment, his name **eludes** me.

allusion, illusion An *allusion* is a casual or indirect reference: The **allusion** was to Shakespeare's *Twelfth Night.* An *illusion* is a false idea or an unreal image: His idea of college is an **illusion.**

alot See **a lot of.**

already See **all ready, already.**

alright See **all right.**

altogether See **all together, altogether.**

a.m., p.m. Use these abbreviations only with figures: The show will begin at 7:00 **p.m.** [COMPARE: The show will begin at seven *in the evening.*]

* **among, between** To follow traditional usage, use *among* with three or more entities (a group): The snorklers swam **among** the fish. Use *between* when referring to only two entities: The rivalry **between** the two teams is intense. Current dictionaries also note the possibility of using *between* to refer to more than two entities, especially when these entities are considered distinct: We have strengthened the lines of communication **between** the various departments.

amoral, immoral *Amoral* means "neither moral nor immoral" or "not caring about right or wrong": Complaining that U.S. schools are **amoral,** the senator proposed the addition of prayer time. *Immoral* means "not moral": Some philosophers consider war **immoral.**

amount of, number of Use *amount of* before nouns that cannot be counted: The **amount of** rain that fell last year was insufficient. Use *number of* with nouns that can be counted: The **number of** students attending college has increased.

and/or This combination denotes three options: one, the other, or both. These options can also be presented separately with *or:* The student's application should be signed by a parent **and/or** a teacher. The student's application should be signed by a parent, a teacher, **or** both.

✳ **angry at, angry with** Both *at* and *with* are commonly used after *angry,* although according to traditional guidelines, *with* should be used when a person is the cause of the anger: She was **angry with** me because I was late.

another, other, the other *Another* is followed by a singular noun: **another** book. *Other* is followed by a plural noun: **other** books. *The other* is followed by either a singular or a plural noun: **the other book, the other books.**

anymore, any more *Anymore* meaning "any longer" or "now" most frequently occurs in negative sentences: Sarah doesn't work here **anymore.** Its use in positive sentences is considered conversational; *now* is generally used instead: All he ever does **anymore** now is watch television. As two words, *any more* appears with *not* to mean "no more": We do not have **any more** time.

anyone, any one *Anyone* means "any person at all": We did not know **anyone.** *Any one* refers to one of a group: **Any one** of the options is better than the current situation.

anyplace, everyplace, someplace According to traditional usage, each of these words should be written as two words (*any place, every place, some place*). Note, however, that *anywhere, everywhere,* and *somewhere* are each written as one word.

anyways, anywheres Unconventional; use *anyway* and *anywhere* instead: We decided to go **anyways.**

as Conversational when used after such verbs as *know, say,* and *see.* Use *that, if,* or *whether* instead: I do not know **as** whether my application is complete. Also considered conversational is the use of *as* instead of *who, which,* or *that:* Many of the performers **as** who have appeared on our program will be giving a concert this evening.

as, because The use of *as* to signal a cause may be vague; if it is, use *because* instead: **As** Because we were running out of gas, we turned around.

✳ **as, like** According to traditional usage, *as* begins either a phrase or a clause; *like* begins only a phrase: My brother drives too fast, just **like** as my father did. Current dictionaries note the informal use of *like* to begin clauses, especially after verbs such as *look, feel,* and *sound.*

assure, ensure, insure *Assure* means "to state with confidence, alleviating any doubt": The flight attendant **assured** us that our flight would arrive on time. *Ensure* and *insure* are usually interchangeable to mean "make certain," but only *insure* means "to protect against loss": The editor

ensured [OR **insured**] that the reporter's facts were accurate. Physicians must **insure** themselves against malpractice suits.

awful, awfully Conversational when used to mean "very."

awhile See **a while, awhile.**

bad Unconventional as an adverb; use *badly* instead. The team played **badly.** However, the adjective *bad* is used after sensory verbs such as *feel, look,* and *smell:* I feel **bad** that I forgot to return your book yesterday.

because See **as, because.**

being as, being that Unconventional; use *because* instead. ~~Being as~~ Because the road was closed, traffic was diverted to another route.

* **beside, besides** According to traditional usage, these two words have different meanings. *Beside* means "next to": The president sat **beside** the prime minister. *Besides* means "in addition to" or "other than": She has written many articles **besides** those on political reform. Current dictionaries report that professional writers regularly use *beside* to convey this meaning, as long as there is no risk of ambiguity.

better, had better *Better* is conversational. Use *had better* instead: We ~~better~~ had better finish the report by five o'clock.

between See **among, between.**

breath, breathe *Breath* is a noun: Take a deep **breath.** *Breathe* is a verb: **Breathe** deeply.

* **bring, take** Both words describe the same action but from different standpoints. *Bring* indicates movement toward the writer: She **brought** me some flowers. *Take* implies movement away from the writer: He **took** my overdue books to the library. Dictionaries report that this distinction is often blurred when the writer's position is ambiguous or irrelevant: He **brought** [OR **took**] her some flowers.

bunch Conversational to refer to a group: A ~~bunch~~ group of students participated in the experiment.

busted Unconventional. Use *broken* instead: Every day he walked past a ~~busted~~ broken vending machine on his way to class.

but that, but what Conversational after expressions of doubt such as *no doubt* or *did not know.* Use *that* instead: I do not doubt ~~but what~~ that they are correct.

* **can, may** *Can* refers to ability, and *may* refers to permission: You **can** [are able to] drive seventy miles an hour, but you **may** not [are not permitted to] exceed the speed limit. Current dictionaries report that in contemporary usage *can* and *may* are used interchangeably to denote possibility or permission, although *may* is used more frequently in formal contexts.

can't hardly, can't scarcely Unconventional. Use *can hardly* or *can scarcely:* The students **can't hardly** wait for summer vacation.

capital, capitol *Capital* means either "a governing city" or "funds": The **capital** of Minnesota is St. Paul. An anonymous donor provided the **capital** for the project. As a modifier, *capital* means "chief" or "principal": This year's election is of **capital** importance. It may also refer to the death penalty: **Capital** punishment is legal in some states. A *capitol* is a statehouse; the *Capitol* is the U.S. congressional building in Washington, DC.

censor, censure, sensor As a verb, *censor* means "to remove or suppress because of immoral or otherwise objectionable ideas": Do you think a ratings board should **censor** films? As a noun, *censor* refers to a person who is authorized to remove material considered objectionable: The **censor** recommended that the book be banned. The verb *censure* means "to blame or criticize"; the noun *censure* is an expression of disapproval or blame. The Senate **censured** Joseph McCarthy. He received a **censure** from the Senate. A *sensor* is a device that responds to a stimulus: The **sensor** detects changes in light.

center around Conversational for "to center on" or "to revolve around": The discussion **centered around on** the public's response to tax reform initiatives.

chair, chairman, chairperson As gender-neutral terms, *chairperson* and *chair* are preferred to *chairman.* See **32d.**

cite, site, sight *Cite* means "to mention": Be sure to **cite** your sources. *Site* is a location: The president visited the **site** for the new library. As a verb, *site* also means "to situate": The builder **sited** the factory near the freeway. *Sight* means "to see": The crew **sighted** land. *Sight* also refers to a view: What an incredible **sight!**

climactic, climatic *Climactic* refers to a climax, or high point: The actors rehearsed the **climactic** scene. *Climatic* refers to the *climate:* Many environmentalists are worried about the recent **climatic** changes.

coarse, course *Coarse* refers to roughness: The jacket was made of **coarse** linen. *Course* refers to a route: Our **course** to the island was indirect. *Course* may also refer to a plan of study: I want to take a **course** in nutrition.

compare to, compare with *Compare to* means "to regard as similar," and *compare with* means "to examine for similarities and/or differences": She **compared** her mind **to** a dusty attic. The student **compared** the first draft **with** the second.

complement, complementary, compliment, complimentary *Complement* means "to complete" or "to balance": Their personalities **complement** each other. They have **complementary** personalities. *Compliment* means "to express praise": The professor **complimented** the students on their first drafts. Her remarks were **complimentary.** *Complimentary* may also mean "provided free of charge": We received **complimentary** tickets.

* **compose, comprise** *Compose* means "to make up": That collection **is composed** of medieval manuscripts. *Comprise* means "to consist of": The anthology **comprises** many famous essays. Dictionary editors have noted the increasing use of *comprise* in the passive voice to mean "to be composed of."

conscience, conscious, consciousness *Conscience* means "the sense of right and wrong": He examined his **conscience** before deciding whether to join the protest. *Conscious* means "awake": After an hour, the patient was fully **conscious.** After an hour, the patient regained **consciousness.** *Conscious* may also mean "aware": We were **conscious** of the possible consequences.

continual, continually, continuous, continuously *Continual* means "constantly recurring": **Continual** interruptions kept us from completing the project. Telephone calls **continually** interrupted us. *Continuous* means "uninterrupted": The job applicant had a record of ten years' **continuous** employment. The job applicant worked **continuously** from 1996 to 2006.

* **convince, persuade** *Convince* means "to make someone believe something": His passionate speech **convinced** us that school reform was necessary. *Persuade* means "to motivate someone to act": She **persuaded** us to stop smoking. Dictionary editors note that many speakers now use *convince* as a synonym for *persuade.*

could care less Unconventional to express complete lack of concern. *Couldn't care less* is used in informal contexts.

could of *Of* is often mistaken for the sound of the unstressed *have:* They **could of** have [OR might **have,** should **have,** would **have**] gone home.

council, counsel A *council* is an advisory or decision-making group: The student **council** supported the new safety regulations. A *counsel* is a legal adviser: The defense **counsel** conferred with the judge. As a verb, *counsel* means "to give advice": The new psychologist **counsels** people with eating disorders.

criteria, criterion *Criteria* is a plural noun meaning "a set of standards for judgment": The teachers explained the **criteria** for the assignment. The singular form is *criterion:* Their judgment was based on only one **criterion.**

* **data** *Data* is the plural form of *datum,* which means "piece of information" or "fact": When the **data are** complete, we will know the true cost. However,

current dictionaries also note that *data* is frequently used as a mass entity (like the word *furniture*), appearing with a singular verb.

desert, dessert *Desert* can mean "a barren land": Gila monsters live in the **deserts** of the Southwest. As a verb, *desert* means "to leave": I thought my friends had **deserted** me. *Dessert* refers to something sweet eaten at the end of a meal: They ordered apple pie for **dessert.**

device, devise *Device* is a noun: She invented a **device** that measures extremely small quantitites of liquid. *Devise* is a verb: We **devised** a plan for work distribution.

dialogue Many readers consider the use of *dialogue* as a verb to be an example of unnecessary jargon. Use *discuss* or *exchange views* instead: The committee members ~~dialogued about~~ discussed the issues.

differ from, differ with *Differ from* means "to be different": A bull snake **differs from** a rattlesnake in a number of ways. *Differ with* means "to disagree": Senator Brown has **differed with** Senator Owen on several issues.

different from, different than *Different from* is generally used with nouns, pronouns, noun phrases, and noun clauses: This school was **different from** most others. The school was **different from** what we had expected. *Different than* is used with adverbial clauses; *than* is the conjunction: We are no **different than** they are.

discreet, discrete *Discreet* means "showing good judgment or self-restraint": His friends complained openly, but his comments were quite **discreet.** *Discrete* means "distinct": The participants in the study came from three **discrete** groups.

disinterested, uninterested *Disinterested* means "impartial": A **disinterested** observer will give a fair opinion. *Uninterested* means "lacking interest": She was **uninterested** in the outcome of the game.

distinct, distinctive *Distinct* means "easily distinguishable or perceived": Each proposal has **distinct** advantages. *Distinctive* means "characteristic" or "serving to distinguish": We studied the **distinctive** features of hawks.

* **due to** Traditionally, *due to* was not synonymous with *because of:* ~~Due to~~ Because of holiday traffic, we arrived an hour late. However, dictionary editors now consider this usage of *due to* acceptable.

dyeing, dying *Dyeing* comes from *dye,* meaning "to color something, usually by soaking it": As a sign of solidarity, the students are **dyeing** their shirts the same color. *Dying* refers to the loss of life: Because of the drought, the plants are **dying.**

effect See **affect, effect.**

elicit, illicit *Elicit* means "to draw forth": He is **eliciting** contributions for a new playground. *Illicit* means "unlawful": The newspaper reported their **illicit** mishandling of public funds.

elude See **allude, elude.**

emigrate from, immigrate to *Emigrate* means "to leave one's own country": My ancestors **emigrated from** Ireland. *Immigrate* means "to arrive in a different country to settle": The Ulster Scots **immigrated to** the southern United States.

eminent, imminent *Eminent* means "distinguished": An **eminent** scholar in physics will be giving a public lecture tomorrow. *Imminent* means "about to happen": The merger of the two companies is **imminent.**

ensure See **assure, ensure, insure.**

especially, specially *Especially* emphasizes a characteristic or quality: Some people are **especially** sensitive to the sun. *Especially* also means "particularly": Wildflowers are abundant in this area, **especially** during May. *Specially* means "for a particular purpose": The classroom was **specially** designed for music students.

etc. Abbreviation of *et cetera,* meaning "and others of the same kind." Use only within parentheses: Be sure to bring appropriate camping gear (tent, sleeping bag, mess kit, **etc.**). Because *and* is part of the meaning of *etc.,* avoid using the combination *and etc.*

eventually, ultimately *Eventually* refers to some future time: She has made so many valuable contributions that I am sure she will **eventually** become the store supervisor. *Ultimately* refers to the final outcome after a series of events: The course was difficult but **ultimately** worthwhile.

everyday, every day *Everyday* means "routine" or "ordinary": These are **everyday** problems. *Every day* means "each day": I read the newspaper **every day.**

everyone, every one *Everyone* means "all": **Everyone** should attend. *Every one* refers to each person or item in a group: **Every one** of you should attend.

everyplace See **anyplace, everyplace, someplace.**

except See **accept, except.**

expect Conversational; use *think* or *believe* instead: I **expect** believe the answer is clear.

explicit, implicit *Explicit* means "expressed clearly and directly": Given his **explicit** directions, we knew how to proceed. *Implicit* means "implied or expressed indirectly": I mistakenly understood his silence to be his **implicit** approval of the project.

farther, further Generally, *farther* refers to geographic distance: We will have to drive **farther** tomorrow. *Further* means "more": If you need **further** assistance, please let me know.

✳ **feel** Traditionally, *feel* was not synonymous with "think" or "believe": I ~~feel~~ **think** that more should be done to protect local habitat. Dictionary editors now consider such a use of *feel* to be a standard alternative.

fewer, less *Fewer* occurs before nouns that can be counted: **fewer** technicians, **fewer** pencils. *Less* occurs before nouns that cannot be counted: **less** milk, **less** support. *Less than* may be used with measurements of time or distance: **less than** three months, **less than** twenty miles.

✳ **first, firstly; second, secondly** Many college instructors prefer the use of *first* and *second*. However, dictionary editors state that *firstly* and *secondly* are also well-established forms.

foreword, forward A *foreword* is an introduction: The **foreword** to the book provided useful background information. *Forward* refers to a frontward direction: To get a closer look, we moved **forward** slowly.

former, latter Used together, *former* refers to the first of two; *latter* to the second of two. John and Ian are both English. The **former** is from Manchester; the **latter** is from Birmingham.

further See **farther, further.**

get Considered conversational in many common expressions: The weather ~~got better~~ **improved** overnight. I did not know what he ~~was getting at~~ **meant.**

go, goes Unconventional for *say(s), respond(s),* and other similar words: My friends say I'm strange, and I ~~go~~ **reply,** "You're right!"

good, well *Good* is an adjective, not an adverb. Use *well* instead: He pitched ~~good~~ **well** last night. *Good* in the sense of "in good health" may be used interchangeably with *well:* I feel **good** [OR **well**] this morning.

had better See **better, had better.**

half A *half a* or *a half an* is unconventional; use *half a/an* or *a half:* You should be able to complete the questionnaire in **a half an** hour.

hanged, hung *Hanged* means "put to death by hanging": The prisoner was **hanged** at dawn. For all other meanings, use *hung:* He **hung** the picture above his desk.

hardly Unconventional when combined with a negative word such as *not.* Depending on the intended meaning, either omit *hardly* or omit the negative word: The drivers could**n't hardly** see the road.

has got, have got Conversational; omit *got:* I **have got** a meeting tomorrow.

he/she, his/her As a solution to the problem of sexist language, these combinations are not universally accepted. Consider using *he or she* and *his or her.* See **32d.**

herself, himself, myself, yourself Unconventional as subjects in a sentence. Joe and ~~myself~~ I will lead the discussion. See **25a(4).**

hopefully Conversational to mean "I hope": ~~Hopefully,~~ I hope the game will not be canceled.

hung See **hanged, hung.**

i.e. Abbreviation of *id est,* meaning "that is." Use only within parentheses: All participants in the study ran the same distance (**i.e.,** six kilometers). Otherwise, replace *i.e.* with the English equivalent, *that is:* Assistance was offered to those who would have difficulty boarding, ~~i.e.~~ that is, the elderly, the disabled, and parents with small children. Do not confuse *i.e.* with *e.g.,* meaning "for example."

illicit See **elicit, illicit.**

illusion See **allusion, illusion.**

immigrate See **emigrate from, immigrate to.**

imminent See **eminent, imminent.**

immoral See **amoral, immoral.**

∗ **impact** Though *impact* is commonly used as a verb in business writing, many college teachers still use it as a noun only: The new tax ~~impacts~~ affects everyone.

implicit See **explicit, implicit.**

imply, infer *Imply* means "suggest without actually stating": Though he never mentioned the statistics, he **implied** that they were questionable. *Infer* means "draw a conclusion based on evidence": Given the tone of his voice, I **inferred** that he found the work substandard.

in regards to Unconventional; see **regard, regarding, regards.**

inside of, outside of Drop *of* when unnecessary: Security guards stood **outside** ~~of~~ the front door.

insure See **assure, ensure, insure.**

irregardless Unconventional; use *regardless* instead.

its, it's *Its* is a possessive form: The committee forwarded **its** recommendation. *It's* is a contraction of *it is:* **It's** a beautiful day.

-ize Some readers object to using this ending to create new verbs: *enronize.* Some of these new verbs, however, have already entered into common usage: *computerize.*

kind of a, sort of a The word *a* is unnecessary: This **kind of a** book sells well. *Kind of* and *sort of* are not conventionally used to mean "somewhat": The report was **kind of** somewhat difficult to read.

later, latter *Later* means "after a specific time" or "a time after now": The concert ended **later** than we had expected. *Latter* refers to the second of two items: Of the two versions described, I prefer the **latter.**

lay, lie *Lay* (*laid, laying*) means "put" or "place": He **laid** the book aside. *Lie* (*lay, lain, lying*) means "rest" or "recline": I had just **lain** down when the alarm went off. *Lay* takes an object (to **lay** something), while *lie* does not. These verbs may be confused because the present tense of *lay* and the past tense of *lie* are spelled the same way.

lead, led As a noun, *lead* means "a kind of metal": The paint had **lead** in it. As a verb, *lead* means "to conduct": A guide will **lead** a tour of the ruins. *Led* is the past tense of the verb *lead*: He **led** the country from 1949 to 1960.

less, less than See **fewer, less.**

liable *Liable* generally means "likely" in an undesirable sense: If they invest money in that stock, they are **liable** to lose money. With her brains, she is **liable** likely to achieve success easily.

lie See **lay, lie.**

like See **as, like.**

literally Conversational when used to emphasize the meaning of another word: I was **literally** nearly frozen after I finished shoveling the sidewalk. *Literally* is conventionally used to indicate that an expression is not being used figuratively: My friend **literally** climbs the walls after work; his fellow rock climbers join him at the local gym.

lose, loose *Lose* is a verb: She does not **lose** her patience often. *Loose* is chiefly used as an adjective: A few of the tiles are **loose.**

lots, lots of Conversational for *many* or *much:* He has **lots of** many friends. We have **lots** much to do before the end of the quarter.

mankind Considered sexist because it excludes women: All **mankind** humanity will benefit from this new discovery.

many, much *Many* is used with nouns that can be counted: **many** stores, too **many** assignments. *Much* is used with nouns that cannot be counted: **much** courage, not **much** time.

may See **can, may.**

may of, might of See **could of.**

maybe, may be *Maybe* is an adverb: **Maybe** the negotiators will succeed this time. *May* and *be* are verbs: The rumor **may be** true.

* **media, medium** According to traditional definitions, *media* is a plural word: The **media** have sometimes created the news in addition to reporting it. The singular form is *medium:* The newspaper is one **medium** that people seem to trust. Dictionary editors note the frequent use of *media* as a collective noun taking a singular verb, but this usage is still considered conversational.

might could Conversational for "might be able to": The director **might could** be able to review your application next week.

most Unconventional to mean "almost": We watch the news **most** almost every day.

much See **many, much.**

myself See **herself, himself, myself, yourself.**

neither . . . or Conventionally, *nor,* not *or,* follows *neither:* The book is **neither** as funny **or** nor as original as critics have reported.

not . . . no/none/nothing The use of multiple negative words is unconventional: I did **not** want **nothing** anything else. Multiple negation may be used for special effect.

nothing like, nowhere near Unconventional; use *not nearly* instead: Her new book is **nowhere near** not nearly as mysterious as her previous novel.

number of When the expression *a number of* is used, the reference is plural: **A number of** positions **are** open. When *the number of* is used, the reference is singular: **The number of** possibilities **is** limited. See also **amount of, number of.**

off of Conversational; omit *of:* He walked **off of** the field.

on account of Conversational; use *because of:* The singer canceled her engagement **on account of** because of a sore throat.

on the other hand Use *however* instead, or make sure that the sentence or independent clause beginning with this transitional phrase is preceded by one starting with *on the one hand.*

other See **another, other, the other.**

owing to the fact that Considered wordy; use *because* instead: **Owing to the fact that** Because more people came to the concert than were expected, the stage crew set up extra chairs in the aisles.

passed, past *Passed* is the past tense of the verb *pass:* Everyone **passed** the test. *Past* means "beyond a time or location": The band marched **past** the bleachers.

per In ordinary contexts, use *a* or *an:* You should drink at least six glasses of water **per** a day.

percent, percentage *Percent* (also spelled *per cent*) is used with a specific number: **Sixty percent** of the students attended the ceremony. *Percentage* refers to an unspecified portion: The **percentage** of high school graduates attending college has increased in recent years.

perspective, prospective *Perspective* means "point of view": We discussed the issue from various **perspectives.** *Prospective* means "likely to become": **Prospective** elementary teachers visited nearby classrooms last Friday.

persuade See **convince, persuade.**

phenomena, phenomenon *Phenomena* is the plural form of *phenomenon:* Natural **phenomena** were given scientific explanations.

plus *Plus* joins nouns or noun phrases to make a sentence seem like an equation: Her endless curiosity **plus** her boundless energy makes her the perfect camp counselor. Note that a singular form of the verb is required (e.g., *makes*). *Plus* is not used to join clauses: I telephoned ~~plus and~~ I sent flowers.

p.m. See **a.m., p.m.**

precede, proceed To *precede* is to "go ahead of ": A moment of silence **preceded** the applause. To *proceed* is to "go forward": After stopping for a short rest, we **proceeded** to our destination.

prejudice, prejudiced *Prejudice* is a noun: They were unaware of their **prejudice.** *Prejudiced* is an adjective: She accused me of being **prejudiced.**

principal, principle As a noun, *principal* means "chief official": The **principal** greeted the students every day. It also means "capital": The loan's **principal** was still quite high. As an adjective, *principal* means "main": Tourism is the country's **principal** source of income. The noun *principle* refers to a rule, standard, or belief: She explained the three **principles** supporting the theory.

proceed See **precede, proceed.**

prospective See **perspective, prospective.**

quotation, quote In academic writing, *quotation,* rather than *quote,* refers to a repeated or copied sentence or passage: She began her speech with a **quote quotation** from *Othello. Quote* expresses an action: My friend sometimes **quotes** lines from television commercials.

raise, rise *Raise* (*raised, raising*) means "to lift or cause to move upward, to bring up or increase": Retailers **raised** prices. *Rise* (*rose, risen, rising*) means "to get up" or "to ascend": The cost of living **rose** sharply. *Raise* takes an object (to **raise** something); *rise* does not.

rarely ever Conversational; omit *ever:* He **rarely** ~~ever~~ goes to the library.

real, really *Really* rather than *real* is used to mean "very": He is from a ~~real~~ **really** small town. To ensure this word's effectiveness, use it sparingly.

* **reason why** Traditionally, this combination was considered redundant: No one explained **the reason why** the negotiations failed. [OR No one explained **the ~~reason~~ why** the negotiations failed.] However, dictionary editors report its use by highly regarded writers.

regard, regarding, regards These forms are used in the following expressions: *in regard to, with regard to, as regards,* and *regarding* [NOT *in regards to, with regards to,* or *as regarding*].

* **relation, relationship** According to traditional definitions, *relation* is used to link abstractions: We studied the **relation** between language and social change. *Relationship* is used to link people: The **relationship** between the two friends grew strong. However, dictionary editors now label as standard the use of *relationship* to connect abstractions.

respectfully, respectively *Respectfully* means "showing respect": The children learned to treat one another **respectfully.** *Respectively* means "in the order designated": We discussed the issue with the chair, the dean, and the provost, **respectively.**

rise See **raise, rise.**

sensor See **censor, censure, sensor.**

sensual, sensuous *Sensual* refers to gratification of the physical senses, often those associated with sexual pleasure: Frequently found in this music are **sensual** dance rhythms. *Sensuous* refers to gratification of the senses in response to art, music, nature, and so on: **Sensuous** landscape paintings lined the walls of the gallery.

shall, will Traditionally, *shall* was used with *I* or *we* to express future tense, and *will* was used with the other personal pronouns, but *shall* has almost disappeared in contemporary American English. *Shall* is still used in legal writing to indicate an obligation.

should of See **could of.**

sight See **cite, site, sight.**

sit, set *Sit* means "to be seated": Jonathon **sat** in the front row. *Set* means "to place something": The research assistant **set** the chemicals on the counter. *Set* takes an object (to **set** something); *sit* does not.

site See **cite, site, sight.**

so *So* intensifies another word when it is used with *that:* He was **so** nervous **that** he had trouble sleeping. Instead of using *so* alone, find a precise modifier: She was **so** intensely focused on her career. See 27f.

someplace See **anyplace, everyplace, someplace.**

sometime, sometimes, some time *Sometime* means "at an unspecified time": They will meet **sometime** next month. *Sometimes* means "at times": **Sometimes** laws are unfair. *Some time* means "a span of time": They agreed to allow **some time** to pass before voting on the measure.

sort of a See **kind of a, sort of a.**

specially See **especially, specially.**

stationary, stationery *Stationary* means "in a fixed position": Traffic was **stationary** for an hour. *Stationery* means "writing paper and envelopes": The director ordered new department **stationery.**

supposed to, used to Be sure to include the frequently unsounded *d* at the end of the verb form: We are **supposed** to leave at 9:30 a.m. We **used to** leave earlier.

take See **bring, take.**

than, then *Than* is used in comparisons: The tape recorder is smaller **than** the radio. *Then* refers to a time sequence: Go straight ahead for three blocks; **then** turn left.

＊ **that, which** *Which* occurs in nonessential (nonrestrictive) clauses: Myanmar, **which** borders Thailand, was formerly called Burma. Both *that* and *which* occur in essential (restrictive) clauses, although traditionally only *that* was considered acceptable: I am looking for an atlas **that** [OR **which**] includes demographic information. (For more information on essential and nonessential clauses, see 35d and 35g.)

＊ **that, which, who** In essential (restrictive) clauses, *who* and *that* refer to people. We want to hire someone **who** [OR **that**] has had experience programming. Traditionally, only *who* was used to refer to people. *That*, as well as *which*, refers to things: He proposed a design **that** [OR **which**] will take advantage of solar energy.

their, there, they're *Their* is the possessive form of *they:* They will give **their** presentation tomorrow. *There* refers to location: I lived **there** for six years. *There* is also used as an expletive (see 34a(3)): **There** is no explanation for the phenomenon. *They're* is a contraction of *they are:* **They're** leaving in the morning.

theirself, theirselves Unconventional; use *themselves.* The students finished the project by **theirself** themselves.

then See **than, then.**

thru *Through* is preferred in academic and professional writing: We drove **thru** through the whole state of South Dakota in one day.

thusly Unconventional; use *thus, in this way,* or *as follows* instead: He accompanied his father on archeological digs and **thusly** discovered his interest in ancient cultures.

time period Readers are likely to consider this combination redundant; use one word or the other, but not both: During this **time period,** the economy was strong.

to, too, two *To* is an infinitive marker: She wanted **to** become an actress. *To* is also used as a preposition, usually indicating direction: They walked **to** the memorial. *Too* means either "also" or "excessively": I voted for her **too.** They are **too** busy this year. *Two* is a number: She studied abroad for **two** years.

toward, towards Although both are acceptable, *toward* is preferred in American English.

try and Conversational for *try to:* The staff will **try and** to finish the project by Friday.

ultimately See **eventually, ultimately.**

uninterested See **disinterested, uninterested.**

* **unique** Traditionally, *unique* meant "one of a kind" and thus was not preceded by a qualifier such as *more, most, quite,* or *very:* Her prose style is **quite** unique. However, dictionary editors note that *unique* is also widely used to mean "extraordinary."

usage, use *Use* is generally preferred to *usage* in nontechnical contexts: He designed the furniture for practical **usage** use.

use, utilize In most contexts, *use* is preferred to *utilize:* We **utilized** used a special dye in the experiment. However, *utilize* may suggest an effort to employ something for a purpose: We discussed how to **utilize** the new equipment we had been given.

used to See **supposed to, used to.**

way Conversational as an intensifier: The movie was **way** utterly depressing.

ways Conversational when referring to distance; use *way* instead: It's a long **ways** way from home.

well See **good, well.**

where Conversational for *that:* I noticed **where** that she had been elected.

where . . . at, where . . . to Conversational; omit *at* and *to:* **Where** is the library **at? Where** are you moving **to?**

which See **that, which** and **that, which, who.**

* **who, whom** *Who* is used as the subject or subject complement in a clause: We have decided to hire Marian Wright, **whom** who I believe is currently

finishing her degree in business administration. [*Who* is the subject in *who is currently finishing her degree in business administration.*] See also **that, which, who**. *Whom* is used as an object: Jeff Kruger, **who** whom we hired in 2004, is now our top sales representative. [*Whom* is the object in *whom we hired.*] Dictionary editors note that in conversation *who* is commonly used as an object as long as it does not follow a preposition. See **25b(5)**.

whose, who's *Whose* is a possessive form: **Whose** book is this? The book was written by a young Mexican-American woman **whose** family still lives in Chiapas. *Who's* is the contraction of *who is:* **Who's** going to run in the election?

will See **shall, will.**

with regards to Unconventional; see **regard, regarding, regards.**

would of See **could of.**

your, you're *Your* is a possessive form: Let's meet in **your** office. *You're* is a contraction of *you are:* **You're** gaining strength.

yourself See **herself, himself, myself, yourself.**

GLOSSARY

OF

TERMS

This glossary provides brief definitions of frequently used terms. Consult the index for references to terms not listed here.

absolute phrase A sentencelike structure containing a subject and its modifiers. Unlike a sentence, an absolute phrase has no verb marked for person, number, or tense: *The ceremony finally over,* the graduates tossed their mortarboards in the air. See **21a(6)**.

acronym A word formed by combining the initial letters or syllables of a series of words and pronounced as a word rather than as a series of letters: *NATO* for North Atlantic Treaty Organization. See **43e**.

active voice See **voice.**

adjectival clause A dependent clause, sometimes called a **relative clause,** that modifies a noun or a pronoun. See **21b(2)**.

adjectival phrase A phrase that modifies a noun or a pronoun. See **20d(3)**.

adjective A word that modifies a noun or a pronoun. Adjectives typically end in suffixes such as *-al, -able, -ant, -ative, -ic, -ish, -less, -ous,* and *-y.* See **20a(4)** and **24a. Coordinate adjectives** are two or more adjectives modifying the same noun and separated by a comma: a *brisk, cold* walk. See **35c(2)**.

adverb A word that modifies a verb, a verbal, an adjective, or another adverb. Adverbs commonly end in *-ly.* Some adverbs modify entire sentences: *Perhaps* the meeting could be postponed. See **20a(5)** and **24a**.

adverbial clause A dependent clause that modifies a verb, an adjective, or an adverb. See **21b(2)**.

alt tags Descriptive lines of text for each visual image in an electronic document. Because these lines can be read by screen-reading software, they can assist visually impaired users. See **6e(1)**.

analysis A separation of a whole into its parts. For example, a literary work may be separated into such elements as setting, plot, and characters. See **3f(4)** and **16e**.

antecedent A word or group of words referred to by a pronoun. See 20a(3) and 25c.

appositive A pronoun, noun, or noun phrase that identifies, describes, or explains an adjacent pronoun, noun, or noun phrase. See 21a(5) and 25b(4).

article A word used to signal a noun. *The* is a definite article; *a* and *an* are indefinite articles. See 20a(4).

asynchronous forum Online means of communication in which a period of time elapses between the sending and the receiving of a message. Internet newsgroups and electronic mailing lists are examples of asynchronous discussion groups. See 6c(1). COMPARE: **synchronous forum.**

attributive tag Short phrase that identifies the source of a quotation: *according to Jones, Jones claims.* See 11d.

auxiliary verb, auxiliary A verb that combines with a main verb. *Be, do,* and *have* are auxiliary verbs when they are used with main verbs. Also called **helping verbs. Modal auxiliaries** include *could, should,* and *may* and are used for such purposes as expressing doubt or obligation and making a request. See 20c and 26a(4).

blog Shortened form of *Web log,* a Web site that is part diary and part community forum in which users regularly post their observations or opinions on self-defined topics, maintain archives, and encourage responses from other users. See 6c(1).

Boolean operators See **logical operators.**

bulletin board See **newsgroup.**

case The form of a pronoun that indicates the relationship of the pronoun to other words in a sentence. Pronouns can be subjects or subject complements (**subjective case**), objects (**objective case**), or markers of possession and other relations (**possessive case**). See 25b.

claim A statement that a writer wants readers to accept; also called a **proposition.** See 8d.

clause A sequence of related words forming an independent unit (**independent clause,** or **main clause**) or an embedded unit (**dependent clause** used as an adverb, adjective, or noun). A clause has both a subject and a predicate. See 21b.

cliché An expression that has lost its power to interest readers because of overuse. See 33b.

clipped form A word that is a shortened form of another word: *bike* for *bicycle.* See 43d(3).

collective noun A noun that refers to a group: *team, faculty, committee.* See **20a(2)**.

collocation Common word combination such as *add to, adept at,* or *admiration for.* See **33c**.

colloquial A label for any word or phrase that is characteristic of informal speech. *Tummy* and *belly* are colloquial words; *stomach* is used in formal contexts. See **32c(2)**.

common noun A noun referring to any or all members of a class or group (*woman, city, holiday*) rather than to specific members (*Susan, Reno, New Year's Day*); also called **generic noun.** COMPARE: **proper noun.** See **20a(2)**.

complement A word or words used to complete the meaning of a verb. A **subject complement** is a word or phrase that follows a linking verb and categorizes or describes the subject. An **object complement** is a word or phrase that categorizes or describes a direct object when it follows such verbs as *make, paint, elect,* and *consider.* See **20d**.

complete predicate See **predicate.**

complete subject See **subject.**

complex sentence A sentence containing one independent clause and at least one dependent clause. See **21d(3)**.

compound-complex sentence A sentence containing at least two independent clauses and one or more dependent clauses. See **21d(4)**.

compound predicate Predicate that has two parts joined by a connecting word such as *and, or,* or *but*: Clara Barton *nursed the injured during the Civil War* and *later founded the American Red Cross.* See **20b**.

compound sentence A sentence containing at least two independent clauses and no dependent clauses. See **21d(2)**.

compound subject Subject that has two parts joined by a connecting word such as *and, or,* or *but*: Students and *faculty* are discussing the issue of grade inflation. See **20b**.

compound word Two or more words functioning as a single word: *ice cream, double-check.* See **40f(1)**.

conditional clause An adverbial clause, usually beginning with *if,* that expresses a condition: *If it rains,* the outdoor concert will be postponed.

conjunction A word used to connect other words, phrases, clauses, or sentences. **Coordinating conjunctions** (*and, but, or, nor, for, so,* and *yet*) connect and relate words and word groups of equal grammatical rank. See

20a(7) and 21c(1). A **subordinating conjunction** such as *although, if,* or *when* begins a dependent clause and connects it to an independent clause. See 20a(7) and 21c(3). COMPARE: **conjunctive adverb.**

conjunctive adverb A word such as *however* or *thus* that joins one independent clause to another. See 21c(4) and 23d. COMPARE: **conjunction.**

convention, conventional Refers to language or behavior that follows the customs of a community such as the academic, medical, or business community.

coordinate adjective See **adjective.**

coordinating conjunction See **conjunction.**

coordination The use of grammatically equivalent constructions to link or balance ideas. See chapter 28.

correlative conjunctions, correlatives Two-part connecting words such as *either . . . or* and *not only . . . but also.* See 20a(7) and 21c(2).

count nouns Nouns naming things that can be counted (*word, student, remark*). See 20a(2). COMPARE: **noncount nouns.**

dangling modifier A word or phrase that does not clearly modify another word or word group in the sentence. See 24d. COMPARE: **misplaced modifier.**

dangling participial phrase A verbal phrase that does not clearly modify another word or word group in the sentence. See 24d.

database An organized collection of related information, usually in electronic form. A full-text database contains the complete, or nearly complete, text of articles. An abstract database contains summaries of articles. A bibliographic database contains limited information such as the subjects, titles, and authors of articles. See 9c(1).

deductive reasoning A form of logical reasoning in which a conclusion is formed after relating a specific fact (minor premise) to a generalization (major premise). See 8h(2). COMPARE: **inductive reasoning.**

demonstratives Four words (*this, that, these,* and *those*) that distinguish one individual, thing, event, or idea from another. Demonstratives may occur with or without nouns: *This* [demonstrative determiner] *law* will go into effect in two years. *This* [demonstrative pronoun] will go into effect in two years.

dependent clause See **clause.**

determiner A word that signals the approach of a noun. A determiner may be an article, a demonstrative, a possessive, or a quantifier: *a reason, this reason, his reason, three reasons.*

direct address See **vocative.**

direct object See **object.**

direct quotation See **quotation.**

electronic mailing list See **listserv.**

ellipsis points Three spaced periods that indicate either a pause or the omission of material from a direct quotation. See **39h.**

elliptical clause A clause missing one or more words that are assumed to be understood. See **21b(2).**

essential element A word or word group that modifies another word or word group, providing information that is essential for identification. Essential elements are not set off by commas, parentheses, or dashes: The woman *who witnessed the accident* was called to testify. Also called a **restrictive element.** COMPARE: **nonessential element.**

ethos One of the three classical appeals; the use of language to demonstrate the writer's trustworthy character, good intentions, and substantial knowledge of a subject. Also called an **ethical appeal.** See **8f(1).** See also **logos** and **pathos.**

exigence The circumstance compelling one to write. See **1b.**

expletive A word signaling a structural change in a sentence, usually used so that new or important information is given at the end of the sentence: *There were over four thousand runners in the marathon.* See **20d(1).**

faulty predication A sentence error in which the predicate does not logically belong with the given subject. See **27d(2).**

figurative language The use of words in an imaginative rather than in a literal sense. See **33a(4).**

file transfer protocol See **ftp.**

first person See **person.**

flaming Heated, confrontational exchanges via e-mail. See **6d.**

ftp Abbreviation for **file transfer protocol.** The guidelines that establish the format in which files can be transmitted from computer to computer.

gender The grammatical label that distinguishes nouns or pronouns as masculine, feminine, or neuter. In English, grammatical gender usually corresponds to natural gender. Gender also describes how people see themselves, or are seen by others, as either male or female. See **25c** and **32d(1).**

generic noun See **common noun.**

genre A literary category, such as drama or poetry, identified by its own conventions. See **16a.**

gerund A verbal that ends in *-ing* and functions as a noun: *Snowboarding* is a popular winter sport. See 21a(3).

gerund phrase A verbal phrase that employs the *-ing* form of a verb and functions as a noun: Some students prefer *studying in the library.* See 21a(3).

helping verb See **auxiliary verb.**

homophones Words that have the same sound and sometimes the same spelling but differ in meaning: *their, there,* and *they're* or *capital* meaning "funds" and *capital* meaning "the top of a pillar." See 40c.

hyperlink A Web address that is embedded in an electronic document and usually highlighted by color and underlining and that allows users to move between Web pages or sites. See 6e(3).

hypertext A computer-based text retrieval system that allows users, by clicking on links in a Web document, to move to other parts of that document or to other Web documents. See 6e(1).

idiom An expression whose meaning often cannot be derived from its elements. *Burning the midnight oil* means "staying up late studying." See 33c.

imperative mood See **mood.**

indefinite article See **article.**

indefinite pronoun A pronoun such as *everyone* or *anything* that does not refer to a specific individual, object, event, and so on. See 25c(1).

independent clause See **clause.**

indicative mood See **mood.**

indirect object See **object.**

indirect question A sentence that includes an embedded question, punctuated with a period instead of a question mark: My friends asked me *why I left the party early.* See 39a(1).

indirect quotation See **quotation.**

inductive reasoning The reasoning process that begins with facts or observations and moves to general principles that account for those facts or observations. See 7h(2). COMPARE: **deductive reasoning.**

infinitive A verbal that consists of the base form of the verb, usually preceded by the infinitive marker *to.* An infinitive is used chiefly as a noun, less frequently as an adjective or adverb: My father likes *to golf.* See 21a(3).

infinitive phrase A verbal phrase that contains the infinitive form of a verb: They volunteered *to work at the local hospital.* See 21(a)3.

inflection A change in the form of a word that indicates a grammatical feature such as number, person, tense, or degree. For example, *-ed* added to a verb indicates the past tense, and *-er* indicates the comparative degree of an adjective or adverb.

intensifier See **qualifier.**

intensive pronoun See **reflexive pronoun.**

interactive media Any type of online media that allows the user to influence and react to it.

interjection A word expressing a simple exclamation: *Hey! Oops!* When used in sentences, mild interjections are set off by commas. See **20a(8)**.

intransitive verb A verb that does not take an object: Everyone *laughed.* See **20e** and **26d(1)**. COMPARE: **transitive verb.**

invention Using strategies to generate ideas for writing. See **3a**.

inversion A change in the usual subject-verb order of a sentence: *Are you ready?* See **20e**.

keywords Specific words used with a search tool (such as Google) to find information. See **9b(1)**.

linking verb A verb that relates a subject to a subject complement. Examples of linking verbs are *be, become, seem, appear, feel, look, taste, smell,* and *sound.* See **20a(1)** and **26d(1)**.

listserv An online discussion forum consisting of a list of subscribers who share information about a specific subject by sending e-mail messages that are automatically distributed to all the other subscribers. Also referred to as an **e-mail list.** See **6c(1)**.

logical operators Words used to broaden or narrow electronic database searches. These include *or, and, not,* and *near.* Also called **Boolean operators.** See **9b(1)**.

logos One of the three classical appeals; the use of language to show clear reasoning. Also called a **logical appeal.** See **8f(1)**. See also **ethos** and **pathos.**

lurk The practice of anonymously observing how users in a given online community write and conduct themselves in order to learn the conventions before joining their discussion. See **6c(1)**.

major premise. See **premise.**

main clause Also called **independent clause.** See **clause.**

minor premise. See **premise.**

misplaced modifier A descriptive or qualifying word or phrase placed in a position that confuses the reader: I read about a wildfire that was out of

control *in yesterday's paper.* [The modifier belongs before *I* or after *read.*]
See 24c.

mixed construction A confusing sentence that is the result of an unintentional shift from one grammatical pattern to another: When police appeared who were supposed to calm the crowds showed up, most people had already gone home. [The sentence should be recast with either *appeared* or *showed up,* not with both.] See 27d(1).

mixed metaphor A construction that includes parts of two or more unrelated metaphors: Her *fiery* personality *dampened* our hopes of a compromise. See 27c.

modal auxiliary See **auxiliary verb.**

modifier A word or word group that describes, limits, or qualifies another. See chapter 24.

mood A set of verb forms or inflections used to indicate how a speaker or writer regards an assertion: as a fact or opinion (**indicative mood**); as a command or instruction (**imperative mood**); or as a wish, hypothesis, request, or condition contrary to fact (**subjunctive mood**). See 26e.

netiquette Word formed from *Internet* and *etiquette* to name a set of guidelines for writing e-mail messages and listserv postings and for online behavior in general. See 6d.

newsgroup An online discussion group that is accessible to anyone and allows users to post messages related to a specific topic (or thread). Messages are kept on a server, organized by topic so that other users can search for, read, and respond to whatever has been discussed by the group. Also called a **bulletin board.** See 6c(1).

nominalization Formation of a noun by adding a suffix to a verb or an adjective: *require, requirement; sad, sadness.*

nominative case Also called **subjective case.** See **case.**

noncount nouns Nouns naming things that cannot be counted (*architecture, water*). See 20a(2). COMPARE: **count nouns.**

nonessential element A word or word group that modifies another word or word group but does not provide essential information for identification. Nonessential elements are set off by commas, parentheses, or dashes: Carol Murphy, *president of the university,* plans to meet with alumni representatives. Also called a **nonrestrictive element.** See 35d. COMPARE: **essential element.**

nonrestrictive element See **nonessential element.**

nonstandard, nonstandardized Refers to speech forms that are not considered conventional in many academic and professional settings. See the **Glossary of Usage.**

noun A word that names a person, place, thing, idea, animal, quality, event, and so on: *Alanis, America, desk, justice, dog, strength, departure.* See also **common noun, proper noun, count noun, noncount noun,** and **collective noun.** See **20a(2).**

noun clause A dependent clause used as a noun. See **21b(2).**

noun phrase A noun and its modifiers. See **21a(1).**

number The property of a word that indicates whether it refers to one **(singular)** or to more than one **(plural).** Number is reflected in the word's form: *river/rivers, this/those, he sees/they see.* See **26b.**

object A noun, pronoun, noun phrase, or noun clause that follows a preposition or a transitive verb or verbal. A **direct object** names the person or thing that receives the action of the verb: I sent the *package.* An **indirect object** usually indicates to whom the action was directed or for whom the action was performed: I sent *you* the package. See **20d(2).** The **object of a preposition** follows a preposition: I sent the package to *you.* See **21a(4).**

object complement See **complement.**

object of a preposition See **object.**

objective case Also called **accusative case.** See **case.**

parenthetical element Any word, phrase, or clause that adds detail to a sentence or any sentence that adds detail to a paragraph but is not essential for understanding the core meaning. Commas, dashes, or parentheses separate these elements from the rest of the sentence or paragraph. See **35e.**

participial phrase A verbal phrase that includes a participle: The stagehand *carrying the trunk* fell over the threshold. See **21a(3).** See also **participle** and **phrase.**

participle A verb form that may function as part of a verb phrase (was *thinking,* had *determined*) or as a modifier (a *determined* effort; the couple, *thinking* about their past). A **present participle** is formed by adding *-ing* to the base form of a verb. A **past participle** is usually formed by adding *-ed* to the base form of a verb (*walked, passed*); however, many verbs have irregular past-participle forms (*written, bought, gone*). See **26a(5).**

particle A word such as *across, away, down, for, in, off, out, up, on,* or *with* that combines with a main verb to form a phrasal verb: *write down, look up.* See **26a(3).**

parts of speech The classes into which words may be grouped according to their forms and grammatical relationships. The traditional parts of speech are verbs, nouns, pronouns, adjectives, adverbs, prepositions, conjunctions, and interjections.

passive voice See **voice.**

past participle See **participle.**

pathos One of the three classical appeals; the use of language to stir the feelings of an audience. Also called an **emotional appeal** or a **pathetic appeal.** See **8f(1).** See also **ethos** and **logos.**

person The property of nouns, pronouns, and their corresponding verbs that distinguishes the speaker or writer **(first person)**, the individuals addressed **(second person)**, and the individuals or things referred to **(third person)**. See **26b(1).**

personal pronoun A pronoun that refers to a specific person, place, thing, and so on. Pronoun forms correspond to three cases: subjective, objective, and possessive. See **25a(1).**

phrasal verb A grammatical unit consisting of a verb and a particle such as *after, in, up, off,* or *out: fill in, sort out.* See **26a(3).**

phrase A sequence of grammatically related words that functions as a unit in a sentence but lacks a subject, a predicate, or both: *in front of the stage.* See **21a.**

point of view The vantage point from which a topic is viewed; also, the stance a writer takes: objective or impartial (third person), directive (second person), or personal (first person).

possessive case See **case.**

predicate The part of a sentence that expresses what a subject is, does, or experiences. The **complete predicate** consists of the main verb, its auxiliaries, and any complements and modifiers. The **simple predicate** consists of only the main verb and any accompanying auxiliaries. See **20b–c.** COMPARE: **subject.**

premise An assumption or a proposition on which an argument or explanation is based. In logic, premises are either **major** (general) or **minor** (specific); when combined correctly, they lead to a conclusion. See **8h(2).** See also **syllogism.**

preposition A word such as *at, in, by,* or *of* that relates a pronoun, noun, noun phrase, or noun clause to other words in the sentence. See **20a(6).**

prepositional phrase A preposition with its object and any modifiers: *at* the nearby airport, *by* the sea. See **21a(4).**

present participle See **participle.**

primary source A source that provides firsthand information. See **9a.** COMPARE: **secondary source.**

pronoun A word that takes the position of a noun, noun phrase, or noun clause and functions as that word or word group does: *it, that, he, them.* See 20a(3) and chapter 25.

proper adjective An adjective that is derived from the name of a person or place: *Marxist* theories. See 41a(9).

proper noun The name of a specific person, place, organization, and so on: *Dr. Pimomo, Fargo, National Education Association.* Proper nouns are capitalized. See 20a(2). COMPARE: **common noun.**

proposition See **claim.**

qualifier A word that intensifies or moderates the meaning of an adverb or adjective: *quite* pleased, *somewhat* reluctant. Words that intensify are sometimes called **intensifiers.**

quotation A **direct quotation** is the exact repetition of someone's spoken or written words. Also called **direct discourse.** An **indirect quotation** is a report of someone's written or spoken words not stated in the exact words of the writer or speaker. See 11d and chapter 38.

reflexive pronoun A pronoun that ends in *-self* or *-selves* (*myself* or *themselves*) and refers to a preceding noun or pronoun in the sentence: *He* added a picture of *himself* to his Web page. When used to provide emphasis, such a pronoun is called an **intensive pronoun:** The president *herself* awarded the scholarships. See 25a(4).

refutation A strategy for addressing opposing points of view by discussing those views and explaining why they are unsatisfactory. See 8e(2) and 8g(3).

relative clause See **adjectival clause.**

relative pronoun A word (*who, whom, that, which,* or *whose*) used to introduce an adjectival clause, also called a **relative clause.** An antecedent for the relative pronoun can be found in the main clause. See 21b(2).

restrictive element See **essential element.**

rhetorical appeal The means of persuasion in argumentative writing, relying on reason, authority, or emotion. See 8f.

Rogerian argument An approach to argumentation that is based on the work of psychologist Carl R. Rogers and that emphasizes the importance of withholding judgment of others' ideas until they are fully understood. See 8f(2).

search engine A Web-based program that enables users to search the Internet for documents containing certain words or phrases. Sometimes called a **search tool.** See 9d.

search tool See **search engine.**

secondary source A source that analyzes or interprets firsthand information. See **9a.** COMPARE: **primary source.**

sentence modifier A modifier related to a whole sentence, not to a specific word or word group within it: *All things considered,* the committee acted appropriately when it approved the amendment to the bylaws.

simple predicate See **predicate.**

simple subject See **subject.**

split infinitive The separation of the two parts of an infinitive form by at least one word: *to completely cover.* See **21a(3).**

squinting modifier A modifier that is unclear because it can refer to words either preceding it or following it: Proofreading *quickly* results in missed spelling errors. See **24c(3).**

Standardized English The usage expected in most academic and business settings. See **Glossary of Usage.**

subject The general area addressed in a piece of writing. See **3a.** COMPARE: **topic.** Also, the pronoun, noun, or noun phrase that carries out the action or assumes the state described in the predicate of a sentence. Usually preceding the predicate, the **complete subject** includes the main noun or pronoun and all determiners and modifiers. A **simple subject** consists of only the main noun or pronoun. See **20b** and **20d(1).** COMPARE: **predicate.**

subject complement See **complement.**

subjective case See **case.**

subjunctive mood See **mood.**

subordinating conjunction See **conjunction.**

subordination The connection of a grammatical structure to another, usually a dependent clause to an independent clause: *Even though customers were satisfied with the product,* the company wanted to improve it. See chapter **28.**

syllogism Method for deductive reasoning consisting of two premises and a conclusion. See **8h(2).** See also **premise.**

synchronous forum Online means of communication in which messages are exchanged in real time; that is, the receiver of a message sees it on the screen right after the sender completes it. Chat rooms are synchronous discussion groups. See **6c(1).** COMPARE: **asynchronous forum.**

synthesis Collecting and connecting information on a topic; usually involves summary, analysis, and interpretation.

tag question A question attached to the end of a related statement and set off by a comma: She came back, *didn't she?*

tense The form of a verb that indicates when and for how long an action or state occurs. See **26b–c.**

theme The main idea of a literary work. See **16b(7).**

thesis The central point or main idea of an essay. See **3c.**

tone The writer's attitude toward the subject and the audience, usually conveyed through word choice and sentence structure. See **4a(3).**

topic The specific, narrowed main idea of an essay. See **3b.** COMPARE: **subject.**

topic sentence A statement of the main idea of a paragraph. See **4c(1).**

Toulmin model A system of argumentation developed by philosopher Stephen Toulmin in which a claim and supporting reasons or evidence depend on a shared assumption. See **8h(3).**

transitions Words, phrases, sentences, or paragraphs that relate ideas by linking sentences, paragraphs, or larger segments of writing. See **4d** and **23c(5).**

transitive verb A verb that takes an object. The researchers *reported* their findings. See **20e** and **26d(1).** COMPARE: **intransitive verb.**

URL Abbreviation for **Uniform Resource Locator,** which identifies an Internet address, including the domain name and often a specific file to be accessed.

usability testing The process of soliciting reactions from potential users of a Web site or other complex electronic document in order to improve the content or design of the document. See **6e(4).**

verb A word denoting action, occurrence, or existence (state of being). See **20a(1)** and chapter **26.**

verb phrase A main verb and any auxiliaries. See **21a(2)** and **26a(4).**

verbal A verb form functioning as a noun, an adjective, or an adverb. See **21a(3).** See also **gerund, infinitive,** and **participle.**

vocative Set off by commas, the name of or the descriptive term for the person or persons being addressed. See **35b(3).**

voice A property of a verb that indicates the relationship between the verb and its subject. The **active voice** is used to show that the subject performs the action expressed by the verb; the **passive voice** is used to show that the subject receives the action. See **26d** and **30e.**

warrant According to the Toulmin model, the underlying assumption connecting a claim and data. See **8h(3).**

Web log See **blog.**

CREDITS

These pages constitute an extension of the copyright page. We have made every effort to trace the ownership of all copyrighted material and to secure permission from copyright holders. In the event of any question arising as to the use of any material, we will be pleased to make the necessary corrections in future printings. Thanks are due to the following authors, publishers, and agents for permission to use the material indicated.

Text and Art

p. 103: Online course: "Coding for Corporate Survival" screen: "Discussion Papers." Courtesy of Jeff Pruchnic.

p. 107: FOR BETTER OR FOR WORSE © 2000 Lynn Johnston Productions. Dist. By Universal Press Syndicate. Reprinted with permission. All rights reserved.

p. 112: Thesis statement and supporting points by Trish Parsons. Reprinted by permission of the author.

p. 122 (Fig. 6.2): Screen shot: newsgroups on programming games, Google Beta Groups. © 2005 Google Corporation. All rights reserved.

p. 123 (Fig. 6.3): CJR Daily Homepage Screen Grab. Courtesy of Columbia Journalism Review, CJRDaily.org. Photo of Protesters outside the United Nations during the U.N. 2005 Summit 9/14/05 on the CJR Daily Homepage © John Smock/AP/Wide World Photos.

p. 124 (Fig. 6.4): Instant messaging screen shot. Courtesy of Stacey Sheriff.

p. 127 (Fig. 6.5): Home page for The Green Belt Movement. Copyright © 2005 The Green Belt Movement.

p. 142 (Fig. 7.1): Cover illustration from *Diary of a Worm* by Doreen Cronin and Harry Bliss, 2003. © 2003 by Harry Bliss. Reprinted by permission of HarperCollins Publishers, Inc.

p. 147 (Fig. 7.5): Cover of 2005 *Virginia Is for Lovers Travel Guide*. Copyright © Scott K. Brown Photography, Inc.

p. 159 (Fig. 7.12): *New York Times* front page, 4/10/03. Copyright © 2003 The New York Times.

p. 165 (Fig. 7.15): Reprinted by permission of JETLOG Corporation, www.jetlog24x7.com.

p. 167 (Fig. 7.18): Line drawing of a printer from PIXMA iP4000/iP3000 Quick Start Guide, 2004. Courtesy of Canon USA, Inc. © 2004 Canon U.S.A., Inc.

pp. 181–182: "Letter from Birmingham Jail" by Martin Luther King, Jr. Reprinted by arrangement with the Estate of Martin Luther King Jr. c/o Writers House as agent for the proprietor, New York, NY. Copyright 1963 Dr. Martin Luther King Jr., copyright renewed 1991 Coretta Scott King.

p. 191: By permission of Gary Varvel and Creators Syndicate, Inc.

p. 192 (top): © The New Yorker Collection 1994 Mick Stevens from cartoonbank.com. All Rights Reserved.

p. 192 (bottom): FOR BETTER OR FOR WORSE © 2000 Lynn Johnston Productions. Dist. By Universal Press Syndicate. Reprinted with permission. All rights reserved.

p. 193: © The New Yorker Collection 1996 Warren Miller from cartoonbank.com. All Rights Reserved.

p. 195 (top): Reprinted by permission of Ed Colley.

p. 195 (bottom): © 2004 by Brian Fairrington. Reprinted by permission of Cagle Cartoons, Inc.

p. 196: Reprinted by permission of Don Landgren, Jr.

p. 213 (Fig. 9.1): Search boxes from university library's Web page. Courtesy of the James E. Brook Library.

p. 214 (Fig. 9.2): Keyword search from university library's Web page. Courtesy of the James E. Brook Library.

p. 218 (Fig. 9.3): OCLC FirstSearch. The FirstSearch Catalog screen captures are used with OCLC's permission. FirstSearch WorldCat and ArticleFirst are registered trademarks of OCLC Online Computer Library Center, Inc. WorldCat and ArticleFirst screens are copyrighted by OCLC and/or its third party database providers.

p. 221 (Fig. 9.4): InfoTrac screen shot. Result screen from InfoTrac® College Edition by Gale Group. Reprinted by permission of The Gale Group.

p. 222 (Fig. 9.5): First page of article found through InfoTrac. Result screen from InfoTrac® College Edition by Gale Group. Reprinted by permission of The Gale Group.

p. 233: Excerpt from "Bad Rapport with Patients to Blame for Most Malpractice Suits." Reprinted by permission of *The University of Chicago Chronicle*.

p. 236 (Fig. 10.1): Nobel e-Museum Web site. From http://www.nobel.se/peace/laureates/1997. Copyright © The Nobel Foundation. Reprinted by permission.

p. 240: "What Is NPR?" from www.npr.org/about/. Reprinted by permission of National Public Radio, Inc.

p. 279 (Fig. 12.1): From PROTECTING AMERICA'S HEALTH by Philip J. Hilts, copyright © 2003 by Philip J. Hilts. Used by permission of Alfred A. Knopf, a division of Random House, Inc.

p. 279 (Fig. 12.2): Reprinted by permission of Bloomsbury, USA.

p. 284 (Fig. 12.3): Page from *American Literary History* 14:3 (Fall 2002), by permission of Oxford University Press.

p. 293 (Fig. 12.4): Home page of Art Institute of Chicago. Reproduced by permission of The Art Institute of Chicago.

p. 294 (Fig. 12.5): New Yorker Web page. From NewYorker.com, November 14, 2003.

p. 298 (Fig. 12.6): Abstract page from ProQuest database. Copyright © 2005 ProQuest.

pp. 326 and 327 (Figs. 13.1 and 13.2): From "Working with People with Learning Disabilities" by David Thomas and Honor Woods. Copyright © 2003 David Thomas and Honor Woods. Reprinted by Permission of Jessica Kingsley Publishers Ltd.

p. 328 (Fig. 13.3): Adapted with permission from *Journal of Applied Social Psychology*, 2003, Vol. 33, No. 2, 423–443. © V. H. Winston & Son, Inc., 360 South Ocean Boulevard, Palm Beach, FL 33480. All rights reserved.

p. 334 (Fig. 13.4): Computer printout of abstract page from EBSCOhost. Copyright © 2005 EBSCO Industries, Inc.

p. 336 (Fig. 13.5): First page of Web article "Ethical Standards for School Counselors." © American School Counselor Association.

p. 341: Graph of sleep stages. From *Good sleep, good learning, good life*, by Piotr Wozniak, July 2000. Retrieved September 19, 2002, from http://www.supermemo.com/articles/sleep.htm. Reprinted with permission.

p. 394: "Portrait" reprinted by permission of Louisiana State University Press from *Girl at the Window* by Pinkie Gordon Lane. Copyright © 1991 by Pinkie Gordon Lane.

p. 419: Reprinted with permission from Blissitt, P. A. Sleep, memory, and learning. *Journal of Neuroscience Nursing*, 33 (4), 208. Copyright © 2001 by the American Association of Neuroscience Nurses.

p. 448: © Reprinted with permission of King Features Syndicate.

pp. 459 and 514: Boboli package directions. The Boboli trademark and directions are used with the permission of Entenmann's Products, Inc. Boboli® is a registered trademark of Entenmann's Products, Inc.

p. 660: By permission. From *Merriam-Webster's Collegiate Dictionary*, Eleventh Edition © 2004 by Merriam-Webster, Incorporated (www.Merriam-Webster.com).

Photos

p. 6: © AFP/Getty Images.

p. 11: Reprinted by permission of MADD.

p. 37: © Jeremy Woodhouse Photodisc/Getty Images.

p. 50: Courtesy of Mercedes-Benz USA.

p. 51: © Britt Erlanson/Getty Images.

p. 52: © Amy Etra/PhotoEdit—All rights reserved.

p. 54: (Kennedy) © Time-Life Pictures/Getty Images; (King) © Flip Schulke/Black Star.

p. 55: © Scott T. Smith/Corbis.

p. 60: Migrant Mother by Dorothea Lange, 1936 Library of Congress, Farm

INDEX

Numbers and letters in color refer to chapters and sections in the handbook; other numbers refer to pages.

(cont.)

(cont.)

(cont.)

CHECKLISTS

CONTENTS

CONTENTS

CONTENTS

CONTENTS

PREFACE

The *Prentice-Hall Handbook* is both a reference for the writer and a text for class use. As a summary of grammar, usage, and elementary rhetoric, it provides essential information. Its format is designed to serve two purposes: (1) to provide the student with a convenient reference for both preparing and reviewing written work; and (2) to assist the instructor in reading papers, allowing him or her to direct attention readily to specific essentials. Ample examples and exercises provide ready help in study, review, or class discussion.

This edition has been revised to retain the full coverage of former editions, to expand several sections, and to add some new material. All changes have been in the interest of ensuring clear, straightforward, and adequate guidance for students.

Though the organization of the book remains essentially the same as that of previous editions, revised and new material appears in various ways. We have made three important changes. Section 1 on sentence sense has been reworked for greater clarity. Sections 4 and 5 have been extensively revised to provide two full sections on the central and often troublesome problems of verbs; Section 4 now addresses verb forms and their problems; Section 5, tense, mood, and voice. Finally, the entire description of internal punctuation has been revised to provide individual sections on each major mark of punctuation and on the punctuation of quoted material. Users of previous editions will want to note the necessary renumbering of Sections 3–5 and Sections 20–26.

In the material on larger elements (Sections 31–33) we have considerably revised Section 31, "The Whole Composition," to emphasize the importance of prewriting and revising and to allow the student to follow a single paper from its conception to its final corrected version with instructor comments. In Section 32, "Effective Paragraphs," the proportion of student paragraphs has been increased. And a new Section 33, "Writing Persuasively," incorporates information from Section 37 of earlier editions and places it more clearly in the context of persuasive writing. Both the revised Sections 31 and 33 display entirely new student papers for study and analysis.

The unit on effective sentences (formerly Sections 33–36, now Sections 34–37) has been extensively reworked. The revised sequence emphasizes the writer's need to generate stronger and more effective sentences rather than merely to avoid weak ones. New material includes information on using coordination as well as subordination as a successful strategy for relating ideas, on using various subordinating words to express different relationships among ideas, and on using appositives, participial phrases, and absolutes as well as subordinate clauses to generate effective sentences. Throughout the sequence, we have tried to stress the value of revising and to offer exercises that will invite students to explore various ways of expressing their ideas.

Throughout the remaining sections of the *Handbook* we have made a number of less basic but we believe nonetheless helpful revisions. In Sections 38–44, "Words," we have continued to emphasize exactness, directness, and appropriateness as the three principles of word choice, but we have tried to sharpen some of the explanations and to compress somewhat the information on dictionaries. In Section 46, "The Research Paper," we have updated all the conventions of research writing to conform to those of the *MLA Handbook* (1977) and have added additional note and bibliographical forms, information on forms commonly used in scientific writing, and new material on handling quotations in research papers. In the final sections of the text, we have revised and somewhat expanded Section 49, now entitled "Writing on the Job: Business Correspondence," to correspond wholly with current practice and to include a brief explanation of memorandum form. In both the usage glossary (Section 43) and the concluding glossary of grammatical terms (Section 50), we have added and revised items, many in accord with suggestions from users of the seventh edition.

Throughout the revision our purpose has been to make material more accessible to students and easier for instructors both to teach from and to refer to. To this end, we have expanded explanations whenever they seemed insufficient, briefly redefined terms when they recur in order to minimize the student's need to consult other sections of the text, and provided ample examples. We have updated and revised exercises through most of the sections of the book. While retaining the very plentiful exercises of previous editions, we have tried to redistribute them to ensure that all important subsections are followed by a set of exercises. Sections addressing the most critical problems, such as those of sentence fragments, pronoun forms and reference, and the like, have additional exercises where possible.

As we indicated earlier, the *Handbook* is consistently designed to be a useful and easy reference guide in preparing, correcting, and revising papers. It classifies the standards and conventions of writing and provides reference to them in three ways: (1) through a full index, (2) through a detailed table of contents, and (3) through the charts on the endpapers of the book. Each major rule is given a number and a symbol, and each subrule is designated by the number of the major rule plus a letter (5a, 16b, 22c, and so on). Thus in writing a paper the student may check readily any convention about which he or she is doubtful. The instructor, in reading papers, may conveniently call attention to a specific convention or a general principle by using either numbers or symbols, so that the student may easily locate the appropriate section in the *Handbook*. For an illustration of these possibilities, see the sample paragraphs on p. 109 and the final corrected draft of the student paper on pp. 220–221.

ACKNOWLEDGMENTS

We continue to be indebted to the many colleagues who over the years have suggested ways to improve each new edition of the *Prentice-Hall Handbook*. In preparing this edition, we have benefited from many perceptive criticisms of the seventh edition and of various sections of the manuscript for this new edition. For their extensive comments on the seventh edition, we are especially grateful to Art Albanese, San Diego State University; James Childs, Middlesex Community College, Connecticut; Robert Cosgrove, Saddleback College; Frank Garratt, Tacoma Community College; Robert Gregory, Carnegie-Mellon University; John Hanes, Duquesne University; Leonard Held, Chemeketa Community College; Thomas N. Huckin, University of Michigan; Gary Keedy, Catonsville Community College; Georgia A. Newman, Polk Community College; Lea Newman, North Adams State College; Robert Newsom, University of California, Irvine; John Reiss, Western Kentucky University; Charles Scarborough, Northern Virginia Community College; Richard Scorza, Broward Community College; Paul Suter, Chemeketa Community College; Mary Waldrop, Tyler Junior College, Texas; Samuel D. Watson, Jr., University of North Carolina at Charlotte; Dennis L. Williams, Central Texas College; and Laura M. Zaidman, South Georgia College. For their thoughtful comments on various parts of the manuscript for this edition, we are grateful to David S. Betts, State University of New York, Oneonta; Pamela Clements, University of Illinois; Macy Creek, Central Piedmont Community College; Ann Fields, Western Kentucky University; Thomas Kelly, State University of New York, College at Cortland; and Gretchen B. Niva, Western Kentucky University.

Special credit goes to two contributing authors who have joined us in this edition. To William Connelly, Middle Tennessee State University, we are indebted for his extensive revision of Sections 31 and 32, "The Whole Composition," and "Paragraphs." To Melinda Kramer, Purdue University, we are indebted for the new Section 33, "Writing Persuasively," which incorporates material from the logic section of earlier editions; and for the full revision of Section 49, "Writing on the Job: Business Correspondence." To both these contributing authors we also express our appreciation for their copious suggestions for improving the seventh edition and the manuscript for this edition.

Special thanks go also to Pamela Clements, University of Illinois, for preparing the text of the *Instructor's Manual* for this edition, and to Mamie Atkins, Purdue University, for preparing the handbook exercise answers incorporated in the *Instructor's Manual.*

Among the many at Prentice-Hall who have helped make this book possible, we want particularly to thank William H. Oliver, our editor, who has always been ready with advice and warm encouragement through this and earlier editions; Virginia Rubens, our production editor, who ensured that a manuscript became a book; and Joyce Perkins, our manuscript editor, who not only made our prose straight when crooked, clear when cluttered, and simple when complicated, but also always did so with grace and tact. Finally, our thanks to Caren Mattice, who through this and two earlier editions has faithfully typed and retyped manuscript and attended to permissions correspondence.

Throughout the *Handbook* we have quoted from copyrighted material and we are grateful to the copyright holders acknowledged below for their permission.

Maya Angelou, *I Know Why the Caged Bird Sings,* New York: Random House, Inc., 1969. By permission of Random House, Inc.

W. H. Auden, *Tales of Grimm and Andersen.* Copyright © 1952 by Random House, Inc.

Toni Cade Bambara, *Tales and Stories for Black Folks,* New York: Doubleday and Company, Inc., 1971. By permission of the author.

Jacques Barzun, *Teacher in America.* By permission of Little, Brown and Company, in association with the Atlantic Monthly Press.

Monroe Beardsley, *Practical Logic.* Copyright © 1950 by Prentice-Hall, Inc.

Isaiah Berlin, *Mr. Churchill in 1940.* By permission of the author and John Murray (Publishers) Ltd.

Pierre Berton, *The Klondike Fever* (Alfred A. Knopf, Inc., 1958).

Newman and Genevieve Birk, *Understanding and Using English.* By permission of the Odyssey Press, Inc.

Daniel J. Boorstin, *The Image.* Atheneum. Copyright © 1971 by Daniel J. Boorstin.

Claude Brown, *Manchild in the Promised Land* (The Macmillan Company, 1965).

Rachel Carson, *Silent Spring* (Houghton Mifflin Company, 1962).

Winston Churchill, *Blood, Sweat and Tears.* By permission of G. P. Putnam's Sons and Cassel and Company Ltd.

John Ciardi, "Confessions of a Crackpot," *Saturday Review,* Feb. 24, 1962.

Walter Van Tilburg Clark, *Track of the Cat.* By permission of Random House, Inc.

R. P. T. Coffin and Alexander Witherspoon, *Seventeenth Century Prose.* By permission of Harcourt, Brace and Company, Inc.

E. E. Cummings, "a man who had fallen among thieves." Copyright 1926 by Horace Liveright; published by Harcourt, Brace and Company, Inc.; used by permission of Brandt and Brandt.

Joan Didion, "On Keeping a Notebook," in *Slouching Toward Bethlehem,* New York: Farrar, Straus & Giroux, 1968. By permission of Farrar, Straus & Giroux.

Annie Dillard, *Pilgrim at Tinker Creek.* Copyright © 1974 by Annie Dillard. By permission of Harper & Row, Publishers, and Blanche C. Gregory, Inc.

Peter Drucker, "How to Be an Employee," *Fortune,* May 1952. Copyright © 1952 by Time, Inc.

Kent Durden, *Flight to Freedom.* Reprinted by permission of Simon & Schuster, Inc.

Loren Eiseley, "Little Men and Flying Saucers," copyright © 1953 by Loren C. Eiseley. Reprinted from *The Immense Journey* by permission of Random House, Inc.

T. S. Eliot, *Collected Poems.* By permission of Harcourt, Brace and Company, Inc.

The Foxfire Book, edited with an Introduction by Eliot Wigginton, Anchor Books, Doubleday & Company, Inc., 1972. By permission of Doubleday & Company, Inc.

William H. Gass, *In the Heart of the Heart of the Country.* Copyright © 1967 by William H. Gass. Reprinted by permission of International Creative Management.

Walker Gibson, *Tough, Sweet, and Stuffy.* Copyright © 1970. Indiana University Press.

From *Language in Thought and Action,* Third Edition, by S. I. Hayakawa, copyright © 1972 by Harcourt Brace Jovanovich, Inc. and reprinted with their permission and the permission of George Allen & Unwin Ltd.

From the book, *How Children Fail* by John Holt. Copyright © 1964 by Pitman Publishing Corporation. Reprinted by permission of Fearon-Pitman Publishers, Inc.

Jane Howard, *Families.* Copyright 1978 by Jane Howard. By permission of Simon and Schuster, a Divison of Gulf & Western Corporation. Reprinted by permission of A. D. Peters & Co. Ltd.

W. H. Ittelson and F. P. Kilpatrick, "Experiments in Perception," *Scientific American,* August 1951.

Jane Jacobs, "How City Planners Hurt Cities," *Saturday Evening Post,* Oct. 14, 1961.

Okakura Kakuzo, *The Book of Tea.* By permission of Charles E. Tuttle Company.

Elaine Kendall, "An Open Letter to the Corner Grocer," *Harper's* Magazine, December 1960. Reprinted by permission.

Jerzy Kosinski, NBC's *Comment.* By permission of Jerzy Kosinski.

Susanne K. Langer, "The Lord of Creation," *Fortune,* January 1944. Copyright © 1944 by Time, Inc.

George Laycock, "Games Otters Play," from *Audubon,* January, 1981. By permission of the National Audubon Society.

Henry S. Leonard, *Principles of Right Reason.* Published by Holt, Rinehart and Winston, Inc.

From p. 16 in *Guests: or How to Survive Hospitality* by Russell Lynes. Copyright 1951 by Harper & Row, Publishers, Inc. By permission of Harper & Row, Publishers, Inc.

William H. MacLeish, "The Year of the Coast," from *Smithsonian,* Sept. 1980.

Margaret Mead, "What Women Want," *Fortune* Magazine, December 1964. Reprinted by permission of the publisher.

H. L. Mencken, "Bryan," from *Selected Prejudices;* and *In Defense of Women.* By permission of Alfred A. Knopf, Inc.

Edmund S. Morgan, "What Every Yale Freshman Should Know," *Saturday Review,* Jan. 23, 1960.

Beth Neman, *Teaching Students to Write,* Columbus, Ohio: Charles E. Merrill Publishing Company, 1980. By permission of Charles E. Merrill Publishing Company.

ACKNOWLEDGMENTS

Russell Nye, *The Unencumbered Muse,* New York: Dial Press, 1970. By permission of Dial Press.

Bernard Pares, *Russia: Its Past and Present.* Copyright 1943, 1949 by The New American Library of World Literature, Inc.

S. J. Perelman, *Keep It Crisp.* By permission of Random House, Inc.

John Radar Platt, *Style in Science.* Reprinted from *Harper's* Magazine, October 1956.

Herbert Read, *The Eye of Memory.* Copyright 1947 by Herbert Read. By permission of Harold Ober Associates, Inc.

James Harvey Robinson, *The Mind in the Making.* By permission of Harper & Brothers.

Lionel Ruby, *The Art of Making Sense.* Copyright © 1968. Reprinted by permission of the publisher, J. B. Lippincott Company.

Herbert H. Sanders, *How To Make Pottery.* Copyright © 1974 by Watson Guptill Publications. Reprinted by permission.

May Sarton, *Plant Dreaming Deep,* New York: W. W. Norton & Co., Inc., 1968. By permission of W. W. Norton & Co., Inc.

Ben Shahn, *The Shape of Content.* By permission of Harvard University Press.

Mina P. Shaughnessy, *Errors and Expectations: A Guide to the Teaching of Basic Writing,* New York: Oxford University Press, 1977. Copyright © 1977 by Mina P. Shaughnessy. By permission of Oxford University Press.

Susan Sontag, *On Photography,* New York: Farrar, Straus, & Giroux, 1973, 1974, 1977. By permission of Farrar, Straus, and Giroux and Penguin Books Ltd.

George Summey, Jr., *American Punctuation.* Copyright 1949 The Ronald Press Company, New York.

Deems Taylor, *Of Men and Music.* By permission of Simon & Schuster, Inc.

James Thurber, *The Years with Ross.* Copyright © 1959 by James Thurber. Published by Atlantic-Little Brown. Originally printed in *The New Yorker.*

Barbara Tuchman, *A Distant Mirror,* New York: Alfred H. Knopf, 1978. By permission of Alfred H. Knopf.

John Updike, from "The Dogwood Tree," in *Five Boyhoods,* edited by Martin Levin (Doubleday). Copyright © 1962 Martin Levin. Reprinted by permission of Martin Levin.

Andrew Ward, "Yumbo." Copyright © 1978 by Andrew Ward. First published in the *Atlantic Monthly,* May, 1977. Excerpted by permission.

Eudora Welty, "Death of a Travelling Salesman," from *A Curtain of Green and Other Stories,* New York: Harcourt Brace Jovanovich 1941. By permission of Harcourt Brace Jovanovich. Reprinted by permission of Russell & Volkening as agents for the author.

E. B. White, *One Man's Meat.* By permission of Harper & Brothers.

A. N. Whitehead, *Science and the Modern World,* copyright 1925. By permission of The Macmillan Company.

William K. Zinsser, *On Writing Well,* New York: Harper & Row Publishers, Inc., 1980. By permission of Harper & Row Publishers, Inc.

INTRODUCTION

All life therefore comes back to the question of our speech, the medium through which we communicate with each other; for all life comes back to the question of our relations with one another.

HENRY JAMES, *The Question of Our Speech*

The growth of English

Like all languages, English changes constantly. Changes in vocabulary are the most rapid and obvious. *Butcher* once meant "a man who slaughters goats"; *neutron* and *proton,* key terms in physics today, were unrecorded fifty years ago; *biofeedback* appeared in dictionaries only in the 1970's. But language changes in more complex ways too. Today educated speakers avoid the multiple negatives of *She won't never do nothing.* But William Shakespeare's *nor this is not my nose neither* was good Elizabethan English. Even the sounds of language change. For Shakespeare, four hundred years ago, *deserts* rhymed with *departs,* and *reason* sounded much like our *raisin;* two hundred years ago, Alexander Pope properly rhymed *join* with *line* and *seas* with *surveys.*

The changes we see if we look back at the history of our language are far more dramatic. English is a Germanic language, descended from the language of the Germanic tribes (Angles, Saxons, and Jutes) who invaded the British Isles in the fifth and sixth centuries. In the centuries following, their language was subjected to a variety of influences. Its structure was loosened by the effects of the Danish invasions in the ninth and tenth centuries and by the Norman Conquest in 1066. To its vocabulary were added thousands of Latin, Scandinavian, and, particularly, French words. Spelling and pronunciation changed. Word meanings were modified or extended.

Perhaps the most important changes were gradual changes in **syntax,** the ways of showing relationships among the words in a sentence. The English of the sixth, seventh, and eighth centuries—Old English—was a highly **inflected** language. That is, it depended largely upon changes in the forms, and particularly the endings, of words to show their relationships to one another. Gradually, **word order** for the most part replaced such endings as the main way to convey sentence syntax. At the same time, **function words**—words like *the, yet, because,* and *with* (articles, conjunctions, and prepositions)—grew in number and importance. Thus, one of the great differences between Old English and English as we know it is this: in Old English, syntax depended heavily upon inflection, whereas syntax in Modern English depends mainly upon word order. Understanding this difference is important to using language well.

Look at the following brief passages to see something of the great changes that occurred between the time of King Alfred in the late ninth century and that of Shakespeare in the late sixteenth century.

Ða   gemette   hie   Æpelwulf   aldorman   on   Englafelda,   ond
Then   met   them   Aethelwulf   alderman   in   Englefield,   and
him   þær   wiþ   gefeaht ond   sige   nam.
them there against   fought   and victory won.

KING ALFRED, *Anglo-Saxon Chronicle,* c. 880

But now, if so be that dignytees and poweris be yyven to gode men,
the whiche thyng is full selde, what aggreable thynges is there in tho
dignytees or power but oonly the goodnesse of folk that usen them?

GEOFFREY CHAUCER, from the translation of *Boethius,* c. 1380

Hit befel in the dayes of Uther Pendragon, when he was kynge of
all Englond, and so regned, that there was a myghty duke in Cornewaill
that helde warre ageynst hym long tyme, and the duke was called the
duke of Tyntagil.   SIR THOMAS MALORY, *Morte d'Arthur,* c. 1470

A Proude Man contemneth the companye of hys olde friendes, and
disdayneth the sight of hys former famyliars, and turneth hys face from
his wonted acquayntaunce.

HENRY KERTON, *The Mirror of Man's Lyfe,* 1576

To us, these passages illustrate a steady development toward the
English we know. But to people living then, the changes often seemed
not growth but chaos. English, it appeared, would not hold still long
enough to have any value as a means of communication. Some, like
Sir Thomas More and Francis Bacon, preferred to write their greatest
works in Latin. But others, like Chaucer and Malory, wrote in their
native language. By doing so, they gave English a somewhat stabilizing
prestige. The development of English printing and the growth of a
national spirit helped even more to dignify and standardize the language. By the end of the sixteenth century, English had become a
national language, as indicated by the great English translation of the
Bible in 1611. Printing, together with the great increase in the number
of people who could read and write, tended to slow change in the
language, particularly in its written form. But though less rapid,
change remains continuous as the language adapts to the changing
needs of those who use it.

As always, change is most easily seen in vocabulary. In its very early
history, the coming of Christianity brought into the language such
Latin words as *angel, candle, priest,* and *school.* From the Danish came
such basic words as the pronouns *they, their,* and *them,* and *skull,
skin, anger, root,* and *ill.* After the Norman Conquest in 1066, French
words poured into the language for nearly three hundred years,
touching nearly every corner of life with words that are part of our
everyday vocabulary: *dance, tax, mayor, justice, faith, battle, paper,
poet, surgeon, gentle, flower, sun*—the list extends to thousands. In the
seventeenth century, when Latin became greatly respected and avidly

studied, thousands upon thousands of Latin words flooded into English. They included not only the words we think of as learned, but also many that are common such as *industry, educate, insane, exist, illustrate, multiply, benefit, paragraph, dedicate,* and the like. And as English reached into other parts of the world, it continued its habit of borrowing. It has played no favorites, drawing on Arabic *(alcohol, assassin),* Hebrew *(cherub, kosher),* East Indian *(jungle, yoga),* Japanese *(jujitsu, tycoon),* Spanish *(adobe, canyon),* and many others.

The borrowing process continues today. But in the past hundred years two other developments have had major consequences for English. The first is the rapid development of mass education and the resulting rise in literacy. The second is advancement in science and technology. Both of these developments have had complex effects upon the language and will doubtless continue to be strong influences. Though the effect of the first is difficult to measure, it is clear that a language that can reach many of its users in print and an even greater number through radio and television will develop differently from a language in which writing is addressed to a special minority or in which speech occurs largely in face-to-face exchange. The effect of the technological revolution and rapid specialization is clearer. It has given us a burgeoning vocabulary of technical terms ranging from the names of drugs to the specialized words in everything from do-it-yourself kits to space engineering.

Changes in grammar since the sixteenth century, though minor compared with the loss of inflections and the accompanying fixing of word order that came earlier, have continued in Modern English. Since the sixteenth century, reliance upon word order and function words has become even greater. Questions in the form of *Consents she?* and negations in the form of *I say not, I run not* have disappeared, to be replaced by the use of the auxiliary verb *do,* as in *Does she consent?, I do not say, I do not run.* Verb forms with *be* in the pattern of *He was speaking, We are going, It is being built* have multiplied greatly. Other changes include an increase in the number of verbs made from verbs combined with adverbs or with prepositions, as in *He looked up the word, He looked over Bill's new house, The fireplace was smoking up the room.* Similarly, nouns used as modifiers of other nouns, as in *college student, radio station, mathematics course, ice-cream stand,* have become more common. Such changes make it clear that the evolution of the language continues.

The following passages, though less strikingly dissimilar than those we saw earlier, demonstrate some of the changes in the language between 1600 and 1900. Many of the differences among these selections are differences of idiom or style rather than of grammar.

I had often before this said, that if the Indians should come, I should chuse rather to be killed by them than taken alive but when it came to the tryal my mind changed; their glittering weapons so daunted my spirit, that I chose rather to go along with those (as I may say) ravenous Bears, then that moment to end my dayes; and that I may better declare what happened to me during that grievous Captivity, I shall particularly speak of the severall Removes we had up and down the Wilderness.

MARY ROWLANDSON, *The Narrative of the Captivity, c.* 1682

About the twelfth year of my age, my Father being abroad, my Mother reproved me for some misconduct, to which I made an Undutifull reply & the next first-day, as I was with my Father returning from Meeting, He told me he understood I had behaved amis to my Mother, and Advised me to be more careful in future.

JOHN WOOLMAN, *The Journal,* 1756

I had stopped in Boston at the Tremont House, which was still one of the first hostelries of the country, and I must have inquired my way to Cambridge there; but I was sceptical of the direction the Cambridge horsecar took when I found it, and I hinted to the driver my anxieties as to why he should be starting east when I had been told that Cambridge was west of Boston.

WILLIAM DEAN HOWELLS, *Literary Friends and Acquaintances,* 1894

Variety and standards

Language not only changes with time, it also varies widely at any given time. It varies from one geographical area to another and from one occupational and social group to another. Further, the language each of us uses varies from situation to situation. The language of conversation differs from that in a public address, and that in turn differs from written language. Even carefully written and edited English varies according to the writer's audience and purpose.

One important variation of language is that between standard and nonstandard English. The term **standard English** is applied to the written language of business, journalism, education, law, public documents, and literature. It is also used to describe speech—the speech of people in the practice of the professions (medicine, teaching, theology, and so on), the speech of courtrooms, the speech of many public functions. In many occupations, competence in its use is necessary.

Nonstandard English describes language that varies in grammar and usage from the standard. Nonstandard commonly differs from standard English in verb and pronoun forms and in the use of double negatives, which are rare in standard. Such forms include *he give, growed, have saw; him and me is, hern, youse; can't never.* Nonstandard is also characterized by a relatively narrow range of vocabulary and a heavy dependence upon a small variety of sentence structures.

Distinctions between standard and nonstandard English are not distinctions between good and bad or right and wrong. The function of language is to communicate, and any language that makes for clear and accurate communication is good language. The reasons nonstandard forms are not used in business and the professions nor, ordinarily, in publications are social and historical rather than because they do not communicate. Nonetheless, standard English is the widely used and understood public language, and competence in its use is almost indispensable to taking part in the public functions in which it is used.

The following passages illustrate standard and one form of nonstandard English. Since nonstandard is primarily spoken, the illustration can only approximate it.

STANDARD

Today, as never before, the sky is menacing. Things seen indifferently last century by the wandering lamplighter now trouble a generation that has grown up to the wail of air-raid sirens and the ominous expectation that the roof may fall at any moment. Even in daytime, reflected light on a floating dandelion seed, or a spider riding a wisp of gossamer in the sun's eye, can bring excited questions from the novice unused to estimating the distance or nature of aerial objects.

LOREN EISELEY, "Little Men and Flying Saucers"

The voice we hear in an ad is not the official voice of the corporation that pays the bill. The voice in the ad is a highly fictitious created person, speaking as an individual in a particular situation. In a bathtub, for instance. No corporation official could ever say, officially, "I never, never bathe without Sardo." The official voice of the corporation appears, I suppose, in its periodic reports to its stockholders, or in its communications with government agencies.

WALKER GIBSON, *Tough, Sweet, & Stuffy*

NONSTANDARD

"I can't tell ya' [how to heal] because it's handed down from th' beginnin'. It's in th' Bible. If y'tell somebody, y'lose yer power—in other words, like a man doin' somethin' t'destroy his rights, y'know.

"In that now, I could learn two women, or three I think it is, and then one of 'em that I'd learnt could learn a man person. So about th' biggest point I get in that is t'add a little mystery t'th' party that don't believe, maybe we'll say, in fire drawin' [laughing].

"I learnt two, an' I studied about it after that. Never asked 'em yet if they've ever tried it t'see if it works. But I think th' one that learnt me said learn somebody not no kin to ya'. Well, these parties wasn't, but they'uz my brother's wives, see? But I've never asked them if they've tried it."   ELIOT WIGGINTON, ed., *The Foxfire Book*

Standard English varies too, according to its use or function. Such varieties are sometimes called **functional varieties.** The most general variation is that between informal and formal. **Informal** describes the English of everyday speaking and writing, casual conversation between friends and associates, personal letters, and writing close to general speech. **Formal** describes the language of scholarly books and articles, the reports of business, industry, and science, most legal writing, and literary prose.

Informal and formal cannot be clearly differentiated, for there are wide ranges of degree in each. In general, as language moves toward casual speech, it becomes more informal. At the extreme of informality is casual speech of educated people in familiar situations and the writing that tries to catch the flavor of such speech. Free use of contractions, loose sentence structures, and the use of informal words and expressions (such as *shape up* and *get going*) characterize informal language.

At the extreme of formality is careful scientific, scholarly, and legal writing, which needs to be exact. Note the elaborate sentence structure, the Latinate vocabulary, and the serious tone in the formal examples below. In the informal examples, the sentences become increasingly relaxed, the vocabulary is everyday, and the tone conversational. But if you catch yourself thinking that one is better than the other, remember that the purpose, subject matter, audience, temperament, and hence style of each author are quite different.

FORMAL

An antibiotic is a chemical substance, produced by microorganisms, which has the capacity to inhibit the growth of and even destroy bacteria and other microorganisms. The action of an antibiotic against microorganisms is selective in nature, some organisms being affected and others not at all or only to a limited degree; each antibiotic is thus characterized by a specific antimicrobial spectrum. The selective action of an antibiotic is also manifested against microbial vs. host cells. Antibiotics vary greatly in their physical and chemical properties and in their toxicity to animals. Because of these characteristics, some antibiotics have remarkable chemotherapeutic potentialities and can be used for the control of various microbial infections in man and in animals.

Quoted in SELMAN A. WAKSMAN, *The Actinomycetes and Their Antibiotics*

Dean Donne in the pulpit of old Paul's, holding his audience spellbound still as he reversed his glass of sands after an hour of exposition and application of texts by the light of the church fathers, of mortification for edification, of exhortation that brought tears to the eyes of himself and his hearers, and of analogies born of the study, but sounding of wings—there was a man who should have had wisdom, surely. For if experience can bring it, this was the man.

R. P. T. COFFIN and A. M. WITHERSPOON, "John Donne," in *Seventeenth Century Prose*

INTRODUCTION

All scientists are not alike. Look at any laboratory or university science department. Professor Able is the kind of man who seizes an idea as a dog seizes a stick, all at once. As he talks you can see him stop short, with the chalk in his fingers, and then almost jump with excitement as the insight grips him. His colleague, Baker, on the other hand, is a man who comes to understand an idea as a worm might understand the same stick, digesting it a little at a time, drawing his conclusions cautiously, and tunneling slowly through it from end to end and back again.   JOHN RADAR PLATT, "Style in Science"

Of all the common farm operations none is more ticklish than tending a brooder stove. All brooder stoves are whimsical, and some of them are holy terrors. Mine burns coal, and has only a fair record. With its check draft that opens and closes, this stove occupies my dreams from midnight, when I go to bed, until five o'clock, when I get up, pull a shirt and a pair of pants on over my pajamas, and stagger out into the dawn to read the thermometer under the hover and see that my 254 little innocents are properly disposed in a neat circle round their big iron mama.   E. B. WHITE, *One Man's Meat*

The colossal success of the supermarkets is based upon the fact that nobody, but nobody, can sell you something as well as you can by yourself. As a result, supermarkets now stock clothing, appliances, plastic swimming pools, and small trees. The theory is that if you succumb to an avocado today, tomorrow you may fall for an electronic range or a young poplar.

      ELAINE KENDALL, "An Open Letter to the Corner Grocer"

The terms *colloquial* and *edited* are often used in discussing varieties of English. **Colloquial** means "spoken." The word is used to describe the everyday speech of educated people and the kind of writing that uses the easy vocabulary, loose constructions, contractions, and other characteristics of that speech. The informal style of E. B. White and Elaine Kendall illustrated above is colloquial. **Edited English** is the written language of many books, magazines, and newspapers. It may be more or less formal or informal, but it is always marked by its observation of conventional spelling, punctuation, grammar, and sentence structure.

The fact that English has such variety means that there can be no unvarying and absolute standard of correctness. But it does not mean that we can do entirely without standards or that what is appropriate for familiar conversation is appropriate for all kinds of communication. If people were to write as naturally as they talk, they might rid their writing of some affectation. But for much of its force, conversational English depends upon the physical presence of the speaker. Personality, gesture, and intonation all contribute to the success of spoken communication. Written English, on the other hand, uses structure, rather than the physical presence of the writer, to achieve clarity. Written English communicates through the precision of its diction, the orderliness of its sentence and paragraph structure, and the relative fullness of its detail. If it is to be taken seriously by a general audience, it must observe the conventions of spelling, punctuation, and grammar. In short, writers do conform to certain standards to get their meaning across.

A handbook somewhat arbitrarily classifies such standards into rules or conventions that cannot always be defended on logical grounds. Rather, they reflect the practices—some old, some new—of English and American writers. Most of these conventions are quite flexible. The rules for punctuation, for instance, permit many variations, and so do the standards for diction, sentence structure, and paragraphing. The truth is that the rules of writing represent "typical" or "normal" practices. Skillful writers interpret them very loosely and occasionally ignore those that seem too restrictive for their purposes. For most writers, however, the rules are a discipline and a security. Observing them does not make writers great, but it does help to make writing clear and orderly. And clarity and order are the marks of good writing.

BASIC GRAMMAR
GR

Good grammar is not merely grammar which is free from unconventionalities, or even from the immoralities. It is the triumph of the communication process, the use of words which create in the reader's mind the thing as the writer conceived it; it is a creative act. . . .

JANET AIKEN, *Commonsense Grammar*

The term *grammar* is used in two ways. In one sense, grammar is the system by which a language works. In this sense, learning to speak a language *is* learning its grammar. If you grew up speaking English, as soon as you learned the difference between such pairs as *toy* and *toys*, *home run* and *run home*, or *tiger tails* and *tiger's tail*, you had learned a good deal of English grammar. And by the time you could put together sentences such as *Howard's father gave him some new toys*, or *See the monkeys jumping around in the cages*, you had learned very complicated things about English grammar.

In another sense, grammar is a description of language. In this sense, grammar is in the same class as physics. Physics describes how light, sound, electricity, and other kinds of energy and matter work. Grammar describes the way a language works. It describes the kinds of words in a language (nouns, verbs, prepositions, and so on) and how users of the language put single words together into meaningful groups.

In the following pages, you will find many of the details of English grammar. One basic concept about language may help you to keep these details in perspective. Any language is composed of individual words and **grammatical devices** for putting them together meaningfully. A series of words such as *age, buggy, the, and, horse* is just a series of isolated English words. Each word makes sense by itself, but they aren't obviously related to one another. But *the horse-and-buggy age* makes a quite different kind of sense; the words have been put together into a meaningful combination. English has several devices for putting words into such combinations. The three most important are word order, function words, and inflections.

In English, grammatical meaning is largely determined by **word order.** *Blue sky* and *sky blue* mean different things: in the first, *blue* describes *sky;* in the second, *sky* describes *blue.* Here is the principle in action:

The thief called the lawyer a liar.
The lawyer called the thief a liar.
The liar called the lawyer a thief.

Our new neighbors bought an old house.
Our old neighbors bought a new house.

See how important word order can be in such a sentence as *The man in the black shoes with the sandy hair knocked on the door.* Word order has *with the sandy hair* describing *shoes,* but common sense tells us that shoes do not have sandy hair.

Function words, sometimes called **grammatical words,** are words such as *the, and, but, in, to, because, while, ought,* and *must.* The main use of function words is to express relationships among other words. Compare the following:

I am lonely *at* dark.   The cook prepared *a* rich feast.
I am lonely *in the* dark.   The cook prepared *the* rich *a* feast.

Inflections, less important in Modern English than they were in earlier stages of the language, are changes in the form of words that indicate differences in grammatical relationship. Inflections account for the differences in the following:

The boy*s* walk slowly.   Stop bother*ing* me.
The boy walk*s* slowly.   Stop*s* bother me.

Being able to control these grammatical devices—word order, function words, and inflections—is essential to writing clearly.

A distinction is sometimes made between grammar and *usage.* Grammar is concerned with generally applicable principles about a language. **Usage,** in contrast, is concerned with choices, particularly with differences between standard and nonstandard English and between formal and informal English. The differences between *tile floor* and *floor tile, he walks* and *he walked, he was biting the dog* and *the dog was biting him* are grammatical differences. The differences between *I saw* and *I seen, he doesn't* and *he don't,* and *let me do it* and *leave me do it* are differences in usage. They may identify the persons who use them, as speakers of standard or nonstandard dialects, but they do not mean different things. Since this book is concerned with providing guidelines for writing standard English, it is concerned with both grammar and usage. And since many questions of grammar and usage overlap, the two are not set apart sharply.

1   SENTENCE SENSE **SS**

Grammar describes the kinds of words in a language and the ways these words are fitted together into meaningful groups. Grammarians describe the words in a language by assigning them to different classes or groups according to their functions. The major kinds of words in English and the functions they usually perform are as follows:

Function	Kinds of Words
Naming	Nouns and pronouns
Predicating (stating or asserting)	Verbs
Modifying	Adjectives and adverbs
Connecting	Prepositions and conjunctions

Of these, nouns and verbs, the naming and stating words, are the basic elements. They are the bones of the sentence, the most important unit of writing. They work together to make our simplest sentences; other kinds of words and word groups expand and refine those simple sentences.

1a Recognizing sentences and their basic words

A **sentence** is a group of words that contains a subject and a predicate and that is not introduced by a connecting word such as *although, because, when,* or *where* that makes it dependent upon another group of words to complete its meaning. *She is studying* and *What is she studying* are sentences. But *although she is studying* is not a sentence because the word *although* makes the whole word group depend upon something else for completion, as in the statement *Although she is studying, she will be finished soon.*

Subjects and predicates. All complete sentences have two main parts, a subject and a predicate. The **subject** names the person, thing, or concept that the sentence is about. The **predicate** makes a statement or asks a question about the subject.

Verbs. The predicate of a sentence *always* contains a **verb**, a word that makes some sort of assertion about the subject. A sentence cannot exist without a verb. Verbs indicate some kind of action, the occurrence of something, or the presence of some condition. Examples of verbs are *ask, eat, give, describe, criticize, seem, appear, become.*

In the simplest English sentences, a verb may stand alone as the predicate: *Lions hunt.* Or it may be followed by a word called its **object,** which indicates who or what receives the action of the verb: *Lions hunt prey.*

Verbs have the following characteristics of form:

1 When verbs indicate present time, they always add *-s* or *-es* to the form listed in the dictionary when their subjects are *he, she,* or *it* or a word for which *he, she,* or *it* can be substituted: *the boys run,* but *the boy* [he] *runs; the logs burn,* but *the log* [it] *burns.*

2 Almost all verbs have a separate form to indicate past tense. Most add *-d* or *-ed* to the form listed in the dictionary: *save, saved;*

walk, walked; repeat, repeated. A few indicate past time in irregular ways: *eat, ate; go, went; run, ran; sleep, slept.* A few verbs do not have a separate form: *cut, put, hit, hurt.*

3   The dictionary form of verbs can always be preceded by any one of the following words: *can, could; may, might; will, would; shall, should;* and *must,* as in *can talk, may go, would leave, should pay,* or *will read.* These words are called **auxiliaries** or **helping verbs** and are used with verbs to convey special shades of meaning. Other forms of the verb can combine with other auxiliaries to form verb phrases, such as *have been eating, will be finished, could have been working,* that express various time relationships as well as other shades of meaning. (For a full discussion of auxiliaries, see Section **4**.)

4   Many verbs have typical endings, called **suffixes,** such as *-ate, -en, -fy,* and *-ize,* as in *implicate, operate, widen, hasten, liquefy, simplify, recognize, modernize.*

Nouns. The subject of a sentence is usually a noun or a pronoun. **Nouns** name or classify things, places, activities, and concepts: *studio, committee, Carl, Detroit, athletics, courage, wealth.* Nouns have the following characteristics:

1   Nouns naming things that can be counted add *-s* or *-es* to make the plural form which indicates more than one: *chair, chairs; car, cars; church, churches; bush, bushes.* A few nouns have irregular plurals: *woman, women; foot, feet; sheep, sheep.* Nouns that name particular people or places *(Dorothy, Omaha)* and nouns that name things not usually counted *(gravel, milk, sugar, courage, honesty)* do not ordinarily have plural forms.

2   Nouns typically serve as the subjects *(The wind blew; Sally arrived; Honesty pays)* and the objects of verbs and prepositions *(Send John to the store).*

3   Many nouns have characteristic endings such as *-ance, -ence, -ism, -ity, -ment, -ness, -tion,* and *-ship: relevance, excellence, realism, activity, argument, darkness, adoption, seamanship.*

Pronouns. Pronouns are words that can substitute for nouns. Thus, pronouns can be subjects or objects of verbs or prepositions. The noun for which a pronoun substitutes is called its **antecedent.** In the sentence *Clara Barton is the woman who founded the American Red Cross,* the pronoun *who* refers to its antecedent, *woman.* In the sentence *Whichever he chooses will be acceptable,* it is impossible to know what *whichever* means. (Only if you saw this sentence in a larger context could you tell what *whichever* refers to.) In such sentences as *He who hesitates is lost,* the meaning of *he* is implied by the context itself; that is, *he* refers to any person who hesitates to take action. **Indefinite**

pronouns, words like *anybody, everybody,* and *somebody,* act as nouns and require no antecedent.

The **personal pronouns** *I, we, he, she,* and *they,* and the pronoun *who,* which is used either to relate one group of words to another or to ask a question, change form in the subjective, possessive, and objective cases; *you* and *it* change form as possessives only. (See Section **2.**)

Basic sentence patterns. All English sentences are built on a limited number of patterns, to which all sentences, no matter how long or complex, can be reduced. The five most basic patterns are described below. In all the patterns the subject remains a simple noun or pronoun. Differences among the patterns lie in the predicate part of the sentence—the verb and what follows it.

The simplest of all English sentence patterns consists of a subject and its verb. Sentences as simple as these are relatively rare in mature writing, yet simple sentences (subject-verb) are the core of all sentences.

PATTERN 1

Subject	*Verb*
Red	fades.
The woman	arrived.
The snow	fell.

The verbs in the second pattern are always action words that can pass their action on to another word called an object, or more exactly, a **direct object.** The direct object is always a noun, a pronoun, or a group of words serving as a noun that answers the question "what" or "whom" after the verb. Verbs that can take objects are called **transitive** verbs.

PATTERN 2

Subject	*Verb*	*Direct Object*
Dogs	eat	bones.
The carpenter	repaired	the roof.
John	prefers	the movies.
Someone	insulted	her.

With a few verbs, such as *appoint, believe, consider, judge, made,* and *name,* the direct object may be followed by another noun or a modifying word that renames or describes the direct object. These are called **object complements,** and they distinguish the third sentence pattern.

PATTERN 3

Subject	Verb	Direct Object	Object Complement
Henry	called	him	a traitor.
They	appointed	Shirley	chairperson.
We	made	the clerk	angry.
People	judged	her	innocent.

The fourth pattern introduces the **indirect object.** After such action verbs as *ask, give, send, tell,* and *teach,* the direct object is often preceded by an **indirect object** that names the receiver of the message, gift, or whatever, and always comes before the direct object.

PATTERN 4

Subject	Verb	Indirect Object	Direct Object
His father	gave	Sam	a car.
The college	found	me	work.
Wellington	brought	England	victory.
John	sold	her	a book.

The same meaning can usually be expressed by a phrase that begins with *to* or *for* and is positioned after the direct object: *Wellington brought victory to England; The college found work for me.*

The fifth pattern occurs only with a special kind of verb, called a **linking verb.** The most common linking verb is *be* in its various forms: *is, are, was, were, has been, might be,* etc. Other common linking verbs include *appear, become, seem* and in some contexts such verbs as *feel, grow, act, look, taste, smell,* and *sound.* Linking verbs are followed by a **complement,** which may be either a **predicate noun** or a **predicate adjective.** A complement following a linking verb, in contrast to an object after a transitive verb, is related to the subject of the sentence. Predicate nouns rename the subject; predicate adjectives modify the subject.

PATTERN 5

Subject	Linking Verb	Complement Predicate Noun	Predicate Adjective
Napoleon	was	a Frenchman.	
My brother	remains	an artist.	
Natalie	may become	president.	
The book	seemed		obscene.
Work	was		scarce.
The fruit	tasted		bitter.

Other sentence patterns. The preceding five sentence patterns are the basis of all English sentence structure. Other kinds of sentences may be thought of either as additional patterns or as changes, called *transformation* by some grammarians, in these basic patterns. Thus, we create questions by inverting the subject and verb, as in *Will he run,* or by using a function word before the basic pattern, as in *Does he run.* We create commands by omitting the subject, as in *Open the can, Know thyself, Keep calm.*

Two kinds of patterns are especially important because they involve changes either in the usual actor-action relation of subject and verb or in the usual order of subject and verb.

The first of these is the **passive sentence.** The passive sentence is made from one of the basic patterns that have a direct object. In its most common form, the original object of the verb becomes the subject, and the original subject may be either omitted or expressed in a phrase beginning with *by.* In the passive sentence the subject no longer names the performer of the action described by the verb, as it does in active patterns. Rather, it names the receiver of the action. This characteristic makes the passive sentence especially useful when we do not know who performs an action. Thus we normally say *He was killed in action* rather than *Someone killed him in action.* (See "Voice," in Section **5.**)

The verb in passive sentences consists of some form of the auxiliary, or helping, verb *be* and the past participle.

ACTIVE

The carpenter *repaired* the roof.
Someone *insulted* her.
Henry *called* him a traitor.
Wellington *brought* England victory.

PASSIVE

Subject	*Passive Verb*	*(Original Subject)*
The roof	was repaired	(by the carpenter).
She	was insulted	(by someone).
He	was called a traitor	(by Henry).
Victory	was brought to England	(by Wellington).

Notice that in all passive sentences the original subject can be expressed by a prepositional phrase, but the sentence is complete without that prepositional phrase.

The second important kind of sentence that involves change in the word order allows us to postpone the subject of the sentence until after the verb by beginning with the **expletive** *there* or *it.*

Expletive	Verb	Complement	Subject
It	is	doubtful	that they will arrive.
There	is		no reply.
There	are		seven students.
There	will be		an opportunity.

EXERCISE 1a Identify the subjects, verbs, direct objects, indirect objects, and complements in the following sentences.

1 Poverty often deprives children of opportunity.
2 Alcoholism is a disease.
3 Television brings us many good movies.
4 The quarterback threw a long pass for a touchdown.
5 Sally bought her brother a new radio.
6 Some foods may cause cancer.
7 Local citizens sent the police many complaints about burglaries in the neighborhood.
8 Our football team was beaten only twice last year.
9 Dictionaries are useful for many kinds of information.
10 There were only seven people at the meeting.

1b Recognizing modifiers, connecting words, and verbals

If all sentences in English were limited to the basic patterns, our writing would be bare and monotonous indeed. Clearly, the variety and complexity of our sentences are not created by variety and complexity in these basic patterns. Rather, they are created by the addition of modifying words and by the use of several different kinds of word groups that can themselves serve as nouns and modifiers.

1 Modifying words: adjectives and adverbs. Modifiers are words or word groups that limit, qualify, make more exact the other words or word groups to which they are attached. Adjectives and adverbs are the principal single-word modifiers in English.

Adjectives modify nouns or pronouns. Typical adjectives are the underlined words in the following: *brown dog, Victorian dignity, yellow hair, one football, reasonable price, sleek boat.* Adjectives have distinctive forms in the **comparative** and **superlative:** *happy, happier, happiest; beautiful, more beautiful, most beautiful; good, better, best.*

Adverbs modify verbs, adjectives, or other adverbs, although they may modify whole sentences. Typical adverbs are the underlined words in the following: *stayed outside, walked slowly, horribly angry, fortunately the accident was not fatal.*

For a discussion of the special forms by which adjectives and adverbs show comparison, and of certain distinctions between the two, see Section **3.**

2 Connecting words: prepositions and conjunctions. Connecting words enable us to link one word or word group with another and to combine them in ways that allow us not only to express our ideas more concisely, but also to express the relationships between those ideas more clearly. We don't need to say *We had coffee. We had toast.* Rather, we can say *We had coffee and toast* or *We had coffee with toast.* We don't need to say *We talked. We played cards. We went home.* Rather, we can say *After we talked and played cards, we went home* or *After talking and playing cards, we went home.* The kinds of words that enable us to make these connections and combinations are prepositions and conjunctions.

A **preposition** links a noun or pronoun (called its **object**) with some other word in the sentence and shows the relationship between the object and the other word. The preposition, together with its object, almost always modifies the other word to which it is linked.

> The dog walks *on* water. [*On* links *water* to the verb *walks; on water* modifies *walks.*]
> The distance *between* us is short. [*Between* links *us* to the noun *distance; between us* modifies *distance.*]

Although a preposition usually comes before its object, in a few constructions it can follow its object.

> *In what town* do you live?
> *What town* do you live *in?*

The most common prepositions are listed below:

about	below	into	through
above	beside	near	to
across	by	next	toward
after	down	of	under
among	during	off	until
around	except	on	up
as	for	out	upon
at	from	over	with
before	in	past	within
behind	inside	since	without

Many simple prepositions combine with other words to form phrasal prepositions, such as *at the point of, by means of, down from, from above, in addition to, without regard to.*

Note that some words, such as *below, down, in, out,* and *up,* occur both as prepositions and as adverbs. Used as adverbs, they never have objects. Compare *He went below* with *He went below the deck.*

Note too that *after, as, before, since,* and *until* also function as subordinating conjunctions. (See below.)

A **conjunction** joins words, phrases, or clauses. Conjunctions show the relationship between the sentence elements that they connect.

Coordinating conjunctions *(and, but, or, nor, for, so, yet)* join words, phrases, or clauses of equal grammatical rank. (See **1d,** "Recognizing Clauses.")

WORDS JOINED	We ate ham *and* eggs.
PHRASES JOINED	Look in the closet *or* under the bed.
CLAUSES JOINED	We wanted to go, *but* we were too busy.

Correlative conjunctions are coordinating words that work in pairs to join words, phrases, clauses, or whole sentences. The most common correlative pairs are *both . . . and, either . . . or, neither . . . nor, not . . . but,* and *not only . . . but also.*

both courageous *and* loyal
either before you go *or* after you get back
neither circuses *nor* sideshows
not only as a child *but also* as an adult

Subordinating conjunctions join clauses that are not equal in rank. A clause introduced by a subordinating conjunction is called a *dependent* or *subordinate* clause (see **1d**) and cannot stand by itself as a sentence; it must be joined to a main, or independent, clause.

We left the party early *because we were tired.*
If the roads are icy, we will have to drive carefully.
Whether we like it or not, oil grows more expensive.

The following are the most common subordinating conjunctions:

after	even if	than	where
although	even though	that	wherever
as	if	though	whether
as if	in order that	unless	while
as though	rather than	until	
because	since	when	
before	so that	whenever	

3 Verbals. Verbals are special verb forms that have some of the characteristics and abilities of verbs but cannot function as predicates by themselves. Verbs make an assertion. Verbals do not; they function as nouns and modifiers. There are three kinds of verbals: infinitives, participles, and gerunds.

Infinitives are usually marked by a *to* before the actual verb *(to eat, to describe)*. They are used as nouns, adjectives, or adverbs.

> *To see* is *to believe*. [Both used as nouns]
> It was time *to leave*. [Used as adjective]
> I was ready *to go*. [Used as adverb]

Participles may be either present or past. The present form ends in *-ing (eating, running, describing)*. The past form usually ends in *-ed (described)*. But note that some end in *-en (eaten)*, and a few make an internal change *(begun, flown)*. Participles are always used as adjectives.

> *Screaming*, I jumped out of bed. [Present participle]
> *Delighted*, we accepted his invitation. [Past participle]

Gerunds have the same *-ing* form as the present participle. The distinctive name *gerund* is given to *-ing* forms only when they function as nouns.

> *Writing* requires effort. [Subject of *requires*]
> You should try *swimming*. [Object of *try*]

Although verbals can never function by themselves as predicates, they can, like verbs, take objects and complements, and like verbs, they are characteristically modified by adverbs. Note the following:

> I prefer *to believe him*. [*Him* is the object of *to believe*.]
> It was time *to leave the house*. [*House* is the object of *to leave*.]
> *Screaming loudly*, I jumped out of bed. [The adverb *loudly* modifies the participle *screaming*.]
> Swimming *in the Atlantic* is refreshing. [The adverb phrase *in the Atlantic* modifies the gerund *swimming*.]

EXERCISE 1b In the following sentences, identify the adjectives, adverbs, prepositions, coordinating conjunctions, subordinating conjunctions, and verbals.

1 Books are powerful weapons against ignorance.
2 Sally soon recovered from her severe injuries.
3 Misreading directions is a common mistake in taking examinations.
4 With the wind blowing furiously from the northeast, the storm raged for two days.
5 A man should never wear his best suit when he goes out to fight for freedom and truth.
6 Because scientists have warned about its dangers, great efforts have been made to control pollution.

7 Some resorts are strangely desolate in winter.
8 Marie would like to go to medical school, but she is concerned about the cost.
9 Nothing disturbs Joe when he is sleeping.
10 Peering into the fog, she could barely see the car in front of her.

1c Recognizing phrases

A **phrase** is a group of related words that has no subject or predicate and is used as a single part of speech. Typical phrases are a preposition and its object *(I fell on the sidewalk),* or a verbal and its object *(I wanted to see the parade).*

Phrases are usually classified as prepositional, infinitive, participial, or gerund phrases.

Prepositional phrases. Prepositional phrases consist of a preposition, its object, and any modifiers of the object *(under the ground, without thinking, in the blue Ford).* Prepositional phrases function as adjectives or adverbs and occasionally as nouns.

He is a man *of action.* [Adjective modifying *man*]
The plane arrived *on time.* [Adverb modifying *arrived*]
We were ready *at the airport.* [Adverb modifying *ready*]
She came early *in the morning.* [Adverb modifying *early*]
Before breakfast is too early. [Noun, subject of *is*]

Infinitive phrases. Infinitive phrases consist of an infinitive, its modifiers, and/or its object *(to see the world, to answer briefly, to earn money quickly).* Infinitive phrases function as nouns, adjectives, or adverbs.

I wanted *to buy the house.* [Noun, object of verb]
It is time *to go to bed.* [Adjective modifying *time*]
We were impatient *to start the game.* [Adverb modifying *impatient*]

Participial phrases. Participial phrases consist of a present or past participle, its modifiers, and/or its object *(lying on the beach, found in the street, eating a large dinner).* Participial phrases always function as adjectives.

The dog *running in the yard* belongs to my mother.
The man *walking his dog* is my father.
Covered with ice, the road was dangerous.
Beaten twice by Susan, Jim fought to win the last game.

Gerund phrases. Gerund phrases consist of a gerund, its modifiers, and/or its object (*telling the truth, knowing the rules, acting bravely*). Gerund phrases always function as nouns.

Collecting stamps is my hobby. [Subject]
She earned more by *working overtime*. [Object of preposition]
He hated *living alone*. [Object of verb]
Making a profit is their only purpose. [Subject]

Note that since both the gerund and the present participle end in *-ing*, they can be distinguished only by their separate functions as nouns or adjectives.

Absolute phrases. Absolute phrases are made up of a noun or pronoun and a participle. Unlike participial phrases, absolute phrases do not modify particular words in the sentence to which they are attached. Rather, they modify the whole sentence.

The whole family sat silent, *their eyes glued to the TV screen.*
Mortgage rates having risen drastically, Isabel gave up searching for a new house.
The old man lay sprawled on the sofa, *eyes closed, arms folded across his chest, his loud snores almost rousing the dog sleeping near him.*

In absolute phrases with the participle *being* followed by an adjective, *being* is often omitted so that the phrase itself consists simply of a noun followed by an adjective and any other modifiers.

Final examinations over, Linda returned to work.
The den was thoroughly inviting, *the lights low, the long sofa and overstuffed chairs luxuriously comfortable, the logs burning brightly in the fireplace,* and *our host open and friendly.*

EXERCISE 1c In the following sentences, identify the verbal phrases by underlining them once and the prepositional phrases by underlining them twice. Note that a prepositional phrase may sometimes be part of a verbal phrase, as in the verbal phrase *lying on the beach,* in which the verbal *lying* is modified by the prepositional phrase *on the beach.*

1 Pears are the most succulent fruit of winter.
2 Having worked late into the night, Mary went to bed.
3 To become independent is the desire of most young men and women.
4 Watching football on TV is the favorite sport of millions.
5 Rising in a graceful arc, the spaceship swung into orbit.
6 Smith wanted to hold the foreman to his promise.
7 Reports of flying saucers grew frequent in the summer.

8 Being loyal to her principles was more important to Jane than gaining approval from her friends.

9 For many years the gap between the rich and poor in South America has been widening.

10 The tornado struck the town, ripping roofs from houses and wrenching trees from the ground.

1d Recognizing clauses

A **clause** is a group of words containing a subject and a predicate. The relation of a clause to the rest of the sentence is shown by the position of the clause or by a conjunction. There are two kinds of clauses: (1) main, or independent, clauses and (2) subordinate, or dependent, clauses.

1   Main clauses. A main clause has both subject and verb, but it is not introduced by a subordinating word. A main clause makes an independent statement. It is not used as a noun or as a modifier.

2   Subordinate clauses. Subordinate clauses are usually introduced by a subordinating conjunction (*as, since, because,* etc.) or by a relative pronoun *(who, which, that)*. Subordinate clauses function as adjectives, adverbs, or nouns. They express ideas that are less important than the idea expressed in the main clause. The exact relationship between the two ideas is indicated by the subordinating conjunction or relative pronoun that joins the subordinate and the main clause.

A   An ADJECTIVE CLAUSE modifies a noun or pronoun.

This is the jet *that broke the speed record.* [The subordinate clause modifies the noun *jet.*]

Anybody *who is tired* may leave. [The subordinate clause modifies the pronoun *anybody.*]

Canada is the nation *we made the treaty with.* [The subordinate clause modifies the noun *nation,* with the relative pronoun *that* understood.]

B   An ADVERB CLAUSE modifies a verb, adjective, or adverb.

The child cried *when the dentist appeared.* [The subordinate clause modifies the verb *cried.*]

I am sorry *he is sick.* [The subordinate clause modifies the adjective *sorry,* with the subordinating conjunction *that* understood.]

He thinks more quickly *than you do.* [The subordinate clause modifies the adverb *quickly.*]

C A NOUN CLAUSE **functions as a noun. It may serve as subject, predicate noun, object of a verb, or object of a preposition.**

What John wants is a better job. [The subordinate clause is the subject of the verb *is.*]

This is *where we came in.* [The subordinate clause is a predicate noun.]

Please tell them *I will be late.* [The subordinate clause is the object of the verb *tell.*]

He has no interest in *what he is reading.* [The subordinate clause is the object of the preposition *in.*]

EXERCISE 1d(1)   Underline the subordinate clauses in the following sentences and identify each as an adjective, adverb, or noun clause.

1 What one thinks at twenty often seems silly at thirty.
2 If success depended only on work, many would be rich.
3 Linda and her friends left before the party was over.
4 The apples that make the best pies are the sour ones.
5 When the lake was calm, we tried the outboard we had just bought.
6 Julie had the quality of intelligence that the director needed.
7 What a man promises is less important than what he does.
8 The clerks who annoyed him the most were those who seemed indifferent.
9 While he was telephoning, the repairman whom he had called knocked on the door.
10 Many people think that education is to be gotten only in school.

EXERCISE 1d(2)   In the following sentences, identify the main and subordinate clauses. Indicate the function of each subordinate clause as adjective, adverb, or noun.

1 Platinum, which was discovered in 1750, is a very valuable metal.
2 The price that John paid for his car was too high.
3 Many unemployed men and women lack the skills that they need for jobs.
4 As the class ended, the teacher sighed with relief.
5 Many people who oppose capital punishment argue that it doesn't reduce crime.
6 Some parents let their children do whatever they please.
7 An educated person is one who knows the limits of his knowledge.
8 When a woman works, she should be paid whatever a man would be paid for the same work.
9 What we would like to do and what we can do are seldom the same thing.
10 One of the most valuable talents a writer can have is that of never using two words when one will do.

Clausal sentence classification. The number of main or subordinate clauses in a sentence determines its classification: simple, compound, complex, or compound-complex.

A **simple sentence** has a single main clause.

The wind blew.

Note that a sentence remains a simple sentence even though the subject, the verb, or both are compounded.

The cat and the dog fought.
The dog barked and growled.
The cat and the dog snarled and fought.

A **compound sentence** has two or more main clauses.

The wind blew and the leaves fell.

A **complex sentence** has one main clause and one or more subordinate clauses.

When the wind blew, the leaves fell.

A **compound-complex sentence** contains two or more main clauses and one or more subordinate clauses.

When the sky darkened, the wind blew and the leaves fell.

EXERCISE 1d(3)   In the following sentences, underline each main clause once, each subordinate clause twice, and indicate whether the sentence is simple, compound, complex, or compound-complex.

1 When the professor told his class he was retiring, they applauded.
2 Teachers advise against cramming for an exam, but it's better than flunking.
3 Though I enjoy the country, bugs scare me and flowers make me sneeze.
4 Before they are elected, politicians always promise to cut taxes, yet after they are elected, they seldom do.
5 The judge wondered why the jury had deliberated so long.
6 An addict needs more and more heroin, and needs it all the time.
7 John and Judy, who enjoy skiing, are disappointed when the snowfall is light.
8 The judge wondered why the members of the jury were deliberating so long and when they would return their verdict.
9 Whenever you leave, please let me know where you are going.
10 Barking and wagging his tail violently, the dog exploded into the room and knocked everything off the table.

2

2 CASE **CA**

Case shows the function of nouns and pronouns in a sentence. In the sentence *He gave me a week's vacation,* the **subjective case** form *he* indicates that the pronoun is being used as the subject; the **objective case** form *me* shows that the pronoun is an object; the **possessive case** form *week's* indicates that the noun is a possessive.

Case endings were important in early English, but Modern English retains only a few remnants of this complicated system. Nouns have only two case forms, the possessive *(student's)* and a common form *(student)* that serves all other functions. The personal pronouns *I, we, he, she,* and *they* and the relative or interrogative pronoun *who* have three forms: subjective, possessive, and objective. The personal pronouns *you* and *it* have distinctive forms in the possessive.

PERSONAL PRONOUNS

	SUBJECTIVE	POSSESSIVE	OBJECTIVE
Singular			
FIRST PERSON	I	my, mine	me
SECOND PERSON	you	your, yours	you
THIRD PERSON	he, she, it	his, her, hers, its	him, her, it
Plural			
FIRST PERSON	we	our, ours	us
SECOND PERSON	you	your, yours	you
THIRD PERSON	they	their, theirs	them

RELATIVE OR INTERROGATIVE PRONOUN

Singular	who	whose	whom
Plural	who	whose	whom

2a

2a Subjective case

We use the subjective pronoun for the subjects of all verbs and for all pronouns after all forms of the verb *be* such as *is, are, were,* or *have been.* Speakers of English are unlikely to say or write "Us are happy" or "Him is going away." But compound subjects and some constructions in which the subject is not easily recognized sometimes cause problems.

1 Use the subjective pronoun form in all parts of a compound subject.

He and *she* wanted to go to the circus.
Jack and *she* went to the circus, but Bill and *I* worked.

2 After the conjunctions *than* and *as*, use the subjective form of the pronoun if it is the subject of an understood verb.

She gets her work done faster than *I*. [*I* is the subject of *get mine done*, which is understood by the reader.]
We are as rich as *they* [are].

3 Use the subjective form of a pronoun in an appositive describing a subject or a subject complement. An appositive is a word or phrase set beside a noun or pronoun that identifies or explains it by renaming it.

We three, *Joe, Mary, and I,* graduated together. [*Joe, Mary, and I* is an appositive describing the subject *We three*.]
We students had worked together for two years. [Not *Us students. Students* is an appositive defining the pronoun *we*.]

4 Use the subjective forms of the relative pronoun *who* and *whoever* when they serve as subjects of a clause.

The man *who* came to dinner stayed a month. [*Who* is the subject of *came* in the clause *who came to dinner*.]
Whoever sees the movie will enjoy it. [*Whoever* is the subject of the verb *sees* in the clause *whoever sees the movie*.]

The form of the pronoun is always determined by its function in its own clause. If it serves as subject of its clause, be sure to use the subjective form even though the whole clause may be the object of a verb or preposition.

No one can predict *who* will be appointed. [*Who* is the subject of *will be appointed*. The clause *who will be appointed* is the object of the verb *predict*.]
The owner offered a reward to *whoever* caught the escaped lion. [The entire clause is the object of the preposition *to*. *Whoever* is the subject of the clause.]

Note that the form of the pronoun used as subject will not be changed when such expressions as *I think* and *he says* come between the subject and its verb.

We invited only the people *who* he said were his friends. [*Who* is the subject of *were*.]

Barbara is a woman *who* I think deserves praise. [*Who* is the subject of *deserves*.]

Who do you think will buy Joe's car? [*Who* is the subject of *will buy*.]

If you are not sure which form to use in sentences such as these, try testing by temporarily omitting the interrupting words.

Barbara is a woman (who, whom) deserves praise.

(Who, whom) will buy Joe's car?

The test will help you determine in each case whether the pronoun *who* is the subject of the verb in the subordinate clause.

5 In writing, use the subjective case of the personal pronoun after forms of the verb *be*, except in dialogue.

It's me, using the objective form of the pronoun, is generally used by speakers in all but the most formal situations, and *it's him, her, us, them* are increasingly common. In writing, these simple conversational constructions seldom occur except in dialogue. When they do, choose between the formal *It's I* and the conversational *It's me* depending upon the character whose speech you are quoting.

Except in dialogue, standard written English requires the subjective case of pronouns after the forms of *be*.

It was *she* who determined the agenda of the committee, not *they,* the other committee members.

It was *they,* however, who determined the final committee recommendations.

6 In writing, use the subjective case for a pronoun following the infinitive *to be* when the infinitive has no expressed subject.

Spoken English commonly uses the objective case of the pronoun in this construction. (See **2c5** for the case of the pronoun after the infinitive when the subject is expressed.)

WRITTEN   I would not want to be *he*. [The infinitive *to be* has no expressed subject.]

SPOKEN   I would not want to be *him*.

EXERCISE 2a   In the following sentences, correct the errors of case in accordance with formal usage. Be ready to give reasons.

1 She and him were both born under the sign of Libra.
2 The senior cheerleaders, Jan, Eli, and me, attended the banquet.

3 After the flood, the Red Cross gave food to whomever needed it.
4 I would like to be them and camp in the mountains.
5 She may be stronger than me, but I'm smarter than her.
6 Aurelio is the kind of student whom is admired by everybody.
7 It was them who found the abandoned copper mine.
8 At the picnic Gary and me shared some ice cream with a stray bulldog.
9 There will be a place in the orchestra for whomever can play the violin as well as her.
10 The man in the blue sweater is him.

2b Possessive case

1 Generally, use the *s*-possessive *(boy's, Jane's)* with nouns naming living things. With nouns naming inanimate things, the *of*-phrase is sometimes preferred, but the *s*-form occurs very often.

ANIMATE	Jane's hair; an outsider's view; inspector's approval
INANIMATE	the point of the joke; the wheel of the aircraft; the name of the paper; the city's newsstands; the magazine's tone

The *s*-possessive is commonly used in expressions that indicate time *(moment's notice, year's labor)* and in many familiar phrases *(life's blood, heart's content)*. Which possessive form to use may also depend on sound or rhythm: The *s*-possessive is more terse than the longer, more sonorous *of*-phrase (the President's signature, the signature of the President).

2 In formal English use the possessive case for a noun or pronoun preceding a gerund. In informal English, however, the objective case rather than the possessive case is often found before a gerund.

FORMAL	What was the excuse for *his* being late?
INFORMAL	What was the excuse for *him* being late?
FORMAL	He complained of *Roy's* keeping the money.
INFORMAL	He complained of *Roy* keeping the money.

Even in formal English the objective case is frequently used with plural nouns.

The police prohibited *children* playing in the street.

The choice of case sometimes depends on the meaning the writer intends to convey.

Imagine *his* playing the violin. [The act of playing the violin is emphasized.]

Imagine *him* playing the violin. [The emphasis is on *him*. *Playing* is here used as a participle modifying *him*.]

And note the difference in the meaning of the following sentences:

I hate that *woman* riding a bicycle.
I hate that *woman's* riding a bicycle.

Revise such sentences to ensure clarity.

I hate that woman who is riding a bicycle.
I hate the way that woman rides a bicycle.

3 Use *which* to refer to impersonal antecedents. However, substitute *whose* where the phrase *of which* would be awkward.

We saw a house *whose* roof was falling in. [Compare: *We saw a house the roof of which was falling in.*]

This is the car *whose* steering wheel broke off when the driver was going seventy miles an hour. [Compare: *This is the car the steering wheel of which broke off when the driver was going seventy miles an hour.*]

2c Objective case

Objective pronoun forms are used for the objects of all verbs, verbals, and prepositions.

OBJECT OF VERB	The doctor sent *her* home.
	Our friends visited *us*.
OBJECT OF VERBAL	Visiting *them* was pleasant. [Object of gerund *visiting*]
	I wanted to send *him* away. [Object of infinitive *to send*]
OBJECT OF PREPOSITION	Forward the mail to *me*.
	She must choose between *us*.

Problems in the use of the objective pronoun forms are likely to occur only with the same kinds of constructions that cause problems in the use of the subjective pronouns. (See **2a**.)

1 Use the objective pronoun forms in all parts of a compound object.

He found Tom and *me* at home. [Not *Tom and I*. *Me* is a part of a compound object of the verb *found*.]

They must choose between you and *me*. [Not *between you and I*. *Me* is a part of a compound object of the preposition *between*.]

2   After the conjunctions *than* and *as,* use the objective pronoun if it is the object of an understood verb.

She needs him more than [she needs] *me*.
I notified him as well as [I notified] *her*.

3   Use the objective form of a pronoun in an appositive describing an object.

Their friends invited them—Jerry and *her*. [*Jerry and her* is an appositive describing *them*.]

4   Standard written English requires *whom* for all objects.

Whom are you discussing? [*Whom* is the object of the verb *are discussing*.]
Whom are you looking for? [*Whom* is the object of the preposition *for*.]

Speakers at all levels of usage commonly use *who* in such constructions unless it immediately follows a preposition.

SPOKEN   Who are you discussing?
SPOKEN   Who are you looking for?
SPOKEN   For whom are you looking?

In subordinate clauses, use *whom* and *whomever* for all objects. Remember that the case of the relative pronoun in a subordinate clause depends upon its function in the clause and not upon the function of the whole clause.

The visitors *whom* we had expected did not come. [*Whom* is the object of the verb *had expected*. The clause *whom we had expected* modifies visitors.]
Whomever we asked wanted more money than we could afford. [*Whomever* is the object of the verb *asked* in the clause *whomever we asked*. The entire clause is the subject of the sentence.]

5   When the infinitive *to be* has an expressed subject, both the subject and the object of the infinitive are in the objective case.

He took *him* to be *me*. [*Him* is the subject of the infinitive; *me* is the object.]

EXERCISE 2b–c   In the following sentences, correct the errors of case in accordance with formal usage. Be ready to give reasons.

1 We appreciated him showing Jill and I the shortest route to Dallas.
2 The shortstop's error allowed Steve and I to score.
3 Just between you and I and the gatepost, her new dog has fleas.
4 The yoga teacher showed the three new students, Ian, Mary, and I, how to do a shoulder stand.
5 Who is Freda playing chess with?
6 Many of we birdwatchers were in the woods before daybreak.
7 I telephoned her as well as he.
8 We enjoyed seeing she and my cousin.
9 I thought them playing golf in a thunderstorm was foolish.
10 The rescue party found Rick and he in a hidden cave.

EXERCISE 2a–c   In the following paragraph, correct the errors in case forms in accordance with formal usage. Be prepared to give reasons for your revisions.

Last night three of we avid moviegoers, Ike, Len, and me, went to the Palace Theater to see Charlie Chaplin's last silent film, *City Lights*. Chaplin, whom Ike and me think is even funnier than Buster Keaton, makes friends with an eccentric millionaire, whom, it seems, is likable only when he is drunk. The other main character, who is more congenial than him, is a blind flower girl who wants a rich, respectable boyfriend and mistakenly takes Charlie, the poor tramp, to be he. There is a sentimental attachment between she and him, at least until she regains her eyesight and sees whom he really is. Ike disagreed with Len and I about which scene was the funniest. Ike liked the opening sequence in which several dignitaries, whom we think are city officials, unveil the Statue to Prosperity and find Charlie, the penniless tramp, asleep on the statue. They are humiliated by him spoiling the ceremony. Len and me liked the scene in which Charlie, whom is driving a Rolls-Royce belonging to the millionaire, stops the car and, not being as proud as him, picks up a discarded cigar butt.

3   ADJECTIVES AND ADVERBS **AD**

Adjectives and adverbs are modifying words; that is, they are words that limit or qualify the meaning of other words. Adjectives modify nouns, and they are usually placed either immediately before or immediately after the word they modify.

Adverbs normally modify verbs, adjectives, and other adverbs, although they may sometimes modify whole sentences. When they modify adjectives or other adverbs, they are adjacent to the words they modify. When they modify verbs, they are frequently, but not always, adjacent to the verbs.

Adverbs qualify the meaning of the words they modify by indicating such things as *when, where, how, why, in what order,* or *how often.*

The office closed *yesterday.* [*Yesterday* indicates when.]

Deliver all mail *here.* [*Here* indicates where.]

She replied *quickly* and *angrily.* [*Quickly* and *angrily* describe how she replied.]

Consequently, I left. [*Consequently* describes why.]

He *seldom* did any work. [*Seldom* indicates how often.]

Most adverbs are distinguished from their corresponding adjectives by the ending *-ly: strong-strongly, happy-happily, doubtful-doubtfully, hasty-hastily, mad-madly.* But the *-ly* ending is not a dependable indication of the adverb since some adverbs have two forms *(quick, quickly; slow, slowly);* others have the same form as adjectives *(fast, much, late, well);* and some adjectives also end in *-ly.* (See Section **39,** "Vocabulary," for a discussion of the ways adjectives are formed from nouns.)

Most uses of adjectives and adverbs are common to both standard and nonstandard English and to all levels. But formal English makes more frequent use of distinctive adverb forms than ordinary conversation does. Since certain distinctions in the use of adjectives and adverbs are especially clear markers of differences between standard and nonstandard, and between formal and informal English, they must be observed closely.

Where there is a choice between a form with *-ly* and a form without it, formal English prefers the *-ly* form—*runs quickly* rather than *runs quick, eats slowly* rather than *eats slow*—even though the shorter forms are widely used in informal English, particularly in such commands as *Drive slow.* Note particularly that *good* and *bad* as adverbs are nonstandard. The sentence *He talks <u>good</u> but writes <u>bad</u>* is nonstandard. Standard English requires *He talks well but writes badly.*

3a   Use an adverb, not an adjective, to modify a verb.

INCORRECT	He writes *careless.*
CORRECT	He writes *carelessly.* [The adverb *carelessly* is needed to modify the verb *writes.*]
INCORRECT	She talks *modest.*
CORRECT	She talks *modestly.* [The adverb is needed to modify the verb.]

3b

3b Use an adverb, not an adjective, to modify another adverb or an adjective.

INCORRECT	He was *terrible* wounded.
CORRECT	He was *terribly* wounded. [The adverb *terribly* is needed to modify the adjective *wounded*.]
INCORRECT	She works *considerable* harder than he does.
CORRECT	She works *considerably* harder than he does. [The adverb *considerably* is needed to modify the other adverb *harder*.]

The use of adjectives in place of adverbs is more common in conversation than in writing. The use of the adjective *real* as an emphatic *very* to modify adjectives and adverbs is heard at all levels of speech.

FORMAL	You will hear from me *very* soon.
COLLOQUIAL*	You will hear from me *real* soon.

3c

3c Use an adjective to modify the subject after a linking verb.

The common **linking verbs** are *be, become, appear, seem* and the verbs pertaining to the senses: *look, smell, taste, sound, feel*. Predicate adjectives after such verbs refer back to the subject and should be in adjective form. In each of the following sentences, for example, the predicate adjective modifies the subject. The verb simply links the two.

Jane looks *tired* tonight. [*Tired* modifies *Jane*.]
The butter smells *sour*. [*Sour* modifies *butter*.]

One of the most frequent errors in this construction is *I feel badly* in place of the correct subject/linking-verb/predicate-adjective form *I feel bad*. Though *badly* is common even in educated speech, *bad* is strongly preferred by many speakers.

FORMAL	He feels *bad* [ill].
COLLOQUIAL	He feels *badly*.
FORMAL	He felt *bad* about it.
COLLOQUIAL	He felt *badly* about it.

*We use the term *colloquial* to signify the qualities of familiar spoken English.

3d Use an adverb after the verb if the modifier describes the manner of the action of the verb.

He looked *suspiciously* at me. [The adverb *suspiciously* modifies the verb *looked*. Contrast *He looked suspicious to me*.]

The thief felt *carefully* under the pillow. [The adverb *carefully* modifies the verb *felt*.]

In these examples the verbs *look* and *feel* express action, and must be modified by adverbs. But in constructions like *She looks tired* or *He feels well*, the verbs serve, not as words of action, but as links between the subject and the predicate adjective. The choice of adjective or adverb thus depends on the function and meaning of the verb—in other words, on whether or not the verb is being used as a linking verb. Ask yourself whether you want a modifier for the subject or for the verb.

EXERCISE 3a–d In the following sentences, correct in accordance with formal usage any errors in the use of adjectives and adverbs.

1 Tom is working regular at the shoe factory.
2 Some medicines taste bitterly.
3 We were reasonable careful using the chain saw.
4 Marie danced very graceful in the ballet.
5 The old couple were utter surprised by the anniversary party.
6 The defendant replied negative to the lawyer's questions.
7 The traffic sounds loudly to the residents of Main Street.
8 A Pawnee scout watched intent the wagon train in the valley.
9 The children were sure happy riding the carousel.
10 A young frog looked curious at the dragonfly.

3e Distinguish between the comparative and superlative forms of adjectives and adverbs.

Adjectives and adverbs show degrees of quality or quantity by means of their positive, comparative, and superlative forms. The **positive** form *(slow, quickly)* expresses no comparison at all. The **comparative,** formed by adding *-er* or by prefixing *more* to the positive form *(slower, more quickly)*, expresses a greater degree or makes a comparison. The **superlative,** formed by adding *-est* or by putting *most* before the positive form *(slowest, most quickly)*, indicates the greatest degree of a quality or quantity among three or more persons or things. Some common adjectives and adverbs retain old irregular forms *(good, better, best; badly, worse, worst)*.

Whether to use *more* or *most* before the adjective or adverb or to add the *-er, -est* endings depends on the number of syllables in the word. Most adjectives and a few adverbs of one syllable form the comparative and superlative with *-er* and *-est*. Adjectives of two syllables often have variant forms *(fancier, more fancy; laziest, most lazy)*. Adjectives and adverbs of three or more syllables always take *more* and *most* *(more beautiful, most regretfully)*. Where there is a choice, select the form that sounds better or that is better suited to the rhythm of the sentence.

Some adjectives and adverbs, such as *unique, empty, dead, perfect, round,* are sometimes thought of as absolute in their meaning and thus not able to be logically compared. Logically, a room is either *empty* or *not empty,* a person is either *dead* or *alive.* Nevertheless, phrases such as "emptier than," "more perfect than," and "more dead than alive" are common in speech and very informal writing.

FORMAL	His diving form is *more nearly perfect* than mine.
INFORMAL	His diving form is *more perfect* than mine.
FORMAL	The new stadium is *more clearly circular* than the old one.
INFORMAL	The new stadium is *more circular* than the old one.

3f In formal usage, use the comparative to refer only to one of two objects; use the superlative to refer only to one of three or more objects.

COMPARATIVE	His horse is the *faster* of the two.
SUPERLATIVE	His horse is the *fastest* in the country.
COMPARATIVE	Ruth is the *more* attractive but the *less* good-natured of the twins.
SUPERLATIVE	Ruth is the *most* attractive but the *least* good-natured of his three daughters.

EXERCISE 3e–f   In the following sentences, correct in accordance with formal usage any errors in the use of the comparative and superlative forms of adjectives and adverbs.

1 The *Sea Sprite* was the faster of the nine sailboats in the regatta.
2 The Green Phantom's crime was more perfect than the police realized.
3 Sarah is reliabler than the other employees.
4 Your excuse for missing this meeting is the most impossible story I have ever heard.
5 Sanibel is the largest of the two offshore islands.

6 Old Granny Hawks says the more dignity people have, the deader they are.
7 The cars with front-wheel drive are successfuler than many earlier models.
8 Professor Blosser directs the world's most unique cyclotron laboratory.
9 Ruth is the best qualified of the two applicants for the job.
10 The reservoir is more empty than it was a year ago.

3g Avoid the excessive use of nouns to modify other nouns.

The use of nouns to modify other nouns in expressions such as *rock garden, steel mill, silver mine,* and *telephone booth* is very common in English. (See **40c.**) When there is no appropriate adjective form and when the nouns used to modify are short, such constructions are usually clear and concise. But when nouns are used to replace appropriate adjectives or when the series of nouns modifying other nouns is long, such expressions are awkward at best, confusing at worst.

1 Prefer an adjective if there is an appropriate one.

AWKWARD *Siberia* railroad line
IMPROVED *Siberian* railroad line

2 Avoid long series of nouns modifying other nouns.

CONFUSING office management personnel report [A report about the management of office personnel? A report by personnel who are managing an office? Something else?]
CONFUSING teacher education program analysis [An analysis of a program for educating teachers? An analysis by teachers of an educational program? Or something else?]

EXERCISE 3a–g In the following sentences, correct in accordance with formal usage any errors in the use of adjectives and adverbs.

1 He felt badly about losing his car keys.
2 Public servants should take their responsibilities serious.
3 According to Uncle Zed, the air didn't smell very well at the Garlic Festival.
4 We stopped at a Canada tourist office for information.
5 Our cat Daniel looks suspicious at all stray dogs.
6 The snow is not near as deep as it was last winter.
7 The tall ships sailed majestic into the harbor.
8 Of the two major types of Pacific storms, the typhoon is the most destructive.
9 This lake is called Round Lake because it is the roundest body of water in central Michigan.
10 I quit drinking the ginger ale very sudden when I saw the fly in the ice cube.

4 VERB FORMS **VB**

Of the several different parts of speech in English, verbs are the most complex. They have more forms than any other kind of word, and they can be divided into a number of different kinds according to their forms and uses. Since the terms used to describe these various forms and kinds are frequently used in discussing problems in their use, it is helpful to know them and to understand the distinctions they describe.

This section covers the various forms and kinds of verbs, their function, and some common problems in their use. Section **5** covers the forms, use, and problems of tense, mood, and voice in verbs.

Forms of the verb

All verbs except *be,* which we will discuss separately, have five forms. The first three of these—the plain form, the past tense, and the past participle—are called the **principal parts** of the verb.

A plain form or infinitive. The plain form, sometimes called the **base form,** of the verb is that listed in the dictionary *(work, begin, choose).* This is the form we use with the pronouns *I, we, you,* and *they,* and with all plural nouns to indicate present time or habitual action *(they work, days always end, we choose).* It is also the form we use after all the helping verbs, such as *will, can, must, should,* etc., except the forms of the verb *be.* When this form functions as an infinitive, it is usually preceded by *to: they wanted to work, we needed money to pay our bills.*

A past tense form. This is the form we use to indicate that the action or state of being indicated by the verb occurred at some time in the past. In most verbs it is formed simply by adding *-d* or *-ed* to the plain form: *smoked, planned, worked.* But in about two hundred verbs it is formed in some irregular way, usually by a vowel change: *grow, grew; swim, swam; drive, drove.* (See **4b.**)

A past participle. This is the form we use when we combine the verb with *has, have,* or *had: has worked, have grown, had driven.* It is also used with the forms of *be* to form the **passive voice:** *is defeated, was being driven, were discovered.* (See Section **5.**) In most verbs the past tense and the past participle have the same form: *played, have played; found, has found; slept, had slept.* But about forty-five verbs, including many very common ones such as *become, do, grow, speak,* and *write,* have separate forms for the past participle. (See **4b.**)

An -s form. This is the form we use with the pronouns *he, she,* and *it,* with all singular nouns, and with certain indefinite pronouns such as *each* or *someone* to indicate present time or habitual action: *she asks, the dog bites, someone always wins.* For all verbs except *be* and *have,* this form is made by adding *-s* to the plain form: *asks, bites, wins.* For the verbs *be* and *have* the *-s* forms are *is* and *has.*

A present participle. This is the form we use after *am, is, are, was,* or *were* to indicate action continuing at the time indicated: *I am working, he is playing, they are eating, the corn was growing.* For all verbs this form is made by adding *-ing* to the plain form.

The five forms of two verbs are summarized below:

		Regular verb	*Irregular verb*
PRINCIPAL PARTS	Plain form	work	begin
	Past tense	worked	began
	Past participle	worked	begun
	-*s* form	works	begins
	Present participle	working	beginning

The verb *be*. The verb *be* is different from any other in having eight forms, three more than any other English verb. Unlike any other verb, it has three present tense forms *(am, are,* and *is),* all different from the plain form *be;* and it has separate singular and plural forms *(was* and *were)* in the past tense. In addition, it has a present participle *(being)* and a past participle *(been).*

Kinds of verbs

Verbs can be divided into various kinds according to main forms and uses.

Regular and irregular verbs. Verbs are either regular or irregular according to the way they form their past tense and past participle.

A **regular verb** forms the past tense and past participle simply by adding *-d* or *-ed* to the plain form: *complete, completed, completed; repeat, repeated, repeated.*

An **irregular verb** forms the past tense and/or past participle in some unusual way, usually by changing an internal vowel. In many irregular verbs, although the internal vowel is changed, the past tense and past participle have the same form: *keep, kept, kept; sleep, slept, slept.* About forty-five, however, have three distinct forms: *freeze, froze, frozen; give, gave, given.* About twenty irregular verbs keep the same form for all three principal parts: *cut, cut, cut; hit, hit, hit.* Although there are in all only about two hundred irregular verbs in modern English, they include a great many we use most frequently. (See **4b** for a list of the most common.)

Main and auxiliary verbs. In a verb phrase such as *is going, had been winning, must have been found,* or *will be helped,* the last verb form indicates the principal meaning and is called the **main verb.** All other verb forms in the phrase indicate special shades of meaning, such as those of time, obligation, and possibility, and are called **auxiliary verbs** or helping verbs.

Auxiliary verbs make up a small group of function words that may be divided into subgroups according to the kinds of function they perform. All auxiliary or helping verbs except *be, have,* and *do* are marked by the fact that they have only one *form.*

1 The forms of *be (am, is, are, was, were, been,* and *being)* and of *have (has, have, had, having)* combine with main verbs to indicate tense and voice (see Section **5**) as in *have worked, were studying, is planned, had been defeated.* The auxiliaries *will* and *shall* are used to indicate future time as in *will go.*

2 The auxiliaries *can, could, may, might, must, ought (to), should,* and *would,* sometimes called **modal auxiliaries,** combine with main verbs to indicate ability, obligation, permission, possibility, etc.: *can go, could have gone, must go.*

3 The auxiliary *do* is used to form questions and negative statements and to give emphasis, as in *Does she work; She did not work yesterday; She does work hard.*

Transitive, intransitive, and linking verbs. Verbs may be grouped as intransitive, transitive, or linking according to whether they do or do not pass their action to another word, called their object, or whether they are followed by a word which refers back to the subject, called a subject complement. (See also Section **1.**)

Intransitive verbs are those that are not followed by any object or complement.

The church bells rang.
The book lay on the table.

Transitive verbs are those that are followed by one or more objects.

> The hurricane struck the coast.
>
> The company gave its workers notice. [*Workers* is an indirect object, *notice* a direct object.]
>
> The storm made the roads impassable. [*Roads* is a direct object, *impassable* an object complement modifying *roads*.]

Linking verbs are those that are followed by a subject complement, that is, a word that renames or describes the subject.

> Mata Hari was a German spy. [*Spy* describes *Mata Hari*.]
>
> His allowance seems generous. [*Generous* describes *allowance*.]
>
> The old man remained active. [*Active* describes *old man*.]

Many verbs may be used as either intransitive or transitive according to the sentence in which they are used.

> He drove the car to work every day.
>
> He always drives carefully.

Finite and nonfinite verbs. A **finite verb** can serve without an auxiliary as the main verb in a sentence; a **nonfinite verb** cannot. We can use *drive* as a main verb; *the men always drive.* But we cannot make a sentence with *infinitives* or *participles,* which are nonfinite verb forms: *the men to drive, the men driving,* and *the men driven* are not sentences. We must add an auxiliary to such forms to make them capable of forming sentences: *the men have to drive, the men are driving, the men were driven.*

It is usually possible to distinguish between finite and nonfinite verb forms by the fact that finite verbs change form in the present tense according to whether their subjects are singular or plural: *the bell rings* but *the bells ring.* In finite verb phrases, the auxiliaries *be, have* and *do* change form according to whether the subject is singular or plural: *the bell is ringing* but *the bells are ringing.* Compare the finite and nonfinite verbs in the following lists. Note particularly that all the word groups containing a finite verb are complete sentences but that none of those containing only nonfinite verbs are. Note also that the nonfinite verb forms remain unchanged.

FINITE	NONFINITE
The man plans his work.	The man planning his work. . .
The men plan their work.	The men planning their work. . .
The dog has eaten.	The dog having eaten. . .
The dogs have eaten.	The dogs having eaten. . .
She defeats her opponents.	The opponent to defeat. . .
They defeat their opponents.	The opponents to defeat. . .

Problems with verb forms

4a

4a Be careful to use the -s and -ed forms of the verb when required.

Standard English requires the *-s* ending on all present-tense verbs whenever the subject is *he, she,* or *it,* a singular noun, or an indefinite pronoun such as *someone.* Similarly, it requires the *-ed* ending on the past tense and the past participle of all regular verbs.

Writers sometimes fail to use these necessary endings, particularly on verbs in which the ending is not clearly pronounced in speaking. When such endings do not form a separate syllable, as in *attacks, attacked,* the final *-s* and *-d* sounds are likely to be almost entirely lost in speech. When the verb endings are immediately followed by a word beginning with a very similar sound, as in *used to, supposed to,* or *asks Steven,* the final sound of the verb is likely to be almost completely obscured.

While these endings may give any writer occasional difficulty, the *-s* ending is likely to be especially troublesome for speakers of dialects that regularly omit it, using such forms as *she go, he work, the man work.* All writers, in their proofreading, should be alert to the possible omission of these endings; speakers of dialects that regularly omit the *-s* ending may have to proofread their writing with special attention to the problem.

EXERCISE 4a In the blank spaces in the following sentences, supply the correct form of the verb or verbs given in parentheses at the end of the sentence. If there are two blanks, use the correct form of the first verb in the first space and the second in the second space.

1. Now that Sally is working, it always _____ her father when she _____ him to have lunch with her. (please, ask)

2. Last year, when we _____ near the airport, the low-flying planes often _____ my mother. (live, frighten)

3. Now she _____ what she _____ to do. (do want)

4. Next year, she _____ to go to law school, so she _____ hard. (hope, work)

5. Bill _____ off during yesterday's lecture even though he _____ hard to stay awake. (doze, try)

4b Distinguish carefully between the principal parts of irregular verbs.

Any writer may occasionally have to check a recent dictionary to be certain of the past tense or the past participle form of an irregular verb he or she seldom uses. But for writers whose spoken dialects regularly use nonstandard verb forms, irregular verbs can be especially troublesome. Such nonstandard forms seldom seriously interfere with meaning: the meaning of *I done, I have did,* or *I have took* is perfectly clear. But nonstandard forms of the irregular verbs are regarded as serious errors, and learning the correct forms is well worth the effort.

Remember that your dictionary lists the principal parts of all irregular verbs, that is, the plain form *(begin),* the past tense *(began),* and the past participle *(begun).* If your dictionary lists only the plain form and one other form *(bend, bent,* for example), the second form will be that of both the past tense and past participle. If the dictionary lists only the plain form, the verb is regular and forms both its past tense and past participle by adding *-d* or *-ed.*

The principal parts of many of the most commonly used irregular verbs are listed below. When two forms are listed, both are acceptable, although the first is that listed first in most dictionaries. Add to the list any other verbs you may have used incorrectly.

Present Infinitive (Plain Form)	*Past Tense*	*Past Participle*
beat	beat	beaten
become	became	become
begin	began	begun
bet	bet	bet
bid	bade, bid	bidden, bid
bite	bit	bitten
blow	blew	blown
break	broke	broken
bring	brought	brought
burst	burst	burst
buy	bought	bought
catch	caught	caught
choose	chose	chosen
come	came	come

Present Infinitive (Plain Form)	Past Tense	Past Participle
cut	cut	cut
dive	dived, dove	dived
do	did	done
draw	drew	drawn
drink	drank	drunk
drive	drove	driven
eat	ate	eaten
fall	fell	fallen
feel	felt	felt
find	found	found
fly	flew	flown
forget	forgot	forgot, forgotten
forgive	forgave	forgiven
freeze	froze	frozen
get	got	got, gotten
give	gave	given
go	went	gone
grow	grew	grown
hang (suspend)	hung	hung
hang (execute)	hanged	hanged
hide	hid	hidden
hit	hit	hit
hurt	hurt	hurt
keep	kept	kept
know	knew	known
lead	led	led
leave	left	left
let	let	let
lose	lost	lost
make	made	made
mean	meant	meant
read	read	read
ride	rode	ridden
ring	rang	rung
rise	rose	risen
run	ran	run
see	saw	seen
shake	shook	shaken
shine	shone	shone
sink	sank, sunk	sunk
speak	spoke	spoken
spin	spun	spun
spring	sprang, sprung	sprung
stand	stood	stood
steal	stole	stolen
stink	stank	stunk

Present Infinitive (Plain Form)	Past Tense	Past Participle
strike	struck	struck
swear	swore	sworn
swim	swam	swum
swing	swung	swung
take	took	taken
teach	taught	taught
tear	tore	torn
tell	told	told
think	thought	thought
throw	threw	thrown
wear	wore	worn
weave	wove, weaved	woven, weaved
weep	wept	wept
win	won	won
wind	wound	wound
write	wrote	written

EXERCISE 4b   In the blanks in the following sentences, supply the correct forms of the verb or verbs in parentheses at the end of the sentence. If there are two blanks, use the correct form of the first verb in the first space and the second in the second space.

1 Plans for the space launch were _____ last spring. (begin)

2 The church bells _____ daily for two hundred years. (ring)

3 Shirley's friends had all _____ before she arrived. (eat)

4 Although many of the guests had _____ several glasses of beer, there was still plenty _____. (drink, leave)

5 Although Jack had _____ much about his topic, he was not satisfied with the report he had _____. (read, write)

6 Before they _____ in the morning, the pond had _____. (wake, freeze)

7 The child might have _____ if rescuers had not been near. (drown)

8 Soon after the fire started, the rats _____ out of the basement. (come)

9 On its first trial last week, the new speedboat _____ a record. (break)

10 Moses _____ his people follow the Ten Commandments. (bid)

4c

4c Make the standard distinctions between *lie* and *lay*, *sit* and *set*.

These two pairs of irregular verbs are often bothersome. *Lie* and *sit* are always intransitive, which means that they cannot take objects or occur in the passive voice. *Lay* and *set* are always transitive and therefore always must either have objects or be in the passive. The distinction between the verbs in the two pairs continues to be carefully observed in written English, though not always in speech.

The principal parts of *lie*, meaning "recline," are *lie, lay, lain*. The principal parts of *lay*, meaning "place," are *lay, laid, laid*.

LIE

PRESENT	*Lie* down for a while and you will feel better.
PAST	The cat *lay* in the shade and watched the dog carefully.
PRESENT PARTICIPLE	His keys were *lying* on the table where he dropped them.
PAST PARTICIPLE	After he *had lain* down for a while, he felt better.

LAY

PRESENT	*Lay* the book on the table and come here.
PAST	He *laid* the book on the table and walked out the door.
PRESENT PARTICIPLE	*Laying* the book on the table, he walked out the door.
PAST PARTICIPLE	*Having laid* the book on the table, he walked out the door.

The principal parts of *sit* (meaning "occupy a seat") are *sit, sat, sat;* the principal parts of *set* (meaning "put in place") are *set, set, set.*

SIT

PRESENT	*Sit* down and keep quiet.
PAST	The little girl *sat* in the corner for half an hour.
PRESENT PARTICIPLE	*Sitting* down quickly, he failed to see the tack in the chair.

| PAST PARTICIPLE | *Having sat* in the corner for an hour, the child was subdued and reasonable. |

SET

PRESENT	*Set* the basket on the table and get out.
PAST	Yesterday he *set* the grocery cartons on the kitchen table; today he *set* them on the porch.
PRESENT PARTICIPLE	*Setting* his spectacles on the table, he challenged John to wrestle.
PAST PARTICIPLE	*Having set* the basket of turnips on the porch, Terry went to play the piano.

EXERCISE 4c In sentences 1, 2, and 3 below, supply the correct forms of *lie* or *lay* in the blanks provided. In sentences 4, 5, and 6, supply the correct forms of *sit* or *set.*

1 The trash _____ on the floor all last week; it has often _____ there before.

2 Every day when we came home from work, he _____ down for half an hour.

3 As they took them off the tree, they _____ the Christmas ornaments carefully on the table, but they did not want them to _____ there very long.

4 When he brought the groceries home, he _____ them on the counter and then _____ down at the table with his wife.

5 He said he was sure that he had _____ the vase on the shelf where his mother had told him to _____ it.

6 They had _____ down in the living room to discuss where they could _____ the new chair, which the delivery men had _____ in the garage.

4d Be sure that the main verb in every sentence you write is a finite verb.

Remember that only finite verbs or verb phrases can make assertions and serve as the main verbs of sentences. Nonfinite verb forms—infinitives *(to steal)*, present participles *(stealing)*, and past participles *(stolen)*—cannot serve as the main verbs of sentences unless they are accompanied by a helping verb. A group of words that has only a nonfinite verb will always be a sentence fragment. (See Section **6** for a full discussion of sentence fragments.)

EXERCISE 4a–c In the blanks in each of the following sentences, supply the correct form of the verb or verbs given in parentheses at the end of the sentence. If there is more than one blank, use the correct form of the first verb in the first blank, the second in the second blank, and so on. If there is more than one blank and only one verb given in parentheses, use the correct forms of that verb in the blanks.

1 Sally had _____ in the sun for an hour when Allen came and

_____ down nearby. (lie or lay)

2 His new shirt _____ badly when he washed it. (shrink)

3 Peter _____ every time he plays poker; he _____ again last night. (win)

4 Betty had _____ three miles daily for two months. (swim)

5 The thief had never _____ anyone where he had _____

the money after he _____ it. (tell, hide, steal)

6 Biff now throws his suit on the chair, but the first year he had it, every

time he _____ it, he _____ it up carefully as soon

as he _____ home. (wear, hang, come)

7 Yesterday I _____ my new car; I wish I could have _____ it last month. (get)

8 After the storm we _____ that the high wind had _____

limbs off several trees and _____ down two others. (find, break, blow)

9 Now she always _____ her father before she _____ the car. (ask, take)

10 The pipes had _____ even though we _____ the

plumber had _____ them when we _____ him to. (freeze, think, fix, ask)

5

5 VERBS: TENSE, MOOD, AND VOICE **T**

The form of a verb or verb phrase tells us three things about the action or state it names. It tells us what time the action occurs (tense); what the attitude of the speaker or writer is (mood); and whether the subject is performing the action or receiving it (voice).

Tense

Tense is the time of the action or state expressed by the verb. Almost all verbs show the difference between **present** and **past** time by a change in the verb form. All verbs show **future** time by using *shall* or *will* before the infinitive, or plain form, of the verb.

	Regular Verb	Irregular Verb
PRESENT	She walks today.	The sun rises today.
PAST	She walked yesterday.	The sun rose yesterday.
FUTURE	She will walk tomorrow.	The sun will rise tomorrow.

A few verbs have only one form for both present and past time: *burst, cast, hurt, split*. By themselves these verbs cannot show time; to do so, they must depend entirely on modifying words *(I split the wood yesterday)* or auxiliary verbs *(I was splitting the wood)*.

In addition to the three tenses, which indicate the natural divisions of time into past, present, and future, all verbs have three **perfect tenses.** The perfect tenses indicate that the action named is completed or finished before a given point in time. Thus, for example, the past perfect tense *(had eaten)* indicates that the action named was completed before another past action: *He had eaten before his sister came home.* The three perfect tenses are formed by using the forms of the auxiliary *have* before the past participle of the main verb. The perfect tense forms of the verbs *work* and *see* are shown in the following:

	Regular Verb	Irregular Verb
PRESENT PERFECT	has or have worked	has or have seen
PAST PERFECT	had worked	had seen
FUTURE PERFECT	will have worked	will have seen

The six tenses, together with the way each is formed, are summarized in the following:

PRESENT	Plain form of verb with *I, we, you, they,* and all plural nouns; *-s* forms of verbs with *he, she, it,* and all singular nouns	I, we, you, they, the men eat he, she, it, the man eats
PAST	Plain form plus *-ed* in regular verbs; internal change in irregular verbs	talked, ate
FUTURE	*Shall* or *will* before plain form of verb	will talk, shall eat
PRESENT PERFECT	*Have* before past participle; *has* with *he, she, it,* and singular nouns	we, you, they, the men have talked/eaten; he, she, it, the man has talked/eaten

| PAST PERFECT | *Had* before past participle | had talked/eaten |
| FUTURE PERFECT | *Shall/will have* before past participle | will have talked/ eaten |

All six tenses can have **progressive-tense** forms. These progressive forms indicate that the action named is continuing at the time indicated. They are made by using the forms of the auxiliary verb *be* with the *-ing* form of the main verb *(is giving, was winning, have been going)*.

The most common uses of the tenses of the active verb forms are as follows:

Tense	*Use*	*Example*
PRESENT	Expressing a present or habitual action	He is *is talking* to the students now. He *talks* to the students at least once every year.
PAST	Expressing an action that was completed in the past	He *talked* to the students yesterday.
FUTURE	Expressing an action yet to come	He *will talk* to the students tomorrow.
PRESENT PERFECT	Usually expressing an action carried out before the present and completed at the present; sometimes expressing an action begun in the past and continuing in the present	He *has talked* to the students before. [Action carried out before the present and now completed] He *has* always *talked* to the students. [Action begun in the past and continuing in the present]
PAST PERFECT	Expressing a past action completed before some other past action	This morning I saw the speaker who *had talked* to the students last month.
FUTURE PERFECT	Expressing an action that will be completed before some future time	He *will have talked* to the students before next Thursday.

For a full synopsis of a regular and an irregular verb, see *Conjugation* in the glossary, p. 516.

Problems with tense

In spite of the relatively complicated tense system, writers whose native language is English ordinarily have few problems in its use. The main problems that occur involve either special uses of the present tense or the choice of the appropriate tense in the subordinate clauses of some complex sentences.

5a Use the present tense to express general truths or accepted facts and to indicate habitual action. Use the present tense in critical writing about literature and the other arts.

GENERAL TRUTHS	All that glitters *is* not gold. Corn *grows* rapidly in warm, humid weather.
HABITUAL ACTION	The old man *exercises* daily. The bank *closes* at four o'clock.
CRITICAL WRITING	In Dickens' novel *David Copperfield,* David's harsh stepfather *sends* him to London where every day David *works* in a warehouse pasting labels on bottles. Jane Austen's use of ironic comment *is* highly effective.

Note that the present tense also often expresses future action, as in *Our trip begins tomorrow.*

5b Be sure that the tenses of verbs are in appropriate sequence.

The term **tense sequence** refers to the relation of the times expressed by the verbs in main and subordinate clauses in a complex sentence. When the verb in the main clause of a complex sentence is in any tense except the past or past perfect, the verb in the subordinate clause will be in whatever tense the meaning requires.

The weather service *predicts* that it *will be* hot again tomorrow. [The prediction occurs in the present but refers to the future.]
Our friends *will* not *know* that we *were* here unless we *leave* them a note. [Future, past, present]

If the verb in a main clause is in the past or past perfect tense, the verb in a subordinate clause following it will usually be in the past or past perfect tense, unless the subordinate clause states a general truth.

She *said* that she *wanted* [not *wants*] to live in an apartment.
He *thought* that he *had left* his coat in the car.

5b

The owners *discovered* later that the fire *had destroyed* their house. [The destruction of the house occurred at a time before the owner's discovery of it.]

BUT   The child *discovered* painfully that fire *burns*. [Here *fire burns* states a general truth. Thus the verb is in the present even though the child's discovery occurred in the past.]

EXERCISE 5a–b In the following sentences, choose the verb form entered in parentheses that is in appropriate sequence. Be prepared to explain your choice.

1 He had never been told that the earth (revolved, revolves) around the sun.
2 They did not know what (has become, had become) of him, for he (has left, had left) over two hours before.
3 Joe made his way slowly down the steep slope, fearing that he (would fall, would have fallen) if he (moved, had moved) faster.
4 I (have been, had been) in college for three terms before I decided to major in computer science.
5 At the party we saw many people we (have seen, had seen) the week before.
6 Many people wished he never (made, had made) the speech.
7 He will be entitled to a vacation as soon as he (finished, has finished) his present assignment.
8 Of the movies I saw last year, *Holocaust* was the one I (enjoyed, have enjoyed) most.
9 We later learned that he (had, had had) to stay at the hospital for an hour even though he (had not been, has not been) injured.
10 In one of his most famous poems, Robert Frost says that good fences (make, made) good neighbors.

5c

5c   **Use present infinitives and participles to express action occurring at the same time as or later than that of the main verb. Use perfect infinitives and past or perfect participles to express action earlier than that of the main verb.**

The infinitive and participle forms are as follows:

	Infinitives	*Participles*
PRESENT	to begin	beginning
PAST	——	begun
PERFECT	to have begun	having begun

Infinitives and participles express only a time that is relative to the time indicated by the main verb of the sentence in which they are used. A present infinitive or participle expresses an action occurring at the same time as or later than that indicated by the main verb. A perfect infinitive or a past or perfect participle expresses a time that is earlier than that indicated by the main verb.

She *wants* [*wanted, had wanted, will want*] *to study* law. [The present infinitive *to study* indicates the same time or time later than that of the main verb *want.*]

She *would have* preferred *to study* [not *to have studied*] law.

She *was* [*is, will be*] glad *to have studied* law. She would like *to have studied* law. [The perfect infinitive *to have studied* indicates that the study occurred earlier than the time indicated by the main verbs *was, is, will be,* or *would like.*]

Wanting to study law, she *works* [*worked, had worked, will work*] hard. [The present participle *wanting* indicates the same time or a time later than that of the main verb.]

Having passed the entrance exam, she is *celebrating* [*has celebrated, will celebrate*]. The perfect participle *having passed* indicates that passing the exam occurs before the celebrating.]

Defeated in the election, the candidate *retired* [*has retired, had retired, will retire*] from politics. [The past participle *defeated* indicates that the defeat occurred before the time indicated by the main verb *retire.*]

EXERCISE 5c In the following sentences, choose the infinitive or participle form that is in appropriate sequence. Be prepared to explain your choice.

1 He would have liked (to finish, to have finished) his work before going to bed.

2 They know him (to be, to have been) a concert pianist before his accident.

3 (Waving, Having waved) his arms wildly, the man standing by the road clearly wanted help.

4 In college, I hope (to study, to have studied) subjects which will be useful to me later.

5 They should not have tried (to drive, to have driven) the entire distance without stopping.

Mood

The mood of a verb indicates whether the speaker or writer regards the action named by the verb as a fact, a command, or a wish, request, or condition contrary to fact.

English has three moods: the **indicative,** used for ordinary statements and questions (*He is happy, Is he happy*); the **imperative,** used for commands (*Be happy*); and the **subjunctive,** used to express conditions contrary to fact (*If he were happy*) and in clauses following certain verbs. Except for the subjunctive, mood causes writers few problems.

Special forms for the subjunctive have almost disappeared from modern English. The few that do survive are those that appear in *if*

5c

clauses expressing unreal conditions; in *that* clauses after verbs expressing requests, recommendations, and demands; and in a few formal idioms.

5d

5d Use the subjunctive to express conditions contrary to fact.

If the rose bush *were* healthy, it would have more buds. [The bush is not healthy.]

Last year, the bush looked as though it *were* going to die. [But it didn't die.]

Helen could settle the argument if she *were* here. [But she isn't here.]

Note that not all clauses beginning with *if* automatically express a condition contrary to fact.

If my experiment is successful, I will prove my point. [Here the clause beginning with *if* merely states a condition that, if met, will prove the point.]

5e

5e Use the subjunctive in *that* clauses after verbs expressing wishes, commands, requests, or recommendations.

I wish I *were* younger. [*That* unexpressed]

The law requires that there *be* a prompt trial.

I move that the meeting *be* adjourned.

Resolved, that Mr. Smith *investigate* our finances.

His parents asked that he *remain* home.

5f

5f Be aware that the subjunctive is called for in a few surviving idioms.

Far be it from me.	Long live the Republic!
Suffice it to say.	Come what may.
Heaven help us!	Be that as it may.

Note that except in surviving idioms even the few remaining uses of the subjunctive observed above are often replaced in speech and informal writing by alternative forms. Compare *I wish I was taller, The law requires a prompt trial,* or *His parents asked him to remain at home* with the examples above. In more formal writing, the subjunctive remains quite firm.

EXERCISE 5d–f In the following sentences, choose the correct verb form. Be prepared to explain your choice.

1 The actor who played Roosevelt made the audience feel as if he (was, were) actually Roosevelt.

2 The crowd demanded that the criminal (is, be) executed.
3 If I (was, were) in Alaska, I would be colder than I am now.
4 If the bill (is, be) unpaid this month, our credit rating will be lowered.
5 My father urged that I (stay, stays) in college for the rest of the term.

Voice

Voice refers to the ability of transitive verbs to show whether the subject performs or receives the action named by the verb. When the subject performs the action, the verb is in the **active voice.** When it receives the action, the verb is in the **passive voice.**

ACTIVE   The elephant *dragged* his trainer.
            The poison *drove* its victim mad.
PASSIVE   The trainer *was dragged* by the elephant.
            The victim *was driven* mad by the poison.

The passive voice is formed by using the appropriate form of the verb *be (am, is, are, was, were, been, being)* with the past participle of the main verb: *was driven, will have been driven, is being driven.* Note that although other auxiliaries may be included in the passive verb phrase, some form of the verb *be* must always come immediately before the past participle of the main verb.

Only **transitive verbs,** that is, verbs that can take an object, can show both active and passive voices. We can say *The student wrote the paper* or *The paper was written by the student,* but only *He talked,* not *He was talked.*

Most sentences in writing use verbs in the active voice, which is almost always more direct, more economical, and more forceful than the passive. But in two situations the passive voice is both useful and natural.

1   Use the passive when the actor is not known. Consider the following:

Peter L. Little was attacked and badly beaten while walking through Eastern Park about 11:15 last night.
The play was first performed in 1591.

In the first of these, since the writer presumably does not know who attacked Peter L. Little, he is forced to use the passive or to resort to some much less economical alternative such as *Some person or persons unknown attacked and badly beat. . . .* The second sentence suggests that though there is a record of the play's performance, there is none of its performers.

2 Use the passive when the receiver of the action is more important than the actor. Consider the following:

The new bridge was completed in April.

The experiment was finished on June 16; on June 17 the conclusions were reviewed by the advisory board and reported immediately to the Pentagon.

In such sentences as these, we have little interest in who completed the bridge or who performed the experiment and reported the results; the important things are the bridge and the experiment.

Problems in the use of voice include awkward and ineffective shifts from one voice to another, and the unnecessary or weak use of the passive. Both are problems of effectiveness in writing rather than of grammar. For awkward shifts in voice, see Section **10a.** For the weak use of the passive voice, see Section **36e.**

EXERCISE 5a–f   In each of the following sentences choose the correct form of the verbs, infinitives, or participles from each of the pairs given in parentheses.

1 The missing girl is reported (to be thumbing, to have been thumbing) a ride on the highway yesterday afternoon.
2 Though she hated (to go, to have gone) back to work, she should not (be, have been) too unhappy, since she (has had, had had) a full month's vacation.
3 Ever since I was ten years old, I (was, have been) riding horses.
4 The instructor will be very frustrated when he (finds, found) that five students have failed (to complete, to have completed) last week's assignment.
5 She was saving her money so that she (can go, could go) to California.
6 They thought it (is, was) better to drive than to go by train.
7 I wish I (was, were) going with you to Mexico.
8 Would he be as willing as he says, if he (was, were) being drafted?
9 The boy learned very early in life that some dogs (bite, bit).
10 (Having walked, walking) several miles, the old woman, exhausted, (decides, decided) to rest.

BASIC SENTENCE FAULTS
SEN FLT

The purpose of writing is to communicate facts, feelings, attitudes, and ideas clearly and effectively. Having something to say, thinking about it clearly, developing general ideas with ample fresh, specific, and accurate details—these are all indispensable to effective writing. So are many details of basic sentence structure and punctuation. Unless sentences observe the limits of English grammar and conform to the conventions of written English, they are not likely to be read, even if the ideas are interesting and the writing vivid. Readers confronted, for instance, with *In Yellowstone Park driving down the road some bears were seen having climbed down from the trees* don't judge effectiveness. They worry about basic grammatical difficulties that make the statement an incoherent mishmash. And writers who wish to be read must worry about them, too.

6

6   SENTENCE FRAGMENT **FRAG**

The usual sentence contains a subject and a verb and at least one independent clause. In writing, we indicate sentences by capitalizing the first word and placing appropriate end punctuation, usually a period, after the last. Any group of words that is set off as a sentence but that lacks a subject, a verb, or an independent clause is a **sentence fragment.**

Such fragments are common in speech, and they are sometimes used for certain special purposes in writing. But in most writing, incomplete sentences, or fragments, are very infrequent. The subject-verb sentence is what readers expect, and they will want some special effectiveness if that expectation is not met.

6a   Avoid punctuating phrases, dependent clauses, and other fragments as sentences.

Most fragments in student writing are phrases, clauses, and occasionally other constructions that depend for their meaning on independent clauses immediately preceding them. The most common types of fragments, together with revisions, are illustrated on pages 61–63. A fragment is usually an improperly punctuated part of the sentence that precedes or follows it. Thus the fragment can almost always be revised by joining it to that sentence, although other revisions may be possible and sometimes desirable.

1 Prepositional phrase. Prepositional phrases consist of a preposition, its object, and any modifiers of the object: *over the mountains, during the long intermission, after eating dinner.* Prepositional phrases usually serve as modifiers. (See **1c**.) The prepositional phrases in the following examples are italicized.

FRAGMENT	Lisa and Sally had just come home. *From their trip to New Orleans, Miami, and Atlanta.*
REVISED	Lisa and Sally had just come home *from their trip to New Orleans, Miami, and Atlanta.*
FRAGMENT	There must always be secrets. *Even between you and me.*
REVISED	There must always be secrets, *even between you and me.*
	There must always be secrets—*even between you and me.*
	[Here both revisions join the prepositional phrase introduced by *between* with the main statement, to which it clearly belongs. But the dash gives greater emphasis to the phrase. See **23b**.]

2 Verbal phrase. Verbal phrases consist of a verbal (infinitive, participle, or gerund), its object, and any modifiers of the object or verbal. (See **1c**.) The verbal phrases in the following examples are italicized.

FRAGMENT	The Dean finally agreed to see me. *To talk about my financial problems.* [Infinitive phrase]
REVISED	The Dean finally agreed to see me *to talk about my financial problems.*
FRAGMENT	The Egyptian pyramids are a remarkable accomplishment. *Showing much knowledge of the laws of physics.* [Participial phrase]
REVISED	The Egyptian pyramids are a remarkable accomplishment, *showing much knowledge of the laws of physics.*
FRAGMENT	The citizens voted against the proposed town budget. *Being angry at the continued tax increases.* [Participial phrase]
REVISED	The citizens voted against the proposed town budget, *being angry at the continued tax increases.*
	The citizens voted against the proposed town budget; they were angry at the continued tax increases.
	[This second revision changes the participial phrase beginning with *being* to an independent clause. Thus the two sentences could be separated by a period, but the semicolon suggests the close relationship between the clauses. See **21b**.]

3 Subordinate clause. Subordinate clauses are usually introduced by such subordinating conjunctions as *after, although, because, when, where, while,* or *until* or by a relative pronoun such as *who, which,* or *that.* Subordinate clauses that occur as fragments are almost always modifiers, which properly belong with the preceding or following sentence. (See **1d.**) Subordinate clauses in the following examples are italicized.

FRAGMENT He took both English and mathematics. *Because both were required.*

REVISED He took both English and mathematics *because both were required.*

He took both English and mathematics; both were required. [Here the fragment has been made independent by dropping the subordinating conjunction *because,* but the close relationship of the second clause to the first is suggested by separating the two with a semicolon rather than a period.]

FRAGMENT The resentment that his attack on the children caused lasted for many years. *Although it was seldom openly expressed.*

REVISED The resentment that his attack on the children caused lasted for many years, *although it was seldom openly expressed.*

FRAGMENT Prospectors invaded the newly discovered gold field. *Which was reported to be the richest yet found.*

REVISED Prospectors invaded the newly discovered gold field, *which was reported to be the richest yet found.*

4 Appositives. Appositives are words or phrases that rename or explain a noun or a pronoun standing immediately before them. The appositives in the following examples are italicized.

FRAGMENT The supervisor on my job was a kind person. *A thorough man, but always sympathetic and thoughtful.*

REVISED The supervisor on my job was a kind person, *a thorough man, but always sympathetic and thoughtful.*

The supervisor on my job was a kind person. He was thorough, but always sympathetic and thoughtful. [Here the fragment has been made independent by adding a subject and verb. This revision gives greater emphasis to the qualities of the supervisor.]

FRAGMENT McBride knew better than to mix ten beers with driving. *Particularly driving in city traffic.*

REVISED | McBride knew better than to mix ten beers with driving, *particularly driving in city traffic.*

McBride knew better than to mix ten beers with driving—*particularly driving in city traffic.* [Here the dash rather than the comma gives greater emphasis to what follows. See **23b.**]

5 Other fragments.

FRAGMENT | She was offered one position in a law office. *And another in the Bureau of Indian Affairs.*

REVISED | She was offered one position in a law office and another in the Bureau of Indian Affairs. [Here the fragment is the second part of a compound object of the verb *offered.*]

FRAGMENT | After packing Saturday night, they left early Sunday morning. *And reached Denver Monday evening.*

REVISED | After packing Saturday night, they left early Sunday morning *and reached Denver Monday evening.*

[Here the fragment is the second part of a compound predicate: *They left . . . and reached . . . .*]

FRAGMENT | *No rain for three months.* The reservoirs were low and the streams were drying up.

REVISED | *With no rain for three months,* the reservoirs were low and the streams were drying up. [This is an uncommon form of fragment. Revision requires either giving the disconnected initial phrase a beginning preposition and joining it to the main clause, as illustrated, or making it into an independent clause, as in *There had been no rain for three months.*]

6b Recognize acceptable incomplete sentences.

Exclamations, commands, and requests have no expressed subject; the subject *you* is always understood. Such sentences as the following are standard sentence patterns rather than incomplete sentences. (See **1a.**)

Look out! | Let the buyer beware!
Close the door. | Please pass the spinach.

Incomplete sentences are common in the questions and answers of speech and in written dialogue, which imitates speech.

"Where do we go tonight?"
"To the movies."
"When?"
"In about an hour."

In most writing, except for the standard sentence patterns of exclamations and commands, incomplete sentences appear only in special situations.

1 Transitional phrases and a few familiar expressions. Sometimes experienced writers indicate the conclusion of one topic and the turning to another by using incomplete sentences.

So much for my first point. Now for my second.

In addition, a few familiar expressions such as *The quicker, the better* and *The more, the merrier* occur as incomplete sentences.

2 Answers to rhetorical questions. A rhetorical question is one to which the answer is obvious or one that the asker of the question intends to answer. Experienced writers sometimes follow such questions with incomplete sentences.

How much does welfare do for the poor? Not enough.
Who is to blame for accidents caused by drunk drivers? The drivers, always.

3 Experienced writers sometimes use incomplete sentences for special purposes. In description, particularly when recording *sense* impressions, writers occasionally rely on verbless sentences, as in the first example below. In expository writing, writers sometimes use a sentence fragment to gain special emphasis, as in the second example.

I watch the cars go by for a while on the highway. Something lonely about them. Not lonely—worse. Nothing. Like the attendant's expression when he filled the tank. Nothing. A nothing curb, by some nothing gravel, at a nothing intersection, going nowhere.

ROBERT M. PIRSIG, *Zen and the Art of Motorcycle Maintenance*

The voice in the ad is a highly fictitious created person, speaking as an individual in a particular situation. In a bathtub, for instance.

WALKER GIBSON, *Tough, Sweet & Stuffy*

EXERCISE 6(1)   In the following sentences, eliminate ineffective fragments by (1) combining them with the main clause or (2) making them into complete sentences.

1 Many young people consider social work as a career. Not for the money, but for the satisfaction it provides.

2 The Beatles decided to stop giving concerts. Just as they were at the peak of their popularity.

3 Violence has become a tool of political dissent. Chiefly because non-violence can be so easily ignored.

4 He visited on Tuesday afternoon. Immediately after he had arrived from Los Angeles.

5 I think we should take the airport bus now. Or take a taxi later.

6 Linda has saved $700. Enough to make a down payment on a car.

7 Congress has investigated the Kennedy assassination several times. Trying to determine whether there was a conspiracy.

8 The hiking party should reach Porcupine Ridge before nightfall. Even with this heavy snow.

9 Winston Churchill is regarded as a great British leader. In war and in peace.

10 I left the Palace Bar when Desert Pete shot down the chandelier. Excusing myself first.

11 Ishmael finally arrived in Nantucket. To find a berth aboard a whaling ship.

12 Pedro has many hobbies. Collecting records, sailing, and skiing.

13 As a physician she had one major ambition. To alleviate pain.

14 Small, hand-held computers cannot handle complex data. Since they have little memory space.

15 The town marshal and the outlaw's daughter rode off into the sunset. And ended the movie.

EXERCISE 6(2)　　In the following paragraph, eliminate ineffective fragments by (1) combining them with the main clause or (2) making them into complete sentences.

　　The Indians of the Great Lakes found many uses for the weeds and wildflowers of the region. Such as food, medicine, and dyes. Plants provided edible berries and seeds. Among them being the cranberry and the wild lily of the valley. And especially sunflower seeds, making a ground-up meal. Which when boiled was used in cooking. And by the Hurons as a hairdressing. Bulbs of the wood lily were eaten like potatoes. The plant also serving as a medicinal charm. White settlers copied the Indian practice of making tea from Labrador tea. An evergreen shrub. Especially during the Revolution. Imported tea being scarce in the war years. The Jack-in-the-pulpit, or Indian turnip, was used medicinally. To treat ulcers and sore eyes. There were many other medicinal plants. Wild iris, hepatica, and the cardinal flower, for example. Indians made a red dye from pokeweed. Sometimes called inkberry. Using the dye to stamp designs on baskets. Yellow dye was made from goldenrod. A weed growing profusely on rocky banks. And on the sand dunes of the Great Lakes. Other plants were useful as articles of trade or as charms. Cranberries and columbine seeds having value in inter-tribal commerce. The columbine and cardinal flower being prized as love charms. The wild lotus was thought to have mystic powers. Some tribes keeping it to protect against evil spirits.

7

7 COMMA SPLICE **CS**
RUN-TOGETHER OR FUSED SENTENCE **FS**

7a

7a Comma splice   CS

Do not connect two main clauses with only a comma. Placing a comma between two main clauses without a coordinating conjunction (*and, but, for, or, nor, so, yet*) results in the **comma fault** or **comma splice.** If two main clauses are joined by a coordinating conjunction, a comma may precede the conjunction. If no conjunction is used, the two clauses must be separated by a semicolon or a period.

Comma splices may be corrected in one of the following ways:

1 Connect the main clauses with a coordinating conjunction.
2 Replace the comma with a semicolon.
3 Make a separate sentence of each main clause.
4 Change one of the main clauses to a subordinate clause.

COMMA SPLICE I was unwilling to testify, I was afraid of the defendant.

REVISED I was unwilling to testify, *for* I was afraid of the defendant.

I was unwilling to testify; I was afraid of the defendant.

I was unwilling to testify. I was afraid of the defendant.

Because I was afraid of the defendant, I was unwilling to testify.

The fourth revision would ordinarily be the most effective, for it not only corrects the comma splice but also indicates a specific relationship between the clauses. A good revision of a comma-splice error often entails reworking the sentence rather than merely inserting a punctuation mark. The kind of revision you choose will depend on the larger context in which the sentences occur.

A comma is sometimes used between main clauses not connected by a coordinating conjunction if two clauses are in balance or in contrast. Commas are also sometimes used between three or more brief and closely connected main clauses that have the same pattern.

A journalist's work is not important, it is indispensable. [Balanced main clauses]

Some people solve problems, others create them. [Contrasting main clauses]

I'm tired, I'm angry, I'm leaving! [Main clauses with the same pattern]

Although such sentences can be very effective, inexperienced writers would be wiser to use semicolons in them.

7b Use a semicolon or a period between two main clauses connected by a conjunctive adverb or a transitional phrase.

Conjunctive adverbs are words such as *accordingly, also, consequently, furthermore, however, instead, likewise, moreover, nevertheless, then, therefore,* and *thus.* Transitional phrases are phrases such as *for example, in fact, on the other hand, in conclusion, in the meantime.* When such words or phrases connect main clauses, they must always be preceded by a semicolon or a period.

Everything seemed quiet; then the explosion came.

John must be sick; otherwise he would be here.

He disliked college; however, he studied every day.

He wanted a job; in fact, he needed a job very badly.

7c Run-together or fused sentence FS

Do not omit punctuation between main clauses. Such omission results in run-together or fused sentences—that is, two grammatically complete thoughts with no separating punctuation. Correct these errors in the same way as the comma splice.

FUSED   Balboa gazed upon the broad Pacific his heart was filled with awe.

REVISED   Balboa gazed upon the broad Pacific, *and* his heart was filled with awe.

Balboa gazed upon the broad Pacific; his heart was filled with awe.

Balboa gazed upon the broad Pacific. His heart was filled with awe.

When Balboa gazed upon the broad Pacific, his heart was filled with awe.

EXERCISE 7(1)   Eliminate comma splices and fused sentences from the following sentences.

1 The racing car crashed headlong into the wall then all was quiet.
2 One way to publicize a movie is to say it's restricted and intended for adults then everyone will want to see it.

3 After the blood transfusion, the patient was comfortable, the doctor left the hospital.

4 "I have not finished the painting," said the artist, "I hope to finish it soon."

5 My brother must be color-blind, he calls all colors blue.

6 General Eisenhower wrote a book about World War II, he called it *Crusade in Europe.*

7 Population continues to increase in most of the world we may not have enough food for all.

8 Most of Hemingway's novels have similar subjects, love and war are two of the most frequent.

9 Water is becoming scarce in many parts of the country, our children may have to ration it.

10 Russia and China were close allies for many years however they are now very suspicious of each other.

11 "The flood of '31 was the worst I can remember," remarked Granny Hawks, "The water in Bear Creek was so high you could walk under it."

12 Lefty Gomez shook his head when the catcher signaled for a fast ball he nodded when the catcher called for a slow curve.

13 Television comedies often emphasize tensions between parents and children, furthermore, they show how their problems can be solved by love and common sense.

14 We are seldom challenged by television, it's much easier to watch the screen than read a book.

15 "Smokey Bear's out to lunch," said the truck driver over his CB radio, "You can drive to the next water hole with the hammer down, this is Fiddle Cat out, good buddy."

EXERCISE 7(2) In the following paragraph, eliminate comma splices and fused sentences.

Since 1965 Mexicans of all ages have enjoyed a comic book called *Kaliman, El hombre increíble* (The incredible man) Kaliman is a handsome, powerful super-hero. Kaliman, whose native country is unspecified, became an orphan while a young boy, afterward he was educated by lamas in Tibet. But his adventures are not confined to Asia, in fact, he roams the universe crusading for justice. His adversaries are plunderers, mad scientists, vampires, and various other villians, they commit outrageous crimes against the innocent and oppressed, at times they plot to destroy Kaliman himself by using poison or deadly weapons. The victim whom he defends often has a beautiful daughter who falls in love with Kaliman, nevertheless he always treats women as innocent persons who should never be hurt or dishonored, occasionally, however, his life is threatened by an exotic villainess with magic powers. Kaliman is not a typical comic book hero defeating injustice with his physical strength or ability to dodge bullets and leap from mountains, instead, he depends mainly on his remarkable powers of mind and great learning to outwit his enemies. He never tries to kill a villain in the most desperate circumstances he uses a blowgun whose darts induce sleep for several hours.

8 FAULTY AGREEMENT **AGR**

Agreement is the grammatical relationship between a subject and a verb or a pronoun and its antecedent or a demonstrative adjective and the word it modifies. Since Modern English nouns and verbs have few inflections, or special endings, agreement usually presents few problems. However, there are some grammatical patterns, such as the agreement in number of a subject and verb, or a pronoun and its antecedent, that you must watch carefully.

8a Make every verb agree in number with its subject.

Sometimes a lack of agreement between subject and verb results from carelessness in composition or revision. But more often, writers use a singular subject with a plural verb or a plural subject with a singular verb, not because they misunderstand the general rule, but because they are uncertain of the number of the subject or because other words coming between the subject and the verb obscure the real subject.

1 Do not be confused by words or phrases that come between the subject and verb. Find the subject and make the verb agree with it.

The first two *chapters* of the book *were* exciting. [The verb agrees with the subject, *chapters,* not with the nearest noun, *book.*]
The *size* of the bears *startles* the spectators.

Singular subjects followed by such expressions as *with, together with, accompanied by,* and *as well as* take singular verbs. The phrases introduced by such expressions are not part of the subject, even though they do suggest a plural meaning.

FAULTY	The *coach,* as well as the players, *were* happy over the victory.
REVISED	The *coach,* as well as the players, *was* happy over the victory.
FAULTY	*Sally,* together with her friends, *were* here.
REVISED	*Sally,* together with her friends, *was* here.

2 Be alert to agreement problems with indefinite pronouns used as subjects.

Indefinite pronouns ending in *-one*, *-body*, and *-thing*, such as *anyone*, *everybody*, and *something*, always take singular verbs. The indefinite pronouns *another*, *each*, *either*, *neither*, and *one* always take a singular verb.

> *Everybody* in the audience *was* enthusiastic.
> *Another* of the pesticides *has* proved harmful to birds.
> *Each* of the students *needs* individual help.
> *Neither* of the books *was* available in the library.

The indefinite pronouns *all, any, most, more, none,* and *some* may take either a singular or a plural verb depending upon the noun they refer to.

> *Some* of the silver *is* missing. [*Some* refers to the singular noun *silver.*]
> *Some* of her ancestors *were* slaves. [*Some* refers to the plural noun *ancestors.*]
> *None* of the work *is* finished. [*None* refers to the singular *work.*]
> *None* of the birds *have* migrated yet. [*None* refers to the plural *birds.*]

A singular verb is sometimes used with *none* even when it refers to a plural noun. The plural is more common, however, in both spoken and written current English.

3 Use a plural verb with two or more subjects joined by *and*.

> A dog and a cat *are* seldom friends.
> The Ohio River and the Missouri River *empty* into the Mississippi.

However, use a singular verb when the two parts of a compound subject refer to the same person or thing.

> My friend and benefactor *was* there to help me.

4 Use a singular verb with two or more singular subjects joined by *or* or *nor*. If the subjects differ in number or person, make the verb agree with the subject nearer to it.

> Either the dean or his assistant *was* to have handled the matter.
> Either you or he *has* to be here.
> Neither the farmer nor the chickens *were* aware of the swooping hawk.

If one of the subjects joined by *or* or *nor* is singular and one plural, as in the last example above, place the plural subject second to avoid awkwardness.

5   When the verb precedes the subject of the sentence, be particularly careful to find the subject and make the verb agree with it.

Do not mistake the expletive *there* as the subject of the verb. (An expletive is a word that signals that the subject will follow the verb. See **1a.**)

> There *are* no *trees* in our yard. [*There* is an expletive. The subject is *trees: No trees are in our yard.*]
>
> On this question, there *remains* no *doubt.* [The subject is *doubt: No doubt remains on this question.*]

When a compound subject comes after the verb in a sentence beginning with the expletive *there,* the singular verb is sometimes used, particularly if the first item of the compound is singular.

> There *is* [or *are*] only a chair and a table left to auction. [The subject is the compound *a chair and a table.*]

Such sentences are best rewritten.

> Only a chair and a table are left to auction.

In some sentences beginning with the adverbs *here* and *there* or with an adverbial word group, the verb comes before the subject.

> There *goes* the *man* I was describing. [*There* is an adverb. The subject is the noun *man.*]
>
> Up the trail *race* the *motorcycles.* [The subject is *motorcycles.*]

6   Use a singular verb with collective nouns when the group is considered as a unit acting together. Use a plural verb when the individual members of the group are acting separately.

Collective nouns have a singular form but name a group of persons or things as a single unit: *audience, bunch, crowd, family, herd, jury,* and the like.

> Our family *goes* out to dinner weekly. [The family acts together as a single unit.]
>
> The family *have been* arriving all morning. [Members of the family arrived at different times.]

The committee *is* meeting today. [The singular verb *is* emphasizes the committee acting as a unit.]

The committee *are* unable to agree on a plan. [The plural verb *are* emphasizes the members of the committee acting separately.]

7   Make the verb agree with its subject, not with a predicate noun.

The best part of the program *is* the vocal duets.

Expensive cars *are* a necessity in his life.

8   When the relative pronouns *who, which*, and *that* are used as subjects, use a singular verb when the antecedent is singular, a plural verb when the antecedent is plural.

They are the women who *deserve* praise. [*Who* refers to the plural noun *women;* thus the verb is plural.]

The book that *was* lost belonged to the library. [*That* refers to the singular noun *book;* thus the verb is singular.]

The phrase *one of the* frequently causes problems in such sentences.

Sanderson is one of the councilmen who *oppose* the plan. [*Who* refers to the plural *councilmen;* several councilmen oppose the plan.]

Sanderson is the only one of the councilmen who *opposes* the plan. [*Who* refers to *one;* there is only one councilman, Sanderson, opposing the plan. Note that the meaning of the sentence would not be changed if the phrase *of the councilmen* were omitted.]

9   When the subject is the title of a novel, a play, or the like, or a word used as a word, use a singular verb even though the form of the subject is plural.

Romeo and Juliet is a Shakespearean play.

Songs and Satires is a book by Edgar Lee Masters.

Women is the plural of *woman.*

10   Use a singular verb with nouns that are plural in form but singular in meaning, such as *economics, news, physics*.

Mathematics *has* always been Betty's downfall.

The financial news *was* favorable last month.

11   Subjects indicating sums of money, distance, measurement, and the like ordinarily take singular verbs.

Three quarters of the money *is* already spent.

Forty years *is* a long time to live in one town.

Four miles *is* too much to jog.

If the items that make up the quantity are thought of as separate parts rather than as a single unit, the verb may be plural.

Forty percent of the trees *were* damaged by the hurricane. [The trees were damaged separately.]

One half of the students *have* finished the examination. [The students finished individually.]

The expression *the number* takes a singular verb, but *a number* takes a plural verb.

The number of candidates for the position *was* large.

A number of candidates *were* applying for the position.

The number of people moving to the Southwest *is* increasing.

A number of business firms *have* moved from New York.

EXERCISE 8a In the following sentences, correct any errors in agreement. Indicate any sentences that might be appropriate in informal English.

1 His only interest are his studies.
2 A fool and his money is soon parted.
3 Among my favorite plays are *Blues for Mister Charlie* by James Baldwin.
4 The burden of sales taxes fall most heavily on low-income families.
5 Taste in dress styles differ greatly.
6 None of his horses are entered in the Kentucky Derby.
7 The farmer and not the city dweller are hurt when food prices fall.
8 Thirty dollars are more than many can afford for a pair of shoes.
9 The white-throated sparrow is one of those field birds that loves to sing.
10 There is a good many reasons for tensions between Arabs and Israelis.

8b Use a singular pronoun in referring to a singular antecedent. Use a plural pronoun in referring to a plural antecedent.

8b

Helen said that *she* wanted to work. [*She* refers to the singular antecedent *Helen.*]

Helium is a tasteless and odorless gas; *it* is one of the most abundant elements. [*It* refers to the singular antecedent *helium.*]

Women should be free to make *their* own decisions. [*Their* refers to the plural antecedent *women.*]

Most problems of agreement between pronouns and their antecedents occur with indefinite pronouns, collective nouns, and compound antecedents.

1 In writing, use singular pronouns to refer to indefinite antecedents such as *person, one, any, each, either, neither*

and compounds ending in *-one,* **-body, and** *-thing,* **such as**
someone, anybody, **and** *everything.* (See also **8a2.**)

Spoken English frequently uses a plural pronoun to refer to indefinite antecedents, but the singular continues to be preferred in writing.

WRITTEN   *Everyone* should be allowed to speak *his* [or *his or her*] own
            mind.

SPOKEN   *Everyone* should be allowed to speak *their* own minds.

WRITTEN   He asked *each* of us to bring *his* [or *his or her*] own lunch.

SPOKEN   He asked *each* of us to bring *our* own lunch.

Historically *he* (*him, his*) has been used to refer to such antecedents
as *one, none, everybody,* and similar indefinite pronouns that designate
either male or female. This "common gender" use of the masculine
pronouns has been widely criticized in recent years. Some critics have
suggested coining new pronouns such as *himmer,* which would refer
to both men and women. Others have urged the regular use of *he or
she* (*him or her, his or hers*) when the reference is general. Language
resists such changes as the first. Sometimes, using the second alternative is awkward, for it creates numerous pronoun references within a
single sentence or paragraph. When awkwardness becomes a problem,
writers who wish to avoid *he, him, his* for common gender can cast
their sentences in the plural or rework sentences to eliminate gender
references.

A careful writer will recast his sentences.
A careful writer will recast his or her sentences.
Careful writers will recast their sentences.

Recasting sentences will eliminate awkward gender references.

**2   With a collective noun as an antecedent, use a singular
pronoun if you are considering the group as a unit and a plural pronoun if you are considering the individual members of
the group separately.**

The *army* increased *its* watchfulness. [The army is acting as a unit.]
The *crew* are going about *their* duties without complaint. [The members
of the crew have separate duties.]

3   If two or more antecedents are joined by *and,* **use a
plural pronoun to refer to them. If two or more singular antecedents are joined by** *or* **or** *nor,* **use a singular pronoun to**

refer to them. **If one of two antecedents joined by** *or* **or** *nor* **is singular and one plural, make the pronoun agree with the nearer.**

Jack and Jim *have* finished *their* work.

Neither Jack nor Jim *has* finished *his* work.

Neither the instructor nor the students *have* finished *their* work.

EXERCISE 8b   In the following sentences, make every pronoun agree with its antecedent in accordance with written usage. Indicate any sentence that would be acceptable in speech.

1 A person should be willing to defend their own principles.
2 Neither of the trucking companies could afford to compromise on their rates.
3 Every American should be free to live wherever they can afford.
4 The Vietnamese family has survived in spite of their tragedies.
5 Everybody has their own solution to the campus parking problem.
6 None of the students in the psychology class could analyze their own dreams.
7 If either a resident or a nonresident were qualified, they would get the job.
8 No child fully appreciates their parents until later in life.
9 The school board disagreed in its opinions about closing the Adams School.
10 The citizens' group submitted their complaint to the town council.

8c   Make sure that a demonstrative adjective *(this, that, these, those)* **agrees in number with the noun it modifies.**

These adjective forms seldom cause difficulty. One frequent error, however, occurs when the demonstrative adjective is used with *kind of* or *sort of* followed by plural nouns. Here you must remember that the demonstrative adjective modifies the singular noun *kind* or *sort* and <u>not</u> the following plural noun. Thus a singular demonstrative is used.

NONSTANDARD	*These kind* of strawberries taste sweet.
STANDARD	*This kind* of strawberry tastes sweet.
NONSTANDARD	*These sort* of watches are expensive.
STANDARD	*This sort* of watch is expensive.

EXERCISE 8a–c   In the following sentences, correct every error of agreement in accordance with written usage.

1 Poverty is one of the major forces that encourages crime.
2 If someone wants to "do their thing," they should be encouraged.
3 These sort of planes can exceed the speed of sound.

8c

4 "Everybody is in a hurry to jump in their car and go some place," said Uncle Zed, "but they can't think of anything to do after they get there."

5 A person can live in a big city and still retain their warm feelings about life in a small town.

6 Two solutions to the state's energy problems have been offered, but neither have been tried.

7 After thirty, one loses both the rebelliousness and the inventiveness of their earlier years.

8 Although everyone wants the right to vote, they don't all exercise that right at election time.

9 If the house is to be sold, either the owner or the buyer must alter their price.

10 The committee on city planning do not approve the plan for a new shopping mall.

9

9 FAULTY REFERENCE OF PRONOUNS **REF**

A pronoun depends for its meaning upon its antecedent, the noun or other pronoun to which it refers. If the antecedents of the pronouns in your writing are not clear, your writing will not be clear. Place pronouns as close to their antecedents as possible and make all pronoun references exact.

9a

9a Make sure that each pronoun refers clearly to a single antecedent.

Pronouns can, of course, refer to compound antecedents in such sentences as *Joan and Karen both believed they had been cheated,* where the pronoun *they* refers to *Joan and Karen.* If, however, a pronoun can refer to either of two possible antecedents, it will be ambiguous.

AMBIGUOUS	When Kathy visited her mother, she was angry. [Who was angry, Kathy or her mother?]
CLEAR	Kathy was angry when she visited her mother. Her mother was angry when Kathy visited her.
AMBIGUOUS	Arthur went with John to the airport, where he took a plane to Phoenix. [Who took the plane?]
CLEAR	After going to the airport with John, Arthur took a plane to Phoenix.
	After Arthur went to the airport with him, John took a plane to Phoenix.

EXERCISE 9a Revise the following sentences by eliminating the ambiguous reference of pronouns.

1 Doris took the guppy out of the bowl while she washed it.
2 He took the shutters off the window frames and painted them.
3 I dropped the camera on the coffee table and damaged it.
4 Marilyn told Susan she should never have married Jim.
5 Andy gave his father a copy of *Huckleberry Finn,* which was one of his favorite books.

9b Avoid making a pronoun refer to a remote antecedent.

In general, the nearer a pronoun is to its antecedent, the more likely it is to be immediately clear. The reader should never have to search for a pronoun's antecedent.

REMOTE   Champlain and his men could hear the sounds of the St. Lawrence rushing past boulders below their camp and the sighing of pines in the morning wind. In the distance was an ominous mountain range. *They* felt alone in the Canadian wilderness. [*Champlain and his men* is the only antecedent to which *They* can sensibly refer, but the pronoun is too remote from its antecedent for clear, easy reading.]

CLEAR   . . . *The explorers* felt alone in the Canadian wilderness. [This revision uses a noun that, in effect, repeats the subject.]

Champlain and his men, who felt alone in the Canadian wilderness, could hear the sounds . . . [The remote reference is eliminated by changing the third sentence into a subordinate clause.]

EXERCISE 9b Revise all sentences in which pronouns are too remote from their antecedents.

1 Old Mission is a small village near the tip of a narrow peninsula that is covered with cherry orchards. Nearby are the east and west arms of Grand Traverse Bay. It has a post office and a grocery store.
2 The accident insurance policy lists the hazards covered and should be clear to the policyholder, since they are fully explained.
3 The delegates arrived in small groups for the emergency session of the UN. *The New York Times* printed a front-page story about the historic meeting. They stopped only to pose for press photographers at the entrance.
4 This house was built with fieldstones by my great-grandfather. The grounds cover several acres and include apple orchards and several outbuildings. It is filled with family heirlooms.
5 In the early spring many wildflowers, such as trillium, hepatica, and Dutchman's-breeches, grow in the woods near Walden Pond. Thoreau liked to ramble about this countryside. He often described them in his journals.

9c

9c Avoid the vague use of *this, that,* and *which* to refer to the general idea of a preceding clause or sentence.

The use of *this, that,* and *which* to refer to an idea stated in a preceding clause or sentence is common in informal English in such sentences as *They keep their promises, which is more than some people do.* Although such broad reference is often used by experienced writers when the meaning is unmistakably clear, it risks confusing the reader unless it is used with great care. Less experienced writers should ordinarily eliminate any vague use of *this, that,* and *which,* either by recasting the sentence to eliminate the pronoun or by supplying a specific antecedent for the pronoun.

> VAGUE Aid to African countries has been very limited, which has angered many black Africans.
>
> REVISED Aid to African countries has been very limited, a fact which has angered many black Africans. [*Fact* supplies a clear antecedent for *which.*]
>
> That aid to African countries has been very limited has angered many black Africans. [The sentence has been recast to eliminate the vague *which.*]
>
> VAGUE Migrant workers are being exploited. Action to prevent this should be taken immediately.
>
> REVISED Action to prevent the exploitation of migrant workers should be taken immediately. [The sentence has been recast to eliminate the vague *this.*]

EXERCISE 9c Revise all sentences in which the reference of pronouns is vague.

1 This is the most productive oil refinery in Louisiana. This was not built overnight.
2 She was self-conscious about her thick glasses, which didn't bother her friends.
3 Martin Luther King, Jr., was dedicated to nonviolence. That influenced his decision to become a minister.
4 The turn signals on this car do not operate, which should be repaired immediately.
5 He is going to a convention in Honolulu, which is exciting.

9d

9d Do not use a pronoun to refer to an unexpressed but implied noun.

To be clear, a pronoun must have a noun or the equivalent of a noun as its specific antecedent. Modifiers, possessives, and other words or phrases that merely suggest an appropriate noun do not provide clear and specific antecedents. Revise faulty sentences so that each pronoun has a specific noun or noun equivalent as antecedent, or otherwise recast the sentence.

FAULTY	Because we put a wire fence around the chicken yard, *they* cannot escape. [*Chicken* here is a noun modifying *yard*. It suggests but does not express the necessary antecedent *chickens*.]
REVISED	Because we put a wire fence around the chicken yard, the chickens cannot escape.
FAULTY	When the president's committee was established, she appointed several student representatives. [The possessive *president's* implies but does not express the antecedent *president*.]
REVISED	When the president established the committee, she appointed several student representatives.
FAULTY	Tom's mother is an engineer, and that is the profession Tom wants to study. [The appropriate antecedent, *engineering*, is implied but needs to be specifically stated.]
REVISED	Tom's mother is an engineer, and engineering is the profession Tom wants to study.

EXERCISE 9d In the following sentences, eliminate all references to unexpressed antecedents.

1 There is a fire station near the school, and we called them when we saw smoke.

2 He had a slight heart attack, but after a month's rest it was as good as ever.

3 When he was young he was a good chess player, but now he seldom has time to play it.

4 When the witness asked for police protection, two of them were assigned to guard him.

5 If children are irresponsible, some of it is probably the fault of their parents.

9e   In writing, avoid the indefinite use of *they* and *it*. Make sure any use of *you* is appropriate.

The indefinite use of *they, it,* and *you* is common at most levels of speech: *In Germany, they drink beer; it says in the dictionary that . . .; you can never find anything where you're looking for it.* In writing, these pronouns all have a much more restricted use.

1 *They* **always requires a specific antecedent in all but the most informal writing.** Correct its use in your writing by substituting an appropriate noun, or revise the sentence.

SPOKEN	In less industrialized areas, *they* do not understand the problems of the city.
WRITTEN	People living in less industrialized areas do not understand the problems of the city.
SPOKEN	*They* said on the late news that Mount St. Helens had erupted again.
WRITTEN	It was reported on the late news that Mount St. Helens had erupted again.

2 *It* **in the phrase** *it says* **referring to information in newspapers, magazines, books, and the like, though common in speech, is unacceptable in writing, except in dialogue.**

SPOKEN	*It* says in the newspaper that Monday will be warmer.
WRITTEN	The newspaper says that Monday will be warmer.

3 *You* **in the sense of people in general is common in informal writing:** *Differences of opinion among friends can be healthy if you don't take them too seriously,* **or** *When you're driving you should always be alert.* **More formal writing ordinarily prefers a general noun such as** *people* **or** *a person,* **or the pronoun** *one.*

INFORMAL	Many suburban towns do not permit *you* to drive more than twenty-five or thirty miles an hour.
FORMAL	Many suburban towns do not permit *people* [or *a person* or *one*] to drive more than twenty-five or thirty miles an hour.

You is always correct in writing directions or in other contexts where the meaning is clearly *you, the reader.*

Before turning on your air conditioner, be sure you have closed all your windows.

When using *you* in the sense of *you, the reader,* be sure that the context is appropriate to such use.

INAPPROPRIATE	In early colonial villages, you had to depend on wood for fuel. [The reader is unlikely to be living in an early colonial village.]

| REVISED | In early colonial villages, *people* [or *a person* or *one*] had to depend on wood for fuel. |
| BETTER | Early colonial villagers had to depend on wood for fuel. |

EXERCISE 9e   Revise the following sentences to avoid the indefinite use of *they, you,* and *it.*

1 In the first few verses of the Bible, it describes the creation of the world.
2 In every society you have to expect that some people will not be able to provide for themselves.
3 You find a generation gap in every generation.
4 In the Victorian era, they never talked about sex in public.
5 Throughout the development of the West, they drove back the Indians and took their land.

9f   Match the relative pronouns *who, which,* and *that* with appropriate antecedents.

In general, use *who* to refer to persons, *which* to refer to things, and *that* to refer to things and sometimes to persons.

Many *students who* major in mathematics today find employment with computer companies.

Arkansas, which became a state in 1836, was earlier a part of Louisiana.

Among the *flowers that* (or *which*) grow most easily are petunias and marigolds.

The possessive *whose* is frequently used to refer to things when the phrase *of which* would be awkward.

Cinderella is a story *whose* ending most of us know. [Compare *the ending of which.*]

The relative *that* can be used only in restrictive clauses, clauses necessary to meaning and thus not set off by commas. *Which* can be used in both restrictive and nonrestrictive clauses, clauses not necessary to meaning and thus set off by commas. (See **20c.**)

The *Equal Rights Amendment, which* was proposed by Congress in 1972, still had not been ratified by thirty-eight states in 1980.

The *amendment that* (or *which*) gave the right to vote to all citizens eighteen years old or older was ratified in less than four months.

Some writers prefer to introduce all restrictive clauses with *that* and to limit the use of *which* entirely to nonrestrictive clauses.

9g

9g Avoid the awkward use of *it* in two or more ways in a sentence.

We use *it* as an expletive to postpone a subject as in *It is sensible to be careful,* in certain idioms such as *it is cold* and such colloquial expressions as *He made it to the finish line,* and of course as a definite pronoun referring to specific antecedents. All of these uses are acceptable when appropriate, but sentences in which two different uses occur are likely to be confusing.

CONFUSING	He put his *car* in the garage because he never leaves *it* out when *it* is bad weather. [The first *it* refers to *car;* the second is idiomatic.]
IMPROVED	He put his car in the garage because he never leaves it out when the weather is bad [or *in bad weather*].

EXERCISE 9a–g Revise the following sentences by eliminating the faulty reference of pronouns.

1 Amy is studying hotel administration because her father owns one.
2 Mark told Bruce that he stayed up too late watching the televised hockey game.
3 We have an annual pumpkin show in my home town, which is open to the public.
4 Earl finished the roll of film by taking two pictures of a rusty Civil War cannon. Then he reloaded it.
5 Brad likes to talk about his wrestling ability, but he isn't a very good one.
6 In our textbook it says that pronouns should have clear antecedents.
7 She left her billfold in one of the stores and couldn't find it when she went back.
8 "The question is not whether God is on our side," said the army chaplain to the ragged band of patriots. They looked up in surprise as they prepared to meet the enemy in the hills near Boston. "It is whether we are on God's side."
9 The twins telephoned their parents nearly every day when they were vacationing in New Orleans.
10 After the hurricane's heavy damage in Haiti, it weakened to a tropical storm.

10

10 SHIFTS

A sentence is kept consistent by using one subject; one tense, voice, and mood in verbs; and one person and number in pronouns, as far as grammar and meaning allow. Unnecessary shifts in any of these elements tend to obscure meaning and make reading more difficult than it has to be. [See **32d(1)** for a discussion of consistency within paragraphs.]

10a Do not shift the subject or the voice of the verb within a sentence unnecessarily.

Particularly in compound and complex sentences, meaning frequently requires the writer to refer to more than one subject, as in the following sentence:

> When the *car* hit their dog, *John* ran home, and *Bill* held the dog until help arrived.

Here the writer is describing an accident involving two boys, their dog, and a car. Meaning clearly requires a shift of subject from one clause to another within the sentence. Such movement of a sentence from one subject to another is perfectly natural.

Less frequently, meaning may justify a shift from active to passive voice within a sentence.

> Three men *escaped* from the state prison yesterday but *were captured* before sundown.

Here the writer could have chosen to write *but the police captured them,* changing the subject but keeping the active voice in both main clauses of a compound sentence. But by choosing to use the compound predicate, *escaped . . . but were captured,* the writer keeps attention focused on the important subject, *three men.*

Unlike the shifts in subject and voice in these sentences, the shifts in the following sentences are unnecessary:

FAULTY   As *the boys approached* the swamp, *frogs could be heard* croaking. [Here the focus of the sentence is on *the boys.* The shift of subject from *the boys* to *frogs* and of the voice of the verb from the active to the passive are unnecessary and distracting.]

REVISED   As *the boys approached* the swamp, *they could hear* frogs croaking.

FAULTY   *Ellen stayed* at a mountain resort, and her *time was spent* largely in reading. [The sentence is about Ellen. The shift of subject from *Ellen* to *time* and the resulting shift from active to passive voice blurs rather than sharpens the sentence.]

REVISED   *Ellen stayed* at a mountain resort *and spent* her time largely in reading.

10a

EXERCISE 10a In the following sentences, correct unnecessary shifts in subject or voice.

1 On the Fourth of July the people paraded down Main Street, and a fireworks display was also enjoyed.
2 Many unknown rings of Saturn were discovered when Voyager I sent back photographs to scientists.
3 If a person attends furniture auctions, bargains in antiques can sometimes be found.
4 The doctor told most patients to exercise daily, but the advice was largely ignored.
5 As we canoed toward the rapids, white water could be seen.

10b

10b Do not shift person or number unnecessarily.

Just as meaning frequently requires us to refer to more than one subject in a single sentence, it may require us to refer to different persons or to combinations of singular and plural subjects, as in the following sentences:

> *I* stayed, but *they* left. [*I* is first person singular; *they* is third person plural.]
> The *snake* held its ground until the *coyotes* finally left. [*Snake* is singular, *coyotes* plural.]

But unless meaning clearly requires such changes, keep person and number within a given sentence consistent.

Unnecessary shifts in person are frequently shifts from the third person (the person being talked about) to the second person (the person being talked to). They occur principally because in English we can make general statements by using either the second person pronoun *you*, the third person pronoun *one*, or one of various third person general nouns such as the singular *a person* or the plural *people*. Thus any one of the following sentences is consistent:

> If *you* want to play games, *you* must learn the rules.
> If *a person* [or *one*] wants to play games, *he* [or *he or she*] must learn the rules.
> If *people* want to play games, *they* must learn the rules.

Failure to follow one of these possible patterns produces faulty shifts, as in the following:

FAULTY   When *a person* has good health, *you* should feel fortunate.
REVISED When *a person* has good health, *he* [or *he or she*] should feel fortunate.
         When *you* have good health, *you* should feel fortunate.
         When *people* have good health, *they* should feel fortunate.

A second kind of unnecessary shift frequently occurs in sentences in which the writer starts with the first person and inconsistently shifts to the second. Such sentences are ordinarily more effective when the writer maintains the first-person point of view.

WEAK   I refuse to go to a movie where you can't buy popcorn.

IMPROVED   I refuse to go to a movie where I can't buy popcorn.

Faulty shifts in number within a sentence usually involve faulty agreement between pronouns and their antecedents. (See **8b.**)

FAULTY   I like *an occasional cup* of coffee, for *they* give me an added lift. [Shift from singular to plural. The pronoun should agree with the singular antecedent *cup.*]

REVISED   I like *an occasional cup* of coffee, for *it* gives me an added lift.

              I like *occasional cups* of coffee, for *they* give me an added lift.

EXERCISE 10b In the following sentences, correct unnecessary shifts in person or number.

1 I enjoy an exciting basketball game, but they leave me emotionally exhausted.
2 If a person lives in a democracy, you have a right to voice your opinions.
3 Sheila often studies in the library, where you can have peace and quiet.
4 Since you can get delicious chili at the Campus Diner, I often eat there.
5 Joyce and I visited the art museum because you could go free.

10c Do not shift tense or mood unnecessarily.

In a sentence such as *Nostalgia is a love of the way things were in our youth,* meaning requires a shift of tense from the present *is* to the past *were.* But except when the meaning or the grammar of a sentence requires such changes in tense, keep the same tense throughout all the verbs in a sentence.

FAULTY   He *sat* down at the desk and *begins* to write. [The verb shifts unnecessarily from past to present tense.]

REVISED   He *sat* down at the desk and *began* to write.

FAULTY   In chapter one of the book, Sally *accepts* her first job, but in chapter three she *resigned* it.

REVISED   In chapter one of the book, Sally *accepts* her first job, but in chapter three she *resigns* it. [In this sentence, the revision uses the present tense in both verbs because it is customary to use the present tense in describing actions in literature. See **5a.**]

10c

Shifts in mood within a single sentence or a series of related sentences are almost never justified. Such shifts most often occur in writing directions. Avoid them by casting directions consistently either in the imperative or the indicative mood.

> FAULTY *Hold* the rifle firmly against your shoulder, and then you *should take* careful aim. [Shift from imperative to indicative mood]
>
> REVISED *Hold* the rifle firmly against your shoulder and then *take* careful aim. [Both verbs are in the imperative mood.]
>
> You *should hold* the rifle firmly against your shoulder and then (you should) take careful aim. [Both verbs are in the indicative. Note that here the second *you should* can be omitted since it will be understood by the reader.]

In general, directions are most economical and effective when they are written throughout in the imperative.

EXERCISE 10c In the following sentences, correct needless shifts in tense or mood.

1 In the early innings the Tigers have a three-run lead, but in the seventh inning they lost it.
2 Henry jogged about a mile; then he sits on a park bench to rest.
3 *Gomer's Ghost* is an entertaining movie, even if the ghost overplayed his part.
4 Stand with your feet together; then you should raise your arms to shoulder height.
5 While shopping, Don saw Goldie Hawn at the frozen food counter, but she only gives him an icy stare.

10d

10d Do not shift from indirect to direct quotation unnecessarily.

Direct quotation reports in quotation marks the exact words of a speaker or writer. Indirect quotation reports what someone has said or written, but not in the exact words.

> DIRECT She said, "I'm tired and ready to leave."
>
> INDIRECT She said that she was tired and ready to leave.

The tense in an indirect quotation should ordinarily be the same as the tense of the main verb. Unnecessary shifts between direct and indirect quotation often cause problems in tense.

> FAULTY Lincoln asked the general *whether his army was well supplied* and *is it ready for battle.* [Shift from indirect to direct quotation. In such mixed constructions, the writer usually omits quotation marks from the direct quotation.]

REVISED   Lincoln asked the general whether his army was well supplied and whether it was ready for battle. [Indirect quotation]

Lincoln asked the general, "Is your army well supplied? Is it ready for battle?" [Direct quotation]

EXERCISE 10a–d Revise the following sentences, correcting all needless shifts in tense, mood, voice, person, and number, and any shifts from indirect to direct quotation. Be prepared to explain your changes.

1 First the surface should be carefully cleaned; then put the glue on.
2 The Sunday drivers were out in full force, and suddenly there is an accident.
3 They said they had a copy of *Science,* and would I like to borrow it.
4 Great supplies of gold are found in South Africa, while Mexico leads in silver mining.
5 A public opinion poll is based on a cross section of the population, but sometimes they have been inaccurate.
6 Mr. Stein put a new fence around the yard, and then the wooden pickets were painted.
7 Ruth wondered whether her mother had left and did she say when she would be back.
8 The manager decided to offer free balloons, and the next day the store is packed with children.
9 When one feels tired, a candy bar will give you quick energy.
10 Careful drivers check the pressure in the spare tire because it is sometimes needed.

11 MISPLACED PARTS **MIS PT**

11

Modern English relies heavily upon word order to show relations among words. The Latin sentences *Puella amat agricolam* and *Agricolam amat puella* have the same literal meaning: *The girl loves the farmer.* Even though the subject and object are reversed, the special endings (*-a* and *-am*) make the meaning of the sentence unmistakable. But if the English words are reversed, so is the English meaning: *The girl loves the farmer; The farmer loves the girl.* Word order is crucial to meaning in English.

Just as word order is the principal way to keep subject-verb-object relations clear, so it is the principal way to keep many modifiers attached to the words they modify. Phrases and clauses that modify nouns require special care, since they normally attach to the nearest noun preceding them. Unless writers are alert, sentences such as these can occur:

He bought a horse from a stranger with a lame hind leg.

We returned to Atlanta after a week's vacation on Monday.

11

Context usually—though not always—allows readers to work out the intended meaning of such sentences. But at best a reader is distracted by the necessary effort.

11a

11a   In writing, place adverbs such as *almost, even, hardly, just, only, nearly* immediately before the words they modify.

In speech we commonly put *only* and similar adverbs before the verb, regardless of what we mean them to modify. To avoid any possible ambiguity in writing, place such modifiers immediately before the words they modify.

SPOKEN	He *only* ran a mile.
WRITTEN	He ran *only* a mile.
SPOKEN	The team didn't *even* score once.
WRITTEN	The team didn't score *even* once.
SPOKEN	She *almost* read the whole book.
WRITTEN	She read *almost* the whole book.

EXERCISE 11a   Revise the following sentences so that the limiting adverbs are placed immediately before the words they modify.

1 He almost seemed amused.
2 The oil spill just occurred off the French coast last week.
3 She only refused our offer of help because she wanted to be independent.
4 The earthquake victims needed the volunteers to bandage their wounds badly.
5 The legislature scarcely provided any funds for maintaining state parks.

11b

11b   Be sure that modifying phrases refer clearly to the words they modify.

Phrases used to modify nouns must ordinarily be placed immediately after the words they are intended to modify.

CONFUSING	Who is the woman who gave you the candy *in the pink dress?* [The writer intends the phrase *in the pink dress* to modify woman, not candy.]
CLEAR	Who is the woman *in the pink dress* who gave you the candy?
CONFUSING	Joan borrowed a bicycle from a friend *with ten speeds.* [The writer intended the phrase *with ten speeds* to modify *bicycle,* not *friend.*]
CLEAR	Joan borrowed a bicycle *with ten speeds* from a friend.

Phrases used as adverbs may usually be placed either within the sentence close to the words they modify or at the beginning or end of the sentence. In some sentences, however, their placement requires special thought.

CONFUSING   The author claims the revolt was caused by corruption *in the first chapter*. [*In the first chapter* seems to modify the noun *corruption* although the writer surely intended it to modify the verb *claims*.]

CLEAR   *In the first chapter*, the author claims the revolt was caused by corruption.

CONFUSING   A huge boulder fell as we rounded the corner *with a crash*. [*With a crash* seems to modify the verb *rounded* although the writer intended it to modify the earlier verb, *fell*.]

CLEAR   A huge boulder fell *with a crash* as we rounded the corner.

EXERCISE 11b   Revise the following sentences so that the modifying phrases refer clearly to the words they are intended to modify.

1 I kept thinking how religious my friends were for the rest of the day.
2 The astronauts looked forward to landing on the moon for several years.
3 The president announced that he would confer with his economic advisors at his press conference yesterday.
4 Hal dropped out of school after a semester's attendance over the weekend.
5 We were rescued after we were nearly drowned by a lifeguard.

11c   Be sure that modifying clauses refer clearly to the words they modify.

Clauses that modify nouns usually begin with *who, which,* or *that* and follow immediately after the words they modify.

CONFUSING   He had a ribbon around his neck *that was tied in a bow*. [The ribbon, not his neck, was tied in a bow.]

CLEAR   Around his neck he had a ribbon *that was tied in a bow*.

CONFUSING   Susan cautiously approached the deserted house by a winding path, *which was said to be haunted*. [The house, not the path, was said to be haunted.]

CLEAR   By a winding path, Susan cautiously approached the house *that was said to be haunted*.

Adverb clauses are introduced by words such as *after, although, because, since,* and *until.* Like adverb phrases, they can usually be placed either within the sentence close to the words they modify or at the beginning or end of the sentence; but they can sometimes be confusing unless writers are careful.

CONFUSING   The police towed the stolen station wagon to the city garage *after it was abandoned.* [The clause *after it was abandoned* is intended to modify the verb *towed* but seems to modify the noun *garage.*]

CLEAR   *After the stolen station wagon was abandoned,* the police towed it to the city garage.

The police towed the stolen station wagon, *after it was abandoned,* to the city garage.

EXERCISE 11c   In the following sentences, place the modifying clauses in clear relationships to the words they modify.

1 She found a large apartment with two windows facing a garden that was well ventilated.
2 I suddenly realized that I had left the tickets at home after we reached the stadium.
3 Marty bought a Great Dane from a neighbor that was too big for the doghouse.
4 She gave an alarm clock to her cousin that was guaranteed for five years.
5 Nick sold his sports car to a used-car dealer that needed overhauling.

11d

11d   Avoid squinting modifiers.

A **squinting modifier** is one that may modify either a preceding word or a following word. It squints at the words on its right and left, and leaves the reader confused.

SQUINTING   His physician told him *frequently* to exercise.
CLEAR   His physician *frequently* told him to exercise.
His physician told him to exercise *frequently.*

SQUINTING   The committee which was studying the matter *yesterday* turned in its report.
CLEAR   The committee that was studying the matter turned in its report *yesterday.*
The committee, *which spent yesterday* studying the matter, turned in its report.

SQUINTING   She promised *on her way home* to visit him.
CLEAR   *On her way home,* she promised to visit him.
She promised to visit him *on her way home.*

EXERCISE 11d Recast the following sentences to eliminate squinting modifiers.

1 The pilot was told constantly to be prepared for emergencies.
2. The story he was reading slowly put Sarah to sleep.
3 A person who succeeds often is ambitious.
4 The speaker told the audience when the lecture was over they could ask questions.
5 The men who were beating on the wall wildly began shooting.

11e Do not split infinitives awkwardly.

An infinitive is split when an adverbial modifier separates the *to* from the verb. There is nothing ungrammatical about splitting an infinitive, and sometimes a split is useful to avoid awkwardness. But most split infinitives are unnecessary.

AWKWARD	She tried not *to* carelessly *hurt* the kitten.
CLEAR	She tried not *to hurt* the kitten carelessly.
AWKWARD	You should try *to*, if you can, *take* a walk every day.
CLEAR	If you can, you should try *to take* a walk every day.

On the other hand, note the following sentence:

The course is designed *to* better *equip* graduates to go into business.

In this case, if *better* is placed before *to equip* it will squint awkwardly between *designed* and the infinitive; after *to equip* it will modify graduates; at the end of the sentence it will be at best awkward and unnatural, if not entirely unclear.

EXERCISE 11e Revise the following sentences by eliminating awkward split infinitives.

1 We agreed to once and for all dissolve our business partnership.
2 The tennis team expects to, if the weather permits, play the match tomorrow.
3 The major nations of the world regularly decide to sometime in the near future reduce their armaments.
4 It's a relief to promptly send in your tax return after the first of the year.
5 You have to willingly accept the idea that you are responsible for the well-being of others, or the human condition will never improve.

11f

11f In general, avoid separating a subject from its predicate, a verb from its object, or the parts of a verb phrase unless separating them makes the sentence more effective.

EFFECTIVE SEPARATION

The captain, *seeing the ominous storm clouds gathering overhead,* ordered the crew to take in the sail.

And so Pilate, *willing to content the people,* released Barabbas unto them, and delivered Jesus, *when he had scourged him,* to be crucified.

MARK 15:15

Only when a man is safely ensconced under six feet of earth, *with several tons of enlauding granite upon his chest,* is he in a position to give advice with any certainty, and then he is silent.

EDWARD NEWTON

AWKWARD SEPARATION

She *found,* after an hour's search, the *money* hidden under the rug.

CLEAR

After an hour's search, she *found* the *money* hidden under the rug.

AWKWARD SEPARATION

At the convention I saw Mary Ward, whom I *had* many years ago *met* in Chicago.

CLEAR

At the convention I saw Mary Ward, whom I *had met* many years ago in Chicago.

EXERCISE 11f Revise the following sentences by eliminating the unnecessary separations of related sentence elements.

1 In a pleasant house in Concord, Emerson, who was a neighbor of Thoreau, lived.

2 Peggy is, despite strong objections from her parents, going to study music and painting.

3 John wrote, after discussing it with his sister, a letter resigning his position.

4 Swenson made, after years of smoking heavily, a great effort to stop.

5 Pollution, as many have discovered, is very hard to control.

Revise the following sentences by eliminating all misplaced parts.

1 We watched the dog show on our TV, which was won by a golden retriever.
2 A farmer's market is located on the edge of the town, which always has fresh fruits and berries.
3 Charley even exercises during his lunch hour.
4 A salesperson who tries often makes a good profit.
5 The minister speaks out against sin every Sunday.
6 Everyone nearly suffers during an economic recession.
7 Linda is, despite her friends' confidence in her ability, going to give up studying music composition.
8 We had lunch at a drive-in, which cost more than it was worth.
9 Religious faith without doubt is a comfort to many people.
10 During the bombing the platoon leader ordered the men to immediately take cover.

12 DANGLING MODIFIERS **DGL**

A modifier must have something to modify. A **dangling modifier** is one that has nothing to modify because what it ought to modify has not been clearly stated in its sentence. For example:

Driving through the mountains, three bears were seen.

Driving through the mountains is a participial phrase that can modify anything that can drive. But there is nothing in the sentence that can do this. The sentence says that the bears were driving, but common sense tells us this can't be so. The writer surely meant that the bears were seen by some person who was driving.

Dangling modifiers may be verbal or prepositional phrases or elliptical clauses **(12d).** They most commonly come at the beginning of a sentence, but they can come at the end as well. To write *There were three bears, driving through the mountains* still leaves the bears apparently doing the driving. Nothing is expressed that *driving* can sensibly modify. Nor is *When a baby, my grandfather gave me a silver cup* improved by moving the clause to the end of the sentence.

Eliminate dangling modifiers by (1) reworking the sentence so that the modifier is clearly attached to the right word or (2) expanding the dangler into a full subordinate clause. The sentence in the illustration, for example, can be revised as follows:

Driving through the mountains, we saw three bears.
When we drove through the mountains, we saw three bears.

12a

12a Avoid dangling participial phrases.

A **participle** is a verb form used as an adjective to modify a noun or pronoun. A participial phrase consists of a participle, its object, and any modifiers of the participle or object. (See **1b** and **1c**.)

DANGLING	Coming home late, the house was dark. [There is nothing in the sentence that can sensibly be coming home. A revision must identify some person.]
REVISED	Coming home late, we found the house dark.
	When we came home late, the house was dark.
DANGLING	Being made of glass, Horace handled the tabletop carefully.
REVISED	Because the tabletop was made of glass, Horace handled it carefully. [The participial phrase is expanded into a subordinate clause.]

EXERCISE 12a   Revise the following sentences to eliminate the dangling participial phrases.

1 Marinated in mustard sauce, the cook served a delicious ham.
2 Spanning the Straits of Mackinac, the engineers realized the bridge would be one of the world's longest suspension bridges.
3 Fierce and uncaged, visitors to wild game preserves must be careful not to arouse the animals.
4 Seated at an outdoor cafe, Paris reveals an exciting panorama.
5 Howling through the treetops, I could hear the wind.

12b

12b Avoid dangling phrases containing gerunds.

A **gerund** is an *-ing* form of a verb used as a noun. A gerund phrase consists of a gerund, its object, and any modifiers of the gerund or object. (See **1b** and **1d**.) In typical dangling phrases containing gerunds, the gerund or gerund phrase serves as the object of a preposition.

DANGLING	Before exploring the desert, our water supply was replenished. [Who replenished it?]
REVISED	Before exploring the desert, we replenished our water supply.
DANGLING	After putting a worm on my hook, the fish began to bite. [A very accommodating fish that will bait the hook for you.]
REVISED	After I put a worm on my hook, the fish began to bite.

EXERCISE 12b Revise the following sentences to eliminate the dangling gerund phrases.

1 In deciding where to live, the distance to one's work should be considered.
2 After releasing the suspect, new evidence was submitted to the police.
3 In preparing the launch, Voyager II was inspected many times.
4 Before transferring to the new school, his mother took Bobby to meet his future teacher.
5 After getting up in the morning, the day began with a good breakfast.

12c Avoid dangling infinitive phrases.

An **infinitive** consists of the infinitive marker *to* followed by the plain form of the verb. An infinitive phrase consists of an infinitive, its object, and any modifiers of the infinitive or object.

DANGLING   To take good pictures, a good camera must be used. [Who will use the camera?]

REVISED   To take good pictures, you must use a good camera.
If you wish to take good pictures, you must use a good camera.

DANGLING   To write effectively, practice is necessary.

REVISED   To write effectively, you [or *one*] must practice.

EXERCISE 12c Revise the following sentences to eliminate the dangling infinitive phrases.

1 To save fuel, the thermostat is turned down.
2 To be a good citizen, some knowledge of local government is necessary.
3 To plan a college program, career goals must be carefully considered.
4 To be a financial success, at least a hundred performances of a Broadway play are essential.
5 To be really secure, the lock on their office door was changed.

12d Avoid dangling elliptical clauses.

An **elliptical clause** is one in which the subject or verb is implied or understood rather than stated. The clause dangles if its implied subject is not the same as the subject of the main clause. Eliminate a dangling elliptical clause by (1) making the dangling clause agree with the subject of the main clause or (2) supplying the omitted subject or verb.

DANGLING   *When a baby,* my grandfather gave me a silver cup.

REVISED   *When a baby, I* was given a silver cup by my grandfather. [The subject of the main clause agrees with the implied subject of the elliptical clause.]
When I was a baby, my grandfather gave me a silver cup. [The omitted subject and verb are supplied in the elliptical clause.]

12d

| DANGLING | *While rowing on the lake,* the boat overturned. |
| REVISED | *While rowing on the lake,* we overturned the boat. [The subject of the main clause agrees with the implied subject of the elliptical clause.]
While we were rowing on the lake, the boat overturned [*or* we overturned the boat]. [The elliptical clause is expanded into a subordinate clause.] |

EXERCISE 12d   Revise the following sentences to eliminate the dangling elliptical clauses.

1 If sighted, astronauts could confirm that there is a man in the moon.
2 While combing her hair, someone knocked at the door.
3 A fish stole the bait off my hook while dozing.
4 If found, we will pay a reward for the lost ring.
5 You may slip on the floor, if highly polished.

EXERCISE 12a–d   Revise the following sentences to eliminate the dangling modifiers.

1 Pacing a mile in 1 minute, $52\frac{1}{5}$ seconds, a world record in harness racing was set by Niatross.
2 When frightened, our thinking is controlled by our emotions.
3 After sharpening his claws on the waterbed, Uncle Zed saw our cat Daniel swimming to safety.
4 Waiting for the fog to lift, the flight to Louisville was finally cancelled.
5 To appreciate the music fully, the volume on the stereo should be high.
6 While riding my unicycle, a large dog chased me.
7 Being a minor, the judge suspended the sentence of the prowler.
8 Relaxing on the shore of the lake, his eyes followed the path of the speedboat.
9 To understand modern civilization, the past must be studied.
10 By collecting postage stamps, much history and geography are learned.

13

13 OMISSIONS **OM**
INCOMPLETE AND ILLOGICAL
COMPARISONS **COMP**

A sentence will be confusing if the writer omits words needed to insure clarity and accuracy. Sometimes, of course, writers omit words through haste or carelessness. This sort of omission can be caught with careful proofreading. Most omissions not caused by carelessness occur in three kinds of construction: (1) some constructions in which the omission of a preposition or conjunction is common in informal speech, (2) some kinds of compound constructions, and (3) comparisons.

13a Proofread your writing carefully to avoid careless omissions.

The sample sentences below are confusing because they omit necessary words.

> The opportunities for people television repair are varied.
> Many millions people were unemployed last depression.
> Learning by imitation is one of the most common in early life.

In the first two examples, the writer has simply failed to write the necessary words: *in* after *people* in the first, and *of* before *people* and *during the* before *last* in the second. The third sentence, although somewhat more complex, clearly requires something like *methods of learning* after *common*. Very probably the writer thought out the sentence with such a phrase and was merely careless in getting the idea down on paper.

13b In writing, spell out relationships left implied in speech.

Some constructions such as *He left Monday* are idiomatic. In speaking we often extend this pattern to such expressions as *We became friends spring semester,* or *The next few years we'll worry about prices.* In writing, such relationships need to be spelled out.

SPOKEN	Space travel *the last few years* has been exciting.
WRITTEN	Space travel *during the last few years* has been exciting.

The omission of *that* can often be confusing.

CONFUSING	He felt completely naked but totally private swimming was indecent.
REVISED	He felt that completely naked but totally private swimming was indecent.

The use of *type, make, brand* and some other similar words immediately before a noun (*this type show, this brand cereal*) is common in speech but is avoided by most writers.

COLLOQUIAL	I have never driven this *make car* before.
WRITTEN	I have never driven this *make of car* before.

13b

EXERCISE 13b In the following sentences, supply the omitted words that are implied but not stated.

1 Columbus Day, a special holiday for Americans of Italian ancestry, is celebrated October.
2 This model camera has an automatic film winder.
3 Rachel received several nice gifts the eight days of Hanukkah.
4 I understood French toast was provided with the American plan.
5 With this type metal detector you can find buried treasure, such as bottle caps and gum wrappers.

13c

13c Include all necessary words in compound constructions.

When we connect two items of the same kind with coordinating conjunctions such as *and* or *but,* we often omit words that unnecessarily duplicate each other: *She could [go] and did go; He was faithful [to] and devoted to his job.* But such omissions work only if the two items are in fact the same. If they are not, the resulting construction will be incomplete (see also the discussion of parallelism in Section **35**). Such incomplete constructions usually result from omitting necessary prepositions or parts of verb phrases.

INCOMPLETE Martha was interested and skillful at photography.

REVISED Martha was interested *in* and skillful *at* photography. [*Interested* idiomatically requires the preposition *in;* if it is not present, we tend to read *interested at.*]

INCOMPLETE My cat never has and never will eat fish.

REVISED My cat never has *eaten* and never will *eat* fish.

INCOMPLETE Tom's ideas were sound and adopted without discussion.

REVISED Tom's ideas were sound and *were* adopted without discussion. [*Were* needs to be repeated here since the two verbs are not parallel; the first *were* is used as the main verb; the second is used as an auxiliary with *adopted.*]

EXERCISE 13c Supply the omitted words in the following sentences.

1 Virginia always has and always will admire her Aunt Kate.
2 The concert was lively and appreciated by the audience.
3 Last year he determined to but finally gave up visiting Japan.
4 In China the major problem has and continues to be overpopulation.
5 He annually resolves to but fails in taking off excess weight.

13d

13d Make all comparisons complete and logical.

A comparison expresses a relation between two things: *A is larger than B.* To make a comparison complete and logical, include both items being compared, include all words necessary to make the relationship clear, and be sure that the two items are in fact comparable.

1   Avoid incomplete comparisons. Sentences such as *Cleanaid is better* or *Weatherall Paint lasts longer* are popular with advertisers because they let the advertiser avoid telling us what the product is better than or lasts longer than. To be complete, a comparison must state both items being compared.

INCOMPLETE   Our new Ford gets better mileage. [Better than what?]

REVISED   Our new Ford gets better mileage than our old one did.

2   Avoid ambiguous comparisons. In comparisons such as *He enjoys watching football more than* [*he enjoys watching*] *baseball,* we can omit *he enjoys watching* because only one meaning is reasonable. But when more than one meaning is possible in such sentences, the comparison will be ambiguous.

AMBIGUOUS   I admire her more than Jane. [More than Jane admires her? More than you admire Jane?]

CLEAR   I admire her more than I admire Jane.
I admire her more than Jane does.

3   Avoid illogical comparisons. A comparison will be illogical if it compares or seems to compare two things that cannot be sensibly compared.

ILLOGICAL   A lawyer's income is greater than a doctor. [The sentence compares an income to a doctor. Logic requires the comparison of income to income or of lawyer to doctor.]

REVISED   A lawyer's income is greater than a doctor's.
A lawyer's income is greater than that of a doctor.
A lawyer has a greater income than a doctor does.

4   Avoid grammatically incomplete comparisons. Comparisons using the expression *as strong as, as good as,* and the like always require the second *as.*

INCOMPLETE   He is as strong, if not stronger than, Bob.

REVISED   He is as strong as, if not stronger than, Bob.
He is as strong as Bob, if not stronger.

In comparisons of items in the same class of things, use *other* or *any other*. In comparisons of items in different classes, use *any*.

INCORRECT	Mt. Everest is higher than *any* Asian mountain.
CORRECT	Mt. Everest is higher than *any other* Asian mountain.
	Mt. Everest is higher than *other* Asian mountains. [We are comparing Mt. Everest, one Asian mountain, to other Asian mountains.]
	Mt. Everest is higher than *any* American mountain. [We are comparing Mt. Everest, an Asian mountain, with American mountains, a different class.]

EXERCISE 13d In the following sentences, make all comparisons complete and logical.

1 The population of Illinois is larger than Iowa.
2 Dennis telephones me more often than Jamie.
3 Graffiti, or words and pictures inscribed on walls, are as old, if not older than, ancient Roman civilization.
4 Lake Ontario is smaller than any of the Great Lakes.
5 For good eyesight, vitamin A is as essential, if not more essential than, other vitamins.

EXERCISE 13a–d The following sentences all contain incomplete constructions. Revise each by supplying words that have been omitted.

1 His eyes are like a frightened chipmunk.
2 Ghetto children deserve to and should be getting better schools.
3 The Nile is longer than any African river.
4 In some countries the people are not as friendly as Italy.
5 His opinions were different from the other committee members.
6 Many people are both afraid and fascinated by snakes.
7 It seemed Thoreau wanted to avoid some of his Concord neighbors.
8 Jill is better than any rebounder on her basketball team.
9 Early Nebraska settlers found sod houses were warmer in winter.
10 Lee is both excited and experienced at mountain climbing.

14

14 AWKWARD OR CONFUSED SENTENCES **AWK**

Sometimes a sentence goes wrong because the predicate says something about the subject that cannot sensibly apply to that subject. Or a sentence goes wrong because it starts with one kind of construction and ends with a different kind of construction. The first of these faults is called **faulty predication;** the second, a **mixed construction.**

14a

14a   Make sure to combine only subjects and predicates that make sense together.

Not all subjects and verbs make sense together. For example, many living things can be subjects for the verb *eat*—*women, boys, ants, panthers.* Figuratively, we can speak of water *eating away* rock. But nouns like *bed, fence,* and *idea* are not likely subjects for *eat.* Sometimes, however, in haste or carelessness, writers construct sentences in which inappropriate verbs create faulty predications.

In each of the following sentences, the subject and the verb do not fit together.

> The *selection* of the committee *was chosen* by the students.
>
> Many *settlers,* moving into a new part of the country, *expanded* into towns.
>
> Any *member* who failed to do his job on the ship *meant* danger for the whole crew.

Illogical combinations of subject and verb are particularly likely to occur when the verb is the linking verb *to be* in its various forms. Linking verbs equate what comes before the verb with what comes after it—the subject with the complement. They say that something equals something else. Thus they cannot be used to connect things that are not equal. *My dog is a beagle* will do, but not *My dog is a reason.*

> FAULTY   The first step in writing is spelling. [*Step* does not equal *spelling.*]
>
> REVISED   The first step in writing is learning to spell.
>
> FAULTY   His first trick was a pack of cards. [*Trick* does not equal *pack.*]
>
> REVISED   His first trick was one with a pack of cards.
>
> FAULTY   Schools are a serious quarrel today.

In the third example, *schools* clearly is not equivalent to *quarrel.* But revision is not really possible because the subject, *schools,* is itself so vague. Perhaps the writer meant something like *Increased taxes for schools cause serious quarrels today.*

A common kind of faulty equation occurs with predicates that begin with *is when* and *is where* and with the expression *the reason is because.* Definitions such as *Drunkenness is when you've had too much to drink* or *Subtraction is where you take one thing from another* are common in speech. Written English, however, ordinarily requires a noun or a word group functioning as a noun as both subject and complement in such definitions. Note the following sentences and their revisions.

FAULTY   A documentary is when a movie or a television drama analyzes news events or social conditions.

REVISED   A documentary is a movie or a television drama that analyzes news events or social conditions.

FAULTY   A hasty generalization is when you jump to conclusions.

REVISED   Hasty generalization involves jumping to conclusions.

               To make a hasty generalization is to jump to conclusions.

Sentences such as *The reason he didn't come was because he was sick* are also common in speech, but *reason is that* is strongly preferred at all levels of writing. *Because* means *for the reason that;* therefore, the expression *the reason is because* is redundant.

FAULTY   The reason he went to Chicago was because he wanted to visit Kareem.

REVISED   The reason he went to Chicago was that he wanted to visit Kareem.

               He went to Chicago because he wanted to visit Kareem.

EXERCISE 14a   Revise the following sentences to eliminate faulty predications.

1 People in the American sun belt, needing protection from intense summer heat, are many flat-roofed, Hispanic-styled houses.
2 Country music is sometimes broken dreams and lost loves.
3 A comic strip is when you have a series of drawings, usually with dialogue and stereotyped characters.
4 The reason some artists live in obscurity and die in poverty is because their work is boring as well as gaudy.
5 Mark Twain said that a camel was where a committee tried to plan a horse.

4b   **14b** **Do not mix constructions.**

A mixed construction is one in which a writer begins a sentence in one construction and then shifts to another. The result is a derailed sentence that must be put back on its track to be clear.

MIXED   With every effort the student made to explain his problem got him more confused.

Here the writer began with a prepositional phrase, but by the time he arrived at his verb *got* he is thinking of *every effort* as his subject. We can untangle the sentence either by giving *got* the subject *he;* or by dropping the preposition *with* and making *every effort* his subject.

REVISED   With every effort the student made to explain his problem he got more confused.

Every effort the student made got him more confused.

Beginnings such as *the fact that, there are,* and *it is* often cause needless complexity and lead to mixed or confusing sentences.

MIXED   The fact that Ben was a good student he had many offers for good jobs. [*The fact that* as a beginning requires something like *results* or *leads to* as a main verb in the sentence. But the writer has forgotten that as the sentence develops.]

REVISED   The fact that Ben was a good student resulted in his having many offers for good jobs.

Because Ben was a good student, he had many offers for good jobs.

EXERCISE 14b   Revise the following sentences to eliminate the mixed constructions.

1 Some of the teams they play, it would make their season a success by beating Notre Dame.
2 Although he read some books about sailing does not mean he is an expert sailor.
3 The culture described by Chicano poets, they often reflect their Aztec origins.
4 By installing smoke alarms in houses will reduce the loss of life and property.
5 The fact that floodwaters covered the valley many farmers lost their wheat crop.

EXERCISE 14a–b   Correct the following sentences to eliminate faulty predications and mixed constructions.

1 By developing solar energy, it could reduce the need for other kinds of energy.
2 As a center for the performing arts, most young actors and actresses yearn to go to New York.
3 Because he forgot the date was why he missed the meeting.
4 My first reaction to being in a large class frightened me.
5 The price of the car cost her over $5,000.
6 The reason for her resignation is because she has been offered a higher salary.
7 Funky music is where the jazz style is derived from work songs, the blues, and gospel tunes.

8 He suffered from asthma is the main reason he moved to the South-west.

9 Dandruff is when your scalp is dry and flakes off after you brush or comb your hair.

10 Having spent more than he expected for rent left him very little money for food.

REVIEW EXERCISE ON BASIC SENTENCE FAULTS (Sections 6–14) Indicate what strikes you as the principal error in each of the following sentences (faulty agreement, faulty reference, misplaced parts, etc.), and then revise the sentence.

1 Having been buried since the 14th century B.C., scientists found the tomb of Egyptian King Tutankhamen in 1922.

2 The letter was mailed an hour ago by the new clerk with the red sweater in the corner mailbox.

3 She likes Marie better than any of the other players.

4 Because Manhattan is an island, you have to take a bridge from New Jersey.

5 Millicent went to work in the theater after being graduated from college as an usherette.

6 When teenage children criticize their parents' friends, they usually feel uncomfortable.

7 In 1934 a well-known criminal wrote to Henry Ford saying he drove more Fords than others and stole them almost exclusively.

8 No matter how much he wanted to get there on time, and with several modes of transportation available.

9 Being too weak to answer the bell for the tenth round, the referee signaled the beaten challenger that the bout was over.

10 Most motorcycle riders consciously or unconsciously relate to their machines, they see them as extensions of their own personalities.

11 The years between 1865 and 1890 is the era of the cowboy, the trail town, and the great cattle drives.

12 The fairy tale is one of the early influences that helps children move from a fantasy world to reality.

13 In popular song lyrics an "outsider" is when a person is antisocial, unstable, arrogant, and often surviving through luck or violence.

14 Many housing projects for the elderly and low-income families are being built, which should emphasize open space and the human feelings of the occupants.

15 Since you can find great bargains at the flea market, I often go there.

16 They only bought a dog because their children wanted one.

17 Uncle Zed took our cat Daniel to a veterinarian that scratched his eye climbing a tree.

18 We intend to, if we can obtain tickets, see next year's Superbowl game.

19 In settling the New World, horses were first introduced by the Spaniards.

20 Children's toys are becoming safer, and some of it is a result of parents' complaints.

MANUSCRIPT MECHANICS
MS

It was very pleasant to me to get a letter from you the other day. Perhaps I should have found it pleasanter if I had been able to decipher it.

THOMAS BAILEY ALDRICH

M any practices of written English are merely conventions. Logic does not justify them; they represent standard ways of doing things. The mechanics of manuscript form, of writing numbers and abbreviations, of word division (syllabication) are such conventions. We observe them chiefly because readers expect writers to observe them. To be ignorant of these conventions or to violate them is not to commit a cardinal sin—it is only to be a nuisance to readers, who expect that any writer seeking their attention will have the graciousness to do the little things properly.

15 MANUSCRIPT FORM **MS**

15a Use suitable materials for your manuscripts.

1 Paper. Your instructor will probably require you to use standard theme paper (8½ by 11 inches) with lines about a half inch apart. Unless specifically told to, do not use narrow-lined notebook paper for themes. If you typewrite your manuscript, use either regular typewriter paper or the unruled side of theme paper. Do not use onionskin paper.

2 Typewriter. Use a black ribbon and keep the keys clean.

3 Pen and ink. Write on only one side of the paper. Use a good pen and black or blue-black ink. Do not write in pencil.

15b Make sure your manuscripts are legible.

1 Typewritten manuscripts. Use double spacing. Leave one space between words and two spaces between sentences.

2 Handwritten manuscripts. Provide adequate spacing between words and between lines. Avoid unnecessary breaks between letters and syllables at the ends of lines. Form all letters distinctly, with clear and conspicuous capitals. Cross all *t*'s. Dot all *i*'s with dots, not with decorative circles or other designs. Avoid artistic flourishes. If your handwriting tends to be large and sprawling or small and cramped or precariously tipped to right or left, make a conscious effort to improve it.

15c   Keep your manuscripts physically uniform and orderly.

1   Margins. Leave a uniform one-and-a-half-inch margin at the top and at the left side of each page and about one inch at the right side and bottom. Resist the temptation to crowd words in at the right or bottom of the page.

2   Title. Center the title about two inches from the top of the page, or on the first line of a handwritten paper. Leave a blank line between the title and the first paragraph. Capitalize the entire title, or if your instructor prefers, capitalize the first word and all other words in the title except the articles, *a, an, the,* and short prepositions or conjunctions. Do not underline the title or put it in quotation marks unless it is an actual quotation. Use no punctuation after titles except when a question mark or exclamation point is required. Do not repeat the title after the first page.

3   Indenting. Indent the first line of each paragraph about an inch, or five spaces on the typewriter. Indent lines of poetry one inch from the regular margin, or center them on the page. If you are typewriting, use single spacing for poetry you are quoting.

4   Paging. Number all pages, after the first, in the upper right-hand corner. Use Arabic numerals (2, 3, 4, etc.).

5   Endorsement. The endorsement usually appears on the outside sheet of the folded composition and includes your name, the course, and the date, plus any other information required by your instructor. Below is a specimen:

Fold here ⟶ | John Doe
English 101, Section A
October 18, 1981
Instructor: Mr. Brown
Class Paper 2

15d   Carefully proofread your manuscripts before submitting them.

Give every manuscript a close, critical reading before turning it in. Allow a cooling-off period between composition and proofreading. If you know you are poor in spelling, punctuation, or some other skill,

15d

give your paper a separate reading for each kind of error. If your proofreading reveals a great many errors, recopy your composition. When recopying is not necessary, make specific changes as follows:

1   If you want to delete words, draw a horizontal line through them. Do not use a series of parentheses to cancel words.

2   If you want to begin a new paragraph within an existing paragraph, put the sign ¶ or *Par.* before the sentence that is to begin the new paragraph. When you want to remove a paragraph division, write *No* ¶ or *No Par.* in the margin.

3   If you want to make a brief insertion, write the new material above the line and indicate the point of insertion by placing a caret (∧) below the line.

15e

15e   **After your instructor has returned a manuscript, make the necessary corrections and submit it again.**

Correcting or rewriting your papers is invaluable practice. If your instructor indicates errors in your writing by using numbers or correction symbols that refer to specific sections of this handbook, study these sections before making revisions. Note that your instructor may not indicate all errors. Try to eliminate all faults before returning your corrected paper. Your instructor may want you to make corrections directly on your paper, particularly when these corrections involve grammar, punctuation, and mechanics. Or he or she may suggest that you try reworking a single paragraph or an entire brief paper.

On page 109 is an example of a paragraph marked by an instructor who has used the abbreviations and symbols listed on the front inside cover pages. The instructor asked the class to respond to the assertion that Freshman Composition should be a required course. Below it is the same paragraph after it has been corrected and revised by a student. Notice that the student has underlined those words and instructions that have been rewritten so that the instructor may easily check the accuracy of the corrections. (On pages 220–221 in Section **31**, "The Whole Composition," is an example of an essay that has been marked with the numbers that appear on the back endpapers of the handbook.)

16

16   NUMBERS **NOS**

Conventions governing the choice between spelling out numbers and using figures vary with the kind of writing. The more scientific or technical the writing, the greater the use of figures as opposed to spelled-out numbers. Most writing intended for the general reader

A paragraph marked with correction symbols

Glos

Freshman Composition should be required of (each and every) student.

Dir

Shift (I) know that in (today's modern society) (I) will need to be able to write

NOS *AB*

to get a good job. [(You) would think that after (4 (yrs.) of high school

awk

English] students would be able to write. But even students who (receive)

T

EX

good grades in high school have trouble (writing out) their ideas and

Shift

SUB feelings. In college there are many other courses that (we) will be re-

Frag quired to write in. [For example an essay exam in history.] So English

Cap (composition will help (me) pass these other courses. My English teachers

EX

always said that writing was (something) which could be learned by anyone

CS

who really worked at it. [I hope this is true. I think I have supported *Shift*

SP

my (arguement) in this paragraph.

The same paragraph rewritten/revised

Freshman Composition should be required of <u>all</u> students. <u>Today</u>
<u>a person needs to be able to write to get a good job.</u> <u>Although</u>
<u>students should be able to write after completing four years of high</u>
<u>school English</u>, even students who <u>received</u> good grades in high school
have trouble <u>expressing</u> their ideas and feelings <u>in writing</u>. In
college there are many other courses, <u>such as history, in which</u>
<u>students will be required to write essay exams</u>. English Composition
will help <u>them</u> pass these courses. My English teachers always said
that writing was <u>a skill that</u> could be learned by anyone who really
worked at it. <u>The experience of many students has proven this true</u>.
<u>These reasons support the argument that composition should be a re-</u>
<u>quired course.</u>

spells out numbers that can be written in two words or less except for special kinds of numbers such as those listed in 16b and 16c below. This is particularly true if the subject requires the use of only a few numbers. If a subject requires the extensive use of numbers, it will ordinarily be clearer if figures are used throughout. In any case, you should be consistent in your use of figures or spelled-out numbers in a given piece of writing. The following guidelines give common conventions for most general writing.

16a

16a   In nonscientific writing spell out numbers or amounts less than one hundred; use figures for other numbers or amounts.

He spent ninety-seven dollars for a camera.

Miriam is twenty-two years old.

The boy saved $4.53.

On their vacation they drove 2,468 miles.

16b

16b   Use figures for dates and addresses.

Dates	*Addresses*	
May 4, 1914	13 Milford Avenue	
July 2, 1847	57 East 121st Street	
1862–1924	Route 1 P.O. Box 353	Apartment 6A
17 B.C. to A.D. 21	Grinnell, Iowa 50122	

The ordinal numbers (first, third, ninth) or the forms 1st, 3rd, 9th may be used in dates if the year is not given: March 1, March first, March 1st.

In formal invitations dates are usually written out: Sunday, September ninth, nineteen hundred and eighty-one. (See **20i** for the punctuation of dates and addresses.)

16c

16c   Ordinarily, use figures for the following:

decimals	8.72 13.27
percentages	72% or 72 percent
mixed numbers and fractions	$27\frac{1}{2}$ $19\frac{1}{4}$
scores and statistics	score of 35–10 a vote of 86–53
identification numbers	Channel 7 Flight number 523
volume, chapter, and page numbers	Volume V, Chapter 7, page 518
act, scene, and line numbers	Act II, scene 4, lines 18–47
figures followed by symbols or abbreviations	$18'' \times 23''$ $6' \times 9'$
	5 cu. ft. 72F 31C 55 mph.
exact amounts of money	$8.93 $29.95 53¢
times	4:30 P.M. 5:45 A.M.
	But *half past four, quarter of six, seven o'clock*

16d Except in legal or commercial writing, do not repeat in parentheses a number that has been spelled out.

COMMERCIAL   The original order was for fifty (50) pumps.

STANDARD   Carol has trained four sopranos in four years.

16e Spell out numbers that occur at the beginning of a sentence.

INAPPROPRIATE   217 bales of hay were lost in the fire.

REVISED   Two hundred seventeen bales of hay were lost in the fire.

If necessary, recast a sentence to eliminate numerals at the beginning.

INAPPROPRIATE   2,655 entries were received in the puzzle contest.

REVISED   In the puzzle contest 2,655 entries were received.

EXERCISE 16a–e   In the following sentences, make any necessary corrections in the use of numbers.

1 John F. Kennedy was inaugurated on January 20th, 1961, at the age of 44.
2 The used stereo receiver was guaranteed for only ninety (90) days.
3 2 pounds of Kentucky bluegrass seed will sow 1,000 square feet of soil.
4 The satellite model measured eleven and nineteen-hundredths inches in circumference.
5 The bus left Mayfield at two-thirty P.M.
6 My breakfast at Pedro's Taco House cost $.95.
7 Labor Day is the 1st Monday in September.
8 There is a twenty percent chance of rain today.
9 Each of us consumers, on the average, uses one hundred and twenty-eight pounds of sugar a year.
10 Channel seven provides continuous television news coverage.

17   ABBREVIATIONS **AB**

With a few standard exceptions, abbreviations are avoided in ordinary writing. The following sections describe standard exceptions, as well as some forms that should not be used.

17a

17a The following abbreviations are appropriate in both formal and informal writing.

1 Titles before proper nouns. Use such abbreviations as *Mr., Mrs., Ms., Dr.* only when the surname is given: *Dr. Hart* or *Dr. F. D. Hart.*

INAPPROPRIATE	He has gone to consult the Dr.
REVISED	He has gone to consult Dr. Hart (*or* the doctor).

Use *St.* (Saint) with a Christian name: *St. James, St. Theresa.*

Use abbreviations such as *Hon., Rev., Prof., Sen.* only when both the surname and given name or initials are given: *The Hon. O. P. Jones,* but not *Hon. Jones.* In more formal usage, spell out these titles and use *The* before *Honorable* and *Reverend.*

INFORMAL	Rev. W. C. Case delivered the sermon.
FORMAL	The Reverend W. C. Case delivered the sermon.

2 Titles after proper names. Use the following abbreviations only when a name is given: *Jr., Sr., Esq., M.D., D.D., LL.D., Ph.D.* You may, however, use academic titles by themselves.

John Nash, Jr., received an M.A.

F. D. Hart, M.D., is now studying for his J.D.

3 Abbreviations with dates and numerals. Use the following abbreviations only when specific dates and numerals are given: B.C.; A.D.; A.M. or a.m.; P.M. or p.m.; No. or no.; $.

4 Latin abbreviations. Latin abbreviations such as *i.e.* (that is), *e.g.* (for example), *etc.* (and so forth) are common in most writing. In formal writing the English equivalent is increasingly used. Do not use *etc.* as a catch-all. It is meaningless unless the extension of ideas it implies is unmistakably clear. Do not write *and etc.;* the *and* becomes redundant.

CLEAR	The citrus fruits—oranges, lemons, etc.—are rich in Vitamin C. [The reader has no difficulty in mentally listing the other citrus fruits.]
INEFFECTIVE	We swam, fished, etc. [The reader has no clues to the implied ideas.]
REVISED	We swam, fished, rode horses, and danced.

5 The names of agencies, organizations, corporations, and people ordinarily referred to by their initials.

Agencies	IRS, FBI, SEC
Organizations	AMA, YWCA, NOW
Corporations	NBC, IBM
People	JFK, FDR

If the name of an organization occurs frequently in a paper or article but is likely to be unfamiliar to readers, it should be spelled out in its first use and the abbreviation given in parentheses. Thereafter the abbreviation may be used: Zimbabwe African National Union (ZANU).

17b Spell out personal names; the names of countries and states; the names of days, months, and holidays; and the names of courses of instruction.

INAPPROPRIATE	Eliz., a student from Eng. who joined our bio class last Wed., expects to go home for Xmas.
REVISED	Elizabeth, a student from England who joined our biology class last Wednesday, expects to go home for Christmas.

The District of Columbia is spelled out when it is used alone but abbreviated, D.C., when it follows the city name, Washington. The United States and the Soviet Union are commonly abbreviated as the USA (or U.S.A.) or the US, and as the USSR (or U.S.S.R.)

17c Spell out the words *street, avenue, company,* and references to a subject, volume, chapter, or page, except in special contexts such as addresses and footnotes.

INAPPROPRIATE	The Perry Coal Co. has an office at Third Ave. and Mott St.
REVISED	The Perry Coal Company has an office at Third Avenue and Mott Street.
INAPPROPRIATE	The p.e. class is reading ch. 3 of the textbook.
REVISED	The physical education class is reading the third chapter (*or* Chapter 3) of the textbook.

Use such abbreviations as Bros., Inc., Co., and the ampersand (& for *and*) only in the names of firms where they are used in the official titles.

Barnes & Noble, Inc.
Sears, Roebuck and Co.

17c

EXERCISE 17a–c   In the following sentences correct all faulty abbreviations.

1 Mister Whitefeather is an artist who paints wildlife in the Cherokee Nat'l. Forest near the border of Tenn. and N. Carolina.

2 He enrolled in the U. of Me. because he wanted to study the culture of northern N. England.

3 The prof. in my comp. class explained how to write a letter of application.

4 The urban renewal project will cover the area between Main St. and Wisc. Ave.

5 Doctor Wilenski told the patient to take a tsp. of cough syrup every six hrs.

6 As we walked along Bourbon St. in N. Orleans we heard a Dixieland band playing "When the Sts. Go Marching In."

7 Gary & Jon Burns are bros. who own a business called Burns Bros. Car Sales.

8 Many writers, e.g. Benj. Franklin and Emma Goldman, have pointed out the dangers of the individual's being submerged in a mass society.

9 Wm. Shakespeare began writing plays during the reign of Queen Eliz. I of Eng.

10 Rev. Dean's sermons reflect her training in phil. and ancient hist.

18

18   SYLLABICATION **SYL**

When you find that you can write only part of a word at the end of a line and must complete the word on the next line, divide the word between syllables and use a hyphen to indicate the break. Always place the hyphen at the end of the line after the first part of a divided word, not at the beginning of the next line on which you complete the word.

When you are in doubt about the syllabication of a word, consult a good dictionary. Desk dictionaries normally use dots to divide words between syllables: *bank·rupt, col·lec·tive, ma·lig·nant, punc·ture.* Note that not every syllable marks an appropriate point at which to divide a word at the end of a line. (See **18b** and **18c.**)

18a

18a   Never divide words of one syllable.

WRONG   thr-ee, cl-own, yearn-ed, plough-ed
REVISED   three, clown, yearned, ploughed

18b

18b   Never divide a word so that a single letter stands alone on a line.

WRONG   wear-y, e-rupt, a-way, o-val
REVISED   weary, erupt, away, oval

18c   When dividing a compound word that already contains a hyphen, make the break where the hyphen occurs.

18c

AWKWARD   pre-Shake-spearean, well-in-formed, Pan-Amer-ican

REVISED   pre-Shakespearean, well-informed, Pan-American

EXERCISE 18a–c   Which of the following words may be divided at the end of a line? Indicate permissible breaks with a hyphen. Refer to your dictionary if you are doubtful.

drowned	enough	walked
swimmer	twelve	automobile
learned	through	exercise
abrupt	acute	open
envelope	ex-President	preeminent

REVIEW EXERCISE ON MANUSCRIPT MECHANICS (Sections 15–18)   Correct the errors in the following sentences.

1 Some stores add a service charge to bills that are not paid within thirty (30) days.
2 On Thursdays Betsy's classes are finished by ten forty-five A.M.
3 The vice-pres. of the Student Council sometimes acts as secy. of the mtgs.
4 The new Center of African Studies is located at the corner of Maple and Main Sts.
5 2 box tops must accompany every request for a free recipe booklet.
6 Paperback books, which once sold for a quarter, now cost as much as six dollars and ninety-five cents.
7 The Campus Theater will show a Bogart film on the 1st. Mon. of every mo.
8 Tourists in N.Y.C. often go to see the Empire State Bldg.
9 Most people voted to extend suffrage to 18 yr. olds.
10 A chimney sweep must have a variety of shovels, buckets, flue brushes, etc.
11 The Moore Mfg. Co. advertised a five percent discount on household appliances.
12 Heavyweight boxers must weigh over 175 lbs.
13 People fishing on Lake Mendota must throw back all perch measuring under five in.
14 Rev. Winters performed the marriage ceremony at the Lutheran Ch.
15 Mr. & Mrs. Hone entered their 3 yr. old filly in the race.

PUNCTUATION
P

Punctuation is far from being a mere mechanical device. It is mechanical as a matter of course, like word-spacing or the use of initial capitals; but punctuation is much more than that. It is an integral part of written composition.

GEORGE SUMMEY, JR.

When we speak, we use pauses and gestures to emphasize meaning, and we vary the tempo, stress, and pitch of our voices to mark the beginning and end of units of thought. In other words, we "punctuate" our speech. We punctuate writing for the same purposes, drawing on a whole set of conventional devices developed to give the reader clues to what we are trying to communicate.

The first of these devices is **spacing:** that is, closing up or enlarging the space between letters or words. For example, we do not runwordstogetherthisway. Instead, we identify a word as a word by setting if off from its neighbors. Spacing is the most basic of all punctuating devices. We use spacing also to set off paragraphs, to list items as in an outline, to mark lines of poetry, and the like.

But spacing, of course, is not the only punctuation we need. What, for example, can you understand from this string of words:

> yes madam jones was heard to say to the owl like old dowager without a doubt the taming of the shrew by shakespeare would be a most appropriate new years present for your husband

To make this passage intelligible, we need to add two other kinds of punctuation: (1) changes in the size and design of letters, namely, **capitals** and **italics;** and (2) marks or points, namely, **periods, commas, quotation marks, apostrophes,** and other special signs.

> "Yes, Madam," Jones was heard to say to the owl-like old dowager, "without a doubt, *The Taming of the Shrew* by Shakespeare would be a most appropriate New Year's present for your husband."

The example shows four functions of punctuation:

1 End punctuation. Capitals, periods, question marks, and exclamation points indicate sentence beginnings and endings.

2 Internal punctuation. Commas, semicolons, colons, dashes, and parentheses within sentences show the relationship of each word or group of words to the rest of the sentence.

3 Direct-quotation punctuation. Quotation marks and brackets indicate speakers and changes of speaker.

4 Word punctuation. Capitals, italics, quotation marks, apostrophes, and hyphens indicate words that have a special character or use.

In questions of punctuation there is often no absolute standard, no authoritative convention to which you can turn for a "correct" answer. But two general rules serve as reliable guides:

1 Punctuation is a part of meaning, not a substitute for clear and orderly sentence structure. Before you can punctuate a sentence properly, you must construct it properly. No number of commas, semicolons, and dashes can rescue a poorly written sentence.

2 Observe conventional practice in punctuation. Though many of the rules are not hard and fast, still there is a community of agreement about punctuating sentences. Learning and applying the punctuation rules that follow will help you observe these conventions.

19 END PUNCTUATION **END P**

Periods, question marks, and exclamation points signal the end of a sentence. Use a period after plain statements or commands; use a question mark after questions; use an exclamation point after strongly emotional expressions. Ordinarily, the character of the sentence dictates the proper end punctuation. Occasionally, however, you must determine for yourself what you intend the meaning of a sentence to be. Notice the different intentions behind these three sentences:

He struck out with the bases loaded.
He struck out with the bases loaded?
He struck out with the bases loaded!

The Period .

19a Use a period to signal the end of a statement, a mild command, or an indirect question.

STATEMENT	She swam the mile with easy strokes.
COMMAND	Swim with easy strokes.
INDIRECT QUESTION	I asked her where she learned to swim with such easy strokes.

19b Use a period after an abbreviation.

Dr.   Mr.   Mrs.   Ms.   R.N.   C.P.A.   Sen.   B.A.

Omit the period after abbreviations that serve as names of organizations or government agencies (NEA, AFL, UNESCO, AMA, TVA).

If you are in doubt about whether to use periods in an abbreviation, consult a good dictionary for the standard practice.

The Question Mark ?

19c Use a question mark after a direct question.

Direct questions often begin with an interrogative pronoun or adverb *(who, when, what, etc.),* and usually have an inverted word order, with the verb before the subject.

> When did you study chemistry?
> Do you ever wonder what your future will be?
> You want to make a good impression, don't you?

19d Use a question mark inside parentheses (?) to indicate doubt or uncertainty about the correctness of a statement.

The device shows that, even after research, you could not establish the accuracy of a fact. It does not serve as a substitute for checking facts.

> John Pomfret, an English poet, was born in 1667 (?) and died in 1702.

Rather than using (?), you may simply use *about:*

> John Pomfret, an English poet, was born about 1667 and died in 1702.

Do not use this mark as a form of sarcasm:

> It was a very charming (?) play.

19e Do not use a question mark after an indirect question.

An **indirect question** is a statement implying a question but not actually asking one. Though the idea expressed is interrogative, the actual phrasing is not.

> They asked me whether I had studied chemistry in high school.
> He asked me whether I wished to make a good impression.
> I wonder what my future will be.

A polite request phrased as a direct question is often followed by a period rather than a question mark.

> Will you please return this book as soon as possible.
> May we hear from you at your earliest convenience.

The Exclamation Point !

19f Use the exclamation point after an interjection or after a statement that is genuinely emphatic or exclamatory.

Fire! Help!
What a vicious war!
The examination has been stolen!

19g Do not overuse the exclamation point.

Used sparingly, the exclamation point gives real emphasis to individual statements. Overused, it either deadens the emphasis or introduces an almost hysterical tone in your writing.

War is hell! Think of what it does to young men to have their futures interrupted and sometimes cut off completely! Think of what it does to their families! Think of what it does to the nation!

EXERCISE 19a–g Supply the appropriate punctuation marks in each of the following sentences. If you feel that a choice of marks is possible, state why you chose the one you did.

1 Could you clarify that remark please
2 Every hotel guest should know where the fire exits are
3 Keep off the grass
4 He has an M A degree in horticulture and works for the U S D A
5 Those kids are hungry already
6 She asked whether our cat Daniel is a good mouser
7 A student group at M I T visited the Smithsonian Institution in Washington, D C
8 Will all passengers please collect their personal belongings before leaving the aircraft
9 Big John tooled his diesel van over to Pete's Diner and asked for the daily special of greasy pork chops and gravy
10 The management asks that people in the balcony refrain from throwing peanut shells on patrons in the lower seats
11 The real-estate investor bought a 450 ft lot on Rt 40
12 I wonder why Granny Hawks always describes anything she likes as "all wool and a yard wide"
13 Laurie has an A B degree and is studying for a Ph D at U C L A
14 The ship's captain ordered the crew to lower the lifeboats immediately
15 She asked the secretary whether there is a standard abbreviation for "chairperson"

20-24 INTERNAL PUNCTUATION **INT P**

End punctuation indicates whether a writer wants you to read a whole sentence as a question, a statement or an expression of emotion. Internal punctuation indicates the relationships and relative importance of elements within the sentence. Five punctuation marks are used for tnis purpose: commas, semicolons, colons, dashes, and parentheses.

The most important uses of these marks, like those of end punctuation, recur again and again. And like all uses of punctuation, they are a vital way of making the meaning of your sentences clear. In studying the following rules, notice not only how each mark is used but also how it contributes to the total meaning of the sentence.

20

20a

20 THE COMMA **,**

20a **Use a comma to separate main clauses joined by a coordinating conjunction.**

The coordinating conjunctions are *and, but, or, nor, for, so,* and *yet.* When any one of these conjunctions is used to connect main clauses, it is always preceded by a comma.

The Mayans of early Mexico were expert weavers, and some of their cotton textiles were mistaken for silk by Spanish explorers.

Emerson said that youthful idealism is often misdirected and even comic, but sometimes young people see faults in society that are hidden from older people.

The backpackers could follow the river valley, or they could risk finding a trail through the mountains.

He lacks the sensitivity of an artist, nor does he have the patience of a scientist.

In the spring thousands of hawks return north after wintering in the United States, for the Canadian forests are their hunting and nesting grounds.

Thrifty housekeepers thaw frozen foods before cooking them, so they can save on utility bills.

Engineers' squares should be completely accurate, yet they tend to get out of line and fail to measure a perfect 90 degrees.

There are, however, two exceptions.

1   Some writers omit the comma before the coordinating conjunction when one or both of the main clauses are very short: *Give a child enough rope and he'll trip you up.* But there is nothing wrong with a comma in such sentences, and since the comma is sometimes necessary for clarity, it is advisable simply to establish the habit of using it regularly.

2   When one or both of the main clauses joined by a coordinating conjunction are long or internally punctuated, use a semicolon before the coordinating conjunction.

> The Canadian Mounted Police were established in the 1870's to assure peaceful settlement of the northwest wilderness; and they became symbols of political and social order.
>
> The Mounties, dressed in red tunics and riding well-trained horses, were a familiar sight on the Canadian frontier; but few people in the United States saw Mounties except in the movies.

EXERCISE 20a   In the following sentences, place a comma before each coordinating conjunction that joins main clauses.

1   In 1215 the Magna Carta became the law of England and it remains the basis for English civil liberties.
2   During the evening, storm clouds gathered overhead yet no rain fell.
3   I have a raspberry seed stuck between two teeth but I think a toothpick will dislodge it.
4   Helicopters are not relatively fast nor are they suited for long-distance travel.
5   The light wave is the transmission medium of the future for it has great message-carrying capacity because it uses glass fibers instead of copper wires.
6   We can walk to the stadium and arrive late for the game or we can take a taxi and see the kickoff.
7   Many young athletes call themselves joggers but others think of them as runners.
8   Solar energy is a promising field of research and many people are discovering its good employment prospects.
9   Dolphins have unusually good memories so they can be trained to perform amazing tricks.
10   The United States has vast reserves of coal and much of it may be converted into methane gas for energy.

20b   Use a comma to separate introductory phrases and clauses from a main clause.

Introductory phrases and clauses may be adverbial, modifying the verb in the main clause or the whole main clause; or they may serve as adjectives, modifying the subject of the main clause. Whatever their function, they should always be separated from the main clause by a comma unless they are very short and there is no possibility of misreading.

INTRODUCTORY PREPOSITIONAL PHRASES

According to legend, Hercules had enormous strength.
After his long exile to France, Charles II returned to England in 1660.
Like any man of sense and good feeling, I abominate work.
ALDOUS HUXLEY

INTRODUCTORY VERBAL PHRASES

To succeed as a long-distance runner, a person must have strong legs.
Announcing a recess, the judge retired to his chambers.
Exhausted by her effort, the swimmer fell back into the pool.
To be quite honest about it, that dog has been known to climb trees.

INTRODUCTORY CLAUSES

As soon as she had finished studying, she left the library.

If your job is to write every day, you learn to do it like every other job.
WILLIAM ZINSSER

Whenever I hear anyone arguing for slavery, I feel a strong impulse to see it tried on him personally. ABRAHAM LINCOLN

Do not confuse verbal modifiers with verbals used as subjects.

VERBAL MODIFIER	*Having been an arbitrator between labor and management for a decade,* he felt confident in tackling one more labor dispute.
VERBAL AS SUBJECT	*Having been an arbitrator between labor and management for a decade* made him feel confident in tackling one more labor dispute.

The comma is frequently omitted after very short introductory clauses or phrases. However, even when the introductory clause or phrase is very short, a comma is necessary if its omission can cause misreading.

CLEAR	When he arrived she was taking the cat out of the piano.
	After his defeat he retired from public life.
CONFUSING	When he returned home was not what it used to be.
	After dark fireflies came in large numbers.

EXERCISE 20b   In the following sentences, insert commas after introductory elements whenever they are required.

1 According to Charlie Brown's philosophy you should dread only one day at a time.
2 Predicting the end of the world the self-styled prophet retired to a mountain cave.
3 To maintain our economic strength we must produce goods that can compete with products from other industrialized societies.
4 In winter storms are frequent in the Atlantic.
5 When people talk about ragtime they usually mean Afro-American folk music improvised on or composed for the piano.
6 As a symbol for modern America the novelist Ken Kesey chose a cuckoo's nest, or mental hospital.
7 To produce exciting or novel recordings rock groups are often dependent on electronic effects created in the sound studio.
8 In the American imagination the astronauts are a modern version of such early heroes as the explorers, pathfinders, and scouts.
9 Since we wanted to have a scenic vacation we traveled by boat from Vancouver through the inland waterways to Alaska.
10 Because of the fog all planes were grounded at the airport.

20c   Use commas to set off nonrestrictive elements. Do not set off restrictive elements.

A **restrictive element**—which may be a clause, a phrase, or a word— is an essential modifier. It defines, limits, or identifies in some way the meaning of whatever it modifies. If it is removed from the sentence, the meaning is changed in some basic way. A **nonrestrictive element** may be interesting, but it is incidental to the basic meaning of the sentence.

An illustration will help make the difference clear.

RESTRICTIVE   A man *who is honest* will succeed.
NONRESTRICTIVE   Jacob North, who is honest, will succeed.

In the first sentence the clause *who is honest* identifies the kind of man who will succeed; it restricts the subject of *will succeed* to men *who are honest* as opposed to men *who are not honest.* In other words, the clause is restrictive. It is thus *not* set off with commas. In the second sentence, however, the proper noun *Jacob North* identifies or designates the particular man who *will succeed;* the fact that Jacob North *is honest* is merely amplifying information about a person already sufficiently identified. The clause is nonrestrictive. It *is* set off with commas.

In the illustration just discussed, the meaning is such that there is no question that the clause *who is honest* is restrictive in one sentence and not restrictive in the other. But sometimes whether a modifying element is restrictive or nonrestrictive depends upon your meaning. In such instances you must decide what you mean. Setting off the modifier or not setting it off is your only way of making your meaning clearer to your reader.

The house, built by my grandfather, faced the mountain. [The phrase *built by my grandfather* is nonrestrictive and is thus set off by commas.]

The house built by my grandfather faced the mountain, and the house built by my father stood only a hundred yards away. [In this compound sentence, the two phrases beginning with *built* limit and define the particular houses, distinguishing them from each other.]

Texans, who have oil wells, can afford high prices. [All Texans have oil wells and can afford high prices.]

Texans who have oil wells can afford high prices. [Some Texans have oil wells; only they can afford high prices.]

Always use *two* commas to set off a nonrestrictive element unless it begins or ends the sentence.

NOT   The old mare, half-blind and lame was hardly able to stand in the traces.

BUT   The old mare, half-blind and lame, was hardly able to stand in the traces.

         Half-blind and lame, the old mare was hardly able to stand in the traces.

1   Set off nonrestrictive clauses and phrases with commas. Do not set off restrictive clauses and phrases.

NONRESTRICTIVE CLAUSE   Elephants use their tusks, *which sometimes grow to ten feet or longer,* to fight, dig, or carry loads.

RESTRICTIVE CLAUSE   Elephants *that are sick or dying* often seek rivers or other water sources.

NONRESTRICTIVE CLAUSE   Akron, Iowa, *where my father grew up,* has a population of only 1242.

RESTRICTIVE CLAUSE   The town *where my father grew up* has a population of only 1242.

NONRESTRICTIVE PHRASE   My father, *on time for a change,* greeted us enthusiastically. [Prepositional]

RESTRICTIVE PHRASES   From the window *on the top floor* we could see the ships *in the harbor.* [Prepositional]

NONRESTRICTIVE PHRASES   Melinda, *determined to save enough money to buy a new car,* stayed home during her vacation. [Participial]

RESTRICTIVE PHRASES   Many houses *constructed with large windows exposed to the north* need a great deal of fuel. [Participial]

NONRESTRICTIVE PHRASES	The blizzard, *driving the heavy snow into deep drifts across the roads,* continued for twenty-seven hours. [Participial and prepositional]
RESTRICTIVE PHRASES	The economics text *lying on the table* was dog-eared. [Participial]

2   Set off nonrestrictive appositives with commas. Do not set off restrictive appositives. An appositive is a noun or a group of words used as a noun that describes or renames another noun, ordinarily the noun that comes immediately before it. Like clauses and phrases, appositives may be either restrictive or nonrestrictive, though appositives of more than one or two words are usually nonrestrictive and therefore set off by commas.

NONRESTRICTIVE APPOSITIVES

Davy Crockett, *the most famous man at the Alamo,* was a former Indian fighter.

No treatment, *not even hypnosis or acupuncture,* helped them stop smoking.

The whale, *a cold-water-dwelling mammal,* is protected by a thick layer of blubber.

"Hello, Mitty. We're having the devil's own time with McMillan, *the millionaire banker and close personal friend of Roosevelt."*   JAMES THURBER

Restrictive appositives limit, define, or designate the noun that they follow in such a way that their absence from the sentence would change its essential meaning. They are often, though by no means always, proper names following a more general noun or identifying phrase.

RESTRICTIVE APPOSITIVES

Robert Frost's poem *"Stopping by Woods on a Snowy Evening"* is one of his best-known poems.

The poet *Bryant* was a leader in New York literary circles.

Do you mean Napoli *the grocer* or Napoli *the doctor?*

The slang term *shrink* is often applied to psychiatrists.

The removal of the restrictive appositives from these sentences would leave such sentences as *Robert Frost's poem is one of his best-known poems* and *Do you mean Napoli or Napoli?*

EXERCISE 20c   In the following sentences, insert commas to set off nonrestrictive elements. Indicate which sentences are correct as written.

  1 The expression "do your thing" was used by Emerson in the 1841 edition of his essay "Self-Reliance."

2 During the days of 19th century "Yellow Journalism," reporters who were unscrupulous created sensational events and paid witnesses to confirm them.

3 Pope John Paul II leader of the world's 563 million Catholics spoke strongly against political forces that degrade the poor.

4 Little Wolf a chief of the Cheyennes led a hunting party into the Powder River country.

5 Recent studies made by international economists predict that the gap between the wealthiest and poorest nations will continue to widen.

6 The heavy rain causing huge puddles on the streets delayed traffic.

7 By the year 2000, Mexico City which attracts many rural residents will have a population of thirty million.

8 In his journal, the voyager Christopher Columbus lamented that there were no nightingales in the New World.

9 Betsy eager to graduate and find a job enrolled in summer classes.

10 In the election of 1896, William McKinley the Governor of Ohio defeated William Jennings Bryan the silver-tongued orator from Nebraska.

20d Use a comma to set off adverb phrases and clauses following the main clause and explaining, amplifying, or offering a contrast to it. Do not set off such clauses if they are closely related to the main clause.

Adverbial phrases and clauses usually *restrict* the meaning of the main clauses to which they are joined. They are therefore essential to the meaning of the main clause and are not set off by a comma when they follow the main clause. When they merely introduce additional *non-restrictive* information, however, a comma is used to indicate that they are not essential to the meaning. The writer must be guided by the logic of his sentence and the meaning he intends. Note the following:

> You will not pass the examination unless you study carefully.
> You did not pass the examination, although I am sure you studied carefully.

The first of the examples sets up *unless you study carefully* as the condition for passing the examination. In the second, the main clause makes an unqualified statement of fact; the *although* clause adds some sympathy, but it doesn't qualify the fact of the main clause.

> Jane loves John because he tolerates her petty moodiness.
> Jane knows that she loves John, because she can tolerate his petty moodiness.

The first of the foregoing examples states that John's tolerance is an essential condition of Jane's love for him. In the second, the *because* clause merely introduces explanatory information about how Jane knows that she loves John.

Note that in some constructions a comma or the lack of one determines whether the reader will understand a phrase or a clause as a modifier of a final noun in the main clause or as an adverbial modifier.

> He has visited all the small towns in Pennsylvania.
> He has visited *all* the small towns, in Pennsylvania, in Ohio, in almost every state of the union.

In the first of these examples, *in Pennsylvania* restricts the location of the small towns and is an adjectival modifier of *towns*. In the second, however, the *in* phrase is additional information amplifying the assertion of the main clause but not essential to it.

EXERCISE 20d In the following sentences, insert commas wherever they are necessary to set off adverbial clauses or phrases.

1 We can get to the wedding on time if we hurry.
2 The hidden gold remains undiscovered since nobody can decipher the pirates' coded map.
3 We won't go out in this blizzard unless one of our neighbors needs help.
4 The climbers finally reached the top of Mt. Fuji although others had climbed to the summit before them.
5 Elisa went to the library after finishing her classes.

20e Use commas to set off all absolute phrases.

Absolute phrases consist of a noun or a pronoun followed by a present or past participle. They modify the entire main clause in which they stand rather than any particular word or words in that clause. They are always nonrestrictive, supplying amplifying or explanatory detail rather than essential information. Thus they should always be set off by commas whether they appear at the beginning or end of a sentence or within it.

> He was stretched out on his reclining chair in the full sun, *his eyes covered, his head thrown back, his arms spread wide.*
> *Other things being equal,* short familiar words are better than long unfamiliar words.
> She was waiting for us, *her figure defined by the light from the half-open door.*
> The mastiff, *teeth bared, ears standing erect, body tensed,* refused to give ground.

EXERCISE 20e Insert commas in the following sentences to mark off absolute phrases.

1 Their faces lined with exhaustion the bicycle racers crossed the finish line.
2 The seagulls soared over the bay their wings spread against the wind.
3 All things considered gardening is a profitable hobby.
4 The bulldog his mouth watering with anticipation waited for the mail carrier to arrive.
5 Darkness rapidly approaching the children returned to their homes.

20f Use commas to set off elements that slightly interrupt the structure of a sentence.

Words, phrases, and clauses that slightly interrupt the structure of a sentence are often called *parenthetical elements*. Although such elements may add to the meaning of the sentence or serve to relate the sentence in which they stand to a preceding sentence or idea, they are not essential to its grammatical structure. Such elements include words of direct address, mild interjections, the words *yes* and *no*, transitional words and expressions, and phrases expressing contrast.

DIRECT ADDRESS	Can you show me, *Kathy,* how to punctuate this sentence?
	Will you speak a little louder, *George?*
MILD INTERJECTIONS	*Well,* no one can do more than his best.
	Oh, I never get A's—only C's and more C's.
TRANSITIONAL WORDS AND PHRASES	Sales taxes, *moreover,* hurt poor people severely.
	Christians, *on the other hand,* are opposed to violence.
	The judge ruled, *nevertheless,* that damages must be paid.
	The result, *in short,* was a complete breakdown of discipline.
CONTRASTED ELEMENTS	He had intended to write 1868, *not 1968.*
	Tractors, *unlike horses,* require gasoline.
	Insecticides and garden sprays now available are effective, *yet safe.*

Note that other elements of a sentence will interrupt its structure and require commas when they are inserted out of their normal grammatical order. Compare the following:

My grandmother always told me that work never killed anyone.
Work, *my grandmother always told me,* never killed anyone.

The exhausted and thirsty construction workers welcomed the cold beer.

The construction workers, *exhausted and thirsty,* welcomed the cold beer.

Always use two commas to set off a parenthetical element unless it begins or ends a sentence.

NOT   She insisted, however that they leave before midnight.

NOT   She insisted however, that they leave before midnight.

BUT   She insisted, however, that they leave before midnight.

       She insisted that they leave before midnight, however.

EXERCISE 20f   Insert commas in the following sentences to set off parenthetical elements.

1 Sherlock Holmes to tell the truth was a very eccentric detective.

2 Well this is my bus stop, so I'll see you later Helen.

3 The main problem about exploring outer space Uncle Zed tells me is what people are going to do after they get there.

4 The traffic light was green officer when I drove through the intersection.

5 The Navaho tribe for instance are developing the energy resources on their reservations in the Southwest.

6 The world's poorer nations moreover must boost food production to sustain increasing numbers of urban industrial workers.

7 Excuse me sir but you are sitting on my hat.

8 Shrewd business management I think can yield profits even in bad times.

9 Peace in the Middle East according to some government experts is the key to solving American energy problems.

10 Radio unlike television cannot use cartoons and puppet shows to attract an audience of children.

20g   Use commas to separate the items in a series.

A series consists of three or more words, phrases, or clauses of equal grammatical rank. The items of such a series are said to be coordinate: they have approximately equal importance. Typical series take the form *a, b,* and *c,* or the form *a, b,* or *c.*

She talked *fluently, wittily,* and *penetratingly.* [Three adverbs]

Some newspapers report sports events in *sailing, cross-country running, swimming,* and *tennis,* as well as other sports. [Four nouns]

Only a generation ago, the Navaho were *horsemen, nomads, keepers of flocks, painters in sand, weavers of wool, artists in silver,* and *singers of the yei-bie-chai.* [Seven nouns, some modified by prepositional phrases]

EDWARD ABBEY

Her sails ripped, her engines dead, and *her rudder broken,* the sailing vessel drifted helplessly. [Three absolute phrases]

The city couldn't *issue birth certificates on time, pay overtime when it was due, maintain its automotive fleets, deliver asphalt to men filling potholes, submit claims for federal and state aid payments, supply diaper pins to obstetric wards,* or *hire key staff.* [Seven predicates, each consisting of a verb and its object]   CHARLES R. MORRIS

After the accident, the driver of the car had no idea of *who he was, where he came from,* or *how the accident happened.* [Three dependent clauses]

Some writers treat three or more short, closely related independent clauses not joined by coordinate conjunctions as a series, separating them by commas rather than semicolons.

Some of the people said the elephant had gone in one direction, some said he had gone in another, some professed not even to have heard of any elephant.   GEORGE ORWELL

Less experienced writers will be safer using semicolons in such a series.

Some writers omit the comma before *and* in simple *a, b,* and *c* series: violins, flutes and cellos; men, women and children. But since the comma is sometimes vital for clarity, it is preferable to establish the habit of always including it.

Note how necessary the final comma is in the following:

Our resort is equipped with comfortable cabins, a large lake with boating facilities, and a nine-hole golf course.

I am interested in a modern, furnished apartment with two bedrooms, kitchenette, living room, bathroom with shower, and garage.

Without the comma after *facilities,* the first sentence seems to suggest that the resort has a lake with a golf course in it. Without the comma after *shower* in the second sentence, the writer seems to be asking for an apartment with a garage in the bathroom.

20h Use commas to separate coordinate adjectives in a series; do not use commas to separate adjectives that are not coordinate.

Adjectives in a series are coordinate if each adjective modifies the noun separately. They are not coordinate if any adjective in the series modifies the total concept that follows it.

COORDINATE	You are a *greedy, thoughtless, insensitive* prig.
NOT COORDINATE	The boys are planning an *exciting holiday canoe* trip.

In the first sentence, each adjective is more or less independent of the other two; the three adjectives might be rearranged without seriously affecting the sense of the sentence: *thoughtless, insensitive, greedy prig; insensitive, greedy, thoughtless prig.* Moreover, the conjunction *and* could be inserted in place of the commas and the basic meaning would remain—*greedy* and *thoughtless* and *insensitive prig.*

But in the second sentence the adjectives are interdependent. Their order may not be changed, nor may *and* be substituted, without making hash of the original meaning—*canoe holiday exciting* trip; *holiday exciting canoe* trip; *exciting* and *holiday* and *canoe* trip. The adjectives in the second sentence constitute, in effect, a *restrictive* phrase, as distinct from the *nonrestrictive* quality of the adjectives in the first sentence, and therefore are not separated from one another by commas.

In actual usage, punctuating coordinate adjectives varies a great deal. Though few writers would punctuate the sentences above differently from the way we have punctuated them, many writers would be unable to choose between the punctuation of the following sentences:

He presented the ambassador with a *dirty, yellowed, gnarled* hand to shake.

He presented the ambassador with a *dirty yellowed gnarled* hand to shake.

Some writers feel that the meaning of the two sentences is slightly different: that the latter sentence suggests a more unified image than the former. That is, they feel that in the latter case the three adjectives intensify one another's qualities—*dirty-yellowed-gnarled* rather than *dirty and yellowed and gnarled.*

EXERCISE 20g–h In the following sentences, supply commas where they are needed to separate sentence elements in series.

1 Television advertising assures us that we can have skin that never wrinkles hair that always shines and dentures that never slip.
2 He brought a cup of strong steaming black coffee to the table.
3 Not all good citizens need endorse baseball hot dogs and apple pie.
4 To be healthy we should eat balanced meals sleep eight hours nightly and exercise daily.
5 Jean attended the Delta Gamma fall semester rush party.
6 Among the innovations brought into the world by Chinese civilization are the sailing ship the printing press and commercial banking.
7 Every year the engineering students sponsor an old time skunk rassle.
8 To the astronauts on the moon, the earth appeared fragile beautiful and alone in a dark universe.

20h

9 Taking off his dingy old white cap lowering his battered black umbrella and scraping his tennis shoes on the doormat he rang the bell.

10 At the Navy swearing-in ceremony Nancy wore something old something new something borrowed and something blue.

20i

20i Follow established conventions for the use of commas in dates, addresses, geographical names, titles, and long numbers.

1 Dates. If a date is written as month-date-year, use a comma between the date and the year. If such a date stands within a sentence, use a comma after the year.

> He left Detroit on July 19, 1967.
> He left Detroit on July 19, 1967, and never returned.

If only the month and year are given, use a comma neither between them nor after the year.

> He left Detroit in July 1967.
> He left Detroit in July 1967 and never returned.

If a date is written as day-month-year, use no commas.

> 17 July 1931   6 August 1982

2 Addresses. Standard comma punctuation of addresses is as follows:

> 205 Hayes Street, San Francisco, California 94102
> 39 West 46th Street, Olean, New York 71402

If geographical names or addresses appear within a sentence, use a comma after the final item. Note that no comma is used before the zip code.

ADDRESSES	He gave 39 West 46th Street, Olean, New York 71402 as his forwarding address.
GEOGRAPHICAL NAMES	He pretended to make the grand tour in three months, but he spent a whole month at Bremen, Germany, and the rest of his time in Tunbridge Wells, Kent, a small village in England.

3 Titles. Use commas to separate names from titles when the title follows the name. If the name followed by a title occurs within a sentence, use a comma after the title as well as between the name and the title.

Katherine Dugald, M.D.   William Harrington, Sr.

The university recently announced the appointment of Katherine Dugald, M.D., to the faculty of the medical school.

4 Large numbers. Ordinarily use commas in large numbers to indicate thousands, but do not use commas in social security numbers, telephone numbers, zip codes, and the like. These latter should be written as stated.

1,249	Social security number 391-07-4855
89,129	Telephone number 515-236-7669
1,722,843	Jamaica Plain, MA 02130

20j Use a comma to prevent misreading.

Sometimes in a sentence two words fall together so that they may be read two ways. In such instances, a comma may be necessary to prevent misreading even though no standard punctuation rule applies.

Long before, she had left everything to her brother.
Pilots who like to see sunbathers, fly low over apartment houses.
Inside the house, cats are sometimes a nuisance.

The omission of a comma after *before* in the first sentence would be momentarily confusing; we get off to a false start by reading *Long before she had left* without interruption. If there were no comma in the second sentence, we might think we were reading about flying sunbathers. A similar difficulty arises in the third sentence if *house* is not separated from *cats*. Often it is best to rewrite such sentences to avoid confusion.

The following sentences present similar problems:

To John, Smith was a puzzle. [Without the comma, the reader will take the introductory phrase to be *To John Smith.*]
People who can, take vacations in the summer. [Without the comma, the reader is likely to assume that the verb is *can take.*]

For the use of commas in quoted material, see **25d–f**.
For the misuse of the comma, see Section **24**.

EXERCISE 20i–j In the following sentences, insert commas where conventional usage requires them or where they are needed to prevent misreading.

1 By age fifteen, the average American child has spent about 20000 hours in front of a television set.

2 Cautiously watching the cat spotted a field mouse in the deep grass.

3 The Great Depression began on Black Thursday October 24 1929 when the New York Stock Exchange began to collapse.

4 Tom made a down payment of $1200 on a new car.

5 On 6 May 1954 at Oxford England Roger Bannister became the first athlete to break the four-minute barrier in the mile run.

6 Above the clouds gathered ominously.

7 The public opinion poll asked 2304 people to name the most urgent problems facing the nation.

8 After July 1 her address will be 321 Rosewood Avenue Kilgore Texas.

9 My sister, who has always loved animals, now has an office with JANE SILVER D.V.M. painted on the door.

10 If you can wait for me after class.

REVIEW EXERCISE ON COMMA USAGE (Section 20) Insert commas where they are needed in the following sentences. Indicate your reasons.

1 According to Benjamin Franklin success depended on practicing such virtues as industry frugality moderation and humility.

2 The Greek Parthenon built in the Fifth Century B.C. as a temple to the goddess Athena is threatened by pollution from countless Athenian automobiles.

3 We were surprised by the early spring snow shower.

4 The word *television* was used in *Scientific American* in 1907.

5 Among the signs of a good farmer are clean fence rows weedless fields and a well-painted barn.

6 *Adios amigo* until we meet again next fall.

7 On July 20 1969 Neil Armstrong and Edwin Aldrin made the first moon landing.

8 For directory assistance within your own telephone area dial 1 555 1212 and tell the operator the city and the name or place you want.

9 The hobo has many enemies including dogs and the police but his worst enemy is rain.

10 Many people criticize boxing as a brutal sport but some champions such as Jack Dempsey and Muhammad Ali have been seen as American folk heroes.

11 All contest entries must be postmarked by Saturday March 30 and mailed to P.O. Box 312 Atlanta Georgia 30300.

12 The college directory lists John A. Ward M.F.A. who teaches creative writing and John B. Ward Ph.D. who teaches biology.

13 Football is the only sport dependent on language for it uses play names color codes and formation numbers.

14 A migraine headache never kills doctors say.

15 As we walked across the dry field we could see the dust sticking to our clothes.

21   THE SEMICOLON ;

21a   Use a semicolon to separate closely related main clauses not joined by a coordinating conjunction.

The main clauses of compound sentences are most commonly joined by a comma and one of the coordinating conjunctions: *and, but, or, nor, for, so,* and *yet.* (See **20a.**) When main clauses expressing closely related ideas are not joined by a comma and a coordinating conjunction, use a semicolon between them. (If the ideas in the main clauses are not closely related, or if you don't intend to direct the reader's attention to their relatedness, treat each main clause as a separate sentence.)

> The rabbit is the all-American game; it is everywhere, and everywhere hunted.   JOHN RANDOLPH

> Good writing is not merely "correct writing"; it is clear, economical, and expressive writing.

> Initiative in the attack is not much in the nature of the tarantula; most species fight only when cornered so that escape is impossible.
>   ALEXANDER PETRUNKEVITCH

> Children begin by loving their parents; as they grow older they judge them; sometimes they forgive them.   OSCAR WILDE

> If employees were late or participated in job actions, the payroll system couldn't dock them; when they were hired, they weren't paid; and when they retired, they would as likely keep on being paid.
>   CHARLES R. MORRIS

A comma is sometimes used to separate very short main clauses not joined by coordinating conjunctions, particularly if the clauses are parallel, as in *She is not a person, she is a legend* or *Some allow it, some don't.* But the semicolon is always correct in such sentences—and much safer for the inexperienced writer.

21b   Use a semicolon to separate main clauses joined by a conjunctive adverb.

Conjunctive adverbs are words like *however, moreover, therefore, consequently, indeed,* and *then* that carry a thought from one main clause to the next. (See p. 517 for a more complete list.)

She applied for the position three weeks after the deadline for applications; *therefore,* she was not considered.

The meeting was long and boring; *nevertheless,* we stayed until the end.

An abnormally hot, dry growing season has parched crops throughout the plains; *consequently,* we may expect higher food prices in the near future.

You can recognize conjunctive adverbs and distinguish them from other kinds of joining words if you remember that they are the only kind of joining word that can be moved from the beginning of the clause in which they stand to another position in that clause without changing the sense.

We could survive without running water; *indeed,* our ancestors survived without any modern conveniences.

We could survive without running water; our ancestors, *indeed,* survived without any modern conveniences.

In contrast, coordinating conjunctions (*and, but,* etc.) or subordinating conjunctions (*although, because, if, since, when,* and the like) cannot move from their positions without changing or destroying meaning.

Coordinating conjunctions must stand between the clauses they connect.

Fido barked, *so* we knew he wanted to go out.

BUT NOT Fido barked, we *so* knew he wanted to go out.

Similarly, subordinating conjunctions must stand at the beginning of the clauses they introduce.

Fido barked *because* he wanted to go out.

BUT NOT Fido barked he *because* wanted to go out.

When a conjunctive adverb comes within the second main clause instead of at the beginning, the clauses still must be separated by a semicolon and the conjunctive adverb set off by commas.

Americans spend millions of dollars for road-building; our roads, however, are rapidly deteriorating.

21c **Use a semicolon to separate main clauses joined by a coordinating conjunction if the clauses are long or internally punctuated.**

The meeting last night, the most argumentative and confusing thus far, lasted until midnight; and unless something unexpected happens in the meantime, the next meeting may last even longer.

When New England was first settled, lobsters were plentiful all along the coast; and since the settlers depended heavily on the sea for their food, especially in the early years, they certainly must have eaten lobster frequently.

In some instances, even when relatively short main clauses are joined by a coordinating conjunction, a semicolon instead of a comma may be used for emphasis.

He could hear the excitement of their talk from the next room; but he could not distinguish what they were saying.

21d Use a semicolon to separate the items of a series if the items themselves contain commas.

The following people were present: John Smith, the doctor; Angelo Martinez, the dentist; and Alice Wilson, the psychiatrist.

The bureaucracy consists of functionaries; the aristocracy, of idols; the democracy, of idolators.   G. B. SHAW

EXERCISE 21a–d In the following sentences, insert semicolons or substitute them for commas wherever needed.

1 Rudy's Steak House is a very busy restaurant you need dinner reservations on the weekend.
2 The badger is only as big as a small dog, however, it is fearless and has sharp teeth and claws.
3 Several centuries before Christopher Columbus sailed to America, Irish sailors, exploring the Atlantic, reached Iceland, and they were followed by Norse sailors, who settled in Greenland.
4 In Latin America, carnivals are a popular form of entertainment they express both the old traditions and the modern culture of the region.
5 Detective-mystery stories are popular with readers of all ages, consequently, one of every four books published in the United States is a detective-mystery.
6 Louis Armstrong was not just a great jazz musician he was an emissary abroad for the creativeness of American music.
7 Older citizens remember the era of the railroad with nostalgia: the great black engines, steam hissing beneath their wheels, the dining car, where flawless waiters served ham soufflé and huckleberry pie, the brass-railed, open-air observation car, often the last car on the train.
8 Richard Cory was rich, handsome, and popular, nevertheless, he went home one summer night and put a bullet through his head.
9 Laurie manages the budget of the Flying Club, she is largely responsible for the group's sound financial practices.
10 Cedar trees are usually only about forty feet in height and about two feet in diameter, therefore, cedar lumber is seldom very long or wide.

11 The decade of the Twenties was the heyday of Babe Ruth, the Yankee slugger, Charles Lindbergh, the Atlantic flyer, and Rudolph Valentino, the movie matinee idol.

12 Some modern societies venerate the machine the automobile, especially, is often viewed as a symbol of efficiency and affluence.

13 Our canoe moved noiselessly across the calm lake, occasionally a splashing fish broke the silence.

14 Television has developed several kinds of western drama, the classic western, however, embodies the clash between frontier and civilization, lawlessness and order.

15 Public opinion polls have become a part of government, indeed, few governmental or political party decisions are made without consulting them.

22 THE COLON :

Whereas the semicolon always indicates a full stop, the colon indicates an addition or expectation. It indicates that what follows will explain, clarify, illustrate, specify detail.

22a Use a colon to separate two main clauses when the second explains, illustrates, or amplifies the first.

It is safe to predict what prices will do in the next decade: they will go up.

Charm, in the abstract, has something of the quality of music: radiance, balance, and harmony. LAURIE LEE

There are two times in a man's life when he should not speculate: when he can't afford it and when he can. MARK TWAIN

22b Use a colon to set off a list or series, including a list or series introduced by *the following* or *as follows*.

For the most part we are an intemperate people: we eat too much when we can, drink too much, indulge our senses too much.
JOHN STEINBECK

Anything is possible on a train: a great meal, a binge, a visit from card players, an intrigue, a good night's sleep, and strangers' monologues framed like Russian short stories. PAUL THEROUX

If you are interested in reading further about usage, we recommend the following books: Evans, *A Dictionary of Contemporary American Usage;* Follet, *Modern American Usage;* and Bernstein, *The Careful Writer*.

22c   Use a colon to introduce a formal quotation.

The sixteenth amendment set up the income tax: "The Congress shall have power to lay and collect taxes on incomes, from whatever source derived, without apportionment among the several states, and without regard to any census or enumeration."

22d   Use a colon according to established conventions to separate items in biblical citations, subtitles and titles, and divisions of time.

BIBLICAL CITATION	Luke 3: 1–4
DIVISIONS OF TIME	9:20 a.m. 10:10 p.m.
SUBTITLES	*Evaluating Writing: Describing, Measuring, Judging*

EXERCISE 22a–d   In the following sentences, insert colons where they are needed.

1 The refugees left their homeland to search for three ideals peace, equality, and opportunity.
2 Thomas Paine stoutly defended the rights of the American colonies, as did others Franklin, Jefferson, John Adams.
3 Only one word can describe my first attempt to water ski splash.
4 One final question how do people learn to be self-confident?
5 Much of life is consumed by routine reading newspapers, riding to work, discussing the weather.
6 To make Paul Bunyan stew, combine the following one steer cut into two-inch cubes, one truckload of mixed carrots and potatoes, and one tanker of crushed tomatoes.
7 The "trouble" in Northern Ireland can be interpreted in an entirely nonreligious way it is a tragedy deriving from a lack of jobs in a dying economy.
8 To this I have made up my mind my own life is somehow related to the lives of all other human beings.
9 We need to preserve the distinct spheres of our environment the city, the rural countryside, and the wilderness.
10 To summarize belief in the magic power of music over the forces of nature prevailed in ancient China and still persists in India and Africa.

23   THE DASH AND PARENTHESES

Both dashes and parentheses are used to set off interrupting comments, explanations, examples, and other similar parenthetical elements from the main thought of the sentence. Commas are ordinarily used when parenthetical or other nonrestrictive elements are closely related in the main thought of the sentence. Dashes and parentheses are used when the interruption is abrupt and the element set off is only loosely related to the main thought of the sentence.

Though the choice between dashes and parentheses is sometimes a matter of taste, dashes emphasize more strongly the element being set off and give it greater importance than parentheses. Parentheses are more commonly used when the element enclosed is an incidental explanatory comment, an aside, or a nonessential bit of information.

A single dash is used following an introductory element or preceding a final sentence element. A pair of dashes is used to enclose an element within a sentence. Parentheses always are used in pairs around the enclosed element. In handwriting, distinguish the dash from the hyphen by making the dash longer. In typewritten copy, use two hyphens without spacing to indicate the dash.

The dash — —

23a Use the dash or a pair of dashes to mark abrupt shifts in sentence structure or thought.

Could he—should he even try to—borrow money from his father?

The police ordered the boys—their authority to do so has been questioned—to stop gathering in front of the store.

23b Use the dash to set off nonrestrictive appositives and other parenthetical elements for emphasis.

At the end of the month, he will go on half time—and half pay.

In any fight against the sun, man—for all his technology—will come out the loser.   *Newsweek*

Each person is born to one possession which overvalues all his others—his last breath.   MARK TWAIN

The student wandered in at 9:30—half an hour after the class began.

The spoken language does not have the same standards as the written language—the tune you whistle is not the orchestra's score.

WILLIAM SAFIRE

23c Use the dash for clarity to set off internally punctuated appositives or other parenthetical elements.

To prevent confusion, use dashes rather than commas to set off compound appositives. In the following sentence it is difficult to determine whether *Bill, Dave, and Blacky* are three additional men—or perhaps dogs or tame bears—or whether these are, in fact, the names of the men who were in the office.

> Three men, Bill, Dave, and Blacky, were sitting in the office with their feet on the desk.

But when the commas are replaced by dashes, the meaning becomes clear:

> Three men—Bill, Dave, and Blacky—were sitting in the office with their feet on the desk.

23d Use the dash to set off introductory lists or summary statements.

> Gather data, tabulate, annotate, classify—the process seemed endless to Jane.
>
> Black flies, horseflies, little triangular flies, ordinary house flies, unidentified kinds of flies—those are what I mean when I say I'm sick of flies.
>
> Pound, Eliot, Williams—these were the poets the course devoted most attention to.

23e Use the dash to show interruption or hesitation in speech.

> "Why don't you—" He stopped abruptly and looked away.
>
> "Well, I—uh—we—some of us really want to drop your plan."

Parentheses ( )

23f Use parentheses to set off parenthetical information, explanation, or comment that is incidental or unimportant to the main thought of the sentence.

> The lawyer contends (and we can see that the contention has some merit) that this client was convicted on doubtful evidence.
>
> In our society (it's the only one I've experienced, so I can't speak for others) the razor of necessity cuts close.   STUDS TERKEL
>
> More than 1,000 years ago, the Hopis (the word means "the peaceful ones") settled in the mesa-dotted farmland of northern Arizona. *Time*
>
> Among the narratives in the text, Maya Angelou's (pp. 58–68) is my favorite.

23g

23g Use parentheses to enclose numerals or letters labeling items listed within sentences.

To check out a book from our library, proceed as follows: (1) check the catalog number carefully; (2) enter the catalog number in the upper left-hand corner of the call slip; (3) fill out the remainder of the call-slip information; and (4) hand in the call slip at the main desk.

EXERCISE 23a–g In the following sentences insert dashes or parentheses wherever needed.

1 They noticed or thought they noticed a figure disappearing in the darkness.

2 The Washington Mall, intended as a grand avenue, became instead oh, so obviously the backyard of official Washington.

3 This is a common impulse among all nations the quest for a happier way of life.

4 Gentleness, devotion, and playfulness all are requirements for a child's first dog.

5 The Wizard of Oz and his friends remember the Scarecrow and the Cowardly Lion? lived in a land of magic.

6 The Zen teacher told the students they should 1 eat when they are hungry, 2 sleep when they are tired, and 3 have quiet minds.

7 Several original plays a comedy, a tragedy, and a melodrama were presented by the Drama Club.

8 Well, I'm not sure that would you please repeat the question?

9 When it was officially designated as a town in 1833, Chicago had fewer than a hundred inhabitants.

10 Some seemingly valueless things old barn boards are an example can unexpectedly become popular and valuable.

24

24 SUPERFLUOUS INTERNAL PUNCTUATION

Careful punctuation helps readers separate words and ideas, helps group related words together, and enables writers to set off words or word groups for emphasis. Inadequate punctuation can force a reader to go over a passage several times to get its meaning. But too many marks of punctuation, marks inserted where they are not necessary or where they separate words that belong together, confuse a reader as much as too few marks.

The following sentence, for example, is jarring because of unnecessary and confusing punctuation.

The people of this company, have, always, been aware, of the need, for products of better quality, and lower prices.

None of the commas in that sentence is necessary.

Use all the punctuation marks that will make the reader's work easier or that are required by convention. But do not insert marks that are superfluous. Especially avoid the misuses of the comma, the semicolon, and the colon described below.

24a Do not separate a single or final adjective from its noun.

NOT   He was a discourteous, greedy, deceitful, boy.

BUT   He was a discourteous, greedy, deceitful boy.

24b Do not separate a subject from its verb unless there are intervening words that require punctuation.

NOT   The worth of real estate, is determined by the demand for it.

BUT   The worth of real estate is determined by the demand for it.

The worth of real estate, tangible property, is determined by the demand for it. [The commas set off an appositive.]

24c Do not separate a verb from its object unless there are intervening words that require punctuation.

NOT   Molly drove, her old car carefully down the road.

BUT   Molly drove her old car carefully down the road.

NOT   The boys always made Peanut, the butt of their pranks.

BUT   The boys always made Peanut the butt of their pranks.

The boys always made Peanut, an undersized and immature smart aleck, the butt of their pranks.

24d Do not separate two words or phrases that are joined by a coordinating conjunction.

NOT   He is very honest, and patient.

BUT   He is very honest and patient.

NOT   I decided to work during the summer, and relax in the fall.

BUT   I decided to work during the summer and relax in the fall.

24e

24e Do not separate an introductory word, brief phrase, or short clause from the main body of the sentence unless clarity requires it.

NOT　　On Wednesday, the ice in the river began to break up.

BUT　　On Wednesday the ice in the river began to break up.

Occasionally, however, a comma must be inserted to prevent misreading. (See **20j.**)

NOT　　Notwithstanding *Drums at Dusk* is a worthy successor to *Black Thunder*.

BUT　　Notwithstanding, *Drums at Dusk* is a worthy successor to *Black Thunder*.

24f

24f Do not separate a restrictive modifier from the main body of the sentence. (See **20c.**)

NOT　　The girl, who slapped my face, also kicked my shins.

BUT　　The girl who slapped my face also kicked my shins.

NOT　　The band, in the park, played the same tired old marches we had heard, for fifteen years.

BUT　　The band in the park played the same tired old marches we had heard for fifteen years.

Note that adverbial phrases and clauses usually *restrict* the meaning of the word or clause to which they are attached. They are therefore essential to the meaning and should *not* be separated by a comma from what they modify. (See also **20d.**)

NOT　　The product is available, in large and small sizes.

BUT　　The product is available in large and small sizes. [The phrase *in large and small sizes* restricts the adjective *available* and is essential to the meaning.]

NOT　　Once darkness fell, over the trees, the dogs began to bark.

BUT　　Once darkness fell over the trees, the dogs began to bark. [The phrase *over the trees* restricts the meaning of the verb *fell*.]

24g Do not separate indirect quotations or directly quoted single words and short phrases from the rest of the sentence.

CORRECT   After drinking ten bottles of pop, Henry said he could drink ten more.

Claude said he was "weary of it all" and that he had "absorbed" his "fill of monotony."

24h Do not separate a preposition from its object.

NOT   Carol went to, New York, Washington, and Atlanta.

BUT   Carol went to New York, Washington, and Atlanta.

24i Do not use a semicolon to separate a main clause from a subordinate clause, a phrase from a clause, or other parts of unequal grammatical rank.

NOT   Mortimer rushed out of the house in his shirt sleeves; although it was raining.

BUT   Mortimer rushed out of the house in his shirt sleeves although it was raining.

NOT   The speaker rambled on and on; making everyone increasingly restless.

BUT   The speaker rambled on and on, making everyone increasingly restless.

24j Do not use a semicolon before a direct quotation or before a list.

NOT   She said to him; "Harry, you have to straighten up and fly right."

BUT   She said to him, "Harry, you have to straighten up and fly right."

NOT   On their trip to "rough it," they took the following; a propane cooking stove, two radios, a portable TV, and a supply of the latest paperbacks.

BUT   On their trip to "rough it," they took the following: a propane cooking stove, two radios, a portable TV, and a supply of the latest paperbacks.

24k

24k Do not use a colon between a verb and its object or complement, or between a preposition and its object.

NOT   My brother hates: snakes, caterpillars, worms, grubs, and all beetles.

BUT   My brother hates snakes, caterpillars, worms, grubs, and all beetles.

NOT   The driver was charged with: driving without a license, driving so as to endanger, and driving an unregistered vehicle.

BUT   The driver was charged with driving without a license, driving so as to endanger, and driving an unregistered vehicle.

EXERCISE 24a–k Eliminate any superfluous commas in the sentences below.

1 The pilot, having received clearances, circled the airport, before landing.

2 Across the river was a protected cove, in which there were two rowboats, and one small sailboat.

3 The meeting began late, because Kelly was not sure where the Regency Hotel was, or when the meeting was scheduled.

4 Sherry decided she could not take the night job, and still take courses in chemistry, accounting, and history, in the mornings.

5 The ice, near the southern bank, was too thin, and soft, for ice skating.

6 Both robins, and phoebes, will build their nests in your backyard, on a shelf nailed to the house, or garage.

7 Chief Justice John Marshall, of Virginia, was a strong Federalist, who shaped our interpretation of the Constitution.

8 Penguins, in the Galapagos Islands, are unafraid of people on land, but they are terrified, if people join them, while swimming in the Pacific.

9 During the Irish Potato Famine, (1845–1849), thousands of Irish people found no food to buy, and fled to Boston, and other cities.

10 The speaker replied slowly, because he had not expected the question, and did not know what to say.

REVIEW EXERCISE ON INTERNAL PUNCTUATION (Sections 20–24) In the following sentences, there are various errors in internal punctuation. Correct all errors, and be prepared to explain the reasons for your corrections.

1 Jeff went shopping Marty went to a movie and Louise stayed home to study.

2 Answering the defense attorney Robbins said angrily he was sure of his evidence.

3 Uranium which is important in atomic processes is found in parts of Africa.

4 Most novelists osteopaths paperhangers and funeral directors have something in common they are self-employed.

5 Every year more than thirteen million people visit the 2300 acre expanse of Walt Disney World in Lake Buena Vista Florida.

6 In the 17th century Newton Galileo and Descartes said that the universe operated according to a constant pattern moreover mathematics was the God-given key to understanding it.

7 Glenn our plumber who can bend iron pipe in his bare hands whistled songs from Gilbert and Sullivan operettas as he fixed our leaking pipes.

8 Common sense is not a common quality those who have it are often sought after.

9 Instead of buying costly pollution control devices some industrialists find it economical to redesign equipment improve products and recycle water and waste material.

10 A quiet stretch of Sudbury farmland, set behind a row of tidy typical colonials is the setting of the story.

11 According to American historians Elihu Burritt 1810–1879 the famous Learned Blacksmith carried a Greek grammar in his hat but they also report that he was not a very good blacksmith.

12 Words words words were all that came out of the meeting.

13 It's relatively easy to borrow money it's much harder to repay it.

14 The bones of birds zoologists report are hollow to improve flight and are much the same in all birds.

15 Jealousy a debilitating emotion can wreck a relationship for without genuine trust there can be no real love.

25–26 THE PUNCTUATION OF QUOTED MATERIAL **Q**

Direct speech and material quoted word for word from other written sources must always be set off distinctly from a writer's own words. Quotation marks usually indicate such distinction, although when quotations from written sources are long, the distinction may be shown with different spacing and indentation. Section 25 describes the conventional uses of quotation marks and special spacing to set off quoted material; the use and punctuation of explanatory words such as *he said;* the conventions controlling the placement of other marks of punctuation with quotation marks; and the special uses of quotation marks in certain titles and with words used as words.

An explanatory comment inserted in a quotation or the omission of some part of the original quotation calls for the use of brackets or the ellipsis mark. These are discussed in Section 26.

25 QUOTATION MARKS " "

Indicating quoted material

25a Use double quotation marks to enclose a direct quotation from speech or writing.

"Don't dive from that rock," she told me.
It was Emerson who wrote, "A foolish consistency is the hobgoblin of little minds."

Note that in dialogue, each change of speaker is indicated by a new paragraph.

"I know I've been here before," he said.
"Don't you remember exactly when?" She looked at him questioningly, and she pointed to something behind and above him. He turned and saw the path into the woods.
"No, I don't remember. Can't you understand? I don't remember when!"

Remember not to set off indirect quotations.

She told me not to dive from that rock.
It was Emerson who wrote that foolish consistency is the hobgoblin of little minds.

25b Use single quotation marks to enclose a quotation within a quotation.

She turned and said, "Remember Grandfather's advice, 'When other people run, you walk.' "

Notice that the end punctuation of the sentence within single quotation marks serves also as the end punctuation for the entire sentence unit of which it is a part.

25c Set off prose quotations of more than four lines and poetry quotations of more than three lines by spacing and indentation.

Long prose quotations. Prose quotations of more than four lines should be displayed—set off from the text of a paper and indented from the left-hand margin. In typewritten papers, leave three line-spaces between the text and the quotation, indent all lines of the quotation ten character-spaces from the left, and single-space it. Do not enclose a displayed quotation in quotation marks. If quotation marks occur *within* material you are setting off, use them as they are in the original: double for double, single for single.

Professor George Summey's comment on the writer's responsibility for accuracy in reporting the words of others is worth quoting:

> Anyone who quotes another person's words has the duty of keeping the words unchanged and continuous or of giving clear notice to the contrary. It is improper to alter wording or punctuation of quoted matter, to italicize words without due notice, or to make any other change. That would misrepresent the meaning of the quoted words in their context.

No careful writer would question the need for such accuracy.

Quoted poetry. Single lines of poetry are ordinarily run into the text and enclosed in quotation marks unless the writer wishes to give them particular emphasis by setting them off.

In the line "A spotted shaft is seen," the hissing *s* sounds echo Dickinson's subject: a snake.

Two or three lines of poetry may be either enclosed in quotation marks and run into the text or indented ten spaces from the left. If they are enclosed in quotation marks and run into the text, divisions between lines are indicated by a slash mark (/).

Blake combines mystical and military images, as in the lines "Bring me my Spear: O clouds unfold! / Bring me my Chariot of fire."

. . . as in the lines
> Bring me my Spear: O clouds unfold!
> Bring me my Chariot of fire.

Poetry quotations of more than three lines should always be set off from the text and indented ten spaces from the left.

EXERCISE 25a–c In the following sentences, insert double or single quotation marks or slash marks wherever needed.

1 I sometimes wonder what life will be like in the next century, Lee said.
2 She recalled, In his Nobel Prize acceptance speech, William Faulkner said, I believe that man will not merely endure: he will prevail.
3 Robert Herrick's lines, Gather ye rosebuds while ye may, Old Time is still a-flying remind us to make the most of our youth, for it passes quickly.
4 This large skylight is a collector to preheat our hot water supply, explained the owner of the solar house.
5 TV newscaster Jessica Savitch reported: When the space shuttle Columbia lifted off at Cape Canaveral, one witness said, It's like a hundred Fourth of Julys rolled into one.
6 The scientist predicted that cold water pumped from the ocean floor will someday be used to generate energy.
7 Uncle Zed smiled and began, Whenever old Buck Owen met a stranger, he would say, Let me tell you how I led a wagon train across the plains to Laramie.
8 For generations, American schoolchildren read Longfellow's poem beginning: Listen, my children, and you shall hear Of the midnight ride of Paul Revere.
9 The old Indian spoke: Listen to me, Little Fox, and I will teach you the good medicine songs of the Chippewas.
10 Geologists said that the eruption of Mount St. Helens in the spring of 1980 was one of the worst volcanic explosions in American history.

Punctuating explanatory words with quotations

25d **In punctuating explanatory words preceding a quotation, be guided by the length and formality of the quotation.**

Explanatory words such as *he said* are ordinarily set off from quotations by a comma when they precede the quotation. However, when the quotation that follows is grammatically closely related, it may be followed by no punctuation, or when it is relatively long and formal it may be followed by a colon.

NO PUNCTUATION	He yelled "Stop!" and grabbed the wheel.
	Auden's poem "In Memory of W. B. Yeats" begins with the line "He disappeared in dead of winter."
	The Preamble begins with the words "We, the people of the United States."
	It was President Franklin Roosevelt who said that "the only thing we have to fear is fear itself."

PUNCTUATION
WITH COMMA

The old man said very quietly, "Under no circumstances will I tell you where the money is
hidden."

The chairman asked him, "Have I stated your
motion correctly?"

PUNCTUATION
WITH COLON

The speaker rose to his feet and began: "The
party in power has betrayed us. It has not only
failed to keep its election promises but has sold
out to the moneyed powers."

**25e Use a comma to separate an opening quotation from the
rest of the sentence unless the quotation ends with a
question mark or an exclamation point.**

"The man is dead," he said with finality.

"Is the man dead?" he asked.

"Oh, no!" he screamed hysterically. "My brother can't be dead."

**25f When a quotation is interrupted by explanatory words (*he
said,* or their equivalent), use a comma after the first part of
the quotation. In choosing the proper punctuation mark to
place after the explanatory words, apply the rules for
punctuating clauses and phrases.**

"I am not unaware," he said, "of the dangers of iceboat racing."

"I have always worked hard," he declared. "I was peddling newspapers
when I was eight years old."

"Jean has great capacities," the supervisor said; "she has energy, brains,
and personality."

EXERCISE 25d–f In the following sentences, insert appropriate punctuation
marks where necessary to separate quotations from the rest of the sentence.

1 Woodrow Wilson's speech began "No matter how often we think of it,
the discovery of America must each time make a fresh appeal to our
imaginations."

2 When Ruth and Bill arrived at the party, we shouted "Surprise!" and
turned on the lights.

3 "When does the next bus leave for Oakland" he asked.

4 "I take the ecological view" she explained "that nature is a process in
which humans are involved with all other life forms."

5 "Look out for the bicycle!" somebody yelled, and the shortshop
dropped the fly ball.

6 "Do you believe in astrology" he inquired.

7 "You can have this rod and reel" the old man said "I never fish any
more."

8 Addressing the Birdwatchers Club, he asked "Did you know that a hummingbird weighs only one-tenth of an ounce?"

9 My favorite limerick begins with the words "There once was a man named Mehaffy."

10 "We intend" the hiker said "to follow the Alaska Pipeline along Richardson Highway to the Gulf of Alaska at Valdez."

Using other marks of punctuation with quotation marks

25g **25g Follow established conventions in placing other punctuation with quotation marks.**

1 Place commas and periods inside quotation marks. Commas are generally used to separate direct quotations from unquoted material.

"There is no use in working," he complained, "when it only makes me more sleepy than usual."

Note that this rule *always* applies, regardless of the reason for using quotation marks.

According to Shakespeare, the poet writes in a "fine frenzy."
While he insisted that he was a "beatnik," I certainly got tired of hearing him say that everything was "cool."

2 Place semicolons and colons outside quotation marks.

According to Shakespeare, the poet writes in a "fine frenzy"; by "fine frenzy" he meant a combination of energy, enthusiasm, imagination, and a certain madness.

3 Place a dash, question mark, or exclamation point inside the quotation marks when it applies only to the quotation; place it outside the quotation marks when it applies to the whole statement.

He said, "Will I see you tomorrow?"
Didn't he say, "I'll see you tomorrow"?
"You may have the car tonight"—then he caught himself abruptly and said, "No, you can't have it; I need it myself."

When a mark applies to both quotation and sentence, use it only once.

Has he ever asked, "May I come in?"

EXERCISE 25g   In the following sentences insert whatever punctuation marks are appropriate for use with quotation marks.

1 In his First Inaugural Address, Thomas Jefferson called for "a wise and frugal government"
2 The Dixieland band played "Do You Know What It Means to Miss New Orleans"
3 Did she say, "Acid rain has ruined the telescope lens"
4 "Excuse me, please" then he blushed with embarrassment and went on, "I know this is silly, but haven't I seen you in the movies"
5 This fishing lure is called the "Frivolous Fly" it is used mostly for trout fishing.

Other uses of quotation marks

25h   Use quotation marks to set off titles of poems, songs, articles, short stories, and other titles that are parts of a longer work. (For the use of italics to set off titles of longer works, see **27a** and **27b**.)

Theodore Roethke's poem "My Papa's Waltz" appeared in his book *The Lost Son and Other Poems.*
"The Talk of the Town" has for many years been the opening column of *The New Yorker.*
Bob Dylan's "A Hard Rain's A-Gonna Fall" is one of his most popular songs.
"Beowulf to Batman: The Epic Hero in Modern Culture," an article by Roger B. Rollin, originally appeared in the journal *College English.*

25i   Words used in a special sense may be set off by quotation marks.

When a new book comes into the library, it is first of all "accessioned."
Is this what you call "functional" architecture?

Do not use quotation marks around common nicknames. Do not use them for emphasis. And do not use them apologetically to enclose slang, colloquialisms, trite expressions, or for imprecise words or phrases when you cannot find the right word. If a word is appropriate, it will stand without apology. If it is not appropriate, it should be replaced.

EXERCISE 25h–i   In the following sentences, insert quotation marks wherever they are needed.

1 W. C. Handy's St. Louis Blues is one of the most popular jazz melodies ever composed.

2 *The Yale Review* begins each issue with a series of book reviews called Reader's Guide.
3 The word karate comes from the Japanese and means empty-handed or, to put it another way, the art of defense without a weapon.
4 Walt Whitman's When Lilacs Last in the Dooryard Bloomed is usually considered the best American poem about the death of Lincoln.
5 Expressions like Take it easy or Have a nice day soon become trite.

26 BRACKETS AND THE ELLIPSIS MARK [ ] . . .

The important uses of brackets and ellipsis marks are to indicate some change that a writer has made in material being quoted. Brackets are used to indicate that a writer has inserted into a quotation some information, comment, or explanation not in the original. The ellipsis mark is used to indicate that something has been omitted from the material being quoted.

26a Use brackets to set off editorial remarks in quoted material.

You will sometimes want to insert an explanatory comment in a statement you are quoting. By enclosing such comments in brackets, you let the reader know at once that *you* are speaking rather than the original author.

> John Dryden, a famous English poet, said, "Those who accuse him [Shakespeare] to have wanted knowledge, give him the greater commendation; he was naturally learned."

> The favorite phrase of their [English] law is "a custom whereof the memory of man runneth not back to the contrary."
>
> RALPH WALDO EMERSON

In bibliographical notations, use brackets to enclose the name of a writer *reputed* to be the author of the work in question.

> [Ned Ward], *A Trip to New England* (1699)

26b Use the word *sic* ("thus it is") in brackets to indicate that a mistake or peculiarity in the spelling or the grammar of a foregoing word appears in the original work.

> The high school paper reported, "The students spoke most respectively [sic] of Mrs. Higginbottom."

26c Use an ellipsis mark (three spaced periods . . .) to indicate an intentional omission from quoted material.

26c

When you wish to quote from an author but wish to omit some word within a sentence or to omit one or more sentences, in fairness to the original author and your readers you must indicate that you have omitted material from the original. Such omissions are indicated by inserting an ellipsis mark at the point of omission. For an omission within a sentence, use three spaced periods, leaving a space before and after each period. When the omission comes at the end of a sentence, use four periods; the first is the usual sentence period, and the last three are the ellipsis mark.

For example, the first selection below is taken without any omission from Russel Nye's *The Unembarrassed Muse* (New York, 1971). It describes the comic-strip world of Walt Disney's Mickey Mouse. The second selection shows how a writer quoting from the original passage might use the ellipsis.

Mickey's is a child's world, safe (though occasionally scary), nonviolent, nonideological, where all the stories have happy endings. Characterization is strong and simple—Mickey is bright and friendly, Minnie eternally feminine, Goofy happily stupid, Donald of the terrible temper a raffish, likeable rascal. No Disney strip ever gave a child bad dreams or an adult anything to ponder.

Mickey's is a child's world, safe . . . nonviolent, nonideological, where all the stories have happy endings. Characterization is strong and simple—Mickey is bright and friendly, Minnie eternally feminine, Goofy happily stupid, Donald of the terrible temper a raffish, likeable rascal. No Disney strip ever gave a child bad dreams. . . .

EXERCISE 26 Supply the appropriate punctuation in each of the following sentences.

1 The letter said tartly, The fault is not with our product but with your skin; it appears to be supersensitive.
2 Perhaps you might like to do a study of Irish ghost stories the professor suggested.
3 How long have you noticed this condition the doctor asked.
4 The editor of the *Weekly Echo* reported that "The Martins recently celebrated their thirtieth year of martial *sic* bliss."
5 He said, When the policeman asked me Where's the fire? I felt like telling him it was in his garage.
6 The song Aquarius is from the musical *Hair*.

7 William Blake wrote the often-quoted lines To see a world in a grain of sand And a heaven in a wildflower Hold infinity in the palm of your hand And eternity in an hour.

8 The salesclerk said, Sir I would exchange this sweater, but he added, it has already been worn.

9 One day, just as I was going out to Rahul's house, I heard her shouting outside the door of the study. The director is a busy man! She was shouting. She had her back against the door and held her arms stretched out; M. stood in front of her and his head was lowered. Day after day you come and eat his life up! she said.

R. PRAWER JHABVALA, "My First Marriage"

10 I climbed up in the bar yelling, Walsh, I'm shot. I'm shot. I could feel the blood running down my leg. Walsh, the fellow who operated the fish-and-chips joint, pushed me off the bar and onto the floor. I couldn't move now, but I was still completely conscious. Walsh was saying, Git outta here, kid. I ain't got no time to play. A woman was screaming, mumbling something about the Lord, and saying, Somebody done shot that poor child.

CLAUDE BROWN, Manchild in the Promised Land

27–30 WORD PUNCTUATION **WORD P**

Italics, capitals, apostrophes, and hyphens identify words that have a special use or a particular grammatical function in a sentence.

> Our two-week reading program, assigned in Wednesday's class, is Shakespeare's *King Lear*.

Here the italics set off the words *King Lear* as a single title. The capitals identify *Wednesday, Shakespeare, King,* and *Lear* as proper names. The apostrophes indicate that *Shakespeare* and *Wednesday* are singular possessives and not plurals. The hyphen between *two* and *week* makes the two words function as a single adjective.

27 ITALICS

In printing, italics are typefaces that slope toward the right. In typed or handwritten manuscript, italics are indicated by underlining.

> On the printed page: *italics*

> In typewritten copy: `italics`

> In handwritten copy: *italics*

27a **Italicize the titles of books, newspapers, magazines, and all publications issued separately.**

"Issued separately" means published as a single work and not as an article or story in a magazine, nor as a chapter or section of a book. (For the proper punctuation of such titles, see **25h**.)

The New York Times   *Commentary*
The Lord of the Flies   *Death of a Salesman*
                    Webster's New Collegiate Dictionary

Be careful not to add the word *The* to titles unless it belongs there and not to omit it if it does belong.

NOT   *The Reader's Digest*   NOT   the *Red Badge of Courage*
BUT   the *Reader's Digest*   BUT   *The Red Badge of Courage*

27b **Italicize the names of ships and aircraft, and the titles of works of art, movies, television and radio programs, and record albums.**

Titanic   *Spirit of St. Louis*
The Thinker   *The Empire Strikes Back*
Barney Miller   *Jethro Tull Live: Bursting Out*

27c **Italicize letters, words, and numbers used as words.**

Your *r*'s look very much like your *n*'s, and I can't tell your *7*'s from your *1*'s.
The early settlers borrowed Indian words like *moccasin, powwow,* and *wigwam.*

Quotation marks are also used to set off words as words in type-written or handwritten manuscripts (see **25i**). However, if the subject you are writing about requires you to set off frequent words as words, underlining (italics) will make your manuscript look less cluttered.

27d **Italicize foreign words and phrases that have not yet been accepted into the English language.**

She graduated *magna cum laude.*
Many of the works of the *fin de siècle* that seemed so sensational when they were written appear to us now as innocent.

You may sometimes feel that a foreign word or phrase expresses your meaning more aptly or concisely than an English one. If you are sure that your readers will understand the expression, use it. But to overuse such words is pedantry. Many foreign words have been accepted into the English language and need no longer be italicized. The following words, for example, do not require italics:

bourgeois   milieu   denouement   liqueur

To determine whether a foreign word should be italiziced, consult a good dictionary. (See the discussion of spelling under "The Uses of a Dictionary," pp. 341–342.)

27e   Use italics to give a word special stress.

The idea that knowledge follows interest is a scandalous half-truth; it is a better-than-half-truth that *interest follows knowledge.*

I heard him say once that in a democracy (a *democracy,* mind you) a division of opinion cannot be permitted to exist.

27f   Avoid the overuse of italics.

Distinguish carefully between a real need for italicizing and the use of italics as a mechanical device to achieve emphasis. The best way to achieve emphasis is to write effective, well-constructed sentences. The overuse of italics will make your writing seem immature and amateurish, as in the following:

Any good education must be *liberal.*

America is a *true* democracy, in every sense of the word.

This book has what I call *real* depth of meaning.

EXERCISE 27a–f   Italicize words where necessary in the following sentences.

1 Robert Redford, who is best known as an actor, received an Oscar as best director for the movie Ordinary People.

2 H. M. S. Queen Elizabeth, for years the flagship of the Cunard Line, was finally retired from service.

3 Are you supposed to pronounce the p in coup de grâce?

4 Some Americans use the word simpatico as though it meant sympathetic, but its meaning is really closer to that of the English word charming.

5 Is T. S. Eliot's The Wasteland included in The Oxford Book of English Verse?

6 His travels had brought him greater understanding of himself and just a touch of savoir-faire.

7 Webster's Third New International Dictionary lists more than half a dozen pronunciations of lingerie.

8 I am constantly forgetting what eclectic means.

9 New Englanders tend to add an r to words that end in a and to omit the r in words that do end in r.

10 Thus, in Boston, Cuba becomes Cuber, while river becomes riva.

28 CAPITALS

Modern writers capitalize less frequently than did older writers, and informal writing permits less capitalization than formal writing. Two hundred years ago, a famous author wrote:

> Being ruined by the Inconstancy and Unkindness of a Lover, I hope a true and plain Relation of my Misfortune may be of Use and Warning to Credulous Maids, never to put much Trust in deceitful Men.
>
> JONATHAN SWIFT, "The Story of the Injured Lady"

A modern writer would eliminate all capitals but the initial *B* and the pronoun *I*.

28a Capitalize the first word of a sentence and the first word of a line of poetry.

Education is concerned not with knowledge but with the meaning of knowledge.

True ease in writing comes from art, not chance,
As those move easiest who have learned to dance.

ALEXANDER POPE, *Essay on Criticism*

Some modern poets ignore the convention of capitalizing each line of poetry, perhaps because they feel that an initial capital letter gives a word unwanted emphasis.

a man who had fallen among thieves
lay by the roadside on his back
dressed in fifteenthrate ideas
wearing a round jeer for a hat

e. e. cummings, "a man who had fallen among thieves"

28b Capitalize the pronoun I and the interjection O.

Do not capitalize the interjection *oh* unless it is the first word of a sentence.

28c Capitalize proper nouns, their derivatives and abbreviations, and common nouns used as proper nouns.

1 Specific persons, races, nationalities, languages.

William	Bob	George A. Smith	Semitic
Asiatic	American	Mongolian	Cuban
Canadian	English	Swahili	Zulu

Usage varies for the term *black (blacks)* designating members of the Negro race. Although it is often not capitalized, and is never capitalized in the phrase "blacks and whites," many authors regularly capitalize other uses in current writing.

2 Specific places.

Dallas	Jamestown	California	Lake Erie
Newfoundland	Iran	Jerusalem	Ohio River

3 Specific organizations, historical events, and documents.

Daughters of the American Revolution	the French Revolution
the Locarno Pact	NAACP
Declaration of Independence	

4 Days of the week, months, holidays, and holy days.

Thursday	April	Christmas	Sunday	Labor Day
Easter	Good Friday	Hanukkah	Ramadan	

5 Religious terms with sacred significance.

the Virgin   Allah   Holy Ghost   the Saviour

6 Titles of books, plays, magazines, newspapers, journals, articles, poems.
Capitalize the first word and all others except articles, and conjunctions and prepositions of fewer than five letters. (See also **25h** and **27a**.)

Gone with the Wind	*The Country Wife*	*Pippa Passes*
Paradise Lost	*Atlantic Monthly*	*War and Peace*
Ebony	*Much Ado About Nothing*	

7   Titles, when they precede a proper noun. Such titles are an essential part of the name and are regularly capitalized.

Professor Wilson	Secretary Hawkins
Dr. Natalie Spence	Mr. Gottschalk
President Reagan	Judge Paul Perry

When titles follow a name, do not capitalize them unless they indicate high distinction:

> Robert F. Jones, president of the National Bank
> J. R. Derby, professor of English

BUT   Abraham Lincoln, President of the United States
> John Marshall, Chief Justice, United States Supreme Court

"High distinction" is, however, becoming more and more broadly interpreted. Some people write forms such as the following:

Robert F. Jones, President of the National Bank
J. R. Derby, Professor of English

8   Common nouns used as an essential part of a proper noun. These are generic names such as *street, river, avenue, lake, county, ocean, college.*

Vine Street	Fifth Avenue	Pacific Ocean Lake Huron
General Motors Corporation		Penn Central Railroad
Hamilton College		Mississippi River

When the generic term is used in the plural, it is not usually capitalized.

Vine and Mulberry streets   Hamilton and Lake counties
the Atlantic and Pacific oceans

28d   Avoid unnecessary capitalization.

28d

A good general rule is not to capitalize unless a specific convention warrants it.

1   Capitalize north, east, south, west only when they come at the beginning of a sentence or refer to specific geographical locations.

> Birds fly south in the winter.

BUT   She lives in the western part of the Old South.

2   The names of seasons need not be capitalized.

fall   autumn   winter   midwinter   spring   summer

3   Capitalize nouns indicating family relationships only when they are used as names or titles or in combination with proper names. Do not capitalize *mother* and *father* when they are preceded by possessive adjectives.

	I wrote to my father		My uncle has ten children.
BUT	I wrote Father	BUT	My Uncle Ben has ten children.

4   Ordinarily, do not capitalize common nouns and adjectives used in place of proper nouns and adjectives.

	I went to high school in Cleveland.
BUT	I went to John Adams High School in Cleveland.
	I am a university graduate.
BUT	I am a Columbia University graduate.
	I took a psychology course in my senior year.
BUT	I took Psychology 653 in my senior year.

EXERCISE 28a–d Capitalize words as necessary in the following sentences. Remove unnecessary capitals.

1 After leaving detroit, we turned North toward Mackinac island for our Summer vacation with uncle Jim.
2 The reverend Martin Luther King, jr., first came to public attention as a leader of the Civil Rights sit-ins in the south.
3 The late Robert Kennedy had been attorney general of the United States before being elected senator from the state of New York.
4 It has been predicted that power in the un will eventually shift from the security council to the general assembly.
5 The Boston symphony orchestra is not to be confused with the Boston pops orchestra.
6 All Math Majors who were preparing to teach Elementary School students were required by the math department to take courses in the New Math.
7 The organization of American states is designed to encourage cooperation and understanding among the nations of the western hemisphere.
8 Annemarie O'hara, president of the student congress, addressed the meeting.
9 Many of the aberdeen angus cattle come from the state of Nebraska.
10 It was the fall of the Roman empire which ushered in the middle ages.

29 APOSTROPHE '

29a Use an apostrophe to show the possessive case of nouns and indefinite pronouns.

1 If a word (either singular or plural) does not end in *s*, add an apostrophe and *s* to form the possessive.

the woman's book   the women's books
the child's book   the children's books
the man's book   the men's book
someone's book   people's books

2 If the singular of a word ends in *s*, add an apostrophe and *s* unless the second *s* makes pronunciation difficult; in such cases, add only the apostrophe.

	Lois's book	James's book
BUT	Moses' leadership	Sophocles' dramas

(The addition of a second *s* would change the pronunciation of *Moses* to *Moseses* and *Sophocles* to *Sophocleses*.)

3 If the plural of a word ends in *s*, add only the apostrophe.

the girls' books
the boys' books
the Smiths' books [Referring to at least two persons named Smith]

4 In compounds, make only the last word possessive.

father-in-law's book [*Singular possessive*]
mothers-in-law's books [*Plural possessive*]
someone else's book

5 In nouns of joint possession, make only the last noun possessive; in nouns of individual possession, make both nouns possessive.

John and Paul's book [*Joint possession*]
John's and Paul's books [*Individual possession*]

29a

Here is a list showing standard singular and plural possessive forms:

Singular	Possessive Singular	Plural	Possessive Plural
child	child's	children	children's
man	man's	men	men's
lady	lady's	ladies	ladies'
father-in-law	father-in-law's	fathers-in-law	fathers-in-law's
passer-by	passer-by's	passers-by	passers-by's

29b Use an apostrophe to indicate the omission of a letter or number.

can't	can not	o'clock	of the clock
doesn't	does not	blizzard of '89	blizzard of 1889
it's	it is	will-o'-the wisp	will of the wisp

In reproducing speech, writers frequently use an apostrophe to show that a word is given a colloquial, or dialectical pronunciation.

"An' one o' the boys is goin' t' be sick," he said.

A too frequent use of the apostrophe for such purposes, however, clutters up the page and annoys the reader.

29c Use an apostrophe and s to form the plurals of letters, numbers, and words used as words.

In such cases, the letters, numbers, and words are also italicized, but the s is not.

Cross your *t*'s and dot your *i*'s.
Count to 10,000 by *2*'s.
Tighten your sentence structure by eliminating unnecessary *and*'s.

These are the only kinds of situations in which the apostrophe is used in forming plurals. It is never used in forming the plurals of proper names or other nouns.

29d Do not use the apostrophe with the possessive form of personal pronouns.

The personal pronouns *his, hers, its, ours, yours, theirs* and the pronoun *whose* are possessives as they stand and do not require the apostrophe.

his father   a book of *hers*   a friend of *theirs*

Be particularly careful not to confuse the possessive pronoun *its* with the contraction *it's* (it is).

We couldn't find *its* nest.
We know *it's* a robin.

EXERCISE 29a–d   Insert apostrophes or apostrophes plus *s* as necessary in the following sentences.

1 One of my most prized possessions is the Supremes first record album.
2 Its hard to believe that in a country as rich as ours, some people still go to bed hungry every night.
3 The chairpersons assistant has assured all members of the department that theyll have their class schedules in two weeks time.
4 Most modern cities havent the resources with which to keep up with their expanding populations.
5 He had asked for a months leave of absence, but he was allowed to take only the three days sick leave that were due him.
6 Hers was the better way, mine was the quicker.
7 Whats the point of experimenting with mind-expanding drugs when they can do terrible damage to ones mind?
8 A rock groups career, as show business goes, is relatively short.
9 The greatest years of *The New Yorker* were those under Harold Ross editorship.
10 Its hard to keep up with the Joneses when you dont have Mr. Jones income.

30   HYPHEN -

30

The hyphen has two distinct uses: (1) to form compound words, and (2) to indicate that a word is continued from one line to the next.

Convention in the latter use of the hyphen, called syllabication or *word division,* is arbitrarily fixed. (See Section **18.**) But convention in the use of hyphens with compounds not only shifts rapidly but is unpredictable. As a noun, *short circuit* is spelled as two words; but the verb *short-circuit* is hyphenated. *Shorthand, shortstop,* and *shortwave* are spelled as single words, but *short cut* is spelled as two words. *Short-term* in *short-term loan* is hyphenated, but in *the loan is short term* it is spelled as two words.

In such a rapidly changing and unpredictable matter, your only safe recourse is to consult a good, up-to-date dictionary. The following uses of the hyphen in forming compound words are widely accepted.

30a

30a Use a hyphen to form compound words that are not yet accepted as single words.

The spelling of compound words that express a single idea passes through successive stages. Originally spelled as two separate words, then as a hyphenated word, a compound word finally emerges as a single word.

> *base ball* became *base-ball* became *baseball*
> *post mark* became *post-mark* became *postmark*

There is no way of determining the proper spelling of a compound at any given moment. Your dictionary is your most authoritative reference.

30b

30b Use a hyphen to join two or more words serving as a single adjective before a noun.

Do not hyphenate such an adjective if it follows the verb as a predicate adjective.

	a well-known speaker
BUT	The speaker was well known.

	a grayish-green coat
BUT	The coat was grayish green.

Omit the hyphen when the first word is an adverb ending in -ly.

	a slow-curving ball		a quick-moving runner
BUT	a slowly curving ball	BUT	a quickly moving runner

30c

30c Use a hyphen to avoid an ambiguous or awkward union of letters.

NOT	recreate [For "create again"]	NOT	belllike
BUT	re-create	BUT	bell-like

In commonly used words, the hyphen is omitted.

> coeducational   coordinate   cooperate   readdress

30d **Use a hyphen to form compound numbers from twenty-one through ninety-nine and to separate the numerator from the denominator in written fractions.**

twenty-nine   fifty-five   two-thirds   four-fifths

30e **Use a hyphen with the prefixes self-, all-, ex-, and the suffix -elect.**

self-important   all-Conference   ex-mayor   governor-elect

Do not capitalize the prefix *ex-* or the suffix *-elect,* even when used in titles that are essential parts of a name.

ex-Mayor Kelley   Governor-elect Jones   ex-President Truman

EXERCISE 30   Insert hyphens as needed.

1 The editor in chief owns a well designed house.
2 He boasts that he is self made and self educated, but he forgets that he is also self centered.
3 My father in law once ran in the hundred meter relay; his team went as far as the semi finals.
4 The life long dream of many Americans is a four bedroom home with a two car garage.
5 He changed a twenty dollar bill into five dollar bills.

REVIEW EXERCISE ON WORD PUNCTUATION (Sections 27–30)   Supply the necessary italics, capitals, apostrophes, and hyphens in the sentences below.

1 magazines such as yankee and vermont life are popular with readers who idealize old time country life.
2 The item appeared in last mondays new york times.
3 its a well known fact that most old age pensions are inadequate for present day needs.
4 sarahs exhusband had been well meaning enough but too self effacing for an out going girls taste.
5 hes got too many ands in his sentences.
6 barbra streisands first big break in show business was in the broadway play i can get it for you wholesale.
7 the four american delegates carefully prepared proposal was rejected by the soviet unions spokesman.

8 although eighteen year olds can now vote, my brothers friend didn't vote until he was twenty-one.

9 the four cylinder sixty horse power car wasnt able to pull Jones custom built limousine out of the ditch.

10 roots, an eight part dramatic series based on alex haleys search for his long buried past, topped all previous tv programs in the nielson ratings.

REVIEW EXERCISES ON PUNCTUATION (Sections 19-30)

EXERCISE A Make all necessary corrections in internal punctuation and in the use of capitals, italics, apostrophes, and hyphens in the following sentences.

1 Her favorite writers joyce carol oates and james dickey are both contemporary.

2 Your faults are an uncontrollable temper inexperience and indifference to your work.

3 Since we had driven the car 87,000 miles we decided to turn it in.

4 If siege is spelled with an ie why is seize spelled with an ei?

5 What we need said mr. blevin the union spokesman is a good days pay for a good days work.

6 Many people perhaps most people do not know from what materials their clothing is made.

7 The government was faced with a difficult task it had to persuade a skeptical frustrated people that the energy shortage was real.

8 Her camera her new dress and her books all of which she left in her car were stolen.

9 I have just received an un-expected letter from the director of the bureau of internal revenue.

10 Ruth wanted a pontiac frances a ford donna a chrysler and alice a raleigh bicycle.

11 The late will rogers favorite saying was ive never met a man i did'nt like.

12 Judy garland is best remembered for her role in the 1930s film the wizard of oz.

13 Does anyone remember who said absolute power corrupts absolutely?

14 I make it a point to read the new york times every day and the new yorker every week only rarely however do i get around to time or newsweek.

15 You can't do that, they shouted from the balcony, you can't you can't.

EXERCISE B In the following sentences, determine which marks of punctuation are used correctly, which marks are used incorrectly, and what additional punctuation is needed. Be prepared to give reasons for your decisions.

1 I've seen the play *The Elephant Man* twice, but I still find it's plot fascinating.

2 We like to think that the spoils system went out with Andrew Jackson, but actually it's still in effect: in federal, state, and municipal government.

3 Is'nt it time we all ignored our own personal problems and cooperated with one another in making this world a better place to live in

4 You watch television all day long; and in the evening too.

5 Should one judge candidates from the speeches they make? from the printed matter they distribute? or from the ideas they generate?

6 Blacks and whites must learn to live and work together; otherwise, this country will suffer civil disorder.

7 The Presidents wifes activities are always reported in the press, so are his childrens.

8 I think I recognize that actor, wasn't he on the television show *The Jeffersons?*

9 I wanted to make that perfectly clear, the speaker said, Have I made it so?

10 D. W. Griffiths *The Birth of a Nation* 1915, was the most important movie in the early history of the film.

LARGER ELEMENTS

If you wish to be a writer, write.

EPICTETUS

Anyone who wishes to become a good writer should endeavor, before he allows himself to be tempted by the more showy qualities, to be direct, simple, brief, vigorous, and lucid.

H. W. FOWLER

31 THE WHOLE COMPOSITION **PLAN**

Whenever you undertake a specific piece of writing, you face two problems: saying what you really mean and making that meaning clear to your readers. For these two problems there are no easy solutions. One thing is certain, though. If a piece of writing is to be effective, you must decide at the outset *what* you want to say, *to whom* you want to say it, and *how* you want to say it. Once the writing is done—whether it be a letter home, or an application for a job, or a term paper—you must look at what you have produced and give honest answers to the following questions: Is the writing readable and clear? Does it convey a sense of purpose? Does it engage the reader in the way you want it to?

To be consistently satisfied with the answers to these questions, you need to develop a somewhat standardized approach to writing assignments, however different in form and purpose they may be. The procedure described in this section is one that many writers—professional and amateur—have found useful. Not all writing assignments require the use of each step in the procedure. Conversely, some assignments may require the addition of a step or two. The basic system provides a methodical way to approach any writing task, not in a rigid, lock-step manner but rather with a flexible framework you can adapt to the demands of the writing task confronting you.

Prewriting

1   Select a topic, then narrow it to fit the length of your writing assignment. (See Sections **31a** and **31b** on selecting and limiting a subject.)

2   Make a list of ideas, assertions, facts, and examples that are related to your subject and work this list into a preliminary outline. (See Section **31c** on taking notes and making a preliminary outline.)

3   Decide on the purpose of your piece of writing and frame a specific thesis statement for that purpose. (See Section **31d** on determining purpose and thesis.)

4   Think carefully about the kind of reader you are writing to; the identity of the reader largely determines *what* you want to say and *how* you want to say it. (See Section **31e** on considering audience.)

5   Decide on the pattern of organization and the methods of development that will best serve your purpose. (See Section **31f** on deciding on a pattern of organization and methods of development.)

6   Identify those items in the preliminary outline that fit your

purpose and support your thesis. Then work these items into an outline. (See Section **31g** on making an outline.)

Writing and revising

7   Begin to write and keep writing until you have completed a rough draft. Don't be concerned with problems of wording and phrasing or grammar and punctuation at this stage. (See Section **31i** on writing a preliminary draft.)

8   Try to think of an illustration, an anecdote, or an example to use for an interesting, engaging opening statement for this first draft. Once you have done so, go through the paper checking especially to make sure the ending is a complete summary of your topic and thesis. (See Section **31h** on beginning and ending the paper.)

9   Go over the entire draft, checking it for correct spelling, punctuation, and grammar. Then reread it carefully for clarity, organization, and sound reasoning. (See Section **31j** on revising the rough draft.)

10   Put your paper aside, if possible for a day or two but for as much time as you can afford. (You will gain perspective about the paper and be better able to spot weaknesses in logic or organization.) Then prepare the final copy. (See Section **31k** on preparing the final draft.)

These ten steps of the writing process comprise two phases: first, the prewriting or planning phase of the paper; second, the writing and revising phase of the paper. The prewriting process—the first six steps listed above—is as important to the quality and success of the final paper as are writing and revising—the final four steps in the list. Effective writing requires careful planning.

31a   Select a topic.

In college writing courses you are sometimes free to choose the topic for a paper; at other times you are assigned a topic. When you are asked to develop your own topic, look for one that interests you and about which you have some knowledge. Begin your search for a topic by examining your own experience, your abilities, your religious and political beliefs. Can you repair cars or lawnmowers? Are you knowledgeable about stereo components? Do you make your own clothes? Can you cook ethnic food? Do you play a sport or a musical instrument? What interesting people have you known as teachers, as religious leaders, as employers, or as fellow employees? Which ones have you liked or admired, and why? Have you recently read a book or seen a film that you liked? Why did you like it? What is your favorite television program, and why? Do you have any strong feelings, favorable or unfavorable, about courses you have taken in high school or college? Do you have political beliefs or allegiances? What are they, and why do you hold them? What kinds of jobs have you had? Which ones did you like or dislike, and why?

Examine your own experience. Every day you spend some time watching television, listening to the radio, perhaps reading a newspaper. What shows do you watch and why? What do you read first in the newspaper—the world news, the sports pages, the comics? Why? Perhaps you are dissatisfied with parking conditions on your campus or with the food served in the university grill. What remedies can you suggest for these problems? As these questions and the ones in the preceding paragraph suggest, the possibilities for finding topics in your own experience are limitless. Reflect on your experience and your interests in order to discover them.

Whether you choose your own topic or are assigned a single topic or a list of topics from which to choose one, the first step in the writing procedure is to select the topic and then narrow it down to fit the length of the paper required. Many students make the mistake of thinking that they have found a topic when, in fact, they have only thought of a general idea. Most of the papers you write in English courses will be 400 to 700 words long, or about 4 to 8 paragraphs. Topics such as "Prejudice is Evil" or "Equal Educational Opportunities for All" cannot be managed in papers of 400 to 700 words. Prejudice may be a good concept to think about, but you need a very limited aspect of prejudice for a short essay. Once you think of such topics as "My Roommate's Prejudices" or "My Prejudice Against Tall Blonds," you are approaching a manageable topic. Once you think of such possibilities as "Handicapped Students Need P.E. Courses Too" or "Why Not Women on the Football Team?" you have a topic you can discuss in a few well-developed paragraphs.

The following lists illustrate the difference between a general idea and a specific topic. Any topic in the *General* column can be narrowed to many different specific topics. Many of the topics in the *Specific* column are phrased as questions because questions often help to determine the purpose of a paper. Some of the specific topics might require further limiting, depending on the length of the paper assigned.

General	*Specific*
1. Controlling Pollution	1. The Cause of Three Recent Fish Kills in the Stones River
2. Technology Today	2. Bathroom Gadgets Unlimited
3. Television	3. The Glamorous Female Private Eye: Sexy and Savvy

General	*Specific*
4. Parents and Children	4. My Father's Unpredictable Moods
5. Advertising	5. "The Man Who Reads *Playboy*": Does He Really Exist?
6. Fashion in Clothes	6. Charlie Daniels: Boots, Jeans, and Big Cowboy Hats
7. Science Fiction	7. Why Ray Bradbury Is My Favorite Author
8. College Administration	8. Do Minority Students Really Need Minority Advisors?
9. College Life	9. Should Thursday Night Keg Parties Be Banned?
10. The College Newspaper	10. More Humor and Fewer Editorials, Please!
11. The Cost of Higher Education	11. Why I Can't Afford Not to Work Part-Time
12. Women's Athletics	12. Equal Funds for Equal Sports?
13. Popular Magazines	13. Why *Omni* Is Necessary to My Well-being
14. Soap Operas	14. The Soaps: How Clean Are They?
15. Military Service	15. Why Is Mom So Hostile Toward the Draft?
16. Solar Energy	16. The Advantages of a Solar Water Heater
17. Racial Prejudice in the U.S.	17. The Klan's Current Appeal to the Younger Generation
18. The Energy Crisis	18. The Economic Advantages of Owning a Subcompact
19. U.S. Middle East Policy	19. Could We Live Without Oil from the Middle East?
20. Urban Congestion	20. Catching a Taxi in New York City

EXERCISE 31a(1) Make a list of five general topics suggested by your interest in television, in movies, and in sports—for example, "Why Are Sitcoms so Popular?" "Why I Like Sci Fi Movies" or "My Weekly Date with Monday Night Football."

EXERCISE 31a(2) Make a list of five general topics suggested by your hobbies or your work—for example, "Refinishing Antique Furniture" or "Selling Ladies' Leisure Wear."

EXERCISE 31a(3) Make a list of five general topics suggested by your taste in music and in books—for example, "Is Country Music Just for Country Folks?" or "Why I Like the Novels of Ray Bradbury."

31b

31b Limit the topic.

Many students assume that writing a 500-word paper is an impossible task. ("How can I write 500 words about a topic? I don't know 500 words about anything.") Yet, as we have suggested, the experience of most freshmen is rich in potential topics. Finding these topics is the difficulty. Suppose your instructor gives you a list of general subjects such as the one in Section 31a and tells you to formulate a specific topic from one of the general subjects, frame a thesis statement about this specific topic, and then write a 500-word essay on the topic you chose. How do you begin? First, examine the list, looking for a subject that interests you or that you can relate to your own experience. With concentration and imagination, you almost certainly can come up with something.

But suppose you can't. You then face not so much the task of *finding* a topic as the challenge of *creating* or *inventing* one. You must go back over the list again, thinking about anything in your personal life that you might be able to connect to one of the general topic areas. Imagine college freshman Kevin McNeil in exactly that situation. An essay has been assigned, and Kevin is sitting in the library staring at the general subjects in Section 31a. Nothing exceptional has occurred in his life in the past few months, he is sure, except for the sporty little subcompact he purchased shortly after high-school graduation to get to work in the summer and to college in the fall. Kevin remembers worrying about whether he could afford a car and still assume some of the costs of college. He also recalls wondering if he would be able to afford gas for a car once he had one. As he thinks about his new car, Kevin suddenly realizes that connections exist between his reasons for buying it and topic 11, "The Cost of Higher Education" and topic 18, "The Energy Crisis." Both subjects were very much on his mind while he was considering what kind of car to buy.

Still, Kevin is uneasy about trying to write a paper that ties the cost of college to his new car or links his car and the high price of gas. Both ideas seem very general in scope and neither seems to have a clear direction or purpose to it. What Kevin recalls most vividly are the long hours he spent shopping for the car and the many conversations he and his parents had about financing the car and buying insurance for it. He feels that he learned a good deal about how to buy a car from the experience, and he thinks that this new knowledge might be best to write about.

So far, Kevin has isolated a subject that might be workable for him. The subject of buying a used car is still a very general one, and it needs further limiting if Kevin is to manage it in 500 words. No instructor wants you to write papers that are nothing more than series of vague generalizations lacking support. Good writing uses concrete details and examples to illustrate and support the main ideas in a paper. The next problem, then, is how to make a topic you have chosen even more specific. To limit a topic, you must define what *you* know about it.

What Kevin knows about used cars is how he shopped for and bought his car. To refresh his memory, he jots down a few notes about what he did when he decided to buy a car:

1 Asked parents for their permission and advice.
2 Stopped by some local dealers to look over their selection.
3 Called the bank to find out current interest rates and payment schedules.
4 Started reading the used car ads.

Looking over his notes, what Kevin sees is what *he* did when *he* wanted to buy a car, not necessarily what all people do when they set out to buy cars. He thinks that he might very well be able to write the following paper: "How I Selected the Used Car That Was Right for Me."

Kevin now has a topic drawn from his personal experience, one that he can write about effectively, one that may be instructive for someone who reads his paper. Kevin has not so much *found* this topic as *created* it. The paper is a long way from being finished, though. There is still much thinking to do about the topic, notes and at least a preliminary outline to prepare.

Thus far, Kevin has decided on a general subject and narrowed it to a manageable topic for a short essay. He has accomplished this much using his own experience and using his knowledge of that experience as it applies to the assignment in his English class. Kevin has discovered that a topic is not found, but rather made. He has engaged in a process called **invention,** a term applied to that aspect of the writing process involving the creation and development of a topic. He has, however, completed only the creation part of the process. Development comes next.

EXERCISE 31b(1) Make a list of five specific topics from the list you made for Exercise 31a(1).

EXERCISE 31b(2) Make a list of five specific topics from the list you made for Exercise 31a(2).

EXERCISE 31b(3) Make a list of five specific topics from the list you made for Exercise 31a(3).

31c

31c Take notes and make a preliminary outline.

To develop a topic, you need to use the methods, **strategies of invention,** that are discussed and illustrated in this section. Invention strategies enable you to formulate a purpose (a thesis) and help you to organize the evidence you plan to use in your essay to support the thesis.

Finding out how much you really know about your selected topic, discovering how much information you can assemble that can be worked into your paper is the next step. Even with a good topic, one you are interested in and know something about, further crafting is necessary if you are to write an organized, coherent, adequately developed essay.

Many inexperienced writers think they are ready to write once they have selected their topics. They assume that all the examples and details an essay requires will spontaneously appear when they take pen in hand. In fact, very few people can simply pour forth coherent, well-constructed writing, even when they are writing about personal experiences. Accordingly, once you have selected a topic, set aside some time for making notes and for working up a preliminary outline or plan of your paper. Otherwise, you may discover too late that your topic is still too general or that you have insufficient information to develop the topic. Using one or more of the strategies of invention can make your work relatively easy.

Perhaps the most common method of inventing material for a topic is to make a list, an inventory of facts, examples, details—of practically anything relating to the topic. Some writers do this gradually, over a period of time. Some think about their topics while they enjoy a quiet cup of coffee, some while they travel to and from work or classes, some while they take an evening walk, jog, or bicycle ride. Other writers sit down with a blank piece of paper and write down ideas for thirty minutes or an hour. This latter technique, **brainstorming,** involves listing anything that comes to mind about the topic during a specified amount of time. One method is not superior to the other; discover for yourself which method you prefer.

Having selected a topic, Kevin needs to explore it further. When his roommate is out for a couple of hours in the morning, Kevin stays in the room and brainstorms. He gets a cup of coffee and sits at the desk to review the notes he made when he was narrowing the topic. Then he writes a list of everything he can remember. After an hour, he is surprised at how much he has written down. Here's what he has:

1 Asked parents for their permission.
2 Asked about methods of financing.

3 Asked about down payment: Should I earn it first? Could I borrow it?

4 Called bank to inquire about car loans and personal loans.

5 Inquired about interest rates and payment schedules.

6 Talked to Mom and Dad and some friends about what kind of car to buy.

7 Looked into advantages of subcompacts.

8 Discovered that some subcompacts were priced higher than many regular-sized cars.

9 Visited local dealers to look over their cars.

10 Inquired about the reputations of certain local dealers. Were they honest? Did they give warranties? What kind?

11 Started looking through the want ads for personal sales.

12 Learned how to check for condition of used cars; read *Consumer Reports.*

13 Learned about financing through a dealer.

14 Would be a cash purchase; no trade-in available.

15 Learned how to compare cars and prices.

As it is, the list looks pretty jumbled; but Kevin certainly has at hand enough information about buying the car to be able to write a 500-word essay. As he studies the notes, he sees a pattern in them—a chronological pattern that begins with his talking with his parents and ends with the actual financing and buying of the car. For the time being, he arranges this pattern into three major headings:

1 How I decided what kind of car to buy
2 How I shopped for and selected the car
3 How I bought and financed the car

This is not an outline for Kevin's paper, but it is a valuable first step toward a workable outline. It establishes at least temporary direction and order.

Another method that can help you to develop a topic is talking with people. Choose someone you can trust to give you an honest opinion about whether the topic is interesting, workable, and worth writing about. Have ready specific questions to ask your listener; it is likely, though, that the person will ask questions about the topic that you have not thought about yet. If possible, talk with someone who already knows something about the topic you have chosen. English instructors are always glad to talk about papers. They have been trained to give valuable assistance when you encounter such problems as developing a topic.

For his paper on buying a car, Kevin talks with his parents and with friends who have bought cars in the recent past. His father reminds him that he told Kevin never to offer a dealer the asking price of a car, but instead to start with a much lower bid. His mother mentions that she suggested having a reputable mechanic check the car before Kevin bought it. Kevin adds this additional information to his notes.

Once you have used one of the strategies of invention, you will realize what a valuable step it is as you prepare to write your paper. Invention results in specific information, and grouping specific information can produce a tentative plan of order for your paper.

EXERCISE 31c(1)   Use one or two methods of invention to generate preliminary notes for two of the specific topics you listed in Exercises 31b(1), (2), or (3).

EXERCISE 31c(2)   Which of the suggested specific topics listed on pp. 176–177 could you use without any further study or research for an essay of 300 to 500 words? Choose two of the topics and use one or two methods of invention to make preliminary notes for them.

31d   Determine your paper's purpose and create a thesis statement reflecting that purpose.

After you have selected and narrowed your subject and listed your ideas on that subject, you have made real progress. But before you can start to write your paper, you need to decide upon a purpose for it. Then you need to frame a thesis; that is, you must create a statement that sums up the paper's controlling idea.

1   Determine a purpose. The purpose of a paper reflects your choice, as the writer, about what you want to do with the topic. But before you can sensibly decide on your purpose, you should know that, for centuries, writing has been categorized according to four types, or **modes:** narration, description, exposition, and argumentation. Each mode sets up its own promises and expectations between writer and reader, and each mode has certain characteristics that differentiate it from the others. This is not to say that the modes are mutually exclusive; in fact, most pieces of writing make use of two or more modes. For example, an attorney's brief may *narrate* the sequence of events in a crime, *describe* the actions of the alleged criminal, and *argue* for the conviction of the defendant. Before you can choose the mode (or modes) best suited to your essay, then, you must understand the uses and characteristics of all four.

A   Narration. The purpose of narration is to tell a story, to recount in sequence a series of occurrences, to tell "what happened." Narration is the form most commonly given to writing meant to entertain: you experience it daily on television, in movies, and in short stories and novels. Its appeal is universal; narration is the first kind of discourse that children learn, in bedtime stories and in the yarns a grandfather spins about growing up long ago. If you have ever been asked to write an essay about what you did on your summer vacation—and who hasn't!—you were asked to write narration.

Usually, the purpose of a piece of narrative writing is not simply to relate a sequence of events. Storytellers almost always construct a story to make a point: to reveal character or to make a statement about human existence. Similarly, when you retell an experience of your own, you often do it in such a way that you reveal something about what you learned in the experience. You relate a certain historical event to compare it with a current political situation. You tell the story of a friend's death in an automobile accident to make a point about the uncertainty of life. See the first paper, p. 223, in the papers for analysis at the end of this chapter. As he recounts an unusual evening with his family, the writer discovers a meaning in the experience for himself and the other members of his family.

B   Description. The purpose of description is to make readers see, feel, hear what the writer has seen or felt or heard. Description is often combined with exposition, argumentation and especially narration. In a narrative, for example, a writer may choose to describe a character's physical attributes in such a way as to suggest the character's moral attributes. In Melville's novel *Moby-Dick,* Captain Ahab's leg becomes a powerful symbol of his crippled moral nature, of his obsession to punish the whale that took part of his humanity from him. The descriptions of Ahab's physical appearance are meant to give insight into his moral nature.

Description can be of two kinds: objective (or technical) and suggestive (or impressionistic). The first requires writers to reproduce what they see as a camera would. An appraiser for a mortgage company provides an objective description of a house:

> Lot size 120 feet wide by 150 feet deep. Exterior dimensions of house: 84 feet by 27 feet. Living area 1,620 square feet; 648 additional square feet in two-car garage. Seven rooms: three bedrooms, living room, dining room, kitchen, den; two baths. One brick fireplace. Central heat (gas); central air (electric). R–19 insulation rating. Three years old.

The appraisal contains no emotional reaction or judgment of the house's appeal. The purpose of the appraiser's objective description is to enable the mortgage company to set a fair loan value on the house.

The homeowner who wishes to sell the same house writes up a description that reads as follows:

> Practically new three-bedroom, two-bath, ranch-style brick home situated on a shade-tree-covered half-acre lot. Over 1600 square feet of living area. Modern kitchen with built-in appliances. Cozy den with old-fashioned red brick fireplace and beamed ceiling. Formal living and

dining rooms for gracious entertaining. Master bedroom suite with adjoining full bath. Oversized two-car garage. Large patio with gas grill. All of this is nestled beneath stately maples and is available on a mortgage with a low $10^1/_2\%$ interest.

This description creates a much different impression than does the appraiser's. The latter description may not be merely the product of the owner's desire to sell the house; it no doubt reflects an emotional attachment to the house.

Another example of descriptive writing, especially of impressionistic description, can be found in the second paper, pp. 224–225, in the papers for analysis. In it the writer reveals the childhood fondness she felt for her uncle's country store as she describes a visit after an absence of several years. Notice how the attention to detail (objective description) intensifies the writer's reactions to and impressions of the old store. The best descriptive writing often fuses the two kinds of description in one piece of writing.

C Exposition. The purpose of exposition is to inform, to explain, to clarify—to make readers know or understand something about a subject. Your most frequent contact with exposition may be television news and the newspaper. The television program *Nova* is a good example of exposition. Exposition may sometimes appeal to emotions, as narration and description often do. For example, a news report of the death of a loved or hated person is likely to provoke strong feelings. But the primary purpose of exposition is to inform, fully and fairly. For this reason, good exposition is clear, concise, and straightforward.

Exposition is the mode used to write a manual for automobile owners, a recipe for southern fried chicken, a booklet on the rules of soccer, the format directions for preparing a paper. When you receive a booklet of instructions about how to register for your classes, you have been given expository prose. If the writers have failed in any of these instances to be clear and precise, the car owner, the cook, the soccer player, and the student suffer the consequences. Learning to write effective expository prose is the most important writing skill you can develop for daily life.

Even when exposition deals with controversial subject matter—gun control, for example—the writer or reporter in effect says to readers: "I'm simply trying to tell you something. I'm not trying to persuade you to believe what I believe or to lead you to value judgments, although there is the possibility that may happen. What I want to do is to make you know or understand something you didn't know or understand before—at least not so well or clearly." In the third paper, pp. 226–228, in the papers for analysis, the writer points out that the science-fiction film *Star Wars* makes use of certain conventions common in western stories and films. He is not arguing that *Star Wars* is a veiled copy of a western movie (although he may, in fact, think so); he is simply pointing out that some popular western elements are used in the film. The writer's purpose is certainly to interest and inform his readers; but he leaves it up to them to evaluate the significance of the information that such "western ingredients" as the "comical sidekick" and the "shoot-out" are a part of *Star Wars.*

D   Argumentation. The purpose of argumentation—or **persuasion,** as it is also called—is to convince readers (or listeners) of the rightness of your point of view (and, usually, the wrongness of an opposing viewpoint). You encounter argumentation in debates and editorials. Most, if not all, political speeches are a form of argumentation.

Because you are usually committed to the arguments you make, you must be careful not to lose control of your reasoning and your emotions when you intend to argue or persuade. Your purpose is to convince readers or listeners, and you can do so only if you present your case fully, objectively, and reasonably. Sound logic and a thorough understanding of the opposing position are prerequisites for effective argumentation.

In the fourth paper, pp. 229–230, in the papers for analysis, the writer uses careful logic as she constructs an interpretation of the E. A. Robinson poem "Richard Cory." She firmly believes that the author intended the story to be viewed in a certain way, and she supports her point of view with specific evidence from the poem itself. Similarly, a prosecuting attorney refers to the evidence of a crime to support an argument for a guilty verdict.

The difference between exposition and argumentation is this: in exposition you inform for the sake of informing, but in argumentation you inform in order to persuade. When you write argumentation, you say in effect: "I know what I believe. You may or may not find what I have to say interesting and informative, but my main purpose is not to inform. My main purpose is to persuade you to believe as I do." (See Section **33** for a discussion of writing persuasively.)

Taking into account the foregoing information on writing modes, Kevin is ready to decide the purpose for his paper on buying a car. Determining the purpose will help him frame a thesis statement for his paper. Remember that he proceeded through a chronology of events after he decided to buy a car. His notes and the very simple outline he made from them indicate the following sequence: he talked with his parents and others to decide what kind of car to buy; he shopped around and eventually found the car he wanted; he called the bank to inquire about loans and to make arrangements for financing the car.

Kevin's paper can certainly take the form of a narrative, but, just to be sure, he considers other possibilities. Description is out; Kevin sees no reason to include the appearance of the car. Argumentation seems unsuited to the topic; Kevin is unwilling to contend that the methods he used to buy a car ought to be followed by everyone who is shopping for a used car. Exposition, however, causes him to think further about what he wants the paper to accomplish. Kevin has to decide whether he simply wants to tell readers what he did or to inform them about a logical and systematic approach to a common dilemma. Kevin imagines a reader being able to use his paper as a guide to selecting a satisfactory used car. He decides that he is more interested in the essay's potential as exposition—informative writing—than as narration. Writing an expository paper will be a challenge, but Kevin feels that if he succeeds he will have written a better and more effective paper than if he were merely to tell the story of buying the car. Having decided to write an expository paper, he is now ready to frame a thesis statement, perhaps the most important step in the prewriting process.

2   Create a thesis statement. A thesis statement sets forth in a sentence the controlling idea and purpose of a paper. It answers the questions, What point does this paper make, what opinion does it offer, what stand does its writer take? A carefully stated thesis sentence introduces and summarizes the entire paper. Like any other sentence, a thesis sentence consists of a subject and a predicate. Once you have successfully limited your subject so that it is narrow and specific enough to manage in your paper, you have found the subject of your thesis sentence. Writing a thesis sentence is a matter of writing a predicate to go with that subject, a matter of deciding what assertion you wish to make about that subject.

For example, suppose you are given the general subject "Mass Media" as a topic to write about. After some thought, you narrow your interest down to television and, after still further thought, you decide to concentrate on television commercials. The next question is, what about television commercials? You need to state some central idea about commercials, to isolate what you wish to assert about them. You can make almost endless assertions about this topic (or any other). Here are a few examples:

> Television commercials are entertaining because of their music, their humor, and their scenery.
>
> Television commercials appeal to our desires for good health, good looks, and good living.
>
> Television commercials make us dissatisfied with our health, our appearance, and our income.
>
> Television commercials are at best misleading and at worst downright dishonest.

Television commercials make financially possible a far greater range of entertainment than would otherwise be possible without their financial support.

Each of the foregoing thesis sentences contains a clearly stated controlling idea, and each gives direction to the whole paper. The first two theses suggest overall expository purposes—to show in what ways commercials are entertaining and to explain how they appeal to certain desires; the last three suggest overall persuasive purposes—to convince the reader that commercials make viewers dissatisfied, to argue that commercials are dishonest, and to prove that they make possible variety in programming.

A well-formed thesis sentence not only gives a paper a clear purpose, it also helps you to keep a paper unified, provided that you stick to the purpose defined in the thesis statement. A good thesis sentence commits you to your purpose. Your task then is to support the thesis, to back it up with details and evidence, to explain what you mean by it, to convince your readers that it is a valid contention. The thesis sentence helps you to organize your paper because it provides the basis for decisions about what to include and what to exclude. What sponsors pay for TV advertising is crucial to your thesis if the point of your paper is that such payments support a broad range of entertainment. The same information, however, is clearly irrelevant to the four other examples of thesis statements; for them, it is information to exclude.

Most importantly, perhaps, a thesis sentence can give your paper an argumentative edge, a kind of dramatic interest. Even in a paper in which the general purpose is to explain or describe, a thesis sentence serves as the writer's commitment, a promise to make a clear point, to show that commercials are, after all, entertaining and not, as the reader thought, boring and frustrating. A good thesis sentence that defines a central idea clearly and precisely and gives a paper confident direction must meet three tests: it must be unified, limited, and specific.

A   A good thesis sentence is unified. A thesis sentence expresses only one central idea. Although it may include a secondary idea, it must subordinate any secondary idea to the central idea. You should be immediately suspicious of any thesis statement that is a compound sentence. Such sentences usually contain two central ideas, thereby defeating the unifying purpose of a thesis statement. Each of the following thesis sentences commits its writer to two main ideas, either of which requires a full paper for adequate development:

Television commercials are entertaining, *and* they help support a great range of programs.

Science fiction often anticipates new scientific developments, *but* it has never had as much appeal as detective stories.

The recent curriculum changes provide increased opportunities for students, *but* they also restrict the students' choices.

Intercollegiate football costs a disproportionate amount of money, *and* it involves many fewer students than other sports.

B A good thesis sentence is limited. Just as you need to narrow any general subject to a limited topic, so you need to narrow *your* assertion about the topic. In other words, just as the subject of a thesis sentence must be limited, so must its predicate. A good thesis must make an assertion that can be supported adequately in the time and space you have.

GENERAL	Good teachers have several different things in common.
LIMITED	Good teachers possess certain qualities: they are *competent* in their subjects, *fair* in their grading, and *imaginative* in presenting their materials.
GENERAL	Magazine advertising varies from magazine to magazine.
LIMITED	A magazine's advertising reflects the *social and economic desires* of its readers.
GENERAL	The selfishness of people can be seen in many ways.
LIMITED	The selfishness of people is at its worst *in a crowded subway.*

C A thesis sentence must be specific. A thesis sentence can be unified and restricted and yet not define a central idea usefully because the predicate is too vague and imprecise to give the paper any clear direction. Predicates that consist of *is* or *are* plus a vague complement such as *good, interesting,* or *a serious problem* are too imprecise to be useful. A sentence such as *The rising cost of higher education is a serious problem,* for example, does not state in what ways the problem is serious. The following examples show how thesis sentences with vague predicates can be made precise:

VAGUE	The rising cost of higher education is a serious problem.
SPECIFIC	The rising cost of higher education *may prevent many good students from attending college.*
	The rising cost of higher education *makes it increasingly difficult for private colleges to survive.*
VAGUE	The neighborhood I grew up in was an unusual place to live.
SPECIFIC	Although the neighborhood in which I grew up was *crowded and noisy, it was always friendly.*

> Although the neighborhood in which I grew up *was open and quiet, it was very lonely.*

VAGUE   My difficulties in biology lab are unbelievable.

SPECIFIC   My difficulties in biology lab *amuse the other students, confuse my instructor, and frustrate me.*

> My difficulties in biology lab *are so serious that they provide a strong argument against requiring all students to take a laboratory science.*

The more unified, limited, and specific you can make a thesis sentence, the better you will have focused your central idea and controlled the purpose of your paper. The more clearly you state your purpose, the better prepared you are to determine what evidence should go in the paper to develop your central idea and how best that evidence should be organized.

Let's return to Kevin's paper on buying a car. Having decided that its purpose will be expository rather than narrative, Kevin must frame a thesis statement that clearly informs readers of the paper's central idea. Kevin should explain the systematic approach he followed in selecting and buying a used car so that anyone who reads his paper will learn this useful information. He also wants to make it clear that the procedure described in his paper is the result of his own experience in buying a used car. What he did in buying a car is going to serve as the supporting evidence for Kevin's thesis.

Kevin does not want to become argumentative about what he learned. He does not want a thesis statement that reads, "Based on my experience, I think that every potential used-car buyer should complete the following steps in purchasing a car." He is writing only from his own experience, too limited a base to prescribe what is best for all other used-car buyers. After several attempts, he finally writes the following thesis sentence: "I learned recently that buying a used car entails thoughtful planning, careful shopping, and sound financing." Something about this sentence satisfies him. Let's see what it is.

Kevin states, "I learned recently. . . ," which implies that his paper will inform readers of what he learned. What did he learn? He learned "that buying a used car entails thoughtful planning, careful shopping, and sound financing." The topic and organization of the paper are clearly stated in this clause. First, the paper will be about buying a *used car* only. Moreover, Kevin prepares readers for three paragraphs of development—on planning, shopping, and financing, in that order. He has composed an effective thesis statement, one that focuses the topic and establishes direction and control for his central idea and purpose.

And that is precisely the point. A good thesis sentence is certainly informative for readers; but at this stage its importance is that it helps the writer to organize and construct an effective essay.

LARGER ELEMENTS

EXERCISE 31d(1)   Identify which writing mode seems most appropriate for each of the five specific topics you made for Exercise 31b(1), (2), (3). Explain what other modes, if any, you might use to supplement the primary mode for each topic.

EXERCISE 31d(2)   Read the papers for analysis, pp. 223–230, at the end of this chapter. Each paper represents one of the four writing modes. Identify the primary mode of each paper and tell what others have been combined with it to achieve the paper's purpose.

EXERCISE 31d(3)   Write two brief essays on the same subject but with different purposes. For example, write a factual, informative essay describing a dormitory room or an apartment, and then write a persuasive essay intended to convince a reader to live in the dormitory room or rent the apartment. Or write an objective report of an automobile accident, and then write a report about the same accident intended to prove that one of the drivers was clearly at fault.

EXERCISE 31d(4)   Some of the following thesis sentences define unified, limited, and specific central ideas. Others are not unified or are too broad or vague to be useful. Indicate which ones you think are satisfactory and explain why. Suggest revisions for those you think are unsuccessful.

1 Cigarette smoking is disgusting to those who don't smoke, harmful to those who do, and should be prohibited in public places.
2 A good coach has many different qualities.
3 Inflation is the most serious problem in the United States today.
4 Professional women athletes deserve benefits equal to those of men.
5 Shooting pool requires steady hands, keen eyes, and great patience.
6 Professor Winslow is a real human being.
7 Soccer is very different from football.
8 Objective examinations are unfair because they rely primarily on memory rather than on the ability to relate facts to one another.
9 There are several sure ways to lose a job.
10 Handicapped persons face many challenges every day.

EXERCISE 31d(5)   Write thesis sentences from the preliminary notes you made when you completed either Exercise 31c(1) or 31c(2).

31e   Consider your reader.

Unless you are taking notes for yourself or writing a diary, your writing is aimed at a reader other than yourself. You must keep these readers in mind as you write, because they—your audience—influence what you write, the way you write, even why you write. Always try to picture a specific reader or some specific group or type of reader. Then ask yourself whether the best presentation for this specific audience is likely to be simple or complex, popular or technical, general or specific. If your intention is truly to communicate, you must adjust your subject matter, your point of view, the kind of detail and explanation you use, even the words you choose to the audience you are writing for.

When you write to parents, brothers or sisters, or close friends, you know their interests and the language they use. These are readers *familiar* to you. When you write to them you use a *personal* tone and style; you do so without even thinking about it. Generally, when you write to a familiar audience, you do so with ease and confidence. On the other hand, you may have experienced some difficulty writing to a reader *unfamiliar* to you. Did you, for example, find yourself uncertain about how to write letters of application to deans of admission when you were applying to college? Have you ever found it agonizing to write a letter of application for a job? If you have, it is because you are writing to an *unfamiliar* audience. When you write to such an audience, you are expected to do so in an *impersonal* tone and style. In such writing you want to appear as mature and responsible as you possibly can.

Imagine that near the end of the current semester Suellen Calley discovers that her grades are not going to be good. In fact, she is probably going to fail at least two courses. The reasons are painfully clear to her: excessive absences, incomplete work, and a lack of serious studying, combined with too many parties and a lot of time on the golf course practicing her game. To break the bad news, she writes the following letter home to her parents before the semester's end:

> Well, I know you're not going to like this one bit, but it looks as if I'm going down the tube in a couple of my courses. I think I told you before that my history instructor didn't like me from the first. And besides, the requirements are superhuman! I mean, how can anyone be expected to write two research papers in one semester, work part-time, study for other classes, and have any fun? As for biology, I think you have to be an Einstein to pass lab. I mean, how can they get away with requiring all that lab time? Half the time I was late for work because I had to stay over in lab to complete some stupid exercise on the circulation system of the great American toad. Don't worry, though, it looks like I'm going to get all A's and B's in my other courses. My PE teacher really likes me; he says I've shown more improvement than anyone else in my putting game.

Sure enough, the report card comes and along with it a notice that Suellen has been placed on academic suspension. If she chooses to appeal, she is told, she may do so by writing the Dean of Admissions and requesting a one-semester period of academic probation. Suellen knows a break when she sees one, so she sits down and writes the following letter to the dean:

> I would respectfully like to appeal my academic suspension and to request a semester's probation. I would like to point out that I only

failed two of the six courses that I took, and both are courses in which failures are common. I would like to emphasize that I made one A, two C's, and a D in my other classes. This should be evidence of my academic ability to do college-level work. I will frankly admit to you that I did not apply myself up to my ability in the two courses I failed. Moreover, I worked part-time last semester to help cover the cost of my education. I'm certain that you understand with today's economy the way it is why I need to help my parents with my college expenses. Maybe I worked too much; I plan to be more careful if I am permitted to return. Considering all these factors, I sincerely hope that you will allow me to return to school next semester.

The differences in the two letters are due to Suellen's perception of their different audiences. Despite the embarrassment of the revelation to her parents, she writes to them in a casual tone of confidence, knowing they will continue to love her despite her failures. To the Dean of Admissions, however, she sets forth her case in a respectful, impersonal tone. Her style is clearly self-conscious, even awkward at times because she is unsure of her audience. Otherwise, why would she write, "I will *frankly* admit *to you* that I did not *apply myself up to my ability*"? Writing to an unfamiliar audience need not result in such awkwardness; the rules and conventions of acceptable written English can help to ease the composition of even the most formal communications.

Specialized versus general audiences

In most of your writing, both for college courses and for later in your professional life, it is useful to think of two broadly different kinds of audience: specialized and general.

A **specialized reader** already knows a good deal about a subject. Attorneys who write articles for the *Harvard Law Review* do not have to define the legal terms they use: readers of the *Harvard Law Review*, other attorneys, already know them. Such writers do not have to attract readers' attention: the subject matter and the publication have already done that. Specialists, however, are not necessarily scholars or doctors or engineers. They can be enthusiasts for almost anything—drag racing, photography, country music, astrology, pottery making, or football. Today, numerous magazines court readers who have highly specialized hobbies and interests: *Antique Monthly, Big Bike Choppers, Fly Fisherman, Idaho Farmer-Stockman, Model Railroader, Nordic Skiing, The Plate Collector, Stamp Show News and Philatelic Review, Videography, Yoga Journal,* and so on.

Articles that appear in such magazines are written with a very specific and specialized audience in mind. Writers can take for granted the audience's interest in and knowledge of the subject matter. Such an audience can make sense of information, ideas, and sometimes even language that would be inappropriate for general readers.

A **general reader** is the reader to whom most writing is addressed. General readers may work in highly specialized professions or enjoy unusual hobbies; but when they turn to general-interest publications such as *Ebony, Psychology Today, Saturday Review,* and *Sports Illustrated,* they expect to be able to understand the articles. This is especially true of such widely read weekly magazines as *Newsweek, Time,* and *U.S. News and World Report.* Your English instructors may be highly educated readers of literature; but when they read *Newsweek,* they expect the section on law and medicine, for example, to be written in standard, nontechnical language that can be readily understood. Because their audience is made up of general readers, writers for such magazines must avoid technical, overspecialized terms. When such terms are used, writers must be careful to define them and to provide examples.

Most writing you do for college classes will be directed to a college-level audience. Admittedly, this is a mixed group, from new freshmen to well-seasoned professors. But this audience shares certain traits and interests. Such readers are interested in keeping up with current events and issues, in learning about new ideas and various life-styles, and in exploring new possibilities in technology. In other words, they are readers who are intelligent and curious, who will give what you write a fair hearing, but who will also scrutinize it carefully. They will expect what you write to be clear, to be specific, and to be honest or authentic. They will expect you to write coherently, to explain adequately, and to use concrete examples to illustrate general statements. Such expectations are not unreasonable; nor are they impossible for you to satisfy.

A word of warning to you in your college writing: do not waste time trying to write what you think the instructor wants. Any attempt to write what you think your instructor is looking for is almost certain to result in an artificial and unsuccessful piece of writing. Most instructors, whatever they teach, try their best to serve as sympathetic general or specialized readers of student papers. They try to judge how well a paper has met the needs of the readers to whom it was directed. The comments of your instructors are intended to explain to you how your paper might have been organized more clearly, how your style might have been sharpened, and how your paper might have been better suited to your readers. But, most of all, what your instructors want is *your* ideas, *your* explanations, *your* reasons. They want you to learn to speak your own mind so that others will listen and respect what you have to say.

EXERCISE 31e(1) Do any of the specific topics you listed for Exercise 31b (1), (2), or (3) seem aimed at specialized readers? What are they? Why are they appropriate for specialized readers?

EXERCISE 31e(2) Write two letters in which you state the need for money. Write the first letter to your parents. Write the second to a loan officer at a local bank. Analyze the differences in the two letters and explain why you wrote them differently.

EXERCISE 31e(3) Go to the library, find a magazine intended for general readers, and copy a paragraph from it. Then find a magazine or journal published for specialized readers and copy a paragraph from it. Analyze and explain the differences in the two paragraphs.

31f

31f Decide on a pattern of organization and on one or more methods of development.

After you have narrowed your topic, used invention to generate a list of notes, decided on your purpose, and framed a thesis statement, the general shape of the paper should be clear to you. You have drawn up the paper's blueprint. You must now think about organization; that is, you must decide how you are going to give the paper internal order and coherence. You must also decide what method or methods of development to use in your paper.

1 Decide on a pattern of organization. The difference between a composition that is not planned and one that is carefully planned is the difference between a collection of parts for a motor and an assembled working motor. The collection of parts lacks organization; it is chaotic. The assembled motor is organized; the parts have been put together according to a design, and they function together as a whole.

Good organization in a composition results from your keeping purpose and thesis clearly in mind and from your arranging ideas and facts in an orderly pattern. Patterns of organization can be grouped into two kinds of order: natural order and logical order. **Natural order** is a pattern inherent in the topic itself. Narration, for example, normally requires that actions be told in the sequence in which they occurred. Description most often requires spatial order. **Logical order,** on the other hand, is imposed; the writer establishes the rationality of the arrangement of material.

A Natural order. The two natural orders are (1) time, or chronological, order and (2) space order. They are the patterns most common to narrative and descriptive writing.

(1) *Time Order.* If your purpose is narration, time order will almost certainly be the pattern appropriate for your paper. If you write about an automobile accident, an athletic contest, or a historcal event, you will very probably relate the events in the same sequence in which they took place. Time order is also the pattern to use for writing instructions about how to set up a campsite, how to dissect a frog, or how to proceed through college registration. In using time order, you organize by laying out information in the sequence in which events occur or should occur. There can, of course, be departures from strict time sequence. For example, in an essay about an automobile accident, the writer might begin with an ambulance shrieking up to an emergency room, then retreat in time to narrate the events of the accident. But it is unlikely that the writer could compose a coherent paper without relying primarily on the order in which events occurred.

The first paper in the papers for analysis at the end of this chapter is an example of a narrative paper that uses time order. In it the writer carefully reconstructs the events at his home one Saturday night when the electricity failed during a storm.

(2) *Space Order.* If your purpose is description, spatial order is probably the appropriate pattern for your paper. If you write a description of your dormitory room, of your front yard, or of the view atop a ridge in the Great Smoky Mountains, you will want readers to develop a mental picture of what you are talking about. You may choose to focus the scene from where you stand and then move outward from left to right or right to left. In describing a house or building, you may first describe its exterior, then the interior. In describing both views, exterior and interior, you must maintain spatial control if the reader is to see the house clearly. Even the physical description of a person makes use of spatial pattern. If you were to write a description of your mother, for example, you would find it virtually impossible to create a sensible impression of her looks if you were to describe her dress, then her hair, then her fingernails, then her eyelashes, then her skin, then her shoes. Spatial order closely follows the order in which eyes see or movie cameras move. One bit of information relates to the next in terms of position.

The second paper in the papers for analysis at the end of this chapter is a descriptive paper that uses space order. In it the writer's focus moves from one side to the other as she describes the cluttered interior of her uncle's old country store. While the paper issues from the writer's experience, her primary purpose is to describe the store as she sees it once again after being away for several years.

B   Logical order. If your purpose is to explain an idea or to persuade a reader, a pattern of organization inherent in the topic itself may not exist. You must, therefore, impose an order on the topic.

You must decide how best to arrange your examples and your reasons. The most common and useful patterns for exposition and argumentation are as follows: (1) the order of climax; (2) general to particular; and (3) particular to general. If you are explaining an idea, you will most often state the *general* idea first in your thesis sentence and then support the general statement with *particular* details and examples that illustrate and develop the idea. The reverse is also possible: instances and examples first, summed up by a general statement. If you are writing to persuade a reader, you should arrange your reasons and evidence from least important to most important. This is order of climax; you save your most persuasive evidence or reason for the end of your argument.

The third of the papers for analysis at the end of this chapter is an example of general to particular order. In it the writer begins with the general statement (or thesis) that the film *Star Wars* contains many characteristics common to western stories and movies. He then lists and discusses particular features in *Star Wars* that bear striking similarities to the plot and characters in westerns.

Paper Four is an example of the order of climax. The writer arranges the reasons for her interpretation of the poem in a pattern of least important to most important, thus building to a logical climax. Note that she arranges the details from the poem to fit the order of her paper rather than simply following the order of their appearance in the poem.

Just as the modes of writing—narration, description, exposition, and argumentation—are often combined in a paper, so too the patterns of organization are often interwoven. Kevin's information about buying a car, for example, is laid out in a chronological series of steps. But he did not talk seriously with the loan officer at the bank or with the insurance agent until he had selected the car. There was no point in Kevin's talking to either party until he could provide the first with a specific amount to be borrowed and the second with a specific make, model, and year. Kevin's essay, then, will combine time order with logical order. He wants to inform readers not only that there are certain steps to take in buying a car, but that there are sound logical reasons to follow these steps in the order in which he presents them.

2 Decide on one or more patterns of development. No matter how coherently you organize a paper, if you hope to satisfy your readers you must develop the paper so that it seems both complete and convincing to them. If you are writing narration, you must recount all the events that are relevant to your thesis. If your paper is description, you must include sufficient details so that your readers have a clear, full picture of the scene or person that you are portraying. If you are writing exposition, you must provide sufficient examples or instructions so that readers can easily understand the idea or follow the steps outlined. If your purpose is argumentation, you must offer ample reasons and evidence if you expect to persuade your readers. Generally, you should provide a minimum of three examples, instances, or reasons to illustrate an idea or to support an argument. Fewer items of what is essentially proof of your thesis may seriously weaken the credibility of your paper.

Methods of development include the following: (1) detail and example; (2) comparison and contrast; (3) analysis and classification; and (4) cause and effect. Even though this discussion separates the processes of organization and development, the two go hand in hand. The choice of an organizational pattern leads quite naturally to a choice of one of these methods of development. The choice of both, of course, issues from your purpose and your thesis.

(1) Detail and example. Many, if not most, papers you write in college will consist of a thesis supported by details and examples. A sharply defined thesis tends to reveal what details and examples you will need to develop the paper adequately. A specific thesis will control both the unity and the coherence (the pattern of order) of the details and examples. Suppose Kevin had decided on the following thesis: "Buying a used car is a time-consuming and frustrating experience." This thesis is not very helpful in identifying, ordering, and developing the details needed for support. On the other hand, the thesis statement that Kevin actually prepared contains the kinds of signals that direct a writer to the examples he or she needs. Look at it again: "I learned recently that buying a used car entails *thoughtful planning, careful shopping,* and *sound financing.*" This sentence calls for examples of how Kevin planned, shopped for, and financed the car. He can go back to the brainstorming list and find exactly the examples he will need to develop the paper.

Notice that all four papers for analysis, even though they have different purposes, contain examples and details. All the writers recognized the need to provide some details and examples in order to support and develop their respective theses adequately. Without such concrete development, a paper becomes merely a collection of general assertions. In the fourth paper, note how the writer uses direct quotations from a poem to support the general assertions about it.

(2) Comparison and contrast. Another common type of development, comparison and contrast, may be more familiar to you than you realize. A history professor compares the causes of one war with the causes of another. An economics exam requires you to compare the economic conditions of the 1980's with those of the 1930's. You use comparison and contrast when you compare high-school courses with college courses or when you debate whether it's best to live in a dormitory or off campus.

The third paper at the end of this chapter is an example of development by contrast and comparison. In it the writer discusses how *Star Wars* is similar to (has points of comparison with) western movies, especially in its characters and plot. The writer refers specifically to a number of western films and television series to support and develop his thesis. The writer has constructed his paper using comparision as a method of development.

(3)   Analysis and classification. Analysis is the conscious process of trying to understand something, usually by taking it apart, breaking it down into its smaller parts. For example, if you have decided on a career in nursing, you must consider what kind of nursing you wish to practice: obstetrics, pediatrics, geriatrics, surgery. If you are assigned to write a paper on the government of the United States, you will quickly realize that the federal government has three parts: the legislative, executive, and judicial branches. It is impossible to understand much about an abstract concept like American government until you understand about the functions, responsibilities, procedures, and powers of these components, the three branches of federal government.

An important adjunct of analysis is classification; analysis, in fact, makes classification possible. You engage in classification when you group items according to a common principle or characteristic. Suppose you were assigned to write an essay on the student body at your university. You would first analyze, then classify. You would have to consider a variety of ways to distinguish one student from another. You could do so in terms of those who study diligently, those who study enough just to get by, and those who demonstrate no interest in their studies. When you assign several individuals to each of these categories, you are classifying according to study habits, a principle common to all students. Notice that a number of classifications are possible. For the same paper you could also divide students according to their place of residence or their choice of career. Whatever classification you select for a paper will depend on your purpose and must derive from careful analysis.

Classification without analysis is called **stereotyping.** You stereotype if you classify a person or a group without systematic and valid analysis. The outcome of stereotyping is often prejudice directed toward members of ethnic, political, racial, or religious groups. For example, almost all of Archie Bunker's opinions are instances of his stereotyping persons or groups rather than analyzing them in any rational manner.

The fourth paper at the end of this chapter shows how analysis and classification can be used to examine another person and his behavior. The writer observes that the townspeople have stereotyped Cory. The writer then examines Cory to try and explain why, since the townspeople thought him so privileged, he should wish to kill himself. The answer lies in a close analysis of what the reader can infer about Cory from the poem.

(4) Cause and effect. If your chemistry professor asks you to discuss the results of combining certain chemicals, you will develop your answer by the cause-and-effect method. You will state that a particular reaction occurs after various substances are combined. Similarly, if your economics professor wants you to discuss the likely consequences of restrictive fiscal policies, you are being asked to explore a cause-and-effect relationship. If your English instructor asks you to write a paper on why you selected the college you attend, you will be expected to develop the paper using an effect-to-cause relationship. The decision is an effect, an already accomplished action; the reasons for your decision are the causes.

Cause-and-effect development quite naturally falls into the pattern of (1) stating causes and describing or arguing what their consequences will be, or (2) identifying a problem or consequence and then explaining the causes. The fourth of the papers for analysis uses such development in the section where the writer states that Richard Cory has committed suicide. The effect is known; what must be explained are its causes. This paper, by the way, effectively incorporates all four methods of development discussed here.

The patterns of organization and the methods of development discussed in this unit are also explained and illustrated with sample paragraphs in Sections **32c** and **32g.**

EXERCISE 31f(1)   Read the papers for analysis, pp. 223–230. List the pattern of organization and the methods of development used in each paper. Then select one paper and write a paragraph in which you explain how the organization and development support the purpose of the paper.

EXERCISE 31f(2)   Study the list of specific topics you made for exercise 31b(1), (2), or (3). Which patterns of organization and methods of development seem best suited to the topics on the list? Explain how the organization and development would support the purpose of the paper.

EXERCISE 31f(3)   Study the thesis sentences that you composed for Exercise 31d(5). Which patterns of organization and methods of development seem appropriate to each statement? Explain how the organization and the development would support the purpose stated in the thesis.

31g   Make an outline or plan for your paper.

Make it a habit to construct an outline for every piece of writing you do. An outline provides you with a working blueprint of your paper's organization and development. An outline helps you to develop a topic in a logical and orderly way, and it enables you to distinguish clearly between more and less important ideas.

Outlines may vary from quickly jotted notes for an essay exam to carefully worked out topic or sentence outlines for long and complex papers. The kind of outline you choose will depend upon your writing assignment. For a brief in-class paper on your high-school English courses, for example, you might have time only for such brief notes as the following:

1 More literature than composition
2 Emphasis on grammar in 10th grade
3 Wrote most papers on literature
4 Research papers in 11th and 12th grades
5 Enjoyed literature more than papers
6 Lack of contemporary literature
7 Not much comment on papers except in 11th grade

Even this limited set of notes provides a guide for your paper. The notes suggest immediately two major divisions into composition and literature, and indicate that the main emphasis in high school was on literature. A glance at the notes suggests a grouping of topics 1, 3, 5, and 6 in one paragraph, 2 and 4 in another. Item 7 may not fit into this essay, or you may be able to use it as a supporting detail in one paragraph. The whole suggests some such thesis statement as *My high-school preparation in English included work in both composition and literature, but the latter was the more thorough as well as the more enjoyable.* With this kind of start and your notes before you as you write, even a brief paper is likely to go more smoothly and logically. Such preliminary outlines are, of course, especially valuable in writing examinations. The five or ten extra minutes you spend on a preliminary outline often pays off with a stronger answer.

The best place to begin an outline is with a carefully crafted thesis sentence because an effective statement of thesis announces the general divisions of your paper. Using the thesis sentence, you can thus establish the general divisions of your outline. In addition, the more notes you have, the easier it is for you to make an outline.

Examine your notes for some pattern of organization—time order, space order, general to specific, order of climax—and arrange your notes according to it. Next, think about what method or methods of development will complement the pattern of order, and arrange your notes according to it. If you follow these two steps, you will discover that making an outline is a much easier task than you supposed.

Make an outline for every paper whether or not your instructor requires one. The guidance an outline provides is especially valuable for in-class essays, which require you to work against a deadline. If you don't prepare an outline, you may discover too late that your paper lacks clear purpose, coherent order, and adequate development.

1   Use a consistent method for numbering and indenting major headings and subheadings. For most outlines, it is unnecessary to divide subheadings more than two degrees. Here is a conventional system of outline notation:

I.   . . . .
   A.   . . . .
      1.   . . . .
         a.   . . . .
         b.   . . . .
      2.   . . . .
   B.   . . . .
II.   . . . .

2   Make your outline logical, clear, and consistent. Do not use single headings or single subheadings in your outline. Any category of heading or subheading must have at least two parts. If you have a I, you must also have a II. If you introduce an *A* under a roman numeral, you must also have a *B* under that roman numeral. If you put 1 under an *A*, you must also put a 2, and so on for any division. This procedure is logical since each new level of the outline is a division of a foregoing larger area, and you cannot logically divide something into just one part. A single subheading reflects poor organization; it should be incorporated into the heading of which it is logically a part. The following example illustrates correct divisions mathematically.

I.   One dollar
   A.   Fifty cents
   B.   Fifty cents
      1.   Twenty-five cents
      2.   Twenty-five cents
II.   One dollar

The same principle requires that each group of subheadings be logically equal to the larger heading under which they fall. If you wish, for instance, to divide the general heading "dogs," you can do so with the subheadings "house dogs" and "working dogs" or "large dogs" and "small dogs" or "poodles," "collies," "spaniels." But each one of these groups represents a different principle of classification. If you were to make your major subheads "house dogs," "small dogs," and "poodles," for example, the outline would be illogical.

3 Use either the topic, the sentence, or the paragraph form throughout an outline. In a topic outline, use for each heading a noun (or a word or phrase used as a noun) and its modifiers. In a sentence outline, which has the same structure as the topic outline, use complete sentences as separate headings. Because it states ideas more fully, a sentence outline is more informative than a topic outline, but a topic outline is easier to read. A paragraph outline gives only a summary sentence for each paragraph in the theme. It does not divide and subdivide headings into subordinate parts. Sentence outlines are the most inclusive of the three types. Topic outlines, however, are probably the most popular with inexperienced writers because they take less time to prepare.

Before you start to outline, decide which type of outline you are going to use and then fulfill the requirements for that type consistently. If, for example, you choose to make a sentence outline, remember that *every* statement in the outline must be expressed as a complete sentence. Remember also to make all parts of the outline parallel in structure. The following outlines illustrate the types. Each one shows consistent structure. A thesis statement for these outlines might read as follows:

> A study of printed advertisements from the eighteenth and nineteenth centuries reveals their rapid growth and changing character.

TOPIC OUTLINE

I. Colonial period
    A. Advertisements in Franklin's *Poor Richard's Almanack*
    B. Advertisements in newspapers
        1. Products and services
        2. Personals
II. Nineteenth century
    A. Appearance of mass circulation publications
        1. General audience newspapers and magazines
        2. Women's magazines
    B. Concentration of advertisements on particular products
        1. Soap and cosmetics
        2. Patent medicines
        3. Bicycles
    C. Introduction of sensational advertisements by P. T. Barnum

SENTENCE OUTLINE

I. Advertisements were printed during the colonial period.
    A. Benjamin Franklin both wrote and published advertisements.
    B. Advertisements appeared frequently in newspapers.
        1. A variety of products and services were advertised.
        2. Personal advertising was also very common.

II. Advertising flourished in the nineteenth century.
    A. Mass circulation publications made their appearance.
        1. Some newspapers and magazines appealed to general audiences.
        2. Some magazines appealed especially to women.
    B. A large proportion of advertisements were concentrated on a narrow range of products.
        1. Soap and cosmetics advertisements proliferated.
        2. Patent medicines were sold to millions as the result of mass advertising.
        3. As bicycles became popular toward the end of the century, competitive advertisements appeared by the hundreds.
    C. An analysis of P. T. Barnum's advertisements shows his introduction of sensational material.

PARAGRAPH OUTLINE

1. A variety of advertisements appeared frequently in newspapers of the colonial period.
2. With the development of mass circulation publications in the nineteenth century, advertisements proliferated in general audience and women's magazines.
3. An analysis of P. T. Barnum's advertisements shows his introduction of sensational material.

4 Use parallel grammatical construction for all items in the outline. Using consistent grammatical form emphasizes the logic of any outline you create and gives that outline clarity and smoothness. Inconsistent form, on the other hand, can make a perfectly rational ordering of items seem illogical. Of the following outlines on tennis, the one on the left is not in parallel grammatical form. The outline on the right is consistent both in form and logic.

THE GAME OF TENNIS	THE GAME OF TENNIS
(nonparallel)	*(parallel)*

I. The playing court	I. The court
A. The surface materials for it	A. Surfaces
1. Made of clay	1. Clay
2. Grass	2. Grass
3. Asphalt surfaces	3. Asphalt
B. Measuring the court	B. Measurements
1. For singles	1. Singles
2. Doubles	2. Doubles
C. Net	C. Net
D. Backstops necessary	D. Backstops

THE GAME OF TENNIS	THE GAME OF TENNIS
(nonparallel)	*(parallel)*

II. Equipment needed	II. The equipment
A. Racket	A. Racket
B. The tennis balls	B. Ball
C. The wearing apparel of players	C. Wearing apparel
III. Rules for playing tennis	III. The rules
A. The game of singles	A. Singles
B. Doubles	B. Doubles
IV. Principal strokes of tennis	IV. The strokes
A. Serving the ball	A. Serve
B. The forehand	B. Forehand
1. Drive	1. Drive
2. Lobbing the ball	2. Lob
C. The backhand stroke	C. Backhand
1. The drive	1. Drive
2. Lob	2. Lob

5 Avoid vague outline headings such as Introduction, Body, and Conclusion. Not only does the outline serve as a guide in your writing; submitted with your paper, it may also serve as a table of contents for your reader. To use such words as *Introduction, Body,* and *Conclusion* as outline headings gives no clue to what material is to come. If your paper is to have an introduction, indicate in the outline what it will include. If your paper is to have a formal conclusion, indicate in the outline what conclusion you will draw.

His composition instructor has not required Kevin McNeil to submit a formal outline with his paper on buying a used car. She has, however, strongly recommended the use of at least an informal outline to help in arranging the order of the paper. In the notes Kevin made while brainstorming, he discovered an arrangement that combines time order and logical order. He stated that order in his thesis sentence. Using the thesis, then, Kevin made these general divisions of his paper: (1) Selecting the car; (2) Shopping for the car; (3) Financing and insuring the car. Next, he arranged his notes according to these three divisions. When he finished putting the pieces together, Kevin's informal outline looked like this:

> Thesis: I learned recently that buying a used car involves thoughtful planning, careful shopping, and sound financing.
>
>   I. Selecting the car
>   A. Sources of information
>   1. Parents
>   2. *Consumer Reports*

  B. Type of car
    1. Standard size
    2. Subcompact
 II. Shopping for the car
  A. Newspaper want ads
  B. Local auto dealers
    1. Types of cars sold
    2. Reputations of dealers
  C. Inspection by a reputable mechanic
 III. Financing the car
  A. Sources of loans
    1. Dealers
    2. Banks
  B. Types of payments
    1. Down payment
    2. Monthly payments
    3. Insurance premiums

  Kevin now has a plan to follow as he writes the paper. His outline provides not only an order for the paper but also the details necessary to develop it adequately. With this outline, he is ready to write a rough draft. Kevin's prewriting process is complete.

EXERCISE 31g(1) Study the following outlines. Are they organized consistently? Do you find any single headings or subheadings? Are all items in parallel grammatical construction? Be prepared to suggest appropriate revisions for each. Write a thesis sentence for one of the outlines; then revise that outline so that it is consistent with the principles of outlining.

THE ADVANTAGES AND DISADVANTAGES
OF A CITY UNIVERSITY

 I. Convenience of location
  A. Transportation
  B. Hotels
  C. People
  D. Stores
  E. Theaters
 II. Advantages
  A. Center of travel
  B. Students learn to be more independent
  C. More types of people
  D. Those who have never been in city get new view
  E. Opportunities for work

III. Disadvantages
    A. Tendency to become interested in other things
    B. Too much for some to cope with
    C. Too close to other schools

THE VALUE OF PUBLIC OPINION POLLS

I. Introduction
    A. Operation of public opinion polls
        1. Selection of an important issue
        2. Constructing a set of questions
            a. Scientific nature of this construction
        3. A cross-section of the population is selected
    B. Replies are tabulated and results summarized
II. Importance of polls' results
        1. Attitudes of public revealed to lawmakers
        2. Power of present groups revealed
        3. Polls are a democratic process
            a. Polls reveal extent of people's knowledge

BAKING YOUR OWN BREAD

I. Introduction: Delicious taste, look, and feel of good bread
II. Bread-making in the past
    A. More difficult than now
    B. Necessary to make own yeast
    C. Kneading difficult
III. Bread-making today is popular
    A. Much easier
        1. Can make a few loaves at a time
        2. Gas and electric ovens are easier to control
    B. Making bread is enjoyable
        1. Sense of satisfaction in kneading own dough
        2. Bread baking in oven smells good
        3. More tasty than most bought breads
IV. Three easy recipes
    A. White bread
    B. Sweetened breads
        1. Raisin
V. Conclusion: Pleasure of sitting down to eat a slice of your own baked bread

EXERCISE 31g(2) Choose one of the papers for analysis (pp. 223–230) and make an outline for it that you think the writer could have followed to produce the paper he or she wrote.

EXERCISE 31g(3) Study the preliminary notes you made in Exercise 31c(1). Make an outline for each of the two sets of notes. Use the same style (topic, sentence, or paragraph) for both outlines. Be sure to construct the outlines in parallel form.

31h Begin and end your paper effectively.

Begin your paper effectively.

The beginning of a paper serves as a springboard into the topic. It should inform as well as catch the reader's interest. These results are almost certain to follow if you write a strong, direct opening.

Important as a good beginning is, don't be concerned about it in your rough draft. After you have written the draft, you may find that your purpose is clearer to you, and writing an opener will then be much easier. You may discover that the first few sentences you wrote in the rough draft were warm-ups and that a little revising will transform the third or fourth sentence into a good beginning.

The length of the introduction depends on the size and the complexity of your subject. A paper of 1,000 or 1,500 words on, say, the merits of a career in the field of mass communications may require a paragraph to state the thesis and to outline the general plan of the paper. Papers of 500 to 600 words, the length you will normally write in your English classes, usually need no more than three to five sentences to get started effectively. You will find more helpful advice in the following comments about ineffective and effective beginnings.

A Ineffective Beginnings

1 Avoid beginnings that are not self-explanatory. Do not make a reader refer to the title to find out the meaning of your paper's opening sentence. Do not begin a paper entitled "Nuclear Energy" with *Everyone is against it;* or a paper giving instructions for building a model airplane with *The first thing to do is to lay all the parts on the table.*

2 Avoid beginnings that start too far back. If you are writing a paper describing last Saturday's football game, get directly to the description; don't begin by explaining how you happened to go to the game. The writer of the following paragraphs meant well but should have begun with the second paragraph:

FATHER KNOWS BEST

You probably wonder from my title what I am going to write about. Well, it's a long story. It started back in 1964 when I was born. My mother announced to my father that I was a boy! "We're going to send him to State University!" my father exclaimed. So here I am at State, a member of the freshman class.

It was my father's idea from the first that I should come to State. He had been a student here in 1957 when he met my mother. . . .

3 Avoid beginnings that complain or apologize. If you want to complain about an assigned topic or apologize for what you have written, do so in a note attached to your paper. Do not use your opening paragraph to do so.

COMPLAINT   Describing a building accurately is a very difficult task. Though it is a good assignment because it makes you look closely and observe details you would not otherwise notice, it takes considerable time and does not leave the student enough time to write the actual paper. I discovered this when I tried to observe and describe the university chapel.

APOLOGY   After trying unsuccessfully to write a paper describing my roommate, and then attempting to gather some new ideas on books I had read during the summer, I gave up and decided to write on my experience in reading *The Grapes of Wrath* by John Steinbeck. I hope this fits the assignment.

B Effective Beginnings

Following are some proven methods of beginning papers effectively. They are almost certain to catch your reader's attention and interest, so they well repay the time you spend to create them.

1 Begin with a statement of fact or an unusual detail.

Mrs. Gardner didn't drink tea; she drank beer.

My grandmother believed in ghosts.

Ninety-two percent of the students at State College live at home and commute.

Lonepine is a little place in Sanders County in western Montana. The people there are farmers.

The world does not much like curiosity. The world says that curiosity killed the cat.

EDMUND S. MORGAN, "What Every Yale Freshman Should Know"

2 Begin with a firm statement of opinion or a directly stated proposition.

I do not believe in studying composition.

Cats are a nuisance, and they should be exterminated.

Television made Alex Haley's book *Roots* into an interesting drama, but the book itself is more powerful.

Because people who rarely talk together talk differently, differences in speech tell what group a man belongs to.

JAMES SLEDD, "Bi-Dialectalism: The Linguistics of White Supremacy"

Every culture develops some kind of art as surely as it develops language. SUSANNE K. LANGER, "The Cultural Importance of Art"

3 Begin with a brief anecdote or incident that leads directly into your main topic.

When Mark Twain left home at an early age, he had no great respect for his father's intelligence. When he returned a few years later, he was astounded at how much his father had learned in the meantime. I have been similarly astonished at how much both my father and mother have learned in the time I have been away from home.

I had a job interview several weeks ago. Friends warned me not to be too aggressive. During the interview, I tried to present myself as a competent candidate, able to "think like a man" and yet not to be a "masculine" female. After fielding several questions relevant to the job, I suddenly heard, "Miss Stern, are you in love?"

PAULA STERN, "The Womanly Image"

4 Begin with a quotation that illustrates or leads into your thesis.

"Courage is what it takes to stand up and speak," Winston Churchill once said, and then added, "Courage is also what it takes to sit down and listen." Churchill was talking about politics. But the advice is sound advice for college students, who often have the courage to stand up and speak but lack the courage to sit down and listen. If we are to learn all we can, we will need to practice both kinds of courage.

"I heartily accept the motto, 'That government is best which governs least'; and I should like to see it acted up to more rapidly and systematically." This quotation from Henry David Thoreau's "Civil Disobedience" expresses exactly how I feel about the government's constant interference in our lives today.

End your paper effectively.

Just as a strong opening gets your paper off to a healthy start, so a decisive conclusion lends it a finished, polished note. An effective ending should echo your introduction and bring your paper to a logical conclusion. A paper on how to build a model airplane might end with this statement: "If you have followed all the directions correctly, you should now have an assembled model ready to hang in your bedroom."

Just as the nature of an introduction depends on the length and the complexity of the paper, so too does the conclusion. A paper of 500 words may require no more than a sentence or two, while a paper two or three times that length will probably need a short paragraph to summarize its contents.

A   Ineffective Endings

1   Don't end your paper with an apology. Statements like the following harm a paper: "This is only my opinion, and I'm probably not really very well qualified to speak" or "I'm sorry this isn't a better paper, but I didn't have enough time." Such statements destroy the effect of whatever you have written. If you say that you have failed, your reader will probably agree with you.

2   Don't end your paper by branching off into another aspect of the topic or by introducing new material. The ending of a paper should conclude what you have said. Readers are distracted and frustrated when you introduce at the paper's end a new, undeveloped idea. Don't conclude a description of how autumn appeals to you with a statement that says: "Even though autumn is a beautiful and exhilarating time of year, spring is still my favorite season." Such a sentence only makes your reader wonder why you wrote about autumn in the first place.

B   Effective Endings

1   Conclude with a restatement of your thesis sentence. A paper called "Father Knows Best" might end: "Now that I have been here and have seen the school for myself, I am convinced that Father *does* know best. I have decided to enroll for the next term at State." Not only does this ending restate the thesis, it also shows that the student has learned something from writing the paper.

2   Summarize the major ideas that you developed in your paper. A summary serves the double purpose of bringing your paper to a conclusion and of reminding your readers once more of the major points that you discussed. A paper on building a model airplane might end: "As I have shown, all you need to build a model plane is a model to assemble, a little ingenuity, and a lot of patience. With these three ingredients you can fill the friendly skies of your bedroom."

3 Draw a conclusion from the facts you present. Especially if your purpose in a paper has been to argue a point of view, you need to write a conclusion that derives from the evidence or reasons you presented. Thus, if you write a paper in which you argue for passage of the Equal Rights Amendment, you might conclude it by saying: "As the foregoing examples and cases have illustrated, true equality and freedom for women will remain an illusion until they enjoy the same rights and privileges under the law as men do." Your conclusion is based squarely on the evidence presented in the paper.

EXERCISE 31h Read the papers for analysis (pp. 223–230) and evaluate the beginning and ending of each paper. Explain why the beginnings and endings are effective or ineffective.

31i Write a rough draft of a paper.

After you have completed the steps in the prewriting process, you are ready to write a rough draft of a paper. Writing a draft offers you the opportunity just to write. Do not concern yourself with grammar, mechanics, punctuation, or spelling. You can attend to these matters when you revise the draft. Take out your notes and your outline and write. Even when you are required to write rough and final drafts in class, most instructors will permit you to bring notes and a working outline with you to aid in writing your paper. Use your notes and your outline as you write a rough draft of your paper. Begin with your thesis sentence and use it as the controlling statement of order and purpose as you write. Start the rough draft as soon as possible after you have completed the prewriting process. You want to allow time to revise the rough draft at least once before you turn the paper in to your instructor.

As you write, give special attention to adequate development of your thesis. Include all the details and examples you can think of. Many papers fail because the writers fill the papers with unsupported general statements rather than with facts and evidence to support and illustrate the thesis. In your rough draft include everything that you can think of that is related to your thesis. You can go back later to rework the paper for unity and coherence.

For his paper on buying a used car, Kevin made numerous notes while brainstorming. Working with these notes and his outline at hand, he produces the following rough draft:

Rough draft

I learned recently that buying a used car involves thoughtful planning, careful shopping, and sound financing. Like any normal teen-ager who had just graduated from high school I wanted a car, my own set of wheels. Somehow my life just wasn't compleat without it. The question was, how do I go about getting it? I had almost no money saved, I had just started a summer job, and to make matters worse I was starting college in the fall. I needed money for that.

Mom and Dad thought a car would be okay for I was planning to work part time after I started college. They wanted me to buy a subcompact because of good gas mileage. They also told me to check out Consumer Reports for ratings on them. Being a teenager of the world, I sure didn't want a subcompact. I wanted a real set of wheels with bucket seats, a four on the floor, and an engine that really turned over the rpm's. But I knew I was being imature and impractical. In a small car I could get to the college and back on about a gallon of gas and work and back twice. Moneywise, a small car was what I needed, it just wasn't what I wanted. But I could afford the gas, go to school and work part-time. So I went to the library and read all I could find about subcompacts in Consumer Reports. I was really suprised at how much info was available. It told all about miles per gallon and how often different models needed to be repaired and what for. This info was sure helpful.

Shopping for the car turned out to be a lot tougher than I thought. I began reading the want ads for used cars and I spent every minute of my spare time on used car lots in town. Boy, subcompacts were sure hard to find. Where are all those imparts when you need one? I told each dealer how much money I could spend on a car and gave them my name and phone number and told them to call me when they got a car that fit the description of what I wanted. I talked to the people at the Better Business Burow to check into how long some dealers had been in business and their reputations. Finally, a salesman called me to say he had the car I wanted. I looked at what the salesman had and you can imagine how I felt when I saw a little red one with black bucket seats and only 23,000 miles on it! After driving it out, I knew it was the car for me, but to make sure it was in good condition I drove it over to the mechanic who took care of my folks car. He said everything was okay, no oil leaks, the breaks were okay, and the tires still had good rubber on them. So I drove it back and told the salesman it was the car I wanted.

As soon as I said that, the salesman asked me if I wanted to finance the car with them. I told him no, that I was going to finance it with the bank that had the loan on my folks car. So the next day I called the bank. I told the lady how much money I needed and she told me the interest rate (which I couldn't believe!) and the amounts of the payments depending on how long I financed the car. It was a recent model, so the bank let me finance it for four years which really helps keep my payments down. Then I called the insurance company and got another shock. Mom and Dad had told me insurance rates would be high, but that it would make me a better driver. Boy, were they right!

So here I am now going to school and work in my own set of wheels. I never guessed that buying a car could be so much work or so expensive. I will have to work hard to make all the payments and still go to school for the next four years.

LARGER ELEMENTS

Kevin's draft has considerable potential. It contains some basic errors and shows some weaknesses in unity and coherence. Rough drafts usually do have rough spots. Kevin's purpose is not clear because he narrates rather than explains what he learned. He has developed the essay well, however. He leaves hardly a stone unturned as he tells the story of the search for a car. The inclusion of so many details will be very helpful when Kevin revises the draft.

After you finish a rough draft, set it aside for at least a day. During this time, give some thought to the way you want to begin and end your paper.

EXERCISE 31i Study the notes you made for Exercise 31c(1) and the outlines you made for Exercise 31g(3). Using these, write a rough draft about one of the two topics.

31j Revise your rough draft.

After you have let a rough draft sit for a day or two, revise it carefully. Important to producing successful papers is understanding that revision is much more than proofreading for and correcting errors in grammar, mechanics, punctuation, and spelling. True revision involves carefully examining your paper for unity, coherence, and adequate development—the principles discussed in this chapter. You should approach revision willing to rethink, restructure, and rewrite, when necessary, to accomplish your purpose.

Many students "revise" simply by copying the rough draft—often transferring the errors in the rough draft to the final draft. Revision requires not only correction of errors in grammar and punctuation but rearrangements and rewriting of phrases, sentences—whole paragraphs if necessary. Revision is thus a two-step process: (1) rethinking and reworking the rough draft and (2) editing and proofreading the rough draft. Applying the following lists of questions to each essay you write will make it relatively simple to revise your papers effectively.

Checklist for revising

1 Are the choice of topic and tone of the paper appropriate for your reader? See Section **31e.**

2 Does your paper have a clearly stated thesis sentence? See Section **31d.** Do all the paragraphs support and develop the thesis sentence? In other words, does the content of the paper show unity, a clear pattern of coherence, and adequate development? See Section **31f.**

3 Does your paper follow the outline you drew up for it? See Section **31g.** If you have departed from your original outline, are the

changes you have made logical, coherent, and effective improvements?

4   Does each paragraph contain a specific topic sentence? See Section **32a.** Do all the sentences in each paragraph relate logically to the topic sentence and support it? See Sections **32b, 32c,** and **32g.**

5   Are all terms clearly defined and all assertions supported? See Section **33.**

6   Do you have an effective opening and a strong conclusion for the paper? See Section **31h.**

Checklist for editing

1   Is each sentence grammatically correct? Are there errors in pronoun or in verb agreement? See Sections **8** and **9.** In tense? See Section **5.**

2   Are the sentences complete? See Section **6a.** Are any sentences joined by a comma or no punctuation at all? See Section **7.**

3   Are any sentences awkward or confusing because of dangling or misplaced phrases? See Sections **11–14.** Are all the sentences logical in their use of subordination, variety, parallelism, and emphasis? See Sections **34–37.**

4   Have you used correctly all commas, semicolons, periods, and other marks of punctuation? See Sections **19–24.**

5   Have you used correctly apostrophes, capitals, italics, abbreviations, and numbers? Are words hyphenated properly? See Sections **15–18** and **27–30.** If you used quoted material, did you quote it correctly? See Sections **25–26.**

6   Are any words misspelled? See Section **44.** Use the dictionary to check spelling! Are there any problems in usage—*lay* versus *lie,* for example? See Section **43.**

7   Are the words in your paper precise and appropriate to the topic? Have you used any slang expressions? See Sections **40–42.**

Not all these questions may apply to every paper you write—you may not have prepared an outline, for example—but most will. Failing to check even one or two of these matters could result in serious weaknesses in a paper.

Checking Kevin McNeil's rough draft for the items in the lists of questions reveals a number of problems. Kevin got carried away telling the story of how he bought the car—that is, with writing narration rather than exposition. Kevin had defined his purpose as wanting to explain what he learned as he went through the process of finding and buying a used car. With only minor shifts in sentences and in his point of view, Kevin can change the story-telling quality of his paper to what he had originally intended—informative explanation. Kevin also notices some problems in unity and coherence. Some sentences really aren't necessary; others need to be moved to conform to the sequence in his outline. He discovers some errors in grammar, especially in splicing sentences together with commas. He has made some spelling errors, too, in his haste to get his ideas down. None of the revisions Kevin needs to make is a cause for concern. No one, not even a professional writer, can produce a polished, finished essay in just one draft.

After Kevin has carefully examined and revised the rough draft, it looks like this:

Revised rough draft

I ~~learned recently~~ *discovered last summer* that buying a used car ~~involves~~ *requires* thoughtful

planning, careful shopping, and sound financing. Like any normal ~~teen-ager who had just graduated from high school~~ *high school graduate,* I wanted a car, *M* ~~my own set of wheels.~~ Somehow my life ~~just~~ wasn't ~~compleat~~ *complete* without it. ~~The question was, how do I go about getting it?~~ *But* I had almost no money

saved, I had just started a summer job, and to make matters worse ~~I was~~ *comma 2*

starting college in the fall. I needed money for ~~that.~~ *my education*

Mom and Dad ~~thought a car would be okay for I was planning~~ *gave their permission for a car since I planned* to work

part time after I started college. ~~They wanted me to buy a subcompact because of good gas mileage. They also told me to check out Consumer Reports for ratings on them.~~ *They advised me to shop for a gas-saving subcompact and to go to the library and read about them in Consumer Reports.* ~~Being a teenager of the world,~~ *But* I ~~sure~~

didn't want a subcompact. I wanted ~~a real set of wheels~~ *a standard size sporty coupe* with bucket

seats, a four on the floor, "*gearshift*" and an engine that ~~really turned over the~~ *with some real power.*

rpm's. But I knew I was being ~~imature~~ *immature* and impractical. In a small car

I could get to ~~the~~ college and back on about a gallon of gas and work *to*

and back twice. Moneywise, *I had to admit that* a small car was what I needed, ~~it just~~

~~wasn't what I wanted. But I could afford the gas, go to school and work part-time.~~ So I went to the library and read all I could find

about subcompacts in *Consumer Reports.* I was ~~really~~ ~~suprised~~ *surprised* ~~at how much info was available. It told all about miles per gallon and how often different models needed to be repaired and what for.~~ *to find that in addition to listing the mileage ratings they also gave you the repair record for the various models.* This

~~info~~ *information* was ~~sure~~ *most* helpful.

Shopping for the car ~~turned out to be a lot tougher than I thought.~~ *proved to be more work than I thought it would.*

I began reading the want ads for used cars and I spent every minute of

my spare time on used car lots in town. ~~Boy, subcompacts were sure hard to find. Where are all those imparts when you need one?~~ *I couldn't find a suitable car in the want ads, so* I told each

dealer how much money I could ~~spend on a car~~ *was willing to spend* and gave them my name and

phone number ~~and told them to call me when they got a car that fit the~~ *The salesmen said they would call me when they traded for a car* description of what I wanted. I ^*also* talked ~~to~~ *with* the people at the Better

Business ~~Burow~~ *Bureau* to ~~check into~~ *find out* how long ~~some~~ *various* dealers had been in business
and *how good* their reputations *were*. ~~Finally,~~ ^*After about two weeks* a salesman called me to say he had the

car I wanted. ~~I looked at what the salesman had and you can imagine how~~
It was *hatchback*
~~I felt when I saw~~ a little red ~~one~~ with black bucket seats and only

23,000 miles on it! ~~After driving it out, I knew it was the car for me,~~
I *mechanical* *comma?*
but to make sure it was in good condition ~~O~~ I drove it over to the mechanic
takes *He looked it over, drove it, and*
who ~~took~~ care of my folks car. ~~He said everything was okay, no oil~~
told me it looked okay to him.
~~leaks, the breaks were okay, and the tires still had good rubber on them.~~
Then *worked out a deal with* *All that was left was*
~~So~~ I drove it back and ~~told the salesman it was the car I wanted.~~
to arrange the financing.
~~As soon as I said that,~~ the salesman asked me if I wanted to finance
the dealer
the car with ~~them~~. I told him no, that I was going to finance it with
visited with a
the bank that had the loan on my folks car. ~~So the next day I called~~
loan officer at *her* *wanted to finance* *what*
the bank. I told ~~the lady~~ *her* how much money I ~~needed~~ *wanted* and she told me ~~the~~
the monthly payments would be
~~interest rate (which I couldn't believe!) and the amounts of the pay-~~
Because it
~~ments~~ depending on how long I financed the car. ~~It~~ was a recent model,
was willing to *lowered my*
~~so the bank let me~~ finance it for four years which really ~~helps keep my~~
monthly payments. *to arrange for*
~~payments down.~~ ~~Then~~ *Finally* I called the insurance company ~~and got another~~
insurance. *and they were right!*
~~shock.~~ Mom and Dad had told me insurance rates would be high, ~~but that~~
I'm sure, though, that the high rates will
~~it would~~ make me a better driver. ~~Boy, were they right!~~
driving *car.*
So here I am ~~now going~~ to school and work in my own ~~set of wheels.~~
Up until last summer *dreamed* *involved* *planning.*
^I never ~~guessed~~ that buying a car ~~could be~~ so much work or ~~so expensive.~~
manage my money carefully to
I will have to ~~work hard~~ to make ~~all~~ the payments and still go to school

for the next four years. *Even though I didn't get the sporty coupe I wanted, I do have bucket seats and a "four on the floor."*

Study the reworked draft carefully. It shows that revision done correctly is a process requiring much more from a writer than just proofreading for grammar, punctuation, and spelling. Notice that both the beginning and the ending of the essay show improvement. Notice that the personal remarks, or "asides," have been deleted. Although not every item in Kevin's outline has been discussed, the revised draft adheres quite well to the plan and order of the outline. Thus the revision is better unified and more coherent than the rough draft. The essay now informs as well as narrates. It is briefer and more to the point. Even though the new version is not perfect, the revised draft is clearly a better essay than the rough draft.

EXERCISE 31j(1)   Read and analyze the papers for analysis (pp. 223–230) using the questions on pp. 214–215. Revise one of the papers according to the notes you make as you analyze.

EXERCISE 31j(2)   Use the questions listed on pp 214–215 to analyze the rough draft you wrote for Exercise 31i(1). Revise the draft according to the notes you make as you analyze it.

31k   Prepare and submit the final draft for evaluation.

When you have finished revising a paper, either recopy it neatly in your own handwriting or type it. Instructors read papers as editors and advisors. They mark errors in grammar and punctuation, and they suggest ways for you to improve your writing in the paper. Instructors read and evaluate your essays to help you become a more confident and competent writer.

On the following pages, Kevin's essay, marked and evaluated, is reproduced. The instructor has marked the essay with numbers that refer to sections of this handbook so that the precise nature of the errors can be identified and so that these errors can be avoided in future essays. In addition, the instructor has made several comments on the essay's unity, coherence, and development; on sentence structure and style; and on the paper's overall purpose. The instructor wrote these comments to point out the particular strengths of the essay and to encourage the continued development of these qualities in future essays.

Final draft

LEARNING TO WHEEL AND DEAL

I discovered last summer that buying a used car requires thoughtful planning, careful shopping, and sound financing. Like any ~~normal~~
high school graduate, ~~I wanted a car.~~ *I felt that my* ~~My~~ life wasn't complete without
~~it.~~ ~~But~~ ∧I had almost no money saved; I had just started a summer job;   *41a*
~~32d⁽⁴⁾~~ *a car However,*
and to make matters worse, I was starting college in the fall. I
needed money for my education.

Mom and Dad gave their permission for a car ~~since~~ I planned to   *24i*
30b work part time after I started college. They advised me to shop for
a gas-saving subcompact and ~~to go to the library and~~ ∧read about them   *8b*
41a   *to*
in Consumer Reports. [But I didn't want a subcompact. I wanted a
standard size sporty coupe with bucket seats, a "four on the floor"
23a gearshift ~~and~~ an engine with some real power. But I knew I was being
drive
immature and impractical.] In a small car I could ~~get~~ to the college
to (35a)
and back on about a gallon of gas and ∧work and back twice. I had to
admit that a small car was what I needed. ~~So~~ I went to the library,
and read all I could find in Consumer Reports about subcompacts. I
learn
was ~~really~~ surprised to ~~find~~ that in addition to listing the mileage
listed
ratings ~~they~~ also gave ~~you~~ the repair record for the different models.
8b [This information was most helpful.] *unnecessary; delete.*

Shopping for the car proved to be more work than I thought it
read
would. I ~~began reading~~ the want ads for used cars, and I spent every
Because/Since
minute of my spare time on used car lots in town. [∧I couldn't find a
salesmen
suitable car in the want ads, ~~so~~ I told ~~each dealer~~ how much I was
willing to spend and gave them my name and phone number.] ~~The salesmen~~
They promised to
~~said they would~~ call me when they traded for a car that fit the de-
41a
scription of what I wanted. I also talked with the people at the
Better Business Bureau to find out how long various dealers had been

32b: Don't these remarks digress from the topic of thoughtful planning? Reverse the order of these two sentences. therefore, 32d(4)

You might consider combining these into one sentence.

9e

10c Keep tense consistent

34c Use logical subordination

You develop this paragraph well and you clearly organize the details and examples you use in it.

in business and how good their reputations were. (After) ~~a~~ about two
weeks ^*later* a salesman called me to say he had the car I wanted. It was
a little red hatchback with black bucket seats and ^*it had* only 23,000 miles
on it! To ~~make~~ *be* sure it was in good mechanical condition, I drove — 42b
it (over) to the mechanic who takes care of my (folks') *parents'* car. He looked (it)
over, drove (it), and told me (it) looked okay to him. Then I drove (it)
back and [worked out a deal] *42a* with the salesman. All that was left was
to arrange the financing.

when
∧ The salesman asked me if I wanted to finance the car with the
dealer. I told him ~~no~~, that I ~~was going~~ *planned* to finance it with the bank
that had the loan on my (folks') car. The next day I visited with a
loan officer at the bank. *when* I told her how much money I wanted to finance,
~~and~~ she told me what the monthly payments would be depending on how long
I financed the car.] Because it was a recent model, the bank was willing
to finance it for four years [*in order to reduce* ~~which really lowered~~ my monthly payments.]
Finally, I called the insurance company ~~to arrange for insurance.~~ [Mom
and Dad told me insurance rates would be high and they were right! I'm
sure, though, that the high rates will make me a better driver.]
to (35a)
So here I am driving to school and ^work in my own car. Up until
last summer I never dreamed that buying a car involved so much work or
planning. I will have to manage my money carefully to make the payments,
and still go to school for the next four years. Even though I didn't
get the sporty coupe I wanted, I do have bucket seats and a "four on the
floor."

*Your thesis is clear, unified, and specific; you develop it well by
using numerous details and examples. You carefully order the paper
as you explain the process of buying the car. However, the second and
fourth paragraphs lack topic sentences that are clearly related to the thesis
sentence. Only the third paragraph contains a clear expository topic sentence.
Your introductory and concluding paragraphs tie the paper together nicely.
You need to be careful not to digress from the topic of a paragraph; see
Section 32 b. In addition, you should study Section 34 to help you with
logical subordination in sentences. This is an interesting essay. I enjoyed
reading it.*

Handwritten margin notes: *9a — you use "it" too often here.* · *Combine into one sentence for logical subordination.* · *34b* · *12a* · *34g* · *41c* · *32b: Again, don't these comments digress from the topic sentence?* · *24d* · *Effective concluding sentence.* · *41a* · *42b*

Instead of using numbers to mark the paper, the instructor could have used the correction symbols and abbreviations listed on the front inside cover pages of the book. A sample paragraph marked with these symbols appears on p. 109 in Section **15e.** No matter what method your instructor uses to mark papers, examine your papers carefully, note especially any comments about errors, and study the appropriate sections of the handbook in order to avoid repeating these errors in future papers. Pay close attention to the comments your instructor makes. Use them as guidelines to help you prepare and write other papers. If you do so, your writing will almost certainly improve with each paper you complete.

Writing a paper requires careful planning, and doing it well demands time and effort on your part. But the reward is worthwhile: a paper that you can be proud to call your own.

EXERCISE 31k(1)   Read the papers for analysis (pp. 223–230). Mark and analyze each paper as though you were the writer's composition instructor. Evaluate and comment on the qualities of unity, coherence, and development in each paper. Evaluate the four papers in terms of overall quality and effectiveness. Explain your ratings.

EXERCISE 31k(2)   Prepare for submission the revised draft that you wrote for Exercise 31j(2). Submit it to your instructor for evaluation. In addition, prepare a second copy of the paper; then mark and analyze it in a way similar to the sample paper on pp. 220–221. Give particular attention to the qualities of unity, coherence, and development in the paper. Comment on the essay's overall effectiveness.

Papers for analysis

Comments about the papers for analysis have been made throughout Section 31, and a number of exercises in this section make use of them. The papers may also be studied independently of the chapter. An analysis of each paper according to the questions on pp. 214–215 will point out differences in quality as well as purpose.

Each paper represents one of the four main types of writing discussed in Section 31d; it also uses at least one other type to support that purpose. The papers incorporate different patterns of organization and different methods of development. (See Section **31f.**) The first paper is narrative in its purpose. The second paper is descriptive; the writer makes use of some narration to clarify the description. The third paper is expository, but with a secondary argumentative purpose. The fourth paper tries to persuade the reader to view a character in a certain way as the basis for understanding the meaning of a poem.

Paper One

THE FAMILY REUNION

Over the past few years my family began to grow apart. Between school, hobbies, and work, there was never time for us as a family to spend together. We were a family that lacked communication. One Saturday something happened that brought my family together.

It was a typical Saturday evening. Both my parents were reading a magazine. My older brother was painting a picture in the basement, while my two younger sisters and brother were watching TV. I was writing a letter. Outside the rain was coming down so hard that I thought it was hailing. The sound of the rain was accompanied by harsh trembling of thunder and flashes of lightening. The lights in our house began to flicker off and on. Then about 8:00 the lights went off. Everything became real quiet. The voices from the TV died. The clocks stopped ticking.

Although we all became temporarily blind, each of us managed to get to the kitchen with only a couple of bruises from running into doors and walls. Each of us took a seat around the table where the candles were lit. My dad began to tell us stories about himself when he was a kid. Eventually, the conversation led up to our futures and what each of us planned to do with it. We all got so caught up with listening to everyone else that when the lights came back on we could not believe it was already 10:00. That night we all went to bed knowing a little more about ourselves and each other.

Paper Two

AN OLD COUNTRY STORE

As I walk up the wooden steps of the old store, I see Jasper, Uncle Ned's lazy hound, stretched out on the front porch basking in the afternoon sun. He raises his head as I pass and then continues his nap. The old men in faded overalls and flannel shirts whittle away at cedar sticks. The faded Coca-Cola sign still hangs on the front of the store. I realize that nothing has changed since I was a little girl scampering up the same steps in hopes of snitching one of Aunt Betty's oatmeal raisin cookoes from one of the big cookie jars on the shelf near the cash register.

As I open the squeaky screen door, I recognize the sweet musty scent which has always filled the room inside the old store. The first thing that catches my eye is the bulky old soft drink cooler under the front windows where Uncle Ned has always kept it. As I lift one of the heavy black lids on the top of the cooler, the cold air rushes out and cools my face. Uncle Ned still lays the bottles on their sides, and I still have to dig through the pile of bottles to get the drink I want. On the floor along the right wall of the store are bushel baskets of white onions, potatoes, fresh green beans, yellow squash, and green and red apples. On the shelves behind the bushels are cans of vegetables and jars of preserves, some of which were made by a lady who lives down the road from Uncle Ned and makes the best strawberry preserves I've ever tasted. Along side the jars of preserves are tins of sorghum molasses which Uncle Ned gets from a man on Sand Mountain. Cloth sacks of flour and sugar are piled on the bottom shelf just behind the bushel baskets.

As I walk toward the back of the store, I see the familiar old white meat case which holds slabs of hoop cheese, bologna, sausage and bacon. I notice that Uncle Ned has a new scale to weigh cheese and meat which is bright white and shiny compared to the dull color of the meat case. Above the meat case, hang several country hams. Next to the meat case in another cooler, Uncle Ned keeps a basket always filled with fresh country eggs and cartons of milk. Against the left wall are such things as catsup, homemade pickles and cans of coffee. Next to these on the wall near the screen door is the usual selection of odds and ends such as shoestrings, nail clippers, pocket knives, rain bonnets, and even a few fishing lures.

My favorite spot was always in the middle of the store where on one particular shelf near Uncle Ned's old antique cash register are boxes and boxes of loose candy in brightly colored wrappers of red, orange, blue, yellow, green, gold, and purple. The floor creaks under my feet just as it did when I was a little girl and tried to snitch a piece of candy before dinner. It was fun to creep across the creaking wooden planks to see if I could reach the candy undetected. And as usual, Uncle Ned spotted me peering over his little spectacles with that familiar grin on his face. Knowing that my sweet tooth has changed about as much as his store has over the years, he reaches for the jar of cookies, removes the lid and hands me a big oatmeal raisin cookie.

Paper Three

COWBOYS OR JEDI KNIGHTS?

The science fiction film <u>Star</u> <u>Wars</u> contains similarities to western movies and television series that do not seem purely coincidental. Even though the terrain of a planet in a distant galaxy and the badlands of the Old West are literally worlds apart, there are a number of coincidences in the settings, the characters, and the plots between <u>Star</u> <u>Wars</u> and westerns. This paper shows how Star Wars is like two of these westerns, <u>True</u> <u>Grit</u> and <u>Gunsmoke</u>.

In the typical western story, the setting is a place without law and order. Lawlessness prevails. The weak and innocent are at the mercy of ruthless outlaws. Similarly, in <u>Star</u> <u>Wars</u> the survival of the galaxy is endangered by the evil Darth Vader and his Imperial Storm Troopers. The opening scenes of both <u>Star</u> <u>Wars</u> and <u>The</u> <u>Empire</u> <u>Strikes</u> <u>Back</u> remind viewers of the Old West. The scenes are desert-like in their loneliness and their sandy, barren appearance. In <u>The</u> <u>Empire</u> <u>Strikes</u> <u>Back</u> Luke Skywalker and Hans Solo ride out like cowboys to patrol the territory on creatures that seem to be a cross-between a camel and a kangaroo. The opening scenes in both movies seem very familiar to the western fan.

In the typical western certain basic character types are evident. They include the "good guy" hero, a damsel in distress, and of course the villain. Very often there is also the humorous "sidekick" who is along to provide comic relief in the story. Luke Skywalker is clearly the "good guy" hero whose youth and innocence are balanced by the not so pure but heroic Hans Solo. It is interesting to note that modern heroes are not always saint-like in virtue, but are a combination of cunning and courage. Skywalker and Solo represent this type of modern hero as they bravely fight for their damsel in distress, Princess Leia. Like Solo, Rooster Cogburn in True Grit is something of an opportunist. He seems more interested in the reward than he is in justice when Mattie asks him to hunt down her father's killer. Yet he does find the killer and even saves Mattie's life after she's been bitten by a poisonous snake. In the ever-popular Gunsmoke, Matt Dillon is frequently called upon to save Miss Kitty from some dastardly and drunken renegade who has taken her hostage.

Whether science fiction or a western, the hero is usually a loner who is handy with a weapon. In most westerns this particular weapon is a six-gun or a rifle; in Star Wars Luke learns from the wise Kenobi to use "the Force." Luke has already lost his parents at the beginning of the film, then loses his aunt and uncle, finding himself alone. Hans Solo translated means "the lonely hand." Likewise, Cogburn and Dillon are men with no family ties. This absence of ties, particularly to females, is important to the image of the science fiction hero as well as to the western hero. However, this is not to say that these heroes aren't in some ways enamored of their damsels in distress. Both Luke and Hans are fond of Princess Leia, even though we know she only has eyes for Luke. Rooster shows a gruff, paternal affection for Mattie, and Dillon's devotion to Miss Kitty is never doubted. The true hero knows his place and keeps his proper distance.

No western would be complete without the "sidekick" who always tags along with the hero. This seems to be LaBoeuf's role in True Grit. And where would Gunsmoke be without Festus? Star Wars has more than its share of sidekicks. Chewbacca is the ever-faithful friend and companion to Hans Solo. But the best moments in the movies go to the two robots, R2D2 and CP30. They remind the viewers of Laurel and Hardy as they get into one mess after another.

The plots of both science fiction stories and western stories depend on these basic character types. Sooner or later the hero must settle the conflict between the forces of good and evil by facing the villain alone in a "shoot-out," relying only on his skillful use of a weapon. Week after week on Gunsmoke Dillon faces a gunman or a gang single-handedly to preserve the law in Dodge City. In an unforgettable scene, Rooster puts his horse's reins in his mouth, a gun in one hand and a rifle in the other, and charges the group of outlaws that have kidnapped Mattie. Luke's courage and use of "the Force" as he rides down the center of the Death Star remind viewers of Rooster's ride into the blazing guns of the outlaws. Even though Luke is lucky to escape from Vader at the end of The Empire Strikes Back, we know that a fateful encounter will come when Luke will destroy Vader and his power once and for all. Until that day, Skywalker and Solo will continue to "ride the range" of space fighting for law and order in the badlands of the galaxy.

Paper Four

"ONE CALM SUMMER NIGHT" . . . BANG!

The speaker of Edwin Arlington Robinson's "Richard Cory" leads us to believe that Richard Cory is the personification of what every man would like to be--the perfect gentleman--and that he has what every man would like to have--unlimited wealth. From this characterization of Richard Cory, we might assume that he is a very content man. However, the surprise ending of the poem indicates differently. We can only deduce from the four stanzas of the poem what may have been Cory's reasons for committing suicide. It is quite possible that despite Richard Cory's calm, civilized appearance he was in reality very frustrated from conforming to the role of a perfect gentleman, having no goals for which to strive, and most importantly, being alienated from those around him.

The references in the poem to Cory's appearance suggest that he looked as regal as a king: "He was a gentleman from sole to crown, / Clean favored, and imperially slim." Although the speaker doesn't actually say that Cory looked like a king, the words "crown" and "imperially" suggest royalty and support such an interpretation. The fact that Cory was "admirably schooled in every grace" is evident in that "he was always quietly arrayed, / And he was always human when he talked." Just as a king is expected to behave in a certain manner, a person who has been taught the social graces may feel compelled to behave as he knows he should. In actuality, Cory may have longed to abandon his knowledge of the stifling rules of etiquette and behave just as those townspeople who so admired him. But having locked himself into this role of "gentleman from sole to crown," he frustrates himself.

Another frustrating aspect of Cory's existence is his wealth. In addition to his perfect demeanor, we find that "he was rich--yes, richer than a king." Had Cory tried to make a living like the townspeople, he may not have been so frustrated with his predicament since there is admittedly a certain amount of satisfaction to be gained from doing a job and accomplishing a task. Receiving money for a job well done also promotes a feeling of self-sufficiency. Admittedly, any job has frustrations, but they seem minor in comparison to the frustration of an existence which seems pointless and futile like Cory's.

Both Richard Cory's social behavior and his wealth set him apart from the townspeople which leads us to perhaps the most significant source of his frustration--unintentional alienation. Although the townspeople admired Cory, they evidently were only aware of his appearance and set him on a pedestal. As the speaker states, "Whenever Richard Cory went down town, / We people on the pavement looked at him." The reference to "people on the pavement" suggests that Cory is not only higher in physical space but figuratively a person of "higher" or special qualities. He was seen as a person who "fluttered pulses when he said, 'Good Morning,' and he glittered when he walked." The townspeople are obviously awed by Cory's presence and "thought that he was eveything / To make us wish that we were in his place." It perhaps never occurs to the townspeople to look beneath Cory's outward appearance; they automatically assume that he is happy. Ironically, they "worked, and waited for the light, / And went without the meat, and cursed the bread," not realizing that compared to Cory who "one calm summer night, / Went home and put a bullet through his head" they were indeed fortunate in that they at least had each other to confide in. Richard Cory had no one.

Richard Cory's frustrations result in his suicide. He is locked behind the appearance of success, yet he is unhappy, and this unhappiness is intensified by his alienation from those who envy and admire him without really knowing him. We have to put ourselves in Richard Cory's place and try to understand him as "one calm summer night" about to explode into a tempestuous storm. When we do so, we become painfully aware of why he took his own life.

32 EFFECTIVE PARAGRAPHS ¶

32

A good paragraph has unity, coherence, and adequate development.

Unity requires that the paragraph have a single, clear, controlling idea, and that all the details introduced into the paragraph contribute to that controlling idea. The controlling or central idea is usually stated in a single sentence of the paragraph, called the **topic sentence**; this sentence often, though not always, is the first sentence of the paragraph. **Coherence** requires that all the sentences in a paragraph be connected in an orderly, clear way so that the reader can easily see how each sentence follows from the previous one, and how all relate to the controlling idea. **Adequate development** requires that there be enough details, facts, examples, evidence, or reasons included in the paragraph to make the controlling idea clear and meaningful to the reader.

For convenience, we discuss these three elements of a good paragraph separately, but all three are interrelated. A coherent paragraph is also unified and adequately developed. In other words, to support a topic sentence clearly and persuasively, you must develop a paragraph adequately and connect its sentences in an orderly way. Making a good paragraph calls for all three skills; no one is sufficient in itself.

UNITY IN THE PARAGRAPH ¶ **UN**

A unified paragraph is one that has a single, clear purpose, and one in which all sentences clearly relate to that purpose.

32a State a paragraph's central idea in one sentence.

32a

Most paragraphs have a **topic sentence**—a sentence that sums up the central idea of the paragraph. Topic sentences in paragraphs serve the same purpose as thesis sentences in papers. They insure that you have defined, both for yourself and your reader, the controlling idea of the paragraph. And by so doing, they serve as a guide to you in developing that idea.

The following paragraphs illustrate various ways of placing the topic sentence.

1   The topic sentence may be the first sentence of the paragraph. Such paragraphs state their central idea first and then add details supporting it. This kind of paragraph is the most common in expository writing, but it also occurs in persuasive and descriptive writing as well.

> *The tea-plant, a native of Southern China, was known from very early times to Chinese botany and medicine.* It is alluded to in the classics under the various names of Tou, Tseh, Chung, Kha, and Ming, and was highly prized for possessing the virtues of relieving fatigue, delighting the soul, strengthening the will, and repairing the eyesight. It was not only administered as an internal dose, but often applied externally in the form of paste to alleviate rheumatic pains. The Taoists claimed it as an important ingredient of the elixir of immortality. The Buddhists used it extensively to prevent drowsiness during their long hours of meditation.   OKAKURA KAKUZE, *The Book of Tea*

> *The* ENCYCLOPAEDIA BRITANNICA, *although a valuable research tool, is difficult to read and hard to handle—hardly designed for the hasty researcher.* Each article is thorough and detailed, but the tiny print is extremely hard to read. To be assured of getting every fact and detail, the researcher needs a strong light and, unless his eyes are keen, a magnifying glass. To pick up a volume in the first place, one needs both hands. One doesn't balance a *Britannica* volume in one hand while scribbling furiously with the other. A table or desk to lay the volume open on is absolutely necessary. But even sitting comfortably at a desk with a *Britannica* presents problems. To avoid crushing or tearing the onion-thin pages requires slow, deliberate, careful moves. Haste or carelessness could easily result in obliterating the whole article one wishes to read. Given these disadvantages to using the *Encyclopaedia Britannica,* fly-by-night researchers should consider other general reference books.
>
> *Student paragraph*

A paragraph's first sentence may combine a transition from the preceding paragraph with the topic statement of the new paragraph. In the example, the references to Dawson's location and size allude to topics in the paragraph preceding the one reproduced here; the clause in italics states the topic of the example paragraph.

> Although it lay in the shadow of the Arctic Circle, more than four thousand miles from civilization, and although it was the only settlement of any size in a wilderness area that occupied hundreds of thousands of square miles, *Dawson was livelier, richer, and better equipped than many larger Canadian and American communities.* It had a telephone service, running water, steam heat, and electricity. It had dozens of hotels, many of them better appointed than those on the Pacific Coast. It had motion-picture theaters operating at a time when the projected motion picture was just three years old. It had restaurants where string orchestras played *Cavalleria Rusticana* for men in tailcoats who ate pâté de fois

gras and drank vintage wines. It had fashions from Paris. It had dramatic societies, church choirs, glee clubs, and vaudeville companies. It had three hospitals, seventy physicians, and uncounted platoons of lawyers. Above all, it had people.   PIERRE BERTON, *The Klondike Fever*

2   The topic sentence may be the last sentence of the paragraph. Such paragraphs give details first and lead up to the main point in the final sentence.

The true problem of city planning and rebuilding in a free society is how to cultivate more city districts that are free, lively and fertile places for the differing plans of thousands of individuals—not planners. Nothing could be farther from the aims of planners today. They have been trained to think of people as interchangeable statistics to be pushed around, to think of city vitality and mixture as a mess. Planners are the enemies of cities because they offer us only the poisonous promise of making every place in a city more like dull and standardized Morningside Heights. They have failed to pursue the main point: to study the success and failure of the real life of the cities. With their eyes on simple-minded panaceas, they destroy success and health. *Planners will become helpful only when they abandon what they have learned about what "ought" to be good for cities.*

JANE JACOBS, "How City Planners Hurt Cities"

Beginning at breakfast with flying globs of oatmeal, spilled juice, and toast that always lands jelly-side down, a day with small children grows into a nightmare of frantic activity, punctuated with shrieks, cries, and hyena-style laughs. The very act of playing turns the house into a disaster area: blankets and sheets that are thrown over tables and chairs to form caves, miniature cars and trucks that race endlessly up and down hallways, and a cat that becomes a caged tiger, imprisoned under the laundry basket. After supper, with more spilled milk, uneaten vegetables, and tidbits fed to the cat under the table, it's finally time for bed. But before they fall blissfully asleep, the children still have time to knock over one more bedtime glass of water, jump on the beds until the springs threaten to break, and demand a last ride to the bathroom on mother's back. *Constant confusion is a way of life for parents of small children.*   *Student paragraph*

3   The topic sentence may appear first and last. In such paragraphs the last sentence repeats the idea of the first, frequently restating it with some amplification or a slightly different emphasis in the light of the intervening details or discussion.

Clearly then, our first step is to convince our students of the importance of working from a thesis. The task is difficult, but we have their original motivation working for us. The students will easily understand that to work from a thesis is the way to please teacher, get a good grade, fulfill the assignment, and so on. If understanding the concept of thesis, finding an effective one, and organizing a paper about it were merely rote skills, this sort of motivation, superficial and temporary though it is, would be sufficient for our initial purposes. Full acceptance will come, and will *only* come, after personal experience has convinced each student that these procedures actually improve writing. Unfortunately for this simple solution, *thesis skills require a logical chain of reasoning and individual reflection.* They cannot be exercised effectively enough to achieve even the required preliminary success without some degree of real commitment on the part of the individual student. So our first task is to bring about in our students a real conversion of idea: *we must genuinely convince them of the persuasive purpose of the thesis and the essentially persuasive nature of all writing.*

BETH NEMAN, Teaching Students to Write

A metal garbage can lid has many uses. In the spring it can be used to catch rainwater in which a small boy can create a world of his own, a world of dead leaves and twigs inhabited by salamanders, small frogs, and worms. In the summer it can be turned on its top, the inside lined with aluminum foil, and used to hold charcoal for a barbecue. In the fall it can be used, with a similar lid, to frighten unsuspecting Halloween "trick-or-treaters." In the winter, if the handle is removed or flattened, the lid can be used by children to speed down snow-packed hills. *A garbage can lid covers garbage most of the time, but with a little imagination, one can uncover new uses for it.* *Student paragraph*

4 The topic sentence may be implied. Narrative and descriptive paragraphs often do not have an explicitly stated topic sentence. But the controlling idea of such paragraphs is clearly implied by its details. In the following paragraph by Joan Didion, for example, the controlling idea might be stated thus: "Though the sources of one's childhood imaginings are long lost, the record of those imaginings perhaps reveals lifelong habits of mind."

My first notebook was a Big Five tablet, given to me by my mother with the sensible suggestion that I stop whining and learn to amuse myself by writing down my thoughts. She returned the tablet to me a few years ago; the first entry is an account of a woman who believed herself to be freezing to death in the Arctic night, only to find, when day broke, that she had stumbled onto the Sahara Desert, where she would die of the heat before lunch. I have no idea what turn of a five-year-old's mind could have prompted so insistently "ironic" and exotic a story, but it does reveal a certain predilection for the extreme which has dogged me into adult life; perhaps if I were analytically inclined I would find it a truer story than any I might have told about Donald Johnson's birthday party or the day my cousin Brenda put Kitty Litter in the aquarium. JOAN DIDION, "On Keeping a Notebook"

EXERCISE 32a What is the topic sentence, expressed or implied, in each of the following paragraphs?

1 Restaurants have always treated children badly. When I was small my family used to travel a lot, and waitresses were forever calling me "Butch" and pinching my cheeks and making me wear paper bibs with slogans on them. Restaurants still treat children badly; the difference is that restaurants have lately taken to treating us all as if we were children. We are obliged to order an Egg McMuffin when we want breakfast, a Fishamajig when we want a fish sandwich, a Fribble when we want a milkshake, a Whopper when we want a hamburger with all the fixings. Some of these names serve a certain purpose. By calling a milkshake a Fribble, for instance, the management need make no promise that it contains milk, or even that it was shaken.

ANDREW WARD, *"Yumbo"*

2 The Civil War was not won by the North; it was won by the South. The main objective of the South was to keep the land south of the Mason-Dixon line a white man's land—and they did just that. It is true that Lincoln, whose main goal was to preserve the Union, proclaimed the slaves free in 1862; but proclamations do not make people equal. That the South had achieved her goal was evident during the reconstruction period which followed the cease-fire. Although blacks were given the vote, they were too intimidated by the whites to cast their ballots. When they did vote, they voted the way the white men told them to—Democratic. The birth of the Ku Klux Klan after the Civil War also kept the black man "in his place." So strong were the South's commitments to the idea of a white man's land that blacks were still in an inferior position as late as 1964. It was not until the sixties, following the Supreme Court decisions on bus and school desegregation, that the black man finally achieved the status of an equal citizen. The South held fast to the idea of the white man's supremacy for one hundred years after the Civil War. *Student paragraph*

3 Through photographs, each family constructs a portrait-chronicle of itself—a portable kit of images that bears witness to its connectedness. It hardly matters what activities are photographed so long as photographs get taken and are cherished. Photography becomes a rite of family life just when, in the industrializing countries of Europe and America, the very institution of the family starts undergoing radical surgery. As that claustrophobic unit, the nuclear family, was being carved out of a much larger family aggregate, photography came along to memorialize, to restate symbolically, the imperiled continuity and vanishing extendedness of family life. Those ghostly traces, photographs, supply the token presence of the dispersed relatives. A family's photograph album is generally about the extended family—and, often, is all that remains of it. SUSAN SONTAG, *"In Plato's Cave"*

4 Every writer has his own ways of getting started, from sharpening pencils, to reading the Bible, to pacing the floor. I often rinse out my mind by reading something, and I sometimes manage to put off getting down to the hard struggle for an unconscionable time. Mostly I am helped through the barrier by music. I play records while I am writing and especially at the start of each day one particular record that accompanies the poem or chapter I am working at. During these last weeks it has been a record by Albinoni for strings and organ. I do not always play that key record, but it is there to draw on—the key to a certain piece of work, the key to that mood. The romantic composers, much as I enjoy listening to them at other times, are no help. Bach, Mozart, Vivaldi—they are what I need—clarity and structure.

MAY SARTON, *"The Art of Writing"*

5 An atmosphere that is a strange mixture of bleakness, tranquillity, and expectancy pervades the downstairs hall of the old gym early in the morning. As I walk from the chilly dawn outdoors into the basement of the old gym, I feel the dry heat on my face; although I assume that I am alone, I am surrounded by the impersonal noises of an antiquated steam-heating system. All the doors, which stand like sentries along the walls of the hallway, are locked, so that the deserted nature of that place and that hour are apparent; pipes hang from above, making the ceiling resemble the ugly, rarely viewed underside of a bizarre animal. I feel peaceful, however, in this lonely place, because of the silence. I know, moreover, that the desertlike heat is a sign that preparation has been made for my arrival and a signal that the day of work is about to begin.

Student paragraph

32b Be sure that every sentence in a paragraph bears on the central subject.

Not only must you have a clear purpose in writing a paragraph, you must also hold to that purpose throughout the paragraph. The writer of the following paragraph, for example, changes his purpose three times in the first three sentences, and he tacks on the last sentence as a kind of afterthought.

Henry James's extensive travel during his early years greatly influenced his later writings. Born in New York in 1843, Henry was destined to become one of the first novelists of the world. He received a remarkable education. His parents took him abroad for a year when he was only an infant. He was educated by tutors until he was twelve, and then taken abroad for three more years by his parents. His father wanted him to absorb French and German culture. His older brother, William, received the same education.

One way of revising this paragraph would be to restrict its subject matter to the one major topic of James's childhood.

Henry James, the novelist, had an unusual childhood. In 1844, while still an infant, he was taken abroad by his parents for a year. Upon his return, he and his older brother, William, were given private tutoring until Henry was twelve. At that time both boys were taken abroad to spend three years absorbing French and German culture.

Be careful not to violate the principle of unity by introducing new topics or points of view at the end of a paragraph. Notice in the following example how the last sentence, in which the writer deserts his earlier objectivity and takes sides in the argument, breaks the unity.

In the years following World War II there was much discussion on the question of lowering the minimum voting age to eighteen. Among people who believed that the age limit should be lowered, the favorite statement was, "If a boy is old enough to die for his country, he's old enough to vote in it." People who wanted the age limit to remain at twenty-one thought eighteen-year-olds would be unduly influenced by local wardheelers who would urge them to vote a "straight ticket." But the young voter who had not had a chance to become a "dyed-in-the-wool" party member tended to weigh the merits of the individual candidate rather than those of the party itself.

Revised, the paragraph might read:

In the years following World War II there was much discussion on the question of lowering the minimum voting age to eighteen. Among people who believed that the age limit should be lowered, the favorite statement was, "If a boy is old enough to die for his country, he's old enough to vote in it." People who wanted the age limit to remain at twenty-one thought eighteen-year-olds would be unduly influenced by the promises of dishonest politicians.

EXERCISE 32b(1)   Each of the following paragraphs opens with a topic sentence, but each violates unity by introducing information not related to the topic. Which sentences in each paragraph are not related to the topic of the paragraph? Could any of the sentences you identify as not related to the topic actually contribute to the topic if their position in the paragraph were changed?

1 (1) Racial discrimination has existed in the United States for many years. (2) It began when the first white settler decided that the Indians were an inferior breed. (3) It was given impetus by the arrival of the first Negro slaves. (4) A civil war was fought largely because the spokesman of the North, Abraham Lincoln, believed that all men are created equal. (5) Slavery was abolished and the Negro set free by act of Congress.

2 (1) The life of Thomas A. Edison illustrates the truth of the old saying "Genius is ten percent inspiration and ninety percent perspiration." (2) Edison was born in Milan, Ohio, and was expelled from school because his teachers thought he was a moron. (3) So Edison was educated at home by his mother, who helped him build a laboratory in the basement. (4) Edison spent long hours here, sometimes working as long as sixteen hours a day.

3 (1) Hardy's *The Return of the Native* is one of the finest novels I have ever read. (2) I was amazed to see how Hardy makes his major and minor episodes culminate in a great climax, and how inextricably he weaves the fortunes of his chief characters with those of his lesser characters. (3) Moreover, his handling of the landscape—gloomy Egdon Heath—is masterful. (4) He makes it a genuine, motivating force in the story. (5) My favorite character, however, was Diggory Venn.

4 (1) The advantages of modern transportation are many. (2) An enormous amount of time is saved by the great speeds at which vehicles of today travel. (3) Cross-country trips are much more comfortable than they were, and they can be made in days rather than months. (4) For land travel today the automobile, motorcycle, and bus have taken the place of the horse and wagon, stagecoach, and mule. (5) The railroad has been developed and extended since the use of the diesel. (6) Sailing ships are now chiefly a hobby and few consider them seriously as a means of transportation.

5 (1) If you intend to plant a strawberry bed, there are several things that you should consider. (2) Strawberries do best in a sandy loam or sandy clay that has been enriched with humus. (3) Blueberries and blackberries are better in acid soils. (4) Strawberries should be set out in an area that receives adequate drainage. (5) Too much moisture in the soil will kill them or interfere with their growth. (6) Other kinds of plants do better in marshy soils. (7) On account of frost dangers it is better to plant strawberries on a hillside or on a relatively high level area. (8) The effects of frost are rather peculiar; in general, plants in low-lying areas are more likely to be harmed by frost than those on hills. (9) The growth of young strawberries is actually increased if one pinches off the runners from the plants.

EXERCISE 32b(2) Following are three topic sentences, each accompanied by a set of statements. Some of the statements are relevant to the topic, some are not. Eliminate the irrelevant ones, and organize the rest into a paragraph.

1 Given my choice I would sooner be in the Air Force than in any other service branch.

I am more interested in flying than in any other military occupation.

Opportunities for advancement are greater in the Air Force.

Wages in certain brackets of the Air Force are higher than in other branches.

There are many opportunities to travel.

My cousin has been in the Navy for two years, and has sailed around the whole world.

I think, though, that I still like the Air Force better.

2 The wreck on Route 64 at Mt. Nixon was caused entirely by careless and reckless driving by the driver of the Buick.

When the wreck occurred the lights were green for the cars coming off the side road.

A heavy truck loaded with hay was pulling out to cross the highway.

The Buick came speeding down the main road, went through the stoplight, and crashed into the truck.

You could hear the screeching of the tires and then the crashing and grinding of metal a quarter of a mile away.

You could hear it in our house up the road.

Both drivers were killed, and I will never forget how awful the accident was.

3 We owe some of our notions of radar to scientific observation of bats.

Most people hate bats.

Bats are commonly considered unattractive, ugly creatures.

They really look more like mice with wings than anything else.

Scientists noticed that bats rarely collided with anything in their erratic flight.

Keen eyesight could not be the reason for their flying the way they do, since bats are blind.

It was found that bats keep sending out noises inaudible to people and that they hear the echoes of those noises.

This principle whereby they fly safely was found to be similar to the main principle of radar.

COHERENCE IN THE PARAGRAPH ¶ **COH**

A paragraph may be unified without being coherent. Unity depends upon selecting details and ideas relevant to the paragraph topic. Coherence depends upon organizing these details and ideas so that the reader can easily see *how* they are relevant. Even though all the sentences of a paragraph bear upon a single point, unless they are knit together and flow into one another so that their relation to that single point is clear, they will not be coherent. A coherent paragraph leads readers easily from sentence to sentence. An incoherent paragraph confronts readers with puzzling jumps in thought, events out of sequence, facts illogically arranged, or points in a discussion omitted. Coherence requires that sentences be logically arranged and clearly connected.

32c Arrange the sentences in a clear order.

To insure coherence in a paragraph, arrange all sentences within the paragraph in some pattern that will create an orderly, natural flow of ideas. Like the arrangement you choose for an essay, the arrangement you choose for a particular paragraph will depend on your materials and your purpose. The common ways of ordering sentences are the methods of arrangement introduced in Section 31f: (1) time order, (2) space order, (3) order of climax, and (4) general to particular or particular to general.

1   Time order. Narrative paragraphs naturally arrange themselves in the order in which the events occur. The following simple paragraph recounts the death of a female eagle.

> On her own, one of the female's bold hunting trips was to prove fatal. The male saw from high above that she was making an attack on a ground squirrel in a dry arroyo. Her path would take her over an embankment at low altitude. Hidden from her view were two hunters walking close to the bluff. The male tensed as he saw his mate approach the men. As her black form swept over the hunters, they whirled and raised their guns. The female saw, but too late. As she banked sharply, two shots sang out and one slug tore through her body, sending her crashing in a crumpled mass. Helpless and distraught, the male watched from above as the hunters stretched out the wings of his mate and examined their prize. With the fear of man reinforced in his mind, he turned away and mounted up to return to the safety of the back country.   KENT DURDEN, *Flight to Freedom*

Specific directions and explanations of processes also arrange themselves naturally in time order. The following directions for mixing powdered clay proceed step by step through the process.

> Clay purchased in powder form is mixed with water to make it a plastic mass. To mix, fill a large dishpan or small tub about one-third full of water, sift clay over [the] water, one handful at a time, until [the] clay settles on top of the water to make a coating about 1 inch think. Cover [the] pan with paper or cloth and let the unstirred mixture set overnight. On the following day mix and stir it thoroughly. If [the] mass is too thick to knead, add more water. If too thin, add dry clay. Clay is in a state to store when it is soft and pliable but does not stick to the hands. Since clay improves with aging in a damp condition, mix as far ahead of time of use as you can. Wrap [the] clay in damp cloth and store in a covered crock for at least one week before using.
>
> HERBERT H. SANDERS, "How to Make Pottery and Ceramic Sculpture"

2   Space order. Many descriptive paragraphs arrange themselves easily according to some spatial order, from east to west, from bottom to top, from near to far, from the center outward, and the like. In the following paragraph, the author is standing at a high point overlooking a valley. The description moves first to the right, then to the left, then straight ahead *(before me)*, and then farther and farther into the distance ahead *(beyond the creek* and *beyond that)*.

> *On my right* a woods thickly overgrown with creeper descended the hill's slope to Tinker Creek. *On my left* was a planting of large shade

trees on the ridge of the hill. *Before me* the grassy hill pitched abruptly and gave way to a large, level field fringed in trees where it bordered the creek. *Beyond the creek* I could see with effort the vertical sliced rock where men had long ago quarried the mountain under the forest. *Beyond that* I saw Hollins Pond and all its woods and pastures; then I saw in a blue haze all the world poured flat and pale between the mountains. ANNIE DILLARD, "Pilgrim at Tinker Creek"

In the following paragraph, the writer is describing the interior of her church's sanctuary. She carefully orders the details, always keeping the relative position of parts clear with such directional words and phrases as *over, above, on each side,* and with such descriptive verbs as *line, hang, guard, flank,* and *arching.*

The sanctuary of the First Presbyterian Church is a study in nineteenth century architecture. The sections of contoured, crescent-shaped oak pews separated by *two main aisles line the wedge-shaped main floor. Over the main floor in the rear hangs a balcony* supported by two Greek columns whose decorative gilt tops complement similar ornamentation at the front upper corners of the auditorium. *Brass rails guard the balcony seats and separate* the raised *podium from the choir loft behind* it. *Above and on each side of the podium* are opera-box windows of beveled glass and brass. *Three stained-glass windows flank each side* of the sanctuary and, gleaming in the sunlight, depict such simple religious subjects as lilies, the cross, and Christ in his roles of Shepherd and Comforter. The most distinctive feature, however, is the *huge fifteen-foot rotunda opening up the center* of the ceiling and arching its way to heaven. *Student paragraph*

3 Order of climax. Many paragraphs can be made coherent as well as more effective by arranging details or examples in order of increasing importance. The writer of the following paragraph arranged its examples—kinds of jobs—in order of climax. Drucker's evidence moves from those jobs in which skill at expressing oneself (the paragraph's subject) is least important to those in which it is most important.

If you work as a soda jerker you will, of course, not need much skill in expressing yourself to be effective. If you work on a machine, your ability to express yourself will be of little importance. But as soon as you move one step up from the bottom, your effectiveness depends on your ability to reach others through the spoken or the written word. And the further away your job is from manual work, the larger the organization of which you are an employee, the more important it will be that you know how to convey your thoughts in writing or speaking. In the very large business organization, whether it is the government, the large corporation, or the Army, this ability to express oneself is perhaps the most important of all the skills a man can possess.

PETER F. DRUCKER, "How to Be an Employee"

4   General to particular or particular to general order. A great many paragraphs begin with a topic sentence that makes a general statement. Sentences that follow support the general statement with details, examples, evidence, and the like. Other paragraphs reverse this order, presenting first a series of details or reasons and concluding with a general statement that summarizes.

In the following paragraph the author begins with a general statement—that readers generally get lost through a writer's carelessness, which can take "any number of forms." The five successive sentences beginning with "perhaps" list five different forms that carelessness can take.

> If a reader is lost, it is generally because the writer has not been careful enough to keep him on the path. This carelessness can take any number of forms. Perhaps a sentence is so excessively cluttered that the reader, hacking his way through the verbiage, simply doesn't know what it means. Perhaps a sentence has been so shoddily constructed that the reader could read it in any of several ways. Perhaps the writer has switched pronouns in mid-sentence, or has switched tenses, so the reader loses track of who is talking or when the action took place. Perhaps sentence B is not a logical sequel to sentence A—the writer, in whose head the connection is clear, has not bothered to provide the missing link. Perhaps the writer has used an important word incorrectly by not taking the trouble to look it up. He may think that "sanguine" and "sanguinary" mean the same thing, but the difference is a bloody big one. The reader can only infer (speaking of big differences) what the writer is trying to imply.   WILLIAM ZINSSER, "On Writing Well"

In the following paragraph, the author begins by asserting that disasters may not be as widespread as records indicate. To support this statement, she contrasts the range of events reported in the news with the relative normalcy of most people's typical day. She then states the "law" she has formulated on the basis of her perception of the true situation. The paragraph thus moves from general to specific back to general.

> Disaster is rarely as pervasive as it seems from recorded accounts. The fact of being on the record makes it appear continuous and ubiquitous whereas it is more likely to have been sporadic both in time and place. Besides, persistence of the normal is usually greater than the effect of disturbance, as we know from our own times. After absorbing the news of today, one expects to face a world consisting entirely of strikes, crimes, power failures, broken water mains, stalled trains, school shutdowns, muggers, drug addicts, neo-Nazis, and rapists. The fact is that one can come home in the evening—on a lucky day—without having encountered more than one or two of these phenomena. This has led me to formulate Tuchman's Law, as follows: "The fact of

being reported multiplies the apparent extent of any deplorable development by five- to tenfold" (or any figure the reader would care to supply).   BARBARA TUCHMAN, *A Distant Mirror*

In contrast to the two preceding paragraphs, the following paragraph moves from particular to general. The writer describes first her former cat, then her present cat, before her final general statement about the obvious difference between the two.

> I do not understand why people confuse my Siamese cat, Prissy, with the one I had several years ago, Henry. The two cats are only alike in breed. Prissy, a quiet, feminine feline, loves me dearly but not possessively. She likes to keep her distance from people, exert her independence, and uphold the cat's right to be finicky. She observes decorum and is never so rude as to beg, lick, or sniff unceremoniously. Her usual posture is sitting upright, eyes closed, perfectly still. Prissy is a very proper cat. Henry, on the other hand, was a disturbingly vocal tom cat who, before he died, loved me dearly but possessively. He was my shadow from morning until night. He expected me to constantly entertain him, and he was a crude, voracious eater. Henry never cared who saw him do anything, whether it was decorous or not, and he usually offended my friends in some way. The cat made himself quite comfortable, be it on top of the television, across strangers' feet or laps, in beds, drawers, sacks, closets, or nooks. The difference between Prissy and Henry is exactly the difference between Barbara Walters and Archie Bunker, and it would certainly take an imperceptive human to mistake those two.   *Student paragraph*

EXERCISE 32c(1)   Write a coherent paragraph that incorporates in your own words all the following information about Thomas Hardy.

He was an English novelist, short story writer, and poet.

He died in 1928, at the age of eighty-eight.

He is considered one of the most important of the writers who revolted against Victorian tradition at the end of the nineteenth century.

He is known for the pessimism of his ideas.

His most important prose works are novels of character and environment.

The Return of the Native, Tess of the D'Urbervilles, and *Jude the Obscure* are among his most important novels.

His best novels are studies of life in the bleak English countryside.

In his best novels individuals are defeated in their struggle against their physical and social environment.

Individuals in his best novels also struggle against the caprices of chance.

EXERCISE 32c(2)   You can see how the order of sentences in a paragraph contributes to its coherence if you examine a paragraph in which the original order has been changed. The following paragraphs were coherent as they were originally written, but the order of sentences has been changed. Rearrange each group of sentences to make a coherent paragraph.

1 (1) Landing a space capsule on Mars is technically complicated. (2) In 1971 one Soviet lander crashed and another stopped sending signals back after 20 seconds. (3) One of the Soviet 1974 attempts just flew past Mars. (4) Descending through Martian atmosphere is much trickier than landing on the airless moon. (5) The Soviets tried to land on Mars four times, twice in 1971 and twice in 1974. (6) Instruments on the second 1974 flight failed during descent, after transmitting usable signals for a few seconds.

2 (1) Language is full of symbols, but we also use signs or images that are not strictly descriptive. (2) Such things are not symbols. (3) We use spoken and written language to express the meaning we want to convey. (4) Although meaningless in themselves, signs have acquired a recognizable meaning through common usage or deliberate intention. (5) Some of these signs are mere abbreviations or strings of initials such as UN or UNESCO. (6) They are signs and do no more than denote the object to which they are attached. (7) Other signs are things such as familiar trademarks, badges, flags, and traffic lights.

3 (1) They fly in magnificent unison as they go further south to escape the cold. (2) The sight of the leaves covering the barren ground, additionally, indicates that cooler weather is approaching. (3) The fact that darkness arrives earlier in the evening makes one finally realize that the fall season has come. (4) There is nothing quite as visually exciting as noticing the signs which indicate fall is approaching. (5) Even during the day, the brisk wind compels a person to move at a quicker pace. (6) Obviously, the splendor of the fall season is unsurpassed. (7) Later in the afternoon, one notices that the birds, as well, are preparing for the onset of fall. (8) During the day one cannot help but notice the transformation in the leaves' colors from various shades of green to deep tones of red, gold, and brown.

32d

32d   Make clear the relationships among sentences.

Coherence requires not only that the sentences within a paragraph be related to each other, but also that their relationship be made clear. You can achieve clear relationships among sentences by the following means: (1) being consistent in point of view, (2) using parallel grammatical structure, (3) repeating words or ideas, and (4) using transitional words or phrases.

1   Maintain a consistent point of view. Avoid unnecessary shifts in person, tense, or number within a paragraph.

UNNECESSARY SHIFT IN PERSON

A pleasant and quiet place to live is essential for a serious-minded college student. If possible, you should rent a room from a landlady with a reputation for keeping order and discipline among her renters. Moreover, a student ought to pick a roommate with the same temperament as his own. Then you can agree to and keep a schedule of study hours.

UNNECESSARY SHIFT IN TENSE

Recently, I saw the movie *9 to 5*. The main characters are played by Jane Fonda, Dolly Parton, and Lily Tomlin. I particularly enjoyed the character who is played by Dolly Parton. She gives an excellent performance as an innocent, happily married woman who was suspected of having an immoral relationship with her boss. Lily Tomlin portrays an efficient, knowledgeable secretary who knew more about running an office than her boss does. Jane Fonda plays the role of a shy, somewhat confused country girl who was awed and rather frightened of the people she works with.

UNNECESSARY SHIFT IN NUMBER

Of great currency at the moment is the notion that education should prepare students for "life." A college graduate no longer goes out into the world as a cultivated gentleman. Instead students feel obliged to prepare themselves for places in the business world. Consequently, we are establishing courses on how to get and keep a mate, how to budget an income, and how to win friends and influence people—that is, how to sell yourself and your product. The study of things not obviously practical to a businessman is coming to be looked upon as unnecessary.

2 Use parallel grammatical structure. Using parallel grammatical structure in successive sentences is one of the most important ways of connecting them. Just as parallel grammatical form in coordinate parts of a single sentence emphasizes the coordinate relationship of the ideas, so parallel structure from sentence to sentence within a paragraph emphasizes the relationship of these sentences to the single idea of the paragraph.

Bowman had just happened to be looking at her. *He set* his cup back on the table in unbelieving protest. A pain pressed at his eyes. *He saw* that she was not an old woman. *She was* young, still young. *He could think* of no number of years for her. *She was* the same age as Sonny, and she belonged to him. *She stood* with the deep dark corner of the room behind her, the shifting yellow light scattering over her head and her grey formless dress, trembling over her tall body when it bent over them in its sudden communication. *She was* young. Her teeth were shining and her eyes glowed. *She turned and walked* slowly and heavily out of the room, and *he heard* her sit down on the cot and then lie down. The pattern on the quilt moved.

EUDORA WELTY, "Death of a Travelling Salesman"

Life has often been described as a game, and if one is to play any game successfully, *he must know how to balance his skills* and blend them into the combination most effective for transferring potential into actual performance. *Regardless of how many times* a guard has held his man scoreless, *if he himself has not scored* for his team, his effort is incomplete. *Regardless of how many points* a forward or center averages per game, *if he has not guarded the lane* at every attempt of penetration by the opposition, he is inefficient. The most valuable player trophy is awarded to the player *who scores considerably, who grabs rebounds mechanically* off the backboard, and *who hustles relentlessly* from the initial center jump until the final buzzer sounds. A successful player at his life's game *must also balance his skills. If he always leads, people may tire* of following; *if he always follows, others may consider* him unworthy of a leadership position when he desires it. The secret, then, is to incorporate the two so that a mediocre character is transformed into an exceptional one.

Student paragraph

3 Repeat key words and phrases. Many well-constructed paragraphs rely on the repetition of key words and phrases, often with slight modification, to emphasize major ideas and carry the thought from sentence to sentence. Pronouns referring back to clearly established antecedents in the previous sentence function in the same way. In the following paragraphs the words and phrases that are repeated to provide clear links from sentence to sentence and produce a closely integrated whole are in italics.

In discussing the pre-Civil War South, it *should be remembered* that the large plantation owners constituted only a small part of the *total Southern population*. By far the greater part of *that population* was made up of *small farmers,* and of course the Negro slaves themselves. Some *small farmers* had acquired substantial acreage, owned three or four slaves, and were relatively prosperous. But most of the *small farmers* were terribly poor. They rented their land and worked it themselves, sometimes side by side with the slaves of the great *landowners.* In everything but *social position* they were worse off than the Negro slaves. But it must *also be remembered* that they were as jealous of that superior *social position* as the wealthy *landowner* himself.   *Student paragraph*

Nonconformity is not only a desirable thing, it is an actual thing. One need only remark that all art is based upon *nonconformity*—a point that I shall undertake to establish—and that every great historic change has been based upon *nonconformity,* has been bought either with the blood or with the reputation of *nonconformists.* Without *nonconformity* we would have had no Bill of Rights nor Magna Carta, no public education system, no nation upon this continent, no continent, no science at all, no philosophy, and considerably fewer religions. All that is *pretty obvious.*

But it seems to be *less obvious* that to *create* anything at all in any field, and especially anything of outstanding worth, requires *nonconformity,* or a want of satisfaction with things as they are. The *creative* person—the *nonconformist*—may be in profound disagreement with the present way of things, or he may simply wish to add his views, to render a personal account of matters.   BEN SHAHN, *The Shape of Content*

4   Use transitional markers. A transitional marker is a word or a phrase placed at or near the beginning of a sentence to indicate its relation to the preceding sentence. The coordinating conjunctions *and, but, or, nor, so,* and *yet* are often used this way, particularly in informal writing, for they provide easy bridges from one sentence to another. But English provides a wide variety of transitional markers, as suggested in the lists below. Good modern writing uses the more formal markers sparingly. Be wary of cluttering your writing with unnecessary *however's, moreover's,* and *consequently's.* But you should be equally careful to know them and to use them when they create clarity.

Here is a list of many of the common transitional words and phrases:

TO INDICATE ADDITION

again, also, and, and then, besides, equally important, finally, first, further, furthermore, in addition, last, likewise, moreover, next, second, third, too

TO INDICATE CAUSE AND EFFECT

accordingly, as a result, consequently, hence, in short, otherwise, then, therefore, thus, truly

TO INDICATE COMPARISON

in a like manner, likewise, similarly

TO INDICATE CONCESSION

after all, although this may be true, at the same time, even though, I admit, naturally, of course

TO INDICATE CONTRAST

after all, although true, and yet, at the same time, but, for all that, however, in contrast, in spite of, nevertheless, notwithstanding, on the contrary, on the other hand, still, yet

TO INDICATE SPECIAL FEATURES OR EXAMPLES

for example, for instance, incidentally, indeed, in fact, in other words, in particular, specifically, that is, to illustrate

TO INDICATE SUMMARY

in brief, in conclusion, in short, on the whole, to conclude, to summarize, to sum up

TO INDICATE TIME RELATIONSHIPS

after a short time, afterwards, as long as, as soon as, at last, at length, at that time, at the same time, before, earlier, immediately, in the meantime, lately, later, meanwhile, of late, presently, shortly, since, soon, temporarily, thereafter, thereupon, until, when, while

Transitional words and phrases are italicized in the following:

As I have remarked, the pilots' association was now the compactest monopoly in the world, perhaps, and seemed simply indestructible. *And yet* the days of its glory were numbered. *First,* the new railroad stretching up through Mississippi, Tennessee, and Kentucky, to Northern railway-centers, began to divert the passenger travel from the steamboats; *next* the war came and almost entirely annihilated the steamboating industry during several years, leaving most of the pilots idle and the cost of living advancing all the time; *then* the treasurer of the St. Louis association put his hand into the till and walked off with every dollar of the ample fund; *and finally,* the railroads intruding everywhere, there was little for steamers to do, when the war was over, but carry freights; *so straightway* some genius from the Atlantic coast introduced the plan of towing a dozen steamer cargoes down to New Orleans at the tail of a vulgar little tugboat; and behold, in the twinkling of an eye, *as it were,* the association and the noble science of piloting were things of the dead and pathetic past!   MARK TWAIN, *Life on the Mississippi*

Sometimes a question may be made still more clear or precise by an indication of the circumstances in which it occurs. *Let us take an example.* I ask, "How wide is this bookcase?" This certainly appears to be a straightforward question that could be answered simply enough by specifying the number of inches across its front. *But* when one undertakes to find the answer, several perplexing considerations may arise. What dimension is wanted: the length of the shelf? the outside dimension? at the widest point? or at some other typical point? *Again,* how accurate a measure is wanted?—for no measurement is entirely accurate; all we can expect is greater or less accuracy. All these questions could be more or less cleared up by indicating the circumstances under which the problem arose. It might be, *for example,* that I contemplate placing the bookcase against a certain wall and desire to know whether or not it is too wide to fit into the position under consideration. *At once* I realize that the widest outside dimension is the one required, and that a relatively high degree of accuracy is necessary only if the width of the wall and that of the bookcase are found to be nearly the same.

HENRY S. LEONARD, *Principles of Right Reason*

EXERCISE 32d(1)   Make a coherent paragraph of the following statements. First, put them in logical order. Second, give them a consistent point of view and link them smoothly with transitional words or phrases. Revise the wording of the statements if necessary, but use all the information given.

(1) This attitude shows a naive faith in the competency of secretaries. (2) Practicing engineers and scientists say they spend half their time writing letters and reports. (3) Many of us foolishly object to taking courses in writing. (4) College students going into business think their secretaries will do their writing for them. (5) A student going into the technical or scientific fields may think that writing is something he seldom has to do. (6) Young businessmen seldom have private secretaries. (7) Our notion that only poets, novelists, and newspaper workers have to know how to write is unrealistic. (8) Other things being equal, a man in any field who can express himself effectively is sure to succeed more rapidly than a man whose command of language is poor.

EXERCISE 32d(2) The following paragraphs and paragraph parts are marred and made incoherent by shifts in person, tense, and number. Rewrite the paragraphs to insure consistency and coherence throughout.

1 Literature is a medium through which a person can convey his ideas toward or protests against different norms of society. Those works that deal with a moral issue are of particular importance in literature; they are written with a particular purpose in mind. A literary work such as Shakespeare's plays with a moral issue will live on to be reinterpreted by different generations. These works involve the reader for he forms his own moral judgment toward the issue. Arthur Miller's *Death of a Salesman* is a play which deals with moral issues.

2 It is difficult to feel compassion for people who do not deserve it. My neighbor, John Carroll, is a poor little rich boy who just can't find happiness and love. He had never been deprived of anything. The one thing he really wanted, a girl who had gone to high school with him, he couldn't get. His mother tells the story in such a way that you feel pity for this man because of this one thing that he couldn't attain. The people who least deserve compassion get more than their share of it.

3 Every time a nation is involved in a war it must face problems about its ex-soldiers after that war. The veteran is entitled to some special considerations from society, but how to treat them with complete fairness is a baffling problem. Livy reports that grants to the former soldier caused some troubles in the early history of Rome. There were many disagreements between them and the early Roman senators.

4 Preparing a surface for new paint is as important a step in the whole process as the application of paint itself. First, be sure that the surface is quite clean. You should wash any grease or grime from the woodwork. The painter may use turpentine or a detergent for this. One must be careful to clean off whatever cleanser they have used. Then sand off any rough or chipped paint.

5 One of the books I read in high school English was Dickens's *Tale of Two Cities*. In it the author tells of some of the horrors of the French Revolution. He spent several pages telling about how the French aristocrats suffered. The climax part of the book tells how a ne'er-do-well who had failed in life sacrifices himself for another. He took his place in a prison and went stoically to the guillotine for him.

PARAGRAPH DEVELOPMENT ¶ **DEV**

32e

32e **Develop every paragraph adequately.**

If you do not pay attention to unity and coherence in writing your paragraphs (and your papers), you will lose your readers. No matter how willing they may be to stay with you, they will soon give up if you include details and reasons that they can't relate to your controlling ideas. And they will give up if they can't follow you from sentence to sentence. Paying attention to unity and coherence helps insure that your thinking is clear and orderly both to yourself and to your readers.

But no matter how careful you are not to introduce irrelevant details or to insure that one sentence follows another with shining clarity, you must develop central ideas with details, examples, evidence, and reasons if you are to inform, persuade, or simply interest your readers. Good topic sentences, no matter how carefully they are constructed to state the controlling ideas of the paragraphs, are relatively general statements. To make readers understand what those statements mean and to keep readers interested, you must explain or support such statements.

The following paragraph does not go far beyond its topic sentence:

It is not always true that a good picture is worth a thousand words. Often writing is much clearer than a picture. It is sometimes difficult to figure out what a picture means, but a careful writer can almost always explain it.

The writer of this paragraph has given us no details that explain why it is not true that pictures are worth more than words, or any reasons for believing his topic sentence. The second sentence merely restates the topic sentence, and the final sentence does very little more. Compare the following paragraph built on the same topic sentence.

It is not always true that a picture is worth a thousand words. Sometimes, in fact, pictures are pretty useless things. Far from being worth more than words, they can be downright frustrating. If you buy a new typewriter, would you rather have a glossy picture of it, or a 1000-word booklet explaining how it works? If your carburetor is clogged, do you need a picture of the carburetor, or an explanation of how to unclog it? If you can't swim and you fall in the river and start gulping water, will you be better off to hold up a picture of yourself drowning, or start screaming "Help!"?

In contrast to the first writer, this writer has given us three concrete examples of how words may in fact be worth more than pictures. We may object that pictures of both the typewriter and the clogged carburetor would be helpful along with the words. But we understand what the writer means. And we've been kept interested.

Each of the following sample paragraphs begins with a satisfactory topic sentence stating the writer's central idea. But each fails to give enough details or reasons to explain that idea to the reader, to make the idea concrete and clear. In short, these paragraphs are not adequately developed.

> The president should be elected for an eight-year term. In a four-year term the president has to spend too much of his time being a politician. He therefore can't carry out his plans.

A reader who is not already convinced that one eight-year presidential term is wiser and safer than two four-year terms is not likely to be persuaded by the two very general reasons the writer gives here.

> Work as a physical therapist is rewarding financially, but more important, it provides the satisfaction of helping others. For example, physical therapists can help handicapped children. They can also help others.

The reader expects more concrete details about the kind of work the physical therapist does, perhaps examples of the kinds of improvement brought to handicapped children, and certainly some more concrete information about who "others" are. He expects, too, some clearer explanation of the idea of satisfaction, which the topic sentence promises.

EXERCISE 32e Choose two of the following topic sentences and develop each into a meaningful paragraph by supporting it with details, examples, evidence, and reasons.

1 A first impression is not always a reliable basis for judgment.
2 A book that is one man's meat may be another man's poison.
3 The first day of college is a nerve-shattering experience.
4 Making homemade furniture is less difficult than it appears.
5 Words are the most powerful drugs used by mankind.
6 There are three great advantages to air travel—speed, comfort, and thrills.
7 Harmony seldom makes the headlines.
8 Keeping a detailed budget is more trouble than it's worth.

32e

9 A good hitter is far more valuable to a baseball team than a good fielder.

10 Fashions in clothes (books, drama, hairdress, slang, etc.) change from one year (decade, century) to the next.

32f

32f Avoid excessively long and excessively short paragraphs.

The length of a paragraph is determined by the nature of the subject, the type of topic sentence, the intention of the writer, and the character of the audience. Ultimately, the length of a paragraph is a matter that you must determine for yourself. In general, however, avoid paragraphs that contain less than six or more than twelve sentences. Too short a paragraph may indicate that you are not developing your topic sentence adequately. Too long a paragraph may indicate that you are permitting excessive detail to obscure your central aim.

Excessively long paragraphs may be revised either by a rigorous pruning of details or by division into two or more paragraphs. Insufficiently developed paragraphs usually show lack of attention to detail and an imperfect command of the full idea of the paragraph. The paragraphs below, for example, are all insufficiently developed. The arguments are undirected, and the generalizations are inadequately supported by reasons, examples, and details. Simply stitching these fragments together would not produce a coherent, unified statement; instead, the entire statement would have to be thought through again and then rewritten.

> I am in favor of lowering the minimum voting age to eighteen. I think the average eighteen-year-old has more good judgment to put to use at the polls than the average middle-aged person.
>
> Among the members of the two major parties there is too much straight-ticket voting. I think the candidate himself and not his party should be voted on. The young voter would weigh the virtues of the candidate and not his party.
>
> It is unlikely that the young voter would be influenced by corrupt politicians. The majority of eighteen-year-olds are high school graduates and would surely have learned enough about current affairs to use good judgment.
>
> If the question of lowering the voting age were put to a nationwide vote, I am sure it would pass.
>
> In conclusion I say give young Americans a chance. I am sure they will make good.

EXERCISE 32f Group the following sentences into two paragraphs. Provide some transitional markers for the sentences, and, when possible, combine sentences.

> Martin Luther King was an ordained minister from Atlanta, Georgia. He gained prominence as a civil-rights leader during the 1950's

and 1960's. In 1956 he led a boycott by Montgomery, Alabama, blacks against segregated city bus lines. After his success in Montgomery, he founded the Southern Christian Leadership Conference. This gave him a base to expand the civil-rights movement in the South and throughout the nation. In 1963 he organized a massive civil-rights march on Washington, D.C., which brought together more than 200,000 people. It was there that he delivered his famous "I Have a Dream" speech. In the years that followed, King broadened his political involvement. He continued to work for civil rights, but he also became an outspoken critic of the Vietnam war. His criticism of the war was based on his belief that the war was contributing to poverty in America. He argued that our valuable national resources were being used to finance the war rather than to fight poverty at home. In 1968 he planned another large-scale march to Washington. It was to be called the Poor People's March. He never fulfilled his wish though. In April of 1968 he went to Memphis, Tennessee, to help settle a strike by sanitation workers. While there he was assassinated.

32g Choose a method of paragraph development suitable to your subject matter and your purpose.

Paragraphs are clear, convincing, and complete to the degree that they are packed with specific, relevant information fleshing out their general controlling ideas, that is, to the degree that those ideas are *developed*. There are many ways of developing paragraphs, and a "best" way depends on the paragraph topic and the way it is related to the other paragraphs in the paper. Most paragraphs can be developed by one of the following methods: (1) by using details, examples, or illustration, (2) by comparing or contrasting, (3) by defining, (4) by explaining causes and effects, or (5) by analyzing or classifying.

1 Details, examples, and illustrations. One of the most common and convincing ways to develop a general statement is to provide concrete and specific details or illustrations that will convey to the reader a clear impression of what the general statement really means to the writer. In fact, a good many of the other methods of development depend more or less on the use of detail and example, for these are virtually indispensable to clear and lively writing.

You may support a topic sentence either by amassing a variety of specific details, by providing a few examples, each stated in a sentence or two, or by describing at greater length a single extended illustration of your topic.

The author of the following paragraph gives us his controlling idea in the first and last sentences: the freedom of Americans today is a limited and licensed freedom. If you don't believe me, he says in effect, look at this list of thirty or forty different things you must have certificates or licenses for. Note how the writer gains coherence in his long list of details by ordering them roughly in the sequence in which they occur from birth to death.

> Americans are still born free but their freedom neither lasts as long nor goes as far as it used to. Once the infant is smacked on the bottom and lets out his first taxable howl, he is immediately tagged, foot-printed, blood-tested, classified, certificated, and generally taken in census. By the time that squawler has drawn the breath of adulthood he must have some clerk's permission to go to school or stay away, ride a bike, drive a car, collect his salary, carry a gun, fish, get married, go into the army or stay out, leave or re-enter the country, fly a plane, operate a power boat or a ham radio, buy a piece of land, build a house or knock one down, add a room to the house he has bought, burn his trash, park his car, keep a dog, run his business, go bankrupt, practice a profession, pick the wildflowers, bury the garbage, beg in the streets, sell whiskey in his store, peddle magazines from house to house, walk across a turnpike from one of his fields to another now that the state has divided him—the list is endless. Even in death his corpse must be certified and licensed before the earth may swallow him legally. Freedom is no longer free but licensed.
>
> JOHN CIARDI, "Confessions of a Crackpot"

In the following paragraph, the writer explains the pitfalls that await the unsuspecting student in a freshman composition course. She arranges the details she uses in the order she meets them in the course of the semester.

> A student rarely becomes convinced in school that he is an accomplished writer. The student must overcome major errors, only to deal with punctuation problems, poor topic sentences, weak structure, and faulty logic. The unsuspecting freshman believes that when he eliminates from his papers comma splices, fragments, faulty agreement, and misspellings, he merits an A. That student has merely reached the point at which his teacher can check his "respectfully submitted" papers for superfluous internal punctuation, misplaced parts, dangling modifiers, and awkwardness. After dealing with these seemingly insurmountable problems, the student is only held accountable for heavier burdens: paragraph unity and coherence, adequate development, consistency of tone, and variety of sentence structure. Should the student write a paper in English 101 that is worthy of being a model, he would only learn that the demands of 102 are more rigorous. No sooner does the student reach the top of one mountain than he sees a taller one before him.   *Student paragraph*

The following paragraph supports its central idea with a discussion of nine brief examples, each consisting of a quotation. All are selected to support the general assertion that popular magazine biographies of celebrities overflow with superlatives.

We can hear ourselves straining. "He's the greatest!" Our descriptions of celebrities overflow with superlatives. In popular magazine biographies we learn that a *Dr. Brinkley* is the "best-advertised doctor in the United States"; *an actor* is the "luckiest man in the movies today"; *a Ringling* is "not only the greatest, but the first real showman in the Ringling family"; *a general* is "one of the best mathematicians this side of Einstein"; *a columnist* has "one of the strangest of courtships"; *a statesman* has "the world's most exciting job"; *a sportsman* is "the loudest and by all odds the most abusive"; *a newsman* is "one of the most consistently resentful men in the country"; *a certain ex-King's mistress* is "one of the unhappiest women that ever lived." But, despite the "supercolossal" on the label, the contents are very ordinary. The lives of celebrities which we like to read, as Leo Lowenthal remarks, are a mere catalogue of "hardships" and "breaks." These men and women are "the proved specimens of the average." DANIEL J. BOORSTIN, *The Image*

In the following paragraph, the writer supports her central idea that college students and graduates with their first job have much in common by citing several ways in which the circumstances of the two are alike.

Why is it that college students envy graduates with full-time jobs, and graduates with full-time jobs envy college students? Except for the direction that the money flows, the two have much in common. Whether a person is beginning college or beginning his first full-time job, he discovers that he is at the lowest level of the institution and that movement toward the top is a slow process. Meanwhile, he must report regularly and monotonously to a given place at a given time. He finds himself besieged with deadlines and relentless demands, and he must continuously fulfill another person's expectations of him. Either as college student or new employee, he is penalized for absences, late work, and indifference to his tasks. His vacation time is fixed by someone in a superior position. When the college student finally graduates and the employee is finally promoted, both sadly discover that the process begins again: the college student needs a Master's degree; the vice-president lacks seniority. Both are again the lowest in the new rank; for both, the next move toward the top again seems a difficult and remote possibility. *Student paragraph*

The central idea of the next paragraph is that scientists who experiment with the world's living space take irresponsible risks with our future. Here the author does not offer several relatively brief examples to support his assertion. Rather he describes more fully a single illustration—an experiment with the little-understood Van Allen

Belt—in which scientists have acted without any foreknowledge of the consequences.

> When the mad professor of fiction blows up his laboratory and then himself, that's O.K., but when scientists and decision-makers act out of ignorance and pretend it is knowledge, they are using the biosphere, the living space, as an experimental laboratory. The whole world is put in hazard. And they do it even when they are told not to. During the International Geophysical Year, *the Van Allen Belt was discovered. The Van Allen Belt* is a region of magnetic phenomena. *Immediately the bright boys decided* to carry out an experiment and explode a hydrogen bomb in the Belt to see if they could produce an artificial aurora. The colorful draperies, the luminous skirts of the aurora, are caused by drawing cosmic particles magnetically through the rare gases of the upper atmosphere. It is called ionization and is like passing electrons through the vacuum tubes of our familiar neon lighting. It was called the Rainbow Bomb. Every responsible scientist in cosmology, radio-astronomy, and physics of the atmosphere protested against this tampering with a system we did not understand. They exploded their bomb. They got their pyrotechnics. We still do not know the price we may have to pay for this artificial magnetic disturbance.
>
> LORD RITCHIE-CALDER, *Polluting the Environment*

2 Comparison and contrast. Some controlling ideas naturally suggest development by comparison and contrast. Consider these topic sentences:

> My brother is a natural student; I am a natural nonstudent.
>
> Women have a long way to go before they have genuinely equal opportunity and recognition, but they have gone some of the distance since my mother finished high school.
>
> Foreign small cars may have virtues, but if we compare them carefully to their American counterparts, we'll choose the American.

Such sentences either directly assert or imply a contrast and almost require the writer to fill out the details of that contrast.

The paragraph that follows compares poetry and advertising, developing the assertion that they are alike in many ways by giving three examples of their similarity. The parallel constructions that mark the successive points of comparison and help give the paragraph coherence are in italics.

> Nevertheless, poetry and advertising have much in common. To begin with, *they both make extensive use* of rhyme and rhythm ("What's the word? Thunderbird!"). *They both use words chosen* for their affective and connotative values rather than for their denotative content ("Take a puff . . . it's springtime! Gray rocks and the fresh green leaves of springtime reflected in a mountain pool. . . . Where else can you find

air so refreshing? And where can you find a smoke as refreshing as Salem's?"). William Empson, the English critic, said in his *Seven Types of Ambiguity* that *the best poems are ambiguous;* they are richest when they have two or three or more levels of meaning at once. *Advertising, too,* although on a much more primitive level, *deliberately exploits ambiguities* and plays on words: a vodka is advertised with the slogan "Leaves you breathless"; an automobile is described as "Hot, Handsome, a Honey to Handle."   S. I. HAYAKAWA, *Language in Thought and Action*

In the following paragraph, the writer compares modern astronauts and the ocean voyagers of centuries ago.

Our modern astronauts are much like the ocean voyagers who sailed the seas five hundred years ago. Like the ocean voyagers, today's astronauts are adventurous men who want to experience the thrill of exploring unconquered areas. After blast-off, the astronauts sail into an unexplored sea of space to find new information about other planets and to contribute to man's understanding of space and of distant planets. Similarly, the ocean voyagers contributed to man's understanding of this planet. They chartered the oceans of the world, discovered its continents, and brought back to the Europeans new knowledge of the world and of other cultures. It takes the same kind of adventurous spirit to explore the unknown seas of outer space that it took to explore the unknown seas of this world.   *Student paragraph*

In the two preceding paragraphs, the similarities between two things constitute the central ideas of the paragraphs. But in many paragraphs the controlling idea, while not stating a comparison or contrast, nonetheless may require some development of a comparison or contrast. In the following paragraph, for example, the author contends that because beginning writers do not know how writing differs from speech, they proceed under false assumptions. Her assertion requires her to explain some of the contrasts between writing and speaking.

Here the problem of unfamiliar forms merges with the second pedagogical problem—that *the beginning writer does not know how writers behave.* Unaware of the ways in which writing is different from speaking, he imposes the conditions of speech upon writing. As an extension of speech, writing does, of course, draw heavily upon a writer's competencies as a speaker—his grammatical intuitions, his vocabulary, his strategies for making and ordering statements, etc., but it also demands new competencies, namely the skills of the encoding process (handwriting, spelling, punctuation) and the skill of objectifying a statement, of looking at it, changing it by additions, subtractions, substitutions, or inversions, taking the time to get as close a fit as possible between what he means and what he says on paper. Writers who are not aware of this tend to think that the point in writing is to get everything right the first time and that the need to change things is a mark of the amateur. (Thus a student who saw a manuscript page of Richard Wright's *Native Son*, with all its original deletions and substitutions, concluded that Wright couldn't have been much of a writer if he made all those "mistakes.") MINA SHAUGHNESSY, *Errors and Expectations*

In any comparison or contrast, it is important to give your careful attention to the clear arrangement of the points of similarity or difference. The more extended the comparison, the more crucial such clear ordering becomes. Note how careful the writer of the two following paragraphs is to keep the same order within the two paragraphs. In each, he speaks first of Roosevelt, then of Churchill; in each he moves back, at the end of the paragraph, to a telling final point of comparison. The careful ordering of the paragraphs helps keep them coherent.

> *Roosevelt,* as a public personality, was a spontaneous, optimistic, pleasure-loving ruler who dismayed his assistants by the gay and apparently heedless abandon with which he seemed to delight in pursuing two or more totally incompatible policies, and astonished them even more by the swiftness and ease with which he managed to throw off the cares of office during the darkest and most dangerous moments. *Churchill* too loves pleasure, and he lacks neither gaiety nor a capacity for exuberant self-expression, together with the habit of blithely cutting Gordian knots in a manner which often upsets his experts; but he is not a frivolous man. *His nature possesses a dimension of depth—and a corresponding sense of tragic possibilities, which Roosevelt's lighthearted genius instinctively passed by.*
>
> *Roosevelt* played the game of politics with virtuosity, and both his successes and his failures were carried off in splendid style; his performance seemed to flow with effortless skill. *Churchill* is acquainted with darkness as well as light. Like all inhabitants and even transient visitors of inner worlds, he gives evidence of seasons of agonized brooding and slow recovery. *Roosevelt might have spoken of sweat and blood, but when Churchill offered his people tears, he spoke a word which might have been uttered by Lincoln or Mazzini or Cromwell but not Roosevelt, greathearted, generous, and perceptive as he was.* ISAIAH BERLIN, "Mr. Churchill"

A special kind of comparison is **analogy.** An analogy draws a parallel between two things that have some resemblance on the basis of which other resemblances are to be inferred. When a comparison is drawn between a large city and an anthill or between a college and a factory or between the human nervous system and a telephone system, that is analogy. Parallels of this sort, although they may be quite inexact in many respects, enable us to visualize ideas or relationships and therefore to understand them better.

In the first of the two paragraphs that follow, the writer compares having a manuscript dissected by a gifted editor to having a skilled mechanic work on one's car. In the second, the writer compares the student's job of managing time to that of the juggler's coordinating multiple tennis balls or Indian clubs.

> Having a manuscript under Ross's scrutiny was like putting your car in the hands of a skilled mechanic, not an automotive engineer with a bachelor of science degree, but a guy who knows what makes a motor go, and sputter, and wheeze, and sometimes come to a dead stop; a man with an ear for the faintest body squeak as well as the loudest engine rattle. When you first gazed, appalled, upon an uncorrected proof of one of your stories or articles, each margin had a thicket of queries and complaints—one writer got a hundred and forty-four on one profile. It was as though you beheld the works of your car spread all over the garage floor, and the job of getting the thing together again and making it work seemed impossible. Then you realized that Ross was trying to make your Model T or old Stutz Bearcat into a Cadillac or Rolls-Royce. He was at work with the tools of his unflagging perfectionism, and, after an exchange of growls or snarls, you set to work to join him in his enterprise.   JAMES THURBER, *The Years with Ross*

> A college student trying to organize his studies and activities is like a juggler trying to manage several tennis balls or Indian clubs at once. Each student takes several courses that have varying types and amounts of required work. He must learn to manage his time so that he can get all his work for each course done on schedule. The task of the student in managing the work of four or five different courses alone is similar to that of the juggler coordinating four or five tennis balls at once. But in addition to his four or five courses, the student must also fulfill his responsibilities to perhaps two or three organizations and manage his social activities with friends. If the student cannot learn to distribute his time wisely among all these different demands, he may begin to feel like the juggler who has lost his coordination; his work and activities may begin to scatter in disarray, like the juggler's tennis balls which fall to the ground around him. In contrast, the student who learns to manage his time effectively keeps his studies and varied activities flowing smoothly, just as the juggler who successfully creates a smooth circle of six or eight flying tennis balls or Indian clubs.   *Student paragraph*

3 Definition. The logic of a paragraph sometimes requires that key objects or terms be defined. Definition is necessary to set the limits within which a topic or a term is used, especially in dealing with abstract matters. Full and exact paragraphs of definition are frequently important parts of papers, essays, and articles. Note that paragraphs of definition many times make use of details and examples, of comparison and contrast, and of restatement, in order to insure clarity.

The following definition first states the two basic elements of the fairy story—"a human hero and a happy ending." The author develops the paragraph by describing the kind of hero and the kind of story pattern that are the special marks of the fairy tale. Italics show the movement of the paragraph, a movement basically controlled by the progress of the hero from beginning to end of the tale.

> *A fairy story,* as distinct from a merry tale, or an animal story, *is a serious tale with a human hero and a happy ending. The progression of its hero is the reverse of the tragic hero's: at the beginning* he is either socially obscure or despised as being stupid or untalented, lacking in the heroic virtues, *but at the end,* he has surprised everyone by demonstrating his heroism and winning fame, riches, and love. *Though ultimately he succeeds, he does not do so without a struggle* in which his success is in doubt, for opposed to him are not only natural difficulties like glass mountains, or barriers of flame, but also hostile wicked powers, stepmothers, jealous brothers, and witches. *In many cases indeed, he would fail were he not* assisted by friendly powers who give him instructions or perform tasks for him which he cannot do himself; that is, in addition to his own powers, he needs luck, but this luck is not fortuitous but dependent upon his character and his actions. *The tale ends with the establishment of justice;* not only are the good rewarded but also the evil are punished.
>
> W. H. AUDEN, Introduction to *Tales of Grimm and Andersen*

In the two paragraphs that follow, John Holt develops a definition of intelligence. Holt relies upon contrast to develop his definition: intelligence is not, Holt tells us, what it is often said to be—an ability to score well or do well. Rather, it is a "way of behaving" in certain situations. We might call the development here a not-this-but-that development.

The three-sentence first paragraph sets the general contrast between the two definitions. The second moves initially to the more specific but quickly returns to the basic pattern. The italicized phrases will help you follow the controlling, not-this-but-that flow of the definition. The two paragraphs here could have been combined. By using two paragraphs, however, Holt is better able to draw attention to his description of how a person acts in a new situation—a description that is very important in clarifying his definition.

> *When we talk about intelligence, we do not mean* the ability to get a good score on a certain kind of test, or even the ability to do well in school; these are at best only indicators of something larger, deeper, and far more important. *By intelligence we mean* a style of life, a way of behaving in various situations, and particularly in new, strange, and perplexing situations. *The true test of intelligence is not how* much we know how to do, *but how* we behave when we don't know what to do.
>
> *The intelligent person, young or old, meeting a new situation or problem,* opens himself up to it; he tries to take in with mind and senses everything he can about it; he thinks about *it,* instead of about himself or what it might cause to happen to him; he grapples with it boldly, imaginatively, resourcefully, and if not confidently at least hopefully; if he fails to master it, he looks without shame or fear at his mistakes and

learns what he can from them. *This is intelligence.* Clearly its roots lie in a certain feeling about life, and one's self with respect to life. *Just as clearly, unintelligence is not* what most psychologists seem to suppose, the same thing as intelligence only less of it. *It is an entirely different* style of behavior, arising out of an entirely different set of attitudes.

JOHN HOLT, Why Children Fail

4   Causes and effects. Some kinds of central ideas invite development by an examination of causes or effects. Pollution and poverty exist. What causes them? What are their effects? What are the effects of television? Of the widespread use of computers? What are the causes behind the movements for equality of women, the popularity of football, the high rate of unemployment?

The initial topic sentence of the following paragraph by Margaret Mead states a general *effect*—that in our society women suffer from lack of stimulation, from loneliness, dullness. Mead then develops the paragraph by detailing specific causes. The paragraph gains clarity and order by the author's division of detailed causes into two main groups—those associated with the pattern of relationships with children and husbands, and those associated with certain "conditions of modern life." The sentence that begins with *Moreover* marks this division.

Women in our society complain of the lack of stimulation, of the loneliness, of the dullness of staying at home. Little babies are poor conversationalists, husbands come home tired and sit reading the paper, and women who used to pride themselves on their ability to talk find on the rare evening they can go out that their words clot on their tongues. As the children go to school, the mother is left to the companionship of the Frigidaire and the washing machine. Yet she can't go out because the delivery man might come, or a child might be sent home sick from school. The boredom of long hours of solitary one-sided communication with things, no matter how shining and streamlined and new, descends upon her. *Moreover,* the conditions of modern life, apartment living, and especially the enormous amount of moving about, all serve to rob women of neighborhood ties. The better her electric equipment, the better she organizes her ordering, the less reason she has to run out for a bit of gossipy shopping at the corner store. The department stores and the moving-picture houses cater to women—alone—on their few hours out. Meanwhile, efficient mending services and cheap ready-made clothes have taken most sensible busy work out of women's hands and left women—still at home—listening to the radio, watching television.   MARGARET MEAD, "What Women Want"

The central idea of the next paragraph, by Jerzy Kosinski, is that television has turned today's students into spectators. Television is the cause, says Kosinski; I have just described the effects. Here the topic sentence—the statement of *cause*—comes in the middle of the paragraph. Kosinski leads up to it by detailing the *effects* he has observed and follows it with his speculative explanation.

> During the last four years, I have taught at Wesleyan, Princeton, and at Yale University. I have often lectured at many schools throughout the country. I am appalled by what I think emerges as the dominant trait of the students of today—their short span of attention, their inability to know or believe anything for more than half an hour. *I feel it was television which turned them into spectators,* since by comparison with the world of television, their own lives are slow and uneventful. When they first believed that what they saw on TV was real, they overreacted, only to feel cheated when the next program demanded a new emotion. Later, they felt simply manipulated by whatever drama they witnessed. By now, they have become hostile, and so they either refuse to watch the TV altogether or they dissect the medium and throw out all that upsets them. JERZY KOSINSKI, NBC *Comment*

In the paragraph that follows, the writer discusses the causes of a problem faced by his father, a high-school teacher, and other teachers. Note how many examples the writer gives of the causes of the "shell shock" that teachers experience every day. The writer makes good use of parallel grammatical structure to reinforce the impact of the examples on the reader.

> My father is a public high-school teacher. He and the other teachers face a growing number of problems that seem to have no solutions. Having observed my father's behavior for several years, I have concluded that high-school teachers are suffering from a disorder formerly associated with war veterans—shell shock. Besides teaching five or six classes a day, teachers are also expected to sponsor clubs, coach athletic teams, raise money, head committees, chaperone dances, arrange parades, light bonfires, publish newspapers, and sell pictures. In my father's work, paper work means more than just grading papers. It also means filling out a never-ending stream of forms that insure racial equality in the classroom, that provide free lunches to the needy, that reassure administrators that everything is in its place, and that even request more forms to be filled out. Discipline has also taken on a new meaning in public schools. Today, discipline means searching for drugs, putting out fires, disarming students, and breaking up gang fights. Faced with these daily problems and demands, it is no wonder that teachers like my father are becoming less like educators and more like soldiers suffering from combat fatigue. *Student paragraph*

5 Analysis and classification. Analysis takes things apart. Classification groups things together on the basis of their differences or similarities. You use them both every day. You break your days into morning, noon, and night; in the supermarket you look for pepper among the spices and hamburger in the meat department, because you know that's the way they're classified. Similarly in writing, both in individual paragraphs and in entire essays, analysis and classification frequently can serve as guides to development and to organization.

In the following paragraph, Lynes develops his explanation of bores by setting up three different classes: the Crashing Bore, the Tinkling Bore, and the Still Waters Run Deep Bore. He also suggests two broader classes: the militant, to which the first two kinds belong, and the passive. The classification provides the pattern for the development of his paragraph and serves as a guide to the kind of detail he will select in describing each.

> The common variety of bores is well known to everyone. Ambrose Bierce said that a bore is "a person who talks when you want him to listen," but as apt as the definition is, the species is a good deal more complicated than that. There are, for example, many gradations of boredom, such as the Crashing Bore whose conversation weighs on you like an actual physical burden that you want to throw off because it is stifling you, and quite a different kind, the Tinkling Bore whose conversation bothers you in the way that an insistent fly does, annoying but not dangerous. There are such types as the Still Waters Run Deep variety who defy you to say anything that will change the expression on their faces much less elicit an encouraging word from them. There you are on the sofa with them, their intense eyes peering at you wth something between hopelessness and scorn, impressing on you the deep reservoir of their self-sufficiency and challenging you to ruffle the waters that lurk there. I cite this merely as an example of the passive as opposed to the militant type (both the Crashing and the Tinkling are militant), for it is those who make you feel like a bore who are the most boring of all.   RUSSELL LYNES, *Guests: or How to Survive Hospitality*

In the following paragraph, the writer humorously analyzes the types of assignments that college students are asked to do during a semester. She classifies each assignment on the basis of the emotional effect it has on the student.

> After his first semester at a university, a student may notice that his assignments can be categorized according to the various emotional states they produce. For example, "The I'll-Do-It-Later-Tonight" assignment is a relatively easy assignment which takes no more than five or ten minutes and causes the student little inconvenience or worry. Related to this type is "The-I-Thought-I-Could-Do-It-Later-Tonight" assignment, which seems simple but is in reality much more than the student bargained for. This type often causes a sleepless night for the panicking student. "The-Impossible-Dream" assignment also causes the student a certain amount of panic. These assignments, also known as semester projects, are designed to take the majority of the semester to complete, and they seem to hang over the student's head like a dark cloud of doom. Much like this assignment, but perhaps even more traumatic, is "The-I'm-Going-To-Fail-This-Course" assignment. The pur-

pose of this one is to rid the instructor of half the class. This assignment may be seriously pursued with genuine interest and yet remain incomprehensible. The student must face the fear of a low grade-point average if he encounters many assignments of this type. Of all the types of assignments, this is the most dreaded. *Student paragraph*

In the next paragraph, Lionel Ruby divides language into three classes on the basis of three different functions that language performs. From such a paragraph, the author could clearly develop successive paragraphs illustrating each function by example or by further subdivision.

Language has more than one purpose. We might say that language operates on different levels, except that the word "levels" suggests higher and lower planes in a scale of value, and this is not intended here. We shall deal with three functions: the informative, the expressive, and the directive. To say that language has these three functions is to say that there are three different reasons for speaking. One reason, or purpose, is to communicate factual information. This is the informative function. We speak also in order to express our feelings, to "blow off steam," or to stir the feelings and attitudes of the person we are talking to. We shall call this the expressive or "emotive" function. And, finally, we speak in order to get people to act. This is the directive function. LIONEL RUBY, *The Art of Making Sense*

EXERCISE 32g(1) Which of the methods of paragraph development discussed in this section seems to be the most appropriate method of developing each of the following topic sentences into a paragraph? Why? After you have answered this question briefly, choose one of the topics and write a paragraph using it. Is your paragraph developed according to your original notion?

1 Attending a small college has disadvantages as well as advantages.
2 To watch a college mixer is to see every type of human being.
3 Wit and humor are not the same thing.
4 Contemporary society places too much emphasis on test scores.
5 Good government begins at the local level.
6 Fraternities have to watch carefully the line between fellowship and snobbishness.
7 Some people come to college wanting to learn, but refusing, at the same time, to change a single idea they came with.
8 A distinction should be drawn between liberty and license.
9 Campus slang is a puzzle to the uninitiated.
10 The differences in education and social conditioning for boys and girls in our society result in the waste of many talented women.
11 If we must reduce the amount of energy we use, we must expect to make great changes in the way we live.
12 We are too much inclined to measure progress by the number of television sets rather than by the quality of television programs.

EXERCISE 32g(2)   *You cannot do wrong without suffering wrong.* Write two separate and unrelated paragraphs to develop this topic sentence. In the first paragraph, define as clearly as you can what you think is meant by *wrong* and *suffering wrong.* In the second, demonstrate the truth or falsity of the statement by giving examples.

EXERCISE 32g(3)   *My reading tastes have changed since I came to college.* Write three separate and unrelated paragraphs to develop this topic sentence. In the first paragraph, show why your tastes have changed. In the second, demonstrate how they have changed. In the third, contrast specifically your reading tastes in high school with your reading tastes in college.

CONSISTENCY OF TONE IN THE PARAGRAPH ¶ **CON**

When you read effective writing, you may be struck by the fact that what seems to hold the sentences together is more than mere adherence to an organizational principle. There is about such writing some inner consistency that unites everything into an authoritative whole. What you are responding to is a kind of consistency of **tone** that pervades the whole of a passage of good writing.

Tone is one of those matters that are clear enough until you try to define them. You know well enough what you mean when, if your neighbor has complained about your barking beagle, you remark that you don't mind his complaining but you don't like his tone. But when you try to describe exactly what it is you don't like, you find it extremely difficult. Tone is produced by an interplay of many elements in speech and writing. Sentence structure, diction, the mode of organization and development chosen, the kinds of examples, illustrations, and details drawn on—these and many other factors are involved in tone.

The best way to increase your awareness of tone in writing is to study carefully a variety of effective paragraphs, asking yourself how you would describe their tone and then trying to determine how the writer has conveyed that tone. A writer's tone can be impersonal or personal, formal or informal, literal or ironic, sentimental or sarcastic, sincere or insincere, enthusiastic or indifferent, dogmatic or doubtful, hostile or friendly, condescending or respectful, modest or authoritative, serious or humorous, and the like. Obviously it can be a level in between any of these extreme pairs, or it can be a complex quality that can be adequately described only by a combination of several of these terms. By careful study of good writing, you can increase your awareness of the many factors that contribute to the control of tone.

32h **32h Choose an appropriate tone and maintain it consistently.**

1 Appropriate tone. An appropriate tone is one that reflects the writer's understanding of and respect for the needs and feelings of readers. It is not easy to state what will create such appropriateness in any particular paragraph or paper; but some things are generally to be avoided. Among them, these are the most important: talking down to your audience by repeating the obvious; talking over the heads of your audience, merely to impress them, by using words or allusions or examples they are unlikely to understand; being excessively dogmatic or sarcastic; being excessively or falsely enthusiastic.

This opening sentence of a student paper illustrates an extreme of inappropriate tone: *No one can tell me that people who vote for the characters on the Democratic ticket aren't putting their own selfish interests ahead of the true good of the country.* Whatever readers may think of the thesis of the writer, his expression of it is offensive. The language is emotional, the writer's attitude dogmatic. Readers have the immediate feeling that there is no point in reading further, since they cannot hope, apparently, for any sort of balanced or reasoned discussion of the sort appropriate to the topic.

2 Consistent tone. Consistency requires that once you have set a particular tone, you maintain it. A jarring shift in tone may ruin the effect of a paragraph even though it otherwise meets the tests of unity, coherence, and adequate development. The following paragraph from a student theme illustrates the point:

> Curiosity has developed ideas that have been vastly beneficial to mankind. We have seen mankind emerge from the age of great darkness into the age of great light. Today every hotrod artist profits from the ideas of past inventors and every housewife has a kitchen full of push-button gadgets that she couldn't have without ideas. Above all, modern scientific theory leads us to a clearer and deeper comprehension of the universe. So we see curiosity is really a helpful tool.

The principal fault of this paragraph is its jarring shifts of tone. The first two sentences and the next to last sentence set a serious, somewhat formal tone by such phrases as *vastly beneficial, we have seen mankind emerge,* the parallel phrases *great age of darkness* and *great age of light,* and *clearer and deeper comprehension of the universe.* But the language of both the third and last sentences, and the examples cited in the third sentence, depart completely from this tone of seriousness and formality. Having been prepared for comment about the great concepts of religion, politics, education, or science, readers are offered *hotrod artists* and *push-button gadgets*. The effect is something like that of a cat meowing in a church service.

EXERCISE 32h   Study the following paragraphs. Describe the tone of each and discuss the factors that contribute to it.

1   Have you ever noticed the detail of the plants in the backgrounds of some Albrecht Dürer prints? They are perfect and finished, as finished as though they are as important as Death or Virtue in the foreground. The ferns have countless lacy fronds, the grasses are heavy-headed with seeds, the succulents are fleshy and ready to ooze viscous fluid if they're grazed by the tip of a lance.   *Student paragraph*

2   For we're always out of luck here. That's just how it is—for instance in the winter. The sides of the buildings, the roofs, the limbs of the trees are gray. Streets, sidewalks, faces, feelings—they are gray. Speech is gray, and the grass where it shows. Every flank and front, each top is gray. Everything is gray: hair, eyes, window glass, the hawkers' bills and touters' posters, lips, teeth, poles and metal signs—they're gray, quite gray. Cars are gray. Boots, shoes, suits, hats, gloves are gray. Horses, sheep, and cows, cats killed in the road, squirrels in the same way, sparrows, doves, and pigeons, all are gray, everything is gray, and everyone is out of luck who lives here.

    WILLIAM H. GASS, "In the Heart of the Heart of the Country"

3   Even though large tracts of Europe and many old and famous States have fallen or may fall into the grip of the Gestapo and all the odious apparatus of Nazi rule, we shall not flag or fail. We shall go on to the end. We shall fight in France, we shall fight in the seas and oceans, we shall fight with growing confidence and growing strength in the air; we shall defend our Island, whatever the cost may be. We shall fight on the beaches, we shall fight on the landing grounds, we shall fight in the fields and in the streets, we shall fight in the hills; we shall never surrender; and even if, which I do not for a moment believe, this Island or a large part of it were subjugated and starving, then our Empire beyond the seas, armed and guarded by the British Fleet, would carry on the struggle, until, in God's good time, the New World, with all its power and might, steps forth to the rescue and liberation of the Old.

    WINSTON CHURCHILL, *Speech at Dunkerque*

4   At one point or another in their college careers, many students find themselves having to cope with the insensitive professor. This creature abounds with irritating habits of disregard. He continually begins class late, leaving the students to wonder whether or not class will indeed be held. When he does arrive, he fills the room with the smoke of the cigar that he chews the duration of the period. He smiles as his students groan over the impossible questions on the mid-term, a test that he assured them would be no problem. He returns papers that bleed with his nasty comments which show no regard for the student ego. And perhaps most irritating to the student, he is never to be found outside of class. When a lucky student does find this professor, he doesn't hesitate to make the student aware of the inconvenience created by him. Obviously not all professors suffer the disease of disregard. If they did, college would be intolerable. *Student paragraph*

5 My education and that of my Black associates were quite different from the education of our white schoolmates. In the classroom we all learned past participles, but in the streets and in our homes the Blacks learned to drop *s*'s from plurals and suffixes from past-tense verbs. We were alert to the gap separating the written word from the colloquial. We learned to slide out of one language and into another without being conscious of the effort. At school, in a given situation, we might respond with "That's not unusual." But in the street, meeting the same situation, we easily said, "It be's like that sometimes."

MAYA ANGELOU, *I Know Why the Caged Bird Sings*

Paragraphs for study

No one can learn to write well simply by following general prescriptions. One of the best ways to develop skill in writing is to develop skill in observing how others write. Reading is an integral part of the process of learning to write, not something entirely separate from it. Test your understanding of the principles of good paragraphs by a close study of the following paragraphs. Analyze each to determine the main points, the topic sentence, the transitions from sentence to sentence, the method or methods of paragraph development and organization, and the tone.

1. By day it [the kitchen] was the scene of intense bustle. The kitchen-maid was down by five o'clock to light the fire; the laborers crept down in stockinged feet and drew on their heavy boots; they lit candles in their horn lanthorns and went out to the cattle. Breakfast was at seven, dinner at twelve, tea at five. Each morning of the week had its appropriate activity: Monday was washing day, Tuesday, ironing, Wednesday and Saturday baking, Thursday "turning out" upstairs and churning, Friday "turning out" downstairs. Every day there was the milk to skim in the dairy—the dairy was to the left of the kitchen, and as big as any other room in the house. The milk was poured into large flat pans and allowed to settle; it was skimmed with horn scoops, like toothless combs. HERBERT READ, *The Eye of Memory*

2. The whole aim of good teaching is to turn the young learner, by nature a little copycat, into an independent, self-propelling creature, who cannot merely learn but study—that is, work as his own boss to the limit of his powers. This is to turn pupils into students, and it can be done on any rung of the ladder of learning. When I was a child, the multiplication table was taught from a printed sheet which had to be memorized one "square" at a time—the one's and the two's and so on

up to nine. It never occurred to the teacher to show us how the answers could be arrived at also by addition, which we already knew. No one said, "Look: if four times four is sixteen, you ought to be able to figure out, without aid from memory, what five times four is, because that amounts to four more one's added to the sixteen." This would at first have been puzzling, *more* complicated and difficult than memory work, but once explained and grasped, it would have been an instrument for learning and checking the whole business of multiplication. We could temporarily have dispensed with the teacher and cut loose from the printed table.   JACQUES BARZUN, *Teacher in America*

3.   Registration is a very frustrating experience for the college freshman. First, a student has to find her advisor to get help in deciding what courses to take and to get the advisor to sign the trial schedule. Usually, the advisor is not in the office because he is either at home, in the gym helping with registration, on a coffee break, or out for an early lunch. After one finally finds her advisor or forges the advisor's signature, the second step is to wait with hundreds of other students for the assigned registration time to arrive. When the right time arrives, the third step is to secure class cards from the different tables on the gym floor. Getting class cards requires standing in long lines, sometimes for an hour. Frequently, the class cards that one needs most are unavailable, in which case one has to make an entirely new schedule. Sometimes, one must even return some class cards already secured and begin to secure new cards. After finally getting the class cards needed, the last step in registration is spending another hour standing in lines to pay fees, get an identification card, and register a car. Having survived registration, the new student usually leaves the gym completely exhausted.   *Student paragraph*

4.   One of the earliest forms of the story that we made up in Africa was the fable. A fable is a tale about animals . . . but really about people. It instructs us; it teaches us something about human behavior. But people do not like to be told straight out about themselves, so the storyteller acts as if he's just talking about buzzards or rabbits or something. When we came to these shores years ago, we brought these tales along. We even made up new ones, for there was much peculiar behavior on the part of people here to talk about and to teach about. So often, while drumming in the yard, we would tell stories about crafty foxes or sly monkeys or big dumb bears. We were often talking about our situation as slaves, trying to survive through our wits, trying to instruct each other through a "code" language.

TONI CADE BAMBERA, "Rappin' About Story Forms"

5.   What men, in their egoism, constantly mistake for a deficiency of intelligence in woman is merely an incapacity for mastering that mass of small intellectual tricks, that complex of petty knowledges, that collection of cerebral rubber-stamps, which constitute the chief mental equipment of the average male. A man thinks that he is more intelligent than his wife because he can add up a column of figures more accurately, or because he is able to distinguish between the ideas of

rival politicians, or because he is privy to the minutiae of some sordid and degrading business or profession. But these empty talents, of course, are not really signs of intelligence; they are, in fact, merely a congeries of petty tricks and antics, and their acquirement puts little more strain on the mental powers than a chimpanzee suffers in learning how to catch a penny or scratch a match.

H. L. MENCKEN, *In Defense of Women*

6. It was all over though. The big cat lay tangled in the willows: his head and shoulder raised against the red stems, his legs reaching and his back arched downward, in the caricature of a leap, but loose and motionless. The great, yellow eyes glared balefully up through the willows. The mouth was a little open, the tongue hanging down from it behind the fangs. The blood was still dripping from the tongue into the red stain it had already made in the snow. High behind the shoulder, the black pelt was wet too, and one place farther down, on the ribs. Standing there, looking at it, Harold felt compassion for the long, wicked beauty rendered motionless, and even a little shame that it should have passed so hard. WALTER V. T. CLARK, *The Track of the Cat*

7. The world does not much like curiosity. The world says that curiosity killed the cat. The world dismisses curiosity by calling it idle, or *mere* idle, curiosity—even though curious persons are seldom idle. Parents do their best to extinguish curiosity in their children, because it makes life difficult to be faced every day with a string of unanswerable questions about what makes fire hot or why grass grows, or to have to halt junior's investigations before they end in explosion and sudden death. Children whose curiosity survives parental discipline and who manage to grow up before they blow up are invited to join the Yale faculty. Within the university they go on asking their questions and trying to find the answers. In the eyes of a scholar, that is mainly what a university is for. It is a place where the world's hostility to curiosity can be defied.

EDMUND S. MORGAN, "What Every Yale Freshman Should Know"

8. As man proceeds toward his announced goal of the conquest of nature, he has written a depressing record of destruction, directed not only against the earth he inhabits but against the life that shares it with him. The history of the recent centuries has its black passages—the slaughter of the buffalo on the western plains, the massacre of the shorebirds by the market gunners, the near-extermination of the egrets for their plumage. Now, to these and others like them, we are adding a new chapter, and a new kind of havoc—the direct killing of birds, mammals, fishes, and indeed practically every form of wildlife by chemical insecticides indiscriminately sprayed on the land.

RACHEL CARSON, *Silent Spring*

9. For years, nuclear-power advocates have claimed that nuclear power is the most economical form of energy available; but in light of a few facts, one begins to doubt this claim. The cost of building the Sequoiah nuclear plant, for example, exceeded a billion dollars. For

this astronomical amount of money, one can expect this reactor to be out of operation approximately thirty percent of the time. After thirty or forty years, it will become too "hot" to operate and will be shut down permanently. Even though the reactor will be shut down, it will still be highly radioactive and will have to be totally encased in concrete and lead—all at a cost of another few million dollars—and guarded virtually forever. Nuclear power is neither cheap nor economical; it is both expensive and wasteful. *Student paragraph*

10. My boyhood was spent in a world made tranquil by two invisible catastrophes: the Depression and World War II. Between 1932, when I was born, and 1945, when we moved away, the town of Shillington changed, as far as I could see, very little. The vacant lot beside our home on Philadelphia Avenue remained vacant. The houses along the street were neither altered nor replaced. The high-school grounds, season after season, continued to make a placid plain visible from our rear windows. The softball field, with its triptych backstop, was nearest us. A little beyond, on the left, were the school and its boiler house, built in the late 1920's of the same ochre brick. In the center a cinder track circumscribed the football field. At a greater distance there were the tennis courts and the poor farm fields and the tall double rows of trees marking the Poorhouse Lane. The horizon was the blue cloud, scarred by a gravel pit's orange slash, of Mount Penn, which overlooked the city of Reading. JOHN UPDIKE, *Five Boyhoods*

11. The definition of equality varies from woman to woman. For some women, equality means being equal to men politically and socially. They feel that the traditional codes of chivalry are no longer applicable and resent men who open their doors, pull out their chairs, and help them with their coats. On the other hand, for some women, equality means that they should have the same opportunities and benefits as men yet also enjoy the tradition of chivalry. These women, although they may hold prestigious positions in government, education or medicine, don't resent a man who opens the door for them. Still for other women, equality is little more than a public interest story which has no effect upon their lives. They are secure in their lifestyles, whether domestic or not, and tend not to question the issue. Perhaps there is no one definition of equality for women but many, since each woman must decide how important equality is to her own self-esteem before she can determine what equality means. *Student paragraph*

12. A sign is anything that announces the existence or the imminence of some event, the presence of a thing or a person, or a change in a state of affairs. There are signs of the weather, signs of danger, signs of future good or evil, signs of what the past has been. In every case a sign is closely bound up with something to be noted or expected in experience. It is always a part of the situation to which it refers, though the reference may be remote in space and time. In so far as we are led to note or expect the signified event we are making correct use of a sign. This is the essence of rational behavior, which animals show in varying degrees. It is entirely realistic, being closely bound up with the

2h

33

actual objective course of history—learned by experience, and cashed in or voided by further experience.

SUSANNE K. LANGER, "The Lord of Creation"

33 WRITING PERSUASIVELY **LOG**

During your lifetime most of your writing, whether in school or on the job, will have a distinctly argumentative character. Your U.S. history exam may require that you write a short essay answering the question "What were the major causes of the Civil War?" Your English professor, explaining possible topics for a research paper, may say, "I don't want to read papers 'all about' a topic. I want you to digest your research and draw your own conclusions about the subject." Your company's regional manager may ask you for a proposal assessing several new sales strategies. The school board may decide to close your child's school, sending her to one in another neighborhood, and you and your neighbors want to write a letter of protest.

All these writing tasks require more than assembling facts and information. They require analysis and logical evaluation so that the information builds a case, so that a stand on the issues can be formed. In short, few of us put words on paper, whether by desire or request, unless we have some point to make, some assertion to present [see Section **31d(2)**]. Making an assertion places us in the realm of argument, because an assertion is a statement that can (or should) be supported with facts, with reasons—in other words, with evidence.

In each of the situations cited above, the audience evaluating the assertion and the supporting argument is clear: the professors, the regional manager, the school board. But even when you do not personally know your readers, making educated guesses about them and assessing their probable characteristics can be as important as thinking about the points you want to present (see Section **31e**).

Assessing the audience helps you decide on an effective approach. What is your readers' average age and level of education? What other factors such as sex, life style, income, type of employment, political or geographic affiliation may make them more or less receptive to your point of view? Most important of all, is your audience likely to agree with you or disagree with you?

If your audience already agrees with you, your problem is clearly not to persuade them further. It is rather to get them to act. When Thoreau delivered his address "Civil Disobedience," he knew his audience was already opposed to slavery; his task was not to convince them of the evils of slavery but to inspire them to act on behalf of the antislavery cause. Thoreau's essay is full of emotionally charged language, passionate in its call for action.

How much emotion you can effectively communicate to readers will depend on the topic and the intensity of belief you and your readers share. Clearly, a fist-shaking, tear-streaming appeal to vote down a proposed $2 increase in club dues is inappropriate. On the other hand, if you fail to express deep feelings when the occasion demands, your appeal will be equally ineffective. "Move us," the audience says to you, "don't talk about a serious problem as if it were a minor inconvenience."

If readers are likely to disagree with you, you must take a different approach. No matter how strongly you believe that abortion is wrong or that welfare should be increased or that writing courses should not be required in college, there are nonetheless persuasive arguments for believing the opposite. You can assume that many of your readers will start out disagreeing with your point of view. If you want these readers to listen to your position, start out by recognizing theirs. If you begin by acknowledging their arguments, even admitting the strength of some of those arguments, you can then move on to suggest their weaknesses, and finally to set your own arguments against them (see Section **33e**).

If you go about the task of persuading with respect for readers' convictions, you will be much more likely to get them to listen. Your purpose is, after all, to persuade. If you say (or even suggest) that your readers are ignorant, stupid, or ridiculous to believe as they do, you will only antagonize them. You will never persuade them.

An effective argument is more, then, than an attempt to persuade readers that what you do or believe is right or just—or what others do or believe is wrong or unjust. At its most fundamental level, an effective argument is a statement of judgment or opinion that is supported with logical and persuasive evidence.

33a Learn to recognize arguable assertions.

It is important to recognize which assertions are arguable and which are not. Trying to argue some assertions is pointless because not all assertions can be supported with valid reasons.

1 *A priori* is a term of logic meaning, roughly, "before examination." Assertions based on an *a priori* premise cannot be argued because such a premise can be neither proved nor disproved; people are simply convinced of its truth or untruth. *A priori* premises are beliefs so deeply held that they have the force of fact, although they cannot be supported by factual evidence.

Many deeply held and widely shared assumptions about human nature are *a priori* premises with cultural, racial, social, and moral or religious roots. If you argue from an *a priori* premise with someone who does not share that premise, you will find yourself arguing in circles or along parallel lines—but never toward resolution—because legitimate proof is not possible. For instance, when people passionately argue that one governmental or social system is better than another, they are often basing their position on different *a priori* premises. If one person believes, *a priori*, that human beings are basically good, altruistic, and trustworthy while the other person believes human nature essentially wicked, selfish, and dishonest, then the two can reach no final conclusion. The premises are not provable, no matter how many examples each person cites.

A priori premises may change or be replaced over time. Such change can be seen in emerging attitudes toward women's roles in American society. *A priori* assumptions underlying assertions about the "weaker sex," a woman's "place," or inherently masculine and feminine characteristics are not nearly as widely shared today.

2   Subjective expressions of taste and nonrational reactions cannot be argued. The Latin *de gustibus non disputandum est,* "there is no disputing about tastes," is another way of saying subjective reactions do not lend themselves to reasoning. No matter how sound your logic that there is no lack of oxygen in an elevator stalled between floors, to a claustrophobic the sense of suffocation is very real. No matter how good for you spinach may be, if you can't stand its taste, nutritional reasons won't convince you to eat it.

3   Matters of fact cannot be argued. If a fact is verifiable, there is no point in debating it. It can either be true (a *bona fide* fact) or false (not a fact), but in neither case is it a matter for argument because the record can be checked. The earth is round, or nearly so. This fact was verified by fifteenth-century explorers and more recently by means of space flights.

4   Statements involving unverifiable facts cannot be argued. While it is interesting to speculate about whether there is life after death, the answer is simply unknowable.

5   Statements based on insufficient facts cannot be argued conclusively. For instance, people enjoy arguing that life exists on other planets. Statistically, the odds favor extraterrestrial life forms. But we have no hard evidence at this point to prove the assertions. All we can say is perhaps; the jury is still out. Should information pointing one way or the other come to light, a conclusion may eventually be drawn. In the meantime, logical reasoning on the topic won't carry us very far.

6   On the other hand, facts are slippery and not necessarily static. What may be accepted as verifiably true this year may be proven false by next. Before sailors circled the globe, the populace accepted as fact that the world was flat. During the Middle Ages the plague that killed

millions was attributed to God's wrath. People had no knowledge that fleas could transmit microorganisms from rats to humans and thus infect the population. What was once the "fact" of God's wrath is now regarded as a lack of adequate hygiene. Correspondingly, what serves as fact today may be tomorrow's quaint, ignorant notion. Time and scientific inquiry have taught us that very little is immutably certain. The best we can do is draw conclusions from available data, deciding to formulate an argument when the supporting data warrant it.

EXERCISE 33a Decide which of the following assertions are arguable and which are not. Be prepared to explain why each assertion does or does not lend itself to argument.

1 The television series "Roots" was watched by more viewers than any network program in television history.
2 Peanut butter cookies taste better than chocolate chip cookies.
3 Killing is wrong.
4 Not all high-school graduates should attend college.
5 One should always tell the truth.
6 Americans own more cars and television sets per capita than citizens of any other country.
7 God created the universe and everything in it in six days.
8 Blue is a prettier, more restful color than orange.
9 A good first-grade teacher is one who keeps the children quiet and in their seats.
10 If the people of this country had believed the Vietnam war was right, we would have won it.

33b **Learn the parts of an argument.**

Because an **assertion** states the stand or point of view on a topic [see Section **31d(2)**], it is sometimes called a thesis, claim, or proposition. But whatever it may be called, it must be supported by valid evidence if the reader is going to believe it.

Evidence is the part of an argument the reader is willing to accept as true without further proof. Most evidence can be categorized as either fact or opinion: that is, (1) a verifiable occurrence or experience or (2) a trusted judgment believed reliable because the source is knowledgeable, prestigious, and authoritative. We have already noted that facts can be slippery **[33a(6)].** In a later section **[33e(l)],** you will see that prestigious opinion also has its pitfalls if the source is not truly knowledgeable. Nevertheless, a plausible argument depends on evidence that is accurate, pertinent to the main assertion, and sufficient to support it.

Evidence often comprises a major portion of an argument, especially if the topic is controversial or complex. There are no hard and fast rules for determining how much evidence is enough. It depends on the nature of your topic and the characteristics of your audience—how likely the readers are to agree or disagree with your assertion.

You have probably experienced the frustration of reading on your English compositions the comments "not enough support" or "more examples needed." Bear in mind the benchmark of shared experience; that is, the more widely shared or commonly acknowledged an experience, the fewer examples you need to convince readers. The sun rises in the east. No one is going to argue with you. If in a paper on the value of home remedies, however, you offer as fact the statement that mustard-plasters are good for curing colds, you will have to cite a wide and representative sampling of incidents as well as testimony from respected medical authorities to convince your audience. Most readers would view your statement not as fact but as an assertion needing proof.

Evidence is only as good as its accuracy and your audience's willingness to accept it. Consequently, persuading the reader means looking at the evidence from the reader's point of view and then supplying an appropriate combination of statistics, illustrations, specific examples, personal experience, or occurences reported by authorities to validate the evidence in your reader's eyes—and thus to support your argument's assertion.

Arguments also contain a third element, sometimes implied rather than stated, that shows the connection between the truth of the supporting evidence and the truth of the assertion. This third element is often called the **warrant.**

> ASSERTION: We can expect college tuition to increase.
> EVIDENCE: The cost of living keeps going up.
> WARRANT: Since colleges are subject to the same economic pressures as everyone else, tuition increases will be necessary to meet rising costs.

Using an implied warrant, and a different order of presentation, the same argument might be written:

> EVIDENCE: Because the cost of living keeps going up,
> ASSERTION: we can expect college tuition to increase as well.

The words "because" and "as well" serve as the warrant, clearly implying the reason why or connection between the truth of the evidence and the truth of the assertion.

EXERCISE 33b Find the assertion, evidence, and warrant in each of the following passages. If any of the parts is implied, point out the words that indicate the implied part or supply the missing words.

1 I have a terrible sinus headache. Whenever the weather changes, I get one of these headaches, so we can expect rain before the day is over.

2 Most people are indifferent to local politics. Oh, they complain a lot about things, but only a minority of registered voters bothers to go to the polls when national candidates are not on the ballot.

3 And they lived happily ever after.

4 America's love affair with the big, flashy, luxury car is over. The energy crisis has seen to that.

5 If you don't behave yourself, Santa Claus won't bring you any presents.

6 The Surgeon General has determined that cigarette smoking is dangerous to your health.

7 National political conventions are merely ritualistic pageants. Their intended function, selecting the party's presidential candidate, has been taken over by the state primaries.

8 Some acreage in California's San Joaquin Valley is suffering from a build-up of salt deposits, the result of irrigation without adequate drainage. Irrigation can bring life to crop lands, but it can also bring slow death.

9 I must be out of shape. Yesterday I painted the bathroom, and this morning I feel as if I had been run over by a truck.

10 Don't touch the baby birds in that nest or their mother will abandon them.

33c Define terms whose exact meaning is essential to clear communication.

Much senseless argument arises because people fail to agree on meanings. Readers have to understand your terms before they can follow your reasonings. The assertion *If the people of this country had believed the Vietnam war was right, we would have won it* is unsatisfactory on several counts, not the least of which is the slippery term *right*. The reader is bound to ask, "What do you mean by 'right'?"

The word *right* is an abstraction, and abstract terms are among the most difficult to define. However, the assertion itself could have provided some useful clues. Consider the statement *A good first-grade teacher is one who keeps the children quiet and in their seats.* This assertion defines *good* by using a concrete example: a teacher whose class is quiet and in place. Definitions, then, supply words or examples more easily understood than the term being defined and show what items should be included or excluded from the category the term covers.

Definition by word substitution. Many terms can be satisfactorily defined by merely offering a synonym the reader is likely to know. This is particularly true for technical or other little-known terms. Often an **appositive**—another noun or a group of words used as a noun—placed immediately after the term will be useful for such a definition.

cardiac arrest, stopping of the heart
aerobic (oxygen-requiring) bacteria

aquifer, a natural underground water reservoir
layette, clothing or equipment for a newborn child

Formal definition. We learn about something new by discovering it resembles things we already know and then noting how it differs from them. Constructing a **formal definition**—sometimes called an *Aristotelian, logical,* or *sentence definition*—requires exactly the same steps. First, we explain the class of things—the **genus**—to which a term belongs, and then we determine how it differs from other things in that class—its **differentiation.** Formal definitions characteristically take the form *x is y;* that is why they are termed *sentence definitions.*

1 The first step in formal definition is to put the term into the class of items to which it belongs. This process is called **classification.**

Term		*Genus*
A carpet	is	a floor covering.
A crumpet	is	a light, soft bread similar to a muffin.

In general, the narrower the classification, the clearer the eventual definition.

NOT	A crumpet is a bread.
BUT	A crumpet is a light, soft bread similar to a muffin.
NOT	A rifle is a weapon.
BUT	A rifle is a firearm.

Indeed, a crumpet is classified as bread, but so is pumpernickel. Though *weapon* is a legitimate classification for *rifle,* the class includes more than is necessary (knives, spears, clubs, and so on).

2 Distinguish the term from other members of its class. This process is called **differentiation.**

Term		*Genus*	*Differentiation*
A carpet	is	a floor covering	of woven or felted fabric usually tacked to a floor.
A crumpet	is	a light, soft bread similar to a muffin	baked on a griddle, often toasted and served with tea.

Defining a term by genus and differentiation is analogous to the comparison and contrast methods of paragraph and essay development (see Sections **31f** and **32g**). The term is first classified according to similarity and then differentiated according to dissimilarity.

3   Use parallel form in stating the term to be defined and its definition. Do not use the phrases *is when* or *is where* in definitions.

NOT   A debate *is when* two people or sides argue a given proposition in a regulated discussion.

BUT   A debate is a regulated discussion of a given proposition between two matched sides.

4   Be sure the definition itself does not contain the name of the thing defined or any derivative of it. John Keats's line "Beauty is truth, truth beauty" is poetic, but not very helpful as a definition. Nothing is achieved when definitions are **circular,** when words are defined in terms of themselves.

NOT   A rifle is a firearm with *rifling* inside its barrel to impart rotary motion to its projectile.

BUT   A rifle is a firearm with spiral grooves inside its barrel to impart rotary motion to its projectile.

NOT   Traditionally, masculinity has been defined as the behavioral *characteristics of men.*

BUT   Traditionally, masculinity has been defined as the behavioral characteristics of courage, forcefulness, and strength.

5   Whenever possible, define a term in words that are familiar to the reader. It doesn't do much good to describe a truffle as "a fleshy, subterranean fungus, chiefly of the genus *Tuber,* often esteemed as food" if your reader won't know the meaning of *subterranean* or *fungus.* This example illustrates why dictionary definitions can sometimes be frustrating and unhelpful. Readers might find "an edible, lumpy plant that grows underground and is related to the mushroom" a much more understandable definition of *truffle.* The complexity of Dr. Samuel Johnson's definition of the simple word *network* is a notorious illustration:

Network: anything reticulated or decussated, at equal distances, with interstices between the intersections.

Ordinarily, of course, you will define terms without being aware of giving them a genus and a differentiation. But it is always possible to check your definition against the criteria given above. Consider the following example from a student paper:

Finally, college is valuable to a person interested in success. By *success* I don't mean what is usually thought of when that word is used. I mean achieving one's goals. Everybody has his own goals to achieve, all of them very different. But whatever they are, college will give one the know-how and the contacts he needs to achieve them successfully.

This definition is obviously unsatisfactory; but the specifications for definition will help clarify why and how it breaks down. If the statement that this paragraph makes about *success* is isolated, it comes out like this: *Success is the successful achievement of goals that know-how and contacts gained at college help one achieve.* First, this statement violates one of the principles of definition because it defines the word in terms of itself: *success is the successful achievement.* Next, the writer does not make clear what he means by *goals,* and the qualifying clause *that know-how and contacts gained at college help one achieve* does nothing to help us grasp his intended meaning because we do not know how he defines *know-how* and *contacts.* Hence, he has failed in both aspects of good definition: he has neither put the terms into an understandable class nor made a real differentiation. What he says is that success means being successful, which is not a definition.

Extended definition. A good many terms, particularly abstract words like *propaganda, democracy, happiness, religion, justice,* and *satisfaction,* require considerably more than a formal definition if their meaning is to be clear. Extended definitions usually have a formal definition at their core but expand upon it using synonyms, examples, analogies, descriptions of operations and results, and various other explanations to show the reader more precisely what is meant. Extended definitions may be one paragraph long or longer; entire articles or even books can be structured as extended definitions.

The following paragraph illustrates a simple extended definition. (For further examples see the sample paper at the end of this section, pp. 292–294.) Note that the first sentence in this definition gives a kind of dictionary definition of *induction. Induction* is put into a class of things—in this case *the art of reasoning.* It differs from other things in that class—in this case by being that kind of reasoning in which we first examine particulars and then draw a conclusion from them. This general definition is then developed in two parts: (1) by explaining the kind of scientific reasoning that is inductive, and (2) by explaining, through a series of specific examples, how our everyday reasoning is inductive.

Induction is the kind of reasoning by which we examine a number of particulars or specific instances and on the basis of them arrive at a conclusion. The scientific method is inductive when the scientist observes a recurrent phenomenon and arrives at the conclusion or hypothesis that under certain conditions this phenomenon will always take place; if in the course of time further observation supports his hypothesis and if no exceptions are observed, his conclusion is generally accepted as truth and is sometimes called a law. In everyday living, too, we arrive at conclusions by induction. Every cat we encounter has claws; we conclude that all cats have claws. Every rose we smell is fragrant; we conclude that all roses are fragrant. An acquaintance has, on various occasions, paid back money he has borrowed; we conclude that he is frequently out of funds but that he pays his debts. Every Saturday morning for six weeks the new paper boy is late in delivering the paper; we conclude that he sleeps on Saturday mornings and we no longer look for the paper before nine o'clock. In each case we have reasoned inductively from a number of instances; we have moved from an observation of some things to a generalization about all things in the same category.

NEWMAN AND GENEVIEVE BIRK, *Understanding and Using English*

Extended definition can be used to clarify terms in an argument, but frequently it constitutes a whole argument—in and of itself—used not only to inform but also to persuade. In such a case the writer is trying to convince readers to share his or her beliefs in addition to clarifying a term. Thoreau wrote "Civil Disobedience" not only to explain the concept but also to justify it as a course of action. Alvin Toffler's book *Future Shock* provided our language with a new term, and the book is an extended definition of that term. But *Future Shock* does more than identify and describe a phenomenon: in Toffler's words, the book's purpose is "to help us cope more effectively with both personal and social change. . . . Toward this end, it puts forward a broad new theory of adaptation." In short, *Future Shock* argues for a set of new attitudes and behavioral patterns.

EXERCISE 33c(1) Examine the following definitions and be prepared to answer the following questions about each. Is the class (genus) to which the term belongs clearly named? Is the class narrow enough to be satisfactory? Does the definition clearly differentiate the term from other things in the class? Does the definition repeat the term it is defining? Is it stated in parallel form?

1 An expert is one who guesses right.
2 A pot party is where everyone is smoking pot.
3 A thermometer measures temperature.
4 Religion is emotion seasoned with morality.
5 A touchdown pass is when the player throws the ball for a touchdown.
6 Analysis means to break something down into its parts.
7 Passive resistance is when people simply refuse to follow orders.
8 A frying pan is a cooking utensil that is large and flat.
9 Inflation is rising prices.
10 "Home is the place where, when you have to go there, they have to take you in." ROBERT FROST

EXERCISE 33c(2) Write formal definitions of two of the following terms.

1 rain check
2 guerrilla
3 jukebox
4 chair
5 examination

33c

EXERCISE 33c(3) Select one of the following terms and write a paragraph of extended definition. Use your first sentence to state a formal definition of the term and then clarify it in the rest of the paragraph.

1 mass media
2 inflation
3 pornography
4 underemployment
5 freedom

33d

33d Be sure your argument is well supported and logically sound. Sound arguments are usually constructed using two major logical processes: induction and deduction.

Inductive reasoning (as you learned from the example of extended definition) proceeds from the particular to the general. If particular facts are shown to be true time after time or if a laboratory experiment yields the same result whenever it is run or if people in a wide and varied sampling respond the same way to a given question, *then* a general conclusion may be drawn. Repeated experimentation and testing led to the conclusion that the Sabin vaccine would prevent polio. Scientists use induction when they test and retest a hypothesis before stating it as a general truth. The whole scientific method proceeds by inductive reasoning.

Deductive reasoning proceeds from the general to the particular. From a general conclusion other facts are deduced. The validity of the deduction, naturally, depends on the truth of the initial conclusion. Because you know that penicillin is an effective weapon against infection, seeking a doctor to administer it to you if you have an infection is valid deductive reasoning.

You should also be aware that there is an induction-deduction cycle of reasoning. Sound conclusions reached through induction may in turn serve as the basis for deduction. For example, over many years the National Safety Council has kept careful records of the occurrence and circumstances of highway accidents and has reached the valid conclusion that the proportion of accidents to cars on the road on holiday weekends is the same as the proportion on weekends that are not holidays. From this conclusion, arrived at inductively, you may deduce that you can travel safely by car to your grandmother's house next Thanksgiving.

In this way, the arguments you construct may use both induction and deduction. Sometimes you reason from conclusions a reader accepts as true; sometimes you must prove the truth of the conclusions themselves. In either case, the assertions you make in the course of the argument should be adequately supported, and there should be no errors in the logic.

A convincing argument presents sufficient evidence to support its assertions and presents it in a manner that is logically error-free. Errors of logic in argument, called **fallacies,** weaken an argument, making it unreliable. Most fallacies fall into two categories: fallacies of oversimplification and fallacies of distortion. Common fallacies of oversimplification are **hasty generalizations, inadequate cause-and-effect relationships, false analogies,** and **either/or fallacies.**

1 Support and qualify all generalizations. A **generalization** asserts that what is true of several particulars (objects, experiences, people) of the same class (genus) is true of most or all particulars of that class. For example, the statement *Drinking coffee in the evening always keeps me awake at night* is a generalization based on several particular experiences on separate evenings. Generalization is essential to thinking; without it, we could not evaluate experience—only accumulate isolated facts. Similarly, generalization is essential to argument, since evaluation is part of the argumentative process. In fact, generalizations often appear as topic sentences in paragraphs (see Section **32a**).

An argument's main assertion may be presented as a generalization: *Most people are indifferent to local politics.* Moreover, because arguments of any length or complexity are comprised of clusters or chains of smaller, related arguments whose proof supports the main assertion, the writer typically uses a number of generalizations in the course of convincing the reader. Thus, generalization is very important—but it has its dangers, as the following discussion reveals.

Avoid hasty generalizations. Do not leap to conclusions on the basis of insufficient evidence. We all tend to generalize from a few striking examples, especially when they accord with what we want to believe. But unless examples are irrefutably typical, they can lead to fallacies, even absurd assertions.

PARTICULAR *A*	Mrs. Jones's son never gets home when his mother tells him to.
PARTICULAR *B*	Sally, the girl down the street, won't go to college though her father wants her to.
PARTICULAR *C*	My brother keeps telling his daughter not to go out with that boy, but she keeps right on doing it.
HASTY GENERALIZATION	Young people today don't obey their parents. [Does this generalization include Henry and John and Mike, who are always home on time? Or Katie, who is in college though she doesn't want to be? Or the brother's other daughter, who married the son of her father's best friend?]

PARTICULAR *A*	I know an Italian who is a bookie.
PARTICULAR *B*	The Italian who runs our neighborhood grocery once short-changed my neighbor.
PARTICULAR *C*	A man named Valenti was a gangster.
HASTY GENERALIZATION	Italians are crooks.

Hasty generalizations are dangerous because they make assertions about groups containing millions of individuals on the basis of three or four examples. And more often than not, the writer knows of examples that don't fit the generalizations but, giving in to the temptation to oversimplify, leaves them out.

To protect an argument's validity, as well as to be fair to your readers, never advance a generalization unless you can support it with sufficient evidence. Sometimes two or three examples may be enough, but sometimes you will need to analyze the evidence in detail. If you can think of exceptions to the generalization, you can be sure your readers will too; so you should prepare a counterargument to handle them (see Section **33e**).

Avoid broad generalizations. Be cautious in using words such as *always, never, all, none, right, wrong* in generalizations. Broad generalizations, like hasty generalizations, arise from inadequate evidence. Sweeping statements invite readers to start thinking of exceptions, to start picking apart your argument even before you've presented your evidence. Many an otherwise reasonable assertion has foundered for lack of *seldom* instead of *never, usually* instead of *always.*

OVERSTATED	Playing football always results in injury.
	Playing football results in injury.
QUALIFIED	Playing football sometimes results in injury.
	Playing football can result in injury.

Note that an overstated generalization need not specifically state that it applies to *all* people. By not making a qualification it clearly implies *all,* as in the second overstatement above. Similarly, words other than modifiers can act as qualifiers. For example, the verbs *can* and *may* prevent overstatements, as in the second qualification above, where *can* implies possibility rather than certainty.

2   Do not assume that a cause-and-effect relationship exists between two facts merely because one follows the other in time. This inadequate assessment of cause and effect results in the fallacy of oversimplification known as **post hoc, ergo propter hoc** ("after this, therefore because of this").

The Navy began allowing women to serve on its ships in the 1970's, and its preparedness has decreased steadily since then. [The newspaper columnist who made this statement ignored other important factors such as cuts in defense spending and a shortage of new vessels and equipment, all of which adversely affected the Navy's military strength.]

I'm not surprised George had a heart attack. We warned him not to take that high-pressure job at company *X*. [While a connection between stress and heart disease has been established, physicians point to diets high in cholesterol, lack of exercise, and smoking—long-term behavior that can contribute to heart attack. George's life style more than likely made him a good candidate for a heart attack long before he changed jobs.]

3 Do not assume that because two circumstances or ideas are alike in some respects, they are alike in all respects. This fallacy, **false analogy**, shares some characteristics of broad generalizations. Because one or two points are analogous, it is very tempting to go overboard and claim two situations or concepts are wholly analogous. Political speeches are full of oversimplified, faulty analogies, and so are moral diatribes.

Of course he'll make a good Secretary of Agriculture. He's lived on a farm all his life and turned a healthy profit raising livestock. [Undoubtedly farming experience is an asset, but success as a cattle grower does not guarantee success as a governmental administrator dealing with a wide variety of agricultural concerns.]

The United States is headed right down the road to oblivion, following in the footsteps of ancient Rome: too much luxury and leisure, too much sex and violence. The Roman orgy and bloody circus have their modern counterparts in American promiscuity and violent television programs. Like the Romans, we'll be conquered by stronger invaders one day. [This analogy fails to take into account vast differences between ancient Rome and modern America—imperial dictatorship versus representative democracy, to mention just one.]

Analogy can be a useful persuasive tool, but keep in mind that while it can clarify, it can never prove a point. Analogy's value increases in direct proportion to the number of parallels you cite and decreases with every difference your reader thinks of.

4 Do not claim there are only two alternatives if, in fact, there are several. Either/or fallacies result if you oversimplify choices, proposing only two when several actually exist. Truth sometimes is an either/or sort of thing: either you passed the examination, or you failed it. But most things about which we argue aren't as clear-cut. Arguing as if only two possibilities exist when the facts justify a variety of possibilities is also known as the **all-or-nothing fallacy** or

false dilemma. (These two fallacies are frequently distinguished from each other, but both involve ignoring alternatives.)

> Students come to college for one of two reasons: they come either to study or to party. Judging by Mack's attendance at campus mixers, I'd say he didn't come to study. [It's possible Mack studies very little, if at all. It's also possible he studies very efficiently and thus has free time to go to dances. Clearly, many combinations of studying and partying, to say nothing of the endless possibilities that include neither studying nor partying, are available to both the prudent and the not-so-prudent college student.]

> A woman can't have it both ways. She has to choose between career and family. [Statistics show that a significant proportion of married women and mothers in this country hold jobs. Somebody obviously has seen through the false dilemma to at least a third alternative.]

EXERCISE 33d Explain what is wrong with the reasoning in the following statements, and try to identify the fallacies of oversimplification that occur.

1 Television is responsible for the violence in society today.
2 That girl my brother is seeing is a very bad influence on him; he met her at Christmas time and within a year he had dropped out of college.
3 Sex education gives kids too many ideas. There has been an increase in teenage pregnancies in our town every year since they started those sex education classes at the high school.
4 Your repeated failure to show up for work on time suggests either you don't like your job or you're lazy.
5 Welfare recipients are a lot like drones in a beehive. While the rest of us work to produce society's goods and services, they just consume and breed.
6 Any member of Congress who goes on a junket is just taking a vacation at the taxpayers' expense.
7 All this emphasis on "career training" has turned the university into an assembly line. Poke the students in at one end, keep piling on the required courses, and out they pop at the other end with a diploma but no individuality or ability to think creatively.
8 If you really loved me, you'd spend our anniversary here at home instead of going on that business trip.
9 World War I started during Wilson's term, World War II started during Roosevelt's term, and the Vietnam War escalated during Johnson's term; if we elect another Democratic president, he'll start another war.
10 Anyone who heads a large corporation got to the top by ruthless maneuvering and looking out for "number one."

33e **33e Be sure your argument answers objections from the opposition without resorting to distortion.**

A successful argument takes into account counterarguments the reader is likely to raise and tries to refute them fairly and reasonably. If counterpoints are indeed valid, the best procedure is to recognize their validity but provide sufficient evidence to substantiate the truth of your assertions over all. The surest way to damage your own position is to ignore counterarguments or, worse yet, divert attention from them by trying to appeal to your reader's prejudices and emotions. You may be successful in your diversion, but you will have avoided the real issues being discussed and failed the test of logical reasoning. In short, your argument will have been distorted and unfair.

One of the most common kinds of argumentative distortion is **slanted language,** words using **connotation** to appeal to emotion and prejudice (see Section **40**). Slanted language "twists out of shape," distorts meaning. For example, today words like *radical, permissive,* and *cover-up* produce negative responses from many people, while words like *freedom, responsibility,* and *efficiency* produce positive responses.

Consequently, the calculated—or careless—use of such words in argument tends to evoke emotional rather than reasoned reactions. If Candidate Jones is described as standing for "free, responsible, and efficient government" while Candidate Smith is described as "a radical with a permissive philosophy," voters are likely to favor Jones over Smith without attempting to learn either candidate's actual position on inflation, government spending, unemployment, or anything else. It's not unusual to find diametrically opposed positions described by the same connotative language. "Fiscal responsibility" can mean a tax cut in one politician's campaign and a tax increase in another's.

Arguments can also be twisted and bent by **fallacies of distortion,** errors that misrepresent all or part of an argument's meaning. Among distortion techniques are **transfer, argument to the man, argument to the people, non sequitur, begging the question,** and **red herring.**

1 Do not associate an idea or term with a famous name in the hope of imbuing the former with characteristics of the latter. The erroneous technique of **transfer (argumentum ad verecundiam)** uses positive or negative association rather than reason as a basis for conclusion. When used negatively, transfer becomes a form of **name calling.** In either case, the hope is that characteristics will transfer, even when logically there is no connection—which explains the notable incongruity of professional football players' endorsing women's pantyhose or popcorn poppers.

> We are the political party of Franklin D. Roosevelt and John Kennedy. Our campaign platform follows in that great democratic tradition.
>
> Schmaltz believes the federal government should decide the issue. He stands for big government, which is just another name for creeping socialism.
>
> If Miss America can get beautiful hair like this using X shampoo, you can too.

2 Do not sidestep an argument by trying to discredit the person who proposed it. Argument to the man (**argumentum ad hominem**) ignores the point being argued and attacks a person's character instead. This distortion technique is similar to that of red herring [see Section **33e(6)**] because it substitutes a false issue for *bona fide* proof. Furthermore, even though discredited for one thing, a person may be right about others.

> Why should you believe what Hartwell says about the needs of our schools? He is suspected of taking bribes. [Quite apart from the fact that Hartwell is only "suspected of taking bribes," what he has to say about school needs may be based upon extensive study and analysis.]
>
> Don't listen to Collins's arguments for abortion. She doesn't even like children. [That Collins doesn't like children says something about her. But her arguments for abortion may stem from deep conviction reached after long experience as a doctor.]

3 Do not sidestep an argument by appealing to the instincts and prejudices of the crowd. Argument to the people (**argumentum ad populum**) arouses emotions people have about institutions and ideas. When politicians evoke God, country, family, or motherhood, they are making such an appeal—as, for example, when candidates say they will protect the interests of the American family.

A slightly different fallacy that uses similar crowd appeal is the **bandwagon** approach. This fallacy says that what is right for the masses is right for the individual: one must go along with the crowd in belief or action. Obviously this is not true, as many incidents of mob rule have shown. Nevertheless, the bandwagon is a favorite ploy among advertisers (and children) who claim "everyone" is buying or doing something.

> Fifty million people can't be wrong! Drink Slurp-o!
>
> But Mom, all the kids are wearing shorts (*or* roller-skates *or* green wigs) to the prom!
>
> The responsible citizens of this state know that a vote for Jenkins is a vote for open and honest government.

4 Do not substitute inference for a logically sound conclusion. A **non sequitur** ("it does not follow") attempts a fallacious leap in logic, omitting proof.

> This is the best play I have seen this year, and it should win the Pulitzer prize. [Unless you have seen all the plays produced this year and are qualified to judge the qualities that make one a Pulitzer prize winner, it doesn't follow that the one you like best should win.]
>
> The problems we face today have been caused by Washington. Elect Green to Congress. [Not only is the first assertion offered without evi-

dence, but certainly we are given no proof that Green can solve the problems. Perhaps his strength lies in the fact that he has been in Omaha rather than Washington for the past four years.]

5 Do not assume the truth of something you are trying to prove. **Begging the question** is a fallacy that occurs when a premise requiring proof is put forward as true. A related fallacy is called **circular argument.**

> This insurance policy is a wise purchase. It covers all expenses related to cancer treatment. [While the policy may pay cancer-related expenses, the statement assumes the buyer will get cancer. If he or she does not, the policy will not have been a wise purchase.]

> His handwriting is hard to read because it is illegible. [This argument does not move from premise to conclusion but merely moves in a circle. *Illegible* means "difficult or impossible to read," so the author has said only that the handwriting is hard to read because it is hard to read.]

6 Do not introduce a false issue in the hope of leading your reader away from a real one. A most graphically termed fallacy, a **red herring,** supplies a false scent in an argument, diverting the hounds from their quarry and leading them down an irrelevant trail. Usually the false issue elicits an emotional reaction, side-tracking the reader's attention from the real issue and the proof it needs.

> American cars really are superior to Japanese imports. After all, we should "buy American" and support our own economy rather than sending our dollars overseas. ["Buying American," a disguised appeal to patriotism, diverts attention from real issues such as mileage ratings, repair records, safety, and so on, exhibited generally by American cars as compared with Japanese cars.]

> I don't think Mary Ann should have been expelled from school for cheating on Professor Thompson's calculus text. Lots of people cheat on exams—they just don't get caught. Besides, everybody knows Thompson's tests are too hard anyway. [Neither the pervasiveness of academic cheating nor the difficulty of calculus tests is relevant to the issue. The author tries to justify Mary Ann's action with two red herrings—a bandwagon appeal and an attack on Thompson—both of which are beside the point.]

EXERCISE 33e Explain the errors in reasoning in the following statements and try to identify the fallacies of distortion that occur.

1 My father raised his children with an iron hand, and we turned out all right. I intend to raise my son the same way. What was good enough for Dad is good enough for me.

2 Norma's house is always a mess. Anyone who's that disorganized at home couldn't possibly organize city government. I certainly wouldn't vote for her for mayor.

3 If you believe in the sanctity of the family, you'll agree that the books used in our schools should be chosen by us parents and not by the teachers. We are the ones who should decide what our children read.

4 He made very good grades in college so he's bound to do well in the business world.

5 The government must cut spending because economy in government is essential.

6 He knew how to run a lathe, but I didn't hire him because he spent a year in reform school and once a criminal, always a criminal.

7 How can you support the Equal Rights Amendment? Do you want women and men sharing the same restrooms?

8 In that TV commercial for Uppity Airlines, Herman Hero says their plane is the safest thing in the sky. He used to be an astronaut, so he must know what he's talking about.

9 Obviously a good golf game is the key to success in this company. Most of the rising young executives play golf, so I'd better practice my putting.

10 Senator Graft wouldn't have been charged with accepting bribes if there weren't some truth to it.

REVIEW EXERCISES ON WRITING PERSUASIVELY (Section 33)

EXERCISE A Prepare a counterargument for at least one of the arguments stated below. Be sure your counterargument exposes any fallacious reasoning you find in the statements and does not itself contain fallacies. Also be sure to anticipate and defuse objections likely to be raised by the opposition.

1 I have been trying to help my nephew with his arithmetic assignments, but he's still getting failing grades on his tests. He must not be paying attention, or else he's just stupid in math.

2 All these unnecessary environmental regulations are really not essential. Besides, the costs of pollution control are aggravating the national decline in productivity and the rise in inflation. The auto industry has suffered severe financial losses in recent years, and the energy crisis has made our country's deposits of high-sulfur coal crucial to our energy supply. What we need now is less environmental regulation, not more.

3 Since 1964 scores on Scholastic Aptitude Tests have been dropping. What's more, students graduating from high school today can neither read nor write nor do arithmetic at their grade level. Clearly, the minimum competency testing program used in Jacksonville, Florida, should be instituted nationwide. If a student can't pass these standardized tests, he or she shouldn't graduate.

4 My roommate will make a terrific veterinarian. She just loves animals. She's always bringing home stray dogs and cats. It really upsets her to see an animal suffer.

5 If a coat or suit becomes old, ragged, and out of style, we don't continue to wear it. We replace it with a new one. Similarly, employees who reach age 65 should be forced to retire to make way for younger people with energy and fresh ideas.

EXERCISE B The following problems are designed to direct your attention to some of the violations of logic that you encounter every day.

1 Analyze several automobile advertisements, several cosmetic or drug advertisements, and several cigarette advertisements in current magazines or on television on the basis of the following questions:

   a What specific appeals are made? (For example, automobile advertising makes wide use of the bandwagon approach; cosmetic advertising often uses transfer methods.) How logical are these appeals?

   b Are all terms clearly defined?

   c What kinds of generalizations are used or assumed? Are these generalizations adequately supported?

   d Is evidence honestly and fairly presented?

   e Are cause-and-effect relationships clear and indisputable?

   f Is slanted, loaded language used? What is the advertiser trying to achieve with the connotative language?

2 Look through copies of your daily newspaper and bring to class letters to the editor or excerpts from political speeches that contain examples of fallacious reasoning. Look for false analogies, unsupported generalizations, name-calling, and prejudices.

3 Read an opinion article in a popular magazine and write a report analyzing the logic underlying the opinions and conclusions it states.

EXERCISE C Read "Disporting at the Olympics," the student paper at the end of this section, and answer the following questions.

1 Which of the four types of writing (narration, description, exposition, argumentation) are represented? (See Section **31d.**)

2 Which type matches the author's apparent purpose?

3 Where does the author use definition?

4 In your own words, what is the essay's main assertion? Which sentence(s) in the essay states this assertion?

5 What generalizations does the author make? Are they supported with adequate evidence?

6 Do any parts of the argument rest on shaky assumptions or *a priori* premises?

7 Does the essay include counterarguments to handle objections likely to be raised by the opposition?

8 Is the author's reasoning sound?

9 Is any of the language unfairly slanted?

10 Do you find the essay persuasive? Why or why not?

Paper for analysis

DISPORTING AT THE OLYMPICS

The word <u>sport</u>, which for most of us means some kind of organized athletic activity like football or tennis, is a shortened form of the word <u>disport</u>, meaning to occupy oneself with diversion or amusement. <u>Disport</u> has its roots in a Latin verb, <u>disporter</u>--to carry away. Every four years sports fans act out the intent if not the knowledge of the Latin root, getting "carried away" by the Olympic Games. In modern times, the Olympics have certainly provided diversion; however, frequently they have not been all that amusing. All too often the Olympics have been a showcase for politics rather than athletics.

Nevertheless, the International Olympic Committee tries to put on a brave face and continues to declare the Olympics apolitical: the old "it's not whether you win or lose, but how you play the game" spirit. This sentiment echoes the words of Baron Pierre de Coubertin, who founded the modern Olympics in 1896: "The essential thing in life is not conquering, but fighting well." Noble sentiments indeed, but the youngest Little Leaguer will tell you they just don't wash. When athletes gather to compete, winning is everything. When athletes representing their nations gather to compete every four years at the Olympics, winning is also political.

But need politics spoil the Olympics? Not necessarily. Not if audiences and the International Olympic Committee stop worrying so much about politics and focus on the true center of the games--the athletes and their skill. We can't ignore the politics, but if we stop paying so much attention to them, we may be able to adjust our perspective so the sports predominate.

The first step in adjusting our perspective is to recognize that the Olympics--both ancient and modern--have always been political. The ancient games were a display of martial strength and ability--running, boxing, wrestling, chariot racing were all combat skills. From 380 B.C. the games even featured a race run in armor. In 364 B.C. the Eleians "forgot" it was "only a game" and actually attacked the Pisates during the Olympics, trouncing them.

The modern Olympics had their own savage counterpart in 1968 at Munich when Arab terrorists kidnapped and killed nine Israeli athletes in the Olympic Village. Less violent incidents include Hitler's use of the 1936 Berlin games to propagandize for Naziism; African boycotts in 1972 and 1976 protesting Rhodesian participation; and the summer games boycott by the United States and 30 other nations in 1980 to protest Russia's invasion of Afghanistan. It's pretty hard to ignore politics like that.

On the other hand, we can stop stewing about it and concentrate on the sports themselves. Every time our news media, the Olympic Committee, or anyone else dwells on politics rather than athletics, the people who would use the games for political ends benefit. The attention feeds on itself and creates more attention, more politics. The cry that the Olympics are too political becomes self-fulfilling prophesy.

Instead, the real story, the real media event, is the athletes, their skill, and the demands of their sport. The mind in concentration, the body in motion--these things are basic and satisfying no matter what training program, sports medicine staff, government, or political persuasion attends them. Athletic ability is fundamentally individual and personal; we can respond to it in an individual and personal way.

A good example is the Russian figure-skating pair, Rodnina and Zeitzev. They participated in the 1980 winter games at Lake Placid, after the Russian invasion of Afghanistan but before the American boycott. As they skated into the ice rink, the television commentator noted the pair had been nervous about their reception by the American crowd. The crowd was polite, but as the pair executed their routine, people became enthusiastic. The audience knew that Irina Rodnina would never skate at another Olympics: she was retiring after these winter games. They also knew her performance was thrilling, nearly flawless. Spinning, jumping, whirling through lifts and spirals with her husband-partner, Rodnina personified grace on ice. That was what brought the crowd to its feet in applause.

Human grace, skill, and achievement--personal talent, endurance, and triumph--these carried Rodnina and Zeitzev beyond politics. If the Olympic Committee, and media, and American audiences focus on these, every four years we can still get "carried away" at the Olympics.

EFFECTIVE SENTENCES
EF

Every sentence is the result of a long probation [and] should read as if its author, had he held a plough instead of a pen, could have drawn a furrow deep and straight to the end.

HENRY DAVID THOREAU

A sentence may be perfectly clear and grammatical without being *effective.* Most effective sentences not only communicate simple facts and ideas, they bring together a number of facts and ideas in ways that show the relationship among them. Such sentences enable the writer to knit into the basic subject-verb-object pattern of a sentence the modifiers that give interest and full meaning to ideas. And the skillful use of such sentences together, in carefully thought out sequence, allows writers to express meaning more exactly.

34   34 COORDINATION AND SUBORDINATION **SUB**

Most effective sentences bring together two or more ideas that they relate to one another by **coordination** and **subordination.** Broadly, **coordination** expresses equality: two things that are coordinate have roughly the same importance, the same rank, the same value. **Subordination** expresses some sort of inequality: when one thing is subordinate, or dependent, upon another, it is in some way of lesser importance or rank or value.

Coordination

When you coordinate two or more words, phrases, or clauses, you tell your reader that they go together and that they are equally important, or approximately so. The simplest kind of coordination occurs when you join two or more phrases or clauses by *and, but, or,* or by one of the other coordinating conjunctions: *workers and managers, working in the city but living in the suburbs, wherever you go or whatever you do.* Like other coordinating conjunctions, **correlative conjunctions**—coordinating conjunctions that work in pairs—indicate that the single words and phrases they link are equally important. The most important of these pairs are *both . . . and, either . . . or, neither . . . nor, not . . . but,* and *not only . . . but also*—as in *both successful and satisfied, neither chemistry nor biology, she not only practiced medicine but also raised English spaniels.* Conjunctive adverbs—words like *consequently, however,* and *nonetheless*—can never connect words, phrases, or dependent clauses, but they allow you to coordinate whole sentences: *He had been warned that a severe storm was coming; nonetheless, he insisted on starting his trip.*

34a Coordinate to bring equal related ideas together.

Coordination allows you to bring equal parts of separate sentences together into single sentences by creating compound subjects, objects, modifiers, or whole predicates. By so connecting them and by putting them in the same grammatical form, you emphasize their equal meaning and importance and express your ideas more clearly and without needless repetition.

> John wanted a new suit. He wanted a new coat. He wanted a new hat. He couldn't afford them.
>
> John wanted a new suit, coat, and hat, but couldn't afford them. [Coordinate objects, *suit, coat,* and *hat;* coordinate verbs, *wanted* and *couldn't afford*]
>
> Susan applied to graduate school. Elaine applied to graduate school. Ted applied to graduate school.
>
> *Susan, Elaine,* and *Ted* all applied to graduate school. [Coordinate subjects]
>
> During the morning the students were studying for their biology exam. They were also studying throughout the afternoon and evening.
>
> The students were studying for their biology exam *not only during the morning but also throughout the afternoon and evening.* [Adverbial phrases coordinated by correlative conjunctions *not only* and *but also*]

But coordination not only allows you to bring together equal parts within sentences; it also allows you to express equal relationships among more complex ideas and information among a series of sentences. Although a series of sentences may set out facts and ideas of roughly equal importance, those sentences often leave readers to puzzle out exact relationships. When the ideas in such sentences are equal and closely related, they can often be brought together by coordination into a single, easy-to-follow sentence that clearly reveals those relationships.

Compare the following:

> Winter is the season when animals get stripped down to the marrow. Humans also do. Animals can take the winter easy by hibernating. Humans are exposed naked to the currents of elation and depression.

> Winter is the season when *both* animals *and* humans get stripped down to the marrow, *but* many animals can hibernate, take the winter easy, as it were; we humans are exposed naked to the currents of elation and depression. — MAY SARTON, *Plant Dreaming Deep*

The information in both versions is much the same. But the first forces the reader to work much harder to discover that animals and humans share the same exposure to winter, but with different effects. May Sarton's original single sentence pulls all the relationships tightly and clearly together by first linking *animals* and *humans* with the co-ordinating pair *both . . . and,* then by establishing the idea of contrast between them with *but,* and carries out the contrast by linking her statements about animals on the one hand and humans on the other by the semicolon, itself a kind of coordinating link.

EXERCISE 34a Combine the following sentences, using coordinating conjunctions either to link the two sentences as a single compound sentence or to link similar elements of the two sentences as compound subjects, objects, predicates, or modifiers.

1 Ryan has made a great deal of money. He still lives simply and unpretentiously.
2 I planned my paper carefully. I wrote it hastily.
3 The four roommates had decorated the fine old Victorian house with furniture that looked expensive. It was inexpensive.
4 You may remain outside in the hot sun. You can go inside and watch TV in an air-conditioned room.
5 The Senator said that he disapproved of the legislation. The Senator said that he would support the legislation.
6 The program indicated that Dr. Thomas would speak at 11:00 A.M. She spoke at 9:30 A.M. We missed her talk.
7 You had better not annoy Bowser, Chuck's dog. You'll wish you hadn't.
8 The bobcat was fearless. The bobcat was vicious.
9 The field was full of rattlesnakes. We were afraid to walk through it.
10 Lois and Guido could afford a trip to Europe. They could afford a new car. They couldn't afford both.

Subordination

Subordination allows you to build into sentences details, qualifications, and other lesser information and ideas while keeping the main statement of the sentence clear and sharply focused. When you coordinate two or more pieces of information, you indicate that they are equally important. When you put information into subordinate constructions—modifying words, phrases, subordinate clauses, and other modifying word groups—you indicate that they are less important than the main statement, even though they may still be vital to the full meaning of the sentence. Subordinating conjunctions, particularly, enable you to express exact relationships among your ideas.

Take a simple example of two factual statements. *He was late. I was angry.* If these two sentences stand as they are or if they are joined coordinately with *and—He was late, and I was angry—*readers will probably guess that the lateness caused the anger. But they can't be sure. They can be sure, however, if the two sentences are combined with a subordinating conjunction that expresses the intended relationship.

> Because he was late, I was angry.
> When he was late, I was angry.
> If he was late, I was angry.

Each of these expresses a different kind of relationship between the two events, but each of them makes the intended relationship explicit. None of them leave the reader to guess at the meaning the writer had in mind.

34b Put your main idea in the main clause; subordinate other information.

The main clause of a sentence should carry your central idea; details, qualifications, and other relevant information that is closely related but less important than that central idea should be put into subordinate constructions.

Consider the following sentence as a possible topic sentence for a paragraph:

> Gorillas have often been killed to permit the capture of their young for zoos, and men have recently been occupying more and more of their habitat and gorillas are now threatened with extinction.

Although the information in that sentence is perfectly clear, it is unclear whether the central concern is with the gorilla's threatened extinction or with the causes for that threat. Readers will probably assume that the principal concern is the threat to the gorilla's existence. But neither writer nor readers can be sure what direction the paragraph that this sentence introduces will take.

Either of the following versions, however, makes the central idea of the writer unmistakably clear:

> Because gorillas have often been killed to permit the capture of their young for zoos and men have recently been occupying more and more of their habitat, *they are now threatened with extinction.*

> Even though gorillas have often been killed to permit the capture of their young and are now threatened with extinction, *men have recently been occupying more and more of their habitat.*

The first version of the sentence makes it clear that the writer's focus is on the threatened extinction of the gorillas; the second, that the

34b

writer's focus is on the current increasing encroachment on the gorilla's habitat.

Here is another example.

> An arms race will be very costly, but we may be forced into one, and many people think it is necessary.

Which is the writer's main idea? That an arms race will be costly? That we may be forced into one? That many people think it is necessary? The following revisions establish one idea as the main idea by expressing it in a main clause and subordinating the other related ideas:

> Although we may be forced into an arms race because many people think it is necessary, *such a race will be very costly.*
>
> Although an arms race may be very costly, *we may be forced into one,* because many people think it is necessary.

Each of these revisions establishes a slightly different idea as the writer's central one, but both knit the three originally separate ideas into a single sentence that clearly distinguishes the writer's main point from subordinate ones. Neither of these sentences is intrinsically better than the other. Which of them the writer chooses must be determined by which point the writer sees as most important.

EXERCISE 34b   Revise the following sentences by making one idea the main clause and subordinating other ideas.

1 We drove onto a gravel road. It led into the woods. It was narrow. We wondered whether it was safe.

2 The house was very old. It was painted yellow. The paint was faded. In some places it was cracked.

3 The bookshelves were too expensive. I went to a lumber yard. I bought some boards. I bought some brackets. I put them up myself.

4 I got up late this morning. I had to wait for a bus. I was late to class.

5 One of the early experimenters with submarines was Robert Fulton. He built the first successful steamboat. He also experimented with torpedoes.

6 I had never smoked marijuana before. I was invited to a pot party. I went. Someone offered me a joint. I took it. The effect was not quite what I had expected. I didn't finish it. I left the party.

7 Late-night TV talk shows are very popular. The hosts are usually very funny. The guests are from many walks of life. Some of them are politicians. Some are show-business celebrities. They talk about various things. The mixture makes for interesting conversation.

8 TV documentaries are very interesting. One showed the plight of the migrant workers. Another showed conditions in the ghetto. Still another showed the helplessness of neglected senior citizens. The one I liked best was entitled "Birth and Death."

9 We decided to take the subway. We didn't know the way. We asked directions. The train agent was very helpful.

10 I studied hard. I read the textbook. I read outside sources. I wrote a 15-page paper. I bought the instructor a Christmas present. I flunked the course.

34c Be aware of the different relationships subordinating words express.

Subordinating conjunctions allow you to express a variety of relationships. The most important of these are cause, condition, concession, purpose, time, and location. These relationships, together with the most common subordinating conjunctions expressing them and examples of their use, are shown below:

CAUSE

because, since

We now controlled the minority vote. We felt sure we could win.

Because we now controlled the minority vote, we felt sure we could win.

CONDITION

if, even if, provided, unless

Many serious diseases can be controlled. We must identify them early enough.

If we identify them early enough, we can control many serious diseases.

Unless we identify them early enough, many serious diseases cannot be controlled.

CONCESSION

although, though, even though

Morgan has always worked conscientiously and carefully. He has never received a very high salary.

Although Morgan has always worked conscientiously and carefully, he has never received a very high salary.

PURPOSE

in order that, so that, that

Shelley had prepared carefully for her bar examination. She wanted to be sure of passing it on her first attempt.

Shelley had prepared carefully for her bar examination so that she could be sure of passing it on her first attempt.

TIME

as long as, after, before, when, whenever, while, until

Terry and Lee were confronted with the evidence and they admitted that they had taken part in the robbery.

After Terry and Lee were confronted with the evidence, they admitted that they had taken part in the robbery.

LOCATION

where, wherever

A new office building stands on the corner of High and Federal Streets. A small cigar factory stood on that corner for years.

A new office building stands on the corner of High and Federal Streets where a small cigar factory stood for years.

The relative pronouns—*who (whose, whom)*, *which*, and *that*—allow you to use adjective clauses for information and details about nouns.

Susan brought me a beautiful piece of jade. She just returned from Mexico.

Susan, who just returned from Mexico, brought me a beautiful piece of jade.

Hemenway was a big burly man. His face was tough and belligerent.

Hemenway, whose face was tough and belligerent, was a big burly man.

The tomb of Tutankhamen was filled with spectacular treasures. It was among the greatest archaeological finds of all time.

The tomb of Tutankhamen, which was among the greatest archaeological finds of all time, was filled with spectacular treasures.

EXERCISE 34c Combine the following pairs of sentences, using a subordinate conjunction that will expess the relationship indicated in parentheses.

1 He rested over the weekend. He would be ready to go back to work on Monday. (purpose)
2 Manuel was given the award. He had the highest score. (cause)
3 Sally will go to college. She can borrow the necessary money. (condition)
4 The children washed the car. Their father was sleeping. (time)
5 Karen had been saving as much money as she could for a year. She still could not afford to go to San Francisco for her vacation. (concession)
6 My neighbors the Cavalettis prefer to heat by gas. They believe it is cheaper and cleaner. (cause)
7 Compensation for women has improved significantly. It is still far from equal to that of men. (concession)

8 The river reaches flood level. Those people living along its banks have to be evacuated. (time)

9 Jim has been betting on the horse races. He needs to borrow money from all his friends. (result)

10 All students must have their schedules approved by an advisor. Then they can get their admission cards for each of their courses. (time)

34d Learn to use such subordinating constructions as appositives, participial phrases, and absolute phrases.

Subordinate clauses, together with single-word modifiers and simple prepositional phrases, are the most common means of subordinating ideas and detail. But writing often uses other constructions that seldom occur in speech. Three of the most useful of these are appositives, participial phrases, and absolute phrases. Understanding these structures and learning to use them when appropriate can help you to improve your sentences.

Appositives

Appositives are words or word groups that rename, further identify, or describe another word. Appositives rename, clarify, identify, or expand the meaning of the word or phrase to which they are attached, but unlike clauses or whole sentences, they have the same grammatical function as the word or phrase they clarify. That is, a word group that serves as an appositive to a sentence subject could also serve as the subject; an appositive to a verb object could also serve as its object. Appositives most often function as nouns or noun word groups, but they may also serve as adjectives.

Appositives often offer an economical alternative to subordinate clauses. You can, for example, combine the following two sentences by putting the information of the second sentence either in a relative clause or in an appositive:

Sven Nilssen has told me much about Sweden.
He is my close friend and an accomplished pianist.
Sven Nilssen, who is my close friend and an accomplished pianist, has told me much about Sweden.

But the combination with an appositive is briefer and moves more quickly:

Sven Nilssen, a close friend and an accomplished pianist, has told me much about Sweden.

In general, any nonrestrictive clause that consists of *who* or *which* as the subject, some form of the verb *to be*, and a complement can be reduced to an appositive, as in the following:

My mother was born in Lincoln, Nebraska.
She was the oldest of seven children.

My mother, the oldest of seven children, was born in Lincoln, Nebraska.

Jim Slade, who is a militant labor organizer, has been repeatedly denied admission to the factory.

Jim Slade, a militant labor organizer, has been repeatedly denied admission to the factory.

Often a series of appositives can be used to bring together several details in a single sentence. In the following passage, each of the last three sentences states a separate observation about the way in which keepers of notebooks are a "different breed altogether."

Keepers of private notebooks are a different breed altogether. They are lonely and resistant rearrangers of things. They are anxious malcontents. They are children afflicted at birth with some presentiment of loss.

But in Joan Didion's original sentence, she has used a series of appositives to combine all these observations into a single smooth, clear, yet packed sentence.

Keepers of private notebooks are a different breed altogether, lonely and resistant rearrangers of things, anxious malcontents, children afflicted at birth with some presentiment of loss.

JOAN DIDION, *On Keeping a Notebook*

Although appositives are most commonly noun groups, they can also be used as adjectives, as in the following:

A lovely hand tentatively rose.
The hand was almost too thin to be seen.

A lovely hand, almost too thin to be seen,
tentatively rose. HERBERT KOHL, *36 Children*

She was about thirty-five years old.
She was dissipated.
She was gentle.

She was about thirty-five years old, dissipated and gentle.

JOHN CHEEVER, "The Sutton Place Story"

Participles and participial phrases

Participles are nonfinite verb forms that can help form verb phrases or function as adjectives. Like finite verbs, they can take objects and modifiers to form participial phrases. Present participles end in *-ing* (living, studying, flowing, driving, eating). Past participles of regular verbs end in *-ed* (lived, studied, wasted); past participles of irregular verbs often end in *-n* or *-en* (blown, driven, eaten) but sometimes have other irregular forms (slept, clung, swum). Together with objects or modifiers, participles may form phrases, as in the following:

Eating their way into the sills of the house, the termites caused great damage.

Dressed in the warmest clothes they could find, Kathie and Mark stepped out into the driving wind.

Participial phrases often provide an alternative way of expressing information or ideas that can be expressed in sentences or dependent clauses. Compare the following:

Writing is a slow process. It requires considerable thought, time and effort.

Writing is a slow process, *which requires considerable thought, time, and effort.*

Writing is a slow process, *requiring considerable thought, time, and effort.*

In contrast to relative clauses, which ordinarily must follow immediately after the nouns they modify, participial phrases can precede the nouns they modify. A participial phrase can usually be placed at more than one point in a sentence.

The old house, *which was deserted twenty years ago and said to be haunted by the ghost of its former owner,* stood halfway up the hill.

Deserted twenty years ago and said to be haunted by the ghost of its former owner, the old house stood halfway up the hill.

The old house, *deserted twenty years ago and said to be haunted by the ghost of its former owner,* stood halfway up the hill.

Since participial phrases are somewhat flexible in their position, they often permit you to vary sentence structure to fit a particular purpose in a given paragraph. You must, however, be careful not to create misplaced modifiers with participial phrases (see Section **12a**).

Participial constructions are especially useful for suggesting action and for describing events that occur at the same time as those in the main clause. Compare the following:

The hikers struggled to the top of the ridge. They were gasping for breath and nearly exhausted.

The hikers, gasping for breath and nearly exhausted, struggled to the top of the ridge.

In the following sentence, notice how Updike uses a pair of present participial phrases to suggest that his walking through the yard and his clutching the child's hand both occur at the same time as his thinking that "It was all superstition."

[It was all] superstition, I thought, walking back through my yard, and clutching my child's hand tightly as a good luck token.

JOHN UPDIKE, "Eclipse"

Absolute phrases

Absolute phrases consist of a subject, usually a noun or a pronoun, and a participle together with any objects or modifiers of the participle. They may be formed from any sentence in which the verb is a verb phrase that contains a form of the verb *be* followed by a present or past participle simply by omitting the *be* form. In other sentences they may be formed by changing the main verb of a sentence into its *-ing* form. Note the following:

SENTENCE	Her lips were trembling.
ABSOLUTE	Her lips trembling . . .
SENTENCE	The wind blew with increased fury, and the drifts rose ever higher.
ABSOLUTE	The wind blowing with increased fury, and the drifts rising ever higher . . .

When the participle of an absolute phrase is a form of the verb *be*, the verb is frequently omitted entirely, so that the absolute consists simply of a noun followed by adjectives.

The pianist played beautifully, her technique flawless, her interpretation sure and sensitive.

The advantages of the absolute phrase are its speed and compression. It allows you to add specific, concrete detail to a general statement with greater economy than most alternative constructions. In addition, its placement in a sentence is extremely flexible. It can be placed at the beginning or end of a sentence, or often in the middle. Note the following examples:

> *The rain having stopped,* we went to the beach.
>
> *Their dinner finished,* the two industrialists were ready to talk business.
>
> We ran into the house, *eyes averted.*
>
> The little boy stood crying beside the road, *his bicycle broken, his knees bruised,* and *his confidence badly shaken.*
>
> The driver of the wrecked car, *one leg trapped beneath the dashboard, body pinned firmly against the steering wheel,* had to be extricated by the rescue squad.

EXERCISE 34d   Revise the following passages, expressing what you consider to be the most important idea in the main clause and using appositives, participial phrases, or absolute phrases to subordinate other ideas.

1 Mrs. James will chair this year's Community Fund drive. She is a vice-president of the City Savings Bank.

2 Jane left home at seven o'clock this morning so that she could avoid the heavy traffic, because she wanted to get to work early.

3 As Jack ran back to throw a pass, he slipped and fell on a patch of gravel.

4 Anne Frank's diary, which she began in 1943 and kept faithfully until her death two years later, became one of the most humane accounts of one of history's least humane periods.

5 Aspirin was first commercially produced in 1899. It is the most common pain reliever known today.

6 Millie Luce was a freshman at State University. She was sitting at her desk. The writing pad before her was blank. The pencil in her hand was badly chewed. The waste basket beside her was overflowing with crumpled sheets of paper.

7 Houdini was the undisputed champion of escapes. He successfully challenged audiences around the world to construct traps from which he could not escape.

8 They were accused of cheating. They tried to lie their way out of it because they had succeeded in doing so once before.

9 The patient quickly got into the dentist's chair. Her jaw was badly swollen and her tooth was aching horribly.

10 The 1974 red Toyota stood in the driveway. Its engine was running smoothly. Its body was dented a bit here and there but it was polished mirror-bright. Inside, the upholstery was carefully protected by covers.

34e   Avoid excessive coordination.

34e

A series of short, simple sentences all of the same or very similar structure will give all your facts and ideas equal weight and importance. Such sentences are sometimes called "primer" sentences because they are like those of children's first reading books. If you find yourself relying heavily on such sentences, examine them, try to determine which ideas are important and which are minor, and rework them into more complex sentences, making appropriate use of both coordination and subordination.

| CHOPPY | He stood on a street corner. The wind was blowing. He peered into the darkness. He was a stranger. He realized that he had no place to go. |
| REVISED | Standing on a windy street corner and peering into the darkness, the stranger realized that he had no place to go. |

| CHOPPY | A plane far off broke the sound barrier. Several windows on the avenue were shattered. The landlords were angry. They complained to the authorities. |
| REVISED | When several windows on the avenue were shattered by a distant plane breaking the sound barrier, the angry landlords complained to the authorities. |

Avoid trying to solve the problem of excessively simple sentences by stringing them together with a series of *and's* and *but's*. Such strings are just as ineffective as a choppy series of simple sentences.

| INEFFECTIVE | We approached the river and we looked down from the bluff, and we could see the silvery stream and it wound below in the valley. |
| REVISED | When we approached the river and looked down from the bluff, we could see the silvery stream winding below in the valley. |

34f   Avoid faulty coordination.

Faulty coordination occurs when two or more facts or ideas that have no apparent logical connection are coordinated.

| FAULTY | The poet John Keats wrote "The Eve of St. Agnes," and he died of tuberculosis. |

Two such unrelated facts would make strange bedfellows even if one were subordinated to the other, unless perhaps they were given some such meaningful context as the following.

He could remember only two facts about John Keats: He wrote "The Eve of St. Agnes" and he died of tuberculosis.

Sometimes faulty coordination occurs when writers leave out important information that is evident to them but not to a reader.

| FAULTY | My father was in the army in World War II, but he didn't have enough money to finish college. |

CLEAR   Although my father's service in World War II entitled him to some education under the G.I. bill for veterans, he didn't have enough money to finish college.

A somewhat different kind of faulty coordination occurs when a writer coordinates items from overlapping classes. In the following sentence, for example, the four-item coordinate series makes it appear that there are four different kinds of animals or birds in the pet show the writer is describing. But clearly there are only three: dogs, parrots, and monkeys. The "mangy cocker spaniel" belongs among the dogs.

CONFUSING   Entered in the pet show were several dogs, two parrots, three monkeys, and a mangy cocker spaniel.

CLEAR   Entered in the pet show were two parrots, three monkeys, and several dogs, one of which was a mangy cocker spaniel.

EXERCISE 34e–f(1)   Revise the following sentences to eliminate excessive or faulty coordination.

1 Their father was an accountant and he worked for the Chase Manhattan Bank and he had moved to New York in 1980.
2 Olson bought his new car only three months ago and he has already had two accidents.
3 John Ciardi published his first book of poems in 1940 and he has written several books of poems and for some years he wrote a column for the *Saturday Review* and he has translated Dante's *Divine Comedy* and has written several other books.
4 Unemployment and declining productivity in our industry are our greatest problems, and we are spending billions for new weapons.
5 He dropped out of high school and he decided to get a job but he couldn't find one and then he decided to go back to school and later he went to college.
6 Her grandfather's will left her a collection of old glass, three clocks, an antique car, and several broken bottles.
7 New York has a first-class harbor and has become the leading American port, and the city has had many financial problems.
8 Hilda has not read the assigned books, so she will not be ready for the examination, so she may have trouble with the course.
9 *Funny Girl* had a long run on Broadway and broke many box office records and was later made into a movie and Barbra Streisand played the leading role.
10 The Indian Highway was formerly an Indian trail, but it is now a major highway, and it is a scenic and important route.

EXERCISE 34e–f(2)   Rewrite the following passages, using both coordination and subordination as appropriate to eliminate choppy sentences.

1 I arrived home at quarter past four. Then I began my reading for the next day. My first assignment took two hours. Then it was time to have

dinner. I was tired. I could not enjoy the steak that we had for dinner. I finished dinner. I went back to finish my reading. At eleven o'clock I went to bed.

2 The setting of most of Edith Wharton's stories is New York or Paris. These cities are world capitals. Their society is wealthy and aristocratic. Perhaps, however, Edith Wharton's best novel is *Ethan Frome.* The story tells the tragic story of a poor farmer. He lived in a remote section of Massachusetts.

34g Avoid excessive subordination.

Excessive subordination occurs when you include in a sentence details that are unessential or only loosely related to the main line of thought in the sentence. It also occurs when successive dependent clauses are strung together, each attached to the preceding one without clear relationship to the main clause. In the following sentence, for example, the italicized clauses are only remotely related to the main direction of the sentence. They clutter rather than clarify what the writer is saying.

EXCESSIVE SUBORDINATION	My fishing equipment includes a casting rod *which my Uncle Henry gave me many years ago* and which is nearly worn out, and an assortment of lines, hooks, and bass flies, which make good bait *when I can get time off from work to go bass fishing* at Hardwood Lake.
REVISED	My fishing equipment includes an old casting rod and an assortment of lines, hooks, and bass flies. The flies make good bait when I can go bass fishing at Hardwood Lake.

In the following sentence, the successive details are all essential, but the structure of successive dependent clauses makes their relationship hard to grasp.

AWKWARD	We walked down Fifth Avenue, which led us to Washington Square, where we saw the memorial arch, which resembles the *Arc de Triomphe* which is in Paris.

Such sentences can often be improved by changing some of the clauses to modifying phrases. Sometimes clarity requires that the sentence be reworked as two separate sentences.

REVISED	We walked down Fifth Avenue to Washington Square, where we saw the memorial arch resembling the *Arc de Triomphe* in Paris.

34h Avoid faulty subordination.

Faulty subordination, sometimes called "upside-down" subordination, occurs when the idea that the reader would normally expect to be the more important is placed in a subordinate clause. In many sentences, determining which ideas to place in a main clause and which to subordinate depends entirely on context. In one context, you might want to write, *While Lincoln was still President, he was shot,* thus emphasizing the assassination itself. In another, you might want to write, *When he was shot, Lincoln was still in office,* thereby making more prominent the fact that he was still in office. There is no way of determining, aside from context, which of these versions is the better sentence.

But in many sentences, the logic of normal expectation works on the reader. A sentence such as *He happened to glance at the sidewalk, noticing a large diamond at his feet* contradicts the reader's sense of the relative importance of the two ideas, glancing at the sidewalk and noticing a diamond. Except in a very unusual situation, the finding of a diamond would be the logically more important fact, and a reader would expect the sentence to say *Happening to glance at the sidewalk, he noticed a large diamond at his feet.*

INEFFECTIVE	The octopus momentarily released its grip, when the diver escaped.
REVISED	The octopus momentarily releasing its grip, the diver escaped.
INEFFECTIVE	He was playing his first major league game, being a better first baseman than some who had been playing for years.
REVISED	Although he was playing his first major league game, he was a better first baseman than some who had been playing for years.
INEFFECTIVE	I visited my home town after being away twenty years, when I was astonished at the change in its appearance.
REVISED	When I visited my home town after being away twenty years, I was astonished at the change in its appearance.
	After being away twenty years, I visited my home town and was astonished at the change in its appearance.

EXERCISE 34g–h Some of the following sentences subordinate their more important ideas. Others contain excessive subordination. Rewrite them, using both coordination and subordination to make them more effective.

1 She pulled the emergency cord, averting a train wreck.

2 According to the popular ballad, Casey Jones attempted to arrive on schedule, being prevented by a head-on collision with another train.

3 The reporters, many of them wearing their press cards pinned to their lapels, flocked to the launch site, where the technicians were giving a last check to the spaceship that was to carry three astronauts, who were just then walking up the ramp, to the moon.

4 Ralph Waldo Emerson was an individualist because he said, "Whoso would be a man must be a nonconformist."

5 *A Clockwork Orange,* which was written by Anthony Burgess, and which was a best seller for many months, was made into a motion picture, directed by Stanley Kubrick, which was very well received by film critics who thought it was one of the year's best movies.

6 Although their salaries remained the same, prices continued to rise.

7 Mrs. Wood opened the door of the cage, when her pet parrot escaped.

8 My sports car, which I bought from a friend of mine, a car enthusiast who buys old cars and then rebuilds them as a hobby, had developed a rumble in the engine which has begun to worry me for I know nothing about repairing cars and haven't the money to go to a mechanic.

9 He fell seven stories and broke eight ribs, puncturing one lung, although he lived to tell the tale.

10 Although Marion graduated with honors, she had to pay most of her own expenses.

35 PARALLELISM II

Grammar requires that when you coordinate two or more elements in a sentence, you make them *parallel,* that is, you state them in the same grammatical form. Noun must be matched with noun, verb with verb, phrase with phrase, and clause with clause.

A lawyer must be *articulate* and *logical.* [Parallel and coordinate adjectives]

She *closed the door, opened the window,* and *threw herself* into the chair. [Three coordinate and parallel predicates, each consisting of verb plus direct object]

The otter's fur is dark-chocolate brown, and *its eyes are small and black.* [Two coordinate and parallel independent clauses]

But parallelism is more than a grammatical requirement; it is a basic rhetorical principle. Equal form reinforces equal meaning. By putting equally important parts of a sentence or of successive sentences into equal grammatical constructions, you emphasize their relationship to one another. Grammar requires the parallelism in each of the examples above. But in each, the parallelism confirms the coordinate relationship, the equal importance of the coordinate parts.

35a Use parallelism to make coordinate relationships clear.

1   In single sentences. Putting equal ideas in a sentence in parallel constructions will help you make their coordinate relationship more immediately clear to your reader. Compare the following sentences:

> If they buy the assigned books, students can usually be successful, but they must read them and careful notes must be taken.
> Students can usually be successful if they *buy the assigned books, read them,* and *take careful notes.*

The first sentence really sets three conditions for a student's success: buying the books, reading them, and taking notes. But the sentence muddies this equal relationship by putting the first in an *if* clause separate from the other two; and although the last two conditions—reading the books and taking notes—are coordinated by *and,* the first is active and the second passive, thus further weakening their coordinate relationship. The revised sentence brings the three conditions neatly and clearly together in a single parallel series of predicates.

2   Among successive sentences. Many times you can increase the coherence of your writing by combining several successive sentences into a single sentence that uses parallelism carefully.

Suppose you are trying to get together your ideas about the things necessary for good writing and that you have written the following in a first draft:

> Logical thinking is one of the things necessary for good writing. Good writers also have to organize their ideas coherently. And finally, anyone who wants to write well must express his ideas clearly.

Look at this closely; *thinking, organizing,* and *expressing* are the main related processes here. Parallel structure can help you knit these together tightly and emphasize them clearly. Compare the following single sentences with the three original sentences:

Thinking logically,
organizing ideas coherently,
and
expressing ideas clearly   are three requirements of good
                                    writing.

or

Logical thought,
coherent organization,
and
clear expression   are the major ingredients of good
                            writing.

or

Anyone who wishes to write well must learn
                                            to think logically,
                                            to organize ideas
                                                coherently,
                                            and
                                            to express them
                                                clearly.

Any of these versions of the first draft pulls the ideas together into a single economical unit and gives emphasis to the three major items.

Notice how parallelism helps to keep the following sentences clear and to emphasize the relation between the ideas.

Strikes, though sometimes necessary, mean
                                            loss of wages for
                                                workers,
                                            interference with
                                                production for
                                                managers,
                                            and
                                            disruption of services
                                                for consumers.

Political language is designed   to make   lies sound truthful
                                                  and
                                                  murder respectable
                                      and
                                      to give an appearance of
                                          solidity to pure wind.

3 In whole paragraphs. Just as you can often make single sentences clearer by coordinating equal ideas and putting them in parallel constructions, so you can often use roughly parallel sentences to increase the coherence of an entire paragraph. [See also Section **32d(2)**.] Study the following paragraph:

> Otters seem to improvise. *When swimming along* in a lake or a stream, *one may push* a leaf or twig ahead of it. *Or it may drop* a pebble, then chase it through the sparkling water, catching it before it touches bottom, only to bring it to the surface and drop it again. *Underwater, it may balance* a rock or mussel on its head as it swims, *or play* cat and mouse games with its prey. *In captivity, it plays* games with every moving object and explores all corners and crevices for string to pull, wires to loosen, latches to open, and new mysteries to solve.
>
> GEORGE LAYCOCK, "Games Otters Play," *Audubon*

The structure of this paragraph is kept unmistakably clear by its careful coordinating and confirming parallelism throughout. The simple topic sentence, "Otters seem to improvise," is developed by a series of details of their improvisation in three situations: in the water, underwater, or in captivity.

EXERCISE 35a Using parallelism and subordination, revise and improve the following passages.

1 The cat is a domestic animal. It is clean. It is also intelligent. Cats like to stay at home. They are fond of playing with people and like to sleep. It enjoys catching mice, too.
2 How she sleeps on that bed is a mystery. The bed is hard. It is lumpy and it slopes. Her diet is also a mystery. And no one understands where she gets her money.
3 Walking in the rain is one way Dan relaxes. He also likes to relax by listening to music. He likes to listen to selections from his large record collection. He also likes classical music on his favorite FM station. In the summer he sometimes gets his relaxation by reading while he sits on the sun deck.
4 Ann Jenkins strode through the lobby of the Warner Building. Next she walked into the elevator. She got off at the sixteenth floor after which she walked into her office. During that whole time she couldn't remember why she was going to her office.
5 Burdo dresses neatly. He does not dress flashily. He always thinks clearly. He has a record of being honest. What's more, he has considerable influence with several of our excellent customers. That's why we hired him—all those things and especially the last one.

35b Use parallelism for elements joined by coordinating or correlative conjunctions.

Coordinating conjunctions. Just as the careful use of parallelism can be an aid to constructing effective sentences, to combining successive sentences for economy and clarity, and to maintaining coherence throughout an entire paragraph, lack of parallelism can throw a reader off and make for particularly ineffective sentences. To keep your sentences clear as well as grammatically correct, let the structure of the first of two or more coordinate elements in a sentence set the pattern for the structure of the remaining elements.

AWKWARD	Mollie enjoys *her work* as a marketing manager during the day and *going* to the theatre in the evening.
PARALLEL	Mollie enjoys *working* as a marketing manager during the day and *going* to the theatre in the evening.
AWKWARD	Desmond is tall, with blue eyes, and has a congenial manner.
PARALLEL	Desmond is tall, blue-eyed, and congenial.

When you are coordinating prepositional phrases or infinitives, clarity will sometimes require you to point up parallel structure by repeating prepositions.

AMBIGUOUS	Sam helps with the work around the house by cooking and ironing his own shirts.
CLEAR	Sam helps with the work around the house *by* cooking and *by* ironing his own shirts.
AMBIGUOUS	Maria wants to write stories that describe the South and study the habits of the Creoles. [stories that study the habits of the Creoles?]
CLEAR	Maria wants *to* write stories that describe the South and *to* study the habits of the Creoles.

Correlative conjunctions. Correlative conjunctions are coordinating pairs: *either . . . or, neither . . . nor, both . . . and, not . . . but, not only . . . but also.* Parallelism requires that the structure following the second part of the correlative be the same as that following the first part.

FAULTY	You are either *late* or *I am early*. [The writer has connected the adjective *late* and the clause *I am early*. Parallelism requires the connection of the two clauses beginning with *You* and *I*.]
PARALLEL	*Either you are late* or *I am early*.
FAULTY	Ellen not only has been outstanding in her studies but also in athletics.
PARALLEL	Ellen has been outstanding not only in her studies but also in athletics.

If you are uncertain of the parallelism with correlative conjunctions, try recasting your sentence as two sentences. Take, for example, the sentence *Not only is Shakespeare famous for his plays but also his sonnets.* Recast as separate sentences, this becomes

Shakespeare is famous for his plays.
Shakespeare is famous for his sonnets.

When you combine the common parts of these two sentences to get *Shakespeare is famous for,* it is clear that the two distinct parts that belong in parallel form are *his plays* and *his sonnets.* The correct forms of the sentence are thus either

Shakespeare is famous for not only his plays but also his sonnets.

or

Shakespeare is famous not only for his plays but also for his sonnets.

35c Avoid faulty parallelism with *and who, and which, and that.*

Do not use an *and who, and which,* or *and that* clause in a sentence unless you have already used a parallel *who, which,* or *that* clause. (So too with *but* and *who, which,* or *that.*)

FAULTY	We met Abner Fulton, a brilliant biologist and who is also an excellent pianist.
REVISED	We met Abner Fulton, who is a brilliant biologist and who is also an excellent pianist.
REVISED	We met Abner Fulton, who is both a brilliant biologist and an excellent pianist.
FAULTY	I like a romantic novel with exciting action and which keeps me guessing.
REVISED	I like a romantic novel that has exciting action and that keeps me guessing.

EXERCISE 35b–c(1) Revise the following sentences to express coordinate ideas in parallel form.

1 The navy promoted all officers who had served two years at sea, or if they had been on shore duty for five years.
2 Hilda has spent three summers in Europe, but she neither speaks German nor French.
3 You make many of your friends angry not only because you cheat but you are such a hypocrite.
4 She is a person who knows how to play tennis and having a knack for dancing.

5 My work consisted of planning the menus, purchasing the food, and supervision of the employees.

6 The students were told to obtain a transcript of their grades and that they could apply for admission.

7 To be a good teacher, one must have patience, liking to help others, and to show a great capacity for learning.

8 Ann not only had applied for the position, but also Warren had applied for it.

9 You must either pass this examination, or you will fail the course.

10 Marcia moved into a new apartment with more space and having air conditioning.

EXERCISE 35b–c(2) Revise the following sentences to express coordinate ideas in parallel form.

1 Being too early, even if it wastes valuable time, is better than to arrive too late.

2 The biography of Stilwell is interesting, lively, and also an informative piece of writing.

3 She bought a new Volvo having a standard transmission and with a radio and heater.

4 Mary has a full-time career, is a member of the school committee, and doing her own yard work.

5 Good politicians not only work well with the public but also they do not compromise their own ideals.

6 The reviewer could not decide whether he should ignore the book or to write an unfavorable review of it.

7 Hemingway's early short stories and novels not only were fresh and vigorous, but he also influenced other writers.

8 The lecture was long, tiresome, and could not be easily understood.

9 They put out the oil well fire by tunneling under the surface, planting some dynamite, and then they exploded it from a distance.

10 Some people neither like popular music or classical music.

36

36 EMPHASIS **EMP**

Effective sentences emphasize main ideas and keep related details in the background. The careful use of coordination, parallelism, and subordination enables you to stress your most important ideas without losing track of less important, related ideas and information. Variety enables you to emphasize important ideas by stating them in sentences that are brief and simple in relation to the other sentences around them. In addition to all these useful strategies, you can also emphasize ideas within a single sentence by controlling the arrangement of elements within the sentence and by the careful use of repetition.

As you revise sentences to achieve the emphasis you want, always keep in mind that any sentence is part of a paragraph and of a larger whole. To determine what to emphasize in a given sentence, you must always think of the sentence in its context.

36a Put important ideas in emphatic positions in the sentence.

The position of a word or idea within a sentence usually determines the emphasis it receives. Generally, the most emphatic place in the sentence is its end; the next most emphatic, its beginning; the least emphatic, its middle. Consider the following sentence:

> Mr. Ellicott, our new plant manager, was inefficient from the start, but always agreeable.

The end position of *always agreeable* gives that fact the heaviest stress in the sentence, a stress further heightened by separating *but always agreeable* with the slight pause of a comma. As, say, a topic sentence of a paragraph that explains Ellicott's combination of inefficiency and agreeableness, with emphasis on the latter, the sentence is well suited to its purpose.

If, however, the sentence introduces a paragraph explaining Ellicott's inefficiency, it must be revised.

> Mr. Ellicott, our new plant manager, though always agreeable, was from the start inefficient.

In this version of the sentence, the statement of Ellicott's agreeableness is subordinated and placed in the middle of the sentence, and the statement of his inefficiency is held for the most emphatic position. Compare the emphasis in the following pairs of sentences:

> Fields was arrested for fraud after he escaped from prison recently.
> Fields, who escaped from prison recently, was arrested for fraud.

> Hispanic-speaking people want to be understood, just as much as other minorities in the country.
> Hispanic-speaking people, just as much as other minorities in the country, want to be understood.

In the latter of each of these pairs of sentences, emphasis on the main clause is increased by placing lesser information within the main clause. Such placement of modifying phrases and clauses delays the predicate for the final emphatic position in the sentence.

Sometimes you can increase the emphasis on a single-word adverb or a brief adverb phrase by moving it to the initial position in a sentence.

> Debra reached sleepily for the alarm clock.
> Sleepily, Debra reached for the alarm clock.

Be careful not to weaken emphasis by placing minor qualifying phrases before your subject or at the end of the sentence.

> Such matters as incorrect spelling and unconventional punctuation can distract a reader from otherwise good writing.
> Incorrect spelling and unconventional punctuation can distract a reader from otherwise good writing.

Be aware, too, that weak qualifying phrases such as *in my opinion, by and large,* and *for the most part* are usually unnecessary. When they are necessary for accuracy, it is usually better to place them within the sentence than at the beginning or end of the sentence.

> WEAK   The history of English vocabulary is the history of English civilization, in many ways.
>
> BETTER   The history of English vocabulary is in many ways the history of English civilization.

EXERCISE 36a   Revise the following sentences by putting important words in an emphatic position.

1 He is an overbearing, egotistical bore, in my opinion.
2 The results of the flood were disastrous, by and large.
3 You are more perceptive and far more sensitive than I am, as a rule.
4 Tolstoy had a profound understanding of people and of the passions that drive them, for the most part.
5 This university would be closed and its faculty fired, if I had my way.
6 Teddy Roosevelt was dynamic and full of life, I have read.
7 Test results prove that smoking seriously impairs the health, in most cases.
8 The lawyer shirked his responsibility and the judge was biased, it seems to me.
9 The day was clear, the sun was shining, and the snow was packed hard; it was a great day for skiing, in my opinion.
10 With its superior technology and its single-minded determination, the United States will definitely win the space race, if everything goes right.

36b   Use periodic sentences for emphasis.

A **periodic sentence** holds its main idea until the end. A **loose sentence,** sometimes called a **cumulative sentence,** completes its main statement and then adds subordinate details.

Strictly speaking, any sentence consisting of a main clause followed by an adverbial phrase or clause is loose and can be made periodic simply by moving the adverbial modifier to the beginning.

LOOSE   Brenda showed great courage and kindness when her mother was in the hospital for two months and her father was on the edge of a breakdown.

PERIODIC   When her mother was in the hospital for two months and her father was on the edge of a breakdown, Brenda showed great courage and kindness.

The balanced sentence is a compound sentence in which the independent clauses are exactly, or very nearly, parallel in all elements.

We always like those who admire us; we do not always like those whom we admire.   LA ROCHEFOUCAULD, *Maxims*

Grammar maps out the possible; rhetoric narrows the possible down to the desirable and effective.

FRANCIS CHRISTENSEN, *Notes Toward a New Rhetoric*

As these two examples illustrate, the balanced sentence is useful in stating contrasts and distinctions.

Both the long periodic sentence and the balanced sentence are planned sentences, the product of careful revision rather than of first drafts. They carry considerable emphasis and should be used only when your subject matter warrants them. Be careful not to fall into the error of the following sentence, in which the writer creates a degree of suspense completely disproportionate to the subject matter.

PERIODIC AND   At the end of a dark alley, three flights down in a
INEFFECTIVE   dark basement full of grim and evil-looking sailors, I ate my lunch.

Often, periodic and loose constructions are more or less equally effective. Your choice must be guided by the particular emphasis you want, and by the relation of your sentence to those before it and after it.

LOOSE   Balboa reached the Pacific after a long, hazardous journey.

PERIODIC   After a long, hazardous journey, Balboa reached the Pacific.

LOOSE   He will be a good kindergarten teacher if enthusiasm is a guarantee of success.

PERIODIC   If enthusiasm is a guarantee of success, he will be a good kindergarten teacher.

EXERCISE 36b   Change these loose sentences into periodic ones.

1 I began seeing a psychiatrist regularly after my marriage broke up.
2 They started a new business and made a million dollars after their first business failed.
3 The wine turned to vinegar, although we tried to keep it in a cool place.
4 The boat neared the finish line, the rowers bending rhythmically and the oars flashing in the sun.
5 They stood the cold for an hour, stamping their feet and blowing on their fingers.
6 I saw two cars crash head-on several years ago on a three-lane highway in Minnesota.
7 Aretha's doctor insisted that she take a vacation after she suffered a severe shoulder dislocation.
8 Your research paper will be accepted if, after you have finished typing it, the footnotes are in good order.
9 I had still not balanced my accounts, although I had checked my figures and added again.
10 Three miles of rough water lay between the ship and the shore.

36c   **36c   Be aware of the arrangement of items in a parallel series.**

When items are arranged in a parallel series, emphasis tends to fall on the last item, simply because it is last. Compare the following:

> You are a coward, a thief, a murderer, and a liar.
> You are a liar, a coward, a thief, and a murderer.

Of these two, the first, by placing *a liar* in the end position, tends to suggest that lying is more important than thievery and murder. The second sentence, in contrast, moves in the order that fits our usual sense of values, suggesting by its arrangement that of all the items named, murder is the most serious. Note that in each of the following sentences the items in the series are arranged in the order of their increasing importance:

> Their lives were brief and tragic.
> I was broke, lonely, and thoroughly discouraged.
> The city was famous for clear signs, wide clean streets, beautiful parks, and well-planned museums.

The arrangement of a series in descending order of importance can sometimes be used for its humor.

> If once a man indulges himself in murder, very soon he comes to think little of robbery; and from robbing he next comes to drinking and Sabbath-breaking, and from that to incivility and procrastination.
>
> THOMAS DE QUINCY

In many series some other principle works together with that of increasing importance to dictate the arrangement of items in a series. In the following sentences, for example, the controlling principle of arrangement is simply the order of events; in the first sentence, events occur in the order we would normally expect, but, as the second sentence illustrates, they might well have occurred in the reverse order.

> At first they were perplexed by the unusual noises, then disturbed, and at last terror-stricken.
>
> At first they were terror-stricken by the unusual noises, then as time wore on merely disturbed, and finally merely perplexed.

In the following sentence, the order of items in each of the series is from large to small, an order that is consistent with the writer's intention to show that even the smallest detail reflected "orderliness."

> The orderliness of their house and their yard mirrored the orderliness of their lives: inside, each chair, each painting, each book had its assigned place; outside, each tree, shrub, and flower seemed planted by design.

EXERCISE 36c   Revise the following sentences by arranging ideas in more logical order.

1 He moved away from the city because he was ill, his rent was high, and he wanted to let his dog run.
2 Most students get bored with school after years of college, high school, and elementary school.
3 They inherited a million dollars, a house, and some jewelry.
4 The play closed after the first week and received terrible reviews.
5 The candidate promised a guaranteed income for all, mingled with people in the street, and smiled at children.
6 Charles is a capable gardener, a famous athlete and a poker player.
7 We find similar psychological reactions in frogs, in guinea pigs, in men, and in rats.
8 During his vacation David acquired some souvenirs, a thoroughbred racehorse, and a bad sunburn.
9 The earthquake caused 100 deaths and toppled several of the buildings in the area.
10 Laurence Olivier is one of the great Shakespearean actors of all time and a director and producer as well.

36d   Repeat key words and ideas for emphasis.

36d

Careless and awkward repetition of words makes sentences weak and flabby (see Section **41d**), but careful repetition of key words can be an effective way of gaining emphasis, as in the following sentences:

> A *moderately* honest man with a *moderately* faithful wife, *moderate* drinkers both, in a *moderately* healthy home: that is the true middle class unit.
>
> G. B. SHAW

Don't *join* too many gangs. *Join* few if any. *Join* the United States and *join* a family—but not much in between, unless a college.

ROBERT FROST

It is the *dull* man who is always *sure,* and the *sure* man who is always *dull.*

H. L. MENCKEN

(For a discussion of ways in which repetition of words and ideas links sentences within a paragraph, see Section **32d.**)

EXERCISE 36d   Discuss the effectiveness of the repetition of words and phrases in each of the sentences below. (Note how frequently effective repetition and effective parallelism reinforce each other.)

1 No one can be perfectly free till all are free; no one can be perfectly moral till all are moral; no one can be perfectly happy till all are happy.

HERBERT SPENCER

2 There is no mistake; there has been no mistake; and there shall be no mistake.

DUKE OF WELLINGTON

3 To know how to say what others only know how to think is what makes men poets or sages; and to dare to say what others only dare to think makes men martyrs or reformers or both.

ELIZABETH CHARLES

4 It is true that you may fool all the people some of the time; you can even fool some of the people all the time; but you can't fool all of the people all the time.

ABRAHAM LINCOLN

36e   Prefer the active to the passive voice.

The **active voice** puts the subject (the actor) first, and follows it with the active verb, and then the object (the receiver of the action): *The cat killed the rat.* The **passive voice** turns things around, putting the receiver in front, then the verb, and finally the original subject: *The rat was killed by the cat.* (See Section **5**.)

Of the two, the active is almost always more direct, more forceful, and more economical. Always prefer it to the passive unless you have good reason not to. When you find yourself using the passive, check yourself to be sure you really need it, that what you want to say cannot in fact be better said in the active voice. More often than not, you will find that you gain both economy and emphasis with the active voice. Note the following examples:

PASSIVE   The pump has been installed in several medical centers and will be tested next week. [15 words]

ACTIVE   Several medical centers have installed the pump and will test it next week. [13 words]

PASSIVE   Two devices for insuring safety are shown in the accompanying illustrations. [11 words]

ACTIVE	The accompanying illustrations show two safety devices. [7 words]
PASSIVE	It was voted by the faculty that all students should be required to take mathematics. [15 words]
ACTIVE	The faculty voted to require mathematics. [6 words]
PASSIVE	Your request has been received and reviewed by the department, but it has been decided that it does not meet the requirement as stated by departmental rules. [27 words]
ACTIVE	We have reviewed your request; it does not meet requirements stated by the department. [14 words]

Careless and unnecessary use of the passive sometimes leads to a shift in a voice that makes your sentences inconsistent (see Section 10a). Note the following:

FAULTY	He boiled the water, and then the spaghetti was added.
REVISED	He boiled the water and then added the spaghetti.
FAULTY	When weasels suck eggs, both yolk and white are sucked out of the shell.
REVISED	When weasels suck eggs, they suck both yolk and white out of the shell.

For situations in which the passive voice is useful and natural, see Section 5.

EXERCISE 36e In the following sentences replace the passive voice with the active.

1 A boomerang can be made to do amazing stunts by a skillful thrower.
2 My ankles were snapped at by an angry dog.
3 The radiator of my car became frozen during the cold spell.
4 Extreme caution is needed if we are to experiment with genetic change.
5 Police procedures were scrutinized by the press.
6 An addition to the house was planned by my parents.
7 The returned astronauts were interviewed by reporters.
8 The menu was selected by the chairman of the refreshments committee.
9 Many major accidents are caused by drunken drivers.
10 Polio vaccine is distributed by the local Department of Health.

37 VARIETY **VAR**

37

A long series of sentences identical or very similar in length and structure is monotonous. But a series of well-written sentences provides more than mere absence of monotony. It reflects the careful molding of form to the writer's thought and the careful choice of length and structure to gain emphasis where the writer wants it.

37a Vary sentence structure and length to create emphasis and accentuate meaning.

Consider the following paragraph by Jane Howard. Notice the variety in length and structure of the eight sentences that make up the paragraph.

> The trouble with the families many of us were born into is not that they consist of meddlesome ogres but that they are too far away. In emergencies we rush across continents and if need be oceans to their sides, as they do to ours. Maybe we even make a habit of seeing them, once or twice a year, for the sheer pleasure of it. But blood ties seldom dictate our addresses. Our blood kin are often too remote to ease us from our Tuesdays to our Wednesdays. For this we must rely on our families of friends. If our relatives are not, do not wish to be, or for whatever reasons cannot be our friends, then by some complex alchemy we must try to transform our friends into our relatives. If blood and roots don't do the job, then we must look to water and branches.
>
> JANE HOWARD, *Families*

The length of these eight sentences ranges from the seven-word *But blood ties seldom dictate our addresses* to the long thirty-three-word sentence beginning *If our relatives are not.* Structure varies from the simple subject-verb-object pattern of the crisp fourth, fifth, and sixth sentences to the much greater complexity of the opening twenty-six-word sentence and the two closing sentences of thirty-three and sixteen words respectively.

Such variety of length and structure is by no means accidental. In the paragraph immediately before this one, Howard has set her thesis: all of us need to belong to a clan, a tribe; if our families don't fit that need, we will find a substitute that does. The quoted paragraph develops that thesis. Its pivotal point falls at the cluster of three sentences—seven, sixteen, and ten words, respectively—that comes at the approximate center of the paragraph: we need "kin . . . to ease us from our Tuesdays to our Wednesdays"; our blood families are usually too remote; for this we need friends.

There is no formula for such a "right" variety of length and form among the sentences of a paragraph or a paper. The variety of Jane Howard's paragraph above comes not from some predetermined pattern she worked out for the paragraph. It comes, rather, from choosing the length and form best suited to the meaning and emphasis she intended.

Such fitting of form to meaning is not likely to come in the first draft of a paragraph or paper. It comes with revision. When you turn to revising the early drafts of your writing, be suspicious if many or most of your sentences are either short or long or if some single structure seems to recur overfrequently. You will need relatively long and complex sentences to relate ideas clearly to one another and to subordinate minor detail; short sentences to give you emphasis where you want it; variety to avoid monotony. Be aware, too, that the kind of sentences that will be appropriate if you are writing a sports column or a set of simple directions will differ from the kind you will need to explain a complex idea. Remember that short sentences can be vigorous and emphatic, but that they are more likely to be effective when placed in contrast to longer sentences.

Most important, always keep in mind that sentence variety is not an end in itself. If you set out to make your sentences alternately short and long, you will end with awkward and artificial writing. If you set out to shift structure with each new sentence without regard to the relationship of one to another, you are more likely to destroy the coherence of the whole than to achieve effective variety. Your choice of length and structure for any one sentence must always depend upon your meaning and upon the relationship of that sentence to those that stand before and after it.

Ways of achieving variety

37b   Use coordination and subordination to combine several short sentences or to improve long compound sentences.

If you find that many of your sentences tend to be short and simple or to fall into strings of short sentences connected by *and*'s and *but*'s, review Sections **34** and **35** and practice using subordination and parallelism to improve your sentences.

INEFFECTIVE	Gail approached the stallion warily. He saw the bridle in her hand. She stood still and the stallion waited. Then she tried to toss the reins over his head. But he galloped away.
REVISED	Gail warily approached the stallion, who saw the bridle in her hand. She stood still, the stallion waiting. But when she tried to toss the reins over his head, the stallion galloped away.
INEFFECTIVE	Gilman was the chief of the volunteer fire department, and he was also the town's only grocer, but he was never too busy in his store to attend a fire.
REVISED	Gilman, the chief of the volunteer fire department and the town's only grocer, was never too busy in his store to attend a fire. [Facts about Gilman in the first two clauses are reduced to an appositive; the last becomes the main clause.]

37b

For practice in combining short sentences and improving long compound sentences, see Exercises **34a** and **34b**.

37c

37c Vary the position of free modifiers.

A modifier that can be moved from one position to another within a sentence without interfering with clarity or meaning is called a **free modifier.** Prepositional phrases, clauses, and single words that modify nouns must ordinarily be placed next to or very close to the nouns they modify; their position is relatively fixed. But adverbs, adverb phrases and clauses, many participial phrases, and absolute phrases can often be placed at different positions in a sentence; these are free modifiers. Moving such modifiers into varying positions in your sentences can help you place the emphasis of your sentence where you want it and increase sentence variety.

ADVERB PHRASES AND CLAUSES

Westerners and Arabs still do not understand each other, *in spite of two thousand years of contact.*

In spite of two thousand years of contact, Westerners and Arabs still do not understand each other.

Westerners and Arabs, *in spite of two thousand years of contact,* still do not understand each other.

The defendant changed his plea to guilty *because the prosecutor had built up such convincing evidence against him.*

Because the prosecutor had built up such convincing evidence against him, the defendant changed his plea to guilty.

The defendant, *because the prosecutor had built up such convincing evidence against him,* changed his plea to guilty.

The bank's vice president kept juggling several customers' large deposits *to cover his own embezzlement.*

To cover his own embezzlement, the bank's vice president kept juggling several customers' large deposits.

The bank's vice president, *to cover his own embezzlement,* kept juggling several customers' large deposits.

PARTICIPIAL PHRASES

The deer, *grazing peacefully in the valley,* were unaware of the approaching hunters.

Grazing peacefully in the valley, the deer were unaware of approaching hunters.

[Being] unaware of the approaching hunters, the deer were grazing peacefully in the valley.

Gasping for air, the diver came to the surface.

The diver, *gasping for air,* came to the surface.

The diver came to the surface, *gasping for air.*

Note that in placing participial modifiers, you must be alert to the possibility of creating a misplaced modifier (see Section **12a**). Participial phrases can almost always be placed either before or after the nouns they modify. But whether they can be more widely separated will depend upon the sentence. In the example above, *gasping for air* can logically modify only *diver,* not *surface;* and since the sentence is brief, the phrase can comfortably be placed at its end. But in the previous example, if the *grazing* phrase were moved to the end of the sentence, it would modify *hunters* rather than *deer.*

Absolute phrases, since they always modify the entire sentence in which they stand, can usually be placed either at the beginning or end of a sentence or within it.

ABSOLUTE PHRASES

His hair cut close, his arms and legs tanned, his face freckled, Jonathan seemed the typical country boy in summer.

Jonathan, *his hair cut close, his arms and legs tanned, his face freckled,* seemed the typical country boy in summer.

Jonathan seemed the typical country boy in summer—*his hair cut close, his arms and legs tanned, his face freckled.*

Sarah settled back for a quiet evening, *the work day over, the bills paid, some letters written.*

The work day over, the bills paid, some letters written, Sarah settled back for a quiet evening.

Sarah, *the work day over, the bills paid, some letters written,* settled back for a quiet evening.

EXERCISE 37c In the following sentences, underline the modifier or modifiers that could be placed in a different position. Write one or if possible two revisions of each sentence. In some sentences you may have to make slight changes in wording when you change the position of the modifier.

1 The workers discovered a leak in the twelve-inch pipeline late last night, after searching for two days.

2 Examining each apple in the bin one by one, Henry chose only the ripest and the reddest ones.

3 Emily, lingering at the window of her apartment, watched the last boat sail out of the harbor.

4 The zebras, warned by the hunter's shots, stampeded across the plain.

5 Their membership expired and their credit exhausted, the four couples were in no position to argue with the club manager.

37c

6 Audrey looked around the living room one last time, her suitcases already packed and her mind firmly made up.

7 To prevent Oswald from complaining and making an unpleasant scene, Doris exchanged seats with him.

8 Ellen had decided that borrowing money was not the answer to their financial troubles, even before Susan brought up the question.

9 Although millions of dollars were expended in one eight-block area of the city's slums, living conditions changed little for most of those living there.

10 Buried for two centuries or more, valuable relics of the early inhabitants' daily life were unearthed when the new subway was constructed.

37d

37d Occasionally vary the normal subject-verb-object sentence pattern.

The subject-verb-object pattern of the basic English sentence is so strongly established that any shift in it causes unusually heavy emphasis. Sentences such as *Over the fence jumped Oscar* or *Siamese cats she adores* are rare in most modern writing. But such **inversion** is possible, and when context justifies it, it can be useful. Consider the following, for example:

> Throughout Dawson's life his great obsession had been to secure wealth, great wealth, wealth that would enable him to indulge his wildest fantasies. Such wealth he constantly dreamed of; and such wealth he was determined to get at all costs.

A more common and much less emphatic inversion occurs when the subject and verb of a sentence are reversed in a sentence opening with a long adverbial modifier, as in the following:

> Across the boulevard where a milk truck scurries to more lucrative fields lies the sea and miles of empty beach.
>
> JOHN J. ROWLAND, *Spindrift*

37e

37e Occasionally vary the types of sentences.

Except in dialogue, the overwhelming majority of sentences in writing are statements. But questions, commands, and occasionally even exclamations are sometimes useful.

Questions at the beginning of a paragraph can point its direction. The following sentence opens a paragraph in which the author argues that TV news coverage is superior to that of all but the best newspapers:

> Why do I think network TV does a better job of informing than [most] newspapers?   MARYA MANNES, "What's Wrong with the Press?"

Or a question may open a paragraph of definition.

> What is civilized man? By derivation, he is one who lives and thinks in a city. — BERNARD IDDINGS BELL

Imperative sentences are the staple sentences of writing that gives directions. But occasionally they are useful in other contexts.

> Observations indicate that the different clusters of galaxies are constantly moving apart from one another. To illustrate by a homely analogy, think of a raisin cake baking in an oven.

EXERCISE 37a–e(1) Rewrite each of the following sentences twice, using the methods suggested in this section to vary the structure.

1 We came home sullen and irritable after fighting traffic for an hour and a half.
2 The child had lost her way but was brought home by a thoughtful neighbor.
3 The coach rushed out on the field to protest the umpire's decision.
4 I knew my hangover had begun because my head ached and my mouth felt dry.
5 The upholsterer, his mouth full of tacks and his magnetic hammer swinging like a piece of machinery, stretched and fastened the chair cover with amazing speed.
6 The Surgeon General has determined that cigarette smoking is dangerous to your health, and that warning is printed on every package of cigarettes.
7 The earthquake caused much loss of life and devastation in the villages and cities of Nicaragua, and the United States quickly offered assistance.
8 Black writers have made important contributions to American literature for more than 150 years, but many educated people are still not aware of that fact.
9 They wanted to dance, and the record player was broken.
10 They bought only old furniture, which they refinished themselves, and were able to furnish their new home at relatively little cost.

EXERCISE 37a–e(2) Revise the following paragraph by introducing greater variety in sentence structure.

> Mark felt better as he slammed the front door. He did not even glance over his shoulder to see if his parents were watching him. He walked to a nearby park. He sat down on a bench. He knew why his parents had yelled at him. He didn't blame them. They had both worked hard at their restaurant to keep him in comfort. They wanted him to have the opportunities that they had missed. They wanted him to be a doctor. But he couldn't seem to concentrate at school. He wanted to sleep in class. He liked most of his teachers but he didn't

really hear them. He brought home very poor marks. He wanted to work with automobiles. He didn't want to be a doctor. The smell of gasoline, the sound of the motor, the shine of the chrome all fascinated him. He would have to face them and tell them that he couldn't be something he didn't want to be. He delayed returning home to tell them and he did not look forward to the scene they would make and the lack of understanding they would show.

REVIEW EXERCISE ON EFFECTIVE SENTENCES (Sections 34–37) Indicate what strikes you as the principal detraction from the effectiveness of each of the following sentences (faulty subordination, lack of emphasis, lack of parallelism, etc.), and then revise the sentence.

1 While Mario was still deeply in debt, he felt that the bargain was too good to let pass.
2 The children were terrified and confused and they fell exhausted on the wet leaves.
3 Robert Frost was a poet. He wrote about rural New England. He also wrote about the human condition.
4 After reading the book, I decided to change my way of life, and my plans for the future also changed.
5 The fighter was very strong and in excellent condition and he was knocked out in the fifth round.
6 Poverty still exists in the United States, and it's a shame because we are the wealthiest nation on earth, and there is no excuse for it, and it's about time we eradicated it.
7 Many countries are suffering badly from overpopulation, and India and Pakistan are but two examples.
8 Some college students regard their education as irrelevant, and not being useful.
9 After working in the Peace Corps for two years, Elizabeth returned to school after refusing several job offers.
10 He leaned back in his chair, closed his eyes, rested his hands on his lap, and sleep came to him.
11 While Chekhov was the principal support of his family, he attended medical school and wrote short stories.
12 The substitute teacher was a married man with a good sense of humor and who loved Russian ardently and conveyed this to his classes.
13 To a naughty child, a scolding parent seems like a giant standing seven feet tall with a large mouth, and having eyes that glared in the dark.
14 Our love of colonial arts and crafts is reflected in our homes and in our home magazines but our love of modern technological skills is also reflected in our homes and magazines.
15 Arizona has the largest United States Indian population and the Hopi, Navajo, and Apache are the names of the Indian tribes there.
16 To become a responsible voter you should know the issues. You should listen to the candidates. You should become familiar with their views. You should learn their weaknesses. You should also come to know their strengths. Then you can make a wise choice.
17 Rachel Carson wrote a great deal about the problems that arise when insecticide is used and she was vigorously opposed by insecticide com-

panies and some people who find insecticides helpful but what about the people who have been poisoned by them?

18 Harlem is reached by walking up Fifth Avenue, the most glamorous street in the richest city in the world, and it is infested with rats and disease.

19 Terror gripped the city of Boston when the Boston Strangler roamed free, and later a movie was made that recalled those days.

20 The space trip was an unqualified success, and the astronauts had been kept in seclusion for weeks before it to guard them against infection.

WORDS
WDS

Dictionaries are like watches; the worst is better than none, and the best cannot be expected to go quite true.

SAMUEL JOHNSON

38 THE DICTIONARY

The study of words begins with the dictionary. A good dictionary is a biography of words. It records spelling, pronunciation, word history, meaning, part of speech, and, when necessary, principal parts, or plurals, or other forms. Frequently it records the level of current usage. Very often the dictionary includes other information as well—lists of abbreviations, rules for punctuation and spelling, condensed biographical and geographical information, the pronunciation and source of many given names, and a vocabulary of rhymes. For writers and readers a dictionary is an indispensable tool.

Unabridged dictionaries

Unabridged dictionaries contain the most complete and scholarly description of English words available. The three most often referred to today are described below.

> *The Oxford English Dictionary.* 13 vols., plus supplements. New York: Oxford Univ. Press, 1933, 1972, 1977. Now also available in a photographically reduced edition of two volumes published in 1971.

Commonly referred to as the *OED,* this is the greatest dictionary of the English language. Containing over 500,000 entries, it traces the progress of each word through the language, giving dated quotations to illustrate its meaning and spelling at particular times in its history. A single word may occupy several pages. *Set,* for example, occupies twenty-three pages, and a single one of its more than 150 definitions is illustrated by thirteen quotations from writings beginning in 1056 and extending to 1893.

> *Webster's New International Dictionary of the English Language.* 3rd ed. Springfield, Mass.: G. & C. Merriam, 1976.

This is the unabridged dictionary that people who live in the United States are most likely to be familiar with. Issued originally in 1909, it was revised in 1934. The current edition, thoroughly revised, was first published in 1961. Though not as exhaustive as the *OED,* its definitions are scholarly and exact and frequently supported by illustrative quotations. Since the 1961 edition uses style labels such as *slang* infrequently and does not use the label *colloquial,* some readers continue to prefer the second edition.

Random House Dictionary of the English Language. New York: Random House, 1966.

With only 260,000 entries, the *Random House Dictionary* is considerably briefer than most unabridged dictionaries. But it is a sound and scholarly dictionary with especially up-to-date entries. It is the only entirely new unabridged dictionary to be published in recent years.

Other unabridged dictionaries of English are the *New Standard Dictionary of the English Language* and the *Dictionary of American English* (four volumes), which is made on the same plan as the *OED* and follows the history of words as they were used by American writers between 1620 and 1900.

The wide resources of an unabridged dictionary are suggested by the entry below. Since dictionaries must say much in little space, they use a great number of abbreviations and seemingly cryptic entries. You will find these troublesome unless you take time to read the explanatory pages and acquaint yourself with the symbols used. It will also be useful to follow through the sample entry below:

¹**howl** \'haùl, *esp before pause or consonant* -aùəl\ *vb* -ED/-ING/ -S [ME *houlen;* akin to MD *hūlen* to howl, MHG *hiulen, hiuweln* to howl, OHG *hūwila* owl, Gk *kōkyein* to shriek, wail, lament, Skt *kauti* he cries out] *vi* **1 :** to utter or emit a loud sustained doleful sound or outcry characteristic of dogs and wolves ⟨wolves ∼*ing* in the arctic night⟩ ⟨the only sound is a melancholy wind ∼*ing* —John Buchan⟩ **2 :** to cry out or exclaim with lack of restraint and prolonged loudness through strong impulse, feeling, or emotion ⟨the scalded men ∼*ing* in agony⟩ ⟨the hungry mob ∼*ed* about the Senate house, threatening fire and massacre —J.A.Froude⟩ ⟨proctors ∼*ing* at the blunder⟩ **3 :** to go on a spree or rampage ⟨this is my night to ∼⟩ **∼** *vt* **1 :** to utter or announce noisily with unrestrained demonstrative outcry ⟨newsboys ∼*ing* the news⟩ **2 :** to affect, effect, or drive by adverse outcry — used esp. with *down* ⟨supporters of the Administration . . . ready to ∼ down any suggestion of criticism —*Wall Street Jour.*⟩ **syn** see ROAR

²**howl** \"\ *n* -s **1 :** a loud protracted mournful rising and falling cry characteristic of a dog or a wolf **2 a :** a prolonged cry of distress **:** WAIL   **b :** a yell or outcry of disappointment, rage, or protest **3 :** PROTEST, COMPLAINT ⟨raise a ∼ over high taxes⟩ ⟨set up a ∼ that he was being cheated⟩ **4 :** something that provokes laughter ⟨his act was a ∼⟩ **5 :** a noise produced in an electronic amplifier usu. by undesired regeneration of alternating currents of audio frequency **:** OSCILLATION — called also *squeal*

By permission. From *Webster's Third New International Dictionary.* © 1981 by G. & C. Merriam Co., Publishers of the Merriam-Webster Dictionaries.

In the example, from *Webster's Third New International,* the two main entries are printed in boldface type and preceded by the superscripts ¹ and ². The first is labeled *vb* for *verb,* the second *n* for *noun.* The -ED/-ING/-S in the first entry and the -S in the second show that the endings of *howl* as verb and as noun are regular. The pronunciation is indicated between slant lines, called **reverse virgules.** For the verb, it is given as follows: \haùl or haùəl\. The note before the second pronunciation explains that it occurs especially when the word is pronounced before a pause (at the end of a sentence, for example) or before a word beginning with a consonant. Inside the front cover or in the prefatory material of the dictionary, a key shows that *au̇* is pronounced like the *ow* in *now* or the *ou* in *loud,* and that ə is a symbol representing the sound of the first and last *a* in *banana.*

The material between the brackets shows the origin or etymology of the word: *howl* comes from a word in Middle English (ME) spelled *houlen,* and is related to Middle Dutch (MD) *hūlen* and Middle High German (MHG) *hiulen* or *hiuweln,* all meaning "to howl"; to the Old High German (OHG) word *hūwila* meaning "owl"; to the Greek (Gk) *kōkyein* meaning "to wail" *or* "lament"; and to the Sanskrit (Skt) word *kauti* meaning "he cries out."

The definitions that follow are divided into various senses by bold-face numerals 1, 2, etc. The first group of these senses under ¹**howl** is preceded by the label *vi,* indicating that these are senses in which the verb is intransitive (not followed by an object). The second group of two meanings is preceded by the label *vt,* indicating that these are meanings in which the verb is transitive (followed by an object). For each sense, enclosed in angle brackets (⟨ ⟩) are quotations typical of the contexts in which the word occurs in the meaning given. These verbal illustrations become a major part of the definition itself by showing an actual context for the word. Those labeled by authors' names or by sources are actual quotations; those not so labeled are typical phrases offered by the dictionary editors. Under meaning 2 as a transitive verb, a usage note states that in this meaning *howl* is used especially with *down* in the phrase *howl down.* A swung dash (∼) replaces the word itself in all such illustrations of the word. The final information, after **syn,** means that in the entry for *roar* is a discussion of the synonyms of *howl.* (See pp. 353–356 for illustration and discussion.)

In the second boldface entry, ²**howl,** the pattern is repeated for the senses in which *howl* occurs as a noun. Since no separate pronunciation or etymology is given, each of these is the same as for the verb. Under *a* and *b* of meaning 2, two different but related senses of that meaning are given. The words in small capitals (WAIL in meaning 2, PROTEST and COMPLAINT in meaning 3, and OSCILLATION in meaning 5) are the other main entries where further related definitions are given.

You can see something of the ways in which dictionaries must change if they are to be contemporary by comparing with the foregoing entry the following entry for the noun *howl* from the second edition, first issued in 1934.

howl, *n.* **1.** The loud, protracted, mournful cry of a dog or a wolf, or other like sound.
2. A prolonged cry of distress; a wail; also, a wild yell of disappointment, rage, or the like; as, *howls* of derision.

As you can see at a glance, the two meanings offered here are very close to those numbered 1 and 2 in the *Third New International.* But meanings 3, 4, and 5 listed in the *Third International* are all missing. They developed after the second edition was compiled.

Desk dictionaries

Although occasionally you may wish or need to refer to an unabridged dictionary in the library, particularly if you are reading older literature or older writing in other fields, a good abridged, or desk, dictionary will ordinarily serve all your needs in daily reading and writing. Although the five desk dictionaries briefly described below differ in important ways, they all contain 150,000 or more entries, provide careful etymologies and basic grammatical information about each entry, and specify distinctions among synonyms. All but *Webster's Collegiate* provide helpful style or usage labels.

1 *Webster's New Collegiate Dictionary.* **8th ed. Springfield, Mass.: G. & C. Merriam Co., 1981.** Based upon the *Third New International,* this desk dictionary profits from its extensive scholarship. The order of definitions under any one word is historical. It has relatively full etymologies, a wide range of synonymies, and full prefatory material. Abbreviations, biographical names, and place names are listed separately at the end of the dictionary. Some users find inconvenient the lack of the label *colloquial* or its equivalent, *informal,* and sparse use of the label *slang.*

> **howl** \\'haủ(ə)l\\ *vb* [ME *houlen;* akin to MHG *hiulen* to howl, Gk *kōkyein* to shriek] *vi* **1 :** to emit a loud sustained doleful sound characteristic of dogs **2 :** to cry loudly and without restraint under strong impulse (as pain or grief) **3 :** to go on a spree or rampage ~ *vt* **1 :** to utter with unrestrained outcry **2 :** to affect, effect, or drive by adverse outcry — used esp. with *down* <~ *ed* down the speaker> — **howl** *n*

2 *Webster's New World Dictionary.* **2nd college ed. New York: Simon & Schuster Inc., 1981.** This dictionary emphasizes simplified definitions even of technical terms and includes a large number of words and phrases that are relatively informal. Usage labels are generously used. Synonymies and etymologies are full and thorough. Common meanings are placed first in the definitions. All words are contained in the main alphabetical list. Identification of Americanisms and attention to the origin of American place names are special features.

howl (houl) *vi.* [ME. *hulen*, akin to G. *heulen* < IE. echoic base *kāu-*, whence Sans. *kāuti*, (it) cries, OHG. *hūwila*, owl] **1.** to utter the long, loud, wailing cry of wolves, dogs, etc. **2.** to utter a similar cry of pain, anger, grief, etc. **3.** to make a sound like this [a *howling* wind] **4.** to shout or laugh in scorn, mirth, etc. —*vt.* **1.** to utter with a howl or howls **2.** to drive or effect by howling —*n.* **1.** a long, loud, wailing cry of a wolf, dog, etc. **2.** any similar sound **3.** [Colloq.] something hilarious; joke —**howl down** to drown out with shouts of scorn, anger, etc. —**one's night to howl** one's time for unrestrained pleasure

With permission. From *Webster's New World Dictionary,* Second College Edition. Copyright © 1981 by Simon & Schuster, Inc.

3 *The American Heritage Dictionary of the English Language.* **New York: American Heritage Publishing Company, Inc.; Boston: Houghton Mifflin Company, 1981.** The distinguishing features of this dictionary are its generous illustrations and its usage notes based upon a consensus of a panel of some 100 writers, editors, poets, and public speakers. Definitions are arranged in this order: the initial definition offers what the editors judge to be the central meaning, and it serves as the base for the arrangement of other senses of the word. Synonymies are generous; etymologies are made somewhat more readable by avoidance of all abbreviations. The single alphabetical listing incorporates abbreviations and biographical and geographical entries. An appendix of Indo-European roots is a special feature.

howl (houl) *v.* **howled, howling, howls.** —*intr.* **1.** To utter or emit a long, mournful, plaintive sound characteristic of wolves or dogs. **2.** To cry or wail loudly and uncontrollably in pain, sorrow, or anger. **3.** *Slang.* **a.** To laugh uproariously. **b.** To go on a carousal or spree. —*tr.* **1.** To express or utter with a howl or howls. **2.** To effect, drive, or force by or as if by howling. —*n.* **1.** The sound of one that howls. **2.** *Slang.* Something uproariously funny or absurd. [Middle English *houlen, howlen,* perhaps from Middle Dutch *hūlen.* See **ul-** in Appendix.*]

© 1981, Houghton Mifflin Company. Reprinted by permission from *The American Heritage Dictionary of the English Language.*

4 *The Random House Dictionary of the English Language.* **College ed. New York: Random House, 1980.** This dictionary is based on the unabridged *Random House Dictionary of the English Language.* Definitions are arranged with the most common given first; recent technical words receive careful attention. A single alphabetical listing incorporates all biographical and geographical as well as other entries. Among its prefaces, that by Raven I. McDavid, Jr., on usage, dialects, and functional varieties of English, is a particularly valuable summary.

howl (houl), *v.i.* **1.** to utter a loud, prolonged, mournful cry, as that of a dog or wolf. **2.** to utter a similar cry in distress, pain, rage, etc.; wail. **3.** to make a sound like an animal howling: *The wind howls through the trees.* **4.** *Informal.* to laugh loudly. —*v.t.* **5.** to utter with howls. **6.** to drive or force by howls (often fol. by *down*): *to howl down the opposition.* —*n.* **7.** the cry of a dog, wolf, etc. **8.** a cry or wail, as of pain, rage, protest, etc. **9.** a sound like wailing: *the howl of the wind.* **10.** a loud, scornful laugh or yell. **11.** something that causes a laugh or a scornful yell, as a joke or funny or embarrassing situation. [ME *hul(en),* D *huilen,* G *heulen,* LG *hülen,* Dan *hyle;* with loss of *h,* Icel *ȳla*]

From *The Random House College Dictionary,* Revised Edition. Copyright © 1980, 1979, and 1975 by Random House, Inc. Reprinted by permission.

5 *Funk & Wagnalls Standard College Dictionary.* **New York: Funk & Wagnalls, 1977.** The reliability of this dictionary is insured by an impressive advisory board, many members of which are leading linguists. It is marked by a convenient type size, by relatively simple and natural definitions, and by particular attention to usage labels for words termed *informal* (which replaces the term *colloquial)* and *slang.* Material on usage is incorporated in some 260 notes. Common meanings are placed first in each entry. The *Standard* runs biographical names and place names into the main body of the dictionary rather than listing them separately. Introductory material in the text edition includes valuable summaries of the history of the language, English grammar, and regional variations in American pronunciation.

howl (houl) *v.i.* **1.** To utter the loud, mournful wail of a dog, wolf, or other animal. **2.** To utter such a cry in pain, grief, or rage. **3.** To make a sound similar to this: The storm *howled* all night. **4.** To laugh loudly: The audience *howled.* — *v.t.* **5.** To utter or express with howling: to *howl* one's disapproval. **6.** To condemn, suppress, or drive away by howling: often with *down.* — *n.* **1.** The wailing cry of a wolf, dog, or other animal. **2.** Any howling sound. [ME *houlen.* Cf. G *heulen.*]

From *Funk & Wagnalls Standard College Dictionary.* Copyright © 1977 by Harper & Row Publishers, Inc. Reprinted by permission of the publisher.

The uses of a dictionary

1 Spelling. The spelling entry of a word in the dictionary uses centered dots between syllables, showing how to separate it properly at the ends of lines (see "Syllabication," Section **18**). It also gives the proper spelling of compound words—properness depending on whether the editors found them more often written as two single words *(half brother),* as a hyphenated compound *(quarter-hour),* or as one word *(drugstore).* Dictionaries also indicate foreign words that require italics (in manuscript, underlining). The *American Heritage* and the *Standard* label such words or phrases as Latin, German, etc.; *Webster's New World* uses a double dagger (‡). *The Random House Dictionary* indicates such words by printing the main entry word in boldface italic type. All dictionaries also indicate whether a word is always or usually capitalized in a particular meaning.

All modern dictionaries list variant spellings of many words, though not all by any means list the same variants or give the same comments about them. For example, all five list *centre* and *theatre* as well as the more common *center* and *theater*. But while *centre* is cited as the British spelling by all, only *Random House* and the *Standard* cite *theatre* as British; the other three leave it unqualified. And all five dictionaries list *licence* as a variant spelling of *license,* but whereas *Webster's Collegiate* and *Random House* have no qualifying note, all others cite *licence* as British. The spelling *knowledgeable* is the first entry in all five dictionaries, but only *Random House* lists the variant spelling *knowledgable.*

Such variation among dictionaries is common, and you must be careful to examine the explanatory material at the front of a dictionary to know exactly what policy is followed. Frequently, though by no means always, if variant spellings are listed, the first will be somewhat more common; the most carefully edited dictionaries sometimes adopt some means of indicating that this is so. *Webster's New Collegiate,* for example, indicates that two variants are equally common by joining them with *or (caddie* or *caddy)* but joins variants the second of which is less common by *also (woolly* also *wooly).* In general, if there is a question about spelling, choose the first listed variant unless there is a special reason for choosing the second.

Whatever dictionary you choose, it will be your authority on all questions of spelling. Refer to it whenever you have any doubt about a correct spelling.

EXERCISE 38(1)   Give the preferred spelling of each word.

aesthetic	enclose	liquorice
catalogue	favour	modeled
catsup	judgement	Shakspere

EXERCISE 38(2)   Rewrite the following compounds, showing which should be written as they are, which hyphenated, and which written as two or more separate words.

castoff	jazzmen	uptodate
easygoing	passkey	wellmarked
horserace	showdown	worldwide

EXERCISE 38(3)   Copy the following foreign words, underlining those that require italics and supplying accents where needed.

bon voyage	dramatis personae	resume
coup d'etat	matinee	sine qua non
creche	nouveau riche	Weltschmertz

2 Pronunciation. Dictionaries indicate the pronunciation of words by respelling them with special symbols and letters. Explanation of the symbols is given either at the bottom of the page on which the entry appears or in the prefatory pages or both.

Dictionaries show frequently occurring variant pronunciations as they do variant spellings. In the sample entry from *Webster's Third New International,* for example, you can see that an unabridged dictionary may even show variant pronunciations for such a simple word as *howl.* Again, as with variant spellings, though the first listed is sometimes said to be "preferred," the statements about pronunciation in most carefully edited modern dictionaries do not bear this out. Usually, unless there is a limiting label or comment attached to one or more variants, they are all equally "correct." Your preference should be determined by the pronunciation you hear in the conversation around you.

EXERCISE 38(4) What is the pronunciation of the following words? If usage is divided for any, which pronunciation seems more acceptable to you? Why? Copy the dictionary pronunciation for each.

adult	exquisite	impotent
cerebral	formidable	mischievous
despicable	greasy	route

3 Etymology. The **etymology** of a word—that is, origin and derivation—often helps clarify its present meaning and spelling. Because the course of history changes, restricts, or extends the meanings of words, however, many original meanings have been lost completely. *Presently,* for example, formerly meant *at once, immediately;* it now usually means *shortly, in a little while.*

EXERCISE 38(5) Trace the etymology ᶠ each of the following:

assassin	familiar	neighbor	shirt
bedlam	fedora	organization	skirt
draggle	lampoon	sandwich	squelch

EXERCISE 38(6) From what specific na ıes have the following words been derived?

ampere	gardenia	shrapnel
boycott	macadam	ulster
chauvinism	quisling	watt

EXERCISE 38(7) From what language did each of the following words come?

almanac	dory	jute	mukluk	trek
cherub	goulash	kerosene	piano	tulip
cockatoo	huckster	moccasin	squadron	typhoon

4 Meaning. Strictly speaking, dictionaries do not *define* words; they record the meaning or meanings that actual usage, past and present, has attached to words. When more than one meaning is recorded for a single word, *Webster's Collegiate* lists them in order of historical use. Most other dictionaries list the more general and present meaning first. Special and technical meanings are clearly labeled. Choosing the appropriate meaning out of the many offered is not difficult if you read them *all* and understand their order of arrangement as indicated in the prefatory pages of the dictionary.

EXERCISE 38(8) How many different meanings can you find for each of the following words?

call	land	run
get	light	set
go	out	turn

EXERCISE 38(9) Trace the changes in meaning that have taken place in each of the following words:

bounty	gossip	machine
complexion	humor	manufacture
engine	intern	sincere
fond	knave	starve
generous	lozenge	virtue

5 Synonyms and antonyms. A **synonym** is a word having the same or almost the same general meaning as the vocabulary entry. An **antonym** is a word having approximately the opposite meaning. In dictionaries, for practical reasons, not all entries show synonyms and antonyms. Well-edited desk dictionaries include paragraph-length discussions of groups of synonyms, defining the different shades of meaning associated with each member of the group. These discussions are located usually at the end of certain entries and cross-referenced at related entries. (For full illustration of synonym entries from various dictionaries, see pp. 354–356.)

6 Grammar. Dictionaries give a good deal of grammatical information about a word. All dictionaries indicate the part of speech to which each word belongs. If a particular word can serve as more than one part of speech, most dictionaries include all its functions and meaning under a single entry, grouping the meanings separately for each function. Thus under the entry for *minor, Webster's New World* and *American Heritage* list its meanings first as an adjective *(adj)*, then as a noun *(n)*, and last as an intransitive verb *(vi* or *intran)*. *Webster's Collegiate,* however, has a separate entry for each part of speech.

Dictionaries also list the inflected forms of words if they are irregular in any way or if they might cause spelling problems. Thus in the entry for the verb *drink,* all dictionaries list the irregular past tense *drank* and past participle *drunk.* Similarly, dictionaries list irregular plural forms of nouns, as in *child, children,* or *alumna, alumnae.* Usually the principal parts of verbs, noun plurals, and the comparative and superlative forms of adjectives are not given if they are formed regularly. Thus verbs that form both their past tense and their past participles by adding *-ed (walk, walked)* are not given unless they raise a spelling question, as in *travel, traveled, traveling* or *travelled, -lling.* Similarly, plurals ending in *-s* or *-es (cats, dishes)* are often not given. And comparatives and superlatives formed by adding *more, most,* or *less, least,* or *-er, -est* are not given unless the addition of the *-er, -est* endings presents a spelling difficulty *(heavy, heavier, heaviest).*

EXERCISE 38(10)   What are the past tense and the present participle of each of these verbs?

broadcast	get	set
focus	lend	teach
dive	shrink	wake

EXERCISE 38(11)   What is the plural (or plurals) of each of the following?

alumnus	crisis	index
bear	daisy	madame
court-martial	fish	stratum

EXERCISE 38(12)   Write the comparative and superlative forms of each of the following:

bad	lengthy	red
ill	much	shyly
little	often	well

7   Labels. Dictionaries label words or particular meanings of words to indicate that they are in some way restricted. Words and meanings not so labeled are appropriate for general use. Although the particular labels dictionaries use vary somewhat, all labels can be divided into four general categories: *geographic* labels, *time* labels, *occupational* or *subject* labels, and *usage* or *style* labels.

   Geographic labels indicate that the word or meaning so labeled is limited to a particular area. Typical labels of this sort are *British, Australian, New England, Southern U.S.,* and the like. Thus *Webster's Collegiate* labels *lift,* in the meaning of *elevator, British,* and *outbye,* meaning *a short distance away, Scottish. Webster's New World* labels *corn pone,* a kind of corn bread, *Southern U.S.* The label *dialectal* or *regional* usually suggests a specialized local or provincial word, often traditional. Thus *larrap,* meaning a *blow* or *to flog,* is labeled *dialectal* by *Webster's Collegiate* and *regional* by *American Heritage.*

Time labels indicate that the labeled word has passed out of use entirely or no longer occurs in ordinary contexts. *Obsolete* means that a word has passed out of use entirely, as *absume* and *enwheel*, words that have not been used for two hundred years. *Archaic* means that the labeled word or meaning is no longer generally used although it may still be seen occasionally in older writing, as *belike*, meaning "probably," or *outland*, meaning "a foreign land."

Subject labels indicate that a word or a particular meaning belongs to a special field such as law, medicine, baseball, finance, mathematics, or psychology. Thus *Webster's New World* identifies *projection* as a psychiatric term *(Psychiatry)* when used to mean the process of assigning one's own undesirable impulses to others and as a photographic term *(Photog.)* when used to mean projecting an image on a screen. *American Heritage* labels as *law* the meaning of *domain* in the sense of ownership and rights of disposal of property.

Style labels indicate that a word or meaning is restricted to a particular level of usage. Typical style labels are *slang, colloquial, informal, nonstandard, substandard, illiterate,* and *vulgar.* Variations among dictionaries are greatest in their choice of labels and in the words and meanings to which they apply them. Nonetheless, there is broad agreement on the meanings of the labels themselves.

Slang indicates that a word, though widely used, has not yet been accepted in the general vocabulary. Slang terms and meanings often are used humorously; are likely to be short-lived, limited to a particular group of people; and are used almost entirely in speech rather than writing. Typical examples are *hangup* (a fixation, an intense preoccupation), *shades* (sunglasses), *snow* (cocaine or heroin), and *megabuck* (a million dollars). Of the dictionaries described, *Webster's Collegiate* is by far the most sparing in its use of the label, allowing many entries labeled *slang* by others to pass without any label.

Colloquial and informal are almost synonymous terms. They both indicate that a word is characteristic of speech or of quite informal, rather than more formal, writing. The *Standard* and the *American Heritage* use the label *informal; Webster's New World* uses *colloquial. Webster's Collegiate* uses neither label and thus may be less useful for those who need to determine how appropriate a word is for a particular writing context. *Webster's New World*, for example, says *fizzle* is colloquial, the *Standard* says it is informal, and *Webster's Collegiate* gives it no label.

Illiterate, substandard, and some other similar terms are labels indicating that a word is limited to uneducated speech, as *drownded* for the past tense of *drown.* Though dictionaries vary somewhat in the particular labels they use (the *Standard* uses *illiterate* to mean about the same thing as *Webster's substandard,* for example), their agreement in classifying a word as being limited to uneducated speech is much greater than their agreement in labeling a word *slang, colloquial,* and so on.

To use your dictionary wisely as a guide to usage, you will have to examine the explanatory notes in it carefully to determine exactly what labels are applied and how they are interpreted by the editors.

EXERCISE 38(13) Which of the following are standard English, which colloquial or informal, and which slang, according to your dictionary? If possible, check more than one dictionary to determine if they agree.

corny	goof	moll
cool	hipster	snollygoster
flap	jerk	wise-up
foul-up	kibitzer	yak

EXERCISE 38(14) In what areas of the world would you be likely to hear the following?

billabong	hoecake	potlatch
chuckwagon	laager	pukka
coulee	petrol	sharpie

EXERCISE 38(15) The following questions are designed to test your ability to use the whole dictionary, not only its vocabulary entries, but also its various appendices. Any of the desk dictionaries discussed in this section will help you find the answers. Look up the meanings of *etymology, homonym, antonym, syllabication,* and *synonym,* if necessary, before answering the questions.

1 What is the etymology of the word *precise?*
2 What are two homonyms for the word *reign?*
3 What are some antonyms for the word *concise?*
4 What is the syllabication of the word *redundant?*
5 What are some synonyms for the adjective *correct?*
6 Give the meanings of these abbreviations: *syn., v. mus., R.C.Ch.*
7 What do the following phrases mean: *finem respice, ars longa vita brevis, de profundis, honi soit qui mal y pense?*
8 What is the population of Birmingham, Michigan?
9 Who was the oldest of the Brontë sisters?
10 From what language does the proper name *Nahum* come?

Special dictionaries

General dictionaries bring together in a single reference all of the information you ordinarily need about a word. Special dictionaries, because they limit their attention to a single kind of information about words or to a single category of words, can give more complete information. Thus a dictionary of slang can devote an entire page to the word *hip,* in contrast to the general dictionary, which can afford no more than four or five lines. Similarly, dictionaries of usage and of synonyms can provide much more complete information of a particular kind than space allows in general dictionaries. Such dictionaries are no substitute for the daily usefulness of a good desk dictionary, but they are extremely useful supplements.

When you need specialized information about words, check one of the following dictionaries:*

Bernstein, Stuart M. *The Careful Writer: A Modern Guide to Usage.* New York: Atheneum, 1977.

Fowler, H. W. *Dictionary of Modern English Usage.* 2nd ed. Rev. and ed. Sir Ernest Gowers. London: Oxford Univ. Press, 1965.

Partridge, Eric. *Origins: A Short Etymological Dictionary of Modern English.* 4th ed. New York: MacMillan, 1966.

Webster's New Dictionary of Synonyms. Springfield, Mass: G. & C. Merriam, 1973.

Wentworth, Harold, and Stuart Berg Flexner. *Dictionary of American Slang.* 2nd supp. ed. New York: Crowell, 1975.

The difference between the right word and the almost-right word is the difference between lightning and the lightning bug.

Attributed to MARK TWAIN

39 VOCABULARY

The English language contains well over a million words. Of these, about two-fifths belong almost exclusively to special fields: e.g., zoology, electronics, psychiatry. Of the remaining, the large dictionaries list about 500,000, the desk dictionaries about 150,000. Such wealth is both a blessing and a curse. On the one hand, many English words are loosely synonymous, sometimes interchangeable, as in *buy* a book or *purchase* a book. On the other hand, the distinctions between synonyms are fully as important as their similarities. For example, a family may be said to be living in *poverty,* or in *penury,* or in *want,* or in *destitution.* All these words are loosely synonymous, but only one will describe the family exactly as you see it and wish your reader to see it. In short, as a writer of English you must use words carefully.

Passive and active vocabulary

In a sense, you have two vocabularies: a **passive,** or **recognition, vocabulary,** which is made up of the words you recognize in the context of reading matter but do not actually use yourself; and an **active** vocabulary, which consists of "working" words—those you use daily in

*See also the lists of reference books in "The Library," Section **45**.

your own writing and speaking. In the passage below, the meaning of the italicized words is fairly clear, or can at least be guessed at, from the context. But how many belong in your *active* vocabulary?

> Has it been duly marked by historians that the late William Jennings Bryan's last *secular* act on this globe of sin was to catch flies? A curious detail, and not without its *sardonic overtones.* He was the most *sedulous* flycatcher in American history, and in many ways the most successful. His *quarry,* of course, was not *Musca domestica* but *Homo neandertalensis.* For forty years he tracked it with coo and bellow, up and down the *rustic* backways of the Republic. Wherever the *flambeau* of Chautauqua smoked and guttered, and the bilge of idealism ran in the veins, the Baptist pastors damned the brooks with the *sanctified,* and men gathered who were weary and heavy laden, and their wives who were full of Peruna and as *fecund* as the shad (*Alosa sapidissima*)—there the *indefatigable* Jennings set up his traps and spread his bait.
>
> H. L. MENCKEN, *Selected Prejudices*

Increasing your vocabulary

There are no shortcuts to word power. A good vocabulary is the product of years of serious reading, of listening to intelligent talk, and of seeking to speak and write forcefully and clearly. All this does not mean that devices and methods for building up your vocabulary are useless. But it does mean that acquiring a good vocabulary is inseparable from acquiring an education.

1 Increasing your recognition vocabulary. English has many words based on a common root form, to which different prefixes or suffixes have been added. The root form *spec-,* for example, from the Latin *specere (to look),* appears in *specter, inspection, perspective, aspect, introspection, circumspect, specimen, spectator.* Knowing the common prefixes and suffixes will help you detect the meaning of many words whose roots are familiar.

Prefixes

Prefix	*Meaning*	*Example*
ab-	away from	absent
ad-*	to *or* for	adverb
com-*	with	combine
de-	down, away from, *or* undoing	degrade, depart, dehumanize
dis-*	separation *or* reversal	disparate, disappoint
ex-*	out of *or* former	extend, ex-president
in-*	in *or* on	input
in-*	not	inhuman

Prefix	Meaning	Example
mis-	wrong	mistake
non-	not	non-Christian, nonsense
ob-*	against	obtuse
pre-	before	prevent
pro-	for *or* forward	proceed
re-	back *or* again	repeat
sub-*	under	subcommittee
trans-	across	transcribe
un-	not	unclean

EXERCISE 39(1) Write words denoting *negation* from the following.

EXAMPLE   movable—able to be moved

immovable—*not* able to be moved

accuracy	conformity	mutable
adorned	distinctive	rational
agreeable	explicable	workable

EXERCISE 39(2) Write words denoting *reversal* from the following.

EXAMPLE   accelerate—to move at increasing speed

decelerate—to move at decreasing speed

increase—to grow larger

decrease—to grow smaller

centralize	integrate	please
do	magnetize	qualify
inherit	persuade	ravel

Suffixes. These fall into three groups: noun suffixes, verb suffixes, adjectival suffixes.

Noun suffixes denoting *act of, state of, quality of* include the following:

Suffix	Example	Meaning
-dom	freedom	*state of* being free
-hood	manhood	*state of* being a man
-ness	dimness	*state of* being dim
-ice	cowardice	*quality of* being a coward
-ation	flirtation	*act of* flirting

*The spelling of these prefixes varies, usually to make pronunciation easier. *Ad* becomes *ac* in *accuse,* *ag* in *aggregate,* *at* in *attack.* Similarly, the final consonant in the other prefixes is assimilated by the initial letter of the root word: *colleague (com + league); illicit (in + licit); offend (ob + fend); succeed (sub + ceed).*

Suffix	Example	Meaning
-ion	intercession	*act of* interceding
-sion	scansion	*act of* scanning
-tion	corruption	*state of* being corrupt
-ment	argument	*act of* arguing
-ship	friendship	*state of* being friends
-ance	continuance	*act of* continuing
-ence	precedence	*act of* preceding
-ancy	flippancy	*state of* being flippant
-ency	currency	*state of* being current
-ism	baptism	*act of* baptizing
-ery	bravery	*quality of* being brave

Noun suffixes denoting *doer, one who* include the following:

Suffix	Example	Meaning
-eer (general)	auctioneer	*one who* auctions
-ist	fascist	*one who* believes in fascism
-or	debtor	*one who* is in debt
-er	worker	*one who* works

Verb suffixes denoting *to make* or *to perform the act of* include the following:

Suffix	Example	Meaning
-ate	perpetuate	*to make* perpetual
-en	soften	*to make* soft
-fy	dignify	*to make* dignified
-ize, -ise	sterilize	*to make* sterile

Adjectival suffixes include the following:

Suffix	Meaning	Example
-ful	full of	hateful
-ish	resembling	foolish
-ate	having	affectionate
-ic, -ical	resembling	angelic
-ive	having	prospective
-ous	full of	zealous
-ulent	full of	fraudulent
-less	without	fatherless
-able, -ible	capable of	peaceable
-ed	having	spirited
-ly	resembling	womanly
-like	resembling	childlike

EXERCISE 39(3) Write words indicating *act of, state of,* or *quality of* from the following words.

advance	deny	promote
calculate	helpless	rebel
disappear	judge	statesman

EXERCISE 39(4) Write nouns indicating *doer* from the following.

advise	communicate	profit
boast	disturb	sail
command	preach	save

EXERCISE 39(5) Write verbs indicating *to make* or *to perform the act of* from the following nouns and adjectives.

beauty	idol	moral
black	liquid	peace
captive	modern	victim

EXERCISE 39(6) Make adjectives of the following words by adding a suffix.

humor	rest	thwart
irony	speed	wasp
mule	talk	whimsey

Combining forms. Linguists refer to the following as **bound forms;** they appear generally, but not always, as prefixes:

Combining Form	Meaning	Example
anthropo	man	*anthropo*logy
arch	rule	*arch*duke, mon*arch*
auto	self	*auto*mobile
bene	well	*bene*ficial
eu	well	*eu*logy
graph	writing	*graph*ic, bio*graphy*
log, logue	word, speech	mono*logue*
magni	great	*magni*ficent
mal	bad	*mal*ady
mono	one	*mono*tone
multi	many	*multi*plication
neo	new	*neo*-classic
omni	all	*omni*bus
pan, pant	all	*pan*hellenic
philo	loving	*philo*sophy
phono	sound	*phono*graph
poly	many	*poly*gamy
pseudo	false	*pseudo*nym
semi	half	*semi*formal

2 Increasing your active vocabulary. Another way to increase word power is to keep transferring words from your recognition vocabulary to your active vocabulary. Make a conscious effort to introduce at least one new word a day into your active vocabulary. At the same time, be alert to opportunities for increasing your recognition vocabulary. A good system is to enter each new word on a small card: write the word on one side, the definition and a sentence illustrating its correct use on the other. Then you can quickly test yourself on the meaning of all the new words you collect.

EXERCISE 39(7) Define each of the following words and use it correctly in a sentence.

compatible	malign	estrangement
demagogue	unscrupulous	promiscuous
intimidate	officious	euphoria
disparage	facetious	corpulent
ostentatious	incentive	transcend
altruistic	ambiguous	pompous
taciturn	pragmatic	finite

3 Strengthening your active vocabulary. Are you sure that *enthusiast, fanatic, zealot,* and *bigot* mean what you think they mean? You know that *deadly, mortal,* and *fatal* are very much alike in meaning—but do you know the exact distinctions among them? All the desk dictionaries listed in Section 38 group synonyms and point out their differences. Unabridged dictionaries carry quite exhaustive discussions of synonyms. The Merriam-Webster *New Dictionary of Synonyms* is devoted exclusively to the grouping and differentiating of synonyms. The various editions of Roget's *Thesaurus* are valuable for the long lists of closely related words they provide, though they must be used cautiously because they give no discussion of distinctions in meaning and offer no guiding examples.

One of the most valuable ways to strengthen your vocabulary is to cultivate the habit of studying dictionary discussions of synonyms. The following examples will give you an idea of the extent to which various dictionaries explore synonyms. The numerals in synonym entries refer to numbered meanings in the definition part of a main entry. For example, "**4.** alleviate, cure, heal" in the *Random House* example means that *alleviate, cure,* and *heal* are all synonyms for *help* when it is used in the sense numbered **4** in the definition part of the main entry. Similarly, *afflict* is an **antonym,** or opposite, for this fourth defined sense of *help.*

From the *Random House,* for *help:*

—**Syn. 1.** encourage, befriend; support, uphold, back, abet.
HELP, AID, ASSIST, SUCCOR agree in the idea of furnishing
another with something needed, esp. when the need comes
at a particular time. HELP implies furnishing anything that
furthers another's efforts or relieves his wants or necessities.
AID and ASSIST, somewhat more formal, imply esp. a fur-
thering or seconding of another's efforts. AID implies a more
active helping; ASSIST implies less need and less help. To
SUCCOR, still more formal and literary, is to give timely help
and relief in difficulty or distress: *Succor him in his hour of
need.* **4.** alleviate, cure, heal. **10.** support, backing. —**Ant.**
4. afflict. **8.** hinder.

From *Webster's Third,* for *howl:*

syn HOWL, ULULATE, BELLOW, BAWL, BLUSTER, CLAMOR,
VOCIFERATE: ROAR suggests the full loud reverberating sound
made by lions or the booming sea or by persons in rage or
boisterous merriment ⟨far away guns *roar* —Virginia Woolf⟩
⟨the harsh north wind ... *roared* in the piazzas —Osbert
Sitwell⟩ ⟨*roared* the blacksmith, his face black with rage
—T.B.Costain⟩ HOWL indicates a higher, less reverberant
sound often suggesting the doleful or agonized or the sounds
of unrestrained laughter ⟨frequent *howling* of jackals and
hyenas —James Stevenson-Hamilton⟩ ⟨how the wind does
howl —J.C.Powys⟩ ⟨*roared* at his subject ... howled at ...
inconsistencies —Martin Gardner⟩ ULULATE is a literary
synonym for HOWL but may suggest mournful protraction and
rhythmical delivery ⟨an *ululating* baritone mushy with
pumped-up pity —E.B.White⟩ BELLOW suggests the loud,
abrupt, hollow sound made typically by bulls or any similar
loud, reverberating sound ⟨most of them were drunk. They
went *bellowing* through the town —Kenneth Roberts⟩ BAWL
suggests a somewhat lighter, less reverberant, unmodulated
sound made typically by calves ⟨a woman *bawling* abuse from
the door of an inn —C.E.Montague⟩ ⟨the old judge was in the
hall *bawling* hasty orders —Sheridan Le Fanu⟩ BLUSTER suggests the turbulent noisiness of gusts of wind; it often suggests
swaggering and noisy threats or protests ⟨expressed her
opinion gently but firmly, while he *blustered* for a time and
then gave in —Sherwood Anderson⟩ ⟨swagger and *bluster* and
take the limelight —Margaret Mead⟩ CLAMOR suggests sustained, mixed and confused noisy outcry as from a number
of agitated persons ⟨half-starved men and women *clamoring*
for food —Kenneth Roberts⟩ ⟨easy ... for critics ... to
clamor for action —Sir Winston Churchill⟩ VOCIFERATE suggests loud vehement insistence in speaking ⟨was not willing to
break off his talk; so he continued to *vociferate* his remarks
—James Boswell⟩

From *Webster's New Collegiate,* for *wit:*

syn WIT, HUMOR, IRONY, SARCASM, SATIRE, REPARTEE *shared meaning element* : a mode of expression intended to arouse amused interest or evoke attention and laughter or a quality of mind that predisposes to such expression. WIT suggests the power to evoke laughing attention by remarks showing verbal felicity or ingenuity and swift perception, especially of the incongruous <true *wit* is nature to advantage dressed, what oft was thought, but ne'er so well expressed —Alexander Pope> HUMOR implies an ability to perceive and effectively express the ludicrous, the comical, or the absurd, especially in human life <the modern sense of *humor* is the quiet enjoyment and implicit expression of the fun of things —Louis Cazamian> IRONY applies to a manner of presentation in which an intended meaning is subtly emphasized by appropriate expression of its opposite <*irony* properly suggests the opposite of what is explicitly stated, by means of peripheral clues — tone of voice, accompanying gestures, stylistic exaggeration . . . thus, for "Brutus is an honorable man" we understand "Brutus is a traitor" —Jacob Brackman> SARCASM applies to savagely humorous expression, frequently in the form of irony, intended to cut and wound <the arrows of *sarcasm* are barbed with contempt —Washington Gladden> SATIRE applies primarily to writing that holds up vices or follies to ridicule and reprobation often by use of irony or caricature <his dry wit and his easy, good-natured *satire* on the follies of the day —Eleanor M. Sickels> REPARTEE applies to the power or art of responding quickly, smoothly, pointedly, and wittily or to an interchange of such response <as for *repartee* . . . , as it is the very soul of conversation, so it is the greatest grace of comedy —John Dryden>

From *Webster's New World,* for *destroy:*

SYN.—destroy implies a tearing down or bringing to an end by wrecking, ruining, killing, eradicating, etc. and is the term of broadest application here *[to destroy* a city, one's influence, etc.*];* **demolish** implies such destructive force as to completely smash to pieces *[the bombs demolished the factories];* **raze** means to level to the ground, either destructively or by systematic wrecking with a salvaging of useful parts; to **annihilate** is to destroy so completely as to blot out of existence *[rights that cannot be annihilated]*

From *Funk & Wagnalls Standard,* for *speech:*

—Syn. 4. *Speech, address, talk, oration, harangue, lecture, discourse, sermon,* and *homily* denote something said to an audience. Any public speaking may be called a *speech.* An *address* is a formal *speech,* as on a ceremonial occasion. *Talk,* on the other hand, suggests informality. An *oration* is an eloquent *address* that appeals to the emotions, while a *harangue* is a vehement *speech,* appealing to the emotions and often intended to spur the audience to action of some sort. A *lecture* is directed to the listener's intellect; it gives information, explanation, or counsel. Any carefully prepared *speech* or writing is a *discourse. Sermon* and *homily* are concerned with religious instruction; a *sermon* is usually an interpretation of Scripture, and a *homily* gives ethical guidance.

From the *American Heritage,* for *curious:*

> **Synonyms:** *curious, inquisitive, snoopy, nosy, intrusive.* These adjectives apply to persons who show a marked desire for information or knowledge. *Curious* more often implies a legitimate desire to enlarge one's knowledge, but can suggest a less commendable urge to concern oneself in others' affairs. *Inquisitive* frequently suggests excessive curiosity and the asking of many questions. *Snoopy* implies an unworthy motive and underhandedness in implementing it. *Nosy* suggests excessive curiosity and impertinence in an adult; applied to a child, it may refer less unfavorably to habitual curiosity. *Intrusive* stresses unwarranted and unwelcome concern with another's affairs.

© 1981, Houghton Mifflin Company. Reprinted by permission from *The American Heritage Dictionary of the English Language.*

EXERCISE 39(8)   Indicate the distinctions in meaning among the words in each of the following groups.

1 neglect, omit, disregard, ignore, overlook
2 costly, expensive, valuable, precious, priceless
3 calm, tranquil, serene, placid, peaceful
4 puzzle, perplex, bewilder, dumbfound
5 fashion, style, vogue, fad, rage, craze
6 conform, adjust, reconcile
7 correct, accurate, exact, precise
8 obstruct, hinder, impede, bar, block, dam
9 design, plan, scheme, plot
10 mock, mimic, copy, ape

Care should be taken, not that the reader may understand, but that he must understand.

QUINTILIAN

40   EXACTNESS **EX**

To write with precision, you must know both the denotation and the connotation of words. **Denotation** is the core of a word's meaning, sometimes called the "dictionary," or literal, meaning; for example, a *tree* is *a woody perennial plant having a single main axis or stem commonly exceeding ten feet in height.* **Connotation** refers to the reader's emotional response to a word and to the associations the word carries with it. Thus, *tree* connotes *shade* or *coolness* or *shelter* or *stillness.*

   You can fail to write what you mean by misunderstanding the denotation of a word you choose. For example, the student who wrote *In thinking biology would be an easy course, I was thinking wistfully* simply chose a wrong word. She meant *wishfully*, not *wistfully*. To write *The men who had risked their lives to rescue the child were praised for their heroics* will not do. *Heroics* means something quite different from *heroism,* and if you use one when you mean the other, you will simply be wrong.

But you are more likely to miss saying exactly what you mean by missing the connotations of the words you use than by missing their denotations. Connotations cannot be fixed precisely, for individual responses to a word differ. But many words nonetheless have quite stable connotations. *Home* generally suggests security, a sense of one's own place. Most of us would prefer a *convertible* to a *jalopy* and would be suspicious of buying either from a *scheming* seller of used cars.

You must take care, of course, that the connotations of the individual words you choose are those you intend. But you must also make sure that your words fit the associations called up by other words in both the individual sentence and the larger context in which they are used. Sentences such as the following go wrong because the words don't fit connotatively:

> *Brandishing* his gun and *angrily demanding* the money, the thief *gaped* at the frightened clerk.
>
> The *timid little* man *sidled* up to the policeman and *glared* at him.

In the first example, the verb *gaped* suggests awe, stupidity, or astonishment, any of which clash sharply with the meaning associated with words like *brandishing* and *angrily demanded.* In the second sentence, *timid* and *sidle* suggest a hesitancy and lack of confidence that don't jibe with the choice of *glare,* which suggests hardness and hostility. Both sentences go wrong because they set up conflicting connotations.

Many words stand for abstractions: *democracy, truth, beauty.* Because the connotations of such words are both vague and numerous, state specifically what you mean when you use them, or make sure that the context clarifies their meaning. Otherwise, readers will misunderstand, or—worse—will think they understand your terms when they do not. (See Section **33a.**)

40a   Distinguish carefully among synonyms.

English is rich in synonyms, groups of words that have nearly the same meaning: *begin, start, commence; female, feminine, womanly; funny, comic, laughable.* But most synonyms differ in connotation, and exact writers choose carefully among them, observing their precise shades of meaning. Occasionally, the difference in meaning between two synonyms is so slight that it makes little difference which you choose: you can *begin a vacation* or *start a vacation*—either will do. But usually the differences will be much greater. To *commence a vacation,* for example, will not do; *commence* means *begin,* but it connotes far more formality than ordinarily goes with vacations. And it makes a much more important difference whether you describe a woman as *female, feminine,* or *womanly,* or a movie as *funny, comic,* or *laughable.*

Exact writing requires that you both increase the number of synonyms you can draw from in writing (see pp. 353–356), and distinguish carefully among them. Knowing that *fashion* and *vogue* are synonyms for *fad,* or that *renowned* and *notorious* are synonyms for *famous,* gives you the chance to make writing more exact. Choosing the synonyms that connote the precise shade of meaning you want makes it more exact.

The careless use of synonyms not only makes writing inexact; it often actually distorts meaning.

> Capone was a *renowned* gangster. [*Renowned* has favorable connotations that the writer probably did not intend. *Famous* would do, but it is not very exact. *Notorious* would be exact.]

EXERCISE 40a(1) Replace the italicized words in the following sentences with more exact ones. Explain why each italicized word is inappropriate.

1 His characters are *garish* and alive; they are people you will remember as old friends.
2 His *obstinacy* in the face of danger saved us all.
3 The ambassador, being treated like a common tourist, sputtered in *displeasure.*
4 We can't blame Margaret for leaving him; certainly she had an ample *pretext.*
5 The school's most honored professor was without fault: a wise mentor to her students, and in addition a scholar recognized as *pedantic* and profound.

EXERCISE 40a(2) Explain the differences in meaning among the italicized words in each of the following groups.

1 an *ignorant,* an *illiterate,* an *unlettered,* an *uneducated* person
2 a *detached,* a *disinterested,* an *indifferent,* an *unconcerned* attitude
3 to *condone,* to *excuse,* to *forgive,* to *pardon* a person's actions
4 an *insurrection,* a *mutiny,* a *rebellion,* a *revolution*
5 a *barbarous,* a *cruel,* a *fierce,* a *ferocious,* an *inhuman,* a *savage* character

40b **Be careful not to confuse words with similar sound or spelling but with different meanings.**

Some words are **homonyms,** that is, they have the same pronunciation but different meanings and different spellings (*idol, idle, idyll; aisle, isle*). Other words are sufficiently similar in sound and spelling to be confusing. Treat all these words as you would any other unfamiliar term: learn the correct spelling and meaning of each as an individual word.

EXERCISE 40b What are the differences in meaning in each of the following groups of words?

1 adapt, adept, adopt
2 alley, ally
3 allude, elude
4 anecdote, antidote
5 anesthetic, antiseptic
6 angel, angle
7 arraign, arrange
8 block, bloc
9 borne, born
10 Calvary, cavalry
11 cannon, canon
12 canvas, canvass
13 carton, cartoon
14 chord, cord
15 climactic, climatic

16 confidently, confidentially
17 costume, custom
18 elicit, illicit
19 epic, epoch
20 flaunt, flout
21 genteel, gentile
22 historic, historical
23 human, humane
24 ingenious, ingenuous
25 marital, martial
26 morality, mortality
27 prescribe, proscribe
28 receipt, recipe
29 statue, statute
30 waive, wave

40c Generally, avoid invented words.

A **coined** word is a new and outright creation (like *gobbledegook, blurb*). A **neologism** is either a new word or a new use of an old word or words (like Madison Avenue's *package plans*). A **nonce-word,** literally **once-word,** is a word made up to suit a special situation and generally not used more than once (*"My son," he said, "suffers from an acute case of televisionitis"*). Though the great majority of neologisms and nonce-words are short-lived, they are among the ways by which new words and new functions for old words are constantly working their way into a changing language.

English is relatively free in shifting words from one part of speech to another. The process is called **functional shift** and is one of the many ways in which our language grows. The noun *iron* is used as an adjective in *iron bar,* and as a verb in *iron the sheets.* The space age gives us *All systems are go,* using the verb *go* as a modifier. *River, paper,* and *sea* are clearly nouns in form (they make plurals with -*s*), but we commonly use them as modifiers in *river bank, paper bag,* and *sea water.*

But the fact that such changes are common in English does not mean that words can freely shift from one function to another. In *He opinioned that Edward was guilty, opinion* is used as a verb, a grammatical function to which it is entirely unaccustomed. The meaning may be roughly clear, but the use is not accepted. We *punish* a person. There is perhaps no good reason why we should not speak of *a punish.* But we don't; if we want a noun, we use *punishment.*

You should devote most of your attention to learning the meanings of words already established by usage, but you should not be afraid to try a new coinage if it seems to suit your purpose. Your instructor will judge whether the experiment is successful. Be careful, however, to avoid "unconscious" inventions—words that you "invent" because of spelling errors or an inexact knowledge of word forms (*understandment* for *understanding, multification* for *multiplication*). If you have any doubt about the accepted grammatical functions of a word, consult your dictionary.

EXERCISE 40c In the following sentences correct the italicized words that seem to you needlessly invented. Check your dictionary when necessary to determine whether a particular word is an accepted form or whether it is used in the way it appears in the sentence in the exercise.

1 One glimpse of the activities of the police or the mobs in urban riots reveals the *savagism* of human nature.
2 Teachers should be strictly *unpolitical;* they should not try to influence their students.
3 Even in our computer age, human behavior is largely *unpredictable.*
4 He displayed *liberalistic* tendencies in economic affairs.
5 That highway is *stoplighted* all the way to town; let's take the turnpike.
6 The cottage is nearly finished; we're going *to roof* it tomorrow.
7 Before we started building it, we had *to bulldoze* a clearing.
8 As each of the kids came out of the pool, I *toweled* him or her dry.
9 This year we're going *to holiday* in Bermuda.
10 Next summer Janine is going *to jeep* her way cross-country.

40d

40d   Be alert to changes in meaning from one form of a word to another.

A roommate whom you *like* is not necessarily a *likable* roommate, nor is a *matter of agreement* an *agreeable matter.* Many words have two, sometimes three, adjectival forms: e.g., a *changeable* personality, a *changing* personality, a *changed* personality. Be careful not to substitute one form for another.

FAULTY   The cook served our *favorable* dessert last night.

STANDARD   The cook served our *favorite* dessert last night.

FAULTY   He is a good student; he has a very *questionable* mind.

STANDARD   He is a good student; he has a very *questioning* mind.

EXERCISE 40d Point out the differences in meaning between the italicized words in each of the following groups.

1 an *arguable* point
   an *argued* point
2 a *practical* solution
   a *practicable* solution
3 a *hated* person
   a *hateful* person
4 a *liberal* foreign minister
   a *liberated* foreign minister
5 a *single* effect
   a *singular* effect
6 an *intelligible* writer
   an *intelligent* writer

7 a *godly* person
a *godlike* person
8 an *informed* teacher
an *informative* teacher
9 a *peaceful* nation
a *peaceable* nation

10 a *workable* arrangement
a *working* arrangement
11 an *amicable* neighbor
an *amiable* neighbor
12 a *yellow* piece of paper
a *yellowed* piece of paper

40e   Use accepted idioms.

An **idiom** is an expression that does not follow the normal pattern of the language or that has a total meaning not suggested by its separate words: *to catch fire, strike a bargain, ride it out, lose one's head, hold the bag.** Such expressions are a part of the vocabulary of native speakers. In fact, we learn them in the same way we learn new words—by hearing them in the speech around us, and by reading them in context. For the most part they give no more, and no less, difficulty than vocabulary itself gives us. Dictionaries usually give the common idiomatic expressions at the end of the definition of a word entry.

For many writers the most troublesome idioms in English are those that require a particular preposition after a given verb or adjective according to the meaning intended. The following list contains a number of such combinations that frequently cause trouble.

ABSOLVED BY, FROM	I was *absolved by* the dean *from* all blame.
ACCEDE TO	He *acceded to* his father's demands.
ACCOMPANY BY, WITH	I was *accompanied by* George. The terms were *accompanied with* a plea for immediate peace.
ACQUITTED OF	He was *acquitted of* the crime.
ADAPTED TO, FROM	This machine can be *adapted to* farm work. The design was *adapted from* a previous invention.
ADMIT TO, OF	He *admitted to* the error. The plan will *admit of* no alternative.
AGREE TO, WITH, IN	They *agreed to* the plan but *disagreed with* us. They *agreed* only *in* principle.
ANGRY WITH, AT	She was *angry with* me and *angry at* the treatment she had received.
CAPABLE OF	He is *capable of* every vice of the ignorant.
CHARGE FOR, WITH	He expected to be *charged for his* purchase, but he didn't expect to be *charged with* stealing something.
COMPARE TO, WITH	He *compared* the roundness of the baseball *to* that of the earth. He *compared* the economy of the Ford *with* that of the Plymouth.

*The term *idiom* is also used to mean the characteristic expression or pattern of a dialect or language. In this sense of the word, we can speak of the *idiom* of speakers from South Boston, or we can compare English *idiom* with German or French.

CONCUR WITH, IN	I *concur with* you *in* your desire to use the revised edition.
CONFIDE IN, TO	He *confided in* me. He *confided to* me that he had stolen the car.
CONFORM TO, WITH CONFORMITY WITH	The specifications *conformed to* (or *with*) his original plans. You must act in *conformity with* our demands.
CONNECT BY, WITH	The rooms are *connected by* a corridor. He is officially *connected with* this university.
CONTEND FOR, WITH	Because she needed to *contend for* her principles, she found herself *contending with* her parents.
DIFFER ABOUT, FROM, WITH	We *differ about* our tastes in clothes. My clothes *differ from* yours. We *differ with* one another.
DIFFERENT FROM*	Our grading system is *different from* yours.
ENTER INTO, ON, UPON	She *entered into* a new agreement and thereby *entered on* (or *upon*†) a new career.
FREE FROM, OF	He was *freed from* his mother's domination and now he is *free of* her.
IDENTICAL WITH	Your reasons are *identical with* his.
JOIN IN, WITH, TO	He *joined in* the fun *with* the others. He *joined* the wire cables *to* each other.
LIVE AT, IN, ON	He *lives at* 14 Neil Avenue *in* a Dutch colonial house. He *lives on* Neil Avenue.
NECESSITY FOR, OF NEED FOR, OF	There was no *necessity (need) for* you to lose your temper. There was no *necessity (need) of* your losing your temper.
OBJECT TO	I *object to* the statement in the third paragraph.
OBLIVIOUS OF	When he held her hand he was *oblivious of* the passing of time.
OVERCOME BY, WITH	I was *overcome by* the heat. I was *overcome with* grief.
PARALLEL BETWEEN, TO, WITH	There is a *parallel between* your attitude and his. This line is *parallel to* (or *with*) that one.
PREFERABLE TO	A leisurely walk is *preferable to* violent exercise.
REASON WITH, ABOUT	Why not *reason with* them *about* the matter?

Different than is colloquially idiomatic when the object of the prepositional phrase is a clause:

FORMAL	This town looks *different from* what I had remembered.
COLLOQUIAL	This town looks *different than* I had remembered it.

†In many phrases, *on* and *upon* are interchangeable: *depend on* or *depend upon*; *enter on* or *enter upon*.

REWARD BY, WITH, FOR	They were *rewarded by* their employer *with* a raise *for* their work.
VARIANCE WITH	This conclusion is at *variance with* your facts.
VARY FROM, IN, WITH	The houses *vary from* one another *in* size. People's tastes *vary with* their personalities.
WAIT FOR, ON	They *waited for* someone to *wait on* them.
WORTHY OF	That candidate is not *worthy of* your trust.

EXERCISE 40e Provide the idiomatic prepositions needed in the following sentences.

1 The students acceded _____ the increased need to conform _____ security regulations.

2 The men were acquitted _____ the charge and absolved _____ all blame for the damage to the building.

3 Price control seems preferable _____ excessive inflation but many businesspeople differ _____ this conclusion.

4 Some critics argue that there was no necessity _____ the resumption of bombing North Vietnam, and that the United States could have entered _____ a ceasefire agreement earlier.

5 I agreed _____ his proposal, which had been adapted _____ one I had made previously.

6 Lois Bowers said she was angry _____ him because his actions did not conform _____ those of a responsible citizen.

7 The fence was built parallel _____ the street and connected _____ their neighbor's stone wall.

8 Having been freed _____ his parents' supervision, he saw no necessity _____ keep (*or* keeping) them informed of his whereabouts.

9 I am not capable _____ budget (*or* budgeting) my own income for I am unable to add 4 and 4 and get 8.

10 We entered _____ a contract to buy the house after Mr. Jones agreed _____ our request for a twenty-year mortgage.

40f **Prefer concrete and specific to abstract and general words.**

40f

Abstract words name qualities, ideas, concepts: *honesty, virtue, poverty, education, wisdom, love, democracy.* **Concrete** words name things we can see, hear, feel, touch, smell. *Sweetness* is abstract; *candy, honey, molasses,* and *sugar* are concrete. To describe people as *reckless* is to describe them abstractly; to say *they ran two traffic lights in the center of* *town, and they drove eighty-five miles an hour in a restricted zone* is to pin that recklessness down, to make it concrete.

General words refer to all members of a class or group. **Specific words** refer to the individual members of a class. *Vegetation* is general; *grass, shrubs, trees, flowers,* and *weeds* are specific. *Animal* is general; *lions, elephants, monkeys, zebras, cats, dogs, mice,* and *rabbits* are specific.

The classes abstract and concrete, and general and specific overlap with each other, and both are relative. The verb *communicate* is both abstract and general. *Speak* is concrete and specific relative to *communicate,* but it is general compared to *gasp, murmur, rant, rave, shout,* and *whisper. Music* is concrete and specific relative to *sound* but general compared to *classical music,* which in turn is general compared to *Beethoven's Fifth Symphony. Dwelling* is a general word; *apartment, cabin, barracks, house, hut, mansion, shack,* and *tent* are specific. But *dwelling* is more specific than *building,* which includes not only *dwelling* but also *church, factory, garage, school,* and *store.*

All effective writing will use both abstract and concrete words, both general and specific. There are no substitutes for such abstractions as *fairness, friendship, love,* and *loyalty.* But all abstractions need to be pinned down by details, examples, and illustrations. When not so pinned down, they remain vague and always potentially confusing. We can all quickly agree that taxes and justice should be *fair.* But until each of us has narrowed down by detail and example what he or she means by *fairness* in these matters, we will not understand each other in any useful way.

Similarly, we cannot do without general terms. We would be hard-pressed to define *cat* if we could not begin by putting cats in the general class *animal.* But immediately we have done so, we must name the specific characteristics and qualities that distinguish cats from, say, armadillos or raccoons. To say *Tom enjoys reading* tells readers very little until they know whether the reading consists of *Sports Illustrated, Popular Mechanics,* and *Wonder Woman* or of Dickens and Dostoyevsky.

Effective writing constantly weaves back and forth between abstract and concrete, between general and specific. It is the writer's use of the abstract and general that guides the reader, but it is the concrete and specific that allow the reader to see, feel, understand, and believe. *This lamp supplies insufficient light* informs us; *this fifteen-watt bulb gives no more light than a firefly in a jam jar* makes us understand what the writer means by *insufficient.*

Whenever you use abstract words, give them meaning with concrete details and examples. Whenever you use general words, tie them down with specific ones. Try constantly to express yourself and your ideas in concrete terms; search for the most specific words you can find.

| GENERAL | The flowers were of different colors. |
| SPECIFIC | The chrysanthemums were bronze, gold, and white. |

GENERAL	The cost of education has increased greatly.
SPECIFIC	Tuition at many private universities has increased as much as 1,000 percent in the past three decades.
MORE SPECIFIC	Tuition at Boston University was $300 in 1947; it was $6,200 in 1982.

| SPECIFIC | Mateo was a stocky man, with clear eyes and a deeply tanned face. His skill as a marksman was extraordinary, even in Corsica, where everyone is a good shot. He could kill a ram at one hundred and twenty paces, and his aim was as accurate at night as in the daytime. |
| MORE SPECIFIC | Picture a small, sturdy man, with jet-black, curly hair, a Roman nose, thin lips, large piercing eyes, and a weather-beaten complexion. His skill as a marksman was extraordinary, even in this country, where everyone is a good shot. For instance, Mateo would never fire on a wild ram with small shot, but at a hundred and twenty paces he would bring it down with a bullet in its head or shoulder, just as he fancied. He used his rifle at night as easily as in the daytime, and I was given the following illustration of his skill, which may seem incredible, perhaps, to those who have never travelled in Corsica. He placed a lighted candle behind a piece of transparent paper as big as a plate, and aimed at it from eighty paces away. He extinguished the candle, and a moment later, in utter darkness, fired and pierced the paper three times out of four. |

PROSPER MÉRIMÉE, *Mateo Falcone*

40g Use figurative language.

Inexperienced writers are likely to think that figurative language is the monopoly of poets. In fact, it plays an important part in much prose and is one of the most effective ways of making meaning concrete. The basis of most figurative language lies in the comparison or association of two things essentially different but nonetheless alike in some underlying and surprising way. The two most common figures of speech are simile and metaphor. **Similes** make direct and explicit comparisons, usually introduced by *like, as, as if,* or *as when,* as in *Jess is as changeable as the New England weather.* **Metaphors** imply comparisons, as in *Prisoned in her laboratory, she ignored the world.*

Both simile and metaphor require that the two things compared be from different classes so that their likeness, when pointed out, will be fresh and surprising. If they are extended, as in the second example below, they must be consistent.

The teacher shook her finger in my face as she might shake a clogged fountain pen.

Up scrambles the car, on all its four legs, like a black beetle straddling past the schoolhouse and the store down below, up the bare rock and over the changeless boulders, with a surge and a sickening lurch to the skybrim, where stands the foolish church.

D. H. LAWRENCE, *Mornings in Mexico*

Apt figures of speech can do much to make writing concrete and vivid, and by making one experience understandable in terms of another, they can often help clarify abstractions. But take care in creating figures of speech. When they strain too hard, as in the first example below, they will miss their mark and fall flat. When two figures get mixed so that they create clashing images in the eye of the reader, they will not only miss their mark, they will be ludicrous, as in the second and third examples below.

Her smile was as warm as an electric blanket.

He had to be on the rocks before he would turn over a new leaf.

Grandmother's tiny fingers seemed to stitch the material with the speed of a pneumatic drill.

EXERCISE 40g Replace the mixed or incongruous figures of speech in the following sentences with fresher, more appropriate comparisons.

1 While he was battling his way through the sea of life, fate stepped in and tripped him up.
2 John brought his big guns to the debate and stifled his opponent.
3 The odor of the flowers on the table shouted a welcome.
4 The young teacher is rapidly gaining a foothold in the eyes of the students.
5 We're skating on thin ice, and if anybody upsets the applecart, we'll all lose our bread and butter.
6 The Senate wanted to plug the loopholes in the tax bill, but they couldn't because too many important people had their fingers in the pie.
7 He worked as busily as a beaver, but one day he got as sick as a dog and decided to turn over a new leaf.
8 I'm as blind as a bat without my glasses, even in my apartment, which I know like the back of my hand.
9 She was head over heels in love with him, but she kept her feet firmly on the ground.
10 He had his back to the wall when he finally hit the nail on the head.

In composing, as a general rule, run your pen through every other word you have written; you have no idea what vigor it will give your style.

SIDNEY SMITH

41 DIRECTNESS **DIR**

The challenge to directness comes from two fronts—wordiness and vagueness. A wordy writer uses more words than are necessary to convey meaning.

WORDY	He attacks the practice of making a profitable business out of college athletics from the standpoint that it has a detrimental and harmful influence on the college students and, to a certain degree and extent, on the colleges and universities themselves.
IMPROVED	He attacks commercialization of college athletics as harmful to the students and even to the universities themselves.

A vague writer fails to convey meaning sharply and clearly.

VAGUE	The report asserts the danger from unguarded machines which may lessen the usefulness of workers in later life as well as reducing their life expectancy.
IMPROVED	The report asserts that unguarded machines may severely injure or even kill workers.

Vagueness and wordiness are sometimes indistinguishable, as in the preceding examples. The weight of unnecessary words tends to obscure meaning. But very often wordiness is just awkwardness; the meaning is clear, but the expression is clumsy.

AWKWARD	The notion that Communists are people who wear long black beards is a very common notion.
IMPROVED	The notion is common that Communists are people who wear long black beards.

41a Eliminate words and phrases that do not add to your meaning.

Good writing says things in as few words as possible without losing clarity or completeness. It makes every word count. You can often make your writing more direct and economical by (1) cutting unnecessary words and phrases and (2) reducing clauses to phrases, and phrases to single words.

41a

1 Cutting unnecessary words and phrases. Often as you revise your writing you will be able to strike out words that are clearly unnecessary, or gain directness by slight changes.

WORDY	When the time to go had arrived, Molly left.
REVISED	When it was time to go, Molly left.
WORDY	After the close of the war, Bob went to college.
REVISED	After the war, Bob went to college.
WORDY	She is attractive in appearance, but she is a rather selfish person.
REVISED	She is attractive, but rather selfish.

Words such as *angle, aspect, factor,* and *situation,* and phrases such as *in the case of, in the line of, in the field of* are almost never necessary. They are common obstacles to directness.

WORDY	John is majoring in the field of biology.
REVISED	John is majoring in biology.
WORDY	Another aspect of the situation that needs to be examined is the matter of advertising.
REVISED	We should also examine advertising.

Be suspicious of sentences beginning with *there are, there is, it is.* They are often roundabout statements.

WORDY	There are many reasons why we have pollution.
REVISED	Pollution has many causes.
WORDY	It is a fact that many students read very little.
REVISED	Many students read very little.

Phrases such as *I believe, I think,* and *in my opinion* are usually unnecessary.

WORDY	In my opinion, we must reduce violence on television.
REVISED	We must reduce violence on television.
WORDY	I believe that nuclear power plants are dangerous.
REVISED	Nuclear power plants are dangerous.

2 Reducing clauses to phrases and phrases to single words. Wordiness often results from using a clause when a phrase will do, or a phrase when a single word will do.

WORDY   There were instances of aggression on the country's frontier in many cases.

REVISED   There were many instances of aggression on the country's frontier.

Aggression was frequent on the country's frontier. [In the first revision the phrase *in many instances* has been reduced to a single adjective modifying *instances*. But note that the second revision is made even more direct by eliminating the *there are* construction.]

WORDY   The shirt, which is made of wool, has worn well for eight years.

REVISED   The woolen shirt has worn well for eight years. [The clause *which was made of wool* has been reduced to the single modifier *woolen*.]

WORDY   The snow that fell yesterday is already melting.

REVISED   Yesterday's snow is already melting. [The clause *that fell yesterday* has been reduced to the single modifier *yesterday's*.]

WORDY   The conclusions that the committee of students reached are summarized in the newspaper of the college that was published today.

REVISED   The conclusions reached by the student committee are summarized in today's college newspaper. [The first *that* clause has been reduced to a participial phrase beginning with *reached*. The second *that* clause has become the single word *today's*. The phrases *of students, in the newspaper,* and *of the college* have all been reduced.]

WORDY   The football captain, who is an All-American player, played his last game today.

REVISED   The football captain, an All-American, played his last game today. [The clause has been reduced to a descriptive noun phrase—an appositive.]

EXERCISE 41a   Rewrite the following sentences to reduce their wordiness.

1 He is an expert in the field of labor relations.
2 The fastest kind of automobile requires the best quality of gasoline.
3 Most Congressmen spend a majority of the hours which they have in each working day attending committtee meetings.
4 In my opinion, Dr. Mackenzie is of greater ability and of greater experience than Dr. Smith.
5 People have to be educated as to how to plan good, inexpensive menus that will meet their nutritional needs.
6 The rain, which has been coming down steadily for two weeks now, is washing away the seeds I planted in the ground at an earlier time.
7 Mrs. Armstrong, who was my history teacher, had a classroom manner that was very dynamic.

41a

8 There are two reasons that I have for not going: the first is that I have an examination to study for; the second is that I have no money.

9 Love and understanding of them are two of the most important things young children need.

10 After several hours of shopping around to buy my niece a gift, I finally decided to give her a check to buy whatever she decided she preferred.

41b

41b Prefer one exact word to two or more approximate words.

Many groups of words are simply roundabout ways of expressing what a single exact word expresses more directly.

Wordy	*Direct*
this day and age	today
of an indefinite nature	indefinite
at this point in time	now
by means of	by
call up on the telephone	telephone
destroy by fire	burn
was made the recipient of	was given

Often we can substitute one precise word for two or more approximate synonyms.

WORDY   His *temperament* and *disposition* are unpleasant.

REVISED   His *disposition* is unpleasant

WORDY   She described her *deeds* and *doings* as a foreign correspondent.

REVISED   She described her *adventures* as a foreign correspondent.

41c

41c Avoid redundancy.

Expressions such as *visible to the eyes* and *audible to the ears* are said to be **redundant;** they say the same thing twice. Typical examples include the following:

Redundant	*Direct*
advance forward	advance
continue on	continue
refer back	refer
combine together	combine
circle around	circle
small in size	small
disappear from view	disappear
throughout the whole	throughout
basic fundamentals	fundamentals
important essentials	essentials

Sometimes sentences become wordy through the writer's careless repetition of the same meaning in slightly different words.

WORDY	As a rule, Susan usually woke up early.
REVISED	Susan usually woke up early.
WORDY	We planned to go at 3 o'clock P.M. in the afternoon.
REVISED	We planned to go at 3 P.M.
WORDY	In their opinion, they think they are right.
REVISED	They think they are right.

41d   Avoid awkward repetition.

Repetition of important words is a useful way of gaining emphasis (see Section **3d**). But careless repetition is awkward and wordy.

AWKWARD	The investigation revealed that the *average teachers teaching* industrial arts in California have an *average* working and *teaching* experience of five years.
REVISED	The investigation revealed that teachers of industrial arts in California have an average of five years experience.
AWKWARD	Gas mileage in the American car is being *improved* constantly in order to *improve* efficiency.
REVISED	Gas mileage in the American car is being improved constantly to increase efficiency.
AWKWARD	The *important subject* on which I am going to speak is career opportunities, a *subject* of *great importance* to college students.
REVISED	I am going to speak on career opportunities, a subject of great importance to college students.

EXERCISE 41b–d   Eliminate redundancies and unnecessary repetition from the following sentences.

1 Because Jill believed exercise was a necessary requirement, her habitual custom was to jog every morning at 7 A.M.
2 This book is intended and designed to explain the basic fundamentals of English.
3 Barbara Linger's limousine sedan, black in color, has been seen a countless number of times parked in front of Blickel's market.
4 It was the consensus of opinion among the students that grades should be abandoned.
5 Teachers should provide several examples to illustrate the grammatical rules they are trying to teach.
6 So far as understanding his meaning is concerned, I would classify Joyce in the category of writers who are very difficult to read.

7 He is an industrial engineering student studying the principles of time-and-motion study.

8 As far as I'm concerned, government should keep out of intervening in private business, in my opinion.

9 A reckless driver is no better than a murderer who goes around killing people.

10 Last night we had to circle all around the block before finding a parking space in which to park the car.

41e Prefer simple, direct expressions to needlessly complex ones.

Never be ashamed to express a simple idea in simple language. The use of complicated language is not in itself a sign of superior intelligence (see Sections **42d** and **42e**).

NEEDLESSLY COMPLEX	Not a year passes without some evidence of the fundamental truth of the statement that the procedures and techniques of education are more complicated and complex than they were two decades ago.
DIRECT	Each year shows that methods of education are more complex than they were twenty years ago.

If alternative forms of the same word exist, prefer the shorter. Choose *truth* and *virtue* rather than *truthfulness* and *virtuousness*. Choose *preventive* rather than *preventative*.

To prefer simplicity does not mean to make *all* writing simple. Naturally, highly complex or technical subjects call at times for complex and technical language.

One of the simplest ways of evolving a favorable environment concurrently with the development of the individual organism, is that the influence of each organism on the environment should be favorable to the *endurance* of other organisms of the same type. Further, if the organism also favors *development* of other organisms of the same type, you have then obtained a mechanism of evolution adapted to produce the observed state of large multitudes of analogous entities, with high powers of endurance. For the environment automatically develops with the species, and the species with the environment.

A. N. WHITEHEAD, *Science and the Modern World* [his italics]

EXERCISE 41e Find a paragraph or two of needlessly complex writing in one of your textbooks. Explain in one or two paragraphs how you think the writing might be made more direct.

41f   Use euphemisms sparingly.

Euphemisms substitute a more pleasant word or phrase for one that is, for any reason, objectionable. They express unpleasant things in less harsh and direct ways: *pass away* for *die, perspire* for *sweat, mortal remains* for *corpse, intoxicated* for *drunk.* Most common euphemisms are associated with the basic facts of existence—birth, age, death, sex, the bodily functions—and often seem necessary for politeness or tact. We are more comfortable describing a good friend as one who *is stout* and *likes to drink* than as a *fat drunk.* And in such contexts these terms are harmless.

But the use of euphemisms to distract us from the realities of work, unemployment, poverty, and war is at best misleading and at worst dishonest and dangerous. Today we take for granted such terms as "sanitation engineer" (plumber), "funeral director" (undertaker), and "maintenance people" (janitors). Such terms perhaps help protect the feelings of individuals and give them status. But the individuals themselves still have to sweat pipes, prepare bodies for burial, and sweep floors—in short, do work that is hard or unpleasant. And if the terms make us forget that reality, they are misleading. It is a short step further to language consciously intended to deceive. Such language gives us "protective reaction" (bombing), "strategic withdrawal" (retreat), "visual surveillance" (spying), and "inoperative statements" (lies). Such phrases are downright dishonest. They are created for the sole purpose of distracting us from realities that we need to know about. Slums and ghettos are no less slums and ghettos because we call them the "inner city." And if you're fired, you're out of a job even if you've been "terminated" or "deselected."

Keep your own writing honest, and be alert to dishonesty in the writing of others. Use euphemism when tact and genuine respect for the feelings of your audience warrant it. Do not use it to deceive.

EXERCISE 41a–f   Each of the sentences below violates a principal of directness. Find and then correct the error.

1 We of the United States cannot expect to spread peace throughout other nations and countries until we can teach and educate our own people to respect each other as equal individuals.
2 Their capacity for hard work makes them capable of working long hours each day.
3 The integration of public schools is a major step forward toward complete equality of all groups.
4 During the entirety of my whole college career, I continually went on thinking about my plan to work my way around the world.

5 It has just been in the past couple of years that black Americans have begun to make clear that they wish to develop their own racial identity by themselves without outside interference.

6 The reason for Nixon's choice of Agnew as a running mate for vice-president stemmed from the fact that he wanted a Southern candidate as nominee.

7 The first settlers in the West were prospectors who explored the new land as they prospected for gold.

8 The actress acted very badly, but the play was played through to the very end and conclusion.

9 He was the handsomest-looking Irish wolfhound I had ever seen before in my life.

10 The increasing filth in our waterways through pollution has bothered and troubled scientists for a period of one and a half decades.

A speech is composed of three things: the speaker, the subject on which he speaks, and the audience he is addressing.

ARISTOTLE, *Rhetoric*

42 APPROPRIATENESS **APPR**

Because the English language is constantly growing, it continues to be a useful vehicle for conveying thought accurately and effectively. Fortunately, words appear, disappear, or shift their meanings slowly so that there is always available a large core of stable, generally used words. Beyond this core are wide ranges of usage: slang, regional expressions, profanity, clichés, jargon, stilted diction. Words from these categories must be used sparingly if at all.

There are no words in the English language that cannot be used somewhere at some time. But when a piece of writing is overloaded with slang or clichés, the question of *appropriateness* arises. You may consider yourself such a casual, easy-going person that you think casual, easy-going language is appropriate to you. It may be—in a letter to close friends about an exciting summer holiday. Even in letter-writing, however, you must also consider your audience and your subject: that letter to friends would necessarily be different if you were expressing your sympathy for an illness in their family. But when you sit down to write papers for your courses, keep your eye on that core of stable, generally used and generally understood words. If you do depart from those words, have a good reason.

42a Ordinarily, avoid slang.

Slang consists of the rapidly changing words and phrases in popular speech that people invent to give language novelty and vigor. Slang often is created by the same processes we use to create most new words: by combining two words (*ferretface, blockhead*); by shortening words (*pro, prof, vet*); by borrowing from other languages (*kaput, spiel*); and by generalizing a proper name (*the real McCoy*). Often slang simply extends the meaning of phrases borrowed from other activities (*lower the boom* from sailing; *tune in, tune out* from radio; *cash in your chips* from poker). A great deal of slang gives a new range of meaning to existing words (*tough, cool, bread, heavy, crash, turned on, joint*).

Slang is a part of the current language. It is spontaneous and direct and helps give color and liveliness to the language. It often contributes directly to the growth of the language as slang terms move gradually into general use. Words like *rascal* and *sham* were originally slang terms; shortened forms such as *A-bomb, ad, gym,* and *phone* are now appropriate to most informal writing. In informal writing, a carefully chosen slang word can be effective:

Has Harold Wilson *Lost His Cool?*   *New York Times* headline

Heaven knows there are large areas where a shrewd eye for the *quick buck* is dominant.   FREDERICK LEWIS ALLEN, *The Big Change*

But slang has serious limitations in writing, and even much conversation. It is imprecise, is often understandable only to a narrow social or age group, and usually changes very rapidly. You may be familiar with the latest slang, but who knows *lollapalooza, balloon juice,* or *twerp?* The fact that *hep* became *hip* within a few years suggests how shortlived slang can be.

Enjoy slang for the life it sometimes gives to speech. But even in conversation, remember that slang expressions may not be understood, that at best a little of it goes a long way, and that if you rely on *hot, cool, lousy,* and *tough* to describe all objects, events, and ideas, you don't communicate much. In writing, use slang only when it serves some special purpose. Except in carefully controlled contexts, slang and standard language make an inappropriate mixture.

Persuading Mrs. McGinnis to be seated, the chairman of the Committee on Indian Affairs asked her politely not to foul up the state's plans to hit pay dirt on Ishimago's claim.

EXERCISE 42a(1) Almost everyone has favorite slang terms. Make a list of your own slang expressions and compare the list with those of your classmates to see how "original" your own slang is.

EXERCISE 42a(2) Can you think of a situation or general context in which the following sentences might be appropriate? Explain.

1 We were invited to a party last night but we couldn't make the scene.
2 The trouble was that my boyfriend was all uptight about his car and I got hung up on a TV show I was watching.

42a

3 I finally told him that he should do his thing and I'd do mine.
4 Anyway, I never got a chance to show off my crazy new hairdo and my really cool fur coat.
5 My boyfriend finally showed up when I was all decked out and he said I was real foxy.
6 I asked him how he was making out with the car and he told me everything was coming up roses.
7 So we decided to blast off and go to a movie.
8 The movie was like dullsville so my boyfriend asked if I wanted to go and tie one on.

42b

42b Avoid regional and nonstandard language.

Regional words (sometimes called **provincialisms** or **localisms**) are words whose use is generally restricted to a particular geographical area. Examples are *tote* for *carry, poke* for *bag, spider* for *frying pan, gumshoes* for *overshoes, draw* for *small valley,* and *woodpussy* for *skunk.* **Nonstandard** words and expressions generally occur only in the speech of uneducated speakers. Examples are *ain't, could of, he done,* and double negatives such as *can't never, scarcely none,* and *don't have no.* Dictionaries label such words *nonstandard* or *illiterate.*

REGIONAL	She *redded up* the house for our *kinfolk.*
GENERAL	She cleaned the house for our relatives.
NONSTANDARD	He *didn't ought to have* spent the money.
STANDARD	He shouldn't have spent the money.
NONSTANDARD	I wish Irving *had of drove more careful.*
STANDARD	I wish Irving had driven more carefully.

EXERCISE 42b(1) List at least five examples of regionalisms (as *The cat wants in*) and describe circumstances under which they could be used appropriately.

EXERCISE 42b(2) If you are a native of the region in which your college is located, ask a classmate from another region to give you a list of ten words or expressions that strike him or her as being regionalisms in your speech. If you come from another region yourself, make up your own list of regionalisms of the college area and compare it with a classmate's.

42c

42c Avoid trite expressions.

A trite expression, sometimes called a **cliché,** or a **stereotyped** or **hackneyed phrase,** is an expression that has been worn out by constant use, as *burning the midnight oil, Father Time, raving beauties, man about town.* Words in themselves are never trite—they are only used tritely. We cannot avoid trite expressions entirely, for they sometimes describe a situation accurately. But writers who burden their language with clichés run the risk of being regarded as trite thinkers. What would be your estimate of the person who wrote this?

> A college education develops a *well-rounded personality* and gives the student an appreciation of *the finer things of life.*

Effectively used, triteness can be humorous. The string of trite expressions in the example below explodes into absurdity when the writer transposes the words in the two clichés in the last clause.

> A pair of pigeons were cooing gently directly beneath my window; two squirrels plighted their troth in a branch overhead; at the corner a handsome member of New York's finest twirled his night stick and cast roguish glances at the saucy-eyed flower vendor. The scene could have been staged only by a Lubitsch; in fact Lubitsch himself was seated on a bench across the street, smoking a cucumber and looking as cool as a cigar.   S. J. PERELMAN, *Keep It Crisp*

Watch for trite words and phrases in your own writing, and replace them with new, original ways of expressing yourself. As you proofread your manuscripts, be as sensitive to clichés as you are to misspellings.

EXERCISE 42c   Copy the following passage. Circle all clichés and all expressions that are longer or more involved than they need be. Suggest more appropriate wordings for each.

> The American Way is the only feasible route for educational personnel to tread in our educational institutions of learning. Despite its humble origins, this child of adversity, born in a log cabin, has beyond a shadow of a doubt reached the summits in this fair country of ours.
> There is too much of a tendency to view this great institution with alarm. But on the other hand people who live in glass houses, which is the type most inclined to cast aspersions and generally be wet blankets, are usually the ones by whom the criticisms are made.
> Now I'm just an ordinary schoolteacher, and don't have any complicated ideas on how our schools should be run, but I know that Abe Lincoln, if he were alive, would disapprove of the newfangled techniques that are making a shambles of our educational system.
> Foreigners are at the bottom of the attack on our American heritage and the American Way in education. These notorious radicals have wreaked havoc with our boys and girls.

42d   Avoid jargon in writing for a general audience.

The term **jargon** has several meanings. In a famous essay, "On Jargon," Sir Arthur Quiller-Couch defined the term as vague and "woolly" speech or writing that consists of abstract words, elegant

42d

variation, and "circumlocution rather than short straight speech." Linguists often define jargon as hybrid speech or dialect formed by a mixture of languages. An example would be the English-Chinese jargon known as pidgin English.

To most people, however, jargon is the technical or specialized vocabulary of a particular trade or profession—for example, engineering jargon or educational jargon. Members of the profession, of course, can use their jargon when they are communicating with one another, for it is their language, so to speak. But the use of technical jargon is inappropriate when you are writing for a general audience.

Unfortunately, jargon impresses a great many people simply because it sounds involved and learned. We are all reluctant to admit that we do not understand what we are reading. What, for example, can you make of the following passage?

THE TURBO-ENCABULATOR IN INDUSTRY

. . . Work has been proceeding in order to bring to perfection the crudely conceived idea of a machine that would not only supply inverse reactive current for use in unilateral phase detractors, but would also be capable of automatically synchronizing cardinal grammeters. Such a machine is the Turbo-Encabulator. . . . The original machine had a base plate of prefabulated amulite surmounted by a malleable logarithmic casing in such a way that the two spurving bearings were in a direct line with the pentametric fan. . . . The main winding was of the normal lotus-o-delta type placed in a panendermic semiboloid slot in the stator, every seventh conductor being connected by a non-reversible tremie pipe to the differential girdlespring on the "up" end of the grammeters. . . .

Reprinted by permission of the publishers,
Arthur D. Little, Inc., Cambridge, Mass.

This new mechanical marvel was a joke, the linquistic creation of a research engineer who was tired of reading jargon.

EXERCISE 42d Make a list of twenty words, terms, or phrases that constitute the jargon in a field that you know. Define these terms in a way that a general reader could understand; then justify the use of the terms among the people in your field.

42e

42e Avoid artificial diction and "fine writing."

Artificiality is not inherent in words themselves but in the use that we make of them. State simple facts and assertions simply and directly, or you run the risk of making your writing sound pompous and self-conscious, as in the following examples.

ARTIFICIAL	The edifice was consumed by fire.
NATURAL	The house burned down.
ARTIFICIAL	We were unable to commence our journey to your place of residence because of inclement weather conditions.
NATURAL	We could not come because it was snowing.

Many inexperienced writers believe, mistakenly, that an artificial diction makes for "good writing." They shift gears when they go from speaking to writing. They try to make their writing sound like the speech of Hollywood's version of a college professor, and once again the results sound stilted.

ARTIFICIAL	The athletic contest commenced at the stipulated time.
NATURAL	The game began on time.
ARTIFICIAL	I informed him that his advice was unsolicited.
NATURAL	I told him to mind his own business.

Your writing may become artificial simply because you are trying too hard to write effectively, because you have grown more concerned with *how* you write than with *what* you write. Writing marked by a continuously artificial diction is called "fine writing."

| FINE WRITING | Whenever the press of daily events and duties relaxes its iron grip on me, whenever the turmoil of my private world subsides and leaves me in quiet and solitide, then it is that I feel my crying responsibility as one of God's creatures and recognize the need to speak out loudly and boldly against the greed and intolerance that carry humanity into the terrible destruction of armed conflict. |
| NATURAL | I am a crusader for international peace. |

EXERCISE 42e Find an example of "fine writing" in a newspaper or magazine and explain in a short paper why you think it ineffective.

EXERCISE 42a–e First assume a specific audience (e.g., classmates, group of businesspeople, parents, etc.); then comment on the appropriateness of the language in the following selection in terms of that audience.

Like many other just plain "guys," I just graduated from high school. Being like most of these other guys, I naturally didn't really accomplish much during my previous school years. Yes, I got fair grades, met lots of swell kids, played football. I guess I'm just one of those guys who had the run of the school and never bothered to study.

No, I'm not bragging. I'm just telling you why high school was never like college.

A lot of people graduate from high school every year. A good percentage go to college and the rest go out and get a job. Four years later, the college student graduates. Does that mean he's going to get a better job than the fellow who went from high school directly to a job?

No. It doesn't mean a thing unless the guy in college really studied and hit the books. What I'm trying to bring out is that a person who goes to college and doesn't study is no better off than a guy who goes out and gets a job immediately after high school graduation.

So college for me is the "big jump." I fooled around in high school, and if I don't get right down and study now, I might as well quit school and start that $150.00 a week job.

Now, I don't have anything against a $150.00 a week job. It's just that twenty years from now, I'd probably still be there getting the same $150.00. This is it, so I guess it's time for me to bear down and study hard. I think this will be the "big jump."

REVIEW EXERCISE ON WORDS (Sections 40–42)   Revise each of the following sentences according to what you have learned in the sections on exactness, directness, and appropriateness.

1 He was trying to keep abreast of company development when the tide turned against him and his reputation ebbed.

2 College students have to invest most of their time with studying if they are going to be successful students.

3 C. B. Brown must have really been on the stick when he polished off six Gothic novels in less than four years.

4 Many neophyte pedagogues in the area of bilingual education are substandard in instructional methodology of teaching.

5 The authorship of the novel has not been authenticated, but the evidence of the extant material that survives points to one Joshua Fiddings.

6 The campus police opinionated that the burglary attempters had entranced through the caf.

7 Although my little subcompact is cute as a button, my face becomes red as a beet when someone leaves me in the dust at a stoplight.

8 Mr. Smith's frequent disregard of his wife's bridge bids was the bane of her existence.

9 It is our intention to supply all your wants, and we intend to make you so comfortable here that you will not be afraid to tell us what you want in the way of comforts.

10 Professor Caitlin's life was poor in terms of meager remunerative values, but more students in the college remember her than any other teacher.

11 Coaches are paid for the type of teams they produce or for the number of winning games per season.

12 The house was square in shape and blue in color, and he decided in his mind that price-wise it was a real good buy.

13 I thought I was doing the best thing when I signed up for the army.

14 I was filled with anger and rage when my precious and expensive stereo equipment was destroyed and ruined by the vandals.

15 By reading *Yachting* I am able to keep abreast with the tide of affairs in the sailing world.

"Awfully nice" is an expression than which few could be sillier: but to have succeeded in going through life without saying it a certain number of times is as bad as to have no redeeming vice.

H. W. FOWLER

43 GLOSSARY OF USAGE **GLOS**

43

Choosing the right word—or not choosing the wrong one—is one of the most difficult problems for writers. General guidelines—such as, be idiomatic, confine colloquial words to speech and very informal writing, avoid nonstandard words—can be helpful, but only if you know the idiom and know what is colloquial and nonstandard. And that knowledge often comes only slowly and with much reading and experience. This glossary is intended to help you with some of the most commonly troublesome words and phrases. But it is necessarily brief; you should keep a good college dictionary at hand and consult it both for words not listed here and for additional information about words that are listed.

For information about labels used in dictionaries, see pp. 345–346. The following two labels are used in this glossary:

COLLOQUIAL	Commonly used in speech but inappropriate in all but the most informal writing
NONSTANDARD	Generally agreed not to be standard English

In addition to specifically labeled words, some words and phrases are included here because, although widely used, they are wordy or redundant (e.g., *but that, inside of, in the case of*); vague and overused (e.g., *level, overall*); or objected to by many readers (e.g., *center around, hopefully* meaning *it is hoped, -wise* as a suffix). A few word pairs often confused (e.g., *imply, infer*) are included, but Section **40b** has a more complete list of such pairs.

a, an *A* is used before words beginning with a consonant sound, even when the sound is spelled with a vowel (*a dog, a European, a unicorn, a habit*). *An* is used before words beginning with a vowel sound or a silent *h* (*an apple, an Indian, an hour, an uproar*).

above, below   *Above* and *below* are standard ways of referring to material preceding or following a particular passage in writing *(the paragraph above, the statistics below)*. Some readers object to the use as stilted and overly formal.

accept, except   To *accept* is to receive. To *except* is to exclude. As a preposition *except* means "with the exclusion of." (He *accepted the list from the chairman. The list excepted George from the slate of candidates. He asked why it included all except George.)*

actually   Like *really*, frequently overworked as an intensifier.

ad   A shortened form of *advertisement*, inappropriate in formal writing. Other clipped forms include *auto, exam, math, phone, photo.*

affect, effect   As verbs, to *affect* is to influence, to *effect* is to bring about. *Effect* is more commonly used as a noun meaning "result." *(Recent tax reforms affect everyone. They are intended to effect a fairer distribution of taxes. The effects have yet to be felt.)*

aggravate   To *aggravate* is to intensify, to make worse *(The hot sun aggravated his sunburn)*. Colloquially it is often used to mean "to annoy, provoke" *(My teasing aggravated him).*

agree to, agree with   To *agree to* is to consent; to *agree with* means "to concur" *(I agree with Gail's opinion, and will therefore agree to the contract).*

ain't   A contraction of *am not*, extended to *is not, are not, has not, have not*. Though often used in speech, it is strongly disapproved by the majority of speakers and writers.

a lot, alot   The correct spelling is *a lot.*

all, all of   Constructions with *all of* followed by a noun can frequently be made more concise by omitting the *of;* usually the *of* is retained before a pronoun or a proper noun; *all of Illinois*, but *all the money, all this confusion.*

allude, refer   To *allude to* is to refer to indirectly; to *refer to* is to direct attention to *(When he spoke of family difficulties, we knew he was alluding to his wife's illness even though he did not refer directly to that).*

allusion, illusion   An *allusion* is an indirect reference; an *illusion* is a false impression *(He was making an allusion to magicians when he spoke of people who were apt at creating illusions).*

already, all ready   *Already* is an adverb meaning "previously" *(We had already left)* or "even now" *(We are already late)*. In the phrase *all ready, all* modifies *ready;* the phrase means "completely prepared" *(We were all ready by eight o'clock).*

alright, all right   *All right* remains the only established spelling. *Alright* is labeled nonstandard in both the *New World* and *Random House* dictionaries, although *Webster's* lists it without a usage label.

also, likewise   Not acceptable substitutes for *and* (*We packed our clothes, our food, and* [not *also* or *likewise*] *our books*).

altogether, all together   *Altogether* means "wholly, completely"; *all together* means "in a group," "everyone assembled" (*She was altogether pleased with her new piano, which she played when we were all together for our reunion*).

alumnus, alumna   An *alumnus* (plural *alumni*) is a male graduate. An *alumna* (plural *alumnae*) is a female graduate. *Alumni* is now usually used for groups including both men and women.

among, between   *Among* implies more than two persons or things; *between* implies only two. To express a reciprocal relationship, or the relationship of one thing to several other things, however, *between* is commonly used for more than two (*She divided the toys among the three children. Jerry could choose between pie and cake for dessert. An agreement was reached between the four companies. The surveyors drove a stake at a point between three trees.*)

amount, number   *Amount* refers to quantity or mass; *number* refers to countable objects (*Large numbers of guests require a great amount of food*).

an   See *a, an.*

and etc.   *Etc.* (Latin *et cetera*) means "and so forth." The redundant *and etc.* means literally "and and so forth." See **17a4.**

and/or   A legalism to which some readers object.

and which, and who   Use only when *which* or *who* is introducing a clause that coordinates with an earlier clause introduced by *which* or *who* (*John is a man who has opinions and who often expresses them*).

ante-, anti-   *Ante-* means "before," as in *antedate*. *Anti-* means "against," as in *anti-American*. The hyphen is used after *anti-* before capital letters, and before *i*, as in *anti-intellectual*.

any more, anymore   Either spelling is correct. Meaning *now* or *nowadays,* the expression is used only in negative contexts (*He doesn't live here any more*). Used in affirmative contexts the expression is regional and should be avoided in writing (*What's the matter with you anymore?*).

anyone, everyone, someone   Not the same as *any one, every one, some one. Anyone* means "any person" (*He will talk to anyone who visits him*). *Any one* means "any single person or thing" (*He will talk to any one of his neighbors at a time, but not more than one at a time*).

anyplace   Colloquial for *any place.*

anyway, any way, anyways *Anyway* means "nevertheless, no matter what else may be true" *(They're going to leave school anyway, no matter what we say).* Do not confuse it with *any way (I do not see any way to stop them). Anyways* is a colloquial form of *anyway.*

anywheres Colloquial for *anywhere.*

apt See *liable.*

around Colloquial as used in *stay around* meaning "stay nearby" and in *come around to see me.* As a synonym for the preposition *about, around* is informal and objected to by some in writing; write *about one hundred* rather than *around one hundred.*

as In introducing adverbial clauses, *as* may mean either "when" or "because." Thus it is best avoided if there is any possibility of confusion. As a substitute for *that* or *whether (He didn't know as he could go)* or for *who (Those as want them can have them), as* is nonstandard. For confusion between *as* and *like,* see *like, as, as if.*

as . . . as, so . . . as In negative comparisons, some authorities prefer *not so . . . as* to *not as . . . as,* but both are generally considered acceptable.

as, like See *like, as.*

as to A wordy substitute for *about (He questioned me about* [not *as to*] *my plans).* At the beginning of sentences, *as to* is standard for emphasizing *(As to writing, the more he worked, the less successful he was).*

at Wordy in such constructions as *"Where are you eating at?"* and *"Where is he at now?*

athletics Plural in form, but often treated as singular in number. See **8a10.**

awful, awfully In formal English *awful* means "inspiring awe" or "causing fear." Colloquially it is used to mean "very bad" or "unpleasant" *(an awful joke, an awful examination). Awfully* is colloquial as an intensifier *(awfully hard, awfully pretty).*

bad, badly Often confused. *Bad* is an adjective and should be used only to modify nouns and as a predicate adjective after linking verbs *(She had a bad cold and felt bad* [not *badly*]). *Badly* is an adverb *(She hurt her leg badly* [not *bad*]).

being that, being as (how) Nonstandard substitutions for the appropriate subordinating conjunctions *as, because, since.*

below See *above, below.*

beside, besides *Beside* is a preposition meaning "by the side of." *Besides* is an adverb or a preposition meaning "moreover" or "in addition to." *(He sat beside her. Besides, he had to wait for John.)*

better See *had better*.

between, among See *among, between*.

blame for, blame on Both are standard idioms, although some writers prefer the first. *(They blamed him for it. They blamed it on him.)*

bunch Colloquial when used to mean a group of people or things *(a bunch of dishes, a bunch of money)*. Used in writing to refer only to things growing or fastened together *(a bunch of bananas, a bunch of celery)*.

bursted, bust, busted The principal parts of the verb are *burst, burst, burst. Bursted* is an old form of the past and past participle, which is no longer considered good usage. *Bust* and *busted* are nonstandard.

but, hardly, scarcely All are negative and should not be used with other negatives. *(He had only* [not *didn't have but] one hour. He had scarcely* [not *hadn't scarcely] finished. He could hardly* [not *couldn't hardly] see.)*

but however, but yet Redundant. Use *but, however,* or *yet* but not two together (I was ill, *but* [not *but yet*] I attended).

but that, but what Wordy equivalents of *that* as a conjunction or relative pronoun *(I don't doubt that* [not *but that* or *but what] you are right)*.

calculate, figure, reckon Colloquial when used to mean "to think" or "to expect."

can, may Informally *can* is used to indicate both ability *(I can drive a car)* and permission *(Can I use the car?)*. In formal English, *may* is reserved by some for permission *(May I use the car?)*. *May* is also used to indicate possibility *(I can go to the movies, but I may not)*.

case, in the case of Wordy and usually unnecessary. See **41al.**

censor, censure To *censor* means "to examine in order to delete or suppress objectionable material." *Censure* means "to reprimand or condemn."

center around, center about Common expressions, but objected to by many as illogical. Prefer *center on (The debate centered on* [not *centered around* or *centered about] the rights of students)*.

character Wordy. *He had an illness of a serious character* means *He had a serious illness.*

complected A colloquial or dialect equivalent of *complexioned* as in *light-complected*. Prefer *light-* or *dark-complexioned* in writing.

complete See *unique*.

consensus of opinion Redundant; omit *of opinion*. *Consensus* means "a general harmony of opinion."

considerable Standard as an adjective *(considerable success, a considerable crowd)*. Colloquial as a noun *(They lost considerable in the flood)*. Nonstandard as an adverb *(They were considerable hurt in the accident)*.

contact Overused as a vague verb meaning "to meet, to talk with, write," etc. Prefer a more specific word such as *interview, consult, write to, telephone*.

continual, continuous *Continual* means "frequently repeated" *(He was distracted by continual telephone calls)*. *Continuous* means "without interruption" *(We heard the continuous sound of the waves)*.

continue on Redundant; omit *on*.

convince, persuade Widely used interchangeably, but many careful writers *convince* people that something is so, but *persuade* them to do something. The distinction seems worth preserving.

could of Nonstandard for *could have*.

couple Colloquial when used to mean "a few" or "several." When used before a plural noun, it is nonstandard unless followed by *of (We had a couple of* [not *couple*] *minutes)*.

credible, creditable, credulous Sometimes confused. *Credible* means "believable" *(Their story seemed credible to the jury)*. *Creditable* means "praiseworthy" *(You gave a creditable violin recital)*. *Credulous* means "inclined to believe on slight evidence" *(The credulous child really believed the moon was made of cheese)*.

criteria See *data*.

cute, great, lovely, wonderful Overworked as vague words of approval. Find a more specific word *(It was an attractive, spacious, compact, convenient, or comfortable house)*.

data, criteria, phenomena Historically *data* is a plural form, but the singular *datum* is now rare. *Data* is often treated as singular, but careful writing still often treats it as plural *(These data* [not *this*] *are* [not *is*] *the most recent)*. *Criteria* and *phenomena* are plurals of the same kind for the singular forms *criterion* and *phenomenon*.

deal Colloquial in the sense of *bargain* or *transaction (the best deal in town); of secret arrangement (I made a deal with the gangsters);* and of *treatment (I had a rough deal from the Dean).* Currently overworked as a slang term referring to any kind of arrangement or situation.

definite, definitely Colloquial as vague intensifiers *(That suit is a definite bargain; it is definitely handsome).* Prefer a more specific word.

differ from, differ with To *differ from* means "to be unlike." To *differ with* means "to disagree."

different from, different than *From* is idiomatic when a preposition is required; *than* introduces a clause. See **40e.**

disinterested, uninterested Now frequently used interchangeably to mean "having no interest." The distinction between the two, however, is real and valuable. *Uninterested* means "without interest"; *disinterested* means "impartial" *(Good judges are disinterested but not uninterested).*

don't A contraction for *do not,* but not for *does not (She doesn't* [not *don't*] *want a new dress).*

doubt but what See *but that.*

due to Some writers object to *due to* as a preposition meaning "because of" or "owing to" *(The festival was postponed because of* [or *owing to,* not *due to*] *rain).* Acceptable when used as an adjective *(My failure was due to laziness).*

due to the fact that Wordy for *because.*

each and every Unnecessarily wordy.

effect See *affect, effect.*

enthuse Colloquial for *show enthusiasm* or *make enthusiastic.*

equally as good The *as* is unnecessary. *Equally good* is more precise.

etc. See *and etc.* and **17a4.**

everyone, every one See *anyone.*

everywheres Nonstandard for *everywhere.*

every which way Colloquial for *in every direction, in great disorder.*

except See *accept, except.*

expect Colloquial when used to mean "suppose" or "believe" *(I suppose* [not *expect*] *I should do the dishes now).*

extra Colloquial when used as an adverb meaning *especially* or *particularly* (*It was a particularly* [not *extra*] *hot summer*).

fact, the fact that Usually wordy for *that* (*I was unaware that* [not *of the fact that*] *they had left*).

factor Wordy and overworked. See **41a1.**

farther, further Some writers prefer to use *farther* to refer to distance and restrict *further* to mean "in addition" (*It was two miles farther to go the way you wished, but I wanted no further trouble*). Dictionaries recognize the forms as interchangeable.

fewer, less *Fewer* refers to numbers, *less* to amounts, degree, or value (*We sold fewer tickets than last year, but our expenses were less*).

field Wordy and overworked. Say, for example, *in atomic energy* not *in the field of atomic energy*. See **41a1.**

figure See *calculate*.

fine As an adjective to express approval (*a fine person*) *fine* is vague and overused. As an adverb meaning "well" (*works fine*) *fine* is colloquial.

flunk Colloquial for *fail*.

folks Colloquial when used to mean *relatives*, and in the phrase *just folks*, meaning "unassuming, not snobbish." Standard in the sense of people in general, or of a specific group (*folks differ, young folks*).

former, latter *Former* refers to the first-named of two; *latter* refers to the last-named of two. *First* and *last* are used to refer to one of a group of more than two.

function As a noun meaning "event" or "occasion," *function* is appropriate only when the event is formal (*a presidential function*). As a verb meaning "work," "operate," *function* is currently overused and jargonish (*I work* [not *function*] *best after I've had a cup of coffee*).

further See *farther, further*.

get A standard verb, but used colloquially in many idioms inappropriate in most writing. (*Get wise to yourself. That whistling gets me. You can't get away with it.*)

good, well *Good* is colloquial as an adverb (*The motor runs well* [not *good*]). *You look good* means "'You look attractive, well dressed," or the like. *You look well* means "You look healthy."

good and Colloquial as a synonym for *very* (*good and hot, good and angry*).

great See *cute*.

graduate Either I *graduated from* college or I *was graduated from* college is acceptable, but I *graduated college* is nonstandard.

had better, had best, better Standard idioms for *ought* and *should,* which are more formal *(You had better* [or *had best] plan carefully).* More formally: *You ought to* [or *should] plan carefully). Better* alone *(You better plan carefully)* is colloquial.

had ought, hadn't ought Nonstandard for *ought* and *ought not.*

hang, hung The principal parts of the verb are *hang, hung, hung,* but when referring to death by hanging, formal English uses *hang, hanged, hanged (We hung the pictures. The prisoners hanged themselves.)*

hardly See *but.*

have, of See *of, have*

he or she See **8b1.**

himself See *myself.*

hisself Nonstandard for *himself.*

hopefully *Hopefully* means "in a hopeful manner" *(They waited hopefully for money).* It is now widely used in the sense of "it is hoped" *(Hopefully, you can send me money).* Some readers object to this use.

hung See *hang, hung.*

idea Often used vaguely for *intention, plan, purpose,* and other more exact words. Prefer a more exact choice. *(My intention* [not *idea] is to become an engineer. The theme* [not *idea] of the movie is that justice is colorblind.)*

ignorant, stupid The distinction is important. An *ignorant* child is one who has been taught very little; a *stupid* child is one who is unable to learn.

illusion See *allusion, illusion.*

imply, infer To *imply* means to suggest without stating; to *infer* means to draw a conclusion. Speakers *imply;* listeners *infer (They implied that I was ungrateful; I inferred that they didn't like me).*

in, into *In* indicates "inside, enclosed, within." *Into* is more exact when the meaning is "toward, from the outside in," although *in* is common in both meanings. *(I left the book in the room, and went back into the room to get it.)*

in back of, in behind, in between Wordy for *back of, behind, between.*

individual, party, person *Individual* refers to one particular person. *Person* refers to any human being as a distinct personality. *Party* refers to a group of people, except in legal language (*Jefferson defended the rights of the individual. Lee is a person* [not *an individual*] *of strong character. You are the person* [not *party*] *I am looking for.*)

infer   See *imply, infer*.

ingenious, ingenuous   *Ingenious* means "clever"; *ingenuous* means "naive" (*Inventors are usually ingenious, but some are too ingenuous to know when they have been cheated*).

in regards to   Nonstandard for *as regards* or *in regard to*.

inside of, outside of   The *of* is unnecessary (*He stayed inside* [not *inside of*] *the house*).

in the case of, in the line of   See *case*.

into   See *in, into*.

irregardless   Nonstandard for *regardless*.

is when, is where, is because   Faulty predications in such sentences as: *A first down is when the football is advanced ten yards in four plays or fewer. A garage is where. . . . The reason is because. . . .* See **14a.**

its, it's   The possessive pronoun has no apostrophe. *It's* is a contraction of *it is.*

-ize   The suffix *-ize* is one of several used to form verbs from nouns and adjectives (*hospitalize, criticize, sterilize*). Writers in government, business, and other institutions have often used it excessively and unnecessarily in such coinages as *finalize, concretize, permanize*. Such coinages are widely objected to; it is best to limit your use of *-ize* words to those that are well established, and resist the temptation to coin new ones.

kind, sort   These are frequently treated as plural in such constructions as *these kind of books* and *those sort of dogs*. Preferred usage in both speech and writing requires singular or plural throughout the construction, as in *this kind of book* or *these kinds of books*.

kind of, sort of   Colloquial when used to mean *somewhat, rather* (*I was rather* [not *kind of*] *pleased*).

kind of a, sort of a   Omit the *a*.

latter   See *former, latter*.

lay, lie   To *lay* means "to place, put down" (*Lay the book on the table*). To *lie* means "to recline" (*The dog lies on the floor*). See **4c.**

learn, teach   To *learn* means "to gain knowledge"; to *teach* means "to give knowledge" (*We learn from experience; experience teaches us much*).

leave, let To *leave* is to depart; to *let* is to permit or allow *(I must leave now. Will you let me go?)*.

less See *fewer, less.*

let See *leave, let.*

level Overworked and unnecessary in such phrases as *at the retail level, at the particular level.* Use only when the idea of rank or degree is clearly meant *(We speak of our education as divided into three levels: elementary, secondary, and college).*

liable, apt, likely Often used interchangeably. But careful writing reserves *liable* for "legally responsible," or "subject to," *likely* for "probably," and *apt* for "having an aptitude for" *(I am likely to drive carefully, for I am not an apt driver, and I know I am liable for any damages).*

lie, lay See *lay, lie,* and see **4d.**

like, as, as if *Like* is a preposition; *as* and *as if* are conjunctions. Though *like* is often used as a conjunction in speech, writing preserves the distinction *(He looks as if* [not *like*] *he were tired).* Note that *as if* is followed by the subjunctive *were.*

likely See *liable.*

loose, lose Loose means "to free." *Lose* means "to be deprived of." *(He will lose the dog if he looses him from his leash.)*

lots, lots of, a lot of Colloquial for *much, many,* or *a great deal (I had a great deal of* [not *lots of*] *money and bought many* [not *lots of* or *a lot of*] *cars).*

lovely See *cute.*

mad Dictionaries recognize *mad* as a synonym for *angry,* or *very enthusiastic,* but some readers object to its use in these meanings.

manner Often unnecessary in phrases like *in a precise manner* where a single adverb *(precisely)* or a "with" phrase *(with precision)* would do.

may See *can, may.*

may of Nonstandard for *may have.*

media A plural form (singular *medium*) requiring a plural verb *(The mass media are* [not *is*] *sometimes guilty of distorting the news).*

maybe, may be *Maybe* means "perhaps"; *may be* is a verb form. Be careful to distinguish between the two.

might of Nonstandard for *might have.*

mighty Colloquial as an intensifier meaning "very" or "extremely" (*mighty tasty, mighty expensive*).

most Colloquial as a substitute for *almost* or *nearly*.

must of Nonstandard for *must have*.

myself, yourself, himself *Myself* is often used in speech as a substitute for *I* or *me* but is not standard in written English. Reserve *myself* for emphatic (*I myself will do the work*) or reflexive use (*I hurt myself*). The same applies to the forms *yourself, himself, herself*, etc.

nice, nice and *Nice* is overused as a vague word of approval meaning "attractive, agreeable, friendly, pleasant," and the like. Use a more exact word. *Nice and* as an intensifier (*The beer was nice and cold*) is colloquial.

nohow Nonstandard for *not at all, in no way*.

none The indefinite pronoun *none* may take either a singular or a plural verb, depending on its context (*None of the gold was stolen; None of the men were absent*). See **8a2.**

nothing like, nowhere near Colloquial for *not nearly* (*I was not nearly* [not *nowhere near*] *as sick as you*).

nowheres Nonstandard for *nowhere*.

number See *amount, number*.

of, have In speech the auxiliary *have* in such combinations as *could have, might have*, etc., sounds very much like *of*, leading some people to write *could of, might of*, etc. All such combinations with *of* are nonstandard. In writing be careful to use *have*.

off of, off from Wordy and colloquial (*The paper slid off* [not *off of*] *the table*.

OK, O.K., okay All are standard forms, but formal writing prefers a more exact word.

on account of Wordy for *because of*. Regional for *because* (*She bought the car because* [not *on account of*] *she needed it*).

outside of Colloquial for *except* (*Nobody was there except* [not *outside of*] *Henry*). See also *inside of*.

overall An overused synonym for *general, complete*, as in *overall prices, overall policy*. Often meaningless, as in *Our overall decision was to buy the car*.

over with Colloquial for *ended, finished, completed*.

party See *individual*.

per Appropriate in business and technical writing *(per diem, per capita, feet per second, pounds per square inch)*. In ordinary writing prefer *a* or *an* *(ninety cents a dozen, twice a day)*.

percent, percentage Both mean "rate per hundred." *Percent* (sometimes written *per cent*) is used with numbers *(fifty percent, 23 percent)*. *Percentage* is used without numbers *(a small percentage)*. Avoid using either as a synonym for *part* *(A small part* [not *percentage*] *of the money was lost)*.

perfect See *unique*.

person See *individual*.

persuade See *convince, persuade*.

phenomena See *data*.

phone Colloquial for *telephone*. In formal writing use the full word.

photo Colloquial for *photograph*. In formal writing use the full word.

plan on Colloquial in such phrases as *plan on going, plan on seeing,* for *plan to go, plan to see*.

plenty Colloquial as an adverb meaning "very, amply" *(I was very* [not *plenty*] *angry)*. Note that as a noun meaning "enough, a large number," *plenty* must be followed by *of (I've had plenty of money)*.

poorly Colloquial or dialectal for *ill, in poor health*.

practical, practicable *Practical* means "useful, not theoretical." *Practicable* means "capable of being put into practice" *(Franklin was a practical statesman; his schemes were practicable)*.

pretty Colloquial and overused as an adverb meaning "somewhat, moderately" *(pretty difficult, pretty sick)*. Use a more specific word.

principal, principle As an adjective *principal* means "chief, main"; as a noun it means "leader, chief officer," or, in finance, "a capital sum, as distinguished from interest or profit." The noun *principle* means "fundamental truth" or "basic law or doctrine." *(What is my principal reason for being here? I am the principal of the local elementary school. That bank pays 5 percent interest on your principal. The textbook explained the underlying principle.)*

provided, providing Both are acceptable as subordinating conjunctions meaning "on the condition" *(I will move to Washington, providing* [or *provided*] *the salary is adequate)*.

raise, rise *Raise, raised, raised* is a transitive verb *(They raised potatoes)*. *Rise, rose, risen* is intransitive *(They rose at daybreak)*.

real Colloquial for *really* or *very* *(real cloudy, real economical)*.

reason is because   See *is when* and **14a.**

reason why   Usually redundant *(The reason* [not *reason why*] *we failed is clear).*

reckon   See *calculate.*

refer   See *allude, refer.*

regarding, in regard to, with regard to   Overused and wordy for *on, about,* or *concerning (We have not decided on* [not *with regard to*] *your admission).*

right   Colloquial or dialectal when used to mean "very" *(right fresh, right happy). Right along* and *right away* are colloquial for *continuously, immediately.*

rise, raise   See *raise, rise.*

round   See *unique.*

said   *Said* in such phrases as *the said paragraph, the said person* occurs frequently in legal writing. Avoid the use in ordinary writing.

scarcely   See *but, hardly, scarcely.*

set, sit   Often confused. See **4c.**

shall, will, should, would   *Will* is now commonly used for all persons *(I, you he, she, it)* except in the first person for questions *(Shall I go?)* and in formal contexts *(We shall consider each of your reasons). Should* is used for all persons when condition or obligation is being expressed *(If he should stay. . . . We should go). Would* is used for all persons to express a wish or customary action *(Would that I had listened! I would ride the same bus every day.)*

shape up   Colloquial for *proceed satisfactorily (Our plans are shaping up).*

should   See *shall.*

should of   Nonstandard for *should have.*

show up   Colloquial when used to mean "appear" *(They did not show up)* or to mean "expose" *(You showed them up for the liars they are).*

since, because   The subordinating conjunction *because* always indicates cause. *Since* may indicate either cause or time *(It has rained since yesterday. Since you need money, I'll lend you some).* Be careful to avoid using *since* in sentences where it could indicate either cause or time and thus be ambiguous. In *since we moved, we have been working longer hours,* it is unclear whether *because we moved* or *from the time we moved* is meant.

sit, set   See *set, sit.*

situation Wordy and unnecessary in expressions like *We have an examination situation.*

so *So* is a loose and often imprecise conjunction. Avoid using it excessively to join independent clauses. For clauses of purpose, *so that* is preferable *(They left so that* [not *so*] *I could study). Because* is preferable when cause is clearly intended *(Because it began to rain, we left* [not *It began to rain, so we left*]).

some Colloquial and vague when used to mean "unusual, remarkable, exciting" *(That was some party. This is some car.).* In writing use a more specific word.

someone, some one See *anyone.*

sometime, some time Use one word in the sense of a time not specified; use two words in the sense of a period of time *(Sometime we shall spend some time together).*

somewheres Nonstandard for *somewhere.*

sort See *kind, sort.*

sort of See *kind of, sort of.*

sort of a See *kind of a.*

straight See *unique.*

stupid See *ignorant, stupid.*

such Colloquial and overused as a vague intensifier *(It was a very* [not *such a*] *hot day).*

sure Colloquial for *surely, certainly (I was surely* [not *sure*] *sick).*

sure and, try and Colloquial for *sure to, try to.*

suspicion Dialectal when used in place of the verb *suspect.*

take and Nonstandard in most uses *(Lou slammed* [not *took and slammed*] *the book down).*

teach, learn See *learn, teach.*

than, then Don't confuse these. *Than* is a conjunction *(younger than John). Then* is an adverb indicating time *(then, not now).*

that Colloquial when used as an adverb *(She's that poor she can't buy food. I didn't like the book that much.)*

that, which *That* always introduces restrictive clauses; *which* may introduce either restrictive or nonrestrictive clauses. See **20c.** Some writers and editors prefer to limit *which* entirely to nonrestrictive clauses *(This is the car that I bought yesterday. This car, which I bought yesterday, is very economical.)*

theirselves   Nonstandard for *themselves.*

then, than   See *than, then.*

there, their, they're   Don't confuse these. *There* is an adverb or an expletive *(He walks there. There are six.). Their* is a pronoun *(their rooms). They're* is a contraction for *they are (They're too eager).*

these kind, these sort   See *kind, sort.*

this here, that there, these here, them there   Nonstandard for *this, that, these, those.*

thusly   Nonstandard for *thus.*

to, too   *To* is a preposition. *Too* is an adverb meaning *also (She laughed too)* or *more than enough (You worked too hard).* In the sense of *indeed* it is colloquial *(She did too laugh).*

toward, towards   Both are correct, though *toward* is more common in the United States, *towards* in Britain.

try and   See *sure and.*

type   Colloquial for *type of (This type of* [not *type*] *research is expensive).* Often used, but usually in hyphenated compounds *(colonial-type architecture, tile-type floors, scholarly-type text).* Omit *type* for such expressions wherever possible.

uninterested   See *disinterested, uninterested.*

unique   Several adjectives such as *unique, perfect, round, straight,* and *complete* name qualities that do not vary in degree. Logically, therefore, they cannot be compared. Formal use requires *more nearly round, more nearly perfect* and the like. The comparative and superlative forms, however, are widely used colloquially in such phrases as *the most unique house, most complete examination, most perfect day.* Their occurrence even in formal English is exemplified by the phrase *more perfect union* in the Constitution. See **3c.**

used to   In writing be careful to preserve the *d (We used to* [not *use to*] *get up at six every morning).*

used to could   Nonstandard for *used to be able.*

wait on   Colloquial when used to mean "wait for"; *wait on* means "to serve, attend" *(We waited for* [not *waited on*] *the clerk to wait on us).*

that you should go. The expressions *want off, want in, want out* are regional and should not be used in writing.

wait on Colloquial when used to mean "wait for"; *wait on* means "to serve, attend" *(We waited for [not waited on] the clerk to wait on us).*

ways Colloquial when used for *way* meaning "distance" *(It is a long way [not ways] to Brownsville).*

well See *good, well.*

where Colloquial when used as a substitute for *that (I read in the mayor's report that [not where] many local crimes are unsolved).*

which For *and which,* see *and which;* for the distinction between *that* and *which,* see *that, which.*

while Used most precisely to indicate time *(He had the radio on while he was studying).* It can also be used with the meaning of *although (While she was always willing to work, she seldom was paid well).* Because both these meanings are possible, be careful not to use *while* when the meaning could be ambiguous. In *While we both worked for the same company, we did not often meet* it is not clear whether the meaning is *when* or *although.*

While is not generally acceptable in the meaning of *and* or *but (Susan is a doctor, and or but [not while] Ray is an engineer).*

will See *shall.*

wise A long-established adverb suffix, *-wise* is used to mean "in a specific direction" *(lengthwise, sidewise)* or "in the manner of" *(crabwise, clockwise).* More recently *-wise* has been widely overworked as a suffix meaning "with regard to, in connection with" *(dollarwise, educationwise).* Many object to the use as jargon and unnecessary, and it is best avoided.

wonderful See *cute.*

would See *shall.*

would of Nonstandard for *would have.*

you all Informal Southern dialect form used as a plural of *you.*

yourself See *myself.*

44

44 SPELLING **SP**

Language existed first as speech, and the alphabet is basically a device to represent speech on paper. When letters of the alphabet have definite values and are used consistently, as in Polish or Spanish, the spelling of a word is an accurate index to its pronunciation, and vice versa. Not so with English. The alphabet does not represent English sounds consistently. The letter *a* may stand for the sound of the vowel in *may, can, care,* or *car; c* for the initial consonant of *carry* or city; *th* for the diphthong in *both* or in *bother.* Different combinations of letters are often sounded alike, as in *rec(ei)ve, l(ea)ve,* or *p(ee)ve.* In many words, moreover, some letters appear to perform no function at all, as in *i(s)land, de(b)t, of(t)en, recei(p)t.* Finally, the relationship between the spelling and the pronunciation of some words seems downright capricious, as in *through, enough, colonel, right.*

Much of the inconsistency of English spelling may be explained historically. English spelling has been a poor index to pronunciation ever since the Norman conquest, when French scribes gave written English a French spelling. Subsequent tampering with English spelling has made it even more complex. Early classical scholars with a flair for etymology added the unvoiced *b* to early English *det* and *dout* because they mistakenly traced these words directly from the Latin *debitum* and *dubitum* when actually both the English and the Latin had derived independently from a common Indo-European origin. Dutch printers working in England were responsible for changing early English *gost* to *ghost.* More complications arose when the pronunciation of many words changed more rapidly than their spelling. The *gh* in *right* and *through,* and in similar words, was once pronounced much like the German *ch* in *nicht. Colonel* was once pronounced *col-o-nel.* The final *e* in words like *wife* and *time* was long ago dropped from actual speech, but it still remains as a proper spelling form.

The English tendency to borrow words freely from Latin and French has given us groups like the native English *sight,* the French *site,* and the Latin *cite.* Our word *regal,* with its hard *g,* comes from the Norman French. Our word *regent,* with *g* sounded as a *j,* comes from Parisian French. Words like *machine, burlesque,* and *suite* come directly from the French, with little change in spelling or pronunciation. *Envelope,* on the other hand, maintains its French spelling but is given an English pronunciation. From Spanish comes the proper noun *Don Quixote;* its Spanish pronunciation (dōn kē·hō′tā) is still frequently heard, but the English adjective *quixotic* is pronounced kwĭks · ot′ĭk.

The complex history of the English language may help to explain why our spelling is illogical, but it does not justify misspelling. Society tends to equate bad spelling with incompetent writing. In fact, only the misspellings tend to be noticed, not the quality of the writing, and correct spellings sometimes render faulty constructions invisible. That particularly American institution, the spelling bee, has for generations put a higher premium on the correct spelling of *phthisis* than on a clearly constructed sentence. To illustrate, test your own attitude. Which of the two selections below seems better?

> Parants should teech children the importence of puntuallity.

> The condition of unpunctuality which exists in the character of a great many members of the younger generation should be eliminated by every means that lies at the disposal of parents who are responsible for them.

On first reading, the first sentence seems inferior to the second. Actually the former is the better sentence—more direct and succinct. But the misspellings make it difficult to take the sentence seriously. Readers have been conditioned to treat misspellings as one of the greatest sins a writer can commit.

44a Avoid secondary and British spellings.

Many words have a secondary spelling, generally British. Though the secondary spelling is not incorrect, as an American writer you should avoid it. Here is a brief list of preferred and secondary spelling forms; consult a good dictionary for others.

1. American **-e**	*British* **-ae, -oe**
anemia	anaemia
anesthetic	anaesthetic
encyclopedia	encyclopaedia
fetus	foetus
2. American **im-, in-**	*British* **em-, en-**
impanel	empanel
incase	encase
inquiry	enquiry
3. American **-ize**	*British* **-ise**
apologize	apologise
4. American **-or**	*British* **-our**
armor	armour
clamor	clamour
color	colour
flavor	flavour

4. *American* **-or** *(cont.)*   *British* **-our** *(cont.)*

labor   labour
odor   odour
vigor   vigour

5. *American* **-er**   *British* **-re**

center   centre
fiber   fibre
somber   sombre
theater   theatre

6. *American* **-o**   *British* **-ou**

mold   mould
plow   plough
smolder   smoulder

7. *American* **-ction**   *British* **-xion**

connection   connexion
inflection   inflexion

8. *American* **-l**   *British* **-ll**

leveled   levelled
quarreled   quarrelled
traveled   travelled

9. *American* **-e** *omitted*   *British* **-e**

acknowledgment   acknowledgement
judgment   judgement

44b

44b Proofread your manuscripts carefully to eliminate misspelling.

In writing a first draft, you are forming words into sentences faster than you can write them down. You are concentrating, not on the words you are actually writing, but on the words to come. A few mistakes in spelling may easily creep into a first draft. Always take five or ten minutes to proofread your final draft to make sure that you do not let misspellings stand uncorrected.

The failure to proofread accounts for the fact that the words most often misspelled are not, for example, *baccalaureate* and *connoisseur,* but *too, its, lose, receive,* and *occurred.* Not trusting ourselves to spell hard words correctly, we consult a dictionary and take pains to get the correct spelling on paper. But most of us think we can spell a familiar word. Either we never bother to check the spelling, or we assume that a word pictured correctly in our minds must automatically spell itself correctly on the paper in front of us. This thinking accounts for such errors as omitting the final *o* in *too,* confusing the possessive *its* with the contraction *it's,* and spelling *loose* when *lose* is meant. You will never forget how to spell *receive* and *occurred* if you will devote just a few moments to memorizing their correct spelling.

On pages 408–410 is a list of 350 words often misspelled. Almost every one of them is a common word; to misspell any of them in a finished paper denotes carelessness.

44c   Cultivate careful pronunciation as an aid to correct spelling.

Some words are commonly misspelled because they are mispronounced. The following list of frequently mispronounced words will help you overcome this source of spelling error.

accident*al*ly		note the *al*
acc*u*rate		note the *u*
can*d*idate		note the first *d*
envir*o*nment		note the *on*
gover*n*ment		note the *n*
incident*al*ly		note the *al*
math*e*matics		note the *e*
prob*ab*ly		note the *ab*
quan*t*ity		note the first *t*
represen*ta*tive		note the *ta*
soph*o*more		note the second *o*
su*r*prise		note the first *r*
a*thl*etics	NOT	ath*el*etics
disas*tr*ous	NOT	disast*er*ous
heigh*t*	NOT	heigh*th*
gr*ie*-vous	NOT	gr*e-vi*-ous
ir-r*el*-e-*v*ant	NOT	ir-rev-e-*l*ant
mis-ch*ie*-vous	NOT	mis-che-*vi*-ous

However, pronunciation is not an infallible guide to correct spelling. Although, for example, the last syllables of *adviser, beggar,* and *doctor* all are pronounced as the same unstressed *ur,* all are spelled differently. Proceed cautiously in using pronunciation as a spelling aid.

44d   Distinguish carefully between the spellings of words that are similar in sound.

English abounds in words whose sound is similar to that of other words but whose spelling is different: for example, *rain, rein, reign.* The most troublesome of such words are listed below.

all ready: everyone is ready
already: by this time

all together: as a group
altogether: entirely, completely

altar: a structure used in worship
alter: to change

ascent: climbing, a way sloping up
assent: agreement; to agree

breath: air taken into the lungs
breathe: to exhale and inhale

capital: chief; leading or governing city; wealth, resources
capitol: a building that houses the state or national lawmakers

cite: to use as an example, to quote
site: location

clothes: wearing apparel
cloths: two or more pieces of cloth

complement: that which completes; to supply a lack
compliment: praise, flattering remark; to praise

corps: a military group or unit
corpse: a dead body

council: an assembly of lawmakers
counsel: advice; one who advises; to give advice

dairy: a factory or farm engaged in milk production
diary: a daily record of experiences or observations

descent: a way sloping down
dissent: disagreement; to disagree

dining: eating
dinning: making a continuing noise

dying: ceasing to live
dyeing: process of coloring fabrics

forth: forward in place or space, onward in time
fourth: the ordinal equivalent of the number 4

loose: free from bonds
lose: to suffer a loss

personal: pertaining to a particular person; individual
personnel: body of persons employed in same work or service

principal: chief, most important; a school official; a capital sum (as distinguished from interest or profit)
principle: a belief, rule of conduct or thought

respectfully: with respect
respectively: in order, in turn

stationery: writing paper
stationary: not moving

their: possessive form of *they*
they're: contraction of *they are*
there: adverb of place

whose: possessive form of *who*
who's: contraction of *who is*

your: possessive form of *you*
you're: contraction of *you are*

44e Familiarize yourself with spelling rules as an aid to correct spelling.

1 Carefully distinguish between *ie* and *ei*. Remember this jingle:

Write *i* before *e*
Except after *c*
Or when sounded like *a*
As in *eighty* and *sleigh*.

i before e	*ei after c*	*ei when sounded like a*
thief	receive	weigh
believe	deceive	freight
wield	ceiling	vein

Some exceptions

leisure
financier
weird

2 Drop the final *e* before a suffix beginning with a vowel but not before a suffix beginning with a consonant.

a. Suffix beginning with a vowel, final *e* dropped:

please + ure = *pleasure*
ride + ing   = *riding*
locate + ion = *location*
guide + ance = *guidance*

EXCEPTIONS:

In some words the final *e* is retained to prevent confusion with other words.

dyeing (to distinguish it from *dying*)

Final *e* is retained to keep *c* or *g* soft before *a* or *o*.

	notice + able	= *noticeable*
	change + able	= *changeable*
BUT	practice + able	= *practicable* (*c* has sound of *k*)

b. Suffix beginning with a consonant, final *e* retained:

sure + ly	= *surely*
arrange + ment	= *arrangement*
like + ness	= *likeness*
entire + ly	= *entirely*
entire + ty	= *entirety*
hate + ful	= *hateful*

EXCEPTIONS:

Some words taking the suffix *-ful* or *-ly* drop final *e:*

awe + ful = *awful*
due + ly = *duly*
true + ly = *truly*

Some words taking the suffix *-ment* drop final *e:*

judge + ment = *judgment*
acknowledge + ment = *acknowledgment*

The ordinal numbers of *five, nine,* and *twelve,* formed with *-th,* drop the final *e. Five* and *twelve* change *v* to *f.*

fifth   ninth   twelfth

3   Final *y* is usually changed to *i* before a suffix, unless the suffix begins with *i*.

	defy + ance	= *defiance*
	forty + eth	= *fortieth*
	ninety + eth	= *ninetieth*
	rectify + er	= *rectifier*
BUT	cry + ing	= *crying* (suffix begins with *i*)

4   A final single consonant is doubled before a suffix beginning with a vowel when (a) a single vowel precedes the consonant, and (b) the consonant ends an accented syllable or a one-syllable word. Unless both these conditions exist, the final consonant is not doubled.

stop + ing	= *stopping* (*o* is a single vowel before consonant *p* which ends word of one syllable.)
admit + ed	= *admitted* (*i* is single vowel before consonant *t* which ends an accented syllable.)

stoop + ing   = *stooping* (*p* ends a word of one syllable but is preceded by double vowel *oo*.)

benefit + ed = *benefited* (*t* is preceded by a single vowel *i* but does not end the accented syllable.)

EXERCISE 44e(1)   Spell each of the following words correctly and explain what spelling rule applies. Note any exceptions to the rules.

argue + ment	= ?	change + able	= ?
beg + ar	= ?	change + ing	= ?
bury + ed	= ?	awe + ful	= ?
conceive + able	= ?	precede + ence	= ?
eighty + eth	= ?	shine + ing	= ?
associate + ion	= ?	busy + ness	= ?
hop + ing	= ?	defer + ed	= ?
droop + ing	= ?	peace + able	= ?

5   Nouns ending in a sound that can be smoothly united with -*s* usually form their plurals by adding -*s*. Verbs ending in a sound that can be smoothly united with -*s* form their third person singular by adding -*s*.

Singular	*Plural*	*Some Exceptions*		*Verbs*	
picture	pictures	buffalo	buffaloes	blacken	blackens
radio	radios	Negro	Negroes	criticize	criticizes
flower	flowers	zero	zeroes	radiate	radiates
chair	chairs				
ache	aches				
fan	fans				

6   Nouns ending in a sound that cannot be smoothly united with -*s* form their plurals by adding -*es*. Verbs ending in a sound that cannot be smoothly united with -*s* form their third person singular by adding -*es*.

Singular	*Plural*
porch	porches
bush	bushes
pass	passes
tax	taxes

7   Nouns ending in *y* preceded by a consonant form their plurals by changing *y* to *i* and adding -*es*. Verbs ending in *y* preceded by a consonant form their third person singular in the same way.

Singular	Plural
pity	pities
nursery	nurseries
carry	carries
mercy	mercies
body	bodies

EXCEPTIONS:

The plural of proper nouns ending in *y* is formed by adding *-s* (*There are three Marys in my history class*).

8 Nouns ending in *y* preceded by *a, e, o,* or *u* form their plurals by adding *-s* only. Verbs ending in *y* preceded by *a, e, o,* or *u* form their third person singular in the same way.

Singular	Plural
day	days
key	keys
buy	buys
guy	guys
enjoy	enjoys

9 The spelling of plural nouns borrowed from French, Greek, and Latin frequently retains the plural of the original language.

Singular	Plural
alumna (*feminine*)	alumnae
alumnus (*masculine*)	alumni
analysis	analyses
basis	bases
crisis	crises
datum	data
hypothesis	hypotheses
phenomenon	phenomena

The tendency now, however, is to give many such words an anglicized plural. The result is that many words have two plural forms, one foreign, the other anglicized. Either is correct.

Singular	Plural (foreign)	Plural (anglicized)
appendix	appendices	appendixes
beau	beaux	beaus
focus	foci	focuses
index	indices	indexes

Singular	Plural (foreign)	Plural (anglicized)
memorandum	memoranda	memorandums
radius	radii	radiuses
stadium	stadia	stadiums

EXERCISE 44e(2) Spell the plural of each of the following words correctly and explain what spelling rule applies. Note any exceptions to the rules.

1	frame	**6**	branch	**11**	echo	**16**	Charles
2	rose	**7**	bass	**12**	stratum	**17**	no
3	dash	**8**	cameo	**13**	church	**18**	potato
4	maze	**9**	fly	**14**	lady	**19**	play
5	table	**10**	box	**15**	mass	**20**	pain

44f Spell compound words in accordance with current usage.

Compound words usually progress by stages from being written as two words, to being hyphenated, to being written as one word. Since these stages often overlap, the correct spelling of a compound word may vary. For the spelling of a compound at any particular moment, take the advice of a good dictionary. (For the general use of the hyphen in compounds, see "Hyphen," Section **30**.)

44g Use drills to help cultivate the habit of correct spelling.

Spelling is primarily a habit. Once you learn to spell a word correctly, you no longer need to think about it; its correct spelling becomes an automatic skill. But if you are a chronic misspeller you have the task not only of learning correct spellings but of unlearning the incorrect spellings you now employ. You must train your fingers to write the word correctly until they do so almost without your thinking about it. Here is a suggested drill that will aid you in learning correct spellings.

1 Look carefully at a word whose spelling bothers you and say it to yourself. If it has more than one syllable, examine each syllable.

2 Look at the individual letters, dividing the word into syllables as you say the letters.

3 Try to visualize the correct spelling before you write the word. If you have trouble, begin again with the *first* step.

4 Write the word without looking at your book or list.

5 Look at your book or list and see whether you wrote the word correctly. If you did, cover the word and write it again. If you write the word correctly the third time, you have probably learned it and will not have to think about it again.

6 If you spell the word incorrectly any one of the three times, look very carefully at the letters you missed. Then start over again and keep on until you have spelled it correctly three times.

44g Spelling lists

The following lists contain many words you are likely to use in writing whose spelling is troublesome. The words are arranged in alphabetized groups for easy reference and for drill.

Group 1	*Group 2*	*Group 3*
1. accidentally	1. arctic	1. apparent
2. accommodate	2. auxiliary	2. appearance
3. accompanied	3. business	3. attendance
4. achieved	4. candidate	4. beggar
5. address	5. characteristic	5. brilliant
6. aggravate	6. chauffeur	6. calendar
7. anxiety	7. colonel	7. carriage
8. barren	8. column	8. conqueror
9. believe	9. cylinder	9. contemptible
10. ceiling	10. environment	10. coolly
11. confident	11. especially	11. descent
12. course	12. exhaust	12. desirable
13. disappear	13. exhilaration	13. dictionary
14. disappoint	14. February	14. disastrous
15. dissipate	15. foremost	15. eligible
16. efficiency	16. ghost	16. equivalent
17. emphasize	17. government	17. existence
18. exaggerate	18. grievous	18. familiar
19. exceed	19. hygiene	19. grammar
20. fiery	20. intercede	20. guidance
21. finally	21. leisure	21. hindrance
22. financial	22. library	22. hoping
23. forehead	23. lightning	23. imaginary
24. foreign	24. literature	24. incredible
25. forfeit	25. mathematics	25. indigestible
26. grief	26. medicine	26. indispensable
27. handkerchief	27. mortgage	27. inevitable
28. hurriedly	28. muscle	28. influential
29. hypocrisy	29. notoriety	29. irresistible
30. imminent	30. optimistic	30. liable
31. incidentally	31. pamphlet	31. marriage
32. innocence	32. parliament	32. momentous
33. intentionally	33. physically	33. naturally
34. interest	34. physician	34. nickel
35. legitimate	35. prairie	35. noticeable
36. likely	36. prejudice	36. nucleus
37. manual	37. pronunciation	37. obedience
38. mattress	38. recede	38. outrageous
39. misspell	39. recognize	39. pageant
40. niece	40. reign	40. permissible
41. occasion	41. rhetoric	41. perseverance

Group 1 (cont.)

42. organization
43. parallel
44. piece
45. psychiatrist
46. psychology
47. receive
48. religious
49. severely
50. villain

Group 4

1. allot
2. allotted
3. barbarian
4. barbarous
5. beneficial
6. benefited
7. changeable
8. changing
9. commit
10. committed
11. committee
12. comparative
13. comparatively
14. comparison
15. compel
16. compelled
17. competent
18. competition
19. compulsion
20. conceivable
21. conceive
22. conception
23. conscience
24. conscientious
25. conscious
26. courteous
27. courtesy
28. deceit
29. deceive
30. deception
31. decide
32. decision
33. defer
34. deference
35. deferred
36. describe
37. description

Group 2 (cont.)

42. rhythm
43. schedule
44. sentinel
45. soliloquy
46. sophomore
47. studying
48. surprise
49. twelfth
50. Wednesday

Group 5

1. hesitancy
2. hesitate
3. instance
4. instant
5. intellectual
6. intelligence
7. intelligent
8. intelligible
9. maintain
10. maintenance
11. miniature
12. minute
13. ninetieth
14. ninety
15. ninth
16. obligation
17. oblige
18. obliged
19. occur
20. occurred
21. occurrence
22. omission
23. omit
24. omitted
25. picnic
26. picnicking
27. possess
28. possession
29. precede
30. precedence
31. preceding
32. prefer
33. preference
34. preferred
35. procedure
36. proceed
37. realize

Group 3 (cont.)

42. persistent
43. pleasant
44. possible
45. prevalent
46. resistance
47. secede
48. strenuous
49. vengeance
50. vigilance

Group 6

1. obstacle
2. operate
3. opinion
4. pastime
5. persuade
6. piece
7. politician
8. practically
9. presence
10. professor
11. propeller
12. quantity
13. recommend
14. region
15. relieve
16. representative
17. reservoir
18. restaurant
19. ridiculous
20. sacrifice
21. sacrilegious
22. safety
23. salary
24. scarcely
25. science
26. secretary
27. seize
28. separate
29. shriek
30. siege
31. similar
32. suffrage
33. supersede
34. suppress
35. syllable
36. symmetry
37. temperament

Group 4 (cont.)

38. device
39. devise
40. discuss
41. discussion
42. dissatisfied
43. dissatisfy
44. equip
45. equipment
46. equipped
47. excel
48. excellent
49. explain
50. explanation

Group 5 (cont.)

38. really
39. refer
40. reference
41. referred
42. repeat
43. repetition
44. transfer
45. transferred
46. tried
47. tries
48. try
49. writing
50. written

Group 6 (cont.)

38. temperature
39. tendency
40. tournament
41. tragedy
42. truly
43. tyranny
44. unanimous
45. unusual
46. usage
47. valuable
48. wholly
49. yoke
50. yolk

Group 7

1. accept
2. across
3. aisle
4. all right
5. amateur
6. annual
7. appropriate
8. argument
9. arrangement
10. association
11. awkward
12. bachelor
13. biscuit
14. cafeteria
15. career
16. cemetery
17. completely

18. convenient
19. cruelty
20. curiosity
21. definite
22. desperate
23. diphtheria
24. discipline
25. disease
26. distribute
27. dormitories
28. drudgery
29. ecstasy
30. eighth
31. eliminate
32. eminent
33. enemy
34. except

35. exercise
36. extraordinary
37. fascinate
38. fraternity
39. furniture
40. grandeur
41. height
42. hypocrite
43. imitation
44. interest
45. livelihood
46. loneliness
47. magazine
48. material
49. messenger
50. mischievous

THE LIBRARY
AND THE
RESEARCH PAPER

Knowledge is of two kinds: We know a subject ourselves, or we know where we can find information
upon it.

A man will turn over half a library to make one book.

SAMUEL JOHNSON

The processes of **research** range from simple fact-digging to the most abstruse speculations. Consequently, there is no one generally accepted definition of the word. *Webster's Dictionary* emphasizes the meaning of the first syllable, *re-:* "critical and exhaustive investigation . . . having for its aim the revision of accepted conclusions, in the light of newly discovered facts." The *New World Dictionary* stresses the meaning of the second syllable, *-search:* "systematic, patient study and investigation in some field of knowledge, undertaken to establish facts or principles." The second definition more closely describes what is expected of you in your first years in college. You will not often revise accepted conclusions or establish new principles. But you can learn to collect, sift, evaluate, and organize information or evidence and come to sound conclusions about its meaning. In doing so you will learn some of the basic methods of modern research, and the ethics and etiquette that govern the use the researcher makes of other people's facts and ideas.

When instructors ask you to prepare a research paper, they are concerned less with the intrinsic value of your findings than with the value you derive from the experience. Writing a research paper demands a sense of responsibility, because you must account for all your facts and assertions. If your results are to be accepted—and that is a large part of your purpose—you must be prepared to show how you got those results.

The citing of sources distinguishes the research paper from the expository essay in popular magazines. Good journalists undertake research to assemble their materials, but readers of magazines or newspapers are primarily concerned with the results of that research. Journalists expect to be accepted on faith. Researchers, however, write for their peers—for readers who can critically evaluate findings; for this reason researchers use footnotes to help readers check the evidence if they wish to do so.

In a research paper, your audience expects you to indicate your sources. It expects you to be thorough—to find and sift the relevant evidence; to be critical of the evidence—to test the reliability of your authorities; to be accurate—to present your facts and cite your sources with precision; to be objective—to distinguish clearly between facts and opinions or generalizations related to those facts.

45 THE LIBRARY

The library is one of the most valuable resources on the college campus. Every successful student draws constantly on its facilities. To use the library efficiently, you must know about its resources: what they are, how to find them, how to use them. Many libraries provide guided tours as well as printed information about their resources and the location of different kinds of books. There is always a reference librarian whose special assignment is to help you. Never feel embarrassed to ask him or her for help if you are confused.

Once you have learned to use the library, you will be able to spend your time on productive study and research rather than in wandering about in the hope of finding random bits of information. Section 45 is designed to help you become familiar with what is in your library and with the ways of finding what you want.

Knowing the library resources

Libraries have three principal kinds of holdings: a general collection of books; a collection of reference works; and a collection of periodicals, bulletins, and pamphlets.

General collection of books. The general collection includes most of the books in the library—all those that are available for general circulation. Small libraries usually place these books on open shelves and make them available to people who have library privileges. Most large university libraries, however, keep these books in stacks, which are closed to everyone except librarians, graduate students, faculty members, and persons holding special permits. If you want to borrow a book from such a library, you submit a call slip bearing the call number of the book you want, the name of its author, and its title to library personnel. (The information that goes on the call slip you obtain from the **card catalog,** which will be discussed later.)

Reference books. Reference books include encyclopedias, dictionaries, indexes, directories, handbooks, yearbooks, atlases, and guides. Most libraries place these books on open shelves in the main reading room and do not allow their removal from the room.

Periodicals, bulletins, pamphlets. A **periodical** is a publication that appears at regular (periodic) intervals. **Bulletins** and **pamphlets** may or may not be periodicals, depending on whether they are issued as parts of a series of publications or as separate, single publications. They are usually kept in the stacks with the main collection of books. Recent issues of magazines and newspapers are usually kept in the open shelves of the reading room. Older issues are bound in volumes and shelved in the stacks.

Finding your way among the library resources

Even a small library may have fifty or sixty thousand books—far too many for you ever to hope to search through for what you need. A large university library will have several hundred thousand books, and perhaps a million or more. The directories and guides that libraries provide will help you find the particular books and articles you want. These include (1) the card catalog, (2) the collection of reference books, and (3) the various indexes to periodicals. With a knowledge of how to use these and occasional help from the reference librarian, you can find your way to the books and articles on any subject.

Using the card catalog. The heart of the library is its **card catalog,** an alphabetical list of all the books and periodicals the library contains. Most libraries have a separate catalog that describes all periodical holdings in detail.

The **classification system** on which a card catalog is based serves as a kind of map of library holdings. In libraries where you have direct access to the shelves, familiarity with the classification system enables you to find classes of books in which you are interested without using the catalog. But the chief purpose of a classification system is to supply a **call number** for every item in the library. When you fill out a slip for a book, be sure to copy the call number exactly as it appears on the card.

American libraries generally follow either the Dewey decimal system or the Library of Congress system in classifying books. The system in use determines the call number of any book.

The Dewey system, used by most smaller libraries, divides books into ten numbered classes:

000–099	General works	500–599	Pure science
100–199	Philosophy	600–699	Useful arts
200–299	Religion	700–799	Fine arts
300–399	Social sciences	800–899	Literature
400–499	Philology	900–999	History

Each of these divisions is further divided into ten parts, as:

800	General literature	850	Italian literature
810	American literature	860	Spanish literature
820	English literature	870	Latin literature
830	German literature	880	Greek literature
840	French literature	890	Other literatures

Each of these divisions is further divided, as:

821	English poetry	826	English letters
822	English drama	827	English satire
823	English fiction	828	English miscellany
824	English essays	829	Anglo-Saxon
825	English oratory		

Further subdivisions are indicated by decimals. *The Romantic Rebels,* a book about Keats, Byron, and Shelley, is numbered 821.09, indicating a subdivision of the 821 English poetry category.

The Library of Congress classification system, used by large libraries, divides books into lettered classes:

A	General works
B	Philosophy, Religion
C	History, Auxiliary sciences
D	Foreign history and topography
E–F	American history
G	Geography, Anthropology
H	Social sciences
J	Political science
K	Law
L	Education
M	Music
N	Fine arts
P	Language and literature
Q	Science
R	Medicine
S	Agriculture
T	Technology
U	Military science
V	Naval science
Z	Bibliography, Library science

Each of these sections is further divided by letters and numbers that show the specific call number of a book. *English Composition in Theory and Practice* by Henry Seidel Canby and others is classified in this system as PE 1408.E5. (In the Dewey decimal system this same volume is numbered 808 C214.)

For most books (not periodicals) you will find at least three cards in the library catalog: an **author card;** a **title card** (no title card is used when the title begins with words as common as "A History of . . ."); and at least one **subject card.** On the following page is a specimen **author card** in the Dewey system; it is filed according to the surname of the author:

1   820.903
    W54
      2   **Wilson, John Harold,** 1900–
              The court wits of the Restoration, an introduction.
          3   Princeton, Princeton Univ. Press, 1948.

              4   vi, 264 p.   ports.   23 cm.

              5   Bibliography : p. ₁218₁–222.

              1. English literature—Early modern (to 1700)—Hist. & crit.
          6   2. English wit and humor—Hist. & crit.   I. Title.

      7   PR437.W54   8   820.903   9   48—4835*

      10   Library of Congress   ₁60b²1₁
                                    11

1   820.903   gives you the call number of the book.
    W54

2   "Wilson, John Harold, 1900–" gives the name of the author and the date of his birth and, because no date follows 1900–, indicates that he was living at the time this card was printed.

3   "The court wits . . . 1948" gives the full title of the book, the place of publication, the name of the publisher, and the date of publication. (Note that library practice in capitalizing titles differs from general practice.)

4   "vi, 264 p. ports. 23 cm." indicates that the book contains 6 introductory pages numbered in Roman numerals and 264 pages numbered in Arabic numerals; that portraits appear in the book; and that the book is 23 centimeters high (an inch is 2.54 centimeters).

5   "Bibliography: p. [218]–222" indicates that the book contains a bibliography that begins on page 218 and ends on page 222. The brackets around 218 mean that the page is not actually numbered but appears between numbered pages 217 and 219.

6   "1. English literature . . . Title" indicates that the book is also listed in the card catalog under two subject headings—English Literature, and English Wit and Humor—and under one title heading, "Court wits of the Restoration. . . ." Notice that the subject heading "English literature" has the subdivision "Early modern (to 1700)" and that this latter heading has the subdivision "Hist. & crit.," the heading under which the first subject card is located. The second subject card comes under a division of "English wit and humor" called "Hist. & crit." The Arabic numerals indicate subject headings; the Roman numeral ("I. Title") indicates a title heading.

7   "PR437.W54" is the Library of Congress call number.

8   "820.903" is the class number under the Dewey system.

9 "48–4835*" is the order number used by librarians when they wish to order a copy of the card itself.

10 "Library of Congress" tells you that a copy of the book is housed in, and has been cataloged by, the Library of Congress.

11 "[60b²1]" is a printer's key to the card.

A **title card** is simply a copy of the author card with the title typed just above the author's name. The title card is filed in the catalog according to the first word of the title that is not an article.

A **subject card** is also a copy of the author card, with the subject typed just above the author's name. It is filed in the catalog alphabetically according to the subject heading (see item 6 above). The subject cards, which are gathered together in one place in the catalog, help you find all or most books on a particular subject. (To find articles on a subject, use the reference tools described on pages 423–426.)

Title and subject cards for Wilson's *The Court Wits* are illustrated below.

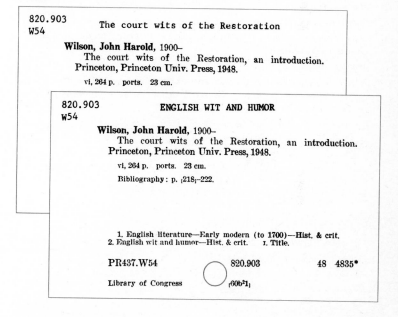

Except for the difference in the call number, catalog cards in libraries that use the Library of Congress system are identical with those in libraries that use the Dewey system. The Library of Congress call number and the Dewey system number appear in the lower line of the card illustrated (items 7 and 8), whereas only that of the system a given library uses is typed in the upper left corner of its catalog cards.

45

Finding the right reference book. Explore the reference section of your library. Become familiar with the kinds of reference works available and with the most important works of each kind. If you cannot find the book you want or if you do not know what book will help you most, consult the reference librarian.

Following is a representative list of reference books available in most libraries.

GUIDES TO REFERENCE BOOKS

Galin, Saul, and Peter Spielberg. *Reference Books: How to Select and Use Them.* 1969.

Gates, Jean Key. *Guide to the Use of Books and Libraries.* 3rd ed. 1973.

Sheehy, Eugene P. *Guide to Reference Books.* 9th ed. 1976.

Shove, Raymond H., *et al. The Use of Books and Libraries.* 10th ed. 1967.

CATALOGS

Books in Print. Author and title indexes for *Publishers' Trade List Annual. Subject Guide to Books in Print.* 2 vols.

Cumulative Book Index. Monthly listing of published books in English. Cumulated annually.

Monthly Catalog of U.S. Government Publications. 1895 to date.

National Union Catalog. Subject and author listings of Library of Congress holdings as well as titles from other libraries, motion pictures, recordings, and film strips.

Union List of Serials in Libraries of the United States and Canada. Lists of periodicals and newspapers. Supplemented monthly by *New Serial Titles.*

Vertical File Index. 1935–. Supplements to date. (Formerly called *Vertical File Service Catalog,* 1935–54.) Monthly, with annual cumulations. Subject and title index to selected pamphlet material.

GENERAL ENCYCLOPEDIAS

Chambers Encyclopedia. New rev. ed. 15 vols. 1975.

Collier's Encyclopedia. 24 vols. 1977.

Encyclopedia Americana. 30 vols. 1977.

Encyclopaedia Britannica. 15th ed. 30 vols. 1979.

Encyclopedia International. 20 vols. 1963–64.

New Columbia Encyclopedia. 1 vol. 1975.

DICTIONARIES, WORD BOOKS

Dictionary of American English on Historical Principles. 4 vols. 1936–44.

Evans, Bergen and Cornelia. *A Dictionary of Contemporary American Usage.* 1957.

Fowler, Henry W. *Dictionary of Modern English Usage.* 2nd ed. Rev. by Sir Ernest Gowers. 1965.

Funk & Wagnalls New Standard Dictionary. Unabridged. 1964.

Oxford Dictionary of English Etymology. 1966.

Oxford English Dictionary. 12 vols. and supplement. 1888–1933. Also known as *New English Dictionary.*

Partridge, Eric. *A Dictionary of Slang and Unconventional English.* 7th ed. 1970.

Random House Dictionary of the English Language. Unabridged. 1973.

Roget's International Thesaurus. Several editions available.

Webster's Dictionary of Proper Names. 1970.

Webster's New Dictionary of Synonyms. 1973.

Webster's Third New International Dictionary. Unabridged. 1976.

Wentworth, Harold, and Stuart B. Flexner. *Dictionary of American Slang.* 2nd ed. 1975.

YEARBOOKS

Americana Annual. 1924–.

Britannica Book of the Year. 1938–.

CBS News Almanac. 1976–.

Congressional Record. 1873–. Issued daily while Congress is in session; revised and issued in bound form at end of the session.

Facts on File. A weekly digest of world events. 1940–.

Information Please Almanac. 1947–.

Negro Almanac. 1967–.

New International Year Book. 1907–.

Reader's Digest Almanac and Yearbook. 1966–.

Statesman's Year Book. 1864–.

Statistical Abstract of the United States. 1878–.

United Nations Statistical Yearbook. 1945–1968. Monthly supplements.

World Almanac and Book of Facts. 1868–.

Year Book of World Affairs. 1947–.

ATLASES AND GAZETTEERS

Columbia-Lippincott Gazetteer of the World. 1962.

Commercial and Library Atlas of the World. Frequently revised.

Encyclopaedia Britannica World Atlas. Frequently revised.

National Geographic Atlas of the World. 4th ed. 1975.

New Cosmopolitan World Atlas. Issued annually.

The Times Atlas of the World. 1975.

Webster's New Geographical Dictionary. 1972.

GENERAL BIOGRAPHY

American Men and Women of Science. 13th ed. 1976.

Biography Index. 1946–. Quarterly. Cumulated annually, with permanent volumes every three years.

Current Biography: Who's News and Why. 1940–. Published monthly with semiannual and annual cumulations.

Dictionary of American Biography. 24 vols. 1922–76.

Dictionary of American Scholars. 6th ed. 1974.

Dictionary of National Biography. (British) 22 vols. 1938. Reprinted 1966 with corrections and additions 1923–63.

Dictionary of Scientific Biography. 1970–.

International Who's Who. 1936–.

Webster's Biographical Dictionary. 1976.

Who's Who. (British) 1849–.

Who's Who in America. 1899–.

Who's Who of American Women. 1958–.

Who Was Who. 1897–1960.

Who Was Who in America, Historical Volume. 1607–1896.

World Who's Who in Science. 1968.

BOOKS OF QUOTATIONS

Bartlett, John. *Familiar Quotations.* 15th ed. 1981.

Evans, Bergen. *Dictionary of Quotations.* 1968.

The Macmillan Book of Proverbs, Maxims, and Famous Phrases. 1965.

Mencken, H. O. *A New Dictionary of Quotations on Historical Principles from Ancient and Modern Sources.* 1942.

Oxford Dictionary of Quotations. 1953.

Stevenson, Burton. *The Home Book of Bible Quotations.* 1949.

——————. *The Home Book of Quotations.* 10th rev. ed. 1967.

MYTHOLOGY AND FOLKLORE

Bullfinch, Thomas. *Bullfinch's Mythology.* 2nd rev. ed. 1970.

Funk & Wagnalls Standard Dictionary of Folklore, Mythology, and Legend. 2 vols. 1949.

Gray, Louis H., ed. *The Mythology of All Races.* 1916–32. Reprinted 1964.

Hammond, N. G., and H. H. Scullord. *The Oxford Classical Dictionary.* 2nd ed. 1970.

Larousse World Mythology. 1968.

LITERATURE, DRAMA, FILM, AND TELEVISION

Aaronson, C. S., ed. *International Television Almanac.* 1956–.

Adelman, Irving, and R. Dworkin. *Modern Drama: A Checklist of Critical Literature on Twentieth Century Plays.* 1967.

Benét, William Rose. *The Reader's Encyclopedia.* 2nd ed. 1965.

Bukalski, Peter J. *Film Research: A Critical Bibliography.* 1972.

Cassell's *Encyclopedia of World Literature.* Rev. ed. 1973.

Cawkwell, Tim, and John Milton Smith, eds. *World Encyclopedia of the Film.* 1972.

Columbia Dictionary of Modern European Literature. 1947.

Dictionary of World Literary Terms. 3rd ed. 1970.

Etheridge, J. M., and Barbara Kopala. *Contemporary Authors.* 1967.

Hart, J. D. *Oxford Companion to American Literature.* 4th ed. 1965.

Hartnoll, Phyllis. *The Oxford Companion to the Theatre.* 3rd ed. 1967.

Harvey, Sir Paul, and J. E. Heseltine. *Oxford Companion to Classical Literature.* 2nd ed. 1937.

_____. *Oxford Companion to English Literature.* 4th ed. 1967.

Hoffman, Daniel, ed. *Harvard Guide to Contemporary American Writing.* 1979.

Hornstein, Lillian H., ed. *The Reader's Companion to World Literature.* Rev. ed. 1973.

International Encyclopedia of the Film. 1972.

Kunitz, S. J., and Vineta Colby. *European Authors, 1000–1900.* 1967.

Kunitz, S. J., and Howard Haycraft. *American Authors, 1600–1900.* 1952.

_____. *British Authors Before 1800.* 1952.

_____. *British Authors of the Nineteenth Century.* 1936.

_____. *Twentieth Century Authors.* 1942. Supplement, 1955.

Literary History of England. 2nd ed. 4 vols. 1967.

Literary History of the United States. 4th ed. 2 vols. 1974.

Millett, Fred B. *Contemporary American Authors.* 1970.

Manly, John M., and Edith Rickert. *Contemporary British Literature.* 1974.

New Cambridge Bibliography of English Literature. 4 vols. 1969–74.

New York Times Film Reviews, 1913–1968. 1970–71.

Whitlow, Roger. *Black American Literature.* 1973.

Woodress, James, ed. *American Fiction 1900–1950: A Guide to Information Sources.* 1974.

HISTORY, POLITICAL SCIENCE

Cambridge Ancient History. Rev. ed. 5 vols. Plates. 1970–75.

Cambridge Medieval History. Rev. ed. 1967–.

Cyclopedia of American Government. 3 vols, 1949.

Dictionary of American History. 3rd ed. 8 vols. 1976.

Encyclopedia of American History. 5th ed. 1976.

Harvard Guide to American History. Rev. ed. 2 vols. 1974.

Johnson, Thomas H. *Oxford Companion to American History.* 1966.

Langer, William L. *An Encyclopedia of World History.* 5th ed. 1972.

New Cambridge Modern History. 14 vols. 1975.

Political Handbook and Atlas of the World. Published annually.

Political Science: A Bibliographical Guide to the Literature. 1965.

Schlesinger, Arthur M., and D. R. Fox, eds. *A History of American Life.* 13 vols. 1927–48.

Smith, Edward C., and Arnold J. Zurcher, eds. *Dictionary of American Politics.* 2nd ed. 1968.

Webster's Guide to American History. 1971.

THE ARTS

Apel, Willi. *Harvard Dictionary of Music.* 2nd ed. 1969.

Bryan, Michael. *Bryan's Dictionary of Painters and Engravers.* 5 vols. 1971.

Canaday, John C. *The Lives of the Painters.* 4 vols. 1969.

Chujoy, Anatole, and P. W. Manchester. *The Dance Encyclopedia.* Rev. ed. 1967.

Dictionary of Contemporary Music. 1974.

Dictionary of Contemporary Photography. 1974.

Encyclopedia of Painting. 3rd ed. 1970.

Encyclopedia of World Art. 15 vols. 1959–1968.

Feather, Leonard. *Encyclopedia of Jazz.* Rev. ed. 1960.

Fletcher, Sir Banister F. *A History of Architecture.* Rev. ed. 1975.

Focal Encyclopedia of Photography. Rev. ed. 2 vols. 1969.

Grove's Dictionary of Music and Musicians. 5th ed. 9 vols. and supplement. 1954.

Myers, Bernard S. *McGraw-Hill Dictionary of Art.* 5 vols. 1969.

Osborne, Harold. *Oxford Companion to Art.* 1970.

Popular Music: An Annotated List of American Popular Songs. 6 vols. 1973.

Scholes, Percy A. *Oxford Companion to Music.* 10th ed. 1970.

Stambler, Eric. *Encyclopedia of Pop, Rock, and Soul.* 1975.

Thompson, Oscar, and N. Slonimsky. *International Cyclopedia of Music and Musicians.* 10th ed. 1975.

Westrup, Jack A., and F. C. Harrison. *The New College Encyclopedia of Music.* 1960.

PHILOSOPHY, RELIGION

Adams, Charles, ed. *A Reader's Guide to the Great Religions.* 1977.

The Concise Encyclopedia of Western Philosophy and Philosophers. 1960.

Encyclopedia Judaica. 16 vols. 1972.

Encyclopedia of Philosophy. 4 vols. 1973.

Encyclopedia of Religion and Ethics. 1908–27. 12 vols. and index. Reissued 1951.

Ferm, Vergilius. *Encyclopedia of Religion.* 1976.

Grant, Frederick C., and H. H. Rowley. *Dictionary of the Bible.* Rev. ed. 1963..

New Catholic Encyclopedia. 15 vols. 1967.

New Schaff-Herzog Encyclopedia of Religious Knowledge. 1949–50. 12 vols. and index.

Twentieth-Century Encyclopedia of Religious Knowledge. 2 vols. 1955.

Universal Jewish Encyclopedia. 10 vols. 1948.

SCIENCE, TECHNOLOGY

Chamber's Technical Dictionary. 3rd ed. Revised with supplement. 1974.

Dictionary of Physics. 1975.

Encyclopedia of Chemistry. 3rd ed. 1973.

Encyclopedia of Physics. 1974.

Gray, Peter, ed. *The Encyclopedia of the Biological Sciences.* 1970.

Handbook of Chemistry and Physics. 1914–.

Harper Encyclopedia of Science. Rev. ed. 1967.

McGraw-Hill Encyclopedia of Science and Technology. 15 vols. 1971.

Speck, G., and B. Jaffe. *A Dictionary of Science Terms.* 1965.

Universal Encyclopedia of Mathematics. 1964.

Van Nostrand's Scientific Encyclopedia. 5th ed. 1978.

SOCIAL SCIENCES

Davis, John P., ed. *The American Negro Reference Book.* 1966.

A Dictionary of Psychology. Rev. ed. 1964.

Encyclopedia of Educational Research. 4th ed. 1969.

Encyclopedia of Human Behavior: Psychology, Psychiatry, and Mental Health. 1975.

Encyclopedia of Social Work. 1965. (Formerly *Social Work Yearbook,* 1929–1960.)

Encyclopedia of the Social Sciences. 15 vols. 1930–35.

Good, Carter V. *Dictionary of Education.* 3rd ed. 1973.

Handbook of Business Administration. 1967.

Handbook of Forms and Model Letters. 1971.

International Encyclopedia of the Social Sciences. 17 vols. 1968.

Klein, Barry T., ed. *Reference Encyclopedia of the American Indians.* 1973–74.

Mitchell, Geoffrey D. *A Dictionary of Sociology.* 1968.

Munn, G. G. *Encyclopedia of Banking and Finance.* 7th ed. 1973.

White, Carl M., et al. *Sources of Information in the Social Sciences.* 2nd ed. 1973.

Using general and special periodical indexes. A library's catalog merely shows what periodicals are available. To locate the articles you may need in those periodicals you must be acquainted with and know how to use the periodical indexes, which are usually shelved in the reference section of the library. Such indexes are usually classed as general or special indexes. **General indexes** list articles on many different kinds of subjects. **Special indexes** limit themselves to articles in specific areas. Representative lists of both kinds of indexes follow.

GENERAL INDEXES

Readers' Guide to Periodical Literature, 1900 to date. Published semimonthly; cumulated every three months and annually. The *Readers' Guide* gives entries under author, title, and subject.

This is the most widely known and used of the general indexes. Because many periodical indexes use systems very similar to that of the *Readers' Guide,* it is worth examining some sample entries below.

The headings for 1 through 5 are **subject entries;** 6 and 7 are **author entries.** Entry 8, a subject entry, indicates that an article indexed under the subject heading *Graffiti* was published in the June 1969 issue of *Science Digest,* volume 65, pages 31 through 33. Titled "Walls Remember," it was illustrated and unsigned. (All abbreviations and symbols used are explained in the first pages of any issue of the *Readers' Guide.*)

The second listing under entry 1 refers the user to a series of articles by D. Wolfle published in *Science* on the subject "Are Grades Necessary?" The first article appeared in the issue of November 15, 1968 (volume 162, pages 745–746); the second and third appeared, respectively, in the issues for April 18 and June 6, 1969. Entry 2, under the subject heading *Graduate students,* indexes a review by D. Zinberg and P. Doty in the May 1969 issue of *Scientific American* of a book, *New Brahmins: Scientific Life in America,* by S. Klaw. The + that follows the page references is an indication that the review is continued on a page or pages past 140. Entries 3, 4, and 7 are cross-references to the places in the *Guide* at which the user can find the subject or author listed.

1 **GRADING and marking (students)**
 Answer to Sally; multiple-choice tests. **W. R. Link.** Ed Digest 34:24-7 My '69
 Are grades necessary? D. Wolfle; discussion. Science 162:745-6; 164:245, 1117-18 N 15 '68, Ap 18, Je 6 '69
 ROTC: under fire but doing fine. il U S News 66:38 My 19 '69

2 **GRADUATE students**
 New Brahmins: scientific life in America, by S. Klaw. Review
 Sci Am 220:139-40+ My '69. D. Zinberg and P. Doty

3 **GRADUATION. See Commencements**

4 **GRADUATION addresses.** See Baccalaureate addresses

5 **GRAEBNER, Clark**
 Profiles. J. McPhee. por New Yorker 45:45-8+ Je 7: 44-8+ Je 14 '69

6 **GRAEF, Hilda**
 Why I remain a Catholic. Cath World 209: 77-80 My '69

7 **GRAF, Rudolf F.** See Whalen, G. J. jt. auth.

8 **GRAFFITI**
 Walls remember. il Sci Digest 65:31-3 Je '69

From *Readers' Guide to Periodical Literature,* July 1969, p. 73. Reproduced by permission of The H. W. Wilson Company.

Two other general indexes are valuable supplements to the *Readers' Guide:*

> *International Index.* 1907–65. Became *Social Sciences and Humanities Index.* 1965–73. Divided into *Social Sciences Index.* 1974–, and *Humanities Index.* 1974–.
>
> *Poole's Index to Periodical Literature,* 1802–81. Supplements through January 1, 1907. This is a subject index to American and English periodicals.

SPECIAL INDEXES

These indexes list articles published in periodicals devoted to special concerns or fields.

> *The Bibliographic Index.* 1938–. Indexes current bibliographies by subject; includes both bibliographies published *as* books and pamphlets and those that appear *in* books, periodical articles, and pamphlets.
>
> *Book Review Digest.* 1905–. Monthly, cumulated annually. Lists books by author and quotes from several reviews for each.
>
> *Essay and General Literature Index.* 1934–. Indexes collections of essays, articles, and speeches.
>
> *New York Times Index.* 1913–. Semimonthly, with annual cumulation. Since this index provides dates on which important events, speeches, and the like, occurred, it serves indirectly as an index to records of the same events in the other newspapers.
>
> *Ulrich's International Periodicals Directory.* 13th ed. 2 vols. 1969–70. Lists periodicals under the subjects they contain, with detailed cross-references and index, thus indicating what periodicals are in a particular field. Also indicates in what other guide or index each periodical is indexed, thus serving indirectly as a master index.

The titles of most of the following special indexes are self-explanatory.

> *Agricultural Index.* 1916 to date. A subject index, appearing nine times a year and cumulated annually.
>
> *Applied Science and Technology Index.* 1958 to date. (Formerly *Industrial Arts Index.*)
>
> *The Art Index.* 1929 to date. An author and subject index.
>
> *Articles on American Literature.* 1900–1950. 1950–1967.
>
> *Biological and Agricultural Index.* 1964–. (Formerly *Agricultural Index.* 1907–64)
>
> Boyd, Anne M. *United States Government Publications.* 3rd ed. 1949.
>
> *Business Periodicals Index.* 1958 to date. Monthly. (Formerly *Industrial Arts Index.*)
>
> *Catholic Periodical Index.* 1930–1933. 1939–. An author and subject index.

Dramatic Index. 1909–1949. Continued in *Bulletin of Bibliography,* 1950 to date. Annual index to drama and theater.

The Education Index. 1929 to date. An author and subject index.

Engineering Index. 1884 to date. An author and subject index.

Granger's Index to Poetry. 6th ed. 1973.

Index to Legal Periodicals. 1908 to date. A quarterly author and subject index.

Industrial Arts Index. 1913–1957. An author and subject index, monthly, with annual cumulations. (In 1958 this index was split into *Applied Science and Technology Index* and *Business Periodicals Index.*)

Monthly Catalog of United States Government Publications. 1905–.

Play Index. 1968.

Popular Periodical Index. 1973. Author and subject guide to about 25 periodicals not otherwise indexed.

Public Affairs Information Service Bulletin. 1915 to date. Weekly, with bi-monthly and annual cumulations. An index to materials on economics, politics, and sociology.

Quarterly Cumulative Index Medicus. 1927 to date. A continuation of the *Index Medicus,* 1899–1926. Indexes books as well as periodicals.

Short Story Index. 1953–. Supplements.

Song Index. 1926. Supplement.

United Nations Documents Index. 1950–.

EXERCISE 45(1) Draw a diagram of the reference room of your library, indicating on it the position of the following reference books and indexes.

1 *Encyclopaedia Britannica*
2 *Encyclopedia of Religion and Ethics*
3 *Jewish Encyclopedia*
4 *Dictionary of American History* (DAH)
5 *Dictionary of American Biography* (DAB)
6 *American Authors, 1600–1900*
7 *Who's Who*
8 *Facts on File*
9 *World Almanac*
10 *New English Dictionary* (NED), often referred to as *Oxford English Dictionary* (OED)
11 *General Card Catalog*
12 *Readers' Guide to Periodical Literature*
13 *The New York Times Index*
14 *The Art Index*
15 *Dramatic Index*

EXERCISE 45(2) Answer each of the following questions by consulting one of the standard reference guides listed in Exercise 45(1).

1 Where can you find information on the significance of the Menorah in Jewish history?

2 Among which tribe of American Indians is the highest development of shamanism found?

3 What did the word *gossip* mean in twelfth-century England?

4 Where can you find listed articles on French stained glass, printed in 1957 and 1958?

5 What was the first invention of Peter Cooper, American inventor, manufacturer, and philanthropist (d. 1883)?

EXERCISE 45(3) Write a brief paper on one of the following subjects. Be sure to answer all the questions raised. Read the prefaces or introductions to the reference works you are asked to describe, check to see how each work is organized, and make a special point of finding out how to use the works efficiently and effectively. If you have difficulty deciding what particular advantage each work has for research, consult Eugene P. Sheehy, *A Guide to Reference Books.*

1 Compare the *Dictionary of National Biography* and *Who's Who in America.* On what basis does each work include biographical data about an individual? Nationality? Contemporaneity? Prominence? What kinds of prominence? What kinds of information can you get about an individual in each work? Which work is more detailed? What particular research value does each have?

2 Compare the *World Almanac* and *Facts on File.* Both works are known as "yearbooks." How do they differ in methods of compilation of material? How does this difference affect the way in which they are organized? How does it determine the types of information included in each? How do you look up an item in each one? Under what circumstances would you consult the *World Almanac* rather than *Facts on File? Facts on File* rather than the *World Almanac?*

3 Compare the *Oxford English Dictionary* (OED) with the *Heritage Dictionary* or *Webster's New World Dictionary.* For illustrative purposes look up the word *kind* in each. What does each work tell you about the derivation of the word? About its history in the English language? How up-to-date is each dictionary? When would you use each one and for what purpose? What does each work tell you about the meaning of *devil* in the phrase *between the devil and the deep blue sea?* What does each work tell you about the sense in which Shakespeare meant the word *prevent?* What does each work tell you about *turbojet?* About *chemist?* About *fancy?*

46 THE RESEARCH PAPER

Choose and limit a subject.

Although your own interest in or curiosity about a topic is a good motivation in choosing a subject for a research paper, common sense requires that you choose a subject appropriate for research and limit it so that you can cope with it satisfactorily in the space and time at your disposal. Subjects developed largely from personal experience will not make satisfactory research topics since they do not require the acquaintance with library resources and the practice of note-taking that are part of the purpose of a research paper. Topics such as "The History of Medicine," "The American Indian," or "Modern Warfare" are far too broad and general for, say, a 1,500-word paper. If they are to be made at all workable, they have to be narrowed to such topics as "The Discovery of Anesthesia," "The Relation of the Mohicans to the Five Nations," "The Rival Claims of Types of Army Rifles in World War II," or similar relatively specific subjects.

Certain other kinds of topic will prove unsatisfactory for less obvious reasons. Some topics offer little practice because all necessary information can easily be found in a single authoritative source. Descriptions of technical or industrial processes ("The Production of Coffee"), narratives of a person's life ("Napoleon's Military Career"), or relatively simple narrative histories ("The History of Baseball") usually fall in this group. Some topics are so controversial and complex that the time and space allowed for a student research paper are not sufficient to permit a careful weighing of evidence for both sides leading to a reasonably objective conclusion. Topics such as "Is the Supreme Court Too Powerful?" and "The Relative Merits of Federal and Local Support of Education" are of this kind.

The most satisfactory topics, then, are those that encourage you to explore the resources of the library and to develop habits of meaningful note-taking. They give you practice in organizing and unifying information drawn from several sources. In your preliminary consideration of possible topics, avoid those that are too personal, too broad, too simple, or too complex to accomplish these aims.

Choosing and limiting a topic require more preliminary work than merely choosing a general topic you are interested in and arbitrarily narrowing it down to something you think you can manage. Unless you have already read widely about the topic you choose, you will need to begin your search for material, discover what material is available in your library, and skim several articles or chapters of books before the direction you will wish to take becomes very clear to you. Even after you have made a preliminary outline and started taking notes, you will still be engaged in more and more clearly limiting and defining your topic as you read. In fact, until you have made a preliminary survey of what is available about your topic, you may have only a very general sense of how you can limit it wisely.

EXERCISE 46(1) If you do not have a topic you are already interested in or curious about and have not been assigned a specific topic, one good way to get started is to select a question and then search out the most accurate possible answer to it. If you lack a topic, select one of the following questions and begin working on a research paper in which you will answer it—or another question to which it leads you. Use your ingenuity to discover exactly what the question means. Check the rest of this section for guidance in finding material and getting it in order.

1 Why did Benedict Arnold turn traitor?
2 Was Billy the Kid a desperado?
3 What progress have women made in securing improved wages and salaries in the past decade?
4 How extensively did the early Algonquins engage in agriculture?
5 Where did American Indians come from?
6 How was Lincoln's "Gettysburg Address" received by his contemporaries?
7 What are some of the important changes that have taken place in the Roman Catholic Church in recent years?
8 Can a pitcher curve a baseball?
9 How are Spanish-speaking children taught English?
10 What happened in the Scopes trial?
11 What are the present theories on the migratory instincts of birds?
12 Have employment opportunities improved for black Americans?
13 What happened to the settlers on Roanoke Island?
14 What was the Teapot Dome scandal?
15 Is the climate growing warmer?
16 What was learned about the moon in the Apollo program?
17 What are the plausible explanations for the statues on Easter Island?
18 Does the legend that Pocahontas saved John Smith's life square with the probable facts in the case?
19 Did Fulton invent the steamboat?
20 Has football supplanted baseball as the national game?
21 Did the Norse make voyages to America before Columbus?
22 What is the present ideological makeup of the Supreme Court?
23 Were Sacco and Vanzetti convicted on the basis of circumstantial evidence?
24 Did Edgar Allan Poe die insane?
25 What are the reasons for the disappearance of the dinosaur?
26 What effects has television had on professional sports?
27 What are the future prospects for a practical electric car?
28 To what extent was politics involved in the 1980 Olympics?
29 What is disco dancing and how did it develop?
30 What accounts for the popularity of country music?

Begin your search for information and start tentative planning.

Make use of bibliographical aids. After your initial choice of subject, research begins with a preliminary search for material and the preparation of a preliminary bibliography—that is, a list of articles, books, newspaper reports, or the like, that you think are relevant to your subject. The sources for your preliminary bibliography are such reference works as the following:

Subject cards in the main card catalog.
Bibliographies at the end of pertinent articles in various encyclopedias.

Readers' Guide to Periodical Literature.

Appropriate special periodical indexes (*Engineering Index, Education Index,* etc.).

The New York Times Index.

Guides to reference books, such as those listed on pages 418–423.

For the research paper reproduced later in this chapter, Annie Guzman decided to investigate the predictions of futurists about life in the year 2000. She began her search for material with the most recent issues of the *Readers' Guide,* and since her interest was in current predictions, she limited herself to the most recently published sources. (If she had been writing about, say, the Great Depression, she probably would have looked through the bound volumes of the *Readers' Guide* starting with 1929.) Annie looked for appropriate articles not only under the heading *Future* but also under likely cross-reference headings such as *Twenty-first century* and *Forecasting.* She then skimmed through five or six articles with promising titles to get a general sense of the topic. Within two or three hours, Annie had decided that at least part of her paper would be concerned with the possibility of some kind of worldwide disaster. She had also realized that there were many aspects of the topic she simply couldn't handle and some she didn't care to pursue. Annie was thus beginning to *limit* her topic intelligently. What had been a vague idea and a hazy interest was now beginning to take a more specific preliminary shape.

In her next visit to the library, after skimming through a few more articles with promising titles, Annie sat back, thought about her topic, and jotted down a very rough outline on a note card:

  I. Possible disasters (Bundy)
     A. War—compare Bradbury story
     B. Famine—controversy re supply of food
     C. Overpopulation—get more data
  II. Optimistic futurists—Buckminster Fuller?—get book
 III. Pessimistic futurists—???

The reminders "get more data" and "get book," as well as the question marks, are indications that Annie is learning how in research one thing leads to another and that it is a mistake to depend on one's memory. As you will see, Annie later decided not to categorize the futurists as optimistic and pessimistic, although she did use those adjectives once or twice. But this very rough outline did lead her to Buckminster Fuller and, in turn, to some important new ideas.

The next session at the library Annie devoted primarily to books. Searching the subject catalog led to several promising titles. Annie jotted down the call numbers, gave them to the desk, and eventually collected the books. She did not make the mistake of starting to read immediately. Instead, she looked first at *all* the tables of contents and indexes, and she skimmed through the prefaces, introductions, and one or two chapters. On this basis she was able to determine that several books had little value for her topic, so she returned them. She did not waste time reading books and articles that later turned out to be useless. As you become a practiced researcher, you will learn not only what to hold on to but also what to send back.

Prepare exact bibliography cards for each source. Annie was careful throughout her preliminary search to make an individual bibliography card for each article, book, or pamphlet she thought she might use. Follow this procedure consistently, even though it may sometimes seem unnecessary. Failure to get all the necessary bibliographic information at the time you are consulting a book or article can delay and inconvenience you later. Return trips to the library, time-consuming in themselves, sometimes result only in finding that a periodical is at the bindery or that a book is not available. At best, omission of a particularly useful piece of information may make it necessary to look through several books or periodicals to relocate an exact source.

The best method of keeping an accurate and useful record of your sources is to make out bibliography cards. The common sizes of cards are $3'' \times 5''$, $4'' \times 6''$, and $5'' \times 8''$. Researchers often use larger sizes for note-taking and the $3'' \times 5''$ size for bibliographic entries.

Make out a separate bibliography card for each source you consult. Although the exact information for various kinds of sources varies, all entries require three basic kinds of information: author, title, and publication information. For magazines, journals, newspapers, and the like, "publication information" includes the title of the magazine or journal, its date, and the pages on which the article you are citing occurs. If your source is a translation or an edited book, you will need the name of the translator or editor as well as that of the author. If your source is a selection in an anthology or a collection, you will need the name of the editor and the title of the collection in addition to the title of your selection and the name of its author.

For your use in later locating each source, place the library call number in the lower left-hand corner of each bibliography card.

The exact details of form for both bibliography entries and documentation notes (footnotes or endnotes) vary among disciplines. The forms given following, as well as those given for documentation on pages 445–453, are those established by the Modern Language Association and described in the *MLA Handbook* (1977), which is the style guide for some eighty professional journals in the languages, humanities, and some social sciences. Use these forms unless your instructor requires otherwise.

46

FORM FOR BIBLIOGRAPHIC ENTRIES

Books

A BOOK WITH ONE AUTHOR	Roszak, Theodore. <u>The Making of a Counter-Culture</u>. Garden City, N.Y.: Anchor Books, 1969.
A BOOK WITH TWO OR THREE AUTHORS	Bryan, Margaret B., and Boyd H. Davis. <u>Writing About Literature and Film</u>. New York: Harcourt Brace Jovanovich, 1975.
A BOOK WITH MORE THAN THREE AUTHORS	Lauer, Janice, et al. <u>Four Worlds of Writing</u>. New York: Harper & Row, 1981.
A BOOK IN AN EDITION OTHER THAN THE FIRST	Ferguson, Mary Anne. <u>Images of Women in Literature</u>. 2nd ed. Boston: Houghton Mifflin, 1973.
A BOOK IN A SERIES	Ryf, Robert S. <u>Henry Green</u>. Columbia Essays on Modern Writers, No. 29. Ed. William York Tindall. New York: Columbia Univ. Press, 1967.
A WORK OF TWO OR MORE VOLUMES	Morison, S. E., and H. S. Commager. <u>The Growth of the American Republic</u>. 3rd ed. 2 vols. New York: Oxford University Press, 1942.
A TRANSLATION	Kazantzakis, Nikos. <u>Zorba the Greek</u>. Trans. Carl Wildman. New York: Simon & Schuster, 1952.
A REPRINT OF AN OLDER EDITION	Lowes, John Livingston. <u>The Road to Xanadu: A Study in the Ways of the Imagination</u>. 2nd ed. 1930; rpt. New York: Vintage-Knopf, 1959.
AN EDITED BOOK	Timko, Michael, ed. <u>Twenty-Nine Short Stories</u>. New York: Knopf, 1975.

A BOOK WITH AN
AUTHOR AND EDITOR

> Melville, Herman. <u>Billy Budd, Sailor</u>.
>
>   Ed. Harrison Hayford and Merton M.
>
>   Sealts, Jr. Chicago: Univ. of
>
>   Chicago Press, 1962.

A SELECTION IN
AN ANTHOLOGY
OR COLLECTION

> Wills, Gary. "The Making of the Yippie
>
>   Culture." In <u>Perspectives for the</u>
>
>   <u>70's</u>. Ed. Robert G. Noreen and
>
>   Walter Graffin. New York: Dodd,
>
>   Mead, 1971.

Encyclopedia Articles

AN UNSIGNED ARTICLE

> "Universities." <u>Encyclopaedia Britan-</u>
>
>   <u>nica: Macropaedia</u>. 1974 ed.

SIGNED ARTICLE

> J[ones], J. K[nox], and D[avid] M.
>
>   A[rmstrong]. "Mammalia." <u>Encyclo-</u>
>
>   <u>paedia Britannica: Macropaedia</u>.
>
>   1974 ed.
>
> Goodwin, George G. "Mammals." <u>Collier's</u>
>
>   <u>Encyclopaedia</u>. 1976 ed.

*Magazine, Journal,
and Newspaper Articles*

AN ARTICLE FROM
A WEEKLY MAGAZINE

> Farrell, Barry. "Second Reading: Bad
>
>   Vibrations from Woodstock." <u>Life</u>,
>
>   5 Sept. 1969, pp. 4-7.

AN ARTICLE FROM
A MONTHLY MAGAZINE

> DeMott, Benjamin. "Looking Back on the
>
>   Seventies: Notes Toward a Cultural
>
>   History." <u>The Atlantic</u>, March 1971,
>
>   pp. 58-64.

AN ARTICLE FROM A
JOURNAL WITH CON-
TINUOUS PAGINATION
THROUGHOUT THE
VOLUME

> Tracy, Philip. "Birth of a Culture."
>
>   <u>Commonweal</u>, 90 (1969), 529-33.

AN ARTICLE FROM
A JOURNAL THAT
PAGES EACH ISSUE
SEPARATELY

> Kopkind, Andrew. "A New Culture of
> Opposition." _Current_, 111 (October
> 1969), pp. 54-57.

AN ARTICLE FROM
A DAILY NEWSPAPER

> Hartnett, Ken. "The Alternative Society,
> Part Two: Disaffected Depend on
> Society They Shun." _Boston Evening_
> _Globe_, 27 April 1971, p. 2 cols 2-5.

A BOOK REVIEW

> Morris, Jan. "Visions in the Wilderness."
> Rev. of _Sands River_, by Peter Matt-
> hiessen. _Saturday Review_, April
> 1981, pp. 68-69.

AN UNSIGNED ARTICLE
OR REVIEW

> "Form and Function in a Post and Beam
> House." _Early American Life_, Oct.
> 1980, pp. 41-43.

A PUBLIC DOCUMENT

> U.S. Department of Health, Education, and
> Welfare. National Center for Educa-
> tional Statistics. _Digest of_
> _Educational Statistics_. Washington,
> D.C.: Government Printing Office, 1968.

AN UNPUBLISHED THESIS
OR DISSERTATION

> Stein, Robert A. "_Paradise Regained_ in
> the Light of Classical and Christian
> Traditions of Criticism and Rhet-
> oric." Diss. Brandeis 1968.

Films, Television,
and Radio Programs

> Boorman, John, dir. _Excalibur_. With
> Nigel Terry, Helen Mirren, Nicholas
> Clay, Cherie Lunghi, Paul Geoffrey,
> and Nicol Williamson. Orion Pic-
> tures, 1981.

> _Casey Stengel_. Writ. Sidney and David
> Carroll. Perf. Charles Durning.
> PBS, Boston, 6 May 1981.

Recordings

> Thomas, Dylan. <u>Dylan Thomas Reading</u>.
>
>   Caedmon, TC-1002, 2 vols., 1952.
>
> Moussorgsky, Modeste. <u>Pictures at an</u>
>
>   <u>Exhibition</u>. Leonard Pennario,
>
>   piano. Capitol Records, P-8323,
>
>   n.d.

Letters

A PUBLISHED LETTER

> Mills, Ralph J. Jr., ed. <u>Selected</u>
>
>   <u>Letters of Theodore Roethke</u>.
>
>   Seattle: Univ. of Washington
>
>   Press, 1968.

A PERSONAL LETTER

> Hall, Donald. Letter to author. 18
>
>   Sept. 1980

INTERVIEWS

> Silber, John R. Personal interview. 5
>
>   June 1979.
>
> Kennedy, Senator Edward. Telephone
>
>   interview. 3 May 1980.

EXERCISE 46(2) Select one or more of the following subjects and list all the likely sources in which you would look for (1) preliminary information and (2) periodical articles on the subject.

1 Bilingual Education for Spanish-Speaking Americans
2 The India-Pakistan Wars
3 Women's Magazines
4 "Black Capitalism"
5 The "Jewish Novel"
6 Acupuncture
7 The Poetry of Robert Frost
8 Jazz in the 1920's
9 The Early Plays of G. B. Shaw
10 Religious Rites of the Navaho Indians
11 The Use of Hypnosis in Medicine
12 Migratory Habits of Birds
13 The Early History of the Teamster's Union
14 Viking Exploration of America
15 Migratory Workers in the Southwest

EXERCISE 46(3) Prepare a short bibliography (on cards) for one of the following topics.

1 Negro Colleges
2 Color Television
3 The Development of Solar Energy
4 The Theatre of the Absurd
5 Organic Foods
6 Medicare
7 Bluegrass Music
8 Pop Art
9 The Assassination of Lincoln
10 Rockets and Interplanetary Travel

EXERCISE 46(4) Prepare a short working bibliography for one of the following persons and hand in a brief biographical sketch with it.

Martin Luther King	Joe Louis
Margaret Fuller	Charles Steinmetz
Henry Kissinger	Anwar Sadat
Marilyn Monroe	Tennessee Williams
Susan B. Anthony	Charles Chaplin
Harry Truman	Georgia O'Keeffe
Pope John XXIII	Louis Armstrong
Winston Churchill	Frank Lloyd Wright
Ralph Nader	Eudora Welty

Start planning your paper.

The processes of choosing and limiting a subject, making a preliminary search of materials available, and gathering bibliographic entries all help you bring your subject gradually into focus. As you begin to read sources, even at the preliminary stage of your research, your plan should slowly become more and more definite and clear. Try to crystallize it into some sort of outline.

Your early outlines may be quite general and will eventually be reworked as you make additions, deletions, even outright changes in direction. Outlines are useful to let you review your own thinking about your topic, to suggest kinds of information you have and do not have, and to help you see possible patterns of final organization that you can work toward.

Annie Guzman was able to expand and refine her preliminary outline after several days of reading, note-taking, and thinking:

I. Summary of Ray Bradbury's "August 2026 . . ."
   A. Technological advances
   B. Nuclear disaster
II. View of Futurists
   A. Technological advances
      1. Automation in home (plenty in Kahn and Wiener)
      2. Transportation—get more
      3. Energy sources—(too complex?)
      4. Daily life—maybe something on family structure
   B. Possibility of disaster
      1. Nuclear war—need for international control
      2. Overpopulation
         a. Optimistic view
         b. Pessimistic view—get Ehrlich book?
      3. Famine—control over food production
III. Cooperation among nations
   A. Energy—????? (too complex?)
   B. Agriculture
   C. Armaments
   D. Population
IV. Conclusion—Buckminster Fuller

This second outline differs greatly both from the first one (p. 430) and from the final one (pp. 458–459). At this point, Annie was satisfied that she knew where she was going. There were still question marks and reminders, and there would be additions, deletions, and revisions, but the paper was nearing the rough-draft stage.

Take careful notes on your reading. Once you have finished the preliminary search to assure yourself that you have a workable subject, have established some sense of the directions you may take, and have jotted down an initial list of possible headings, you will begin to take notes on everything you read that seems at all pertinent to your topic. Do not be afraid of taking too many notes. It is much easier to lay aside notes that turn out to be superfluous than it is to return to the library to search again for sources you have already gone to the trouble of finding once.

Develop the habit of entering your reading notes on standard-size cards. They are easier to carry than a notebook, easier to refer to than full sheets of paper, and easy to rearrange as you experiment with various possible structures. In taking notes, observe the same principles that you observed in writing out your bibliography cards: Make sure that all your notes are accurate and complete. Be especially careful that you know the exact source from which you took each piece of information. Be *very* careful to distinguish between information you are summarizing or paraphrasing and information you are quoting. Place quotation marks around *all* material you take word for word from any source. In general, force yourself to summarize, paraphrase, and record relevant facts rather than quote. Reserve exact quotation for particularly telling phrases or for information that must be rendered exactly as you found it.

Use a separate card for each note. Each card should contain notes from only one source, and all notes on any one card should be about a single subject. Do not include on a single card notes on more than one subtopic in your outline. The usefulness of your cards depends greatly on the convenience with which they can be arranged in differing sequences.

To make arrangements and rearrangements easier, place a subject heading on each card. Think of a heading as a title for what you have just read. Carefully expressing the heading in your own words, not in words copied from the source, will help you be certain that you understand the material you have read.

Cards with separate notes can easily be combined when you are experimenting with arrangements for your first draft. Cards that combine two or more notes on somewhat different items will prevent you from doing this.

Annie Guzman prepared the note cards on page 439 for her research paper. The first is an exact quotation. The second is a brief summary of several pages of her reading. The third records a short quotation and then summarizes the article's conclusion. Study these cards as well as those given with the text of the research paper. They do not represent the only way to take notes, but they are good notes and, more than anything else, are responsible for the success of the paper itself.

Understand what to acknowledge. One of the purposes of keeping accurate bibliography cards and careful notes that record all your sources and distinguish carefully between direct quotation and paraphrase is to provide you with all the information you will need for documenting in footnotes or endnotes all the material you have gathered in researching your topic. Your own contributions in a research paper are your exact definition of the topic or problem you are studying; the order you impose upon the material you have collected; and the insights, interpretations, judgments, and conclusions you arrive at through your reading in a variety of sources. But in the nature of research, your own final judgments and conclusions grow out of the facts, ideas, and opinions of the various authors whose books and articles you have read and taken notes on. And all those facts, ideas, interpretations, opinions, and conclusions of others that you incorpo-

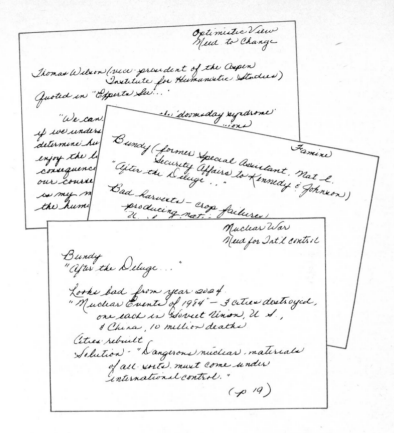

rate in your own paper you must always acknowledge by documenting the sources.

Always acknowledge in documentation notes all direct quotations, charts, diagrams, tables, and the like, that you reproduce wholly or in part in your paper. Always acknowledge also your paraphrases and summaries of the interpretations, opinions, and conclusions of authors you have read. Keep in mind that the interpretations and conclusions reached by other writers are in many ways more important contributions on their part than the bald facts they may have gathered and therefore even more deserving of acknowledgment.

You do not have to provide documentation for facts that are common knowledge. "Common knowledge" consists of standard historical and literary information available in many different reference books—the date of Lincoln's assassination, the birth and death dates of John F. Kennedy, the fact that Charles Dickens created such characters as Uriah Heep and Mr. Micawber, or that Faulkner's novels are set in the South, or that Darwin's theory of evolution was the subject of great intellectual debate in the nineteenth century. Such information is considered common knowledge as far as documentation is concerned, even though it may be far from the tip of your tongue at the moment, even though you may, in fact, have learned it for the first time when you began your research. In contrast, common sense will tell you that highly specialized facts—the cost of a six-room house in the 1830's, the number of Polaroid cameras sold between 1970 and 1980, the estimated population of Mongolia in 1950, the highest recorded tide in San Francisco Bay, or the number of earthquakes in Peru during the nineteenth century—are unlikely to be common knowledge.

In addition to information that is widely available and undisputed, facts agreed upon by nearly all writers discussing a particular subject are considered common knowledge. As soon as you read in any subject to some depth, you will quickly come to see that certain material is taken as established fact while other material is disputed or has been established by some special investigation. A student writing on Wordsworth for the first time, for example, may not have known at the start that the *Preface to the Lyrical Ballads* was first published in 1800. But it will not take long to discover that everyone writing on the subject accepts this as an established fact. Such information will not need to be acknowledged. In contrast, the exact date of a particular poem may be a matter of dispute or may have been established by a scholar's diligent research. Information of this kind must be acknowledged.

Be careful to avoid plagiarism. Plagiarism consists of passing off other people's ideas, opinions, conclusions, facts, and words as your own. Always acknowledge direct quotations, charts, diagrams, tables, and discussions that paraphrase or summarize the ideas, interpretations, opinions, and conclusions of others.

The most obvious kind of plagiarism occurs when you appropriate whole paragraphs or longer passages from another writer into your own paper. Long word-for-word quotations are rarely appropriate to a paper, but if they ever are, you must indicate clearly that they *are* quotations and indicate their exact source in a note. No less dishonest is the use of all or most of a single sentence or an apt figure of speech appropriated without acknowledgment from another writer.

Suppose, for example, that you are working on a paper about families and have read a book by Jane Howard entitled *Families*. You have a note card on which you have written the partial sentence "Good families have a switchboard operator—someone who cannot help but keep track of what all the others are up to . . ." Your notes indicate that this is a quotation. But when you turn to writing your paper, this and other phrases from the same source seem so apt to your purposes in a slightly different context that you yield to temptation and write, as if in your own words, "All families need at least two things: someone around whom others cluster and someone who cannot help but keep track of what all the others are up to—a kind of switchboard operator." You have plagiarized just as badly as the writer who has appropriated a whole paragraph. The words are not yours, they are Jane Howard's, and honesty requires that you give her credit for them.

You are unlikely to copy directly from another writer without being consciously dishonest as you do so. But even though you acknowledge the source in a note, you are also plagiarizing when you incorporate in your paper faultily paraphrased or summarized passages from another author in which you follow almost exactly the original's sentence patterns and phrasing. Paraphrasing and summarizing require that you fully digest an author's ideas and interpretations and restate them in your own words. It is not enough simply to modify the original author's sentences slightly, to change a word here and there. Consider the following original together with the sample paraphrases and summary:

ORIGINAL   The craft of hurricane forecasting advanced rapidly in the Sixties and early Seventies, thanks to fast computers and new atmospheric modeling techniques. Now there is a lull in the progress, strangely parallel to the lull in the storm cycle. The Center shoots for a 24-hour warning period, with 12 daylight hours for evacuation. At that remove, it can usually predict landfall within 100 miles either way. Longer lead times mean much larger landfall error and that is counterproductive. He who misses his predictions cries wolf.

WILLIAM H. MACLEISH, "Our Barrier Islands," *Smithsonian*, Sept. 1980, p. 54.

FAULTY   Hurricane forecasting made rapid progress in the
PARAPHRASE   sixties and seventies due to fast computers and new atmospheric techniques, but there is now a lull in the progress. The Warning Center tries for a 24-hour warning period, including 12 hours of daylight. That close to a storm, it can usually predict landfall within 100 miles either way. If lead times are longer, there will be a much larger error, which will be counterproductive.[7]

Even though the writer acknowledges the author, as indicated by the footnote at the end of the paragraph, this is a clear example of plagiarism. The author has combined the first two sentences of the original and changed a few words here and there but in no way indicated that most of the paragraph's structure and phrasing is almost exactly that of the original.

IMPROVED New techniques, together with computers, have
PARAPHRASE significantly increased the accuracy of hurricane forecasting. Now it is possible to predict where a hurricane will hit land with an error of not more than 100
miles if a warning of 24 hours is allowed. If more
than 24 hours is required, the error will be propor-
tionately greater.[7]

This paraphrase successfully puts the information in the words of
the researcher. Both the sentence structure and the phrasing are
clearly the researcher's, not the original author's. But such a full paraphrase of a relatively simple passage is probably much more complete
than someone researching hurricane warning problems and developments in a variety of sources would need. In many contexts, a simple,
brief summary statement like the following might well be sufficient:

SUMMARY With computers and new techniques, forecasters can
now provide a 24-hour hurricane warning and predict
within 100 miles either way where a storm will hit.[7]

Learn when and how to use quotations. A research paper
sprinkled with quotations or consisting of long quotations stitched
loosely together with brief comments will almost always be an unsatisfactory paper. The point of research is to present in your own words
the interpretations and judgments you have come to as a result of
your reading, making clear and accurate references to the sources you
have learned from.

Nonetheless, since such a paper requires evidence from your
sources for the conclusions you have reached, it is likely to lead to
more frequent direct quotations than you would ordinarily use in an
essay presenting your personal, unresearched views. A carefully researched paper on the changing roles of the family in the past three
decades will present more occasions for quotation from outside
sources than a personal essay on your changing relationship with your
own family.

Learning to use quotations wisely when you have good reason and
learning how to fit them easily, naturally, and logically into your own
writing are the tricks of effective use of quotation. Your *use* of a quotation, not the quotation itself, is your research contribution. When
readers come upon a quotation, they should never feel that it has been
dropped upon them suddenly, but rather that it is an intrinsic part of
the whole weave of what they are reading.

Many contexts can justify the use of brief and—less frequently—
long quotations. But the contexts in which they are most likely to be
preferable to paraphrase or summary are those in which the original
phrasing is striking or memorable; the force of the writer's statement
is important and would be lost in paraphrase; the quotation is an

example of what is being discussed; or, in writing about a writer or a literary work, the quotations exemplify the writer's style or typify a character, theme, or the like.

In general, long quotations are less useful and less justified than short ones. Annie Guzman, the writer of the research paper in this section, uses two quotations long enough to require setting off by indentation (see Section **25c**). The two present typical situations in which such quotations are useful. The first gives Ray Bradbury's portrait of a frightening future, which Annie quotes in the opening paragraph of her paper. Here, the quotation immediately establishes a scenario—one kind of possible future—a description it would have been difficult, perhaps impossible, to paraphrase without losing the force of Bradbury's original.

The second long quotation in the paper comes on p. 467, where Annie reproduces some nine lines of direct quotation from Paul Ehrlich, an authority who sees overpopulation as the greatest threat to the future. Although perhaps less well justified than the quotation from Bradbury, the force of Ehrlich's language is important to the paper's purpose and would have been hard to preserve in paraphrase.

Annie provides a fairly formal introduction to each of her long quotations, making clear the purpose of each. Annie has also been selective in both long quotations: as the ellipses indicate, she has left out material by the original authors that is extraneous to her purpose. Such omissions are permissible as long as they do not change the meaning of the original.

In most papers, you are likely to have more occasion to use brief quotations than long ones. Short quotations, well used and not overused, can often give concreteness and a sense of authenticity to your research. Occasional short quotations, carefully chosen and wisely used in a paper in which paraphrase and summary predominate, testify to the fact that you have read thoroughly and carefully, digested your sources well, and identified telling phrases and statements. Such brief quotations need always to be fitted naturally into the syntax of your own sentences and the flow of your thought.

Study the following examples, noticing how their student writers have worked the quotations smoothly into their own sentences or introduced them with such natural phrases as "John Frederick Nims remarks," "reports that," "in Mary McCarthy's words," or "in the words of one man."

> Not all Victorian women were the shy, timid, modest beings they are sometimes imagined to be. Elizabeth Barrett Browning once submitted a poem about women as sex objects which her editor rejected "for indecency."[6] As John Frederick Nims remarks, "Who would have expected such a poem from a Victorian lady with three names?"[7]

Any study of the music of Bela Bartok can well begin by taking note of the commanding presence of the man himself. Yehudi Menuhin, describing his first meeting with the composer, reports than he "felt at once that I was facing someone pared down to the essential core."[1]

The book which is most informative about Mary McCarthy as a person is perhaps her *Memories of a Catholic Girlhood,* which reflects, in part, her early life with her great-aunt, who, in McCarthy's words, "had a gift for turning everything sour and ugly."[5]

Distrust of and distaste for "new-fangled inventions" is long. English writers of the nineteenth century denounced the arrival of the railroad in their beloved Lake country. Fifty years ago, H. L. Mencken recorded in characteristically pungent language his dislike for automobiles, phonographs, and movies, and observed that although he saw "potentialities" for the radio, he was convinced they would never be realized "so long as the air is laden and debauched by jazz, idiotic harangues by frauds who do not know what they are talking about, and the horrible garglings of ninth-rate singers."[6]

There is nothing like a time of inflation, declining productivity, burgeoning government expenditures, and increasing taxes to unleash a flood of conflicting economic theory. Our own period is fertile ground for such debate, and we find ourselves choosing sides between those who believe that only a return to the virtues of old-line capitalism can save us, preaching that we must untax the rich so that they may invest, since "the creation of wealth is the only salvation of the poor,"[1] and those who tell us that only a "fundamental restructuring of American society"[2] will keep us from going down.

Whenever you make use of direct quotations in your writing, be sure to transcribe them accurately. Make it a rule to check and recheck each quotation, including its punctuation. Make sure that you understand the mechanical conventions of quoting material. Indicate omissions from a quotation by using ellipses (see **26c**), and make sure that what you retain is grammatically coherent. If you insert words of your own in the original, indicate your insertion by placing brackets around it (see **26a**). If the quotation contains a mistake or peculiarity of spelling or grammar, retain it in your quotation but indicate that it appears in the original by using *sic* (thus it is) in brackets immediately following it (see **26b**).

Follow standard forms for documentation notes. Note form, as used in professional scholarship and research, is complex and varied. Most forms have evolved in meeting the demands of formal scholarship, itself a precise and exacting business. Furthermore, conventions of documentation differ from discipline to discipline. If you have occasion to write research papers in a field other than English, you are likely to find that the discipline has its own established conventions that you will be expected to follow. Consult the style of the publications in the field, study the conventions, and adhere to them exactly.

Even though you are now chiefly concerned with adding to your *own* knowledge, you are expected to adopt the habits of the professional scholar and follow an established set of conventions. The conventions described here, like those for bibliographic entries on pp. 432–435, are based on those established by the Modern Language Association and set forth in the *MLA Handbook* (1977).

Number notes consecutively throughout a paper. Indicate that you are providing a note by placing a raised number at the end of the statement to be documented. Always place the raised note number outside whatever punctuation goes with the sentence or paragraph to which it refers, and always at the end of the statement, never at the beginning. Then repeat the raised figure at the beginning of the note itself. Do not use periods, other marks of punctuation, diagonals, or parentheses with note numbers. After the raised numeral, leave a space (one space, if you are typing), then begin the note.

In typewritten papers, double-space all notes. Start each note on a new line, indented five spaces. If the note extends for more than one line, begin the second and later lines flush to the margin.

TEXT of these about 100 were independent, over 106 more were

church-related, and more than 500 were public institu-

tions.[1]

NOTE [1] Paul Woodring, The Higher Learning in America:

A Reassessment (New York: McGraw T. McGraw, 1968), p.

32.

In the first full draft of your paper, it sometimes helps you keep track of notes if you include each one as you write, directly after the reference to it, setting it off from the text itself by lines, as in the following. Then in the final draft you can place the notes in their correct position.

TEXT "College teachers," writes Professor Seymour E. Harris,

"do not primarily seek high economic rewards, or they

would not have chosen teaching in the first place."[2]

NOTE [2] Higher Education: Resources and Finance (New

York: McGraw-Hill, 1962), p. 637.

TEXT It becomes increasingly apparent, however, that many who

might otherwise have

In the final copy of your paper, notes may be placed either at the bottom of pages on which references fall—**footnotes**—or collected at the end of the paper on a separate page or pages. Placed at the end, they are called **endnotes** or simply **notes.** The *MLA Handbook,* whose guidelines we are following, recommends that in research papers of the sort you are doing, all notes be collected at the end of the paper, as in Annie Guzman's paper in this section. Notes gathered at the end of the paper begin on a separate page entitled *Notes.* These notes are typed consecutively, double-spaced, on as many pages as are necessary; the note pages are numbered consecutively with those of the paper; the first page is often not numbered. The same is true for the bibliography (see also p. 480–481).

Footnotes, too, are typed in consecutive order, double-spaced, with at least a two-line space separating text from footnote. Some instructors prefer you to use a straight line to separate text from footnotes (see an example on p. 445).

The sample note forms that follow are the forms you should use the first time you refer to a particular source you are using in your paper. If you refer to the same source again in your paper, you may often use a shorter form (see pp. 450–451).

FORM FOR NOTES CITING A REFERENCE FOR THE FIRST TIME

Books

A BOOK WITH ONE AUTHOR

[1] Theodore Roszak, <u>The Making of a Counter-Culture</u> (Garden City, N.Y.: Anchor Books, 1969), pp. 47–48.

A BOOK WITH TWO OR THREE AUTHORS

[2] Margaret B. Bryan and Boyd H. Davis, <u>Writing About Literature and Film</u> (New York: Harcourt Brace Jovanovich, 1975), pp. 37–38.

A BOOK WITH MORE THAN THREE AUTHORS

[3] Janice Lauer et al., <u>Four Worlds of Writing</u> (New York: Harper & Row, 1981), pp. 170–71.

A BOOK IN AN EDITION OTHER THAN THE FIRST

[4] Mary Anne Ferguson, <u>Images of Women in Literature</u>, 2nd ed. (Boston: Houghton Mifflin, 1973), p. 268.

A BOOK IN A SERIES

[5] Robert S. Ryf, <u>Henry Green</u>, Columbia Essays on Modern Writers, No. 29, ed. William York Tindall (New York, Columbia Univ. Press, 1967), pp. 22-23.

A WORK OF TWO OR MORE VOLUMES

[6] S. E. Morison and H. S. Commager, <u>The Growth of the American Republic</u>, 3rd ed. (New York: Oxford Univ. Press, 1942), II, 75.

A TRANSLATION

[7] Nikos Kazantzakis, <u>Zorba the Greek</u>, trans. Carl Wildman (New York: Simon & Schuster, 1952), pp. 121-22.

A REPRINT OF AN OLDER EDITION

[8] John Livingston Lowes, <u>The Road to Xanadu: A Study in the Ways of the Imagination</u>, 2nd ed. (1930; rpt. New York: Vintage-Knopf, 1959), p. 231.

AN EDITED BOOK

[9] Michael Timko, ed., <u>Twenty-Nine Short Stories</u> (New York: Knopf, 1975), p. ix.

A BOOK WITH AN AUTHOR AND AN EDITOR

[10] Herman Melville, <u>Billy Budd, Sailor</u>, ed. Harrison Hayford and Merton M. Sealts, Jr. (Chicago: Univ. of Chicago Press, 1962), pp. 27-29.

A SELECTION IN AN ANTHOLOGY OR COLLECTION

[11] Gary Wills, "The Making of the Yippie Culture," in <u>Perspectives for the 70's</u>, ed. Robert G. Noreen and Walter Graffin (New York: Dodd, Mead, 1971), p. 57.

Encyclopedia Articles

AN UNSIGNED ARTICLE

[12] "Universities," <u>Encyclopaedia Britannica</u>: <u>Macropaedia</u>, 1974 ed.

A SIGNED ARTICLE

[13] J. K[nox] J[ones], Jr., and D[avid] M. A[rmstrong], "Mammalia," Encyclopaedia Britannica: Macropaedia, 1974 ed.

[14] George G. Goodwin, "Mammals," Collier's Encyclopaedia, 1976 ed.

Magazine, Journal, and Newspaper Articles

AN ARTICLE FROM A WEEKLY MAGAZINE

[15] Barry Farrell, "Second Reading: Bad Vibrations from Woodstock," Life, 5 September 1969, p. 4.

AN ARTICLE FROM A MONTHLY MAGAZINE

[16] Benjamin DeMott, "Looking Back on the Seventies: Notes Toward a Cultural History," The Atlantic, March 1971, p. 60.

AN ARTICLE FROM A JOURNAL WITH CONTINUOUS PAGINATION THROUGHOUT THE VOLUME

[17] Philip Tracy, "Birth of a Culture," Commonweal, 90 (1969), 532.

AN ARTICLE FROM A JOURNAL THAT PAGES EACH ISSUE SEPARATELY

[18] Andrew Kopkind, "A New Culture of Opposition," Current, 111 (October 1969), 56.

AN ARTICLE FROM A DAILY NEWSPAPER

[19] Ken Hartnett, "The Alternative Society, Part Two: Disaffected Depend on Society They Shun," Boston Evening Globe, 27 April 1971, Sec. 3, p. 2, col. 2.

A BOOK REVIEW

[20] Jan Morris, "Visions in the Wilderness," rev. of Sands River, by Peter Matthiessen, Saturday Review, April, 1981, p. 69.

AN UNSIGNED ARTICLE OR REVIEW

21 "Form and Function in a Post and Beam House,"

Early American Life, October, 1980, p. 42.

A PUBLIC DOCUMENT

22 U.S. Department of Health, Education, and Welfare, National Center for Educational Statistics,

Digest of Educational Statistics (Washington, D.C.:

Government Printing Office, 1968), p. 69.

AN UNPUBLISHED THESIS OR DISSERTATION

23 Robert A. Stein, "Paradise Regained in the Light

of Classical and Christian Traditions of Criticism and

Rhetoric," Diss. Brandeis 1968, p. 73.

Films, Television, and Radio Programs

24 John Boorman, dir., Excalibur, with Nigel Terry,

Helen Mirren, Nicholas Clay, Cherie Lunghi, Paul Geoffrey,

and Nicol Williamson, Orion Pictures, 1981.

25 Casey Stengel, writ. Sidney and David Carroll,

performed by Charles Durning, PBS, Boston, 6 May, 1981.

Recordings

26 Dylan Thomas, "Fern Hill," Dylan Thomas Reading,

Vol, I, Caedmon, TC-1002, 1952.

27 Modeste Moussorgsky, Pictures at an Exhibition,

Leonard Pennario, piano, Capitol Records, P-8323, n.d.

Letters

A PUBLISHED LETTER

28 "To Kenneth Burke," 6 Sept. 1949, Selected

Letters of Theodore Roethke, ed. Ralph J. Mills, Jr.

(Seattle: Univ. of Washington Press, 1968), pp. 154-55.

A PERSONAL LETTER

^{29} Letter received from Donald Hall, 18 Sept. 1980.

Interviews

^{30} Personal Interview with John Silber, President,
Boston University, 5 June 1979.

^{31} Telephone interview with Senator Edward Kennedy,
3 May 1980.

FORM FOR SECOND AND SUBSEQUENT
REFERENCES TO A SOURCE

A first note must be detailed because certain information is necessary to distinguish one source from all others. Later notes can—and should—be brief and simple.

Current practice, as encouraged by the *MLA Handbook,* is as follows:

1 If only one work by a given author is used, cite only the author's last name and the appropriate page reference in subsequent notes.

^{1} Theodore Roszak, The Making of a Counter-
Culture (Garden City, N.Y.: Anchor Books, 1969), p. 61.

^{4} Roszak, p. 110.

2 If two or more works by the same author are used, cite the author's last name and a shortened title, as follows:

^{1} Benjamin DeMott, "Looking Back on the Seventies:
Notes Toward a Cultural History," The Atlantic, March
1971, p. 60.

^{3} Benjamin DeMott, "The Sixties: A Cultural Revolution," New York Times Magazine, 14 December 1969, p. 4.

^{5} DeMott, "Looking Back," p. 62.

^{8} DeMott, "The Sixties," p. 4.

If your reference is to one volume of a work in two or more volumes be careful to indicate the volume number in subsequent notes, even if the reference is to the same volume.

⁴ S. E. Morison and H. S. Commager, <u>The Growth of</u>

<u>the American Republic</u>, 3rd ed. (New York: Oxford Univ.

Press, 1942), II, 75.

⁹ Morison and Commager, II, 183.

Although the forms described above for note references after the first are now widely used, some editors and instructors continue to prefer the use of the Latin abbreviation *ibid.,* meaning "the same title as the one cited in the previous note," when a subsequent reference to a given work immediately follows the first citation.

¹ Mary Anne Ferguson, <u>Images of Women in Litera-</u>

<u>ture</u>, 2nd ed. (Boston: Houghton Mifflin, 1973), p. 268.

² Ibid., p. 249.

If the second reference in the example above were to a work other than Ferguson's *Images of Women in Literature, ibid.* could not be used.

When a second reference cites exactly the same page, only *ibid.* is used; otherwise the appropriate page number is given.

Be aware that documentation forms vary among disciplines. The preferred forms of notes and bibliographic entries vary considerably among disciplines. The style described in the *Publication Manual of the American Psychological Association* describes the style used in psychology and, with slight differences, in several other fields. Each of the natural sciences, the American Medical Association, such fields as linguistics, and many other groups and disciplines have their own preferred styles, each of which is described in detail in the particular group's style manual.

Although these manuals differ in exact detail from discipline to discipline, all sciences use basically one of two systems that may be described as the name and year system and the number system. In both of these systems, the work cited is referenced parenthetically within the text, and the full description of the work appears only at the end of the paper in a *List of References* or *Literature Cited* section.

The **name and year system** places, in parentheses, the last name of the author and the year of publication at the point a source is mentioned in the text. If the author's name is mentioned in the text itself, only the year of publication is given in parentheses.

> Bilkovsky (1979) finds no correlation between the growth of the spores and temperature changes of no more than 10°. Therien (1981), however, finds slight changes in the growth rate with changes greater than 7°.

If the author's name is not mentioned in the text itself, it is enclosed in parentheses together with the publication date.

> One study (Speisman, 1978) showed Nardil to produce significant changes in the depressive patterns of men over 40, even when the drug was given in a dosage no greater than 30 mg daily.

When page numbers are important, they may be inserted within the parentheses.

> Gonzales (1977: 23–25) has calculated the memory properties of the alloy Nitinol.

When this system is used, all references are listed alphabetically by the author's last name at the end of the paper. If two or more studies by the same author are cited, they are listed in chronological sequence by year. The information given on each work in the listing is essentially the same as that required by the MLA form exemplified in this text—author, title, and publication information—but the entries differ in the order in which the information is arranged and in some mechanical details. Only the last name and initials of the author are given, and only the first word of the title is capitalized.

```
Perkins, J.  Neurotic characteristics as predictors of

    author success.  Englewood Cliffs, N.J.:  Prentice-

    Hall, 1981.

Strethman, C. P.  Achievement and longevity.  New York:

    John Wiley, 1978.
```

In the **number system** of documentation, if the author's name is mentioned in the text itself, the reference is indicated only by a number in parentheses. If the author's name is not mentioned, the reference given parenthetically includes the author's last name followed by the appropriate number. References are numbered in this way sequentially throughout the text. In the *List of References* or *Works Cited* section at the end of the paper, each item is given a corresponding number and listed in the order of its occurrence in the text. In the text the reference will appear as follows:

> Oliver (11) finds that only one type of halophyte, *Salicornia europa*, or pickleweed, will germinate in water with a saline content of 36 parts per thousand.

The list of references would then show this entry:

11. Oliver, W. H. <u>Salinity tolerance among halophytes</u>.

New York: Academic Press, 1978.

Abbreviations

As recommended by the *MLA Handbook* and other style manuals, researchers currently use many fewer abbreviations than they once did. Several abbreviations, however, such as ed., rev., n.d., and the like, are still commonly used, and others occur frequently in earlier research you may read. The following list contains most of those you are likely to meet:

anon.	anonymous
art., arts.	article(s)
c., ca.	*circa* (about); used with approximate dates
cf.	*confer* (compare)
ch., chs. (*or* chap., chaps.)	chapter(s)
col., cols.	column(s)
diss.	dissertation
ed., edn.	edition
ed., eds.	editor(s)
e.g.	*exempli gratia* (for example)
et al.	*et alii* (and others)
f., ff.	and the following page(s)
ibid.	*ibidem* (in the same place)
i.e.	*id est* (that is)
illus.	illustrator, illustrated by, illustration
introd.	introduction
l., ll.	line(s)
loc. cit.	*loco citato* (in the place cited)
ms, mss	manuscript(s)
n.b.	*nota bene* (take notice, mark well)
n.d.	no date (of publication) given
n.p.	no place (of publication) given
n. pag.	no pagination
no., nos.	number, numbers
numb.	numbered
op. cit.	*opere citato* (in the work cited)
p., pp.	page(s)
passim	throughout the work, here and there
q.v.	*quod vide* (which see)
rev.	revised

rpt.	reprint, reprinted
trans., tr.,	translator, translated, translation
univ.	university
v.	*vide* (see)
vol., vols.	volume(s)

Prepare your final bibliography.

Your last task, when you have completed the final draft of your paper and made sure your notes are all in proper order, is to prepare your final bibliography. Use the cards you prepared as you were working on your paper. Arrange them in alphabetical order by the last name of each author. If you have sources for which no author is given, their position in your alphabetical listing should be determined by the first word of their titles, excluding initial articles *a, an,* and *the.* That is, "A Guide to Course Studies" should be included at its appropriate position under the letter *G.*

Begin your bibliography on a separate page headed *Works Cited, Bibliography,* or *Bibliography of Works Cited* according to your instructor's requirement. Include all items you have referred to in notes or in your text, but unless your instructor requests, do not include any works you may have consulted but have not referred to. Begin each item of your bibliography flush with the left-hand margin. Whenever an item runs to more than one line, indent the second and later lines five spaces. Double-space the bibliography throughout. See the bibliography at the end of the sample research paper for an example.

Sample research paper

Annie Guzman's research paper, presented in this section, is a successful student paper. For this assignment Annie had to choose a topic that interested her, gather authoritative information about it from a number of sources, and organize the information clearly in a paper of about 1,500 words that would both report the information and make some evaluation of it. She was also required to submit a thesis statement, a sentence outline, a bibliography in proper form, and endnotes to document all evidence in appropriate note form. The Commentary accompanying this paper directs attention to some of the problems of writing and documentation Annie faced and solved.

The format. The title of each part (outline, paper, bibliography, endnotes) is centered one inch below the top of the page. The text is double-spaced, with well-balanced left and right margins of about one inch. Small Roman numerals number the thesis and outline pages. Consecutive Arabic numerals number the pages of the paper itself, including the bibliography and endnotes.

The title page, thesis statement, and sentence outline. The first three sections give a quick summary of this research paper. This prefatory material falls into three divisions: (1) *the title,* which is a very general statement; (2) *the thesis statement,* which explains briefly what the paper attempts to do; and (3) *the outline,* which is a rather full statement.

THE FASCINATING AND FRIGHTENING WORLD

OF THE FUTURISTS

By

Annie Guzman

English 101, Section Q

Mr. G. Lapin

April 4, 1982

i

Outline

Thesis: Although all those studying the future recognize the threat

of worldwide disaster, often portraying it vividly, many

believe that through cooperation and technology we can es-

cape doomsday and enjoy major innovations in the ways we live.

I. Ray Bradbury's science-fiction story "August 2026: There Will

Come Soft Rains" gives a fascinating and frightening glimpse

into the future.

II. Most futurists believe we can escape doomsday through technol-

ogy and cooperation among nations.

A. We can escape the doomsday threats of nuclear war, famine,

and overpopulation through technology and cooperation.

1. Nuclear war: Such a war would have nightmarish con-

sequences, but international control of nuclear

weapons can prevent it.

2. Famine: Crop failures could result in the death of

many millions, but some futurists believe that ad-

vanced technology can provide enough food for everyone.

3. Overpopulation: Uncontrolled population growth could

bring humanity to "the brink of extinction," but most

futurists believe we still have time to institute

population control, and may be able to do so without

restricting individual freedom.

    B. Cooperation among nations will be an absolute necessity if we are to solve our problems.

        1. We can expect more global interdependence in the future.

        2. We in the United States may have to cut back on our standard of living, but life will be far from unpleasant.

III. Futurists predict major changes in our daily lives.

    A. In our daily lives we will make use of many technical innovations, for which we will find the necessary resources and energy sources.

    B. We can expect other changes in family size and housing.

    C. We will be healthier and live longer as medical science makes major breakthroughs.

 IV. There is still time to avert oblivion and instead fulfill the dream of a peaceful, prosperous world, and even dare to work toward a future Utopia.

Commentary

Paragraph 1

This introductory paragraph, the summary of the science-fiction story, not only is interesting—research papers do not have to be boring—but it also serves as a framework to the paper as a whole. It leads to the two key questions asked in paragraph 2 and it serves as a continuing motif in paragraphs 8, 9, and 11. Annie summarizes the story effectively in a few sentences and selects a good quotation to dramatize the situation.

The long quotation is indented ten spaces from the left and double-spaced and does not use quotation marks at beginning and end. Note also the use of ellipsis—three spaced periods after the sentence period.

1

THE FASCINATING AND FRIGHTENING WORLD

OF THE FUTURISTS

In 1950 Ray Bradbury, the famous science-fiction writer, published the short story "August 2026: There Will Come Soft Rains." The main character is a fully automated, almost human house full of mechanical devices. Meals are prepared automatically according to an established schedule; listening devices are programmed to recognize and respond to people's voices; and the house's own "voice" entertains by reading poetry aloud. Bridge tables miraculously appear in time for card games, and tiny automated cleaning animals resembling robot mice continually keep the house spotless. The house seems to function without the aid of any human beings, and early in the story we are told that that is indeed the case:

> The house stood alone in a city of rubble and ashes. . . .
> At night the ruined city gave off a radioactive glow which
> could be seen for miles. . . . The entire west face of the
> house was black, save for five places. Here the silhouette
> in paint of a man mowing a lawn. Here, as in a photograph,
> a woman bent to pick flowers. Still farther over, their
> images burned on wood in one titanic instant, a small boy,
> hands flung into the air; higher up, the image of a thrown
> ball, and opposite him a girl, hands raised to catch a ball
> which never came down.[1]

Paragraph 2

Using the story as a link, Annie introduces the two questions she will answer in her paper. Paragraphs 3, 4, 5, and 6 will deal with the possibility of disaster, and paragraphs 8, 9, and 10 will deal with possible technological advances. Annie has divided her paper into two parts—"the fascinating" and "the frightening," or "the hopes" and "the fears." The reader, given a good direct statement about the intention and limits of the paper, knows exactly what to expect.

Paragraph 3

This paragraph is a general answer to the first question and will be developed in greater detail in the following three paragraphs. Some readers might question Annie's statement about "most futurists." How can she arrive at such a conclusion on the basis of necessarily limited reading? Her defense would be that she felt she had looked at a reasonably large body of material, had noted that a few authorities had also written that "most" futurists felt that way, and that her judgment was based on objective reading of what she believed were representative viewpoints.

Annie tells us something about the authorities she cites—Wilson is "of the Aspen Institute"; in paragraph 4 Bundy is "a former White House aide"; in paragraph 5 Abelson is "editor of *Science Magazine*." Such identification is important because it provides evidence that the authorities cited are really authorities.

Paragraph 4

In a good opening sentence, Annie introduces the three elements of the first part of her paper—the answer to the first question. She then begins discussion of the first element, "nuclear war." In her research, Annie had gathered a good deal of material about the horrors of nuclear war, and in the first draft of the paper she had devoted a complete paragraph to that subject. But then she decided that she was belaboring the point and was in danger of losing sight of her thesis statement.

Her decision to remove the paragraph from the final draft was a good one. Writers must learn to resist the temptation to include all their researched material; and they must learn to be discriminating in their revisions.

2   Bradbury's imaginative glimpse into the future is both fascinating and frightening. The future, the story seems to say, holds out the possibility of tremendous technological advances, but also the threat of total destruction. Today both the hopes and the fears concern not only the science-fiction writers but also the scientists and scholars--- "futurists"---whose studies cover a very wide range of interests. My own interest in this subject I have limited to the two questions raised by Bradbury's story: How real is the threat of worldwide disaster? And if we do have a future, what kind of technological and other advances can the average American really expect?

3   As for the first question, most futurists believe we can avoid the kind of catastrophe described in the story. Thomas Wilson, of the Aspen Institute for Humanistic Studies, seems to sum up this view: "We can ward off the 'doomsday syndrome' if we understand that human decisions determine human conditions. . . . We have the ability to change our course---our social values---and this is my main cause for optimism about the human predicament."[2]

4   The three most frequently mentioned causes of a future doomsday are nuclear war, famine, and overpopulation. Former White House aide McGeorge Bundy, taking an imaginative look backward from the year 2024, speaks of the "Nuclear Events of 1984" in which three great cities were destroyed, one each in the Soviet Union, China, and the United States, with the loss of ten million lives. But he sees this nightmarish pro-

Paragraph 5

Annie moves neatly to the second element, and again cites Bundy to point out the possible consequences. This time, however, Annie presents the views of two additional authorities. She felt she had to do so because she herself was surprised to read that experts were so optimistic about food production. Again, she exercised good judgment. (There is no need to belabor a point, to indulge in "documentation overkill"; but when it is necessary to prove a point, do not hesitate to use more than one source.) In addition, Annie realized that she had relied entirely on Bundy in her discussion of nuclear disaster. Though he had proved a good authority, she recognzed the need to support her point with additional authorities.

By comparing the note cards below with the text, you can see how effectively Annie paraphrases the Piel quotation and how she works the Abelson statement into the structure of her sentence.

3

phesy not as leading to the end of the world but as a terrible lesson
that teaches the leaders of the nations to do something about international control of nuclear weapons.[3] Certainly such a scenario can by
no means be described as "optimistic"--although other possibilities in
thermonuclear, gas, and biological warfare are more horrifying. What
futurists are saying is that if we realize how utterly destructive
future wars can be, perhaps we will learn in time to prevent such wars.

5   The second doomsday nightmare is famine in large parts of the
world. In Bundy's scenario, famines resulting from crop failures in
the grain-producing countries cause a death toll of sixty-five million.[4]
Bundy then imagines the creation of an international "World Food Commission" with the power to prevent future famines.[5] But other futurists
are even more confident that famine can be averted. Gerard Piel, key-
note speaker at the 1976 annual meeting of the American Institute of
Biological Sciences, was optimistic about the ability of advanced technology to provide enough food for everyone, and he cited one agricultural expert who estimated that India alone could feed the world.[6]
Philip H. Abelson, editor of Science Magazine, believes that the United
States is technically capable of feeding a "population ten to one
hundred times as great as our present one." But as do others, Abelson
recognizes that the basic problem is not insufficient food but overpopulation.[7]

Paragraph 6

Annie introduces the third element, but this time she gives the first words to the more pessimistic view of Ehrlich. Ideally, she should have gone to Ehrlich's book, since Hilsman in his footnote tells us where he got the quotation. The reason the original source is better is that readers can then go to the source and make a judgment about whether or not the quoted writer has been treated fairly. Does the quotation truly represent his view? Is it taken out of context? Have important ideas or modifications been left out?

Annie's defense was, "What am I supposed to do—spend my whole life in the library?" It's hard to argue with the writer of a good paper, but still . . .

In the last sentence, Annie recapitulates the three doomsday possibilities by mentioning once again the Bundy scenario.

Note the *three* spaced periods indicating ellipsis within a sentence in the quoted paragraph, and the use of brackets to indicate a change Annie made in the Hilsman quotation.

4

6   And here the futurists come to the third possible doomsday--
overpopulation. But again the views of most futurists are more optimistic than one might expect. Roger Hilsman, for example, does not see the
future as bleakly as Paul R. Ehrlich, who wrote in 1970:

> The explosive growth of the human population is the most
> significant terrestrial event of the past million millennia.
> Three and one half billion people now inhabit the Earth, and
> every year this number increases by 70 million. . . . Man-
> kind itself may stand on the brink of extinction; in its
> death throes it could take with it most of the other passen-
> gers of Spaceship Earth. No geological event in a billion
> years . . . has posed a threat to terrestrial life comparable
> to that of human overpopulation.[8]

Hilsman believes that mankind can solve this problem, and that even
with a population of seven billion in the year 2000, there is still
hope to slow down the rate of growth and to find the food, resources,
and energy to support that population. Hilsman admits he is "alarmed"
by the present threat of overpopulation, but he believes that humans
"will eventually solve [the] problem."[9] And Dennis Gabor believes this
can be done "without any dictatorial interference with the family and
with the institutionalized religions."[10] It is interesting to note

Paragraph 7

This paragraph serves both as a commentary on the doomsday section and as a transition to the second part of the paper—the answer to the second question. Here again, Annie had much more material than she used. She put in the Waldheim quotation because of his authoritative position as Secretary General of the United Nations, and she summarized Barber's ideas because he said so succinctly what other futurists were saying. Here are some of the cards she worked with:

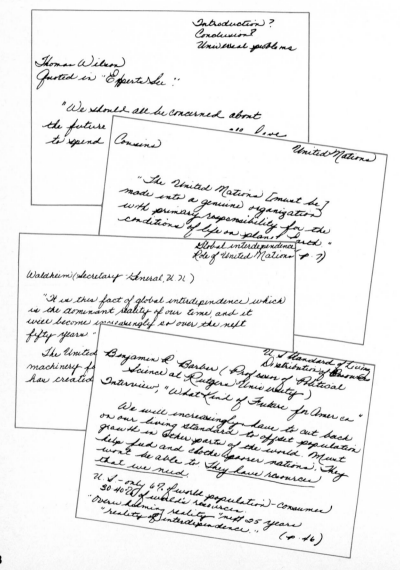

5

that in Bundy's futuristic scenario, population control is tied to the program to end hunger, and thus, together with international control of nuclear weapons, the world finds solutions to the three major problems it faces.[11]

7   If there is one thing that futurists agree upon, it is that cooperation among nations will be an absolute necessity. Kurt Waldheim, Secretary General of the United Nations, states, "It is this fact of global interdependence which is the dominant reality of our times, and it will become increasingly so over the next fifty years."[12] Such interdependence may very well result, as one authority pointed out in an interview, in the need for us in the United States to cut back on our standard of living. A nation that has six percent of the world's population cannot continue to use forty percent of the world's resources.[13] But, although life may change in a number of ways, future inhabitants of the United States will find life not at all unpleasant.

8   According to at least one prediction, the automation described in Bradbury's science-fiction story will probably be part of daily life in the United States by the year 2000. In a list of one hundred "very likely" technical innovations, the authors include such items as "Automated or more mechanized housekeeping and home maintenance . . . automated grocery and department stores . . . extensive use of robots

Paragraph 8

Annie begins discussion of the second part of the report. Here the three elements are not so clearly marked as in the first part, but material does not always lend itself to clear-cut divisions or categories. Annie does well in organizing and condensing what she does have. Wisely, she anticipates a question from the reader: Where will the energy for all this automation come from? And wisely, she resists the temptation to get deeply involved in the controversy over energy resources, not because she cannot find any answers but because there are just too many for her to make use of in this paper.

Paragraph 9

Annie continues with the discussion by presenting material from several sources. This catch-all paragraph could have been strengthened by the introduction of more sociological data, more predictions about "the home" rather than the house of the future. But the paragraph is well organized and begins and ends with effective transitional devices.

The bit about the contoured bathtub Annie did not find in the library. She just ran across it while reading the newspaper. This is not unusual, since good researchers give themselves plenty of time and often happen upon useful material in unexpected places.

6

and machines 'slaved' to humans."[14] Such large-scale mechanization
would of course require unprecedented demands for energy and resources,
but futurists seem to be optimistic about the possibility of discovering new resources and energy sources. Rene Dubos stated in an interview that "resources don't exist until we invent them. . . . A
resource is something that each generation learns to extract and use."
For example, he suggests that new technologies will make it possible
for us to make use of much that we now consider industrial and domestic
waste.[15] In addition, we will make considerable use of new sources of
energy such as solar electrical power and geothermic energy.[16]

9

But of course a house--even a science-fiction house--is not a home.
And here, too, futurists see changes in the years to come. Families
will be smaller; there will be more single people and childless
couples.[17] Actually, the citizen of the future is unlikely to live in
a single-family dwelling, as in the Bradbury story, since such housing
will not only be too expensive for the average person but will also become a symbol of wastefulness and thus "socially unacceptable."[18] Instead, the condominium will replace the single-family home.[19] Heating
of buildings will be made more efficient, and even bathtubs may be contoured to the body to avoid wasting hot water.[20]

Paragraph 10

This is a well-written paragraph. It begins with a good topic sentence, provides links between sentences, and contains a good mix of paraphrase, summary, and direct quotation. The information is derived from five different sources, but the paragraph flows smoothly from beginning to end.

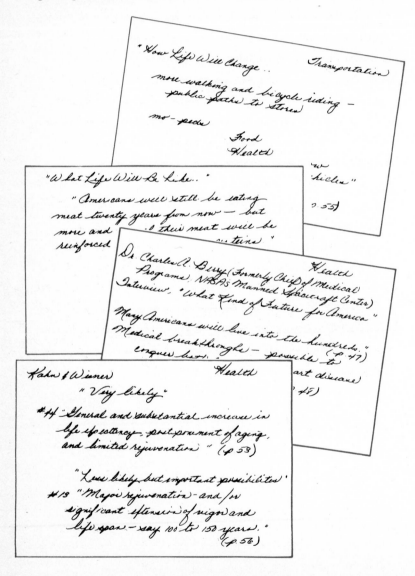

10   Conservation of energy will also probably result in a healthier lifestyle. Since we will be less likely to use automobiles—we will see more bicycles, mopeds, and trolleys[21]—people will do more walking. A reduction of meat in our diet will also be healthier for us, and the meat we do eat will be reinforced with vegetable proteins.[22] The fact that we will be eating less and less meat is suggested by a headline "Remember Chickens?" in "Clippings from Tomorrow's Newpaper: News Stories of 2024" by scientist and science-fictionist Isaac Asimov.[23] More important, Kahn and Wiener list as "very likely" such advancements as "general substantial increase in life expectancy, postponement of aging, and limited rejuvenation" and as an "important possibility" a life span of between 100 and 150 years.[24] Dr. Charles A. Berry, the "astronauts' doctor," stated in an interview that he believes many people will have a life span of one hundred years, and the future will also bring major medical breakthroughs, including the conquest of both cancer and heart disease.[25]

11   Number 87 in Kahn and Wiener's list of one hundred very likely innovations is "stimulated and planned and perhaps programmed dreams."[26] This sounds like science-fiction material (what Andrew A. Spekke calls "Buck Rogers stuff"),[27] but in a way it summarizes what most futurists

Paragraph 11

Annie spent a great deal of time on her final paragraph. It is a good one. It summarizes the paper; it reminds us of the science-fiction story and contrasts the story's conclusion with the vision of Buckminster Fuller. Annie came across his name many times while doing her research, and she decided very early that she would end her paper with a quotation from his works.

It is worthwhile comparing Annie's final draft of the last four sentences with her first two drafts. The time she spent on the rewriting was clearly worth it.

FIRST DRAFT

R. Buckminster Fuller, who is regarded by many as the "prophet" among futurists, is more optimistic than Ray Bradbury. Bradbury seems to say that even if we attain a technical Utopia we will end in oblivion. But Fuller writes: "This moment of realization that it soon must be Utopia or Oblivion coincides exactly with the discovery by man that for the first time in history Utopia is, at least, physically possible of human attainment." Not only futurists but all people hope that he is right.

SECOND DRAFT

R. Buckminster Fuller, the "Prophet," is optimistic about making the dream come true. He believes that Utopia is possible, but it will not come unless we choose it. Bradbury offers Utopia and then Oblivion, but Fuller speaks for the many futurists who feel there is still time for mankind to come to its senses. He believes that "for the first time in history Utopia is, at least, physically possible of human attainment."

are saying. If we hope to achieve the dream of a peaceful, prosperous

world, we will have to stimulate our imaginations and plan and program

our course of action. R. Buckminster Fuller, perhaps the most respected

"prophet" among the futurists, believes that the chances of fulfilling

that dream are good. He is not afraid to speak of a future Utopia.

Whereas Bradbury seems to offer both Utopia and oblivion, Fuller speaks

for those who feel there is still time for us to come to our senses

and choose our future. He writes: "This moment of realization that it

soon must be Utopia or Oblivion coincides exactly with the discovery by

man that for the first time in history Utopia is, at least, physically

possible of human attainment."[28]

Documentation notes. Note 1 follows MLA style for a first reference to a short story in an edited collection. The author's name is not given in the note since it was mentioned in the text. Giving the edition makes it possible for the reader to find the documented material; editions often differ considerably.

Note 2 follows MLA style for an unsigned article in a weekly magazine. "Quoted in" makes clear that Thomas Wilson is not the author of the article.

Note 3, like note 2, follows the form for a weekly magazine. Since the author was identified in the text, his name is omitted from the note.

Notes 4 and 5 require only the name of the author and the page references since they refer to the source cited in note 3.

Note 6 is in MLA style for an article in a journal with continuous pagination throughout the volume.

Note 7 is MLA form for a signed article in a book by several contributors and an editor.

Note 10 refers to the publisher, Alfred A. Knopf, simply as Knopf. MLA style recommends the use of shortened forms of publisher names. Such shortened forms may be used in bibliographic entries too.

Note 14 follows MLA form for a book written by two authors. It also contains a brief documented comment that Annie did not incorporate into the text. Editors and teachers disagree about notes of this type, called **substantive notes.** Some readers of research papers find substantive notes a useful way to include material that is relevant but too digressive to include in the text itself. Others feel that if material is not significant enough to be in the text, it should not appear in the paper at all. Check with an instructor before you use substantive notes, and never use them simply to cram in all the leftover bits of your research.

NOTES

[1] <u>An Introduction to Literature</u>, ed. Sylvan Barnet, Morton Berman, and William Burto, 6th ed. (Boston: Little, Brown, 1977), pp. 270-71.

[2] Quoted in "Experts See World Perils Ahead--But 'Humanity Will Survive,'" <u>U. S. News & World Report</u>, 23 June 1975, p. 64.

[3] "After the Deluge, the Covenant," <u>Saturday Review/World</u>, 24 Aug. 1974, p. 19.

[4] Bundy, pp. 18-19.

[5] Bundy, p. 20.

[6] Quoted in "The Next 200 Could Be Best," <u>BioScience</u>, 26 (1976), 431.

[7] "The Continuing Scientific Revolution," in <u>Man and the Future</u>, ed. James E. Gunn (Lawrence, Kansas: The Univ. Press of Kansas, 1968), p. 57.

[8] Quoted in Roger Hilsman, <u>The Crouching Future</u> (Garden City, N. Y.: Doubleday, 1975), pp. 503-04.

[9] Hilsman, p. 504.

[10] <u>Inventing the Future</u> (New York: Knopf, 1964), p. 210.

[11] Bundy, p. 20.

[12] "Toward Global Interdependence," <u>Saturday Review/World</u>, 24 Aug. 1974, p. 63,

[13] Benjamin R. Barber, in "What Kind of Future for America?" <u>U. S. News & World Report</u>, 7 July 1975, p. 46.

[14] Herman Kahn and Anthony J. Wiener, <u>The Year 2000: A Framework for Speculation on the Next Thirty-Three Years</u> (New York: Macmillan, 1967), pp. 52, 53, 54. Some of these predictions seem to have come

Note 16 indicates a summary of six pages. Annie had four separate note cards with information about various sources of energy but ultimately decided that all she could spare was a one-sentence statement.

Note 19 gives a shortened form of the title first documented in note 17.

Note 20 provides information about the columns the newspaper article can be found in as well as the page and section.

In note 28, Annie refers to a work she did not actually use in her paper. Although she took notes from this collection, she found no direct use for the material. She did feel, however, that the book was interesting enough to mention to readers of her research paper who might want to look deeper into the topic for themselves.

true already. Robot mail carts and an electronic library are in use.
A. R. Roalman, "A Practical Approach to Predicting the Future," Science
Digest, Nov. 1976, 75.

[15] "Looking into the Future," Current, 171 (Mar. 1975), 40.

[16] Gabor, pp. 95-100.

[17] "How Life Will Change for Americans in Years Ahead," U. S. News
& World Report, 12 Jan. 1976, p. 54.

[18] Rene Dubos, "Recycling Social Man," Saturday Review/World, 24
Aug. 1974, p. 10.

[19] "How Life Will Change . . .," p. 54.

[20] "Contoured Bathtub--Energy Saver of the Future," The Boston
Globe, 14 Feb. 1977, Sec. 2, p. 6, cols. 3-7.

[21] "How Life Will Change . . .," p. 55.

[22] "What Life Will Be Like 20 Years in the Future," U. S. News &
World Report, 14 Jan. 1974, p. 74.

[23] Saturday Review/World, 24 Aug. 1974, p. 78.

[24] Kahn and Wiener, pp. 53, 56.

[25] "What Kind of Future for America?" pp. 47-48.

[26] Kahn and Wiener, p. 55.

[27] "America: The Next 200 Years," Intellect, 105 (1976), 50.

[28] Utopia or Oblivion: The Prospects for Humanity (New York:
Bantam, 1969), p. 292. For some informative discussion about Buckmin-
ster Fuller's ideas as well as selections from his writings, see
Patricia Wallace Garlan, Maryjane Dunstan, and Dyan Howell Pike, Star
Sight: Visions of the Future (Englewood Cliffs, N.J.: Prentice-Hall,
1977), pp. 107-45.

WORKS CITED

Asimov, Isaac. "Clippings from Tomorrow's Newspapers: News Stories
     of 2024." <u>Saturday Review/World</u>, 24 Aug. 1974, pp. 78, 80.

Bradbury, Ray. "August 2026: There Will Come Soft Rains." <u>An Intro-
     duction to Literature</u>. Ed. Sylvan Barnet, Morton Berman, and
     William Burto. 6th ed. Boston: Little, Brown, 1977.

Bundy, McGeorge. "After the Deluge, the Covenant." <u>Saturday Review/
     World</u>, 24 Aug. 1974, pp. 18-20, 112-114.

"Contoured Bathtub--Energy Saver of the Future." <u>The Boston Globe</u>, 14
     Feb. 1977, Sec. 2, p. 6, cols. 3-7.

Dubos, Rene. "Recycling Social Man." <u>Saturday Review/World</u>, 24 Aug.
     1974, pp. 8-10. 102-06.

"Experts See World Perils Ahead--But 'Humanity Will Survive.'" <u>U. S.
     News & World Report</u>, 23 June 1975, pp. 64-65.

Fuller, R. Buckminster. <u>Utopia or Oblivion: The Prospects for Human-
     ity</u>. New York: Bantam, 1969.

Gabor, Dennis. <u>Inventing the Future</u>. New York: Knopf, 1964.

Garlan, Patricia Wallace, Maryjane Dunstan, and Dyan Howell Pike.
     <u>Star Sight: Visions of the Future</u>. Englewood Cliffs, N.J.:
     Prentice-Hall, 1977.

Gunn, James E., ed. <u>Man and the Future</u>. Lawrence, Kansas: The Univ.
    Press of Kansas, 1968.

Hilsman, Roger. <u>The Crouching Future</u>. Garden City, N. Y.: Doubleday,
    1975.

"How Life Will Change for Americans in Years Ahead." <u>U. S. News &</u>
    <u>World Report</u>, 12 Jan. 1976, pp. 54-56.

Kahn, Herman, and Anthony J. Wiener. <u>The Year 2000: A Framework for</u>
    <u>Speculation on the Next Thirty-Three Years</u>. New York: Macmillan,
    1967.

"Looking Into the Future." <u>Current</u>, 171 (Mar. 1975), 24-46.

Roalman, A. R. "A Practical Approach to Predicting the Future."
    <u>Science Digest</u>, Nov. 1976, pp. 74-79.

Spekke, Andrew A. "America: The Next 200 Years." <u>Intellect</u>, 105
    (1976), 49-50.

Waldheim, Kurt. "Toward Global Interdependence." <u>Saturday Review/</u>
    <u>World</u>, 24 Aug. 1974, pp. 63-64, 122.

"What Kind of Future for America?" <u>U. S. News & World Report</u>, 7
    July 1975, pp. 44-50.

"What Life Will Be Like 20 Years in the Future." <u>U. S. News & World</u>
    <u>Report</u>, 14 Jan. 1974, pp. 72-75.

WRITING SUMMARIES
AND ESSAY EXAMS

47 SUMMARIES

The ability to summarize effectively—to strip a paragraph or a chapter down to its central meaning without distorting the author's original thought and approach—is extremely useful. Writing such summaries is an excellent way to study. Having such summaries available is invaluable for later reference and review.

Preparing summaries can also help you to read with greater accuracy and to write with greater conciseness and directness. You cannot summarize effectively if you have not read carefully, discriminating between principal and subordinate ideas. Such discrimination, in turn, will help you to sharpen your own style and to avoid the wordiness that creeps into careless writing.

Before you try to summarize a passage, read it carefully to discover the author's purpose and point of view. As you read, pick out the central ideas and notice how they are arranged. Be on the lookout for the author's own compact summaries, either at the beginning or end of a passage or at points of transition.

After studying the passage, you are ready to organize your summary, or **précis.** Ordinarily you will be able to reduce a paragraph—or sometimes a whole group of paragraphs—to a single sentence. Very complex paragraphs, however, may require more than one sentence.

Use a simple or complex sentence rather than a compound sentence to summarize a paragraph—unless the original paragraph itself is poorly organized. A compound sentence implies that there are two or more equally dominant ideas in the paragraph. If you find that you have written a compound summarizing sentence, recheck the paragraph to make sure that the author did not imply some subordinating relationship that you have missed. In determining the author's intent, be alert to such writing techniques as parallel clauses and phrases, which indicate ideas of equal weight, and transitional words and phrases, which show relationships among ideas.

Summarize the author's ideas in the order in which they have been presented, but avoid following the exact wording too closely. If you are overly scrupulous in trying to preserve the flavor of the original, your summary will be far too long. Do not hesitate, however, to pick up the author's key terms and phrases, for they are useful in binding the précis together. Discard any figures of speech, digressions, or discussions that are not essential to the "trunk and main branches." When you are all through, you should find that you have reduced the material to not over one-third of its original length. Study the following example:

We very rarely consider, however, the process by which we gained our convictions. If we did so, we could hardly fail to see that there was usually little ground for our confidence in them. Here and there, in this department of knowledge or that, some one of us might make a fair claim to have taken some trouble to get correct ideas of, let us say, the situation in Russia, the sources of our food supply, the origin of the Constitution, the revision of the tariff, the policy of the Holy Roman Apostolic Church, modern business organization, trade unions, birth control, socialism, the League of Nations, the excess-profits tax, pre-paredness, advertising in its social bearings; but only a very exceptional person would be entitled to opinions on all of even these few matters. And yet most of us have opinions on all these, and on many other questions of equal importance, of which we may know even less. We feel compelled, as self-respecting persons, to take sides when they come up for discussion. We even surprise ourselves by our omniscience. Without taking thought we see in a flash that it is most righteous and expedient to discourage birth control by legislative enactment, or that one who decries intervention in Mexico is clearly wrong, or that big advertising is essential to big business and that big business is the pride of the land. As godlike beings why should we not rejoice in our omni-science? JAMES HARVEY ROBINSON, *The Mind in the Making*

Notice that this paragraph hinges on the sentence beginning *And yet most of us have opinions on all these. . . .* This sentence suggests the pattern that your summarizing sentence should probably take. The central idea of the paragraph is that we do not ordinarily take pains in forming our convictions on important matters, but we nevertheless express our opinions as a matter of right and even take delight in our apparent omniscience. The main clause of your summarizing sentence will express the second part of the central idea, retaining the author's ironic approach.

We are godlike beings who delight in our ability to form and express convictions on birth control, on intervention in Mexico, or on the role of big business, without a moment's thought.

To preserve the author's qualification in the first part of the para-graph, however, you must precede the main clause with a subordinate clause.

Although the few pains we take to understand such things as the situation in Russia, the sources of our food supply, the origin of the Constitution, the revision of the tariff, the policy of the Holy Roman Apostolic Church, modern business organization, trade unions, birth control, socialism, the League of Nations, the excess-profits tax, pre-paredness, and advertising in its social bearings give us little reason to have confidence in our opinions on these matters, we are godlike beings who delight in our ability to form and express convictions on birth control, on intervention in Mexico or on the role of big business, without a moment's thought.

But this "summary" is almost half as long as the original. To reduce it further, replace the specific examples with general terms.

> Although the few pains we take to understand such things as social, political, economic, religious, and medical issues give us little reason to have confidence in our convictions on these matters, we are godlike beings who delight in our ability to form and express such convictions without a moment's thought.

This summary, less than one-third the length of the original, would be acceptable for most purposes, but occasionally even a shorter summary is desirable.

> Although we have little reason to trust our convictions on the important issues of life, we delight in forming and expressing such opinions without a moment's thought.

Clearly this last sentence does not express everything in Robinson's paragraph, where the concreteness and the vigor of the short sentences are perhaps even more striking than its central thought. But a summary is concerned only with the central thought, not necessarily with retaining the author's style, and the central thought is preserved even in the shortest statement above.

EXERCISE 47(1) Write a two-sentence summary of the paragraph by Jacques Barzun, on pp. 268–69, beginning "The whole aim of good teaching."

EXERCISE 47(2) Write a one-sentence summary of the same paragraph.

EXERCISE 47(3) Try to write a one-sentence summary of the following paragraph. Does the effort tell you anything about the weakness of the paragraph itself?

> Among the many interesting aspects of dietary training is the living together of the students. This allows each to get acquainted with people from all over the States and to exchange ideas and viewpoints from different sections of the country. By living in such a home, many girls grow into more mature individuals. It proves a good chance for girls who have always lived at home to become more independent. It also helps to establish feelings of self-sufficiency in those who have never before been on their own.

EXERCISE 47(4) Write the briefest summary you can of the paragraph below.

Great care and attention is given in the organization of pageants and other popular feasts, and of these a Russian crowd is particularly appreciative, throwing itself wholeheartedly into the enjoyment of every detail. The "crowd sense," which is just another expression of the corporate instinct, is peculiarly strong in Russia, and it is often curiously reminiscent of an English crowd, particularly in its broad and jolly sense of humor. But Russians of any class have a much stronger artistic sense than we have. This was so before the revolution, and it comes out in the organization of these festivals. They are all out to enjoy themselves, and anything particularly clever or pretty gets them at once. In Kiev, still as always a beautiful city on its lovely site, in the late summer of 1936, I saw a march past of all the wards in turn. They swung past with splendid vigor, squads of men or of women—one squad of women had in the middle of it a fine old man with a long beard who looked very pleased with his company. There were flowers and dancing everywhere; each ward was preceded by a dancing band of girl skirmishers in the picturesque Ukrainian costume, sometimes singing the charming Ukrainian folk songs. At one point various forms of recreation and amusement were represented: the fishermen carrying long fishing rods with colored paper fish hooked to them, the chess players carrying enormous cardboard knights, bishops, and castles. Interspersed between the detachments came curious and fanciful constructions, sometimes very ingenious; an effigy of Trotsky with long nose and black eyes and curls made an excellent Mephistopheles. It was a family feast of old and young, and we all exchanged our comments as each new surprise went past. With the usual courtesy to guests there was a chair set for me, and when I wanted to let a lady have it, I was genially told "that I had to submit to the will of the majority." At one time a torrent of rain came down, but the marchers swung past with all the more vigor and enjoyment. And so it was with the on-lookers. After several hours of it, I asked a neighboring policeman whether I couldn't go away: "No," he said very nicely, "you must stay and enjoy it." And enjoy it they certainly did, for in spite of more downpours of rain, from my room in the hotel I could hear them singing and dancing on the square outside till two in the morning. The one thing that fell below the level of all the rest was the exhausting reiteration of the portraits of Stalin and the other "big noises" of Communism. There must have been about forty of Stalin alone: one ten foot high, of the face alone. I noticed a sympathetic cheer when there came past a single portrait of Lenin.   BERNARD PARES, *Russia: Its Past and Present*

48   ESSAY EXAMS

What you have learned from this handbook about effective writing applies to the special problem of writing essays for exams. You will be expected to write standard English, to organize material intelligently, and to provide evidence and detail to support generalizations. When you have several days to write a paper or a take-home exam, you spend a good part of the time on prewriting—choosing and limiting your subject, thinking about it, gathering material, and outlining. You also have time to make important changes after your first draft—revising paragraphs and sentences, substituting more precise words, and proofreading. You cannot expect to do all this in the half-hour, hour, or even two hours you have for an in-class exam. You are writing under pressure; you have so much time and no more. Therefore, it saves time to go into essay exams knowing how to proceed.

Preparation

Most of your prewriting must be done before you go to the exam. How can you accomplish that when you don't know what questions will be asked? You will not be able to choose a subject; it will be chosen for you—or, at best, you will be allowed to choose from among two or three. You know the *general subject* of the exam, however: it is the subject matter of the course or of part of the course. Your goal, then, is to go to the exam having in mind a rough outline of the course segments. This process of outlining begins with the first lecture or reading assignment and continues uninterrupted to the day of the exam. Take notes during lectures, underline key passages and make marginal notations in your textbooks, summarize your reading, look over your gathered material from time to time, evaluate it, and structure it. You will then be ready to study and review for the exam. As you study, prepare a more formal outline based on an overview of the course material and any guidelines suggested by your instructor. Writing such an outline and studying it helps fix the general subject in your mind.

Prewriting

As soon as you see the specific questions in an exam, your subject is limited for you. Say, for example, your general subject was the history of Europe from 1815 to 1848—the segment of the course on which you are being examined. Now you are given fifty minutes to answer four questions, the first of which is: *What were the four major political and social developments in Europe during the period of 1815–1848?* Or, your general subject was three stories by Nathaniel Hawthorne and two by Herman Melville—the stories you discussed in class. Now you are given fifty minutes to answer two questions, the first of which is: *Hawthorne has been called a "moralist-psychologist." Define the term and eval-*

uate Hawthorne's effectiveness as moralist-psychologist by making specific reference to two of his tales.

Read the examination question carefully. Never start writing without thinking about what you are being asked to do. Are you being asked to summarize or to analyze? Are you expected to present information or to interpret? Are you being asked to comment on a given statement, possibly disagree with it, or to prove it by providing supporting evidence?

The European history question directs you to furnish information (what *are* the four major developments?). You have only about ten minutes to answer the question, so you will not be able to go into great detail. Don't try to fill up half a blue book with everything you know about the subject. In the second question, you are asked to define and evaluate; you must make a critical judgment on the basis of specific evidence in Hawthorne's stories. You have approximately twenty-five minutes to organize and write the essay. Make it a rule to take a minute or two to think about the question, and answering it will be easier.

Having done this, gather material and prepare a rough outline of the limited topic. Typical notes for the history question could include the following:

1815—Congress of Vienna
1848—Revolutions
Nationalism—C. of V. denied rights to Poles, Belgians, Greeks, etc.
Conservative—Liberal Conflict—Cons. anti-reform. Lib. underground
Industrial Expansion—Intro. of machines. Transportation—railroads, steam transport, etc.
Class conflict—Lower class vs. middle class

An answer to the question on Hawthorne could develop from the following notes:

How human beings behave (psych.) and how they ought/ought not to (moral)
"Ambitious Guest"—psychological study of human ambitions—moralistic application
"Wakefield"—integration of psych. and moral—people tied to systems

After briefly studying such notes, you have only to number them in the order you wish to present them—and you have an outline.

As in all outlining, you should not feel rigidly bound to the material and its structure. As you write, other ideas may come to you and a better structure may suggest itself. The student who answered the Hawthorne question, for example, decided to write on "Egotism" rather than "The Ambitious Guest." With time looking over your shoulder, though, you probably cannot afford to change your plans more than once.

Cover statement

On the basis of your notes you should now be able to begin your examination essay by writing a sentence or two that will serve as a thesis statement. The students who answered the above questions began as follows:

> Although there were no major conflicts among the European powers between the Congress of Vienna (1814–1815) and the Revolutions of 1848, important developments were taking place that would affect the future history of Europe. Four of these developments were the rise of nationalism, the conflict between the conservatives and the liberals, the conflict between the lower and middle classes, and the expansion of industry.

> Hawthorne is a moralist-psychologist who is concerned not only with *how* people behave but also with how they *ought* or *ought not* to behave. He is most successful when he integrates the two approaches, as in "Wakefield," and least successful when his moralizing gets away from him, as in "Egotism; or, The Bosom Serpent."

Often, of course, the pressure of the exam keeps you from composing such a thorough cover statement. If coming up with a good cover statement is delaying you, limit your opening to what is specifically required by the question (e.g., Define "moralist-psychologist"), then develop your ideas, and then conclude, after looking over what you have written, with the summary or evaluation (e.g., "Hawthorne, then, is most successful when. . . ."). In some examinations you will not be in the position to summarize or evaluate until you have addressed yourself to a number of particulars in the body of your answer. Whether you begin your answer with a cover statement or not, resist the temptation, so powerful during the first few minutes of an exam, to start writing down everything you know. Don't begin to write until you know what direction you want your answer to take. And remember, your audience is your instructor: he or she knows the subject, so don't waste valuable time on writing background information or overexplaining facts.

Development

Provide supporting evidence, reasoning, detail, or example. Nothing weakens a paper so much as vagueness, unsupported generalizations, and wordiness. Don't talk about "how beautiful Hawthorne's images are and what a pleasure it was to read such great stories," etc., etc. If necessary, go back to your jotted notes to add supporting material. If you have written a cover statement, look at it again and then jot down some hard evidence in the space at the top of the page.

Say you have been asked to discuss the proper use of the I.Q. score by a teacher. Your notes read: *Intelligence—capacity for learning. Must interpret carefully. Also child's personality. Score not permanent. Measures verbal ability.* You have formulated this cover statement: *"Intelligence" is a vague term used to describe an individual's capacity for learning. The teacher must remember that I.Q. scores tell only part of the story and that they are subject to change.* Now you must provide the material for development. Think about specific I.Q. tests, specific studies that support your generalizations. Such notes as the following will help you develop your essay:

> 10% of children significant change after 6 to 8 years
>
> High motivation often more important than high I.Q.
>
> Stanford-Binet—aptitude rather than intelligence
>
> Verbal ability—children from non-English-speaking families—culturally deprived—low verbal score
>
> N.Y. study—remedial courses, etc.—40% improvement in scores

You now have some raw material to work with, material you can organize and clearly relate to your cover statement.

You still have some hard thinking to do, but at least you have something to think about. Even if you do not fully succeed in integrating your data into a perfectly coherent and unified essay, you will have demonstrated that you read the material and have some understanding of it. Padding, wordiness, and irrelevancies prove only that you can fill up pages.

Must you never toss in a few interesting tidbits not specifically called for by the question? There is nothing wrong with beginning a discussion of the significance of the Jefferson-Adams correspondence with: "In their 'sunset' correspondence of more than 150 letters, Jefferson and Adams exchanged their ideas on world issues, religion, and the nature and future of American democratic society, almost until the day they both died—July 4, 1826." While only the middle third of this sentence is a direct response to the question, the other information is both relevant and interesting. Such details cannot *substitute* for your answer, but they can enhance it, just as they would an out-of-class essay.

Last look

Try to leave time at the end of the exam to read what you've written. Check to see if you have left out words or phrases. See if you can add an additional bit of detail or evidence; you can make insertions in the margins. Correct misspellings and awkward sentences. See if your cover statement can be improved. You are not expected to write a perfectly polished essay in an exam, but make your essay as readable as you can in the time you have left.

EXERCISE 48 Evaluate an essay exam answer you have written. Place pluses (+) and minuses (−) in the margins, and make a list of strengths and weaknesses. Look over your lecture notes, textbooks, and other material, and then revise your examination until you are satisfied it merits a higher grade.

WRITING ON THE JOB: BUSINESS CORRESPONDENCE

49

49 WRITING ON THE JOB: BUSINESS CORRESPONDENCE

A frequent complaint voiced by college students goes like this: "What good will knowing how to write a 500-word essay do me after I've graduated? How does my research paper on Hawthorne's short stories prepare me to compose a business letter to a customer or a memo to my boss?"

These are reasonable questions, and they deserve a thoughtful reply. The assumption is that if you write well in one context, let's say the research paper on Hawthorne, you will be able to write well in other contexts, too. The assumption is generally correct. Your ability to construct clear, purposeful, effective sentences and paragraphs will stand the test of almost any writing task. The organizing and writing skills you need to construct a 500-word essay are those you need, on the job, to write letters, memos, and reports.

Another way of saying it is that both academic and business writing require attention to the same elements of composition: purpose, audience, tone, style, grammar, mechanics, and organization. Business correspondence may *look* special because it uses a special format (with headings, salutations, and so forth), but it is really governed by the same principles as your college writing assignments. Indeed, the biggest difference between academic and business writing is that your business associates, if anything, will be *less* tolerant than your teachers of errors, poor organization, windy language, and time-wasting failure to present ideas clearly. Because its fundamental purpose is to help get things done, the hallmark of good business writing is its efficiency.

Memos and letters

The most common types of business correspondence are the memorandum (memo) and the letter. The principal difference between the two is really only a matter of audience: a memo is *internal* correspondence written to your fellow employees; a letter is *external* correspondence written to someone outside your company or organization. A memo reflects this difference in its **routing information.** Instead of the return and inside addresses, salutation, complimentary close, and signature found on a letter, a memo provides this "sender-receiver" information in abbreviated form at the upper left of its first page.

```
TO:       Marian Kaufman
FROM:     Jon Carter  JC
DATE:     March 13, 1982
SUBJECT:  April Sales Meeting Agenda

As we agreed on the phone yesterday, the April
meeting should be used to develop strategies
for improving sales of our summer sportswear
line. Historically, the most unprofitable
territory has been New England, even though
```

Because people in the same organization ordinarily have the same address, full addresses are superfluous. When writer and recipient know each other, titles and departments can be omitted, though they may be used if the writer and the recipient have not corresponded often.

```
TO:       William H. Whalen, Director of
          University Publications
FROM:     Cinda Brandt, Management Business
          Representative
DATE:     December 5, 1983
SUBJECT:  Bid for Undergraduate Catalog
```

You may have noticed that Jon Carter's memo contains his signed initials next to his name. Although initialing a memo is not mandatory, to do so indicates that the sender has reread and approved the memo after it was typed.

In most other respects, memos differ little from letters. Both are single-spaced with double-spacing between paragraphs and sections, both may use block or indented paragraphs, and both may contain headings and enumeration as visual cues to guide the reader through the contents.

Visual cues are important in business correspondence. As the sample letters illustrate, paragraphs tend to be shorter than in an essay, research paper, or novel. Lists are sometimes presented vertically, and series may include bullets (see sample letter 1) or numbers that would probably be omitted in an essay. The reason has to do with the way business letters and memos are used. As part of its function of getting a job done, business correspondence often serves as a reference document. Consequently, the reader must be able to find items quickly. By dividing the discussion more frequently into subtopics and by providing more visual cues, the writer aids not only the reader's understanding but also a fast, easy reference to specific portions of the document.

49 Parts of a business letter

The standard business letter has six parts: (1) the heading, which includes the return address and date; (2) the inside address; (3) the salutation; (4) the body; (5) the complimentary close; and (6) the signature. The first sample letter (p. 502) illustrates a widely used format for these parts and provides a model you can follow. The content of that letter describes the arrangement of the parts and the special conventions of punctuation.

A more unusual business letter format, but one that is growing in popularity, is known as the simplified letter format. Simplified letters use full block style, with all parts flush at the left margin. The salutation and complimentary close are eliminated. A subject line appears where the salutation ordinarily would be placed. This format is easy to type because no tab stops are needed, the subject is immediately clear, and the lack of salutation resolves problems when the name of the recipient is not known. Sample letter 3 (p. 504) shows the simplified format.

The following comments explain appropriate selection of the heading, salutation, complimentary close, and other details pertaining to the parts of business letters.

The heading. Two parts comprise the heading of a business letter: the return address and the date. Although you may have seen a writer's name included as part of the heading, usually the first line, this practice is incorrect. It may be the result of the writer's copying the appearance of letterhead stationary.

Most businesses use letterhead stationery on which the company's name, address, and sometimes the writer's name have been printed or engraved. When using letterhead stationery, you need supply only the date portion of the heading. Sample letter 4 (p. 505) illustrates correspondence typed on letterhead stationery.

The salutation. The content of the salutation, or greeting, depends somewhat on the relationship between writer and reader. Commonly the title and last name of the addressee are used: *Dear Mr. Meade, Dear Professor Connelly, Dear Miss* [or *Mrs.*] *Shearer. Dear Ms. Shearer* is now widely used, not only when a woman's title is not known, but also because many women prefer it. If a woman to whom you are writing identifies herself as Miss or Mrs., however, always address her in the same way.

What if you know the recipient's name but not whether that person is male or female, as may happen if a letter is signed with initials *(S.S. Fleming)* or with a name popular for both sexes *(Lee Hunter)?* Rather than annoying your recipient by guessing incorrectly, it is better—and never wrong—to use the addressee's full name in the salutation: *Dear Lee Hunter.*

Formerly, the conventions governing standard business letters called for *Dear Sir* or *Gentlemen* when writing to organizations or persons you do not know. Because the reader may very likely be a woman, this greeting is inappropriate. Although *Dear Sir or Madame* or *Dear Ladies and/or Gentlemen* is acceptable, another alternative is to use the recipient's title, avoiding gender-specific designations entirely: *Dear Personnel Director; Dear Department Manager.* Avoid *To whom it may concern.*

For appropriate forms of salutation and inside addresses for letters to government officials, military personnel, and the like, check your desk dictionary for guidance. If you are answering a letter, use the same forms as those in the letter to which you are replying.

How should you address a person you know well or with whom you have corresponded before? If you would address that person by his or her first name when speaking face to face or on the telephone, it is more than likely appropriate to use the first name in your letter's salutation as well.

The complimentary close. The majority of business letters close simply and courteously with *Sincerely.* Less common but quite acceptable are the following closes: *Yours truly; Very truly yours; Sincerely yours.* Business letters addressed to people with whom there is frequent and friendly correspondence often use *Cordially* or *Cordially yours.* Closings such as *Respectfully yours* and *Yours respectfully* are reserved for formal circumstances where they seem appropriate as, for example, in addressing a letter to the president of your university or to a high government official.

Note that the first word of a complimentary close is always capitalized, but *only* the first.

The signature. Both the handwritten and the typewritten signature are important. If appropriate, the typewritten signature may be followed by the writer's official capacity, but neither professional titles nor degrees should be used with the signature.

Sincerely yours,

William H. Oliver

William H. Oliver
Editor

A woman may, if she wishes, place *(Ms.), (Miss),* or *(Mrs.)* before her typed name. A married woman may choose to add, in parentheses, below her typed name *Mrs.* followed by her husband's name.

Sincerely,

Katherine Carlone

(Ms.) Katherine Carlone

Yours truly,

Elizabeth Phillips

Elizabeth Phillips
(Mrs. Charles Phillips)

As with the salutation, in letters to people with whom you are on a first-name basis, it is perfectly appropriate to sign only your first name. The typewritten signature should use your full professional name.

Cordially,

Melinda

Melinda G. Kramer
Communications Director

Reference initials. Business letters that have been typed by someone other than the sender frequently identify the sender and the typist by their initials. In the same area—the lower left—you will find information about other material enclosed with the letter and the names of people who have received copies of the letter. Such information is typed flush with the left margin, as follows:

INITIALS OF SENDER AND OF TYPIST	RLW/cwm
ENCLOSURE	Enc.: Color chart
RECIPIENT OF A COPY	cc: Patrick Q. Jay, Manager

Kinds of business letters*

Request letters. Perhaps the most common kind of business letter most of us write is that asking someone to do something: give us information, send us something we have seen advertised, or correct a mistake. Such letters should be direct, businesslike, and courteous, even when you are registering a complaint.

Above all they must be clear. They must directly state what you want the reader to do, and they must give the exact information the reader needs to meet your request. You will notice that sample letters 2 and 3 (pp. 503 and 504) conclude by telling the readers just what the writers want, what results Kevin Lawry and Marilyn Conway expect. Conclusions of this type are appropriately called **action endings.**

Request letters can be grouped into two categories: (1) those with reader benefit and (2) those without reader benefit. In other words, if fulfilling the sender's request does the recipient some good, the request has reader benefit. Sample letter 3, although registering a complaint, falls in the reader-benefit category because the company clearly

---

*Some of the sample letters on pp. 502–507 are adapted from P.D. Hemphill, *Business Communications* (Englewood Cliffs, N.J.: Prentice-Hall, 1976).

gains when its customers are satisfied and loses when they are unhappy.

Requests without reader benefit are somewhat problematic. Why should your reader do what you want if he or she has nothing to gain from it? In such cases you are really relying on your reader's good will. Besides writing clearly, you should take up as little of the reader's time as possible, make your request reasonable, and—if you can—encourage the reader's good will, perhaps by paying an honest compliment. Requests for information can frequently be handled in this way, as sample letter 2 shows.

Verification letters and letters of transmittal. The purpose of much business correspondence is to let readers know information has been received or is being sent and to ensure that it has been understood accurately. Verification letters do what their name suggests: they verify. If an associate telephones you to arrange a meeting, you may want to send him or her a verification letter confirming time and place and the topics to be discussed. Following that meeting, either of you might write another letter summarizing the discussion and substantiating any agreement reached. Participants thus have a record of pertinent information and can verify mutual understanding.

Letters of transmittal (also called **cover letters**) typically accompany other materials, especially documents such as reports. A transmittal letter identifies for the reader the material it accompanies and explains why the sender is transmitting the material to the recipient. When a report or document is involved, a transmittal letter may briefly summarize its contents—highlighting the most important findings, conclusions, and recommendations.

A transmittal letter is not nearly as superfluous as it may seem. Consider the number and variety of tasks confronting a business person in the course of a week or month, and imagine what could happen if a fifty-page report appeared in the morning mail without its transmittal letter: "Now what in the world is this?" Eventually the recipient would remember he or she had commissioned a study to be passed along to Jones in Consumer Affairs—but not before wasting time in puzzlement and frustration. Meanwhile, the report idles between the sender and the people who need it. Sample letter 4 (p. 505) shows an example of a transmittal letter.

Letters of application. Though letters requesting information, registering complaints, and the like, are probably those you will write most often, letters in which you apply for a job you want are almost certainly among the most important you will write. When writing such letters, keep the following advice in mind:

1   Application letters usually fit either of two categories: solicited

applications and prospecting applications. When you know an opening for a position actually exists because you have heard about the vacancy or seen it advertised, you will write a solicited application letter (see sample letter 5). In addition to specifying the position, in this case identify the advertisement or mention the source from whom you obtained the information about the job opening. If a specific person suggested you write, mention that fact. When you have no direct knowledge that a job opening exists but you want to be considered if a position is available, your application letter is a prospecting application (see sample letter 6). In this case you will identify the type of position you desire and mention why you are interested in working for the company you are addressing.

2   Describe any part of your education or previous work experience that you believe prepares you for the job you want. Be brief, direct, and factual, but at the same time present the information to your advantage. Use your education and experience to show the prospective employer how you are qualified to contribute to the company. Remember that the employer is the "buyer," and you are "marketing" your credentials and skills. Although the tone of your letter should not be egotistical, neither should it sound apologetic or pleading. Do not beg. Write a letter that is informative, courteous, and confident.

3   Provide references if at all possible, but remember that useful and relevant references must come from people who actually know your work at first hand. People for whom you have worked successfully and instructors with whom you have taken relevant courses are often among your best references. Remember that a potential employer consulting one of your references will want to know specific things about the quality of your work, your overall ability—and your reliability. Be sure to get permission from persons whose names you intend to use before you list them as references.

4   An application letter is similar to a request letter: you are asking the reader to do something—consider you for a job. Consequently, you should use an action ending. Since the next step in the employment process is typically a job interview, you can end your letter by asking the reader to let you know when it would be convenient for you to come for an interview. Always tell the reader when, where, and how you can be reached if you are not available at your return address during business hours.

5   For many part-time or temporary positions, it is sufficient to describe your experience and other qualifications in the body of your letter, as the writer of sample letter 5 does. But for full-time positions, and particularly if your background, qualifications, and references are fairly extensive, it is wiser to present information in clear, quickly readable form on a personal data sheet, or resumé, as does the writer of sample letter 6. This enables you to use your application letter to highlight in summary form particularly important information and to

provide any additional persuasive details, while conveniently presenting necessary factual information on the resumé. Be sure to mention your resumé in your letter.

Following the sample letters are two resumés showing effective formats. The first format is widely used and fairly traditional. The second format organizes information according to skills and may be a good choice if you want to emphasize your capabilities. For people whose work experience is varied or not continuous, or whose education is not obviously applicable to the job they are seeking, the format of the second resumé is the more effective.

Remember, too, that experience need not be only jobs for which you received pay. Volunteer work, community service, and other activities may have added skills relevant to the job you are seeking. Similarly, you may want to list education that did not result in a degree. Consider for your resumé and your application letter evening classes, classes taken at the YMCA or community center—in fact, any training that is relevant to the employment you desire.

Use action verbs to describe your experience: *organized, developed, assisted,* instead of *duties included.* . . . Talk about what you accomplished, goals you met or exceeded, skills you learned or demonstrated. Like your application letter, your resumé should be persuasive.

The personal data you include on your resumé should be only that which is pertinent to the job. For example, height and weight, hair or eye color are not likely to be the least bit relevant. Laws forbidding job discrimination based on marital status, age, sex, race, or religion have also changed the personal data appearing on resumés; employers cannot require this type of information from job applicants. For instance, if you are seeking a sales position that involves extended periods on the road or a job with a company that routinely transfers managers among its several plants around the country, you might list willingness to travel or relocate under personal data; but you need not indicate whether you are male or female, single or married.

Sample letter 1: modified block style without indented paragraphs

521 Lake Street
Tucson, Arizona 85702
April 29, 1983

Mr. Peter B. McHenry
Business Manager
University of Texas
Austin, Texas 78752

Dear Mr. McHenry:

Business letters appear in several formats. The most common ones are full block style, modified block style either with or without indented paragraphs, and simplified style. This letter uses modified block style without indented paragraphs.

- All parts of the letter except the heading, the complimentary close, and the signature are placed flush with the left margin.

- Paragraphs are not indented.

- Within the body of the letter, portions for which special emphasis is desired may be indented.

- The heading is placed approximately flush with the right margin; note that it includes the date.

- The complimentary close is aligned with the heading.

If you are using letterhead stationary, the date may be typed three or four spaces below the letterhead and either centered or placed flush with either margin. In what is called the full block style, all parts of the letter are placed flush with the left margin.

The punctuation in the heading and inside address of this letter is open. That is, no punctuation is placed at the end of lines, although internal punctuation between city and state and between day and year is retained. The salutation and complimentary close, however, are followed by a colon and a comma, respectively. In fully open punctuation, no punctuation is used after the salutation and close.

Note that spacing in the letter is an important part of its appearance. Two or three spaces should be left between the date and the inside address. Double spacing should be used between all other main parts of the letter, and always between paragraphs. It is wise to allow four spaces between the complimentary close and your typed signature.

The appearance is well served also by the picture frame placement used in this letter, which maintains uniform and generous margins. In addition, the bullets denoting the principal characteristics of modified block style draw the reader's attention to the information, making it easy to spot. The purpose of a business letter format is to increase efficiency and effectiveness in transmitting information.

Sincerely,

Dan Portillo

Dan Portillo

Sample letter 2: full block style

416 Wabash Avenue
West Point, Indiana 47963
April 23, 1983

Clark Equipment Company
Public Relations Department
Circle Drive
Buchanan, Michigan 49107

Dear Sir or Madam:

An assignment for my college business-writing class requires that I
write a research report on a company for whom I might like to work
after graduation. Clark Equipment Company is my choice for this
report.

Preliminary research in our business school's library has convinced me
that Clark is a solid performer in the heavy equipment industry. Because I am a construction management major, I am familiar with your
construction machinery and its excellent reputation.

Please send me a copy of Clark's 1982 annual report together with any
other descriptive information you may have about Clark Equipment Company, particularly the construction machinery division. I would also
appreciate a few issues of the company's employee magazine. Thank you.

Sincerely,

Kevin Lawry

Kevin Lawry

Sample letter 3: simplified style

444 West Wilson Street
Madison, Wisconsin 53715
July 9, 1982

Cambridge Camera Exchange, Inc.
7th Avenue and 13th Street
New York, N.Y. 10011

INCOMPLETE SHIPMENT

The Minolta SRT 201 camera outfit I ordered from you on June 21 arrived today and appears to be in good working order. However, your advertisement in The New York Times for Sunday, June 16, listed six items as being supplied with this outfit, including a film holder and a sun shade. Neither of these items was included in the package I have just received, nor do I find any notice that they will be sent at a later date.

I am sure that this omission is unintentional and that you will correct it. Will you please let me know when I may expect to receive the film holder and sun shade, as advertised. If there is a dealer in the immediate area, I would be happy to get them from him if you will authorize me to do so at your expense.

Marilyn S. Conway

Marilyn S. Conway

Sample letter 4: modified block style with indented paragraphs

November 10, 1981

Ms. Roberta Basave
Employee Training and Development
Precision Engineering Incorporated
3116 Garson Blvd.
Greenbelt, Tennessee 37401

Dear Ms. Basave:

The enclosed proposal outlines a six-week training program to assist your staff with technical writing. Following your request on October 1 that I evaluate Precision Engineering's technical publications, reports, and correspondence, I reviewed writing samples collected by the company's six department heads. Besides analyzing the samples for grammatical correctness, clarity, tone, style, and organization, I also used the Gunning-Fogg Index to assess the readability level.

The conclusions detailed in the proposal indicate that your employees write correct, grammatical English. However, they need to work on reducing their use of jargon, editing for wordiness, and simplifying their sentence structure--particularly in the company's instruction manuals.

The proposal describes a training program designed to help your staff improve specific skills, enabling them to communicate more effectively with your customers.

Working with you and your staff during the past month has been a pleasure. I look forward to continued association with Precision Engineering. Once the proposal is approved, we can begin arrangements for the training program, perhaps holding the initial session shortly after the first of the year.

Cordially,

Ruthann Schlar

(Mrs.) Ruthann Schlar

RS/bo
Enc. proposal

Sample letter 5: modified block style without indented paragraphs

3481 Mountain Road
Bellevue, Washington 98004
April 14, 1982

Dr. Winthrop D. Pierce
Professor of Marketing
University of Washington
Seattle, Washington 98105

Dear Professor Pierce:

Through your bulletin posted at the University of Washington placement
service I learned that you are looking for students to work part time
for you next year in various marketing research projects. I think my
educational background and my experience working with people could be
put to good advantage in such work.

In early June I expect to receive my A.A. degree with a marketing
specialty from Bellevue Community College. Courses I have taken
include Marketing, Advertising, Business Writing, Business Law,
Accounting, and Computer Programming. I plan to continue my study at
the University of Washington next year.

I have been holding two part-time jobs, one as an assistant to
Professor John Leonard in the Business Department at Bellevue Community College, and one as a night dispatch clerk in the Bellevue
Trucking Company. I believe I work well with people. In my position
with Professor Leonard I supervise three other part-time students, and
my work at the Bellevue Trucking Company requires me to deal constantly
with other workers.

Both Professor John Leonard and Mr. Oscar Malenko, manager of the
Bellevue Trucking Company, have assured me they could recommend me to
you. I believe you know Professor Leonard. Mr. Malenko can be reached
by telephone at (206) 555-5437.

Please let me know when we can meet for an interview. I can arrange to
come to Seattle at your convenience. You can reach me or leave a message for me at my home phone (206) 555-7654.

Sincerely,

Ralston Phillips

Ralston Phillips

Sample letter 6: modified block style with indented paragraphs

848 Plains Street
Fort Pierre, South Dakota   57067
August 15, 1982

John Stafford
Curator
W.H. Over Museum
University of South Dakota
Vermillion, South Dakota   57069

Dear Mr. Stafford:

I have been an active volunteer at museums throughout most of my adult life and am now looking for permanent employment in a museum. As the enclosed resume shows, I have experience in many areas of museum operations ranging from collecting and cataloging specimens to arranging exhibits to managing funds and staff.

My love for museum work began in college when I helped with children's programs at a small natural history museum. Later I served a very exciting six years on the governing board of the Tippecanoe County Historical Association in Indiana.

During that time we supervised the County Historical Museum, located in the Victorian home of the city's founder, and oversaw the archeological exploration of a seventeenth-century settlement along the Wabash River. In addition, the Association-sponsored Feast of the Hunter's Moon, a re-creation of a frontier harvest festival, doubled its annual attendance while I was handling its publicity.

Since moving to South Dakota, I have visited your museum several times and am impressed by the quality of its exhibits, particularly those on mining and native Americans. While participating in the Fort Quiatenon archeological excavations, I gained expertise in Indian artifacts, which I want to broaden.

I would like to talk with you about employment possibilities at the W.H. Over Museum. Please call me at (605) 555-30859.

Sincerely yours,

Joanne Lewkowski

Joanne Lewkowski

<u>PERSONAL DATA SHEET</u>

JOANNE LEWKOWSKI

848 Plains Street
Fort Pierre, South Dakota 57067
(605) 555-0859

POSITION SOUGHT: MUSEUM CURATOR'S ASSISTANT

<u>Education</u>	B.A., Earlham College, Richmond, Indiana, 1970 Major: history Minor: biology Graduate study, State University of New York, 1971-72. Courses in researching, cataloging, mounting exibits.
<u>Experience</u>	Board of governors, Tippecanoe County Historical Association (TCHA), Lafayette, Indiana, 1975-81. Association owns and operates County Historical Museum; operates block house at Fort Quiatenon; sponsors and organizes annual Feast of the Hunter's Moon, a two-day re-enactment of the 17th-century French settlers' life; is granting agency for archeological dig at original Quiatenon site.
	Chairwoman, TCHA Quiatenon Committee, 1976-80. Handled major funds and grants, worked with federal and local agencies and Michigan State University anthropology faculty and students. Excavation volunteer at Quiatenon dig, summers 1976-80.
	Docent, Tippecanoe County Historical Museum, 1974-75. Researched and prepared exhibits, presented historical lectures and guided tours.
	Student volunteer, Joseph Moore Museum, Earlham College, 1968-70. Assisted director of small natural history museum, identified and cataloged specimens, maintained exhibits, organized museum tours for school children.
<u>Personal Data</u>	Speak and write French. Interests include travel and photography.
<u>References</u>	Martin Ferguson, administrative assistant, Tippe- canoe County Historical Association, 909 South St., Lafayette, Indiana 47905
	Professor Norris Vernon, Department of Anthropology, Michigan State University, East Lansing, Michigan 48824
	Professor Jack Copeland, Biology Department, Earlham College, Richmond, Indiana 47374

RESUME

JOANNE LEWKOWSKI   OBJECTIVE: MUSEUM MANAGEMENT

848 Plains Street
Fort Pierre, South Dakote   57067
(605) 555-0859

Qualifications	Familiar with all aspects of museum work from preparing exhibits to fund-raising and publicity. Proven skills in research, exhibit design, financial management, staff supervision, and communications.
Museum Management	As member of Tippecanoe County Historical Association (TCHA) board of governors, 1975-80, directly involved in operation of County Historical Museum: preparing annual budget, approving acquisitions and events, hiring staff.
Research and Field Work	Learned research methods and field techniques during two years as undergraduate volunteer at Earlham College's Joseph Moore Museum and during part-time graduate study in New York. Applied these skills while a docent at County Historical Museum, 1974-75. Researched and mounted Museum's highly successful "Victorian Christmas" exhibit in 1975. Gained further experience at Fort Quiatenon archeological digs run by TCHA and anthropologists from Michigan State University, summers 1976-80.
Fundraising	Obtained four major federal grants and raised over $15,000 locally when chairing TCHA Quiatenon Committee, 1976-80.
Public Relations	Prepared publicity campaign for Feast of the Hunter's Moon, annual re-enactment of 17th century settler's life at Fort Quiatenon, 1976-77. Wrote news releases, secured state and local media coverage. Feast attendance increased by 10,000 in 1977. While docent at County Historical Museum developed a four-lecture series on city's founding fathers attracting largest lecture audiences in museum's history. During second year with Joseph Moore natural history museum took "touchable" traveling exhibit to local elementary schools.
Education	B.A. Earlham College, Richmond, Indiana, 1970. Major: history Minor: biology Graduate Study, State University of New York, 1971-72. Courses in researching, cataloging, mounting exhibits, and photography.

References available upon request

A GLOSSARY
OF GRAMMATICAL
TERMS

50

This glossary provides brief definitions of the grammatical terms used in this text. Cross references refer you to pertinent sections of the text. For further text references to terms defined, as well as for references to terms not included in the glossary, consult the index.

absolute phrase   Absolute constructions modify the entire remainder of the sentence in which they stand. They differ from other modifying word groups in that (1) they lack any connective joining them to the rest of the sentence and (2) they do not modify any individual word or word group in the sentence. Compare *Seeing the bears, we stopped the car,* in which the participial phrase modifies *we,* with *The rain having stopped, we saw the bears,* in which the construction *the rain having stopped* is an absolute modifying the rest of the sentence. The basic pattern of the absolute phrase is a noun or pronoun and a participle. *(She having arrived,* we all went to the movies. We left about ten o'clock, *the movie being over.)* Such phrases are sometimes called **nominative absolutes,** since pronouns in them require the nominative case.

Absolute phrases may also be prepositional phrases *(In fact,* we had expected rain) or verbal phrases (It often rains in April, *to tell the truth. Generally speaking,* July is hot.)

For the punctuation of absolute phrases see **20e.**

abstract noun   See *noun.*

active voice   See *voice.*

adjectival   Any word or word group used to modify a noun. Some modern grammars limit the meaning of **adjective** strictly to words that can be compared by adding *-er* and *-est (new, newer, newest; high, higher, highest).* Such grammars apply the term **adjectival** to other words that ordinarily modify nouns, and to any other word or word group when it is used as an adjective. In such grammars the italicized words below may be called **adjectivals.**

LIMITING ADJECTIVES	*my* suit, *a* picture, *one* day
NOUNS MODIFYING NOUNS	*school* building, *home* plate, *government* policy
PHRASES MODIFYING NOUNS	man *of the hour*
CLAUSES MODIFYING NOUNS	girl *whom I know*

adjective   A word used to describe or limit the meaning of a noun or its equivalent. According to their position, adjectives may be (1) **attributive,** i.e., placed next to their nouns *(vivid* example; *a* boy, *strong* and *vigorous),* or (2) **predicative,** i.e., placed in the predicate after a linking verb (She was *vigorous).*

According to their meaning, adjectives may be (1) **descriptive,** naming some quality (*white* house, *small* child, *leaking* faucet); (2) **proper,** derived from proper nouns (*Roman* fountain, *French* custom); or (3) **limiting.** Limiting adjectives may indicate possession *(my, his),* may point out *(this, former),* may number *(three, second),* or may be articles *(a, the).*

See **1b(1)** and Section **3.**

adjective clause   A subordinate, or dependent, clause used as an adjective.

> The man *who lives here* is a biologist. [The adjective clause modifies the noun *man.*]
>
> Dogs *that chase cars* seldom grow old. [The adjective clause modifies the noun *dogs.*]

See also **1d.**

adjective phrase   See *phrase.*

adverb   A word used to describe or limit the meaning of a verb, an adjective, another verb, or a whole sentence.

According to function, adverbs may (1) modify single words (went *quickly, quite* shy, *nearly* all men); (2) modify whole sentences (*Maybe* he will go); (3) ask questions (*When* did he go? *Where* is the book?); or (4) connect clauses and modify their meaning (see *conjunctive adverb*).

According to meaning, adverbs may indicate (1) manner (*secretly* envious); (2) time (*never* healthy); (3) place (*outside* the house); or (4) degree (*quite* easily angered).

See **1b(1)** and Section **3.**

adverb clause   A subordinate, or dependent, clause used as an adverb.

> *When you leave,* please close the door. [The adverb clause, indicating time, modifies the verb *close.*]
>
> The sheep grazed *where the grass was greenest.* [The adverb clause, indicating place, modifies the verb *grazed.*]

Adverb clauses also indicate manner, purpose, cause, result, condition, concession, and comparison.

See **1d.**

adverb phrase   See *phrase.*

adverbial   A term used to describe any word or word group used as an adverb. Common adverbials are nouns in certain constructions (She went *home*), phrases (She went *in a great hurry*), or clauses (She went *when she wanted to go*). Compare *adjectival.*

adverbial objective   Sometimes applied to nouns used as adverbials. (They slept *mornings.* He ran a *mile.*)

agreement   A correspondence or matching in the form of one word and that of another. Verbs agree with their subjects in number and person (in

She runs, both *she* and *runs* are singular and third person). Pronouns agree with their antecedents in person, number, and gender (in *He wanted his way, he* and *his* are both third person singular, and masculine). Demonstrative adjectives match the nouns they modify in number *(this kind, these kinds).* See Section **8.**

antecedent   A word or group of words to which a pronoun refers.

> She is a *woman who* seldom writes letters. [*Woman* is the antecedent of the pronoun *who.*]
> *Uncle Henry* came for a brief visit, but *he* stayed all winter. [*Uncle Henry* is the antecedent of the pronoun *he.*]

appositive   A word or phrase set beside a noun, a pronoun, or a group of words used as a noun, that identifies or explains it by renaming it.

> John, my *brother*   Albany, that is, *New York's state capital*
> His hobby, *playing handball*   modifiers, *words that describe or limit*

The appositives illustrated above are **nonrestrictive:** they explain the nouns they follow but are not necessary to identify them. When appositives restrict the meaning of the nouns they follow to a specific individual or object, they are **restrictive:** *my sister Ilene* (that is, *Ilene,* not *Dorothy* or *Helen*); *Huxley the novelist* (not *Huxley the scientist*). See **20c(2).**

article   The words *a, an,* and *the* are articles. *A* and *an* are **indefinite** articles; *the* is a **definite** article. Articles are traditionally classed as limiting adjectives, but since they always signal that a noun will follow, some modern grammars call them **determiners.**

auxiliary   A verb form used with a main verb to form a verb phrase. Auxiliaries are commonly divided into two groups. The first group is used to indicate tense and voice. This group includes *shall, will,* and the forms of *be, have,* and *do* (*shall* give, *will* give, *has* given, *had* given, *does* give, *is* giving, *was* given).

The second group, called **modal auxiliaries,** includes *can, could, may, might, must, ought, should,* and *would.* These are used to indicate ability, obligation, permission, possibility, etc., and they do not take inflectional endings such as *-s, -ed,* and *-ing.* See Section **4.**

cardinal numbers   Numbers such as *one, three, twenty,* used in counting. Compare *ordinal numbers.*

case   The inflectional form of pronouns or the possessive form of nouns to indicate their function in a group of words. Pronouns have three cases: (1) **nominative or subjective** *(we, she, they),* used for the subject of a verb, or a subjective complement; (2) the **possessive,** used as an adjective *(their dog, anybody's guess);* and (3) the **objective** *(us, her, them),* used for objects of verbs, verbals, and prepositions. Possessive pronouns may also stand alone (The car is *his*). Nouns have only two cases: (1) a **common** case (*woman, leopard*) and (2) a **possessive** case (*woman's, leopard's*). See Section **2.**

clause   A group of words containing a subject and a predicate. Clauses are of two kinds: main, or independent; and subordinate, or dependent. **Main clauses** make independent assertions and can stand alone as sentences. **Subordinate clauses** depend on some other element within a sentence; they function as nouns, adjectives, or adverbs, and cannot stand alone.

MAIN	*The moon shone,* and *the dog barked.*[Two main clauses, either of which could be a sentence]
SUBORDINATE	*When the moon shone,* the dog barked. [Adverb clause] *That he would survive* is doubtful. [Noun clause]

See **1d.**

collective noun   A noun naming a collection or aggregate of individuals by a singular form (*assembly, army, jury*). Collective nouns are followed by a singular verb when the group is thought of as a unit and a plural verb when the component individuals are in mind (the majority *decides;* the majority *were* slaves). See **8a(6)** and **8b.**

comma splice   A sentence error in which two independent clauses are joined only by a comma without a coordinating conjunction. See Section **7.**

common noun   See *noun.*

comparison   Change in the form of adjectives and adverbs to show degree. English has three degrees: (1) **positive,** the form listed in dictionaries (*loud, bad, slowly*); (2) **comparative** (*louder, worse, more slowly*); and **superlative** (*loudest, worst, most slowly*). See **3e.**

complement   In its broadest sense, a term for any word, excluding modifiers, that completes the meaning of a verb (direct and indirect objects), a subject (subject complements), or an object (object complements).

VERB COMPLEMENTS	Give *me* the *money.* [*Money* and *me* are direct and indirect objects, respectively.]
SUBJECT COMPLEMENTS	Helen is a *singer.* She is *excellent.* [The noun *singer* and the adjective *excellent* refer to the subject.]
OBJECT COMPLEMENTS	We elected Jane *secretary.* That made Bill *angry.* [*Secretary* and *angry* refer to the direct objects *Jane* and *Bill.*]

complete predicate   See *predicate.*

complete subject   See *subject.*

complex sentence   See *sentence.*

compound Made up of more than one word but used as a unit, as in compound noun (*redhead, football*), compound adjective (*downcast, matter-of-fact*), or compound subject (Both *patience* and *practice* are necessary).
See also *sentence.*

compound-complex See *sentence.*

concrete noun See *noun.*

conjugation A list of inflected forms for a verb, displaying the forms for first, second, and third person singular and plural for each tense, voice, and mood. A synopsis of the third person singular (*he, she, it,* and singular nouns) forms for a regular and an irregular verb is shown below.

	Simple Form	*Progressive Form*
Active Voice		
PRESENT	*he/she* asks/drives	*he/she* is asking/driving
PAST	*he/she* asked/drove	*he/she* was asking/driving
FUTURE	*he/she* will ask/drive	*he/she* will be asking/driving
PRESENT PERFECT	*he/she* has asked/driven	*he/she* has been asking/driving
PAST PERFECT	*he/she* had asked/driven	*he/she* had been asking/driving
FUTURE PERFECT	*he/she* will have asked/driven	*he/she* will have been asking/driving
Passive Voice		
PRESENT	*he/she* is asked/driven	*he/she* is being asked/driven
PAST	*he/she* was asked/driven	*he/she* was being asked/driven
FUTURE	*he/she* will be asked/driven	*he/she* will be being asked/driven
PRESENT PERFECT	*he/she* has been asked/driven	*he/she* has been being asked/driven
PAST PERFECT	*he/she* had been asked/driven	*he/she* had been being asked/driven
FUTURE PERFECT	*he/she* will have been asked/driven	*he/she* will have been being asked/driven

Forms for first and second person singular and all plural forms may be described briefly as follows:
The present tense forms for other persons are *I/you/we/they* ask/drive.
The past and future tense forms for all persons are the same as those shown for the third person.

All perfect tense and passive voice forms that use *has* as an auxiliary in the third person use *have* in all other persons.

All perfect tense and passive voice forms that use *is/was* in the third person use *am/was* for the first person *(I)* and *were* in all other persons.

conjunction　A part of speech used to join and relate words, phrases, and clauses. Conjunctions may be either coordinating or subordinating.

Coordinating conjunctions connect words, phrases, and clauses of equal grammatical rank: *and, but, or, nor, for.*

Subordinating conjunctions join dependent clauses to main clauses: *after, although, as if, because, since, when.*

See **1b(2).**

conjunctive adverb　An adverb used to relate and connect main clauses in a sentence. Common conjunctive adverbs are *also, consequently, furthermore, hence, however, indeed, instead, likewise, moreover, nevertheless, otherwise, still, then, therefore, thus.* **Conjunctive adverbs,** unlike **coordinating** and **subordinating conjunctions,** are movable and can thus occupy different positions within the main clause in which they stand. See **21b.**

connective　A general term for any word or phrase that links words, phrases, clauses, or sentences. **Connective** thus includes conjunctions, prepositions, and conjunctive adverbs. See **1b(2).**

construction　A general term describing any related groups of words such as a phrase, a clause, or a sentence.

coordinate　Having equal rank, as two main clauses in a compound sentence. See Section **34.**

coordinating conjunction　See *conjunction.*

correlatives　Coordinating conjunctions used in pairs to join sentence elements of equal rank. Common correlatives are *either . . . or; neither . . . nor; not only . . . but also; whether . . . or; both . . . and.* See **1b(2).**

dangling construction　A subordinate construction that cannot easily and unambiguously be linked to another word or group of words it modifies. See Section **12.**

declension　See *inflection* and *case.*

degree　See *comparison.*

demonstratives　*This, that, these,* and *those* are called **demonstratives** when used as pointing words. (*This* dinner is cold. *That* is the man.)

dependent clause　See *clause.*

derivational suffix　See *suffix.*

determiner A word such as *a, an, the, his, our, your,* which indicates that one of the words following it is a noun.

direct address A noun or pronoun used parenthetically to point out the person addressed, sometimes called **nominative of address** or **vocative.** (*George,* where are you going? I suppose, *gentlemen,* that you enjoyed the lecture.)

direct and indirect quotation A direct quotation is an exact quotation of a speaker's or writer's words (sometimes called **direct discourse**). In **indirect discourse** the speaker's or writer's thought is summarized without direct quotation.

DIRECT He said, "I must leave on the eight o'clock shuttle."

INDIRECT He said that he had to leave on the eight o'clock shuttle.

direct object See *object* and *complement.*

double negative The use of two negative words within the same construction. In certain forms, two negatives are used in the same statement in English to give a particular emphasis to a positive idea. (He was *not* entirely *un*prejudiced). In most instances, the double negative is nonstandard. (He *didn't* do *no* work. We *didn't* see *no*body.) See **42b.**

elliptical construction An omission of words necessary to the grammatical completeness of an expression but assumed in the context. The omitted words in elliptical expressions are understood (*He is older than I* [am]. *Our house is small, his* [house is] *large*).

expletive The word *it* or *there* used to introduce a sentence in which the subject follows the verb.

It is doubtful that he will arrive today. [The clause *that he will arrive today* is the subject of the verb *is.*]

There are two ways of solving the problem. [The noun *ways* is the subject of *are.*]

faulty predication A grammatical fault that results when a subject and its verb or a subject and its complement in a subject/linking verb/complement construction are mismatched in meaning. See Section **14.**

finite verb A verb form that makes an assertion about its subject. Verbals (infinitives, participles, gerunds) are not finite forms. All finite verbs can add -*s* in the third person singular of the present tense to show agreement with their subject. Nonfinite verb forms cannot make this inflectional change. See Section **4.**

function words A term used to describe the words, such as articles, auxiliaries, conjunctions, and prepositions, that are more important for their part in the structure of the sentence than for their meaning. They indicate the function of other words in a sentence and the grammatical relations between those words.

gender The classification of nouns and pronouns as masculine *(man, he)*, feminine *(woman, she)*, and neuter *(desk, it)*. A few English nouns have special forms to indicate gender *(salesman, saleswoman; hero, heroine)*.

genitive case The possessive case. See Section **2**.

gerund A verbal that ends in *-ing* and is used as a noun. Gerunds may take complements, objects, and modifiers. See **1c(3)**.

idiom An expression established by usage and peculiar to a particular language. Many idioms have unusual grammatical construction and make little sense if taken literally. Examples of English idioms are *by and large, catch a cold, lay hold of, look up an old friend*. See **40f**.

imperative See *mood*.

indefinite pronoun A pronoun, such as *anybody, anyone, someone*, that does not refer to a specific person or thing.

independent clause See *clause*.

independent element An expression that has no grammatical relation to other parts of the sentence. See *absolute*.

indicative See *mood*.

indirect object See *object*.

infinitive A verbal usually consisting of *to* followed by the present form of the verb. With a few verbs *to* may be omitted (heard her *tell;* made it *work*). Infinitives can serve as nouns (*To swim* is to relax), as adjectives (I have nothing *to say*), or as adverbs (We were ready *to begin*). See **1b(3)**.

inflection Variation in the form of words to indicate case *(he, him)*, gender *(he, she, it)*, number *(mouse, mice)*, tense *(walk, walked)*, etc. **Declension** is the inflection of nouns and pronouns; **conjugation** the inflection of verbs; and **comparison** is the inflection of adjectives and adverbs.

inflectional suffix See *suffix*.

intensifier A term applied to such modifiers as *much, so, too*, and *very*, which merely add emphasis to the words they modify. Words such as *actually, mighty, pretty*, and *really* often occur as vague intensifiers in colloquial English.

intensive pronoun Any compound personal pronoun ending with *-self* used for emphasis. (I did it *myself*. The Dean *himself* wrote the letter.)

interjection A word or group of words that is grammatically independent and used to show mild, strong, or sudden emotion. (*Ych*. I hate caterpillars. *Say!* Let's rob a bank.)

intransitive verb   See *verb.*

inversion   A reversal of normal word order. *(Dejected, he left the witness stand. The verdict he clearly foresaw.)*

irregular verb   A verb that forms its past tense and past participle by a change in an internal vowel, or by some other individualized change, as opposed to the usual addition of *-d* or *-ed* to the basic form of so-called **regular verbs,** as in *walk, walked, walked (begin, began, begun; do, did, done; fall, fell, fallen).* See Section **4.**

kernel sentence   A term used in some contemporary grammars to describe one of a limited number of basic sentence patterns from which all grammatical structures can be derived. See **1a.**

lexical word   Nouns, verbs, adjectives, and adverbs are sometimes termed lexical words, that is, words that carry most of the meaning in English, in contrast to *function words,* which indicate relationships among lexical words. Compare *function word.*

linking verb   A verb that shows the relation between the subject of a sentence and a complement. *(He seems timid. The cake tastes sweet. He is a thief.)* The chief linking verbs are *be, become, appear, seem,* and the verbs pertaining to the senses *(look, smell, taste, sound, feel).*

mixed construction   A grammatical fault that consists of joining as a sentence two or more parts that do not fit in grammar or meaning. See Section **14.**

modal auxiliary   See *auxiliary.*

modification   Describing or limiting the meaning of a word or group of words. Adjectives and adjective phrases or clauses modify nouns; adverbs and adverb phrases or clauses modify verbs, adjectives, or adverbs. See Section **3.**

modifier   A general term given to any word or word group that is used to limit, qualify, or otherwise describe the meaning of another word or word group. Adjectives, adverbs, preposition and verbal phrases, and subordinate clauses are the usual modifiers in English. See Section **3** for adjectives and adverbs and Section **1** for various word groups as modifiers.

mood   The form of a verb used to show how the action is viewed by the speaker. English has three moods: (1) **indicative,** stating a fact or asking a question (The wheat *is* ripe. *Will* he *go?*); (2) **imperative,** expressing a command or a request (*Report* at once. Please *clear* your desk); and (3) **subjunctive,** expressing doubt, wish, or condition contrary to fact. (The grass looks as if it *were* dying. I wish he *were* more friendly.) See Section **5.**

nominal   A word or word group used as a noun. (The *blue* seems more suitable. *Eating that pie* will not be easy.) Compare *adjectival.*

nominative case See *case.*

nonrestrictive modifier A modifying phrase or clause that is not essential to pointing out or identifying the person or thing modified.

Smith, *who was watching the road,* saw the accident.
The Wankel engine, *new to the market,* is promising.

See Section **20c.**

noun A word, like *man, horse, carrot, trip, theory,* or *capitalism,* that names a person, place, thing, quality, concept, or the like. Nouns usually form plurals by adding *-s,* and possessives by adding *'s,* and most frequently function as subjects and complements, although they also function in other ways. See **1a.**

Nouns are divided into various subclasses according to their meaning. The most common classes are the following:

Class	*Meaning*	*Examples*
common	general classes	*tiger, house, idea*
proper	specific names	*Chicago, Burma, Lee*
abstract	ideas, qualities	*liberty, love, emotion*
concrete	able to be sensed	*apple, smoke, perfume*
collective	groups	*herd, bunch, jury*
count	able to be counted	*chicken, slice, book*
mass	not ordinarily counted (not used with *a, an*)	*salt, gold, equality*

noun clause A subordinate clause used as a noun. (*What I saw* was humiliating. I shall accept *whatever he offers.*) See **1d.**

number The form of a noun, pronoun, verb, or demonstrative adjective to indicate one (singular) or more than one (plural).

object A general term for any word or word group that is affected by or receives action of a transitive verb or verbal, or of a preposition. A **direct object** receives the action of the verb. (I followed *him.* Keep *whatever you find.*) An **indirect object** indicates to or for whom or what something is done. (Give *me* the money). The **object of a preposition** follows the preposition and is related to another part of the sentence by the preposition (We rode across the *beach*). See also *complement* and **1a** and **2c.**

object complement See *complement.*

objective case See *case.*

ordinal numbers Numbers such as *first, third, twentieth,* used to indicate order. Compare *cardinal numbers.*

paradigm An illustration of the systematic inflection of a word such as a pronoun or a verb, showing all its forms.

parenthetical expression An inserted expression that interrupts the thought of a sentence. (His failure, *I suppose,* was his own fault. I shall arrive—*this will surprise you*—on Monday.)

participial phrase See *participle* and *phrase.*

participle A verbal used as an adjective. As an adjective, a participle can modify a noun or pronoun. The present participle ends in *-ing (running, seeing, trying).* The past participle ends in *-d, -ed, -t, -n, -en,* or changes the vowel *(walked, lost, seen, rung).* Though a participle cannot make an assertion, it is derived from a verb and can take an object and be modified by an adverb *(Swimming the river, completely beaten).*

parts of speech The classes into which words may be divided on the basis of meaning, form, and function. The traditional parts of speech are: noun, pronoun, verb, adjective, adverb, preposition, conjunction, and interjection. See **1a** and **1b** and separate entries in this glossary.

passive voice See *voice.*

person The form of a pronoun and verb used to indicate the speaker (first person—*I am*); the person spoken to (second person—*you are*); or the person spoken about (third person—*she is*).

personal pronoun See *pronoun.*

phrase A group of related words lacking both subject and predicate and used as a single part of speech. Phrases may be classified as follows:

PREPOSITIONAL	We walked *across the street.*
PARTICIPIAL	The man *entering the room* is my father.
GERUND	*Washing windows* is tiresome work.
INFINITIVE	*To see the sunset* was a pleasure.
VERB	He *has been educated* in Europe.

See **1c.**

plain form A term often used for the infinitive or dictionary form of a verb, as *run, stand, pounce.* See Section **4.**

possessive See *case.*

predicate The part of a sentence or clause that makes a statement about the subject. The *complete predicate* consists of the verb and its complements and modifiers. The *simple predicate* consists of only the verb and its auxiliaries. See **1a.**

predicate adjective An adjective serving as a subject complement (He was *silent*). See *complement.*

predicate noun A noun serving as a subject complement (He was a *hero*). See *complement.*

prefix   One or more syllables, such as *a-*, *mis-*, *sub-*, or *un-*, that can be added at the beginning of a word or root to change or modify its meaning: *a* + moral = amoral; *mis* + print = misprint; *sub* + standard = substandard; *un* + zipped = unzipped.

preposition   A word used to relate a noun or pronoun to some other word in the sentence. A preposition and its object form a **prepositional phrase.** (The sheep are *in* the meadow. He dodged *through* the traffic.) See **1c.**

prepositional phrase   See *phrase* and *preposition.*

principal clause   A main or independent clause. See *clause.*

principal parts   The three forms of a verb from which the various tenses are derived; the **present infinitive** *(join, go)*, the **past tense** *(joined, went)*, and the **past participle** *(joined, gone)*. See Section **4.**

progressive   The form of the verb used to describe an action occurring, but not completed, at the time referred to. (I *am studying.* I *was studying.*) See Section **4.**

pronoun   A word used in place of a noun. The noun for which a pronoun stands is called its **antecedent.** (See **1a** and **8b.**) Pronouns are classified as follows:

PERSONAL	*I, you, he, she, it, etc.*
RELATIVE	*who, which, that* I am the man *who* lives here. We saw a barn *that* was burning.
INTERROGATIVE	*who, which, what* *Who* are you? *Which* is your book?
DEMONSTRATIVE	*this, that, these, those*
INDEFINITE	*one, any, each, anyone, somebody, all,* etc.
RECIPROCAL	*each other, one another*
INTENSIVE	*myself, yourself, himself,* etc. I *myself* was afraid. You *yourself* must decide.
REFLEXIVE	*myself, yourself, himself,* etc. I burned *myself.* You are deceiving *yourself.*

proper noun   See *noun.*

reciprocal pronoun   See *pronoun.*

regular verb   See *irregular verb.*

relative clause   A subordinate clause introduced by a relative pronoun. See *pronoun.*

relative pronoun   See *pronoun.*

restrictive modifier A modifying phrase or clause that is essential to pointing out or identifying the person or thing modified. (People *who live in glass houses* shouldn't throw stones. The horse *that won the race* is a bay mare.) See **20c.**

sentence A complete unit of thought containing a subject and a predicate. Sentences can be classified according to their form as **simple, compound, complex,** and **compound-complex.**

SIMPLE	They rested. [One main clause]
COMPOUND	They rested and we worked. [Two main clauses]
COMPLEX	They rested while we worked. [One main clause, one subordinate clause]
COMPOUND-COMPLEX	They rested while we worked, but we could not finish. [Two main clauses, one containing a subordinate clause]

sentence fragment A group of words capitalized and punctuated as a sentence but not containing both a subject and a finite verb. See Section **6.**

.subject The person or thing about which the predicate of a sentence or clause makes an assertion or asks a question. The *simple subject* is the word or word group with which the verb of the sentence agrees. The *complete subject* is the simple subject together with all its modifiers. In *The donkey that Jones keeps in the back yard brays all the time, donkey* is the simple subject, and *the donkey that Jones keeps in the back yard* is the complete subject. See Section **1.**

subject complement See *complement.*

subjunctive mood See *mood.*

subordinate clause See *clause.*

substantive A word or group of words used as a noun. Substantives include pronouns, infinitives, gerunds, and noun clauses.

substantive clause A noun clause. See *clause.*

suffix An ending that modifies the meaning of the word to which it is attached. Suffixes may be **inflectional,** such as the *-s* added to nouns to form plurals *(rug, rugs)* or the *-ed* added to verbs to indicate past tense *(call, called).* Or they may be called **derivational,** such as *-ful, -less,* or *-ize (hope, hopeful; home, homeless; union, unionize).* Derivational suffixes often, though not always, change the part of speech to which they are added. See *inflection* and item **1** in Section **39.**

superlative See *comparison.*

syntax   The part of grammar that describes the structure and function of meaningful word groups such as phrases, clauses, and sentences, as opposed to **morphology,** the part of grammar that describes the formation, function, and classification of words.

transitive verb   See *verb.*

verb   A word, like *confide, raise, see,* which indicates action or asserts something. (See **1a.**) Verbs are inflected and combine with auxiliaries to form **verb phrases.** Verbs may be **transitive,** requiring an object (He *made* a report), or **intransitive,** not requiring an object (They *migrated*). Many can function both transitively and intransitively. (The wind *blew.* They *blew* the whistle.) **Linking verbs,** such as *be, become,* and *appear,* are followed by complements that refer back to the subject. See Section **4.**

verb complement   See *complement.*

verb phrase   See *phrase.*

verbal   A word derived from a verb and able to take objects, complements, modifiers, and sometimes subjects but unable to stand as the main verb in a sentence. See *gerund, infinitive,* and *participle.* See also **1b(3)** and **1c.**

voice   The form of the verb that shows whether the subject acts **(active voice)** or is acted upon **(passive voice).** Only transitive verbs can show voice. A transitive verb followed by an object is **active** (They *bought* flowers). In the **passive** the direct object is made into the subject (The flowers *were bought*). See **1a,** and Section **5.**

word order   The order of words in a sentence or smaller word group. Word order is one of the principal grammatical devices in English.

INDEX

Note: Numbers in boldface refer to section designations; other numbers refer to pages. Thus, for example, the entry **40f:**363 refers to Section 40f on page 363.

INDEX

Homonyms, **40b:**358
hopefully, **42:**389
hung, hanged, **43:**389
Hyphen, **30:**167-69
  with adjectives, **30b:**168
  to avoid ambiguity in spelling, **30c:**168
  in compound words, **30:**167-68
  with prefixes and suffixes, **30e:**169
  in syllabication, **18:**114

I

I, **28b:**161
ibid., **36:**451
idea, **43:**389
Ideas, expressing, in composition:
  emphasizing, **36:**318-25
  relating, by coordination, **34:**296-98
  relating, by parallelism, **35:**312-17
  relating, by subordination, **34a-d:**298-307
identical with, **40e:**362
Idioms, **40e:**361-63, **50:**519
if, **5d:**56
ignorant, stupid, **43:**389
Illiterate usage, **38(7):**346
illusion, allusion, **43:**382
Imperative mood, **5c:**55, **50:**520
Imperative sentence, **37e:**331
imply, infer, **43:**389
in, into, **43:**389
in back of, in behind, in between, **43:**389
Impersonal construction *(it is, there is, there are)*. *See* Expletive
Incomplete constructions:
  comparisons, **13d:**98-100
  omissions, **13a-c:**97-98
  sentence fragments, **6a-b:**60-64
Indefinite article, **50:**514
Indefinite pronoun:
  defined, **50:**519
  as subject, and agreement, **8a(2):**70
  use, **1a:**15-16
  Indention of manuscripts, **15c(3):**107
Independent element, **50:**519
Indexes. *See* Periodical indexes
Indicative mood, **5c:**55, **50:**520
Indirect discourse, **50:**518
Indirect object:
  defined, **50:**521
  sentence pattern, **1a:**17
Indirect question, punctuation, **19a:**119, **19e:**120
Indirect quotation:
  defined, **50:**518
  no punctuation for, **25a:**150
  shifting improperly, **10d:**86-87
individual, party, person, **43:**389
Inductive reasoning, **33d:**282
infer, imply, **43:**389
Infinitive(s):
  defined, **1b(3):**22, **50:**519
  form of, **4:**40

perfect, and tense, **5c:**54-55
present, and tense, **5c:**54-55
split, **11e:**91
Infinitive phrase:
  dangling, **12c:**95
  defined, **50:**522
  function, **1c:**23
Inflection:
  defined, **50:**519
  function, 13
Inflectional suffix, **50:**524
Informal English, 7-8, **38(7):**346
ingenious, ingenuous, **43:**390
in regards to, **43:**390
in regard to, **43:**394
Insertion sign (caret), **15d:**108
inside of, **43:**390
Intensifier, **50:**519
Intensive pronoun, **50:**519
Interjection:
  defined, **50:**519
  exclamation point after, **19f:**121
Internal punctuation, **19:**118
  superfluous, **24:**144-48
Interrogative sentence. *See* Question
in the case of, **43:**385
Intransitive verb, **4:**42, **50:**525
Introductory elements, comma after, **20b:**123-24
Invention (of topic), **31b:**179
  strategies of, **31c:**180-82
Inversion, sentence, **37d:**330, **50:**520
irregardless, **43:**390
Irregular verb:
  defined, **4:**41-42, **50:**520
  principal parts (table), **4b:**45-47
is when, is where, is because, **14a:**101-2, **33c:**279, **43:**390
it:
  ambiguous use, **9g:**82
  as expletive, **1a:**18, **9g:**82
  indefinite use, **9e:**79-80
Italics:
  for emphasis, **27e:**160
  for foreign words, **27d:**159-60
  function, **19:**118
  for letters and words as words, **27c:**159
  overuse of, **27f:**160
  for titles, **27a-b:**159
its, it's, **29d:**167, **43:**390
-ize, **43:**390

J

Jargon, **42d:**377-78
join in, with, to, **40e:**362
just, **11a:**88

K

Kernel sentence, **50:**520
kind, **43:**390

INDEX